Real business cycles

The Real Business Cycle model has become the dominant mode of business analysis within the new classical school of macroeconomic thought. It has been the focus of a great deal of debate and controversy, and yet, to date, there has been no single source for material on real business cycles, much less one which provides a balanced account of both sides of the debate.

This volume fills the gap by presenting a collection of the essential articles that define and develop the real business cycle school, as well as those that criticize it. Key areas covered include:

- the establishment of the real business cycle program
- the aims and methods of the real business cycle school
- analysis of the statistics and econometrics of the calibration techniques advocated by real businesss cycle modelers
- assessment of the empirical success of the real business cycle model from a variety of methods and perspectives
- the measurement of technology shocks in business cycle models (the Solow residual).

A detailed Introduction assesses the strengths and weaknesses of real business cycle theory from a critical perspective and includes a non-technical User's Guide to the formulation and solution of models which will aid understanding of the articles and issues discussed.

Offering a thorough assessment of the real business cycle program, this volume will be a vital resource for students and professionals in macroeconomics.

James E. Hartley is Assistant Professor of Economics at Mount Holyoke College, Massachusetts. **Kevin D. Hoover** is Professor of Economics at the University of California, Davis. **Kevin D. Salyer** is Associate Professor of Economics, also at the University of California, Davis.

Real business cycles

A Reader

Edited by

James E. Hartley,
Kevin D. Hoover,
and
Kevin D. Salyer

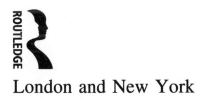

London and New York

First published 1998 by Routledge
11 New Fetter Lane, London EC4P 4EE

Simultaneously published in the USA and Canada
by Routledge
29 West 35th Street, New York, NY 10001

Typeset in Times by
J&L Composition Ltd, Filey, North Yorkshire
Printed and bound in Great Britain by
TJ International Ltd, Padstow Cornwall

British Library Cataloguing in Publication Data
A catalogue record for this book is available from the British Library

Library of Congress Cataloging in Publication Data
Real business cycles/[edited by] James E. Hartley, Kevin D. Hoover,
and Kevin D. Salyer.
p.   cm.
Includes bibliographical references and index.
1. Business cycles. I. Hartley, James E., 1966– . II. Hoover,
Kevin D., 1955– . III. Salyer, Kevin D., 1954– .
HB3711.R35 1998   97–40397
                               CIP

ISBN 0–415–16568–7 (hbk)
ISBN 0–415–17154–7 (pbk)

"It is thus that the existence of a common standard of judgment leads physicists, who are no more saintly than economists, to question their own best work."

Steven Weinberg

Contents

Acknowledgements

The editors have benefited from the help of a number of people in putting this volume together. We thank: John Muellbauer for comments on a draft of Chapter 1; Michael Campbell for bibliographic work; Jeannine Henderson for her careful work in preparing camera-ready copy of the articles reproduced here; Alan Jarvis, Alison Kirk, and Laura Large of Routledge for their encouragement and help with the production details; Colin Cameron, Timothy Cogley, Martin Eichenbaum, Robert Feenstra, Andrew Harvey, Dale Heien, Richard Howitt, Finn Kydland, Martine Quinzii, Steven Sheffrin, and Gregor Smith for helping us to obtain copies of the articles suitable for the reproduction in the volume.

We also acknowledge the following permissions to reprint:

The Econometric Society and Dickey and Fuller for a table from "Likli-hood Ratio Statistics for Auto-regression Time Series with a Unit Root" in *Econometrica*, 49, 1981, pp. 12–26. The Econometric Society and N.E. Savin and K.J. White for a table from "The Durbin–Watson Test for Serial Correlation with Extreme Small Samples or Many Regressors", *Econometrica*, 45, 1977, 1989–1986 as corrected by R.W. Farbrother, *Econometrica*, 48, September 1980, p. 1554. The American Economic Association and Finn E. Kydland and Edward C. Prescott for "The Computational Experiment: An Econometric Tool" in *Journal of Economic Perspectives*, vol. 10: 1, Winter 1996, pp. 69–86. The American Economic Association and Lars Peter Hansen and James H. Heckman for "The Empirical Foundations of Calibration" in *Journal of Economic Perspectives*, vol. 10: 1, Winter 1996, pp. 87–104. The American Economic Association and Gary D. Hansen and Edward C. Prescott for "Did Technology Shocks Cause the 1990–1991 Recession" in *American Economic Review*, vol. 83: 2, May 1993, pp. 280–286. The American Economic Association and Lawrence J. Christiano and Martin Eichenbaum for "Current Real-Business Cycle Theories and Aggregate Labour Market Functions" in *American Economic Review*, vol. 82: 3, June 1992, pp. 430–450. The American Economic

Association and Thomas F. Cooley and Gary D. Hansen for "The Inflation Tax in a Real Business Cycle Model" in *American Economic Review*, vol. 79: 4, September 1989, pp. 733–748. The Econometric Society and Finn E. Kydland and Edward C. Prescott for "Time to Build and Aggregate Fluctuations", in *Econometrica*, vol. 50: 6, November 1982, pp. 1345–1369. Reed Elsevier Plc and Edward C. Prescott for "Theory Ahead of Business Cycle Measurement" in *Federal Reserve Bank of Minneapolis Quarterly Review*, vol. 10: 4, Fall 1986, pp. 9–22. Reed Elsevier Plc and Lawrence H. Summers for "Some Sceptical Observations On Real Business Cycle Theory" in *Federal Reserve Bank of Minneapolis Quarterly Review*, vol. 10: 4, Fall 1986, pp. 23–27. Reed Elsevier Plc and Edward C. Prescott for "Response to a Sceptic" in *Federal Reserve Bank of Minneapolis Quarterly Review*, vol. 10: 4, Fall 1986, pp. 28–33. Elsevier Science BV, The Netherlands and Robert G. King, Charles I. Plosser and Sergio T. Rebelo for "Production, Growth and Business Cycles I: The Basic Neoclassical Model" in *Journal of Monetary Economics*, vol. 21: 2, March 1988, pp. 195–232. Elsevier Science BV, The Netherlands and Gary D. Hansen for "Indivisible Labour and the Business" in *Journal of Monetary Economics*, vol. 16: 3, November 1985, pp. 309–328. Reed Elsevier Plc and Gary D. Hansen and Randall Wright for "The Labour Market in Real Business Cycle Theory" in *Federal Reserve Bank of Minneapolis Quarterly Review*, Spring 1992, pp. 2–12. Basil Blackwell Ltd and Finn E. Kydland and Edward C. Prescott for "The Econometrics of the General Equilibrium Approach to Business Cycles" in *Scandinavian Journal of Economics*, vol. 93: 2, 1991, pp. 161–178. Oxford University Press Journals and Kevin D. Hoover for "Facts and Artifacts: Calibration and the Empirical Assessment of Real-Business Cycle Models" in *Oxford Economic Papers*, vol. 47: 1, March 1995, pp. 24–44. The American Statistical Association and Allan W. Gregory and Gregor W. Smith for "Calibration as Testing: Inference in Simulated Macroeconomic Growth Models" in *Journal of Business and Economic Statistics*, vol. 9: 3, July 1991, pp. 297–303. University of Chicago Press Journals and Mark W. Watson for "Measures of Fit for Calibrated Models" in *Journal of Political Economy*, vol. 101: 6, December 1993, pp. 1011–1041. John Wiley & Sons Ltd and Fabio Canova for "Statistical Inference in Calibrated Models" in *Journal of Applied Econometrics*, 9, 1994, pp. 123–144. University of Pennsylvania and Fabio Canova for "Sensitivity Analysis and Model Evaluation in Simulated Dynamic General Equilibrium Economies" in *International Economic Review*, vol. 36: 2, May 1995, pp. 477–501. Reed Elsevier Plc and Finn E. Kydland and Edward C. Prescott for "Business Cycles: Real Facts and a Monetary Myth" in *Federal Reserve Bank of Minneapolis Quarterly Review*, vol. 14: 2, Spring 1990, pp. 3–18. University of Pennsylvania and Sumru Altuğ for "Time-to-Build and Aggregate Fluctuations", in *International Economic Review*, vol. 30: 4, November 1989, pp. 889–920.

Fabio Canova, M. Finn, and A.R. Pagan for "Evaluating a Real Business Cycle Model" © Colin P. Hargreaves1994, reprinted from *Nonstationary Time Series Analysis and Cointegration*, edited by C. Hargreaves (1994) by permission of Oxford University Press. Elsevier Science BV, The Netherlands and Robert G. King and Charles I. Plosser for "Real Business Cycles and the Test of the Adelmans" in *Journal of Monetary Economics*, vol. 33: 2, April 1989, pp. 405–438. Louisiana State University Press and James E. Hartley, Kevin D. Salyer and Steven M. Sheffrin for "Calibration and Real Business Cycle Models: An Unorthodox Experiment" in *Journal of Macroeconomics*, vol. 19: 1, Winter 1997, pp. 1–17. Elsevier Science BV, The Netherlands and Martin Eichenbaum for "Real Business Cycle Theory: Wisdom or Whimsy", *Journal of Economic Dynamics and Control*, vol. 15: 4, October 1991, pp. 607–626. MIT Press Journals and Robert M. Solow for "Technical Change and the Aggregate Production Function" in Review of Economics and Statistics, 39, August 1957, pp. 312–320. The American Economic Association and N. Gregory Mankiw for "Real Business Cycles: A New Keynesian Perspective" in *Journal of Economic Perspectives*, vol. 3: 3, Summer 1989, pp. 79–90. The American Economic Association and Zvi Griliches for "The Discovery of the Residual: A Historical Note", *Journal of Economic Literature*, vol. 34: 3, September 1996, pp. 1330–1334. The American Economic Association and Timothy Cogley and James M. Nason for "Output Dynamics in Real Business Cycle Models" in *American Economic Review*, vol. 85: 3, June 1995, pp. 492–511. Ohio State University Press and Robert J. Hodrick and Edward C. Prescott "Postwar US Business Cycles: An Empirical Investigation", in *Journal of Money Credit and Banking*, vol. 29: 1, February 1997, pp. 1–16. John Wiley & Sons Ltd and A.C. Harvey and A. Jaeger for "Detrending, Stylized Facts and the Business Cycle" in *Journal of Applied Econometrics*, 8, 1993, pp. 231–247. Elsevier Science BV and Timothy Cogley and James M. Nason for "Effects of the Hodrick-Prescott Filter on Trend and Difference Stationary Time Series: Implications for Business Cycle Research", *Journal of Economic Dynamics and Control*, vol. 19: 1–2, January-February 1995, pp. 253–278.

Part I

Introduction

Chapter 1

The limits of business cycle research

"That wine is not made in a day has long been recognized by economists." With that declaration in Kydland and Prescott's "Time to Build and Aggregate Fluctuations" (1982 [3]: 1345),* the real business cycle school was born. Like wine, a school of thought is not made in a day. Only after it has matured is it possible to judge whether it is good and to separate the palatable portions from the dregs. The literature on real business cycle models has now sufficiently aged, ready for the connoisseurs to pass judgment.

To facilitate those judgments, we have collected together in this volume thirty-one previously published articles relevant to real business cycle models. While there has been no shortage of commentaries on the real business cycle program, the commentaries have been widely scattered and have often focused on narrow aspects of the models or represented partisan positions. Until now, there has not been an easily accessible means for students of business cycles to assess the real business cycle program on the basis of the original sources from the perspectives of the critics as well as the proponents. To date, the most systematic accounts of the real business cycle program are found in the works of active proponents, particularly in Thomas Cooley's (ed.) *Frontiers of Business Cycle Research* (1995b), and in the programmatic manifestoes of Kydland and Prescott (1991 [12], 1996 [13]). Yet the critical literature is burgeoning.

The present volume brings together the important articles which make the case for and against real business cycle models. The articles begin with the classics of the real business cycle school, starting with Kydland and Prescott's (1982 [3]) seminal model. In addition, we include articles on the methodology of real business cycle models, particular aspects of the program (e.g., calibration, the measurement of technology shocks, methods of

---

* Throughout Chapters 1 and 2, the bold numbers in the square brackets within the text references refer to later chapters in this volume. However, all page numbers in these references are the page numbers from the original article.

detrending), as well as articles that attempt to evaluate the empirical success of the real business cycle model.

The real business cycle program is still a very active one. We therefore hope that this anthology will prove useful to students and professional macroeconomists working on real business cycle models — bringing some perspective to the literature and pointing the way to further research. As an aid to research, the articles are reprinted here as facsimiles rather than reset. The preservation of the original pagination, facilitating authoritative citations, more than compensates, we believe, for the loss of an aesthetically pleasing typographical consistency.

It is difficult for the neophyte in any area of economics to jump into the middle of a literature that was meant to advance the current interests of established economists, rather than a didactic purpose. In the remainder of this introductory chapter, we aim to provide a segue from the common knowledge of the advanced student of macroeconomics (or of the nonspecialist professional) to the essential elements of the real business cycle program. The objective is to provide a clear, accessible background to the literature that avoids unnecessary technical complications. At the same time, in this introductory essay we present our own assessment of the successes and failures of the real business cycle program. It is an assessment with which many economists will strongly disagree. We nevertheless hope that it will be easier for others to articulate their own assessments against the background of our effort. The articles reprinted in the volume provide the necessary raw materials.

The technical demands of real business cycle models are often very high. As a further aid to the neophyte reader of the literature, and to the potential user of the models, the second introductory chapter to the volume is a user's guide to real business cycle models, which provides a step-by-step account of how to formulate, solve, and simulate a real business cycle model.

So much for preliminaries; let us turn now to the background of the real business cycle program and to the assessment of its successes and failures.

I THE REAL BUSINESS CYCLE CONJECTURE

The philosopher of science Karl Popper (1959, 1972) argued that science progresses through a series of bold conjectures subjected to severe tests. Most conjectures are false and will be refuted. The truth, by definition, will survive the ordeal of testing and emerge unrefuted at the end of inquiry in an infinitely distant future. The boldest conjectures are often the most fruitful, because, making the strongest claims, they are the most readily refuted and their refutation narrows the universe of acceptable conjectures most rapidly. We argue that real business cycle models are bold conjectures in the Popperian mold and that, on the preponderance of the evidence (to use a legal phrase), they are refuted. It is not, however, straightforward to see this, because the real business cycle conjecture is advanced jointly with a claim that models should be assessed using a novel strategy. We must therefore evaluate the conjecture and the assessment strategy simultaneously.

Since the publication of Kydland and Prescott's "Time to Build and Aggregate Fluctuations" (1982 [3]), the paradigm real business cycle model, a large and active group of new classical macroeconomists have elaborated and developed the real business cycle model. As important as these developments are to the real business cycle program, none of them fundamentally affects the critical points that we will make.[1] Our assessment will, therefore, focus on the original Kydland and Prescott model and its successor models in a direct line. We will also refer frequently to the programmatic statements and methodological reflections of Kydland, Prescott and Lucas, the most articulate defenders of the aims and methods of equilibrium business cycle models.

(i) Equilibrium business cycles

To common sense, economic booms are good and slumps are bad. Economists have attempted to capture common sense in disequilibrium models: full employment is modeled as an equilibrium: that is, as a situation in which each worker's and each producer's preferences (given his or her constraints) are satisfied, while anything less than full employment represents a failure of workers or employers or both to satisfy their preferences. The real business cycle model is an extraordinarily bold conjecture in that it describes each stage of the business cycle — the trough as well as the peak — as an equilibrium (see, for example, Prescott, 1986a [4]: 21). This is not to say that workers and producers prefer slumps to booms. We all prefer good luck to bad.[2] Rather it is to deny that business cycles represent failures of markets to work in the most desirable ways. Slumps represent an undesired, undesirable, and unavoidable shift in the constraints that people face; but, given those constraints, markets react efficiently and people succeed in achieving the best outcomes that circumstances permit.

Some other models have come close to the real business cycle conjecture. Models of coordination failure treat booms and slumps as two equilibria and posit mechanisms that push the economy to one equilibrium or the other (e.g., Cooper and John, 1988; Bryant, 1983). Since the boom equilibrium is the more desirable, policies might seek to affect the mechanism in a way that improves the chances of ending in the boom state. The Phillips-curve models of Milton Friedman (1968) and Robert Lucas (1972, 1973) envisage people achieving their preferences conditional on an incorrect understanding of the true situation. Booms occur when workers believe that real wages are higher than they really are, inducing them to supply more labor than they would if they knew the truth; slumps occur when workers believe that real wages are lower than they really are. Were people fully informed, there would be no booms or slumps.[3]

The real business cycle model is starker. As with Lucas's monetary model, every stage of the business cycle is a Pareto-efficient equilibrium, but the source of the fluctuations is not misperceptions about prices or the money supply, but objective changes in aggregate productivity (so-called *technology shocks*). Thus, in the midst of a slump (i.e., a bad draw), given the objective situation and full information, every individual, and the economy as a whole, would choose to be in a slump.

Contrary to the claims of some proponents of the real business cycle (e.g., Hodrick and Prescott, 1997 [31]: 1), there is no pre-Keynesian historical precedent for viewing business cycles as equilibria. Kydland and Prescott (1991 [12]) see such a precedent in the business cycle models of Ragnar Frisch (1933), while Lucas (1977: 215; 1987: 47 *inter alia*) sees such a precedent in the work of Hayek (1933, 1935) and other members of the Austrian School. Hoover (1988, ch. 10; 1995 [15]) demonstrates that these precedents are, at best, superficial. Frisch's business cycle models are aggregative and do not involve individual optimization, even of a representative agent. Some Austrians reject the notion of equilibrium altogether. Hayek, who is not among these, accepts dynamic equilibrium as an ideal case, but sees business cycles as the result of mismatches of capital type and quantity to the needs of production transmitted to unemployment through a failure of wages and prices to adjust to clear markets in the short run — clearly a disequilibrium explanation.[4] The real business cycle model advances a novel conjecture as well as a bold one.

(ii) The novelty of the real business cycle model

Novel in their bold conjecture, real business cycle models nonetheless have precursors. The primary antecedent is Robert Solow's (1956, 1970) neoclassical growth model. In this model, aggregate output (Y) is produced according to a constant-returns-to-scale production function $\Phi(\bullet)$ using aggregate capital (K), aggregate labor (L), and a production technology indexed by Z:[5]

$$Y = \Phi(K, L, Z). \tag{1.1}$$

Consumption follows a simple Keynesian consumption function:

$$C = (1 - s)Y, \tag{1.2}$$

where s is the marginal propensity to save. Since Solow was interested in long-term growth, he ignored the aggregate demand pathologies that concerned earlier Keynesian economists and assumed that people's plans were coordinated so that savings (S) equaled investment (I) *ex ante* as well as *ex post*:

$$I = S. \tag{1.3}$$

Capital depreciates at rate δ and grows with investment:

$$\dot{K} = I - \delta K = sY - \delta K, \tag{1.4}$$

where $\dot{K}$ indicates the rate of change of capital. Labor grows exogenously at a rate n per cent per unit time, and labor-augmenting technology (Z) improves at a rate ζ percent per unit time, so that *effective labor* grows at $n + \zeta$.

Under these circumstances, the economy will converge to a *steady state* in which the growth of capital after compensating for depreciation is just enough to match the growth of effective labor. Along the steady-state growth path both capital and effective labor grow at a rate $n + \zeta$; and, since both inputs to production are growing at that steady rate, so is output itself.

In the Solow growth model we need to distinguish between equilibrium and steady state. The model is always in equilibrium, because *ex ante* savings always equals *ex ante* investment (equation (1.3)). But the model need not be in steady state (i.e., growing at $n + \zeta$). Any change in the data that drives the economy away from the steady state (for example, a change in s or n) will also produce changes in capital and output (adjustments to a new steady state), but the economy remains in continuous equilibrium along the adjustment path.

Lucas (1975) employed the Solow growth model to solve a difficulty in his own analysis of business cycles. Lucas (1972, 1973) explained the business cycle as the reaction of workers and producers to expectational errors induced by monetary policy. The difficulty was to explain why such expectational mistakes should not be corrected quickly so that business cycles were short week-to-week, month-to-month, or quarter-to-quarter fluctuations rather than the five- to six-year cycles typically observed. Lucas's solution was to distinguish, in Ragnar Frisch's (1933) useful terminology, between *impulses* that begin a business cycle and *propagation mechanisms* that perpetuate a cycle. Expectational errors were the impulses. These impulses drove the economy away from steady state. *Ex post* the economy was seen to be in disequilibrium until the expectational errors were corrected. But even when they had been corrected, the economy was returned to an equilibrium away from the steady state. The process of adjusting capital in order to regain the steady state would be a relatively slow one. This was the propagation mechanism.

In keeping with the new classical agenda of reducing macroeconomics to microeconomic foundations, Lucas replaced the stripped-down demand behavior of the Solow growth model with the assumption that the behavior of the aggregate economy can be described by the utility-maximizing choices of a *representative* agent, who chooses consumption and labor supply by solving a dynamic, intertemporal optimization problem. In effect, the simple consumption function (equation (1.2)) was replaced by a permanent-income (or life-cycle) consumption function, and investment was replaced by a neoclassical investment function in which the opportunity cost of capital determines the rate of investment. Unlike in the Solow model, the factors important to the savings decision now enter separately from those important to the investment decision. Aggregate demand pathologies are, nonetheless, impossible, because in Lucas's model the same agents make both the savings and the investment decision, which insures *ex ante* coordination, and the agents have *rational expectations*, which insures that mistakes about the future course of the economy are necessarily unsystematic. Furthermore, the supply of labor responds elastically to temporarily high real wages: workers make hay while the sun shines.

Kydland and Prescott's (1982 [3]) seminal real business cycle model is a direct outgrowth of Lucas's monetary growth model. It differs from the Lucas model in that there is no monetary sector; technology shocks (i.e., deviations of Z in equation (1.1) from trend) supply the impulse to business cycles. The model does not rely on expectational errors. There is no need. Lucas originally posited expectational errors as a way of permitting changes in the stock of money to have real effects on the economy without violating the assumption that money is neutral in the long run. In Kydland and Prescott's model, technological change has real effects regardless of whether it is anticipated. While some of the variability in aggregate output, consumption, investment, and labor supply in Kydland and Prescott's model is attributable to the unexpectedness of technology shocks, the aggregate variables would fluctuate even if technological change were perfectly anticipated.

In a recent summary of the real business cycle methodology, Kydland and Prescott (1997: 210) state that "we derive the business cycle implications of growth theory." Seen in context, this is misleading. Historically, it is not the use of the growth model that distinguishes the real business cycle model from earlier business cycle models. Rather it is finding the impulses in technology shocks, and modeling the economy in continuous equilibrium. Both in their theoretical development and (as we shall see presently) in their quantitative implementation, real business cycle models abstract from the traditional concerns of growth theory. They provide no analysis of the steady-state rate of growth at all, but take the factors that determine it as exogenously given.[6] Instead, the focus is on the deviations from the steady state. Only if growth theory were synonymous with *aggregate* general equilibrium models with an optimizing representative agent would it be fair to say that their behavior is the implication of growth theory. But

Solow's growth model is an example of an aggregate general equilibrium model that does not posit an optimizing representative agent. Technology shocks would be propagated in a Solow growth model, though rather slowly, for the convergence time to steady state is long in a realistically parameterized Solow model (cf. Sato, 1966). The characteristic business cycle behavior in real business cycle models comes from the shocks and from the optimizing model itself (of which more presently), rather than from the fact that these are embedded in a growth model.

(iii) A quantified idealization

Real business cycle models are implemented by giving specific functional forms to the equations of the optimal growth model. This is most easily seen for production; equation (1.1) is replaced by a specific function, very often the Cobb-Douglas production function:

$$Y = ZL^{\theta}K^{1-\theta}, \tag{1.1'}$$

where θ is the share of labor in national output. An equation such as (1.1') could be estimated as it stands or jointly with the other equations in the model to determine the value of θ. Real business cycle proponents do not typically estimate the parameters of their models. Instead, they assign values to them on the basis of information from sources outside the model itself. This is known as *calibration* of the model. The value chosen for θ is usually the average value that the labor share takes in suitably adapted national accounts.[7] The value of the depreciation rate (δ) is calibrated similarly. As we mentioned already equations (1.2) and (1.3), which represent aggregate demand in the Solow growth model, are replaced in real business cycle models by an optimization problem for a representative agent who is both consumer and producer. The representative agent maximizes a utility function:

$$U = U(\{C_t\}, \{L_t\}), \tag{1.5}$$

subject to current and future production constraints given by equation (1.1'), and linked together by equation (1.4), which governs the evolution of the capital stock. The set $\{C_t\}$ is the set of current and future levels of consumption, and $\{L_t\}$ is the set of current and future supplies of labor (the time subscript $t = 0, 1, 2, \ldots, \infty$). The utility function must be calibrated as well. This is usually done with reference to the parameters estimated in unrelated microeconomic studies.[8]

The calibrated model is nonlinear. To solve the model its equations are typically reformulated as linear approximations around the unknown steady state. This is the technical sense in which real business cycle models abstract from the concerns of traditional growth theory; for no explanation of the steady state is sought — the focus is on (equilibrium) deviations from the steady state. The solution to the linearized model is a set of linear equations for output, consumption, labor, and investment of the form:

$$y = \gamma_{11}z + \gamma_{12}k, \tag{1.6-1}$$
$$c = \gamma_{21}z + \gamma_{22}k, \tag{1.6-2}$$
$$l = \gamma_{31}z + \gamma_{32}k, \tag{1.6-3}$$
$$i = \gamma_{41}z + \gamma_{42}k, \tag{1.6-4}$$

where the lower-case letters are the deviations from steady state of the logarithms of the analogous upper-case variables. The coefficients γ_{ij} are combinations of the calibrated parameters determined by solving the model.[9]

The right-hand variables in equations (1.6–1) to (1.6–4) are called *state variables*. They summarize the past evolution of the model economy and are exogenous in the sense that the representative agent takes them as given data and conditions his choices upon them (z is exogenous and k is determined from choices made in previous periods). Equations (1.6–1) to (1.6–4) detail the outcomes of those choices, that is, how the preferences of the representative agent interact with the constraints he faces, including the current state of z and k, to determine output, capital, labor, and investment.

In the original Kydland and Prescott (1982 [3]) model, the technology shock, z, was modeled as a random process with parameters chosen to cause the model to mimic the variance of GNP in the US economy. Since z was artificial, there was no chance of direct period-by-period or historical comparisons of the modeled time series in equations (1.6–1) to (1.6–4)with their real-world equivalents. Kydland and Prescott, however, wished only to compare the covariances among the modeled time series to those among the actual series, so this did not seem problematic. Nevertheless, as Lucas (1987: 43–45; cf. Prescott, 1986b [6]: 31) noticed, *constructing* the predicted output series to mimic actual output does not provide an *independent* test of the model.[10] Beginning with Prescott (1986a [4]), real business cycle models have taken a different tack (cf. Kydland and Prescott, 1988). Solow (1957 [27]) attempted to quantify technical change by using a production function with constant returns to scale (such as equation (1.6)) to compute Z. Typically, real business cycle models use the Cobb-Douglas production function (equation (1.1')) as follows:

$$\log(Z) = \log(Y) - \theta\log(L) - (1 - \theta)\log(K). \tag{1.7}$$

This empirical measure of the technology parameter is known as the *Solow residual*. When estimated using actual data, the Solow residual, like the series used to compute it, has a trend (implying $\zeta \neq 0$), and so must be detrended before being used as an input to the real business cycle model. Detrended $\log(Z)$ is the state-variable z.[11]

(iv) The limits of idealization

The real business cycle model does not present a descriptively realistic account of the economic process, but a highly stylized or idealized account. This is a common feature of many economic models, but real business cycle practitioners are bold in their conjecture that such models nevertheless provide useful *quantifications* of the actual economy. While idealizations are inevitable in modeling exercises, they do limit the scope of the virtues one can claim for a model.

In particular, the real business cycle program is part of the larger new classical macroeconomic research program. Proponents of these models often promote them as models that provide satisfactory microfoundations for macroeconomics in a way that Keynesian models conspicuously fail to do (e.g., Lucas and Sargent, 1979). The claim for providing microfoundations is largely based on the fact that new classical models in general, and real business cycle models in particular, model the representative agent as solving a single dynamic optimization problem on behalf of all the consumers, workers, and firms in the economy. However, the claim that representative agent models are innately superior to other sorts of models is unfounded. There is no a priori reason to accord real business cycle models a presumption of accuracy because they look like they are based on microeconomics. Rather, there are several reasons to be theoretically skeptical of such models.[12]

Most familiar to economists is the problem of the fallacy of composition, which Samuelson's (1948) introductory economics text prominently addresses. It is difficult to deny that what is true for an individual may not be true for a group, yet, representative agent models explicitly embody the fallacy of composition. The central conceptual achievement of *political* economy was to analogize from the concerns of Robinson Crusoe — alone in the world — to those of groups of people meeting each other in markets. The complexities of economics from Adam Smith's invisible hand to Arrow and Debreu's general equilibrium model and beyond have largely been generated from the difficulties of coordinating the behavior of millions of individuals. Some economists have found the source of business cycles precisely in such coordination problems. By completely eliminating even the possibility of problems relating to coordination, representative agent models are inherently incapable of modeling such complexities.

Problems of aggregation are similar to problems arising from the fallacy of composition. Real business cycle models appear to deal with disaggregated agents, but, in reality, they are aggregate models in exactly the same way as the Keynesian models upon which they are meant to improve. The conditions under which a representative agent could legitimately represent the aggregate consequences of, and be deductively linked to, the behavior individuals are too stringent to be fulfilled: essentially all agents must be alike in their marginal responses.[13] Because it is impracticable, no one has ever tried to derive the aggregate implications of 260 million people attempting to solve private optimization problems. The real business cycle model thus employs the formal mathematics of microeconomics, but applies it in a theoretically inappropriate circumstance: it provides the simulacrum of microfoundations, not the genuine article. It is analogous to modeling the behavior of a gas by a careful analysis of a single molecule *in vacuo*, or, of a crowd of people by an analysis of the actions of a single android. For some issues, such models may work well; for many others, they will miss the point completely.[14]

A significant part of the rhetorical argument for using real business cycle methodology is an appeal to general equilibrium theory. However, because the models do not reach a microfoundational goal of a separate objective function for every individual and firm, the models are at best highly idealized general equilibrium models. Real business cycle theorists do not appear to be aware of the degree to which this undermines certain sorts of claims that can be made for their models. The fact that they do not provide genuine microfoundations essentially removes any prior claims that real business cycle models are superior to Keynesian or other aggregate models.

It is not difficult to understand why general equilibrium theory has such allure for economists in general and macroeconomists in particular. The theory provides for an extensive model of the economy with individual consumers maximizing utility and individual firms maximizing profits, all interacting in competitive markets, and despite all this complexity, it can be shown that an equilbrium exists. However, knowing that an equilibrium point exists is all well and fine, but it doesn't get you very far. What else can we tell about the economy from the general equilibrium framework? The answer to that question turned out to be quite depressing; as Kirman (1989) subtitled a paper about this state of affairs, "The Emperor Has No Clothes."

After showing that an equilibrium point existed, people became interested in the question of whether it could be shown that the equilibrium was either unique or stable. In order to answer this question, the shape of the aggregate excess demand curve had to be determined. In a remarkable series of papers, Sonnenschein (1973, 1974), Mantel (1974, 1976), Debreu (1974) and Mas-Colell (1977) showed that in an economy in which every individual has a well-behaved excess demand function, the only restrictions on the aggregate excess demand function are that it is continuous, homogenous of degree zero in prices, and satisfies Walras' Law. *Nothing* else can be inferred. Any completely arbitrary function satisfying those three properties can be an aggregate excess demand function for an economy of well-behaved individuals. Having an economy in which every single agent obeys standard microeconomic rules of behavior tells us virtually nothing about the aggregate economy. For example, not even something as basic as the Weak Axiom of Revealed Preference carries over from the microeconomic level to the macroeconomic level. (See Shafer and Sonnenschein (1982) for a complete, technical discussion of this literature and Kirman (1989) or Ingrao and Israel (1990) for good nontechnical discussions.)

The implication can be stated in two ways. Even if we know that the microeconomy is well behaved, we know very little about the aggregate excess demand function. Or, given a completely arbitrary aggregate excess demand function satisfying the three characteristics above, we can find a well-behaved microeconomy that generates that aggregate function.

Kirman's (1992) article in the *Journal of Economic Perspectives* was largely centered on showing how these results invalidated the use of a representative agent model. There is simply no theoretical justification for assuming that the excess demand function of a representative agent bears any resemblance to the excess demand function for an aggregate economy. If we want to justify the notion that macroeconomics needs microfoundations by pointing to general equilibrium theory, then these results derived by general equilibrium theorists unambiguously demonstrate that the representative agent is flawed. Oddly, we seem to be simultaneously seeing a situation in which macroeconomists point to general equilibrium theory as a justification for representative agent models at the same time as general equilibrium theorists are prominently noting that the representative agent has no home in the theory.

Thus the implicit claim in real business cycle theory that their representative agent models provide rigorous microfoundations is incorrect. Starting with first principles, or general equilibrium theory, only, we can derive all sorts of macroeconomics. Some form of *aggregate* structure must be provided.

Beyond this, Kydland and Prescott argue that the models are designed to capture some features of the economy while ignoring or even distorting other features. They hold this to be one of their virtues, and argue that their failure to capture features that they were not designed to model should not count against them (Kydland and Prescott, 1991 [12]). We take this claim seriously. It should, nevertheless, be noted that it undermines the argument that we trust the answers which the models give us on some dimensions because they have been successful on other dimensions (Lucas, 1980: 272). Kydland and Prescott (1996 [13]: 72) make exactly this claim with regard to using the Solow growth model to explore the business cycle. However, if the dimensions on which we need answers are ones on which, because of their idealized natures, the models are false, the success on other dimensions is irrelevant. As a point of logic, rigorous deductions are useful only if they start with true premises.[15] Idealized models are useful because they are tractable, but only if they remain true in the features relevant to the problem at hand. Kydland and Prescott want idealized real business cycle models to provide quantitative conclusions about the economy. There is nothing in their construction that insures that they will succeed in doing so.

Thus, part of the boldness of the real business cycle conjecture is the seriousness with which it takes the idealization of a representative agent. Although economists, at least since Alfred Marshall, have sometimes used representative agents as a modeling tool, new classical (and real business cycle) models expect the representative agent to deliver far more than earlier economists thought possible. For example, Friedman's (1957) explication of the permanent-income hypothesis begins with something that looks like a representative agent, but Friedman uses the agent only as a means of thinking through what sorts of variables belong in the aggregate consumption function. He makes no attempt to derive an aggregate consumption function from his agent; in fact, he takes pains to note how different the aggregate function will look from the individual's function.

Real business cycle models, on the other hand, take the functions of the representative agent far more seriously, arguing that "we deduce the quantitative implications of theory for business cycle fluctuations" (Kydland and Prescott, 1997: 211). However, for the reasons described above, these deductions are not the rigorous working out of microeconomic principles combined with a serious analysis of heterogeneity and aggregation.

There is nothing in the construction of real business cycle models which insures that they will succeed in providing accurate quantitative conclusions. There is nothing that guarantees a priori their superiority. The proof of the pudding is in the eating: the real business cycle model must be tested and evaluated empirically.

II TESTING

(i) What are the facts about business cycles?

Before real business cycle models can be tested, we must know precisely what they are meant to explain. Following Prescott (1986a [4]), advocates of real business cycle models have redefined the explanandum of business cycles. As observed already, common sense and the traditional usage of most economists holds that recessions are periods in which the economy is suboptimally below its potential. Business cycle theory has thus traditionally tried to explain what causes output to fall and then rise again. To be sure, this is not just a matter of output declining: when output declines, one expects employment, income, and trade to decline as well, and these declines to be widespread across different sectors.[16] Nevertheless, the central fact to be explained was believed to be the decline and the subsequent recovery, and not the comovements of aggregate time series.

Even before the first real business cycle models, new classical macroeconomics shifted the focus to the comovements. Sargent (1979: 256) offers one definition: "the business cycle is the phenomenon of a number of important economic aggregates (such as GNP, unemployment and lay-offs) being characterized by high pairwise covariances at the low business cycle frequencies [two- to eight-year range]. . . . This definition captures the notion of the business cycle as being a condition symptomizing the common movements of a set of aggregates." Lucas (1977: 217) argues that the movements of any single economic aggregate are irregular, and "[t]hose regularities which are observed are in the *comovements* among different aggregative time series."[17]

Real business cycle models view the business cycle in precisely the same way as Sargent and Lucas. The things to be explained are the correlations between time series, and the typical assessment of the success or failure of a model is to compare the correlations of the actual time series to those that result from simulating the model using artificially generated series for the technology shock (Z). Formal statistical measures of the closeness of the model data to the actual data are eschewed. Prescott (1986a [4]), for example, takes the fact that the model approximates much of the behavior of the actual aggregates as an indicator of its success. In the case in which the model data predict an empirical elasticity of output to labor greater than the theory, Prescott (1986a [4]: 21) argues "[a]n important part of this deviation could very well disappear if the economic variables were measured more in conformity with theory. That is why I argue that theory is now ahead of business cycle measurement."

Kydland and Prescott (1990 [20]) make similar arguments in opposing "business cycle facts" to "monetary myths." For example, the real business cycle model predicts that the real wage is procyclical: a positive technology shock (an upward shift of the production function), which is a positive impulse to output, increases the marginal product of labor, and workers are paid their marginal products. In contrast, monetary business cycle models (Keynesian and monetarist) predict countercyclical real wages: a monetary shock, which is a positive impulse to output, increases aggregate demand and therefore the demand for labor, which requires a lower marginal product of labor (a movement along the production function). Kydland and Prescott (1990 [20]: 13–14) argue that a correlation of 0.35 between money lagged one period and current output is too low to support the view that money leads output; while a correlation of 0.35 between the real wage and output is high enough to support the view that the real wage is procyclical. They argue that if measurements were made in closer conformity to theory, the second correlation would be higher.[18] But, even as it stands, they take the "business cycle facts" as supporting the real business cycle model.

Theory may be ahead of measurement. It is well understood that as science progresses, theoretical advances improve measurements. Thermo-meters were originally atheoretical devices that rested on some simple untested assumptions, such as the linearity of the relationship between temperature and the expansion of materials. In time, as the theory of heat developed, better thermometers were possible because theoretical understanding permitted corrections for departures from the initial assumptions and new methods of measurement that, among other things, permitted the range of temperature measurements to be increased to near absolute zero, at one end, and to millions of degrees, at the other.

Given the best data in the world, however, simply mimicking the data is a weak test. Indeed, logically it is fallacious to argue that theory A implies that data behave as B, data in fact behave as B, therefore A is true. This is the fallacy of *affirming the consequent*. It is a fallacy because there is nothing to rule out incompatible theories C, D, and E also implying B. Popper's concentration on refutations is a reaction to this fallacy in the form in which it was exposed by David Hume (1739): there is no logic that allows one to move inductively from particular instances to a general rule; there is no inductive logic analogous to deductive logic. It is a correct inference that theory A implies data behavior B, data fail to behave as B, therefore A is false. At best, the data limit the class of theories that are acceptable. One learns very little from knowing that a theory mimics the data — especially if it was designed to mimic the data. One needs to know that the data cannot be mimicked by rival theories. Although real business cycle models are often shown (without any formal metric) to mimic actual data, they have rarely been tested against rivals.[19]

It is usually regarded as a more stringent test of a model that it performs well on a set of data different from the one used in its formulation. Most often this means that models are formulated on one sample and then tested against a completely different sample. Kydland and Prescott (1997: 210) offer a different argument: real business cycle models are formulated using the "stylized facts" of *long-run growth theory* and are then tested, not against a completely different data set, but for their ability to mimic the *short-run business cycle behavior* of the same data. While there is clearly merit in deriving empirically supported implications of one set of facts for another, this particular test provides very weak support for the real business cycle model. Many models that are fundamentally different from the real business cycle model, in that they posit neither continuous equilibrium nor impulses arising from technology shocks, are consistent with the "stylized facts" of growth (e.g., the constancy of the labor share in national income or the constancy of the capital–output ratio).[20]

(ii) Do real business cycle models fit the facts?

Although it is a weak test to check whether models mimic the facts, it is a useful starting point. The fact that real business cycle models are idealized presents some difficulties in judging them even on such a standard. As

Kydland and Prescott (1991 [12]: 169) stress, the real business cycle model is unrealistic in the sense that it aims only to capture certain features of the data rather than to provide a complete explanation. The econometric ideal is to provide predictions of dependent variables on the basis of all of the relevant independent variables, so that whatever errors are left are truly random and independent of any omitted variables. In contrast, real business cycle models are driven by a single variable, the technology shock, and aim to explain the relationships among a number of series (as in equations (1.6–1) to (1.6–4)) on the basis of this single shock. The success of the model is to be judged, in Kydland and Prescott's view, on its ability to capture selected correlations in the actual data. There is no claim that it will do well in explaining correlations it was not designed to capture; nor is there any claim that its errors will be truly random, either in being mean zero and symmetrically (e.g., normally) distributed or in being independent from omitted variables.

The dilemma is this: Theories are interpretable, but too simple to match all features of the data; rich econometric specifications are able to fit the data, but cannot be interpreted easily. The coefficients of a statistically well-specified econometric equation indicate the effects on the dependent variable *ceteris paribus* of a change in the independent variables. In general, these effects depend in a complicated way on the parameters of the deep relations that connect the variables together and generate the observed data. Lucas (1976) in his famous "critique" of policy analysis noticed the lack of autonomy of econometrically estimated coefficients and argues, in particular, that the values of the coefficients would not remain stable in the face of changes in monetary and fiscal policy regimes.

One solution to the Lucas critique might be to identify the complex structure of the estimated coefficients. Hansen and Sargent (1980) map out a strategy for doing this. Essentially, the model is taken to be true and used, in the classic manner of textbook econometric identification, to disentangle the "deep" parameters (i.e., the parameters of the theory) from the estimated coefficients.[21] The central difficulty with this strategy as a means of providing support for real business cycle models is that it does not work. In the case in which the model imposes more relationships among the parameters than there are parameters to identify, the model is said to be over-identified. Statistical tests can be used to assess whether these redundant relationships can be rejected empirically. Altuğ (1989 [21]) estimated an econometric version of the real business cycle model and tested its over-identifying restrictions. They were clearly rejected. This should not be surprising. An idealized model abstracts from too many of the features of the world for the resulting specification to meet the econometric ideal. Not only is it likely that the errors will not show irreducible randomness and the appropriate symmetry, but they are unlikely to be independent of omitted variables. One may, of course, add additional variables into the regression equations. An econometric specification with many free parameters (i.e., many independent variables) will invariably fit better than a calibrated business cycle model. But then one loses the mapping of the theory onto the estimated coefficients that helped to disentangle the deep parameters.

Kydland and Prescott advocate a second solution: eschew econometric estimation altogether. They believe that the advantage of the calibrated model is that it refers to theoretically interpretable parameters, so that counterfactual experiments can be given precise meanings: for example, the effects of a change in the persistence of the technology shock or in the relative risk aversion of consumers or, in richer real business cycle models, of government-policy rules (e.g., tax rates) have precise analogues in the calibrated model. A good model, in Kydland and Prescott's view, is unrealistic, in the sense that it will not fit the data in the manner of a statistically well-specified econometric model, but it will fit with respect to certain features of interest. Calibration and model structure are adjusted until the models do well against those features of the data that are of interest.

The development of the labor market in early real business cycle models provides an illustration of the strategy. Table 1.1 reproduces from Hansen (1985 [8]) some statistics for actual data and data generated from simulating two real business cycle models. Model I is a simple model similar to Kydland and Prescott (1982 [3]) in which labor is supplied in continuously variable amounts. The standard deviations of hours worked and productivity are nearly equal in Model I; while, in the actual data, hours worked are over 50 percent more variable. Model II is a modification of Model I in which, to capture the fact that workers typically must either work a full day or not work, labor must be supplied in indivisible eight-hour units. Model II was created in part as an attempt to add realism to capture a feature that was not well described in Model I. In fact, it succeeds rather too well: hours are nearly three times as variable as productivity in Model II. Further developments of the real business cycle model (see, e.g., Hansen and Wright, 1992 [9]) aim in part to refine the ability to mimic the data on this point.

A serious case can be made for choosing Kydland and Prescott's strategy for dealing with the Lucas critique and favoring idealized models at the expense of achieving the econometric ideal of complete description of the data (see Hoover, 1995 [15]). The gain is that one preserves theoretical interpretability — though only at the cost of a limited understanding of the actual economy. Real business cycle modelers might respond that the choice is between limited understanding and no genuine understanding at all. But this would be too glib. There are at least two barriers to declaring the triumph of the real business cycle approach on the basis of the methodological virtues of idealization.

Table 1.1. Summary statistics for actual US data and for two real business cycle models

| | Actual US data | | Artificial economy | | | |
| | 1953.3–1984.1 | | Divisible labor | | Indivisible labor | |
Series	Standard deviation	Correlation with output	Standard deviation	Correlation with output	Standard deviation	Correlation with output
Output	1.76	1.00	1.35 (0.16)	1.00 (0.00)	1.76 (0.21)	1.00 (0.00)
Consumption	1.29	0.85	0.42 (0.06)	0.89 (0.03)	0.51 (0.08)	0.87 (0.04)
Investment	8.60	0.92	4.24 (0.51)	0.99 (0.00)	5.71 (0.70)	0.99 (0.00)
Capital stock	0.63	0.04	0.36 (0.07)	0.06 (0.07)	0.47 (0.10)	0.05 (0.07)
Hours	1.66	0.76	0.70 (0.08)	0.98 (0.01)	1.35 (0.16)	0.98 (0.01)
Productivity	1.18	0.42	0.68 (0.08)	0.98 (0.01)	0.50 (0.07)	0.87 (0.03)

Source: Hansen (1985 [8]), table 1; standard deviations in parentheses.

First, most of the assessments of the success or failure of real business cycle models have been made in the casual manner exemplified by our previous discussion of Hansen's (1985 [8]) divisible and indivisible labor models, using data no more precise than that of Table 1.1. The standard is what might be called "aesthetic R^2": whether Models I or II in Table 1.1 are too far from the actual data or close enough is a purely subjective judgment without a good metric.

One response might be that no formal metric is possible, but that a more rigorous subjective evaluation would go some way to providing the missing standards. King and Plosser (1989 [23]) take this tack. They revive the method of Adelman and Adelman (1959), first used to evaluate the Klein–Goldberger econometric macromodel. King and Plosser simulate data from a real business cycle model and evaluate it using the business cycle dating procedures developed by Burns and Mitchell at the National Bureau of Economic Research. These techniques aim to characterize the repetitive features of the economy by averaging over historical business cycles normalized to a notional cycle length.[22] Both the actual data and the simulated data from the real business cycle model are processed using Burns and Mitchell's procedures. King and Plosser observe that it is difficult to discriminate between these two sets of data. But they note that the results "leave us uncomfortable," because the same claims can be made on behalf of the Keynesian Klein–Goldberger model. Despite the greater detail in this study compared to typical assessments of real business cycle models, it is still wedded to aesthetic R^2.

In a similar vein, Hartley, Salyer, and Sheffrin (1997 [24]) examine the ability of the standard informal methods of assessment of real business cycle models to discriminate between alternative accounts of the actual economy. Hartley *et al.* use the Fair macroeconometric model of the US economy, a model in the tradition of Keynesian macroeconomic forecasting models such as the Brookings model or the Federal Reserve–University of Pennsylvania–Social Science Research Council model, to simulate data for a "Keynesian" economy in which demand shocks and disequilibrium are important.[23] Calibrating a real business cycle to be consistent with the relevant parameters of the Fair model, they ask whether the real business cycle model, which is driven by technology shocks (these are calculated from the simulated data from the Fair model) and continuous equilibrium, can mimic a "Keynesian" economy. They find out that it can to at least as high a degree as it mimics the actual economy on the usual standards used by real business cycle modelers. One interpretation of this result is that it is very bad news for the real business cycle model, because it shows that it has no power of discrimination; its key assumptions do not restrict the sort of economies it can fit.

A real business cycle modeler, however, might riposte that the Fair model is a typical Keynesian model with many free parameters, so that it gives a good statistical description of the economy, even as it fails to model the true underlying mechanisms. Thus the fact that the real business cycle model "works" for simulations from the Fair model means nothing more than that it works for the actual economy. To check this interpretation, Hartley *et al.* alter two key parameters, those governing the interest elasticities of money demand and investment, changes which makes the simulations of the Fair model (particularly, the cross-correlations stressed by real business cycle analysts) behave more like European economies than like the US economy (see Backus and Kehoe, 1992). The real business cycle model is poor at mimicking the data from the altered Fair model. One might conclude that the real business cycle model is, in fact, discriminating. However, for a modeling strategy that takes pride in its grounding in fundamental and universal economic theory (the Solow growth model is not country-specific), this is hardly an attractive conclusion. Although European business cycles may be substantially different from American business cycles because of important institutional differences, real business cycle models typically seek to explain business cycles abstracting from those very institutional details.

A second barrier to declaring the triumph of the real business cycle model on the basis of the methodological virtues of idealization is that, even if idealized models cannot be expected to fit as well as traditional econometric specifications under the best of circumstances, the conclusion that econometric estimation is irrelevant to the real business cycle model would be unwarranted. Calibration might be regarded as a form of estimation (Gregory and Smith, 1990; 1991 [16]). The problem is how to judge the performance of calibrated models against an empirical standard. Watson (1993 [17]) develops an asymmetrical measure of goodness of fit that is useful for real business cycle models precisely because their idealized nature makes it likely that the errors in fitting them to actual data are systematic rather than random. Even using his goodness of fit measure, Watson fails to produce evidence of high explanatory power for real business cycle models.

Kydland and Prescott's (1991 [12]) objection to traditional econometrics, what they call the "systems of equations" approach, is that an idealized model will not provide the necessary restrictions to permit the accurate estimation of its own parameters on actual data, because of the many features of the data that it systematically and intentionally ignores. Canova, Finn and Pagan (1994 [22]) undertake a somewhat less demanding test. Where Altuğ (1989 [21]) had tested restrictions that were strong enough to identify all the parameters of the real business cycle model and, therefore, to eliminate the need for calibration, Canova *et al.* examine the implications of a previously calibrated real business cycle model for the dynamic behavior of various time series. They observe that the various time series can be described by a *vector autoregression (VAR)* in which each series is regressed on its own lagged values and the lagged values of each of the other series. What is more, if the real business cycle model is an accurate description of the actual data, then a number of restrictions must hold among the estimated parameters of the VAR.

The real business cycle model implies three sets of restrictions on the VAR of two distinct types. First, various time series should be *cointegrated*. Two series are cointegrated when a particular linear combination of them is stationary (i.e., when its mean, variance, and higher moments are constant), even though the series are not separately stationary. There are two sets of such cointegration restrictions: (1) the state variables (the analogues of Z and K, the non-detrended counterparts to the state variables in equations (1.6–1) to (1.6–4)) must stand in particular linear relationships; (2) state variables and predicted values for various time series (e.g., the left-hand variables in equations (1.6–1) to (1.6–4)) to must also stand in particular linear relationships. Finally, once one has accounted for the cointegrating relationships among these time series and concentrates on their behavior about their common trends, there is a third set of restrictions (second type), which are the particular implications of the real business cycle model for the parameters of the VAR.

Canova *et al.* use a calibrated real business cycle model with a considerably richer specification than Kydland and Prescott's early models to derive the necessary restrictions on the VAR. These restrictions are then compared to the data. Canova *et al.* show that the restrictions do not hold. A particularly interesting finding is that the real business cycle model imputes too much importance to the productivity shock.

Canova *et al.*'s imposition of a specific numerical calibration of the real business cycle model might limit the generality of their results: it might be said that the real business cycle model is correct in principle, but Canova *et al.* have failed to calibrate it correctly. In defense of their test, their choice of parameters is not at all atypical. What is more, they examine a limited range of alternative choices of parameters, asking the question: What parameters would it take to make the model agree with the data? Their results along these lines, however, are not nearly as comprehensive as they would need to be to close the case.

Eichenbaum (1991 [25]) examines the issue of parameter choice more systematically. He begins by noting that the numerical values of the underlying parameters used to calibrate a real business cycle model are simply estimates of the true values. We do not *know* the true values of things like the depreciation rate or the variance of the shock to the Solow residual. Instead, we estimate these numbers from sample data, and there is a sampling error associated with every estimate. (Hansen and Heckman, 1996 [14]: 95, make a similar argument.)

Eichenbaum finds that altering most of the parameters within the range of their sampling error does little to alter the behavior of the real business cycle model. The notable exceptions are the parameters associated with the Solow residual, which have large standard errors. He finds that at standard levels of statistical significance (5 percent critical values), technology shocks may account for as little as 5 percent and as much as 200 percent of the variance in output. Eichenbaum's results suggest that, even if real business cycle models had no other problems, we cannot reject the view that technology shocks in conjunction with a real business cycle model explain only a small fraction of aggregate fluctuations.

Although not decisive, conventional econometric tests of real business cycle models are not kind to the theory. Canova et al.'s investigation of alternative real business cycle specifications, like Hartley et al.'s investigation of alternative data-generating processes, reminds us that no test of the real business cycle is likely on its own to provide a decisive Popperian refutation. The very fact that the models are idealized implies that the actual data alone provide at best a weak standard. More important than simply fitting the data is the *relative* performance of alternative models. Canova et al. and Hartley et al. push in the right direction, though not terribly far. Of course, the advocates of real business cycle models have always judged them relatively against other models in their class. Hansen's (1985 [8]) model with indivisible labor was judged superior to his model with divisible labor. Cooley and Hansen (1989 [11]) present a real business cycle model with a monetary sector and additional monetary shocks; Christiano and Eichenbaum (1992 [10]) present one with a government sector and fiscal policy shocks. Other models have included household production (Benhabib, Rogerson, and Wright, 1991) or variable capacity utilization (Greenwood, Hercowitz, and Huffman, 1988).

All of these models, however, retain the common core of the original Kydland and Prescott real business cycle model. The only substantial comparison between a real business cycle model and one with quite different principles of construction is found in Farmer's (1993) model of an economy with increasing returns to scale and shocks to "animal spirits." In Farmer's model there are multiple equilibria. The economy ends up in one equilibrium or another depending upon the self-fulfilling expectations of consumers. Farmer argues that his model performs better than the real business cycle model using Kydland and Prescott's standard of mimicking the relative correlations of actual data. He also claims that his model captures the dynamics of the economy more accurately. He estimates vector autoregressions for the actual economy and then uses the estimated equations to generate the path the economy would follow as the result of shocks to the various variables (i.e., *impulse response functions*). He then compares the impulse response functions of the real business cycle model and of his model with multiple equilibria to each other and to those of the estimated VARs. He finds that the impulse responses of the real business cycle model are very different from his model and that his model is more like those from the VAR. Once again, the appeal is to aesthetic R^2. Further work on standards of comparison is much to be desired.[24]

(iii) Testing the elements of the real business cycle model: the impulse mechanism

Rather than assessing the performance of the real business cycle model directly against the data, we can ask how well its fundamental components succeed. As we noted earlier, one of two distinguishing features of the real business cycle model is that it locates the impulse to business cycles in technology shocks. The overarching question is: What evidence do we have that technology shocks are the principal impulse driving the business cycle?

Before we can answer that question, however, another more basic one must be answered: What are technology shocks? This is a question that has plagued real business cycle research from the beginning (see, e.g., Summers, 1986 [5]). At the formal level, technology shocks are just the deviations of the parameter Z in the aggregate production function (e.g., equations (1.1) or (1.1') above) from its steady-state growth path: we represented these shocks earlier as z. By analogy to the microeconomic production function for individual products, one might naturally interpret z as a measure of physical technique or organizational ability.

An aggregate measure should average out shocks to particular technology, so that z should measure shocks that have widespread effects across the economy. Such averaging should reduce the variability of the aggregate shocks relative to the underlying shocks to individual technologies. However, in order to make the real business cycle model match the variability of US output, the technology shocks must be relatively large and persistent: Kydland and Prescott (1982 [3]) model z as an autoregressive process with a half-life of about 14 quarters and a standard deviation of 2.9 percent of trend real per capita GDP. Our calculations for the period 1960:1 to 1993:1 are similar, yielding a standard deviation for z of 2.8 percent and for GDP per capita of 4.4 percent about trend.

Although technology is improving over time, Kydland and Prescott's assumptions about the variability of z imply that technology must sometimes regress. But as Calomiris and Hanes (1995: 369–70) write: "Technological regress does not appear to correspond to any event in Western economic history since the fall of the Roman Empire." Elsewhere they point to the large literature on the introduction and diffusion of particularly important technologies through history: even for such crucial technological developments as the steam engine, the electric motor, and the railroad, the speed of diffusion is relatively slow, so that new technologies take decades rather than quarters to spread through the economy. Calomiris and Hanes (1995: 369):

conclude that the diffusion of any one technological innovation could not increase aggregate productivity by more than a trivial amount from one year to the next. If no single innovation can make much of a difference, it seems extremely unlikely that the aggregate rate of improvement could vary *exogenously* over cyclical frequencies to an important degree.

In the face of such objections, proponents of real business cycle models have broadened the scope of technology to include "changes in the legal and regulatory system within a country" (Hansen and Prescott, 1993 [26]: 281). Fair enough; such changes may be important to the economy and may plausibly be negative; but are they likely to justify quarter-to-quarter variation in z of the required amount? Furthermore, as Calomiris and Hanes (1995: 370) point out, regulatory and legal intervention in the US economy was substantially smaller before World War I when business cycles themselves were more variable.[25]

Debates over the size and frequency of technology shocks are difficult to resolve because the shocks are not directly observable. Real business cycle models have largely adopted the biblical criterion "by their fruits ye shall know them" and used the Solow residual (equation (1.7) above) as a proxy for technology shocks. The Solow residual attributes to technology any change in output that cannot be explained by changes in factor inputs. Jorgenson and Griliches (1967) and Griliches (1996 [29]) point out that the Solow residual measures more than underlying technological change (a fact recognized by Solow, 1957 [27]: 312, himself), picking up among other things variability in capital utilization and labor hoarding.[26] Summers (1986 [5]) and Mankiw (1989 [28]) reiterate these points in the context of real business cycle models. Hall (1986, 1990) notes that calibrating the parameters of the Cobb–Douglas production function (equation (1.1′)), θ and $(1-\theta)$, as the shares of labor and capital in output in the calculation of the Solow residual (as in equation (1.7)) requires the assumption of perfect competition so that firms and workers are paid their marginal products and factor shares exactly exhaust output. But if firms have market power so that price exceeds marginal cost, factor shares will no longer coincide with the technological parameters θ and $(1-\theta)$, and z will reflect variations in markups across the business cycle as well as true technology shocks. Hall (1990) also demonstrates that if there are increasing returns to scale, the Solow residual will move with things other than pure technology shocks.

Jorgenson, Griliches and Hall conclude that the Solow residual captures a great deal besides technology. Hartley (1994) provides evidence that the Solow residual may not reliably capture even genuine technology shocks. The evidence is found in simulated economies constructed using Hansen and Sargent's (1990) flexible, dynamic linear-quadratic equilibrium macromodel. This model permits a richer specification of the underlying production technology than typical of real business cycle models: there are multiple sectors, including intermediate and final goods, and parameters representing multiple aspects of the production process. Hartley was able to generate series for output, capital, and labor based on shocks to specific parts of the production process. Because these were simulations, he could be assured that the variability in these series reflected only technology shocks and not market power, labor hoarding, and the like. He then calculated Solow residuals from the simulated series using equation (1.7) and asked whether these accurately reflected the size and direction of the underlying true technology shocks. For a wide range of plausible parameters, Hartley found an extremely low correlation between his controlled technology shocks and the calculated Solow residuals. Often the correlation was not even positive. The failure of the Solow residual to capture the underlying process accurately appears to reflect the fact that the Cobb–Douglas production function, implicit in the calculation of Solow residuals, is a poor approximation to the rich production details of Hansen and Sargent's model: the Solow residuals largely reflect specification error, rather than technological change on a quarter-by-quarter horizon. Hansen and Sargent's model is rich relative to the typical idealized real business cycle model, but is itself an extreme idealization of the real production process. Hartley's simulation results, a fortiori, call the Solow residual into question as a measure of actual technology shocks.

(iv) Testing the elements of the real business cycle model: the propagation mechanism

The propagation mechanism of a business cycle model should transmit and amplify the impulses to the various cyclical aggregates. Together with the shocks themselves it should account for the pattern of fluctuations in each series and for their comovements. Real output is generally taken as the marker series for the business cycle. The balance of evidence is that real business cycle models add relatively little to the pattern of fluctuations in real output beyond what is implicit in the technology shocks themselves. Watson (1993 [17]) uses spectral analysis to decompose the power of the real business cycle model to match movements in output at different frequencies or (equivalently) time horizons. He finds that the spectral power of the real business cycle model is high at low frequencies (corresponding to trend or long-term growth behavior), but low at business cycle frequencies (approximately two to eight years). Cogley and Nason (1995b [30]) compare the dynamic pattern of the technology shocks fed into the real business cycle model with the predicted time series for output generated by the model. Again, they find that it is the dynamic properties of the exogenous inputs that determine the properties of the output, with the model itself contributing almost nothing. In one sense, these results should not be surprising: the Solow growth model, the foundational model of the real business cycle model, was originally meant to capture secular change. It is bold to conjecture that, unaltered, it would also model the business cycle. What is more surprising is that it took relatively long to document its low value-added with respect to business cycles.

Part of the reason that the real business cycle model has appeared to do well is that its proponents — sometimes for good methodological reasons — have relied on standards of assessment that are not particularly discriminating and have failed to develop more discriminating ones (see section II (ii) above). Part of the reason has to do with the standard practices of real business cycle models with respect to handling data. The real business cycle model predicts values for output, consumption, investment, and other time series expressed as deviations from the steady state. In order to compare these with actual data, an estimate of the steady state must be removed from these variables, which typically are trending. The Solow growth model suggests that all these variables should grow at rates related to the steady-state growth rate. Unfortunately, that is not observable. In practice, real business cycle models follow one of two strategies to generate detrended data. They sometimes remove a constant exponential trend, which is linear in the logarithm of the series, and so is known as *linear* detrending (e.g., King, Plosser and Rebelo, 1988 [7]). This would be precisely correct if the growth model were in fact true and the rate of growth of the labor force (n) and of technology (ζ) were constant over time, so that the steady-state growth rate ($n + \zeta$) were also constant over time. But there is no reason to think that this is so. An alternative strategy is to use a slowly varying trend that effectively allows the steady-state growth rate to be variable. This is the most popular option and it is typically implemented using the Hodrick–Prescott (HP) filter (Hodrick and Prescott, 1997 [31]).[27] The HP filter is a nonlinear regression technique that acts like a two-side moving average. As we noted, and as Prescott (1986a [4]) asserts, one should in principle model growth and cycles jointly (see also Kydland and Prescott, 1996 [13]). In practice, however, real business cycle models express the interrelationships of data as deviations from the steady state. So, in effect, the HP filter provides an atheoretical estimate of the steady-state growth path.

Harvey and Jaeger (1993 [32]) analyze the usefulness of the HP filter in accomplishing this task. They compare the cyclical component for output generated from an HP filter to that from a structural time-series model in which the trend and the cyclical component are estimated jointly. (This is closer to what Kydland and Prescott advocate in principle than to what they actually practice.) For US GDP, both detrending methods produce similar cyclical components. Harvey and Jaeger, however, demonstrate that the HP filter is wildly different from the structural time-series model for several other countries. This underscores the previously cited finding of Hartley *et al.* (1997 **[24]**) that the real business cycle model matches US data — at least on the standard of aesthetic R^2 typically employed by real business cycle modelers — but not artificial data of a more "European" character.

Harvey and Jaeger also show that the HP filter and the structural time-series model differ substantially when applied to other US time series — particularly in the case of U.S. prices and the monetary base. Given Kydland and Prescott's impassioned attack on the "monetary myths" of the business cycle, it is obviously critical to know whether the facts about money and prices are independent of the filtering process. Furthermore, Harvey and Jaeger demonstrate that in small samples the HP filter can induce apparent cyclical fluctuations and apparent correlations between series even when the prefiltered series are independent and serially uncorrelated. As they point out, these results are in the same spirit as Slutsky's and Yule's analyses of spurious cyclical behavior (Yule (1926), Slutsky ([1927] 1937); more recently, see Nelson and Kang, 1981). This phenomenon has been long known if not fully appreciated. Simon Kuznets, for example, "discovered" long cycles in US data that had first been transformed through two separate moving averages and first differencing. It can be shown that purely random data subjected to such transformations present precisely the same twenty-year cycles that Kuznets reported: they are nothing but an artifact of the filtering (see Sargent, 1979: 249–51). The analogy between the HP filter and Kuznets's transformations is close because the HP filter acts as a type of two-sided moving average.

Cogley and Nason (1995a **[33]**) reinforce Harvey and Jaeger's analysis; they demonstrate that prefiltered data do not generate cycles in a real business cycle model, while HP filtered data do. Furthermore, when the input data are highly serially correlated (a correlation coefficient of unity, or nearly so, between current and lagged values of the variable: i.e., a unit root or near unit root), the HP filter not only generates spurious cycles but also strongly increases the correlation among the predicted values for output, consumption, investment, hours of work, and other predicted values from the real business cycle model. The model itself — that is, the propagation mechanism — does little of the work in generating the cyclical behavior; the HP filter does the lion's share.

On the one hand, the use of the HP filter calls into question the very facts of the business cycle. Kydland and Prescott (1990 **[20]**) document the intercorrelations among HP filtered time series. These correlations are held by real business cycle modelers to provide strong prima facie support for the real business cycle model (Kydland and Prescott's (1990 **[20]**) subtitle to their paper is "Real Facts and a Monetary Myth"). For example, they show that the correlation between HP-filtered real GDP and HP-filtered prices is −0.50, and claim that this contradicts the prediction of Keynesian models that prices are procyclical. Harvey and Jaeger (1993

[32]) not only show that the HP filter can induce such correlations, but they also show that it adds statistical noise, so that a genuine correlation would, in a sample size of one hundred, have to exceed 0.40 before we could be sure that it was statistically significant at the standard 5 percent critical value. If such correlations are really artifacts of a filtering procedure, with no particular grounding in the economics of the business cycle, then the support of the "real facts" for the real business cycle model is substantially weakened.

Prescott (1986a [4]: 10) wrote: "If the business cycle facts were sensitive to the detrending procedure used, there would be a problem. But the key facts are not sensitive to the procedure if the trend curve is smooth." The weight of evidence since Prescott wrote this suggests that he is incorrect: the facts are sensitive to the type of filtering that defines the trend.

On the other hand, while there is good reason to find some way to detrend the technology-shock series used as an input into the real business cycle model, it is also standard practice to HP filter the predicted series generated by the real business cycle model before checking their intercorrelations and comparing them to the HP filtered actual data. Harvey and Jaeger's and Cogley and Nason's analyses suggest that this practice raises the correlations among these series artificially.

Kydland and Prescott (1996 [13]: 76–77 n) defend the use of the HP filter against critics who have argued that it induces spurious cycles by stating that deviations from trends defined by the HP filter "measure nothing," but instead are "nothing more than well-defined statistics"; and, since "business cycle theory treats growth and cycles as being integrated, not as a sum of two components driven by different factors . . . talking about the resulting statistics as imposing spurious cycles makes no sense." The logic of Kydland and Prescott's position escapes us. It is true that real business cycle theory treats the business cycle as the equilibrium adjustments of a neoclassical growth model subject to technology shocks. But, as we have previously noted, the real business cycle model does not, in practice, model the steady state. The HP filter is an atheoretical method of extracting it prior to the economic modeling of the deviations from the steady state. The implicit assumption is that the extracted trend is a good approximation of the steady state, for which no evidence is offered. This does not say that the steady state could not be modeled jointly with the deviations in principle. That it is not actually modeled jointly in practice, however, means that the objection to the HP filter raised by many critics remains cogent. The work of Harvey and Jaeger and Cogley and Nason (see also Canova, 1991), which Kydland and Prescott wish to dismiss, demonstrates that the choice of which ad hoc method is used to extract the balanced-growth path greatly affects the stochastic properties of the modeled variables and their relationships with the actual data.

One way of reading Watson (1993 [17]) and Cogley and Nason (1995a

[30]) is that, while a model driven by a technology shocks fits output well, it is the technology shocks not the model which are responsible for that fact. The picture painted is one of the real business cycle model as a slightly wobbly transmission belt converting the time-series characteristics of the technology shocks into the model's predictions for real output. But in the end there is a good fit between the model and real output. King (1995) and Hoover (1997) suggest that if the Solow residual is taken as the proxy for technology shocks, then this success is an illusion.

Despite having rejected in earlier work the relevance of direct comparisons to historical data, real business cycle models have recently made precisely such comparisons.[28] Hansen and Prescott (1993 [26]) ask whether technology shocks can explain the 1990–91 recession in the United States, while Cooley (1995a) asks whether they can explain the "Volcker recessions" of 1980–82. In each case, the predictions of a real business cycle model are compared directly to the historical path of real output.[29]

Again the standard is one of aesthetic R^2, and the pitfalls of this standard are easily seen Hansen and Prescott's (1993 [26]: 285) figure 4 (see p. 538 below). Hansen and Prescott cite the fact that the output predicted from their real business cycle model tracks actual output as favorable evidence for its explanatory power. In particular, they note that the model catches the fall in output in 1990–91. But look more closely. Actual GNP peaks in the first quarter of 1990, while model GNP peaks in the fourth quarter; actual GNP bottoms out in the first quarter of 1991, while model GNP bottoms out in the second quarter. Furthermore, the model predicts two earlier absolute falls in GNP, while, in fact, there are no other recessions in the data. One of these predicted falls is actually on a larger scale than the genuine recession of 1990–91: the model shows that GNP peaks in the first quarter of 1986 and falls 2.3 percent to a trough in the fourth quarter of 1986, where in reality GNP rose the entire time. The actual fall in GNP in the 1990–91 recession is only 1.6 percent.

The difficulties of using aesthetic R^2 to one side, these graphical measures or their more statistical counterparts (e.g., see Smith and Zin, 1997) offer no support for the real business cycle model. To see the difficulty, consider a simple version of a real business cycle model in which we abstract from time trends. Initially, let labor be supplied inelastically. Capital is inherited from the previous period. The Solow residual (z_t) can be calculated in log-linear form:

$$\log(z_t) = \log(Y_t) - (1 - \theta)\log(K_t) - \theta\log(L_t). \tag{1.8}$$

The log-linear version of the production function is given by

$$\log(Y_s) = \log(z_t) + (1 - \theta)\log(K_t) + \theta\log(L_s), \tag{1.9}$$

where the s subscripts refer to variables determined in the model. From the inelastic supply of labor we know that $L_s = L_t$. Substituting this fact and the Solow residual into equation (1.9),

$$\log(Y_s) = \log(Y_t) - (1 - \theta)\log(K_t) - \theta\log(L_t)$$
$$+ (1 - \theta)\log(K_t) + \theta\log(L_t)$$
$$= \log(Y_t) \qquad (1.10)$$

or

$$Y_s = Y_t \qquad (1.10')$$

Our model fits perfectly; the correlation between predicted and actual output is unity. Does anyone believe that this is a demonstration of its goodness?

Real business cycle models do not fit perfectly, as this little exercise suggests. The reason is that the inputs to their production function do not recapitulate the capital and labor measures used to calculate the Solow residual. In particular, the labor input (L_s) is determined by other features of the model — in fact, by features that are considered the most characteristic of real business cycle models, such as intertemporal substitutability of labor and optimal investment and consumption planning.[30] So, it is natural to relax our assumption of an inelastic labor supply. Then equation (1.10) becomes

$$\log(Y_s) = \log(Y_t) - (1 - \theta)\log(K_t) - \theta\log(L_t)$$
$$+ (1 - \theta)\log(K_t) + \theta\log(L_s)$$
$$= \log(Y_t) - \theta[\log(L_t) - \log(L_s)] \qquad (1.11)$$

How well predicted output fits actual output is seen to depend on how well predicted labor fits actual labor. Still, there is an artifactual element to the correlation between predicted and actual output. Notice that the share parameter θ is not given in nature, but is a modeling choice. If θ is calibrated to be close to zero, then the predicted and actual output are again nearly perfectly correlated. Now, it might be objected that we *know* θ is not close to zero but close to 0.69 (Hansen and Prescott's (1993 [26]) assumption). We agree. But information about the true size of θ comes from the calibrator's supply of exogenous information and has nothing to do with the fit of the model to historical data or with traditional econometrics. It underscores Kydland and Prescott's advocacy of external sources of information to pin down free parameters. We must not forget that whether θ is zero, 0.69, or one, actual output shows up on the right-hand side of equation (1.11) only because we put it there in the construction of the Solow residual, not because the model generated it by closely matching the structure of the economy.[31]

Of course, it would be a marvelous testament to the success of the model if the right-hand side of equation (1.11) turned out to be very nearly $\log(Y_t)$. That would occur because the model's predicted labor was very nearly the actual labor. The true measure of such success is not found indirectly in the comparison of Y_s to Y_t, but in the direct comparison of L_s to L_t.

Even a test based on modeling labor conditional on the Solow residual is likely to suffer from spurious success at fitting historical labor, since the Solow residual also contains current labor information by construction. Truly revealing tests of the success of the real business cycle model at capturing the true propagation mechanism based on comparisons of the predictions of the model against historical time series should then concentrate on those series (e.g., consumption) the current values of which play no part in the construction of measures of the technology shocks.

To give up the comparison of historical and predicted output (or labor) is not to give up the comparison of historical and predicted data altogether. One might ask different questions of the model: for example, if one knew actual output and capital, what would the model imply that consumption and labor would have to be? These conditional predictions are measures of consumption and labor that are uncorrupted by actual labor in their construction. Historical comparisons on these dimensions would be useful tests of the model: a close fit would then be a genuine accomplishment of the real business cycle model, and not an artifact of the construction of the Solow residual.[32] We know of no work to date that has systematically investigated the propagation mechanism of the real business cycle model in this manner independently of the Solow residual.

III REFUTATION?

The history of real business cycle models illustrates a fact well known to philosophers and historians of science: It is rare for a conjecture — however bold — to be refuted *simpliciter* on the basis of a single experiment or a single observation, as in Popper's ideal case. Accumulated evidence may, nonetheless, render the intellectual cost of persisting in a particular conjecture (model or theory) higher than the cost of abandoning or modifying it. To some extent, it does not appear to be controversial that the evidence weighs against the real business cycle program narrowly construed. Even the best-known advocates of real business cycle models have tended to move away from models of perfectly competitive representative agents driven by technology shocks only (see n. 1). While these models are direct descendants of the real business cycle model and remain in the broader class of equilibrium business cycle models, they represent an abandonment of the strongest form of the real business cycle conjecture. The balance of the evidence presented here is that they are right to do so. Although there can be no objection to investigating just how far these new models can be pushed, there is little in the evidence with respect to the narrower real business cycle conjecture that would warrant much optimism about their success.

The case against the real business cycle conjecture has several parts. First, the propagation mechanism (i.e., the Solow growth model), while it provides, to a first approximation, a reasonable account of long-term growth, has virtually no value added with respect to business cycles. The growth model will transmit fluctuations at business cycle frequencies from impulses that are already cyclical, but it will not generate them from non-cyclical impulses.

The putative impulse mechanism is the fluctuation of technology. In the model itself this amounts to shifts in a disembodied parameter (Z). The proponents of real business cycle models have given very little account of what features of the world might correspond to Z and fluctuate in the way needed to produce business cycles. Z is an unexplained residual in every sense of the word: it is whatever it has to be to make the real business cycle model behave in an appropriate manner, and it cannot be independently observed. If measured as the Solow residual, "technology" means whatever bit of output that cannot be accounted for by capital and labor inputs. Using this residual output as an impulse cannot yield predicted values for output that provide a logically sound independent comparison between the model and the actual data on the dimension of output.

While valid comparisons might be made on other dimensions, the actual evidence in favor of real business cycles is weak in the sense that it does not provide discriminating tests: alternative models do as good a job in mimicking the data on the usual aesthetic standards as does the real business cycle model. Both the facts to be explained and the ability of the models to match those facts are themselves frequently distorted by the common data-handling techniques (particularly the HP filter). These data problems, combined with the fact that the highly idealized nature of the real business cycle models limits the ambitions that their advocates have for matching the actual data, insulate the model from decisive refutation, but equally well undercut the role of empirical evidence in lending positive support to them.

The real business cycle model has for fifteen years dominated the agenda of business cycle research. On balance, however, there is little convincing empirical evidence that favors it over alternative models. To its advocates, the paucity of evidence may not be of too much concern, for Kydland and Prescott (1991 [12]: 171) argue that the confidence one places in a model to answer economic question cannot "be resolved by computing some measure of how well the model economy mimics historical data. . . . The degree of confidence in the answer depends on the confidence that is placed in the economic theory being used." But anyone who believes that theories must be warranted by evidence has little reason to date to place much confidence in real business cycle models.

NOTES

1 As will become clear below, our focus is on real business cycles narrowly construed as perfectly competitive representative agent models driven by *real* shocks. A number of recent developments have extended models with roots in Kydland and Prescott (1982 **[3]**) to include monetary factors, limited heterogeneity among agents, non-Walrasian features, and imperfect competition. These models are ably surveyed in chapters 7–9 of Cooley (1995b). One way to view this literature is as a constructive response to some of the difficulties with the narrow real business cycle model that we evaluate.

2 Lucas (1978: 242).

3 Friedman's monetarist model is distinguished from Lucas's new classical monetary model in that Friedman imagines that people can be systematically mistaken about the true state of real wages for relatively long periods, while Lucas argues that people have rational expectations (i.e., they make only unsystematic mistakes) and, therefore, correct their judgments about the real wage quickly.

4 Lucas (in Snowden, Vane and Wynarczyk, 1994: 222) accepts that his previous characterization of the Austrians as precursors to new classical business cycle theory was incorrect.

5 Equation (1.1) is a snapshot of the economy at a particular time. In fact, variables in the model are growing. We could indicate this with subscripts indexing the relevant time, but this would simply clutter the notation unnecessarily.

6 There is a large literature on endogenous growth models (see, e.g., the symposium in the *Journal of Economic Perspectives*, 1994).

7 Cooley and Prescott (1995, sec. 4) discusses the issues related to establishing an appropriate correspondence between the real business cycle model and the national accounts to permit the calibration of the model.

8 It is actually a debated question whether microeconomic studies do in fact provide the necessary parameters. Prescott (1986a **[4]**: 14) cites Lucas's (1980: 712) argument that we have "a wealth of inexpensively available data" of this sort. However, Hansen and Heckman (1996 **[14]**: 93–94) argue that in this regard Prescott is wrong. As evidence they point to Shoven and Whalley (1992: 105), who rather candidly admit that "it is surprising how sparse (and sometimes contradictory) the literature is on some key elasticity values. And although this procedure might sound straightforward, it is often exceedingly difficult because each study is different from every other." (Cf. the debate between Summers (1986 **[5]**) and Prescott (1986b **[6]**) about whether the parameters used in Prescott (1986a **[4]**) are the appropriate ones.)

9 Details on how to solve these sorts of models are provided in Chapter 2.

10 Despite this argument, Lucas's view of real business cycle models is rather favorable. See, e.g., the discussion in Manuelli and Sargent (1988).

11 Although we refer to z as "the technology shock," this terminology is not universal. Generally, z will be a persistent process; for example, $z_t = \rho z_t + \varepsilon_t$, with $\rho > 0$ and ε_t an independent, identically distributed random variable. Some economists identify ε_t as "the technology shock." Similarly, some economists identify z_t rather than Z_t as the "Solow residual."

12 These reasons are elaborated in Hartley (1997).

13 The classic reference is Gorman (1953); the literature is summarized in Stoker (1993).

14 Coleman (1990) calls this the micro-to-macro transition and provides an

extensive and illuminating discussion about what is involved in making this transition properly.

15 This seems to be Friedman's (1997: 210) point when he criticizes Kydland and Prescott's (1996 [13]) standards of empirical evaluation for calibrated models, saying, "There is a world of difference between mimicking and explaining, between 'can or may' and 'does'."

16 The official definition of a business cycle used by the National Bureau of Economic Research in the United States emphasizes that recessions are unfavorable movements across a breadth of economic aggregates; see Geoffrey Moore quoted in Hall (1981).

17 Prescott (1986a [4]: 10) argues that the noun "business cycle" should be avoided as it encourages people to believe incorrectly that there is an entity to be explained, independently of economic growth, which is characterized by a deterministic cycle. Instead, "business cycle" should be used as an adjective, as in "business cycle phenomena," that points to the volatility and comovements of various economic series. Lucas (1987, sec. V) acknowledges the difference between defining the business cycle, as common usage does, as recurrent fluctuations in unemployment and, as he and real business cycle models typically do, as equilibrium comovements. He recognizes that, to the extent that one is interested in questions of unemployment, models that aim to explain the comovements alone are silent on an important question — although he argues that this is a limitation, not a fault.

18 Harvey and Jaeger (1993) present evidence that the HP filter which is used to detrend the series analyzed by Kydland and Prescott (1990 [20]) distorts the correlations among them, suggesting that the "facts" might be artifacts of the statistical processing after all (see section II (v) below).

19 Farmer (1993) is an exception, see section II (ii) below.

20 Both the term "stylized facts" and the facts themselves are due to Kaldor (1961). Also see Kaldor (1957) in which the facts themselves are discussed with the name "stylized."

21 Manuelli and Sargent (1988) criticize the real business cycle literature for backing away from following procedures along these lines.

22 Kydland and Prescott (1990 [20]) and Burns and Mitchell (1946).

23 See Fair (1990) for a description of the model.

24 A strategy for the assessment of idealized models is discussed in Hoover (1994).

25 This claim is controversial. Romer (1986a, b; 1989) argues that postwar business cycles are not substantially less variable than those of the nineteenth century. Weir (1986) and Balke and Gordon (1989) challenge Romer's revisionism. The debate is updated and assessed in Siegler (1997), which, on the basis of better estimates of nineteenth-century GNP, supports the traditional view that modern business cycles are in fact smoother than those of the nineteenth century.

26 Solow (1956 [27]: 314, 320) explicitly observes that idle capacity biases the measure and that the measure hinges on the assumption of factors being paid their marginal products, but that a similar measure could be created for monopolistic factor markets. Looking back over thirty years later, Solow (1990: 225) argues that he never intended the Solow residual as a suitable measure of anything but the *trend* in technology: "the year-to-year behavior of the residual could be governed by all sorts of 'technologically' irrelevant short-run forces. I still think that. . . . "

27 The HP filter is defined as follows: Let $x_t = \bar{x}_t + \hat{x}_t$, where $\bar{x}_t$ denotes the trend

component and $\hat{x}_t$ denotes the deviation from trend. The HP filter chooses this decomposition to solve the following problem:

$$\min \left\{ (1/T) \sum_{t=1}^{T} \hat{x}_t^2 + (\lambda/T) \sum_{t=2}^{T-1} \left[(\bar{x}_{t+1} - \bar{x}_t) - (\bar{x}_t - \bar{x}_{t-1}) \right]^2 \right\}.$$

T is the number of observations and λ is a parameter that controls the amount of smoothness in the series: if $\lambda = 0$, then the smooth series is identical to the original series; if $\lambda = \infty$, the smoothed series is just a linear trend. Hodrick and Prescott use a value of $\lambda = 1600$ for quarterly data on the ground that this replicates the curve a business cycle analyst might fit freehand to the data. With no better justification than this, $\lambda = 1600$ has become the standard choice for the smoothing parameter in the real business cycle literature.

28 For example, Prescott (1986a [4]: 16) argues against comparing the model output to the path of actual US output.

29 Christiano (1988) seems to have been the first real business cycle modeler to employ such a test.

30 Additionally, independently detrending the Solow residual and the other inputs to the production function may introduce discrepancies between actual and model-generated data.

31 Hoover and Salyer (1996) provide simulation evidence that the Solow residual does not convey useful information about technology shocks, and that the apparent success of real business cycle models in matching historical data for output is wholly an artifact of the use of current output in the construction of the Solow residual.

32 If, for instance, we were to condition on actual output, inherited capital and the government expenditure shock, then we could back out another measure of z_S. But, given that we have nothing independent to compare it with, the more interesting point is that we can back out some other series, say, labor conditional on actual output and capital, which can then be compared to its actual counterpart.

REFERENCES

Adelman, Irma and Frank L. Adelman (1959) "The Dynamic Properties of the Klein–Goldberger Model," *Econometrica*, 27(4): 596–625.

Altuğ, Sumru (1989) "Time-to-Build and Aggregate Fluctuations: Some New Evidence," *International Economic Review*, 30(4), November: 889–920, reprinted here in Chapter 21.

Backus, David K. and Patrick J. Kehoe (1992) "International Evidence on the Historical Properties of Business Cycles," *American Economic Review*, 82(4): 864–88.

Balke, Nathan S. and Robert J. Gordon (1989) "The Estimation of Prewar Gross National Product: Methodology and New Evidence," *Journal of Political Economy*, 97(1): 38–92.

Benhabib, Jess, Richard Rogerson, and Randall Wright (1991) "Homework in Macroeconomics: Household Production and Aggregate Fluctuations," *Journal of Political Economy*, 99(6), December: 1166–87.

Bryant, John (1983) "A Simple Rational Expectations Keynes-type Model," *Quarterly Journal of Economics*, 98(3), August: 525–28.

Burns, Arthur F. and Wesley C. Mitchell (1946) *Measuring Business Cycles*, New York: National Bureau of Economic Research.

Calomiris, Charles W. and Christopher Hanes (1995) "Historical Macroeconomics and Macroeconomic History," in Kevin D. Hoover (ed.) *Macroeconometrics: Developments, Tensions, and Prospects*, Dordrecht: Kluwer: 351–416.

Canova, Fabio (1991) "Detrending and Business Cycle Facts," unpublished typescript, Department of Economics, European University Institute, Florence, Italy, July 20.

Canova, Fabio, M. Finn, and A. R. Pagan (1994) "Evaluating a Real Business Cycle Model," in C. Hargreaves (ed.) *Nonstationary Time Series Analysis and Cointegration*, Oxford: Oxford University Press: 225–55, reprinted here in Chapter 22.

Christiano, Lawrence J. (1988) "Why Does Inventory Investment Fluctuate So Much?" *Journal of Monetary Economics*, 21(2): 247–80.

Christiano, Lawrence J. and Martin Eichenbaum (1992) "Current Real Business Cycle Theories and Aggregate Labor Market Fluctuations," *American Economic Review*, 82(3), June: 430–50, reprinted here in Chapter 10.

Cogley, Timothy and James M. Nason (1995a) "Effects of the Hodrick–Prescott Filter on Trend and Difference Stationary Time Series: Implications for Business Cycle Research," *Journal of Economic Dynamics and Control*, 19(1–2), January–February: 253–78, reprinted here in Chapter 33.

Cogley, Timothy and James M. Nason (1995b) "Output Dynamics in Real Business Cycle Models," *American Economic Review*, 85(3), June: 492–511, reprinted here in Chapter 30.

Coleman, James S. (1990) *Foundations of Social Theory*, Cambridge, Mass.: The Belknap Press.

Cooley, Thomas F. (1995a) "Contribution to a Conference Panel Discussion: What Do We Know about How Monetary Policy Affects the Economy?" paper given at the 19th Annual Economic Policy Conference, Federal Reserve Bank of St Louis. *Federal Reserve Bank of St Louis Review*, 77(3): 131–37.

Cooley, Thomas F. (ed.) (1995b) *Frontiers of Business Cycle Research*, Princeton: Princeton University Press.

Cooley, Thomas F. and Gary D. Hansen (1989) "The Inflation Tax in a Real Business Cycle Model," *American Economic Review*, 79(4), September: 733–48, reprinted here in Chapter 11.

Cooley, Thomas F. and Edward C. Prescott (1995) "Economic Growth and Business Cycles," in Cooley (1995b): 1–38.

Cooper, Russell and Andrew John (1988) "Coordinating Coordination Failures," *Quarterly Journal of Economics*, 103(3), August: 441–64.

Debreu, Gerard (1974) "Excess Demand Functions," *Journal of Mathematical Economics*, 1(1), March: 15–23.

Eichenbaum, Martin (1991) "Real Business Cycle Theory: Wisdom or Whimsy?" *Journal of Economic Dynamics and Control*, 15(4), October: 607–26, reprinted here in Chapter 25.

Fair, Ray C. (1990) *Fairmodel: User's Guide and Intermediate Workbook*, Southborough, Mass.: Macro Incorporated.

Farmer, Roger E. A. (1993) *The Macroeconomics of Self-fulfilling Prophecies*, Cambridge, Mass.: MIT Press.

Friedman, Milton (1957) *A Theory of the Consumption Function*, Princeton: Princeton University Press.

Friedman, Milton (1968) "The Role of Monetary Policy," *American Economic Review*, 58(1): 1–17.

Friedman, Milton (1997) "Computational Experiments," *Journal of Economic Perspectives*, 11(1), Winter: 209–10.

Frisch, Ragnar (1933) "Propagation Problems and Impulse Response Problems in Dynamic Economics," in *Economic Essays in Honour of Gustav Cassel: October 20, 1933*, London: George Allen & Unwin.

Gorman, W. M. (1953) "Community Preference Fields," *Econometrica*, 21(1): 63–80.

Greenwood, Jeremy, Zvi Hercowitz, and Gregory W. Huffman (1988) "Investment, Capacity Utilization and the Real Business Cycle," *American Economic Review*, 78(3), June: 402–17.

Gregory, Allan W. and Gregor W. Smith (1990) "Calibration as Estimation," *Econometric Reviews*, 9(1): 57–89.

Gregory, Allan W. and Gregor W. Smith (1991) "Calibration as Testing: Inference in Simulated Macroeconomic Models," *Journal of Business and Economic Statistics*, 9(3), July: 297–303, reprinted here in Chapter 16.

Griliches, Zvi (1996) "The Discovery of the Residual: A Historical Note," *Journal of Economic Literature*, 34(3): 1324–30, reprinted here in Chapter 29.

Hall, Robert E. (1981) "Just a Peak and Trough," National Bureau of Economic Research (downloaded from World Wide Web site: nber.harvard.edu).

Hall, Robert E. (1986) "Market Structure and Macroeconomics Fluctuations," *Brookings Papers on Economic Activity*, no. 2: 265–338.

Hall, Robert E. (1990) "Invariance Properties of Solow's Productivity Residual," in Peter Diamond (ed.) *Growth/Productivity/Unemployment: Essays to Celebrate Bob Solow's Birthday*, Cambridge, Mass.: MIT Press: 71–112.

Hansen, Gary D. (1985) "Indivisible Labor and the Business Cycle," *Journal of Monetary Economics,* 16(3), November: 309–28, reprinted here in Chapter 8.

Hansen, Gary D. and Edward C. Prescott (1993) "Did Technology Shocks Cause the 1990–1991 Recession?" *American Economic Review*, 83(2), May: 280–86, reprinted here in Chapter 26.

Hansen, Gary D. and Thomas J. Sargent (1988) "Straight Time and Overtime in Equilibrium," *Journal of Monetary Economics*, 21(2), March: 281–308.

Hansen, Gary D. and Randall Wright (1992) "The Labor Market in Real Business Cycle Theory," *Federal Reserve Bank of Minneapolis Quarterly Review*, 16(2), Spring: 2–12, reprinted here in Chapter 9.

Hansen, Lars Peter and James J. Heckman (1996) "The Empirical Foundations of Calibration," *Journal of Economic Perspectives*, 10(1), Winter: 87–104, reprinted here in Chapter 14.

Hansen, Lars Peter and Thomas J. Sargent (1980) "Formulating and Estimating Dynamic Linear Rational Expectations Models," *Journal of Economic Dynamics and Control*, 2(1), February, reprinted in Robert E. Lucas, Jr. and Thomas J. Sargent (eds) (1981) *Rational Expectations and Econometric Practice*, London: George Allen & Unwin: 91–125.

Hansen, Lars Peter and Thomas J. Sargent (1990) "Recursive Linear Models of Dynamic Economies," National Bureau of Economic Research, Working Paper Series, no. 3479.

Hartley, James E. (1994) "Technology in Macroeconomic Models," doctoral dissertation, University of California, Davis.

Hartley, James E. (1997) *The Representative Agent in Macroeconomics*, London: Routledge.

Hartley, James E., Kevin D. Salyer, and Steven M. Sheffrin (1997) "Calibration and Real Business Cycle Models: An Unorthodox Experiment," *Journal of Macroeconomics*, 19(1): 1–17, reprinted here in Chapter 24.

Harvey, A. C. and A. Jaeger (1993) "Detrending, Stylized Facts and the Business Cycle," *Journal of Applied Econometrics*, 8(3): 231–47, reprinted here in Chapter 32.

Hayek, Friedrich A. von (1933) *Monetary Theory and the Trade Cycle*, trans. Nicholas Kaldor and H. M. Croome, London: Jonathan Cape.

Hayek, Friedrich A. von (1935) *Prices and Production*, 2nd ed., London: Routledge & Kegan Paul.

Hodrick, Robert J. and Edward C. Prescott (1997) "Postwar US Business Cycles: An Empirical Investigation," *Journal of Money, Credit, and Banking*, 29(1), February: 1–16, reprinted here in Chapter 31.

Hoover, Kevin D. (1988) *The New Classical Economics: A Sceptical Inquiry*, Oxford: Blackwell.

Hoover, Kevin D. (1994) "Six Queries About Idealization in an Empirical Context," *Poznan Studies in the Philosophy of Science and the Humanities*, 38: 43–53.

Hoover, Kevin D. (1995) "Facts and Artifacts: Calibration and the Empirical Assessment of Real-Business-Cycle Models," *Oxford Economic Papers*, 47(1), March: 24–44, reprinted here in Chapter 15.

Hoover, Kevin D. (1997) "Comments on Smith and Zin's 'Real Business Cycle Realizations, 1925–1995'," *Carnegie–Rochester Series in Public Policy*, forthcoming.

Hoover, Kevin D. and Kevin D. Salyer (1996) "Technology Shocks or Colored Noise? Why Real Business Cycle Models Cannot Explain Actual Business Cycles," unpublished manuscript.

Hume, David ([1739] 1888) *A Treatise of Human Nature*, Oxford: Clarendon Press.

Ingrao, Bruna and Giorgio Israel (1990) *The Invisible Hand: Economic Equilibrium in the History of Science*, trans. Ian McGilvray, Cambridge, Mass.: MIT Press.

Jorgenson, Dale W. and Griliches, Zvi (1967) "The Explanation of Productivity Change," *Review of Economic Studies*, 34(3), July: 249–83.

Journal of Economic Perspectives (1994) Symposium on "New Growth Theory," 8(1): 3–72.

Kaldor, Nicholas (1957) "A Model of Economic Growth," *Economic Journal*, 67(4), December: 591–624.

Kaldor, Nicholas (1961) "Capital Accumulation and Economic Growth," in Friedrich A. Lutz and Douglas C. Hague (eds) *The Theory of Capital: Proceedings of a Conference Held by the International Economics Association*, London: Macmillan.

King, Robert G. (1995) "Quantitative Theory and Econometrics," *Federal Reserve Bank of Richmond Economic Quarterly*, 81(3), Summer: 53–105.

King, Robert G. and Charles I. Plosser (1989) "Real Business Cycles and the Test of the Adelmans," *Journal of Monetary Economics*, 33(2), April: 405–38, reprinted here in Chapter 23.

King, Robert G., Charles I. Plosser and Sergio T. Rebelo (1988) "Production, Growth, and Business Cycles I: The Basic Neoclassical Model," *Journal of Monetary Economics*, 21(2), March: 195–232, reprinted here in Chapter 7.

Kirman, Alan P. (1989) "The Intrinsic Limits of Modern Economic Theory: The Emperor Has No Clothes," *The Economic Journal*, 99 (Conference): 126–39.

Kirman, Alan P. (1992) "Whom or What Does the Representative Individual Represent?" *Journal of Economic Perspectives*, 6(2), Spring: 117–36.

Kydland, Finn E. and Edward C. Prescott (1982) "Time to Build and Aggregate

Fluctuations," *Econometrica*, 50(6), November: 1345–69, reprinted here in Chapter 3.

Kydland, Finn E. and Edward C. Prescott (1988) "The Workweek of Capital and Its Cyclical Implications," *Journal of Monetary Economics*, 21(2): 343–60.

Kydland, Finn E. and Edward C. Prescott (1990) "Business Cycles: Real Facts and a Monetary Myth," *Federal Reserve Bank of Minneapolis Quarterly Review*, 14(2), Spring: 3–18, reprinted here in Chapter 20.

Kydland, Finn E. and Edward C. Prescott (1991) "The Econometrics of the General Equilibrium Approach to Business Cycles," *Scandinavian Journal of Economics*, 93(2): 161–78, reprinted here in Chapter 12.

Kydland, Finn E. and Edward C. Prescott (1996) "The Computational Experiment: An Econometric Tool," *Journal of Economic Perspectives*, 10(1), Winter: 69–86, reprinted here in Chapter 13.

Kydland, Finn E. and Edward C. Prescott (1997) "A Response [to Milton Friedman]," *Journal of Economic Perspectives*, 11(1), Winter: 210–11.

Lucas, Robert E., Jr. (1972) "Expectations and the Neutrality of Money," *Journal of Economic Theory*, 4(2), April: 103–24, reprinted in Lucas (1981): 66–89.

Lucas, Robert E., Jr. (1973) "Some Output–Inflation Tradeoffs," *American Economic Review*, 63(3), June: 326–34, reprinted in Lucas (1981): 131–45.

Lucas, Robert E., Jr. (1975) "An Equilibrium Model of the Business Cycle," *Journal of Political Economy*, 83(6): 1113–44, reprinted in Lucas (1981): 179–214.

Lucas, Robert E., Jr. (1976) "Econometric Policy Evaluation: A Critique," in Karl Brunner and Allan H. Meltzer (eds) *The Phillips Curve and Labor Markets*, vol. 1 of Carnegie–Rochester Conference Series on Public Policy, Amsterdam: North Holland, 19–46, reprinted in Lucas (1981): 104–30.

Lucas, Robert E., Jr. (1977) "Understanding Business Cycles," in Karl Brunner and Allan H. Meltzer (eds) *Stabilization of the Domestic and International Economy*, Carnegie–Rochester Conference Series in Public Policy, Amsterdam: North Holland, 7–29, reprinted in Lucas (1981): 215–39.

Lucas, Robert E., Jr. (1978) "Unemployment Policy," *American Economic Review*, 68(2), May: 353–57, reprinted in Lucas (1981): 240–47.

Lucas, Robert E., Jr. (1980) "Methods and Problems in Business Cycle Theory," *Journal of Money, Credit and Banking*, 12(4), pt. 2, November: 696–713, reprinted in Lucas (1981): 271–96.

Lucas, Robert E., Jr. (1981) *Studies in Business Cycle Theory*, Cambridge, Mass.: MIT Press.

Lucas, Robert E., Jr. (1987) *Models of Business Cycles*, Oxford: Blackwell.

Lucas, Robert E., Jr., and Thomas J. Sargent (1979) "After Keynesian Macroeconomics," *Federal Reserve Bank of Minneapolis Quarterly Review*, 3(2), reprinted in Robert E. Lucas, Jr. and Thomas J. Sargent (eds) (1981) *Rational Expectations and Econometric Practice*, Minneapolis: The University of Minnesota Press, 295–319.

Mankiw, N. Gregory (1989) "Real Business Cycles: A New Keynesian Perspective," *Journal of Economic Perspectives*, 3(3), Summer: 79–90, reprinted here in Chapter 28.

Mantel, R. (1974) "On the Characterization of Aggregate Excess Demand," *Journal of Economic Theory*, 7(3): 348–53.

Mantel, R. (1976) "Homothetic Preferences and Community Excess Demand Functions," *Journal of Economic Theory*, 12(2): 197–201.

Manuelli, Rodolfo and Thomas J. Sargent (1988) "*Models of Business Cycles*: A Review Essay," *Journal of Monetary Economics*, 22: 523–42.

Mas-Collel, A. (1977) "On the Equilibrium Price Set of an Exchange Economy," *Journal of Mathematical Economics*, 4(2): 117–26.

Nelson, Charles R. and H. Kang (1981) "Spurious Periodicity in Inappropriately Detrended Time Series," *Econometrica*, 49(3), May: 741–51.

Popper, Karl (1959) *The Logic of Scientific Discovery*, London: Hutchinson.

Popper, Karl (1972) *Conjectures and Refutations: The Growth of Scientific Knowledge*, 4th ed., London: Routledge.

Prescott, Edward C. (1986a) "Theory Ahead of Business Cycle Measurement," in *Federal Reserve Bank of Minneapolis Quarterly Review,* 10(4), Fall: 9–22, reprinted here in Chapter 4.

Prescott, Edward C. (1986b) "Response to a Skeptic," *Federal Reserve Bank of Minneapolis Quarterly Review*, 10(4), Fall: 28–33, reprinted here in Chapter 6.

Romer, Christina (1986a) "Is the Stabilization of the Postwar Economy a Figment of the Data?" *American Economic Review*, 76(3), June: 314–34.

Romer, Christina (1986b) "New Estimates of Prewar Gross National Product and Unemployment," *Journal of Economic History*, 46: 341–52.

Romer, Christina (1989) "The Prewar Business Cycle Reconsidered: New Estimates of Gross National Product, 1869–1908," *Journal of Political Economy*, 97(1), February: 1–37.

Samuelson, Paul A. (1948) *Economics: An Introductory Analysis*, New York: McGraw–Hill.

Sargent, Thomas J. (1979) *Macroeconomic Theory*, New York: Academic Press.

Sato, R. (1966) "On the Adjustment Time in Neo-Classical Growth Models," *Review of Economic Studies*, 33, July: 263–68.

Shafer, Wayne and Hugo Sonnenschein. (1982) "Market Demand and Excess Demand Functions," in K. J. Arrow and M. D. Intriligator (eds) *Handbook of Mathematical Economics*, vol. 2, Amsterdam: North-Holland: 671–93.

Shoven, John B. and John Whalley (1992) *Applying General Equilibrium*, New York: Cambridge University Press.

Siegler, Mark V. (1997) "Real Output and Business Cycle Volatility, 1869–1993: US Experience in International Perspective," doctoral dissertation, University of California, Davis.

Slutsky, Eugen E. ([1927] 1937) "The Summation of Random Causes as the Source of Cyclic Processes", *Econometrica*, 5: 105–46. Originally published in Russian in 1927.

Smith, Gregor and Stanley Zin (1997) "Real Business Cycle Realizations, 1925–1995," *Carnegie–Rochester Series in Public Policy*, forthcoming.

Snowdon, Brian, Howard Vane, and Peter Wynarczyk (eds) (1994) *A Modern Guide to Macroeconomics*, Aldershot: Edward Elgar.

Solow, Robert M. (1956) "A Contribution to the Theory of Economic Growth," *Quarterly Journal of Economics*, 70(1), February: 65–94.

Solow, Robert M. (1957) "Technical Change and the Aggregate Production Function," *Review of Economics and Statistics*, 39(3), August: 312–20, reprinted here in Chapter 27.

Solow, Robert M. (1970) *Growth Theory: An Exposition*, Oxford: Blackwell.

Solow, Robert M. (1990) "Reactions to Conference Papers," in Peter Diamond (ed.) *Growth/Productivity/Unemployment: Essays to Celebrate Bob Solow's Birthday*, Cambridge, Mass.: MIT Press: 221–29.

Sonnenschein, Hugo (1973) "Do Walras' Law and Continuity Characterize the Class of Community Excess Demand Functions?" *Journal of Economic Theory*, 6(4): 345–54.

Sonnenschein, Hugo (1974) "Market Excess Demand Functions," *Econometrica*, 40(3), May: 549–63.

Stoker, Thomas M. (1993) "Empirical Approaches to the Problem of Aggregation over Individuals," *Journal of Economic Literature*, 21(4), December: 1827–74.

Summers, Lawrence H. (1986) "Some Skeptical Observations on Real Business Cycle Theory," *Federal Reserve Bank of Minneapolis Quarterly Review*, 10(4), Fall: 23–27, reprinted here in Chapter 5.

Watson, Mark W. (1993) "Measures of Fit for Calibrated Models," *Journal of Political Economy*, 101(6), December: 1011–41, reprinted here in Chapter 17.

Weir, David (1986) "The Reliability of Historical Macroeconomic Data for Comparing Cyclical Stability," *Journal of Economic History,* 46(2), June: 353–65.

Yule, G. Udny (1926) "Why Do We Sometimes Get Nonsense-Correlations between Time-Series?" *Journal of the Royal Statistical Society*, 89(1): 1–65. Reprinted in David F. Hendry and Mary S. Morgan (eds) *The Foundations of Econometric Analysis*. Cambridge: Cambridge University Press, 1995, ch. 9.

Chapter 2

A user's guide to solving real business cycle models

The typical real business cycle model is based upon an economy populated by identical infinitely lived households and firms, so that economic choices are reflected in the decisions made by a single representative agent. It is assumed that both output and factor markets are characterized by perfect competition. Households sell capital, k_t, to firms at the rental rate of capital, and sell labor, h_t, at the real wage rate. Each period, firms choose capital and labor subject to a production function to maximize profits. Output is produced according to a constant-returns-to-scale production function that is subject to random technology shocks. Specifically $y_t = z_t f(k_t, h_t)$, where y_t is output and z_t is the technology shock. (The price of output is normalized to one.) Households' decisions are more complicated: given their initial capital stock, agents determine how much labor to supply and how much consumption and investment to purchase. These choices are made in order to maximize the expected value of lifetime utility. Households must forecast the future path of wages and the rental rate of capital. It is assumed that these forecasts are made rationally. A rational expectations equilibrium consists of sequences for consumption, capital, labor, output, wages, and the rental rate of capital such that factor and output markets clear.

While it is fairly straightforward to show that a competitive equilibrium exists, it is difficult to solve for the equilibrium sequences directly. Instead, an indirect approach is taken in which the Pareto optimum for this economy is determined (this will be unique given the assumption of representative agents). As shown by Debreu (1954), the Pareto optimum as characterized by the optimal sequences for consumption, labor, and capital in this environment will be identical to that in a competitive equilibrium. Furthermore, factor prices are determined by the marginal products of capital and labor evaluated at the equilibrium quantities. (For a detailed exposition of the connection between the competitive equilibrium and Pareto optimum in a real business cycle model, see Prescott, 1986 [4].) We now provide an example of solving such a model.

I DERIVING THE EQUILIBRIUM CONDITIONS

The first step in solving for the competitive equilibrium is to determine the Pareto optimum. To do this, the real business cycle model is recast as the following social planner's problem:

$$\max E_1 \left[\sum_{t=1}^{\infty} \beta^{t-1}(c_t, \ 1-h_t) \right]$$

subject to: $\qquad\qquad\qquad\qquad\qquad\qquad\qquad\qquad$ (2.1)

$$c_t + i_t = z_t f(k_t, \ h_t) \equiv y_t.$$

$$k_{t+1} = k_t (1 - \delta) + i_t.$$

$$z_{t+1} = z_t^{\rho} \varepsilon_{t+1}.$$

k_1 *is given.*

where $E_1[\cdot]$ denotes expectations conditional on information at $t = 1$, $0 < \beta < 1$ is agents' discount factor, c_t denotes consumption, $(1-h_t)$ is leisure (agents' endowment of time is normalized to one), i_t is investment, and $0 < \delta < 1$ is the depreciation rate of capital. The exogenous technology shock is assumed to follow the autoregressive process given in the last equation; the autocorrelation parameter is $0 \le \rho \le 1$ and the innovation to technology is assumed to have a mean of one and standard deviation σ_{ε}. The first two constraints in equation (2.1) are the economy-wide resource constraint, and the second is the law of motion for the capital stock.

Dynamic programming problem

This infinite horizon problem can be solved by exploiting its recursive structure. That is, the nature of the social planner's problem is the same every period: given the beginning-of-period capital stock and the current technology shock, choose consumption, labor, and investment. Note that utility is assumed to be time-separable: that is, the choices of consumption and labor at time t do not affect the marginal utilities of consumption and leisure in any other time period. Because of this recursive structure, it is useful to cast the maximization problem as the following dynamic programming problem (for a discussion of dynamic programming, see Sargent (1987)):

state variables at time t: $(k_t, \ z_t)$.

control variables at time t: $(c_t, \ h_t, \ k_{t+1})$.

$$v(k_t, z_t) = \max_{(c_t, k_{t+1}, h_t)} \{U(c_t, 1 - h_t) + \beta \ E_t[v(k_{t+1}, z_{t+1})]\}$$

subject to $c_t + k_{t+1} = z_t f(k_t, z_t) + k_t(1 - \delta)$ $\qquad\qquad$ (2.2)

and $\qquad z_{t+1} = z_t^{\rho} \varepsilon_{t+1}$

(Note that investment has been eliminated by using the law of motion for the capital stock.) A solution to this problem must satisfy the following necessary conditions and resource constraint:

(N1) $U_{2,t} = U_{1,t}z_t f_{2,t}.$

(N2) $U_{1,t} = \beta E_t \{ U_{1,t+1} [z_{t+1} f_{1,t+1} + (1 - \delta)] \}.$

(RC) $k_{t+1} = z_t f(k_t, h_t) + k_t(1 - \delta) - c_t.$

Where the notation $U_{i,t}$; i=1, 2 denotes the derivative of the utility function with respect to the ith argument evaluated at the quantities $(c_t, 1 - h_t)$; $f_{i,t}$; i=1,2 has an analogous interpretation. N1 represents the intratemporal efficiency condition (the labor–leisure tradeoff). It implies that the marginal rate of substitution between labor and consumption must equal the marginal product of labor. The second condition, N2, represents the intertemporal efficiency condition. The left-hand side represents the marginal cost in terms of utility of investing in more capital, while the right-hand side represents the expected marginal utility gain; at an optimum, these costs and benefits must be equal.

To simplify the analysis (again, see Prescott (1986 [4]) for a justification), assume the following functional forms:

$$U(c_t, 1 - h_t) = \ln c_t + A(1 - h_t); f(k_t, 1 - h_t) = k_t^\alpha h_t^{1-\alpha}.$$

(The assumption that utility is linear in leisure is based on Hansen's (1985 [8]) model.) Then the three equilibrium conditions become:

$c_t = [(1 - \alpha)z_t k_t^\alpha h_t^{-\alpha}/A].$

$c_t^{-1} = \beta E_t \{ c_{t+1}^{-1} [\alpha z_{t-1} k_{t+1}^{\alpha-1} h_{t+1}^{1-\alpha} + (1 - \delta)] \}.$ (2.3)

$k_{t+1} = z_t k_t^\alpha h_t^{1-\alpha} + k_t(1 - \delta) - c_t.$

A steady-state equilibrium for this economy is one in which the technology shock is assumed to be constant, so that there is no uncertainty: that is, $z_t = 1$ for all t, and the values of capital, labor, and consumption are constant, $k_t = \bar{k}$, $h_t = \bar{h}$, $c_t = \bar{c}$ for all t. Imposing these steady-state conditions in equation (2.3), the steady-state values are found by solving the following steady-state equilibrium conditions:

(SS1) $\bar{c} = ((1 - \alpha)/A) \bar{k}^\alpha \bar{h}^{-\alpha}.$

(SS2) $\beta^{-1} - 1 + \delta = \alpha \bar{k}^{\alpha-1} \bar{h}^{1-\alpha} = \alpha (\bar{y}/\bar{k}).$

(SS3) $\delta \bar{k} = \bar{k}^\alpha \bar{h}^{1-\alpha} - \bar{c} = \bar{y} - \bar{c}.$

In the above expressions, $\bar{y}$ denotes the steady-state level of output.

Calibration

The next step in solving the model is to choose parameter values for the model. This is done through *calibration*: the set of parameters (δ, β, A, α) are chosen so that the steady-state behavior of the model matches the long-run characteristics of the data. The features of the data which do not exhibit cyclical characteristics are:

1    $(1 - \alpha)$ = labor's average share of output.
2    $\beta^{-1} - 1$ = average risk-free real interest rate.
3   Given (α, β) choose δ so that the output–capital ratio (from (SS2) is consistent with observation.
4   The parameter A determines the time spent in work activity. To see this, multiply both sides of (SS1) by $\bar{h}$ and rearrange the expression to yield: $\bar{h} = \left[(1 - \alpha)/A\right](\bar{y}/\bar{c})$. But the steady-state resource constraint, (SS3), implies that $\bar{y}/\bar{c} = \left[1 - \delta(\bar{k}/\bar{y})\right]^{-1}$, so that the output–consumption ratio is implied by the parameter values chosen in the previous three steps. Hence, the choice of A directly determines $\bar{h}$.

Typical parameter values based on postwar US data (see Hansen and Wright (1992 [9])) are: $\alpha = 0.36$ implying labor's share is 64 percent, $\beta = 0.99$ implying an annual riskless interest rate of 0.04 percent, $\delta = 0.025$ implying the capital–output ratio (where output is measured on a quarterly basis) of roughly 10, and $A = 3$ which implies that roughly 30 percent of time is spent in work activity. (These values will be used in Section IV below.)

II LINEARIZATION

The solution to the social planner's problem is characterized by a set of policy functions for capital, consumption, and labor; moreover, the solution exists and is unique (see Prescott (1986 [4])). There is, however, no analytical solution. To make the model operational, therefore, an approximate numerical solution is found. One of the simplest methods is to take a linear approximation (i.e., a first-order Taylor series expansion) of the three equilibrium conditions and the law of motion of the technology shock around the steady-state values ($\bar{c}$, $\bar{k}$, $\bar{h}$, $\bar{z}$). Provided the stochastic behavior of the model does not push the economy too far from the steady-state behavior, the linear approximation will be a good one. (The discussion below follows closely that of Farmer (1993).) This technique is demonstrated below.[1]

Intratemporal efficiency condition

The optimal labor–leisure choice is represented by condition *N1*:

$$c_t = \left[(1 - \alpha)/A\right] z_t k_t^{\alpha} h_t^{-\alpha}.$$

Linearizing around the steady-state values ($\bar{c}$, $\bar{k}$, $\bar{h}$, $\bar{z}$):

$$(c_t - \bar{c}) = \alpha \left[(1 - \alpha)/A\right] \bar{k}^{\alpha-1} \bar{h}^{-\alpha}(k_t - \bar{k}) - \alpha \left[(1 - \alpha)/A\right] \bar{k}^{\alpha} \bar{h}^{-\alpha-1}(h_t - \bar{h})$$

$$+ \left[(1 - \alpha)/A\right] \bar{k}^{\alpha} \bar{h}^{-\alpha}(z_t - \bar{z}) \qquad (2.4)$$

$$= \alpha \left[(1 - \alpha)/A\right] \bar{k}^{\alpha} \bar{h}^{-\alpha} \frac{(k_t - \bar{k})}{\bar{k}} - \alpha \left[(1 - \alpha)/A\right] \bar{k}^{\alpha} \bar{h}^{-\alpha} \frac{(h_t - \bar{h})}{\bar{h}}$$

$$+ \left[(1 - \alpha)/A\right] \bar{k}^{\alpha} \bar{h}^{-\alpha} \frac{(z_t - \bar{z})}{\bar{z}} .$$

Note that in the last expression, all variables have been expressed as percentage deviations from the steady state (the first two terms modify the respective derivatives while the last term uses the fact that $\bar{z} = 1$ in steady state). Consumption can be expressed as a percentage deviation from steady state by using the steady-state condition $\bar{c} = \left[(1 - \alpha)/A\right] \bar{k}^{\alpha} \bar{h}^{-\alpha}$; dividing both sides of the equation by this expression and denoting percentage deviations from steady state as $\tilde{x}$, equation (2.4) can be written as:

$$\tilde{c}_t = \alpha \, \tilde{k}_t - \alpha \, \tilde{h}_t + \tilde{z}_t. \qquad (2.5)$$

Intertemporal efficiency condition

This efficiency condition is given by $N2$:

$$c_t^{-1} = \beta E_t \left\{ c_{t+1}^{-1} \left[\alpha \, z_{t+1} k_{t+1}^{\alpha-1} h_{t+1}^{1-\alpha} + (1 - \delta) \right] \right\}.$$

Again, linearizing around the steady state, and expressing all variables as percentage deviations from steady state, yields:

$$- \bar{c}^{-1} \tilde{c}_t = - \beta \bar{c}^{-1} \left[\alpha \bar{k}^{\alpha-1} \bar{h}^{1-\alpha} + (1 - \delta) \right] E_t (\tilde{c}_{t+1}) + \beta \bar{c}^{-1} \alpha (\alpha - 1) \bar{k}^{\alpha-1} \bar{h}^{1-\alpha} E_t (\tilde{k}_{t+1})$$
$$+ \beta \bar{c}^{-1} \alpha (1 - \alpha) \bar{k}^{\alpha-1} \bar{h}^{1-\alpha} \, E_t (\tilde{h}_{t+1}) + \beta \bar{c}^{-1} \alpha \, \bar{k}^{\alpha-1} \bar{h}^{1-\alpha} \, E_t (\tilde{z}_{t+1}).$$

Multiplying each side of the equation by $\bar{c}$ and using the steady-state condition ($SS2$) that

$$1 = \beta \left[\alpha \, \bar{k}^{\alpha-1} \, \bar{h}^{1-\alpha} + (1 - \delta) \right]$$

yields:

$$- \tilde{c}_t = - E_t (\tilde{c}_{t+1}) + \beta (\alpha - 1) \alpha \, \bar{k}^{\alpha-1} \bar{h}^{1-\alpha} E_t (\tilde{k}_{t+1}).$$

$$+ \beta (1 - \alpha) \alpha \, \bar{k}^{\alpha-1} \bar{h}^{1-\alpha} E_t (\tilde{h}_{t+1}) \qquad (2.6)$$

$$+ \beta \, \alpha \, \bar{k}^{\alpha-1} \bar{h}^{1-\alpha} E_t (\tilde{z}_{t+1}).$$

Resource constraint

Following the same procedure as before, linearizing the resource constraint around the steady state yields:

$$\tilde{k}_{t+1} = \left[\alpha\, \bar{k}^{\alpha-1}\bar{h}^{1-\alpha} + (1-\delta)\right]\tilde{k}_t + (1-\alpha)\bar{k}^{\alpha-1}\bar{h}^{-\alpha}\tilde{h}_t + \bar{k}^{\alpha-1}\bar{h}^{1-\alpha}\tilde{z}_t$$
$$- (\bar{c}/\bar{k})\tilde{c}_t. \tag{2.7}$$

Technology shock process

The critical difference between the steady-state model and the real business cycle model is the assumption that technology shocks are random — the shocks follow the autoregressive process described in equation (2.1). Linearizing the autoregressive process for the technology shock results in:

$$\tilde{z}_{t+1} = \rho\tilde{z}_t + \tilde{\varepsilon}_{t+1}. \tag{2.8}$$

Taking expectations of both sides:

$$E_t(\tilde{z}_{t+1}) = \rho\tilde{z}_t. \tag{2.9}$$

III SOLUTION METHOD

The equations that define a rational expectations equilibrium (equations (2.5), (2.6), (2.7), and (2.9)) can be written as a vector expectational difference equation. Let

$$\mathbf{u}_t = \begin{bmatrix} \tilde{c}_t \\ \tilde{k}_t \\ \tilde{h}_t \\ \tilde{z}_t \end{bmatrix}$$

where bold print denotes a vector, then the linear system of equations can be written as:

$$\mathbf{A}\mathbf{u}_t = \mathbf{B}E_t(\mathbf{u}_{t+1}). \tag{2.10}$$

The matrices $\mathbf{A}$ and $\mathbf{B}$ are:

$$\mathbf{A} = \begin{bmatrix} 1 & -\alpha & \alpha & -1 \\ -1 & 0 & 0 & 0 \\ -\bar{c}/\bar{k} & \alpha\,\bar{k}^{\alpha-1}\bar{h}^{1-\alpha} + 1 - \delta & (1-\alpha)\bar{k}^{\alpha-1}\bar{h}^{1-\alpha} & \bar{k}^{\alpha-1}\bar{h}^{1-\alpha} \\ 0 & 0 & 0 & \rho \end{bmatrix}$$

$$\mathbf{B} = \begin{bmatrix} 0 & 0 & 0 & 0 \\ -1 & \beta(\alpha-1)\alpha\,\bar{k}^{\alpha-1}\bar{h}^{1-\alpha} & \beta(1-\alpha)\alpha\,\bar{k}^{\alpha-1}\bar{h}^{1-\alpha} & \beta\alpha\,\bar{k}^{\alpha-1}\bar{h}^{1-\alpha} \\ 0 & 1 & 0 & 0 \\ 0 & 0 & 0 & 1 \end{bmatrix}$$

Premultiplying both sides of equation (2.10) by $\mathbf{A}^{-1}$ yields:

$$\mathbf{u}_t = \mathbf{A}^{-1}\mathbf{B}\, E_t(\mathbf{u}_{t+1}). \tag{2.11}$$

The matrix $\mathbf{A}^{-1}\mathbf{B}$ can be decomposed as (see Hamilton (1994) for details):

$$\mathbf{A}^{-1}\mathbf{B} = \mathbf{Q}\Lambda\mathbf{Q}^{-1}. \tag{2.12}$$

where $\mathbf{Q}$ is a matrix whose columns are the eigenvectors of $\mathbf{A}^{-1}\mathbf{B}$ and Λ is a diagonal matrix whose diagonal elements are the eigenvalues of $\mathbf{A}^{-1}\mathbf{B}$. Using this decomposition and premultiplying both sides of the resulting expression in equation (2.11) by $\mathbf{Q}^{-1}$ yields:

$$\mathbf{Q}^{-1}\mathbf{u}_t \equiv \mathbf{d}_t = \Lambda\, E_t(\mathbf{d}_{t+1}) = \Lambda\, E_t(\mathbf{Q}^{-1}\mathbf{u}_{t+1}). \tag{2.13}$$

Note that the elements of the defined (4×1) column vector $\mathbf{d}_t$ are constructed from a linear combination of the elements in the rows of the (4×4) matrix $\mathbf{Q}^{-1}$ and the elements of the (4×1) column vector $\mathbf{u}_t$. Since Λ is a diagonal matrix, equation (2.13) implies four independent equations:

$$d_{i,t} = \lambda_i E_t(d_{i,t+1}); \; i = 1,2,3,4. \tag{2.14}$$

Since the equations in equation (2.14) must hold every period, it is possible to recursively substitute the expressions forward for T periods to yield:

$$d_{i,t} = \lambda_i^{\mathrm{T}} E_t(d_{i,t+\mathrm{T}}); \; i = 1,2,3,4. \tag{2.15}$$

The λ_i are four distinct eigenvalues associated with the four equilibrium conditions (equations (2.5)–(2.8)). Since one of these conditions is the law of motion for the exogenous technology shock (equation (2.8)), one of the eigenvalues will be ρ^{-1}. Also, the first rows of the matrices $\mathbf{A}$ and $\mathbf{B}$ are determined by the intratemporal efficiency condition; since this is not a dynamic relationship, one of the eigenvalues will be zero. The remaining two eigenvalues will bracket the value of unity as is typical for a saddle path equilibrium implied by the underlying stochastic growth framework. As implied by equation (2.15), the stable, rational expectations solution to the expectational difference equation is associated with the eigenvalue with a value less than one. That is, if $\lambda_i > 1$, then iterating forward implies $d_{i,t} \to \infty$ which is not a permissible equilibrium. Furthermore, for equation (2.15) to hold for all T (again taking the limit of the right-hand side), in the stable case when, $\lambda < 1$, it must be the true that $d_{i,t} = 0$; this restriction provides the desired solution. That is, $d_{i,t} = 0$ imposes the linear restriction on $(\tilde{c}_t, \tilde{k}_t, \tilde{h}_t, \tilde{z}_t)$, which is consistent with a rational expectations solution. (Recall that $d_{i,t}$ represents a linear combination between the elements of a particular row of $\mathbf{Q}^{-1}$ and the elements of the vector $\mathbf{u}_t$.)

IV A PARAMETRIC EXAMPLE

In this section, a parameterized version of the RBC model described above is solved. The following parameter values are used: ($\beta = 0.99$, $\alpha = 0.36$,

$\delta = 0.025$, $A = 3$). These imply the following steady-state values: ($\bar{c} = 0.79, \bar{k} = 10.90, \bar{h} = 0.29, \bar{y} = 1.06$). Note that these values imply that agents spend roughly 30 percent of their time in work activities and the capital–output ratio is approximately 10 (output is measured on a quarterly basis); both of these values are broadly consistent with US experience (see McGrattan, 1994).

The remaining parameter values determine the behavior of the technology shock. These are estimated by constructing the Solow residual[2] and then detrending that series linearly. Specifically, the Solow residual is defined as $Z_t = \ln y_t - \alpha \ln k_t - (1 - \alpha) \ln h_t$. The Z_t series can then be regressed on a linear time trend (which is consistent with the assumption of constant technological progress) and the residual is identified as the technology shock z_t. Using this procedure on quarterly data over the period 60.1–94.4 resulted in an estimate of the serial correlation of z_t (the parameter ρ) to be 0.95. The variance of the shock to technology (i.e., the variance of ε_t in equation (2.8)) was estimated to be 0.007. Note that the variance of the technology shock is not relevant in solving the linearized version of the model — however, when the solution of the model is used to generate artificial time series in the simulation of the economy, this parameter value must be stipulated.

These values generated the following entries into the **A** and **B** matrices:

$$
\begin{bmatrix}
1 & -0.36 & 0.36 & -1 \\
-1 & 0 & 0 & 0 \\
-0.072 & 1.010 & 0.062 & 0.098 \\
0 & 0 & 0 & 0.95
\end{bmatrix}
\begin{bmatrix}
\tilde{c}_t \\
\tilde{k}_t \\
\tilde{h}_t \\
\tilde{z}_t
\end{bmatrix}
=
\begin{bmatrix}
0 & 0 & 0 & 0 \\
-1 & -0.022 & 0.022 & 0.035 \\
0 & 1 & 0 & 0 \\
0 & 0 & 0 & 1
\end{bmatrix}
E_t
\begin{bmatrix}
\tilde{c}_{t+1} \\
\tilde{k}_{t+1} \\
\tilde{h}_{t+1} \\
\tilde{z}_{t+1}
\end{bmatrix}
$$

Following the steps described in the previous section (premultiplying by $\mathbf{A}^{-1}$) yields the following:

$$
\begin{bmatrix}
\tilde{c}_t \\
\tilde{k}_t \\
\tilde{h}_t \\
\tilde{z}_t
\end{bmatrix}
=
\begin{bmatrix}
1 & 0.022 & -0.022 & -0.035 \\
0.23 & 0.94 & -0.0051 & -0.27 \\
-2.55 & 0.87 & 0.057 & 2.75 \\
0 & 0 & 0 & 1.05
\end{bmatrix}
E_t
\begin{bmatrix}
\tilde{c}_{t+1} \\
\tilde{k}_{t+1} \\
\tilde{h}_{t+1} \\
\tilde{z}_{t+1}
\end{bmatrix}
$$

Next, decomposing $\mathbf{A}^{-1} \mathbf{B}$ into $\mathbf{Q \Lambda Q}^{-1}$ and then premultiplying by $\mathbf{Q}^{-1}$ yields

$$
\mathbf{Q}^{-1}\mathbf{u}_t =
\begin{bmatrix}
-2.18 & -0.048 & 0.048 & 24.26 \\
0 & 0 & 0 & 23.01 \\
-2.50 & 1.36 & 0.056 & 1.10 \\
-2.62 & 0.94 & -0.94 & 2.62
\end{bmatrix}
\begin{bmatrix}
\tilde{c}_t \\
\tilde{k}_t \\
\tilde{h}_t \\
\tilde{z}_t
\end{bmatrix}
= \Lambda E_t \left(\mathbf{Q}^{-1}\mathbf{u}_{t+1} \right)
$$

$$
=
\begin{bmatrix}
1.062 & 0 & 0 & 0 \\
0 & 1.05 & 0 & 0 \\
0 & 0 & 0.93 & 0 \\
0 & 0 & 0 & 0
\end{bmatrix}
E_t
\left\{
\begin{bmatrix}
-2.18 & -0.048 & 0.048 & 24.26 \\
0 & 0 & 0 & 23.01 \\
-2.50 & 1.36 & 0.056 & 1.10 \\
-2.62 & 0.94 & -0.94 & 2.62
\end{bmatrix}
\begin{bmatrix}
\tilde{c}_{t+1} \\
\tilde{k}_{t+1} \\
\tilde{h}_{t+1} \\
\tilde{z}_{t+1}
\end{bmatrix}
\right\}
$$

The entries in the matrix Λ (i.e., the eigenvalues of $\mathbf{A}^{-1}\mathbf{B}$) determine the solution. Note that the second diagonal entry is (accounting for rounding error) ρ^{-1}. The fourth row of Λ is associated with the intratemporal efficiency condition. These values are proportional to those given in the first row of the $\mathbf{A}$ matrix; consequently, dividing all entries by (-2.62) returns the original intratemporal efficiency condition. The remaining two entries in the Λ matrix are those related to the saddle path properties of the steady-state solution. Since a stable rational expectations solution is associated with an eigenvalue less than unity, the third row of the $\mathbf{Q}^{-1}$ matrix provides the linear restriction we are seeking. That is, the rational expectations solution is:

$$-2.50\tilde{c}_t + 1.36\tilde{h}_t + 0.056\tilde{k}_t + 10.1\tilde{z}_t = 0,$$

or:

$$\tilde{c}_t = 0.54\tilde{h}_t + 0.02\tilde{k}_t + 0.44\tilde{z}_t. \tag{2.16}$$

The law of motion for the capital stock (the parameter values are given in the third row of the $\mathbf{A}$ matrix) and the intratemporal efficiency condition provides two more equilibrium conditions:

$$\tilde{k}_{t+1} = -0.07\tilde{c}_t + 1.01\tilde{k}_t + 0.06\tilde{h}_t + 0.10\tilde{z}_t. \tag{2.17}$$

$$\tilde{h}_t = -2.78\tilde{c}_t + \tilde{k}_t + 2.78\tilde{z}_t. \tag{2.18}$$

A random number generator can next be used to produce a sequence of technology shocks. The above equilibrium equations can then be used to produce time series for capital, consumption, labor, and output.

V ANALYZING OUTPUT FROM THE ARTIFICIAL ECONOMY

The solution to the model is characterized by equations (2.16)–(2.18). Given initial values for capital, and next generating a path for the exogenous technology shock ($\tilde{z}_t$), these equations will produce time series for ($\tilde{c}_t$, $\tilde{k}_t$, $\tilde{h}_t$). Two other series that most macroeconomists are interested in, namely, output and investment, can be generated by linearizing the production function and the resource constraint, respectively.

Specifically, for output, linearizing the assumed Cobb-Douglas production function (i.e., $y_t = z_t k_t^\alpha h_t^{1-\alpha}$ and using the calibrated value that $\alpha = 0.36$) yields the following equation:

$$\tilde{y}_t = \tilde{z}_t + 0.36\,\tilde{k}_t + 0.64\,\tilde{h}_t. \tag{2.19}$$

Finally, a linear approximation of the condition that, in equilibrium, output must equal the sum of consumption and investment, can be expressed in the form of a percentage deviation from the steady state as:

$$\tilde{\imath}_t = \frac{\bar{y}}{\bar{\imath}} \, \tilde{y}_t - \frac{\bar{c}}{\bar{\imath}} \tilde{c}_t. \tag{2.20}$$

Using the steady-state values employed in the numerical solution, the investment equation becomes:

$$\tilde{\imath}_t = \frac{1.06}{0.27} \, \tilde{y}_t - \frac{0.79}{0.27} \, \tilde{c}_t = 3.92 \, \tilde{y}_t - 2.92 \tilde{c}_t. \tag{2.21}$$

Hence, equilibrium in this economy is described by the following set of equations:

$$\tilde{c}_t = 0.54 \tilde{h}_t + 0.02 \tilde{k}_t + 0.44 \tilde{z}_t$$

$$\tilde{k}_{t+1} = -0.07 \tilde{c}_t + 1.01 \tilde{k}_t + 0.06 \tilde{h}_t + 0.10 \tilde{z}_t$$

$$\tilde{h}_t = -2.78 \tilde{c}_t + \tilde{k}_t + 2.78 \tilde{z}_t$$

$$\tilde{y}_t = \tilde{z}_t + 0.36 \, \tilde{k}_t + 0.64 \tilde{h}_t$$

$$\tilde{\imath}_t = 3.92 \, \tilde{y}_t - 2.92 \tilde{c}_t$$

$$\tilde{z}_t = 0.95 \, \tilde{z}_{t-1} + \tilde{\varepsilon}_t.$$

To generate the time series implied by the model, it is necessary first to generate a series for the innovations to the technology shock, i.e., $\tilde{\varepsilon}_t$. These

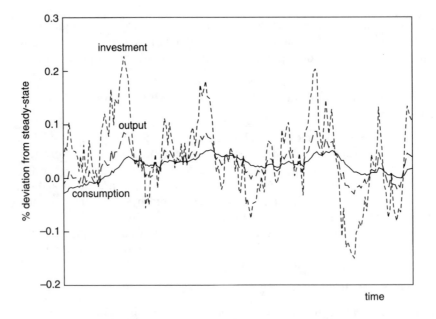

Figure 2.1 Output, Consumption, and Investment in RBC Model

Table 2.1 Descriptive Statistics for US and RBC model

		Relative volatility	Corr (x, y)
Consumption	Model	0.52	0.82
	US data	0.49	0.76
Investment	Model	2.86	0.95
	US data	3.02	0.80
Labor	Model	0.65	0.89
	US data	0.96	0.88

Source: Statistics for US data are taken from Kydland and Prescott (1990 [20]), tables I and II, pp. 10–11.

are assumed to have a mean of zero and a variance that is consistent with the observed variance for the innovations, which, as mentioned above, is roughly 0.007. Then, initializing $\tilde{z}_t = 0$ and using a random number generator in order to generate the innovations, a path for the technology shocks is created. Next, assuming that all remaining values are initially at their steady state (which implies that all initial values are set to zero), the system of equations above can be solved to produce the time path for the endogenous variables.

We generate artificial time paths for consumption, output, and investment (3000 observations were created and only the last 120 were examined), and these are shown in Figure 2.1. It is clear from Figure 2.1, as is also true in the actual data, that the volatility of investment is greater than that of output, which is greater than that of consumption. To see this more precisely, the standard deviation of consumption, labor, and investment relative to output is reported in Table 2.1, along with the correlations of these series with output.

NOTES

1 Recall that the general form for the Taylor series expansion of a function around a point x^* is:

$$f(x) - f(x^*) = f'(x^*)(x - x^*) + f''(x^*) \frac{(x - x^*)^2}{2!} + f'''(x^*) \frac{(x - x^*)^3}{3!} + \dots$$

where $N!$ denotes factorial.

2 The use of the Solow residual as a measure of technology shocks is discussed in Hoover and Salyer (1996).

REFERENCES

Debreu, Gerard (1954) "Valuation Equilibrium and Pareto Optimum," *Proceedings of the National Academy of Science*, 40: 588–92.

Farmer, Roger E. A. (1993) *The Macroeconomics of Self-fulfilling Prophecies*, Cambridge, Mass.: MIT Press.

Hamilton, James D. (1994) *Time Series Analysis*, Princeton: Princeton University Press.

Hansen, Gary D. (1985) "Indivisible Labor and the Business Cycle," *Journal of Monetary Economics,* 16(3), November: 309–28, reprinted here in Chapter 8.

Hansen, Gary D. and Randall Wright (1992) "The Labor Market in Real Business Cycle Theory," *Federal Reserve Bank of Minneapolis Quarterly Review*, 16(2), Spring: 2–12, reprinted here in Chapter 9.

Hoover, Kevin D. and Kevin D. Salyer (1996) "Technology Shocks or Colored Noise? Why Real Business Cycle Models Cannot Explain Actual Business Cycles," unpublished manuscript.

Kydland, Finn E. and Edward C. Prescott (1990) "Business Cycles: Real Facts and a Monetary Myth," *Federal Reserve Bank of Minneapolis Quarterly Review,* 14(2), Spring: 3–18, reprinted here in Chapter 20.

McGratten, Ellen R. (1994) "A Progress Report on Business Cycle Models," *Federal Reserve Bank of Minneapolis Quarterly Review*, 18(4), Fall: 2–16.

Prescott, Edward C. (1986) "Theory Ahead of Business Cycle Measurement," Federal Reserve Bank of Minneapolis Quarterly Review, 10(4), Fall: 9–22, reprinted here in Chapter 4.

Sargent, Thomas J. (1987) *Dynamic Macroeconomic Theory*, Cambridge, Mass.: Harvard University Press.

Part II

The foundations of real business cycle modeling

ECONOMETRICA

VOLUME 50   NOVEMBER, 1982   NUMBER 6

TIME TO BUILD AND AGGREGATE FLUCTUATIONS

By Finn E. Kydland and Edward C. Prescott[1]

The equilibrium growth model is modified and used to explain the cyclical variances of a set of economic time series, the covariances between real output and the other series, and the autocovariance of output. The model is fitted to quarterly data for the post-war U.S. economy. Crucial features of the model are the assumption that more than one time period is required for the construction of new productive capital, and the non-time-separable utility function that admits greater intertemporal substitution of leisure. The fit is surprisingly good in light of the model's simplicity and the small number of free parameters.

1. INTRODUCTION

THAT WINE IS NOT MADE in a day has long been recognized by economists (e.g., Böhm–Bawerk [6]). But, neither are ships nor factories built in a day. A thesis of this essay is that the assumption of multiple-period construction is crucial for explaining aggregate fluctuations. A general equilibrium model is developed and fitted to U.S. quarterly data for the post-war period. The co-movements of the fluctuations for the fitted model are quantitatively consistent with the corresponding co-movements for U.S. data. In addition, the serial correlations of cyclical output for the model match well with those observed.

Our approach integrates growth and business cycle theory. Like standard growth theory, a representative infinitely-lived household is assumed. As fluctuations in employment are central to the business cycle, the stand-in consumer values not only consumption but also leisure. One very important modification to the standard growth model is that multiple periods are required to build new capital goods and only finished capital goods are part of the productive capital stock. Each stage of production requires a period and utilizes resources. Half-finished ships and factories are not part of the productive capital stock. Section 2 contains a short critique of the commonly used investment technologies, and presents evidence that single-period production, even with adjustment costs, is inadequate. The preference-technology-information structure of the model is presented in Section 3. A crucial feature of preferences is the non-time-separable utility function that admits greater intertemporal substitution of leisure. The exogenous stochastic components in the model are shocks to technology and imperfect indicators of productivity. The two technology shocks differ in their persistence.

The steady state for the model is determined in Section 4, and quadratic approximations are made which result in an "indirect" quadratic utility function that values leisure, the capital goods, and the negative of investments. Most of

[1] The research was supported by the National Science Foundation. We are grateful to Sean Becketti, Fischer Black, Robert S. Chirinko, Mark Gersovitz, Christopher A. Sims, and John B. Taylor for helpful comments, to Sumru Altug for research assistance, and to the participants in the seminars at the several universities at which earlier drafts were presented.

the relatively small number of parameters are estimated using steady state considerations. Findings in other applied areas of economics are also used to calibrate the model. For example, the assumed number of periods required to build new productive capital is of the magnitude reported by business, and findings in labor economics are used to restrict the utility function. The small set of free parameters imposes considerable discipline upon the inquiry. The estimated model and the comparison of its predictions with the empirical regularities of interest are in Section 5. The final section contains concluding comments.

2. A CRITIQUE OF CONVENTIONAL AGGREGATE INVESTMENT TECHNOLOGIES

There are two basic technologies that have been adopted in empirical studies of aggregate investment behavior. The first assumes a constant-returns-to-scale neoclassical production function F with labor L and capital K as the inputs. Total output $F(K, L)$ constrains the sum of investment and consumption, or $C + I \leq F(K, L)$, where $C, I, K, L \geq 0$. The rate of change of capital, $\dot{K}$, is investment less depreciation, and depreciation is proportional with factor δ to the capital stock, that is, $\dot{K} = I - \delta K$. This is the technology underlying the work of Jorgenson [19] on investment behavior.

An implication of this technology is that the relative price of the investment and consumption goods will be a constant independent of the relative outputs of the two goods.[2] It also implies that the shadow price of existing capital will be the same as the price of the investment good.[3] There is a sizable empirical literature that has found a strong association between the level of investment and a shadow price of capital obtained from stock market data (see [26]). This finding is inconsistent with this assumed technology as is the fact that this shadow price varies considerably over the business cycle.

The alternative technology, which is consistent with these findings, is the single capital good adjustment cost technology.[4] Much of that literature is based upon the problem facing the firm and the aggregation problem receives little attention. This has led some to distinguish between internal and external adjustment costs. For aggregate investment theory this is not an issue (see [29]) though for other questions it will be. Labor resources are needed to install capital whether the acquiring or supplying firm installs the equipment. With competitive equilibrium it is the aggregate production possibility set that matters. That is, if the Y_j are the production possibility sets of the firms associated with a given industrial organi-

---

[2] This, of course, assumes neither C nor I is zero. Sargent [32], within a growth context with shocks to both preferences and technology, has at a theoretical level analyzed the equilibrium with corners. Only when investment was zero did the price of the investment good relative to that of the consumption good become different from one and then it was less than one. This was not an empirical study and Sargent states that there currently are no computationally practical econometric methods for conducting an empirical investigation within that theoretical framework.

[3] The shadow price of capital has been emphasized by Brunner and Meltzer [7] and Tobin [36] in their aggregate models.

[4] See [1, 17] for recent empirical studies based on this technology.

zation and Y_j' for some other industrial organization, the same aggregate supply behavior results if $\sum Y_j = \sum Y_j'$.

The adjustment cost model, rather than assuming a linear product transformation curve between the investment and consumption goods, imposes curvature. This can be represented by the following technology:

$$G(C, I) \leq F(K, L), \qquad \dot{K} = I - \delta K,$$

where G like F is increasing, concave, and homogeneous of degree one. Letting the price of the consumption good be one, the price of the investment good q_t, the rental price of capital r_t, and the wage rate w_t, the firm's problem is to maximize real profits, $C_t + q_t I_t - w_t L_t - r_t K_t$, subject to the production constraint. As constant returns to scale are assumed, the distribution of capital does not matter, and one can proceed as if there were a single price-taking firm. Assuming an interior solution, given that this technology displays constant returns to scale and that the technology is separable between inputs and outputs, it follows that $I_t = F(K_t, L_t) h(q_t) \equiv Z_t h(q_t)$, where Z_t is defined to be aggregate output. The function h is increasing, so high investment-output ratios are associated with a high price of the investment good relative to the consumption good. Figure 1 depicts the investment-consumption product transformation curve and Figure 2 the function $h(q)$. For any I/Z, the negative of the slope of the transformation curve in Figure 1 is the height of the curve in Figure 2. This establishes that a higher q will be associated with higher investment for this technology. This restriction of the theory is consistent with the empirical findings previously cited.

There are other predictions of this theory, however, which are questionable. If we think of the q-investment curve h depicted in Figure 2 as a supply curve, the short- and the long-run supply elasticities will be equal. Typically, economists argue that there are specialized resources which cannot be instantaneously and costlessly transferred between industries and that even though short-run elasticities may be low, in the long run supply elasticities are high. As there are no specialized resources for the adjustment cost technology, such considerations are absent and there are no penalties resulting from rapid adjustment in the relative outputs of the consumption and investment good.

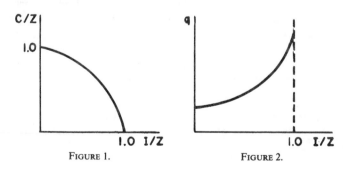

FIGURE 1.   FIGURE 2.

To test whether the theory is a reasonable approximation, we examined cross-section state data. The correlations between the ratios of commercial construction to either state personal income or state employment and price per square foot[5] are both -0.35. With perfectly elastic supply and uncorrelated supply and demand errors, this correlation cannot be positive. To explain this large negative correlation, one needs a combination of high variability in the cross-sectional supply relative to cross-sectional demand plus a positive slope for the supply curve. Our view is that, given mobility of resources, it seems more plausible that the demand is the more variable. Admitting potential data problems, this cross-sectional result casts some doubt upon the adequacy of the single capital good adjustment cost model.

At the aggregate level, an implication of the single capital good adjustment cost model is that when the investment-output ratio is regressed on current and lagged q, only current q should matter.[6] The findings in [26] are counter to this prediction.

In summary, our view is that neither the neoclassical nor the adjustment cost technologies are adequate. The neoclassical structure is inconsistent with the positive association between the shadow price of capital and investment activity. The adjustment cost technology is consistent with this observation, but inconsistent with cross-sectional data and the association of investment with the lagged as well as the current capital shadow prices. In addition, the implication that long- and short-run supply elasticities are equal is one which we think a technology should not have.

Most destructive of all to the adjustment-cost technology, however, is the finding that the time required to complete investment projects is not short relative to the business cycle. Mayer [27], on the basis of a survey, found that the average time (weighted by the size of the project) between the decision to undertake an investment project and the completion of it was twenty-one months. Similarly, Hall [13] found the average lag between the design of a project and when it becomes productive to be about two years. It is a thesis of this essay that periods this long or even half that long have important effects upon the serial correlation properties of the cyclical components of investment and total output as well as on certain co-movements of aggregate variables.

The technological requirement that there are multiple stages of production is not the delivery lag problem considered by Jorgenson [19]. He theorized at the firm level and imposed no consistency of behavior requirement for suppliers and demanders of the investment good. His was not a market equilibrium analysis and there was no theory accounting for the delivery lag. Developing such a market theory with information asymmetries, queues, rationing, and the like is a challenging problem confronting students of industrial organization.

---

[5] The data on commercial construction and price per square foot were for 1978 and were obtained from F. W. Dodge Division of McGraw-Hill.

[6] This observation is due to Fumio Hayashi.

Our technology assumes that a single period is required for each stage of construction or that the time required to build new capital is a constant. This is not to argue that there are not alternative technologies with different construction periods, patterns of resource use, and total costs. We have found no evidence that the capital goods are built significantly more rapidly when total investment activity is higher or lower. Lengthening delivery lags (see [9]) in periods of high activity may be a matter of longer queues and actual construction times may be shorter. Premiums paid for earlier delivery could very well be for a more advanced position in the queue than for a more rapidly constructed factory. These are, of course, empirical questions, and important cyclical variation in the construction period would necessitate an alternative technology.

Our time-to-build technology is consistent with short-run fluctuations in the shadow price of capital because in the short run capital is supplied inelastically. It also implies that the long-run supply is infinitely elastic, so on average the relative price of the investment good is independent of the investment-output ratio.

3. THE MODEL

Technology

The technology assumes time is required to build new productive capital. Let s_{jt} be the number of projects j stages or j periods from completion for $j = 1, \ldots, J - 1$, where J periods are required to build new productive capacity. New investment projects initiated in period t are s_{Jt}. The recursive representation of the laws of motion of these capital stocks is

$$(3.1) \qquad k_{t+1} = (1 - \delta)k_t + s_{1t},$$

$$(3.2) \qquad s_{j,t+1} = s_{j+1,t} \qquad (j = 1, \ldots, J - 1).$$

Here, k_t is the capital stock at the beginning of period t, and δ is the depreciation rate. The element s_{Jt} is a decision variable for period t.

The final capital good is the inventory stock y_t inherited from the previous period.[7] Thus, in this economy, there are $J + 1$ types of capital: inventories y_t, productive capital k_t, and the capital stocks j stages from completion for $j = 1, \ldots, J - 1$. These variables summarize the effects of past decisions upon current and future production possibilities.

Let φ_j for $j = 1, \ldots, J$ be the fraction of the resources allocated to the investment project in the jth stage from the last. Total non-inventory investment in period t is $\sum_{j=1}^{J} \varphi_j s_{jt}$. Total investment, i_t, is this amount plus inventory

---

[7] All stocks are beginning-of-the-period stocks.

investment $y_{t+1} - y_t$, and consequently

$$(3.3) \qquad i_t = \sum_{j=1}^{J} \varphi_j s_{jt} + y_{t+1} - y_t.$$

Total output, that is, the sum of consumption c_t and investment, is constrained as follows:

$$(3.4) \qquad c_t + i_t \le f(\lambda_t, k_t, n_t, y_t),$$

where n_t is labor input, λ_t a shock to technology, and f is a constant-returns-to-scale production function to be parameterized subsequently.

Treating inventories as a factor of production warrants some discussion. With larger inventories, stores can economize on labor resources allocated to restocking. Firms, by making larger production runs, reduce equipment down time associated with shifting from producing one type of good to another. Besides considerations such as these, analytic considerations necessitated this approach. If inventories were not a factor of production, it would be impossible to locally approximate the economy using a quadratic objective and linear constraints. Without such an approximation no practical computational method currently exists for computing the equilibrium process of the model.

The production function is assumed to have the form

$$(3.5) \qquad f(\lambda, k, n, y) = \lambda n^\theta \big[(1 - \sigma) k^{-\nu} + \sigma y^{-\nu} \big]^{-(1-\theta)/\nu}$$

where $0 < \theta < 1$, $0 < \sigma < 1$, and $0 < \nu < \infty$. This form was selected because, among other things, it results in a share θ for labor in the steady state. The elasticity of substitution between capital and inventory is $1/(1 + \nu)$. This elasticity is probably less than one which is why ν is required to be positive.

Preferences

The preference function, whose expected value the representative household maximizes, has the form $\sum_{t=0}^{\infty} \beta^t u(c_t, \alpha(L)l_t)$, where $0 < \beta < 1$ is the discount factor, l_t leisure, L the lag operator, and $\alpha(L) = \sum_{i=0}^{\infty} \alpha_i L^i$. Normalizing so that one is the endowment of time, we let $n_t = 1 - l_t$ be the time allocated to market activity. The polynomial lag operator is restricted so that the α_i sum to one, and $\alpha_i = (1 - \eta)^{i-1} \alpha_1$ for $i \ge 1$, where $0 < \eta \le 1$. With these restrictions,

$$\alpha(L)l_t = 1 - \alpha(L)n_t = 1 - \alpha_0 n_t - (1 - \alpha_0)\eta \sum_{i=1}^{\infty} (1 - \eta)^{i-1} n_{t-i}.$$

By defining the variable $a_t = \sum_{i=1}^{\infty} (1 - \eta)^{i-1} n_{t-i}$, the distributed lag has the following recursive representation:

$$\alpha(L)l_t = 1 - \alpha_0 n_t - \eta(1 - \alpha_0)a_t, \quad \text{and}$$

$$(3.6) \qquad a_{t+1} = (1 - \eta)a_t + n_t.$$

The variable a_t summarizes the effects of all past leisure choices on current and future preferences. If $n_s = n_t$ for all $s \leq t$, then $a_t = n_t/\eta$, and the distributed lag is simply $1 - n_t$.

The parameters α_0 and η determine the degree to which leisure is intertemporally substitutable. We require $0 < \eta \leq 1$ and $0 < \alpha_0 \leq 1$. The nearer α_0 is to one, the less is the intertemporal substitution of leisure. For α_0 equal to one, time-separable utility results. With η equal to one, a_t equals n_{t-1}. This is the structure employed in [33]. As η approaches zero, past leisure choices have greater effect upon current utility flows.

Non-time-separable utility functions are implicit in the empirical study of aggregate labor supply in [25]. Grossman [12] and Lucas [24] discuss why a non-time-separable utility function is needed to explain the business cycle fluctuations in employment and consumption. A micro justification for our hypothesized structure based on a Beckerian household production function is as follows.[8] Time allocated to non-market activities, that is l_t, is used in household production. If there is a stock of household projects with varying output per unit of time, the rational household would allocate l_t to those projects with the greatest returns per time unit. If the household has allocated a larger amount of time to non-market activities in the recent past, then only projects with smaller yields should remain. Thus, if a_t is lower, the marginal utility value of l_t should be smaller.

Cross-sectional evidence of households' willingness to redistribute labor supply over time is the lumpiness of that supply. There are vacations and movements of household members into and out of the labor force for extended periods which are not in response to large movements in the real wage. Another observation suggesting high intertemporal substitutability of leisure is the large seasonal variation in hours of market employment. Finally, the failure of Abowd and Ashenfelter [2] to find a significant wage premium for jobs with more variable employment and earnings patterns is further evidence. In summary, household production theory and cross-sectional evidence support a non-time-separable utility function that admits greater intertemporal substitution of leisure—something which is needed to explain aggregate movements in employment in an equilibrium model.

The utility function in our model is assumed to have the form

$$u\big(c_t, \alpha(L)l_t\big) = \Big[c_t^{1/3}\big(\alpha(L)l_t\big)^{2/3} \Big]^\gamma / \gamma,$$

where $\gamma < 1$ and $\gamma \neq 0$. If the term in the square brackets is interpreted as a composite commodity, then this is the constant-relative-risk-aversion utility function with the relative degree of risk aversion being $1 - \gamma$. We thought this composite commodity should be homogeneous of degree one as is the case when there is a single good. The relative size of the two exponents inside the brackets is

---

[8] We thank Nasser Saïdi for suggesting this argument.

motivated by the fact that households' allocation of time to nonmarket activities is about twice as large as the allocation to market activities.

Information Structure

We assume that the technology parameter is subject to a stochastic process with components of differing persistence. The productivity parameter is not observed but the stand-in consumer does observe an indicator or noisy measure of this parameter at the beginning of the period. This might be due to errors in reporting data or just the fact that there are errors in the best or consensus forecast of what productivity will be for the period. On the basis of the indicator and knowledge of the economy-wide state variables, decisions of how many new investment projects to initiate and of how much of the time endowment to allocate to the production of marketed goods are made. Subsequent to observing aggregate output, the consumption level is chosen with inventory investment being aggregate output less fixed investment and consumption.

Specifically, the technology shock, λ_t, is the sum of a permanent component, λ_{1t}, and a transitory component,[9] λ_{2t}:

$$(3.7) \qquad \lambda_t = \lambda_{1t} + \lambda_{2t} + \bar{\lambda}.$$

In the spirit of the Friedman-Muth permanent-income model, the permanent component is highly persistent so

$$(3.8) \qquad \lambda_{1,t+1} = \rho\lambda_{1t} + \zeta_{1t},$$

where ρ is less than but near one and ζ_{1t} is a permanent shock.[10] The transitory component equals the transitory shock so

$$(3.9) \qquad \lambda_{2,t+1} = \zeta_{2t}.$$

The indicator of productivity, π_t, is the sum of actual productivity λ_t and a third shock ζ_{3t}:

$$(3.10) \qquad \pi_t = \lambda_t + \zeta_{3t} = \lambda_{1t} + \lambda_{2t} + \zeta_{3t} + \bar{\lambda}.$$

The shock vectors $\zeta_t = (\zeta_{1t}, \zeta_{2t}, \zeta_{3t})$ are independent multivariate normal with mean vector zero and diagonal covariance matrix.

The period-t labor supply decision n_t and new investment project decision s_{jt} are made contingent upon the past history of productivity shocks, the λ_k for $k < t$, the indicator of productivity π_t, the stocks of capital inherited from the past, and variable a_t. These decisions cannot be contingent upon λ_t for it is not

---

[9] The importance of permanent and transitory shocks in studying macro fluctuations is emphasized in [8].

[10] The value used for ρ in this study was 0.95. The reason we restricted ρ to be strictly less than one was technical. The theorem we employ to guarantee the existence of competitive equilibrium requires stationarity of the shock.

observed or deducible at the time of these decisions. The consumption-inventory investment decision, however, is contingent upon λ_t for aggregate output is observed prior to this decision and λ_t can be deduced from aggregate output and knowledge of inputs.

The state space is an appropriate formalism for representing this recursive information structure. Because of the two-stage decision process, it is not a direct application of Kalman filtering. Like that approach the separation of estimation and control is exploited. The general structure assumes an unobservable state vector, say x_t, that follows a vector autoregressive process with independent multivariate normal innovations:

$$(3.11) \quad x_{t+1} = A x_t + \epsilon_{0t}, \quad \text{where} \quad \epsilon_{0t} \sim N(0, V_0).$$

Observed prior to selecting the first set of decisions is

$$(3.12) \quad p_{1t} = B_1 x_t + \epsilon_{1t}, \quad \text{where} \quad \epsilon_{1t} \sim N(0, V_1).$$

The element B_1 is a matrix and the ϵ_{1t} are independent over time. Observed prior to the second set of decisions and subsequent to the first set is

$$(3.13) \quad p_{2t} = B_2 x_t + \epsilon_{2t}, \quad \text{where} \quad \epsilon_{2t} \sim N(0, V_2).$$

Equations (3.11)–(3.13) define the general information structure.

To map our information structure into the general formulation, let $x_t' = (\lambda_{1t}, \lambda_{2t})$, $B_1 = [1\ 1]$, $B_2 = [1\ 1]$,

$$A = \begin{bmatrix} \rho & 0 \\ 0 & 0 \end{bmatrix}, \qquad V_0 = \begin{bmatrix} \text{var}(\zeta_1) & 0 \\ 0 & \text{var}(\zeta_2) \end{bmatrix},$$

$V_1 = [\text{var}(\zeta_3)]$, and $V_2 = [0]$. With these definitions, the information structure (3.7)–(3.10) viewed as deviations from the mean and the representation (3.11)–(3.13) are equivalent.

Let m_{0t} be the expected value and Σ_0 the covariance of the distribution of x_t conditional upon the $p_k = (p_{1k}, p_{2k})$ for $k < t$. Using the conditional probability laws for the multivariate normal distribution (see [28, p. 208]) and letting m_{1t} and Σ_1 be the mean and covariance of x_t conditional upon p_{1t} as well, we obtain

$$(3.14) \quad m_{1t} = m_{0t} + (B_1 \Sigma_0)'(B_1 \Sigma_0 B_1' + V_1)^{-1}(p_{1t} - B_1 m_{0t}), \quad \text{and}$$

$$(3.15) \quad \Sigma_1 = \Sigma_0 - (B_1 \Sigma_0)'(B_1 \Sigma_0 B_1' + V_1)^{-1} B_1 \Sigma_0.$$

Similarly, the mean vector m_{2t} and covariance matrix Σ_2 conditional upon p_{2t} as well are

$$(3.16) \quad m_{2t} = m_{1t} + (B_2 \Sigma_1)'(B_2 \Sigma_1 B_2' + V_2)^{-1}(p_{2t} - B_2 m_{1t}), \quad \text{and}$$

$$(3.17) \quad \Sigma_2 = \Sigma_1 - (B_2 \Sigma_1)'(B_2 \Sigma_1 B_2' + V_2)^{-1} B_2 \Sigma_1.$$

Finally, from (3.11),

(3.18) $m_{0,t+1} = A m_{2t}$,   and

(3.19) $\Sigma_0 = A \Sigma_2 A' + V_0$.

The covariances Σ_0, Σ_1, and Σ_2 are defined recursively by (3.15), (3.17), and (3.19). The matrix V_0 being of full rank along with the stability of A are sufficient to insure that the method of successive approximations converges exponentially fast to a unique solution.

The covariance elements Σ_0, Σ_1, and Σ_2 do not change over time and are therefore not part of the information set. The m_{0t}, m_{1t}, and m_{2t} do change but are sufficient relative to the relevant histories for forecasting future values of both the unobserved state and the observable p_τ, $\tau > t$, and for estimating the current unobserved state.

Equilibrium

To determine the equilibrium process for this model, we exploit the well-known result that, in the absence of externalities, competitive equilibria are Pareto optima. With homogeneous individuals, the relevant Pareto optimum is the one which maximizes the welfare of the stand-in consumer subject to the technology constraints and the information structure. Thus, the problem is to

$$\text{maximize } E \sum_{t=0}^{\infty} \beta^t u \big[c_t, 1 - \alpha_0 n_t - \eta(1 - \alpha_0) a_t \big]$$

subject to constraints (3.1)–(3.4), (3.6), and (3.11)–(3.13), given k_0, $s_{10}, \ldots, s_{J-1,0}$, a_0, and that $x_0 \sim N(m_0, \Sigma_0)$. The decision variables at time t are n_t, s_{Jt}, c_t, and y_{t+1}. Further, n_t and s_{Jt} cannot be contingent upon p_{2t} for it is observed subsequent to these decisions.

This is a standard discounted dynamic programming problem. There are optimal time-invariant or stationary rules of the form

$$n_t = n(k_t, s_{1t}, s_{2t}, \ldots, s_{J-1,t}, y_t, a_t, m_{1t}),$$

$$s_{Jt} = s(k_t, s_{1t}, s_{2t}, \ldots, s_{J-1,t}, y_t, a_t, m_{1t}),$$

$$c_t = c(k_t, s_{1t}, s_{2t}, \ldots, s_{Jt}, y_t, a_t, n_t, m_{2t}),$$

$$y_{t+1} = y(k_t, s_{1t}, s_{2t}, \ldots, s_{Jt}, y_t, a_t, n_t, m_{2t}).$$

It is important to note that the second pair of decisions are contingent upon m_{2t} rather than m_{1t} and that they are contingent also upon the first set of decisions s_{Jt} and n_t.

The existence of such decision rules and the connection with the competitive allocation is established in [31]. But, approximations are necessary before equilibrium decision rules can be computed. Our approach is to determine the steady state for the model with no shocks to technology. Next, quadratic approximations are made in the neighborhood of the steady state. Equilibrium decision rules for the resulting approximate economy are then computed. These rules are linear, so in equilibrium the approximate economy is generated by a system of stochastic difference equations for which covariances are easily determined.

4. STEADY STATE, APPROXIMATION, AND COMPUTATION OF EQUILIBRIUM

Variables without subscript denote steady state values. The steady state interest rate is $r = (1 - \beta)/\beta$, and the steady state price of (non-inventory) capital $q = \sum_{j=1}^{J}(1 + r)^{j-1}\varphi_j$. The latter is obtained by observing that φ_1 units of consumption must be foregone in the current period, φ_2 units the period before, etc., in order to obtain one additional unit of capital for use next period.

Two steady state conditions are obtained by equating marginal products to rental rates, namely $f_y = r$ and $f_k = q(r + \delta)$. These imply $f_k/f_y = q(r + \delta)/r$. For production function (3.5), this reduces to

$$(4.1) \qquad y = \left[\frac{r + \delta}{r} q \frac{\sigma}{1 - \sigma} \right]^{1/(\nu+1)} k \equiv b_1 k.$$

Differentiating the production function with respect to capital, substituting for y from (4.1), and equating to the steady-state rental price, one obtains

$$(1 - \theta)(1 - \sigma)b_2^{-(1-\theta-\nu)/\nu}\lambda n^{\theta}k^{-\theta} = q(r + \delta),$$

where $b_2 = 1 - \sigma + \sigma b_1^{-\nu}$. Solving for k as a function of n yields

$$(4.2) \qquad k = \left[\frac{(1 - \theta)(1 - \sigma)}{q(r + \delta)} b_2^{-(1-\theta-\nu)/\nu} \right]^{1/\theta} \lambda^{1/\theta}n \equiv b_3 \lambda^{1/\theta}n.$$

Steady-state output as a function of n is $f = b_2^{-(1-\theta)/\nu}b_3^{1-\theta}\lambda^{1/\theta}n \equiv b_4\lambda^{1/\theta}n$. In the steady state, net investment is zero, so

$$(4.3) \qquad c = b_4\lambda^{1/\theta}n - \delta k = (b_4 - \delta b_3)\lambda^{1/\theta}n.$$

The steady-state values of c, k, and y are all proportional to $\lambda^{1/\theta}n$. We also note that the capital-output ratio is b_3/b_4, and that consumption's share to total steady-state output is $1 - (\delta b_3/b_4)$.

Turning now to the consumer's problem and letting μ be the Lagrange multiplier for the budget constraint and w_t the real wage, first-order conditions are

$$\frac{1}{3} c_t^{(\gamma/3) - 1}(\alpha(L)l_t)^{2\gamma/3} = \mu, \quad \text{and}$$

$$\frac{2}{3} \sum_{i=0}^{\infty} \beta^i \alpha_i c_{t+i}^{\gamma/3}(\alpha(L)l_{t+i})^{(2\gamma/3)-1} = \mu w_t.$$

In the steady state, $c_t = c$, $l_t = l$, and $w_t = w$ for all t. Making these substitutions and using the fact that the α_i sum to one, these expressions simplify to

$$\frac{1}{3}(c^{1/3}l^{2/3})^\gamma = \mu c, \quad \text{and} \quad \frac{2}{3}(c^{1/3}l^{2/3})^\gamma \sum_{i=1}^{\infty} \beta^i \alpha_i = \mu w l.$$

Eliminating μ from these equations yields $2c\sum_{i=0}^{\infty} \beta^i \alpha_i = wl$. Since $\sum_{i=0}^{\infty} \beta^i \alpha_i = \alpha_0 + (1 - \alpha_0)\eta/(r + \eta)$ and $l = 1 - n$, this in turn implies

(4.4) $\qquad 2c(\alpha_0 + (1 - \alpha_0)\eta/(r + \eta)) = w(1 - n)$.

Returning to the production side, the marginal product of labor equals the real wage:

(4.5) $\qquad w = f_n = \dfrac{\theta}{n} f = \theta b_4 \lambda^{1/\theta}$.

Using (4.3) and (4.5), we can solve (4.4) for n:

$$n = \left[1 + 2\frac{\alpha_0 r + \eta}{\theta(r + \eta)}(1 - (\delta b_3/b_4))\right]^{-1}.$$

That n does not depend upon average λ matches well with the American experience over the last thirty years. During this period, output per man-hour has increased by a few hundred per cent, yet man-hours per person in the 16–65 age group has changed but a few per cent.

Approximation About the Steady State

If the utility function u were quadratic and the production function f linear, there would be no need for approximations. In equilibrium, consumption must be equal to output minus investment. We exploit this fact to eliminate the nonlinearity in the constraint set by substituting $f(\lambda, k, n, y) - i$ for c in the utility function to obtain $u(f(\lambda, k, n, y) - i, n, a)$. The next step is to approximate this function by a quadratic in the neighborhood of the model's steady state. As investment i is linear in the decision and state variables, it can be eliminated subsequent to the approximation and still preserve a quadratic objective.

Consider the general problem of approximating function $u(x)$ near $\bar{x}$. The approximate quadratic function is

$$U(x) = u(\bar{x}) + b'(x - \bar{x}) + (x - \bar{x})'Q(x - \bar{x}),$$

where $x, b \in \mathbb{R}^n$ and Q is an $n \times n$ symmetric matrix. We want an approximation that is good not only at $\bar{x}$ but also at other x in the range experienced during the sample period. Let z^i be a vector, all of whose components are zero except for $z_i^i > 0$. Our approach is to select the elements b_i and q_{ii} so that the approximation error is zero at the $\bar{x} + z^i$ and $\bar{x} - z^i$, where the z_i^i selected correspond to the approximate average deviations of the x_i from their steady state values $\bar{x}_i$. The values of $z_i^i/\bar{x}_i$ used for λ, k, y, n, i, and a were 3, 1, 2, 3, 8, and 0.5 per cent, respectively.[11]

The approximation errors being zero at the $\bar{x} + z^i$ and $\bar{x} - z^i$ requires that

$$b_i = \left[u(\bar{x} + z^i) - u(\bar{x} - z^i) \right]/2z_i, \quad \text{and}$$

$$q_{ii} = \left[u(\bar{x} + z^i) - u(\bar{x}) + u(\bar{x} - z^i) - u(\bar{x}) \right]/2z_i^2 .$$

The elements q_{ij}, $i \neq j$, are selected to minimize the sum of the squared approximation errors at $\bar{x} + z^i + z^j$, $\bar{x} + z^i - z^j$, $\bar{x} - z^i + z^j$, and $\bar{x} - z^i - z^j$. The approximation error at the first point is

$$u(\bar{x} + z^i + z^j) - u(\bar{x}) - b_i z_i - b_j z_j - q_{ii} z_i^2 - q_{jj} z_j^2 - 2q_{ij} z_i z_j .$$

Summing over the square of this error and the three others, differentiating with respect to q_{ij}, setting the resulting expression equal to zero and solving for q_{ij}, we obtain

$$q_{ij} = \left[u(\bar{x} + z^i + z^j) - u(\bar{x} + z^i - z^j) - u(\bar{x} - z^i + z^j) \right.$$
$$\left. + u(\bar{x} - z^i - z^j) \right]/8z_i z_j$$

for $i \neq j$.

Computation of Equilibrium

The equilibrium process for the approximate economy maximizes the welfare of the representative household subject to the technological and informational constraints as there are no externalities. This simplifies the determination of the equilibrium process by reducing it to solving a linear-quadratic maximization problem. For such mathematical structure there is a separation of estimation and control. Consequently, the first step in determining the equilibrium decision rules for the approximate economy is to solve the following deterministic problem:

$$\max \sum_{t=0}^{\infty} \beta^t U(k_t, n_t, y_t, \lambda_t, i_t, a_t)$$

[11] We experimented a little and found that the results were essentially the same when the second order Taylor series approximation was used rather than this function. Larry Christiano [10] has found that the quadratic approximation method that we employed yields approximate solutions that are very accurate, even with large variability, for a structure that, like ours, is of the constant elasticity variety.

subject to

$$(4.6) \quad k_{t+1} = (1 - \delta)k_t + s_{1t},$$

$$(4.7) \quad s_{j,t+1} = s_{j+1,t} \quad (j = 1, \ldots, J - 1),$$

$$(4.8) \quad x_{t+1} = Ax_t,$$

$$(4.9) \quad a_{t+1} = (1 - \eta)a_t + n_t,$$

$$(4.10) \quad i_t = \sum_{j=1}^{J} \varphi_j s_{jt} + y_{t+1} - y_t,$$

$$(4.11) \quad \lambda_t = x_{1t} + x_{2t}.$$

At this stage, the fact that there is an additive stochastic term in the equation determining x_{t+1} is ignored as is the fact that x_t is not observed for our economy. Constraints (4.6)–(4.9) are the laws of motion for the state variables. The free decision variables are n_t, s_{Jt}, and y_{t+1}. It was convenient to use inventories taken into the subsequent period, y_{t+1}, as a period t decision variable rather than i_t because the decisions on inventory carry-over and consumption are made subsequent to the labor supply and new project decisions n_t and s_{Jt}.

For notational simplicity we let the set of state variables other than the unobserved x_t be $z_t = (k_t, y_t, a_t, s_{1t}, \ldots, s_{J-1,t})$ and the set of decision variables $d_t = (n_t, s_{Jt}, y_{t+1})$. The unobserved state variables $x_t = (x_{1t}, x_{2t})$ are the permanent and transitory shocks to technology. Finally, $v(x, z)$ is the value of the deterministic problem if the initial state is (x, z). It differs from the value function for the stochastic problem by a constant.

Using constraints (4.10) and (4.11) to substitute for i_t and λ_t in the utility function, an indirect utility function $U(x, z, d)$ is obtained. The value function, $v(x, z)$, was computed by the method of successive approximations or value iteration. If $v_j(x, z)$ is the jth approximation, then

$$v_{j+1}(x_t, z_t) = \max_{d_t} \left[U(x_t, z_t, d_t) + \beta v_j(x_{t+1}, z_{t+1}) \right]$$

subject to constraints (4.6)–(4.9). The initial approximation, $v_0(x, z)$, is that function which is identically zero.

The function U is quadratic and the constraints are linear. Then, if v_j is quadratic, v_{j+1} must be quadratic. As v_0 is trivially quadratic, all the v_j are quadratic and therefore easily computable. We found that the sequence of quadratic functions converged reasonably quickly.[12]

---

[12] The limit of the sequence of value functions existed in every case and, as a function of z, was bounded from above, given x. This, along with the stability of the matrix A, is sufficient to ensure that this limit is the optimal value function and that the associated policy function is the optimal one (see [30]).

The next step is to determine the optimal inventory carry-over decision rule. It is the *linear* function $y_{t+1} = y(x_t, z_t, n_t, s_{Jt})$ which solves

$$(4.12) \qquad \max_{y_{t+1}} \left[U(x_t, z_t, n_t, s_{Jt}, y_{t+1}) + \beta v(x_{t+1}, z_{t+1}) \right]$$

subject to (4.6)–(4.9) and both n_t and s_{Jt} given. Finally, the solution to the program

$$\max_{s_{Jt}, n_t} v_2(x_t, z_t, n_t, s_{Jt}),$$

where v_2 is the value of maximization of (4.12), is determined. The linear functions $s_{Jt} = s(x_t, z_t)$ and $n_t = n(x_t, z_t)$ which solve the above program are the optimal decision rules for new projects and labor supply.

Because of the separation of estimation and control in our model, these decision rules can be used to determine the motion of the stochastic economy. In each period t, a conditional expectation, m_{0t}, is formed on the basis of observations in previous periods. An indicator of the technology shock is observed, which is the sum of a permanent and a transitory component as well as an indicator shock. The conditional expectation, m_{1t}, of the unobserved x_t is computed according to equation (3.14), and s_{Jt} and n_t are determined from

$$(4.13) \qquad s_{Jt} = s(m_{1t}, z_t),$$

$$(4.14) \qquad n_t = n(m_{1t}, z_t),$$

where x_t has been replaced by m_{1t}. Then the technology shock, λ_t, is observed, which changes the conditional expectation of x_t. From (3.16), this expectation is m_{2t}, and the inventory carry-over is determined from

$$(4.15) \qquad y_{t+1} = y(m_{2t}, z_t, s_{Jt}, n_t).$$

To summarize, the equilibrium process governing the evolution of our economy is given by (3.1)–(3.3), (3.6), (3.11)–(3.14), (3.16), (3.18), and (4.13)–(4.15).

5. TEST OF THE THEORY

The test of the theory is whether there is a set of parameters for which the model's co-movements for *both* the smoothed series and the deviations from the smoothed series are *quantitatively* consistent with the observed behavior of the corresponding series for the U.S. post-war economy. An added requirement is that the parameters selected not be inconsistent with relevant micro observations, including reported construction periods for new plants and cross-sectional observations on consumption and labor supply. The closeness of our specification of preferences and technology to those used in many applied studies facilitates such comparisons.

The model has been rigged to yield the observations that smoothed output, investment, consumption, labor productivity, and capital stocks all vary roughly proportionately while there is little change in employment (all variables are in per-household terms) when the technology parameter λ grows smoothly over time. These are just the steady state properties of the growth model with which we began.

Quantitatively explaining the co-movements of the deviations is the test of the underlying theory. For want of better terminology, the deviations will be referred to as the cyclical components even though, with our integrated approach, there is no separation between factors determining a secular path and factors determining deviations from that path. The statistics to be explained are the covariations of the cyclical components. They are of interest because their behavior is stable and is so different from the corresponding covariations of the smoothed series. This is probably why many have sought separate explanations of the secular and cyclical movements.

One cyclical observation is that, in percentage terms, investment varies three times as much as output does and consumption only half as much. In sharp contrast to the secular observations, variations in cyclical output are principally the result of variations in hours of employment per household and not in capital stocks or labor productivity.

The latter observation is a difficult one to explain. Why does the consumption of market produced goods and the consumption of leisure move in opposite directions in the absence of any apparent large movement in the real wage over the so-called cycle? For our model, the real wage is proportional to labor's productivity, so the crucial test is whether most of the variation in cyclical output arises from variations in employment rather than from variations in labor's productivity.

We chose not to test our model versus the less restrictive vector autoregressive model.[13] This most likely would have resulted in the model being rejected, given the measurement problems and the abstract nature of the model. Our approach is to focus on certain statistics for which the noise introduced by approximations and measurement errors is likely to be small relative to the statistic. Failure of the theory to mimic the behavior of the post-war U.S. economy with respect to these stable statistics with high signal-noise ratios would be grounds for its rejection.

Model Calibration

There are two advantages of formulating the model as we did and then constructing an approximate model for which the equilibrium decision rules are linear. First, the specifications of preferences and technology are close to those used in many applied studies. This facilitates checks of reasonableness of many parameter values. Second, our approach facilitates the selection of parameter values for which the model steady-state values are near average values for the American economy during the period being explained. These two considerations

---

[13] Sims [34] has estimated unrestricted aggregate vector autoregressive models.

reduce dramatically the number of free parameters that will be varied when searching for a set that results in cyclical covariances near those observed. In explaining the covariances of the cyclical components, there are only seven free parameters, with the range of two of them being severely constrained a priori.

Capital for our model reflects all tangible capital, including stocks of plant and equipment, consumer durables and housing. Consumption does not include the purchase of durables but does include the services from the stock of consumer durables. Different types of capital have different construction periods and patterns of resource requirements. The findings summarized in Section 2 suggest an average construction period of nearly two years for plants. Consumer durables, however, have much shorter average construction periods. Having but one type of capital, we assume, as a compromise, that four quarters are required, with one-fourth of the value put in place each quarter. Thus $J = 4$ and $\varphi_1 = \varphi_2 = \varphi_3 = \varphi_4 = 0.25$.

Approximately ten per cent of national income account GNP is the capital consumption allowance and another ten per cent excise tax. To GNP should be added the depreciation of consumer durables which has the effect of increasing the share of output going to owners of capital. In 1976, compensation to employees plus proprietary income was approximately 64 per cent of GNP plus consumer durables depreciation less indirect business tax, while owners of capital received about 36 per cent. As labor share is θ, we set $\theta = 0.64$.

Different types of capital depreciate more rapidly than others, with durables depreciating more rapidly than plant and housing, and land not depreciating at all. As a compromise, we set the depreciation rate equal to 10 per cent per year. We assume a subjective time discount rate of four per cent and abstract from growth. This implies a steady-state capital to annual output ratio of 2.4. Of total output 64 per cent is wages, 24 per cent depreciation, and 12 per cent return on capital which includes consumer durables.

The remaining parameters of technology are average λ, which we normalize to one by measuring output in the appropriate units, and parameters σ and ν, which determine the shares of and substitution between inventories and capital. Inventories are about one-fourth of annual GNP so we require ν and σ to be such that $k/y = 10$. A priori reasoning indicates the substitution opportunities between capital and inventory are small, suggesting that ν should be considerably larger than zero. We restricted it to be no less than two, but it is otherwise a free parameter in our search for a model to explain the cyclical covariances and autocovariances of aggregate variables. Given ν and the value of $b_1 = y/k$, σ is implied. From (4.1) it is $\sigma = [1 + q(r + \delta)/(rb_1^{\nu+1})]^{-1}$. For purposes of explaining the covariances of the percentage deviation from steady state values, ν is the only free parameter associated with technology.

The steady state real interest rate r is related to the subjective time discount rate, $\rho = \beta^{-1} - 1$, and the risk aversion parameter, γ, by the equation $r = \rho + (1 - \gamma)(\dot{c}/c)$, where $\dot{c}/c$ is the growth rate of per capita consumption. We have assumed ρ is four per cent per year (one per cent per quarter). As the growth rate of per capita consumption has been about two per cent and the real return on physical capital six to eight per cent, the risk aversion parameter, γ, is constrained to be between minus one and zero.[14]

The parameters α_0 and η which affect intertemporal substitutability of leisure will be treated as free parameters for we could find no estimate for them in the labor economics literature. As stated previously, the steady-state labor supply is independent of the productivity parameter $\bar{\lambda}$. The remaining parameters are those specifying the process on λ_t and the variance of the indicator. These three parameters are $\text{var}(\zeta_1)$, $\text{var}(\zeta_2)$, and $\text{var}(\zeta_3)$. Only two of these are free parameters, however. We restricted the sum of the three variances to be such that the estimate of the variance of cyclical output for the model equalled that of cyclical output for the U.S. economy during the sample period.

In summary, the parameters that are estimated from the variance-covariance properties of the model are these variances plus the parameter ν determining substitutability of inventories and capital, the parameters α_0 and η determining intertemporal substitutability of leisure, and the risk aversion parameter γ. For each set of parameter values, means and standard deviations were computed for several statistics which summarize the serial correlation and covariance properties of the model. These numbers are compared with those of the actual U.S. data for the period 1950:1 to 1979:2 as reported in Hodrick and Prescott [18]. A set of parameter values is sought which fits the actual data well. Having only six degrees of freedom to explain the observed covariances imposes considerable discipline upon the analysis.

The statistics reported in [18] are not the only way to quantitatively capture the co-movements of the deviations.[15] This approach is simple, involves a minimum of judgment, and is robust to slowly changing demographic factors which affect growth, but are not the concern of this theory.[16] In addition, these statistics are robust to most measurement errors, in contrast to, say, the correlations between the first differences of two series. It is important to compute the same statistics for the U.S. economy as for the model, that is, to use the same function of the data. This is what we do.

A key part of our procedure is the computation of dynamic competitive equilibrium for each combination of parameter values. Because the conditional forecasting can be separated from control in this model, the dynamic equilibrium decision rules need only be computed for each new combination of the parame-

---

[14] Estimates in [16] indicate γ is near zero.

[15] With the Hodrick-Prescott method, the smooth path $\{s_t\}$ for each series $\{y_t\}$ minimized

$$\sum_{t=1}^{T} (y_t - s_t)^2 + 1600 \sum_{t=1}^{T} [(s_{t+1} - s_t) - (s_t - s_{t-1})]^2.$$

The deviations for series $\{y_t\}$ are $\{y_t - s_t\}$. The number of observations, T, was 118. The solution to the above program is a linear transformation of the data. Thus, the standard deviations and correlations reported are well-defined statistics.

[16] See, for example, [11].

TABLE I

MODEL PARAMETERS[a]

Preference Parameters:	$\alpha_0 = 0.50$, $\eta = 0.10$, $\gamma = -0.50$, $\beta = 0.99$
Technology Parameters:	$\nu = 4.0$, $\theta = 0.64$, $\sigma = 0.28 \times 10^{-5}$, $\varphi_1 = \varphi_2 = \varphi_3 = \varphi_4 = 0.25$, $\delta = 0.10$, $\bar{\lambda} = 1.0$
Shock Variances:	$\text{var}(\zeta_1) = 0.0090^2$, $\text{var}(\zeta_2) = 0.0018^2$, $\text{var}(\zeta_3) = 0.0090^2$

[a] For parameters with a time dimension, the unit of time is a quarter of a year.

ters ν, α_0, η, and γ. Similarly, the conditional expectations of the permanent and transitory shocks which enter the decision rules depend only on the variances of the three shocks and not upon the parameters of preferences and technology.

For each set of parameter values the following statistics are computed: the autocorrelation of cyclical output for up to six periods, standard deviations of the cyclical variables of interest, and their correlations with cyclical output. In [18] the variables (except interest rates) are measured in logs while we use the levels rather than the logs. This is of consequence only in the measurement of amplitudes, so in order to make our results comparable to theirs, our standard deviations (except for interest rates) are divided by the steady states of the respective variables. One can then interpret the cyclical components essentially as percentage deviations as in [18].

The parameter values that yielded what we considered to be the best fit are reported in Table I. They were determined from a grid search over the free parameters. In the case of ν, we tried the values 2, 3, 4, and 5. The parameters α_0 and η were just constrained to be between zero and one. Only the values -1, -0.5, and -0.1 were considered for the risk aversion parameter γ. The last value is close to the limiting case of $\gamma = 0$ which would correspond to the logarithmic utility function.

Results

All reported statistics refer to the cyclical components for both the model and the U.S. economy. Estimated autocorrelations of real output for our model along with sample values for the U.S. economy in the post-war period are reported in Table II. The fit is very good, particularly in light of the model's simplicity.

Table III contains means of standard deviations and correlations with output for the model's variables. Table IV contains sample values of statistics for the post-war U.S. economy as reported in [18].

The variables in our model do not correspond perfectly to those available for the U.S. economy so care must be taken in making comparisons. A second problem is that there may be measurement errors that seriously bias the estimated correlations and standard deviations. A final problem is that the estimates for the U.S. economy are subject to sampling error. As a guide to the magnitude

1364   F. E. KYDLAND AND E. C. PRESCOTT

TABLE II
AUTOCORRELATIONS OF OUTPUT[a]

Order of Autocorrelations	Model Means (Standard Deviations) of Sample Distribution	U.S. Economy Sample Values for 1950 : 1–1979 : 2
1	.71 (.07)	.84
2	.45 (.12)	.57
3	.28 (.13)	.27
4	.19 (.12)	−.01
5	.02 (.11)	−.20
6	−.13 (.12)	−.30

[a] The length of the sample period both for the model and for the U.S. economy is 118 quarters.

of this variability, we report the standard deviations of sample distributions for the model's statistics which, like the estimates for the U.S. economy, use only 118 observations. These are the numbers in the parentheses in Tables II and III.

The model is consistent with the large (percentage) variability in investment and low variability in consumption and their high correlations with real output. The model's negative correlation between the capital stock and output is consistent with the data though its magnitude is somewhat smaller.

Inventories for our model correspond to finished and nearly finished goods while the inventories in Table IV refer to goods in process as well. We added half

TABLE III
MODEL'S STANDARD DEVIATIONS AND CORRELATIONS WITH REAL OUTPUT[a]

Variable	Standard Deviations: Means (Standard Deviations) of Sample Distribution[b]	Correlations with Output: Means (Standard Deviations) of Sample Distribution
Real Output	1.80 (.23)	—
Consumption	.63 (.09)	.94 (.01)
Investment	6.45 (.62)	.80 (.04)
Inventories	.89 (.06)	−.15 (.11)
Inventories plus	2.00 (.20)	.39 (.06)
Capital Stock	.63 (.08)	−.07 (.06)
Hours	1.05 (.13)	.93 (.01)
Productivity	.90 (.10)	.90 (.02)
Real Interest Rate (Annual)	.23 (.02)	.47 (.10)

[a] The length of the sample period both for the model and for the U.S. economy is 118 quarters.
[b] Measured in per cent.

TABLE IV

SAMPLE STANDARD DEVIATIONS AND CORRELATIONS WITH REAL OUTPUT
U.S. ECONOMY 1950 : 1–1979 : 2

	Standard Deviations (per cent)	Correlations with Real Output
Output	1.8	—
Total Consumption	1.3	.74
Services	0.7	.62
Non-Durables	1.2	.71
Durables	5.6	.57
Investment Fixed	5.1	.71
Capital Stock		
Durable Mfg.	1.2	− .21
Non-durable Mfg.	0.7	− .24
Inventories	1.7	.51
Hours	2.0	.85
Productivity	1.0	.10

the value of uncompleted capital goods to the model's inventory variable to obtain what we call inventories plus. This corresponds more closely to the U.S. inventory stock variable, with its standard deviation and correlation with real output being consistent with the U.S. data.

In Table III we include results for the implicit real interest rate given by the expression $r_t = (\partial u/\partial c_t)/(\beta E(\partial u/\partial c_{t+1})) - 1$. The expectation is conditional on the information known when the allocation between consumption and inventory carry-over is made.

The model displays more variability in hours than in productivity, but not by as much as the data show. In light of the difficulties in measuring output and, in particular, employment, we do not think this discrepancy is large. For example, all members of the household may not be equally productive, say due to differing stocks of human capital. If there is a greater representation in the work force of the less productive, for example less experienced youth, when output is high, hours would be overestimated. The effects of such errors would be to bias the variability of employment upwards. It also would bias the correlation between productivity and output downwards, which would result in the model being nearly consistent with the data. Measurement errors in employment that are independent of the cycle would have a similar effect on the correlation between output and productivity.

Another possible explanation is the oversimplicity of the model. The shocks to technology, given our production function, are pure productivity shocks. Some shocks to technology alter the transformation between the consumption and investment goods. For example, investment tax credits, accelerated depreciation, and the like, have such effects, and so do some technological changes. Further, some technological change may be embodied in new capital, and only after the capital becomes productive is there the increment to measured productivity. Such shocks induce variation in investment and employment without the variability in productivity. This is a question that warrants further research.

We also examined lead and lag relationships and serial correlation properties of aggregate series other than output. We found that, both for the post-war U.S. economy and the model, consumption and non-inventory investment move contemporaneously with output and have serial correlation properties similar to output. Inventory and capital stocks for the model lag output, which also matches well with the data. Some of the inventory stock's cross-serial correlations with output deviate significantly, however, from those for the U.S. economy. The one variable whose lead-lag relationship does not match with the data is productivity. For the U.S. economy it is a leading indicator, while there is no lead or lag in the model. This was not unexpected in view of our discussion above with regard to productivity. Thus, even though the overall fit of the model is very good, it is not surprising, given the level of abstraction, that there are elements of the fine structure of dynamics that it does not capture.

The Smoothed Series

The smoothed output series for the U.S. post-war data deviated significantly from the linear time trend. During the 118-quarter sample period this difference had two peaks and two troughs. The times between such local extremes were 30, 31, and 32 quarters, and the corresponding differences in values at adjacent extremes were 5.00, 7.25, and 5.90 per cent, respectively.

These observations match well with the predictions of the model. The mean of the model's sampling distribution for the number of peaks and troughs in a 118-quarter period is 4.0—which is precisely the number observed. The mean of the number of quarters between extremes is 26.1 with standard deviation 9.7, and the mean of the vertical difference in the values at adjacent extremes is 5.0 with standard deviation 2.9. Thus, the smoothed output series for the U.S. economy is also consistent with the model.

Sensitivity of Results to Parameter Selection

With a couple of exceptions, the results were surprisingly insensitive to the values of the parameters. The fact that the covariations of the aggregate variables in the model are quite similar for broad ranges of many of the parameters suggests that, even though the parameters may differ across economies, the nature of business cycles can still be quite similar.

We did find that most of the variation in technology had to come from its permanent component in order for the serial correlation properties of the model to be consistent with U.S. post-war data. We also found that the variance of the indicator shock could not be very large relative to the variance of the permanent technology shock. This would have resulted in cyclical employment varying less than cyclical productivity which is inconsistent with the data.

Of particular importance for the model is the dependence of current utility on past leisure choices which admits greater intertemporal substitution of leisure. The purpose of this specification is not to contribute to the persistence of output changes. If anything, it does just the opposite. This element of the model is crucial in making it consistent with the observation that cyclical employment fluctuates substantially more than productivity does. For the parameter values in Table I, the standard deviation of hours worked is 18 per cent greater than the deviation of productivity. The special case of $\alpha_0 = 1$ corresponds to a standard time-separable utility function. For this case, with the parameters otherwise the same as in Table I, the standard deviation of hours is 24 per cent less than the deviation of productivity.

Importance of Time to Build

Of particular interest is the sensitivity of our results to the specification of investment technology. The prominent alternative to our time-to-build technology is the adjustment-cost structure. If only one period is required for the construction of new productive capital, we can write the law of motion for the single capital good as $k_{t+1} = (1 - \delta)k_t + s_t$, where s_t is the amount of investment in productive capital in period t. We can then introduce cost of adjustment into the model by modifying the resource constraint (3.4) as follows:

$$c_t + i_t + \xi(s_t - \delta k_t)^2 \leq f(\lambda_t, k_t, n_t, y_t),$$

where the parameter ξ is nonnegative. The model in Section 3 implied that the price of investment goods, i_t, relative to consumption goods, c_t, must be one. This price will now of course generally not equal one, but our cost-of-adjustment formulation insures that it is one when net investment is zero.

The magnitude of the adjustment cost can probably best be judged in terms of the effect it has on this relative price of investment goods which differs from one by the amount $2\xi(s_t - \delta k_t)$. If, for example, the parameter ξ is 0.5, and the economy is near its steady state, a one per cent increase in the relative price of the investment good would be associated with a four per cent increase in gross investment which is approximately one per cent of GNP.

Even when the adjustment cost is of this small magnitude, the covariance properties of the model are grossly inconsistent with the U.S. data for the post-war period. In particular, most of the fluctuation of output in this model is caused by productivity changes rather than changes in work hours. The standard deviation of hours is 0.60, while the standard deviation of productivity is 1.29. This is just the opposite of what the U.S. data show.

Further evidence of the failure of the cost-of-adjustment model is that, relative to the numbers reported in Table III for our model, the standard deviation is nearly doubled for consumption and reduced by a factor of two for investment expenditures, making the amplitudes of these two output components much too close as compared with the data. In addition, the standard deviation of capital stock was reduced by more than one half. The results were even worse for larger values of ξ.

The extreme case of $\xi = 0$ corresponds to the special case of $J = 1$ in our model. Thus, neither time to build nor cost of adjustment would be an element of the model. The biggest changes in the results for this version as compared with Table III are that the correlation between capital stock and output becomes positive and of sizable magnitude (0.43 if the parameters are otherwise the same as in Table I), and that the correlation between inventory stock and output becomes negative (-0.50 for our parameter values). Both of these correlations are inconsistent with the observations. Also, the persistence of movements in investment expenditures as measured by the autocorrelations was substantially reduced.

For our model with multiple periods required to build new capital, the results are not overly sensitive to the number of periods assumed. With a three or five-quarter construction period instead of four, the fit is also good.

6. CONCLUDING COMMENTS

A competitive equilibrium model was developed and used to explain the autocovariances of real output and the covariances of cyclical output with other aggregate economic time series for the post-war U.S. economy. The preference-technology environment used was the simplest one that explained the *quantitative* co-movements and the serial correlation properties of output. These results indicate a surprisingly good fit in light of the model's simplicity.

A crucial element of the model that contributed to persistence of output movements was the time-to-build requirement.[17] We experimented with adjustment costs, the standard method for introducing persistence (e.g., [4, 33]), and found that they were not a substitute for the time-to-build assumption in explaining the data.[18] One problem was that, even with small adjustment costs, employment and investment fluctuations were too small and consumption fluctuations too large to match with the observations.

There are several refinements which should improve the performance of the model. In particular, we conjecture that introducing as a decision variable the hours per week that productive capital is employed, with agents having prefer-

---

[17] Capital plays an important role in creating persistence in the analysis of Lucas [23] as well as in those of Blinder and Fischer [5] and Long and Plosser [22]. In [23] gradual diffusion of information also plays a crucial role. This is not the case in our model, however, as agents learn the value of the shock at the end of the period. Townsend [37] analyzes a model in which decision makers forecast the forecasts of others, which gives rise to confounding of laws of motion with forecasting problems, and results in persistence in capital stock and output movements.

[18] An alternative way of obtaining persistence is the use of long-term staggered nominal wage contracts as in [35].

ences defined on hours worked per week, should help. Introducing more than a single type of productive capital, with different types requiring different periods for construction and having different patterns of resource requirement, is feasible. It would then be possible to distinguish between plant, equipment, housing, and consumer durables investments. This would also have the advantage of permitting the introduction of features of our tax system which affect transformation opportunities facing the economic agents (see, e.g., [14]). Another possible refinement is in the estimation procedure. But, in spite of the considerable advances recently made by Hansen and Sargent [15], further advances are needed before formal econometric methods can be fruitfully applied to testing this theory of aggregate fluctuations.

Models such as the one considered in this paper could be used to predict the consequence of a particular policy rule upon the operating characteristics of the economy.[19] As we estimate the preference-technology structure, our structural parameters will be invariant to the policy rule selected even though the behavioral equations are not. There are computational problems, however, associated with determining the equilibrium behavioral equations of the economy when feedback policy rules, that is, rules that depend on the aggregate state of the economy, are used. The competitive equilibrium, then, will not maximize the welfare of the stand-in consumer, so a particular maximization problem cannot be solved to find the equilibrium behavior of the economy. Instead, methods such as those developed in [20] to analyze policy rules in competitive environments will be needed.

Carnegie-Mellon University
and
University of Minnesota

Manuscript received January, 1981; revision received January, 1982.

[19] Examples of such policy issues are described in [21]. See also Barro (e.g., [3]), who emphasizes the differences in effects of temporary and permanent changes in government expenditures.

REFERENCES

[1] ABEL, A. B.: "Empirical Investment Equations: An Integrated Framework," in *On The State of Macroeconomics*, ed. by K. Brunner and A. H. Meltzer. Amsterdam: North-Holland, 1979.
[2] ABOWD, J., AND O. ASHENFELTER: "Unemployment and Compensating Wage Differentials," in *Studies in Labor Markets*, ed. by S. Rosen. Chicago: University of Chicago Press, 1981.
[3] BARRO, R. J.: "Intertemporal Substitution and the Business Cycle," in *Supply Shocks, Incentives and National Wealth*, ed. by K. Brunner and A. H. Meltzer. Amsterdan: North-Holland, 1981.
[4] BLACK, F.: "General Equilibrium and Business Cycles," Working Paper, Massachusetts Institute of Technology, revised November, 1979.
[5] BLINDER, A. S., AND S. FISCHER: "Inventories, Rational Expectations, and the Business Cycle," *Journal of Monetary Economics*, 8(1981), 227–304.
[6] BÖHM-BAWERK, E. VON: *Positive Theory of Capital*, trans. by W. Smart. London: Macmillan, 1891.
[7] BRUNNER, K., AND A. H. MELTZER: "Money, Debt, and Economic Activity," *Journal of Political Economy*, 80(1972), 951–977.

[8] BRUNNER, K., A. CUKIERMAN, AND A. H. MELTZER: "Stagflation, Persistent Unemployment and the Permanence of Economic Shocks," *Journal of Monetary Economics*, 6(1980), 467–492.

[9] CARLTON, D. W.: "Contracts, Price Rigidity, and Market Equilibrium," *Journal of Political Economy*, 87(1979), 1034–1062.

[10] CHRISTIANO, L. J.: "On the Accuracy of Linear Quadratic Approximations: An Example," Working Paper, University of Chicago, September, 1981.

[11] DENISON, E. F.: *Accounting for United States Economic Growth 1929–1969*. Washington, D.C.: Brookings Institution, 1974.

[12] GROSSMAN, H. I.: "Aggregate Demand, Job Search, and Employment," *Journal of Political Economy*, 81(1973), 1353–1369.

[13] HALL, R. E.: "Investment, Interest Rates, and the Effects of Stabilization Policies," *Brookings Papers on Economic Activity*, 6(1977), 61–100.

[14] HALL, R. E., AND D. W. JORGENSON: "Tax Policy and Investment Behavior," *American Economic Review*, 57(1967), 391–414.

[15] HANSEN, L. P., AND T. J. SARGENT: "Formulating and Estimating Dynamic Linear Rational Expectations Models," *Journal of Economic Dynamics and Control*, 2(1980), 7–46.

[16] HANSEN, L. P., AND K. J. SINGLETON: "Generalized Instrumental Variables Estimation of Nonlinear Rational Expectations Models," *Econometrica*, 50(1982), 1269–1286.

[17] HAYASHI, F.: "Tobin's Marginal q and Average q: A Neoclassical Interpretation," *Econometrica*, 50(1982), 213–224.

[18] HODRICK, R. J., AND E. C. PRESCOTT: "Post-War U.S. Business Cycles: An Empirical Investigation," Working Paper, Carnegie-Mellon University, revised November, 1980.

[19] JORGENSON, D. W.: "Anticipations and Investment Behavior," in *The Brookings Quarterly Econometric Model of the United States*, ed. by J. S. Duesenberry et al. Chicago: Rand McNally, 1965.

[20] KYDLAND, F. E.: "Analysis and Policy in Competitive Models of Business Fluctuations," Working Paper, Carnegie-Mellon University, revised April, 1981.

[21] KYDLAND, F. E., AND E. C. PRESCOTT: "A Competitive Theory of Fluctuations and the Feasibility and Desirability of Stabilization Policy," in *Rational Expectations and Economic Policy*, ed. by S. Fischer. Chicago: University of Chicago Press, 1980.

[22] LONG, J. B., JR., AND C. I. PLOSSER: "Real Business Cycles," Working Paper, University of Rochester, November, 1980.

[23] LUCAS, R. E., JR.: "An Equilibrium Model of the Business Cycle," *Journal of Political Economy*, 83(1975), 1113–1144.

[24] ———: "Understanding Business Cycles," in *Stabilization of the Domestic and International Economy*, ed. by K. Brunner and A. H. Meltzer. New York: North-Holland, 1977.

[25] LUCAS, R. E., JR, AND L. A. RAPPING: "Real Wages, Employment and Inflation," *Journal of Political Economy*, 77(1969), 721–754.

[26] MALKIEL, B. G., G. M. VON FURSTENBERG, AND H. S. WATSON: "Expectations, Tobin's q, and Industry Investment," *Journal of Finance*, 34(1979), 549–561.

[27] MAYER, T.: "Plant and Equipment Lead Times," *Journal of Business*, 33(1960), 127–132.

[28] MOOD, A. M., AND F. A. GRAYBILL: *Introduction to the Theory of Statistics*, 2nd ed. New York: McGraw-Hill, 1963.

[29] MUSSA, M.: "External and Internal Adjustment Costs and the Theory of Aggregate and Firm Investment," *Economica*, 44(1977), 163–178.

[30] PRESCOTT, E. C.: "A Note on Dynamic Programming with Unbounded Returns," Working Paper, University of Minnesota, 1982.

[31] PRESCOTT, E. C., AND R. MEHRA: "Recursive Competitive Equilibrium: The Case of Homogeneous Households," *Econometrica*, 48(1980), 1365–1379.

[32] SARGENT, T. J.: "Tobin's q and the Rate of Investment in General Equilibrium," in *On the State of Macroeconomics*, ed. by K. Brunner and A. H. Meltzer. Amsterdam: North-Holland, 1979.

[33] ———: *Macroeconomic Theory*. New York: Academic Press, 1979.

[34] SIMS, C. A.: "Macroeconomics and Reality," *Econometrica*, 48(1980), 1–48.

[35] TAYLOR, J. B.: "Aggregate Dynamics and Staggered Contracts," *Journal of Political Economy*, 88(1980), 1–23.

[36] TOBIN, J.: "A General Equilibrium Approach to Monetary Theory," *Journal of Money, Credit, and Banking*, 1(1969), 15–29.

[37] TOWNSEND, R. M.: "Forecasting the Forecasts of Others," Working Paper, Carnegie-Mellon University, revised August, 1981.

Edward C. Prescott
Theory Ahead of Measurement

Theory Ahead of Business Cycle Measurement*

Edward C. Prescott
Adviser
Research Department
Federal Reserve Bank of Minneapolis
and Professor of Economics
University of Minnesota

Economists have long been puzzled by the observations that during peacetime industrial market economies display recurrent, large fluctuations in output and employment over relatively short time periods. Not uncommon are changes as large as 10 percent within only a couple of years. These observations are considered puzzling because the associated movements in labor's marginal product are small.

These observations should not be puzzling, for they are what standard economic theory predicts. For the United States, in fact, given people's ability and willingness to intertemporally and intratemporally substitute consumption and leisure and given the nature of the changing production possibility set, it would be puzzling if the economy did not display these large fluctuations in output and employment with little associated fluctuations in the marginal product of labor. Moreover, standard theory also correctly predicts the amplitude of these fluctuations, their serial correlation properties, and the fact that the investment component of output is about six times as volatile as the consumption component.

This perhaps surprising conclusion is the principal finding of a research program initiated by Kydland and me (1982) and extended by Kydland and me (1984), Hansen (1985a), and Bain (1985). We have computed the competitive equilibrium stochastic process for variants of the constant elasticity, stochastic growth model. The elasticities of substitution and the share parameters of the production and utility functions are restricted to those that generate the growth observations. The process governing the technology parameter is selected to be consistent with the measured technology changes for the American economy since the Korean War. We ask whether these artificial economies display fluctuations with statistical properties similar to those which the American economy has displayed in that period. They do.[1]

I view the growth model as a paradigm for macro analysis—analogous to the supply and demand construct of price theory. The elasticities of substitution and the share parameters of the growth model are analogous to the price and income elasticities of price theory. Whether or not this paradigm dominates, as I expect it will, is still an open question. But the early results indicate its power to organize our knowledge. The finding that when uncertainty in the rate of technological change is incorporated into the growth model it

*This paper was presented at a Carnegie-Rochester Conference on Public Policy and will appear in a volume of the conference proceedings. It appears here with the kind permission of Allan H. Meltzer, editor of that volume. The author thanks Finn E. Kydland for helpful discussions of the issues reviewed here, Gary D. Hansen for data series and some additional results for his growth economy, Lars G. M. Ljungqvist for expert research assistance, Bruce D. Smith and Allan H. Meltzer for comments on a preliminary draft, and the National Science Foundation and the Minneapolis Federal Reserve Bank for financial support. The views expressed herein are those of the author alone.

[1]Others [Barro (1981) and Long and Plosser (1983), for example] have argued that these fluctuations are not inconsistent with competitive theory that abstracts from monetary factors. Our finding is much stronger: standard theory predicts that the economy will display the business cycle phenomena.

displays the business cycle phenomena was both dramatic and unanticipated. I was sure that the model could not do this without some features of the payment and credit technologies.

The models constructed within this theoretical framework are necessarily highly abstract. Consequently, they are necessarily false, and statistical hypothesis testing will reject them. This does not imply, however, that nothing can be learned from such quantitative theoretical exercises. I think much has already been learned and confidently predict that much more will be learned as other features of the environment are introduced. Prime candidates for study are the effects of public finance elements, a foreign sector, and, of course, monetary factors. The research I review here is best viewed as a very promising beginning of a much larger research program.

The Business Cycle Phenomena

The use of the expression *business cycle* is unfortunate for two reasons. One is that it leads people to think in terms of a time series' business cycle component which is to be explained independently of a growth component; our research has, instead, one unifying theory of both of these. The other reason I do not like to use the expression is that it is not accurate; some systems of low-order linear stochastic difference equations with a nonoscillatory deterministic part, and therefore no cycle, display key business cycle features. (See Slutzky 1927.) I thus do not refer to business cycles, but rather to business cycle *phenomena*, which are nothing more nor less than a certain set of statistical properties of a certain set of important aggregate time series. The question I and others have considered is, Do the stochastic difference equations that are the equilibrium laws of motion for the stochastic growth display the business cycle phenomena?

More specifically, we follow Lucas (1977, p. 9) in defining the business cycle phenomena as the recurrent fluctuations of output about trend and the co-movements among other aggregate time series. Fluctuations are by definition deviations from some slowly varying path. Since this slowly varying path increases monotonically over time, we adopt the common practice of labeling it *trend*. This trend is neither a measure nor an estimate of the unconditional mean of some stochastic process. It is, rather, defined by the computational procedure used to fit the smooth curve through the data.

If the business cycle facts were sensitive to the detrending procedure employed, there would be a problem. But the key facts are not sensitive to the procedure if the trend curve is smooth. Our curve-fitting method is to take the logarithms of variables and then select the trend path $\{\tau_t\}$ which minimizes the sum of the squared deviations from a given series $\{Y_t\}$ subject to the constraint that the sum of the squared second differences not be too large. This is

$$\min_{\{\tau_t\}_{t=1}^T} \sum_{t=1}^T (Y_t - \tau_t)^2$$

subject to

$$\sum_{t=2}^{T-1} [(\tau_{t+1} - \tau_t) - (\tau_t - \tau_{t-1})]^2 \leq \mu.$$

The smaller is μ, the smoother is the trend path. If $\mu = 0$, the least squares linear time trend results. For all series, μ is picked so that the Lagrange multiplier of the constraint is 1600. This produces the right degree of smoothness in the fitted trend when the observation period is a quarter of a year. Thus, the sequence $\{\tau_t\}$ minimizes

$$\sum_{t=1}^T (Y_t - \tau_t)^2 + 1600 \sum_{t=2}^{T-1} [(\tau_{t+1} - \tau_t) - (\tau_t - \tau_{t-1})]^2.$$

The first-order conditions of this minimization problem are linear in Y_t and τ_t, so for every series, $\tau = A Y$, where A is the same $T \times T$ matrix. The deviations from trend, also by definition, are

$$Y_t^d = Y_t - \tau_t \quad \text{for } t = 1, \ldots, T.$$

Unless otherwise stated, these are the variables used in the computation of the statistics reported here for both the United States and the growth economies.

An alternative interpretation of the procedure is that it is a high pass linear filter. The facts reported here are essentially the same if, rather than defining the deviations by $Y^d = (I-A)Y$, we filtered the Y using a high pass band filter, eliminating all frequencies of 32 quarters or greater. An advantage of our procedure is that it deals better with the ends of the sample problem and does not require a stationary time series.

To compare the behaviors of a stochastic growth economy and an actual economy, only identical statistics for the two economies are used. By definition, a *statistic* is a real valued function of the raw time series. Consequently, if a comparison is made, say, between the standard deviations of the deviations, the date t deviation for the growth economy must be the same function of the data generated by that model as the date t deviation for the American economy is of that

Edward C. Prescott
Theory Ahead of Measurement

economy's data. Our definitions of the deviations satisfy this criterion.

Figure 1 plots the logs of actual and trend output for the U.S. economy during 1947–82, and Figure 2 the corresponding percentage deviations from trend of output and hours of market employment. Output and hours clearly move up and down together with nearly the same amplitudes.

Table 1 contains the standard deviations and cross serial correlations of output and other aggregate time series for the American economy during 1954–82. Consumption appears less variable and investment more variable than output. Further, the average product of labor is procyclical but does not vary as much as output or hours.

The Growth Model

This theory and its variants build on the neoclassical growth economy of Solow (1956) and Swan (1956). In the language of Lucas (1980, p. 696), the model is a "fully articulated, artificial economic system" that can be used to generate economic time series of a set of important economic aggregates. The model assumes an aggregate production function with constant returns to scale, inputs labor n and capital k, and an output which can be allocated either to current consumption c or to investment x. If t denotes the date, $f: R^2 \rightarrow R$ the production function, and z_t a technology parameter, then the production constraint is

$$x_t + c_t \leq z_t f(k_t, n_t)$$

where $x_t, c_t, k_t, n_t \geq 0$. The model further assumes that the services provided by a unit of capital decrease geometrically at a rate $0 < \delta < 1$:

$$k_{t+1} = (1-\delta)k_t + x_t.$$

Solow completes the specification of his economy by hypothesizing that some fraction $0 < \sigma < 1$ of output is invested and the remaining fraction $1 - \sigma$ consumed and that n_t is a constant—say, $\bar{n}$—for all t. For this economy, the law of motion of capital condition on z_t is

$$k_{t+1} = (1-\delta)k_t + \sigma z_t f(k_t, \bar{n}).$$

Once the $\{z_t\}$ stochastic process is specified, the stochastic process governing capital and the other economic aggregates are determined and realizations of the stochastic process can be generated by a computer.

This structure is far from adequate for the study of

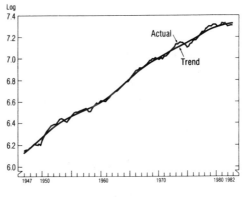

Figure 1

Actual and Trend Logs of U.S. Gross National Product

Quarterly, 1947–82

Source of basic data: Citicorp's Citibase data bank

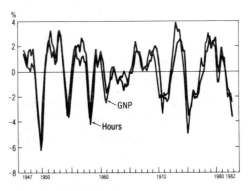

Figure 2

Deviations From Trend of Gross National Product and Nonfarm Employee Hours in the United States

Quarterly, 1947–82

Source of basic data: Citicorp's Citibase data bank

the business cycle because in it neither employment nor the savings rate varies, when in fact they do. Being explicit about the economy, however, naturally leads to

Table 1

Cyclical Behavior of the U.S. Economy
Deviations From Trend of Key Variables, 1954:1–1982:4

Variable x	Standard Deviation	Cross Correlation of GNP With		
		x(t−1)	x(t)	x(t+1)
Gross National Product	1.8%	.82	1.00	.82
Personal Consumption Expenditures				
Services	.6	.66	.72	.61
Nondurable Goods	1.2	.71	.76	.59
Fixed Investment Expenditures	5.3	.78	.89	.78
Nonresidential Investment	5.2	.54	.79	.86
Structures	4.6	.42	.62	.70
Equipment	6.0	.56	.82	.87
Capital Stocks				
Total Nonfarm Inventories	1.7	.15	.48	.68
Nonresidential Structures	.4	−.20	−.03	.16
Nonresidential Equipment	1.0	.03	.23	.41
Labor Input				
Nonfarm Hours	1.7	.57	.85	.89
Average Weekly Hours in Mfg.	1.0	.76	.85	.61
Productivity (GNP/Hours)	1.0	.51	.34	−.04

Source of basic data: Citicorp's Citibase data bank

the question of what determines these variables, which are central to the cycle.

That leads to the introduction of a stand-in household with some explicit preferences. If we abstract from the labor supply decision and uncertainty (that is, $z_t = \bar{z}$ and $n_t = \bar{n}$), the standard form of the utility function is

$$\sum_{t=0}^{\infty} \beta^t u(c_t) \text{ for } 0 < \beta < 1$$

where β is the subjective time discount factor. The function $u: R_+ \to R$ is twice differentiable and concave. The commodity space for the deterministic version of this model is l_∞, infinite sequences of uniformly bounded consumptions $\{c_t\}_{t=0}^{\infty}$.

The theorems of Bewley (1972) could be applied to establish existence of a competitive equilibrium for this l_∞ commodity-space economy. That existence argument, however, does not provide an algorithm for computing the equilibria. An alternative approach is to use the competitive welfare theorems of Debreu (1954). Given local nonsaturation and no externalities, competitive equilibria are Pareto optima and, with some additional conditions that are satisfied for this economy, any Pareto optimum can be supported as a competitive equilibrium. Given a single agent and the convexity, there is a unique optimum and that optimum is the unique competitive equilibrium allocation. The advantage of this approach is that algorithms for computing solutions to concave programming problems can be used to find the competitive equilibrium allocation for this economy.

Even with the savings decision endogenous, this economy has no fluctuations. As shown by Cass (1965)

Edward C. Prescott
Theory Ahead of Measurement

and Koopmans (1965), the competitive equilibrium path converges monotonically to a unique rest point or, if z_t is growing exponentially, to a balanced growth path. There are multisector variants of this model in which the equilibrium path oscillates. (See Benhabib and Nishimura 1985 and Marimon 1984.) But I know of no multisector model which has been restricted to match observed factor shares by sector, which has a value for β consistent with observed interest rates, and which displays oscillations.

When uncertainty is introduced, the household's objective is its expected discounted utility:

$$E\left\{\textstyle\sum_{t=0}^{\infty} \beta^t u(c_t)\right\}.$$

The commodity vector is now indexed by the history of shocks; that is, $\{c_t(z_1, \ldots, z_t)\}_{t=0}^{\infty}$ is the commodity point. As Brock and Mirman (1972) show, if the $\{z_t\}$ are identically distributed random variables, an optimum to the social planner's problem exists and the optimum is a stationary stochastic process with $k_{t+1} = g(k_t, z_t)$ and $c_t = c(k_t, z_t)$. As Lucas and Prescott (1971) show, for a class of economies that include this one, the social optimum is the unique competitive equilibrium allocation. They also show that for these homogeneous agent economies, the social optimum is also the unique sequence-of-markets equilibrium allocation. Consequently, there are equilibrium time-invariant functions for the wage $w_t = w(k_t, z_t)$ and the rental price of capital $r_t = r(k_t, z_t)$, where these prices are relative to the date t consumption good. Given these prices, the firm's period t problem is

$$\max\nolimits_{k_t,\, n_t \geq 0}\left\{y_t - r_t k_t - w_t n_t\right\}$$

subject to the output constraint

$$y_t \leq z_t f(k_t, n_t).$$

The household's problem is more complicated, for it must form expectations of future prices. If a_t is its capital stock, its problem is

$$\max E \textstyle\sum_{t=0}^{\infty} \beta^t u(c_t)$$

subject to

$$c_t + x_t \leq w_t \bar{n} + r_t a_t$$

$$a_{t+1} \leq (1-\delta)a_t + x_t$$

and given $a_0 - k_0$. In forming expectations, a household knows the relation between the economy's state (k_t, z_t) and prices, $w_t = w(k_t, z_t)$ and $r_t = r(k_t, z_t)$. Further, it knows the process governing the evolution of the per capita capital stock, a variable which, like prices, is taken as given.

The elements needed to define a *sequence-of-markets equilibrium* are the firm's policy functions $y(k_t, z_t)$, $n(k_t, z_t)$, and $k(k_t, z_t)$; the household's policy functions $x(a_t, k_t, z_t)$ and $c(a_t, k_t, z_t)$; a law of motion of per capita capital $k_{t+1} = g(k_t, z_t)$; and pricing functions $w(k_t, z_t)$ and $r(k_t, z_t)$. For equilibrium, then,

- The firm's policy functions must be optimal given the pricing functions.

- The household's policy functions must be optimal given the pricing functions and the law of motion of per capita capital.

- Spot markets clear; that is, for all k_t and z_t

$$\bar{n} = n(k_t, z_t)$$

$$k_t = k(k_t, z_t)$$

$$x(k_t, k_t, z_t) + c(k_t, k_t, z_t) = y(k_t, z_t).$$

(Note that the goods market must clear only when the representative household is truly representative, that is, when $a_t = k_t$.)

- Expectations are rational; that is,

$$g(k_t, z_t) = (1-\delta)k_t + x(k_t, k_t, z_t).$$

This definition still holds if the household values productive time that is allocated to nonmarket activities. Such time will be called *leisure* and denoted l_t. The productive time endowment is normalized to 1, and the household faces the constraints

$$n_t + l_t \leq 1$$

for all t. In addition, leisure is introduced as an argument of the utility function, so the household's objective becomes the maximization of

$$E \textstyle\sum_{t=0}^{\infty} \beta^t u(c_t, l_t).$$

Now leisure—and therefore employment—varies in equilibrium.

13

The model needs one more modification: a relaxation of the assumption that the technology shocks z_t are identically and independently distributed random variables. As will be documented, they are not so distributed. Rather, they display considerable serial correlation, with their first differences nearly serially uncorrelated. To introduce high persistence, we assume

$$z_{t+1} = \rho z_t + \epsilon_{t+1}$$

where the $\{\epsilon_{t+1}\}$ are identically and independently distributed and ρ is near 1. With this modification, the recursive sequence-of-markets equilibrium definition continues to apply.

Using Data to Restrict the Growth Model

Without additional restrictions on preferences and technology, a wide variety of equilibrium processes are consistent with the growth model. The beauty of this model is that both growth and micro observations can be used to determine its production and utility functions. When they are so used, there are not many free parameters that are specific to explaining the business cycle phenomena and that cannot be measured independently of those phenomena. The key parameters of the growth model are the intertemporal and intratemporal elasticities of substitution. As Lucas (1980, p. 712) emphasizes, "On these parameters, we have a wealth of inexpensively available data from census cohort information, from panel data describing the reactions of individual households to a variety of changing market conditions, and so forth." To this list we add the secular growth observations which have the advantage of being experiments run by nature with large changes in relative prices and quantities and with idiosyncratic factors averaged out.[2] A fundamental thesis of this line of inquiry is that the measures obtained from aggregate series and those from individual panel data must be consistent. After all, the former are just the aggregates of the latter.

Secularly in the United States, capital and labor shares of output have been approximately constant, as has r, the rental price of capital. However, the nation's real wage has increased greatly—more than 100 percent since the Korean War. For these results to hold, the model's production function must be approximately Cobb-Douglas:

$$z_t f(k_t, n_t) = z_t k_t^{1-\theta} n_t^{\theta}.$$

The share parameter θ is equal to labor's share, which has been about 64 percent in the postwar period, so $\theta = 0.64$. This number is smaller than that usually obtained because we include services of consumer durables as part of output. This alternative accounting both reduces labor's share and makes it more nearly constant over the postwar period.

The artificial economy has but one type of capital, and it depreciates at rate δ. In fact, different types of capital depreciate at different rates, and the pattern of depreciation over the life of any physical asset is not constant. Kydland and I (1982, 1984) simply pick $\delta = 0.10$. With this value and an annual real interest rate of 4 percent, the steady-state capital–annual output ratio is about 2.6. That matches the ratio for the U.S. economy and also implies a steady-state investment share of output near the historically observed average. Except for parameters determining the process on the technology shock, this completely specifies the technology of the simple growth model.

A key growth observation which restricts the utility function is that leisure per capita l_t has shown virtually no secular trend while, again, the real wage has increased steadily. This implies an elasticity of substitution between consumption c_t and leisure l_t near 1. Thus, the utility function restricted to display both constant intertemporal and unit intratemporal elasticities of substitution is

$$u(c_t, l_t) = ([c_t^{1-\phi} l_t^{\phi}]^{1-\gamma} - 1)/(1 - \gamma)$$

where $1/\gamma > 0$ is the elasticity of substituting between different date composite commodities $c_t^{1-\phi} l_t^{\phi}$. This leaves γ and the subjective time discount factor β [or, equivalently, the subjective time discount rate $(1/\beta) - 1$] to be determined.

The steady-state interest rate is

$$i = (1/\beta) - 1 + \gamma(\dot{c}/c).$$

As stated previously, the average annual real interest rate is about 4 percent, and the growth rate of per capita consumption $\dot{c}/c$ has averaged nearly 2 percent. The following studies help restrict γ. Tobin and Dolde (1971) find that a γ near 1.5 is needed to match the life cycle consumption patterns of individuals. Using individual portfolio observations, Friend and Blume (1975) estimate γ to be near 2. Using aggregate stock market and consumption data, Hansen and Singleton (1983) estimate γ to be near 1. Using international data, Kehoe

---

[2]See Solow 1970 for a nice summary of the growth observations.

(1984) also finds a modest curvature parameter γ. All these observations make a strong case that γ is not too far from 1. Since the nature of fluctuations of the artificial economy is not very sensitive to γ, we simply set γ equal to 1. Taking the limit as $\gamma \to 1$ yields

$$u(c_t, l_t) = (1-\phi) \log c_t + \phi \log l_t.$$

This leaves β and ϕ still to be determined.

Hansen (1985b) has found that growing economies—that is, those with z_t having a multiplicative, geometrically growing factor $(1+\lambda)^t$ with $\lambda > 0$—fluctuate in essentially the same way as economies for which $\lambda = 0$. This justifies considering only the case $\lambda = 0$. If $\lambda = 0$, then the average interest rate approximately equals the subjective time discount rate.[3] Therefore, we set β equal to 0.96 per year or 0.99 per quarter.

The parameter ϕ is the leisure share parameter. Ghez and Becker (1975) find that the household allocates approximately one-third of its productive time to market activities and two-thirds to nonmarket activities. To be consistent with that, the model's parameter ϕ must be near two-thirds. This is the value assumed in our business cycle studies.

Eichenbaum, Hansen, and Singleton (1984) use aggregate data to estimate this share parameter ϕ, and they obtain a value near five-sixths. The difference between two-thirds and five-sixths is large in the business cycle context. With $\phi = 2/3$, the elasticity of labor supply with respect to a temporary change in the real wage is 2, while if $\phi = 5/6$, it is 5. This is because a 1 percent change in leisure implies a $\phi/(\phi-1)$ percent change in hours of employment.

We do not follow the Eichenbaum-Hansen-Singleton approach and treat ϕ as a free parameter because it would violate the principle that parameters cannot be specific to the phenomena being studied. What sort of science would economics be if micro studies used one share parameter and aggregate studies another?

The Nature of the Technological Change

One method of measuring technological change is to follow Solow (1957) and define it as the changes in output less the sum of the changes in labor's input times labor share and the changes in capital's input times capital share. Measuring variables in logs, this is the percentage change in the technology parameter of the Cobb-Douglas production function. For the U.S. economy between the third quarter of 1955 and the first quarter of 1984, the standard deviation of this change is 1.2 percent.[4] The serial autocorrelations of these

changes are $\rho_1 = -0.21$, $\rho_2 = -0.06$, $\rho_3 = 0.04$, $\rho_4 = 0.01$, and $\rho_5 = -0.05$. To a first approximation, the process on the percentage change in the technology process is a random walk with drift plus some serially uncorrelated measurement error. This error produces the negative first-order serial correlation of the differences.

Further evidence that the random walk model is not a bad approximation is based on yearly changes. For the quarterly random walk model, the standard deviation of this change is 6.63 times the standard deviation of the quarterly change. For the U.S. data, the annual change is only 5.64 times as large as the quarterly change. This, along with the negative first-order serial correlation, suggests that the standard deviation of the persistent part of the quarterly change is closer to $5.64/6.63 = 0.85$ than to 1.2 percent. Some further evidence is the change over four-quarter periods—that is, the change from a given quarter of one year to the same quarter of the next year. For the random walk model, the standard deviation of these changes is 2 times the standard deviation of the quarterly change. A reason that the standard deviation of change might be better measured this way is that the measurement noise introduced by seasonal factors is minimized. The estimate obtained in this way is 0.95 percent. To summarize, Solow growth accounting finds that the process on the technology parameter is highly persistent with the standard deviation of change being about 0.90.[5]

The Solow estimate of the standard deviation of technological change is surely an overstatement of the variability of that parameter. There undoubtedly are non-negligible errors in measuring the inputs. Since the capital input varies slowly and its share is small, the most serious measurement problem is with the labor input. Fortunately there are two independent measures of the aggregate labor input, one constructed from a survey of employers and the other from a survey of households. Under the assumption of orthogonality of their measurement errors, a reasonable estimate of the variance of the change in hours is the covariance between the changes in the two series. Since the household survey is not used to estimate aggregate output, I

---

[3] Actually, the average interest rate is slightly lower because of risk premia. Given the value of γ and the amount of uncertainty, the average premium is only a fraction of a percent. See Mehra and Prescott 1985 for further details.

[4] I use Hansen's (1984) human capital–weighted, household hour series. The capital stock and GNP series are from Citicorp's Citibase data bank.

[5] The process $z_{t+1} = .9z_t + \epsilon_{t+1}$ is, like the random walk process, highly persistent. Kydland and I find that it and the random walk result in essentially the same fluctuations.

use the covariance between the changes in household hours and output as an estimate of the covariance between aggregate hours and output. Still using a share parameter of $\theta = 0.75$, my estimate of the standard deviation of the percentage change in z_t is the square root of $\mathrm{var}(\Delta\hat{y}) - 2\theta\,\mathrm{cov}(\Delta\hat{h}_1, \Delta\hat{y}) + \theta^2\,\mathrm{cov}(\Delta\hat{h}_1, \Delta\hat{h}_2)$, where the caret (˄) denotes a measured value. For the sample period my estimate is 0.763 percent. This is probably a better estimate than the one which ignores measurement error.

Still, my estimate might under- or overstate the variance of technological change. For example, the measurement of output might include significant errors. Perhaps measurement procedures result in some smoothing of the series. This would reduce the variability of the change in output and might reduce the covariance between measured hours and output.

Another possibility is that changes in hours are associated with corresponding changes in capital's utilization rate. If so, the Solow approach is inappropriate for measuring the technology shocks. To check whether this is a problem, I varied θ and found that $\theta = 0.85$ yields the smallest estimate, 0.759, as opposed to 0.763 for $\theta = 0.75$. This suggests that my estimate is not at all sensitive to variations in capital utilization rates.

To summarize, there is overwhelming evidence that technological shocks are highly persistent. But tying down the standard deviation of the technology change shocks is difficult. I estimate it as 0.763. It could very well be larger or smaller, though, given the accuracy of the measurements.

The Statistical Behavior of the Growth Models
Theory provides an equilibrium stochastic process for the growth economy studied. Our approach has been to document the similarities and differences between the statistical properties of data generated by this stochastic process and the statistical properties of American time series data. An alternative approach is to compare the paths of the growth model if the technological parameters $\{z_t\}$ were those experienced by the U.S. economy. We did not attempt this because theory's predictions of paths, unlike its predictions of the statistical properties, are sensitive to what Leamer (1983, p. 43) calls "whimsical" modeling assumptions. Another nontrivial problem is that the errors in measuring the innovations in the z_t process are as large as the innovations themselves.

The Basic Growth Model
With the standard deviation of the technology shock equal to 0.763, theory implies that the standard devia-

tion of output will be 1.48 percent. In fact, it is 1.76 percent for the post–Korean War American economy. For the output of the artificial economy to be as variable as that, the variance of the shock must be 1.0, significantly larger than the estimate. The most important deviation from theory is the relative volatility of hours and output. Figure 3 plots a realization of the output and employment deviations from trend for the basic growth economy. A comparison of Figures 2 and 3 demonstrates clearly that, for the American economy, hours in fact vary much more than the basic growth model predicts. For the artificial economy, hours fluctuate 52 percent as much as output, whereas for the American economy, the ratio is 0.95. This difference appears too large to be a result of errors in measuring aggregate hours and output.

The Kydland-Prescott Economy
Kydland and I (1982, 1984) have modified the growth model in two important respects. First, we assume that a distributed lag of leisure and the market-produced good combine to produce the composite commodity good valued by the household. In particular,

$$u\big(c_t, \textstyle\sum_{i=0}^{\infty} \alpha_i l_{t-i}\big) = (1/3)\log c_t$$
$$+ (2/3)\log \textstyle\sum_{i=0}^{\infty} \alpha_i l_{t-i}$$

where $\alpha_{i+1}/\alpha_i = 1 - \eta$ for $i = 1, 2, \ldots$ and $\sum_{i=0}^{\infty} \alpha_i = 1$.

Figure 3

Deviations From Trend of GNP and Hours Worked in the Basic Growth Economy

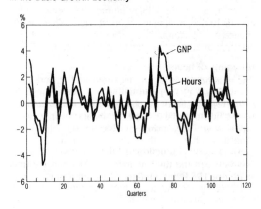

Edward C. Prescott
Theory Ahead of Measurement

Table 2

Cyclical Behavior of the Kydland-Prescott Economy*

Variable x	Standard Deviation	Cross Correlation of GNP With		
		$x(t-1)$	$x(t)$	$x(t+1)$
Gross National Product	1.79%	.60	1.00	.60
	(.13)	(.07)	(—)	(.07)
Consumption	.45	.47	.85	.71
	(.05)	(.05)	(.02)	(.04)
Investment	5.49	.52	.88	.78
	(.41)	(.09)	(.03)	(.03)
Inventory Stock	2.20	.14	.60	.52
	(.37)	(.14)	(.08)	(.05)
Capital Stock	.47	−.05	.02	.25
	(.07)	(.07)	(.06)	(.07).
Hours	1.23	.52	.95	.55
	(.09)	(.09)	(.01)	(.06)
Productivity (GNP/Hours)	.71	.62	.86	.56
	(.06)	(.05)	(.02)	(.10)
Real Interest Rate (Annual)	.22	.65	.60	.36
	(.03)	(.07)	(.20)	(.15)

*These are the means of 20 simulations, each of which was 116 periods long. The numbers in parentheses are standard errors.

Source: Kydland and Prescott 1984

Kydland (1983) provides justification for this preference ordering based on an unmeasured, household-specific capital stock that, like c_t and l_t, is an input in the production of the composite commodity. The economy studied has $\alpha_0 = 0.5$ and $\eta = 0.1$. This increases the variability of hours.

The second modification is to permit the workweek of capital to vary proportionally to the workweek of the household. For this economy, increases in hours do not reduce the marginal product of labor as much, so hours fluctuate more in response to technology shocks of a given size.

The statistical properties of the fluctuations for this economy are reported in Table 2. As is clear there, hours are now about 70 percent as variable as output. This eliminates much of the discrepancy between theory and measurement. If the standard deviation of the technology shock is 0.72 percent, then fluctuations in the output of this artificial economy are as large as those experienced in the U.S. economy.

A comparison of Tables 1 and 2 shows that the Kydland-Prescott economy displays the business cycle phenomena. It does not quite demonstrate, however, that there would be a puzzle if the economy did not display the business cycle phenomena. That is because the parameters α_0 and η have not been well tied down by micro observations.[6] Better measures of these parameters could either increase or decrease significantly the amount of the fluctuations accounted for by the uncertainty in the technological change.

---

[6]Hotz, Kydland, and Sedlacek (1985) use annual panel data to estimate α_0 and η and obtain estimates near the Kydland-Prescott assumed values.

The Hansen Indivisible Labor Economy

Labor economists have estimated labor supply elasticities and found them to be small for full-time prime-age males. (See, for example, Ashenfelter 1984.) Heckman (1984), however, finds that when movements between employment and nonemployment are considered and secondary workers are included, elasticities of labor supply are much larger. He also finds that most of the variation in aggregate hours arises from variation in the number employed rather than in the hours worked per employed person.

These are the observations that led Hansen (1985a) to explore the implication of introducing labor indivisibilities into the growth model. As shown by Rogerson (1984), if the household's consumption possibility set has nonconvexities associated with the mapping from hours of market production activities to units of labor services, there will be variations in the number employed rather than in the hours of work per employed person. In addition, the aggregate elasticity of labor supply will be much larger than the elasticity of those whose behavior is being aggregated. In this case aggregation matters, and matters greatly.

There certainly are important nonconvexities in the mapping from hours of market activities to units of labor services provided. Probably the most important nonconvexity arises from the considerable amount of time required for commuting. Other features of the environment that would make full-time workers more than twice as productive as otherwise similar half-time workers are not hard to imagine. The fact that part-time workers typically are paid less per hour than full-time workers with similar human capital endowments is consistent with the existence of important nonconvexities.

Hansen (1985a) restricts each identical household to either work $\bar{h}$ hours or be unemployed. His relation is as depicted by the horizontal lines in Figure 4. This assumption is not as extreme as it appears. If the relation were as depicted by the curved line, the behavior of the economy would be the same. The key property is an initial convex region followed by a concave region in the mapping from hours of market activity to units of labor service.

With this modification, lotteries that specify the probability of employment are traded along with market-produced goods and capital services. As before, the utility function of each individual is

$$u(c, l) = (1/3) \log c + (2/3) \log l.$$

Figure 4

Relation Between Time Allocated to Market Activity and Labor Service

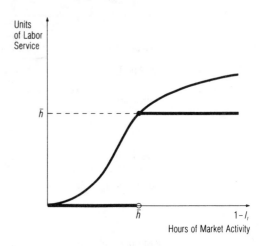

Units of Labor Service

$\bar{h}$

$\bar{h}$

$1 - l_t$

Hours of Market Activity

If an individual works, $l = 1 - \bar{h}$; otherwise, $l = 1$. Consequently, if π is the probability of employment, an individual's expected utility is

$$E\{u(c, l)\} = (1/3) \log c + (2/3) \pi \log (1-\bar{h}).$$

Given that per capita consumption is $\bar{c}$ and per capita hours of employment $\bar{n}$, average utility over the population is maximized by setting $c = \bar{c}$ for all individuals. If $\bar{l}$, which equals $1 - \pi\bar{h}$, denotes per capita leisure, then maximum per capita utility is

$$U(\bar{c}, \bar{l}) = (1/3) \log \bar{c} + (2/3) [(1-\bar{l})/\bar{h}] \log (1 - \bar{h}).$$

This is the utility function which rationalizes the per capita consumption and leisure choices if each person's leisure is constrained to be either $1 - \bar{h}$ or 1. The aggregate intertemporal elasticity of substitution between different date leisures is infinity independent of the value of the elasticity for the individual (in the range where not all are employed).

Hansen (1985a) finds that if the technology shock standard deviation is 0.71, then fluctuations in output for his economy are as large as those for the American

Edward C. Prescott
Theory Ahead of Measurement

economy. Further, variability in hours is 77 percent as large as variability in output. Figure 5 shows that aggregate hours and output for his economy fluctuate together with nearly the same amplitude. These theoretical findings are the basis for my statement in the introduction that there would be a puzzle if the economy did not display the business cycle phenomena.

Empirical Labor Elasticity

One important empirical implication of a shock-to-technology theory of fluctuations is that the empirical labor elasticity of output is significantly larger than the true elasticity, which for the Cobb-Douglas production function is the labor share parameter. To see why, note that the capital stock varies little cyclically and is nearly uncorrelated with output. Consequently, the deviations almost satisfy

$$y_t = \theta h_t + z_t$$

where y_t is output, h_t hours, and z_t the technology shock. The empirical elasticity is

$$\eta = \text{cov}(h_t, y_t)/\text{var}(h_t)$$

which, because of the positive correlation between h_t and z_t, is considerably larger than the model's θ, which is 0.64. For the basic, Kydland-Prescott, and Hansen growth economies, the values of η are 1.9, 1.4, and 1.3, respectively.

Because of measurement errors, the empirical elasticity for the American economy is not well-estimated by simply computing the ratio of the covariance between hours and output and dividing by the variance of hours. The procedure I use is based on the following probability model:

$$\hat{y}_t = y_t + \epsilon_{1t}$$

$$\hat{h}_{1t} = h_t + \epsilon_{2t}$$

$$\hat{h}_{2t} = h_t + \epsilon_{3t}$$

where the caret (⁀) denotes a measured value. The ϵ_{it} are measurement errors. Here, the $\hat{h}_{1t}$ measure of hours uses the employer survey data while the $\hat{h}_{2t}$ measure uses the household survey data. Since these are independent measures, a maintained hypothesis is that ϵ_{2t} and ϵ_{3t} are orthogonal. With this assumption, a reasonable estimate of $\text{var}(h_t)$ is the sample covariance between $\hat{h}_{1t}$ and $\hat{h}_{2t}$. Insofar as the measurement of

Figure 5

Deviations From Trend of GNP and Hours Worked in Hansen's Indivisible Labor Economy

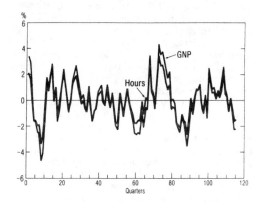

Source: Gary D. Hansen, Department of Economics, University of California, Santa Barbara

output has small variance or ϵ_{1t} is uncorrelated with the hours measurement errors or both, the covariance between measured output and either measured hours series is a reasonable estimate of the covariance between output and hours. These two covariances are 2.231×10^{-4} and 2.244×10^{-4} for the sample period, and I take the average as my estimate of $\text{cov}(h_t, y_t)$ for the American economy. My estimate of the empirical labor elasticity of output is

$$\hat{\eta} = [\text{cov}(\hat{h}_{1t}, \hat{y}_t) + \text{cov}(\hat{h}_{2t}, \hat{y}_t)]/2 \, \text{cov}(\hat{h}_{1t}, \hat{h}_{2t})$$

$$= 1.1.$$

This number is considerably greater than labor's share, which is about 0.70 when services of consumer durables are not included as part of output. This number strongly supports the importance of technological shocks in accounting for business cycle fluctuations. Nevertheless, the number is smaller than those for the Kydland-Prescott and Hansen growth economies.

One possible reason for the difference between the U.S. economy and the growth model empirical labor elasticities of output is cyclical measurement errors in output. A sizable part of the investment component of output is hard to measure and therefore not included in the U.S. National Product Accounts measure of output, the gross national product (GNP). In particular, a firm's major maintenance expenditures, research and development expenditures, and investments in human capital are not included in GNP. In good times—namely, when output is above trend—firms may be more likely to undertake major repairs of a not fully depreciated asset, such as replacing the roof of a 30-year-old building which has a tax life of 35 years. Such an expenditure is counted as maintenance and therefore not included in GNP even though the new roof will provide productive services for many years. The incentive for firms to do this is tax savings: by expensing an investment rather than capitalizing it, current tax liabilities are reduced. Before 1984, when a railroad replaced its 90-pound rails, the expenditure was treated as a maintenance expense rather than an investment expenditure. If these and other types of unmeasured investment fluctuate in percentage terms more than output, as do all the measured investment components, the volatility of GNP is larger than measured. We do know that investment in rails was highly procyclical and volatile in the postwar period. A careful study is needed to determine whether the correction for currently unmeasured investment is small or large.

Another reason to expect the American economy's labor elasticity to be less than the model's is that the model shocks are perfectly neutral with respect to the consumption and investment good transformation. Persistent shocks which alter the product transformation frontier between these goods would cause variation in output and employment but not in the productivity parameters. For fluctuations so induced, the empirical labor elasticity of output would be the true elasticity. Similarly, relatively permanent changes in the taxing of capital—such as altering depreciation rates, the corporate income tax rate, or the investment tax credit rate—would all result in fluctuations in output and employment but not in the productivity parameters.

A final reason for actual labor elasticity to be less than the model's is the way imports are measured. An increase in the price of imported oil, that is, an increase in the quantity of output that must be sacrificed for a given unit of that input, has no effect on measured productivity. From the point of view of the growth model, however, an oil price increase is a negative technology shock because it results in less output, net of the exports used to pay for the imported oil, available for domestic consumption and investment. Theory predicts that such shocks will induce variations in employment and output, even though they have no effect on the aggregate production function. Therefore, insofar as they are important, they reduce the empirical labor elasticity of output.

Extensions

The growth model has been extended to provide a better representation of the technology. Kydland and I (1982) have introduced a technology with more than one construction period for new production capacity.[7] We have also introduced inventory as a factor of production. This improves the match between the model's serial correlation properties and the U.S. postwar data, but has little effect on the other statistics.

Kydland (1984) has introduced heterogeneity of labor and found that if there are transfers from high human capital people to low human capital people, theory implies that hours of the low fluctuate more than hours of the high. It also implies a lower empirical labor elasticity of output than the homogeneous household model.

Bain (1985) has studied an economy that is richer in sectoral detail. His model has manufacturing, retailing, and service-producing sectors. A key feature of the technology is that production and distribution occur sequentially. Thus there are two types of inventories—those of manufacturers' finished goods and those of final goods available for sale. With this richer detail, theory implies that different components of aggregate inventories behave in different ways, as seen in the data. It also implies that production is more volatile than final sales, an observation considered anomalous since inventories can be used to smooth production. (See, for example, Blinder 1984.)

Much has been done. But much more remains to be explored. For example, public finance considerations could be introduced and theory used to predict their implications. As mentioned above, factors which affect the rental price of capital affect employment and output, and the nature of the tax system affects the rental price of capital. Theory could be used to predict the effect of temporary increases in government expenditures such as those in the early 1950s when defense expenditures increased from less than 5 to more than 13 percent of GNP. Theory of this type could also be used to predict the effect of terms-of-trade shocks. An implication of such an exercise most likely will be that economies with persistent terms-of-trade shocks fluctu-

---

[7] Altug (1983) has introduced two types of capital with different gestation periods. Using formal econometric methods, she finds evidence that the model's fit is improved if plant and equipment investment are not aggregated.

Edward C. Prescott
Theory Ahead of Measurement

ate differently than economies with transitory shocks. If so, this prediction can be tested against the observations.

Another interesting extension would be to explicitly model household production. This production often involves two people, with one specializing in market production and the other specializing in household production while having intermittent or part-time market employment. The fact that, cyclically, the employment of secondary wage earners is much more volatile than that of primary wage earners might be explained.

A final example of an interesting and not yet answered question is, How would the behavior of the Hansen indivisible labor economy change if agents did not have access to a technology to insure against random unemployment and instead had to self-insure against unemployment by holding liquid assets? In such an economy, unlike Hansen's, people would not be happy when unemployed. Their gain of more leisure would be more than offset by their loss as an insurer. Answering this question is not straightforward, because new tools for computing equilibria are needed.

Summary and Policy Implications

Economic theory implies that, given the nature of the shocks to technology and people's willingness and ability to intertemporally and intratemporally substitute, the economy will display fluctuations like those the U.S. economy displays. Theory predicts fluctuations in output of 5 percent and more from trend, with most of the fluctuation accounted for by variations in employment and virtually all the rest by the stochastic technology parameter. Theory predicts investment will be three or more times as volatile as output and consumption half as volatile. Theory predicts that deviations will display high serial correlation. In other words, theory predicts what is observed. Indeed, if the economy did not display the business cycle phenomena, there would be a puzzle.

The match between theory and observation is excellent, but far from perfect. The key deviation is that the empirical labor elasticity of output is less than predicted by theory. An important part of this deviation could very well disappear if the economic variables were measured more in conformity with theory. That is why I argue that theory is now ahead of business cycle measurement and theory should be used to obtain better measures of the key economic time series. Even with better measurement, there will likely be significant deviations from theory which can direct subsequent

theoretical research. This feedback between theory and measurement is the way mature, quantitative sciences advance.

The policy implication of this research is that costly efforts at stabilization are likely to be counterproductive. Economic fluctuations are optimal responses to uncertainty in the rate of technological change. However, this does not imply that the amount of technological change is optimal or invariant to policy. The average rate of technological change varies much both over time within a country and across national economies. What is needed is an understanding of the factors that determine the average rate at which technology advances. Such a theory surely will depend on the institutional arrangements societies adopt. If policies adopted to stabilize the economy reduce the average rate of technological change, then stabilization policy is costly. To summarize, attention should be focused not on fluctuations in output but rather on determinants of the average rate of technological advance.

References

Altug, S. 1983. Gestation lags and the business cycle. Working paper, Carnegie-Mellon University.

Ashenfelter, O. 1984. Macroeconomic analyses and microeconomic analyses of labor supply. In *Essays on macroeconomic implications of financial and labor markets and political processes*, ed. K. Brunner and A. H. Meltzer. Carnegie-Rochester Conference Series on Public Policy 21: 117–55. Amsterdam: North-Holland.

Bain, I. R. M. 1985. A theory of the cyclical movements of inventory stocks. Ph.D. dissertation, University of Minnesota.

Barro, R. J. 1981. Intertemporal substitution and the business cycle. In *Supply shocks, incentives and national wealth*, ed. K. Brunner and A. H. Meltzer. Carnegie-Rochester Conference Series on Public Policy 14: 237–68. Amsterdam: North-Holland.

Benhabib, J., and Nishimura, K. 1985. Competitive equilibrium cycles. *Journal of Economic Theory* 35: 284–306.

Bewley, T. F. 1972. Existence of equilibria in economies with infinitely many commodities. *Journal of Economic Theory* 4: 514–40.

Blinder, A. S. 1984. Can the production smoothing model of inventory behavior be saved? Working paper, Princeton University.

Brock, W. A., and Mirman, L. J. 1972. Optimal economic growth and uncertainty: The discounted case. *Journal of Economic Theory* 4: 479–513.

Cass, D. 1965. Optimum growth in an aggregative model of capital accumulation. *Review of Economic Studies* 32: 233–40.

Debreu, G. 1954. Valuation equilibrium and Pareto optimum. *Proceedings of the National Academy of Science* 70: 558–92.

Eichenbaum, M. S.; Hansen, L. P.; and Singleton, K. S. 1984. A time series analysis of representative agent models of consumption and leisure choice under uncertainty. Working paper, Carnegie-Mellon University.

Friend, I., and Blume, M. E. 1975. The demand for risky assets. *American Economic Review* 65: 900–22.

Ghez, G. R., and Becker, G. S. 1975. The allocation of time and goods over the life cycle. New York: National Bureau of Economic Research.

Hansen, G. D. 1984. Fluctuations in total hours worked: A study using efficiency units. Working paper, University of Minnesota.

————. 1985a. Indivisible labor and the business cycle. *Journal of Monetary Economics* 16: 309–27.

————. 1985b. Growth and fluctuations. Working paper, University of California, Santa Barbara.

Hansen, L. P., and Singleton, K. J. 1983. Stochastic consumption, risk aversion, and the temporal behavior of asset returns. *Journal of Political Economy* 91: 249–65.

Heckman, J. 1984. Comments on the Ashenfelter and Kydland papers. In *Essays on macroeconomic implications of financial and labor markets and political processes*, ed. K. Brunner and A. H. Meltzer. Carnegie-Rochester Conference Series on Public Policy 21: 209–24. Amsterdam: North-Holland.

Hotz, V. S.; Kydland, F. E.; and Sedlacek, G. L. 1985. Intertemporal preferences and labor supply. Working paper, Carnegie-Mellon University.

Kehoe, P. J. 1984. Dynamics of the current account: Theoretical and empirical analysis. Working paper, Harvard University.

Koopmans, T. C. 1965. On the concept of optimal economic growth. In *The econometric approach to development planning*. Chicago: Rand-McNally.

Kydland, F. E. 1983. Nonseparable utility and labor supply. Working paper, Hoover Institution.

————. 1984. Labor-force heterogeneity and the business cycle. In *Essays on macroeconomic implications of financial and labor markets and political processes*, ed. K. Brunner and A. H. Meltzer. Carnegie-Rochester Conference Series on Public Policy 21: 173–208. Amsterdam: North-Holland.

Kydland, F. E., and Prescott, E. C. 1982. Time to build and aggregate fluctuations. *Econometrica* 50–70.

————. 1984. The workweek of capital and labor. Research Department Working Paper 267, Federal Reserve Bank of Minneapolis.

Leamer, E. E. 1983. Let's take the con out of econometrics. *American Economic Review* 73: 31–43.

Long, J. B., and Plosser, C. I. 1983. Real business cycles. *Journal of Political Economy* 91: 39–69.

Lucas, R. E., Jr. 1977. Understanding business cycles. In *Stabilization of the domestic and international economy*, ed. K. Brunner and A. H. Meltzer. Carnegie-Rochester Conference Series on Public Policy 5: 7–29. Amsterdam: North-Holland.

————. 1980. Methods and problems in business cycle theory. *Journal of Money, Credit and Banking* 12: 696–715. Reprinted in *Studies in business-cycle theory*, pp. 271–96. Cambridge, Mass.: MIT Press, 1981.

Lucas, R. E., Jr., and Prescott, E. C. 1971. Investment under uncertainty. *Econometrica* 39: 659–81.

Marimon, R. 1984. General equilibrium and growth under uncertainty: The turnpike property. Discussion Paper 624. Northwestern University, Center for Mathematical Studies in Economics and Management Science.

Mehra, R. and Prescott, E. C. 1985. The equity premium: A puzzle. *Journal of Monetary Economics* 15: 145–61.

Rogerson, R. D. 1984. Indivisible labor, lotteries and equilibrium. In *Topics in the theory of labor markets*, chap. 1. Ph.D. dissertation, University of Minnesota.

Slutzky, E. 1927. The summation of random causes as the source of cyclic processes. In *Problems of Economic Conditions*, ed. Conjuncture Institute, Moskva (Moskow), vol. 3, no. 1. Revised English version, 1937, in *Econometrica* 5: 105–46.

Solow, R. M. 1956. A contribution to the theory of economic growth. *Quarterly Journal of Economics* 70: 65–94.

————. 1970. *Growth theory*. Oxford: Oxford University Press.

Swan, T. W. 1956. Economic growth and capital accumulation. *Economic Record* 32: 334–61.

Tobin, J., and Dolde, W. 1971. Wealth, liquidity and consumption. In *Consumer spending and monetary policy: The linkages*. Monetary Conference Series 5: 99–146. Boston: Federal Reserve Bank of Boston.

Federal Reserve Bank of Minneapolis
Quarterly Review Fall 1986

Some Skeptical Observations on Real Business Cycle Theory*

Lawrence H. Summers
Professor of Economics
Harvard University
and Research Associate
National Bureau of Economic Research

The increasing ascendancy of real business cycle theories of various stripes, with their common view that the economy is best modeled as a floating Walrasian equilibrium, buffeted by productivity shocks, is indicative of the depths of the divisions separating academic macroeconomists. These theories deny propositions thought self-evident by many academic macroeconomists and all of those involved in forecasting and controlling the economy on a day-to-day basis. They assert that monetary policies have no effect on real activity, that fiscal policies influence the economy only through their incentive effects, and that economic fluctuations are caused entirely by supply rather than demand shocks.

If these theories are correct, they imply that the macroeconomics developed in the wake of the Keynesian Revolution is well confined to the ashbin of history. And they suggest that most of the work of contemporary macroeconomists is worth little more than that of those pursuing astrological science. According to the views espoused by enthusiastic proponents of real business cycle theories, astrology and Keynesian economics are in many ways similar: both lack scientific support, both are premised on the relevance of variables that are in fact irrelevant, both are built on a superstructure of nonoperational and ill-defined concepts, and both are harmless only when they are ineffectual.

The appearance of Ed Prescott's stimulating paper, "Theory Ahead of Business Cycle Measurement," affords an opportunity to assess the current state of real business cycle theory and to consider its prospects as a foundation for macroeconomic analysis. Prescott's paper is brilliant in highlighting the appeal of real business cycle theories and making clear the assumptions they require. But he does not make much effort at caution in judging the potential of the real business cycle paradigm. He writes that "if the economy did not display the business cycle phenomena, there would be a puzzle," characterizes without qualification economic fluctuations as "optimal responses to uncertainty in the rate of technological change," and offers the policy advice that "costly efforts at stabilization are likely to be counterproductive."

Prescott's interpretation of his title is revealing of his commitment to his theory. He does not interpret the phrase *theory ahead of measurement* to mean that we lack the data or measurements necessary to test his theory. Rather, he means that measurement techniques have not yet progressed to the point where they fully corroborate his theory. Thus, Prescott speaks of the key deviation of observation from theory as follows: "An important part of this deviation could very well disappear if the economic variables were measured more in conformity with theory. That is why I argue that theory is now ahead of business cycle measurement. . . ."

The claims of real business cycle theorists deserve

---

*An earlier version of these remarks was presented at the July 25, 1986, meeting of the National Bureau of Economic Research Economic Fluctuations Group.

serious assessment, especially given their source and their increasing influence within the economics profession. Let me follow Prescott in being blunt. My view is that real business cycle models of the type urged on us by Prescott have nothing to do with the business cycle phenomena observed in the United States or other capitalist economies. Nothing in Prescott's papers or those he references is convincing evidence to the contrary.

Before turning to the argument Prescott presents, let me offer one lesson from the history of science. Extremely bad theories can predict remarkably well. Ptolemaic astronomy guided ships and scheduled harvests for two centuries. It provided extremely accurate predictions regarding a host of celestial phenomena. And to those who developed it, the idea that the earth was at the center seemed an absolutely natural starting place for a theory. So, too, Lamarckian biology, with its emphasis on the inheritance of acquired characteristics, successfully predicted much of what was observed in studies of animals and plants. Many theories can approximately mimic any given set of facts; that one theory can does not mean that it is even close to right.

Prescott's argument takes the form of the construction of an artificial economy which mimics many of the properties of actual economies. The close coincidence of his model economy and the actual economy leads him to conclude that the model economy is a reasonable if abstract representation of the actual economy. This claim is bolstered by the argument that the model economy is not constructed to fit cyclical facts but is parameterized on the basis of microeconomic information and the economy's long-run properties. Prescott's argument is unpersuasive at four levels.

Are the Parameters Right?

First, Prescott's claim to have parameterized the model on the basis of well-established microeconomic and long-run information is not sustainable. As one example, consider a parameter which Prescott identifies as being important in determining the properties of the model, the share of household time devoted to market activities. He claims that is one-third. Data on its average value over the last century indicate, as Martin Eichenbaum, Lars Hansen, and Kenneth Singleton (1986) have noted, an average value of one-sixth over the past 30 years. This seems right—a little more than half the adult population works, and those who work work about a quarter of the time. I am unable to find evidence supporting Prescott's one-third figure in the cited book by Gilbert Ghez and Gary Becker (1975). To take another example, Prescott takes the average real

interest rate to be 4 percent. Over the 30-year period he studies, it in fact averaged only about 1 percent. This list of model parameters chosen somewhat arbitrarily could be easily extended.

A more fundamental problem lies in Prescott's assumption about the intertemporal elasticity of substitution in labor supply. He cites no direct microeconomic evidence on this parameter, which is central to his model of cyclical fluctuations. Nor does he refer to any aggregate evidence on it. Rather, he relies on a rather selective reading of the evidence on the intertemporal elasticity of substitution in consumption in evaluating the labor supply elasticity. My own reading is that essentially all the available evidence suggests only a minimal response of labor to transitory wage changes. Many studies (including Altonji 1982; Mankiw, Rotemberg, and Summers 1985; and Eichenbaum, Hansen, and Singleton 1986) suggest that the intertemporal substitution model cannot account at either the micro or the macro level for fluctuations in labor supply.

Prescott is fond of parameterizing models based on long-run information. Japan has for 30 years enjoyed real wage growth at a rate four times the U.S. rate, close to 8 percent. His utility function would predict that such rapid real wage growth would lead to a much lower level of labor supply by the representative consumer. I am not aware that this pattern is observed in the data. Nor am I aware of data suggesting that age/hours profiles are steeper in professions like medicine or law, where salaries rise rapidly with age.

Prescott's growth model is not an inconceivable representation of reality. But to claim that its parameters are securely tied down by growth and micro observations seems to me a gross overstatement. The image of a big loose tent flapping in the wind comes to mind.

Where Are the Shocks?

My second fundamental objection to Prescott's model is the absence of any independent corroborating evidence for the existence of what he calls *technological shocks*. This point is obviously crucial since Prescott treats technological shocks as the only driving force behind cyclical fluctuations. Prescott interprets all movements in measured total factor productivity as being the result of technology shocks or to a small extent measurement error. He provides no discussion of the source or nature of these shocks, nor does he cite any microeconomic evidence for their importance. I suspect that the vast majority of what Prescott labels technology shocks are in fact the observable concomi-

24

Lawrence H. Summers
Skeptical Observations

tants of labor hoarding and other behavior which Prescott does not allow in his model.

Two observations support this judgment. First, it's hard to find direct evidence of the existence of large technological shocks. Consider the oil shocks, certainly the most widely noted and commented on shocks of the postwar period. How much might they have been expected to reduce total factor productivity? In one of the most careful studies of this issue, Ernst Berndt (1980, p. 85) concludes that "energy price or quantity variations since 1973 do not appear to have had a significant direct role in the slowdown of aggregate labor productivity in U.S. manufacturing, 1973–77." This is not to deny that energy shocks have important effects. But they have not accounted for large movements in measured total factor productivity.

Prescott assumes that technological changes are irregular, but is unable to suggest any specific technological shocks which presage the downturns that have actually taken place. A reasonable challenge to his model is to ask how it accounts for the 1982 recession, the most serious downturn of the postwar period. More generally, it seems to me that the finding that measured productivity frequently declines is difficult to account for technologically. What are the sources of technical regress? Between 1973 and 1977, for example, both mining and construction displayed negative rates of productivity growth. For smaller sectors of the economy, negative productivity growth is commonly observed.

A second observation casting doubt on Prescott's assumed driving force is that while technological shocks leading to changes in total factor productivity are hard to find, other explanations are easy to support. Jon Fay and James Medoff (1985) surveyed some 170 firms on their response to downturns in the demand for their output. The questions asked were phrased to make clear that it was exogenous downturns in their output that were being inquired about. Fay and Medoff (1985, p. 653) summarize their results by stating that "the evidence indicates that a sizeable portion of the swings in productivity over the business cycle is, in fact, the result of firms' decisions to hold labor in excess of regular production requirements and to hoard labor." According to their data, the typical plant in the U.S. manufacturing sector paid for 8 percent more blue-collar hours than were needed for regular production work during the trough quarter of its most recent downturn. After taking account of the amount of other worthwhile work that was completed by blue-collar employees during the trough quarter, 4 percent of the blue-collar hours paid for were hoarded. Similar conclusions have been reached in every other examination of microeconomic data on productivity that I am aware of.

In Prescott's model, the central driving force behind cyclical fluctuations is technological shocks. The propagation mechanism is intertemporal substitution in employment. As I have argued so far, there is no independent evidence from any source for either of these phenomena.

What About Prices? . . .

My third fundamental objection to Prescott's argument is that he does price-free economic analysis. Imagine an analyst confronting the market for ketchup. Suppose she or he decided to ignore data on the price of ketchup. This would considerably increase the analyst's freedom in accounting for fluctuations in the quantity of ketchup purchased. Indeed, without looking at the price of ketchup, it would be impossible to distinguish supply shocks from demand shocks. It is difficult to believe that any explanation of fluctuations in ketchup sales that did not confront price data would be taken seriously, at least by hard-headed economists.

Yet Prescott offers us an exercise in price-free economics. While real wages, interest rates, and returns to capital are central variables in his model, he never looks at any data on them except for his misconstrual of the average real interest rate over the postwar period. Others have confronted models like Prescott's to data on prices with what I think can fairly be labeled dismal results. There is simply no evidence to support any of the price effects predicted by the model. Prescott's work does not resolve—or even mention—the empirical reality emphasized by Robert Barro and Robert King (1982) that consumption and leisure move in opposite directions over the business cycle with no apparent procyclicality of real wages. It is finessed by ignoring wage data. Prescott's own work with Rajnish Mehra (1985) indicates that the asset pricing implications of models like the one he considers here are decisively rejected by nearly 100 years of historical experience. I simply do not understand how an economic model can be said to have been tested without price data.

I believe that the preceding arguments demonstrate that real business cycle models of the type surveyed by Prescott do not provide a convincing account of cyclical fluctuations. Even if this strong proposition is not accepted, they suggest that there is room for factors other than productivity shocks as causal elements in cyclical fluctuations.

. . . And Exchange Failures?

A fourth fundamental objection to Prescott's work is that it ignores the fact that partial breakdowns in the exchange mechanism are almost surely dominant factors in cyclical fluctuations. Consider two examples. Between 1929 and 1933, the gross national product in the United States declined 50 percent, as employment fell sharply. In Europe today, employment has not risen since 1970 and unemployment has risen more than fivefold in many countries. I submit that it defies credulity to account for movements on this scale by pointing to intertemporal substitution and productivity shocks. All the more given that total factor productivity has increased more than twice as rapidly in Europe as in the United States.

If some other force is responsible for the largest fluctuations that we observe, it seems quixotic methodologically to assume that it plays no role at all in other smaller fluctuations. Whatever mechanisms may have had something to do with the depression of the 1930s in the United States or the depression today in Europe presumably have at least some role in recent American cyclical fluctuations.

What are those mechanisms? We do not yet know. But it seems clear that a central aspect of depressions, and probably economic fluctuations more generally, is a breakdown of the exchange mechanism. Read any account of life during the Great Depression in the United States. Firms had output they wanted to sell. Workers wanted to exchange their labor for it. But the exchanges did not take place. To say the situation was constrained Pareto optimal given the technological decline that took place between 1929 and 1933 is simply absurd, even though total factor productivity did fall. What happened was a failure of the exchange mechanism. This is something that no model, no matter how elaborate, of a long-lived Robinson Crusoe dealing with his changing world is going to confront. A model that embodies exchange is a minimum prerequisite for a serious theory of economic downturns.

The traditional Keynesian approach is to postulate that the exchange mechanism fails because prices are in some sense rigid, so they do not attain market-clearing levels and thereby frustrate exchange. This is far from being a satisfactory story. Most plausible reasons why prices might not change also imply that agents should not continue to act along static demand and supply curves. But it hardly follows that ignoring exchange failures because we do not yet fully understand them is a plausible strategy.

Where should one look for failures of the exchange

26

process? Convincing evidence of the types of mechanisms that can lead to breakdowns of the exchange mechanism comes from analyses of breakdowns in credit markets. These seem to have played a crucial role in each of the postwar recessions. Indeed, while it is hard to account for postwar business cycle history by pointing to technological shocks, the account offered by, for example, Otto Eckstein and Allen Sinai (1986) of how each of the major recessions was caused by a credit crunch in an effort to control inflation seems compelling to me.

Conclusion

Even at this late date, economists are much better at analyzing the optimal response of a single economic agent to changing conditions than they are at analyzing the equilibria that will result when diverse agents interact. This unfortunate truth helps to explain why macroeconomics has found the task of controlling, predicting, or even explaining economic fluctuations so difficult. Improvement in the track record of macroeconomics will require the development of theories that can explain why exchange sometimes works well and other times breaks down. Nothing could be more counterproductive in this regard than a lengthy professional detour into the analysis of stochastic Robinson Crusoes.

Lawrence H. Summers
Skeptical Observations

References

Altonji, Joseph G. 1982. The intertemporal substitution model of labour market fluctuations: An empirical analysis. *Review of Economic Studies* 49 (Special Issue): 783–824.

Barro, Robert J., and King, Robert G. 1982. Time-separable preferences and intertemporal-substitution models of business cycles. Working Paper 888. National Bureau of Economic Research.

Berndt, Ernst R. 1980. Energy price increases and the productivity slowdown in United States manufacturing. In *The decline in productivity growth*, pp. 60–89. Conference Series 22. Boston: Federal Reserve Bank of Boston.

Eckstein, Otto, and Sinai, Allen. 1986. The mechanisms of the business cycle in the postwar era. In *The American business cycle: Continuity and change*, ed. Robert J. Gordon, pp. 39–105. National Bureau of Economic Research Studies in Business Cycles, vol. 25. Chicago: University of Chicago Press.

Eichenbaum, Martin S.; Hansen, Lars P.; and Singleton, Kenneth J. 1986. A time series analysis of representative agent models of consumption and leisure choice under uncertainty. Working Paper 1981. National Bureau of Economic Research.

Fay, Jon A., and Medoff, James L. 1985. Labor and output over the business cycle: Some direct evidence. *American Economic Review* 75 (September): 638–55.

Ghez, Gilbert R., and Becker, Gary S. 1975. *The allocation of time and goods over the life cycle*. New York: National Bureau of Economic Research.

Mankiw, N. Gregory; Rotemberg, Julio J.; and Summers, Lawrence H. 1985. Intertemporal substitution in macroeconomics. *Quarterly Journal of Economics* 100 (February): 225–51.

Mehra, Rajnish, and Prescott, Edward C. 1985. The equity premium: A puzzle. *Journal of Monetary Economics* 15 (March): 145–61.

Federal Reserve Bank of Minneapolis
Quarterly Review Fall 1986

Response to a Skeptic

Edward C. Prescott
Adviser
Research Department
Federal Reserve Bank of Minneapolis
and Professor of Economics
University of Minnesota

New findings in science are always subject to skepticism and challenge. This is an important part of the scientific process. Only if new results successfully withstand the attacks do they become part of accepted scientific wisdom. Summers (in this issue) is within this tradition when he attacks the finding I describe (in this issue) that business cycles are precisely what economic theory predicts given the best measures of people's willingness and ability to substitute consumption and leisure, both between and within time periods. I welcome this opportunity to respond to Summers' challenges to the parameter values and the business cycle facts that I and other real business cycle analysts have used. In challenging the existing quality of measurement and not providing measurement inconsistent with existing theory, Summers has conceded the point that theory is ahead of business cycle measurement.

Miscellaneous Misfires

Before responding to Summers' challenges to the measurements used in real business cycle analyses, I will respond briefly to his other attacks and, in the process, try to clarify some methodological issues in business cycle theory as well as in aggregate economic theory more generally.

Prices

Summers asks, Where are the prices? This question is puzzling. The mechanism real business cycle analysts use is the one he and other leading people in the field of aggregate public finance use: competitive equilibrium. Competitive equilibria have relative prices. As stated in the introduction of "Theory Ahead of Business Cycle Measurement" (in this issue), the business cycle puzzle is, Why are there large movements in the time allocated to market activities and little associated movements in the real wage, the price of people's time? Along with that price, Kydland and I (1982, 1984) examine the rental price of capital. An infinity of other relative prices can be studied, but these are the ones needed to construct national income and product accounts. The behavior of these prices in our models conforms with that observed.

In competitive theory, an economic environment is needed. For that, real business cycle analysts have used the neoclassical growth model. It is the preeminent model in aggregate economics. It was developed to account for the growth facts and has been widely used for predicting the aggregate effects of alternative tax schemes as well. With the labor/leisure decision endogenized, it is the appropriate model to study the aggregate implications of technology change uncertainty. Indeed, in 1977 Lucas, the person responsible for making business cycles again a central focus in economics, defined them (p. 23) as deviations from the neoclassical growth model—that is, fluctuations in hours allocated to market activity that are too large to be accounted for by changing marginal productivities of labor as reflected in real wages. Lucas, like me and virtually everyone else, assumed that, once characterized, the competitive equilibrium of the calibrated neoclassical growth economy would display much smaller fluctuations than do the actual U.S. data. Exploiting advances in theory and computational methods, Kydland and I (1982, 1984) and Hansen (1985) computed and studied the competitive equilibrium process for this model economy. We were surprised to find the predicted fluctuations roughly as large as those experienced by the U.S. economy since the Korean War.

Some economists have been reluctant to use the competitive equilibrium mechanism to study business cycle fluctuations because they think it is contradicted by a real-world observation: some individuals who are not employed would gladly switch places with similarly skilled individuals who are. Solow (1986, p. S34), for example, predicted that "any interesting and useful solution to that riddle will almost certainly involve an equilibrium concept broader, or at least different from, price-mediated market-clearing." Rogerson (1984) proved him wrong. If the world had no nonconvexities or moral hazard problems, Solow would be correct. But the mapping between time allocated to market activities and units of labor service produced does have nonconvexities. Time spent commuting is not producing labor services, yet it is time allocated to market activity. With nonconvexities, competitive equilibrium theory implies that the commodities traded or priced are complicated contracted arrangements which can include employment lotteries with both winners and losers. As shown by Hansen (1985), competitive theory accounts well for the observation that the principal margin of adjustment in aggregate hours is the number of people employed rather than the number of hours worked per person—as well as for the observation of so-called involuntary unemployment.

Technology Shocks

Another Summers question is, Where are the technology shocks? Apparently, he wants some identifiable shock to account for each of the half dozen postwar recessions. But our finding is not that infrequent large shocks produce fluctuations; it is, rather, that small shocks do, every period. At least since Slutzky (1927), some stable low-order linear stochastic difference equations have been known to generate cycles. They do not have a few large shocks; they have small shocks, one every period. The equilibrium allocation for the calibrated neoclassical growth model with persistent shocks to technology turns out to be just such a process.

My Claims

Summers has perhaps misread some of my review of real business cycle research (in this issue). There I do not argue that the Great American Depression was the equilibrium response to technology shocks as predicted by the neoclassical growth model. I do not argue that disruptions in the payment and credit system would not disrupt the economy. That theory predicts one factor has a particular nature and magnitude does not imply that theory predicts all other factors are zero. I only claim that technology shocks account for more than half the fluctuations in the postwar period, with a best point estimate near 75 percent. This does not imply that public finance disturbances, random changes in the terms of trade, and shocks to the technology of exchange had no effect in that period.

Neither do I claim that theory is ahead of macroeconomic measurement in all respects. As Summers points out, Mehra and I (1985) have used the representative agent construct to predict the magnitude of the average risk premium of an equity claim over a real bill. Our predicted quantity is small compared to the historically observed average difference between the yields of the stock market and U.S. Treasury bills. But this is not a failure of the representative agent construct; it is a success. We used theory to predict the magnitude of the average risk premium. That the representative agent model is poorly designed to predict differences in borrowing and lending rates—to explain, for example, why the government can borrow at a rate at least a few percentage points less than the one at which most of us can borrow—does not imply that this model is not well designed for other purposes—for predicting the consequences of technology shocks for fluctuations at the business cycle frequencies, for example.

Measurement Issues

Summers challenges the values real business cycle analysts have selected for three model parameters. By arguing that historically the real U.S. interest rate is closer to 1 percent than to the model economy's approximately 4 percent, he is questioning the value selected for the subjective time discount factor. He explicitly questions our value for the leisure share parameter. And Summers' challenge to the observation that labor productivity is procyclical is implicitly a challenge to my measure of the technology shock variance parameter.

Real Interest Rate

Summers points out that the real return on U.S. Treasury bills over the last 30 years has been about 1 percent, which is far from the average real interest rate of the economies that Kydland and I have studied. But for the neoclassical growth model, the relevant return is not the return on T-bills. It is the return on tangible capital, such things as houses, factories, machines, inventories, automobiles, and roads. The return on capital in the U.S. business sector is easily calculated from the U.S. National Income and Product Accounts, so we use it as a proxy for the return on U.S. capital more generally. This number is obtained by dividing the income of capital net of the adjusted capital consumption allowance by the capital stock in the business sector. For the postwar years, the result is approximately 4 percent, about the average real return for the model economies.

Preferences

Summers also questions the value of the leisure share parameter and argues that it is not well tied down by micro observation at the household level, as we claim. This is a potentially important parameter. If it is large, the response of labor supply to temporary changes in the real wage is large. Only if that response is large will large movements in employment be associated with small co-movements in the real wage.

Kydland and I conclude that the leisure share parameter is not large based on findings reported by Ghez and Becker (1975). They report (p. 95) that the annual productive time endowment of U.S. males is 5,096 hours. They also say (p. 95) that U.S. females allocate about 75 hours per week to personal care, leaving 93 hours of production time per week. This multiplied by 52 is 4,836 hours, the annual productive time endowment of females. Ghez and Becker also report the average annual hours of employment for noninstitutionalized, working-age males as about 2,000 hours (pp. 85–91). If females allocate half as many hours to market employment as do males, the average fraction of time the U.S. working-age population spends in employment is about 0.30. Adding to this the time spent commuting yields a number close to those for our models. (They are all between 0.30 and 0.31 in Kydland and Prescott 1982 and 1984.)

Initially Kydland and I used time additive preferences, and the predictions of theory for productivity movements were as large in percentage terms as aggregate hour movements. This is inconsistent with observations, so I did not take seriously the prediction of theory that a little over half the aggregate output fluctuations in the postwar period were responses to technology shocks. At that time, measurement was still

ahead of theory. Then, the prediction of theory would have been consistent with the relative movement of productivity and aggregate hours, and technology shocks would have accounted for the business cycle phenomena, if the leisure share parameter were five-sixths. With the discipline we used, however, this share parameter had to be consistent with observations on household time allocation. That we are now debating about a theory of aggregate phenomena by focusing on household time allocation is evidence that economic theory has advanced. Now, like physical scientists, when economists model aggregate phenomena, the parameters used can be measured independently of those phenomena.

In our 1982 paper, Kydland and I did claim that fluctuations of the magnitude observed could plausibly be accounted for by the randomness in the technological change process. There we explored the implications of a distributed lag of leisure being an argument of the period utility function rather than just the current level of leisure. Like increasing the leisure share parameter, this broadening results in larger fluctuations in hours in response to technology shocks. Kydland (1983) then showed that an unmeasured household-specific capital stock could rationalize this distributed lag. In addition, the lag was not inconsistent with good micro measurement, and these parameters could be measured independently of the business cycle phenomena. The distributed lag was a long shot, though, so we did not claim that theory had caught up to measurement.

Since then, however, two panel studies found evidence for a distributed lag of the type we considered (Hotz, Kydland, and Sedlacek 1985; Eckstein and Wolpin 1986). With this development, theory and measurement of the business cycle became roughly equal.

Subsequently, an important advance in aggregate theory has made moot the issue of whether Kydland's and my assumed preferences for leisure are supported by micro measurement. Given an important nonconvexity in the mapping between time allocated to market activities and units of labor service produced, Rogerson (1984) showed that the aggregate elasticity of labor supply to temporary changes in the real wage is large independent of individuals' willingness to intertemporally substitute leisure. This nicely rationalized the disparate micro and macro labor findings for this elasticity—the microeconomists' that it is small (for example, Ashenfelter 1984) and the macroeconomists' that it is large (for example, Eichenbaum, Hansen, and

Singleton 1984). Hansen (1985) introduced this nonconvexity into the neoclassical growth model. He found that with this feature theory predicts that the economy will display the business cycle phenomena even if individuals' elasticity of labor supply to temporary changes in the real wage is small. Further, with this feature he found theory correctly predicts that most of the variation in aggregate hours of employment is accounted for by variation in the number of people employed rather than in the number of hours worked per person.

Technology
☐ Uncertainty

In our 1982 paper, Kydland and I searched over processes for the technological change process. We did sensitivity analysis with the other parameters, but found the conclusions relatively insensitive to their assumed values (except for the distributed lag of leisure parameters just discussed). The parameters of the technological change process did affect our predictions of the aggregate implications of uncertainty in the technology parameter. In fact, Lucas (1985, p. 48) criticized us for searching for the best fit. In "Theory Ahead of Business Cycle Measurement," I directly examined the statistical properties of the technology coefficient process. I found that the process is an approximate random walk with standard deviation of change in the logs approximately 0.00763 per quarter. When this number is used in the Hansen model, fluctuations predicted are even larger than those observed. In Kydland's and my model (1984), they are essentially equal to those observed.

Some, on the basis of theory, think that the factors producing technological change are small, many, and roughly uncorrelated. If so, by the law of large numbers, these factors should average out and the technological change process should be very smooth. I found (in this issue) empirical evidence to the contrary. Others have too. Summers and Heston (1984) report the annual gross national products for virtually every country in the postwar period. They show huge variation across countries in the rate of growth of per capita income over periods sufficiently long that business cycle variations are a minor consideration. Even individual countries have large variation in the decade growth rates of per capita output. Given Solow's (1957) finding that more than 75 percent of the changes in per capita output are accounted for by changes in the technology parameter, the evidence for variation in the rate of technological advance is strong.

Obviously, economists do not have a good theory of the determinants of technological change. In this regard, measurement is ahead of theory. The determinants of the rate of technological change must depend greatly on the institutions and arrangements that societies adopt. Why else should technology advance more rapidly in one country than in another or, within a country, more rapidly in one period than in another? But a theory of technological change is not needed to predict responses to technological change.

The key parameter is the variance of the technology shock. This is where better measurement could alter the prediction of theory. Is measuring this variance with Solow's (1957) method (as I did) reasonable? I showed that measures of the technology shock variance are insensitive to cyclical variations in the capital utilization rate. Even if that rate varies proportionately to hours of employment and the proportionality constant is selected so as to minimize the measured standard deviation of the technology shock, that measured deviation is reduced only from 0.00763 to 0.00759. Further, when the capital utilization rate varies in this way for the model, the equilibrium responses are significantly larger. Variation in the capital utilization rate does not appear to greatly bias my estimate of the importance of technological change variance for aggregate fluctuations.

Perhaps better measurement will find that the technological change process varies less than I estimated. If so, a prediction of theory is that the amount of fluctuation accounted for by uncertainty in that process is smaller. If this were to happen, I would be surprised. I can think of no plausible source of measurement error that would produce a random walk–like process for technological change.

☐ Labor Hoarding

Summers seems to argue that measured productivity is procyclical because measurement errors are cyclical. To support his argument, he cites a survey by Fay and Medoff (1985), which actually has little if anything to say about cyclical movements. Fay and Medoff surveyed more than 1,000 plant managers and received 168 usable responses. One of the questions asked was, How many extra blue-collar workers did you have in your recent downturn? They did not ask, How many extra workers did you have at the trough quarter and at the peak quarter of the most recent business cycle? Answers to those questions are needed to conclude how the number of extra blue-collar workers reported by managers varies over the cycle. Even if these questions had been asked, though, the response to them would not be a good measure of the number of redundant workers. Such questions are simply too ambiguous for most respondents to interpret them the same way.

The argument that labor hoarding is cyclical is not supported by theory either. The fact that labor is a quasi-fixed factor of production in the sense of Oi (1962) does not imply that more workers will be hoarded in recessions than in expansions. In bad times a firm with low output may be less reluctant to lay off workers than in good times because the worker is less likely to be hired by another firm. This argument suggests that labor hoarding associated with firm-specific output variations should be procyclical. Leisure consumed on the job also may be less in bad times than in good because work discipline may be greater. That is, an entrepreneur might be less reluctant to fire a worker in bad times because the worker can more easily be replaced. One might reasonably think, therefore, that labor's quasi-fixed nature makes measured productivity less, not more, cyclically volatile than productivity really is.

There is another, better reason to think that. In the standard measures of aggregate hours of employment, the hours of an experienced MBA from one of the best business schools are treated the same as those of a high school dropout. Yet these hours do not on average command the same price in the market, which is evidence that they are not the same commodity. In the neoclassical growth model, the appropriate way to aggregate hours is in terms of effective units of labor. That is, if the MBA's productivity is five times that of the high school dropout, then each hour of the MBA's time is effectively equivalent to five hours of the high school dropout's time. The work of Kydland (1984) suggests this correction is an important one. The more educated and on average more highly paid have much less variability in annual hours of employment than do the less educated. Kydland (1984, p. 179) reports average hours and average wages as well as sensitivity of hours to the aggregate unemployment rate for adult males categorized by years of schooling. His figures imply that a 1 percentage point change in the aggregate unemployment rate for adult males is associated with a 1.24 percent change in equally weighted hours. When those hours are measured as effective units of labor, the latter change is only 0.65 percent. This is strong evidence that if the labor input were measured correctly, the measure of productivity would vary more.

To summarize, measurement of the labor input needs to be improved. By questioning the standard measures, Summers is agreeing that theory is ahead of business cycle measurement. More quantitative theoretic work is also needed, to determine whether abstracting from the fact that labor is a partially fixed factor affects any of the real business cycle models' findings. Of course, introducing this feature—or others—into these models may significantly alter their predictions of the aggregate implications of technology uncertainty. But respectable economic intuition must be based on models that have been rigorously analyzed.

To Conclude

Summers cannot be attacking the use of competitive theory and the neoclassical growth environment in general. He uses this standard model to predict the effects of alternative tax policies on aggregate economic behavior. He does not provide criteria for deciding when implications of this model should be taken seriously and when they should not be. My guess is that the reason for skepticism is not the methods used, but rather the unexpected nature of the findings. We agree that labor input is not that precisely measured, so neither is technological uncertainty. In other words, we agree that theory is ahead of business cycle measurement.

References

Ashenfelter, O. 1984. Macroeconomic analyses and microeconomic analyses of labor supply. In *Essays on macroeconomic implications of financial and labor markets and political processes*, ed. K. Brunner and A. H. Meltzer. Carnegie-Rochester Conference Series on Public Policy 21: 117–55. Amsterdam: North-Holland.

Eckstein, Zvi, and Wolpin, Kenneth I. 1986. Dynamic labor force participation of married women and endogenous work experience. Manuscript. Tel Aviv University and Ohio State University.

Eichenbaum, Martin S.; Hansen, Lars P.; and Singleton, Kenneth J. 1984. A time series analysis of representative agent models of consumption and leisure choice under uncertainty. Working paper, Carnegie-Mellon University.

Fay, Jon A., and Medoff, James L. 1985. Labor and output over the business cycle: Some direct evidence. *American Economic Review* 75 (September): 638–55.

Ghez, Gilbert R., and Becker, Gary S. 1975. *The allocation of time and goods over the life cycle.* New York: National Bureau of Economic Research.

Hansen, Gary D. 1985. Indivisible labor and the business cycle. *Journal of Monetary Economics* 16 (November): 309–27.

Hotz, V. S.; Kydland, F. E.; and Sedlacek, G. L. 1985. Intertemporal preferences and labor supply. Working paper, Carnegie-Mellon University.

Kydland, Finn E. 1983. Nonseparable utility and labor supply. Working paper, Hoover Institution.

—————. 1984. Labor-force heterogeneity and the business cycle. In *Essays on macroeconomic implications of financial and labor markets and political processes*, ed. K. Brunner and A. H. Meltzer. Carnegie-Rochester Conference Series on Public Policy 21: 173–208. Amsterdam: North-Holland.

Kydland, Finn E., and Prescott, Edward C. 1982. Time to build and aggregate fluctuations. *Econometrica* 50 (January): 1345–70.

—————. 1984. The workweek of capital and labor. Research Department Working Paper 267. Federal Reserve Bank of Minneapolis.

Lucas, Robert E., Jr. 1977. Understanding business cycles. In *Stabilization of the domestic and international economy*, ed. K. Brunner and A. H. Meltzer. Carnegie-Rochester Conference Series on Public Policy 5: 7–29. Amsterdam: North-Holland.

—————. 1985. Models of business cycles. Manuscript prepared for the Yrjo Jahnsson Lectures, Helsinki, Finland. University of Chicago.

Mehra, Rajnish, and Prescott, Edward C. 1985. The equity premium: A puzzle. *Journal of Monetary Economics* 15 (March): 145–61.

Oi, Walter Y. 1962. Labor as a quasi-fixed factor. *Journal of Political Economy* 70 (December): 538–55.

Rogerson, R. D. 1984. Indivisible labor, lotteries and equilibrium. Economics Department Working Paper 10. University of Rochester.

Slutzky, Eugen. 1927. The summation of random causes as the source of cyclic processes. In *Problems of economic conditions*, ed. Conjuncture Institute, Moskva (Moscow), vol. 3, no. 1. Revised English version, 1937, in *Econometrica* 5: 105–46.

Solow, Robert M. 1957. Technical change and the aggregate production function. *Review of Economics and Statistics* 39 (August): 312–20.

—————. 1986. Unemployment: Getting the questions right. *Economica* 53 (Supplement): S23–S34.

Summers, Robert, and Heston, Alan. 1984. Improved international comparisons of real product and its composition: 1950–1980. *Review of Income and Wealth* 30 (June): 207–62.

Journal of Monetary Economics 21 (1988) 195–232. North-Holland

PRODUCTION, GROWTH AND BUSINESS CYCLES
I. The Basic Neoclassical Model

Robert G. KING, Charles I. PLOSSER and Sergio T. REBELO*

University of Rochester, Rochester, NY 14627, USA

Received September 1987, final version received December 1987

This paper presents the neoclassical model of capital accumulation augmented by choice of labor supply as the basic framework of modern real business cycle analysis. Preferences and production possibilities are restricted so that the economy displays steady state growth. Then we explore the implications of the basic model for perfect foresight capital accumulation and for economic fluctuations initiated by impulses to technology. We argue that the neoclassical approach holds considerable promise for enhancing our understanding of fluctuations. Nevertheless, the basic model does have some important shortcomings. In particular, substantial persistence in technology shocks is required if the model economy is to exhibit periods of economic activity that persistently deviate from a deterministic trend.

1. Introduction and summary

Real business cycle analysis investigates the role of neoclassical factors in shaping the character of economic fluctuations. In this pair of essays, we provide an introduction to the real business cycle research program by considering the basic concepts, analytical methods and open questions on the frontier of research. The focus of the present essay is on the dynamic aspects of the basic neoclassical model of capital accumulation. This model is most frequently encountered in analyses of economic growth, but we share Hicks' (1965, p. 4) perspective that it is also a basic laboratory for investigating more general dynamic phenomena involving the choice of consumption, work effort and investment.

Our use of the neoclassical model of capital accumulation as the engine of analysis for the investigation of economic fluctuations raises a number of central issues. First, what role does economic growth play in the study of

*The authors acknowledge financial support from the National Science Foundation. King and Plosser have joint affiliations with the Department of Economics and the W.E. Simon Graduate School of Business, University of Rochester. Rebelo is affiliated with the Department of Economics, University of Rochester and the Department of Economics, Portuguese Catholic University. We have benefited from the comments of Andrew Abel and Larry Christiano, as well as from those of seminar participants at the Federal Reserve Bank of Richmond, Brasenose College, Oxford, Institute for International Economic Studies, University of Stockholm, Northwestern University, Yale University, and Columbia University.

economic fluctuations? More precisely, does the presence of economic growth restrict the preference and production specifications in ways that are important for the analysis of business cycles? Second, what analytical methods can be employed to study the time series implications of the neoclassical model? Third, what are the dynamics of the neoclassical model in response to technology shocks? Finally, does the neoclassical model – driven by technology shocks – replicate important features of macroeconomic time series? The analysis of these issues forms the core of the present paper and establishes the building blocks of real business cycle theory.

Real business cycle theory, though still in the early stages of development, holds considerable promise for enhancing our understanding of economic fluctuations and growth as well as their interaction. The basic framework developed in this essay is capable of addressing a wide variety of issues that are commonly thought to be important for understanding business cycles. While we focus here on models whose impulses are technological, the methods can be adapted to consider shocks originating from preferences or other exogenous factors such as government policies and terms of trade. Some of these extensions to the basic framework are developed in the companion essay.

To many readers it must seem heretical to discuss business cycles without mentioning money. Our view, however, is simply that the role of money in an equilibrium theory of economic growth and fluctuations remains an open area for research. Further, real disturbances generate rich and neglected interactions in the basic neoclassical model that may account for a substantial portion of observed fluctuations. The objective of real business cycle research is to obtain a better understanding of the character of these real fluctuations. Without an understanding of these real fluctuations it is difficult *a priori* to assign an important role to money.

The organization of the paper follows the sequence of questions outlined above. We begin in section 2 by describing the preferences, endowments and technology of the basic (one-sector) neoclassical model of capital accumulation.[1] In contrast to the familiar textbook presentation of this model, however, work effort is viewed as a choice variable. We then discuss the restrictions on production possibilities and preferences that are necessary for steady state growth. On the production side, with a constant returns to scale production function, technical progress must be expressible in labor augmenting (Harrod neutral) form. In a feasible steady state, it follows that consumption, investment, output and capital all must grow at the exogenously specified rate of technical change. On the other hand, since the endowment of time is constant, work effort cannot grow in the steady state. Thus, preferences must be restricted so that there is no change in the level of effort on the steady state

---

[1]A more detailed and unified development of the material is presented in the technical appendix, available from the authors on request.

growth path despite the rise in marginal productivity stemming from technical progress, i.e., there must be an exact offset of appropriately defined income and substitution effects.

Section 3 concerns perfect foresight dynamic competitive equilibria, which we analyze using approximations near the steady state. Using a parametric version of the model, with parameters chosen to match the long-run U.S. growth experience, we study the interaction between intertemporal production possibilities and the equilibrium quantity of labor effort. Off the steady state path, we find that capital and effort are negatively related despite the fact that the marginal product of labor schedule is positively related to the capital stock. That is, in response to the high real rate of return implied by a low capital stock, individuals will substitute intertemporally to produce additional resources for investment.

Working from a certainty equivalence perspective, section 4 considers how temporary productivity shocks influence economic activity, generating 'real business cycles' in the terminology of Long and Plosser (1983). Again there is an important interaction between variation in labor input – this time in response to a productivity shock – and the intertemporal substitution in production permitted by capital accumulation. Purely temporary technology shocks call forth an expansion of labor input once the Long and Plosser (1983) assumption of complete depreciation is replaced by a more realistic value,[2] since more durable capital increases the feasibility of intertemporal substitution of goods and leisure. Nevertheless, with purely temporary productivity shocks, we find that there are important deficiencies of the basic neoclassical model. Although there is substantial serial correlation in consumption and capital as a consequence of consumption smoothing, there is effectively no serial correlation in output or employment. This lack of propagation reflects two basic properties of the parameterized model: (i) a negative relation between capital and effort along the transition path and (ii) the minor effect of a purely temporary technology shock on a large and durable capital stock. Thus, the basic neoclassical capital accumulation mechanism is important for permitting intertemporal substitution of goods and leisure, but it does not generate serial correlation in output and employment close to that exhibited by macroeconomic data.

It is necessary, therefore, to incorporate substantial serial correlation in productivity shocks [as in Kydland and Prescott (1982), Long and Plosser (1983), Hansen (1985), and Prescott (1986)] if the basic neoclassical model is to generate business fluctuations that resemble those in post-war U.S. experience. Since serial correlation involves movements in productive opportunities that are more persistent in character, labor input responds less elastically to a

---

[2] By a purely temporary shock, we mean one that lasts for a single time period, which is taken to be a quarter in our analysis.

given size shock, but its response remains positive. On the other hand, with more persistent productivity shocks, consumption responds more elastically in accord with the permanent income theory.

In section 5, we show that the basic neoclassical model – with persistent technology shocks – captures some key features of U.S. business cycles. For example, the model replicates observed differences in volatility across key series. Measured as a percentage of the standard deviation of output, there is an identical ordering of the model's implications for investment, wages, consumption and hours, and the U.S. time series: investment is most volatile, followed by wages, consumption and then hours. But there are also aspects of the data that are poorly captured by the single-shock model. For example, consumption, investment and hours are much more highly correlated with output in the model than in the data.

Professional interest in real business cycle analysis has been enhanced by the comparison of moments implied by neoclassical models with those of U.S. time series, as initiated by Kydland and Prescott (1982). Our implications for moments differ from those of Hansen (1985) and Prescott (1986), principally because we do not filter actual and model-generated time series to remove slow-moving components. For example, in Hansen's and Prescott's analyses, filtered hours and output have virtually identical volatilities, in both the model and the transformed data. By contrast, in our analysis, the volatility of hours is about half that of output (both in our model and post-war detrended U.S. data). These differences occur despite the fact that there is little economic difference in the models under study.

Section 6 provides a brief summary and some concluding remarks.

2. The basic neoclassical model

Our analysis of economic growth and fluctuations starts by summarizing the key features of the basic one-sector, neoclassical model of capital accumulation. Much of the discussion in this section will be familiar to readers of Solow (1956), Cass (1965), Koopmans (1965) and subsequent textbook presentations of their work, but it is important to build a base for subsequent developments.

2.1. Economic environment

We begin by considering the preferences, technology and endowments of the environment under study.

Preferences. We consider an economy populated by many identical infinitely-lived individuals with preferences over goods and leisure represented by

$$U = \sum_{t=0}^{\infty} \beta^t u(C_t, L_t), \qquad \beta < 1, \tag{2.1}$$

where C_t is commodity consumption in period t and L_t is leisure in period t. Consumption and leisure are assumed throughout to be goods, so that utility is increasing in C_t and L_t.[3]

Production possibilities.   There is only one final good in this economy and it is produced according to a constant returns to scale neoclassical production technology given by

$$Y_t = A_t F(K_t, N_t X_t), \tag{2.2}$$

where K_t is the predetermined capital stock (chosen at $t-1$) and N_t is the labor input in period t.[4] We permit temporary changes in total factor productivity through A_t. Permanent technological variations are restricted to be in labor productivity, X_t, for reasons that we discuss below.

Capital accumulation.   In this simple neoclassical framework the commodity can be either consumed or invested. The capital stock evolves according to

$$K_{t+1} = (1 - \delta_K) K_t + I_t, \tag{2.3}$$

where I_t is gross investment and δ_K is the rate of depreciation of capital.[5]

Resource constraints.   In each period, an individual faces two resource constraints: (i) total time allocated to work and leisure must not exceed the endowment, which is normalized to one, and (ii) total uses of the commodity must not exceed output. These conditions are

$$L_t + N_t \leq 1, \tag{2.4}$$

$$C_t + I_t \leq Y_t. \tag{2.5}$$

Naturally, there are also the non-negativity constraints $L_t \geq 0$, $N_t \geq 0$, $C_t \geq 0$ and $K_t \geq 0$.

---

[3] Momentary utility, $u(\cdot)$, is assumed to be strictly concave and twice continuously differentiable. Further, it satisfies the Inada conditions, namely that $\lim_{c \to 0} D_1 u(c, L) = \infty$ and $\lim_{c \to \infty} D_1 u(c, L) = 0$, $\lim_{L \to 0} D_2 u(c, L) = \infty$ and $\lim_{L \to 1} D_2 u(c, L) = 0$, where $D_i u(\cdot)$ is the first partial derivative of $u(\cdot)$ with respect to the function's ith argument.

[4] By neoclassical, we mean that the production function is concave, twice continuously differentiable, satisfies the Inada conditions, and that both factors are essential in production.

[5] We abstract from adjustment costs to capital accumulation throughout the analysis, as these seem to us to be basically a restricted formulation of the two-sector neoclassical model.

2.2. Individual optimization and competitive equilibrium

The standard neoclassical analysis focuses on the optimal quantities chosen by a 'social planner' or representative agent directly operating the technology of the economy. Since our setup satisfies the conditions under which the second welfare theorem is valid, optimal capital accumulation will also be realized in a competitive equilibrium.[6] In the companion essay, we discuss departures from the strict representative agent model including government expenditures and distorting taxes, productive externalities, and heterogeneity of preferences and productivities. In these contexts, we will need to be more precise about distinguishing between individual choices and competitive outcomes.

2.3. Steady state growth

A characteristic of most industrialized economies is that variables like output per capita and consumption per capita exhibit sustained growth over long periods of time. This long-run growth occurs at rates that are roughly constant over time within economies but differ across economies. We interpret this pattern as evidence of steady state growth, by which we mean that the levels of certain key variables grow at constant – but possibly different – rates, at least some of which are positive. Additional restrictions on preferences and technologies are required if the system is to exhibit steady state growth.

Restrictions on production.   For a steady state to be feasible, Swan (1963) and Phelps (1966) show that permanent technical change must be expressible in a labor augmenting form, which rationalizes our specification in (2.2) above. To make for an easier comparison with other studies, we adopt the Cobb–Douglas production process for the bulk of our analysis,

$$Y_t = A_t K_t^{1-\alpha} (N_t X_t)^{\alpha}, \tag{2.6}$$

where the quantity $N_t X_t$ is usually referred to as effective labor units.[7]

Since variation in A_t is assumed temporary, we can ignore it for our investigation of steady state growth. The production function (2.6) and the accumulation equation (2.3) then imply that the steady state rates of growth of output, consumption, capital and investment per capita are all equal to the

---

[6] The basic reference is Debreu (1954). See also Prescott and Lucas (1972).

[7] We note, however, that if technological change is labor augmenting, then the observed invariance of factor shares to the scale of economic activity cannot be used to rationalize the restriction to the Cobb–Douglas form. In the presence of labor augmenting technological progress the factor shares are constant for *any* constant returns to scale production function.

growth rate of labor augmenting technical progress.[8] Denoting one plus the growth rate of a variable Z as γ_Z (i.e., Z_{t+1}/Z_t), then any feasible steady state requires

$$\gamma_Y = \gamma_C = \gamma_K = \gamma_I = \gamma_X, \tag{2.7a}$$

and the growth rate of work effort to be zero, i.e.,

$$\gamma_N = 1. \tag{2.7b}$$

Since time devoted to work N is bounded by the endowment, it cannot grow in the steady state (2.7b). Thus, the only admissible constant growth rate for N is zero.

In any such feasible steady state, the marginal product of capital and the marginal product of a unit of labor input in efficiency units are constant. The levels of the marginal products, however, depend on the ratio of capital to effective labor, which is not determined by the restriction to a feasible steady state.

Restrictions on preferences. Eqs. (2.7a) and (2.7b) describe the technologically feasible steady state growth rates. If these conditions are not compatible with the efficiency conditions of agents in the economy, then they are of little interest since they would never be an equilibrium outcome. We can insure that the feasible steady state is compatible with an (optimal) competitive equilibrium, however, by imposing two restrictions on preferences: (i) the intertemporal elasticity of substitution in consumption must be invariant to the scale of consumption and (ii) the income and substitution effects associated with sustained growth in labor productivity must not alter labor supply.

The first condition must hold because the marginal product of capital, which equals one plus the real interest rate in equilibrium, must be constant in the steady state. Since consumption is growing at a constant rate and the ratio of discounted marginal utilities must equal one plus the interest rate, the intertemporal elasticity of substitution must be constant and independent of the level of consumption.

The second condition is required because hours worked cannot grow ($\gamma_N = 1$) in the steady state. To reconcile this with a growing marginal productivity of labor – induced by labor augmenting technical change (X_t) – income and substitution effects of productivity growth must have exactly offsetting effects on labor supply (N).[9]

---

[8] This result, in fact, holds for any constant returns to scale production function.

[9] Effective labor (NX_t) will continue to grow at rate γ_X.

These conditions imply the following class of admissible utility functions:[10]

$$u(C, L) = \frac{1}{(1 - \sigma)} C^{1 - \sigma} v(1 - N) \qquad (2.8a)$$

for $0 < \sigma < 1$ and $\sigma > 1$, while for $\sigma = 1$,

$$u(C, L) = \log(C) + v(1 - N). \qquad (2.8b)$$

Some additional restrictions are necessary to assure that (i) consumption and leisure are goods and (ii) that utility is concave.[11] The constant intertemporal elasticity of substitution in consumption is $1/\sigma$ for these utility functions. For the remainder of our analysis we restrict ourselves to utility functions of this class.

The requirement that preferences be compatible with steady state growth has important implications for the study of economic fluctuations. If there is no capital [i.e., if the production function is just of the form $A_t(N_t X_t)^\alpha$], then there will be no response of hours to variation in X_t or A_t in general equilibrium. This arises because (i) utility implies that the income and substitution effects of wage changes just offset and (ii) with no intertemporal substitution in production, income effects must be fully absorbed within any decision period [as in Barro and King (1984)]. Thus, in all of the parameterizations of the neoclassical model that we consider, variations in work effort are associated with intertemporal substitution made possible in equilibrium by capital accumulation.

2.4. Stationary economies and steady states

The standard method of analyzing models with steady state growth is to transform the economy into a stationary one where the dynamics are more amenable to analysis. In the context of the basic neoclassical model, this transformation involves dividing all variables in the system by the growth component X, so that $c = C/X$, $k = K/X$, $i = I/X$, etc. This economy is identical to a simple 'no-growth' economy with two exceptions. First the capital accumulation equation, $K_{t+1} = (1 - \delta_K)K_t + I_t$, becomes $\gamma_X k_{t+1} = (1 - \delta_K)k_t + i_t$. Second, transforming consumption in the preference specifica-

---

[10] See the technical appendix for a demonstration of the necessity of these conditions and that they imply (2.8a) and (2.8b).

[11] When momentary utility is additively separable (2.8b), all that we require is that $v(L)$ is increasing and concave. When momentary utility is multiplicatively separable, then we require that $v(L)$ is (i) increasing and concave if $\sigma < 1$ and (ii) decreasing and convex if $\sigma > 1$. Defining $D^n v(L)$ as the nth total derivative of the function $v(L)$, we further require that $-\sigma[LD^2 v(L)/Dv(L)] > (1 - \sigma)[LDv(L)/v(L)]$ to assure overall concavity of $u(\cdot)$.

tion generally alters the effective rate of time preference. That is,

$$U = \left(X_0^{1-\sigma} \right) \sum_{t=0}^{\infty} (\beta^*)^t \left[\frac{1}{(1-\sigma)} c_t^{1-\sigma} v(L_t) \right] \quad \text{for} \quad \sigma \neq 1, \qquad (2.9a)$$

$$U = \sum_{t=0}^{\infty} (\beta^*)^t \left[\log(c_t) + v(L_t) + \log(X_t) \right] \quad \text{for} \quad \sigma = 1, \qquad (2.9b)$$

where $\beta^* = \beta(\gamma_X)^{1-\sigma}$ and $\beta^* < 1$ is required throughout to guarantee finiteness of lifetime utility. Thus, unless $\sigma = 1$, $\beta^* \neq \beta$. By suitable selection of X_0, we can in either case make the objective $\sum_{t=0}^{\infty}(\beta^*)^t u(c_t, L_t)$. Combining the resource constraints, we form the Lagrangian

$$\mathscr{L} = \sum_{t=0}^{\infty} (\beta^*)^t u(c_t, 1 - N_t)$$

$$+ \sum_{t=0}^{\infty} \Lambda_t \left[A_t F(k_t, N_t) - c_t - \gamma_X k_{t+1} + (1 - \delta_K) k_t \right]. \qquad (2.10)$$

The efficiency conditions for the transformed economy are (2.11)–(2.15). In these expressions, D_i is the first partial derivative operator with respect to the ith argument. For convenience, we discount the Lagrange multipliers, i.e., $\lambda_t = \Lambda_t / (\beta^*)^t$.

$$D_1 u(c_t, 1 - N_t) - \lambda_t = 0, \qquad (2.11)$$

$$D_2 u(c_t, 1 - N_t) - \lambda_t A_t D_2 F(k_t, N_t) = 0, \qquad (2.12)$$

$$\beta^* \lambda_{t+1} \left[A_{t+1} D_1 F(k_{t+1}, N_{t+1}) + (1 - \delta_K) \right] - \lambda_t \gamma_X = 0, \qquad (2.13)$$

$$A_t F(k_t, N_t) + (1 - \delta_K) k_t - \gamma_X k_{t+1} - c_t = 0, \qquad (2.14)$$

$$\lim_{t \to \infty} (\beta^*)^t \lambda_t k_{t+1} = 0, \qquad (2.15)$$

where (2.11)–(2.14) must hold for all $t = 1, 2, \ldots \infty$ and (2.15) is the so-called transversality condition. The economy's initial capital stock, k_0, is given.

Optimal per capita quantities for this economy – for a given sequence $\{A_t\}_{t=0}^{\infty}$ of technology shifts – are sequences of consumption $\{c_t\}_{t=0}^{\infty}$, effort $\{N_t\}_{t=0}^{\infty}$, capital stock $\{k_t\}_{t=0}^{\infty}$, and shadow prices $\{\lambda_t\}_{t=0}^{\infty}$ that satisfy the efficiency conditions (2.11)–(2.15). Under our assumptions about preferences and production possibilities, conditions (2.11)–(2.15) are necessary and sufficient for an optimum.[12]

The prices that decentralize the optimal solution as a competitive equilibrium can be computed using the technology shifts $\{A_t\}_{t=0}^{\infty}$ and the optimal sequences $\{N_t\}_{t=0}^{\infty}$, $\{k_t\}_{t=0}^{\infty}$ and $\{\lambda_t\}_{t=0}^{\infty}$. For instance, in a complete initial date markets framework the sequence of equilibrium prices of labor and the final good are, respectively, $\{\lambda_t A_t D_2 F(k_t, N_t)\}_{t=0}^{\infty}$ and $\{\lambda_t\}_{t=0}^{\infty}$. Under perfect foresight (rational expectations), a regime of sequential loan markets and spot markets in labor services also supports the optimal solution as a competitive equilibrium. In this market structure, the relevant prices are the real interest rate between t and $t+1$, r_t, and the real wage rate, w_t. It is easy to demonstrate that these are given by $(1 + r_t) = \gamma_X \lambda_t / \lambda_{t+1} \beta^*$ and $w_t = A_t D_2 F(k_t, N_t)$.

3. Perfect foresight capital accumulation

A major feature of the basic one sector neoclassical model with stationary technology is that the optimal capital stock converges monotonically to a stationary point.[13] While qualitative results such as the monotonicity property are important, we wish to undertake quantitative analyses of capital stock dynamics. This requires that we exploit the fact that (2.11)–(2.14) can be reduced to a non-linear system of first-order difference equations in k and λ or a second-order equation in k only. The two boundary conditions of this system are the transversality condition (2.15) and the initial capital stock, k_0. We focus on approximate linear dynamics in the neighborhood of the steady state denoted by $(A, k, N, c \text{ and } y)$.[14]

3.1. Approximation method

The initial step in obtaining the system of linear difference equations is to approximate (2.11)–(2.14) near the stationary point. To do this, we express each condition in terms of the percentage deviation from the stationary value, which we indicate using a circumflex [e.g., $\hat{c}_t = \log(c_t/c)$, $\hat{k}_t = \log(k_t/k)$, etc.]. Then, we linearize each condition in terms of deviations from the stationary

---

[12] See Weitzman (1973) and Romer and Shinotsuka (1987).

[13] In the fixed labor case, which is the most thoroughly studied, this property has been shown to derive principally from preferences, in that the concavity of $u(\cdot)$ is sufficient for monotonicity so long as there is a maximum sustainable capital stock [Boyd (1986) and Becker et al. (1986)]. In environments such as ours, where the production function is strictly concave in capital (for fixed labor), monotonicity also insures that capital approaches a unique stationary point.

[14] The technical appendix discusses solution methods in considerable detail. The linear approximation method, it should be noted, rules out certain phenomena that may arise in the basic neoclassical model, such as a humped shaped transition path for investment [see King (1987)].

point. The results for the first two conditions can be written as follows:

$$\xi_{cc}\hat{c}_t - \xi_{cl}\frac{N}{1-N}\hat{N}_t - \hat{\lambda}_t = 0, \tag{3.1}$$

$$\xi_{lc}\hat{c}_t - \frac{N}{1-N}\xi_{ll}\hat{N}_t - \hat{\lambda}_t - \hat{A}_t - (1-\alpha)\hat{k}_t + (1-\alpha)\hat{N}_t = 0, \tag{3.2}$$

where ξ_{ab} is the elasticity of the marginal utility of a with respect to b.[15]

Approximation of the intertemporal efficiency condition (2.13) implies that

$$\hat{\lambda}_{t+1} + \eta_A\hat{A}_{t+1} + \eta_k\hat{k}_{t+1} + \eta_N\hat{N}_{t+1} = \hat{\lambda}_t, \tag{3.3}$$

where η_A is the elasticity of the gross marginal product of capital with respect to A evaluated at the steady state, etc.[16] Finally, approximation of the resource constraint (2.14) implies

$$\hat{y}_t = \hat{A}_t + \alpha\hat{N}_t + (1-\alpha)\hat{k}_t$$

$$= s_c\hat{c}_t + s_i\phi\hat{k}_{t+1} - s_i(\phi-1)\hat{k}_t, \tag{3.4}$$

where s_c and s_i are consumption and investment shares in output and $\phi = K_{t+1}/I_t = \gamma_X/[\gamma_X - (1-\delta_K)] > 1$.

As in other linear optimal control settings, expressions (3.1) and (3.2) can be solved to give optimal decisions $\hat{c}_t$, $\hat{N}_t$ as functions of the state variables $\hat{k}_t$, $\hat{A}_t$ and the co-state (shadow price) $\hat{\lambda}_t$. Further, given these (conditionally) optimal decisions, expressions (3.3) and (3.4) imply a first-order dynamic system in $\hat{\lambda}$ and $\hat{k}$,

$$\begin{bmatrix} \hat{k}_{t+1} \\ \hat{\lambda}_{t+1} \end{bmatrix} = W\begin{bmatrix} \hat{k}_t \\ \hat{\lambda}_t \end{bmatrix} + R\hat{A}_{t+1} + Q\hat{A}_t, \tag{3.5}$$

where W is a 2×2 matrix and R and Q are 2×1 vectors. To compute the solution to this difference equation and to examine its properties, we use the decomposition $W = P\mu P^{-1}$, where P is the matrix of characteristic vectors of W and μ is a diagonal matrix with the characteristic roots on the diagonal. Ordering the roots (μ_1, μ_2) in increasing absolute value, it can be shown that

---

[15] When the utility function is additively separable, it follows that $\xi_{cc} = -1$, $\xi_{cl} = \xi_{lc} = 0$ and $\xi_{ll} = LD^2v(L)/Dv(L)$. When the utility function is multiplicatively separable, it follows that $\xi_{cc} = -\sigma$, $\xi_{cl} = LDv(L)/v(L)$, $\xi_{lc} = 1-\sigma$ and $\xi_{ll} = LD^2v(L)/Dv(L)$.

[16] With the Cobb–Douglas assumption, it follows that $\eta_A = [\gamma_X - \beta^*(1-\delta_K)]/\gamma_X$, $\eta_k = -\alpha\eta_A$ and $\eta_N = \alpha\eta_A$.

$0 < \mu_1 < 1 < \beta^{*-1} < \mu_2$. The general solution to the difference equation for specified initial conditions $\hat{\lambda}_0$ and $\hat{k}_0$ is given by

$$\begin{bmatrix} \hat{k}_t \\ \hat{\lambda}_t \end{bmatrix} = W^t \begin{bmatrix} \hat{k}_0 \\ \hat{\lambda}_0 \end{bmatrix} + \sum_{h=0}^{t} W^h R \hat{A}_{t-h+1} + \sum_{h=0}^{t} W^h Q \hat{A}_{t-h}. \qquad (3.6)$$

Since $W^t = P\mu^{\prime t}P^{-1}$ and the root μ_2 exceeds $(\beta^*)^{-1} > 1$, it follows that the system is on an explosive path and thus violates the transversality condition for arbitrary $\hat{\lambda}_0$. There is a specific value of the initial shadow price $\hat{\lambda}_0$, however, that results in (3.6) satisfying the transversality condition (2.15). This particular solution specifies the unique optimal (and competitive equilibrium) time path of capital accumulation $\{\hat{k}_t\}_{t=0}^{\infty}$ and shadow prices $\{\hat{\lambda}_t\}_{t=0}^{\infty}$. Given these optimal sequences, consumption $\{\hat{c}_t\}_{t=0}^{\infty}$ and effort $\{\hat{N}_t\}_{t=0}^{\infty}$ can be computed from (3.1) and (3.2). It is also direct to compute variations in output, investment, real wages and real interest rates. For example, output variations are given by $\hat{y}_t = \hat{A}_t + \alpha \hat{N}_t + (1-\alpha)\hat{k}_t$ in (3.4). With Cobb–Douglas production, real wages are proportional to labor productivity, so that $\hat{w}_t = \hat{y}_t - \hat{N}_t$.

In general, optimal decisions for consumption, capital, effort, etc. depend on the entire sequence $\{\hat{A}_t\}_{t=0}^{\infty}$. As demonstrated in the technical appendix, the time path of efficient capital accumulation may be written in the form

$$\hat{k}_{t+1} = \mu_1 \hat{k}_t + \psi_1 \hat{A}_t + \psi_2 \sum_{j=0}^{\infty} \mu_2^{-j} \hat{A}_{t+j+1}, \qquad (3.7)$$

where ψ_1 and ψ_2 are complicated functions of the underlying parameters of preferences and technology. The dynamics of capital accumulation depend on the previous period's capital stock with coefficient μ_1. In addition, with time-varying total factor productivity, the optimal solution for capital accumulation depends on the current productivity level ($\hat{A}_t$) and on the entire future time path of displacements to productivity 'discounted' by μ_2.

3.2. Transition path dynamics

In order to provide a quantitative evaluation of the dynamic properties of the neoclassical model we choose a set of parameters values that match the average U.S. growth experience. The properties of the transition paths to the steady state capital stock (k) can then be numerically investigated by setting $A_t = A$ for all t. In this case, the (approximately) optimal sequence of transformed capital stocks described by (3.7) reduces to the first-order difference equation $\hat{k}_{t+1} = \mu_1 \hat{k}_t$, with $|\mu_1| < 1$. Given an initial condition $k_0 = K_0/X_0$, the transformed economy's capital stock approaches its steady state value more quickly the closer μ_1 is to zero. In addition, the variations in consumption, investment, output, work effort, the real wage and the real interest rate are determined according to linear relations:

$$\hat{c}_t = \pi_{ck}\hat{k}_t, \qquad \hat{i}_t = \pi_{ik}\hat{k}_t, \qquad \hat{y}_t = \pi_{yk}\hat{k}_t,$$

$$\hat{N}_t = \pi_{Nk}\hat{k}_t, \qquad \hat{w}_t = \pi_{wk}\hat{k}_t, \qquad r_t - r = \pi_{rk}\hat{k}_t, \tag{3.8}$$

where r is the steady state real interest rate, $r = \gamma_X/\beta^* - 1$. Except for π_{rk}, the π coefficients should be interpreted as the elasticities of the flow variables with respect to deviations of the capital stock from its stationary value. The transition paths of these flow variables, therefore, are simply scaled versions of the capital stock's transition path. In general, the values of μ_1 and the π coefficients are complicated functions of the underlying parameters of the model, i.e., α, σ, δ_K, β and γ_X.

3.2.1. A fixed labor experiment

Within the neoclassical model with fixed labor, variations in σ alter substitution over time. Table 1 summarizes the quantitative effects of varying σ on the adjustment parameter μ_1 and the π coefficients.[17] The values of the underlying parameters assume that the time interval is a quarter and are summarized in the table. Labor's share $\alpha = 0.58$ is the average ratio of total employee compensation to GNP for the period 1948 to 1986; γ_X is one plus the common trend rate of growth of output, consumption and investment, which is 1.6% per year in the post-war era.[18] The value for $\beta^* = \gamma_X/(1 + r)$ is chosen to yield a return to capital of 6.5% per annum, which is the average real return to equity from 1948 to 1981.[19] Finally, the depreciation rate is set at 10% per annum, which leads to a share of gross investment of 0.295.

In the fixed labor model, some of the π coefficients are invariant to σ. The elasticities of output and real wages with respect to capital are simply determined by $\pi_{yk} = \pi_{wk} = (1 - \alpha)$ which is 0.42 in our table 1 example. The value of $\pi_{rk} = \eta_k$ is also invariant to σ and takes the value -0.024. This means that output and real wages move directly with capital and real interest rates inversely with capital.

In the case of log utility ($\sigma = 1$), the table shows that the adjustment coefficient (μ_1) is 0.966 which implies that one-half of any initial deviation from the stationary state is worked off in 20 quarters or 5 years. If the capital

---

[17] Tedious algebra shows that $\pi_{ck} = [(1 - \alpha) - (\gamma_X\mu_1 - (1 - \delta_K))(k/y)]/s_c$ and $\pi_{ik} = [(\gamma_X\mu_1 - (1 - \delta_K))(k/y)]/s_i$. It is direct that $\pi_{Nk} = 0$ and $\pi_{yk} = (1 - \alpha)$. Finally, μ_1 is the smaller root of the quadratic equation $\mu^2 - [1/\beta^* - s_c\eta_K/\sigma s_i\phi + 1]\mu + 1/\beta^*$.

[18] Details of this computation and the data used are discussed in section 5.2.

[19] Note that while β^* is invariant with respect to σ under the assumption that $\beta^* = \gamma_X/(1 + r)$, β is not since $\beta^* = \beta\gamma_X^{1-\sigma}$.

Table 1

Effects of intertemporal substitution in consumption on near steady state dynamics (fixed labor model).

	Lower substitution						Higher substitution		
σ	10	5	2	1.5	1.0	0.67	0.5	0.2	0.1
μ_1	0.992	0.987	0.977	0.973	0.966	0.958	0.950	0.919	0.886
π_{lk}	0.726	0.557	0.213	0.066	−0.179	−0.474	−0.729	−1.798	−2.963
π_{ck}	0.292	0.363	0.507	0.568	0.670	0.793	0.900	1.346	1.832
Half-life[a] (in quarters)	86	54	30	25	20	16	14	8	6

Baseline parameter values:

Labor's share (α)	0.58
Rate of depreciation (δ_K)	0.025
Utility discount rate (β^*)	0.988
Technological growth rate ($\gamma_X - 1$)	0.004

Implied value of:

$-\eta_k$	0.024
c/k	0.069
i/y	0.295
$r = [\gamma_X/\beta^* - 1]$	0.016

[a] Half-life is defined by the solution to $\mu_1^n = 0.5$, rounded to the nearest integer.

stock is initially below its steady state value, then investment is above its steady state rate ($\pi_{ik} = -0.176 < 0$) and consumption is below its steady state rate ($\pi_{ck} = 0.670 > 0$).

Alternative values of σ change π_{ck}, π_{ik} and μ_1 in intuitive ways. For example, when σ is large the representative agent is less willing to substitute intertemporally and thus desires very smooth consumption profiles. Hence, there is little reaction of consumption to a shortfall in capital (π_{ck} small). Consequently the adjustment to the steady state is slower (μ_1 closer to 1.0) than when $\sigma = 1.0$. When σ is small, there is more willingness to substitute consumption intertemporally and thus a given capital shortfall occasions a larger reduction in consumption. There is thus a more rapid adjustment of capital (μ_1 further from 1.0) than with $\sigma = 1$.

3.2.2. Varying work effort

We are also interested in the pattern of efficient variation in work effort along the transition path, how the labor–leisure margin alters the speed of capital stock adjustment (μ_1) and the responses of the price and quantity variables. To investigate these effects quantitatively, we reinstate labor as a choice variable and suppose that the utility function has the simple form $u(c, L) = \log(c) + \theta_l \log(L)$. The parameter θ_l is chosen so that stationary hours are 0.20.[20] Our choice of this value is based on the average percentage of time devoted to market work in the U.S. during the period 1948–1986.[21]

The resulting value of μ_1 is 0.953, implying a half-life of just under 14 quarters for deviations of the capital stock from its stationary level. This is a slightly more rapid pace of adjustment than the comparable fixed labor case with $\sigma = 1$ in table 1, since work effort provides an additional margin along which agents can respond. The values of the elasticities are $\pi_{ck} = 0.617$, $\pi_{ik} = -0.629$, $\pi_{Nk} = -0.294$, $\pi_{yk} = 0.249$, $\pi_{wk} = 0.544$ and $\pi_{rk} = -0.029$. Transition paths of the key variables are plotted in fig. 1. Starting from an initially low capital stock, there is a sustained period in which output and consumption are low, but rising, while work effort and investment are high, but declining. Temporary variation in work effort is efficient even though steady state hours are invariant to growth.

The economic mechanisms behind these transition paths are important. The initially low capital stock has three implications for the representative consumer in the transformed economy. First, non-human wealth is low relative to its stationary level. Second, the marginal product of labor (shadow real wage)

---

[20] In our computations, we directly specify that $N = 0.20$ in the linear expressions (3.1) and (3.2), noting that logarithmic utility implies zero cross elasticities and unitary own elasticities. This implicitly specifies the utility function parameter θ_l.

[21] This value is equal to the average work week as a fraction of total weekly hours for the period 1948 to 1986.

210   R.G. King et al., Production, growth and business cycles I

TRANSITION DYNAMICS

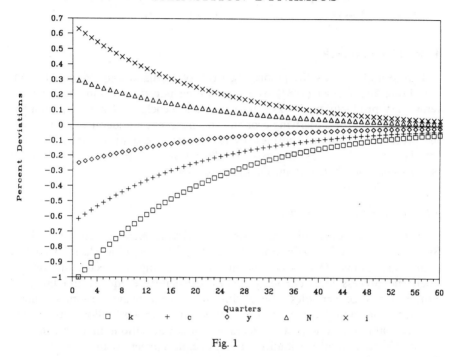

Fig. 1

is low relative to the stationary level. Third, the marginal product of capital (shadow real interest rate) is high relative to its stationary level. The first and third factors induce the representative consumer to work additional hours; the second factor exerts the opposite influence. With the particular preferences and technology under study, the former factors dominate, resulting in hours that are high – relative to the stationary level – along the transition path from a low initial capital stock.

It is beyond the scope of this paper to undertake a detailed sensitivity analysis of how the μ and π coefficients change with parameters of the environment. However, we have studied how the root μ_1 depends on a list of parameter values by computing an elasticity of μ_1 with respect to each parameter.[22] The elasticities are quite small ranging from -0.11 for labor's share (α) to -0.001 for the rate of technological progress ($\gamma_X - 1$).[23] Our

[22] We thank Adrian Pagan for pushing us to conduct these experiments.

[23] The elasticity for steady state hours (N) is 0.003; for depreciation (δ_K) is -0.03 for the intertemporal elasticity of substitution (σ) is 0.03, and for the elasticity of the marginal utility of leisure ($LD^2 v(L)/Dv(L)$) is 0.003.

conclusion is that the speed of adjustment is not highly sensitive to the choice of parameter values.

4. Real business cycles

This section follows the pioneering work of Kydland and Prescott (1982) and Long and Plosser (1983) by incorporating uncertainty – in the form of temporary productivity shocks – into the basic neoclassical model. Although other aspects of the underlying economic environment are identical to those of the preceding section, the business cycle analysis is in marked contrast to the standard 'growth theory' analysis, in which time variation in technology is taken to be smooth, deterministic and permanent.

4.1. Linear business cycle models

In principle, quantitative analyses of stochastic elements should follow Brock and Mirman's (1972) seminal analysis of the basic neoclassical model under uncertainty. One would begin by postulating a specific stationary stochastic process for technology shocks, calculate the equilibrium laws of motion for state variables (the capital stock) and related optimal policy functions for controls (consumption, investment and work effort). It would then be natural to interpret observed business fluctuations in terms of the economy's stationary distribution. The principle barrier to the execution of this strategy is computational. The equilibrium laws of motion for capital and for flows cannot be calculated exactly for models of interest, but must be approximated with methods that are computationally burdensome.[24] Furthermore, computational strategies for approximate suboptimal equilibria are not well developed.

In our analysis we invoke certainty equivalence, employing a linear systems perspective. Our use of certainty equivalence methods in the study of real business cycles builds on prior work by Kydland and Prescott (1982), but the details of our procedures are different.[25] An advantage of our method is that it

---

[24] Examples include Sargent (1980) and Greenwood, Hercowitz and Huffman (1986).

[25] Kydland and Prescott (1982) eliminate non-linearities in constraints (such as the production function) by substituting resource constraints into the utility function and taking a quadratic approximation to the resulting return function. We derive efficiency conditions under certainty and approximate these to obtain linear decision rules. These two procedures are equivalent for the class of models we consider when standard Taylor series approximations are used with each procedure. The only substantive difference between our approximation method and Kydland and Prescott's is that while they search for an approximation based on a likely range of variation of the different variables, we center our linearizations on the steady state. According to Kydland and Prescott (1982, p. 1357, 11) this difference in approximation techniques has little impact on their results. Our procedure yields formulas that have a transparent economic interpretation and allows us to replicate exactly the Long and Plosser (1983) closed form solution.

is readily extended to the study of suboptimal dynamic equilibria, as we show in our second essay. Nevertheless, a detailed analysis of the overall accuracy of these approximation methods in a business cycle context remains to be undertaken.

For the basic neoclassical model, our strategy works as follows. We develop approximate solutions for capital and other variables near the stationary point of the transformed economy as in the previous section. Then, working from a certainty equivalence perspective, we posit a particular stochastic process for $\hat{A}$ and replace the sequence $\{\hat{A}_{t+j}\}_{j=0}^{\infty}$ with its conditional expectation given information available at t. In particular, suppose that $\hat{A}_t$ follows a first-order autoregressive process with parameter ρ. Then, given (3.7), the state dynamics are given by the linear system

$$s_{t+1} \equiv \begin{bmatrix} \hat{k}_{t+1} \\ \hat{A}_{t+1} \end{bmatrix} = \begin{bmatrix} \mu_1 & \pi_{kA} \\ 0 & \rho \end{bmatrix} \begin{bmatrix} \hat{k}_t \\ \hat{A}_t \end{bmatrix} + \begin{bmatrix} 0 \\ \varepsilon_{A,t+1} \end{bmatrix} = Ms_t + \varepsilon_{t+1}, \qquad (4.1)$$

where $\pi_{kA} = \psi_1 + \psi_2 \rho/(1 - \rho\mu_2^{-1})$ and $s_t' \equiv (\hat{k}_t, \hat{A}_t)$ is the state vector.

Additional linear equations specify how consumption, work effort, investment, shadow prices and output depend on the state variables s_t. Let the vector $z_t' = (\hat{c}_t, \hat{N}_t, \hat{y}_t, \hat{i}_t)$ be a vector of controls and other flow variables of interest. Then the linear equations relating flows to states are

$$z_t = \begin{bmatrix} \hat{c}_t \\ \hat{N}_t \\ \hat{y}_t \\ \hat{i}_t \\ \hat{w}_t \\ r_t - r \end{bmatrix} = \begin{bmatrix} \pi_{ck} & \pi_{cA} \\ \pi_{Nk} & \pi_{NA} \\ \pi_{yk} & \pi_{yA} \\ \pi_{ik} & \pi_{iA} \\ \pi_{wk} & \pi_{wA} \\ \pi_{rk} & \pi_{rA} \end{bmatrix} \begin{bmatrix} \hat{k}_t \\ \hat{A}_t \end{bmatrix} = \Pi s_t, \qquad (4.2)$$

where the π coefficients are determined, as in section 3, by requiring that the shadow prices and elements of z_t satisfy the linearized first-order conditions.[26]

---

[26] This state space formulation (4.1) and (4.2) can be solved to obtain the vector autoregressive-moving average (ARMA) representation of the endogenous variables z. In the basic neoclassical model with persistent technology shocks ($\rho \neq 0$), each element of z_t is ARMA (2,1) with common autoregressive but different moving average polynomials. Following Zellner and Palm (1974) and Orcutt (1948), the evolution of states can be expressed as follows

$$\det(I - MB)s_t = \mathrm{adj}(I - MB)\varepsilon_t,$$

where B is the backshift operator, $\det(I - MB)$ is the determinant of the 2×2 matrix defined by $I - MB$, and $\mathrm{adj}(I - MB)$ is the adjoint of $I - MB$. From inspection of (4.1) it is clear that, for $\rho \neq 0$, the determinant of $(I - MB)$ is a second-order polynomial $(1 - \mu_1 B)(1 - \rho B)$. There are moving average terms of at most order 1 in $\mathrm{adj}(I - MB)$. Further, since $z_t = \Pi s_t$, the elements of z_t inherit the ARMA (2,1) structure of the state vector. The relatively simple ARMA structure of the individual elements of z is a result of the dimensionality of the state vector. In a model with many state variables the order of the polynomial $\det(I - MB)$ could become quite large, implying more complex ARMA representations for the elements of z.

This formulation facilitates computation of (i) impulse response functions for the system and (ii) population moments of the joint (z_t, s_t) process.

Impulse responses. Impulse response functions provide information on the system's average conditional response to a technology shock at date t, given the posited stochastic process. The response of the system in period $t + k$ to a technology impulse at date $t + 1$ is

$$s_{t+k} - \mathrm{E}s_{t+k}|s_t = M^{k-1}\varepsilon_{t+1},$$

$$z_{t+k} - \mathrm{E}z_{t+k}|s_t = \Pi M^{k-1}\varepsilon_{t+1},$$

where $\varepsilon'_{t+1} = (0, \varepsilon_{A, t+1})$.

Population moments. Population moments provide additional, unconditional properties of the time series generated by the model economy. We stress that although there is a single shock to the economic model under study, the dynamic character of the model means that the unconditional time series will, in general, not be perfectly correlated. The linear character of the system implies that it is relatively straightforward to calculate population moments. For example, given the variance–covariance matrix of the states, $\Sigma_{ss} = \mathrm{E}(s_t s'_t)$, it is easy to calculate the autocovariance of z at lag j, $\mathrm{E}(z_t z'_{t-j}) = \Pi M^j \Sigma_{ss} \Pi'$. In our analysis below, we will be concerned with how these properties of the model change as we alter parameters of preferences and technology.

4.2. Alternative parameterizations of the basic neoclassical model.

We explore four alternative parameterizations of the basic neoclassical model, obtained by varying certain aspects of preferences and technology. Though far from exhaustive, these parameterizations shed some light on important aspects of neoclassical models. Table 2 summarizes the parameter values that are employed in our four versions of the neoclassical model. Throughout, as in table 1, we use production parameter values for labor's share as $\alpha = 0.58$ and the growth of exogenous technical progress as $(\gamma_X - 1) = 0.004$ per quarter. In all specifications, we take the momentary utility function to be of the additively separable form, $u(c, L) = \log(c) + \theta_l v(L)$. This specification implies zero cross-elasticities ($\xi_{lc} = \xi_{cl} = 0$) and unitary elasticity in consumption ($\sigma = -\xi_{cc} = 1$), while leaving the elasticity of the marginal utility of leisure with respect to leisure (ξ_{ll}) as a parameter to be specified. The parameter θ_l in all parameterizations is adjusted so as to yield a steady state value for N equal to 0.20, the average time devoted to market work in the U.S. during the period 1948–1986. In all of these formulations, the values of σ, γ_X and β combine to yield a steady state real interest rate of 6.5% per annum.

Table 2

Alternative model parameterizations.

Key parameters	(1) Long–Plosser with 100% depreciation	(2) Long–Plosser with realistic depreciation	(3) Panel data labor supply elasticity	(4) Infinite labor supply elasticity
Preference parameters				
Elasticity of marginal utility of consumption with respect to:				
Consumption (ξ_{cc})	−1	−1	−1	−1
Leisure (ξ_{cl})	0	0	0	0
Elasticity of marginal utility of leisure with respect to:				
Consumption (ξ_{lc})	0	0	0	0
Leisure (ξ_{ll})	−1	−1	−10	0
Steady state fraction of time worked (N)	0.20	0.20	0.20	0.20
Utility discount rate (β)	0.988	0.988	0.988	0.988
Technological parameters				
Labor's share of production (α)	0.58	0.58	0.58	0.58
Technological growth rate ($\gamma_X - 1$)	0.004	0.004	0.004	0.004
Depreciation rate of capital (δ_K)	1	0.025	0.025	0.025

Our point of departure is the parameterization of Long and Plosser (1983). The key features of this specification are additively separable, logarithmic preferences, a Cobb–Douglas production function and 100% depreciation. This specification is instructive because there is an exact closed-form solution that enables us to establish a benchmark for judging our approximation methods. The second specification alters the Long–Plosser formulation by assuming less than 100% depreciation. This alteration is sufficient to obtain stochastic properties for key variables that are more compatible with common views of economic fluctuations. We refer to this case as the 'baseline' model – it is closely related to the divisible labor economy studied by Hansen (1985).[27] The next two experiments consider some perturbations of the elasticity of labor supply. The third parameterization uses an 'upper bound' labor supply elasticity from the panel data studies reviewed by Pencavel (1986). This elasticity is ten times smaller than that imposed by the logarithmic preferences of the baseline mode.[28] The fourth parameterization illustrates the consequences of infinite intertemporal substitutability of leisure or, equivalently, the indivisibility of individual labor supply decisions stressed by Rogerson (1988) and Hansen (1985).

4.3. Quantitative linear business cycle models

The reference point for our discussion is table 3, which summarizes the linear systems representation given in eqs. (4.1) and (4.2). That is, table 3 provides the coefficients, μ_1, ρ, π_{kA} of the matrix M and the coefficients of the Π matrix under two assumptions about persistence of technology shocks ($\rho = 0$ and $\rho = 0.9$).

Long–Plosser with complete depreciation. Applying the exact solutions found in Long and Plosser (1983), the capital stock for this parameterization evolves

---

[27] There are at least three differences between our methodology and that employed by Hansen (1985) which make our results not directly comparable. First, we use a different linearization technique, as discussed above. Second, we compute the population movements rather than estimate them through Monte Carlo simulation. Third, we do not filter the series with the Hodrick and Prescott (1980) filter. See footnote 31 for a discussion of differences in parameter values and of the effects of the Hodrick and Prescott filter.

[28] For preferences separable in consumption and leisure, the elasticity of labor supply is $(1 - 1/N)/\xi_{ll}$, where N is the steady state fraction of time devoted to work. Thus if the elasticity of labor supply is 0.4 and $N = 0.20$, then $\xi_{ll} = -10.0$.

We are reluctant to adopt this economy as our benchmark given the difficulty in interpreting the disparity between the elasticity of labor supply of women and men in the context of our representative agent economy. Furthermore, Rogerson (1988) has demonstrated that, in the presence of indivisibility in individual labor supply decisions, an economy with finite elasticity of labor supply may behave as if this elasticity were infinite. Hence, our fourth parameterization has preferences consistent with an infinite elasticity of labor supply ($\xi_{ll} = 0$).

Table 3

Parameter values of the linear system (4.1)–(4.2).

	ρ	μ_1	π_{kA}	π_{ck}	π_{cA}	π_{Nk}	π_{NA}	π_{yk}	π_{yA}	π_{ik}	π_{iA}	π_{wk}	π_{wA}	π_{rk}	π_{rA}
Long–Plosser with complete depreciation	0	0.420	1.000	0.420	1.000	0.000	0.000	0.420	1.000	0.420	1.000	0.420	1.000	−0.244	−0.580
	0.9	0.420	1.000	0.420	1.000	0.000	0.000	0.420	1.000	0.420	1.000	0.420	1.000	−0.244	0.320
Long–Plosser with realistic depreciation	0	0.953	0.166	0.617	0.108	−0.294	1.332	0.249	1.773	−0.629	5.747	0.544	0.441	−0.029	−0.005
	0.9	0.953	0.137	0.617	0.298	−0.294	1.048	0.249	1.608	−0.629	4.733	0.544	0.560	−0.029	0.055
Panel data labor supply elasticity	0	0.963	0.111	0.654	0.075	−0.080	0.317	0.374	1.184	−0.296	3.830	0.454	0.867	−0.025	−0.003
	0.9	0.963	0.097	0.654	0.235	−0.080	0.262	0.374	1.152	−0.296	3.341	0.454	0.890	−0.025	0.040
Rogerson–Hansen infinite labor supply elasticity	0	0.947	0.206	0.598	0.130	−0.424	2.071	0.174	2.201	−0.838	7.143	0.598	0.130	−0.032	−0.007
	0.9	0.947	0.164	0.598	0.337	−0.424	1.579	0.174	1.916	−0.838	5.683	0.598	0.337	−0.032	0.065

according to the stochastic difference equation,

$$\hat{k}_{t+1} = (1 - \alpha)\hat{k}_t + \hat{A}_t = \sum_{j=0}^{\infty} (1 - \alpha)^j \hat{A}_{t-j}, \tag{4.3}$$

which indicates that in our approximation it should be the case that $\mu_1 = (1 - \alpha)$ and $\pi_{kA} = 1.0$. As emphasized by Long and Plosser, (4.3) illustrates that even without long-lived commodities, capitalistic production enables agents to propagate purely transitory productivity shocks forward in time in keeping with their preferences for smooth consumption.

The solutions of Long and Plosser also imply that there are simple log-linear relations for the flow variables ($\hat{y}$, $\hat{c}$, $\hat{i}$ and $\hat{N}$),

$$\hat{y}_t = \hat{i}_t = \hat{c}_t = (1 - \alpha)\hat{k}_t + \hat{A}_t = \sum_{j=0}^{\infty} (1 - \alpha)^j \hat{A}_{t-j}, \tag{4.4}$$

$$\hat{N}_t = 0. \tag{4.5}$$

In percent deviations from steady state, output, consumption, and investment all share the stochastic structure of the capital stock. Work effort, on the other hand, is constant (i.e., $\hat{N}_t = 0$). With work effort constant, real wages (proportional to output per man hour) move just like output. With $\sigma = 1$, interest rates are equal to the expected change in consumption ($r_t - r = E_t\hat{c}_{t+1} - \hat{c}_t$). Thus, in terms of (4.2), $\pi_{yk} = \pi_{ck} = \pi_{ik} = \pi_{wk} = (1 - \alpha)$, $\pi_{yA} = \pi_{cA} = \pi_{iA} = \pi_{Nk} = 1$, and $\pi_{Nk} = \pi_{NA} = 0$. Finally, $\pi_{rk} = -\alpha(1 - \alpha)$ and $\pi_{rA} = (\rho - \alpha)\hat{A}_t$.

Turning to the approximate solutions reported in table 3, we see that these match the exact solutions (4.3)–(4.5) for the parameter values in table 2. For example, with $\alpha = 0.58$, the coefficient $\mu_1 = (1 - \alpha) = 0.42$ as required by eq. (4.1) above. Further, we see that there are two special features of this parameterization previously noted by Long and Plosser in their consideration of multi-sector, log-linear business cycle models. First, the solution involves no influence of expected future technological conditions on the properties of the endogenous variables. This conclusion follows from the observation that the linear systems coefficients linking quantity variables to technology (π_{kA}, π_{cA}, π_{NA}, etc.) are invariant to the persistence (ρ) in the technology shock process. Second, the relation between work effort and the state variables (π_{Nk} and π_{NA}) indicates that the approximation method preserves the other special implications of complete depreciation, namely that effort is unresponsive to the state of the economy ($\pi_{NA} = \pi_{Nk} = 0$).

Fundamentally, each of these invariance results reflects a special balancing of income and substitution effects. For example, more favorable technology conditions ($\hat{A}_{t+j} > 0$) exert two offsetting effects on accumulation: (i) an income effect (since there will be more outputs at given levels of capital input) that operates to lower saving and capital accumulation and (ii) a substitution effect (arising from an increased marginal reward to accumulation) that operates to raise saving. With complete depreciation and logarithmic utility, income and substitution effects exactly offset.

With respect to real interest rates, the complete depreciation model also helps indicate how serial correlation in $\hat{A}$ alters the model's implications. The coefficient $\pi_{rA} = (\rho - \alpha)$, so that with $\rho = 0$ diminishing returns predominates and an impulse to A lowers the rate of return. But with high persistence ($\rho > \alpha$), interest rates rise due to the shift up in the future marginal reward to investment.

Long-Plosser with realistic depreciation.   Adopting a more realistic depreciation rate ($\delta_K = 0.025$ or 10% per year) dramatically alters the properties of the basic neoclassical model. The adjustment parameter μ_1 rises from 0.42 to 0.953, indicating that the capital stock adjusts more slowly. Second, π_{kA} falls from 1.0 to 0.166 when $\rho = 0$ and is no longer invariant to serial correlation properties of $\hat{A}$.

These responses can be explained in terms of the basic economics of lowering the depreciation rate. First, when there is a lower depreciation rate, it follows that there is a higher steady state capital stock and a lower output–capital ratio. As δ_K goes from 1.0 to 0.025, y/k falls from 2.4 to 0.10. This suggests a substantial decline in the elasticity π_{kA}. Second, the change in μ_1 and the sensitivity of π_{kA} to ρ reflect implications that δ_K has for the relative importance of wealth and intertemporal substitution effects. With lower depreciation, the intertemporal technology – linking consumption today and consumption tomorrow – becomes more linear near the stationary point.[29] This means that the representative agent faces less sharply diminishing returns in intertemporal production possibilities and will choose a temporally smooth consumption profile that requires more gradual elimination of deviations of the capital stock from its stationary level (μ_1 rises from 0.42 when $\delta_K = 1$ to 0.953 when $\delta_K = 0.025$). The depreciation rate also impinges on the relative importance of substitution and wealth effects associated with future shifts in technology ($\hat{A}_{t+j}$ for $j > 0$). In particular, the dominance of the wealth effect is indicated by a comparison of purely temporary ($\rho = 0$) with more persistent technology shocks. Capital accumulation is less responsive to technological conditions when the shocks are more persistent (i.e., π_{kA} falls from 0.166 to 0.137 when ρ rises from 0 to 0.9). For the same reason, more persistent technology shocks imply that consumption is more responsive ($\pi_{cA} = 0.108$ when $\rho = 0$ and $\pi_{cA} = 0.298$ when $\rho = 0.9$) and investment is less responsive

---

[29] There is a marked decline in the elasticity of the gross marginal product of capital schedule, $AD_1 F(k, N) + (1 - \delta_K)$, with respect to capital. It falls from $-\eta_k = 0.58$ to 0.023.

($\pi_{iA} = 5.747$ when $\rho = 0$ and $\pi_{iA} = 4.733$ when $\rho = 0.9$). The persistence of shocks also has implications for the response of relative prices to technology shifts. Real wages respond more elastically, since there is a smaller variation in effort when shifts are more permanent. As in the model with complete depreciation, real interest rates respond positively to technology shifts when these are highly persistent.

Altering the character of intertemporal tradeoffs also has implications for labor supply via intertemporal substitution channels. When technology shifts are purely temporary ($\rho = 0$), a one percent change in total factor productivity calls forth a 1.33 percent change in hours. This impact is attenuated, but not eliminated, when shifts in technology are more persistent ($\pi_{NA} = 1.05$ when $\rho = 0.9$). The nature of these intertemporal substitution responses is perhaps best illustrated by examining impulse response functions, which are derived from the coefficients presented in table 3. The two parts of fig. 2 contain impulse responses under our alternative assumptions about the persistence of shocks. In panel A, when technology shifts are purely temporary, intertemporal substitution in leisure is very evident. In the initial period, with positive one percent technology shock, there is a major expansion of work effort. The initial period output response is more than one-for-one with $\hat{A}$ ($\pi_{yA} = 1.77$) because of the expansion in work effort. The bulk of the output increase goes into investment with a smaller percentage change in consumption.

In subsequent periods, after the direct effect of the technology shift has dissipated, the only heritage is a capital stock higher than its steady state value. The change in the capital stock induced by the initial period technology shock is 'worked off' via a combination of increased consumption and reduced effort. The impacts on output are smaller, in percentage terms, than the impacts on consumption or capital, because the transition path back toward the stationary point is associated with negative net investment and negative response of effort. This means that the response function after one period in fig. 2, panel A, is determined by the internal transition dynamics given in fig. 1. The only difference is that in fig. 2 the experiment is a positive increment to the capital stock of 0.166 instead of the negative increment of -1.0 in fig. 1.

In panel B of fig. 2, when technology shifts are more persistent, the impulse responses involve a combination of exogenous ($\hat{A}$) and endogenous dynamics ($\hat{k}$). There is now a protracted period in which technology shocks serve to introduce positive comovements of hours, output, consumption and investment. The magnitudes of these responses are altered by the fact that agents understand the persistent character of technological shifts. In comparison with the case where technology shifts are purely temporary, consumption is more responsive to $\hat{A}$ while effort is less.

Other labor supply elasticities. First, when we restrict preferences to be consistent with an 'upper bound' labor supply elasticity of 0.4 for prime age

DYNAMIC RESPONSE FUNCTIONS

Panel A: Uncorrelated Technology Shocks

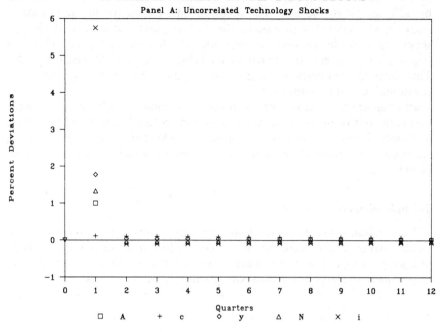

Panel B: Serially Correlated Shocks

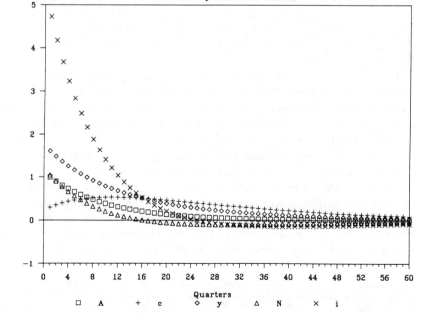

Fig. 2

males reported by Pencavel (1986), we obtain an economy whose dynamics are broadly similar to those of the baseline model except for the amplitude of response to technology shocks. In the case of purely temporary production shocks ($\rho = 0$), the elasticity of response of labor to shocks in technology (π_{NA}) is 0.317, roughly one fourth of the value of π_{NA} for the baseline model. This reduced variability in labor is accompanied by smaller variability in consumption and investment.[30]

Second, when the labor supply elasticity is infinite, we have an economy that is the mirror image of the previous one in terms of amplitude of response to shocks. In the case of purely temporary shocks, the values of π_{cA} and π_{iA} are roughly 1.2 times those of the baseline model, while π_{NA} is fifty percent higher.

5. Implications for time series

This section develops some of the predictions that the basic neoclassical model makes about economic time series when it is driven by a single technology shock. Using the model's organizing principles, we also present some summary statistics for post-war quarterly U.S. time series.

5.1. Variability of components of output

A major feature of economic fluctuations is the differential variability in the use of inputs (labor and capital) and in the components of output (consumption and investment). Table 4 presents some selected population moments for the four alternative parameterizations that summarize the models' implications for relative variability.

The specification with complete depreciation has implications that are readily traced to the simple structure of (4.3) and (4.4). First, output, consumption and investment have identical variances. Second, with complete depreciation, investment and capital differ only in terms of timing, so that capital and output are equally variable.

When realistic depreciation is imposed ($\delta_K = 0.025$), differences in the relative variability of the components of output are introduced. Further, these implications depend on the stochastic process for the technology shifts, since the moments of time series depend on the linear system coefficients reported in table 3 (which are dependent on the persistence parameter ρ). With purely temporary shocks, consumption is much less variable than output (about two tenths as variable) and investment is far more variable (more than three times

---

[30]A productivity shock induces intertemporal substitution of leisure by raising the productivity of current versus future labor and intratemporal substitution by increasing the opportunity cost of leisure in terms of consumption. Both the elasticity of intertemporal substitution of leisure and the elasticity of intratemporal substitution are smaller in this economy than in the baseline model. The reduction in the degree of substitution contributes to a reduced variability of consumption.

Table 4

Selected population moments for four alternative parameterizations.

	ρ	Standard deviation relative to technology ($\hat{A}$)				Standard deviation relative to output ($\hat{y}$)			Correlation with output ($\hat{y}$)		
		$\hat{y}$	$\hat{c}$	$\hat{i}$	$\hat{N}$	$\hat{c}$	$\hat{i}$	$\hat{N}$	$\hat{c}$	$\hat{i}$	$\hat{N}$
Long–Plosser with complete depreciation	0	1.10	1.10	1.10	0.0	1.0	1.0	0.0	1.0	1.0	—
	0.9	1.64	1.64	1.64	0.0	1.0	1.0	0.0	1.0	1.0	—
Long–Plosser with realistic depreciation	0	1.78	0.35	5.76	1.34	0.20	3.24	0.75	0.38	0.99	0.98
	0.9	1.86	0.19	4.28	0.89	0.64	2.31	0.48	0.82	0.92	0.79
Panel data labor supply elasticity	0	1.19	0.28	3.83	0.32	0.23	3.21	0.27	0.39	0.99	0.97
	0.9	1.46	1.01	3.17	0.23	0.69	2.17	0.16	0.85	0.92	0.75
Infinite labor supply elasticity	0	2.20	0.41	7.16	2.09	0.18	3.25	0.95	0.37	0.99	0.98
	0.9	2.11	1.30	5.01	1.32	0.62	2.38	0.63	0.80	0.93	0.81

as variable). Labor input is much more variable than consumption and about three fourths as variable as output.

When shifts in technology become more persistent ($\rho = 0.9$), there are important changes in implications for relative variabilities. Consumption is now six tenths as volatile as output, which accords with the permanent income perspective and with the altered linear systems coefficients discussed previously. Labor input is less than half as volatile as output, which fundamentally reflects diminished desirability of intertemporal substitution of effort with more persistent shocks.[31]

Alterations in the labor supply elasticity exert predictable effects on relative variability of labor input and output, while having relatively minor implications for the relative variability of the components of output. Relative to the baseline model, the reduction in labor supply elasticity to the level suggested by the panel data studies results in a decline of the variability of labor both in absolute terms and in relation to the variability of output. The relative volatility of the labor input in terms of output implied by the model is 0.27, roughly half of the standard deviation of hours relative to detrended output in the U.S. for the period 1948–1986.[32]

In table 5 we present some additional time series implications of our baseline neoclassical model. One notable feature is that $\hat{y}$, $\hat{i}$ and $\hat{N}$ exhibit almost no serial correlation in the absence of serially correlated technology shocks. This is not true for consumption, wages or interest rates, however, which are smoother and correlated with lagged values of output.

---

[31] The baseline model is structurally identical to the divisible labor economy studied by Hansen (1985). It differs, however, in values assigned to parameters. In our notation, Hansen's economy involves $\alpha = 0.64$, $\beta^* = 0.99$, $\gamma_X = 1.00$; $N = 0.33$ and $\delta_K = 0.025$. These alternative parameter values have implications for the moments reported in tables 4 and 5. Using a persistence parameter $\rho = 0.90$, the model's relative volatility measures (standard deviations of variables relative to standard deviation of output) are as follows: consumption (0.62), investment (2.67) and hours (0.41). Basically, relative to table 4 these results reflect the decline in labor supply elasticity implied by $N = 1/3$ rather than $N = 1/5$. The contemporaneous correlations with output are as follows: consumption (0.81), investment (0.92) and hours (0.81). If we filter the population moments with the Hodrick–Prescott (HP) filter, then the relative variabilities and correlations are altered. For consumption these are (0.25) and (0.80), respectively, for investment they are (3.36) and (0.99) and for hours they are (0.55) and (0.98). These alterations occur because the effect of the HP filter is to give less weight to low frequencies, downplaying persistent but transient aspects of the series in question. [See the graph of the transfer function of the HP filter in Singleton (1988).] For example, the correlation of output at the yearly interval (lag 4) is 0.72 in the unfiltered Hansen parameterization and it is 0.08 in the filtered version. It is this sensitivity of results to filtering that makes us hesitant to undertake detailed comparisons with results reported by Hansen.

[32] The inability of the model to generate a sufficiently high variation in labor when the elasticity of labor supply is restricted to be consistent with panel data studies has stimulated several extensions to the basic neoclassical model. Kydland (1984) demonstrates that introducing agent heterogeneity in the model can increase the relative volatility of the average number of hours worked with respect to the volatility of labor productivity. Rogerson (1988) establishes that, in the presence of indivisibility in individual labor supply, an economy with finite elasticity of labor supply behaves as if it had an infinite elasticity of labor supply. This motivates our interest in the fourth parameterization. As Hansen (1985), we find that in this economy labor is too volatile relative to output.

Table 5

Population moments: Baseline model.

Variable	Std. dev.	Std. dev. relative to $\hat{y}$	Autocorrelations			Cross-correlations with $\hat{y}_{t-j}$										
			1	2	3	12	8	4	2	1	0	−1	−2	−4	−8	−12
						Panel A: $\rho = 0.0$, $\sigma(\hat{A}) = 1.0$										
$\hat{y}$	1.78	1.0	0.03	0.03	0.03	0.02	0.02	0.02	0.03	0.03	1.0	0.03	0.03	0.02	0.02	0.02
$\hat{c}$	0.35	0.20	0.95	0.91	0.87	0.21	0.26	0.31	0.34	0.36	0.38	0.08	0.07	0.07	0.05	0.05
$\hat{i}$	5.76	3.24	−0.01	−0.01	−0.01	−0.01	−0.02	−0.02	−0.02	−0.02	0.99	0.02	0.02	0.02	0.01	0.01
$\hat{N}$	1.34	0.75	−0.02	−0.02	−0.02	−0.03	−0.03	−0.04	−0.04	−0.05	0.98	0.01	0.01	0.01	0.01	0.01
$\hat{w}$	0.53	0.30	0.44	0.42	0.40	0.12	0.15	0.18	0.20	0.21	0.87	0.06	0.06	0.05	0.04	0.04
r	0.02	0.01	0.95	0.91	0.87	−0.21	−0.26	−0.31	−0.34	−0.36	−0.38	−0.08	−0.07	−0.07	−0.05	−0.05
						Panel B: $\rho = 0.9$, $\sigma(\hat{A}) = 2.29$										
$\hat{y}$	4.26	1.0	0.93	0.86	0.80	0.42	0.55	0.74	0.86	0.93	1.0	0.93	0.86	0.74	0.55	0.42
$\hat{c}$	2.73	0.64	0.99	0.98	0.97	0.76	0.82	0.86	0.85	0.84	0.82	0.76	0.71	0.61	0.47	0.36
$\hat{i}$	9.82	2.31	0.88	0.77	0.67	0.11	0.26	0.52	0.70	0.80	0.92	0.85	0.79	0.68	0.50	0.38
$\hat{N}$	2.04	0.48	0.86	0.73	0.62	−0.11	0.04	0.32	0.52	0.65	0.79	0.73	0.67	0.57	0.42	0.31
$\hat{w}$	2.92	0.69	0.98	0.96	0.94	0.69	0.78	0.85	0.88	0.90	0.90	0.84	0.78	0.67	0.51	0.39
r	0.11	0.03	0.87	0.76	0.66	−0.47	−0.34	−0.07	0.14	0.28	0.43	0.40	0.36	0.30	0.22	0.16

5.2. Some empirical issues and observations

Since the early part of this century, with the NBER studies of business cycles and economic growth under the leadership of Wesley Mitchell and Simon Kuznets, it has become commonplace for macroeconomic researchers to design models to replicate the principal features of the business cycles isolated by the NBER researchers. More recently, the development of statistical and computing technology has led individual researchers to define analogous sets of 'stylized facts' about economic fluctuations that models are then designed to emulate.

Our perspective is that the development of stylized facts outside of a circumscribed class of dynamic models is difficult at best.[33] First, models suggest how to organize time series. Further, it is frequently the case that stylized facts are sensitive to the methods of detrending or prefiltering. In this investigation we take the perspective that the basic neoclassical model has implications for untransformed macroeconomic data and not some arbitrary or prespecified transformation or component that is defined outside the context of the model [cf. Hicks (1965 p. 4)]. Although we do not perform formal statistical tests of model adequacy, the manner in which we proceed with data analysis is dictated by the models under study.

We have considered deterministic labor augmenting technological change that grows at a constant proportionate rate as the source of sustained growth (trend). The neoclassical model then predicts that all quantity variables (with the exception of work effort) grow at the same rate γ_X. The non-deterministic components of consumption, output and investment ($\hat{y}$, $\hat{c}$ and $\hat{i}$) are then

$$\hat{y}_t = \log(Y_t) - \log(X_t) - \log(y),$$

$$\hat{c}_t = \log(C_t) - \log(X_t) - \log(c),$$ $$\quad (5.1)$$

$$\hat{i}_t = \log(I_t) - \log(X_t) - \log(i),$$

where y, c and i are the steady state values in the transformed economy. Labor augmenting technical progress, $\log(X_t)$, can be expressed as the simple linear trend

$$\log(X_t) = \log(X_0) + t \cdot \log(\gamma_X).$$ $$\quad (5.2)$$

Thus, in the language of Nelson and Plosser (1982), the implied time series are trend stationary. Moreover, they possess a common deterministic trend. Therefore, the model instructs us to consider deviations of the log levels of GNP, consumption and investment from a common linear trend as empirical counterparts to $\hat{y}$, $\hat{c}$ and $\hat{i}$. Work effort, on the other hand, possess no trend and, thus, $\hat{N}$ is simply deviation of the log of hours from its mean.

---

[33] See also Koopmans (1947) and Singleton (1988).

In order to provide some perspective on the models' properties, we summarize some of the corresponding sample moments of the U.S. time series. The series we consider are the quarterly per capita values of real GNP, consumption of non-durables and services (*CNS*), gross fixed investment (*GFI*) and average weekly hours per capita.[34] Following the structure (5.1) and (5.2), we detrend the log levels of each of the first three series by computing deviations from a common estimated linear time trend. The estimated common trend, which corresponds to an estimate of $\log(\gamma_X) \approx (\gamma_X - 1)$, is 0.4% per quarter.[35] The real wage is the gross average hourly earnings of production or non-supervisory workers on non-agricultural payrolls. We chose not to study interest rates because of the well-known difficulties of obtaining measures of expected real interest rates.

Plots of our empirical counterparts to $\hat{y}$, $\hat{c}$, $\hat{i}$ and $\hat{N}$ are presented in fig. 3. Their properties are summarized in table 6 in a manner analogous to the summary of the baseline model in table 5. Our sample period is the first quarter of 1948 (1948.1) to the fourth quarter of 1986 (1986.4). Deviations of output from the common deterministic trend, which are plotted as a benchmark in each of the panels in fig. 3, have a standard deviation of 5.6% and range in value from −13.0% to 10%. The sample autocorrelations in table 6 indicate substantial persistence, suggesting that there may be a non-stationary component to the series not eliminated by removing a common deterministic trend.

The panels A and B show empirical counterparts to $\hat{c}$ and $\hat{i}$, plotted against the reference variable $\hat{y}$. Consumption and investment are highly correlated with output. Table 6 reports estimated correlation coefficients of 0.85 for consumption and 0.60 for investment over the 1948.1–1986.4 sample period. Consumption is less volatile than output, with a sample standard deviation of 3.9% (versus 5.6% for output) and a sample range of −7.8% to 7.4%. Investment is more volatile than output, with a sample standard deviation of 7.6% and sample range of −20.7% to 16.3%. Further, the autocorrelation statistics in table 6 indicate substantial serial correlation in both consumption and investment.

Panel C of fig. 3 contains a plot of the empirical counterpart of per capita hours as well as that of output. This labor input measure has a standard deviation of 3.0%, with a maximum value of 6.5% and a minimum value of

---

[34] All series are taken from the CITIBASE database. *GNP*, *CNS* and *GFI* are quarterly values. Population (*P*) is the total civilian non-institutional population 16 years of age and older. Employment (*E*) is total workers employed as taken from the Household Survey, Bureau of Labor Statistics. Average weekly hours of all workers (*H*) is also from the Household Survey. Average hours per capita is then calculated as $E \cdot H/P$ and averaged for the quarter. The wage rate is gross average hourly earnings of production workers.

[35] This is the source of the estimate of γ_X we use to parameterize the basic model in section 3. We choose not to impose the common trend assumption on wage rates because it involves a specific assumption about market structure.

ESTIMATED DEVIATIONS FROM COMMON TREND

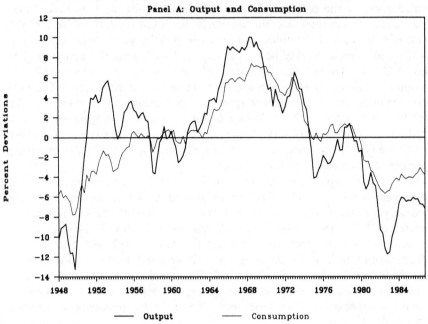

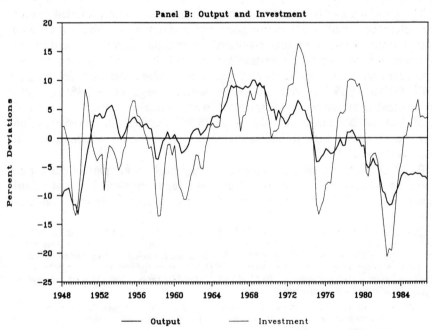

Fig. 3

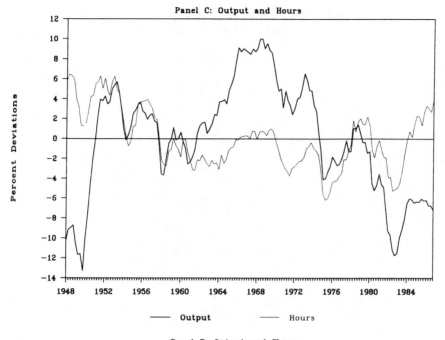

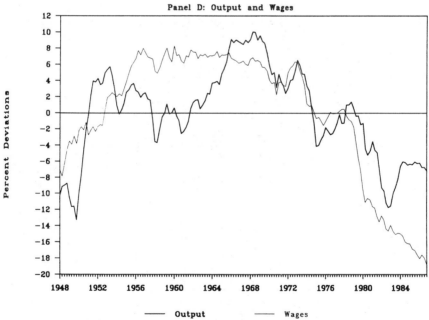

Fig. 3 (continued)

Table 6

Sample moments: Quarterly U.S. data, 1948.1–1986.4.[a]

Variable	Std. dev.	Relative std. dev.[b]	Autocorrelations			Cross-correlations with y_{t-j}										
			1	2	3	12	8	4	2	1	0	−1	−2	−4	−8	−12
$\hat{y}$	5.62	1.00	0.96	0.91	0.85	0.35	0.53	0.79	0.91	0.96	1.0	0.96	0.91	0.79	0.53	0.35
$\hat{c}$	3.86	0.69	0.98	0.95	0.93	0.59	0.68	0.78	0.83	0.84	0.85	0.82	0.78	0.69	0.43	0.26
$\hat{\imath}$	7.61	1.35	0.93	0.78	0.62	0.18	0.20	0.38	0.51	0.57	0.60	0.59	0.55	0.43	0.22	0.08
$\hat{N}$	2.97	0.52	0.94	0.85	0.74	−0.44	−0.31	−0.07	0.03	0.06	0.07	0.07	0.05	−0.01	0.01	0.08
$\hat{w}$	6.49	1.14	0.97	0.93	0.89	0.60	0.63	0.68	0.72	0.74	0.76	0.72	0.69	0.62	0.42	0.25

[a] All variables are taken from the National Income Accounts.
[b] Relative standard deviation of z is $\sigma(\hat{z})/\sigma(\hat{y})$.

-6.2% over the post-war period. The correlation between output and hours reported in table 6 is essentially zero! Inspection of the plot, however, appears to suggest that this relation is closer if one visually corrects for the periods in which output is on average high or low. In fact, if one splits the sample into subperiods of approximately 5 years each, the correlation between output and hours is never less than 0.30 and averages 0.77. Thus, when we permit the sample mean to vary (which is what looking at subperiods effectively does), the correlation between hours and output appears much higher.[36] It is important to stress that there is no theoretical justification for looking at data in subperiods. The basic neoclassical model that we have been discussing has a single source of low frequency variation (the deterministic trend in labor productivity) which has been removed from the time series under study. The sensitivity of these results to the sample period suggests the possibility of a low frequency component not removed by the deterministic trend. This is consistent with the highly persistent autocorrelation structure of output noted above.

The practice of removing low frequency variation in economic data plays an important role in empirical research on business fluctuations. NBER business cycle research has generally followed Mitchell's division of time series into cyclical episodes, removing separate cycle averages for individual series. Our belief is that this methodology is likely to remove important low frequency aspects of the relations between time series, in a manner broadly similar to the computation of correlations over subperiods. Most modern empirical analyses of cyclical interactions have also followed the practice of removing low frequency components from actual and model-generated time series.[37] Studying the impact of such low frequency filtering on economic time series generated by our baseline model, King and Rebelo (1987) find that there are major distortions in the picture of economic mechanisms presented by low frequency filtering. Among these are two that are particularly relevant to the labor–output relation. First, in the theoretical economy analyzed by King and Rebelo, application of a low frequency filter raises the correlation between output and labor input. Second, a low frequency filter dramatically reduces the correlation between output and capital.

Panel D of fig. 3 contains a plot of our empirical measure of $\hat{w}$. While the correlation with output is positive (0.76), it is not as strong as predicted by

---

[36] The subperiod results for the other variables are qualitatively similar to the overall sample. We have also explored the use of another hours series to insure that this finding was not an artifact of our data. Using an adjusted hours series developed by Hansen (1985), which covers only the 1955.3 to 1984.1 period, the correlation is 0.28 compared to 0.48 for our series for the same period. Breaking this shorter sample into subperiods also yields higher correlations than those for the overall period for the Hansen data.

[37] For example, Kydland and Prescott (1982) filter both the data *and* the output of their model using a filter proposed by Hodrick and Prescott (1980). Hansen (1985) follows this practice as well.

the model. Moreover, the positive correlation seems to arise primarily from the association at lower frequencies.

There are two main conclusions we draw from this cursory view of the data. The first, and most important, is that the one sector neoclassical model that we use as our baseline specification is not capable of generating the degree of persistence we see in the data without introducing substantial serial correlation into the technology shocks. The second is that the data suggest the related possibility of a low frequency component not captured by the deterministic trend. This motivates our interest in models with stochastic growth in the companion essay.

6. Conclusions

This paper has summarized the growth and business cycle implications of the basic neoclassical model. When driven by exogenous technical change at constant rates, the model possesses a steady state growth path under some restrictions on preferences for consumption and leisure. Although these restrictions imply that labor effort is constant in the steady state, they do not imply that effort is constant along transition paths of capital accumulation or in response to temporary technology shocks. Rather, the intertemporal substitution made feasible by capital accumulation applies to both consumption and effort in general equilibrium.

When driven by highly persistent technology shocks, the basic neoclassical model is capable of replicating some stylized facts of economic fluctuations. First, the model generates procyclical employment, consumption and investment. Second, the model generates the observed rankings of relative volatility in investment, output and consumption. But along other dimensions, the basic model seems less satisfactory. In particular, the principle serial correlation in output – one notable feature of economic fluctuations – derives mainly from the persistence of technology shocks. On another level, as McCallum (1987) notes, the model abstains from discussing implications of government and the heterogeneity of economic agents.

Perhaps the most intriguing possibility raised by the basic model is that economic fluctuations are just a manifestation of the process of stochastic growth. In the companion essay, we discuss current research into this possibility, along with issues concerning the introduction of government and heterogeneity.

References

Barro, R. and R. King, 1984, Time separable preferences and intertemporal substitution models of business cycles, Quarterly Journal of Economics 99, 817–839.

Becker, R., J. Boyd III and C. Foias, 1986, The existence of Ramsey equilibrium, Working paper (University of Rochester, Rochester, NY).

232   *R.G. King et al., Production, growth and business cycles I*

Boyd III, J., 1986, Recursive utility and the Ramsey problem, Working paper no. 60 (Center for Economic Research, University of Rochester, Rochester, NY).

Brock, W. and L. Mirman, 1972, Optimal economic growth and uncertainty: The discounted case, Journal of Economic Theory 4, 479–513.

Cass, D., 1965, Optimum growth in an aggregative model of capital accumulation, Review of Economic Studies 32, 223–240.

Debreu, G., 1954, Valuation equilibrium and Pareto optimum, Proceedings of the National Academy of Sciences of the U.S.A. 38, 886–893.

Greenwood, J., Z. Hercowitz and G. Huffman, 1986, Investment, capacity utilization and the real business cycle, Working paper (University of Western Ontario, London, Ont.).

Hansen, G., 1985, Indivisible labor and the business cycle, Journal of Monetary Economics 16, 309–327.

Hicks, J., 1965, Capital and growth (Oxford University Press, New York).

Hodrick, R. and E. Prescott, 1980, Post-war U.S. business cycles: An empirical investigation, Working paper (Carnegie-Mellon University, Pittsburgh, PA).

King, R., 1987, Business cycles and economic growth, Lecture notes on macroeconomics (University of Rochester, Rochester, NY).

King, R. and S. Rebelo, 1987, Low frequency filtering and real business cycles, in progress (University of Rochester, Rochester, NY).

Koopmans, T., 1947, Measurement without theory, Review of Economics and Statistics 29, 161–172.

Koopmans, T., 1965, On the concept of optimal economic growth, in: The econometric approach to development planning (Rand-McNally, Chicago, IL).

Kydland, F., 1984, Labor force heterogeneity and the business cycle, Carnegie–Rochester Conference Series on Public Policy 21, 173–208.

Kydland, F. and E. Prescott, 1982, Time to build and aggregate fluctuations, Econometrica 50, 1345–1370.

Long, J. and C. Plosser, 1983, Real business cycles, Journal of Political Economy 91, 1345–1370.

McCallum, B.T., 1987, Real business cycles, Unpublished manuscript (Carnegie-Mellon University, Pittsburgh, PA).

Nelson, C. and C. Plosser, 1982, Trends and random walks in macroeconomic time series: Some evidence and implications, Journal of Monetary Economics 10, 139–167.

Orcutt, G., 1948, A study of the autoregressive nature of the time series used for Tinbergen's model of the economic system of the United States, 1919–1932, Journal of the Royal Statistical Society B 10, 1–45.

Pencavel, J. 1986, Labor supply of men: A survey, in: Orley Ashenfelter and Richard Layard, eds., Handbook of labor economics (North-Holland, Amsterdam).

Phelps, E., 1966, Golden rules of economic growth (Norton, New York).

Prescott, E., 1986, Theory ahead of business cycles measurement, Carnegie–Rochester Conference Series on Public Policy 25, 11–66.

Prescott, E. and R. Lucas, 1972, A note on price systems in infinite dimensional space, International Economic Review 13, 416–422.

Rogerson, R., 1988, Indivisible labor, lotteries and equilibrium, Journal of Monetary Economics 21, 3–16.

Romer, P. and T. Shinotsuka, 1987, The Kuhn–Tucker theorem implies the transversality condition at infinity, Unpublished paper (University of Rochester, Rochester, NY).

Sargent, T., 1980, Tobin's 'q' and the rate of investment in general equilibrium, Carnegie–Rochester Conference Series on Public Policy 12, 107–154.

Singleton, K., 1988, Econometric issues in the analysis of equilibrium business cycle models, Journal of Monetary Economics, this issue.

Solow, R., 1956, A contribution to the theory of economic growth, Quarterly Journal of Economics 70, 65–94.

Swan, T., 1963, On golden ages and production functions, in: Kenneth Berril, ed., Economic development with special references to southeast Asia (Macmillan, London).

Weitzman, M., 1973, Duality theory for infinite time horizon convex models, Management Science 19, 738–789.

Zellner, A. and F. Palm, 1974, Time series analysis and simultaneous equations models, Journal of Econometrics 2, 17–54.

Part III

Some extensions

Journal of Monetary Economics 16 (1985) 309–327. North-Holland

INDIVISIBLE LABOR AND THE BUSINESS CYCLE

Gary D. HANSEN*

University of California, Santa Barbara, CA 93106, USA

A growth model with shocks to technology is studied. Labor is indivisible, so all variability in hours worked is due to fluctuations in the number employed. We find that, unlike previous equilibrium models of the business cycle, this economy displays large fluctuations in hours worked and relatively small fluctuations in productivity. This finding is independent of individuals' willingness to substitute leisure across time. This and other findings are the result of studying and comparing summary statistics describing this economy, an economy with divisible labor, and post-war U.S. time series.

1. Introduction

Equilibrium theories of the business cycle, such as Kydland and Prescott (1982) or Lucas (1977), have been criticized for failing to account for some important labor market phenomena. These include the existence of unemployed workers, fluctuations in the rate of unemployment, and the observation that fluctuations in hours worked are large relative to productivity fluctuations. Equilibrium models have also been criticized for depending too heavily on the willingness of individuals to substitute leisure across time in response to wage or interest rate changes when accounting for the last observation. This criticism is based at least partially on the fact that micro studies using panel data on hours worked by individuals have not detected the intertemporal substitution necessary to explain the large aggregate fluctuations in hours worked [see Ashenfelter (1984)].

In this paper, a simple one-sector stochastic growth model with shocks to technology is constructed in which there is high variability in the number employed and total hours worked even though individuals are relatively unwilling to substitute leisure across time. The model differs from similar models, such as Kydland and Prescott (1982), in that a non-convexity (indivisible labor) is introduced. Indivisible labor is modeled by assuming that individ-

*This paper is part of my doctoral dissertation written while a student at the University of Minnesota. I have benefited from conversations with many people including Robert King, Thomas Sargent, Christopher Sims, Neil Wallace, Sumru Altug, Patrick Kehoe, Ramon Marimon, Ian Bain, and Rody Manuelli. I owe my greatest debt, however, to my advisor, Edward Prescott. I wish to also acknowledge the Federal Reserve Bank of Minneapolis which has provided support for this research. All errors, of course, are mine.

uals can either work some given positive number of hours or not at all – they are unable to work an intermediate number of hours. This assumption is motivated by the observation that most people either work full time or not at all. Therefore, in my model, fluctuations in aggregate hours are the result of individuals entering and leaving employment rather than continuously employed individuals adjusting the number of hours worked, as in previous equilibrium models. This is consistent with an important feature of U.S. post-war data: most fluctuation in aggregate hours worked is due to fluctuation in the number employed as opposed to fluctuation in hours per employed worker. This is a fact that previous equilibrium theories have not tried to account for.[1]

Existing equilibrium models have also failed to account for large fluctuations in hours worked along with relatively small fluctuations in productivity (or the real wage). Prescott (1983), for example, finds that for quarterly U.S. time series, hours worked fluctuates about twice as much (in percentage terms) as productivity. In this paper it is shown that an economy with indivisible labor exhibits very large fluctuations in hours worked relative to productivity. This stands in marked contrast to an otherwise identical economy that lacks this non-convexity. In this economy hours worked fluctuates about the same amount as productivity.[2]

Equilibrium theories of the business cycle have typically depended heavily on intertemporal substitution of leisure to account for aggregate fluctuations in hours worked.[3] The willingness of individuals to substitute intertemporally is measured by the elasticity of substitution between leisure in different time periods implied by an individual's utility function. However, the theory developed here is able to account for large aggregate fluctuations in hours worked relative to productivity without requiring that this elasticity be large. This follows because the utility function of the 'representative agent' in our model implies an elasticity of substitution between leisure in different periods that is infinite.[4] This result does not depend on the elasticity of substitution implied by the preferences of the individuals who populate the economy. Thus, the theory presented here is in principle consistent with the low estimates of this elasticity found from studying panel data [see Altonji (1984) or MaCurdy (1981)].

---

[1] The fact that existing equilibrium models are inconsistent with this observation has been stressed by Heckman (1983) and Coleman (1984).

[2] Kydland and Prescott (1982) attempt to explain the above fact by including past leisure as an argument in the individual's utility function so as to enhance the intertemporal substitution response to a productivity shock. However, even after introducing this feature, Kydland and Prescott were still unable to account for this observation.

[3] This is true for the technology shock theories, such as Kydland and Prescott's (1982), as well as the monetary shock theories of Lucas and Barro [see Lucas (1977)].

[4] In this model there is a crucial distinction between the utility function of the 'representative agent' and the utility function of an individual or household.

The paper is divided as follows: The next section provides a more detailed explanation and motivation of the indivisible labor assumption. In section 3 the artificial economies to be studied are constructed. The first is a standard stochastic growth model where labor is divisible, and the second introduces indivisible labor to that economy. The second economy is a stochastic growth version of a static general equilibrium model developed by Rogerson (1984). Lotteries are added to the consumption set (following Rogerson) which makes it possible to study a competitive equilibrium by solving a representative agent problem, as in Lucas and Prescott (1971). The addition of the lotteries also implies that the firm is providing full unemployment insurance to the workers.

The fourth section explains how the equilibrium decision rules and laws of motion are calculated, as well as how the parameter values used when simulating the model were chosen. Since the representative agent's problem is not one for which a closed form solution is available, in order to calculate decision rules a quadratic approximation of this problem is derived using the method described in Kydland and Prescott (1982). These equilibrium decision rules are a set of stochastic difference equations from which the statistical properties of the time series generated by the artificial economies can be determined. The statistics studied are a set of standard deviations and correlations discussed in section 5. In this section, the statistics computed using the artificial time series are compared to the same statistics computed using U.S. time series. Some concluding remarks are contained in section 6.

2. Motivation

Existing equilibrium theories of the business cycle analyze individuals who are free to adjust continuously the number of hours worked (the 'intensive margin') and who are always employed. There are no individuals entering or leaving employment (the 'extensive margin'). However, the extensive margin seems important for explaining some aspects of labor supply at both the micro and macro levels. Heckman and MaCurdy (1980), for example, discuss the importance of the extensive margin for explaining female labor supply. At the aggregate level, over half of the variation in total hours worked is due to variation in the number of individuals employed rather than variation in average hours worked by those employed. Consider the following decomposition of variance involving quarterly data:

$$\text{var}(\log H_t) = \text{var}(\log h_t) + \text{var}(\log N_t) + 2\,\text{cov}(\log h_t, \log N_t),$$

where H_t is total hours worked, h_t is average hours worked, and N_t is the number of individuals at work, where all variables are deviations from trend.[5]

---

[5] The data used for this analysis is available from the Bureau of Labor Statistics' Labstat data tape. The series I used were collected from households using the *Current Population Survey*. For a description of the detrending method, see footnote 18.

Using this decomposition, 55% of the variance of H_t is due to variation in N_t, while only 20% of this variance can be directly attributed to h_t. The remainder is due to the covariance term.[6]

Most people either work full time or not at all. This might be ascribed to the presence of non-convexities either in individual preferences for leisure or in the technology. For example, the technology may be such that the marginal productivity of an individual's work effort is increasing during the first part of the workday or workweek, and then decreasing later on. That is, the individual faces a production function which is convex at first and then becomes concave. This could be due to individuals requiring a certain amount of 'warm up' time before becoming fully productive. Such a technology could induce individuals to work a lot or not at all.

Another possibility is that the non-convexity is a property of individuals' preferences. If the utility function exhibited decreasing marginal utility of leisure at low levels of leisure and increasing marginal utility at higher levels, individuals would tend to choose a low level of leisure (work a lot) or use their entire time endowment as leisure (not work at all). These preferences may be interpreted as 'indirect' preferences which reflect costs associated with working each period, such as driving a long distance to work or enduring the hassle of putting on a suit and tie. Bearing these fixed costs makes an individual less likely to choose to work only half a day.

In this paper the non-convexity is assumed to be a property of preferences.[7] However, to make the model tractable, the non-convexity introduced – indivisible labor – is an extreme version of the non-convexity described above. Individuals are assumed to have preferences that are defined only at two levels of leisure – one level corresponding to working full time and the other corresponding to not working at all. This is modeled by assuming that the consumption possibilities set consists of only two levels of leisure. This assumption implies that an individual can only adjust along the extensive margin.

Of course fluctuations along both the extensive and intensive margins are observed in the actual economy, as the above evidence indicates. However, by studying two economies – one that exhibits fluctuations only along the intensive margin and another with fluctuations only along the extensive margin – we can determine the importance of non-convexities for explaining labor variability in business cycles. If it turns out that both economies exhibit the same cyclical behavior, then it seems likely that a model that incorporated both margins would also exhibit similar behavior. In fact, non-convexities of this

---

[6] Coleman (1984) comes to a similar conclusion using establishment data.

[7] One advantage of modeling the non-convexity as a feature of the technology is that it would likely explain why part-time workers are paid less than full-time workers, in addition to accounting for features of the data discussed in this paper.

G.D. Hansen, Indivisible labor and the business cycle   313

sort could probably be safely abstracted from when studying business cycle phenomena. However, it happens that the two models have very different implications and that the non-convexity improves our ability to account for U.S. aggregate time series data.

3. Two economies

3.1. A one-sector stochastic growth model with divisible labor

The economy to be studied is populated by a continuum of identical infinitely lived households with names on the closed interval [0, 1]. There is a single firm with access to a technology described by a standard Cobb–Douglas production function of the form

$$f(\lambda_t, k_t, h_t) = \lambda_t k_t^\theta h_t^{1-\theta}, \tag{1}$$

where labor (h_t) and accumulated capital (k_t) are the inputs and λ_t is a random shock which follows a stochastic process to be described below. Agents are assumed to observe λ_t before making any period t decisions. The assumption of one firm is made for convenience. Since the technology displays constant returns to scale – implying that firms make zero profit in equilibrium – the economy would behave the same if there were many firms.

Output, which is produced by the firm and sold to the households, can either be consumed (c_t) or invested (i_t), so the following constraint must be satisfied:

$$c_t + i_t \le f(\lambda_t, k_t, h_t). \tag{2}$$

The law of motion for the capital stock is given by

$$k_{t+1} = (1 - \delta)k_t + i_t, \qquad 0 \le \delta \le 1, \tag{3}$$

where δ is the rate of capital depreciation. The stock of capital is owned by the households who sell capital services to the firm.

The technology shock is assumed to follow a first-order Markov process. In particular, λ_t obeys the following law of motion:

$$\lambda_{t+1} = \gamma\lambda_t + \varepsilon_{t+1}, \tag{4}$$

where the ε_t's are iid with distribution function F. This distribution is assumed to have a positive support with a finite upper bound, which guarantees that output will always be positive. By requiring F to have mean $1 - \gamma$, the unconditional mean of λ_t is equal to 1.

This technology shock is motivated by the fact that in post-war U.S. time series there are changes in output (GNP) that can not be accounted for by changes in the inputs (capital and labor). We follow Solow (1957) and Kydland and Prescott (1982) in interpreting this residual as reflecting shocks to technology.

Households in this economy maximize the expected value of $\sum_{t=0}^{\infty} \beta^t u(c_t, l_t)$, where $0 < \beta < 1$ is the discount factor and c_t and l_t are consumption and leisure in period t, respectively. The endowment of time is normalized to be one, so $l_t = 1 - h_t$. Utility in period t is given by the function

$$u(c_t, l_t) = \log c_t + A \log l_t, \qquad A > 0. \tag{5}$$

We now have a complete specification of the preferences, technology, and stochastic structure of a simple economy where individuals are able to supply any level of employment in the interval $[0, 1]$. Each period three commodities are traded: the composite output commodity, labor, and capital services. It is possible to consider only this sequence of spot markets since there is no demand for intertemporal risk sharing which might exist if households were heterogeneous.

Households solve the following problem, where w_t is the wage rate at time t and r_t is the rental rate of capital:

$$\max E \sum_{t=0}^{\infty} \beta^t u(c_t, 1 - h_t), \text{ given } k_0 \text{ and } \lambda_0, \tag{6}$$

subject to

$$c_t + i_t \leq w_t h_t + r_t k_t \quad \text{and} \quad (3).$$

Agents are assumed to make period t decisions based on all information available at time t (which includes r_t and w_t). They have rational expectations in that their forecasts of future wages and rental rates are the same as those implied by the equilibrium laws of motion. The first-order conditions for the firm's profit maximization problem imply that the wage and rental rate each period are equal to the marginal productivity of labor and capital, respectively.

Since there are no externalities or other distortions present in this economy, the equal-weight Pareto optimum can be supported as a competitive equilibrium. Since agents are homogeneous, the equal-weight Pareto optimum is the solution to the problem of maximizing the expected welfare of the representative agent subject to technology constraints. This problem is the following:

$$\max E \sum_{t=0}^{\infty} \beta^t u(c_t, 1 - h_t), \quad \text{given } k_0 \text{ and } \lambda_0, \tag{7}$$

subject to

$$(1)-(4) \quad \text{and} \quad \varepsilon_t \sim \text{c.d.f. } F.$$

The state of the economy in period t is described by k_t and λ_t. The decision variables are h_t, c_t, and i_t.

This problem can be solved using dynamic programming techniques.[8] This requires finding the unique continuous function $V: S \to \mathbb{R}$ (where S is the state space) that satisfies Bellman's equation (primes denote next period values)

$$V(k, \lambda) = \max\{u(c, 1-h) + \beta E[V(k', \lambda')|\lambda]\}, \tag{8}$$

where the maximization is over c and h and is subject to the same constraints as (7). The value function, $V(k, \lambda)$, is the maximum obtainable expected return over all feasible plans. It turns out that since the utility function is concave and the constraint set convex, the value function is also concave. This implies that the problem (8) is a standard finite-dimensional concave programming problem.

Unfortunately, this problem is not one which can be solved analytically. There is no known explicit functional form for the value function, V. In principle this problem could be solved using numerical methods [see Bertsekas (1976)], but a cheaper method – which does enable one to solve for closed form decision rules – is to approximate this problem by one which consists of a quadratic objective and linear constraints, as in Kydland and Prescott (1982). This method will be explained briefly in section 4.

3.2. An economy with indivisible labor

The assumption of indivisible labor will now be added to the above stochastic growth model. This will give rise to an economy where all variation in the labor input reflects adjustment along the extensive margin. This differs from the economy described above where all variation in the labor input reflects adjustment along the intensive margin. In addition, the utility function of the 'representative agent' for this economy will imply an elasticity of substitution between leisure in different periods that is infinite and independent of the elasticity implied by the utility function of the individual households.

Indivisibility of labor is modeled by restricting the consumption possibilities set so that individuals can either work full time, denoted by h_0, or not at all.[9]

---

[8] For a detailed presentation of dynamic programming methods, see Lucas, Prescott and Stokey (1984).

[9] This is consistent with the interpretation given in section 2. An alternative interpretation of indivisible labor assumes that households can work one of two possible (non-zero) number of hours, h_1 or h_2. This interpretation is consistent with an environment where each household consists of two individuals, at least one of whom works at all times. When only one member works, the household is working h_1 hours, and when both members work the household is working h_2 hours.

In order to guarantee [using Theorem 2 of Debreu (1954)] that the solution of the representative agent's problem can be supported as a competitive equilibrium, it is necessary that the consumption possibilities set be convex. However, if one of the commodities traded is hours worked (as in the above model), the consumption possibilities set will be non-convex. To circumvent this problem, we convexify the consumption possibilities set by requiring individuals to choose lotteries rather than hours worked, following Rogerson (1984).[10] Thus, each period, instead of choosing manhours, households choose a probability of working, α_t.[11] A lottery then determines whether or not the household actually works. After changing the economy in this manner, we make it possible for the competitive equilibrium to be derived by solving a concave programming problem, just as for the economy with divisible labor.

The new commodity being introduced is a contract between the firm and a household that commits the household to work h_0 hours with probability α_t. The contract itself is being traded, so the household gets paid whether it works or not. Therefore, the firm is providing complete unemployment insurance to the workers. Since all households are identical, all will choose the same contract – that is, the same α_t. However, although households are ex ante identical, they will differ ex post depending on the outcome of the lottery: a fraction α_t of the continuum of households will work and the rest will not.[12]

Using (5), expected utility in period t is given by $\alpha_t(\log c_t + A \log(1 - h_0)) + (1 - \alpha_t)(\log c_t + A \log 1)$.[13] This simplifies to the following function $U: \mathbb{R}_+ \times [0,1] \to \mathbb{R}$,

$$U(c_t, \alpha_t) = \log c_t + A\alpha_t \log(1 - h_0). \tag{9}$$

[10] In Rogerson's paper, a static economy with indivisible labor is studied and lotteries are introduced to solve the problem introduced by this non-convexity. Readers may wish to consult Rogerson's paper for a rigorous general equilibrium formulation of this type of model.

[11] Adding lotteries to the consumption set increases the choices available to households when labor is indivisible. If lotteries were not available, households would only be able to choose to not work (corresponding to $\alpha = 0$) or to work h_0 (corresponding to $\alpha = 1$). Therefore, adding lotteries can only make individuals better off.

[12] The lottery involves drawing a realization of a random variable z_t from the uniform distribution on [0,1]. Each individual $i \in [0,1]$ is now 'renamed' according to the following rule:

$$x_t(i,z) \equiv i + z_t \quad \text{if} \quad i + z_t \le 1,$$
$$\equiv i + z_t - 1 \quad \text{otherwise.}$$

The amount worked by agent x in period t is equal to

$$h_t(x) = 0 \quad \text{if} \quad x_t(i,z) \le 1 - \alpha_t,$$
$$= h_0 \quad \text{if} \quad x_t(i,z) > 1 - \alpha_t.$$

This provides a mechanism for dividing the continuum of agents into two subsets, one where each individual works zero hours and another where individuals work h_0. The first will have measure $(1 - \alpha_t)$ and the other measure α_t. This follows from the easily verified fact that $\text{Prob}[x_t(i,z) \le 1 - \alpha_t]$ is equal to $1 - \alpha_t$ for each i.

[13] This uses the fact that, since preferences are separable in consumption and leisure, the consumption level chosen in equilibrium is independent of whether the individual works or not.

Since a fraction α_t of households will work h_0 and the rest will work zero, per capita hours worked in period t is given by

$$h_t = \alpha_t h_0. \tag{10}$$

The other features of this economy are exactly the same as for the economy with divisible labor. These include the technology and the description of the stochastic process for the technology shock. These features are described by eqs. (1) through (4).

Firms in the economy, as in the previous economy, will want to employ labor up to the point where $f_h(\lambda_t, k_t, h_t) = w_t$. However, due to the fact that lottery contracts are being traded, households are not paid for the time they actually spend working, but are instead paid for the *expected* amount of time spent working. This implies that each worker is paid as if he worked h_t [as defined in (10)] rather than for the amount he actually does work. Therefore, the budget constraint of a typical household differs from the budget constraint for the economy where labor is divisible (6) and is given by

$$c_t + i_t \leq w_t \alpha_t h_0 + r_t k_t. \tag{11}$$

Thus, the problem solved by a typical household is

$$\max E \sum_{t=0}^{\infty} \beta^t U(c_t, \alpha_t), \quad \text{given } k_0 \text{ and } \lambda_0, \tag{12}$$

subject to

(11) and (3).

This problem is equivalent to the problem solved by households in a slightly different economy where agents trade man-hours and actuarially fair insurance contracts, rather than the type of contracts traded in the economy studied here. In this alternative economy, which is described in more detail in the appendix, households only get paid for the time they actually spend working. However, if a household has purchased unemployment insurance, it will receive compensation if the lottery determines that the household does not work. In the appendix it is shown that households will choose to insure themselves fully. Therefore, in equilibrium, the households will have full unemployment insurance, just like the households populating the economy described in this section. This implies that the equilibrium allocations for these two economies are the same.

The following is the representative agent's problem that must be solved to derive the equilibrium decision rules and laws of motion:

$$\max E \sum_{t=0}^{\infty} \beta^t U(c_t, \alpha_t), \quad \text{given } k_0 \text{ and } \lambda_0, \tag{13}$$

subject to

$$(1)-(4), (10) \quad \text{and} \quad \varepsilon_t \sim \text{c.d.f. } F.$$

Like problem (7), this is a standard concave discounted dynamic programming problem. The state of the economy in period t is described by k_t and λ_t. The decision variables are α_t, c_t, and i_t.

A key property of this economy is that the elasticity of substitution between leisure in different periods for the 'representative agent' is infinite. To understand this result, first substitute $h_t = 1 - l_t$ into (10) and solve for α_t. After substituting this expression for α_t into (9) one obtains the following utility function for the representative agent (ignoring the constant term):

$$U(c_t, l_t) = \log c_t + B l_t, \tag{14}$$

where $B = -A(\log(1 - h_0))/h_0$. Since this utility function is linear in leisure it implies an infinite elasticity of substitution between leisure in different periods. This follows no matter how small this elasticity is for the individuals populating the economy. Therefore, the elasticity of substitution between leisure in different periods for the *aggregate* economy is infinite and independent of the willingness of individuals to substitute leisure across time.[14]

4. Solution method and calibration

The problems (7) and (13) are not in the class of problems for which it is possible to solve analytically for decision rules. This special class of problems includes those with quadratic objectives and linear constraints, as well as some other structures. For this reason, approximate economies are studied for which the representative agent's problem is linear-quadratic [see Kydland and Prescott (1982)]. It is then possible to obtain explicit decision rules for these approximate economies.

By making appropriate substitutions, one can express problems (7) and (13) as dynamic optimization problems with decision variables i_t and h_t and state variables λ_t and k_t. The constraints for these problems are linear although the

[14] The fact that in this type of model the representative agent's utility function is linear in leisure was originally shown by Rogerson (1984) for his model. This result depends, however, on the utility function being additively separable across time.

G.D. Hansen, Indivisible labor and the business cycle   319

objective functions are non-linear. For each of these problems, Kydland and Prescott's procedure is used to construct a quadratic approximation of the objective function to be accurate in a neighborhood of the steady state for the appropriate model after the technology shock has been set equal to its unconditional mean of one.[15] The reader may consult Kydland and Prescott (1982) for details on the algorithm used for forming these approximations.[16]

To actually compute these quadratic approximations, solve for an equilibrium, and generate artificial time series, it is necessary to choose a distribution function, F, and specific parameter values for θ, δ, β, A, γ, and h_0. Kydland and Prescott (1982, 1984) follow a methodology for choosing parameter values based on evidence from growth observations and micro studies. This methodology will also be followed here. In fact, since they study a similar economy, some of the above parameters (θ, δ, β) also appear in their model. This enables me to draw on their work in selecting values for these parameters, thereby making it easier to compare the results of the two studies.

The parameter θ corresponds to capital's share in production. This has been calculated using U.S. time series data by Kydland and Prescott (1982, 1984) and was found to be approximately 0.36. The rate of depreciation of capital, δ, is set equal to 0.025 which implies an annual rate of depreciation of 10 percent. Kydland and Prescott found this to be a good compromise given that different types of capital depreciate at different rates. The discount factor, β, is set equal to 0.99, which implies a steady state annual real rate of interest of four percent.

The parameter A in the utility function (5) is set equal to 2. This implies that hours worked in the steady state for the model with divisible labor is close to $1/3$. This more or less matches the observation that individuals spend $1/3$ of

---

[15] Let the steady states for the certainty version of these models be denoted by the variable's symbol without any subscript. Eq. (3) implies that investment in the steady state is given by $i = \delta k$. Expressions for k and h can be determined by deriving the Euler equations for the appropriate representative agent problem and setting $h_t = h$, $k_t = k$, and $i_t = i = \delta k$ for all t. For both economies, the steady state capital stock is given by

$$k = [(\rho + \delta)/\theta]^{1/(\theta-1)} h \quad \text{where} \quad \rho = (1/\beta) - 1.$$

Hours worked in the steady state for the economy with divisible labor is given by $h = (1 - \theta) \times (\rho + \delta)/[3(\rho + \delta) - \theta(\rho + 3\delta)]$; and for the economy with indivisible labor, $h = (1 - \theta)(\rho + \delta)/[\psi(\rho + \delta - \theta\delta)]$ where $\psi = -A[\log(1 - h_0)]/h_0$.

[16] Kydland and Prescott's method for approximating this problem requires choosing a vector of average deviations, $z \in \mathbb{R}^4$, which determines the size of the neighborhood around the steady state within which the approximation is accurate. The four components of z are average deviations from trend of the four variables, $x_t = (\lambda_t, k_t, i_t, h_t)$, as found in U.S. time series data. This implies that along those dimensions where there is more variability, the approximation will be accurate in a larger neighborhood around the steady state $(\bar{x})$. For the exercise carried out in this paper $\{z_i/\bar{x}_i\}_{i=1}^4 = (0.012, 0.006, 0.08, 0.017)$, reflecting the average standard deviations of these series as reported in the next section. Although attention was paid to specifying this vector in a reasonable way, it turns out that the results are not altered when the z_i components are decreased by a factor of ten.

their time engaged in market activities and 2/3 of their time in non-market activities.

To determine the parameter h_0, I set the expressions for hours of work in the steady state for the two models equal to each other. Since steady state hours worked in the model with divisible labor is fully determined by the parameters θ, δ, A, and β for which values have already been assigned (see footnote 15), it is possible to solve for h_0. This implies a value for h_0 of 0.53.

The distribution function F along with the parameter γ determine the properties of the technology shock, λ_t. The distribution of ε_t is assumed to be log normal with mean $(1 - \gamma)$, which implies that the unconditional mean of λ_t is 1. The parameter γ is set equal to 0.95 which is consistent with the statistical properties of the production function residual.[17] The standard deviation of ε_t, σ_ε, is difficult to measure from available data since this number is significantly affected by measurement error. A data analysis suggests that σ_ε could reasonably be expected to lie in the interval $[0.007, 0.01]$. A value of 0.007, for example, would imply that a little over half of the variability in ε_t is being attributed to measurement error, which is probably not unreasonable. The actual value used for the simulations in this paper is 0.00712. This particular value was chosen because it implies that the mean standard deviation of output for the economy with indivisible labor is equal to the standard deviation of GNP for the U.S. economy (see next section).

All parameters of the two models have now been determined. We are now ready to study and compare the statistical properties of the time series generated by these two models.

5. Results

For the purposes of this study, the statistical properties of the economies studied are summarized by a set of standard deviations and correlations with output that are reported in table 1.

The statistics for the U.S. economy are reported in the first two columns of the table. Before these statistics were calculated, the time series were logged and deviations from trend were computed. Detrending was necessary because the models studied abstract from growth. The data were logged so that standard deviations can be interpreted as mean percentage deviations from

---

[17] The production function residual is measured, using U.S. time series, by

$$\log \lambda_t = \log y_t - \theta \log k_t - (1 - \theta)\log h_t,$$

where data on GNP, capital stock (nonresidential equipment and structures), and hours worked is obtained from a standard econometric data base. The first-order autocorrelation coefficient for λ_t is about 0.95, indicating high serial correlation in this series. The parameter θ was assumed to be equal to 0.36 for calculating this residual. A more detailed study of the statistical properties of this technology shock is planned but has not yet been carried out.

Table 1

Standard deviations in percent (a) and correlations with output (b) for U.S. and artificial economies.

Series	Quarterly U.S. time series[a] (55.3–84.1)		Economy with divisible labor[b]		Economy with indivisible labor[b]	
	(a)	(b)	(a)	(b)	(a)	(b)
Output	1.76	1.00	1.35 (0.16)	1.00 (0.00)	1.76 (0.21)	1.00 (0.00)
Consumption	1.29	0.85	0.42 (0.06)	0.89 (0.03)	0.51 (0.08)	0.87 (0.04)
Investment	8.60	0.92	4.24 (0.51)	0.99 (0.00)	5.71 (0.70)	0.99 (0.00)
Capital stock	0.63	0.04	0.36 (0.07)	0.06 (0.07)	0.47 (0.10)	0.05 (0.07)
Hours	1.66	0.76	0.70 (0.08)	0.98 (0.01)	1.35 (0.16)	0.98 (0.01)
Productivity	1.18	0.42	0.68 (0.08)	0.98 (0.01)	0.50 (0.07)	0.87 (0.03)

[a] The U.S. time series used are real GNP, total consumption expenditures, and gross private domestic investment (all in 1972 dollars). The capital stock series includes nonresidential equipment and structures. The hours series includes total hours for persons at work in non-agricultural industries as derived from the *Current Population Survey*. Productivity is output divided by hours. All series are seasonally adjusted, logged and detrended.

[b] The standard deviations and correlations with output are sample means of statistics computed for each of 100 simulations. Each simulation consists of 115 periods, which is the same number of periods as the U.S. sample. The numbers in parentheses are sample standard deviations of these statistics. Before computing any statistics each simulated time series was logged and detrended using the same procedure used for the U.S. time series.

trend. The 'detrending' procedure used is the method employed by Hodrick and Prescott (1980).[18]

Since much of the discussion in this section centers on the variability of hours worked and productivity (output divided by hours worked), some discussion of the hours series is appropriate. The time series for hours worked used in constructing these statistics is derived from the *Current Population Survey*, which is a survey of households. This series was chosen in preference to the other available hours series which is derived from the establishment survey. The hours series based on the household survey is more comprehensive than

---

[18] This method involves choosing smoothed values $\{s_t\}_{t=1}^T$ for the series $\{x_t\}_{t=1}^T$ which solve the following problem:

$$\min\left\{ (1/T)\sum_{t=1}^{T}(x_t - s_t)^2 + (\lambda/T)\sum_{t=2}^{T-1}\left[(s_{t+1} - s_t) - (s_t - s_{t-1})\right]^2\right\},$$

where $\lambda > 0$ is the penalty on variation, where variation is measured by the average squared second difference. A larger value of λ implies that the resulting $\{s_t\}$ series is smoother. Following Prescott (1983), I choose $\lambda = 1600$. Deviations from the smooth series are formed by taking $d_t = x_t - s_t$.

This method is used in order to filter out low frequency fluctuations. Although other methods (spectral techniques, for example) are available, this method was chosen because of its simplicity and the fact that other methods lead to basically the same results [see Prescott (1983)].

322   *G.D. Hansen, Indivisible labor and the business cycle*

the establishment series since self-employed workers and unpaid workers in family-operated enterprises are included. Another advantage is that the household series takes into account only hours actually worked rather than all hours paid for. That is, it doesn't include items such as paid sick leave. A disadvantage is that the household series begins in the third quarter of 1955, which prevented me from using data over the entire post-war period.

Sample distributions of the summary statistics describing the behavior of the artificial economies were derived using Monte Carlo methods. The model was simulated repeatedly to obtain many samples of artificially generated time series. Each sample generated had the same number of periods (115) as the U.S. time series used in the study. Before any statistics were computed, the data were logged and the same filtering procedure applied to the U.S. data was applied to these time series. One hundred simulations were performed and sample statistics were calculated for each data set generated. The sample means and standard deviations of these summary statistics are reported in the last four columns of table 1.

When comparing the statistics describing the two artificial economies, one discovers that the economy with indivisible labor displays significantly larger fluctuations than the economy with divisible labor. This shows that indivisible labor increases the volatility of the stochastic growth model for a given stochastic process for the technology shock. In fact, it is necessary to increase σ_ε by 30 percent (from 0.00712 to 0.00929) in order to increase the standard deviation of output for the divisible labor economy so that it is equal to the standard deviation of GNP for the actual economy, which is 1.76. It is still the case that 0.00929 is in the interval suggested by the data (see paragraph on measuring σ_ε in the previous section). However, since it is likely that there is significant measurement error in our empirical estimate of the production function residual, one should prefer the lower value of σ_ε.

Another conclusion drawn from studying this table is that the fluctuations in most variables are larger for the actual economy than for the indivisible labor economy. It is my view that most of this additional fluctuation (except in the case of the consumption series) is due to measurement error. Work in progress by the author attempts to correct for measurement error in the hours series (and hence some of the measurement error in the productivity series).[19] Preliminary findings seem to suggest that the above hypothesis is correct. In addition, the fact that the consumption series fluctuates much more in the actual economy than in the artificial economy can probably be explained by the fact that nothing corresponding to consumer durables is modeled in the economies studied here.

---

[19] The work referred to is a chapter of my dissertation. Copies will soon be available upon request.

Perhaps the most significant discovery made by examining table 1 is that the amount of variability in hours worked relative to variability in productivity is very different for the two model economies. This relative variability can be measured by the ratio of the standard deviation in hours worked to the standard deviation in productivity. For the economy with indivisible labor, this ratio is 2.7, and for the economy without this feature the ratio is not significantly above 1.[20] For the U.S. economy the ratio is equal to 1.4, which is between these two values.

As explained in the introduction, accounting for the large variability in hours worked relative to productivity has been an open problem in equilibrium business cycle theory. Kydland and Prescott (1982) study a version of the stochastic growth model where labor is divisible and the utility function of individuals is non-time-separable with respect to leisure. This non-time-separability property is introduced to make leisure in different periods better substitutes. However, this feature enables these authors to report a value for this ratio of only 1.17, which is still much too low to account for the fluctuations found in U.S. data.

On the other hand, the economy with indivisible labor studied here has exactly the opposite problem Kyland and Prescott's model has. The ratio implied by this model is much larger than the ratio implied by the data. However, this should not be surprising. In fact, it would be bothersome if this were *not* the case. After all, we do observe some adjustment along the intensive margin in the real world. Examples include workers who work overtime in some periods and not in others or salesmen who work a different number of hours each day. Since indivisible labor implies that *all* fluctuations are along the extensive margin, one would expect – even without looking at statistics calculated from the data – that the ratio discussed above should be somewhere between the one implied by an indivisible labor economy and a divisible labor economy.

6. Conclusion

A dynamic competitive equilibrium economy with indivisible labor has been constructed with the aim of accounting for standard deviations and correlations with output found in aggregate economic time series. Individuals in this economy are forced to enter and exit the labor force in response to technology shocks rather than simply adjusting the number of hours worked while remaining continuously employed. Therefore, this is an equilibrium model which exhibits unemployment (or employment) fluctuations in response to aggregate shocks. Fluctuations in employment seem important for fluctuations

---

[20] This ratio is still not significantly different from one even when σ_ε is increased to 0.00929.

in hours worked over the business cycle since most of the variability in total hours is unambiguously due to variation in the number employed rather than hours per employed worker.

An important aspect of this economy is that the elasticity of substitution between leisure in different periods for the aggregate economy is infinite and independent of the elasticity of substitution implied by the individuals' utility function. This distinguishes this model, or any Rogerson (1984) style economy, from one without indivisible labor. These include the model presented in section 3.1 and the economy studied by Kydland and Prescott (1982). In these divisible labor models, the elasticity of substitution for the aggregate economy is the same as that for individuals.

This feature enables the indivisible labor economy to exhibit large fluctuations in hours worked relative to fluctuations in productivity. Previous equilibrium models of the business cycle, which have all assumed divisible labor, have been unsuccessful in accounting for this feature of U.S. time series. This is illustrated in this paper by showing that a model with divisible labor fails to exhibit large fluctuations in hours worked relative to productivity while the model with indivisible labor displays fluctuations in hours relative to productivity which are much larger than what is observed. This seems to indicate that a model which allowed for adjustment along both the extensive margin as well as the intensive margin would have a good chance for successfully confronting the data.

In conclusion, this study demonstrates that non-convexities such as indivisible labor may be important for explaining the volatility of hours relative to productivity even when individuals are relatively unwilling to substitute leisure across time. They are also useful for increasing the size of the standard deviations of all variables relative to the standard deviation of the technology shock. Therefore, a smaller size shock is sufficient for explaining business cycle fluctuations than was true for previous models such as Kydland and Prescott's (1982). In addition, these non-convexities make it possible for an equilibrium model of the business cycle to exhibit fluctuations in employment. Therefore, non-convexities will inevitably play an important role in future equilibrium models of the cycle.

Appendix: A market for unemployment insurance

The purpose of this appendix is to show that the equilibrium of the economy presented in section 3.2 is equivalent to the equilibrium of an economy where labor is still indivisible but households are able to purchase any amount of unemployment insurance they choose. In the original economy, agents are assumed to buy and sell contracts which specify a probability of working in a given period as opposed to buying and selling hours of work. A lottery determines which households must work and which do not. A household is paid according to the probability that it works, not according to the work it actually does. In other words, the firm is automatically providing full unemployment insurance to the households.

In this appendix, households choose a probability of working each period and a lottery is held to determine which households must work, just as in the original economy. Also, preferences, technology, and the stochastic structure are exactly the same as for the original model. However, this economy is different in that households only get paid for the work they actually do – unemployed individuals get paid nothing by the firm. But, the household does have access to an insurance market which preserves the complete markets aspect of the original model. It is shown below that the equilibrium of this economy is equivalent to that of the original economy since individuals will choose to be fully insured in equilibrium. This is shown by proving that the problem solved by households is the same as the problem solved by households (12) in the original model.

The problem solved by the households can be described as follows: Each period, households choose a probability of working, α_t, a level of unemployment compensation, y_t, and consumption and investment contingent on whether the household works or not, c_{st} and i_{st} ($s = 1, 2$). These are chosen to solve the following dynamic programming problem (primes denote next period values):

$$\max V(\lambda, K, k) = \alpha\{u(c_1) + \nu(1 - h_0) + \beta \, EV(\lambda', K', k_1')\}$$

$$+ (1 - \alpha)\{u(c_2) + \nu(1) + \beta \, EV(\lambda', K', k_2')\},$$

$$(A.1)$$

subject to

$$c_1 + i_1 \leq w(\lambda, K)h_0 + r(\lambda, K)k - p(\alpha)y, \tag{A.2}$$

$$c_2 + i_2 \leq y + r(\lambda, K)k - p(\alpha)y, \tag{A.3}$$

$$k_s' = (1 - \delta)k + i_s, \qquad s = 1, 2. \tag{A.4}$$

The function $V(\lambda, K, k)$ is the value function which depends on the household's state. The state vector includes the capital owned by the household, plus the economy wide state variables λ and K, where K is the per capita capital stock.[21] The functions $w(\lambda, K)$ and $r(\lambda, K)$ are the wage rate and rental rate

---

[21]Since we are allowing households to choose any level of unemployment insurance they wish, we have to allow for the heterogeneity that may come about because different households will have different income streams. This is why the distinction is made between the per capita capital stock, K, and the households accumulated capital stock, k. However, this heterogeneity will disappear in equilibrium since all households will choose full insurance, so $K = k$ in equilibrium.

of capital respectively, and $p(\alpha)$ is the price of insurance, which is a function of the probability that the household works. Also, since individuals' preferences are the same as for the original model, $u(c) = \log c$ and $v(l) = A \log l$.

The insurance company in this economy maximizes expected profits which are given by $p(\alpha)y - (1 - \alpha)y$. That is, the firm collects revenue $p(\alpha)y$ and pays y with probability $1 - \alpha$. To guarantee that profits are bounded, $p(\alpha) = (1 - \alpha)$. Therefore, the price the household must pay for insurance equals the probability that the household will collect on the insurance.

One can now substitute this expression for p into constraints (A.2) and (A.3). After eliminating the constraints by substituting out i_s and c_s ($s = 1, 2$), one can write the following first-order necessary conditions for k'_s and $\cdot y$:

$$u'(c_s) = \beta \, E V_{k'}(\lambda', K', k'_s), \qquad s = 1, 2, \tag{A.5}$$

$$u'(c_1) = u'(c_2). \tag{A.6}$$

Eq. (A.6) implies, given the strict concavity of u, that $c_1 = c_2$. This plus eq. (A.5) imply that $k'_1 = k'_2$. This, in turn, implies that $i_1 = i_2$. Therefore, the left-hand sides of eqs. (A.2) and (A.3) are identical. Since these constraints will be binding in equilibrium, y will be chosen so that the right-hand sides are equal as well. This means that $y = wh_0$ in equilibrium. That is, households will choose to insure themselves fully. This has the implication that all households will choose the same sequence of capital stocks, so $K = k$.

Substituting these results into the household's optimization problem (A.1) yields the following problem: Households choose c, i, k', and α to

$$\max V(\lambda, k) = u(c) + \alpha v(1 - h_0) + (1 - \alpha)v(1) + \beta \, E V(\lambda', k'),$$

$$\tag{A.7}$$

subject to

$$c + i \leq \alpha w(\lambda, k)h_0 + r(\lambda, k)k,$$

$$k' = (1 - \delta)k + i.$$

This problem is identical to problem (12). Therefore, the equilibrium allocation for the original economy, where the firm provides full unemployment insurance to workers by assumption, is equivalent to the equilibrium allocation for an economy where households get paid by the firm only for work done but have access to a risk-neutral insurance market. This result, of course, depends crucially on the probability α being publicly observable and the contract being enforceable. That is, it must be the case that the agent announces the same α to both the firm and the insurance company, and if the agent loses the lottery (that is, has to work) this is known by all parties. For example, this result would not hold if α depended on some underlying choice variable like effort that was not directly observed by the insurance company. In this case a difficult moral hazard problem would arise.

References

Altonji, J.G., 1984, Intertemporal substitution in labor supply: Evidence from micro data, Unpublished manuscript (Columbia University, New York).

Ashenfelter, O., 1984, Macroeconomic analyses and microeconomic analyses of labor supply, Carnegie–Rochester Conference Series on Public Policy 21, 117–156.

Bertsekas, D.P., 1976, Dynamic programming and stochastic control (Academic Press, New York).

Coleman, T.S., 1984, Essays on aggregate labor market business cycle fluctuations, Unpublished manuscript (University of Chicago, Chicago, IL).

Debreu, G., 1954, Valuation equilibrium and Pareto optimum, Proceedings of the National Academy of Sciences 40, 588–592.

Heckman, J.J., 1984, Comments on the Ashenfelter and Kydland papers, Carnegie–Rochester Conference Series on Public Policy 21, 209–224.

Heckman, J.J. and T.E. MaCurdy, 1980, A life cycle model of female labor supply, Review of Economic Studies 47, 47–74.

Hodrick, R.J. and E.C. Prescott, 1980, Post-war U.S. business cycles: An empirical investigation, Working paper (Carnegie-Mellon University, Pittsburgh, PA).

Kydland, F.E. and E.C. Prescott, 1982, Time to build and aggregate fluctuations, Econometrica 50, 1345–1370.

Kydland, F.E. and E.C. Prescott, 1984, The workweek of capital and labor, Unpublished manuscript (Federal Reserve Bank of Minneapolis, Minneapolis, MN).

Lucas, R.E., Jr., 1977, Understanding business cycles, Carnegie–Rochester Conference Series on Public Policy 5, 7–29.

Lucas, R.E., Jr. and E.C. Prescott, 1971, Investment under uncertainty, Econometrica 39, 659–681.

Lucas, R.E., Jr., E.C. Prescott and N.L. Stokey, 1984, Recursive methods for economic dynamics, Unpublished manuscript (University of Minnesota, Minneapolis, MN).

MaCurdy, T.E., An empirical model of labor supply in a life-cycle setting, Journal of Political Economy 89, 1059–1085.

Rogerson, R., Indivisible labour, lotteries and equilibrium, Unpublished manuscript (University of Rochester, Rochester, NY).

Prescott, E.C., Can the cycle be reconciled with a consistent theory of expectations? or a progress report on business cycle theory, Unpublished manuscript (Federal Reserve Bank of Minneapolis, Minneapolis, MN).

Solow, R.M., Technical change and the aggregate production function, The Review of Economics and Statistics 39, 312–320.

Federal Reserve Bank of Minneapolis
Quarterly Review Spring 1992

The Labor Market in Real Business Cycle Theory*

Gary D. Hansen
Professor of Economics
University of California,
Los Angeles

Randall Wright
Senior Economist
Research Department
Federal Reserve Bank of Minneapolis
and Professor of Economics
University of Pennsylvania

The basic objective of the real business cycle research program is to use the neoclassical growth model to interpret observed patterns of fluctuations in overall economic activity. If we take a simple version of the model, calibrate it to be consistent with long-run growth facts, and subject it to random technology shocks calibrated to observed Solow residuals, the model displays short-run cyclical behavior that is qualitatively and quantitatively similar to that displayed by actual economies along many important dimensions. For example, the model predicts that consumption will be less than half as volatile as output, that investment will be about three times as volatile as output, and that consumption, investment, and employment will be strongly positively correlated with output, just as in the postwar U.S. time series.[1] In this sense, the real business cycle approach can be thought of as providing a benchmark for the study of aggregate fluctuations.

In this paper, we analyze the implications of real business cycle theory for the labor market. In particular, we focus on two facts about U.S. time series: the fact that hours worked fluctuate considerably more than productivity and the fact that the correlation between hours worked and productivity is close to zero.[2] These facts and the failure of simple real business cycle models to account for them have received considerable attention in the literature. [See, for example, the extended discussion by Christiano and Eichenbaum (1992) and the references they provide.] Here we first document the facts. We

The Editorial Board for this paper was V. V. Chari, Preston J. Miller, Richard Rogerson, and Kathleen S. Rolfe.

then present a baseline real business cycle model (essentially, the divisible labor model in Hansen 1985) and compare its predictions with the facts. We then consider four extensions of the baseline model that are meant to capture features of the world from which this model abstracts. Each of these extensions has been discussed in the literature. However, we analyze them in a unified framework with common functional forms, parameter values, and so on, so that they can be more easily compared and evaluated in terms of how they affect the model's ability to explain the facts.

The standard real business cycle model relies exclusively on a single technology shock to generate fluctuations, so the fact that hours worked vary more than productivity implies that the short-run labor supply elasticity must be large. The first extension of the model we consider is to recognize that utility may depend not only on leisure today but also on past leisure; this possibility leads us to introduce *nonseparable pref-*

---

*This paper is also available in Spanish in *Cuadernos Economicos de ICE*, a quarterly publication of the Ministerio de Economía y Hacienda. The paper appears here with the permission of that publication's editor, Manuel Santos.

[1] These properties are also observed in other countries and time periods. See Kydland and Prescott 1990 for an extended discussion of the postwar U.S. data, and see Blackburn and Ravn 1991 or Backus and Kehoe, forthcoming, for descriptions of other countries and time periods.

[2] Although we concentrate mainly on these cyclical facts, we also mention an important long-run growth fact that is relevant for much of our discussion: total hours worked per capita do not display trend growth despite large secular increases in average productivity and real wages.

Gary D. Hansen, Randall Wright
Real Business Cycle Theory

erences, as in Kydland and Prescott 1982.[3] This extension of the baseline model has the effect of increasing the relevant elasticity, by making households more willing to substitute leisure in one period for leisure in another period in response to short-run productivity changes. At the same time, with these preferences, households do not increase their work hours in response to permanent productivity growth. Thus, the nonseparable leisure model generates an increased standard deviation of hours worked relative to productivity without violating the long-run growth fact that hours worked per capita have not increased over long periods despite large increases in productivity.

The second extension of the baseline real business cycle model we consider is to assume that labor is *indivisible,* so that workers can work either a fixed number of hours or not at all, as in Hansen 1985. In this version of the model, all variation in the labor input must come about by changes in the number of employed workers, which is the opposite of the standard model, where all variation comes about by changes in hours per worker. Although the data display variation along both margins, the indivisible labor model is perhaps a better abstraction, since the majority of the variance in the labor input in the United States can be attributed to changes in the number of employed workers. In the equilibrium of the indivisible labor model, individual workers are allocated to jobs randomly, and this turns out to imply that the aggregate economy displays a large labor supply elasticity even though individual hours do not respond at all to productivity or wage changes for continuously employed workers. The large aggregate labor supply elasticity leads to an increased standard deviation of hours relative to productivity, as compared to the baseline model.

Neither nonseparable utility nor indivisible labor changes the result that the real business cycle model implies a large positive correlation between hours and productivity while the data display a near-zero correlation. This result arises because the model is driven by a single shock to the aggregate production function, which can be interpreted as shifting the labor demand curve along a stable labor supply curve and inducing a very tight positive relationship between hours and productivity. Hence, the next extension we consider is to introduce *government spending* shocks, as in Christiano and Eichenbaum 1992. If public consumption is an imperfect substitute for private consumption, then an increase in government spending has a negative wealth effect on individuals, which induces them to work more if leisure is a normal good. Therefore, government spending shocks can be interpreted as shifting the labor supply curve along the labor demand curve. Depending on the size of and the response to the two shocks, with this extension the model can generate a pattern of hours

versus productivity closer to that found in the data.

The final extension we consider is to introduce *household production* as in Benhabib, Rogerson, and Wright 1991. The basic idea is to recognize that agents derive utility from home-produced as well as market-produced consumption goods and derive disutility from working in the home as well as in the market. In this version of the model, individuals, by working less at home, can increase hours of market work without reducing leisure as much. Therefore, the addition of household production increases the short-run labor supply elasticity and the standard deviation of hours relative to productivity. Furthermore, to the extent that shocks to household production are less than perfectly correlated with shocks to market production, individuals will have an incentive to substitute between home and market activity at a point in time. This is in addition to the standard incentive to substitute between market activity at different dates. Therefore, home production shocks, like government spending shocks, shift the labor supply curve and can generate a pattern of hours versus productivity closer to that found in the data.

Our basic finding is that each of these four extensions to the baseline real business cycle model improves its performance quantitatively, even though the extensions work through very different economic channels. As will be seen, some of the resulting models seem to do better than others along certain dimensions, and some depend more sensitively than others on parameter values. Our goal here is not to suggest that one of these models is best for all purposes; which is best for any particular application will depend on the context. Rather, we simply want to illustrate here how incorporating certain natural features into the standard real business cycle model affects its ability to capture some key aspects of labor market behavior.

The Facts

In this section, we document the relevant business cycle facts. We consider several measures of hours worked and productivity and two sample periods (since some of the measures are available only for a shorter period). As in Prescott 1986, we define the *business cycle* as fluctuations around some slowly moving trend. For any given data series, we first take logarithms and then use the Hodrick-Prescott filter (as described in Prescott 1986) to remove the trend.

Table 1 contains some summary statistics for quarterly U.S. data that are computed from deviations constructed in this manner. The sample period is from 1955:3 to 1988:2. The variables are y = output, c = consumption (nondurables plus services), i = fixed investment, h = hours worked, and w

---

[3]Note that these preferences are nonseparable between leisure in different periods; they may or may not be separable between leisure and consumption in a given period.

Tables 1 and 2

Cyclical Properties of U.S. Time Series

Table 1   1955:3–1988:2

Data Series*	Variable j	% S.D. σ_j	Variable vs. Output		Hours vs. Productivity	
			σ_j/σ_y	$cor(j,y)$	σ_h/σ_w	$cor(h,w)$
Output	y	1.74	1.00	1.00	—	—
Consumption	c	.84	.48	.75	—	—
Investment	i	5.48	3.16	.90	—	—
Labor Market:						
1. Household Survey (All Industries)						
Hours Worked	h	1.42	.82	.87	1.64	.10
Productivity	w	.87	.50	.58		
2. Establishment Survey (Nonag. Industries)						
Hours Worked	h	1.63	.94	.88	1.95	−.13
Productivity	w	.84	.48	.36		
3. Nonag. Industries From Household Survey						
Hours Worked	h	1.75	1.01	.76	1.44	−.35
Productivity	w	1.21	.70	.34		
4. Efficiency Units From Hansen 1991						
Hours Worked	h	1.66	.96	.74	1.37	−.30
Productivity	w	1.22	.70	.41		

Table 2   1947:1–1991:3

Data Series*	Variable j	% S.D. σ_j	Variable vs. Output		Hours vs. Productivity	
			σ_j/σ_y	$cor(j,y)$	σ_h/σ_w	$cor(h,w)$
Output	y	1.92	1.00	1.00	—	—
Consumption	c	.86	.45	.71	—	—
Investment	i	5.33	2.78	.73	—	—
Labor Market:						
1. Household Survey (All Industries)						
Hours Worked	h	1.50	.78	.82	1.37	.07
Productivity	w	1.10	.57	.63		
2. Establishment Survey (Nonag. Industries)						
Hours Worked	h	1.84	.96	.90	2.15	−.14
Productivity	w	.86	.45	.31		

*All series are quarterly, are in 1982 dollars, and have been logged and detrended with the Hodrick-Prescott filter. The output series, y, is the gross national product; c is consumption of nondurables and services; and i is fixed investment. Productivity is $w = y/h$.

Sources: Citicorp's Citibase data bank and Hansen 1991

4

Gary D. Hansen, Randall Wright
Real Business Cycle Theory

= average productivity (output divided by hours worked).[4] For each variable j, we report the following statistics: the (percent) standard deviation σ_j, the standard deviation relative to that of output σ_j/σ_y, and the correlation with output $cor(j,y)$. We also report the relative standard deviation of hours to that of productivity σ_h/σ_w and the correlation between hours and productivity $cor(h,w)$.

We present statistics for four measures of h and w. Hours series 1 is total hours worked as recorded in the household survey and covers all industries. Hours series 2 is total hours worked as recorded in the establishment survey and covers only nonagricultural industries. These two hours series could differ for two reasons: they are from different sources, and they cover different industries.[5] To facilitate comparison, we also report, in hours series 3, hours worked as recorded in the household survey but only for nonagricultural industries. Finally, hours series 4 is a measure of hours worked in efficiency units.[6]

The reason for the choice of 1955:3–1988:2 as the sample period is that hours series 3 and 4 are only available for this period. However, the other series are available for 1947:1–1991:3, and Table 2 reports statistics from this longer period for the available variables.

Both Table 1 and Table 2 display the standard business cycle facts. All variables are positively correlated with output. Output is more variable than consumption and less variable than investment. Hours are slightly less variable than or about as variable as output, with σ_h/σ_y ranging between 0.78 and 1.01, depending on the hours series and the period. Overall, all variables are more volatile in the longer period, but the relative volatilities of the variables are about the same in the two periods. (An exception is investment, which looks somewhat less volatile relative to output in the longer period.)

We want to emphasize two things. First, hours fluctuate more than productivity, with the magnitude of σ_h/σ_w ranging between 1.37 and 2.15, depending on the series and the period. Second, the correlation between hours and productivity is near zero or slightly negative, with $cor(h,w)$ ranging between –0.35 and 0.10, depending on the series and the period. Chart 1 shows the scatter plot of h versus w from hours series 1 for the longer sample period. (Plots from the other hours series look similar.)

The Standard Model

In this section, we present a standard real business cycle model and investigate its implications for the facts just described.

The model has a large number of homogeneous households. The representative household has preferences defined over stochastic sequences of consumption c_t and leisure l_t, described by the utility function

$$(1) \qquad U = E\sum_{t=0}^{\infty} \beta^t u(c_t, l_t)$$

where E denotes the expectation and β the discount factor, with $\beta \in (0,1)$. The household has one unit of time each period to divide between leisure and hours of work:

$$(2) \qquad l_t + h_t = 1.$$

The model has a representative firm with a constant returns-to-scale Cobb-Douglas production function that uses capital k_t and labor hours h_t to produce output y_t:

$$(3) \qquad y_t = f(\tilde{z}_t, k_t, h_t) = \exp(\tilde{z}_t) k_t^\theta h_t^{1-\theta}$$

where θ is the capital share parameter and $\tilde{z}_t$ is a stochastic term representing random technological progress. In general, we would assume that $\tilde{z}_t = z_t + \bar{z}t$, where $\bar{z}$ is a constant yielding exogenous deterministic growth and z_t evolves according to the process

$$(4) \qquad z_{t+1} = \rho z_t + \varepsilon_t$$

where $\rho \in (0,1)$ and ε_t is independent and normally distributed with mean zero and standard deviation σ_ε. However, in this paper, we abstract from exogenous growth by setting $\bar{z} = 0$.[7] Capital evolves according to the law of motion

$$(5) \qquad k_{t+1} = (1-\delta)k_t + i_t$$

where δ is the depreciation rate and i_t investment. Finally, the economy must satisfy the resource constraint

$$(6) \qquad c_t + i_t = y_t.$$

We are interested in the competitive equilibrium of this economy. Since externalities or other distortions are not part of this model (or the other models that we consider), the com-

---

[4]We use the letter w because average productivity is proportional to marginal productivity (given our functional forms), which equals the real *wage* rate in our models.

[5]The establishment series is derived from payroll data and measures hours paid for, while the household series is taken from a survey of workers that attempts to measure hours actually worked. These two measures could differ, for example, because some workers may be on sick leave or vacation but still get paid. The household series is a better measure of the labor input, in principle, but because it is based on a survey of workers rather than payroll records, it is probably less accurate.

[6]Efficiency units are constructed from hours series 3 by disaggregating individuals into age and sex groups and weighting the hours of each group by its relative hourly earnings; see Hansen 1991 for details.

[7]Adding exogenous growth does not affect any of the statistics we report (as long as the parameters are recalibrated appropriately) given the way we filter the data; therefore, we set $\bar{z} = 0$ in order to simplify the presentation. See Hansen 1989.

petitive equilibrium is efficient. Hence, we can determine the equilibrium allocation by solving the social planner's problem of maximizing the representative agent's expected utility subject to feasibility constraints. That problem in this case is to maximize U subject to equations (2)–(6) and some initial conditions (k_0,z_0). The solution can be represented as a pair of stationary decision rules for hours and investment, $h_t = h^*(k_t,z_t)$ and $i_t = i^*(k_t,z_t)$, that determine these two variables as functions of the current capital stock and technology shock. The other variables, such as consumption and output, can be determined from the decision rules using the constraints, while prices can be determined from the relevant marginal conditions.

Standard numerical techniques are used to analyze the model. We choose functional forms and parameter values and substitute the constraint $c_t + i_t = f(z_t,k_t,h_t)$ into the instantaneous return function u to reduce the problem to one of maximizing an objective function subject to linear constraints. Then we approximate the return function with a quadratic return function by taking a Taylor's series expansion around the deterministic steady state. The resulting linear-quadratic problem can be easily solved for optimal linear decision rules, $h_t = h(k_t,z_t)$ and $i_t = i(k_t,z_t)$; see Hansen and Prescott 1991 for details. Using these decision rules, we simulate the model, take logarithms of the artificially generated data, apply the Hodrick-Prescott filter, and compute statistics on the deviations (exactly as we did to the actual time series). We run 100 simulations of 179 periods (the number of quarters in our longer data set) and report the means of the statistics across these simulations.

Preferences are specified so that the model is able to capture the long-run growth fact that per-capita hours worked display no trend despite large increases in productivity and real wages. When preferences are time separable, capturing this fact requires that the instantaneous utility function satisfy

(7) $u(c,l) = \log(c) + v(l)$

or

(8) $u(c,l) = c^\sigma v(l)/\sigma$

where σ is a nonzero parameter and $v(l)$ is an increasing and concave function. (See King, Plosser, and Rebelo 1987, for example.) Intuitively, the growth facts imply that the wealth and substitution effects of long-run changes in productivity cancel, so the net effect is that hours worked do not change.[8] We consider only preferences that satisfy (7) or (8); in fact, for convenience, we assume that

(9) $u(c,l) = \log(c) + A\log(l)$.

Parameter values are calibrated as follows. The discount factor is set to $\beta = 0.99$ so as to imply a reasonable steady-state real interest rate of 1 percent per period (where a period is one quarter). The capital share parameter is set to $\theta = 0.36$ to match the average fraction of total income going to capital in the U.S. economy. The depreciation rate is set to $\delta = 0.025$, which (given the above-mentioned values for β and θ) implies a realistic steady-state ratio of capital to output of about 10 and a ratio of investment to output of 0.26. The parameter A in the utility function (9) is chosen so that the steady-state level of hours worked is exactly $h = 1/3$, which matches the fraction of discretionary time spent in market work found in time-use studies (for example, Juster and Stafford 1991). Finally, the parameter ρ in (4) is set to $\rho = 0.95$, and the standard deviation of ε is set to $\sigma_\varepsilon = 0.007$, which are approximately the values settled on by Prescott (1986).

We focus on the following statistics generated by our artificial economy: the standard deviation of output; the standard deviations of consumption, investment, and hours relative to the standard deviation of output; the ratio of the standard deviation of hours to the standard deviation of productivity; and the correlation between hours and productivity. The results are shown in Table 3, along with the values for the same statistics from our longer sample from the U.S. economy (from Table 2). We emphasize the following discrepancies between the simulated and actual data. First, the model has a predicted standard deviation of output which is considerably less than the same statistic for the U.S. economy in either period. Second, the model predicts that σ_h/σ_w is less than one, while it is greater than one in the data. Third, the correlation between hours and productivity in the model is far too high.

The result that output is not as volatile in the model economy as in the actual economy is not too surprising, since the model relies exclusively on a single technology shock, while the actual economy is likely to be subject to other sources of uncertainty as well. The result that in the model hours worked do not fluctuate enough relative to productivity reflects the fact that agents in the model are simply not sufficiently willing to substitute leisure in one period for leisure in other periods. Finally, the result that hours and productivity are too

---

[8]Other specifications can generate a greater short-run response of hours worked to productivity shocks; but while this is desirable from the point of view of explaining cyclical observations, it is inconsistent with the growth facts. For example, the utility function used in Greenwood, Hercowitz, and Huffman 1988, $u(c,l) = v(c+Al)$, has a zero wealth effect and hence a large labor supply elasticity, but implies that hours worked increase over time with productivity growth. This specification is consistent with balanced growth if we assume the parameter A grows at the same average rate as technology. Although such an assumption may seem contrived, it can be justified as the reduced form of a model with home production in which the home and market technologies advance at the same rate on average, as shown in Greenwood, Rogerson, and Wright 1992.

Gary D. Hansen, Randall Wright
Real Business Cycle Theory

Table 3

Cyclical Properties of U.S. and Model-Generated Time Series

Type of Data or Model	% S.D. of Output σ_y	Variable vs. Output				Hours vs. Productivity	
		Consumption σ_c/σ_y	Investment σ_i/σ_y	Hours σ_h/σ_y	Productivity σ_w/σ_y	σ_h/σ_w	cor(h,w)
U.S. Time Series*							
Output	1.92	.45	2.78	—	—	—	—
Hours Worked:							
1. Household Survey (All Industries)	—	—	—	.78	.57	1.37	.07
2. Establishment Survey (Nonag. Industries)	—	—	—	.96	.45	2.15	−.14
Models*							
Standard	1.30	.31	3.15	.49	.53	.94	.93
Nonseparable Leisure	1.51	.29	3.23	.65	.40	1.63	.80
Indivisible Labor	1.73	.29	3.25	.76	.29	2.63	.76
Government Spending	1.24	.54	3.08	.55	.61	.90	.49
Home Production	1.71	.51	2.73	.75	.39	1.92	.49

*U.S. data here are the same as those in Table 2; they are for the longer time period: 1947:1–1991:3.

**The standard deviations and correlations computed from the models' artificial data are the sample means of statistics computed for each of 100 simulations. Each simulation has 179 periods, the number of quarters in the U.S. data.

Source: Citicorp's Citibase data bank

highly correlated in the model reflects the fact that the only impulse driving the system is the aggregate technology shock.

Chart 2 depicts the scatter plot between h and w generated by the model. Heuristically, Chart 2 displays a stable labor supply curve traced out by a labor demand curve shifting over time in response to technology shocks. This picture obviously differs from that in Chart 1.

Nonseparable Leisure

Following Kydland and Prescott (1982), we now attempt to incorporate the idea that instantaneous utility might depend not just on current leisure, but rather on a weighted average of current and past leisure. Hotz, Kydland, and Sedlacek (1988) find evidence in the panel data that this idea is empirically plausible. One interpretation they discuss concerns the fact that individuals need to spend time doing household chores, making repairs, and so on, but after doing so they can neglect these things for a while and spend more time working in the market until the results of their home work depreciate. The important impact of a nonseparable utility specification for

our purposes is that, if leisure in one period is a relatively good substitute for leisure in nearby periods, then agents will be more willing to substitute intertemporally, and this increases the short-run labor supply elasticity.

Assume that the instantaneous utility function is $u(c_t, L_t) = \log(c_t) + A\log(L_t)$, where L_t is given by

$$(10) \quad L_t = \sum_{i=0}^{\infty} a_i l_{t-i}$$

and impose the restriction that the coefficients a_i sum to one. If we also impose the restriction that

$$(11) \quad a_{i+1} = (1-\eta)a_i$$

for $i = 1, 2, ...$, so that the contribution of past leisure to L_t decays geometrically at rate η, then the two parameters a_0 and η determine all of the coefficients in (10). Since L_t, and not simply l_t, now provides utility, individuals are more willing to intertemporally substitute by working more in some periods and less in others. (At the same time, in a deterministic steady

7

Charts 1–5

Hours Worked vs. Productivity in the Data and the Models

Percentage Deviations From Trend

Chart 1   The U.S. Data, 1947:1–1991:3
Based on the Household Survey

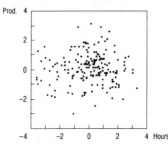

Chart 2   The Standard Model

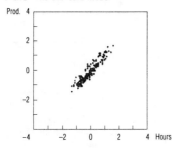

Chart 3   The Nonseparable Leisure Model

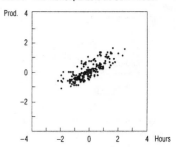

Chart 4   The Government Spending Model
Without Technology Shocks . . .

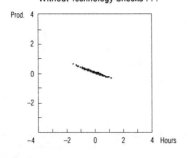

Chart 5   . . . And With Technology Shocks

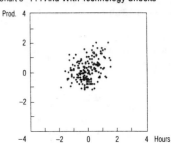

Source of basic data: Citicorp's Citibase data bank

Gary D. Hansen, Randall Wright
Real Business Cycle Theory

state or along a deterministic balanced growth path, this model delivers the correct prediction concerning the effect of productivity growth on hours worked.)

The equilibrium can again be found as the solution to a social planner's problem, which in this case maximizes U subject to (2)–(6), (10)–(11), and initial conditions.[9] The parameter values we use for the preference structure are $a_0 = 0.35$ and $\eta = 0.10$, which are the values implied by the estimates in Hotz, Kydland, and Sedlacek 1988; other parameter values are the same as in the preceding section.

The results are in Table 3. Notice that output is more volatile here than in the standard model, with σ_y increasing from 1.30 to 1.51. Also, the standard deviation of hours worked relative to that of productivity has increased considerably, to $\sigma_h/\sigma_w = 1.63$, and the correlation between hours and productivity has decreased somewhat to 0.80. Chart 3 depicts the scatter plot of h versus w generated by this model. Although these points trace out a labor supply curve that is flatter than the one in Chart 2, the model still does not generate the cloud in Chart 1. We conclude that introducing nonseparable leisure improves things in terms of σ_h/σ_w, but does little for $cor(h,w)$.

Indivisible Labor

We now take up the indivisible labor model of Hansen (1985), in which individuals are constrained to work either zero or $\hat{h}$ hours in each period, where $0 < \hat{h} < 1$. Adding this constraint is meant to capture the idea that the production process has important nonconvexities or fixed costs that may make varying the number of employed workers more efficient than varying hours per worker. As originally shown by Rogerson (1984, 1988), in the equilibrium of this model, individuals will be randomly assigned to employment or unemployment each period, with consumption insurance against the possibility of unemployment. Thus, this model generates fluctuations in the number of employed workers over the cycle. As we shall see, it also has the feature that the elasticity of total hours worked increases relative to the standard model.

Let π_t be the probability that a given agent is employed in period t, so that $H_t = \pi_t \hat{h}$ is per-capita hours worked if we assume a large number of ex ante identical agents. Also, let c_{0t} denote the consumption of an unemployed agent and c_{1t} the consumption of an employed agent. As part of the dynamic social planning problem, π_t, c_{0t}, and c_{1t} are chosen to maximize

$$(12) \quad Eu(c_t,l_t) = \pi_t u(c_{1t}, 1-\hat{h}) + (1-\pi_t)u(c_{0t}, 1)$$

in each period, subject to the following constraint:

$$(13) \quad \pi_t c_{1t} + (1-\pi_t)c_{0t} = c_t$$

where c_t is total per-capita consumption. When $u(c,l) = \log(c) + A\log(l)$, the solution can be shown to imply that $c_{1t} = c_{0t} = c_t$.[10]

Therefore, in the case under consideration, expected utility can be written

$$(14) \quad Eu(c_t,l_t) = \log(c_t) + \pi_t A\log(1-\hat{h}) = \log(c_t) - BH_t$$

where $B \equiv -A\log(1-\hat{h})/\hat{h} > 0$ and, as defined above, H_t is hours worked per capita. Therefore, the indivisible labor model is equivalent to a divisible labor model with preferences described by

$$(15) \quad \tilde{U} = E\sum_{t=0}^{\infty}\beta^t \tilde{u}(c_t,H_t)$$

where $\tilde{u}(c_t,H_t) = \log(c_t) - BH_t$. Based on this equivalence, we can solve the indivisible labor model as if it were a divisible labor model with a different instantaneous utility function, by maximizing $\tilde{U}$ subject to (2)–(6) and initial conditions.[11]

Two features of the indivisible labor economy bear mention. First, as discussed earlier, fluctuations in the labor input come about by fluctuations in employment rather than fluctuations in hours per employed worker. This is the opposite of the standard model and is perhaps preferable, since the majority of the variance in total hours worked in the U.S. data is accounted for by variance in the number of workers.[12] Second, the indivisible labor model generates a large intertemporal substitution effect for the representative agent because instantaneous utility, $\tilde{u}(c,H)$, is linear in H, and therefore the indifference curves between leisure in any two periods are linear. This is true despite the fact that hours worked are constant for a continuously employed worker.

Return to Table 3 for the results of our simulations of this model.[13] The indivisible labor model is considerably more volatile than the standard model, with σ_y increasing from 1.30 to 1.73. Also, σ_h/σ_w has increased from 0.94 to 2.63, actually

---

[9]For the solution techniques that we use, this problem is expressed as a dynamic program. The stock of accumulated past leisure is defined to be X_t, and we write

$$L_t = a_0 l_t + \eta(1-a_0)X_t,$$
$$X_{t+1} = (1-\eta)X_t + l_t.$$

These equations replace (10) and (11) in the recursive formulation.

[10]This implication follows from the fact that u is separable in c and l and does not hold for general utility functions; see Rogerson and Wright 1988.

[11]Since the solution to the planner's problem in the indivisible labor model involves random employment, we need to use some type of lottery or sunspot equilibrium concept to support it as a decentralized equilibrium; see Shell and Wright, forthcoming.

[12]See Hansen 1985 for the U.S. data. Note, however, that European data display greater variance in hours per worker than in the number of workers; see Wright 1991, p. 17.

[13]The new parameter B is calibrated so that steady-state hours are again equal to 1/3; the other parameters are the same as in the standard model.

somewhat high when compared to the U.S. data. Of course, this model is extreme in the sense that all fluctuations in the labor input result from changes in the number of employed workers, and models in which both the number of employed workers and the number of hours per worker vary fall somewhere between the standard divisible labor model and the indivisible labor model with respect to this statistic. (See Kydland and Prescott 1991 or Cho and Cooley 1989, for example.) Finally, the model implies that $\text{cor}(h,w) = 0.76$, slightly lower than the models discussed above but still too high. For the sake of brevity, the scatter plot between h and w is omitted; for the record, it looks similar to the one in Chart 3, although the indivisible labor model displays a little more variation in hours worked.

Government Spending

We now introduce stochastic government spending, as in Christiano and Eichenbaum 1992. (That paper also provides motivation and references to related work.)

Assume that government spending, g_t, is governed by

(16) $\log(g_{t+1}) = (1-\lambda)\log(\bar{g}) + \lambda\log(g_t) + \mu_t$

where $\lambda \in (0,1)$ and μ_t is independent and normally distributed with mean zero and standard deviation σ_μ. Furthermore, as in Christiano and Eichenbaum 1992, assume that μ_t is independent of the technology shock. Also assume that government spending is financed by lump-sum taxation and that it enters neither the utility function nor the production function.[14] Then the equilibrium allocation for the model can be found by solving the planner's problem of maximizing U subject to (16), (2)–(5), and, instead of (6), the new resource constraint

(17) $c_t + i_t + g_t = y_t$.

An increase in g_t is a pure drain on output here. Since leisure is a normal good, the negative wealth effect of an increase in g_t induces households to work more. Intuitively, shocks to g_t shift the labor supply curve along the demand curve at the same time that technology shocks shift the labor demand curve along the supply curve. This first effect produces a negative relationship between hours and productivity, while the second effect produces a positive relationship. The net effect on the correlation between hours and productivity in the model depends on the size of the g_t shocks and on the implied wealth effect, which depends, among other things, on the parameter λ in the law of motion for g_t (because temporary shocks have a smaller wealth effect than permanent shocks). Hence, the calibration of this law of motion is critical. An ordinary least squares regression based on equation (16) yields estimates for λ and σ_μ of 0.96 and 0.021, respec-

tively. (In addition, the average of g_t/y_t in our sample, which is 0.22, is used to calibrate $\bar{g}$.)

For the results, turn again to Table 3. The government spending model actually behaves very much like the standard model, except that the correlation between hours and productivity decreases to $\text{cor}(h,w) = 0.49$, which is better than the previous models although still somewhat larger than the U.S. data. Chart 4 displays the scatter plot generated by the model with only government spending shocks (that is, with the variance in the technology shock set to $\sigma_\varepsilon = 0$), and Chart 5 displays the scatter plot for the model with both shocks. These charts illustrate the intuition behind the results: technology shocks shift labor demand and trace out the labor supply curve, government shocks shift labor supply and trace out the labor demand curve, and both shocks together generate a combination of these two effects. The net results will be somewhat sensitive to the size of and the response to the two shocks; however, for the estimated parameter values, this model generates a scatter plot that is closer to the data than does the standard model.[15]

Home Production

We now consider the household production model analyzed in Benhabib, Rogerson, and Wright 1991. (That paper also provides motivation and references to related work.)

Instantaneous utility is still written $u(c,l)=\log(c)+A\log(l)$, but now consumption and leisure have a different interpretation. We assume that

(18) $c_t = [ac_{Mt}^e + (1-a)c_{Ht}^e]^{1/e}$

(19) $l_t = 1 - h_{Mt} - h_{Ht}$

---

[14] A generalization is to assume that instantaneous utility can be written $u(C,l)$, where $C = C(c,g)$ depends on private consumption and government spending. The special case where $C = c$ is the one we consider here, while the case where $C = c + g$ can be interpreted as the standard model, since then increases in g can be exactly offset by reductions in c and the other variables will not change. Therefore, the model with $C = c + g$ generates exactly the same values of all variables, except that $c + g$ replaces c. The assumption that c and g are perfect substitutes implies that they are perfectly negatively correlated, however. A potentially interesting generalization would be to assume that

$$C(c,g) = [\alpha c^\varphi + (1-\alpha)g^\varphi]^{1/\varphi}$$

where $1/(1-\varphi)$ is the elasticity of substitution.

[15] The size of the wealth effect depends on the extent to which public consumption and private consumption are substitutes. For example, if they were perfect substitutes, then a unit increase in g would simply crowd out a unit of c with no effect on hours worked or any of the other endogenous variables. We follow Christiano and Eichenbaum 1992 in considering the extreme case where g does not enter utility at all. Also, the results depend on the (counterfactual) assumption that the shocks to government spending and technology are statistically independent. Finally, the results depend on the estimates of the parameters in the law of motion (16). The estimates in the text are from the period 1947:1–1991:3 and are close to the values used in Christiano and Eichenbaum 1992. Estimates from our shorter sample period, 1955:3–1988:2, imply a higher λ of 0.98 and a lower σ_μ of 0.012, which in simulations yield $\text{cor}(h,w) = 0.65$.

Gary D. Hansen, Randall Wright
Real Business Cycle Theory

where c_{Mt} is consumption of a market-produced good, c_{Ht} is consumption of a home-produced good, h_{Mt} is hours worked in the market sector, and h_{Ht} is hours worked in the home, all in period t. Notice that the two types of work are assumed to be perfect substitutes, while the two consumption goods are combined by an aggregator that implies a constant elasticity of substitution equal to $1/(1-e)$.

This model has two technologies, one for market production and one for home production:

$$(20) \quad f(z_{Mt}, k_{Mt}, h_{Mt}) = \exp(z_{Mt}) k_{Mt}^{\theta} h_{Mt}^{1-\theta}$$

$$(21) \quad g(z_{Ht}, k_{Ht}, h_{Ht}) = \exp(z_{Ht}) k_{Ht}^{\eta} h_{Ht}^{1-\eta}$$

where θ and η are the capital share parameters. The two technology shocks follow the processes

$$(22) \quad z_{Mt+1} = \rho z_{Mt} + \varepsilon_{Mt}$$

$$(23) \quad z_{Ht+1} = \rho z_{Ht} + \varepsilon_{Ht}$$

where the two innovations are normally distributed with standard deviations σ_M and σ_H, have a contemporaneous correlation $\gamma = \text{cor}(\varepsilon_{Mt}, \varepsilon_{Ht})$, and are independent over time. In each period, a capital constraint holds: $k_{Mt} + k_{Ht} = k_t$, where total capital evolves according to $k_{t+1} = (1-\delta) k_t + i_t$. Finally, the constraints

$$(24) \quad c_{Mt} + i_t = f(z_{Mt}, k_{Mt}, h_{Mt})$$

$$(25) \quad c_{Ht} = g(z_{Ht}, k_{Ht}, h_{Ht})$$

imply that all new capital is produced in the market sector.

The parameters β, θ, δ, and ρ are set to the values used in the previous sections. The two utility parameters A and a are set to deliver steady-state values of $h_M = 0.33$ and $h_H = 0.28$, as found in the time-use studies (Juster and Stafford 1991), and the capital share parameter in the household sector is set to $\eta = 0.08$, implying a steady-state ratio of c_H/c_M of approximately $1/4$.[16] The variances of the two shocks are assumed to be the same: $\sigma_H = \sigma_M = 0.007$. The parameter e, which determines the elasticity of substitution between c_M and c_H, and γ, which is the correlation between ε_M and ε_H, are set to the benchmark values used in Benhabib, Rogerson, and Wright 1991: $e = 0.8$ and $\gamma = 2/3$.

The results are at the bottom of Table 3. In the home production model, output is more volatile than in the standard model and about as volatile as in the indivisible labor model. The standard deviation of hours relative to productivity has increased considerably compared to the standard model, to

$\sigma_h/\sigma_w = 1.92$. And $\text{cor}(h, w)$ has decreased to 0.49, the same as in the model with government spending.[17]

The intuition behind these results is that agents substitute in and out of market activity more in the home production model than in the standard model because they can use non-market activity as a buffer. The degree to which agents do this depends on their willingness to substitute c_M for c_H, as measured by e, and on their incentive to move production between the two sectors, as measured by γ. (Lower values of γ entail more frequent divergence between z_M and z_H and, hence, more frequent opportunities to specialize over time.) Note that some aspects of the results do not actually depend on home production being stochastic.[18] However, the correlation between productivity and market hours does depend critically on the size of the home technology shock, exactly as it depends on the size of the second shock in the government spending model. We omit the home production model's scatter plot between h and w, but it looks similar to that of the model with government shocks.

Conclusion

We have presented several extensions to the standard real business cycle model and analyzed the extent to which they help account for the U.S. business cycle facts, especially those facts concerning hours and productivity. Introducing nonseparable leisure, indivisible labor, or home production increases the elasticity of hours worked with respect to short-run productivity changes. Introducing a second shock, either to government spending or to the home production function, reduces the correlation between hours worked and productivity.[19]

Note that our goal has not been to convince you that any of these models is unequivocally to be preferred. Our goal has been simply to explain some commonly used real business cycle models and compare their implications for the basic labor market facts.

---

[16]The two parameters θ and η can be calibrated to match the observed average levels of market capital (producer durables and nonresidential structures) and home capital (consumer durables and residential structures) in the U.S. economy. This requires a lower value for θ and a higher value for η than used here, as discussed in Greenwood, Rogerson, and Wright 1992.

[17]The exact results are somewhat sensitive to changes in the parameters e and γ, for reasons discussed in the next paragraph.

[18]Even if the variance of the shock to the home technology is set to zero, shocks to the market technology will still induce relative productivity differentials across sectors. And even if the two shocks are perfectly correlated and of the same magnitude, agents will still have an incentive to switch between sectors over time because capital is produced exclusively in the market. It is these effects that are behind the increase in the labor supply elasticity.

[19]Other models can be constructed by combining the extensions considered here. Other extensions not considered here can also affect the implications of the model for the labor market facts, including distorting taxation as in Braun 1990 or McGrattan 1991 and nominal contracting as in Cho and Cooley 1990.

References

Backus, David K., and Kehoe, Patrick J. Forthcoming. International evidence on the historical properties of business cycles. *American Economic Review.*

Benhabib, Jess; Rogerson, Richard; and Wright, Randall. 1991. Homework in macroeconomics: Household production and aggregate fluctuations. *Journal of Political Economy* 99 (December): 1166–87.

Blackburn, Keith, and Ravn, Morten O. 1991. Contemporary macroeconomic fluctuations: An international perspective. Memo 1991-12. University of Aarhus Center for International Economics.

Braun, R. Anton. 1990. The dynamic interaction of distortionary taxes and aggregate variables in postwar U.S. data. Working Paper. University of Virginia.

Cho, Jang-Ok, and Cooley, Thomas F. 1989. Employment and hours over the business cycle. Working Paper 132. Rochester Center for Economic Research. University of Rochester.

_____. 1990. The business cycle with nominal contracts. Working Paper 260. Rochester Center for Economic Research. University of Rochester.

Christiano, Lawrence J., and Eichenbaum, Martin. 1992. Current real-business-cycle theories and aggregate labor-market fluctuations. *American Economic Review* 82 (June): 430–50.

Greenwood, Jeremy; Hercowitz, Zvi; and Huffman, Gregory W. 1988. Investment, capacity utilization and the real business cycle. *American Economic Review* 78 (June): 402–17.

Greenwood, Jeremy; Rogerson, Richard; and Wright, Randall. 1992. Household production in real business cycle theory. Manuscript. University of Western Ontario.

Hansen, Gary D. 1985. Indivisible labor and the business cycle. *Journal of Monetary Economics* 16 (November): 309–27.

_____. 1989. Technical progress and aggregate fluctuations. Department of Economics Working Paper 546. University of California, Los Angeles.

_____. 1991. The cyclical and secular behavior of the labor input: Comparing efficiency units and hours worked. Manuscript. University of California, Los Angeles.

Hansen, Gary D., and Prescott, Edward C. 1991. Recursive methods for computing equilibria of business cycle models. Discussion Paper 36. Institute for Empirical Macroeconomics (Federal Reserve Bank of Minneapolis).

Hotz, V. Joseph; Kydland, Finn E.; and Sedlacek, Guilherme L. 1988. Intertemporal preferences and labor supply. *Econometrica* 56 (March): 335–60.

Juster, F. Thomas, and Stafford, Frank P. 1991. The allocation of time: Empirical findings, behavioral models, and problems of measurement. *Journal of Economic Literature* 29 (June): 471–522.

King, Robert G.; Plosser, Charles I.; and Rebelo, Sergio T. 1987. Production, growth and cycles: Technical appendix. Manuscript. University of Rochester.

Kydland, Finn E., and Prescott, Edward C. 1982. Time to build and aggregate fluctuations. *Econometrica* 50 (November): 1345–70.

_____. 1990. Business cycles: Real facts and a monetary myth. *Federal Reserve Bank of Minneapolis Quarterly Review* 14 (Spring): 3–18.

_____. 1991. Hours and employment variation in business cycle theory. *Economic Theory* 1: 63–81.

McGrattan, Ellen R. 1991. The macroeconomic effects of distortionary taxation. Discussion Paper 37. Institute for Empirical Macroeconomics (Federal Reserve Bank of Minneapolis).

Prescott, Edward C. 1986. Theory ahead of business cycle measurement. *Federal Reserve Bank of Minneapolis Quarterly Review* 10 (Fall): 9–22.

Rogerson, Richard. 1984. Topics in the theory of labor markets. Ph.D. dissertation. University of Minnesota.

_____. 1988. Indivisible labor, lotteries and equilibrium. *Journal of Monetary Economics* 21 (January): 3–16.

Rogerson, Richard, and Wright, Randall. 1988. Involuntary unemployment in economies with efficient risk sharing. *Journal of Monetary Economics* 22 (November): 501–15.

Shell, Karl, and Wright, Randall. Forthcoming. Indivisibilities, lotteries and sunspot equilibria. *Economic Theory.*

Wright, Randall. 1991. The labor market implications of unemployment insurance and short-time compensation. *Federal Reserve Bank of Minneapolis Quarterly Review* 15 (Summer): 11–19.

Current Real-Business-Cycle Theories and Aggregate Labor-Market Fluctuations

By Lawrence J. Christiano and Martin Eichenbaum[*]

Hours worked and the return to working are weakly correlated. Traditionally, the ability to account for this fact has been a litmus test for macroeconomic models. Existing real-business-cycle models fail this test dramatically. We modify prototypical real-business-cycle models by allowing government consumption shocks to influence labor-market dynamics. This modification can, in principle, bring the models into closer conformity with the data. Our empirical results indicate that it does. (JEL E32, C12, C52, C13, C51)

In this paper, we assess the quantitative implications of existing real-business-cycle (RBC) models for the time-series properties of average productivity and hours worked. We find that the single most salient shortcoming of existing RBC models lies in their predictions for the correlation between these variables. Existing RBC models predict that this correlation is well in excess of 0.9, whereas the actual correlation is much closer to zero.[1] This shortcoming leads us to add to the RBC framework aggregate demand shocks that arise from stochastic movements in government consumption. According to our empirical results, this change substantially improves the models' empirical performance.

The ability to account for the observed correlation between the return to working and the number of hours worked has traditionally been a litmus test for aggregate economic models. Thomas J. Sargent (1987 p. 468), for example, states that one of the primary empirical patterns casting doubt on the classical and Keynesian models has been the observation by John T. Dunlop (1938) and Lorie Tarshis (1939) "alleging the failure of real wages to move countercyclically." The classical and Keynesian models share the assumption that real wages and hours worked lie on a stable, downward-sloped marginal productivity-of-labor curve.[2] Consequently, they both counterfactually predict a strong negative correlation between real wages and hours worked. Modern versions of what Sargent (1987 p. 468) calls the "Dunlop–Tarshis observation" continue to play a central role in assessing the empirical plausibility of different business-cycle models.[3] In discussing Stanley Fischer's (1977)

*Christiano: Federal Reserve Bank of Minneapolis, Minneapolis, MN 55480; Eichenbaum: Northwestern University, Evanston, IL 60208, National Bureau of Economic Research, and Federal Reserve Bank of Chicago. This paper is a substantially revised version of NBER Working Paper No. 2700, "Is Theory Really Ahead of Measurement? Current Real Business Cycle Theories and Aggregate Labor Market Fluctuations." We thank Rao Aiyagari, Paul Gomme, Finn Kydland, Ed Prescott, and Mark Watson for helpful conversations. Any views expressed here are ours and not necessarily those of any part of the Federal Reserve System.

[1] This finding is closely related to Bennett McCallum's (1989) observation that existing RBC models generate grossly counterfactual predictions for the correlation between average productivity and output.

[2] As John Maynard Keynes (1935 p. 17) says, "...I am not disputing this vital fact which the classical economists have (rightly) asserted as indefeasible. In a given state of organisation, equipment and technique, the real wage earned by a unit of labour has a unique (inverse) correlation with the volume of employment."

[3] For example, Robert J. Barro and Herschel I. Grossman (1971) cite the Dunlop–Tarshis observation to motivate their work on disequilibrium theories. Also, Edmund S. Phelps and Sidney G. Winter, Jr. (1970 p. 310) and Franco Modigliani (1977 p. 7) use this observation to motivate their work on noncompetitive approaches to macroeconomics. Finally, Robert E. Lucas, Jr. (1981 p. 13) cites the Dunlop–Tarshis observation in motivating his work on capacity and overtime.

sticky-wage business-cycle model, for example, Bennett McCallum (1989 p. 191) states that

> ...the main trouble with the Fischer model concerns its real wage behavior. In particular, to the extent that the model itself explains fluctuations in output and empløyment, these should be inversely related to real wage movements: output should be high, according to the model, when real wages are low. But in the actual U.S. economy there is no strong empirical relation of that type.

In remarks particularly relevant to RBC models, Robert E. Lucas (1981 p. 226) says that "observed real wages are not constant over the cycle, but neither do they exhibit consistent pro- or countercyclical tendencies. This suggests that any attempt to assign systematic real wage movements a central role in an explanation of business cycles is doomed to failure." Existing RBC models fall prey to this (less well-known) Lucas critique. Unlike the classical and Keynesian models, which understate the correlation between hours worked and the return to working, existing RBC models grossly overstate that correlation. According to existing RBC models, the only impulses generating fluctuations in aggregate employment are stochastic shifts in the marginal product of labor. Loosely speaking, the time series on hours worked and the return to working are modeled as the intersection of a stochastic labor-demand curve with a fixed labor-supply curve. Not surprisingly, therefore, these theories predict a strong positive correlation between hours worked and the return to working.[4]

Several strategies exist for modeling the observed weak correlation between measures of these variables. One is to consider models in which the return to working is unaffected by shocks to agents' environments, regardless of whether the shocks are to aggregate demand or to aggregate supply. Pursuing this strategy, Olivier Jean Blanchard and Stanley Fischer (1989 p. 372) argue that the key assumption of Keynesian macro models—nominal wage and price stickiness—is motivated by the view that aggregate demand shocks affect employment but not real wages. Another strategy is simply to abandon one-shock models of aggregate fluctuations and suppose that the business cycle is generated by a variety of impulses. Under these conditions, the Dunlop–Tarshis observation imposes no restrictions per se on the response of real wages to any particular type of shock. Given a specific structural model, however, it does impose restrictions on the relative frequency of different types of shocks. This suggests that one strategy for reconciling existing RBC models with the Dunlop–Tarshis observation is to find measurable economic impulses that shift the labor-supply function.[5] With different impulses shifting the labor-supply and labor-demand functions,

---

[4]Although Finn E. Kydland and Edward C. Prescott (1982) and Prescott (1986) never explicitly examine the hours/real-wage correlation implication of existing RBC models, Prescott (1986 p. 21) does implicitly acknowledge that the failure to account for the Dunlop–Tarshis observation is the key remaining deviation between economic theory and observations: "The key deviation is that the empirical labor elasticity of output is less than predicted by theory." To see the connec-

tions, denote the empirical labor elasticity by η. By definition, $\eta \equiv \text{corr}(y,n)\sigma_y/\sigma_n$, where $\text{corr}(i,j)$ is the correlation between i and j, σ_i is the standard deviation of i, y is the logarithm of detrended output, and n is the logarithm of hours. Simple arithmetic yields $\text{corr}(y-n,n) = [\eta - 1](\sigma_n/\sigma_{y-n})$. If, as Prescott claims, RBC models do well at reproducing the empirical estimates of σ_n/σ_{y-n}, then saying that the models overstate η is equivalent to saying that they overstate $\text{corr}(y-n,n)$. In Prescott's model and with his assumed market structure, $\text{corr}(y-n,n)$ is exactly the same as the correlation between real wages and hours worked. (Also, under log detrending, $y - n$ is log detrended productivity.)

[5]An alternative strategy is pursued by Valerie R. Bencivenga (1992), who allows for shocks to labor suppliers' preferences. Matthew D. Shapiro and Mark W. Watson (1988) also allow for unobservable shocks to the labor-supply function. Jess Benhabib et al. (1991) and Jeremy Greenwood and Zvi Hercowitz (1991) explore the role of shocks to the home production technology.

432   THE AMERICAN ECONOMIC REVIEW   JUNE 1992

there is no a priori reason for hours worked to be correlated in any particular way with the return to working.

Candidates for such shocks include tax rate changes, innovations to the money supply, demographic changes in the labor force, and shocks to government spending. We focus on the last of these. By ruling out any role for government-consumption shocks in labor-market dynamics, existing RBC models implicitly assume that public and private consumption have the same impact on the marginal utility of private spending. Robert J. Barro (1981, 1987) and David Alan Aschauer (1985) argue that if $1 of additional public consumption drives down the marginal utility of private consumption by less than does $1 of additional private consumption, then positive shocks to government consumption in effect shift the labor-supply curve outward. With diminishing labor productivity, but without technology shocks, such impulses will generate a negative correlation between hours worked and the return to working in RBC models.

In our empirical work, we measure the return to working by the average productivity of labor rather than real wages. We do this for both empirical and theoretical reasons. From an empirical point of view, our results are not very sensitive to whether the return to working is measured by real wages or average productivity: Neither displays a strong positive correlation with hours worked, so it seems appropriate to refer to the low correlation between the return to working and hours worked as the *Dunlop–Tarshis observation*, regardless of whether the return to working is measured by the real wage or average productivity. From a theoretical point of view, a variety of ways exist to support the quantity allocations emerging from RBC models. By using average productivity as our measure of the return to working, we avoid imposing the assumption that the market structure is one in which real wages are equated to the marginal product of labor on a period-by-period basis. Also, existing parameterizations of RBC models imply that marginal and average productivity of labor are pro-

portional to each other. For the calculations we perform, the two are interchangeable.

Our empirical results show that incorporating government into the analysis substantially improves the RBC models' performance. Interestingly, the impact of this perturbation is about as large as allowing for nonconvexities in labor supply of the type stressed by Gary D. Hansen (1985) and Richard Rogerson (1988). Once government is incorporated into the analysis, we cannot reject the hypothesis that a version of the Hansen-Rogerson indivisible-labor model is consistent with both the observed correlation between hours worked and average productivity and the observed volatility of hours worked relative to average productivity. This is not true if government is excluded from the analysis.

The paper is organized as follows. In Section I, we describe a general equilibrium model that nests as special cases a variety of existing RBC models. In Section II, we present our econometric methodology for estimating and evaluating the empirical performance of the model. In Section III, we present our empirical results. In Section IV, we offer some concluding remarks.

I. Two Prototypical Real-Business-Cycle Models

In this section, we present two prototypical real-business-cycle models. One is a stochastic version of the one-sector growth model considered by Kydland and Prescott (1980 p. 174). The other is a version of the model economy considered by Hansen (1985) in which labor supply is indivisible. In both of our models, we relax the assumption implicit in existing RBC models that public and private spending have identical effects on the marginal utility of private consumption.

We make the standard RBC assumption that the time series on the beginning-of-period-t per capita stock of capital (k_t), private time-t consumption (c_t^p) and hours worked at time t (n_t) correspond to the solution of a social-planning problem which can be decentralized as a Pareto-optimal competitive equilibrium. The following problem nests both our models as special cases. Let N be a positive scalar that denotes the time-t endowment of the representative consumer, and let γ be a positive scalar. The social planner ranks streams of consumption services (c_t), leisure $(N - n_t)$, and publicly provided goods and services (g_t) according to the criterion function

$$(1) \quad E_0 \sum_{t=0}^{\infty} \beta^t \{\ln(c_t) + \gamma V(N - n_t)\}.$$

Following Barro (1981, 1987), Roger C. Kormendi (1983), and Aschauer (1985), we suppose that consumption services are related to private and public consumption as follows:

$$(2) \quad c_t = c_t^p + \alpha g_t$$

where α is a parameter that governs the sign and magnitude of the derivative of the marginal utility of c_t^p with respect to g_t.[6] Throughout, we assume that agents view g_t as an uncontrollable stochastic process. In addition, we suppose that g_t does not depend on the current or past values of the endogenous variables in the model.[7]

We consider two specifications for the function $V(\cdot)$. In the *divisible-labor model*, $V(\cdot)$ is given by

$$(3) \quad V(N - n_t) = \ln(N - n_t) \qquad \text{for all } t.$$

In the *indivisible-labor model*, $V(\cdot)$ is given

by

$$(4) \quad V(N - n_t) = N - n_t \qquad \text{for all } t.$$

This specification can be interpreted in at least two ways. One is that the specification simply reflects the assumption that individual utility functions are linear in leisure. The other interpretation builds on the assumption that labor supply is indivisible. Under this second interpretation, individuals can either work some positive number of hours or not work at all. Assuming that agents' utility functions are separable across consumption and leisure, Rogerson (1988) shows that a market structure in which individuals choose lotteries rather than hours worked will support a Pareto-optimal allocation of consumption and leisure. The lottery determines whether individuals work or not. Under this interpretation, (4) represents a reduced-form preference-ordering that can be used to derive the Pareto-optimal allocation by solving a fictitious social-planning problem. This is the specification used by Hansen (1985).

Per capita output y_t is produced using the Cobb-Douglas production function

$$(5) \quad y_t = (z_t n_t)^{(1-\theta)} k_t^\theta$$

where $0 < \theta < 1$ and z_t is an aggregate shock to technology that has the time-series representation

$$(6) \quad z_t = z_{t-1} \exp(\lambda_t).$$

Here λ_t is a serially uncorrelated independent and identically distributed process with mean λ and standard error σ_λ. The aggregate resource constraint is given by

$$(7) \quad c_t^p + g_t + k_{t+1} - (1-\delta)k_t \le y_t.$$

That is, per capita consumption and investment cannot exceed per capita output.

At time 0, the social planner chooses contingency plans for $\{c_t^p, k_{t+1}, n_t : t \ge 0\}$ to maximize (1) subject to (3) or (4), (5)–(7), k_0, and a law of motion for g_t. Because of the nonsatiation assumption implicit in (1),

---

[6] We can generalize the criterion function (1) by writing it as $\ln(c_t) + \gamma V(N - n_t) + \phi(g_t)$, where $\phi(\cdot)$ is some positive concave function. As long as g_t is modeled as an exogenous stochastic process, the presence of such a term has no impact on the competitive equilibrium. However, the presence of $\phi(g_t) > 0$ means that agents do not necessarily feel worse off when g_t is increased. The fact that we have set $\phi(\cdot) \equiv 0$ reflects our desire to minimize notation, not the view that the optimal level of g_t is zero.

[7] Under this assumption, g_t is isomorphic to an exogenous shock to preferences and endowments. Consequently, existing theorems which establish that the competitive equilibrium and the social-planning problem coincide are applicable.

we can, without loss of generality, impose strict equality in (7). Substituting (2), (5), and this version of (7) into (1), we obtain the following *social-planning problem*: maximize

$$(8) \quad E_0 \sum_{t=0}^{\infty} \beta^t \Big\{ \ln\big[(z_t n_t)^{(1-\theta)} k_t^\theta$$

$$+ (1-\delta) k_t - k_{t+1}$$

$$+ (\alpha - 1) g_t \Big]$$

$$+ \gamma V(N - n_t) \Big\}$$

subject to k_0, a law of motion for g_t, and $V(\cdot)$ given by either (3) or (4), by choice of contingency plans for $\{k_{t+1}, n_t : t \ge 0\}$.

It is convenient to represent the social-planning problem (8) in a way such that all of the planner's decision variables converge in nonstochastic steady state. To that end, we define the following detrended variables:

$$(9) \qquad \bar{k}_{t+1} = k_{t+1} / z_t$$

$$\bar{y}_t = y_t / z_t$$

$$\bar{c}_t = c_t / z_t$$

$$\bar{g}_t = g_t / z_t .$$

To complete our specification of agents' environment, we assume that $\bar{g}_t$ evolves according to

$$(10) \qquad \ln(\bar{g}_t) = (1 - \rho)\ln(\bar{g})$$

$$+ \rho \ln(\bar{g}_{t-1}) + \mu_t$$

where $\ln(\bar{g})$ is the mean of $\ln(\bar{g}_t)$, $|\rho| < 1$, and μ_t is the innovation in $\ln(\bar{g}_t)$ with standard deviation σ_μ. Notice that g_t has two components, z_t and $\bar{g}_t$. Movements in z_t produce permanent changes in the level of government consumption, whereas movements in $\bar{g}_t$ produce temporary changes in g_t. With this specification, the factors giving rise to permanent shifts in government consumption are the same as those that perma-

nently enhance the economy's productive ability.

Substituting (9) into (8), we obtain the criterion function:

$$(11) \quad \kappa + E_0 \sum_{t=0}^{\infty} \beta^t r\left(n_t, \bar{k}_t, \bar{k}_{t+1}, \bar{g}_t, \lambda_t \right)$$

where

$$(12) \quad r\left(n_t, \bar{k}_t, \bar{k}_{t+1}, \bar{g}_t, \lambda_t \right)$$

$$= \Big\{ \ln\big[n_t^{(1-\theta)} \bar{k}_t^\theta \exp(-\theta \lambda_t)$$

$$+ \exp(-\lambda_t)(1-\delta)\bar{k}_t$$

$$- \bar{k}_{t+1} + (\alpha - 1)\bar{g}_t \big]$$

$$+ \gamma V(N - n_t) \Big\}$$

and where $\kappa = E_0 \sum_{t=0}^{\infty} \beta^t \ln(z_t)$ and $V(\cdot)$ is given by either (3) or (4). Consequently, the original planning problem is equivalent to the problem of maximizing (11), subject to $\bar{k}_0$, (10), and (12), and $V(\cdot)$ is given by either (3) or (4). Since κ is beyond the planner's control, it can be disregarded in solving the planner's problem.

The only case in which an analytical solution for this problem is possible occurs when $\alpha = \delta = 1$ and the function $V(\cdot)$ is given by (3). John B. Long, Jr., and Charles I. Plosser (1983) provide one analysis of this case. Analytical solutions are not available for general values of α and δ. We use Christiano's (1988) log-linear modification of the procedure used by Kydland and Prescott (1982) to obtain an approximate solution to our social-planning problem. In particular, we approximate the optimal decision rules with the solution to the linear-quadratic problem obtained when the function r in (12) is replaced by a function R, which is quadratic in $\ln(n_t)$, $\ln(\bar{k}_t)$, $\ln(\bar{k}_{t+1})$, $\ln(\bar{g}_t)$, and λ_t. The function R is the second-order Taylor expansion of $r[\exp(A_1), \exp(A_2), \exp(A_3), \exp(A_4), A_5]$ about the point

$$[A_1, A_2, A_3, A_4, A_5]$$

$$= \big[\ln(n), \ln(\bar{k}), \ln(\bar{k}), \ln(\bar{g}), \lambda \big].$$

Here n and $\bar{k}$ denote the steady-state values of n_t and k_t in the nonstochastic version of (11) obtained by setting $\sigma_\lambda = \sigma_\mu = 0$.

Results in Christiano (1988) establish that the decision rules which solve this problem are of the form

$$(13) \quad \bar{k}_{t+1} = \bar{k}\left(\bar{k}_t / \bar{k}\right)^{r_k}\left(\bar{g}_t / \bar{g}\right)^{d_k}$$

$$\times \exp\left[e_k(\lambda_t - \lambda)\right]$$

and

$$(14) \quad n_t = n\left(\bar{k}_t / \bar{k}\right)^{r_n}\left(\bar{g}_t / \bar{g}\right)^{d_n} \exp\left[e_n(\lambda_t - \lambda)\right].$$

In (13) and (14), r_k, d_k, e_k, r_n, d_n, and e_n are scalar functions of the model's underlying structural parameters.[8]

To gain intuition for the role of $\bar{g}_t$ in aggregate labor-market fluctuations, it is useful to discuss the impact of three key parameters (α, ρ, and γ) on the equilibrium response of n_t to $\bar{g}_t$. This response is governed by the coefficient d_n.

First, notice that when $\alpha = 1$ the only way c_t^p and g_t enter into the social planner's preferences and constraints is through their sum, $c_t^p + g_t$. Thus, exogenous shocks to g_t induce one-for-one offsetting shocks in c_t^p, leaving other variables like y_t, k_{t+1}, and n_t unaffected. This implies that the coefficients d_n and d_k in the planner's decision rules for k_{t+1} and n_t both equal zero. Consequently, the absence of a role for g_t in existing RBC models can be interpreted as reflecting the assumption that $\alpha = 1$.

Second, consider what happens when $\alpha < 1$. The limiting case of $\alpha = 0$ is particularly useful for gaining intuition. Government consumption now is formally equivalent to a pure resource drain on the economy; agents respond to an increase in government consumption as if they had suf-

fered a reduction in their wealth. (As footnote 6 indicates, this does not imply that they have suffered a reduction in utility.) The coefficient d_n is positive, since we assume that leisure is a normal good. That is, increases in $\bar{g}_t$ are associated with increases in n_t and decreases in y_t / n_t. Continuity suggests that d_n is decreasing in α. The same logic suggests that d_n is an increasing function of ρ, since the wealth effect of a given shock to $\bar{g}_t$ is increasing in ρ. For a formal analysis of the effects of government consumption in a more general environment than the one considered here, see S. Rao Aiyagari et al. (1990).

Finally, consider the impact of γ on aggregate labor-market fluctuations. In several experiments, we found that e_n and d_n were increasing in γ (for details, see Christiano and Eichenbaum [1990a]). To gain intuition into this result, think of a version of the divisible-labor model in which the gross investment decision rule is fixed exogenously. In this simpler model economy, labor-market equilibrium is the result of the intersection of static labor-supply and labor-demand curves. Given our assumptions regarding the utility function, the response of labor supply to a change in the return to working is an increasing function of γ; that is, the labor-supply curve becomes flatter as γ increases. By itself, this makes the equilibrium response of n_t to λ_t (which shifts the labor-demand curve) an increasing function of γ. This relationship is consistent with the finding that e_n is increasing in γ in our model. With respect to d_n, it is straightforward to show that, in the static framework, the extent of the shift in the labor-supply curve induced by a change in $\bar{g}_t$ is also an increasing function of γ. This is also consistent with the finding that d_n is an increasing function of γ in our model.

That e_n and d_n are increasing in γ leads us to expect that the volatility of hours worked will also be an increasing function of γ. However, we cannot say a priori what impact larger values of γ will have on the Dunlop–Tarshis correlation, because larger values of e_n drive that correlation up, but larger values of d_n drive it down.

---

[8]Christiano (1987a, 1988 footnotes 9, 18) discusses the different properties of the log-linear approximation that we use here and linear approximations of the sort used by Kydland and Prescott (1982).

II. Econometric Methodology

In this section, we describe three things: our strategy for estimating the structural parameters of the model and various second moments of the data, our method for evaluating the model's implications for aggregate labor-market fluctuations, and the data used in our empirical analysis. While similar in spirit, our empirical methodology is quite different from the methods typically used to evaluate RBC models. Much of the existing RBC literature makes little use of formal econometric methods, either when model parameter values are selected or when the fully parameterized model is compared with the data. Instead, the RBC literature tends to use a variety of informal techniques, often referred to as *calibration*. In contrast, we use a version of Lars Peter Hansen's (1982) generalized method-of-moments (GMM) procedure at both stages of the analysis. Our estimation criterion is set up so that, in effect, estimated parameter values equate model and sample first moments of the data. It turns out that these values are very similar to the values used in existing RBC studies. An important advantage of our GMM procedures, however, is that they let us quantify the degree of uncertainty in our estimates of the model's parameters. This turns out to be an important ingredient of our model-evaluation techniques.

A. *Estimation*

Now we will describe our estimation strategy. The parameters of interest can be divided into two groups. Let Ψ_1 denote the model's eight structural parameters:

$$(15) \quad \Psi_1 = \{\delta, \theta, \gamma, \rho, \bar{g}, \sigma_\mu, \lambda, \sigma_\lambda\}.$$

The parameters N, β, and α were not estimated. Instead, we fixed N at 1,369 hours per quarter and set the parameter β so as to imply a 3-percent annual subjective discount rate; that is, $\beta = (1.03)^{-0.25}$. Two alternative values of α were considered: $\alpha = 0$ and $\alpha = 1$.

Given estimated values of $\Psi_1, \hat{\Psi}_{1,T}$, and distribution assumptions on μ_t and λ_t, our model provides a complete description of the data-generating process. (Here T denotes the number of observations in our sample.) This can be used to compute the second moments of all the variables of the model. Suppose, for the time being, that we can abstract from sampling uncertainty in $\hat{\Psi}_{1,T}$, say, because we have a large data sample. Then the second moments implied by $\hat{\Psi}_{1,T}$ will coincide with the second moments of the stochastic process generating the data only if the model has been specified correctly.

This observation motivates our strategy for assessing the empirical plausibility of the model. First we calculate selected second moments of the data using our model evaluated at $\hat{\Psi}_{1,T}$. Then we estimate the same second moments directly, without using the model. Our test then compares these two sets of second moments and determines whether the differences between them can be accounted for by sampling variation under the null hypothesis that the model is correctly specified.

To this end, it is useful to define Ψ_2 to be various second moments of the data. Our measures of c_t^p, dk_t, k_t, y_t, $(y/n)_t$, and g_t all display marked trends, so some stationarity-inducing transformation of the data must be adopted for second moments to be well defined. (Here dk_t denotes gross investment.) The transformation we used corresponds to the Hodrick and Prescott (HP) detrending procedure discussed by Robert J. Hodrick and Prescott (1980) and Prescott (1986). We used the HP transformation because many researchers, especially Kydland and Prescott (1982, 1988), G. Hansen (1985), and Prescott (1986), have used it to investigate RBC models. Also, according to our model, the logarithms of c_t^p, dk_t, k_t, y_t, $(y/n)_t$, and g_t are all difference-stationary stochastic processes. That the HP filter is a stationarity-inducing transformation for such processes follows directly from results of Robert G. King and Sergio T. Rebelo (1988). We also used the first-difference filter in our analysis. Since the results are not substantially different from those reported here, we refer the reader to Christiano and Eichenbaum (1990a) for details. The parameters in Ψ_2 are

(16) $\Psi_2 = \{\sigma_{c^p}/\sigma_y, \sigma_{dk}/\sigma_y, \sigma_n,$

$\sigma_n/\sigma_{y/n}, \sigma_g/\sigma_y, \text{corr}(y/n, n)\}$

where σ_x denotes the standard deviation of the variable x, with $x = \{c^p, y, dk, n, y/n, g\}$, and $\text{corr}(y/n, n)$ denotes the correlation between y/n and n.

1. *The Unconditional Moments Underlying Our Estimator of Ψ_1.*—The procedure we used to estimate the elements of Ψ_1 can be described as follows. Our estimator of δ is, roughly, the rate of depreciation of capital implicit in the empirical capital-stock and investment series. The estimators of θ and γ are designed to allow the model to reproduce the average value of the capital:output ratio and hours worked observed in the data. The point estimates of ρ, $\bar{g}$, and σ_μ are obtained by applying ordinary least squares to data on g_t/z_t, where z_t is constructed using the estimated value of θ. Finally, our point estimates of λ and σ_λ are the mean growth rate of output and the standard deviation of the growth rate of z_t, respectively. We map these estimators into a GMM framework to get an estimate of the sampling distribution of our estimator of Ψ_1. We need that estimate for our diagnostic procedures.

To use GMM, we express the estimator of Ψ_1, $\hat{\Psi}_{1,T}$, as the solution to the sample analog of first-moment conditions. We now describe these conditions. According to our model, $\delta = 1 + (dk_t/k_t) - (k_{t+1}/k_t)$. Let δ^* denote the unconditional mean of the time series $[1 + (dk_t/k_t) - (k_{t+1}/k_t)]$; that is,

(17) $E\{\delta^* - [1 - (dk_t/k_t)$

$- (k_{t+1}/k_t)]\} = 0.$

We identify δ with a consistent estimate of the parameter δ^*.

The social planner's first-order necessary condition for capital accumulation requires

that the time-t expected value of the marginal rate of substitution of goods in consumption equals the time-t expected value of the marginal return to physical investment in capital. Therefore,

(18) $E\{\beta^{-1} - [\theta(y_{t+1}/k_{t+1}) + 1 - \delta]c_t/c_{t+1}\} = 0.$

This is the moment restriction that underlies our estimate of θ.

The first-order necessary condition for hours worked requires that, for all t, the marginal productivity of hours times the marginal utility of consumption equals the marginal disutility of working. This implies the condition $\gamma = (1 - \theta)(y_t/n_t)/[c_t V'(N - n_t)]$ for all t. Let γ^* denote the unconditional expected value of the time series on the right side of that condition; that is,

(19) $E\{\gamma^* - (1 - \theta)(y_t/n_t)/[c_t V'(N - n_t)]\} = 0.$

We identify γ with a consistent estimate of the parameter γ^*.

Next, consider the random variable

$\lambda_t = ln(z_t/z_{t-1})$

$= (1 - \theta)^{-1} \Delta ln(y_t)$

$- \Delta ln(n_t) - \theta(1 - \theta)^{-1} \Delta ln(k_t).$

Here Δ denotes the first-difference operator. Under the null hypothesis of balanced growth, $\lambda \equiv E\lambda_t$, the unconditional growth rate of output. Therefore,

(20) $E[\Delta ln(y_t) - \lambda] = 0$

$E[(\lambda_t - \lambda)^2 - \sigma_\lambda^2] = 0.$

The relations in (20) summarize the moment restrictions underlying our estimators of λ and σ_λ.

Our assumptions regarding the stochastic process generating government consumption imply the unconditional moment re-

438   *THE AMERICAN ECONOMIC REVIEW*   *JUNE 1992*

strictions:

(21) $E[\ln(\bar{g}_t) - (1-\rho)\ln(\bar{g})$

$$- \rho\ln(\bar{g}_{t-1})] = 0$$

$E[\ln(\bar{g}_t) - (1-\rho)\ln(\bar{g})$

$$- \rho\ln(\bar{g}_{t-1})]\bar{g}_{t-1} = 0$$

$E\{[\ln(\bar{g}_t) - (1-\rho)\ln(\bar{g})$

$$- \rho\ln(\bar{g}_{t-1})]^2 - \sigma_\mu^2\} = 0.$$

These moment restrictions can be used to estimate ρ, $\bar{g}$, and σ_μ.

Equations (17)–(21) consist of eight unconditional moment restrictions involving the eight elements of Ψ_1. These can be summarized as

(22) $E\mathbf{H}_{1,t}(\Psi_1^0) = 0$ for all $t \geq 0$

where Ψ_1^0 is the true value of Ψ_1 and $\mathbf{H}_{1,t}(\Psi_1)$ is the 8×1 random vector which has as its elements the left sides of (17)–(21) before expectations are taken.

2. *The Unconditional Moments Underlying Our Estimator of* Ψ_2.—Our estimator of the elements of Ψ_2 coincides with standard second-moment estimators. We find it convenient to map these into the GMM framework. The first-moment conditions we use are

(23) $E\{y_t^2(\sigma_x/\sigma_y)^2 - x_t^2\} = 0$

$$x_t = [c_t^p, dk_t, g_t]$$

$E[n_t^2 - \sigma_n^2] = 0$

$E\{(y/n)_t^2(\sigma_n/\sigma_{y/n})^2 - n_t^2\} = 0$

$E\{[\sigma_n^2/(\sigma_n/\sigma_{y/n})]\mathrm{corr}(y/n, n)$

$$- (y/n)_t n_t\} = 0.$$

In (23) we have used the fact that, by construction, HP-filtered data have a zero mean.

Equations (23) consist of six unconditional moment restrictions involving the six elements of Ψ_2. These restrictions can be summarized as

(24) $E\mathbf{H}_{2,t}(\Psi_2^0) = 0$ for all $t \geq 0$

where Ψ_2^0 is the true value of Ψ_2 and $\mathbf{H}_{2:t}(\Psi_2)$ is the 6×1 vector-valued function which has as its elements the left sides of (23) before expectations are taken.

In order to discuss our estimator, it is convenient to define the 14×1 parameter vector $\Psi = [\Psi_1 \ \Psi_2]'$ and the 14×1 vector-valued function $\mathbf{H}_t = [\mathbf{H}'_{1,t} \ \mathbf{H}'_{2,t}]'$. With this notation, the unconditional moment restrictions (22) and (24) can be written as

(25) $E\mathbf{H}_t(\Psi^0) = 0$ for all $t \geq 0$

where $\Psi^0 = [\Psi_1^0 \ \Psi_2^0]'$, the vector of true values of Ψ. Let $\mathbf{g}_T$ denote the 14×1 vector-valued function

(26) $\mathbf{g}_T(\Psi) = (1/T)\sum_{t=0}^{T}\mathbf{H}_t(\Psi).$

Our model implies that $\mathbf{H}_t(\Psi^0)$ is a stationary and ergodic stochastic process. Since $\mathbf{g}_T(\cdot)$ has the same dimension as Ψ, it follows from L. Hansen (1982) that the estimator Ψ_T, defined by the condition $\mathbf{g}_T(\hat{\Psi}_T) = 0$, is consistent for Ψ^0.

Let $\mathbf{D}_T$ denote the matrix of partial derivatives

(27) $$\mathbf{D}_T = \frac{\partial\mathbf{g}_T(\Psi)}{\partial\Psi'}$$

evaluated at $\Psi = \Psi_T$. It then follows from results in L. Hansen (1982) that a consistent estimator of the variance-covariance matrix of $\hat{\Psi}_T$ is given by

(28) $\mathrm{Var}(\hat{\Psi}_T) = [\mathbf{D}_T]^{-1}\mathbf{S}_T[\mathbf{D}'_T]^{-1}/T.$

Here, $\mathbf{S}_T$ is a consistent estimator of the spectral density matrix of $\mathbf{H}_t(\mathbf{\Psi}^0)$ at frequency zero.[9]

B. *Testing*

Now we describe how a Wald-type test statistic described in Eichenbaum et al. (1984) and Whitney K. Newey and Kenneth D. West (1987) can be used to assess formally the plausibility of the model's implications for subsets of the second moments of the data. Our empirical analysis concentrates on assessing the model's implications for the labor-market moments, $[\mathrm{corr}(y/n), \sigma_n/\sigma_{y/n}]$.[10] Here, we describe our procedure for testing this set of moments, a procedure which can be used for any finite set of moments.

Given a set of values for $\mathbf{\Psi}_1$, our model implies particular values for $[\mathrm{corr}(y/n), \sigma_n/\sigma_{y/n}]$ in population. We represent this relationship by the function f that maps $\mathbb{R}^8$ into $\mathbb{R}^2$:

$$(29) \quad f(\mathbf{\Psi}_1) = [f_1(\mathbf{\Psi}_1), f_2(\mathbf{\Psi}_1)].$$

Here, $f_1(\mathbf{\Psi}_1)$ and $f_2(\mathbf{\Psi}_2)$ denote the model's implication for $\mathrm{corr}(y/n, n)$ and $\sigma_n/\sigma_{y/n}$ in population, conditional on the model parameters, $\mathbf{\Psi}_1$. The function $f(\cdot)$ is highly nonlinear in $\mathbf{\Psi}_1$ and must be computed using numerical methods. We use the spectral technique described in Christiano and Eichenbaum (1990b).

Let $\mathbf{A}$ be the 2×14 matrix composed of zeros and ones with the property that

$$(30) \quad \mathbf{A}\mathbf{\Psi} = \left[\mathrm{corr}(y/n, n), \sigma_n/\sigma_{y/n} \right]'$$

and let

$$(31) \quad F(\mathbf{\Psi}) = f(\mathbf{\Psi}_1) - \mathbf{A}\mathbf{\Psi}.$$

Under the null hypothesis that the model is correctly specified,

$$(32) \quad F(\mathbf{\Psi}^0) = 0.$$

If our data sample were large, then $\hat{\mathbf{\Psi}}_T = \mathbf{\Psi}^0$ and (32) could be tested by simply comparing $F(\hat{\mathbf{\Psi}}_T)$ with a 2×1 vector of zeros. However, $F(\hat{\mathbf{\Psi}}_T)$ need not be zero in a small sample, because of sampling uncertainty in $\hat{\mathbf{\Psi}}_T$. To test (32), then, we need the distribution of $F(\hat{\mathbf{\Psi}}_T)$ under the null hypothesis. Taking a first-order Taylor-series approximation of $F(\hat{\mathbf{\Psi}}_T)$ about $\mathbf{\Psi}^0$ yields

$$(33) \quad F(\hat{\mathbf{\Psi}}_T) \cong F(\mathbf{\Psi}^0)$$
$$+ F'(\mathbf{\Psi}^0)\left[\hat{\mathbf{\Psi}}_T - \mathbf{\Psi}^0\right]'.$$

It follows that a consistent estimator of the variance-covariance matrix of $F(\hat{\mathbf{\Psi}}_T)$ is given by

$$(34) \quad \mathrm{Var}\left[F(\hat{\mathbf{\Psi}}_T)\right] = \left[F'(\hat{\mathbf{\Psi}}_T)\right]$$
$$\times \mathrm{Var}(\hat{\mathbf{\Psi}}_T)\left[F'(\hat{\mathbf{\Psi}}_T)\right]'.$$

An implication of results in Eichenbaum et al. (1984) and Newey and West (1987) is that the test statistic

$$(35) \quad J = F(\hat{\mathbf{\Psi}}_T)'\mathrm{Var}\left[F(\hat{\mathbf{\Psi}}_T)\right]^{-1}F(\hat{\mathbf{\Psi}}_T)$$

---

[9] Let $\mathbf{S}_0 = \sum_{k=-\infty}^{\infty} E[\mathbf{H}_{t+k}(\mathbf{\Psi}^0)][\mathbf{H}_t(\mathbf{\Psi}^0)]'$ denote the spectral density matrix of $\mathbf{H}_t(\mathbf{\Psi}^0)$ at frequency zero. Our estimator of $\mathbf{S}_0$, $\mathbf{S}_T$, uses the damped, truncated covariance estimator discussed by Eichenbaum and Hansen (1990). The results we report were calculated by truncating after six lags. Strictly speaking, HP-filtered data do not satisfy the Eichenbaum and Hansen (1990) assumption that $\mathbf{S}_0$ be nonsingular. This is because our model implies that data need to be differenced only once to induce stationarity, while the results of King and Rebelo (1988) show that the HP filter differences more than once. We think this is not a serious problem from the perspective of asymptotic-distribution theory. This is because our numerical results would have been essentially unchanged had we worked with a version of the HP filter in which the extra unit roots were replaced by roots arbitrarily close to 1. Then, the Eichenbaum and Hansen (1990) analysis would apply without caveat. What the small-sample properties are in the presence of unit roots in the data-generating process remains an open and interesting question.

[10] Our formal test does not include σ_n/σ_y because this is an exact function of $[\mathrm{corr}(y/n, n), \sigma_n/\sigma_{y/n}]$. To see this, let $b = \sigma_n/\sigma_{y/n}$ and $c = \mathrm{corr}(y/n, n)$. Then, after some algebraic manipulation,

$$\sigma_n/\sigma_y = b/(1 + 2cb + b^2)^{1/2}.$$

is asymptotically distributed as a chi-square random variable with two degrees of freedom. We used this fact to test the null hypothesis (32).

C. The Data

Next we describe the data used in our analysis. In all of our empirical work, private consumption, c_t^p, was measured as quarterly real expenditures on nondurable consumption goods plus services plus the imputed service flow from the stock of durable goods. The first two time series came from the U.S. Department of Commerce's *Survey of Current Business* (various issues). The third came from the data base documented in Flint Brayton and Eileen Mauskopf (1985). Government consumption, g_t, was measured by real government purchases of goods and services minus real investment of government (federal, state, and local).[11]

A measure of government investment was provided to us by John C. Musgrave of the U.S. Bureau of Economic Analysis. This measure is a revised and updated version of the measure discussed in Musgrave (1980). Gross investment, dk_t, was measured as private-sector fixed investment plus government fixed investment plus real expenditures on durable goods.

The capital-stock series, k_t, was chosen to match the investment series. Accordingly, we measured k_t as the sum of the stock of consumer durables, producer structures and equipment, government and private residential capital, and government nonresidential capital.

Gross output, y_t, was measured as c_t^p plus g_t plus dk_t plus time-t inventory investment. Given our consumption series, the

difference between our measure of gross output and the one reported in the *Survey of Current Business* is that ours includes the imputed service flow from the stock of consumer durables but excludes net exports.

We used two different measures of hours worked and average productivity. Our first measure of hours worked corresponds to the one constructed by G. Hansen (1984) which is based on the household survey conducted by the U.S. Department of Labor. A corresponding measure of average productivity was constructed by dividing our measure of gross output by this measure of hours. For convenience, we refer to this measure of n_t and $(y/n)_t$ as *household* hours worked and *household* productivity.

A potential problem with our measure of household average productivity is that gross output covers more sectors than does the household hours data (for details, see appendix 1 of Christiano and Eichenbaum [1988]). In order to investigate the quantitative impact of this problem, we considered a second measure of hours worked and productivity which covers the same sectors: output per hour of all persons in the nonagricultural business sector (CITIBASE mnemonic LBOUTU) and per capita hours worked by wage and salary workers in private nonagricultural establishments as reported by the U.S. Department of Labor (Bureau of Labor Statistics, IDC mnemonic HRSPST). For convenience, we refer to this measure of n_t and $(y/n)_t$ as *establishment* hours worked and *establishment* productivity.

All data, except those for $(y/n)_t$, were converted to per capita terms using an efficiency-weighted measure of the population. The data cover the period from the third quarter of 1955 through the fourth quarter of 1983 (1955:3–1983:4) (for further details on the data, see Christiano [1987b, 1988]).

III. Empirical Results

In this section, we report our empirical results. Subsection A discusses the results obtained using the household data while Subsection B presents results based on the establishment data. In each case, our results

---

[11] It would be desirable to include in g_t a measure of the service flow from the stock of government-owned capital, since government capital is included in our measure of k_t. Unfortunately, we know of no existing measures of that service flow. This contrasts with household capital, for which there are estimates of the service flow from housing and the stock of consumer durables. The first is included in the official measure of consumption of services, and the second is reported by Brayton and Mauskopf (1985).

TABLE 1—MODEL PARAMETER ESTIMATES (AND STANDARD ERRORS) GENERATED BY
THE HOUSEHOLD DATA SET

	Model			
	Without government ($\alpha = 1$)		With government ($\alpha = 0$)	
Parameter	Divisible labor	Indivisible labor	Divisible labor	Indivisible labor
N	1,369	1,369	1,369	1,369
δ	0.0210 (0.0003)	0.0210 (0.0003)	0.0210 (0.0003)	0.0210 (0.0003)
β	$1.03^{-0.25}$	$1.03^{-0.25}$	$1.03^{-0.25}$	$1.03^{-0.25}$
θ	0.339 (0.006)	0.339 (0.006)	0.344 (0.006)	0.344 (0.006)
γ	2.99 (0.03)	0.00285 (0.00003)	3.92 (0.05)	0.00374 (0.00005)
λ	0.0040 (0.0015)	0.0040 (0.0015)	0.0040 (0.0015)	0.0040 (0.0015)
σ_ε	0.018 (0.001)	0.018 (0.001)	0.018 (0.001)	0.018 (0.001)
$\bar{g}$	186.0 (10.74)	186.0 (10.74)	190.8 (7.09)	190.8 (7.09)
ρ	0.96 (0.028)	0.96 (0.028)	0.96 (0.029)	0.96 (0.029)
σ_μ	0.020 (0.001)	0.020 (0.001)	0.021 (0.001)	0.021 (0.001)

Notes: Standard errors are reported in parentheses only for estimated parameters. Other parameters were set a priori.

are presented for four models. These correspond to versions of the model in Section II with V given by (3) or (4) and $\alpha = 1$ or 0. We refer to the model with V given by (3) and $\alpha = 1$ as our *base model*.

A. Results for the Household Data

Table 1 reports our estimates of Ψ_1 along with standard errors for the different models. (We report the corresponding equilibrium decision rules in Christiano and Eichenbaum [1990a].) Table 2 documents the implications of our estimates of Ψ_1 for various first moments of the data. To calculate these, we used the fully parameterized models to simulate 1,000 time series, each of length 113 (the number of observations in our data set). First moments were calculated on each synthetic data set. Table 2

reports the average value of these moments across synthetic data sets as well as estimates of the corresponding first moments of the data.

As can be seen, all of the models do extremely well on this dimension. This is not surprising, given the nature of our estimator of Ψ_1. Notice that the models predict the same mean growth rate for c_t^p, k_t, g_t, and y_t. This prediction reflects the balanced-growth properties of our models. This prediction does not seem implausible given the point estimates and standard errors reported in Table 2.[12] The models also pre-

[12] The large standard error associated with our estimate of the growth rate of g_t may well reflect a break in the data around 1970. For example, the sample

TABLE 2—SELECTED FIRST-MOMENT PROPERTIES, HOUSEHOLD DATA SET

| | Model | | | | |
| | Without government ($\alpha = 1$) | | With government ($\alpha = 0$) | | U.S. data |
Variable	Divisible labor	Indivisible labor	Divisible labor	Indivisible labor	(1955:4–1983:4)
c_t^p / y_t	0.56 (0.012)	0.56 (0.012)	0.56 (0.010)	0.56 (0.010)	0.55 (0.003)
g_t / y_t	0.177 (0.007)	0.178 (0.007)	0.176 (0.006)	0.177 (0.006)	0.177 (0.003)
dk_t / y_t	0.260 (0.009)	0.260 (0.010)	0.264 (0.009)	0.264 (0.009)	0.269 (0.002)
k_{t+1} / y_t	10.54 (0.268)	10.54 (0.260)	10.68 (0.307)	10.68 (0.293)	100.62 (0.09)
n_t	315.60 (3.01)	314.24 (4.09)	315.19 (4.47)	314.12 (5.74)	320.02 (10.51)
$\Delta \log c_t^p$	0.0040 (0.0017)	0.0040 (0.0016)	0.0040 (0.0016)	0.0040 (0.0016)	0.0045 (0.0007)
$\Delta \log k_t$	0.0040 (0.0015)	0.0040 (0.0016)	0.0040 (0.0015)	0.0040 (0.0016)	0.0047 (0.0005)
$\Delta \log g_t$	0.0040 (0.0019)	0.0040 (0.0019)	0.0040 (0.0019)	0.0040 (0.0019)	0.0023 (0.0017)
$\Delta \log y_t$	0.0040 (0.0017)	0.0040 (0.0017)	0.0040 (0.0017)	0.0040 (0.0017)	0.0040 (0.0017)
$\Delta \log n_t$	0.00001 (0.0002)	0.00002 (0.0003)	0.00001 (0.0003)	0.00001 (0.0005)	0.00002 (0.0013)

Notes: Numbers in the columns under the "model" heading are averages, across 1,000 simulated data sets, each with 113 observations, of the sample average of the variables in the first column. Numbers in parentheses are the standard deviations across data sets. The last column reports empirical averages, with standard errors in parentheses.

dict that the unconditional growth rate of n_t will be zero. This restriction also seems reasonably consistent with the data.

Table 3 displays estimates of a subset of the second moments of the household data, as well as the analog model predictions. All of the models do reasonably well at matching the estimated values of σ_{c^p} / σ_y, σ_{dk} / σ_y, σ_g / σ_y, and σ_y. Interestingly, introducing government into the analysis (i.e., moving from $\alpha = 1$ to $\alpha = 0$) actually improves the

performance of the models with respect to σ_{c^p} / σ_y, σ_{dk} / σ_y, and σ_g / σ_y but has little impact on their predictions for σ_y. The models do not do well, however, at matching the volatility of hours worked relative to output (σ_n / σ_y). Not surprisingly, incorporating government into the analysis ($\alpha = 0$) generates additional volatility in n_t, as does allowing for indivisibilities in labor supply. Indeed, the quantitative impact of these two perturbations to the base model (divisible labor with $\alpha = 1$) is similar. Nevertheless, even when both effects are operative, the model still underpredicts the volatility of n_t relative to y_t. Similarly, allowing for non-convexities in labor supply and introducing government into the analysis improves the

---

average of the growth rate of g_t between 1955:2 and 1970:1 is 0.0060, whereas between 1970:1 and 1984:1 it is -0.0018.

TABLE 3—SECOND-MOMENT PROPERTIES AFTER HP-DETRENDING MODELS ESTIMATED USING
THE HOUSEHOLD DATA SET

| | Model | | | | |
| Statistic | Without government ($\alpha = 1$) | | With government ($\alpha = 0$) | | U.S. data (1955:4–1983:4) |
	Divisible labor	Indivisible labor	Divisible labor	Indivisible labor	
σ_{cp}/σ_y	0.57 (0.085)	0.53 (0.076)	0.49 (0.049)	0.46 (0.05)	0.44 (0.027)
σ_{dk}/σ_y	2.33 (0.16)	2.45 (0.17)	2.11 (0.16)	2.24 (0.17)	2.24 (0.062)
σ_n/σ_y	0.36 (0.004)	0.50 (0.006)	0.46 (0.02)	0.62 (0.03)	0.86 (0.060)
$\sigma_n/\sigma_{y/n}$	0.54 (0.01)	0.96 (0.03)	0.79 (0.07)	1.36 (0.14)	1.21 (0.11)
σ_g/σ_y	1.76 (0.24)	1.55 (0.21)	1.66 (0.20)	1.44 (0.16)	1.15 (0.23)
σ_y	0.020 (0.0026)	0.023 (0.003)	0.021 (0.003)	0.025 (0.003)	0.019 (0.001)
corr($y/n, n$)	0.95 (0.014)	0.92 (0.022)	0.81 (0.058)	0.73 (0.074)	−0.20 (0.11)

Notes: All of the statistics in this table are computed after first logging and then detrending the data using the Hodrick-Prescott filter. Here, σ_i is the standard deviation of variable i detrended in this way and corr(x,w) is the correlation between detrended x and detrended w. Numbers in the columns under the "model" heading are averages, across 1,000 simulated data sets, each with 113 observations, of the sample average of the variables in the first column. Numbers in parentheses are the standard deviations across data sets. The last column reports results for U.S. data with associated standard errors, computed as discussed in the text, in parentheses.

model's performance with respect to the volatility of n_t relative to y_t/n_t. In fact, the model that incorporates both of these effects actually overstates the volatility of n_t relative to y_t/n_t.[13]

Next we consider the ability of the different models to account for the Dunlop–Tarshis observation. Table 3 shows that the prediction of the base model is grossly inconsistent with the observed correlation between average productivity and hours worked. Introducing nonconvexities in labor supply has almost no impact on the model's prediction for this correlation.[14] However, introducing government into the analysis ($\alpha = 0$) does reduce the prediction some, at least moving it in the right direction. But not nearly enough: the models with $\alpha = 0$ still substantially overstate the correlation

[13]These results differ in an important way from those of G. Hansen (1985). Using data processed with the HP filter, he reports that the indivisible labor model with $\alpha = 1$ implies a value of $\sigma_n/\sigma_{y/n}$ equal to 2.7 (Hansen, 1985 table 1). This is more than twice the corresponding empirical quantity. Our version of this model ($\alpha = 1$) underpredicts $\sigma_n/\sigma_{y/n}$ by more than 20 percent. The reason for the discrepancy is that Hansen models innovations to technology as having a transient effect on z_t, whereas we assume that their effect is permanent. Consequently, the intertemporal substitution effect of a shock to technology is considerably magnified in Hansen's version of the model.

[14]To gain intuition into this result, consider a static version of our model, with no capital, in which the wage is equated to the marginal product of labor in each period. In that model, introducing indivisibilities can be thought of as flattening the labor-supply schedule, thereby increasing the fluctuations of hours worked relative to the wage. However, as long as the only shocks are to technology, the correlation between hours worked and the wage will still be strongly negative, regardless of the slope of labor supply.

444   THE AMERICAN ECONOMIC REVIEW   JUNE 1992

TABLE 4—DIAGNOSTIC RESULTS WITH THE TWO DATA SETS

			Model			
			Without government $(\alpha = 1)$		With government $(\alpha = 0)$	
Data set	Statistic	U.S. data	Divisible labor	Indivisible labor	Divisible labor	Indivisible labor
A. Households	corr($y/n, n$)	−0.20 (0.11)	0.951 (0.11) [10.56]	0.915 (0.11) [10.23]	0.818 (0.14) [7.10]	0.737 (0.15) [6.17]
	$\sigma_n / \sigma_{y/n}$	1.21 (0.11)	0.543 (0.11) [5.87]	0.959 (0.11) [2.13]	0.785 (0.12) [3.67]	1.348 (0.12) [1.16]
	J		168.84 {0}	119.29 {0}	62.18 {0}	41.46 {0}
B. Establishments	corr($y/n, n$)	0.16 (0.08)	0.946 (0.08) [9.43]	0.915 (0.08) [9.02]	0.659 (0.22) [2.30]	0.575 (0.22) [1.84]
	$\sigma_n / \sigma_{y/n}$	1.64 (0.16)	0.605 (0.16) [6.45]	0.959 (0.16) [4.23]	0.951 (0.18) [3.75]	1.437 (0.19) [1.07]
	J		131.35 {0}	100.53 {0}	14.55 {0.0007}	3.48 {0.176}

Notes: All results are based on data detrended by the Hodrick-Prescott filter. The numbers in the "U.S. data" column are point estimates based on U.S. data for the statistic. The portion of this column in panel A is taken directly from Table 3. The numbers in parentheses are the associated standard-error estimates. The numbers in the columns under the "model" heading are the probability limits of the statistics implied by the indicated model at its estimated parameter values; the numbers in parentheses are the standard errors of the discrepancy between the statistic and its associated sample value, reported in the U.S. data column. This standard error is computed by taking the square root of the appropriate diagonal element of equation (34). The numbers in brackets are the associated t statistics. The J statistic is computed using equation (35), and the number in braces is the probability that a chi-square with two degrees of freedom exceeds the reported value of the associated J statistic.

between average productivity and hours worked.

Panel A in Table 4 reports the results of implementing the diagnostic procedures discussed in Section II. The last row of the panel (labeled "J") reports the statistic for testing the joint null hypothesis that the model predictions for both corr($y/n, n$) and $\sigma_n / \sigma_{y/n}$ are true. As can be seen, this null hypothesis is overwhelmingly rejected for every version of the model. Notice also that the t statistics (given in brackets in the table) associated with corr($y/n, n$) are all larger than the corresponding t statistics associated with $\sigma_n / \sigma_{y/n}$. This is consistent with our claim that the single most striking

failure of existing RBC models lies in their implications for the Dunlop–Tarshis observation, rather than the relative volatility of hours worked and average productivity.

B. *Results Based on Establishment Data*

There are at least two reasons to believe that the negative correlation between hours worked and average productivity reported above is spurious and reflects measurement error. One potential source of distortion lies in the fact that gross output covers more sectors than household hours. The other potential source of distortion is that household hours data may suffer from classical

TABLE 5—MODEL PARAMETER ESTIMATES (AND STANDARD ERRORS) GENERATED BY
THE ESTABLISHMENT DATA SET

	Model			
	Without government ($\alpha = 1$)		With government ($\alpha = 0$)	
Parameter	Divisible labor	Indivisible labor	Divisible labor	Indivisible labor
δ	0.0210 (0.0003)	0.0210 (0.0003)	0.0210 (0.0003)	0.0210 (0.0003)
θ	0.339 (0.006)	0.339 (0.006)	0.344 (0.006)	0.344 (0.006)
γ	3.92 (0.03)	0.00353 (0.00003)	5.15 (0.05)	0.00463 (0.00005)
λ	0.0040 (0.0015)	0.0040 (0.0015)	0.0040 (0.0015)	0.0040 (0.0015)
σ_ϵ	0.012 (0.0008)	0.012 (0.0008)	0.012 (0.0008)	0.012 (0.0008)
$\bar{g}$	144.9 (22.30)	144.9 (22.30)	148.9 (19.65)	148.9 (19.65)
ρ	0.98 (0.003)	0.98 (0.003)	0.98 (0.003)	0.98 (0.003)
σ_μ	0.016 (0.001)	0.016 (0.001)	0.016 (0.001)	0.016 (0.001)

Notes: Standard errors are reported (in parentheses) only for estimated parameters. Other parameters were set a priori.

measurement error. Classical measurement error in n will bias standard estimates of corr($y/n, n$) downward.

In order to investigate the quantitative impact of the coverage problem, we redid our analysis using establishment hours worked and establishment average productivity. An important virtue of these measures is that they cover the same sectors. With these data, the estimated value of corr($y/n, n$) becomes positive: 0.16 with a standard error of 0.08. This result is consistent with the view that the negative correlation reported in panel A of Table 4 reflects, in part, coverage problems with the household data. Interestingly, our estimate of $\sigma_n / \sigma_{y/n}$ is also significantly affected by the move to the new data set. This increases to 1.64 with a standard error of 0.16. Thus, while the models' performance with respect to the Dunlop–Tarshis observation ought to be enhanced by moving to the new data set,

it ought to deteriorate with respect to the relative volatility of hours worked and output per hour. Therefore, the net effect of the new data set on overall inference cannot be determined a priori.

To assess the net impact on the models' performance, we reestimated the structural parameters and redid the diagnostic tests discussed in Section II. The new parameter estimates are reported in Table 5. The data used to generate these results are the same as those underlying Table 1, with two exceptions. One has to do with the calculations associated with the intratemporal Euler equation, that is, the third element of $\mathbf{H}_t(\cdot)$. Here we used our new measure of average productivity, which is actually an index. This measure of average productivity was scaled so that the sample mean of the transformed index coincides with the sample mean of our measure of y_t divided by establishment hours. The other difference is that, apart from the calculations involving y_t/n_t, we measured n_t using establishment hours.

The new second-moment implications, with the exception of those pertaining to σ_y, corr(y/n, n), and $\sigma_n/\sigma_{y/n}$, are very similar to those reported in Table 3. The new values of σ_y are 0.013 (0.0017) and 0.014 (0.002) for the versions of the divisible-labor model without government ($\alpha = 1$) and with government ($\alpha = 0$), respectively, and 0.015 (0.0019) and 0.016 (0.002) for the versions of the indivisible-labor model without and with government. (Numbers in parentheses are standard deviations, across synthetic data sets.) The fact that these values are all lower than those in Table 3 primarily reflects our finding that the variance of the innovation to the Solow residual is lower with the establishment hours data.

The results of our diagnostic tests are summarized in panel B of Table 4. Notice that, for every version of the model, the J statistic in panel B is lower than the corresponding entry in panel A. Nevertheless, as long as government is not included (i.e., when $\alpha = 1$), both versions of the model are still rejected at essentially the zero-percent significance level. However, this is no longer true when government is added (when $\alpha = 0$). Then, we cannot reject the indivisible labor model at even the 15-percent significance level.

To understand these results, we first consider the impact of the new data set on inference regarding the correlation between hours worked and average productivity. Comparing the $\alpha = 0$ models in panels A and B of Table 4, we see a dramatic drop in the t statistics (the bracketed numbers there). There are two principal reasons for this improvement. The most obvious reason is that $\overline{\text{corr}}(y/n, n)$ is positive in the new data set (0.16), while it is negative in the old data set (-0.20). In this sense, the data have moved toward the model. The other reason for the improved performance is that the new values of $\hat{\Psi}_{1,T}$ generate a smaller value for corr($y/n, n$). For example, in the indivisible-labor model with $\alpha = 0$, corr($y/n, n$) drops from 0.737 to 0.575. In part, this reflects the new values of $\hat{\rho}$ and $\hat{\gamma}$. Consider $\hat{\rho}$ first. With the household data

set, $\hat{\rho}$ is 0.96 (after rounding) for all of the models; with the establishment data set, $\hat{\rho}$ is 0.98 (after rounding). As we emphasized in Section I, increases in ρ are associated with decreases in the correlation between y_t/n_t and n_t.[15] Next consider $\hat{\gamma}$. With the establishment data, the estimates of γ are consistently larger than we obtained with the household data.[16] For example, in the indivisible-labor model with $\alpha = 0$, $\hat{\gamma}$ was 0.00374; now $\hat{\gamma} = 0.00463$. As we noted in Section I, the impact of a change in γ on corr($y/n, n$) cannot be determined a priori. As it turns out, the increase in $\hat{\gamma}$ contributes to a drop in these statistics.[17]

We now examine the impact of the establishment data on inference regarding the relative volatility of hours worked and average productivity. Comparing panels A and B of Table 4, we see that in all cases but one, the t statistics rise. In the exceptional case, that is, the indivisible-labor model with $\alpha = 0$, the change is very small. Three factors influence the change in these t statistics. First, the point estimate of $\sigma_n/\sigma_{y/n}$ is larger with the establishment data. Other things equal, this hurts

---

[15]Consistent with this relationship, corr($y/n,n$) = 0.644 in the indivisible-labor model with $\alpha = 0$, when it is evaluated at the parameter values in Table 1 except with ρ set to 0.98.

[16]To see why the establishment data set generates a higher value of $\hat{\gamma}$, it is convenient to concentrate on the divisible-labor model. The parameter θ is invariant to which data set or model is used. In practice, our estimator of $\hat{\gamma}$ is approximately $\hat{\gamma} \cong [(1-\theta)/(c/y)][(N/n)-1]$, where c/y denotes the sample average of $(c_t^p + \alpha g_t)/y_t$ and N/n denotes the sample average of N/n_t. Obviously, $\hat{\gamma}$ is a decreasing function of n. The value of n with the household data set is 320.4, and the implied value of n/N is 0.23. With the establishment data set, $n = 257.7$, and the implied value of n/N is 0.19. Our estimates of γ are different from the one used by Kydland and Prescott (1982). This is because Kydland and Prescott deduce a value of γ based on the assumption that $n/N = 0.33$. In defending this assumption, Prescott (1986 p. 15) says that "[Gilbert R.] Ghez and [Gary S.] Becker (1975) find that the household allocates approximately one-third of its productive time to market activities and two-thirds to nonmarket activities." We cannot find any statement of this sort in Ghez and Becker (1975).

[17]For example, in the indivisible labor model with $\alpha = 0$ evaluated at the parameter estimates in Table 1, but with γ increased to 0.0046, corr($y/n,n$) = 0.684.

the empirical performance of all the models, except the indivisible-labor model with $\alpha = 0$. Second, these statistics are estimated less precisely with the establishment data, and this contributes to a reduction in the t statistics. Third, the new parameter estimates lead to an increase in each model's implied value of $\sigma_n / \sigma_{y/n}$. For example, the value of $\sigma_n / \sigma_{y/n}$ implied by the indivisible-labor model with $\alpha = 0$ rises to 1.437 from 1.348. In part, this reflects the new values of $\hat{\rho}$ and $\hat{\gamma}$. When we evaluate the indivisible-labor model with $\alpha = 0$ at the parameter estimates in Table 1, with ρ increased to its Table 5 value of 0.98, the value of $\sigma_n / \sigma_{y/n}$ equals 1.396. The analog experiment with γ increases the value of this statistic to 1.436.

Comparing panels A and B of Table 4, we see that inference about the importance of the role of government consumption appears to hinge sensitively on which data set is used. On the one hand, the household data suggest that the role of government consumption is minimal. This is because both the divisible-labor and indivisible-labor models are rejected, regardless of whether $\alpha = 0$ or 1. On the other hand, the establishment data suggest an important role for government consumption. While the divisible-labor model is rejected in both its variants, the indivisible-labor model cannot be rejected at conventional significance levels as long as $\alpha = 0$.

In Christiano and Eichenbaum (1990a), we argue that the sensitivity of inference to which data set is used is resolved once we allow for classical measurement error in hours worked. The basic idea is to assume, as in Prescott (1986), that the measurement errors in the logarithm of household and establishment hours worked are uncorrelated over time and with each other, as well as with the logarithm of true hours worked. In Christiano and Eichenbaum (1990a), we show how to estimate the parameters of the models considered here, allowing for this kind of measurement error. In addition, we did the diagnostic tests that we have discussed in this paper. The main findings can be briefly summarized as follows. First, allowing for measurement error, the indi-

visible-labor model cannot be rejected at conventional significance levels as long as government is incorporated into the analysis. This is true regardless of whether household or establishment hours data are used. Second, the divisible-labor model continues to be rejected for both data sets, regardless of whether government is included in the analysis. Therefore, with this model of measurement error, inference is not sensitive to which measure of hours worked is used. Regardless of whether household or establishment hours data are used, incorporating government into the analysis substantially improves the empirical performance of the indivisible-labor model.

In Christiano and Eichenbaum (1990a), we also present evidence that the plausibility of the divisible-labor model with government is affected by the choice of stationarity-inducing transformation. In particular, there is substantially less evidence against that model with $\alpha = 0$ when the diagnostic tests are applied to growth rates of the establishment hours data set and measurement error is allowed for.

IV. Concluding Remarks

Existing RBC theories assume that the only source of impulses to postwar U.S. business cycles are exogenous shocks to technology. We have argued that this feature of RBC models generates a strong positive correlation between hours worked and average productivity. Unfortunately, this implication is grossly counterfactual, at least for the postwar United States. This led us to conclude that there must be other quantitatively important shocks driving fluctuations in aggregate U.S. output. We have focused on assessing the importance of shocks to government consumption. Our results indicate that, when aggregate demand shocks arising from stochastic movements in government consumption are incorporated into the analysis, the model's empirical performance is substantially improved.

Two important caveats about our empirical results should be emphasized. One has to do with our implicit assumption that public and private capital are perfect substi-

448   *THE AMERICAN ECONOMIC REVIEW*   *JUNE 1992*

tutes in the aggregate production function. Some researchers, including most prominently Aschauer (1989), have argued that this assumption is empirically implausible. To the extent that these researchers are correct, and to the extent that public-investment shocks are important, our assumption makes it easier for our model to account for the Dunlop–Tarshis observation. This is because these kinds of shocks have an impact on the model similar to technology shocks, and they contribute to a positive correlation between hours worked and productivity. The other caveat has to do with another implicit assumption: that all taxes are lump-sum. We chose this strategy in order to isolate the role of shocks to government consumption per se.

We leave to future research the important task of incorporating distortionary taxation into our framework. How this would affect our model's ability to account for the Dunlop–Tarshis observation is not clear. Recent work by R. Anton Braun (1989) and Ellen R. McGrattan (1991) indicates that randomness in marginal tax rates enhances the model on this dimension. However, some simple dynamic optimal-taxation arguments suggest the opposite. Suppose, for example, that it is optimal for the government to increase distortionary taxes on labor immediately in response to a persistent increase in government consumption. This would obviously reduce the positive employment effect of an increase in government consumption. Still, using a version of our divisible-labor model, V. V. Chari et al. (1991) show that this last effect is very small. In their environment, introducing government into the analysis enhances the model's overall ability to account for the Dunlop–Tarshis observation. In any event, if it were optimal for the government to increase taxes with a lag, we suspect that this type of distortionary taxation would actually enhance the model's empirical performance.

REFERENCES

Aiyagari, S. Rao, Christiano, Lawrence J. and Eichenbaum, Martin, "The Output, Employment, and Interest Rate Effects of Government Consumption," Discussion Paper No. 25, Institute for Empirical Macroeconomics (Federal Reserve Bank of Minneapolis and University of Minnesota), 1990.

Aschauer, David Alan, "Fiscal Policy and Aggregate Demand," *American Economic Review*, March 1985, *75*, 117–27.

_____, "Does Public Capital Crowd Out Private Capital?" *Journal of Monetary Economics*, September 1989, *24*, 171–88.

Barro, Robert J., "Output Effects of Government Purchases," *Journal of Political Economy*, December 1981, *89*, 1086–1121.

_____, "Government Purchases and Public Services," in Robert J. Barro, *Macroeconomics*, 2nd Ed., New York: Wiley, 1987, pp. 307–39.

_____, **and Grossman, Herschel I.,** "A General Disequilibrium Model of Income and Employment," *American Economic Review*, March 1971, *61*, 82–93.

Bencivenga, Valerie R., "An Econometric Study of Hours and Output Variation with Preference Shocks," *International Economic Review*, 1992 (forthcoming).

Benhabib, Jess, Rogerson, Richard and Wright, Randall, "Homework in Macroeconomics: Household Production and Aggregate Fluctuations," *Journal of Political Economy*, December 1991, *6*, 1166–81.

Blanchard, Olivier Jean and Fischer, Stanley, *Lectures on Macroeconomics*, Cambridge, MA: MIT Press, 1989.

Braun, R. Anton, "The Dynamic Interaction of Distortionary Taxes and Aggregate Variables in Postwar U.S. Data," unpublished manuscript, University of Virginia, 1989.

Brayton, Flint and Mauskopf, Eileen, "The MPS Model of the United States Economy," unpublished manuscript, Board of Governors of the Federal Reserve System, Division of Research and Statistics, Washington, DC, 1985.

Chari, V. V., Christiano, Lawrence J. and Kehoe, Patrick J., "Optimal Fiscal Policy in a Business Cycle Model," Research Department Working Paper No. 465, Federal Reserve Bank of Minneapolis, 1991.

Christiano, Lawrence J., (1987a) "Dynamic Properties of Two Approximate Solutions to a Particular Growth Model," Research Department Working Paper No. 338, Federal Reserve Bank of Minneapolis, 1987.

_____, (1987b) Technical Appendix to "Why Does Inventory Investment Fluctuate So Much?" Research Department Working Paper No. 380, Federal Reserve Bank of Minneapolis, 1987.

_____, "Why Does Inventory Investment Fluctuate So Much?" *Journal of Monetary Economics*, March/May 1988, *21*, 247–80.

_____ and Eichenbaum, Martin, "Is Theory Really Ahead of Measurement? Current Real Business Cycle Theories and Aggregate Labor Market Fluctuations," National Bureau of Economic Research (Cambridge, MA) Working Paper No. 2700, 1988.

_____ and _____, (1990a) "Current Real Business Cycle Theories and Aggregate Labor Market Fluctuations," Discussion Paper No. 24, Institute for Empirical Macroeconomics (Federal Reserve Bank of Minneapolis and University of Minnesota), 1990.

_____ and _____, (1990b) "Unit Roots in Real GNP: Do We Know, and Do We Care?" *Carnegie-Rochester Conference Series on Public Policy*, Spring 1990, *32*, 7–61.

Dunlop, John T., "The Movement of Real and Money Wage Rates," *Economic Journal*, September 1938, *48*, 413–34.

Eichenbaum, Martin and Hansen, Lars Peter, "Estimating Models With Intertemporal Substitution Using Aggregate Time Series Data," *Journal of Business and Economic Statistics*, January 1990, *8*, 53–69.

_____, _____ and Singleton, Kenneth J., Appendix to "A Time Series Analysis of Representative Agent Models of Consumption and Leisure Under Uncertainty," unpublished manuscript, Northwestern University, 1984.

Fischer, Stanley, "Long-Term Contracts, Rational Expectations, and the Optimal Money Supply Rule," *Journal of Political Economy*, February 1977, *85*, 191–205.

Ghez, Gilbert R. and Becker, Gary S., *The Allocation of Time and Goods Over the Life Cycle*, New York: National Bureau of Economic Research, 1975.

Greenwood, Jeremy and Hercowitz, Zvi, "The Allocation of Capital and Time Over the Business Cycle," *Journal of Political Economy*, December 1991, *6*, 1188–1214.

Hansen, Gary D., "Fluctuations in Total Hours Worked: A Study Using Efficiency Units," working paper, University of Minnesota, 1984.

_____, "Indivisible Labor and the Business Cycle," *Journal of Monetary Economics*, November 1985, *16*, 309–27.

Hansen, Lars Peter, "Large Sample Properties of Generalized Method of Moments Estimators," *Econometrica*, July 1982, *50*, 1029–54.

Hodrick, Robert J. and Prescott, Edward C., "Post-War U.S. Business Cycles: An Empirical Investigation," unpublished manuscript, Carnegie Mellon University, 1980.

Keynes, John Maynard, *The General Theory of Employment, Interest and Money*, New York: Harcourt Brace, 1935.

King, Robert G. and Rebelo, Sergio T., "Low Frequency Filtering and Real Business Cycles," unpublished manuscript, University of Rochester, 1988.

Kormendi, Roger C., "Government Debt, Government Spending, and Private Sector Behavior," *American Economic Review*, December 1983, *73*, 994–1010.

Kydland, Finn E. and Prescott, Edward C., "A Competitive Theory of Fluctuations and the Feasibility and Desirability of Stabilization Policy," in Stanley Fischer, ed., *Rational Expectations and Economic Policy*, Chicago: University of Chicago Press, 1980, pp. 169–87.

_____ and _____, "Time to Build and Aggregate Fluctuations," *Econometrica*, November 1982, *50*, 1345–70.

_____ and _____, "The Workweek of Capital and Its Cyclical Implications," *Journal of Monetary Economics*, March/May 1988, *21*, 343–60.

Long, John B., Jr., and Plosser, Charles I., "Real Business Cycles," *Journal of Political Economy*, February 1983, *91*, 39–69.

Lucas, Robert E., Jr., *Studies in Business-Cycle Theory*, Cambridge, MA: MIT Press, 1981.

McCallum, Bennett, *Monetary Economics:*

Theory and Policy, New York: Macmillan, 1989.

McGrattan, Ellen R., "The Macroeconomic Effects of Distortionary Taxation," Discussion Paper No. 37, Institute for Empirical Macroeconomics (Federal Reserve Bank of Minneapolis and University of Minnesota), 1991.

Modigliani, Franco, "The Monetarist Controversy or, Should We Forsake Stabilization Policies?" *American Economic Review*, March 1977, *67*, 1–19.

Musgrave, John C., "Government-Owned Fixed Capital in the United States, 1925–79," *Survey of Current Business*, March 1980, *60*, 33–43.

Newey, Whitney K. and West, Kenneth D., "A Simple, Positive Semi-definite, Heteroskedasticity and Autocorrelation Consistent Covariance Matrix," *Econometrica*, May 1987, *55*, 703–8.

Phelps, Edmund S. and Winter, Sidney G., Jr., "Optimal Price Policy under Atomistic Competition," in Edmund S. Phelps, ed.,

Microeconomic Foundations of Employment and Inflation Theory, New York: Norton, 1970, pp. 309–37.

Prescott, Edward C., "Theory Ahead of Business Cycle Measurement," *Federal Reserve Bank of Minneapolis Quarterly Review*, Fall 1986, *10*, 9–22.

Rogerson, Richard, "Indivisible Labor, Lotteries and Equilibrium," *Journal of Monetary Economics*, January 1988, *21*, 3–16.

Sargent, Thomas J., *Macroeconomic Theory*, 2nd Ed., New York: Academic Press, 1987.

Shapiro, Matthew D. and Watson, Mark W., "Sources of Business Cycle Fluctuations," National Bureau of Economic Research (Cambridge, MA) Working Paper No. 2589, 1988.

Tarshis, Lorie, "Changes in Real and Money Wages," *Economic Journal*, March 1939, *49*, 150–4.

Survey of Current Business, Washington, DC: U.S. Department of Commerce, various issues.

The Inflation Tax in a Real Business Cycle Model

By THOMAS F. COOLEY AND GARY D. HANSEN*

Money is incorporated into a real business cycle model using a cash-in-advance constraint. The model economy is used to analyze whether the business cycle is different in high inflation and low inflation economies and to analyze the impact of variability in the growth rate of money. In addition, the welfare cost of the inflation tax is measured and the steady-state properties of high and low inflation economies are compared.

Current controversies in business cycle theory have much in common with the macroeconomic debates of the 1960s. Twenty years ago Milton Friedman and Walter Heller debated the issue of whether "money matters." In the ensuing years the methods of business cycle research have changed dramatically but the questions have remained much the same. In particular, the issue of how much money matters is as timely now as it was when Friedman and Heller discussed it. In this paper we take the question of whether money matters to mean three things: does money and the form of the money supply rule affect the nature and amplitude of the business cycle? how does anticipated inflation affect the long-run values of macroeconomic variables? and, what are the welfare costs associated with alternative money supply rules? These are quite different questions and each implies a distinct sense in which money can affect the economy. Herein we describe a model economy

that can be used to address these sorts of questions. The setting is similar to one suggested by Robert Lucas (1987) where money is held due to a cash-in-advance constraint. We use it to provide estimates of the welfare cost of the inflation tax and to study the effect of anticipated inflation on the characteristics of aggregate time-series.

Early equilibrium business cycle models were influenced greatly by the monetarist tradition and the empirical findings of Milton Friedman and Anna Schwartz. They were models where unanticipated changes in the money supply played an important role in generating fluctuations in aggregate real variables and explaining the correlation between real and nominal variables (for example, Lucas, 1972). More recently, business cycle research has been focused on a class of models in which fluctuations associated with the business cycle are the equilibrium outcome of competitive economies that are subject to exogenous technology shocks. In these real business cycle models, as originally developed by Finn Kydland and Edward Prescott (1982) and John Long and Charles Plosser (1983), there is a complete set of contingent claims markets and money does not enter. Considering the importance attributed to money in earlier neoclassical and monetarist business cycle theories, it is perhaps surprising that these real models have been able to claim so much success in replicating the characteristics of aggregate data while abstracting from a role for money. This does not imply that money is unimportant for the evolution of real economic variables, but it is true that the exact role for

*W. E. Simon Graduate School of Management and Department of Economics, University of Rochester, Rochester, NY 14627 and Department of Economics, University of California, Los Angeles, CA 90024, respectively. We would like to acknowledge helpful comments from Steve LeRoy, David I. Levine, Bob Lucas, Bennett McCallum, Ellen McGrattan, Seonghwan Oh, Ed Prescott, Kevin Salyer, Tom Sargent, Bruce Smith, three anonymous referees, and participants in the Northwestern University Summer Research Conference, August 1988. Earlier versions of this paper were titled "The Inflation Tax and the Business Cycle." The first author acknowledges the support of the John M. Olin Foundation.

money in these models is an open and somewhat controversial question.

Not surprisingly, given that the correlation between money and output is a time-honored statistical regularity, the absence of money in real business cycle models has been a source of discomfort for many macroeconomists. One reaction to this, for example, by Ben Bernanke (1986) and Martin Eichenbaum and Kenneth Singleton (1986) among others, has been to reexamine the evidence that money "causes" changes in output. Another approach has been to construct models where money plays an essentially passive role but in which the money output correlation can be explained by distinguishing different roles for money (for example, inside and outside money) as in King and Plosser (1984) and Jeremy Greenwood and Gregory Huffman (1987). Yet another reaction has been to argue that there is some role for money over and above technology shocks. This argument is pursued in Lucas (1987).

In this paper we study the quantitative importance of money in a real business cycle model where money is introduced in a way that emphasizes the influence on real variables of *anticipated inflation* operating through the inflation tax. Money can have important real effects in this setting: anticipated inflation will cause people to substitute away from activities that require cash, such as consumption, for activities that do not require cash, such as leisure. Nevertheless, this structure does not provide any role for unanticipated money or "sticky price" mechanisms, which many believe to be the most important channel of influence of money on the real economy. We analyze the consequence of the distortion due to anticipated inflation for real variables and estimate the magnitude of the welfare losses that result.

In the following sections we describe, calibrate, and simulate a simple one-sector stochastic optimal growth model with a real economy identical to that studied by Gary Hansen (1985). The real time-series generated by the model fluctuate in response to exogenous technology shocks. The model incorporates indivisible labor and an employ-

ment lottery that permits some agents to be unemployed. With the latter features, the model implies a degree of intertemporal substitution that is consistent with observed fluctuations without contradicting microeconomic evidence from panel studies. In addition, the indivisible labor assumption is consistent with the observation that most of the fluctuation in aggregate hours worked is due to fluctuations in employment rather than fluctuations in the average hours worked of an employed worker.

Money is introduced into the model using a cash-in-advance constraint. Economies with this feature have been studied extensively by Alan Stockman (1981), Lucas (1982), Lucas and Nancy Stokey (1983,1987) and Lars Svensson (1985). The cash-in-advance constraint applies only to the consumption good. Leisure and investment in our model are credit goods. Thus, if agents in this economy wish to reduce cash holdings in response to higher inflation, they can only do so by reducing consumption.

In the next section of the paper we lay out the details of our model and describe the competitive equilibrium. Solving for an equilibrium in this economy is more difficult than in other real business cycle economies because the inefficiency imposed by the cash-in-advance constraint rules out the use of invisible hand arguments based on the second welfare theorem. In Section III we describe how we solve for an equilibrium directly using a method described in Kydland (1987).

In Section IV of the paper we present the results of some simulations of the model under various assumptions about the behavior of the monetary growth rate. Our purpose here is to use our model as an experimental device to study the effect of certain parameter interventions.[1] We take a model whose statistical properties have been studied previously and examine how injections of money, operating through a cash-in-advance constraint, alter the conclusions derived from

---

[1] See Thomas Cooley and Stephen LeRoy (1985) for a discussion of parameter and variable interventions.

this purely real economy. In this model, when money is supplied optimally, the real economy and its associated steady-state paths and cyclical characteristics are identical to those in Hansen (1985). This follows from the fact that when money is supplied optimally, the cash-in-advance constraint is not binding. By varying the rate of growth of the money supply we can study how the real allocation and the comovements among variables are altered. In addition we are able to measure the welfare costs of the inflation tax.

The results of the experiments just described are easily summarized. When money is supplied according to a constant growth rate rule that implies positive nominal interest rates, individuals substitute leisure for goods, output and investment fall, and the steady-state capital stock is lower. The features of the business cycle are unchanged by these constant growth rates. We also report the results of experiments in which money is supplied not at a constant rate but erratically with characteristics that mimic historical experience. In these simulations, the cyclical behavior of real variables are altered slightly: consumption becomes more variable relative to income and the price level becomes quite volatile. In addition, the correlations between these variables and output become smaller in absolute value. It is encouraging that with these changes the cyclical properties of the model more closely match U.S. postwar experience.

Using definitions described in Section IV we estimate the welfare cost due to the inflation tax of a sustained moderate (10 percent) inflation to be about 0.4 percent of GNP using $M1$ as the relevant definition of money and a quarter as the period over which it must be held. This is very close to estimates that have been suggested by others. We find the welfare costs to be much lower, about 0.1, when the relevant definition of money is the monetary base and the period over which it is constrained to be held is a month.

Perhaps the most striking implication of our model for the steady-state behavior of economic aggregates is that employment rates should be lower in the long run in high

inflation economies. This possibility, stated somewhat differently as the proposition that in the long run the Phillips curve slopes upward, has been suggested by others, most notably by Friedman (1977). We present evidence that, for a cross section of developed economies during the period 1976–1985, average inflation rates and average employment rates are negatively correlated.

The conclusions drawn from our simulations reflect *only* the costs and consequences of money that are due to the inflation tax: there are no informational problems created by the money supply process. We conclude that if money does have a *major* effect on the cyclical properties of the real economy it must be through channels that we have not explored here.

I. A Cash-in-Advance Model with Production

The economy studied is a version of the indivisible labor model of Hansen (1985) with money introduced via a cash-in-advance constraint applied to consumption. That is, consumption is a "cash good" while leisure and investment are "credit goods," in the terminology of Lucas and Stokey (1983, 1987). In this section we describe the economy and define a competitive equilibrium. In the next section we describe how an equilibrium can be computed using a linear-quadratic approximation of the economy.

We assume a continuum of identical households with preferences given by the utility function,

$$(1) \qquad E_0 \sum_{t=0}^{\infty} \beta^t (\log c_t + A \log \ell_t),$$

$$0 < \beta < 1,$$

where c_t is consumption and ℓ_t is leisure in time t. Households are assumed to be endowed with one unit of time each period and supply labor to a firm which produces the goods. Households are also engaged in accumulating capital which they rent to the firm.

We assume that households enter period t with nominal money balances equal to m_{t-1} that are carried over from the previous period. In addition, these balances are augmented with a lump-sum transfer equal to

$(g_t - 1)M_{t-1}$, where M_t is the per capita money supply in period t. The money stock follows a law of motion

$$(2) \qquad M_t = g_t M_{t-1}.$$

In this paper, we study two economies. In the first, the gross growth rate of money, g_t, is assumed to be constant. In the other economy, the log of the gross growth rate of the money supply evolves according to an autoregression of the form:

$$(3) \qquad \log(g_{t+1}) = \alpha \log(g_t) + \xi_{t+1}.$$

In equation (3), ξ_t is an iid random variable with mean $\log(\bar{g})(1-\alpha)$ and variance σ_ξ^2, where $\log \bar{g}$ is the unconditional mean of the logarithm of the growth rate g_t. It is assumed that g_t is revealed to all agents at the beginning of period t.

Households are required to use these previously acquired money balances to purchase the nonstorable consumption good. That is, a household's consumption choice must satisfy the constraint,

$$(4) \qquad p_t c_t \leq m_{t-1} + (g_t - 1)M_{t-1},$$

where p_t is the price level at time t. In this paper, attention is focused on examples where this constraint always holds with equality. A sufficient condition for this constraint to be binding is that the gross growth rate of money, g_t, always exceeds the discount factor, β. Our examples will satisfy this condition.[2] In our view this assumption is not unreasonable given the observed behavior of the actual money supply.[3]

As in Hansen (1985), labor is assumed to be indivisible. This means that households can work some given positive number of hours, $h_0 < 1$, or not at all. They are not allowed to work an intermediate number of

hours.[4] Under usual market interpretations, this assumption implies that the consumption set of households is nonconvex. However, following Richard Rogerson (1988), we convexify the economy by assuming that agents trade employment lotteries. That is, households sell contracts which specify a probability of working in a given period, π_t, rather than selling their labor directly. Since all agents are identical, they will all choose the same π_t. Thus, a fraction π_t of the households will work h_0 hours and the remaining $(1 - \pi_t)$ households will be unemployed during period t. A lottery determines which of the households work and which do not. Thus, per capita hours worked in period t is given by

$$(5) \qquad h_t = \pi_t h_0.$$

The market structure described above implies that the period utility function of the representative household as a function of consumption and hours worked is given by[5]

$$U(c_t, h_t) = \log c_t + \pi_t A \log(1 - h_0)$$
$$+ (1 - \pi_t) A \log(1)$$
$$= \log c_t + h_t A \big(\log(1 - h_0)/h_0 \big).$$

---

[2] It can be shown from the first-order conditions of the household's problem that the cash-in-advance constraint will be binding (the Lagrange multiplier associated with constraint (3) will be positive) if and only if $E_t(1/g_{t+1}) < 1/\beta$. This condition follows from the use of log utility and the timing assumptions.

[3] In addition, to relax this assumption would considerably complicate our solution procedure, forcing us to consider the possibility of both corner and interior solutions.

[4] The indivisible labor assumption implies that all changes in total hours worked are due to changes in the number of workers. Although over half of the variance in total hours in the United States is unambiguously due to fluctuations in employment, there is still a significant percentage that is due to fluctuation in average hours. A model that allows for adjustment along both of these margins is studied in J. O. Cho and Cooley (1988).

[5] This derivation makes use of the fact that consumption is the same whether or not the household is employed. This result, which holds in equilibrium, follows from the separability of (1) in consumption and leisure and is shown formally in Hansen (1985). It is possible to have unemployed agents consume less than employed without significantly affecting the results obtained from the model by assuming a nonseparable utility function (see Hansen, 1986). A more robust feature of this model is that utility is higher for unemployed individuals than for employed. Rogerson and Randall Wright (1988) show that this implication can be reversed if leisure is assumed to be an inferior good. It is unclear how one would reverse this implication without significantly affecting the other results obtained from the model.

We rewrite this as,

(6) $U(c_t, h_t) = \log c_t - B h_t,$

where

$$B = - A\big(\log(1 - h_0)/h_0\big).$$

In the remainder of this section, we will discuss the problem faced by a representative agent with preferences given by (6) as a stand-in for the individual household with preferences given by (1) who is subject to the labor indivisibility restriction.

This representative household must choose consumption, investment (x_t), and nominal money holdings subject to the following budget constraint:[6]

(7) $c_t + x_t + m_t/p_t \le w_t h_t + r_t k_t$

$$+ \big(m_{t-1} + (g_t - 1) M_{t-1}\big)/p_t.$$

In this equation, w_t and r_t are the wage rate and rental rate of capital, respectively. Investment is undertaken to augment the capital stock (k_t) owned by the household. The capital stock obeys the following law of motion:

(8) $k_{t+1} = (1 - \delta)k_t + x_t,\quad 0 \le \delta \le 1.$

The firm in our economy produces output (Y_t) using the constant returns to scale technology:

(9) $Y_t = \exp(z_t) K_t^\theta H_t^{1-\theta},\quad 0 \le \theta \le 1.$

Capital letters are used to distinguish per capita variables that a competitive household takes as parametric from individual-specific variables that are chosen by the

household.[7] The variable z_t is an exogenous shock to technology that follows a law of motion given by

(10) $z_{t+1} = \gamma z_t + \varepsilon_{t+1},\quad 0 \le \gamma \le 1,$

where ε_t is an *iid* random variable with mean 0 and variance σ_ε^2. We assume that z_t, like g_t, is revealed to all agents at the beginning of period t.

The firm seeks to maximize profit, which is equal to $Y_t - w_t H_t - r_t K_t$. The first-order conditions for the firm's problem yield the following functions for the wage rate and rental rate of capital:

(11) $w(z_t, K_t, H_t)$

$$= (1 - \theta)\exp(z_t) K_t^\theta H_t^{-\theta},$$

(12) $r(z_t, K_t, H_t)$

$$= \theta \exp(z_t) K_t^{\theta-1} H_t^{1-\theta}.$$

A change in variables is introduced so that the problem solved by the households will be stationary. That is, let $\hat{m}_t = m_t/M_t$ and $\hat{p}_t = p_t/M_t$. In addition, let $V(z, g, \hat{m}, K, k) = V(z_t, g_t, \hat{m}_{t-1}, K_t, k_t)$ be the equilibrium maximized present value of the utility stream of the representative household who enters the period with a fraction of per capita money balances equal to $\hat{m}$ and a capital stock equal to k when the aggregate state is described by z, g, and K. Implicit in the functional form of V are the equilibrium aggregate decision rules (H and X) and the pricing function ($\hat{p}$) as functions of the aggregate state, which is taken as given by the households. The function V must satisfy Bellman's equation (primes denote next period values)[8]

(13) $V(z, g, \hat{m}, K, k)$

$$= \max\{U(c, h) + \beta E[V(z', g',$$

$$\hat{m}', K', k')|z, g, \hat{m}, K, k]\}$$

---

[6] This budget constraint incorporates the fact that consumption and investment sell at the same price even though one is a cash good and the other a credit good. This is because, from the point of view of the seller, sales of both credit goods and cash goods result in cash that will be available for spending at the same time in the following period. Although cash good sales in a given period result in cash receipts in the same period, this cash can not be spent until the next period.

[7] In equilibrium these will be the same.
[8] Note that the solution to the firm's profit maximization problem has been substituted into this problem through the functions $w(\ )$ and $r(\ )$.

subject to

$$(14) \quad c + x + \hat{m}'/\hat{p}$$

$$= w(z, K, H)h + r(z, K, H)k$$

$$+ (\hat{m} + g - 1)/(\hat{p}\,g)$$

$$(15) \quad c = (\hat{m} + g - 1)/(\hat{p}\,g)$$

$$(16) \quad z' = \gamma z + \varepsilon \quad g' = g \quad \text{(economy 1) or}$$

$$(17) \quad \log(g') = \alpha \log(g) + \xi \quad \text{(economy 2)}$$

$$(18) \quad K' = (1 - \delta)K + X$$

$$(19) \quad k' = (1 - \delta)k + x$$

and c, x, $\hat{m}'$ nonnegative and $0 \le h \le 1$. In addition, X, H, and $\hat{p}$ are given functions of (z, g, K).

A *stationary competitive equilibrium* for this economy consists of a set of decision rules, $c(s)$, $x(s)$, $\hat{m}'(s)$, and $h(s)$ (where $s = (z, g, \hat{m}, K, k)$, a set of aggregate decision rules, $X(S)$ and $H(S)$ (where $S = (z, g, K)$), a pricing function $\hat{p}(S)$, and a value function $V(s)$ such that:

(i) the functions V, X, H, and $\hat{p}$ satisfy (13) and c, x, $\hat{m}'$, and h are the associated set of decision rules;

(ii) $x = X$, $h = H$, and $\hat{m}' = 1$ when $k = K$ and $\hat{m} = 1$; and

(iii) the functions $c(s)$ and $x(s)$ satisfy $c(s) + x(s) = Y(S)$ for all s.

II. Solution Method

In Hansen (1985) it was possible to compute an equilibrium indirectly by solving for the (unique) equal weight Pareto optimal allocation and invoking the second welfare theorem. In order to obtain an analytic solution to the problem, a linear-quadratic approximation to this nonlinear problem was formed, making it possible to compute linear decision rules. Unfortunately, it is not possible to invoke the second welfare theorem to compute an equilibrium for the economy studied in this paper. This is because money introduces a "wedge of inefficiency" (in the words of Lucas, 1987) that forces one to

solve for an equilibrium directly. To get around this, we apply the method described in Kydland (1987) to compute an equilibrium for our cash-in-advance economy.[9]

Kydland's method involves computing a linear-quadratic approximation to the household's problem (13). This dynamic programming problem is then solved by iterating on Bellman's equation, requiring that the second equilibrium condition (refer to the above definition of equilibrium) hold at each step of this recursive procedure. In the remainder of this section, we outline in more detail how this procedure is implemented in our particular case.

The first step is to substitute the nonlinear constraints, (14) and (15), into the household's utility function (6). This is done by first eliminating c by substituting (15) into (14) and (6). The resulting budget constraint is

$$(20) \quad x + \hat{m}'/\hat{p}$$

$$= w(z, K, H)h + r(z, K, H)k.$$

Because of the constant returns to scale technology, requiring that the functions w and r be of the form (11) and (12) guarantees that equilibrium condition (iii) is satisfied.

The constraint (20) can be substituted into the utility function (6) by eliminating h. However, we must first eliminate H. This is done by aggregating (20) and solving for H. Using (11) and (12), this implies

$$(21) \quad H = \left[\frac{X + (1/\hat{p})}{\exp(z)K^\theta} \right]^{\frac{1}{1-\theta}}.$$

Equation (21) can be substituted into (20), and the result substituted into (6). The re-

[9] This method is similar to the method of Kydland and Prescott (1977), which is described in some detail in Thomas Sargent (1981) and Charles Whiteman (1983). In addition to Kydland's method, a number of other approaches to solving dynamic equilibrium models with distortions have been recently proposed in the literature. Examples include papers by David Bizer and Kenneth Judd (1988), Marianne Baxter (1988), and Wilbur Coleman (1988).

turn function for the household's dynamic programming problem is now given by the following expression:

$$(22) \quad \log\left[\frac{\hat{m} + g - 1}{\hat{p}\, g}\right]$$

$$- B\left[\frac{\left[x + \frac{\hat{m}'}{\hat{p}} - \theta\left(x + \frac{1}{\hat{p}}\right)\frac{k}{K}\right]\left(X + \frac{1}{\hat{p}}\right)^{\frac{\theta}{1-\theta}}}{(1-\theta)(\exp(z)K^\theta)^{\frac{1}{1-\theta}}}\right]$$

In order to obtain an analytic solution to this problem, the above nonlinear return function (22) is approximated by a quadratic function in the neighborhood of the steady state of the certainty problem. This approximation technique is described in detail in Kydland and Prescott (1982). The state vector of the resulting linear-quadratic dynamic programming problem is $s = (1, z, g, \hat{m}, K, k)^T$ and the individuals' decision (or control) vector is $u = (\hat{m}', x)^T$. In addition, the economywide variables $U = (\hat{p}, X)^T$ also enter the quadratic return function. Thus, after computing the quadratic approximation of (22), Bellman's equation for the household's problem (13) become[10]

$$(23) \quad s^T V s = \max\left\{[s^T \quad U^T \quad u^T]\, Q\right.$$

$$\left. \times \begin{bmatrix} s \\ U \\ u \end{bmatrix} + \beta s'^T V s'\right\}$$

subject to (16)–(19) and a linear function that describes the relationship between U and $S = (1, z, g, K)^T$ perceived by the agents in the model.

To solve for an equilibrium, we iterate on this quadratic version of Bellman's equation. This procedure must involve choosing a candidate for the perceived linear function relat-

ing U to S. We start with a guess for the matrix V, call it V_0, and consider the maximization problem on the right side of (23). Once the laws of motion, (16) through (19), have been substituted into the objective, we obtain from the first-order condition for u the linear decision rule

$$(24) \quad u = D_1 s + D_2 U.$$

By imposing the equilibrium conditions, $x = X$, $\hat{m}' = \hat{m} = 1$, and $k = K$; we can obtain, from (24), a linear expression for U in terms of S that we take as our candidate. That is, we obtain

$$(25) \quad U = D_3 S.$$

To compute the value function for the next iteration, we evaluate the objective function on the right side of (23) using our initial guess V_0, the function relating U to S (25) and the household's decision rule (24).[11] This provides a quadratic form, $s^T V_1 s$, that is used as the value function for the next iteration. This procedure is repeated until V_{j+1} is sufficiently close to V_j to claim that the iterations have converged.

Once this process has converged, we obtain the following equilibrium expressions for X and $\hat{p}$ ($\hat{p}$ is equal to the inverse of consumption in an equilibrium where the cash-in-advance constraint is always binding):

$$(26) \quad X = d_{10} + d_{11}z + d_{12}\log g + d_{13}K,$$

$$(27) \quad \hat{p} = d_{20} + d_{21}z + d_{22}\log g + d_{23}K.$$

Examples of these decision rules for particular parameterizations of the money sup-

---

[10] This form for Bellman's equation incorporates both certainty equivalence and the fact that the value function will be quadratic.

[11] For the parameterizations studied in this paper it is not always possible to invert the first-order conditions to obtain an expression like (24). However, it is always possible to obtain equation (25). Therefore, when evaluating (23), we used (25) and, in place of (24) the equilibrium expressions for the components of u ($\hat{m}' = 1$ and $x = X$). The first-order conditions are satisfied given the way in which (25) is constructed and the fact that the coefficients on k and $\hat{m}$ always turn out to equal zero in these first-order conditions.

ply rule are given in the Appendix. These equations, which determine investment and consumption, along with the laws of motion (16) through (18), the expression for hours worked (21), and the technology (9), are used to simulate artificial time-series for various parameterizations of the g_t process. These experiments are discussed in the next section.

III. Results

We use the artificial economy just described to study the interaction between money and the real sector of the economy. We first describe the cyclical behavior of our economy under various money supply rules. We then use the model to measure the welfare costs of anticipated inflation. Finally, we look for confirmation of the implied steady-state behavior of high and low inflation economies in cross-section data on several developed countries.

A. *Cyclical Properties*

Statistics summarizing the cyclical behavior of our model economy under various money supply rules, as well as statistics summarizing the cyclical behavior of actual U.S. time-series, are presented in Table 1. We will begin by describing how these statistics are computed and then proceed to interpret our results.

The first panel of Table 1 shows the (percent) standard deviations of the set of endogenous variables and their correlations with output that characterize recent U.S. quarterly data. These provide some basis for comparison with the results of our experiments although we wish to stress that ours is *not* a data matching exercise but an experimental simulation of a model economy. We use quarterly data from 1955,3 to 1984,1 on real GNP, consumption, investment, capital stock, hours worked, productivity, and two measures of the price level, the CPI and GNP deflator.[12] Before computing statistics,

the data (both actual and simulated) are logged and detrended using the Hodrick-Prescott filter. The use of this detrending procedure enables us to maintain comparability with prior real business cycle studies by Kydland and Prescott (1982) and Hansen (1985).

In order to derive results from the artificial economies, we follow Kydland and Prescott (1982) by choosing parameter values based on growth observations and the results of studies using microeconomic data. In order to make comparisons with Hansen (1985) meaningful, we set the parameters describing preferences and technology to the same values used in that study. Those values, which were chosen under the assumption that the length of a period is one quarter, are $\beta = 0.99$, $\theta = 0.36$, $\delta = 0.025$, B = 2.86, and $\gamma = 0.95$. The standard deviation of ε, σ_e, is set equal to 0.00721 so that the standard deviation of the simulated output series is close to the standard deviation of the actual output series. We experiment with different values for the parameters describing the money supply process.

Given a set of parameter values, simulated time-series with 115 observations (the number of observations in the data sample) are computed using the method described in the previous section. These series are then logged and filtered and summary statistics calculated. We simulate the economy 50 times and the averages of the statistics over these simulations are reported. In addition, we report the sample standard deviations of these statistics, which are given in parentheses.

The columns of the second panel of Table 1 show the percent standard deviations and correlations that result from all of the simu-

---

[12] The series for real GNP, investment, hours worked, and the price level were taken from the Citibase database. The hours series is based on information from the *Current Population Survey*. Productivity is output divided by hours worked. The data on the capital stock include government capital stock and private capital stock (housing) as well as producers' durables and structures. The consumption series includes nondurables and services plus an imputed flow of services from the stock of durables. The consumption and capital stock series were provided by Larry Christiano.

TABLE 1—STANDARD DEVIATIONS IN PERCENT AND CORRELATIONS WITH OUTPUT FOR
U.S. AND ARTIFICIAL ECONOMICS

Series	Quarterly U.S. Time Series[a] (1955.3–1984.1)		Economy with Constant Growth Rate ($\bar{g} = 0.99$–1.15)[b]	
	Standard Deviation	Correlation with Output	Standard Deviation	Correlation with Output
Output	1.74	1.00	1.76 (0.22)	1.00 (0.00)
Consumption	0.81	0.65	0.51 (0.07)	0.87 (0.02)
Investment	8.45	0.91	5.71 (0.74)	0.99 (0.00)
Capital Stock	0.38	0.28	0.48 (0.09)	0.07 (0.07)
Hours	1.41	0.86	1.34 (0.18)	0.98 (0.00)
Productivity	0.89	0.59	0.51 (0.07)	0.87 (0.03)
Price Level { CPI	1.59	−0.48	0.51 (0.07)	−0.87 (0.02)
Price Level { GNP Deflator	0.98	−0.53		

Series	Economy with Autoregressive Growth Rate ($\bar{g} = 1.015$)[b]		Economy with Autoregressive Growth Rate ($\bar{g} = 1.15$)[b]	
	Standard Deviation	Correlation with Output	Standard Deviation	Correlation with Output
Output	1.73 (0.22)	1.00 (0.00)	1.74 (0.22)	1.00 (0.00)
Consumption	0.62 (0.07)	0.72 (0.07)	0.65 (0.07)	0.70 (0.05)
Investment	5.69 (0.76)	0.97 (0.01)	5.69 (0.77)	0.97 (0.01)
Capital Stock	0.48 (0.10)	0.06 (0.07)	0.48 (0.10)	0.06 (0.06)
Hours	1.33 (0.17)	0.98 (0.01)	1.33 (0.17)	0.98 (0.01)
Productivity	0.50 (0.07)	0.87 (0.03)	0.50 (0.07)	0.87 (0.03)
Price Level	1.70 (0.34)	−0.27 (0.16)	1.93 (0.27)	−0.25 (0.16)

[a] The U.S. time-series reported on are real GNP, consumption of nondurables and services, plus the flow of services from durables, gross private domestic investment (all in 1982 dollars). The capital stock series includes nonresidential equipment and structures, residential structures, and government capital. The hours series is total hours for persons at work in nonagricultural industries as derived from the *Current Population Survey*. Productivity is output divided by hours. All series are seasonally adjusted, logged, and detrended. The output, investment, hours, and price-level series were taken from the Citibase database. The consumption and capital stock series were provided by Larry Christiano.

[b] The percent standard deviations and correlations with output are sample means of statistics computed for each of 50 simulations. Each simulation is 115 periods long, which is the same number of periods as the U.S. sample. The sample standard deviations of these statistics are in parentheses. Each simulated time-series was logged and detrended using the same procedure applied to the U.S. sample before the statistics were calculated.

lations of our model economy where the money supply grows at a constant rate. These results confirm that when money is supplied at a constant growth rate, even one that implies a high average inflation rate, the features of the business cycle are unaffected. In particular, the statistics summarizing the behavior of the real variables are the same as would be obtained in the same model without money—the "indivisible labor" model of Hansen (1985).

The remaining two panels of Table 1 show the results of simulations with an erratic money supply. That is, we assume a money supply rule of the form (3). We calibrate this money supply process (that is, choose values for α and σ_ξ) so that the money supply varies in a way that is broadly consistent with postwar experience. We proceed by assuming that the Fed draws money growth rates from an urn with the draws being serially correlated, as in equation (3). We determined the characteristics of that urn from data on $M1$ and the regression (standard errors in parentheses)

$$\Delta \log(M1)_t = 0.00798 + 0.481 \Delta \log(M1)_{t-1}$$
$$\quad\quad\quad (0.0014) \quad (0.082)$$

$$\hat{\sigma} = 0.0086$$

where $M1$ is the average quarterly value. We intentionally averaged to smooth the data somewhat and increase the implied persistence.[13] The results of this regression lead us to set α equal to 0.48 and σ_ξ equal to 0.009. To ensure that the gross rate of money growth always exceeds the discount factor, as is required for the cash-in-advance constraint to be always binding, we draw ξ_t from a lognormal distribution. This implies that $\log(g_t)$ will never become negative.

The statistics reported in Table 1 show that volatility of the money supply has a small but significant impact on the cyclical characteristics of the economy. Virtually all the effect of volatility in the money supply is in the standard deviations of consumption and prices and their correlation with output. In particular, consumption and prices become more volatile and their correlation with output becomes smaller in absolute value. It is worth noting that the numbers in these panels are more in keeping with historical experience (see first panel) than are the results from constant growth rate economies. In addition, comparing the third and fourth panels we find that, although the price level does become more volatile, increases in the average growth rate of money has little effect on the cyclical properties of the real variables.

B. Welfare Costs of the Inflation Tax

In this section estimates of the welfare costs of the inflation tax are presented that are derived by comparing steady states of our growth model assuming different growth rates of the money supply.[14] Measuring the welfare costs of anticipated inflation is an old issue in macroeconomics. Martin Bailey (1956) provided a classic answer to this question by considering the area under the demand curve for money, the welfare triangle, evaluated at an interest rate embodying the steady-state rate of inflation as a measure of the net loss to individuals from the inflation tax. Stanley Fischer (1981) and Robert Lucas (1981) updated Bailey's estimates and they supply a thoughtful discussion of some of the awkward assumptions underlying the welfare triangle approach (for example, that government expenditures are financed by non-distorting taxes). They also discuss some of the subsidiary costs of inflation that are ignored by those calculations.

We chose to measure the welfare costs by comparing steady states because, as explained above, the cyclical characteristics of this economy are unaffected by the average growth rate of the money stock. Thus, our discussion of welfare is based on the steady-state properties of a version of our economy where the money supply grows at a constant rate and the technology shock in equation (9) is replaced by its unconditional mean.

The welfare costs for various annual inflation rates, along with the associated steady-state values for output, consumption, investment, the capital stock, and hours worked, are presented in Table 2. We show results based on two different assumptions on the length of time that the cash-in-advance constraint is binding. The numbers displayed in the top panel reflect the assumption that the relevant period over which individuals are constrained to hold money is a quarter. This is consistent with the calibration of the model in the previous section. In addition, if we assume a unitary velocity as is implied by our model and if we assume that the "cash good" corresponds to consumption of non-durables and services then this would be

---

[13] This equation is open to criticism as a description of the historical sample. Although we cannot reject its adequacy, there may be a leftover moving average piece in the residuals. This in turn could imply that some portion of the innovation in the money growth rate is permanent. See, for example, G. William Schwert (1987). We chose to ignore this because the estimated autoregression seems to capture the features that are appropriate for our experiment.

[14] A somewhat similar approach to that taken here appears in a recent paper by Jean Pierre Danthine, John Donaldson, and Lance Smith (1987). Their model differs from ours in that money appears directly in the utility function and they do not include labor in their model. In addition, they assume that capital depreciates fully each period. They also demonstrate a decline in welfare with inflation, but do so using simulations of their economy rather than comparing steady states.

TABLE 2—STEADY STATES AND WELFARE COSTS ASSOCIATED WITH VARIOUS ANNUAL
GROWTH RATES OF MONEY

Quarterly Constraint		Annual Inflation Rate				
		−4 Percent	0.0 Percent	10 Percent	100 Percent	400 Percent
	$g =$	β	1.0	1.024	1.19	1.41
Steady State:	Output	1.115	1.104	1.077	0.927	0.783
	Consumption	0.829	0.821	0.801	0.690	0.582
	Investment	0.286	0.283	0.276	0.238	0.201
	Capital Stock	11.432	11.318	11.053	9.511	8.027
	Hours	0.301	0.298	0.291	0.250	0.211
Welfare Costs:	$\Delta C/C \times 100$	0.0	0.144	0.520	4.014	10.215
	$\Delta C/Y \times 100$	0.0	0.107	0.387	2.984	7.596
Monthly Constraint						
	$g =$	β	1.0	1.008	1.06	1.12
Steady State:	Output	0.387	0.386	0.383	0.364	0.345
	Consumption	0.286	0.285	0.283	0.269	0.255
	Investment	0.101	0.101	0.100	0.095	0.090
	Capital Stock	12.663	12.624	12.524	11.910	11.272
	Hours	0.303	0.302	0.300	0.285	0.270
Welfare Costs:	$\Delta C/C \times 100$	0.0	0.040	0.152	0.981	2.137
	$\Delta C/Y \times 100$	0.0	0.030	0.112	0.724	1.578

consistent with defining money as $M1$, based on evidence from the 1980s.[15]

The results given in the bottom panel of Table 2 are based on the assumption that the relevant period over which individuals are constrained to hold money is a month. It turns out that monthly consumption of nondurables and services corresponds roughly to the monetary base during the 1980s. The steady states in this second panel were computed using different parameter values for the discount factor and depreciation rate of capital in order to maintain comparability to the quarterly results. The values assigned were $\beta = 0.997$ and $\delta = 0.008$, which are the monthly rates that correspond to the quarterly rates assumed above. We also scale the production function to reflect monthly output levels by multiplying the right-hand side

of equation (9) by $1/3$. The values for the gross growth rate of the money supply (g) that correspond to the desired annual inflation rates are also different for the monthly model. We indicate these values in the table.

The welfare measure we use is based on the increase in consumption that an individual would require to be as well off as under the Pareto optimal allocation. The Pareto optimal allocation for our economy is equivalent to the equilibrium allocation for the same economy without the cash-in-advance constraint, or, equivalently, for a version of the model where the money supply grows at a rate such that the cash-in-advance constraint is never binding. It turns out that for the model studied in this paper, the cash-in-advance constraint is not binding if the gross growth rate of money is equal to the discount factor, β.[16] To obtain a measure of

---

[15] This conclusion is based on the fact that the ratio of the stock of $M1$ to quarterly consumption of nondurables and services has been close to one since the late 1970s. Unfortunately, this result does not hold over a long period of time—the ratio has been as high as 3 early in the postwar period. The same caveat applies to the observation concerning the monetary base made below.

[16] We restrict the growth rate, g, to be greater than or equal to β. This ensures that nominal interest rates will not be negative (see Lucas and Stokey, 1987). When we set $g = \beta$, the initial price level is no longer uniquely determined. However, the real allocation and rate of inflation are uniquely determined and the allocation is Pareto optimal.

the welfare loss associated with growth rates that are larger than β, we solve for ΔC in the equation

$$(28) \quad \overline{U} = [\ln(C^* + \Delta C) - 2.86H^*],$$

where $\overline{U}$ is the level of utility attained (in the steady state) under the Pareto optimal allocation ($g = \beta$), and C^* and H^* are the steady-state consumption and hours associated with the growth rate in question (some $g > \beta$).

The results of the welfare calculations expressed as a percent of steady-state real output ($\Delta C / Y$) and steady-state real consumption ($\Delta C / C$) are shown in the bottom rows of both panels of Table 2. The welfare cost of a moderate (10 percent) inflation is 0.387 percent of GNP when the period over which individuals are constrained is a quarter. This magnitude may be compared to the estimates of 0.3 percent provided by Stanley Fischer or 0.45 percent obtained by Robert Lucas based on an approximation of the area under a money demand function.[17] It is interesting that their exercise, which holds output constant but allows velocity to vary, yields the same answer as our exercise which holds velocity constant but allows output to vary. While an estimate of roughly 0.4 percent of GNP *sounds* small, at current levels of GNP it would amount to $15.2 billion of real GNP. The welfare costs of very high inflation rates, which are not uncommon throughout the world, seem extremely high.

If the relevant period over which individuals are constrained is a month then the welfare costs are considerably reduced being only 0.11 percent at a 10 percent annual inflation rate and slightly more than 1.5 percent at a 400 percent annual inflation rate. Evidently the period over which individuals are constrained, and by implication the definition of the money balances on which individuals are taxed, make a big difference in the welfare costs of inflation.

Since there is a big difference in the estimates it is worth considering what some of the biases might be. Our larger estimates come from assuming that individuals are constrained for one quarter, which is roughly consistent with assuming that the appropriate monetary aggregate is $M1$. However, a large part of $M1$ consists of checkable deposits. To the extent that these earn competitive interest they will be shielded from the inflation tax. At the other extreme, the monetary base consists of currency and reserves. Since these are clearly subject to the inflation tax, the monthly data provides a lower bound on the magnitude of the welfare loss. It seems reasonable that in economies with sustained high inflations many individuals will be able to shield themselves against the inflation tax. If the institutions did not exist to facilitate this, one would expect them to evolve in very high inflation economies. For this reason, our model may not be very reliable for analyzing hyperinflation. On the other hand these estimates abstract from many of the subsidiary costs of inflation that are believed to be important. Among these are distortions caused by nonneutralities in the tax system and adjustment costs or confusion caused by the variability of inflation.

C. Steady-State Implications of Inflation

As shown in Table 2, anticipated inflation has a significant influence on the steady-state path of the economy. Steady-state consumption, output, hours, investment, and the capital stock are all lower whenever the growth rate of the money supply exceeds the optimal level ($g = \beta$). The consumption of leisure increased because agents substitute this "credit good" for the consumption good in the face of a positive inflation tax on the latter. Lower hours worked leads to lower output and therefore lower consumption, investment, and capital stock. The share of output allocated to investment does not change with higher inflation. This result is obtained despite the fact that consumption is a cash good and investment is a credit good since, in the steady state, investment

---

[17]Fischer and Lucas use different definitions of money (high-powered money and $M1$, respectively) and different estimates of the interest elasticity.

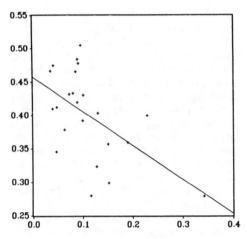

FIGURE 1. AVERAGE EMPLOYMENT AND INFLATION
RATES, 1976–1985

sion of employment rates on inflation rates. There is a statistically significant negative correlation between inflation rates and employment rates. The coefficient of the inflation rate in a regression of the employment rate on the inflation rate and a constant is −0.5 with a standard error of 0.17. The most extreme observation in the graph pertains to Chile. When that is eliminated the conclusions are essentially unchanged; the coefficient of inflation is −0.44 with a standard error 0.22. These results suggest that the phenomenon displayed in our model economy may not be counterfactual.

IV. Conclusions

In this paper we incorporate an interesting paradigm for money holding, the cash-in-advance model, in a stochastic optimal growth model with an endogenous labor leisure decision. We have shown that the solution and simulation of such a model is quite tractable. The model and solution procedure provide a basis for studying the influence of inflation on the path of the real economy and its cyclical characteristics. In addition, the solution procedure we have used could be employed to study the effects of other distortions as well.

We have used this model as the basis for estimating the welfare cost of the inflation tax and studying the long-run features of economies with different inflation rates. The fact that our estimates are well within the range of estimates obtained by other methods and that the empirical implications are confirmed in cross-sectional data is very encouraging. This suggests to us that the approximations and simplifications we have made in writing down a tractable model of a competitive economy incorporating money may not be too serious. This is not to argue that econometric estimation of many of the

will provide consumption in the future that will be subject to exactly the same inflation tax as consumption today.

A striking implication of higher inflation rates in our model economy is that they are accompanied by lower employment rates.[18] The "menu of choices" available to the monetary authority involves giving up low inflation only to obtain higher unemployment. This result, that the operational Phillips curve is upward sloping, is also obtained by Greenwood and Huffman (1987) for their model economy. Friedman (1977) in his Nobel lecture presented some evidence for this phenomenon by plotting data from several countries. Here we present some statistical evidence that supports the negative correlation between employment rates and inflation rates using a cross section of countries.

Figure 1 shows the relation between the average rate of employment and the average rate of inflation from 1976 to 1985 for 23 countries.[19] The solid line depicts the regres-

---

[18] The variable HOURS in Table 2, which corresponds to per capita hours worked, is actually the employment rate multiplied by a constant (h_0), given the assumption of indivisible labor.

[19] The countries are Austria, Belgium, Denmark, Finland, France, W. Germany, Greece, Ireland, Italy,

Netherlands, Norway, Portugal, Spain, Sweden, Switzerland, UK, Canada, United States, Australia, New Zealand, Japan, Chile, and Venezuela. Population data are taken from Summers and Allan Heston (1988) and the remainder of the data are taken from the International Labor Office (1987).

parameters we have simply specified might not yield further insights into these problems. What we find appealing about this approach is that all the features of the economy, from the decision rules to the specification of technology and preferences are explicit. Nothing is hidden. This makes it a valuable environment for experimental exercises like those considered here, and for positive exercises, for example where one would model the behavior of the monetary authority.

Although we have shown that anticipated inflation can have significant effects on the long-run values of real variables, our model economy predicts that the business cycle will be the same in a high inflation economy as in a low inflation economy. When money is supplied erratically, the characteristics of the business cycle are altered somewhat. These changes in the characteristics of the cycle occur solely because of changes in allocations that result from the changing conditional expectation of inflation. Unexpected inflation has no role in this model. However, we speculate that the most important influence of money on short-run fluctuations are likely to stem from the influence of the money supply process on expectations of relative prices, as in the natural rate literature. That is, if money does have a significant effect on the characteristics of the cycle it is likely to come about because the behavior of the monetary authority has serious informational consequences for private agents.

APPENDIX

Decision Rules for Selected Cases

Constant Growth Rate

$\bar{g} = 0.99$

$$\hat{P} = 1.84778 - 0.56736\,Z - 0.05610\,K$$

$$X = 0.66517 + 1.77463\,Z - 0.03318\,K$$

$\bar{g} = 1.00$

$$\hat{P} = 1.86644 - 0.57309\,Z - 0.05724\,K$$

$$X = 0.65852 + 1.75688\,Z - 0.03318\,K$$

$\bar{g} = 1.15$

$$\hat{P} = 2.14634 - 0.65911\,Z - 0.07569\,K$$

$$X = 0.57260 + 1.52768\,Z - 0.03318\,K$$

Autoregressive Growth Rate

$\bar{g} = 1.015$

$$\hat{P} = 1.88633 - 0.58175\,Z$$
$$+ 0.55474\log g - 0.05898\,K$$

$$x = 0.64419 + 1.73073\,Z$$
$$+ 0.30219\log g - 0.03318\,K$$

$\bar{g} = 1.15$

$$\hat{P} = 2.07319 - 0.66585\,Z$$
$$+ 0.63537\log g - 0.07726\,K$$

$$X = 0.52716 + 1.51216\,Z$$
$$+ 0.26423\log g - 0.03318\,K$$

REFERENCES

Bailey, Martin J., "The Welfare Cost of Inflationary Finance," *Journal of Political Economy*, April 1956, *64*, 93–110.

Baxter, Marianne, "Approximating Suboptimal Dynamic Equilibria: A Euler Equation Approach," reproduced, University of Rochester, 1988.

Bernanke, Ben S., "Alternative Explanations of the Money-Income Correlation," *Carnegie-Rochester Conference on Public Policy*, K. Brunner and A. Meltzer, eds., Autumn 1986, *25*, 49–99.

Bizer, David and Judd, Kenneth, "Capital Accumulation, Risk, and Uncertain Taxation," reproduced, University of Chicago, 1988.

Cho, Jang-Ok and Cooley, Thomas F., "Employment and Hours Over the Business Cycle," reproduced, University of Rochester, 1988.

Citibank, "Citibase Economic Database," New York: Citibank, 1978.

Coleman, Wilbur, "Money, Interest, and Capital in a Cash-in-Advance Economy," reproduced, Board of Governors of the Federal Reserve System, 1988.

Cooley, Thomas F. and LeRoy, Stephen F., "Atheoretical Macroeconomics: A Critique," *Journal of Monetary Economics*, November 1985, *16*, 283–308.

Danthine, Jean Pierre, Donaldson, John and Smith, Lance, "On the Superneutrality of Money in a Stochastic Dynamic Macroeconomic Model," *Journal of Monetary Economics*, July 1987, *20*, 475–500.

Eichenbaum, Martin and Singleton, Kenneth, "Do Equilibrium Real Business Cycle Theories Explain Post-War U.S. Business Cycles?" in *Macroeconomics Annual*, Stanley Fischer, ed., Vol. I, 1986, Cambridge: MIT Press.

Fischer, Stanley, "Towards an Understanding of The Costs of Inflation," *Carnegie-Rochester Conference on Public Policy*, K. Brunner and A. Meltzer, eds. Autumn 1981, *15*, 5–42.

Friedman, Milton, "Nobel Lecture: Inflation and Unemployment," *Journal of Political Economy*, June 1977, *85*, 451–72.

_____, _____, and Heller, Walter W., *Monetary vs. Fiscal Policy*, New York: Norton, 1969.

_____, _____, and Schwartz, Anna J., *A Monetary History of the United States, 1967–1960*, Princeton: Princeton University Press, 1963.

Greenwood, Jeremy and Huffman, Gregory, "A Dynamic Equilibrium Model of Inflation and Unemployment," *Journal of Monetary Economics*, March 1987, *19*, 203–28.

Hansen, Gary D., "Indivisible Labor and the Business Cycle," *Journal of Monetary Economics*, November 1985, *16*, 309–28.

_____, "Growth and Fluctuations," reproduced, UCLA, 1986.

International Labour Office, *Yearbook of Labour Statistics*, 1987, Geneva.

King, Robert and Plosser, Charles, "Money, Credit, and Prices in a Real Business Cycle Economy," *American Economic Review*, June 1984, *74*, 363–80.

Kydland, Finn E., "The Role of Money in a Competitive Model of Business Fluctuations," reproduced, Carnegie-Mellon University, 1987.

_____ and Prescott, Edward C., "Rules Rather Than Discretion: The Inconsistency of Optimal Plans," *Journal of Political Economy*, June 1977, *85*, 473–91.

_____ and _____, "Time to Build and Aggregate Fluctuations," *Econometrica*, November 1982, *50*, 1345–70.

Long, John and Plosser, Charles, "Real Business Cycles," *Journal of Political Economy*, February 1983, *91*, 39–69.

Lucas, Robert E., Jr., "Expectations and the Neutrality of Money," *Journal of Economic Theory*, April 1972, *4*, 103–24.

_____, "Discussion of Towards an Understanding of the Costs of Inflation: II." *Carnegie-Rochester Conference on Public Policy*, K. Brunner and A. Meltzer, eds., Autumn 1981, *15*, 43–52.

_____, "Interest Rates and Currency Prices in a Two-Country World," *Journal of Monetary Economics*, November 1982, *12*, 335–60.

_____, *Models of Business Cycles*, New York: Basil Blackwell, 1987.

_____ and Stokey, Nancy L., "Optimal Fiscal and Monetary Policy in an Economy Without Capital," *Journal of Monetary Economics*, July 1983, *12*, 55–93.

_____, "Money and Interest in a Cash-in-Advance Economy," *Econometrica*, May 1987, *55*, 491–514.

Prescott, Edward C., "Can The Cycle Be Reconciled with a Consistent Theory of Expectations?," reproduced, Federal Reserve Bank of Minneapolis, 1983.

_____, "Theory Ahead of Business Cycle Measurement," *Federal Reserve Bank of Minneapolis Quarterly Review*, Fall 1986, *10*, 9–22.

Rogerson, Richard, "Indivisible Labor, Lotteries and Equilibrium," *Journal of Monetary Economics*, January 1988, *21*, 3–16.

_____ and Wright, Randall, "Involuntary Unemployment in Economies with Efficient Risk Sharing," *Journal of Monetary Economics*, November 1988, *22*, 501–15.

Sargent, Thomas, "Lecture Notes on Filtering, Control, and Rational Expectations," reproduced, University of Minnesota, 1981.

Schwert, G. William, "The Effects of Model Specification on Some Tests for Unit Roots," *Journal of Monetary Economics*, July 1987, *20*, 73–103.

Stockman, Alan C., "Anticipated Inflation and the Capital Stock in a Cash-in-Advance

Economy," *Journal of Monetary Economics*, November 1981, *8*, 387–93.

Summers, Robert and Heston, Alan, "A New Set of International Comparisons of Real Product and Prices for 130 Countries, 1950–1985," *Review of Income and Wealth*, March 1988, *34*, Supplement, 1–25.

Svensson, Lars E.O., "Money and Asset Prices in a Cash-in-Advance Economy," *Journal of Political Economy*, October 1985, *93*, 919–44.

Whiteman, Charles, *Linear Rational Expectations Models: A User's Guide*, Minneapolis: University of Minnesota Press, 1983.

Part IV

The methodology of equilibrium business cycle models

Scand. J. of Economics 93(2), 161–178, 1991

The Econometrics of the General Equilibrium Approach to Business Cycles*

Finn E. Kydland

Carnegie-Mellon University, Pittsburgh PA, USA

Edward C. Prescott

Federal Reserve Bank and University of Minnesota, Minneapolis MN, USA

Abstract

The founding fathers of the Econometric Society defined econometrics to be quantitative economic theory. A vision of theirs was the use of econometrics to provide quantitative answers to business cycle questions. The realization of this dream required a number of advances in pure theory — in particular, the development of modern general equilibrium theory. The econometric problem is how to use these tools along with measurement to answer business cycle questions. In this essay, we review this econometric development and contrast it with the econometric approach that preceded it.

I. Introduction

Early in this century American institutionists and members of the German historical school attacked — and rightfully so — neoclassical economic theory for not being quantitative. This deficiency bothered Ragnar Frisch and motivated him, along with Irving Fisher, Joseph Schumpeter, and others, to organize the Econometric Society in 1930. The aim of the society was to foster the development of quantitative economic theory — that is, the development of what Frisch labeled *econometrics*. Soon after its inception, the society started the journal *Econometrica*. Frisch was the journal's first editor and served in this capacity for 25 years.

In his editorial statement introducing the first issue of *Econometrica* (1933), Frisch makes it clear that his motivation for starting the Econo-

---

*We acknowledge useful comments of Javier Díaz-Giménez on an early draft. This research was partly supported by a National Science Foundation Grant. The views expressed herein are those of the authors and not necessarily those of the Federal Reserve Bank of Minneapolis or the Federal Reserve System.

metric Society was the "unification of theoretical and factual studies in economics" (p. 1). This unification of statistics, economic theory, and mathematics, he argues, is what is powerful. Frisch points to the bewildering mass of statistical data becoming available at that time, and asserts that in order not to get lost "we need the guidance and help of a powerful theoretical framework. Without this no significant interpretation and coordination of our observations will be possible" (*ibid.*, p. 2).

Frisch speaks eloquently about the interaction between theory and observation when he says "theory, in formulating its abstract quantitative notions, must be inspired to a larger extent by the technique of observation. And fresh statistical and other factual studies must be the healthy element of disturbance that constantly threatens and disquiets the theorist and prevents him from coming to rest on some inherited, obsolete set of assumptions" (*ibid.*). Frisch goes on to say that

> this mutual penetration of quantitative economic theory and statistical observation is the essence of econometrics. (*ibid.*, p. 2).

To summarize the Frisch view, then, econometrics is quantitative neoclassical theory with a basis in facts.

Forty years after founding the Econometric Society, Frisch (1970) reviewed the state of econometrics. In this review he discusses what he considers to be "econometric analysis of the genuine kind" (p. 163), and gives four examples of such analysis. None of these examples involve the estimation and statistical testing of some model. None involve an attempt to discover some true relationship. All use a model, which is an abstraction of a complex reality, to address some clear-cut question or issue.

It is interesting to note that, in his 1933 editorial statement, Frisch announced that each year *Econometrica* would publish four surveys of "the significant developments within the main fields that are of interest to the econometrician" (*ibid.*, p. 3). These fields are general economic theory (including pure economics), business cycle theory, statistical technique, and, finally, statistical information. We find it surprising that business cycle theory was included in this list of main fields of interest to econometricians. Business cycles were apparently phenomena of great interest to the founders of the Econometric Society.

Frisch's (1933) famous, pioneering work, which appears in the Cassel volume, applies the econometric approach he favors to the study of business cycles. In this paper, he makes a clear distinction between sources of shocks on the one hand, and the propagation of shocks on the other. The main propagation mechanism he proposes is capital-starting and carry-on activities in capital construction, both of them features of the production technology. Frisch considers the implications for duration and amplitude of the cycles in a model that he calibrates using available micro data to select the numerical values for the parameters. Making the production technology with capital accumulation a central element of the theory has its parallel in modern growth theory.

There are many other papers dating from the 1930s that study business cycle models. In these papers, however, and in those of the 1940s and 1950s, little progress was made beyond what Frisch had already done. The main reason was that essential theoretical tools, in particular Arrow–Debreu general equilibrium theory, statistical decision theory, modern capital theory, and recursive methods had yet to be developed. The modern electronic computers needed to compute the equilibrium processes of dynamic stochastic model economies were also unavailable. Only after these developments took place could Frisch's vision be carried out.

In this paper, we review the development of econometric business cycle theory, with particular emphasis on the general equilibrium approach (which was developed later). Crucial to this development was the systematic reporting of national income and product accounts, along with time series of aggregate inputs and outputs of the business sector. Section II is a review of this important development in factual studies. In Section III we review what we call the system-of-equations approach to business cycle theory. With this approach, a theory of the business cycle is a system of dynamic equations which have been measured using the tools of statistics.

Section IV is a review of the general equilibrium approach to business cycle theory. General equilibrium models have people or agents who have preferences and technologies, and who use some allocation mechanism. The crucial difference between the general equilibrium and the system-of-equations approaches is that which is assumed invariant and about which we organize our empirical knowledge. With the system-of-equations approach, it is behavioral equations which are invariant and are measured. With the general equilibrium approach, on the other hand, it is the willingness and ability of people to substitute that is measured. In Section V we illustrate the application of this econometric approach to addressing specific quantitative questions in the study of business cycles. Section VI contains some concluding comments.

II. National Income and Product Accounts

An important development in economics is the Kuznets–Lindahl–Stone national income and product accounts. Together with measures of aggregate inputs to the business sector, these accounts are the aggregate time series that virtually define the field of macroeconomics — which we see as concerned with both growth and business cycle fluctuations. The Kuznets–Lindahl–Stone accounting system is well-matched to the general equilibrium framework because there are both household and business sectors, with measures of factor inputs to the business sector and of goods produced by the business sector, as well as measures of factor incomes and expenditures on products.

An examination of these time series reveals some interesting regularities — in particular, a number of ratios which remain more or less constant. These growth facts led Robert Solow to develop a neoclassical growth model which simply and elegantly rationalized these facts. Solow's structure was not fully neoclassical, however, because the consumption-savings decision was behaviorally determined rather than being the result of maximizing behavior subject to constraints. With the consumption-savings decision endogenized, Solow's growth model does become fully neoclassical, with agents' maximizing subject to constraints and market clearing. This structure can be used to generate time series of national income and product accounts.

Aggregate data present other features that are of interest to economists, such as the more volatile movements in the time series. During the 1950s and 1960s, neoclassical theory had not evolved enough to allow economists to construct computable general equilibrium models with fluctuations. Lacking the necessary tools, economists adopted an empirical approach and searched for laws of motion governing these variables. They hoped this research procedure would result in empirically determined laws which would subsequently be rationalized within the neoclassical paradigm. In the natural sciences, for example, empirically determined laws have often subsequently been rationalized at a deeper theoretical level, and it was hoped that this would also be the case in macroeconomics. In the following section we briefly review the econometrics of this approach to business cycle fluctuations.

III. The System-of-Equations Approach

Tjalling Koopmans, who was influenced by Frisch and might even be considered one of his students, argued forcefully in the late 1940s for what he called the econometric approach to business cycle fluctuations. At the time, it was the only econometric approach. The general equilibrium approach to the study of business cycles had yet to be developed. But since the approach Koopmans advocated is no longer the only one, another name is needed for it. As it is the equations which are invariant and measured, we label this approach the system-of-equations approach.[1]

---

[1] Koopmans subsequently became disillusioned with the system-of-equations approach. When asked in the late 1970s by graduate students at the University of Minnesota in what direction macroeconomics should go, Koopmans is reported by Zvi Eckstein to have said they should use the growth model.

The econometrics of the general equilibrium approach 165

In the 1930s, there were a number of business cycle models or theories. These logically complete theories were a dynamic set of difference equations that could be used to generate time series of the aggregate variables of interest. Notable examples include Frisch's (1933) model in Cassel's volume, Tinbergen's (1935) suggestions on quantitative business cycles, and Samuelson's (1939) multiplier-accelerator model. One problem with this class of models is that the quantitative behavior of the model depended upon the values of the coefficients of the variables included in the equations. As Haberler (1949) points out in his comment on Koopmans' (1949) paper, the stock of cyclical models (theories) is embarrassingly large. Give any sophomore "a couple of lags and initial conditions and he will construct systems which display regular, damped or explosive oscillation…as desired" (p. 85). Pure theory was not providing sufficient discipline, and so it is not surprising that Koopmans advocated the use of the statistics discipline to develop a theory of business fluctuations.

System-of-Equations Models

As Koopmans (1949, p. 64) points out, the main features of the system-of-equations models are the following: First, they serve as theoretical exercises and experiments. Second, the variables involved are broad aggregates, such as total consumption, the capital stock, the price level, etc. Third, the models are "logically complete, i.e., they consist of a number of equations equal to the number of variables whose course over time is to be explained". Fourth, the models are dynamic, with equations determining the current values of variables depending not only on current values of other variables but also on the values of beginning-of-period capital stocks and on lagged variables. Fifth, the models contain, at most, four kinds of equations, which Koopmans calls *structural equations*. The first type of equations are *identities*. They are valid by virtue of the definition of the variables involved. The second type of equations are *institutional rules*, such as tax schedules. The third type are binding *technology constraints*, that is, production functions. The final type are what Koopmans calls *behavioral equations*, which represent the response of groups of individuals or firms to a common economic environment. Examples are a consumption function, an investment equation, a wage equation, a money demand function, etc. A model within this framework is a system-of-equations. Another requirement, in addition to the one that the number of variables equal the number of equations, is that the system have a unique solution. A final requirement is that all the identities implied by the accounting system for the variables in the model hold for the solution to the equation system; that is, the solution must imply a consistent set of national income and product accounts.

Statistical Measurement of Equations

The behavior of these models depends crucially on the numerical magnitudes of the coefficients of the variables and of the time lags. This leads to attempts to estimate these parameters using time series of the variables being modeled. Given that the estimation of these coefficients is a statistical exercise, a probability model is an additional completeness requirement. For that purpose, a residual random disturbance vector typically is added, with one component for each behavioral equation. For statistical completeness, the probability distribution of this disturbance vector must be specified up to some set of parameters. Only then can statistical methods be applied to estimating the coefficients of the behavioral equations and the parameters of the disturbance distribution. The crucial point is that the equations of the macroeconometric model are the organizing principle of the system-of-equations approach. What is measured is the value of the coefficients of the equations. The criterion guiding the selection of the values of the coefficients is essentially the ability of the resulting system of equations to mimic the historical time series. The issue of which set of equations to estimate is settled in a similar fashion. The criterion guiding the selection of equations is in large part how well a particular set can mimic the historical data. Indeed, in the 1960s a student of business cycle fluctuations was successful if his particular behavioral equation improved the fit of, and therefore replaced, a currently established equation.

The Rise and the Fall of the System-of-Equations Approach

With the emergence of a consensus on the structure of the system of equations that best described the behavior of the aggregate economy, the approach advocated by Koopmans became totally dominant in the 1960s. This is well-illustrated by the following statement of Solow's, quoted by Brunner (1989, p. 197):

> I think that most economists feel that the short run macroeconomic theory is pretty well in hand... The basic outlines of the dominant theory have not changed in years. All that is left is the trivial job of filling in the empty boxes [the parameters to be estimated] and that will not take more than 50 years of concentrated effort at a maximum.

The reign of this system-of-equations macroeconomic approach was not long. One reason for its demise was the spectacular predictive failure of the approach. As Lucas and Sargent (1978) point out, in 1969 these models predicted high unemployment would be associated with low inflation. Counter to this prediction, the 1970s saw a combination of both high unemployment and high inflation. Another reason for the demise of this approach was the general recognition that policy-invariant behavioral equations are inconsistent with the maximization postulate in dynamic settings. The principal reason for the abandonment of the system-of-equations approach, however, was advances in neoclassical theory that permitted the application of the paradigm in dynamic stochastic settings. Once the neoclassical tools needed for modeling business cycle fluctuations existed, their application to this problem and their ultimate domination over any other method was inevitable.

IV. The General Equilibrium Approach

A powerful theoretical framework was developed in the 1950s and 1960s that built upon advances in general equilibrium theory, statistical decision theory, capital theory, and recursive methods. Statistical decision theory provided a logically consistent framework for maximization in a dynamic stochastic environment. This is what was needed to extend neoclassical theory, with its maximization assumption, to such environments. Another crucial development was the extension of general equilibrium theory to dynamic stochastic models, with the simple yet important insight that commodities could be indexed not only by type, but also by date and event. This important insight was made by Arrow and Debreu (1954), who had important precursors in the work of Hicks (1939) and, particularly, in that of Lindahl (1929) — who had previously effectively extended competitive theory to dynamic environments. Subsequently, recursive methods, with their Markovian structure, were developed. These methods simplified the use of this dynamic framework and, in particular, its extension to stochastic general equilibrium analyses; see, for example, Stokey and Lucas (1989).

Perhaps just as important as the development of tools for carrying out aggregate equilibrium analysis was the access to better and more systematic national income and product accounts data. In his review of growth theory, Solow (1970) lists the key growth facts which guided his research in growth theory in the 1950s. These growth facts were the relative constancy of investment and consumption shares of output, the relative constancy of labor and capital income shares, the continual growth of the real wage and output per capita, and the lack of trend in the return on capital. Solow (1956), in a seminal contribution, developed a simple model economy that accounted for these facts. The key to this early theory was the neoclassical production function, which is a part of the general equilibrium language. Afterwards the focus of attention shifted to preferences, with the important realization that the outcome of the Cass–Koopmans optimal growth model could be interpreted as the equilibrium of a competitive economy in which the typical consumer maximizes utility and the markets for both factors and products clear at every date.

168   *F. E. Kydland and E. C. Prescott*

General Equilibrium Models

By general equilibrium we mean a framework in which there is an explicit and consistent account of the household sector as well as the business sector. To answer some research questions, one must also include a sector for the government, which is subject to its own budget constraint. A model within this framework is specified in terms of the parameters that characterise preferences, technology, information structure, and institutional arrangements. It is these parameters that must be measured, and not some set of equations. The general equilibrium language has come to dominate in business cycle theory, as it did earlier in public finance, international trade, and growth. This framework is well-designed for providing quantitative answers to questions of interest to the business cycle student.

One of these important questions, which has occupied business cycle theorists since the time of Frisch and Slutzky, is how to determine which sources of shocks give rise to cycles of the magnitudes we observe. To provide reliable answers to this and similar questions, abstractions are needed that describe the ability and willingness of agents to substitute commodities, both intertemporally and intratemporally, and within which one can bring to bear statistical or factual information. One of these abstractions is the neoclassical growth model. This model has proven useful in accounting for secular facts. To understand business cycles, we rely on the same ability and willingness of agents to substitute commodities as those used to explain the growth facts. We are now better able than Frisch was more than 50 years ago to calibrate the parameters of aggregate production technology. The wealth of studies on the growth model have shown us the way. To account for growth facts, it may be legitimate to abstract from the time allocation between market and nonmarket activities. To account for business cycle facts, however, the time allocation is crucial. Thus, good measures of the parameters of household technology are needed if applied business cycle theory is to provide reliable answers.

The Econometrics of the General Equilibrium Approach

The econometrics of the general equilibrium approach was first developed to analyze static or steady-state deterministic models. Pioneers of this approach are Johansen (1960) and Harberger (1962). This framework was greatly advanced by Shoven and Whalley (1972), who built on the work of Scarf (1973). Development was impeded by the requirement that there be a set of excess-demand functions, which are solved to find the equilibrium allocations. This necessitated that preference and technology structures have very special forms for which closed-form supply and demand functions existed. Perhaps these researchers were still under the influence of the system-of-equations approach and thought a model had to be a system

The econometrics of the general equilibrium approach   169

of supply and demand functions. These researchers lacked the time series needed to estimate these equations. Given that they could not estimate the equations, they calibrated their model economy so that its static equilibrium reproduced the sectoral national income and product accounts for a base year. In their calibration, they used estimates of the elasticity parameters obtained in other studies.

Their approach is ill-suited for the general equilibrium modeling of business fluctuations because dynamics and uncertainty are crucial to any model that attempts to study business cycles. To apply general equilibrium methods to the quantitative study of business cycle fluctuations, we need methods to compute the equilibrium processes of dynamic stochastic economies, and specific methods for the stochastic growth model economy. Recursive competitive theory and the use of linear-quadratic economies are methods that have proven particularly useful. These tools make it possible to compute the equilibrium stochastic processes of a rich class of model economies. The econometric problem arises in the selection of the model economies to be studied. Without some restrictions, virtually any linear stochastic process on the variables can be rationalized as the equilibrium behavior of some model economy in this class. The key econometric problem is to use statistical observations to select the parameters for an experimental economy. Once these parameters have been selected, the central part of the econometrics of the general equilibrium approach to business cycles is the computational experiment. This is the vehicle by which theory is made quantitative. The experiments should be carried out within a sensible or appropriate model economy that is capable of addressing the question whose answer is being sought. The main steps in econometric analyses are as follows: defining the question; setting up the model; calibrating the model; and reporting the findings.

Question

To begin with, the research question must be clearly defined. For example, in some of our own research we have looked at quantifying the contribution of changes in a technology parameter, also called Solow residuals, as a source of U.S. postwar business cycles. But we refined it further. The precise question asked is how much variation in aggregate economic activity would have remained if technology shocks were the only source of variation. We emphasize that an econometric, that is, quantitative theoretic analysis, can be judged only relative to its ability to address a clear-cut question. This is a common shortcoming of economic modeling. When the question is not made sufficiently clear, the model economy is often criticized for being ill-suited to answer a question it was never designed to answer.

170   *F. E. Kydland and E. C. Prescott*

Model Economy

To address a specific question one typically needs a suitable model economy for addressing the specified question. In addition to having a clear bearing on the question, tractability and computability are essential in determining whether the model is suitable. Model-economy selection depends on the question being asked. Model-economy selection should not depend on the answer provided. Searching within some parametric class of economies for the one that best fits some set of aggregate time series makes little sense. Unlike the system-of-equations approach, no attempt is made to determine the true model. All model economies are abstractions and are by definition false.

Calibration

The model has to be calibrated. The necessary information can sometimes be obtained from data on individuals or households. An example of such information is the average fraction of discretionary time household members who are, or who potentially are, labor market participants actually spent in market activity. In many other cases, the required information easily can be obtained from aggregate nonbusiness-cycle information. The task often involves merely computing some simple averages, such as growth relations between aggregates. This is the case for inventory-output and capital-output ratios, and long-run fractions of the various GNP components to total output, among others.

In some cases, history has provided sufficiently dramatic price experiments which can be used to determine, with a great deal of confidence, an elasticity of substitution. In the case of labor and capital as inputs in the aggregate business production function, and also in the case of consumption and leisure as inputs to household production, the large real-wage increase over several decades in relation to the prices of the other input, combined with knowledge about what has happened to the expenditure shares on the respective inputs, provides this kind of information. Because the language used in these business cycle models is the same as that used in other areas of applied economics, the values of common parameters should be identical across these areas and typically have been measured by researchers working in these other areas. One can argue that the econometrics of business cycles described here need not be restricted to general equilibrium models. In fact it is in the stage of calibration where the power of the general equilibrium approach shows up most forcefully. The insistence upon internal consistency implies that parsimoniously parameterized models of the household and business sector display rich dynamic behavior through the intertemporal substitution arising from capital accumulations and from other sources.

Scand. J. of Economics 1991

The econometrics of the general equilibrium approach   171

Computational Experiments

Once the model is calibrated, the next step is to carry out a set of computational experiments. If all the parameters can be calibrated with a great deal of accuracy, then only a few experiments are needed. In practice, however, a number of experiments are typically required in order to provide a sense of the degree of confidence in the answer to the question. It often happens that the answer to the research question is robust to sizable variations in some set of parameters and conclusions are sharp, even though there may be a great degree of uncertainty in those parameters. At other times, however, this is not the case, and without better measurement of the parameters involved, theory can only restrict the quantitative answer to a large interval.

Findings

The final step is to report the findings. This report should include a quantitative assessment of the precision with which the question has been answered. For the question mentioned above, the answer is a numerical estimate of the fraction of output variability that would have remained if variations in the growth of the Solow residual were the only source of aggregate fluctuation. The numerical answer to the research question, of course, is model dependent. The issue of how confident we are in the econometric answer is a subtle one which cannot be resolved by computing some measure of how well the model economy mimics historical data. The degree of confidence in the answer depends on the confidence that is placed in the economic theory being used.

V. Two Applications to Business Cycle Theory

We illustrate the econometrics of the general equilibrium approach to business cycle theory with two examples. The first example, credited to Lucas (1987) and Imrohoroglu (1989), addresses the question of quantifying the costs of business cycle fluctuations. An important feature of the quantitative general equilibrium approach is that it allows for explicit quantitative welfare statements, something which was generally not possible with the system-of-equations approach that preceded it. The second example investigates the question of how large business cycle fluctuations would have been if technology shocks were the only source of fluctuations. This question is also important from a policy point of view. If these shocks are quantitatively important, an implication of theory is that an important component of business cycle fluctuations is a good, not a bad.

172   *F. E. Kydland and E. C. Prescott*

Costs of Business Cycle Fluctuations

The economy Lucas uses for his quantitative evaluation is very simple. There is a representative or stand-in household and a random endowment process of the single consumption good. The utility function is standard, namely, the expected discounted value of a constant relative risk aversion utility function. Equilibrium behavior is simply to consume the endowment. Lucas determines how much consumption the agent is willing to forgo each period in return for the elimination of all fluctuations in consumption. Even with an extreme curvature parameter of 10, he finds that when the endowment process is calibrated to the U.S. consumption behavior, the cost per person of business cycle fluctuations is less than one-tenth of a per cent of per-capita consumption.

This model abstracts from important features of reality. There is no investment good, and consequently no technology to transform the date t consumption good into the date $t + 1$ consumption good. As the costs of fluctuation are a function of the variability in consumption and not in investment, abstracting from capital accumulation is appropriate relative to the research question asked. What matters for this evaluation is the nature of the equilibrium consumption process. Any representative-agent economy calibrated to this process will give the same answer to the question, so it makes sense to deal with the simplest economy whose equilibrium consumption process is the desired one. This is what Lucas does. Introducing the time-allocation decision between market and nonmarket activities would change the estimate, since the agent would have the opportunity to substitute between consumption and leisure. The introduction of these substitution opportunities would result in a reduction in the estimated cost of business cycle fluctuations as leisure moves countercyclically. But, given the small magnitude of the cost of business cycle fluctuations, even in a world without this substitution opportunity, and given that the introduction of this feature reduces the estimate of this cost, there is no need for its inclusion.

In representative-agent economies, all agents are subject to the same fluctuations in consumption. If there is heterogeneity and all idiosyncratic risk is allocated efficiently, the results for the representative and hetero-geneous agent economies coincide. This would not be the case if agents were to smooth consumption through the holding of liquid assets as is the case in the permanent income theory. Imrohoroglu (1989) examines whether the estimated costs of business cycle fluctuations are significantly increased if, as is in fact the case, people vary their holdings of liquid assets in order to smooth their stream of consumption. She modifies the Lucas economy by introducing heterogeneity and by giving each agent access to a technology that allows that agent to transform date t consumption into date $t + 1$ consumption. Given that real interest rates were near zero in the

The econometrics of the general equilibrium approach   173

fifty-odd years from 1933 to 1988, the nature of the storage technology chosen is that one unit of the good today can be transferred into one unit of the good tomorrow. She calibrates the processes on individual endowments to the per-capita consumption process, to the variability of annual income across individuals, and to the average holdings of the liquid asset — also across individuals. For her calibrated model economy, she finds the cost of business cycles is approximately three times as large as that obtained in worlds with perfect insurance of idiosyncratic risk. But three times a small number is still a small number.

Technology Shocks as Source of Fluctuations

One source of shocks suggested as far back as in Wicksell (1907) is fluctuations in technological growth. In the 1960s and 1970s, this source was dismissed by many as being unlikely to play much of a role in the aggregate. Most researchers accepted that there could be considerable variation in productivity at the industry level, but they believed that industry-level shocks would average out in the aggregate. During the 1980s, however, this source of shocks became the subject of renewed interest as a major source of fluctuations, in large part supported by quantitative economic theory. The question addressed, then, was how much would the U.S. postwar economy have fluctuated if technological shocks were the only source of aggregate fluctuations?

Our selection of a model economy to address this question follows. First we extended the neoclassical growth model to include leisure as an argument of the stand-in household's utility function. Given that more than half of business cycle fluctuations are accounted for by variations in the labor input, introducing this element is crucial. Next we calibrated the deterministic version of the model so that its consumption-investment shares, factor income shares, capital output ratios, leisure-market time shares, and depreciation shares matched the average values for the U.S. economy in the postwar period. Throughout this analysis, constant elasticity structures were used. As uncertainty is crucial to the question, computational considerations led us to select a linear-quadratic economy whose average behavior is the same as the calibrated deterministic constant elasticity of substitution economy.

We abstracted from public finance considerations and consolidated the public and private sectors. We introduced Frisch's (1933) assumption of time-to-build new productive capital. The construction period considered was four periods, with new capital becoming productive only upon completion, but with resources being used up throughout its construction. Given the high volatility of inventory investment, inventory stocks were included as a factor of production. We found, using the variance of Solow residuals estimated by Prescott (1986), that the model economy's output variance is 55 per cent as large as the corresponding variance for the U.S. economy in the postwar period.

In the early 1980s, there was much discussion in the profession about the degree of aggregate intertemporal substitution of leisure. The feeling was that this elasticity had to be quite high in order for a market-clearing model to account for the highly volatile and procyclical movements in hours. This discussion may have started with the famous paper by Lucas and Rapping (1969). Realizing that the standard utility function implied a rather small elasticity of substitution, they suggested the possibility that past leisure choices may directly affect current utility. Being sympathetic to that view, we considered also a non-time-separable utility function as a tractable way of introducing this feature. When lags on leisure are considered, the estimate of how volatile the economy would have been if technology shocks were the only disturbance increases from 55 to near 70 per cent. But, until there is more empirical support for this alternative preference structure, we think estimates obtained using the economy with a time-separable utility function are better. Unlike the system-of-equations approach, the model economy which better fits the data is not the one used. Rather, currently established theory dictates which one is used.

Probably the most questionable assumption of this theory, given the question addressed, is that of homogeneous workers, with the additional implication that all variation in hours occurs in the form of changes in hours per worker. According to aggregate data for the U.S. economy, only about one-third of the quarterly fluctuations in hours are of this form, while the remaining two-thirds arise from changes in the number of workers; see Kydland and Prescott (1989, Table 1).

This observation led Hansen (1985) to introduce the Rogerson (1988) labor indivisibility construct into a business cycle model. In the Hansen world all fluctuations in hours are in the form of employment variation. To deal with the apparent nonconvexity arising from the assumption of indivisible labor, the problem is made convex by assuming that the commodity points are contracts in which every agent is paid the same amount whether that agent works or not, and a lottery randomly chooses who in fact works in every period. Hansen finds that with this labor indivisibility his model economy fluctuates as much as did the U.S. economy. Our view is that, with the extreme assumption of only fluctuations in employment, Hansen overestimates the amount of aggregate fluctuations accounted for by Solow residuals in the same way as our equally extreme assumption of only fluctuations in hours per worker lead us to an underestimation.

In Kydland and Prescott (1989), the major improvement on the 1982 version of the model economy is to permit variation both in the number of workers and in the number of hours per worker. The number of hours a

The econometrics of the general equilibrium approach   175

plant is operated in any given period is endogenous. The model also treats labor as a quasi-fixed input factor by assuming costs of moving people into and out of the business sector. Thus, in this model there is what we interpret to be labor hoarding.

Without the cost of moving workers in and out of the labor force, a property of the equilibrium turns out to be that all the hours variation is in the form of employment change and none in hours per worker. In that respect, it is similar to Hansen's (1985) model. For this economy with no moving costs, the estimate is that Solow residuals account for about 90 per cent of the aggregate output variance. For this economy with moving costs, we calibrated so that the relative variations in hours per worker and number of workers matched U.S. data. With this degree of labor hoarding, the estimate of the fraction of the cycle accounted for by Solow residuals is reduced to 70 per cent.

A widespread and misguided criticism of our econometric studies, for example, McCallum (1989), is that the correlation between labor productivity and the labor input is almost one for our model economy while it is approximately zero for the U.S. postwar economy. If we had found that technology shocks account for nearly all fluctuations and that other factors were unimportant, the failure of the model economy to mimic the data in this respect would cast serious doubt on our findings. But we did not find that the Solow technology shocks are all-important. We estimate that these technology shocks account for about 70 per cent of business cycle fluctuations. If technology shocks account for 70 per cent, and some other shocks which are orthogonal to technology shocks account for 30 per cent, theory implies a correlation between labor productivity and the labor input near zero. Christiano and Eichenbaum (1990) have established this formally in the case that the other shock is variations in public consumption. But the result holds for any shock that is orthogonal to the Solow technology shocks. The fact that this correlation for our model economy and the actual data differ in the way they do adds to our confidence in our findings.

The estimate of the contribution of technology shocks to aggregate shocks has been found to be robust to several modifications in the model economy. For example, Greenwood, Hercowitz, and Huffman (1988) permit the utilization rate of capital to vary and to affect its depreciation rate, while all technology change is embodied in new capital; Danthine and Donaldson (1989) introduce an efficient-wage construct; Cooley and Hansen (1989) consider a monetary economy with a cash-in-advance constraint; and Rios-Rull (1990) uses a model calibrated to life cycle earnings and consumption patterns. King, Plosser, and Rebelo (1988) have non-zero growth. Gomme and Greenwood (1990) have heterogenous agents with recursive preferences and equilibrium risk allocations. Benhabib, Rogerson, and Wright (1990) incorporate home production.

Hornstein (1990) considers the implications of increasing returns and monopolistic competition. In none of these cases is the estimate of the contribution of technology shocks to aggregate fluctuations significantly altered.

VI. Concluding Remarks

Econometrics is by definition quantitative economic theory — that is, economic analyses which provide quantitative answers to clear-cut questions. The general equilibrium econometric methodology is centered around computational experiments. These experiments provide answers to the questions posed in the model economies whose equilibrium elements have been computed. The model economy selected should quantitatively capture people's ability and willingness to substitute and the arrangements employed which are relevant to the question. We base our quantitative economic intuition on the outcome of these experiments.

The dramatic advances in econometric methodology over the last 25 years have made it possible to apply fully neoclassical econometrics to the study of business cycles. Already there have been several surprising findings. Contrary to what virtually everyone thought, including the authors of this review, technology shocks were found to be an important contributor to business cycle fluctuations in the U.S. postwar period.

Not all fluctuations are accounted for by technology shocks, and monetary shocks are a leading candidate to account for a significant fraction of the unaccounted-for aggregate fluctuations. The issue of how to incorporate monetary and credit factors into the structure is still open, with different avenues under exploration. When there is an established monetary theory, we are sure that general equilibrium methods will be used econometrically to evaluate alternative monetary and credit arrangements.

References

Arrow, Kenneth J. & Debreu, Gerard: Existence of an equilibrium for a competitive economy. *Econometrica 22* (3), 265–90, 1954.

Benhabib, Jess, Rogerson, Richard & Wright, Randall: Homework in Macroeconomics I: Basic Theory, mimeo, 1990.

Brunner, Karl: The disarray in macroeconomics. In Forrest Capie & Geoffrey E. Wood (eds.), *Monetary Economics in the 1980s*, MacMillan Press, New York, 1989.

Christiano, Lawrence J. & Eichenbaum, Martin: Current real business cycle theories and aggregate labor market fluctuations. DP 24, Institute for Empirical Macroeconomics, Federal Reserve Bank of Minneapolis and University of Minnesota, 1990.

Cooley, Thomas F. & Hansen, Gary D.: The inflation tax in a real business cycle model. *American Economic Review 79* (4), 733–48, 1989.

The econometrics of the general equilibrium approach   177

Danthine, Jean-Pierre & Donaldson, John B.: Efficiency wages and the real business cycle. Cahier 8803, Départment d'économétri et d'économie politique, Université de Lausanne, 1988; forthcoming in *European Economic Review.*

Frisch, Ragnar: Propagation problems and impulse problems in dynamic economics. In *Economic Essays in Honor of Gustav Cassel,* London, 1933.

Frisch, Ragnar: Econometrics in the world of today. In W. A. Eltis, M. F. G. Scott & J. N. Wolfe (eds.), *Induction, Growth and Trade: Essays in Honour of Sir Roy Harrod,* Clarendon Press, Oxford, 152–66, 1970.

Greenwood, Jeremy, Hercowitz, Zvi & Huffman, Gregory W.: Investment, capacity utilization and the business cycle. *American Economic Review 78,* 402–18, June 1988.

Gomme, Paul & Greenwood, Jeremy: On the cyclical allocation of risk. WP 462, Research Department, Federal Reserve Bank of Minneapolis, 1990.

Harberger, Arnold C.: The incidence of the corporation income tax. *Journal of Political Economy 70* (3), 215–40, 1962.

Haberler, Gottfried: "Discussion" of the econometric approach to business fluctuations by Tjalling C. Koopmans. *American Economic Review 39,* 84–8, May 1949.

Hansen, Gary D.: Indivisible labor and the business cycle. *Journal of Monetary Economics 16* (3), 309–27, 1985.

Hicks, John R.: *Value and Capital: An Inquiry into Some Fundamental Principles of Economic Theory.* Clarendon Press, Oxford, 1939.

Hornstein, Andreas: Monopolistic competition, increasing returns to scale, and the importance of productivity changes. WP, University of Western Ontario, 1990.

Imrohoroglu, Ayse: Costs of business cycles with indivisibilities and liquidity constraints. *Journal of Political Economy 97,* 1364–83, Dec. 1989.

Johansen, Leif: *A Multi-sectoral Study of Economic Growth.* North-Holland, Amsterdam, 1960.

King, Robert G., Plosser, Charles I. & Rebelo, Sergio T.: Production, growth and business cycles II: New directions. *Journal of Monetary Economics 21,* 309–41, March/May 1988.

Koopmans, Tjalling C.: The econometric approach to business fluctuations. *American Economic Review 39,* 64–72, May 1949.

Kydland, Finn E. & Prescott, Edward C.: Time to build and aggregate fluctuations. *Econometrica 50,* 1345–70, 1982.

Kydland, Finn E. & Prescott, Edward C.: Hours and employment variation in business cycle theory. DP 17, Institute for Empirical Macroeconomics, Federal Reserve Bank of Minneapolis and University of Minnesota, 1989; forthcoming in *Economic Theory.*

Kydland, Finn E. & Prescott, Edward C.: Business cycles: Real facts and a monetary myth. *Federal Reserve Bank of Minneapolis Quarterly Review,* 3–18, Spring 1990.

Lindahl, Erik: Prisbildningsproblemets uppläggning från kapitalteoretisk synpunkt. *Ekonomisk Tidskrift 31,* 31–81, 1929. Translated as: The place of capital in the theory of price, in *Studies in the Theory of Money and Capital,* Farrar and Reinhart, New York, 269–350, 1929.

Lucas, Robert E., Jr.: *Models of Business Cycles.* Yrjö Jahnsson Lectures, Basil Blackwell, Oxford and New York, 1987.

Lucas, Robert E., Jr. & Rapping, Leonard A.: Real wages, employment and inflation. *Journal of Political Economy 77,* 721–54, Sept./Oct. 1969.

Lucas, Robert E., Jr. & Sargent, Thomas J.: After Keynesian macroeconomics. In *After the Phillips Curve: Persistence of High Inflation and High Unemployment,* Conference Series No. 19, Federal Reserve Bank of Boston, 49–72, 1978.

McCallum, Bennett T.: Real business cycle models. In R. J. Barro (ed.), *Modern Business Cycle Theories,* Harvard University Press, Boston, 16–50, 1989.

Prescott, Edward C.: Theory ahead of business cycle measurement. *Carnegie-Rochester Conference Series on Public Policy 25,* 11–44, 1986.

178   *F. E. Kydland and E. C. Prescott*

Rios-Rull, Jose Victor: Life cycle economies and aggregate fluctuations. Preliminary draft, Carnegie-Mellon University, June 1990.

Rogerson, Richard: Indivisible labor, lotteries and equilibrium. *Journal of Monetary Economics 21*, 3–16, Jan. 1988.

Samuelson, Paul A.: Interaction between the multiplier analysis and the principle of acceleration. *Review of Economic and Statistics 29*, 75–8, May 1939.

Scarf, Herbert (with the collaboration of T. Hansen): *Computation of Economic Equilibria.* Yale University Press, New Haven, 1973.

Schumpeter, Joseph: The common sense of econometrics. *Econometrica 1*, 5–12, Jan. 1933.

Shoven, John B. & Whalley, John: A general equilibrium calculation of the effects of differential taxation of income from capital in the U.S. *Journal of Public Economics 1* (3/4), 281–321, 1972.

Solow, Robert M.: A contribution to the theory of economic growth. *Quarterly Journal of Economics 70* (1), 65–94, 1956.

Solow, Robert M.: Technical change and the aggregate production function. *Review of Economics and Statistics 39* (3), 312–20, 1957.

Solow, Robert M.: *Growth Theory: An Exposition.* Radcliffe Lectures, Clarendon Press, Oxford, 1970.

Stokey, Nancy & Lucas, Robert E., Jr., with Prescott, Edward C.: *Recursive Methods in Economic Dynamics.* Harvard University Press, Cambridge, MA, 1989.

Tinbergen, Jan: Annual survey: Suggestions on quantitative business cycle theory. *Econometrica 3*, 241–308, July 1935.

Wicksell, Knut: Krisernas gåta. *Statsøkonomisk Tidsskrift 21*, 255–70, 1907.

Journal of Economic Perspectives—Volume 10, Number 1—Winter 1996—Pages 69–85

The Computational Experiment: An Econometric Tool

Finn E. Kydland and Edward C. Prescott

In a computational experiment, the researcher starts by posing a well-defined quantitative question. Then the researcher uses both theory and measurement to construct a model economy that is a computer representation of a national economy. A model economy consists of households, firms and often a government. The people in the model economy make economic decisions that correspond to those of their counterparts in the real world. Households, for example, make consumption and savings decisions, and they decide how much to work in the market. The researcher then calibrates the model economy so that it mimics the world along a carefully specified set of dimensions. Finally, the computer is used to run experiments that answer the question.[1]

Such experiments have become invaluable tools in quantitative aggregate theory.[2] They are being used, for example, to estimate the quantitative effects of trade liberalization policies, measure the welfare consequences of changes in the tax system and quantify the magnitude and nature of business cycle fluctuations induced by different types of shocks. In this paper, we review the use of the computational experiment in economics.

---

[1] Lucas (1980), in his paper on methods and problems in business cycle theory, explains the need for computational experiments in business cycle research.

[2] Shoven and Whalley (1972) were the first to use what we call the computational experiment in economics. The model economies that they used in their experiments are static and have many industrial sectors.

■ *Finn E. Kydland is Professor of Economics, Carnegie-Mellon University, Pittsburgh, Pennsylvania, and Research Associate, Federal Reserve Bank of Cleveland, Cleveland, Ohio. Edward C. Prescott is Professor of Economics, University of Minnesota, and Research Associate, Federal Reserve Bank of Minneapolis, both in Minneapolis, Minnesota.*

One immediate question that arises is whether the computational experiment should be regarded as an econometric tool (for example, Gregory and Smith, 1993). In the modern (narrow) sense of the term it is not, since it isn't used in the "measurement of economic relations" (Marschak, 1948, p. 1). Yet it is an econometric tool in the original (broad) sense of the term (which we prefer), since computational experiments are used to derive the quantitative implications of economic theory (Frisch, 1933a, p. 1). In Kydland and Prescott (1991a), we develop the position that the computational experiment is an econometric tool, but here, we avoid this largely semantic debate. Instead, we will simply state that the task of deriving the quantitative implications of theory differs from that of measuring economic parameters.

Computational experiments are not unique to economic science—they are heavily used in the physical sciences as well. In one crucial respect, however, they do differ across the two disciplines. Unlike theory in the physical sciences, theory in economics does not provide a law of motion. Rather, economic theory provides a specification of people's ability and willingness to substitute among commodities. Consequently, computational experiments in economics include the additional step of computing the equilibrium process in which all of the model's people behave in a way that is in each person's best interest—that is, economists must *compute* the equilibrium law of motion or process of the model economy. Given the process governing the system, both economic and physical science use the computer to generate realizations of this process.

If the model is deterministic, only one possible equilibrium realization exists for the path of the model economy. If the model economy has aggregate uncertainty—as it must, for example, if the phenomena of interest are business cycle fluctuations—then the model will imply a process governing the random evolution of the economy. In the case of uncertainty, the computer can generate any number of independent realizations of the equilibrium stochastic process, and these realizations, along with statistical estimation theory, are then used to measure the sampling distribution of any desired set of statistics of the model economy.

Steps in an Economic Computational Experiment

Any economic computational experiment involves five major steps: pose a question; use a well-tested theory; construct a model economy; calibrate the model economy; and run the experiment. We will discuss each of these steps in turn.

Pose a Question

The purpose of a computational experiment is to derive a quantitative answer to some well-posed question. Thus, the first step in carrying out a computational experiment is to pose such a question. Some of these questions are concerned with policy evaluation issues. These questions typically ask about the welfare and distributive consequences of some policy under consideration. Other questions are con-

Table 1

Examples of Well-Posed Questions in Studies Using the Computational Experiment

Studies Using Theory	Question
Auerbach and Kotlikoff (1987)	What are the effects of the current U.S. social security system on capital formation and intergenerational equity?
Brown, Deardorff and Stern (1994)	What are the potential welfare, wage rate and terms-of-trade effects of NAFTA on Canada, Mexico and the United States?
Gravelle and Kotlikoff (1995)	What are the welfare consequences of the 1986 U.S. tax reform?
Harris (1984)	What are the welfare gains for a small open economy with scale effects and imperfect competition?
Hopenhayn and Rogerson (1993)	What are the welfare costs of a job destruction tax on firms equal to one year's wages?
İmrohoroğlu (1992)	What are the welfare costs of inflation if insurance is imperfect?

Studies Developing Theory	Question
Backus, Kehoe and Kydland (1994)	Does theory imply the J-curve pattern of covariance between terms of trade and the trade balance?
Christiano and Eichenbaum (1992b) and Chang (1995)	What is the contribution of public finance shocks to aggregate fluctuations?
Finn (1995)	What is the contribution of oil shocks to business cycle fluctuations?
Greenwood, Hercowitz and Huffman (1988)	Does nonneutrality of technology shocks with respect to the consumption and investment good change the estimate of the contribution of technology shocks to business cycle fluctuations?
Hornstein (1993)	Does the introduction of monopolistic competition into real business cycle models alter the estimate of technology shocks contribution?
Kydland and Prescott (1982)	What is the quantitative nature of fluctuations induced by technology shocks?

cerned with the testing and development of theory. These questions typically ask about the quantitative implications of theory for some phenomena. If the answer to these questions is that the predictions of theory match the observations, theory has passed that particular test. If the answer is that there is a discrepancy, a deviation from theory has been documented. Still, other experiments are concerned with the sensitivity of previous findings to the introduction of some feature of reality from which previous studies have abstracted. Table 1 offers some examples of computational experiments that seek to answer each of these types of questions. That table highlights the fact that judging whether a model economy is a "good" abstraction can be done only relative to the question posed.

Use Well-Tested Theory

With a particular question in mind, a researcher needs some strong theory to carry out a computational experiment: that is, a researcher needs a theory that has been tested through use and found to provide reliable answers to a class of questions. Here, by theory we do not mean a set of assertions about the actual economy. Rather, following Lucas (1980), economic theory is defined to be "an explicit set of instructions for building . . . a mechanical imitation system" to answer a question. If the question is quantitative in nature, a computer representation of the imitation system or economy is used, and extensive computations are required to answer the posed question.

As one example, the computational experiments often carried out in modern business cycle theory build upon the neoclassical growth framework. Central to neoclassical growth theory is its use of an aggregate production function, with the output of goods resulting from inputs of labor and capital.[3] This framework has served well when dealing with growth within reasonably stable economic institutions. With an explicit description of the household sector, including its focus on the time-allocation decision, the neoclassical growth model becomes an internally consistent framework for addressing business cycle questions, as well as other questions of interest to macroeconomists. The theory implies that when a model economy is confronted with technology, public finance and terms-of-trade shocks, it should display business cycle fluctuations of a quantitative nature similar to those actually observed. In other words, modern business cycle models are stochastic versions of neoclassical growth theory. And the fact that business cycle models do produce normal-looking fluctuations adds dramatically to our confidence in the neoclassical growth theory model—including the answers it provides to growth accounting and public finance questions.

We recognize, of course, that although the economist should choose a well-tested theory, every theory has some issues and questions that it does not address well. In the case of neoclassical growth theory, for example, it fails spectacularly when used to address economic development issues. Differences in stocks of reproducible capital stocks cannot account for international differences in per capita incomes. This does not preclude its usefulness in evaluating tax policies and in business cycle research.

Construct a Model Economy

With a particular theoretical framework in mind, the third step in conducting a computational experiment is to construct a model economy. Here, key issues are the amount of detail and the feasibility of computing the equilibrium process. Often, economic experimenters are constrained to deal with a much simpler model

---

[3] Neoclassical growth theory also represents a good example of the importance of interaction between factual studies and theory development. Solow (1970) lists several growth facts that influenced the development of neoclassical growth theory. Once the main ingredients of the theory were established—such as the production function—new light was thrown on the data.

economy than they would like because computing the equilibrium of a more complicated model would be impossible, given currently available tools.

This situation is no different from that in the physical sciences, where, as in economics, the computational experiment has become accepted as an invaluable scientific tool. For example, in his overview of climate modeling, Schneider (1987, p. 72) states: "Although all climate models consist of mathematical representations of physical processes, the precise composition of a model and its complexity depend on the problem it is designed to address." And later (p. 72): "Often it makes sense to attack a problem first with a simple model and then employ the results to guide research at higher resolution." In the physical sciences, as in economics, confidence in a particular framework or approach is gained through successful use.

So far, most of the model environments that macroeconomists have used share certain characteristics. The environments are inhabited by a large number of people whose decision problems are described explicitly. Both the household and business sectors play a central role. For some questions, government or foreign sectors must be included as well. In some models everyone is alike; in others, such as those designed to address questions where demographic changes are important, heterogeneous people must be used.

This description may sound somewhat indefinite or abstract, but we reemphasize that an abstraction can be judged only relative to some given question. To criticize or reject a model because it is an abstraction is foolish: all models are necessarily abstractions. A model environment must be selected based on the question being addressed. For example, heterogeneity of people is crucial in the Auerbach and Kotlikoff (1987) model, which predicts the consequences of the population's changing age distribution on savings. However, Ríos-Rull (1994) demonstrates that such life cycle features, even when combined with elements of market incompleteness, are not quantitatively important to business cycle findings regarding issues such as the contribution of technology shocks to business cycle fluctuations. The features of a given model may be appropriate for some question (or class of questions) but not for others.[4]

The selection and construction of a particular model economy should not depend on the answer provided. In fact, searching within some parametric class of economies for the one that best fits a set of aggregate time series makes little sense, because it isn't likely to answer an interesting question. For example, if the question is of the type, "how much of fact X is accounted for by Y," then choosing the parameter values in such a way as to make the amount accounted for as large as

---

[4] We will not debate the legitimacy of these methods, since such debates generally serve to define schools rather than to produce agreement. Such debates are almost nonexistent during normal science, but tend to recur during scientific revolutions. As stated by Kuhn (1962, p. 145), "Few philosophers of science still seek absolute criteria for the verification of scientific theories." All historically significant theories have agreed with the facts, but only to a degree. No more precise answer can be found to the question of how well an individual theory fits the facts. Using probabilistic verification theories that ask us to compare a given scientific theory with all others that might fit the same data is a futile effort. We agree with Kuhn (p. 146) that "probabilistic theories disguise the verification situation as much as they illuminate it."

possible according to some metric is an attempt to get a particular—not a good—answer to the question.

Calibrate the Model Economy

Now that a model has been constructed, the fourth step in carrying out a computational experiment is to calibrate that model. Originally, in the physical sciences, *calibration* referred to the graduation of measuring instruments. For example, a Celsius thermometer is calibrated to register zero degrees when immersed in water that contains ice and 100 degrees when immersed in boiling water. A thermometer relies on the theory that mercury expands (approximately) linearly within this range of temperatures. Related theory also tells us how to recalibrate the thermometer if the measurements are made in Denver or Mexico City rather than at sea level. In a sense, model economies, like thermometers, are measuring devices. Generally, some economic questions have known answers, and the model should give an approximately correct answer to them if we are to have any confidence in the answer given to the question with unknown answer. Thus, data are used to calibrate the model economy so that it mimics the world as closely as possible along a limited, but clearly specified, number of dimensions.

Note that calibration is not an attempt at assessing the size of something: it is not estimation. *Estimation* is the determination of the approximate quantity of something. To estimate a parameter, for example, a researcher looks for a situation in which the signal-to-noise ratio is high. Using the existing data and some theory, the researcher then constructs a probability model. An estimator is developed that is robust, relative to the parameter that is to be estimated, to the questionable features of the maintained hypothesis. As a second example of estimation, a computational experiment itself is a type of estimation, in the sense that the quantitative answer to a posed question is an estimate. For example, the quantitative theory of a computational experiment can be used to measure the welfare implications of alternative tax policies.

It is important to emphasize that the parameter values selected are not the ones that provide the best fit in some statistical sense. In some cases, the presence of a particular discrepancy between the data and the model economy is a test of the theory being used. In these cases, absence of that discrepancy is grounds to reject the use of the theory to address the question.

One such example is the use of standard theory to answer the question of how volatile the postwar U.S. economy would have been if technology shocks had been the only contributor to business cycle fluctuations. To answer this question, a model economy with only technology shocks was needed. Using the standard neoclassical production function, standard preferences to describe people's willingness to substitute intra- and intertemporally between consumption and leisure, and an estimate of the technology shock variance, we found that the model economy displays business cycle fluctuations 70 percent as large as did the U.S. economy (Kydland and Prescott, 1991b). This number is our answer to the posed question.

Some have questioned our finding, pointing out that on one key dimension real business cycle models and the world differ dramatically: the correlation between hours worked and average labor productivity is near one in the model economy and approximately zero in U.S. postwar observations (McCallum, 1989). The detractors of the use of standard theory to study business cycles are correct in arguing that the magnitude of this correlation in the world provides a test of the theory. They are incorrect in arguing that passing this test requires the value of this correlation in the model and in the real world to be approximately equal. An implication of the theory is that this correlation is a function of the importance of technology shocks relative to other shocks. In particular, the less is the relative importance of technology shocks, the smaller this correlation should be. The reason for this is that the factors other than technology shocks that give rise to variation in the labor input result in productivity being low when hours are high.[5] Given that the estimated contribution of technology shocks to fluctuations is 70 percent, the correlation between hours and labor productivity being near one in the data would have been grounds for dismissing our answer. (For further elaboration on this point, see Kydland and Prescott, 1991b, p. 79; Aiyagari, 1994.)

Run the Experiment

The fifth and final step in conducting a computational experiment is to run the experiment. Quantitative economic theory uses theory and measurement to estimate how big something is. The instrument is a computer program that determines the equilibrium process of the model economy and uses this equilibrium process to generate equilibrium realizations of the model economy. The computational experiment, then, is the act of using this instrument. These equilibrium realizations of the model economy can be compared with the behavior of the actual economy in some period as follows.

If the model economy has no aggregate uncertainty, then it is simply a matter of comparing the equilibrium path of the model economy with the path of the actual economy. If the model economy has aggregate uncertainty, first a set of statistics that summarize relevant aspects of the behavior of the actual economy is selected. Then the computational experiment is used to generate many independent realizations of the equilibrium process for the model economy. In this way, the sampling distribution of this set of statistics can be determined to any degree of accuracy for the model economy and compared with the values of the set of statistics for the actual economy. In comparing the sampling distribution of a statistic for the model economy to the value of that statistic for the actual data, it is crucial that the same statistic be computed for the model and the real world. If, for

---

[5] Christiano and Eichenbaum (1992a) have established formally this possibility in the case where the other shock is variations in public consumption, but the result holds for any shock that is approximately orthogonal to the technology shocks.

example, the statistic for the real world is for a 50-year period, then the statistic for the model economy must also be for a 50-year period.

The Computational Experiment in Business Cycle Research

Business cycles, that is, the recurrent fluctuations of output and employment about trend, puzzled economists for a long time. Understanding business cycles required the development of methods that made possible the use of computational experiments to answer questions concerned with the behavior of dynamic economies with uncertainty. Prior to the development of these methods, business cycle fluctuations were viewed as deviations from theory, and very little progress was made in understanding them. Subsequent to the development of those methods, computational experiments have been extensively used in business cycle research. The results of these experiments forced economists to revise their old views, and business cycle fluctuations are now seen as being, in fact, predicted by standard theory. For these reasons, we choose business cycle theory to illustrate the use of computational experiments in economic research.

Posing Questions about the Business Cycle

In the 1970s, a common assumption behind research on the business cycle was that one set of factors, most likely monetary shocks, was behind the cyclical component and that an entirely different set of factors, mainly the growth of productivity and inputs summarized by the neoclassical growth model, accounted for the movement of the long-run growth component.

But there was also an earlier view, tracing as far back as work by Wicksell (1907), that suggested that fluctuation in technological growth could produce broad economic fluctuations. In the 1960s and 1970s, this source was dismissed by many as being unlikely to play much of a role in the aggregate. Most researchers believed that considerable variation could exist in productivity at the industry level, but they believed that industry-level shocks would average out in the aggregate. During the 1980s, however, technology shocks gained renewed interest as a major source of fluctuations, supported largely by computational experiments and quantitative economic theory. As a consequence, business cycle theory treats growth and cycles as being integrated, not as a sum of two components driven by different factors.[6]

---

[6] An operational way of defining the trend empirically is described in Hodrick and Prescott (1980), who used standard curve-fitting techniques to define a growth component as being the curve that best fits a time series in a least-square sense, subject to a penalty on the sum of the second differences squared. The larger this penalty parameter, the smoother the fitted curve. For quarterly series, they found that a penalty parameter of 1600 made the fitted curve mimic well the one that business cycle analysts would draw. Given the finding that business cycle fluctuations are quantitatively just what neoclassical growth theory predicts, the resulting deviations from trend are nothing more than well-defined statistics. We emphasize that given the way the theory has developed, these statistics measure nothing. Business cycle theory treats growth and cycles as being

Thus, the fundamental question here is the extent to which neoclassical growth theory can account for business cycle fluctuations, as well as long-term growth trends. A particular question addressed was, "How much would the U.S. postwar economy have fluctuated if technology shocks had been the only source of fluctuations?" Computational experiments are well suited to tackle this question.

The Theory Used in Model Selection

The basic theory used in the modern study of business cycles is the neoclassical growth model. The basic version of this model can best be understood as based on five relationships.

The first relationship is an aggregate production function that sets total output equal to $A_t F(K_t, H_t)$, where F is a constant returns to scale function where the inputs are capital and labor, and A_t is the technology level that grows at random rates. In the simplest case, aggregate output is divided between consumption C and investment I. Under the assumption that factors are paid their marginal product, we obtain the identity that GNP and income are equal: $C + I = wH + rK$, where w and r are factor rental prices.

The second relationship in the model economy describes the evolution of the capital stock. Each time period, the existing capital stock depreciates at a constant rate δ, but is replenished by new investment I_t. Thus $K_{t+1} = (1-\delta) K_t + I_t$.

The third relationship describes the evolution of the technology parameter A_t. Given that a structure that displays persistence is needed, a typical form would be $A_{t+1} = \rho A_t + \epsilon_{t+1}$, where ρ is large but less than one, and the shocks ϵ_{t+1} are identically and independently distributed. In other words, the technology level for any given period depends on the technology level in the previous period, plus a random disturbance. The technology described by these relations specifies people's ability to substitute.

The fourth relationship needed for a fully specified economy is a specification of people's willingness to substitute between consumption and leisure, both intertemporally and intratemporally. For this purpose, our model economy has a stand-in household with utility function that depends on consumption and leisure.[7] For simplicity, one can assume that the households own the capital stock directly and rent it to the firms.

---

integrated, not as a sum of two components driven by different factors. For that reason, talking about the resulting statistics as imposing spurious cycles makes no sense. The Hodrick-Prescott filter is simply a statistical decomposition that summarizes in a reasonable way what happens at business cycle frequencies. The representation has proven useful in presenting the findings and judging the reliability of the answer, as well as a way of demonstrating remaining puzzles or anomalies relative to theory.

[7] More explicitly, the function can take the general form

$$E \sum_{t=0}^{\infty} \beta^t U(C_t, 1-H_t),$$

where we normalize so that market and nonmarket productive time add to one. For a complete specification of the model, values of the parameters β, δ and ρ are needed, as well as the explicit utility function U and the production function F.

The final required element is an equilibrium concept. The one used is the competitive equilibrium, which equates marginal rates of substitution and transformation to price ratios. This involves equilibrium decision functions for consumption, investment and labor input as functions of the capital stock and productivity level during that time period: $C(K_t, A_t)$, $I(K_t, A_t)$ and $H(K_t, A_t)$, respectively. In other words, using dynamic programming methods, the decisions can be computed as functions of the list of state variables that provide sufficient information about the position of the economy.

Through this theory, business cycle theorists make contact with other fields of economics. Macroeconomics is no longer largely separate from the rest of economics. The utility and production functions used by business cycle theorists are similar to those used by public finance researchers (for example, Auerbach and Kotlikoff, 1987). The introduction of household production illustrates the close connection with the work of labor economists (for example, Benhabib, Rogerson and Wright, 1991; Greenwood and Hercowitz, 1991). When these models are expanded to consider international trade explicitly, they draw upon work in that field (Backus, Kehoe and Kydland, 1994).

The choice of a model, as already noted, must be governed both by the question at hand and by what is computable.

As an example of altering the model to suit the posed question, consider a contrast between two otherwise similar models. Benhabib, Rogerson and Wright (1991) and Greenwood and Hercowitz (1991) both consider household production in addition to market production, but the two studies are motivated by somewhat different questions. Both use capital and labor as inputs in nonmarket production. Benhabib and his coauthors divide the time allocation of households into three uses: market and nonmarket production time and leisure time. The model is designed to capture the household decision to combine its labor with machines, such as stoves and washing machines, to produce household consumption services. The authors argue that houses do not need to be combined with labor, at least not to the same extent that household machines do, so they exclude housing capital from their concept of household capital. Greenwood and Hercowitz, on the other hand, distinguish only between market and nonmarket time and include the stock of housing, along with consumer durables, in their concept of household capital.[8] This example illustrates the important point that even the definition of particular variables in relation to the model economy may depend on the question.

If a model environment is not computable, then it cannot be used for a computational experiment. This restriction can be a severe one, and the development of appropriate computable methods must therefore be given high priority. Fortunately, there has been considerable progress in this area over the last 30 or 40 years.

---

[8] To be consistent, they then subtract gross housing product (the measure of the service flow from the economy's housing stock) from GNP and add it to the consumer durables component of personal consumption expenditures.

In cases involving uncertain intertemporal behavior, the development of statistical decision theory has provided a consistent way for people to make decisions under uncertainty. Another significant development is the Arrow-Debreu general equilibrium theory, which extends equilibrium theory to uncertain environments.[9] More recently, Ríos-Rull (1995) offers an overview of the expansion in computable general equilibrium models that incorporate heterogeneity in the household sector—a category that has expanded dramatically over the last few years.

Calibration

Often, calibration involves the simple task of computing a few averages. For example, if the standard Cobb-Douglas production function is used—that is, if we let $F(K,H) = K^{1-\theta}H^{\theta}$—then a numerical value for the parameter θ can be obtained by computing the average labor share of total output over a period of years. Several other growth relations map more or less directly into parameter values for typical models within the neoclassical growth framework, at least if the functional forms have been chosen with calibration in mind. Most growth relations have not changed much, on average, from one cycle to the next for several decades. As a consequence, computational experiments replicate the key long-term or growth relations among model aggregates.

Exceptions do exist, where long-term relationships are not stable. For example, the inventory stock as a fraction of GNP has declined steadily. Durables expenditures as a fraction of total output have risen. For some purposes these changes can be ignored, since that feature does not significantly affect the answer to the question posed. At other times, depending on the associated pattern in the corresponding relative price, such information enables the researcher to obtain a quite precise estimate of some elasticity of substitution, which can then be built into the model.

A good example of this sort of issue is the fact that hours of work per household are about the same now as four decades ago, in spite of a large rise in the real wage rate over the same period. This fact indicates that the elasticity of substitution between consumption and nonmarket time is near one. Still, many business cycle models abstract from the long-run productivity growth that is required to imply this sort of wage growth, because the answer to the questions addressed in those studies would have been essentially the same, as shown by Hansen (1986).[10]

To calibrate a utility function for the household sector of the economy, it is common to rely on averages across large numbers of the relevant population in the actual economy. For example, some model environments employ a utility function in consumption and leisure that, like the Cobb-Douglas production function above,

---

[9] Also important is the development of recursive methods for the study of economic dynamics, because these methods allow economists to use the computational experiment to generate time series disciplined by factual studies (Stokey and Lucas, 1989).

[10] Hansen (1986) compares otherwise identical model economies and permits growth in one version and not in the other. The model without growth needs a slight adjustment in the capital depreciation rate to be calibrated to the investment share of output and the observed capital/output ratio. With this adjustment, both models estimate the same role of technological shocks (more precisely, Solow residuals) for cyclical fluctuations.

has a share parameter. In this case, the weight that should be placed on consumption turns out to be approximately equal to the average fraction of time spent in market activity. This fraction, in principle, can be obtained from panel data for large samples of individuals. Ghez and Becker (1975) offer a careful measurement study—making reasonable and thoughtful judgments about factors like age limits of the population sample and definition of total time allocated to market and nonmarket activities, including treatment of sleep and personal care.

In calibration, we sometimes make the model economy inconsistent with the data on one dimension so that it will be consistent on another. For example, İmrohoroğlu (1992) explores the welfare consequences of alternative monetary arrangements in worlds where agents are liquidity constrained, while Cooley and Hansen (1989) explore the welfare consequences in worlds where people use money for transaction purposes. These are two very different environments, each of which abstracts from the main feature of the other. İmrohoroğlu calibrates her model economy to yield a stock of money held per household that is in line with U.S. observations. In her model, however, people hold money because they do not have access to an insurance technology to insure against randomness in the market value of their time. Equivalently, if they do have access to such an insurance technology, they find it so costly that, in equilibrium, they do not employ it. This is the only reason, in her model, for people to hold money; if she had calibrated the model to the amount of variation in individual income found in panel data, the model would have implied that average household holdings of liquid assets were about half of those actually held.

Of course, households have other reasons for holding liquid assets that earn much less than the average return on physical capital. For instance, such assets can be used as a down payment on a house at some future date, as a substitute for insurance against sickness and accidents, or for transaction purposes, as in the Cooley and Hansen (1989) environment. These and other factors are abstracted from in the world of İmrohoroğlu (1992), which led her to introduce greater variation in the market value of households' time so as to make per capita holdings of money in the model match actual holdings. This calibration is reasonable, given the question she addresses. Her implicit assumption is that it is unimportant which liquidity factor gives rise to these holdings. Subsequent research will either support this working hypothesis or disprove it and, in the process, lead to better model economies for evaluating monetary and credit policy arrangements. This sequence is how economic science progresses.

Running Experiments

With explicit functional forms for the production and utility functions, with values assigned to the parameters, and with a probability distribution for the shocks, a researcher can use the model economy to perform computational experiments. The first step is to compute the equilibrium decision rules, which are functions of the state of the economy. The next step is to generate equilibrium realizations of the economy. The computer begins each period with a given level of the state variables, for example, the capital stock and the technology level. The values of the state variables along with the equilibrium decision and pricing functions determine the equilibrium realization for that period. Equilibrium investment and the new technology shocks determine next period's state. In the next and subsequent periods, this procedure is repeated until time series of the desired length are obtained. The resulting model time series can then be summarized by a suitable set of statistics.

In Kydland and Prescott (1982), we built a model economy where all fluctuations could be traced back to technology shocks. We began by extending the neoclassical growth model to include leisure as an argument of the stand-in household's utility function. Given that more than half of business cycle fluctuations are accounted for by variations in the labor input, introducing this element was crucial. We then calibrated the deterministic version of the model so that its consumption-investment shares, factor income shares, capital/output ratios, leisure/market-time shares and depreciation shares matched the average values for the U.S. economy in the postwar period. We abstracted from public finance considerations and consolidated the public and private sectors. We introduced Frisch's (1933b) assumption of time to build new productive capital. The construction period considered was four quarters, with new capital becoming productive only upon completion, but with resources being used up throughout the construction period. Given the high volatility of inventory investment, inventory stocks were included as a factor of production. In our computational experiments, using technology shock variance estimated from production function residuals (Prescott, 1986), we found that the model economy's output variance was 55 percent as large as the corresponding variance for the U.S. economy in the postwar period.

Probably the most questionable assumption of this theory is that of homogeneous workers, with the additional implication that all variation in hours occurs in the form of changes in hours per worker. According to aggregate data for the U.S. economy, only about one-third of the quarterly fluctuations in market hours are of this form, while the remaining two-thirds arise from changes in the number of workers (Kydland and Prescott, 1990, Table 1).

This observation led Hansen (1985) to introduce the Rogerson (1988) labor indivisibility construct into a business cycle model. In the Hansen world, all fluctuations in hours are in the form of employment variation. To deal with the apparent nonconvexity arising from the assumption of indivisible labor, Hansen makes the problem convex by assuming that the commodity points are contracts in which every agent is paid the same amount whether that agent works or not, and that a lottery randomly chooses who actually works in every period. He finds that with this labor indivisibility, his model economy fluctuates as much as did the U.S. economy. Our view is that with the extreme assumption of fluctuations only in employment, Hansen overestimates the amount of aggregate fluctuations accounted for by Solow residuals in the same way that our equally extreme assumption of fluctuations solely in hours per worker led to an underestimation.

In Kydland and Prescott (1991b), the major improvement on the 1982 version of the model economy is that variation is permitted in both the number of workers and the number of hours per worker. The number of hours in which a plant is operated in any given period is endogenous.

Because the cost of moving workers in and out of the labor force is not included, a property of the equilibrium is that all of the hours variation is in the form of employment change and none in hours per worker. In that respect, the Kydland and Prescott (1991b) model is identical to Hansen's (1985) model. Using the economy with no moving costs, technology shocks are estimated to account for about 90 percent of the aggregate output variance. For the economy with moving costs, we calibrated it so that relative variations in hours per worker and the number of workers matched U.S. data. The estimate of the fraction of the cycle accounted for by technology shocks is then reduced to 70 percent.

These estimates of the contribution of technology shocks to aggregate fluctuations have been found to be robust in several modifications of the model economy. For instance, Greenwood, Hercowitz and Huffman (1988) permit the utilization rate of capital to vary and affect its depreciation rate and assume all technology change is embodied in new capital. Danthine and Donaldson (1990) introduce an efficiency-wage construct, while Cho and Cooley (1995) permit nominal-wage contracting. Ríos-Rull (1994) uses a model calibrated to life cycle earnings and consumption patterns. Gomme and Greenwood (1995) incorporate heterogeneous agents with recursive preferences and equilibrium risk allocations. In none of these cases is the estimate of the contribution of technology shocks to aggregate fluctuations significantly altered.

The computational experiment is also being used to derive the quantitative implications of monetary shocks for business cycle fluctuations if money is used for transaction purposes only. In these experiments, money may be held either because it is required in advance of purchasing cash goods (Lucas and Stokey, 1987; Cooley and Hansen 1989, 1992) or because real cash balances economize on time (Kydland, 1989). Models of this type have been used to evaluate monetary policy.

At this stage, we are less confident in these model economies than those designed to evaluate the contribution of technology shocks. There are three related reasons. The first is that, unlike actual economies, these model economies fail to display the sluggishness of the inflation rate's response to changes in the growth rate of money (Christiano and Eichenbaum, 1992b). The second is that people seem to hold far larger monetary assets than are needed for transaction purposes—in the postwar period, for example, U.S. households' holdings of M2 have exceeded half of annual GNP—which implies that the transaction rationale for holding money is not well understood. The third reason is that the evaluation of monetary policy appears to be sensitive to the reason people hold these liquid assets. İmrohoroğlu (1992) has constructed a model economy in which people vary their holdings of liquid assets as their income varies to smooth their consumption.[11] She finds that if a transaction-cost model is calibrated to data generated by her model econ-

---

[11] İmrohoroğlu and Prescott (1991) introduce a banking technology to intermediate government debt.

omy and the calibrated economy is used to estimate the cost of inflation, this estimate would grossly underestimate the true cost of inflation for her model world. This result is surprising and bothersome. Typically, how some feature is introduced is unimportant as long as the aggregate substitution elasticities and quantities match. We currently do not have the tools for computing equilibria of models with both the features of the neoclassical growth model and the idiosyncratic shocks that result in people holding money for precautionary reasons. One may say that stronger theory is needed when it comes to evaluating the contribution of monetary policy shocks to business cycle fluctuations.

Summary

With the general equilibrium approach, empirical knowledge is organized around preferences and technologies. Given the question and given existing economic theory and measurement, a researcher creates a model economy. This researcher then determines a quantitative answer to the posed question for the model economy. If the theory is strong and the measurements good, we have confidence that the answer for the model economy will be essentially the same as for the actual economy.

Of course, sometimes measurement is not very good, and a series of computational experiments reveals that different plausible values of some parameter give very different answers to the posed question. If so, this parameter—which measures some aspect of people's willingness and ability to substitute—must be more accurately measured before theory can provide an answer in which we have confidence. Or sometimes the theory relative to the question is weak or nonexistent, and the answer depends upon which of the currently competing theories is used to construct the model economy. If so, these competing theories must be subjected to further tests before there is a good basis for choosing among them. At still other times, the computational tools needed to derive the implications of the theory do not exist, so better computational methods or more powerful computers are needed.

Earlier in this article, we quoted the Lucas (1980) definition of "theory" as being an explicit set of instructions for building an imitation economy to address certain questions and not a collection of assertions about the behavior of the actual economy. Consequently, statistical hypothesis testing, which is designed to test assertions about actual systems, is not an appropriate tool for testing economic theory.

One way to test a theory is to determine whether model economies constructed according to the instructions of that theory mimic certain aspects of reality. Perhaps the ultimate test of a theory is whether its predictions are confirmed—that is, did the actual economy behave as predicted by the model economy, given the policy rule selected? If a theory passes these tests, then it is tested further, often by conducting a computational experiment that includes some feature of reality not previously included in the computational experiments. More often than not, introducing this feature does not change the answers, and currently established theory becomes stronger. Occasionally, however, the new feature turns out to be important, and established theory must then be expanded and improved. In this way, economic science progresses.

Given the infeasibility of controlled experiments with national economies, the computational experiment is the tool of quantitative economic theory, whether the primary concern be with theory use or with theory development and testing.

■ *We thank Graham Candler, Javier Díaz-Giménez, Tryphon Kollintzas, Jim Schmitz and Nancy Stokey for helpful discussions and the National Science Foundation for financial support. The views expressed herein are those of the authors and not necessarily those of the Federal Reserve Banks of Cleveland or Minneapolis, nor of the Federal Reserve System.*

References

Aiyagari, S. Rao, "On the Contribution of Technology Shocks to Business Cycles," *Quarterly Review, Federal Reserve Bank of Minneapolis,* Winter 1994, *18,* 22–34.

Auerbach, Alan J., and Laurence J. Kotlikoff, *Dynamic Fiscal Policy.* Cambridge, U.K.: Cambridge University Press, 1987.

Backus, David K., Patrick J. Kehoe, and Finn E. Kydland, "Dynamics of the Trade Balance and the Terms of Trade: The J-curve?," *American Economic Review,* March 1994, *84,* 84–103.

Benhabib, Jess, Richard Rogerson, and Randall Wright, "Homework in Macroeconomics: Household Production and Aggregate Fluctuations," *Journal of Political Economy,* December 1991, *99,* 1166–87.

Brown, Drussilla K., Alan V. Deardorff, and Robert M. Stern, "Estimates of a North American Free Trade Agreement," manuscript, Federal Reserve Bank of Minneapolis, 1994.

Chang, Ly-June, "Business Cycles with Distorting Taxes and Disaggregate Capital Markets," *Journal of Economic Dynamics and Control,* July/September 1995, *19,* 985–1010.

Cho, Jong Ok, and Thomas F. Cooley, "The Business Cycle with Nominal Contracts," *Economic Theory,* June 1995, *6,* 13–34.

Christiano, Lawrence J., and Martin Eichenbaum, "Current Real-Business-Cycle Theories and Aggregate Labor-Market Fluctuations," *American Economic Review,* June 1992a, *82,* 430–50.

Christiano, Lawrence J., and Martin Eichenbaum, "Liquidity Effects, Monetary Policy, and the Business Cycle." Working Paper No. 4129, National Bureau of Economic Research, 1992b.

Cooley, Thomas F., and Gary D. Hansen, "The Inflation Tax in a Real Business Cycle Model," *American Economic Review,* September 1989, *79,* 733–48.

Cooley, Thomas F., and Gary D. Hansen, "Tax Distortions in a Neoclassical Monetary Economy," *Journal of Economic Theory,* December 1992, *58,* 290–316.

Danthine, Jean-Pierre, and John B. Donaldson, "Efficiency Wages and the Business Cycle Puzzle," *European Economic Review,* November 1990, *34,* 1275–1301.

Finn, Mary G., "Variance Properties of Solow's Productivity Residual and their Cyclical Implications," *Journal of Economic Dynamics and Control,* July/September 1995, *19,* 1249–82.

Frisch, Ragnar, "Editorial," *Econometrica,* January 1933a, *1,* 1–5.

Frisch, Ragnar, "Propagation Problems and Impulse Problems in Dynamic Economics." In *Economic Essays in Honour of Gustav Cassel.* London: G. Allen & Unwin Ltd., 1933b, pp. 171–205.

Ghez, Gilbert R., and Gary S. Becker, *The Allocation of Time and Goods over the Life Cycle.* New York: Columbia University Press, 1975.

Gomme, Paul, and Jeremy Greenwood, "On the Cyclical Allocation of Risk," *Journal of Economic Dynamics and Control,* January/February 1995, *19,* 91–124.

Gravelle, Jane G., and Laurence J. Kotlikoff, "Corporate Taxation and the Efficiency Gains of the 1986 Tax Reform Act," *Economic Theory,* June 1995, *6,* 51–82.

Greenwood, Jeremy, and Zvi Hercowitz, "The Allocation of Capital and Time Over the Business Cycle," *Journal of Political Economy,* December 1991, *99,* 1188–214.

Greenwood, Jeremy, Zvi Hercowitz, and Gregory W. Huffman, "Investment, Capacity Utilization, and the Real Business Cycle," *American Economic Review,* June 1988, *78,* 402–18.

Gregory, Allan W., and Gregory W. Smith, "Statistical Aspects of Calibration in Macroeconomics." In Maddala, G. S., C. R. Rao, and H. D. Vinod, eds., *Handbook of Statistics.* Vol. 2, New York: Elsevier Science, 1993, pp. 703–19.

Hansen, Gary D., "Indivisible Labor and the Business Cycle," *Journal of Monetary Economics,* November 1985, *16,* 309–27.

Hansen, Gary D., "Growth and Fluctuations." In "Three Essays on Labor Indivisibility and the Business Cycle," Ph.D. dissertation, University of Minnesota, 1986.

Harris, Richard, "Applied General Equilibrium Analysis of Small Open Economies with Scale Economies and Imperfect Competition," *American Economic Review,* December 1984, *18,* 1016–32.

Hodrick, Robert J., and Edward C. Prescott, "Post-War U.S. Business Cycles: An Empirical Investigation." Discussion Paper No. 451, Carnegie-Mellon University, 1980.

Hopenhayn, Hugo, and Richard Rogerson, "Job Turnover and Policy Evaluation: A General Equilibrium Analysis," *Journal of Political Economy,* October 1993, *101,* 915–38.

Hornstein, Andreas, "Monopolistic Competition, Increasing Returns to Scale and the Importance of Productivity Change," *Journal of Monetary Economics,* June 1993, *31,* 299–316.

İmrohoroğlu, Ayşe, "The Welfare Cost of Inflation Under Imperfect Insurance," *Journal of Economic Dynamics and Control,* January 1992, *16,* 79–91.

İmrohoroğlu, Ayşe, and Edward C. Prescott, "Seigniorage as a Tax: A Quantitative Evaluation," *Journal of Money, Credit and Banking,* August 1991, *23,* 462–75.

Kuhn, Thomas S., *The Structure of Scientific Revolutions.* Chicago: University of Chicago Press, 1962.

Kydland, Finn E., "The Role of Money in a Business Cycle Model." Discussion Paper No. 23, Institute for Empirical Macroeconomics, Federal Reserve Bank of Minneapolis, 1989.

Kydland, Finn E., and Edward C. Prescott, "Time to Build and Aggregate Fluctuations," *Econometrica,* November 1982, *50,* 1345–70.

Kydland, Finn E., and Edward C. Prescott, "Business Cycles: Real Facts and a Monetary Myth," *Quarterly Review, Federal Reserve Bank of Minneapolis,* Spring 1990, *14,* 3–18.

Kydland, Finn E., and Edward C. Prescott, "The Econometrics of the General Equilibrium Approach to Business Cycles," *Scandinavian Journal of Economics,* 1991a, *93*:2, 161–78.

Kydland, Finn E., and Edward C. Prescott, "Hours and Employment Variation in Business Cycle Theory," *Economic Theory,* January 1991b, *1,* 63–81.

Lucas, Robert E., Jr., "Methods and Problems in Business Cycle Theory," *Journal of Money, Credit and Banking,* November 1980, *12,* 696–715.

Lucas, Robert E., Jr., and Nancy L. Stokey, "Money and Interest in a Cash-in-Advance Economy," *Econometrica,* May 1987, *55,* 491–513.

Marschak, Jacob, "Introduction to Econometrics," hectographed lecture notes, University of Buffalo, 1948.

McCallum, Bennett T., "Real Business Cycle Models." In Barro, Robert J., ed., *Modern Business Cycle Theory.* Cambridge, Mass.: Harvard University Press, 1989, pp. 16–50.

Prescott, Edward C., "Theory Ahead of Business Cycle Measurement," *Quarterly Review, Federal Reserve Bank of Minneapolis,* Fall 1986, *10,* 9–22; also in Brunner, Karl, and Allan H. Meltzer, eds., *Real Business Cycles, Real Exchange Rates, and Actual Policies, Carnegie-Rochester Conference Series on Public Policy.* Vol. 25, Amsterdam: North-Holland, 1986, pp. 11–44.

Ríos-Rull, José-Víctor, "On the Quantitative Importance of Market Completeness," *Journal of Monetary Economics,* December 1994, *34,* 462–96.

Ríos-Rull, José-Víctor, "Models with Heterogeneous Agents." In Cooley, T. F., ed., *Frontiers of Business Cycle Research.* Princeton, N.J.: Princeton University Press, 1995.

Rogerson, Richard, "Indivisible Labor, Lotteries and Equilibrium," *Journal of Monetary Economics,* January 1988, *21,* 3–16.

Schneider, Stephen H., "Climate Modeling," *Scientific American,* May 1987, *256,* 72–80.

Shoven, John B., and J. Whalley, "A General Equilibrium Calculation of the Differential Taxation of Income from Capital in the U.S.," *Journal of Public Economics,* November 1972, *1,* 281–321.

Solow, Robert M., *Growth Theory: An Exposition.* Oxford: Clarendon Press, 1970.

Stokey, Nancy L., and Robert E. Lucas, Jr. (with Edward C. Prescott), *Recursive Methods in Economic Dynamics.* Cambridge, Mass.: Harvard University Press, 1989.

Wicksell, Knut, "Krisernas gåta," *Statsøkonomisk Tidsskrift,* 1907, *21,* 255–70.

Journal of Economic Perspectives—Volume 10, Number 1—Winter 1996—Pages 87–104

The Empirical Foundations of Calibration

Lars Peter Hansen and James J. Heckman

General equilibrium theory provides the intellectual underpinnings for modern macroeconomics, finance, urban economics, public finance and numerous other fields. However, as a paradigm for organizing and synthesizing economic data, it poses some arduous challenges. A widely accepted empirical counterpart to general equilibrium theory remains to be developed. There are few testable implications of general equilibrium theory for a time series of aggregate quantities and prices. There are a variety of ways to formalize this claim. Sonnenschein (1973) and Mantel (1974) show that excess aggregate demand functions can have "arbitrary shapes" as long as Walras' Law is satisfied. Similarly, Harrison and Kreps (1979) show that a competitive equilibria can always be constructed to rationalize any arbitrage-free specification of prices. Observational equivalence results are pervasive in economics. There are two responses to this state of affairs. One can view the flexibility of the general equilibrium paradigm as its virtue. Since it is hard to reject, it provides a rich apparatus for interpreting and processing data.[1] Alternatively, general equilibrium theory can be dismissed as being empirically irrelevant because it imposes no testable restrictions on market data.

Even if we view the "flexibility" of the general equilibrium paradigm as a virtue, identification of preferences and technology is problematic. Concern about the

---

[1] Lucas and Sargent (1988) make this point in arguing that early Keynesian critiques of classical economics were misguided by their failure to recognize this flexibility.

■ *Lars Peter Hansen is Homer J. Livingston Professor of Economics, and James Heckman is Henry Schultz Distinguished Service Professor of Economics and Director of the Center for Social Program Evaluation at the Irving B. Harris School of Public Policy Studies, all at the University of Chicago, Chicago, Illinois.*

lack of identification of aggregate models has long troubled econometricians (for example, Liu, 1960; Sims, 1980). The tenuousness of identification of many models makes policy analysis and the evaluation of the welfare costs of programs a difficult task and leads to distrust of aggregate models. Different models that "fit the facts" may produce conflicting estimates of welfare costs and dissimilar predictions about the response of the economy to changes in resource constraints.

Numerous attempts have been made to circumvent this lack of identification, either by imposing restrictions directly on aggregate preferences and technologies, or by limiting the assumed degree of heterogeneity in preferences and technologies. For instance, the constant elasticity of substitution specification for preferences over consumption in different time periods is one of workhorses of dynamic stochastic equilibrium theory. When asset markets are sufficiently rich, it is known from Gorman (1953) that these preferences can be aggregated into the preferences of a representative consumer (Rubinstein, 1974). Similarly, Cobb-Douglas aggregate production functions can be obtained from Leontief micro technologies aggregated by a Pareto distribution for micro productivity parameters (Houthakker, 1956). These results give examples of when simple aggregate relations can be deduced from relations underlying the micro behavior of the individual agents, but they do *not* justify using the constructed aggregate relations to evaluate fully the welfare costs and benefits of a policy.[2]

Micro data offer one potential avenue for resolving the identification problem, but there is no clear formal statement that demonstrates how access to such data fully resolves it. At an abstract level, Brown and Matzkin (1995) show how to use information on individual endowments to obtain testable implications in exchange economies. As long as individual income from endowments can be decomposed into its component sources, they show that the testability of general equilibrium theory extends to production economies. Additional restrictions and considerable price variation are needed to identify microeconomic preference relations for data sets that pass the Brown-Matzkin test.

Current econometric practice in microeconomics is still far from the nonparametric ideal envisioned by Brown and Matzkin (1995). As shown by Gorman (1953), Wilson (1968), Aigner and Simon (1970) and Simon and Aigner (1970), it is only under very special circumstances that a micro parameter such as the intertemporal elasticity of substitution or even a marginal propensity to consume out of income can be "plugged into" a representative consumer model to produce an empirically concordant aggregate model. As illustrated by Houthakker's (1956) result, microeconomic technologies can look quite different from their aggregate counterparts. In practice, microeconomic elasticities are often estimated by reverting to a partial

---

[2] Gorman's (1953) results provide a partial justification for using aggregate preferences to compare alternative aggregate paths of the economy. Even if one aggregate consumption-investment profile is preferred to another via this aggregate preference ordering, to convert this into a Pareto ranking for the original heterogeneous agent economy requires computing individual allocations for the path—a daunting task.

equilibrium econometric model. Cross-market price elasticities are either assumed to be zero or are collapsed into constant terms or time dummies as a matter of convenience. General equilibrium, multimarket price variation is typically ignored in most microeconomic studies.

Battle lines are drawn over the issue of whether the microeconometric simplifications commonly employed are quantitatively important in evaluating social welfare and assessing policy reforms. Shoven and Whalley (1972, 1992) attacked Harberger's use of partial equilibrium analysis in assessing the effects of taxes on outputs and welfare. Armed with Scarf's algorithm (Scarf and Hansen, 1973), they computed fundamentally larger welfare losses from taxation using a general equilibrium framework than Harberger computed using partial equilibrium analysis. However, these and other applications of general equilibrium theory are often greeted with skepticism by applied economists who claim that the computations rest on weak empirical foundations. The results of many simulation experiments are held to be fundamentally implausible because the empirical foundations of the exercises are not secure.

Kydland and Prescott are to be praised for taking the general equilibrium analysis of Shoven and Whalley one step further by using stochastic general equilibrium as a framework for understanding macroeconomics.[3] Their vision is bold and imaginative, and their research program has produced many creative analyses. In implementing the real business cycle program, researchers deliberately choose to use simple stylized models both to minimize the number of parameters to be "calibrated" and to facilitate computations.[4] This decision forces them to embrace a rather different notion of "testability" than used by the other general equilibrium theorists, such as Sonnenschein, Mantel, Brown and Matzkin. At the same time, the real business cycle community dismisses conventional econometric testing of parametric models as being irrelevant for their purposes. While Kydland and Prescott advocate the use of "well-tested theories" in their essay, they never move beyond this slogan, and they do not justify their claim of fulfilling this criterion in their own research. "Well tested" must mean more than "familiar" or "widely accepted" or "agreed on by convention," if it is to mean anything.

Their suggestion that we "calibrate the model" is similarly vague. On one hand, it is hard to fault their advocacy of tightly parameterized models, because such models are convenient to analyze and easy to understand. Aggregate growth coupled with uncertainty makes nonparametric identification of preferences and technology extremely difficult, if not impossible. Separability and homogeneity restrictions on preferences and technologies have considerable appeal as identifying assumptions. On the other hand, Kydland and Prescott never provide a coherent

---

[3] The earlier work by Lucas and Prescott (1971) took an initial step in this direction by providing a dynamic stochastic equilibrium framework for evaluating empirical models of investment.

[4] The term "real business cycle" originates from an emphasis on technology shocks as a source of business cycle fluctuations. Thus, real, as opposed to nominal, variables drive the process. In some of the recent work, both real and nominal shocks are used in the models.

framework for extracting parameters from microeconomic data. The same charge of having a weak empirical foundation that plagued the application of deterministic general equilibrium theory can be lodged against the real business cycle research program. Such models are often elegant, and the discussions produced from using them are frequently stimulating and provocative, but their empirical foundations are not secure. What credibility should we attach to numbers produced from their "computational experiments," and why should we use their "calibrated models" as a basis for serious quantitative policy evaluation? The essay by Kydland and Prescott begs these fundamental questions.

The remainder of our essay is organized as follows. We begin by discussing simulation as a method for understanding models. This method is old, and the problems in using it recur in current applications. We then argue that model calibration and verification can be fruitfully posed as econometric estimation and testing problems. In particular, we delineate the gains from using an explicit econometric framework. Following this discussion, we investigate current calibration practice with an eye toward suggesting improvements that will make the outputs of computational experiments more credible. The deliberately limited use of available information in such computational experiments runs the danger of making many economic models with very different welfare implications compatible with the evidence. We suggest that Kydland and Prescott's account of the availability and value of micro estimates for macro models is dramatically overstated. There is no filing cabinet full of robust micro estimates ready to use in calibrating dynamic stochastic general equilibrium models. We outline an alternative paradigm that, while continuing to stress the synergy between microeconometrics and macro simulation, will provide more credible inputs into the computational experiments and more accurate assessments of the quality of the outputs.

Simulation as a Method for Understanding Models

In a simple linear regression model, the effect of an independent variable on the dependent variable is measured by its associated regression coefficient. In the dynamic nonlinear models used in the Kydland-Prescott real business cycle research program, this is no longer true. The dynamic nature of such models means that the dependent variable is generated in part from its own past values. Characterizing the dynamic mechanisms by which exogenous impulses are transmitted into endogenous time series is important to understanding how these models induce fluctuations in economic aggregates. Although there is a reliance on linearization techniques in much of the current literature, for large impulses or shocks, the nonlinear nature of such models is potentially important. To capture the richness of a model, the analyst must examine various complicated features of it. One way to do this is to simulate the model at a variety of levels of the forcing processes, impulses and parameters.

The idea of simulating a complex model to understand its properties is not a new principle in macroeconomics. Tinbergen's (1939) simulation of his League of Nations model and the influential simulations of Klein and Goldberger (1955) and Goldberger (1959) are but three of a legion of simulation exercises performed by previous generations of economists.[5] Fair (1994) and Taylor (1993) are recent examples of important studies that rely on simulation to elucidate the properties of estimated models.

However, the quality of any simulation is only as good as the input on which it is based. The controversial part of the real business cycle simulation program is the method by which the input parameters are chosen. Pioneers of simulation and of economic dynamics like Tinbergen (1939) and Frisch (1933) often guessed at the parameters they used in their models, either because the data needed to identify the parameters were not available, or because the econometric methods were not yet developed to fully exploit the available data (Morgan, 1990). At issue is whether the state of the art for picking the parameters to be used for simulations has improved since their time.

Calibration versus Estimation

A novel feature of the real business cycle research program is its endorsement of "calibration" as an alternative to "estimation." However, the distinction drawn between calibrating and estimating the parameters of a model is artificial at best.[6] Moreover, the justification for what is called "calibration" is vague and confusing. In a profession that is already too segmented, the construction of such artificial distinctions is counterproductive. It can only close off a potentially valuable dialogue between real business cycle research and other research in modern econometrics.

Since the Kydland-Prescott essay is vague about the operating principles of calibration, we turn elsewhere for specificity. For instance, in a recent description of the use of numerical models in the earth sciences, Oreskes, Shrader-Frechette and Belitz (1994, pp. 642, 643) describe calibration as follows:

> In earth sciences, the modeler is commonly faced with the inverse problem: The distribution of the dependent variable (for example, the hydraulic head) is the most well known aspect of the system; the distribution of the independent variable is the least well known. The process of tuning the model—that is, the manipulation of the independent variables to obtain a

---

[5] Simulation is also widely used in physical science. For example, it is customary in the studies of fractal dynamics to simulate models in order to gain understanding of the properties of models with various parameter configurations (Peitgen and Richter, 1986).

[6] As best we can tell from their essay, Kydland and Prescott want to preserve the term "estimation" to apply to the outputs of their computational experiments.

match between the observed and simulated distribution or distributions of a dependent variable or variables—is known as calibration.

Some hydrologists have suggested a two-step calibration scheme in which the available dependent data set is divided into two parts. In the first step, the independent parameters of the model are adjusted to reproduce the first part of the data. Then in the second step the model is run and the results are compared with the second part of the data. In this scheme, the first step is labeled "calibration" and the second step is labeled "verification."

This appears to be an accurate description of the general features of the "calibration" method advocated by Kydland and Prescott. For them, data for the *first step* come from micro observations and from secular growth observations (see also Prescott, 1986a). Correlations over time and across variables are to be used in the *second step* of verification.

Econometricians refer to the first stage as *estimation* and the second stage as *testing*. As a consequence, the two-stage procedure described by Oreskes, Shrader-Frechette and Belitz (1994) has a straightforward econometric counterpart.[7]

From this perspective, the Kydland-Prescott objection to mainstream econometrics is simply a complaint about the use of certain loss functions for describing the fit of a model to the data or for producing parameter estimates. Their objection does not rule out econometric estimation based on other loss functions.

Econometric estimation metrics like least squares, weighted least squares or more general method-of-moments metrics are traditional measures of fit. Difference among these methods lie in how they weight various features of the data; for example, one method might give a great deal of weight to distant outliers or to certain variables, causing them to pull estimated trend lines in their direction; another might give less weight to such outliers or variables. Each method of estimation can be justified by describing the particular loss function that summarizes the weights put on deviations of a model's predictions from the data. There is nothing sacred about the traditional loss functions in econometrics associated with standard methods, like ordinary least squares. Although traditional approaches do have rigorous justifications, a variety of alternative loss functions could be explored that weight particular features of a model more than others. For example, one could estimate with a loss function that rewarded models that are more successful in predicting turning points. Alternatively, particular time series frequencies could be deemphasized in adopting an estimation criterion because misspecification of a model is likely to contaminate some frequencies more than others (Dunsmuir and Hannan, 1978; Hansen and Sargent, 1993; Sims, 1993).

---

[7] See Christiano and Eichenbaum (1992) for one possible econometric implementation of this two-step approach. They use a generalized method of moments formulation (for example, Hansen, 1982) in which parameters are estimated by a first stage, exactly identified set of moment relations, and the model is tested by looking at another set of moment restrictions. Not surprisingly, to achieve identification of the underlying set of parameters, they are compelled to include more than just secular growth relations in the first-stage estimation, apparently violating one of the canons of current calibration practice.

The real business cycle practitioners adopt implicit loss functions. In looking at economic aggregates, their implicit loss functions appear to focus on the model predictions for long-run means, to the exclusion of other features of the data, when selecting parameter estimates. It is unfortunate that we are forced to guess about the rationale for the loss functions implicit in their research. There is little emphasis on assessing the quality of the resulting calibration. Formalizing the criteria for calibration and verification via loss functions makes the principle by which a particular model is chosen easier to understand. A clear statement would lead to more fruitful and focused conversations about the sources and reliability of estimated parameters.

As Oreskes, Shrader-Frechette and Belitz (1994) emphasize, the distinction between calibration and verification is often contrived. In many circumstances the verification step should really be considered part of the "calibration" step. The absence of a sharp distinction between these two stages is consistent with the difficulty of obtaining testable implications from the general equilibrium paradigm. Model testing serves as a barometer for measuring whether a given parametric structure captures the essential features of the data. When cleverly executed, it can pinpoint defective features of a model. Applied statistical decision theory and conventional statistical practice provide a formalism for conducting this endeavor. While this theory can be criticized for its rigidity or its naiveté, it seems premature to scrap it altogether without putting in place some other clearly stated criterion for picking the parameters of a model and assessing the quality of that selection.

The rational agents in a model of the Kydland-Prescott type rely explicitly on loss functions. After all, their rational decision making is based on the application of statistical decision theory, and part of the Kydland-Prescott line of research is to welcome the application of this theory to modern macroeconomics. But the idea of a loss function is also a central concept in statistical decision theory (LeCam and Yang, 1990). The rational agents in real business cycle models use this theory and, as a consequence, are assumed to process information in a highly structured way. Why should the producers of estimates for the real business cycle models act differently?

Although Kydland and Prescott are not precise in this essay in stating how calibration should be done in practice, there is much more specificity in Prescott (1986a, p. 14), who writes: "The key parameters of the growth model are the intertemporal and intratemporal elasticities of substitution. As Lucas (1980, p. 712) emphasizes, 'On these parameters, we have a wealth of inexpensively available data from census and cohort information, from panel data describing market conditions and so forth.'"

It is instructive to compare Prescott's optimistic discussion of the ease of using micro data to inform calibration with the candid and informative discussion of the same issue by Shoven and Whalley (1992, p. 105), who pioneered the application of calibration methods in general equilibrium analysis. They write:

> Typically, calibration involves only one year's data or a single observation represented as an average over a number of years. Because of the reliance on a single observation, benchmark data typically does not identify a unique set of values for the parameters in any model. Particular values for the relevant

elasticities are usually required, and are specified on the basis of other research. These serve, along with the equilibrium observation, to uniquely identify the other parameters of the model. This typically places major reliance on literature surveys of elasticities; as many modelers have observed in discussing their own work, it is surprising how sparse (and sometimes contradictory) the literature is on some key elasticity values. And, although this procedure might sound straightforward, it is often exceedingly difficult because each study is different from every other.

What is noteworthy about this quotation is that the authors are describing a deterministic general equilibrium model based on traditional models of factor demand, sectoral output, product supply, labor supply and demand for final products, which have been the focus of numerous micro empirical studies. There have been many fewer micro empirical studies of the sectoral components of the stochastic general equilibrium models used in real business cycle theory. If there are few well-tested models that Shoven and Whalley can pull off the shelf, is it plausible that the shelf is unusually rich in models estimated assuming the relevant economic agents are operating in the more general economic environments considered in real business cycle theory?

Shoven and Whalley (1992, p. 106) come close to acknowledging the fundamental underidentification of general equilibrium systems from time series data when they write:

[I]n some applied models many thousands of parameters are involved, and to estimate simultaneously all of the model parameters using time-series methods would require either unrealistically large numbers of observations or overly severe identifying restrictions. . . . Thus far, these problems have largely excluded complete econometric estimation of general equilibrium systems in applied work.

Current real business cycle models often require many fewer parameters to be calibrated, because they are highly aggregated. However, the extraction of the required elasticities from microeconometric analyses is more problematic, because the implicit economic environments invoked to justify microeconometric estimation procedures seldom match the dynamic stochastic single-agent models for which the micro estimates act as inputs. Microeconomic studies rarely estimate models that can be directly applied to the aggregates used in real business cycle theory. Moreover, as the specification of the real business cycle models become richer, they will inevitably have to face up to the same concerns that plague Shoven and Whalley.[8]

---

[8] This problem has already surfaced in the work of Benhabib, Rogerson and Wright (1991). They try to identify the parameters of a household production function for the services from durable goods using Panel Survey of Income Dynamics data, but without data on one of the inputs (the stock of durable goods), poor data on the other input (time spent by the household required to make durable goods productive) and no data on the output.

The Real Business Cycle Empirical Method In Practice

Kydland and Prescott, along with other real business cycle practitioners, endorse the use of time series averages—but not correlations—in calibrating models. In their proposed paradigm for empirical research, correlations are to be saved and used to test models, but are not to be used as a source of information about parameter values. It has become commonplace in the real business cycle research program to match the steady-state implications of models to time series averages. To an outsider, this looks remarkably like a way of doing estimation without accounting for sampling error in the sample means. In fact, the real business cycle "calibration" estimator of the Cobb-Douglas share parameter is a classical econometric estimator due to Klein (Klein, 1953; Nerlove, 1965). The only difference is that the Klein estimator usually is presented with a standard error.

Why is it acceptable to use sample means as a valid source of information about model parameters and not sample autocorrelations and cross correlations? Many interesting parameters cannot be identified from population means alone. Although the real business cycle literature provides no good reason for not using other sample moments, some reasons could be adduced. For example, one traditional argument for using sample means is that they are robust to measurement error in a way that sample variances and covariances are not as long as the errors have mean zero. Another possible rationale is that steady-state relations are sometimes robust with respect to alternative specifications of the short-run dynamics of a model. In these cases, a calibration fit to sample means will be consistent with a class of models that differ in their implications for short-run dynamics. However, the other side of this coin is that long-term means identify the short-run dynamics of a model only in very special circumstances. Moreover, as pointed out by Sargent (1989), even with measurement error, time series correlations and cross correlations can still provide more information about a model than is conveyed in sample means.

Since the models considered by Kydland and Prescott are stochastic, it is not in general possible to calibrate all of the parameters of a model solely from the means of macro time series. Computational experiments make assumptions about the correlation among the stochastic inputs to the model. Information about shocks, such as their variances and serial correlations, are needed to conduct the computational experiments. In a related vein, macroeconomic correlations contain potentially valuable information about the mechanism through which shocks are transmitted to macro time series. For models with richer dynamics, including their original "time-to-build" model, Kydland and Prescott (1982) envision fully calibrating the transmission mechanisms from micro evidence; but they provide no defense for avoiding the use of macro correlations in that task.

Recently, Cogley and Nason (1995) have criticized models in the literature spawned by Kydland and Prescott for failing to generate business cycle dynamics (see also Christiano, 1988; Watson, 1993; Cochrane, 1994). Since matching the full set of dynamics of the model to the dynamics in the data is not an essential part of calibration methodology, these models survive the weak standards for verification imposed by the calibrators. A much more disciplined and systematic exploration of the intertemporal and cross correlations, in a manner now routine in time series econometrics, would have shifted the focus from the empirical successes to the empirical challenges. We agree with Oreskes, Shrader-Frechette and Belitz (1994) that the distinction between calibration and verification is commonly blurred in practice. In the case of real business cycle research, such blurring is likely to be all the more prevalent as the models are redesigned to incorporate richer transient dynamics and additional sources of uncertainty.

As Kydland and Prescott emphasize, one of the most important questions for macroeconometrics is the quantitative importance of alternative sources of business cycle fluctuations. This classical problem has not yet been definitively answered (Morgan, 1990, pt. I). Using intuition from factor analysis, it is impossible to answer this question from a single time series. From two time series, one can isolate a single common factor. (Intuitively, two random variables can always be decomposed into a common component and two uncorrelated components.) Only using multiple time series is it possible to sort out multiple sources of business cycle shocks. The current emphasis in the literature on using only a few "key correlations" to check a model's implications makes single-factor explanations more likely to emerge from real business cycle analyses.[9] The idiosyncratic way Kydland and Prescott quantify the importance of technology shocks unfortunately makes it difficult to compare their answers to those obtained from the "innovation accounting" methods advocated by Sims (1980) and used extensively in empirical macroeconomics or to those obtained using the dynamic factor models of Geweke (1977) and Sargent and Sims (1977). Kydland and Prescott's answer to the central question of the importance of technology shocks would be much more credible if it were reinforced by other empirical methodologies.

A contrast with John Taylor's approach to investigating the properties of models is instructive. Taylor's research program includes the use of computational experiments. It is well summarized in his recent book (Taylor, 1993). Like Kydland and Prescott, Taylor relies on fully specified dynamic models and imposes rational expectations when computing stochastic equilibria. However, in fitting linear models he uses all of the information on first and second moments available in the macro data when it is computationally possible to do so. The econometric methods used in parameter estimation are precisely described. Multiple sources of business cycle shocks are admitted into the model at the outset, and rigorous empirical testing of models appears throughout his analyses.[10]

---

[9] In private correspondence, John Taylor has amplified this point: "I have found that the omission of aggregate price or inflation data in the Kydland-Prescott second moment exercise creates an artificial barrier between real business cycle models and monetary models. To me, the Granger causality from inflation to output and vice versa are key facts to be explained. But Kydland and Prescott have ignored these facts because they do not fit into their models."

[10] Fair (1994) presents an alternative systematic approach to estimation and simulation, but unlike Taylor, he does not impose rational expectations assumptions.

If the Kydland and Prescott real business cycle research program is to achieve empirical credibility, it will have to provide a much more comprehensive assessment of the successes and failures of its models. To convince a wide audience of "outsiders," the proclaimed successes in real business cycle calibration should not be intertwined with an idiosyncratic and poorly justified way of evaluating models. We sympathize with Fair (1992, p. 141), who writes:

Is the RBC [real business cycle] approach a good way of testing models? At first glance it might seem so, since computed paths are being compared to actual paths. But the paths are being compared in a very limited way in contrast to the way that the Cowles Commission approach would compare them. Take the simple RMSE [root mean square error[11]] procedure. This procedure would compute a prediction error for a given variable for each period and then calculate the RMSE from another structural model or from an autoregressive or vector autoregressive model.

I have never seen this type of comparison done for a RBC model. How would, say, the currently best-fitting RBC model compare to a simple first-order autoregressive equation for real GNP in terms of the RMSE criterion? My guess is very poorly. Having the computed path mimic the actual path for a few selected moments is a far cry from beating even a first-order autoregressive equation (let alone a structural model) in terms of fitting the observations well according to the RMSE criterion. The disturbing feature of the RBC literature is there seems to be no interest in computing RMSEs and the like. People generally seem to realize that the RBC models do not fit well in this sense, but they proceed anyway.

Specification Uncertainty Underlies the Estimates

One of the most appealing features of a research program that builds dynamic macroeconomic models on microeconomic foundations is that it opens the door to the use of micro empirical evidence to pin down macro parameter values. Kydland and Prescott and the entire real business cycle community pay only lip service to the incompatibility between the macroeconomic model used in their computational experiments and the microeconometric models used to secure the simulation parameters.

It can be very misleading to plug microeconometric parameter estimates into a macroeconomic model when the economic environments for the two models are fundamentally different. In fact, many of the micro studies that the "calibrators" draw upon do not estimate the parameters required by the models being simulated.

---

[11] RMSE is the square root of the mean of the squared discrepancies between predicted and actual outcomes.

This creates specification uncertainty (Leamer, 1978). To adequately represent this uncertainty, it is necessary to incorporate the uncertainty about model parameters directly into the outputs of simulations. Standard errors analogous to those presented by Christiano and Eichenbaum (1992) and Eichenbaum (1991) are a useful first step, but do not convey the full picture of model uncertainty. What is required is a sensitivity analysis to see how the simulation outputs are affected by different choices of simulation parameters. Trostel (1993) makes effective use of such a methodology.

Consider using the estimates of intertemporal labor supply produced by Ghez and Becker (1975) for simulation purposes.[12] Ghez and Becker (1975) estimate the intertemporal substitution of leisure time assuming perfect credit markets, no restrictions on trade in the labor market and no fixed costs of work. This study is important, but like all empirical work in economics, the precise estimates are enveloped by some uncertainty. Moreover, different estimation schemes are required to secure this parameter if there is uninsurable uncertainty in the environment (MaCurdy, 1978). Even looking only at estimates of the intertemporal substitution of leisure based on models that assume that workers can perfectly insure, the point estimates reported in the literature are very imprecisely determined (MaCurdy, 1981; Altonji, 1986). Further, it is not clear how the estimates should be modified to be compatible with the other economic environments including settings that allow for uninsurable uncertainty, transactions costs and restrictions on trades in the market.

Current practices in the field of calibration and simulation do not report either estimation error and/or model-specification error. Nor is it a standard feature of real business cycle practice to present formal analyses that explore how sensitive the simulations are to different parameter values. Precise numerical outputs are reported, but with no sense of the confidence that can be placed in the estimates. This produces a false sense of precision.

Observationally Equivalent Models Offer Different Predictions about Policy Interventions

While putting on empirical "blinders" permits a particular line of research to proceed, looking at too narrow of a range of data makes identification problems more severe. A disturbing feature of current practice in the real business cycle

[12] Kydland and Prescott cite Ghez and Becker (1975) as a prime example of the value of microeconomic empirical work. However, their citation misses two central aspects of that work. First, Ghez and Becker (1975) use synthetic cohort data, not panel data as stated by Kydland and Prescott. Second, the interpretation of the Ghez-Becker estimates as structural parameters is predicated on a list of identifying assumptions. These assumptions coupled with the resulting estimates are the most important part of their investigation, not their observation that people sleep eight hours a day, which is what Kydland and Prescott emphasize.

literature is that models with the same inputs can produce fundamentally different computed values of welfare loss and quantitative assessments of alternative economic policies.

Consider the following developments in the field of empirical finance. A frequently noted anomaly is that the observed differences in returns between stocks and bonds are too large to be consistent with models of the preferences commonly used in real business cycle analysis (Hansen and Singleton, 1983; Mehra and Prescott, 1985; Cochrane and Hansen, 1992; Kocherlakota, 1996). One response to these asset-pricing anomalies has been the modification to preferences developed by Epstein and Zin (1989), which breaks the tight link between intertemporal substitution and risk aversion that was maintained in the preceding literature. A parallel advance has been the introduction of intertemporal complementarities such as habit persistence in the preference orderings of consumers (Constantinides, 1990). Hansen, Sargent and Tallarini (1995) find that models with Epstein-Zin type preferences and models without this form of risk sensitivity explain the same quantity data but have fundamentally different implications for the market price of risk (the slope of the mean-standard deviation frontier for asset returns).[13] These "observationally equivalent" preference specifications produce very different estimates of the welfare losses associated with hypothetical policy interventions. The decision by other researchers such as Epstein and Zin to look more broadly at available data and to emphasize model defects instead of successes provoked quantitatively important advances in economic theory.

Another competing explanation for the equity premium puzzle is the presence of incomplete markets and transactions costs in asset markets. This explanation is consistent with Prescott's (1986b, p. 29) earlier argument for ignoring asset market data in real business cycle calibrations: "That the representative agent model is poorly designed to predict differences in borrowing and lending rates . . . does not imply that this model is not well suited for other purposes—for predicting the consequences of technology shocks for fluctuations in business cycle frequencies, for example."

Heaton and Lucas (1995) quantify the magnitude of transaction costs needed to address the equity-premium puzzle (see also Aiyagari and Gertler, 1991). Prescott may be correct that such models will not help to match "key" correlations in economic aggregates, but this requires documentation. Even if there is robustness of the form hoped for by Prescott, the presence of transactions costs of the magnitude suggested by Heaton and Lucas (1995) are likely to alter the welfare comparisons across different policy experiments in a quantitatively important way.[14] This is so because transactions costs prevent heterogeneous consumers from equating marginal rates of substitution and put a wedge between marginal rates of substitution and marginal rates of transformation.

[13] Recent work by Campbell and Cochrane (1995) and Boldrin, Christiano and Fisher (1995) suggests a similar conclusion for models with strong intertemporal complementarities.
[14] This sensitivity actually occurs in the "bothersome" experiment of İmrohoroğlu (1992) mentioned by Kydland and Prescott.

A More Constructive Research Program

The idea of using micro data to enrich the information in macro time series dates back at least to the writings of Tobin (1950). A careful reading of the literature that accompanied his suggestion reveals that his idea was inherently controversial, especially if the micro information is based on cross-section data, and if the behavioral equations are dynamic (Aigner and Simon, 1970; Simon and Aigner, 1970). This issue was revived in the late 1970s and early 1980s when numerous economists attempted to estimate micro labor supply equations to test the Lucas and Rapping (1969) intertemporal substitution hypothesis. The hypothesis rests critically on consumer responses to expected real discounted future wage movements relative to current wages. By providing well-focused economic questions, the Lucas-Rapping model advanced the development of empirical microeconomics by challenging economists to supply answers. Numerous micro studies of labor supply were conducted with an eye toward confirming or disconfirming their hypothesis (Altonji and Ashenfelter, 1980; MaCurdy, 1981; Ham, 1982; Altonji, 1986).

However, these studies reveal that even with large micro samples, it is not possible to estimate the parameter of interest precisely. Measurement error in micro data and selection problems often limit the value of the information in the micro data. Macro time series or aggregated cross sections can sometimes solve selection problems that are intractable in micro data (Heckman and Robb, 1985, pp. 168–169, 210–213). Different micro survey instruments produce fundamentally different descriptions of the same phenomena (Smith, 1995). Micro data are no panacea. Moreover, the recent movement in empirical microeconomics away from economic models to "simple descriptive" estimation schemes has reduced the supply of new structural parameters.

It is simply not true that there is a large shelf of micro estimates already constructed for different economic environments that can be plugged without modification into a new macro model. In many cases, estimators that are valid in one economic environment are not well suited for another. Given the less-than-idyllic state of affairs, it seems foolish to look to micro data as the primary source for many macro parameters required to do simulation analysis. Many crucial economic parameters— for example, the effect of product inputs on industry supply—can only be determined by looking at relationships among aggregates. Like it or not, time series evidence remains essential in determining many fundamentally aggregative parameters.

A more productive research program would provide clearly formulated theories that will stimulate more focused microeconomic empirical research. Much recent micro research is atheoretical in character and does not link up well with macro general equilibrium theory. For example, with rare exceptions, micro studies treat aggregate shocks as nuisance parameters to be eliminated by some trend or dummy variable procedure.[15] A redirection of micro empirical work toward providing input

---

[15] For an exception see Heckman and Sedlacek (1985), who show how cross-section time dummies can be used to estimate the time series of unobserved skill prices in a market model of self-selection.

into well-defined general equilibrium models would move discussions of micro evidence beyond discussions of whether wage or price effects exist, to the intellectually more important questions of what the micro estimates mean and how they can be used to illuminate well-posed economic questions. "Calibrators" could make a constructive contribution to empirical economics by suggesting a more symbiotic relationship between the macro general equilibrium model as a synthesizing device and motivating vehicle and the micro evidence as a source of robust parameter values.

Recently there has been considerable interest in heterogeneous agent models in the real business cycle literature; Ríos-Rull (1995) offers a nice summary. To us, one of the primary reasons for pushing this line of research is to narrow the range of specification errors in calibrating with microeconomic data. Microeconometric estimates routinely incorporate heterogeneity that is often abstracted from the specification of dynamic, stochastic general equilibrium models. It is remarkable to us that so little emphasis has been given to the transition from micro to macro in the real business cycle literature, given that understanding the distribution of heterogeneity is central to making this transition (Stoker, 1993).

The Kydland and Prescott program is an intellectually exciting one. To date, however, the computations produced from it have only illustrated some of the qualitative properties of some dynamic stochastic models and demonstrated the possibility of executing an array of interesting calculations. The real business cycle modeling effort would be more beneficial if it shifted its focus to micro predictions and in this way helped to stimulate research on empirical models that would verify or contradict the macro models.

We envision a symbiotic relationship between calibrators and empirical economists in which calibration methods like those used by Frisch, Tinbergen, and Kydland and Prescott stimulate the production of more convincing micro empirical estimates by showing which gaps in our knowledge of micro phenomenon matter and which gaps do not. Calibration should only be the starting point of an empirical analysis of general equilibrium models. In the absence of firmly established estimates of key parameters, sensitivity analyses should be routine in real business cycle simulations. Properly used and qualified simulation methods can be an important source of information and an important stimulus to high-quality empirical economic research.

The research program we advocate is not an easy one. However, it will be an informative one. It will motivate micro empirical researchers to focus on economically interesting questions; it will secure the foundations of empirical general equilibrium theory; and, properly executed, it will demonstrate both the gaps and strengths of our knowledge on major issues of public policy.

■ *We thank Jennifer Boobar, John Cochrane, Marty Eichenbaum, Ray Fair, Chris Flinn, John Heaton, Bob Lucas, Tom Sargent, Jeff Smith, Nancy Stokey, John Taylor and Grace Tsiang for their valuable comments on this draft. Hansen's research is supported in part by NSF SBR-94095–01; Heckman is supported by NSF 93–048–0211 and grants from the Russell Sage Foundation and the American Bar Foundation.*

References

Aigner, Dennis, and Julian L. Simon, "A Specification BIAS Interpretation of Cross-Section vs. Time-Series Parameter Estimates," *Western Economic Journal,* June 1970, *22,* 144–61.

Aiyagari, S. Rao, and Mark Gertler, "Asset Returns with Transitions Costs and Uninsured Individual Risk," *Journal of Monetary Economics,* June 1991, *27,* 311–31.

Altonji, Joseph G., "Intertemporal Substitution in Labor Supply: Evidence from Micro Data," *Journal of Political Economy,* June 1986, *94:3,* Part 2, S176–S215.

Altonji, Joseph G., and Orley Ashenfelter, "Wage Movements and the Labour Market Equilibrium Hypothesis," *Economica,* August 1980, *49,* 783–824.

Benhabib, J., R. Rogerson, and R. Wright, "Homework in Macroeconomics: Household Production and Aggregate Fluctuations," *Journal of Political Economy,* December 1991, *99,* 1166–87.

Boldrin, Michele, Lawrence J. Christiano, and J. D. M. Fisher, "Asset Pricing Lessons for Modeling Business Cycles," manuscript, August 1995.

Brown, D. J., and R. L. Matzkin, "Testable Restrictions on the Equilibrium Manifold," manuscript, April 1995.

Campbell, John, and John H. Cochrane, "By Force of Habit: A Consumption-Based Explanation of Aggregate Stock Market Behavior." National Bureau of Economic Research Working Paper No. 4995, 1995.

Christiano, Lawrence J., "Why Does Inventory Investment Fluctuate So Much?," *Journal of Monetary Economics,* March/May 1988, *21,* 247–80.

Christiano, Lawrence J., and Martin Eichenbaum, "Current Real Business Cycle Theories and Aggregate Labor Market Fluctuations," *American Economic Review,* June 1992, *82,* 430–50.

Cochrane, John H., "Shocks," *Carnegie-Rochester Conference. Series on Public Policy,* Spring 1994, *41,* 295–364.

Cochrane, John H., and Lars Peter Hansen, "Asset Pricing Explorations for Macroeconomics." In Blanchard, O. J., and S. Fischer, eds., *NBER Macroeconomics Annual 1992.* Cambridge, Mass.: Massachusetts Institute of Technology Press, 1992, pp. 115–69.

Cogley, T., and J. M. Nason, "Effects of the Hodrick-Prescott Filter on Trend and Difference Stationary Time Series Implications for Business Cycle Research," *Journal of Economic Dynamics and Control,* January/February 1995, *19,* 253–78.

Constantinides, George M., "Habit Formation: A Resolution of the Equity Premium Puzzle," *Journal of Political Economy,* June 1990, *98,* 519–43.

Dunsmuir, W., and E. J. Hannan, "Vector Linear Time Series Models," *Advances in Applied Probability,* 1978, *8:2,* 339–64.

Eichenbaum, M., "Real Business Theory: Wisdom or Whimsy," *Journal of Economic Dynamics and Control,* October 1991, *15,* 607–26.

Epstein, Larry G., and Stanley E. Zin, "Substitution, Risk Aversion, and the Temporal Behavior of Consumption and Asset Returns: A Theoretical Framework," *Econometrica,* July 1989, *57,* 937–69.

Fair, Ray, "The Cowles Commission Approach, Real Business Cycle Theories, and New-Keynesian Economics." In Belongia, M. T., and M. R. Garfinkel, eds., *The Business Cycle: Theories and Evidence.* Boston: Kluwer Academic, 1992, pp. 133–47.

Fair, Ray, *Testing Macroeconomic Models.* Cambridge: Harvard University Press, 1994.

Frisch, Ragnar, "Propagation Problems and Impulse Problems in Dynamic Economics." In *Economic Essays in Honor of Gustav Cassel.* London: Allen and Unwin, 1933, pp. 171–205.

Geweke, John, "The Dynamic Factor Analysis of Economic Time Series Models." In Aigner, D. J., and A. S. Goldberger, eds., *Latent Variables in Socio-Economic Models.* Amsterdam: North-Holland, 1977, pp. 365–83.

Ghez, G., and Gary Becker, *The Allocation of Time and Goods Over the Life Cycle.* New York: National Bureau of Economic Research, 1975.

Goldberger, Arthur, *Impact Multipliers and Dynamic Properties of the Klein-Golberger Model.* Amsterdam: North-Holland, 1959.

Gorman, William M., "Community Preference Fields," *Econometrica,* January 1953, *21,* 63–80.

Ham, John C., "Estimation of a Labour Supply Model with Censoring Due to Unemployment and Underemployment," *Review of Economic Studies,* July 1982, *49,* 335–54.

Hansen, Lars Peter, "Large Sample Properties of Generalized Method of Moments Estimators," *Econometrica,* July 1982, *50,* 1029–54.

Hansen, Lars Peter, and Thomas J. Sargent, "Seasonality and Approximation Errors in Rational Expectations Models," *Journal of Econometrics,* January/February 1993, *55,* 21–55.

Hansen, Lars Peter, and K. J. Singleton, "Stochastic Consumption, Risk Aversion, and the Temporal Behavior of Asset Returns," *Journal of Political Economy,* 1983, *91:2,* 249–65.

Hansen, Lars Peter, Thomas J. Sargent, and

T. D. Tallarini, "Pessimism and Risk in General Equilibrium," manuscript, 1995.

Harrison, J. Michael, and David M. Kreps, "Martingales and Arbitrage in Multiperiod Securities Markets," *Journal of Economic Theory*, June 1979, *20*, 381–408.

Heaton, John, and D. Lucas, "Evaluating the Effects of Incomplete Markets on Risk Sharing and Asset Pricing," *Journal of Political Economy*, forthcoming, June 1996.

Heckman, James, and Richard Robb, Jr., "Alternative Methods for Evaluating the Impact of Interventions." In Heckman, J., and Burton Singer, eds., *Longitudinal Analysis of Labor Market Data*. Cambridge, U.K.: Cambridge University Press, 1985, pp. 156–245.

Heckman, James J., and Guilherme Sedlacek, "Heterogeneity, Aggregation, and Market Wage Functions: An Empirical Model of Self-Selection in the Labor Market," *Journal of Political Economy*, December 1985, *93*, 1077–125.

Houthakker, Hendrik, "The Pareto Distribution and the Cobb-Douglas Production Function," *Review of Economic Studies*, 1956, *23*:1 27–31.

İmrohoroğlu, Ayşe, "The Welfare Costs of Inflation Under Imperfect Insurance," *Journal of Economic Dynamics and Control*, January 1992, *16*, 79–91.

Klein, L. R., *A Textbook of Econometrics*. Evanston, Ill.: Row, Peterson and Company, 1953.

Klein, L. A., and A. S. Goldberger, *An Econometric Model of the United States, 1929–52*. Amsterdam: North-Holland, 1955.

Kocherlakota, N., "The Equity Premium: It's Still a Puzzle," *Journal of Economic Literature*, forthcoming 1996.

Kydland, Finn E., and Edward C. Prescott, "Time to Build and Aggregate Fluctuations," *Econometrica*, 1982, *50*:6, 1345–70.

Leamer, E. E., *Specification Searches: Ad Hoc Inference with Nonexperimental Data*. New York: John Wiley & Sons, 1978.

LeCam, L., and G. Yang, *Asymptotics in Statistics: Some Basic Concepts*. Berlin: Springer-Verlag, 1990.

Liu, T. C., "Underidentification, Structural Estimation, and Forecasting," *Econometrica*, October 1960, *28*, 855–65.

Lucas, Robert E., Jr., "Methods and Problems in Business Cycle Theory," *Journal of Money, Credit and Banking*, November 1980, *12*, 696–715; reprinted in Lucas, R. E., ed., *Studies in Business Cycle Theory*. Cambridge, Mass.: Massachusetts Institute of Technology Press, 1981, pp. 271–96.

Lucas, Robert E., Jr., and Edward C. Prescott,

"Investment Under Uncertainty," *Econometrica*, 1971, *39*:5, 659–81.

Lucas, Robert E., Jr., and Leonard A. Rapping, "Real Wages, Employment, and Inflation," *Journal of Political Economy*, September/October 1969, *77*, 721–54.

Lucas, Robert E., Jr., and Thomas J. Sargent, "After Keynesian Macroeconomics," *Quarterly Review, Federal Reserve Bank of Minneapolis*, Spring 1979, *3*, 1–16.

MaCurdy, Thomas, "Econometric Model of the Labor Supply in a Life Setting," Ph.D. dissertation, University of Chicago, 1978.

MaCurdy, Thomas, "An Empirical Model of Labor Supply in a Life Cycle Setting," *Journal of Political Economy*, 1981, *89*:6, 1059–85.

Mantel, Rolf R., "On the Characterization of Aggregate Excess Demand," *Journal of Economic Theory*, March 1974, *7*, 348–55.

Mehra, Rajnish, and Edward C. Prescott, "The Equity Premium: A Puzzle," *Journal of Monetary Economics*, March 1985, *15*, 145–61.

Morgan, M. S., *The History of Econometrics Ideas*. Cambridge: Cambridge University Press, 1990.

Nerlove, M., *Estimation and Identification of Cobb-Douglas Production Functions*. Chicago: Rand McNally, 1965.

Oreskes, Naomi, Kristen Shrader-Frechette, and Kenneth Belitz, "Verification, Validation, and Confirmation of Numerical Models in the Earth Sciences," *Science*, February 4, 1994, *263*, 641–46.

Peitgen, H.-O., and P. Richter, *The Beauty of Fractals*. Berlin: Springer-Verlag, 1986.

Prescott, Edward, "Theory Ahead of Business-Cycle Measurement," *Carnegie-Rochester Conference on Public Policy*, 1986a, *25*, 11–44; reprinted in *Quarterly Review, Federal Reserve Bank of Minneapolis*, Fall 1986, *10*, 9–22.

Prescott, Edward, "Response to a Skeptic," *Quarterly Review, Federal Reserve Bank of Minneapolis*, Fall 1986b, *10*, 28–33.

Ríos-Rull, José-Víctor, "Models with Heterogeneous Agents." In Cooley, T. F., ed., *Frontiers of Business Cycle Research*. Princeton, N.J.: Princeton University Press, 1995, pp. 98–125.

Rubinstein, Mark, "An Aggregation Theorem for Securities Markets," *Journal of Financial Economics*, September 1974, *1*, 225–44.

Sargent, Thomas J., "Two Models of Measurements, and the Investment Accelerator," *Journal of Political Economics*, 1989, *97*:2, 251–87.

Sargent, Thomas J., and Christopher A. Sims, "Business Cycle Modeling Without Pretending to Have Too Much A Priori Economic Theory." In Sims, Christopher, ed., *New Methods in Business Cycle Research*. Minneapolis: Federal Reserve Bank, 1977, pp. 45–110.

Scarf, Herbert, and T. Hansen, *The Computation of Economic Equilibria.* New Haven: Yale University Press, 1973.

Shoven, John B., and John Whalley, "A General Equilibrium Calculation of the Effects of Differential Taxation of Income from Capital in the U.S.," *Journal of Public Economics,* November 1972, *1,* 281–322.

Shoven, John B., and John Whalley, *Applying General Equilibrium.* New York: Cambridge University Press, 1992.

Simon, Julian L., and Dennis J. Aigner, "Cross Sectional Budget Studies, Aggregate Time Series Studies and the Permanent Income Hypothesis," *American Economic Review,* June 1970, *60:*2, 526–41.

Sims, Christopher A., "Macroeconomics and Reality," *Econometrica,* 1980, *48:*1, 1–48.

Sims, Christopher A., "Rational Expectations Modeling with Seasonally Adjusted Data," *Journal of Econometrics,* January/February 1993, *55,* 9–19.

Smith, J., "A Comparison of the Earnings Patterns of Two Samples of JTPA Eligibles," unpublished paper, University of Western Ontario, London, Canada, August 1995.

Sonnenschein, H., "Do Walres Identity and Continuity Characterize the Class of Community Excess Demand Functions?," *Journal of Economic Theory,* August 1973, 6, *345–54.*

Stoker, T. M., "Empirical Approaches to the Problem of Aggregation over Individuals," *Journal of Economic Literature,* December 1993, *31:*4, 1827–74.

Taylor, John B., *Macroeconomic Policy in a World Economy: From Econometric Design to Practical Operation.* New York: W. W. Norton and Company, 1993.

Tinbergen, J., *Statistical Testing of Business Cycle Theories.* Vol. 2, Business Cycles in the USA, 1919-1932, Geneva: League of Nations, 1939.

Tobin, James, "A Statistical Demand Function for Food in the USA," *Journal of the Royal Statistical Society,* 1950, *113,* Series A, Part II, 113–41.

Trostel, P. A., "The Effect of Taxation on Human Capital," *Econometrica,* April 1993, *101,* 327–50.

Watson, M. W., "Measures of Fit for Calibrated Models," *Journal of Political Economy,* 1993, *101:*6, 1011–41.

Wilson, Robert B., "The Theory of Syndicates," *Econometrica,* January 1968, *36,* 119–32.

Oxford Economic Papers 47 (1995), 24–44

FACTS AND ARTIFACTS: CALIBRATION AND THE EMPIRICAL ASSESSMENT OF REAL-BUSINESS-CYCLE MODELS

By KEVIN D. HOOVER

Department of Economics, University of California, Davis, California 95616-8578, USA

1. Whither quantitative macroeconomics?

THE RELATIONSHIP between theory and data has been, from the beginning, a central concern of the new-classical macroeconomics. This much is evident in the title of Robert E. Lucas's and Thomas J. Sargent's landmark edited volume, *Rational Expectations and Econometric Practice* (1981). With the advent of real-business-cycle models, many new classical economists have turned to calibration methods. The new classical macroeconomics is now divided between calibrators and estimators. But the debate is not a parochial one, raising, as it does, issues about the relationships of models to reality and the nature of econometrics that should be important to every school of macroeconomic thought, indeed to all applied economics. The stake in this debate is the future direction of quantitative macroeconomics. It is, therefore, critical to understand the root issues.

Lucas begins the second chapter of his *Models of Business Cycles* with the remark:

> Discussions of economic policy, if they are to be productive in any practical sense, necessarily involve *quantitative* assessments of the way proposed policies are likely to affect resource allocation and individual welfare. (Lucas 1987, p. 6; emphasis added)

This might appear to be a clarion call for econometric estimation. But appearances are deceiving. After mentioning Sumru Altug's (1989) estimation and rejection of the validity of a variant of Finn E. Kydland and Edward C. Prescott's (1982) real-business-cycle model (a model which takes up a large portion of his book), Lucas writes:

> ... the interesting question is surely not whether [the real-business-cycle model] can be accepted as 'true' when nested within some broader class of models. Of course the model is not 'true': this much is evident from the axioms on which it is constructed. We know from the onset in an enterprise like this (I would say, in *any* effort in positive economics) that what will emerge—at *best*—is a workable approximation that is useful in answering a limited set of questions. (Lucas 1987, p. 45)

Lucas abandons not only truth but also the hitherto accepted standards of empirical economics. Models that clearly do not fit the data, he argues, may nonetheless be calibrated to provide useful quantitative guides to policy.

Calibration techniques are commonly applied to so-called 'computable general-equilibrium' models. They were imported into macroeconomics as a means of quantifying real-business-cycle models, but now have a wide range of applications. Some issues raised by calibration are common to all computable general-equilibrium models; the concern of this paper, however, is with real-business-cycle models and related macroeconomic applications; and, as will appear presently, these raise special issues. A model is calibrated when its parameters are quantified from casual empiricism or unrelated econometric studies or are chosen to guarantee that the model precisely mimics some particular feature of the historical data. For example, in Kydland and Prescott (1982), the coefficient of relative risk aversion is justified on the basis of microeconomic studies, while the free parameters of the model are set to force the model to match the variance of GNP without any attempt to find the value of empirical analogues to them.

Allan W. Gregory and Gregor W. Smith (1991, p. 3) conclude that calibration '... is beginning to predominate in the quantitative application of macro-economic models'. While indicative of the importance of the calibration methodology, Gregory and Smith's conclusion is too strong. Aside from the new classical school, few macroeconomists are staunch advocates of calibration. Within the new classical school, opinion remains divided. Even with reference to real-business-cycle models, some practitioners have insisted that calibration is at best a first step, which must be followed '... by setting down a metric (e.g. one induced by a likelihood function) and estimating parameters by finding values that make the metric attain a minimum' (Gary Hansen and Sargent 1988, p. 293).[1]

Sargent advocates estimation or what Kydland and Prescott (1991) call the 'system-of-equations approach'. Estimation has been the standard approach in macroeconometrics for over 40 years. Sargent and like-minded new classical economists modify the standard approach only in their insistence that the restrictions implied by dynamic-optimization models be integrated into the estimations. The standard of empirical assessment is the usual one: how well does the model fit the data statistically? Lucas and Kydland and Prescott reject statistical goodness of fit as a relevant standard of assessment. The issue at hand might then be summarized: who is right—Lucas and Kydland and Prescott, or Sargent?

The answer to this question is not transparent. Estimation is the *status quo*. And, although enthusiastic advocates of calibration already announce its triumph, its methodological foundations remain largely unarticulated. An uncharitable interpretation of the calibration methodology might be that the advocates of real-business-cycle models are so enamored of their creations that they would prefer to abandon commonly accepted, neutral standards of empirical evaluation (i.e. econometric hypothesis testing) to preserve their

[1] Despite the joint authorship of the last quotation, I regard Sargent and not Hansen as the preeminent proponent of the necessity of estimation, because I recall him forcefully insisting on it in his role as discussant of a paper by Thomas F. Cooley and Hansen (1989) at the Federal Reserve Bank of San Francisco's Fall Acacemic Conference; see also Manuelli and Sargent (1988, pp. 531–4).

models. This would be an *ad hoc* defensive move typical of a degenerating research program.

This interpretation is not only uncharitable, it is wrong. Presently, we shall see that Herbert Simon's (1969) *Sciences of the Artifical* provides the materials from which to construct a methodological foundation for calibration, and that calibration is compatible with a well-established approach to econometrics that is nonetheless very different from the Cowles Commission emphasis on the estimation of systems of equations. Before addressing these issues, however, it will be useful to describe the calibration methodology and its place in the history and practice of econometrics in more detail.

2. The calibration methodology

2.1. *The paradigm case*

Kydland and Prescott (1982) is the paradigm new-classical equilibrium, real-business-cycle model. It is neoclassical optimal-growth model with stochastic shocks to technology which cause the equilibrium growth path to fluctuate about its steady state.[2] Concrete functional forms are chosen to capture some general features of business cycles. Production is governed by a constant-elasticity-of-substitution production function in which inventories, fixed capital, and labor combine to generate a single homogeneous output that may either be consumed or reinvested. Fixed capital requires a finite time to be built before it becomes a useful input. The constant-relative-risk-aversion utility function is rigged to possess a high degree of intertemporal substitutability of leisure. Shocks to technology are serially correlated. Together the structure of the serial correlation of the technology shocks and the degree of intertemporal substitution in consumption and leisure choices govern the manner in which shocks are propagagated through time and the speed of convergence back towards the steady state.

Once the model is specified, the next step is to parameterize its concrete functional forms. Most of the parameters of the model are chosen from values culled from other applied econometric literatures or from general facts about national-income accounting. For example, Thomas Mayer (1960) estimated the average time to construct complete facilities to be 21 months; Robert E. Hall (1977) estimated the average time from start of projects to beginning of production to be two years. Citing these papers, but noting that consumer durable goods take considerably less time to produce, Kydland and Prescott (1982, p. 1361) assume that the paramters governing capital formation are set to imply steady construction over four quarters.[3] The values for depreciation

---

[2] For general descriptions of the details and varieties of real-business-cycle models see Lucas (1987), Kevin D. Hoover (1988, ch. 3), and Bennett T. McCallum (1989). Steven M. Sheffrin (1989, ch. 3, especially pp. 80, 81), gives a step-by-step recipe for constructing a prototypical real-business-cycle model.

[3] Mayer's estimates were for complete projects only, so that new equipment installed in old plants, which must have a much shorter time-to-build than 21 months, was not counted.

rates and the capital/inventory ratio are set to rough averages from the national-income accounts. Ready estimates from similar sources were not available for the remaining six paramters of the model, which include parameters governing intertemporal substitution of leisure and the shocks to technology. These were chosen by searching over possible parameter values for a combination that best reproduced certain key variances and covariances of the data. In particular, the technology shock variance was chosen in order to exactly match the variance of output in the postwar US economy.

To test the model's performance, Kydland and Prescott generate a large number of realizations of the technology shocks for 118 periods corresponding to their postwar data. They then compute the variances and covariances implied by the model for a number of important variables: output, consumption, investment, inventories, the capital stock, hours worked, productivity, and the real rate of interest.[4] These are then compared with the corresponding variances and covariances of the actual US data.[5]

Kydland and Prescott offer no formal measure of the success of their model. They do note that hours are insufficiently variable with respect to the variability of productivity to correspond accurately to the data, but otherwise they are pleased with the model's ability to mimic the second moments of the data.

Real-business-cycle models, treated in the manner of Kydland and Prescott, are a species of the genus computable (or applied) general-equilibrium models. The accepted standards for implementing computable general-equilibrium models, as codified, for example, in Ahsan Mansur and John Whalley (1984), do not appear to have been adopted in the real-business-cycle literature. For example, while some practitioners of computable general-equilibrium models engage in extensive searches of the literature in order to get some measure of the central tendency of assumed elasticities, Kydland and Prescott's (1982)

---

[4] In fact, it is not clear in Kydland and Prescott (1982) that these are calculated from the cross-section of a set of realizations or from a single time-series realization. In a subsequent paper that extends their results, Kydland and Prescott (1988, p. 353) are quite precise about using a cross-section of many realizations. Because they are interested only in the moments of the variables and not in particular time-series, Kydland and Prescott initialize variables to their steady-state values or, equivalently in the context of detrended data, to zero. In order to generate a time path that can be compared to the history of a particular series, it is necessary, as in Hansen and Prescott (1993), to initialize at some actual historical benchmark.

[5] Despite my referring to Kydland and Prescott's model as a growth model, the model for which they calculate the variances and covariances does not possess an exogenous source of trend growth. Thus, to make comparisons, Kydland and Prescott (1982, p. 1362) detrend the actual data using the Hodrick-Prescott filter. The particular choice of filter is not defended in any detail. Prescott (1983, p. 6) simply asserts that it produces 'about the right degree of smoothness, when fit to the logarithm of the real GNP series' without any indication by what standard rightness is to be judged. Kydland and Prescott (1990, p. 9) claim that it generates a trend close to the trend that students of business cycles would draw by hand through a plot of actual GNP. Although the Hodrick-Prescott filter is almost universally adopted in comparing real-business-cycle models to actual data, Fabio Canova (1991b) shows that the use of Hodrick-Prescott filters with different choices for the values of a key parameter or of several entirely different alternative filters radically alters the cyclical characteristics of economic data (also see Timothy Cogley and James Nason, 1993).

choice of parameterization appears almost casual. Similarly, although Kydland and Prescott report some checks on robustness, these appear to be perfunctory.[6]

In the context of computable general-equilibrium models, calibration is preferred in those cases in which, because of extensive disaggregation, the number of parameters is too large relative to the available data set to permit econometric estimation.[7] Since typical real-business-cycle models are one-good, one-agent models, there is no difficulty in estimating them using standard methods such as maximum likelihood or generalized method of moments. Indeed, since the practitioners are often interested principally in matching selected second moments, method-of-moments estimators can concentrate on the moments of interest to the exclusion of others (see Watson 1993, p. 1037).

As noted earlier, Altug (1989) estimates and rejects a close relative of Kydland and Prescott's model using maximum likelihood. The central problem of this paper can be restated: is there a case for ignoring Altug's rejection of the Kydland and Prescott model? The case must be something other than the standard one of too many parameters found in the literature on computable general-equilibrium models.

2.2. Calibration as estimation

Various authors have attempted to tame calibration and return it to the traditional econometric fold. Manuelli and Sargent (1988), Gregory and Smith (1990a), Canova (1991a), and Bansal et al. (1991) interpret calibration as a form of 'estimation by simulation'. In such a procedure, parameters are chosen, and the relevant features of the simulated output of the calibrated model are compared to the analogous features of the actual data. Such a procedure differs from standard estimation methods principally in that it allows the investigator to expand or restrict the range of features considered to be relevant.

Lucas's argument, however, is that any form of estimation is irrelevant. In their early writings, Kydland and Prescott were not in fact as explicit as Lucas about the irrelevance of estimation. They merely argued that it would be premature to apply techniques to their model, such as those developed by Lars Peter Hansen and Sargent (1980), to account for the systemic effects of rational expectations (Kydland and Prescott, 1982, p. 1369). Prescott (1983, pp. 8–11)

---

[6] Canova (1991a) suggests a formal methodology and provides an example in which sensitivity analysis is conducted with respect to distributions for parameter values constructed from the different values reported in unrelated studies or from *a priori* information on the practically or theoretically admissible range of parameter values.

[7] Lawrence J. Lau (1984) notices that any model that can be calibrated can also be estimated. He uses 'calibration', however, in a narrow sense. A model is calibrated when its parameters are chosen to reproduce the data of a benchmark period. Thus, parameterization on the basis of unrelated econometric studies does not count as calibration for him. Lau's usage is diametrically opposed to that of Gregory and Smith (1991) for whom calibration is only the assignment of parameter values from unrelated sources. We use 'calibration' in both Lau's and Gregory and Smith's senses. Lau and, similarly, James MacKinnon (1984) make strong pleas for estimation instead of, or in addition to, calibration, and for subjecting computable general-equilibrium models to statistical specification tests.

was more pointed: real-business-cycle models are tightly parameterized. They will almost inevitably be rejected against a weakly restricted alternative hypothesis, but such alternative hypotheses arise from the introduction of arbitrary stochastic processes and, so, are not suitable benchmarks for economic inference. 'A model may mimic the cycle well but not perfectly' (Prescott 1983, p. 10). Similarly, Kydland and Prescott (1991, p. 174) write:

> Unlike the system-of-equations approach, the model economy which better fits the data is not [necessarily?] the one used. Rather, currently established theory dictates which one is used.

The dominance of theory in the choice of models lies at the heart of the difference between estimators and calibrators. To throw the difference into high relief, one can think of estimators pursuing a competitive strategy and calibrators pursuing an adaptive strategy. Under the competitive strategy, theory proposes, estimation and testing disposes. In fine, alternative theories compete with one another for the support of the data. The adaptive strategy begins with an unrealistic model, in the sense of one that is an idealized and simplified product of the core theory. It sees how much mileage it can get out of that model. Only then does it add any complicating and more realistic feature. Unlike the competitive strategy, the aim is never to test and possibly reject the core theory, but to construct models that reproduce the economy more and more closely within the strict limits of the basic theory.

The distinction between the competitive and adaptive strategies is sharply drawn and somewhat stylized, but focuses nonetheless on a genuine difference. On the one hand, the competitive strategy is the received view of econometricians, taught in an idealized form in most econometric textbooks, even if more honored in the breach than the observance by applied economists. The competitive strategy is explicit in Gregory and Smith's (1990b) 'Calibration as Testing'. Even if in practice no theory is ever decisively rejected through a test based on an econometric estimation, the theory is nonetheless regarded as at risk and contingent—even at its core. On the other hand, the real-business-cycle modeller typically does not regard the core theory at risk in principle. Like the estimators, the calibrators wish to have a close fit between their quantified models and the actual data—at least in selected dimensions. But the failure to obtain a close fit (statistical rejection) does not provide grounds for rejecting the fundamental underlying theory. Adaptation in the face of recalcitrant data is adaptation of peripheral assumptions, not of the core. Thus, the inability of Kydland and Prescott's (1982) original real-business-cycle model to match the data prompted more complicated versions of essentially the same model that included, for example, heterogeneous labor (Kydland 1984), a banking sector (Robert G. King and Charles I. Plosser 1984), indivisible labor (Gary Hansen 1985), separate scales for straight-time and overtime work (Gary Hansen and Sargent 1988), and variable capital intensity (Kydland and Prescott 1988).

One consequence of these strategies is that esimators possess a common ground, the performance of each theoretically-based specification against actual data, on which to judge the performance of competing models. For the calibrators, however, data help discriminate only between different adaptations of the common core. The core theory itself is not questioned, so that, unintentially perhaps, the core theory becomes effectively a Lakatosian hardcore (Lakatos 1970, 1978; Blaug 1992, ch. 2). Calibration does not provide a method that could in principle decide between fundamentally different business-cycle models (e.g. real-business-cycle models or Keynesian business-cycle models) on the basis of empirical evidence derived from the calibration exercise itself.[8] Critics of real-business-cycle models who attempt such comparisons fall back either on attacking the discriminating power of calibration methods (e.g. Hartley *et al.* 1993) or on adaptations of standard econometric techniques (e.g. Canova *et al.* 1993). Kydland and Prescott are explicit in rejecting these applications of estimation techniques as missing the point of the calibration method. The aim of this paper is partly to explicate and appraise their view.[9]

2.3. *The mantel of Frisch*

Calibrators radically reject the system-of-equations approach. But Kydland and Prescott, at least, do not reject econometrics. Rather, they argue that econometrics is not coextensive with estimation; calibration is econometrics. Kydland and Prescott (1991, pp. 161, 162) point out that for Ragnar Frisch, Irving Fisher, and Joseph Shumpeter, the founders of the Econometric Society, 'econometrics' was the unification of statistics, economic theory, and mathematics. Unacknowledged by Kydland and Prescott, Mary Morgan's (1990) brilliant history of econometrics supports and elaborates their point. According to Morgan, even before the term 'econometrics' had wide currency, the econometric ideal had been to weld mathematical, deductive economics to statistical, empirical economics to provide a substitute for the experimental methods of the natural sciences appropriate to the study of society. This ideal collapsed with the rise of the system-of-equations approach in the wake of the Cowles Commission.

Kydland and Prescott point to Frisch's (1933) article, 'Propagation Problems and Impulse Response Problems in Dynamic Economics' as a precursor to both their own real-business-cycle model and to calibration methods. Frisch argues that quantitative analysis requires complete models: i.e. general-equilibrium models in a broad sense. He considers a sequence of models, starting with a very simple one, and then adding complications. He models the time-to-build feature of capital formation. He distinguishes between the impulses that start business cycles and the dynamic mechansims that amplify and propagate them. He quantifies his models using calibration techniques. And,

---

[8] This is not to say that there could not be some other basis for some decision.

[9] Hoover 1994a (as well as work in progress) outlines a possible method of using econometric techniques in a way that respects the idealized nature of the core models without giving up the possibility of empirical discrimination.

precisely like Kydland and Prescott (1982), Frisch marvels at how well a very simple model can capture the features of actual data.

Although Kydland and Prescott are correct to see the affinities between Frisch's work and their own, they ignore the very real differences between Frisch and themselves. Frisch's approach is wholly macroeconomic. Frisch writes:

> In order to attack these problems on a macro-dynamic basis so as to explain the movement of the system taken in its entirety, we must deliberately disregard a considerable amount of the details of the picture. We may perhaps start by throwing all kinds of production into one variable, all consumption into another, and so on, imagining that the notions 'production', 'consumption', and on, can be measured by some sort of total indices. (1933, p. 173)

While his flight to aggregates parallels the practice of the new classical real-business-cycle model, Frisch does not suggest that this is a way station on the road to microfoundations. His article does not hint at the desirability of microfoundations, even of the pseudo-microfoundations of the representative-agent model: there is not an optimization problem to be found. Frisch appears to use calibration mainly for purposes of illustration, and not to advocate it as a preferred technique. He writes:

> At present I am guessing very roughly at these parameters, but I believe that it will be possible by appropriate statistical methods to obtain more exact information about them. I think, indeed, that the statistical determination of such structural parameters will be one of the main objectives of the economic cycle analysis of the future. (1933, p. 185)

Precisely which statistical methods are appropriate appears to be an open question.[10]

More generally, although Frisch stresses the importance of theory, there is no hint that his interpretation is limited to 'maximizing behavior subject to constraints' (Kydland and Prescott 1991, p. 164). Frisch does not define 'theory' in 'Propagation Problems...', but the examples he produces of theories are not of an obviously different character from the structures employed by Jan Tinbergen, Lawrence Klein, James Dusenberry, and the other 'Keynesian' macromodelers who are the special bugbears of the advocates of new-classical, real-business-cycle models.

Schumpeter (co-founder with Frisch of the Econometric Society) provides typically prolix discussions of the meaning of 'economic theory' in his magisteral *History of Economic Analysis* (1954). For Schumpeter (1954, pp. 14,

---

[10] Frisch's own shifting views illustrate how open a question this was for him. By 1936, he had backtracked on the desirability of estimating calibrated models. In 1938, he argued that structural estimation was impossible because of pervasive multicollinearity. In its place he proposed estimating unrestricted reduced forms (see Morgan, 1990, p. 97; also see Aldrich 1989, section 2). In this he comes much closer to Christopher Sims (1980) program of vector autoregressions without 'incredible' identifying restrictions. I am grateful to an anonymous referee for reminding me of this point. Hoover (1992) identifies Sims's program as one of three responses to the Lucas (1976) critique of policy invariance. Calibration and the systems-of-equations approach each possess a analogous response.

15), theories are, on the one hand, 'synonomous with Explanatory Hypotheses', and on the other hand, 'the sum total of the gadgets', such as '"marginal rate of substitution", "marginal productivity", "multiplier", "accelerator"', including 'stragegically useful assumptions', 'by which results may be extracted from the hypothesis'. Schumpeter concludes: 'In Mrs. Robinson's unsurpassingly felicitous phrase, economic theory is a box of tools'. Later Schumpeter defends the theoretical credentials of Wesley C. Mitchell, the subject of Tjalling Koopman's (1947) famous attack on 'Measurement without Theory':

> . . . in intention as well as in fact, he was laying the foundations for a 'theory', a business cycle theory as well as a general theory of the economic process, but for a different one. (1954, p. 1166)

Kydland and Prescott (1991, p. 164) argue that the system-of-equations approach flourished in the 1950s only because economists lacked the tools to construct stochastic computable general-equilibrium models. They proclaim the death of the system-of-equations approach:

> The principal reason for the abandonment of the system-of-equations approach, however, was the advances in neoclassical theory that permitted the application of the paradigm in dynamic stochastic settings. Once the neoclassical tools needed for modeling business cycle fluctuations existed, their application to this problem and their ultimate domination over any other method was inevitable. (1991, p. 167)

This is an excessively triumphalist and whiggish history of the development of econometric thought. First, the work of Frisch and others in the 1930s provides no support for Kydland and Prescott's narrowing of the meaning of 'theory' to support such tendentious statements as: 'To summarize the Frisch view, then, econometrics is quantitative *neoclassical* theory with a basis in facts' (Kydland and Prescott 1991, p. 162; emphasis added). (A model is 'neoclassical' for Kydland and Prescott (1991, p. 164) when it is constructed from '. . . agents maximizing subject to constraints and market clearing'.) Second, the declaration of the death of the system-of-equations approach is premature and greatly exaggerated. Allegiance to the system-of-equations approach motivates the many efforts to interpret calibration as a form of estimation. Third, the calibration methodology is not logically connected to Kydland and Prescott's preferred theoretical framework. The example of Frisch shows that calibration can be applied to models that are not stochastic dynamic optimal-growth models. The example of Lars Peter Hansen and Sargent (1980) shows that, even those who prefer such models, can use them as the source of identification for systems of equations—refining rather than supplanting the traditional econometrics of estimation.

3. The quantification of theory

Although Kydland and Prescott overstate the degree to which Frisch and the econometrics of the 1930s foreshadowed their work, they are nonetheless correct to note many affinities. But such affinities, even if they were more complete than they turn out to be, do not amount to an argument favoring calibration over estimation. At most, they are an illicit appeal to authority. To date, no compelling defence of the calibration methodology has been offered. An interpretation of the point of calibration and an assessment of its merits can be constructed, however, from hints provided in Lucas's methodological writings of the 1970s and early 1980s.

3.1. *Models*

'Model' is a ubiquitous term in economics, and a term with a variety of meanings. One commonly speaks of an econometric model. Here one means the concrete specification of functional forms for estimation. I call these observational models. The second main class of models are evaluative or interpretive models. An obvious subclass of interpretive/evaluative models are toy models.

A toy model exists merely to illustrate or to check the coherence of principles or their interaction. An example of a toy model is the overlapping-generations model with money in its simplest incarnations. No one would think of drawing quantitative conclusions about the working of the economy from it. Instead one wants to show that models constructed on its principles reproduce certain known qualitative features of the economy and suggest other qualitative features that may not have been known or sufficiently appreciated (cf. Diamond 1984, p. 47). Were one so rash as to estimate such a model, it would surely be rejected, but that would be no reason to abandon it as a testbed for general principles.

Is there another subclass of interpretive/evaluative models, one that involves quantification? Lucas seems to think so:

> One of the functions of theoretical economics is to provide fully articulated, artificial economic systems that can serve as laboratories in which policies that would be prohibitively expensive to experiment within actual economies can be tested out at much lower cost. (Lucas 1980, p. 271)

Let us call such models benchmark models. Benchmark models must be abstract enough and precise enough to permit incontrovertible answers to the questions put to them. Therefore,

> ... insistence on the 'realism' of an economic model subverts its potential usefulness in thinking about reality. Any model that is well enough articulated to give clear answers to the questions we put to it will necessarily be artificial, abstract, patently unreal. (Lucas 1980, p. 271)

On the other hand, only models that mimic reality in important respects will be useful in analyzing actual economies.

> The more dimensions in which the model mimics the answers actual economies give to simple questions, the more we trust its answers to harder questions. This is the sense in which more 'realism' in a model is clearly preferred to less. (Lucas 1980, p. 272)

Later in the same essay, Lucas emphasizes the quantitative nature of such model building:

> Our task ... is to write a FORTRAN program that will accept specific economic policy rules as 'input' and will generate as 'output' statistics describing the operating characteristics of time series we care about, which are predicted to result from these policies. (p. 288)

For Lucas, Kydland and Prescott's model is precisely such a program.[11]

One might interpret Lucas's remarks as making a superficial contribution to the debate over Milton Friedman's 'Methodology of Positive Economics' (1953): must the assumptions on which a theory is constructed be true or realistic or is it enough that the theory predicts 'as if' they were true? But this would be a mistake. Lucas is making a point about the architecture of models and not about the foundations of secure prediction. Lucas refers to a model as fully 'realistic' when it fully accounts for all the factors that determine the variables of interest. Lucas makes two points. Uncontroversially, he argues that toy models convey deep understanding of economic principles. More interestingly, he argues that benchmark models have an advantage over estimation. This is controversial because estimators believe that fully articulated specifications are required for accurate quantification. This is expressed in their concern for specification error, omitted variable bias, and so forth. Their view is widely shared. The point is not that estimated models are necessarily more realistic in Lucas's sense than calibrated models, nor that estimation is the only or even the most reliable way to quantify a model or its components.[12] Rather it is that any method of quantification that does not aspire to full articulation is likely to mislead. Lucas denies this, and the interesting issues are how to appraise his position, and, if his position is sustainable, how to appraise quantified benchmark models themselves.

To make this clear, consider Lucas's (1987, pp. 20–31) cost-benefit analysis of the policies to raise GNP growth and to damp the business cycle. Lucas's model considers a single representative consumer with a constant-relative-risk-aversion utility function facing an exogenous consumption stream. The model is calibrated by picking reasonable values for the mean and variance of consumption, the subjective rate of discount, and the constant coefficient of relative risk aversion. Lucas then calculates how much extra consumption consumers would require to compensate them in terms of utility for a cut in the growth of consumption and how much consumption they would be willing to give up to secure smoother consumption streams. Although the answers that Lucas seeks are quantitative, the model is not used to make predictions that might be subjected to statistical tests. Indeed, it is a striking illustration of why calibration should not be interpreted as estimation by simulation. Lucas's model is used to set upper bounds to the benefits that might conceivably be gained in the real world. Its parameters must reflect some truth about the world

---

[11] Kydland and Prescott do not say, however, whether it is actually written in FORTRAN.

[12] For example, to clarify a point raised by an anonymous referee, if the central bank had direct knowledge of it money supply function, that would be better than estimating it.

K. D. HOOVER   35

if it is to be useful, but they could not be easily directly estimated. In that sense, the model is unrealistic.[13]

3.2. *Artifacts*

In a footnote, Lucas (1980, p. 272, fn. 1) cites Simon's *Sciences of the Artificial* (1969) as an 'immediate ancestor' of his 'condensed' account. To uncover a more fully articulated argument for Lucas's approach to modelling, it is worth following up the reference.

For Simon, human artifacts, among which he must count economic models,

> can be thought of as a meeting point—an 'interface'...—between an 'inner' environment, the substance and organization of the artifact itself, and an 'outer' environment, the surroundings in which it operates. (Simon 1969, pp. 6, 7)

An artifact is useful, it achieves its goals, if its inner environment is appropriate to its outer environment.

The distinction between the outer and inner environments is important because there is some degree of independence between them. Clocks tell time for the outer environment. Although they may indicate the time in precisely the same way, say with identical hands on identical faces, the mechanisms of different clocks, their inner environments, may be constructed very differently. For determining when to leave to catch a plane, such differences are irrelevant. Equally, the inner environments may be isolated from all but a few key features of the outer environment. Only light entering through the lens for the short time that its shutter is open impinges on the inner environment of the camera. The remaining light is screened out by the opaque body of the camera, which is an essential part of its design.

Simon factors adaptive systems into goals, outer environments and inner environments. The relative independence of the outer and inner environments means that

> [w]e might hope to characterize the main properties of the system and its behavior without elaborating the detail of *either* the outer or the inner environments. We might look toward a science of the artificial that would depend on the relative simplicity of the interface as its primary source of abstraction and generality. (Simon 1969, p. 9)

Simon's views reinforce Lucas's discussion of models. A model is useful only if it foregoes descriptive realism and selects limited features of reality to reproduce. The assumption upon which the model is based do not matter, so long as the model succeeds in reproducing the selected features. Friedman's 'as if' methodology appears vindicated.

---

[13] Of course, Lucas's approach might be accepted in principle and still rejected in detail. For example, McCallum (1986, pp. 411, 412) objects to the characterization of consumption as fluctuating symmetrically about trend that is implicit in Lucas's use of a mean/variance model. If the fluctuations of consumption are better described as varying degrees of shortfall relative to the trend of potential maximum consumption, then the benefits of consumption smoothing will be considerably higher than Lucas's finds.

But this is to move too fast. The inner environment is only relatively independent of the outer environment. Adaptation has its limits.

> In a benign environment we would learn from the motor only what it had been called upon to do; in a taxing environment we would learn something about its internal structure—specifically, about those aspects of the internal structure that were chiefly instrumental in limiting performance. (Simon 1969, p. 13)[14]

This is a more general statement of principles underlying Lucas's (1976) critique of macroeconometric models. A benign outer environment for econometric models is one in which policy does not change. Changes of policy produce structural breaks in estimated equations: disintegration of the inner environment of the models. Economic models must be constructed like a ship's chronometer, insulated from the outer environment so that '... it reacts to the pitching of the ship only in the negative sense of maintaining an invariant relation of the hands on its dial to real time, independently of the ship's motions' (Simon 1969, p. 9). Insulation in economic models is achieved by specifying functions whose parameters are invariant to policy. The independence of the inner and outer environments is not something which is true of arbitrary models; rather it must be built into models. While it may be enough in hostile environments for models to reproduce key features of the outer environment 'as if' reality was described by their inner environments, it is not enough if they can do this only in benign environments. Thus, for Lucas, the 'as if' methodology interpreted as an excuse for complacency with respect to modeling assumptions must be rejected. Simon's notion of the artifact helps justify Lucas's both rejecting realism in the sense of full articulation and at the same time, insisting that only through carefully constructing the model from invariants — tastes and technology, in Lucas's usual phrase—can the model secure the benefits of a useful abstraction and generality.

Recognizing that a model must be constructed from invariants does not itself tell us how to quantify it. The emphasis on a maintained theory or inner environment presents a generic risk for quantified idealized models (see Section 2.2 above). The risk is particularly severe for the calibration methodology with its adaptive strategy. Gregory and Smith (1991, p. 30) observe that '[s]etting parameter values (i.e. calibrating), simulating a model and comparing properties of simulations to those of data often suggests fruitful modifications of the model'. Generally, such modifications leave the essential core theory intact and attempt to better account for the divergences from the ideal, to better account for the fudge factors need to link the output of the model to the phenomenal laws. The risk, then, is that the core of the model becomes completely insulated from empirical confirmation or disconfirmation—even in the weakest senses of

---

[14] Haavelmo (1944, p. 28) makes a similar point in his well-known example of the failure of autonomy: the relationship between the speed of a car and the amount of throttle may be well-defined under uniform conditions, but would break down immediately the car was placed in a different setting. To understand how the car will perform on the track as well as on the road requires us to repair to the deeper principles of its operation.

those terms. Kydland and Prescott (1991, p. 171) explicitly deny that the confidence in the answers a model gives to policy questions can '... be resolved by computing some measure of how well the model economy mimics historical data'. Rather, '[t]he degree of confidence in the answer depends on the confidence that is placed in the economic theory being used'. Kydland and Prescott do not explain what alternative sources there might be to justify our confidence in theory; the adaptive strategy of the calibration approach almost guarantees that empirical evidence will not be among those sources.

3.3. *Quantification without history*

Calibrators of real-business-cycle models typically concentrate on matching selected second moments of variables rather than, say, matching the actual historical evolution of the modeled variables. Why? Lucas (1977, p. 218) observes that 'business cycles are all alike', not in exact detail but qualitatively. An informative test of a model's ability to capture business-cycle behavior is not, therefore, its fit to some historical time series, which is but one of many possible realizations, but rather its ability to characterize the distribution from which that realization was drawn. Lucas (1977, pp. 219, 234) advocates the test of Irma Adelman and Frank L. Adelman (1959). The Adelmans asked the question, could one distinguish data generated by simulating a model (in their case, the Klein-Goldberger macroeconometric model) from actual data describing the economy, in the absence of knowledge of which was which? The Adelmans' test compares the distribution of outcomes of the model to the actual economy. Once a close relation is established, to experiment with alternative policy rules is an easy next step. Even though government is not modelled in Kydland and Prescott's initial models, policy analysis is their ultimate goal (Kydland and Prescott, 1982, p. 1369). Concentration on the second moments of variables can be seen as the practical implementation of the Adelmans' standard: one eschews the particular realization in favor of a more general characterization of the distribution of possible outcomes.[15]

One reason, therefore, not to apply a neutral statistical test for the match between model and reality is that it is along only selected dimensions that one cares about the model's performance at all. This is completely consistent with Simon's account of artifacts. New classical economics has traditionally been skeptical about discretionary economic policies. New classical economists are, therefore, more concerned to evaluate the operating characteristics of policy rules. For this, the fit of the model to a particular historical realization is largely irrelevant, unless it assures it will also characterize the future distribution of

---

[15] The Adelmans themselves examine the time-series properties of a single draw, rather than the characteristics of repeated draws. This probably reflects, in part, the computational expense of simulating a large macroeconometric model with the technology of 1959. It also reflects the application of Burns and Mitchell's techniques for characterizing the repetitive features of business cycles through averaging over historical cycles all normalized to a notional cycle length. King and Plosser (1989) attempt to apply precisely Burns and Michell's techniques to outcomes generated by a real-business-cycle model.

outcomes. The implicit claim of most econometrics is that it does assure a good characterization. Probably most econometricians would reject calibration methods as coming nowhere close to providing such assurance. Substantial work remains to be done in establishing objective, comparative standards for judging competing models.

4. Aggregation and general equilibrium[16]

Whether calibrated or estimated, real-business-cycle models are idealizations along many dimensions. The most important dimension of idealization is the the models deal in aggregates while the economy is composed of individuals. After all, the distinction between microeconomics and macroeconomics is the distinction between the individual actor and the economy as a whole. All new classical economists believe that one understands macroeconomic behavior only as an outcome of individual rationality. Lucas (1987, p. 57) comes close to adopting the *Verstehen* approach of the Austrians.[17] The difficulty with this approach is that there are millions of people in the economy and it is not practical—nor is it ever likely to become practical—to model the behavior of each of them.[18] Universally, new classical economists adopt representative-agent models, in which one agent or a few types of agents, stand in for the behavior of all agents.[19] The conditions under which a single agent's behavior can accurately represent the behavior of an entire class are onerous and almost certainly never fulfilled in an actual economy.

One interpretation of the use of calibration methods in macroeconomics is that the practitioners recognize that highly aggregated theoretical models must be descriptively false, so that estimates of them are bound to fit badly in comparison to atheoretical econometric models, which are able to exploit large numbers of free parameters. The theoretical models are nonetheless to be preferred because policy evaluation is possible only within their structure. In this, they are exactly like Lucas's benchmark consumption model (see Section 3.1, above).

Calibractors appeal to microeconomic estimates of key parameters because information about individual agents is lost in the aggregatation process. Estimators, in contrast, could argue that the idealized representative-agent

[16] Aggregation and the problems it poses for macroeconomics are the subject of a voluminous literature. The present discussion is limited to a narrow set of issues most relevant to the question of idealization.

[17] For a full discussion of the relationship between new classical and Austrian economics see Hoover (1988, ch. 10).

[18] In Hoover (1984, pp. 64–6; and 1988, pp. 218–20), I refer to this as the 'Cournot problem' since it was first articulated by Augustin Cournot ([1838] 1927, p. 127).

[19] Some economists reserve the term 'representative-agent models' for models with a single, infinitely-lived agent. In a typical overlapping-generations model the new young are born at the start of every period, and the old die at the end of every period, and the model has infinitely many periods; so there are infinitely many agents. On this view, the overlapping-generations model is not a representative-agent model. I, however, regard it as one, because within any period one type of young agent and one type of old agent stand in for the enormous variety of people, and the same types are repeated period after period.

model permits better use of other information. Lars Peter Hansen and Sargent (1980, pp. 91, 92), for example, argue that the strength of their estimation method is that it accounts consistently for the interrelationships between constituent parts of the model—i.e. that is a general-equilibrium method. Calibrators respond, however, that it is precisely the importance of general equilibrium that supports their approach. Kydland and Prescott write:

> ... it is in the stage of calibration where the power of the general equilibrium approach shows up most forcefully. The insistence on internal consistency implies that parsimoniously parameterized models of the household and business sector display rich dynamic behavior through the intertemporal substitution arising from capital accumulation and from other sources. (1991, p. 170)

The trade-off between the gains and losses of the two methods is not clear cut. Lucas (1987, pp. 46, 47) and Prescott (1986, p. 15) argue that the strength of calibration is that it uses multiple sources of information, supporting the belief that it is structured around true invariants. This argument would appear to appeal to the respectable, albeit philosophically controversial view, that a theory is better supported when tested on information not used in its formulation (see Lipton 1991, ch. 8; Hoover 1994b). Unfortunately, it is not clear that calibration relies on independent information nor that it avoids estimation altogether. Parameters are sometimes chosen for calibrated business-cycle models because they mimic so-called 'stylized facts'. That the models then faithfully reproduce such facts is not independent information. Other parameters are chosen from microeconomic studies. This introduces estimation through the back door, but without any but a subjective, aesthetic metric to judge model performance.

Furthermore, since all new classical, equilibrium business-cycle models rely on the idealization of the representative agent, both calibrated and estimated versions share a common disability: using the representative-agent model in any form begs the question by assuming that aggregation does not fundamentally alter the structure of the aggregate model. Physics may provide a useful analogy. The laws that relate pressure, temperature, and volumes of gases are macrophysics. The 'ideal-gas laws' can be derived from a micromodel: gas molecules are assumed to be point masses, subject to conservation of momentum, with a distribution of velocities. An aggregate assumption is also needed: the probability of the gas molecules moving in any direction is taken to be equal.

Direct estimation of the ideal gas laws shows that they tend to break down—and must be corrected with fudge factors—when pushed to extremes. For example, under high pressures or low temperatures the ideal laws must be corrected according to van der Waals' equation. This phenomenal law, a law in macrophysics, is used to justify alterations of the micromodel: when pressures are high one must recognize that forces operate between individual molecules.

The inference of the van der Waals' force from the macrophysical behavior of gases has an analogue in the development of real-business-cycle models. Gary Hansen (1985), for example, introduces the microeconomic device of indivisible labor into a real-business cycle model, not from any direct reflection on the nature of labor markets at the level of the individual firm or worker, but as an attempt to account for the macroeconomic failure of Kydland and Prescott's (1982) model to satisfactorily reproduce the relative variabilities of hours and productivity in the aggregate data.[20] Of course, direct estimation of Kydland and Prescott's model rather than calibration may have pointed in the same direction.[21]

Despite examples of macro to micro inference analogous to the gas laws, Lucas's (1980, p. 291) more typical view is that we must build our models up from the microeconomic to the macroeconomic. Unlike gases, human society does not comprise homogeneous molecules, but rational people, each choosing constantly. To understand (*verstehen*) their behavior, one must model the individual and his situation. This insight is clearly correct, it is not clear in the least that it is adequately captured in the heroic aggregation assumptions of the representative-agent model. The analogue for physics would be to model the behavior of gases at the macrophysical level, not as derived from the aggregation of molecules of randomly distributed momenta, but as a single molecule scaled up to observable volume—a thing corresponding to nothing ever known to nature.[22]

5. Calibration and macroeconomic practice

The calibration methodology has both a wide following and a substantial opposition within the new classical school. I have attempted to give it a sympathetic reading—both in general and in its specific application to real-business-cycle models. I have concentrated on Kydland and Prescott, as its most prolific practitioners, and on Lucas, an articulate advocate. Although calibration is consistent with appealing accounts of the nature and role of models in science and economics, of their quanfication and idealization, its practical implementation in the service of real-business-cycle models with representative agents is less than compelling.

Does the calibration methodology amount to a repudiation of econometric estimation altogether? Clearly not. At some level, econometrics still helps to supply the values of the parameters of the models. Beyond that, whatever has been said in favor of calibration methods to the contrary notwithstanding, the

---

[20] Canova (1991b, p. 33) suggests that the particular covariance that Hansen's modification of Kydland and Prescott's model was meant to capture is an artifact of the Hodrick-Prescott filter, so that Hansen's model may be a product of misdirected effort rather than a progressive adaptation.

[21] This, rather than collegiality, may account for Kydland and Prescott's (1982, p. 1369) tolerant remark about the future utility of Lars Peter Hansen and Sargent's (1980) econometric techniques as well as for Lucas's (1987, p. 45) view that there is something to be learned from Altug's estimations of the Kydland and Prescott model—a view expressed in the midst of arguing in favour of calibration.

[22] A notable, non-new-classical attempt to derive macroeconomic behavior from microeconomic behavior with appropriate aggregation assumptions is Durlauf (1989). In a different, but related context, Stoker (1986) shows that demand systems fit the data only if distributional variables are included in the estimating equations. He takes this macroeconomic evidence as evidence for the failure of the microeconomic conditions of exact aggregation.

misgivings of econometricians such as Sargent are genuine. The calibration methodology, to date, lacks any discipline as stern as that imposed by econometric methods. For Lucas (1980, p. 288) and Prescott (1983, p. 11), the discipline of the calibration method comes from the paucity of free parameters. But one should note that theory places only loose restrictions on the values of key parameters. In practice, they are actually pinned down from econometric estimation at the microeconomic level or accounting considerations. Thus, in some sense, the calibration method would appear to be a kind of indirect estimation. Thus, although as was pointed out earlier, it would be a mistake to treat calibration as simply an alternative form of estimation, it is easy to understand why some critics interpret it that way. Even were there less flexibility in the parameterizations, the properties ascribed to the underlying components of the idealized real-business-cycle models (the agents, their utility functions, production functions, and constraints) are not subject to as convincing cross checking as the analogous components in physical models usually are. The fudge factors that account for the discrepancies between the ideal model and the data look less like van der Waals' equation than like special pleading. Above all, it is not clear on what standards competing, but contradictory, models are to be compared and adjudicated.[23] Some such standards are essential if any objective progress is to be made in economics.[24]

ACKNOWLEDGEMENTS

I thank Thomas Mayer, Kevin Salyer, Steven Sheffrin, Roy Epstein, Nancy Cartwright, Gregor Smith, Edward Prescott, Adrian Pagan, and two anonymous referees for helpful comments on an earlier draft. The earliest version of this paper, entitled 'Calibration versus Estimation: Standards of Empirical Assessment in the New Classical Macroeconomics', was presented at the American Economic Association meetings in Washington, DC, December 1990.

[23] Prescott (1983, p. 12) seems oddly, to claim that inability of a model to account for some real events is a positive virtue—in particular, that the inability of real-business-cycle models to account for the Great Depression is a point in their favour. He writes: 'If any observation can be rationalized with some approach, then that approach is not scientific'. This seems to be a confused rendition of the respectable Popperian notion that a theory is more powerful the more things it rules out. But one must not mistake the power of a theory with its truth. Aside from issues of tractability, a theory that rationalizes only and exactly those events that actually occur, while ruling out exactly those events that do not occur is the perfect theory. In contrast, Prescott seems inadvertently to support the view that the more exceptions the better rule.

[24] Watson (1993) develops a goodness-of-fit measure for calibrated models. It takes into account that, since idealization implies differences between model and reality that may be systematic, the errors-in-variables and errors-in-equations statistical models are probably not appropriate. Also see Gregory and Smith (1991, pp. 27–8), Canova (1991a), and Hoover (1994a).

REFERENCES

ADELMAN, I. and ADELMAN, F. L. (1959). 'The Dynamic Properties of the Klein-Goldberger Model', *Econometrica*, **27**, 596–625.

ALDRICH, J. (1989). 'Autonomy', *Oxford Economic Papers*, **41**, 15–34.

ALTUG, S. (1989). 'Time-to-Build and Aggregate Fluctuations: Some New Evidence', *International Economic Review*, **30**, 889–920.

BANSAL, R. and GALLANT, R. A., HUSSEY, R., and TAUCHEN, G. (1991). 'Nonparametric Structural Estimation of Models for High-Frequency Currency Market Data', unpublished typescript.

BLAUG, M. (1992). *The Methodology of Economics: Or How Economists Explain*, Cambridge University Press, Cambridge, 2nd ed.

CANOVA, F. (1991a). 'Sensitivity Analysis and Model Evalution in Simulated Dynamic General Equilibrium Economies', unpublished typescript, Department of Economics, European University Institute, Florence, Italy.

CANOVA, F. (1991b). 'Detrending and Business Cycle Facts', unpublished typescript, Department of Economics, European University Institute, Florence, Italy.

CANOVA, F., FINN, M., and PAGAN, A. R. (1992). 'Evaluating a Real Business Cycle Model', unpublished typescript.

COGLEY, T. and NASON, J. M. (1993). 'Effects of the Hodrick-Prescott Filter on Trend and Difference Stationary Time Series: Implications for Business Cycle Research', unpublished typescript.

COOLEY, T. F. and HANSEN, G. D. (1989). 'Welfare Consequences of Monetary and Fiscal Policy', paper presented to the Federal Reserve Bank of San Francisco's Fall Academic Conference, 1 December.

COURNOT, A. [1838] (1927). *Researches into the Mathematical Principles of the Theory of Wealth*, Nathaniel T. Bacon (trans,), Macmillan, New York.

DIAMOND, P. A. (1984). *A Search-Equilibrium Approach to the Micro Foundations of Macroeconomics: The Wicksell Lectures, 1982*, MIT Press, Cambridge, MA.

DURLAUF, S. N. (1989). 'Locally Interacting Systems, Coordination Failure, and the Behavior of Aggregate Activity', unpublished typescript.

FRIEDMAN, M. (1953). 'The Methodology of Positive Economics', in *Essays in Positive Economics*, Chicago University Press, Chicago, IL.

FRISCH, R. (1933). 'Propagation Problems and Impulse Response Problems in Dynamic Economics', in *Economic Essays in Honour of Gustav Cassel: October 20th 1933*, George Allen and Unwin, London.

GREGORY, A. W. and SMITH, G. W. (1990a). 'Calibration as Estimation', *Econometric Reviews*, 9, 57–89.

GREGORY, A. W. and SMITH, G. W. (1990b). 'Calibration as Testing: Inference in Simulated Macroeconomic Models' in *Journal of Business and Economic Statistics*, forthcoming.

GREGORY, A. W. and SMITH, G. W. (1991). 'Calibration in Macroeconomics', in G. S. Maddala and C. R. Rao (eds), *Handbook of Statistics*, 10: *Econometics*, forthcoming.

HAAVELMO, T. (1944). 'The Probability Approach in Econometrics', *Econometrica*, 12 (supplement).

HALL, R. E. (1977). 'Investment, Interest Rates, and the Effects of Stabilization Policies' *Brookings Papers on Economic Activity*, 6, 61–100.

HANSEN, G. D. (1985). 'Indivisible Labor and the Business Cycle', *Journal of Monetary Economics*, 16, 309–28.

HANSEN, G. D. and PRESCOTT, E. C. (1993). 'Did Technology Shocks Cause the 1990–1991 Recession', *American Economic Review*, 83, 280–6.

HANSEN, G. D. and SARGENT, T. J. (1988), 'Straight Time and Overtime in Equilibrium', *Journal of Monetary Economics*, 21, 281–308.

HANSEN, L. P. and SARGENT, T. J. (1980). 'Formulating and Estimating Dynamic Linear Rational Expectations Models', in R. E. Lucas, Jr. and T. J. Sargent (eds), *Rational Expectations and Econometric Practice*, George Allen & Unwin, London, 1981.

HARTLEY, J. , SALYER, K., and SHEFFRIN, S. (1992). 'Calibration and Real Business Cycle Models: Two Unorthodox Tests', unpublished typescript.

HOOVER, K. D. (1984). 'Two Types of Monetarism', *Journal of Economic Literature*, 22, 58–76.

HOOVER, K. D. (1988). *The New Classical Macroeconomics: A Skeptical Inquiry*, Blackwell, Oxford.

HOOVER, K. D. (1992). 'The Rational Expectations Revolution: An Assessment', *The Cato Journal*, 12, 81–96.

HOOVER, K. D. (1994a). 'Six Queries About Idealization in an Empirical Context', *Poznan Studies in the Philosphy of Science and the Humanities*, 38, 43–53.

K. D. HOOVER   43

Hoover, K. D. (1994b). 'In Defence of Datamining: Some Preliminary Throughts', in K. D. Hoover
    and S. M. Sheffrin (eds), *Monetarism and the Methodology of Econmics: Essays in Honor of
    Thomas Mayer*, Elgar, Aldershot, forthcoming.
King, R. G. and Plosser, C. I. (1984). 'Money, Credit and Prices in a Real Business Cycle',
    American Economic Review, **74**, 363–80.
King, R. G. and Plosser, C. I. (1989). 'Real Business Cycle Models and the Test of the Adelmans',
    paper presented to the Federal Reserve Bank of San Francisco's Fall Academic Conference,
    1 December 1989.
Koopmans, T. C. (1947). 'Measurement without Theory', *Review of Economics and Statistics*, **29**,
    161–72.
Kydland, F. E. (1984). 'Labor-force Heterogeneity and the Business Cycle' in K. Brunner
    and A. H. Meltzer (eds), *Essays on Macroeconomic Implications of Financial and Labor
    Markets and Political Processes*, Carnegie-Rochester Conference Series on Public Policy,
    21.
Kydland, F. E. and Prescott, E. C. (1982). 'Time to Build and Aggregate Fluctuations',
    Econometrica, **50**, 1345–70.
Kydland, F. E. and Prescott, E. C. (1988). 'The Workweek of Capital and Its Cyclical
    Implication' *Journal of Monetary Economics*, **21**, 243–60.
Kydland, F. E. and Prescott, E. C. (1990). 'Business Cycles: Real Facts and a Monetary
    Myth', *Federal Reserve Bank of Minneapolis Quartly Review*, **14**, 3–18.
Kydland, F. E. and Prescott, E. C. (1991). 'The Econometrics of the Great Equlibrium Approach
    to Business Cycles', *Scandinavian Journal of Economics*, **93**, 161–78.
Lakatos, I. (1970). 'Falsification and the Methodology of Scientific Research Programmes', in I.
    Lakatos and A. Musgrave (eds), *Criticism and the Growth of Knowledge*, Cambridge University
    Press, Cambridge.
Lakatos, I. (1978). 'History of Science and Its Rational Reconstructions' in J. Worrall and G.
    Currie (eds), *The Methodology of Scientific Research Programmes: Philosphical Papers*, **I**,
    Cambridge University Press, Cambridge.
Lau, L. J. (1984). 'Comments', in H. E. Scarf and J. B. Shoven (eds), *Applied General Equilibrium
    Analysis*, Cambridge University Press, Cambridge.
Lipton, P. (1991). *Inference to the Best Explanation*, Routlege, London.
Lucas, R. E., Jr. (1976). 'Econometric Policy Evaluaton: A Critique', in *Studies in Business-Cycle
    Theory*, Oxford, Blackwell, 1981.
Lucas, R. E., Jr. (1977). 'Understanding Business Cycles', in *Studies in Business-Cycle Theory*,
    Blackwell, Oxford, 1981.
Lucas, R. E., Jr. (1980) 'Methods and Problems in Business Cycle Theory', in *Studies in
    Business-Cycle Theory*, Blackwell, Oxford, 1981.
Lucas, R. E. Jr. (1986). 'Adapttive Behavior and Economic Theory', *Journal of Business*, **59**,
    S401–26.
Lucas, R. E., Jr. (1987), *Models of Business Cycles*, Blackwell, Oxford.
Lucas, R. E., Jr. and Sargent, T. J. C. (eds) (1981). *Rational Expectations and Econometric
    Practice*, George Allen and Unwin, London.
MacKinnon, J. (1984). 'Comments', in H. E. Scarf and J. B. Shoven (eds), *Applied General
    Equilibrium Analysis*, Cambridge University Press, Cambridge.
Mansur, A. and Walley, J. (1984). 'Numerical Specification of Applied General-equilibrium
    models: Estimation, Calibration, and Data', in H. E. Scarf and J. B. Shoven (eds.), *Applied
    General Equilibrium Analysis*, Cambridge University Press, Cambridge.
Manuelli, R. and Sargent, T. J. (1988). 'Models of Business Cycles: A Review Essay' *Journal of
    Monetary Economics*, **22**, 523–42.
Mayer, T. (1960). 'Plant and Equipment Lead Times' *Journal of Business*, **33**, 127–32.
McCallum, B. T. (1986). 'On "Real" and "Sticky-Price" Theories of the Business Cycle', *Journal
    of Money, Credit and Banking*, **18**, 397–414.
McCallum, B. T. (1989). 'Real Business Cycle Models', in R. J. Barro (ed.), *Modern Business
    Cycle Theory*, Blackwell, Oxford.

Part V

The critique of calibration methods

Journal of Business & Economic Statistics, July 1991, Vol. 9, No. 3

Calibration as Testing: Inference in Simulated Macroeconomic Models

Allan W. Gregory and Gregor W. Smith
Department of Economics, Queen's University, Kingston, Ontario, K7L 3N6, Canada

A stochastic macroeconomic model with no free parameters can be tested by comparing its features, such as moments, with those of data. Repeated simulation allows exact tests and gives the distribution of the sample moment under the null hypothesis that the model is true. We calculate the size of tests of the model studied by Mehra and Prescott. The approximate size of their test (which seeks to match model-generated, mean, risk-free interest rates and equity premia with historical values) is 0 although alternate, empirical representations of this model economy or alternate moment-matching tests yield large probabilities of Type I error.

KEY WORDS: Equity premium; Monte Carlo; Simulation; Type I error.

Calibration in macroeconomics is concerned primarily with testing a model by comparing population moments (or perhaps some other population measure) to historical sample moments of actual data. If the correspondence between some aspect of the model and the historical record is deemed to be reasonably close, then the model is viewed as satisfactory. If the distance between population and historical moments is viewed as too great, then the model is rejected, as in the widely cited equity-premium puzzle of Mehra and Prescott (1985). A drawback to the procedure as implemented in the literature is that no metric is supplied by which closeness can be judged. This leads to tests with unknown acceptance and rejection regions.

This article provides a simple way to judge the degree of correspondence between the population moments of a simulated macroeconomic model and observed sample moments and develops a framework for readily calculating the size (probability of Type I error) of calibration tests. We apply this method to the well-known equity-premium case. This article is *not* concerned with a "solution" to the equity-premium puzzle. Rather it evaluates the probability of falsely rejecting a true macroeconomic model with calibration methods. One finding is that the size of the test considered by Mehra and Prescott (which seeks to match mean risk-free interest rates and equity premia) is 0, so the model with their parameter settings is unlikely to have generated the observed historical moments. Some alternate versions of the consumption-based asset-pricing model or alternate moment-matching tests yield large probabilities of Type I error.

Section 1 characterizes calibration as testing. A simple formalization of calibration as Monte Carlo testing allows exact inference. Section 2 contains an application to the test conducted by Mehra and Prescott (1985). Section 3 concludes.

1. CALIBRATION AS TESTING

Calibration in macroeconomics has focused on comparing observed historical moments with population moments from a fully parameterized simulation model—that is, one with no free parameters. One might elect to simulate a model because of an analytical intractability or because a forcing variable is unobservable. In macroeconomics, examples of unobservable forcing variables include productivity shocks in business-cycle models or consumption measurement errors in asset-pricing models.

Consider a population moment θ, which is restricted by theory, with corresponding historical sample moment $\bar{\theta}_T$ for a sample of size T. Call the moment estimator $\bar{\theta}_T$. Assume that $\bar{\theta}_T$ is consistent for θ. The population moment is a number, the sample moment is the realization of a random variable (an estimate), and the estimator is a random variable. The calibration tests applied in the literature compare θ and $\bar{\theta}_T$ and reject the model if θ is not sufficiently close to $\bar{\theta}_T$. In some calibration studies, attempts are made to exactly match the population moment to the sample moment (there must be some leeway in parameter choice to make this attempt nontrivial). Such matching imposes unusual test requirements because θ and $\bar{\theta}_T$ can differ even when the model is true due to sampling variability in $\bar{\theta}_T$. Moreover, judging closeness involves the sampling distribution of the estimator $\bar{\theta}_T$. Standard hypothesis testing procedures may be unavailable because the exact or even asymptotic distribution of the estimator is unknown.

One prominent advantage in the calibration of macroeconomic models that has not been exploited fully is that the complete data-generating process is specified. Thus the sampling variability of the *simulated* moment can be used to evaluate the distance between θ and $\bar{\theta}_T$.

298   Journal of Business & Economic Statistics, July 1991

Call N the number of simulated observations. We construct tests by repeatedly simulating the fully parameterized model (or artificial economy) and calculating the proportion of times $\hat{\theta}_N$ lies in a set Θ (bounded by $\bar{\theta}_T$). Current calibration studies do simulate repeatedly, but they typically average over a small number of replications and then quote the averages of various properties. Our approach involves treating the historical moment $\bar{\theta}_T$ as a critical value to give the probability (prob) value (i.e., marginal significance level) or size of the test implicit in comparing moments. If simulations use the same number of observations as are used in calculating the historical sample moment so that $N = T$, then the test will be exact. Moreover, confidence intervals can be constructed for $\hat{\theta}_N$ (as opposed to the population moment θ) to determine whether $\bar{\theta}_T$ lies within the interval.

Barnard (1963) suggested basing exact inference on repeated generation of artificial series. Monte Carlo testing was refined by Hope (1968) and Marriott (1979) and applied in economics by Theil, Shonkwiler, and Taylor (1985) and Theil and Shonkwiler (1986). Simulation methods also can be used for estimation, as described for macroeconomic models by Lee and Ingram (1991) and Gregory and Smith (1990).

Suppose one wishes to find the probability with which a model with population moment θ generates a sample moment $\bar{\theta}_T > \theta$. Our suggested procedure is to simulate N observations from the economy, with $N = T$, R times and calculate $\hat{\theta}_N$ at each replication. The proportion of replications with which the simulated moment exceeds the corresponding sample moment is the (one-sided) prob value associated with the historical moment

$$R^{-1} \cdot \sum_{r=1}^{R} I(\hat{\theta}_{Nr} - \bar{\theta}_T), \qquad (1)$$

in which the indicator function I is defined to be equal to 1 if its argument is positive and 0 otherwise.

Simulations involve a finite number of replications, so measures of test size or confidence intervals are themselves random variables. Standard errors for test size may be calculated from the binomial distribution or, if R is large, the normal distribution. Although we have described treating the historical moments as critical values, one also could select a test size and estimate the corresponding critical value (i.e., the quantile) from the order statistics of the Monte Carlo sample of moments.

In some cases one might be interested in the entire probability density of the sample moment under the null hypothesis that the model is true. Although it is simpler to work with the empirical density function, tests also could be based on the density estimated nonparametrically from simulations [denoted by $\hat{f}(\hat{\theta}_N)$], and approximate measures of size could be calculated. There are many estimators available (see Silverman 1986 or Tapia and Thompson 1978), but if we assume that the density is absolutely continuous, then kernel estimators provide an easy way to smooth the empirical density. One advantage in applying kernel estimators is that they are available in an IMSL subroutine.

In the application in Section 2, we calculate prob values in two ways. The first way is the simplest and uses the empirical distribution as in Equation (1). The second way estimates the density nonparametrically with a quartic kernel and, following Silverman (1986), a robust, variable window width given by $.698 \min [s, \text{IQR}/1.34]$, in which s is the empirical standard deviation and IQR the interquartile range. Under weak conditions the empirical distribution function and the nonparametric density consistently estimate the true cumulative distribution function and density, respectively. In the simulations in Section 2, the results from the two methods usually are identical, which suggests using the simpler calculation in Equation (1).

As N becomes large, sample moments converge to population moments by ergodicity. For fixed N, sample moments have distributions; as the number of replications R increases, the estimated distribution function converges to the true finite-sample distribution. One could examine the sensitivity of findings to alternative windows, kernels, and numbers of replications because the speed of convergence may be slow. For example, many replications may be necessary for accurate estimates of tail-area probabilities (i.e., test size), where by definition events are rare in a sampling experiment.

Finally, one also could study tests based on matching properties other than moments, by analogy with the estimation results of Smith (1989), who considered matching properties of misspecified models or linear regressions in simulated and historical data. Naylor and Finger (1971, p. 159) listed other validation criteria, such as matching properties of turning points.

2. APPLICATION: TYPE I ERROR IN THE EQUITY–PREMIUM PUZZLE

As an example, consider the exchange economy described by Mehra and Prescott (1985). A representative consumer has preferences characterized by the utility functional

$$E_t \sum_{s=0}^{\infty} \beta^s u(c_{t+s}), \qquad (2)$$

in which E_t denotes the expectation conditional on information at time t, $\beta \in (0,1)$ is a discount factor, $u(c) = c^{1-\alpha}/(1 - \alpha)$ [$\log(c)$ if $\alpha = 1$], and α is a positive, constant coefficient of relative risk aversion. The consumer's nonstorable endowment y_t evolves exogenously according to

$$y_{t+1} = x_{t+1} \cdot y_t, \qquad (3)$$

in which the growth rate, x_t, follows a process that is Markov on a discrete state space $\Lambda = \{\lambda_1, \lambda_2, \ldots, \lambda_J\}$.

This process is stationary and ergodic, with transition matrix ϕ,

$$\phi_{ij} = \Pr[x_{t+1} = \lambda_j \mid x_t = \lambda_i],$$
$$i, j = 1, 2, \ldots, J. \quad (4)$$

The equilibrium or unconditional probabilities are given by $\phi_i = \Pr[x_t = \lambda_i]$ for all t.

An equilibrium in this economy is characterized by a set of prices for which consumption equals the endowment at all times and in all states. Relative prices are calculated by equating them to marginal rates of substitution. The price of a one-period, risk-free discount bond that provides one unit of the endowment at time $t + 1$ is given by

$$p_t^f = \beta E_t u'(y_{t+1})/u'(y_t), \quad (5a)$$

and the price of an equity claim to the endowment stream is given by

$$p_t^e = \beta E_t[u'(y_{t+1})/u'(y_t)] \cdot (y_{t+1} + p_{t+1}^e). \quad (5b)$$

Thus if the current state is (y_t, λ_i), then the prices (relative to one unit of the commodity at time t) of the two assets are

$$p^f(\lambda_i, y_t) = \beta E_t(y_{t+1}^{-\alpha}/y_t^{-\alpha}) = \beta \sum_{j=1}^{J} \phi_{ij} \lambda_j^{-\alpha}, \quad (6a)$$

and

$$p^e(\lambda_i, y_t) = \beta E_t(y_{t+1}^{-\alpha}/y_t^{-\alpha}) \cdot (y_{t+1} + p^e(\lambda_j, y_{t+1}))$$
$$= \beta \sum_{j=1}^{J} \phi_{ij} \lambda_j^{-\alpha} (\lambda_j y_t + p^e(\lambda_j, \lambda_j y_t)). \quad (6b)$$

The challenge posed of this model by Mehra and Prescott has been the following: With a risk-aversion parameter α between 0 and 10, a discount factor β between 0 and 1, and the Markov per capita consumption growth-rate process matching the sample mean, variance, and first-order autocorrelation of the U.S. series for 1889–1978, can the model (with two or three states) generate a population mean risk-free rate of return and mean equity premium that match the annual U.S. sample values (.8% and 6.2%, respectively) of these measures? Mehra and Prescott compared the 6.2% average equity premium from the full sample (90 observations) to an average premium from their model of at most .35%. These two values were judged not to be close, and hence there is a puzzle.

One could try to gauge closeness with a standard asymptotic hypothesis test. For example, the test statistic implicit in Mehra and Prescott's (1985, p. 156) quotation of the estimated average equity premium and its standard error is $(\bar{\theta}_T - \theta)/\mathrm{se}(\bar{\theta}_T) \sim N(0, 1)$ asymptotically. In this test one could correct the standard error of the average equity premium to allow for dependence and heterogeneity with the methods of Newey and West (1987) or Andrews (1988). The heterogeneity does not matter in a test with no regressors (as in a comparison of means), but the serial correlation does.

Cecchetti, Lam, and Mark (1990) constructed an asymptotic test statistic for matching a moment: $W = (\theta - \bar{\theta}_T)(\hat{\Omega}^{-1})(\theta - \bar{\theta}_T) \overset{a}{\sim} \chi^2(1)$, where $\hat{\Omega}$ is the Newey–West estimate of the variance of the sample moment. To allow for uncertainty about parameters that are estimated, they assumed that the two sources of uncertainty are independent and amended the statistic to $W = (\theta - \bar{\theta}_T)(\hat{\Omega}^{-1} + \hat{V}^{-1})(\theta - \bar{\theta}_T) \overset{a}{\sim} \chi^2(1)$, where $\hat{V}$ is the variance due to parameter uncertainty. Kocherlakota (1990) conducted a Monte Carlo experiment of tests of consumption-based asset-pricing models that use asymptotic 5% critical values and examined the small-sample size of such tests with simulated data. He found that size most closely approximates asymptotic size when parameters are set rather than estimated. Finding a consistent estimate even of the asymptotic standard error for many estimated moments can be very

Table 1. Asset-Pricing Models and Joint Tests

Cases	Parameter settings	Prob value
1. Mehra–Prescott: $\alpha = 1.5$, $\beta = .99$, $\lambda_1 = .982$, $\lambda_2 = 1.054$		
	$\phi = \begin{bmatrix} .43 & .57 \\ .57 & .43 \end{bmatrix}$	.00
2. Rietz: $\alpha = 7.05$, $\beta = .997$, $\lambda_1 = .985$, $\lambda_2 = 1.0512$, $\lambda_3 = .5092$		
	$\phi = \begin{bmatrix} .423 & .5762 & .0008 \\ .5762 & .423 & .0008 \\ .5 & .5 & \end{bmatrix}$	.59
3. Asymmetric growth: $\alpha = 10$, $\beta = .99$, $\lambda_1 = .972$, $\lambda_2 = 1.069$		
	$\phi = \begin{bmatrix} .5 & .5 \\ .70 & .30 \end{bmatrix}$	.14
4. Extreme risk aversion: $\alpha = 25$, $\beta = .99$, $\lambda_1 = .989$, $\lambda_2 = 1.069$		
	$\phi = \begin{bmatrix} .65 & .35 \\ .90 & .10 \end{bmatrix}$	.95

NOTE: The prob value is the marginal significance level of the joint one-sided test that the population mean equity premium is at least 6.2% and the population mean risk-free rate is less than 4%.

Table 2.   Sample and Population Moments: Case 1, Symmetric (Mehra–Prescott)

Variable	Moment	History	Pop.	p value Emp	p value Np	95% confidence interval Emp	95% confidence interval Np
Consumption	μ	1.83	1.8			(1.2, 2.4)	(1.2, 2.4)
	σ	3.57	3.60			(3.6, 3.6)	(3.6, 3.6)
	ρ	−.14	−.14			(−.4, .7)	(−.4, .7)
Risk-free	μ	.80	3.51	.00	.00[a]	(3.4, 3.6)	(3.4, 3.6)
rate	σ	5.67	.8	.00	.00[b]	(.8, .8)	(.7, .8)
	ρ		−.14			(−.4, .7)	(−.4, .7)
Equity-premium	μ	6.18	.20	.00	.00[b]	(−.6, 1.0)	(−.7, 1.1)
rate	σ	16.67	3.9	.00	.00[b]	(3.7, 4.0)	(3.7, 4.0)
	ρ		−.001			(−.3, .2)	(−.2, .2)

NOTE: The symbols μ, σ, and ρ denote mean, variance, and first-order autocorrelation. Sample moments in the third column are based on the full sample. The sample autocorrelations for the risk-free and equity-premium rates were not given in Mehra and Prescott's table 1 (1985, p. 147). Pop. denotes population moments from the model. Emp denotes measures constructed from the empirical density function and Np those constructed from the nonparametrically estimated density function, each based on $R = 1,000$ replications. Confidence intervals run from the .025 to .975 quantiles.
[a] Prob values for $\hat{\theta}_N < \bar{\theta}_T$.
[b] Prob values for $\hat{\theta}_N > \bar{\theta}_T$.

difficult, however. Moreover, some of the historical samples considered by Mehra and Prescott have as few as 10 observations and hence should not be studied with asymptotic methods. On the other hand, the procedure outlined in Section 1 is appropriate for inference in such sample sizes using the sampling variability inherent in fully parameterized models.

To investigate the size of the moment-matching exercise considered by Mehra and Prescott, suppose that their model is true. What is the probability of observing an equity premium of at least 6.2%? To answer this question, we simulate the fully parameterized model, estimate the probability density functions for the random variables that it restricts, and measure tail-area probabilities. We follow the same procedure for four different representations of the transition density for the Markov chain and of risk aversion. These are shown in Table 1. The first representation is that considered by Mehra and Prescott. The second representation is that used by Rietz (1988), in which there is a small probability of a "crash" in growth rates; the source is Rietz's example 1, table 3, row 1. The third representation involves an asymmetry in growth transitions, and

the fourth representation involves a degree of risk aversion greater than that considered by Mehra and Prescott.

The explicit joint test considered by Mehra and Prescott (1985, p. 154) is to generate a population equity premium of at least 6.2% *and* a population risk-free rate less than 4%. For each model we estimate the prob value associated with this joint test. These measures are based on bivariate empirical distributions with $R = 1,000$ replications and on $N = 90$ observations, just as in the annual sample. The results are shown in Table 1. For the Mehra–Prescott model of case 1, the prob value is 0. The other models generate the historical sample-mean rates of return with positive probabilities. The prob values are .59 for case 2, .14 for case 3, and .95 for case 4.

Tables 2–5 give the sample mean, variance, and first-order autocorrelation of consumption growth, the risk-free rate, and the equity premium for the annual data used by Mehra and Prescott and the corresponding population values for the four simulation models described in Table 1. The autocorrelations of the risk-free rate and consumption growth are equal as an analytical

Table 3.   Sample and Population Moments: Case 2, Crash (Rietz)

Variable	Moment	History	Pop.	p value Emp	p value Np	95% confidence interval Emp	95% confidence interval Np
Consumption	μ	1.83	1.80			(1.0, 2.4)	(1.0, 2.4)
	σ	3.57	3.60			(3.3, 6.3)	(3.3, 6.3)
	ρ	−.14	−.15			(−.4, .1)	(−.4, .1)
Risk-free	μ	.80	.30	.94	.92[a]	(−.2, 1.0)	(−.2, 1.0)
rate	σ	5.67	3.2	.00	.00[b]	(3.1, 3.3)	(3.1, 3.3)
	ρ		−.15			(−.4, .1)	(−.4, .1)
Equity-premium	μ	6.18	6.37	.59	.61[b]	(5.1, 7.5)	(5.1, 7.6)
rate	σ	16.67	6.17	.00	.00[b]	(5.8, 8.5)	(5.9, 8.5)
	ρ		−.064			(−.3, .1)	(−.3, .1)

NOTE: See note to Table 2.
[a] Prob values for $\hat{\theta}_N < \bar{\theta}_T$.
[b] Prob values for $\hat{\theta}_N > \bar{\theta}_T$.

Table 4. Sample and Population Moments: Case 3, Asymmetric

Variable	Moment	History	Pop.	p value		95% confidence interval	
				Emp	NP	Emp	Np
Consumption	μ	1.83	1.20			(.4, 2.1)	(.4, 2.0)
	σ	3.57	4.78	.00	.00[a]	(4.6, 4.9)	(4.6, 4.8)
	ρ	−.14	−.2			(−.4, .0)	(−.4, .0)
Risk-free	μ	.80	2.82	.01	.00[a]	(1.4, 4.2)	(1.4, 4.3)
rate	σ	5.67	8.1	1.0	1.0[b]	(7.8, 8.3)	(7.9, 8.3)
	ρ		−.2			(−.4, .0)	(−.4, .0)
Equity-premium	μ	6.18	4.71	.10	.11[b]	(2.4, 6.9)	(2.3, 7.1)
rate	σ	16.67	11.69	.00	.00[b]	(11.4, 12.0)	(11.4, 12.0)
	ρ		−.09			(−.03, .1)	(−.3, .1)

NOTE: See note to Table 2.
[a] Prob values for $\hat{\theta}_N < \bar{\theta}_T$.
[b] Prob values for $\hat{\theta}_N > \bar{\theta}_T$.

property of the model. For each model we construct 95% confidence intervals for a sample size of 90 observations. We also estimate the densities nonparametrically and calculate corresponding approximate intervals. Tables 2–5 also give size results for some univariate, one-sided tests of each model's ability to match individual moments.

For example, Table 2 shows that for one of the Mehra–Prescott parameter settings (given in Table 1) the equity premium has a mean of .20. The estimated probability of observing a premium greater than 6.2% is 0; the 95% confidence interval is (−.6, 1.0) at N = 90 observations. One can also see that the puzzle extends to second moments, because the variances of historical risk-free rates and equity premia lie outside the confidence intervals generated by the theoretical model. Mehra and Prescott (1985, p. 146) did note that their model was poorly suited for asset-price volatility issues. The confidence intervals for autocorrelation coefficients are generally wide and would rationalize a wide range of observed sample values.

The Rietz model (2) in Table 3 is consistent with the sample mean equity premium of 6.18% and, in fact, would be consistent with an even larger premium; the 95% confidence interval is (5.1, 7.5) at N = 90 observations and the prob value (from the simulated empirical density) is .59. Like model 1, it fails to match the variances of the risk-free rate and equity premium. The model with asymmetric growth (3) in Table 4 generates larger variances for the two returns but still cannot match the variance of the equity-premium rate. Model 3 is consistent with the sample mean-equity premium in that it generates the sample value with a prob value of .10, but it also gives a consumption growth variance that is too large relative to the sample variance. In Table 5, model 4, in which α = 25, gives 95% confidence intervals that include the historical values for all moments except the variance of the risk-free rate. Although models 1 and 2 underpredict the variance of the risk-free rate, models 3 and 4 overpredict it. Finally, for model 4, Figure 1 illustrates the nonparametrically estimated density function of the mean equity premium from which the confidence interval in the last column of Table 5 is taken.

In Tables 2–5 the confidence intervals and size estimates from the empirical densities and the nonparametrically estimated densities are virtually identical. We also have used the same method with a sample size of N = 10 for comparison with sample values reported by Mehra and Prescott (1985, table 1) for 1959–1968. Naturally the intervals for the smaller simulated sample size are wider. We also have investigated the effects of in-

Table 5. Sample and Population Moments: Case 4, Extreme Risk Aversion

Variable	Moment	History	Pop.	p value		95% confidence interval	
				Emp	Np	Emp	Np
Consumption	μ	1.83	1.01			(.5, 1.7)	(.6, 1.8)
	σ	3.57	3.59	.44	.41[a]	(3.2, 3.9)	(3.2, 3.9)
	ρ	−.14	−.25			(−.4, −.1)	(−.4, −.1)
Risk-free	μ	.80	2.25	.06	.07[a]	(.3, 4.3)	(.4, 4.3)
rate	σ	5.67	11.5	1.0	1.0[b]	(10.3, 12.3)	(10.3, 12.3)
	ρ		−.25			(−.4, −.1)	(−.4, −.1)
Equity-premium	μ	6.18	8.45	.94	.94[b]	(5.4, 11.2)	(5.4, 11.4)
rate	σ	16.67	16.75	.57	.57[b]	(15.3, 17.7)	(15.3, 17.8)
	ρ		−.22			(−.4, −.1)	(−.4, −.1)

NOTE: See note to Table 2.
[a] Prob values for $\hat{\theta}_N < \bar{\theta}_T$.
[b] Prob values for $\hat{\theta}_N > \bar{\theta}_T$.

302   Journal of Business & Economic Statistics, July 1991

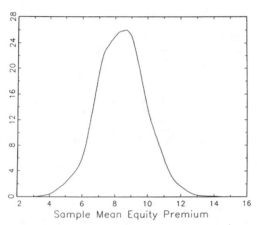

Figure 1. The Nonparametrically Estimated Density Function (based on 1,000 replications) of the Mean Equity Premium in Simulated Samples of 90 Observations, From the Model Economy (4), With Extreme Risk Aversion. Parameter settings are given in Table 1.

creasing the number of replications to $R = 2,000$. This increase has no appreciable effect on the confidence intervals. Although faster convergence in R might be possible with the use of control or antithetic variates to reduce sampling variability in estimated test sizes and confidence intervals, such methods do not seem vital in this application.

In constructing the tests in the tables, we do not rule out applying other criteria to evaluate versions of this asset-pricing model. For example, one might discard the fourth case because of its large risk aversion or the second case because its growth-transition matrix includes elements never observed (see Mehra and Prescott 1988). We are agnostic on these points. The proposed procedure simply allows one to gauge the sampling variability of the moment estimator when the model is assumed to be true and thus permits formal comparisons of historical and population (model) moments. Kwan (1990) and Watson (1990) have proposed alternative measures of the goodness of fit of calibrated models (or closeness of moments) in which the parameterized economic model is not the null hypothesis.

3. CONCLUSION

Calibration in macroeconomics involves simulating dynamic models and comparing them to historical data. This type of comparison can be seen as a test of the model. A natural issue in the use of this method concerns the distribution of the sample moment under the null hypothesis that the model is true. For fully parameterized model economies, one can use repeated simulation to estimate the probability of falsely rejecting a true economic model (Type I error) and to construct confidence intervals using comparisons of moments. The

empirical frequency estimator works well in both cases and is very simple to apply.

As an application we consider the asset-pricing model and parameter settings of Mehra and Prescott, for which the test of mean rates of return has no probability of Type I error; their rejection of the model appears to be statistically sound. Our results can be used to find the sizes of other moment-matching tests of this model. If other parameter settings are admitted, then the model will generate an equity premium of 6.2% more than 5% of the time. The method can be applied directly to extensions of the asset-pricing economy discussed previously (see, for example, Abel 1990; Benninga and Protopapadakis 1990; Cecchetti et al. 1990; Labadie 1989) and to business-cycle models, as Devereux, Gregory, and Smith (1990) demonstrated.

ACKNOWLEDGMENTS

We thank the Social Sciences and Humanities Research Council of Canada for financial support. We thank David Backus, Jean-Marie Dufour, James MacKinnon, Adrian Pagan, Simon Power, Tom Rietz, Jeremy Rudin, the editor, an associate editor, a referee, and numerous seminar participants for helpful comments.

[Received April 1990. Revised January 1991.]

REFERENCES

Abel, A. B. (1990), "Asset Prices Under Habit Formation and Catching up With the Joneses," American Economic Review, 80, 38–42.

Andrews, D. W. K. (1988), "Heteroskedasticity and Autocorrelation Consistent Covariance Matrix Estimation," Cowles Foundation Discussion Paper 877R, Yale University, Dept. of Economics.

Barnard, G. A. (1963), Discussion of "The Spectral Analysis of Point Process," by M. S. Bartlett, Journal of the Royal Statistical Society, Ser. B, 25, 294.

Benninga, S., and Protopapadakis, A. (1990), "Leverage, Time Preference, and the 'Equity Premium Puzzle,' " Journal of Monetary Economics, 25, 49–58.

Cecchetti, S. G., Lam, P., and Mark, N. C. (1990), "The Equity Premium and the Risk Free Rate: Matching the Moments," mimeo, Ohio State University, Dept. of Economics.

Devereux, M. B., Gregory, A. W., and Smith, G. W. (1990), "Realistic Cross-Country Consumption Correlations in a Two-County Equilibrium Business Cycle Model," IER Discussion Paper 774, Queen's University, Dept. of Economics.

Gregory, A. W., and Smith, G. W. (1990), "Calibration as Estimation," Econometric Reviews, 9, 57–89.

Hope, A. C. A. (1968), "A Simplified Monte Carlo Significance Test Procedure," Journal of the Royal Statistical Society, Ser. B, 30, 582–598.

Kocherlakota, N. R. (1990), "On Tests of Representative Consumer Asset Pricing Models," Journal of Monetary Economics, 26, 285–304.

Kwan, Y.-K. (1990), "Bayesian Model Calibration With An Application to a Non-Linear Rational Expectations Two-Country Model," mimeo, University of Chicago, Graduate School of Business.

Labadie, P. (1989), "Stochastic Inflation and the Equity Premium," Journal of Monetary Economics, 24, 277–298.

Lee, B.-S., and Ingram, B. F. (1991), "Simulation Estimation of Time Series Models," Journal of Econometrics, 47, 197–205.

Marriott, F. H. C. (1979), "Barnard's Monte Carlo Tests: How Many Simulations?" *Applied Statistics, 28*, 75–77.

Mehra, R., and Prescott, E. C. (1985), "The Equity Premium: A Puzzle," *Journal of Monetary Economics, 15*, 145–161.

——— (1988), "The Equity Risk Premium: A Solution?" *Journal of Monetary Economics, 22*, 133–136.

Naylor, T. H., and Finger, J. M. (1971), "Validation," in *Computer Simulation Experiments With Models of Economic Systems,* ed. T. H. Naylor, New York: John Wiley, pp. 153–164.

Newey, W. K., and West, K. D. (1987), "A Simple, Positive Semi-definite, Heteroskedasticity and Autocorrelation Consistent Covariance Matrix," *Econometrica, 55*, 703–708.

Rietz, T. (1988), "The Equity Risk Premium: A Solution," *Journal of Monetary Economics, 22*, 117–131.

Silverman, B. W. (1986), *Density Estimation for Statistics and Data Analysis,* London: Chapman & Hall.

Smith, A. (1989), "Estimation of Dynamic Economic Models by Simulation: A Comparison of Two Approaches," mimeo, Duke University, Dept. of Economics.

Tapia, R. A., and Thompson, J. R. (1978), *Nonparametric Probability Density Estimation,* Baltimore: The Johns Hopkins University Press.

Theil, H., and Shonkwiler, J. S., (1986), "Monte Carlo Tests of Autocorrelation," *Economics Letters, 20*, 157–160.

Theil, H., Shonkwiler, J. S., and Taylor, T. G. (1985), "A Monte Carlo Test of Slutsky Symmetry," *Economics Letters, 19*, 331–332.

Watson, M. W. (1990), "Measures of Fit for Calibrated Models," mimeo, Northwestern University, Dept. of Economics.

Measures of Fit for Calibrated Models

Mark W. Watson

Northwestern University and Federal Reserve Bank of Chicago

This paper suggests a new procedure for evaluating the fit of a dynamic structural economic model. The procedure begins by augmenting the variables in the model with just enough stochastic error so that the model can exactly match the second moments of the actual data. Measures of fit for the model can then be constructed on the basis of the size of this error. The procedure is applied to a standard real business cycle model. Over the business cycle frequencies, the model must be augmented with a substantial error to match data for the postwar U.S. economy. Lower bounds on the variance of the error range from 40 percent to 60 percent of the variance in the actual data.

I. Introduction

Economists have long debated appropriate methods for assessing the empirical relevance of economic models. The standard econometric approach can be traced back to Haavelmo (1944), who argued that an economic model should be embedded within a complete probability model and analyzed using statistical methods designed for conducting inference about unknown probability distributions. In the modern literature, this approach is clearly exemplified in work such as that of L. Hansen and Sargent (1980) or McFadden (1981). However, many economic models do not provide a realistic and complete

This paper has benefited from constructive comments by many seminar participants; in particular I thank John Cochrane, Marty Eichenbaum, Jon Faust, Lars Hansen, Robert Hodrick, Robert King, and Robert Lucas. Two referees also provided valuable constructive criticism and suggestions. The first draft of this paper was written while I was visiting the University of Chicago, whose hospitality is gratefully acknowledged. This research was supported by the National Science Foundation through grants SES-89-10601 and SES-91-22463.

[*Journal of Political Economy*, 1993, vol. 101, no. 6]

probability structure for the variables under consideration. To analyze these models using standard econometric methods, they must first be augmented with additional random components. Inferences drawn from these expanded models are meaningful only to the extent that the additional random components do not mask or change the salient features of the original economic models.

Another approach, markedly different from the standard econometric approach, has become increasingly popular for evaluating dynamic macroeconomic models. This approach is clearly articulated in the work of Kydland and Prescott (1982) and Prescott (1986). In a general sense, the approach asks whether data from a real economy share certain characteristics with data generated by the artificial economy described by an economic model. There is no claim that the model explains all the characteristics of the actual data, nor is there any attempt to augment the model with additional random components to more accurately describe the data. On the one hand, the results from this approach are easier to interpret than the results from the standard econometric approach since the economic model is not complicated by additional random elements added solely for statistical convenience. On the other hand, since the economic model does not provide a complete probability structure, inference procedures lack statistical foundations and are necessarily ad hoc. For example, a researcher may determine that a model fits the data well because it implies moments for the variables under study that are "close" to the moments of the actual data, even though the metric used to determine the distance between the moments is left unspecified.

This paper is an attempt to put the latter approach on a less ad hoc foundation by developing goodness-of-fit measures for the class of dynamic econometric models whose endogenous variables follow covariance stationary processes. It is not assumed that the model accurately describes data from the actual economy; the economic model is not a null hypothesis in the statistical sense. Rather, the economic model is viewed as an approximation to the stochastic processes generating the actual data, and goodness-of-fit measures are proposed to measure the quality of this approximation. A standard device—stochastic error—is used to motivate the goodness-of-fit measures. These measures answer the question, How much random error would have to be added to the data generated by the model so that the autocovariances implied by the model + error match the autocovariances of the observed data?

The error represents the degree of abstraction of the model from the data. Since the error cannot be attributed to a data collection procedure or to a forecasting procedure, for instance, it is difficult a priori to say much about its properties. In particular, its covariance with the observed data cannot be specified by a priori reasoning. Rather than make a specific assumption about the error's covariance properties, I construct a representation that minimizes the contribution of the error in the complete model. Thus, in this sense, the error process is chosen to make the model as close to the data as possible.

Many of the ideas in this paper are close to, and were motivated by, ideas in Altug (1989) and Sargent (1989). Altug (1989) showed how a one-shock real business cycle model could be analyzed using standard dynamic econometric methods, after first augmenting each variable in the model with an idiosyncratic error. This produces a restricted version of the dynamic factor analysis or unobserved index models developed by Sargent and Sims (1977) and Geweke (1977). Sargent (1989) discusses two models of measurement error: in the first the measurement error is uncorrelated with the data generated by the model, and in the second the measurement error is uncorrelated with the sample data (see also G. Hansen and Sargent 1988). While similar in spirit, the approach taken in this paper differs from that of Altug and Sargent in two important ways. First, in this paper, the error process is not assumed to be uncorrelated with the model's artificial data or with the actual data. Rather, the correlation properties of the error process are determined by the requirement that the variance of the error is as small as possible. Second, the joint data-error process is introduced to motivate goodness-of-fit measures; it is not introduced to describe a statistical model that can be used to test statistical hypotheses, at least in the standard sense. Rather, the analysis in this paper is similar to the analysis in Campbell and Shiller (1988), Durlauf and Hall (1989), Hansen and Jagannathan (1991), and Cochrane (1992). Each of these papers uses a different approach to judge the goodness of fit of an economic model by calculating a value or an upper bound on the variance of an unobserved "noise" or a "marginal rate of substitution" or a "discount factor" in observed data.

The minimum approximation error representation developed in this paper motivates two sets of statistics that can be used to evaluate the goodness of fit of the economic model. First, like the variance of the error in a regression model, the variance of the approximation error can be used to form an R^2 measure for each variable in the model. This provides an overall measure of fit. Moreover, spectral methods can be used to calculate this R^2 measure for each frequency so that the fit can be calculated over the "business cycle," "growth," or other specific frequency bands. A second set of statistics can be constructed by using the minimum error representation to form fitted values of the variables in the economic model. These fitted values show how well the model explains specific historical episodes; for example, can a real business cycle model simultaneously explain the growth in the United States during the 1960s and the 1981–82 recession?

The paper is organized as follows. Section II develops the minimum approximation error representation and goodness-of-fit measures. Section III calculates these goodness-of-fit statistics for a standard real business cycle model using postwar U.S. macroeconomic data on output, consumption, investment, and employment. Section IV concludes the paper by providing a brief discussion of some tangential issues that arise from the analysis.

II. Measures of Fit

Consider an economic model that describes the evolution of an $n \times 1$ vector of variables $\mathbf{x}_t$. Assume that the variables have been transformed, say by first-differencing or forming ratios, so that $\mathbf{x}_t$ is covariance stationary. As a notational device, it is useful to introduce the autocovariance generating function (ACGF) of $\mathbf{x}_t$, $A_{\mathbf{x}}(z)$. This function completely summarizes the unconditional second-moment properties of the process. In what follows, "economic model" and "$A_{\mathbf{x}}(z)$" will be used interchangeably; that is, the analysis considers only the unconditional second-moment implications of the model. Nonlinearities and variation in conditional second and higher moments are ignored to help keep the problem tractable. The analysis will also ignore the unconditional first moments of $\mathbf{x}_t$; modifying the measures of fit for differences in the means of the variables is straightforward.

The empirical counterparts of $\mathbf{x}_t$ are denoted $\mathbf{y}_t$. These variables differ from $\mathbf{x}_t$ in an important way. The variables making up $\mathbf{x}_t$ correspond to the variables appearing in the theorist's simplification of reality; in a macroeconomic model they are variables such as "output," "money," and the "interest rate." The variables making up $\mathbf{y}_t$ are functions of raw data collected in a real economy; they are variables such as "per capita gross domestic product in the United States in 1987 dollars" or "U.S. M2" or "the yield on 3-month U.S. Treasury bills."

The question of interest is whether the model generates data with characteristics similar to those of the data generated by the real economy. Below, goodness-of-fit measures are proposed to help answer this question. Before I introduce these new measures, it is useful to review standard statistical goodness-of-fit measures to highlight their deficiencies for answering the question at hand.

Standard statistical goodness-of-fit measures use the size of sampling error to judge the coherence of the model with the data. They are based on the following: First, $A_y(z)$, the population ACGF for $\mathbf{y}_t$, is unknown but can be estimated from sample data. Discrepancies between the estimator $\hat{A}_y(z)$ and $A_y(z)$ arise solely from sampling error in $\hat{A}_y(z)$, and the likely size of the error can be deduced from the stochastic process that generated the sample. Now, if $A_y(z) = A_x(z)$, sampling error also accounts for the differences between $\hat{A}_y(z)$ and $A_x(z)$. Standard goodness-of-fit measures show how likely it is that $A_y(z) = A_x(z)$, on the basis of the probability that differences between $\hat{A}_y(z)$ and $A_x(z)$ arise solely from sampling error. If the differences between $\hat{A}_y(z)$ and $A_x(z)$ are so large as to be unlikely, standard measures of fit suggest that the model fits the data poorly, and vice versa if the differences between $\hat{A}_y(z)$ and $A_x(z)$ are not so large as to be unlikely. The key point is that the differences between $\hat{A}_y(z)$ and $A_x(z)$ are judged by how informative the sample is about the population moments of $\mathbf{y}_t$. This is a sensible procedure for judging the coherence of a null hypothesis, $A_y(z) = A_x(z)$, with the data. It is arguably less sensible when this null hypothesis is known to be false.

Rather than rely on sampling error, the measures of fit that are developed here are based on the size of the stochastic error required to reconcile the autocovariances of $\mathbf{x}_t$ with those of $\mathbf{y}_t$. In particular, let $\mathbf{u}_t$ denote an $n \times 1$ error vector; then the importance of a difference between $A_x(z)$ and $A_y(z)$ will be determined by asking, How much error would have to be added to $\mathbf{x}_t$ so that the autocovariances of $\mathbf{x}_t + \mathbf{u}_t$ are equal to the autocovariances of $\mathbf{y}_t$? If the variance of the required error is large, then the discrepancy between $A_x(z)$ and $A_y(z)$ is large, and conversely if the variance of $\mathbf{u}_t$ is small. The vector $\mathbf{u}_t$ is the approximation error in the economic model interpreted as a stochastic process. It captures the second-moment characteristics of the observed data that are not captured by the model. Loosely speaking, it is analogous to the error term in a regression in which the set of regressors is interpreted as the economic model. The economic model might be deemed a good approximation to the data if the error term is small (i.e., the R^2 of the regression is large) and might be deemed a poor approximation if the error term is large (i.e., the R^2 of the regression is small).

To be more precise, assume that $\mathbf{x}_t$ and $\mathbf{y}_t$ are jointly covariance stationary, and define the error $\mathbf{u}_t$ by the equation

$$\mathbf{u}_t = \mathbf{y}_t - \mathbf{x}_t, \tag{1}$$

so that

$$A_u(z) = A_y(z) + A_x(z) - A_{xy}(z) - A_{yx}(z), \tag{2}$$

where $A_u(z)$ is the ACGF of $\mathbf{u}_t$, $A_{xy}(z)$ is the cross ACGF between $\mathbf{x}_t$ and $\mathbf{y}_t$, and so forth. From the right-hand side of (2), three terms are needed to calculate $A_u(z)$. The first, $A_y(z)$, can be consistently estimated from sample data; the second, $A_x(z)$, is completely determined by the model; but the third, $A_{xy}(z)$, is not determined by the model, and it cannot be estimated from the data (since this would require a sample drawn from the *joint* $(\mathbf{x}_t, \mathbf{y}_t)$ process). To proceed, an assumption is necessary.

A common assumption used in econometric analysis is that $A_{xy}(z) = A_x(z)$ so that $\mathbf{x}_t$ and $\mathbf{u}_t$ are uncorrelated at all leads and lags. Equation (1) can then be interpreted as the dynamic analogue of the classical errors-in-variables model. Sargent (1989) discusses this assumption and an alternative assumption, $A_{xy}(z) = A_y(z)$. He points out that under this latter assumption, $\mathbf{u}_t$ can be interpreted as signal extraction error, with $\mathbf{y}_t$ an optimal estimate of the unobserved "signal" $\mathbf{x}_t$.[1] In many applications, these covariance restrictions follow from the way the data were collected or the way expectations are formed. For example, if $\mathbf{x}_t$ represented the true value of the U.S. unemployment rate and $\mathbf{y}_t$ the value published by the U.S. Department of Labor, then $\mathbf{y}_t$ would differ from $\mathbf{x}_t$ because of the sampling error inherent in the monthly Current Population Survey from which $\mathbf{y}_t$ is derived. The sample design underlying the survey implies that the error term, $\mathbf{u}_t$, is statistically independent of $\mathbf{x}_t$. Similarly, if $\mathbf{y}_t$ denoted a rational expectation of $\mathbf{x}_t$, then the error would be uncorrelated with $\mathbf{y}_t$. Neither of these assumptions seems appropriate in the present context. The error is not the result of imprecise measurement. It is not a forecast or signal extraction error. Rather, it represents approximation or abstraction error in the economic model. Any restriction used to identify $A_{xy}(z)$, and hence $A_u(z)$, is arbitrary.[2]

It is possible, however, to calculate a lower bound for the variance of $\mathbf{u}_t$ without imposing any restrictions on $A_{xy}(z)$. When this lower bound on the variance of $\mathbf{u}_t$ is large, then under any assumption on $A_{xy}(z)$, the model fits the data poorly. If the lower bound on the variance of $\mathbf{u}_t$ is small, then there are possible assumptions about $A_{xy}(z)$ that imply that the model fits the data well. Thus the bound is potentially useful for rejecting models on the basis of their empirical

[1] The reader familiar with work on data revisions will recognize these two sets of assumptions as the ones underlying the "news" and "noise" models of Mankiw, Runkle, and Shapiro (1984) and Mankiw and Shapiro (1986).

[2] It is interesting to note that it is possible to determine whether the dynamic errors-in-variables model or the signal extraction error model is consistent with the model and the data. The dynamic errors-in-variables model implies that $A_y(z) - A_x(z) \geq 0$ for $|z| = 1$, so that the spectrum of $\mathbf{y}_t$ lies everywhere above the spectrum of $\mathbf{x}_t$; the signal extraction error model implies the converse. If the spectrum of $\mathbf{x}_t$ lies anywhere above the spectrum of $\mathbf{y}_t$, the errors-in-variables model is inappropriate; if the spectrum of $\mathbf{y}_t$ lies anywhere above the spectrum of $\mathbf{x}_t$, the signal extraction model is inappropriate. If the spectra of $\mathbf{x}_t$ and $\mathbf{y}_t$ cross, neither model is appropriate.

fit. Needless to say, models that appear to fit the data well using this bound require further scrutiny.

The bound is calculated by choosing $A_{xy}(z)$ to minimize the variance of u_t subject to the constraint that the implied joint ACGF for x_t and y_t is positive semidefinite. Equivalently, since the spectrum is proportional to the ACGF evaluated at $z = e^{-i\omega}$, the cross spectrum between x_t and y_t, $(2\pi)^{-1}A_{xy}(e^{-i\omega})$, must be chosen so that the spectral density matrix of $(x_t'\ y_t')'$ is positive semidefinite at all frequencies.

Since the measures of fit proposed in this paper are based on the solution to this minimization problem, it is useful to discuss the problem and its solution in detail. Rather than move directly to the solution of the general problem, we shall first solve two simpler problems. This helps develop intuition for the general solution. In the first problem, x_t and y_t are serially uncorrelated scalars, and the representation follows by inspection. In the second problem, x_t and y_t are serially uncorrelated $n \times 1$ vectors, and the solution is slightly more difficult to derive. Finally, in the last problem, x_t and y_t are allowed to be serially correlated.

Model 1

Suppose that x_t, y_t, and u_t are scalar serially uncorrelated random variables. The problem is to choose σ_{xy} to minimize the variance of u_t, $\sigma_u^2 = \sigma_x^2 + \sigma_y^2 - 2\sigma_{xy}$, subject to the constraint that the covariance matrix of x_t and y_t remains positive semidefinite, that is, $|\sigma_{xy}| \leq \sigma_x\sigma_y$. By inspection, the solution sets $\sigma_{xy} = \sigma_x\sigma_y$ and yields $\sigma_u^2 = (\sigma_x - \sigma_y)^2$ as the minimum. Since $\sigma_{xy} = \sigma_x\sigma_y$, x_t and y_t are perfectly correlated with

$$x_t = \gamma y_t, \tag{3}$$

where $\gamma = \sigma_x/\sigma_y$. Equation (3) is important because it shows how to calculate fitted values of x_t, given data on y_t. Variants of equation (3) will hold for all the models considered. In each model, the minimum approximation error representation makes $\{x_t\}$ perfectly correlated with $\{y_t\}$. In each model, the analogue of (3) provides a formula for calculating the fitted values of the variables in the model, given data from the actual economy.

Model 2

Now suppose that x_t and y_t are serially uncorrelated random vectors with covariance matrices Σ_x and Σ_y, respectively. Let $\Sigma_u = \Sigma_x + \Sigma_y - \Sigma_{xy} - \Sigma_{yx}$ denote the covariance matrix of u_t. Since Σ_u is a matrix, there is not a unique way to judge how "small" it is. A convenient measure of the size of $\mathbf{u}_t$ is the trace of $\mathbf{\Sigma}_\mathbf{u}$, $\text{tr}(\mathbf{\Sigma}_\mathbf{u}) = \sum_{i=1}^n \mathbf{\Sigma}_{\mathbf{u},ii}$, where $\mathbf{\Sigma}_{\mathbf{u},ij}$ denotes the ijth element of $\mathbf{\Sigma}_\mathbf{u}$. While convenient, this measure is not always ideal since it weights all variables equally. Below, we shall find a representation that minimizes $\text{tr}(\mathbf{W}\mathbf{\Sigma}_\mathbf{u})$, where $\mathbf{W}$ is a prespecified $n \times n$ matrix. When all variables are equally important, $\mathbf{W} = I_n$, and unequal weighting can be implemented by making $\mathbf{W}$ diagonal with the desired weights as the diagonal elements. The matrix $\mathbf{W}$ can also be used to focus attention on specific linear combinations of the variables that may be particularly interesting. For example, let $\mathbf{G}$ denote an $n \times n$ matrix and suppose that the researcher is primarily interested in the variables $\mathbf{Gx}_t$ and $\mathbf{Gy}_t$. Then since $\text{tr}(\mathbf{G}\mathbf{\Sigma}_\mathbf{u}\mathbf{G}') = \text{tr}(\mathbf{G}'\mathbf{G}\mathbf{\Sigma}_\mathbf{u})$, $\mathbf{W}$ can be chosen as $\mathbf{G}'\mathbf{G}$.

The problem then is to choose $\mathbf{\Sigma}_\mathbf{xy}$ to minimize $\text{tr}(\mathbf{W}\mathbf{\Sigma}_\mathbf{u})$ subject to the constraint that the covariance matrix of $(\mathbf{x}_t'\ \mathbf{y}_t')'$ is positive semidefinite. The solution is given below for the case in which $\mathbf{\Sigma}_\mathbf{x}$ has rank $k \leq n$. This occurs, for example, in economic models in which the number of variables exceeds the number of shocks. The solution is summarized in the following proposition.

PROPOSITION. Assume (i) $\text{rank}(\mathbf{\Sigma}_\mathbf{x}) = k \leq n$, (ii) $\text{rank}(\mathbf{W}\mathbf{\Sigma}_\mathbf{x}\mathbf{W}') = \text{rank}(\mathbf{\Sigma}_\mathbf{x})$, and (iii) $\text{rank}(\mathbf{\Sigma}_\mathbf{y}) = n$. Let $\mathbf{C}_\mathbf{y}$ denote an arbitrary $n \times n$ matrix square root of $\mathbf{\Sigma}_\mathbf{y}$ (i.e., $\mathbf{\Sigma}_\mathbf{y} = \mathbf{C}_\mathbf{y}\mathbf{C}_\mathbf{y}'$), and let $\mathbf{C}_\mathbf{x}$ denote an arbitrary $n \times k$ matrix square root of $\mathbf{\Sigma}_\mathbf{x}$ (i.e., $\mathbf{\Sigma}_\mathbf{x} = \mathbf{C}_\mathbf{x}\mathbf{C}_\mathbf{x}'$). Let $\mathbf{USV}'$ denote the singular value decomposition of $\mathbf{C}_\mathbf{y}'\mathbf{W}\mathbf{C}_\mathbf{x}$, where $\mathbf{U}$ is an $n \times k$ orthogonal matrix ($\mathbf{U}'\mathbf{U} = I_k$), $\mathbf{S}$ is a $k \times k$ diagonal matrix, and $\mathbf{V}$ is a $k \times k$ orthonormal matrix. Then $\mathbf{\Sigma}_\mathbf{xy} = \mathbf{C}_\mathbf{x}\mathbf{VU}'\mathbf{C}_\mathbf{y}'$ is the unique matrix that minimizes $\text{tr}(\mathbf{W}\mathbf{\Sigma}_\mathbf{u})$ subject to the constraint that the covariance matrix of $(\mathbf{x}_t'\ \mathbf{y}_t')'$ is positive semidefinite.

The proof is given in the Appendix.

One important implication of this solution is that, like the scalar example, the joint covariance matrix $(\mathbf{x}_t'\ \mathbf{y}_t')'$ is singular and $\mathbf{x}_t$ can be represented as

$$\mathbf{x}_t = \Gamma\mathbf{y}_t, \tag{4}$$

where $\Gamma = \mathbf{C}_\mathbf{x}'\mathbf{VU}'\mathbf{C}_\mathbf{y}^{-1}$. (Since $\mathbf{U}'\mathbf{U} = \mathbf{VV}' = I_k$, this simplifies to the scalar result when x_t and y_t are scalars.)

Model 3

This same approach can be used in a dynamic multivariate model with slight modifications; when $\mathbf{u}_t$ is serially correlated, the weighted trace of the spectral density matrix rather than the covariance matrix can be minimized.

To motivate the approach, it is useful to use the Cramer representations for $\mathbf{x}_t$, $\mathbf{y}_t$, and $\mathbf{u}_t$ (see, e.g., Brillinger 1981, sec. 4.6). Assume that $\mathbf{x}_t$, $\mathbf{y}_t$, and $\mathbf{u}_t$ are jointly covariance stationary with mean zero; the Cramer representation can be written as

$$\mathbf{x}_t = \int_0^{2\pi} e^{i\omega t} dz_{\mathbf{x}}(\omega),$$

$$\mathbf{y}_t = \int_0^{2\pi} e^{i\omega t} dz_{\mathbf{y}}(\omega), \tag{5}$$

$$\mathbf{u}_t = \int_0^{2\pi} e^{i\omega t} dz_{\mathbf{u}}(\omega),$$

where $dz(\omega) = (dz_{\mathbf{x}}(\omega)'\ dz_{\mathbf{y}}(\omega)'\ dz_{\mathbf{u}}(\omega)')'$ is a complex valued vector of orthogonal increments, with $E(dz(\omega)\overline{dz(\lambda)'}) = \delta(\omega - \lambda)\mathbf{S}(\omega)d\omega d\lambda$, where $\delta(\omega - \lambda)$ is the dirac delta and $\mathbf{S}(\omega)$ is the spectral density matrix of $(\mathbf{x}_t'\ \mathbf{y}_t'\ \mathbf{u}_t')'$ at frequency ω. Equation (5) represents $\mathbf{x}_t$, $\mathbf{y}_t$, and $\mathbf{u}_t$ as the integral (sum) of increments $dz_{\mathbf{x}}(\omega)$, $dz_{\mathbf{y}}(\omega)$, and $dz_{\mathbf{u}}(\omega)$, which are uncorrelated across frequencies and have variances and covariances given by the spectra and cross spectra of $\mathbf{x}_t$, $\mathbf{y}_t$, and $\mathbf{u}_t$. Since the spectra are proportional to the ACGFs evaluated at $z = e^{-i\omega}$, $E(dz_{\mathbf{x}}(\omega)\overline{dz_{\mathbf{x}}(\omega)'})$ is proportional to $A_{\mathbf{x}}(e^{-i\omega})$, $E(dz_{\mathbf{x}}(\omega)\overline{dz_{\mathbf{y}}(\omega)'})$ is proportional to $A_{\mathbf{xy}}(e^{-i\omega})$, and so forth.

Now consider the problem of choosing $A_{\mathbf{xy}}(z)$ to minimize the variance of $\mathbf{u}_t$. Since $\mathbf{u}_t$ can be written as the integral of the uncorrelated increments $dz_{\mathbf{u}}(\omega)$, the variance of $\mathbf{u}_t$ can be minimized by minimizing the variance of $dz_{\mathbf{u}}(\omega)$ for each ω. Since the increments are uncorrelated across frequency, the minimization problems can be solved independently for each frequency. Thus the analysis carried out for model 2 carries over directly, with spectral density matrices replacing covariance matrices. The minimum trace problem for model 2 is now solved frequency by frequency using the spectral density matrix.

Like models 1–2, the solution yields

$$dz_{\mathbf{x}}(\omega) = \Gamma(\omega)dz_{\mathbf{y}}(\omega), \tag{6}$$

where $\Gamma(\omega)$ is the complex analogue of Γ from (4). Equation (6) implies

$$A_{\mathbf{xy}}(e^{-i\omega}) = \Gamma(\omega)A_{\mathbf{y}}(e^{-i\omega}) \tag{7}$$

and

$$A_{\mathbf{u}}(e^{-i\omega}) = A_{\mathbf{x}}(e^{-i\omega}) + A_{\mathbf{y}}(e^{-i\omega}) - A_{\mathbf{xy}}(e^{-i\omega}) - A_{\mathbf{xy}}(e^{i\omega})'. \tag{8}$$

The autocovariances of $\mathbf{u}_t$ follow directly from (8). Moreover, since $dz_{\mathbf{x}}(\omega)$ and $dz_{\mathbf{y}}(\omega)$ are perfectly correlated from (7), $\mathbf{x}_t$ can be represented as a function of leads and lags of $\mathbf{y}_t$:

$$\mathbf{x}_t = \beta(L)\mathbf{y}_t, \tag{9}$$

where $\beta(L) = \sum_{-\infty}^{\infty} \beta_j L^j$, with $\beta_j = \int_{-\pi}^{\pi} \Gamma(\omega)e^{i\omega j}d\omega$. Thus fitted values of $\mathbf{x}_t$ can be calculated from leads and lags of $\mathbf{y}_t$.

An Example

The model considered in the next section describes the dynamic properties of output, consumption, investment, and employment as functions of a single productivity shock. To demonstrate the mechanics of the minimum approximation error representation for that model, assume that $\mathbf{x}_t$ and $\mathbf{y}_t$ are $n \times 1$ vectors and that $\mathbf{x}_t$ is driven by a single iid$(0, 1)$ shock ϵ_t:

$$\mathbf{x}_t = \boldsymbol{\alpha}(L)\epsilon_t, \tag{10}$$

where $\boldsymbol{\alpha}(L)$ is an $n \times 1$ matrix polynomial in the lag operator, L. Assume that the Wold representation for the data is given by

$$\mathbf{y}_t = \boldsymbol{\Theta}(L)\mathbf{e}_t, \tag{11}$$

where $\boldsymbol{\Theta}(L)$ is an $n \times n$ matrix polynomial in L, and $\mathbf{e}_t$ is an $n \times 1$ serially uncorrelated vector with mean zero and identity covariance matrix.

The minimum error representation can then be computed directly from the matrix expressions given in the proposition. From (10), $A_{\mathbf{x}}(z) = \boldsymbol{\alpha}(z)\boldsymbol{\alpha}(z^{-1})'$ and, from (11), $A_{\mathbf{y}}(z) = \boldsymbol{\Theta}(z)\boldsymbol{\Theta}(z^{-1})'$. Suppose that the weighting matrix is $\mathbf{W} = I_n$, so that the trace of the spectral density of $\mathbf{u}_t$ is to be minimized for each frequency. In terms of the matrices in the proposition, $\mathbf{C}_{\mathbf{x}}(\omega) = \boldsymbol{\alpha}(e^{-i\omega})$ and $\mathbf{C}_{\mathbf{y}}(\omega) = \boldsymbol{\Theta}(e^{-i\omega})$. Thus the cross spectrum/cross ACGF for $\mathbf{x}_t$ and $\mathbf{y}_t$ is chosen as $A_{\mathbf{xy}}(e^{-i\omega}) = \boldsymbol{\alpha}(e^{-i\omega})\mathbf{V}(\omega)\mathbf{U}(\omega)'\boldsymbol{\Theta}(e^{i\omega})'$, where $\mathbf{U}(\omega)\mathbf{S}(\omega)\mathbf{V}(\omega)'$ is the singular value decomposition of $\boldsymbol{\Theta}(e^{i\omega})'\boldsymbol{\alpha}(e^{-i\omega})$. (Since $\mathbf{U}(\omega)$ and $\mathbf{V}(\omega)$ are complex matrices, $\mathbf{V}(\omega)'$ and $\mathbf{U}(\omega)'$ denote the transpose conjugates of $\mathbf{V}(\omega)$ and $\mathbf{U}(\omega)$, respectively.) The ACGF for $\mathbf{u}_t$ follows from $A_{\mathbf{u}}(e^{-i\omega}) = A_{\mathbf{x}}(e^{-i\omega}) + A_{\mathbf{y}}(e^{-i\omega}) - A_{\mathbf{xy}}(e^{-i\omega}) - A_{\mathbf{yx}}(e^{-i\omega})$. Finally, to compute fitted values of $\mathbf{x}_t$ from the $\mathbf{y}_t$ realization, note that $dz_{\mathbf{x}}(\omega) = \Gamma(\omega)dz_{\mathbf{y}}(\omega)$, where $\Gamma(\omega) = \boldsymbol{\alpha}(e^{-i\omega})\mathbf{V}(\omega)\mathbf{U}(\omega)'\boldsymbol{\Theta}(e^{-i\omega})^{-1}$.

Relative Mean Square Approximation Error

A bound on the relative mean square approximation error for the economic model can be calculated directly from (8). The bound—analogous to a lower bound on $1 - R^2$ from a regression—is

$$r_j(\omega) = \frac{[A_{\mathbf{u}}(z)]_{jj}}{[A_{\mathbf{y}}(z)]_{jj}}, \quad z = e^{-i\omega}, \tag{12}$$

where $[A_u(z)]_{jj}$ and $[A_y(z)]_{jj}$ are the jth diagonal elements of $A_u(z)$ and $A_y(z)$, respectively. Thus $r_j(\omega)$ is the variance of the jth component of $dz_u(\omega)$ relative to the jth component of $dz_y(\omega)$, that is, the variance of the error relative to the variance of the data for each frequency. A plot of $r_j(\omega)$ against frequency shows how well the economic model fits the data over different frequencies. Integrating the numerator and denominator of $r_j(\omega)$ provides an overall measure of fit. (Note that since u_t and x_t are correlated, $r_j(\omega)$ can be larger than one; i.e., the R^2 of the model can be negative.)[3]

One advantage of $r_j(\omega)$ is that it is unaffected by time-invariant linear filters applied to the variables. Filtering merely multiplies both the numerator and denominator of $r_j(\omega)$ by the same constant, the squared gain of the filter. So, for example, $r_j(\omega)$ is invariant to "Hodrick-Prescott" filtering (see Hodrick and Prescott 1980; King and Rebelo 1993) or standard linear seasonal adjustment filters.[4] The integrated version of the relative mean square approximation error is not invariant to filtering since it is a ratio of averages of both the numerator and denominator across frequencies. When the data are filtered, the integrated version of $r_j(\omega)$ changes because the weights implicit in the averaging change. Frequencies for which the filter has a large gain are weighted more heavily than frequencies with a small gain.

III. Measures of Fit for a Real Business Cycle Model

In this section, a standard real business cycle model is evaluated using the measures of fit developed in the last section. The model, which derives from Kydland and Prescott (1982), is the "baseline" model of King, Plosser, and Rebelo (1988b). It is a one-sector neoclassical growth model driven by an exogenous stochastic trend in technology.[5]

---

[3] The measure $r_j(\omega)$ is not technically a metric since it does not satisfy the triangle inequality.

[4] Standard seasonal adjustment filters such as the linear approximation to Census X-11 have zeros at the seasonal frequencies, so that $r_j(\omega)$ is undefined at these frequencies for the filtered data.

[5] This model is broadly similar to the model analyzed in Kydland and Prescott (1982). While the baseline model does not include the complications of time to build, inventories, time-nonseparable utility, and a transitory component to technology contained in the original Kydland and Prescott model, these complications have been shown to be reasonably unimportant for the empirical predictions of the model (see Hansen 1985). Moreover, the King, Plosser, and Rebelo baseline model appears to fit the data better at the very low frequencies than the original Kydland and Prescott model since it incorporates a stochastic trend rather than the deterministic trend present in the Kydland and Prescott formulation.

1022   JOURNAL OF POLITICAL ECONOMY

This baseline model is analyzed, rather than a more complicated variant, for several reasons. First, the calibration/simulation exercises reported in King, Plosser, and Rebelo suggest that the model explains the relative variability of aggregate output, consumption, and investment, and it produces series with serial correlation properties broadly similar to the serial correlation properties of postwar U.S. data. Second, King, Plosser, Stock, and Watson (1991) show that the low-frequency/cointegration implications of the model are broadly consistent with similar postwar U.S. data. Finally, an understanding of where this baseline model fits the data and where it does not fit may suggest how the model should be modified.

Only a brief sketch of the model is presented; a thorough discussion is contained in King, Plosser, and Rebelo (1988a, 1988b). The details of the model are as follows:

preferences: $E_t \sum_{t=0}^{\infty} \beta^t u(C_t, L_t)$,   with $u(C_t, L_t) = \log(C_t) + \theta \log(L_t)$;

technology: $Q_t = K_t^{1-\alpha}(A_t N_t)^{\alpha}$,

$$\log(A_t) \equiv a_t = \gamma_a + a_{t-1} + \epsilon_t, \quad \epsilon_t \text{ iid}(0, \sigma_\epsilon^2),$$

$$K_t = (1 - \delta)K_{t-1} + I_t;$$

constraints: $Q_t = C_t + I_t$,

$$1 = N_t + L_t,$$

where C_t denotes consumption, L_t is leisure, Q_t is output, K_t is capital, N_t is employment, I_t is investment, and A_t is the stock of technology, with $\log(A_t)$ assumed to follow a random walk with drift γ_a and innovation ϵ_t.

To analyze the model's empirical predictions, the equilibrium of the model must be calculated as a function of the parameters β, θ, α, γ_a, σ_ϵ^2, and δ. This equilibrium implies a stochastic process for the variables C_t, L_t, N_t, K_t, I_t, and Q_t, and these stochastic processes can then be compared to the stochastic processes characterizing U.S. postwar data. As is well known, the equilibrium can be calculated by maximizing the representative agent's utility function subject to the technology and the resource constraints. In general, a closed-form expression for the equilibrium does not exist, and numerical methods must be used to calculate the stochastic process for the variables corresponding to the equilibrium. A variety of numerical approximations have been proposed (see Taylor and Uhlig [1990] for a survey); here I use the log linearization of the Euler equations proposed by King, Plosser, and Rebelo (1987). A formal justification for approximating the equilibrium of this stochastic nonlinear model near its deterministic steady state using linear methods is provided in Woodford (1986, theorem 2).

The approximate solution yields a vector autoregression (VAR) for the logarithms of Q_t, C_t, K_t, I_t, and N_t. (As in the standard convention, these logarithms will be denoted by lowercase letters.) All of the variables except n_t are nonstationary but can be represented as stationary deviations about a_t, the logarithm of the stock of technology, which by assumption follows an integrated process. Thus q_t, c_t, i_t, and k_t are cointegrated with a single common trend, a_t. Indeed, not only are the variables in the VAR cointegrated, they are singular; the singularity follows since ϵ_t is the only shock to the system. The coefficients in the VAR are complicated functions of the structural parameters β, θ, α, γ_a, σ_ϵ^2, and δ. Values for these parameters are the same as those used by King, Plosser, and Rebelo (1988b): when the variables are measured quarterly, the parameter values are $\alpha = .58$, $\delta = .025$, $\gamma_a = .004$, $\sigma_\epsilon = .010$, and $\beta = .988$, and θ is chosen so that the steady-state value of N is .20. These parameter values were chosen so that the model's steady-state behavior matches postwar U.S. data.[6] With these values for the parameters, the VAR describing the equilibrium can be calculated and the ACGF of $\mathbf{x}_t = (\Delta q_t \ \Delta c_t \ \Delta i_t \ n_t)'$ follows directly.[7]

These autocovariances will be compared to the autocovariances of postwar data for the United States. The data used here are the same data used by King, Plosser, Stock, and Watson (1991). The output measure is total real private GNP, defined as total real GNP less government purchases of goods and services. The measure of consumption is total real consumption expenditures, and the measure of investment is total real fixed investment. The measure of employment is total labor hours in private nonagricultural establishments. All variables are expressed in per capita terms using the total civilian noninstitutional population over the age of 16.[8] Let $\bar{q}_t$ denote the logarithm

[6] The choice of parameter values is described in King, Plosser, and Rebelo (1988a). The value of α was chosen to equal the average value of labor's share of gross national product over 1948–86. The value of γ_a was chosen as the common average quarterly rate of growth of per capita values of real GNP, consumption of nondurables and services, and gross fixed investment. The depreciation rate was chosen to yield a gross investment share of GNP of approximately 30 percent. The parameter θ was chosen so that the model's steady-state value of N matched the average workweek as a fraction of total hours over 1948–86. The discount rate β was chosen so that the model's steady-state annual interest rate matched the average rate of return on equity over 1948–81. The value of $\sigma_\epsilon = .01$ appears to have been chosen as a convenient normalization. This value is used here because it does a remarkably good job matching the very low frequency movements in output, consumption, and investment.

[7] Of course, this not the only possible definition of $\mathbf{x}_t$. The only restriction on $\mathbf{x}_t$ is covariance stationarity, so, e.g., $c_t - q_t$ and $i_t - q_t$ could be included as elements.

[8] All data are taken from Citibase. With the Citibase labels, the precise variables used were gnp82 − gge82 for output, gc82 for consumption, and gif82 for investment. The

of per capita private output, $\bar{c}_t$ the logarithm of per capita consumption expenditures, and so forth. Then the data used in the analysis can be written as $\mathbf{y}_t = (\Delta \bar{q}_t \, \Delta \bar{c}_t \, \Delta \bar{\imath}_t \, \bar{n}_t)'$.

The analysis presented in the last section assumed that the ACGF/spectrum of $\mathbf{y}_t$ was known. In practice, of course, this is not the case, and the spectrum must be estimated. In this work, the spectrum of $\mathbf{y}_t$ was estimated in two different ways. First, an autoregressive spectral estimator was used, calculated by first estimating a VAR for the variables and then forming the implied spectral density matrix. As in King, Plosser, Stock, and Watson (1991), the VAR was estimated imposing a cointegration constraint between output, consumption, and investment. Thus the VAR was specified as the regression of $\mathbf{w}_t = (\Delta \bar{q}_t, \, \bar{q}_t - \bar{c}_t, \, \bar{q}_t - \bar{\imath}_t, \, \bar{n}_t)'$ onto a constant and six lags of $\mathbf{w}_t$. The parameters of the VAR were estimated using data for 1950–88. (Values before 1950 were used as lags in the regression for the initial observations.) Second, a standard nonparametric spectral estimator was also calculated. The spectrum was estimated by a simple average of 10 periodogram ordinates after prewhitening employment with the filter $1 - .95L$. These two estimators yielded similar values for the measures of fit, and to conserve space only the results for the autoregressive spectral estimator are reported.

For each variable, figure 1 presents the spectrum implied by the model, the spectrum of the data, and the spectrum of the error required to reconcile the model with the data.[9] The error process was chosen to minimize the unweighted trace of the error spectral density matrix, subject to the positive semidefiniteness constraint discussed in the last section. Thus the objective function weighted all the variables equally. For output, consumption, and investment, the model and data spectra differ little for very low frequencies (periods greater than 50 quarters) and for output and investment at high frequencies (periods less than five quarters). There are significant differences between the model and data spectra for periods typically associated with the business cycle; the largest differences occur at a frequency corresponding to approximately 20 quarters. The spectra of Δn_t and $\Delta \bar{n}_t$ are quite different. In addition to large differences at business cycle frequencies, the spectra are also very different at low frequencies. The model implies that employment is stationary so that its

---

measure of total labor hours was constructed as total employment in nonagricultural establishments (lhem) less total government employment (lpgov) multiplied by average weekly hours (lhch). The population series was P16.

[9] Figure 1 is reminiscent of figures in Howrey (1971, 1972), who calculated the spectra implied by the Klein-Goldberger and Wharton models. A similar exercise is carried out in Soderlind (1993), who compares the spectra of variables in the Kydland-Prescott model to the spectra of postwar U.S. data.

growth rate has a spectrum that vanishes at frequency zero. In contrast, the data suggest significant low-frequency variation in postwar U.S. employment.[10]

The figure shows that relatively little error is needed to reconcile the model and the data for output, consumption, and investment over the very low frequencies. On the other hand, error with a variance on the order of 40–50 percent of the magnitude of the variance of the series is necessary for the components of output, consumption, and investment with periods in the 6–32-quarter range. At higher frequencies, the model is able to match the stochastic process describing investment, but not the processes describing the other series.

Table 1 provides a summary of the relative mean square approximation error (RMSAE) for a variety of weighting functions and filters. Each panel shows the RMSAE for the variables for five different minimum error representations. Column 1 presents results for the representation that obtains when the unweighted trace of the spectrum is minimized; this is the representation used to construct the error spectra shown in figure 1. Column 2 summarizes the results for the representation that minimizes the output error, with no weight placed on the other variables. Column 3 summarizes results for the representation that minimizes the consumption error, and so forth. Panel A presents the results for the differences of the data integrated across all frequencies, panel B shows results for the levels of the series detrended by the Hodrick-Prescott filter integrated across all frequencies, and panel C presents results for the levels of the series integrated over business cycle frequencies (6–32 quarters). The trade-off inherent in the different representations is evident in all panels. For example, in panel A, with the minimum output error representation, the RMSAE for output is 26 percent, and the RMSAE for consumption is 78 percent; when the minimum consumption error representation is chosen, the RMSAE for consumption falls to 21 percent but the RMSAE for output rises to 75 percent. When all the variables are equally weighted, the RMSAE is 52 percent for output and 66 percent for consumption. Panel C shows that most of this trade-off occurs at the high frequencies, at least for output, consumption, and investment; over the business cycle frequencies their RMSAEs are in the 40–60 percent range.

As explained in Section II, fitted values of the model's variables can be constructed using the minimum error representation together

---

[10] The figures do not include standard errors for the spectra estimated from these data. These standard errors are large—approximately one-third the size of the estimated spectra. The standard errors for the RMSAE, averaged across frequencies, are considerably smaller. These are included in tables 1 and 2 below.

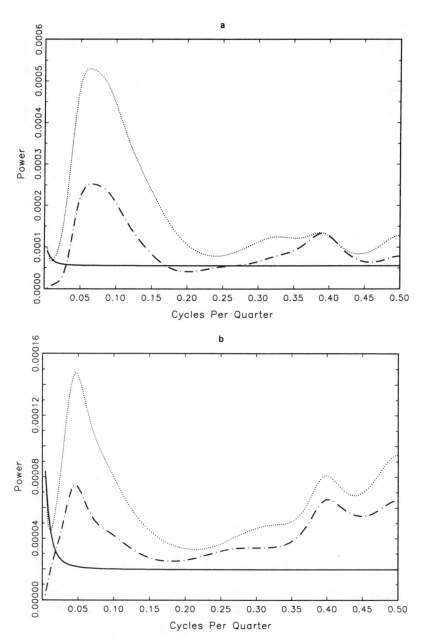

Fig. 1.—Decomposition of spectra: *a*, output; *b*, consumption; *c*, investment; *d*, employment. Dotted lines refer to the data, dashed lines to the model, and solid lines to approximation error.

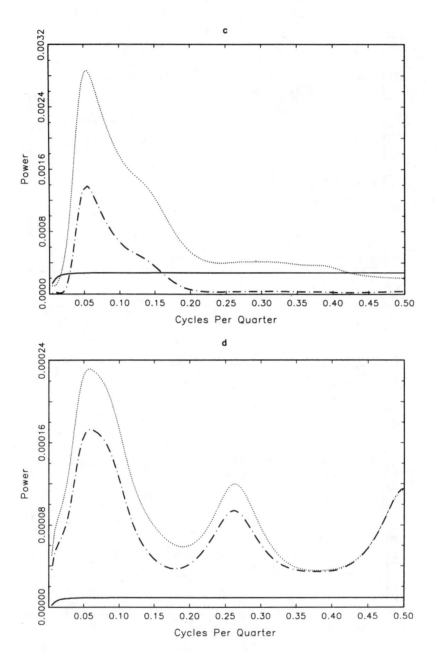

Fɪɢ. 1.—*Continued*

TABLE 1

RELATIVE MEAN SQUARE APPROXIMATION ERROR

VARIABLE	Equal Weight (1)	Output (2)	Consumption (3)	Investment (4)	Employment (5)
A. First Differences: All Frequencies					
Output	.52 (.04)	.26 (.06)	.75 (.06)	.64 (.05)	.79 (.07)
Consumption	.66 (.06)	.78 (.08)	.21 (.05)	.75 (.08)	1.00 (.10)
Investment	.29 (.06)	.63 (.05)	.75 (.07)	.27 (.06)	.79 (.07)
Employment	.78 (.04)	.81 (.04)	.92 (.04)	.81 (.04)	.50 (.04)
B. Hodrick-Prescott Detrended Levels: All Frequencies					
Output	.43 (.05)	.37 (.07)	.58 (.04)	.46 (.04)	.63 (.05)
Consumption	.53 (.04)	.55 (.05)	.29 (.09)	.57 (.05)	.81 (.09)
Investment	.40 (.08)	.48 (.05)	.61 (.04)	.39 (.08)	.63 (.04)
Employment	.73 (.03)	.75 (.03)	.85 (.04)	.74 (.03)	.59 (.06)
C. Levels: 6–32 Quarters					
Output	.43 (.06)	.39 (.07)	.55 (.05)	.44 (.05)	.61 (.05)
Consumption	.51 (.05)	.51 (.06)	.32 (.09)	.53 (.05)	.77 (.08)
Investment	.42 (.08)	.46 (.06)	.59 (.04)	.42 (.08)	.61 (.05)
Employment	.72 (.03)	.74 (.03)	.84 (.04)	.73 (.03)	.61 (.06)

NOTE.—Relative mean square approximation error is the lower bound of the variance of the approximation error divided by the variance of the series. Each column represents the relative mean square approximation error of the row variable constructed from the representation that minimizes the weighted trace of the error spectrum. The weights are summarized by the column headings. For example, col. 1 is the equally weighted trace, col. 2 puts all the weight on the output error, etc. The numbers in parentheses are standard errors based on the sampling error in the estimated VAR coefficients used to estimate the data spectrum.

with the observed data. Since the measurement error model represents $\mathbf{y}_t$ as $\mathbf{x}_t$ plus error, the standard signal extraction formula can be used to extract $\{\mathbf{x}_t\}$ from $\{\mathbf{y}_t\}$. In general, of course, signal extraction methods will yield an estimate of $\mathbf{x}_t$, say $\hat{\mathbf{x}}_t$, that is not exact in the sense that $E[(\mathbf{x}_t - \hat{\mathbf{x}}_t)^2] \neq 0$. In the present context, the estimate will be exact since the measurement error process is chosen so that $dz_{\mathbf{x}}(\omega)$ and $dz_{\mathbf{y}}(\omega)$ are perfectly correlated for all ω.[11] Figure 2 shows the realizations of the data and the realizations of the variables in the model calculated from the data using the equally weighted minimum output error representation.[12]

In figure 2a, which shows the results for output, the model seems capable of capturing the long swings in the postwar U.S. data but not capable of capturing the cyclical variability in the data. Private per capita GNP fell by 8.4 percent from the cyclical peak in 1973 to the trough in 1975 and by 6.8 percent from the peak in 1979 to the trough in 1982. In contrast, the corresponding drops in Q_t—output in the model—were 3.1 percent and 3.0 percent, respectively. The dampened cyclical swings in consumption and investment, shown in figure 2b and c, are even more dramatic. Finally, figure 2d shows that the model predicts changes in employment that have little to do with the changes observed in the United States during the postwar period.[13]

One possible explanation for the relatively poor fit of the model is that the "calibrated" values of the parameters are wrong. In particular, Christiano and Eichenbaum (1990) show that the model's predictions change in an important way when the technology process changes from a random walk to a stationary AR(1). Table 2 shows how the model fares for a range of values of the AR(1) coefficient for technology, denoted by ρ_a. Panel A of the table shows the results for first differences of the variables across all frequencies, panel B presents results for the Hodrick-Prescott detrended levels of the series, and panel C shows the results for the levels of the series over the "business cycle" frequencies. From panel A, the value of ρ_a has

[11] More precisely, the estimate is exact in the sense that $\text{Proj}(\mathbf{x}_t | \mathbf{y}_{t-j}, \ldots, \mathbf{y}_{-1}, \mathbf{y}_0, \mathbf{y}_1, \ldots, \mathbf{y}_{t+j})$ converges in mean square to $\mathbf{x}_t$ as $j \rightarrow \infty$.

[12] As shown in eq. (9), $\mathbf{x}_t$ can be calculated as $\beta(L)\mathbf{y}_t$, where $\beta(L)$ is the inverse Fourier transform of $\Gamma(\omega)$. To calculate the estimates shown in the figure, $\Gamma(\omega)$ was calculated at 128 equally spaced frequencies between zero and π. Since $\beta(L)$ is two-sided, pre- and postsample values of $\mathbf{y}_t$ are required to form $\beta(L)\mathbf{x}_t$. These pre- and postsample values were replaced with the sample means of the $\mathbf{y}_t$ data. The first differences, $\mathbf{x}_t$ and $\mathbf{y}_t$, were then accumulated to form the levels series shown in the figure.

[13] The calculations required to construct figs. 1 and 2 and the results in table 1 are easily carried out. For this example, the model spectrum, data spectrum, RMSAEs, and fitted values were calculated in less than a minute on a standard desktop computer. A GAUSS program for these calculations is available from the author.

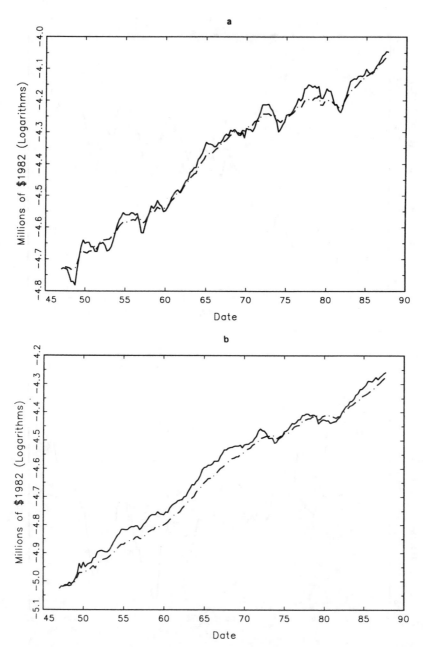

Fig. 2.—Data: *a*, output; *b*, consumption; *c*, investment; *d*, employment. Solid lines refer to U.S. data and dashed lines to realizations from the model.

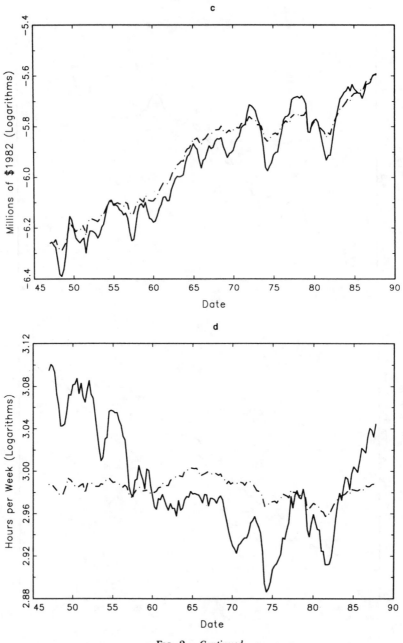

c

d

FIG. 2.—*Continued*

TABLE 2

RELATIVE MEAN SQUARE APPROXIMATION ERROR AS A FUNCTION OF THE AR(1)
COEFFICIENT FOR TECHNOLOGY

| | ρ_a | | | |
| | 1.0 | .98 | .95 | .90 |
VARIABLE	(1)	(2)	(3)	(4)
	A. First Differences: All Frequencies			
Output	.52 (.04)	.52 (.04)	.53 (.05)	.54 (.06)
Consumption	.66 (.06)	.69 (.06)	.71 (.05)	.74 (.05)
Investment	.29 (.06)	.21 (.05)	.18 (.05)	.20 (.04)
Employment	.78 (.04)	.74 (.05)	.73 (.07)	.75 (.09)
	B. Hodrick-Prescott Detrended Levels: All Frequencies			
Output	.43 (.05)	.40 (.05)	.37 (.05)	.36 (.05)
Consumption	.53 (.04)	.58 (.04)	.63 (.04)	.67 (.04)
Investment	.40 (.08)	.29 (.08)	.21 (.08)	.17 (.08)
Employment	.73 (.03)	.64 (.04)	.58 (.04)	.55 (.04)
	C. Levels: 6–32 Quarters			
Output	.43 (.06)	.38 (.06)	.35 (.06)	.33 (.06)
Consumption	.51 (.05)	.56 (.05)	.61 (.05)	.66 (.05)
Investment	.42 (.08)	.30 (.09)	.22 (.09)	.17 (.09)
Employment	.72 (.03)	.63 (.04)	.56 (.05)	.52 (.05)

NOTE.—Relative mean square approximation error is the lower bound of the variance of the approximation error divided by the variance of the series. Each column represents the relative mean square approximation error of the row variable constructed from the representation that minimizes the weighted trace of the error spectrum. The column headings represent the AR(1) coefficient for the process of the logarithm of productivity in the model. For example, col. 1 represents results for the model with random walk technological progress. The numbers in parentheses are standard errors based on the sampling error in the estimated VAR coefficients used to estimate the data spectrum.

little effect on the fit of the model averaged across all frequencies. In particular, as ρ_a falls from 1.0 to .90, the RMSAE increases slightly for consumption, falls for investment, and changes little for output and employment. In contrast, the value of ρ_a has a significant effect on the fit of the model over business cycle frequencies. For example, panel C shows that as ρ_a falls from 1.0 to .90, the RMSAE falls for output (.43 to .33), for investment (.42 to .17), and for employment (.72 to .52); it increases for consumption (.52 to .66).

The source of the changes in the RMSAEs can be seen in figure 3, which plots the spectra of the variables in models with $\rho_a = 1$ and $\rho_a = .90$. The largest difference between the spectra of the models is the increase in variance in output, investment, and employment as ρ_a falls from 1.0 to .90. The economic mechanism behind this increased variance is the increase in intertemporal substitution in response to a technology shock. When $\rho_a = .90$, technology shocks are transitory, and they can be exploited only by large transitory increases in employment and investment. It is interesting to note that while this mechanism increases the variance of the growth rates in employment, investment, and output, it has little effect on their autocorrelations. That is, as ρ_a changes from 1.0 to .90, the shape of the spectra changes little.

Before we leave this section, six additional points deserve mention. First, the fitted values in figure 2 are quantitatively and conceptually similar to figures presented in Christiano (1988) and Plosser (1989). They calculated the Solow residual from actual data and then simulated the economic model using this residual as the forcing process. Implicitly, they assumed that the model and data were the same in the terms of their Solow residual, and then asked whether the model and data were similar in other dimensions. Figure 2 is constructed by making the model and data as close as possible in one dimension (in this case the trace of the variance of the implied approximation error) and then asking whether the model and data are similar in other dimensions. The difference between the two approaches can be highlighted by considering the circumstances in which they would produce exactly the same figure. If the Solow residual computed from the actual data followed exactly the same stochastic process as the change in productivity in the model, and if the approximation error representation was constructed by minimizing the variance of the difference between the Solow residual in the data and productivity growth in the model, then the two figures would be identical. Thus the figures will differ if the stochastic process for the empirical Solow residual is not the same as assumed in the model, or the approximation error representation is chosen to make the model and data close in some dimension other than productivity growth.

Second, the inability of the model to capture the business cycle properties of the data is not an artifact of the minimum measurement error representation used to form the projection of $\mathbf{x}_t$ onto $\mathbf{y}_\tau$, $\tau = 1, \ldots, n$. Rather, it follows directly from a comparison of the spectra of $\mathbf{x}_t$ and $\mathbf{y}_t$. The fitted values are constrained to have an ACGF/spectra given by the economic model. Figure 1 shows that, for all the variables, the spectral power over the business cycle frequencies is significantly less for the model than for the data. Therefore, fitted values from the model are constrained to have less cyclical variability than the data.

Third, the ability of the model to mimic the behavior of the data depends critically on the size of the variance of the technology shock. The value of σ_ϵ used in the analysis is two and one-half times larger than the drift in the series. Thus if the ϵ_t were approximately normally distributed, the stock of technology A_t would fall in one out of three quarters on average. Reducing the standard deviation of the

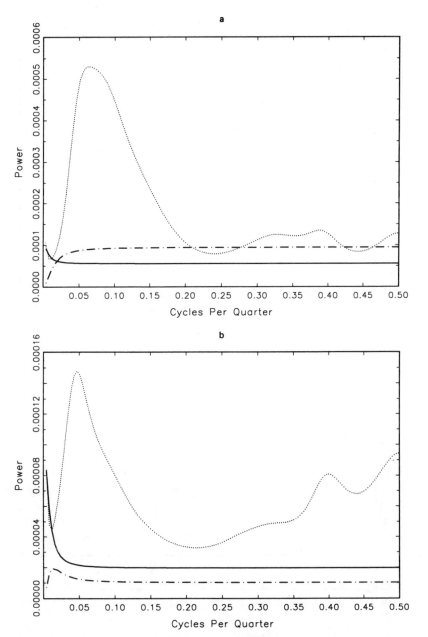

Fig. 3.—Data and model spectra: *a*, output; *b*, consumption; *c*, investment; *d*, employment. Dotted lines refer to the data, solid lines to the model with $\rho_a = 1.00$, and dashed lines to the model with $\rho_a = .90$.

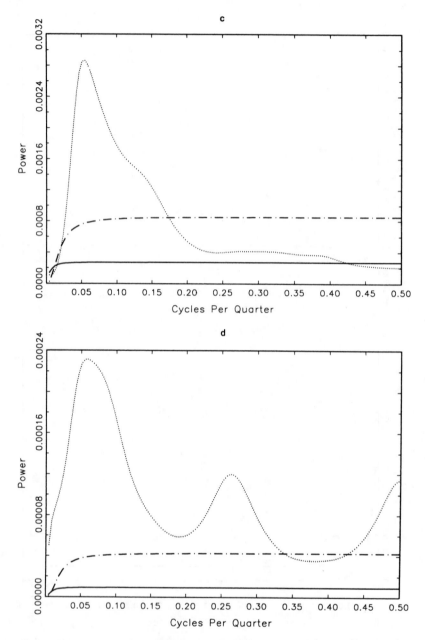

FIG. 3.—*Continued*

technology shock so that it equals the average growth in a_t drastically increases the size of the measurement error necessary to reconcile the model with the data. For example, integrated across all frequencies, the RMSAE for output increases from 52 percent to 74 percent.

Fourth, there is nothing inherent in the structure of the model that precludes the use of classical statistical procedures. Altug (1989) used maximum likelihood methods to study a version of the model that is augmented with serially correlated classical measurement errors. Singleton (1988) and Christiano and Eichenbaum (1992) pointed out that generalized method of moments procedures can be used to analyze moment implications of models like the one presented above. In the empirical work of Christiano and Eichenbaum the singularity in the probability density function of the data that is implied by the model was finessed in two ways. First, limited information estimation and testing methods were used, and second, the authors assumed that their data on employment were measured with error.

Fifth, many if not all of the empirical shortcomings of this model have been noted by other researchers. King, Plosser, and Rebelo clearly show that the model is not capable of explaining the variation in employment that is observed in the actual data. The implausibility of the large technology shocks is discussed in detail in Summers (1986), Mankiw (1989), and McCallum (1989).

Finally, the analysis above has concentrated on the ability of the model to explain the variability in output, consumption, investment, and employment across different frequencies. While it is possible to analyze the covariation of these series using the cross spectrum of the measurement error, such an analysis has not been carried out here. This is a particularly important omission since this is the dimension in which the baseline real business cycle model is typically thought to fail. For example, Christiano and Eichenbaum (1992) and Rotemberg and Woodford (1992) use the model's counterfactual implication of a high correlation between average productivity and output growth as starting points for their analysis, and the empirical literature on the intertemporal capital asset pricing model beginning with Hansen and Singleton (1982) suggests that the asset pricing implications of the model are inconsistent with the data. It would be useful to derive simple summary statistics based on the cross spectra of the measurement error and the data to highlight the ability of the model to explain covariation among the series.

IV. Discussion

The discussion thus far has assumed that the parameter values of the economic model are known. A natural question is whether the measures of fit discussed in this paper can form the basis for estimators of these parameters. Does it make sense, for example, to estimate unknown parameters by minimizing some function of the relative mean square error, $r_j(\omega)$ given in equation (12)? This certainly seems sensible. For example, a researcher may want to "calibrate" his model with a value of $\rho_a = .90$ rather than 1.0, because this value produces spectra closer to the estimated spectra of data over the business cycle frequencies. Yet dropping the standard statistical assumption that the economic model is correctly specified raises a number of important issues. Foremost among these is the meaning of the parameters. If the model does not necessarily describe the data, then what do the parameters measure? Presumably, the model is meant to describe certain characteristics of the data's stochastic process (the business cycle or the growth properties, for example), while ignoring other characteristics. It then makes sense to define the model's parameters as those that minimize the differences between the model and the data's stochastic process in dimensions that the model is attempting to explain. So, for example, it seems sensible to define the parameters of a growth model as those that minimize $r_j(\omega)$ over very low frequencies, or to define the parameters of a business cycle model as those that minimize $r_j(\omega)$ over business cycle frequencies. Given this definition of the parameters, constructing an analog estimator (see Manski 1988) by minimizing $\hat{r}_j(\omega)$ corresponds to a standard statistical practice.

Of course, the parameters may also be defined using other characteristics of the model and the stochastic process describing the data. For example, in standard "calibration" estimation exercises, many of the parameters are implicitly defined in terms of first moments of the data. Parameters are chosen so that the first moments of the variables in the model's steady state match the first moments of the data.

Two final points deserve mention. First, since the measures of fit developed in this paper are based on a representation that minimizes the discrepancy between the model and the data, they serve only as a bound on the fit of the model. Models with large RMSAEs do not fit the data well. Models with small RMSAEs fit the data well given certain assumptions about the correlation properties of the noise that separates the model and the data, but may fit the data poorly given other assumptions about the noise.

Finally, while this paper has concentrated on measures of fit motivated by a model of measurement error, other measures are certainly possible. For example, one measure, which like the measures in this paper uses only the autocovariances implied by the model and the data, is the expected log likelihood ratio using the normal probability density function (pdf) of the data and the model. More precisely, if $g(x)$ denotes the normal pdf constructed from the autocovariances of the data, $f(x)$ denotes the normal pdf constructed for the autocovariances implied by the model, and E_g is the expectation operator taken with respect to $g(x)$, the expected log likelihood ratio $I(g, f) = E_g\{\log[g(x)/f(x)]\}$ can be used to measure the distance between the densities $f(\cdot)$ and $g(\cdot)$; $I(g, f)$ is the Kullback-Leibler information criterion (KLIC), which plays an important role in the statistical literature on model selection (e.g., Akaike 1973) and quasi–maximum likelihood estimation (White 1982). Unfortunately, the KLIC will not be defined when $f(x)$ is singular and $g(x)$ is not; the KLIC distance between the two densities is infinite. Thus, for example, it would add no additional information on the fit of the real business cycle model analyzed in Section III beyond pointing out the singularity.

Arguably, one of the most informative diagnostics presented in this paper is the plot of the model and data spectra. For example, figures 1 and 2 show that the data spectra have mass concentrated around the business cycle frequencies, but the model spectra do not. Any metric comparing the data and model spectra may serve as a useful measure of fit. The RMSAE proposed here has the advantage that it can be interpreted like $1 - R^2$ from a regression, but any summary statistic discards potentially useful information contained in plots such as figures 1 and 2. Some practical advice, therefore, is to present both model and data spectra as a convenient way of comparing their complete set of second moments.

Appendix

To prove the proposition, first parameterize Σ_x, Σ_y, and Σ_{xy} as

$$\Sigma_x = C_x C_x', \tag{A1}$$

$$\Sigma_y = GG' + \Sigma, \tag{A2}$$

$$\Sigma_{xy} = C_x G', \tag{A3}$$

where C_x is $n \times k$ with full column rank, G is $n \times k$, and Σ is positive semidefinite. Since $\Sigma_u = \Sigma_x + \Sigma_y - \Sigma_{xy} - \Sigma_{yx}$, minimizing $\text{tr}(W\Sigma_u)$ with Σ_x and Σ_y given is equivalent to maximizing $\text{tr}(W\Sigma_{xy}) = \text{tr}(WC_xG')$. Given an arbitrary factorization of Σ_x of the form (A1), the problem is to find the $n \times k$ matrix G to maximize $\text{tr}(WC_xG')$ subject to the constraint that $\Sigma_y - GG' = \Sigma$ is positive semidefinite.

Let $\hat{G} = C_y^{-1}G$. Then $\Sigma_y - GG'$ is positive semidefinite if and only if $I_n - \hat{G}\hat{G}'$ is positive semidefinite, which in turn is true if and only if all the eigenvalues of $\hat{G}\hat{G}'$ are less than or equal to one. Since the eigenvalues of $\hat{G}\hat{G}'$ are the same as those of $\hat{G}'\hat{G}$, the problem can be written as

$$\max_{\hat{G}} \text{tr}[\hat{G}'(C_y'WC_x)] \quad \text{subject to} \quad \lambda_i(\hat{G}'\hat{G}) \le 1, \quad i = 1, \dots, k, \tag{A4}$$

where $\lambda_i(\hat{\mathbf{G}}'\hat{\mathbf{G}})$ denotes the ith eigenvalue of $\hat{\mathbf{G}}'\hat{\mathbf{G}}$, and I have used the fact that $\text{tr}(\mathbf{AB}) = \text{tr}(\mathbf{BA})$ for conformable matrices $\mathbf{A}$ and $\mathbf{B}$.

Let $\mathbf{QDR}'$ denote the singular value decomposition of $\hat{\mathbf{G}}$, where $\mathbf{Q}$ is an $n \times k$ orthogonal matrix, $\mathbf{R}$ is a $k \times k$ orthonormal matrix, and $\mathbf{D}$ is a $k \times k$ diagonal matrix with elements d_{ij}. Since $\text{tr}[\hat{\mathbf{G}}'(\mathbf{C}_y'\mathbf{WC}_x)] = \text{tr}[\mathbf{RDQ}'(\mathbf{C}_y'\mathbf{WC}_x)]$ $= \text{tr}[\mathbf{DQ}'(\mathbf{C}_y'\mathbf{WC}_x)\mathbf{R}]$, and since $\lambda_i(\hat{\mathbf{G}}'\hat{\mathbf{G}}) = d_{ii}^2$, the solution to (A4) is seen to require that $\lambda_i(\hat{\mathbf{G}}'\hat{\mathbf{G}}) = 1$, $i = 1, \ldots, k$. This implies that $\hat{\mathbf{G}}'\hat{\mathbf{G}} = I$. Write the singular value decomposition of $\mathbf{C}_y'\mathbf{WC}_x$ as $\mathbf{USV}'$; then $\text{tr}[\hat{\mathbf{G}}'(\mathbf{C}_y'\mathbf{WC}_x)] = \text{tr}(\hat{\mathbf{G}}'\mathbf{USV}') = \text{tr}(\mathbf{V}'\hat{\mathbf{G}}'\mathbf{US}) = \text{tr}(\overline{\mathbf{G}}'\mathbf{US})$, where $\overline{\mathbf{G}} = \hat{\mathbf{G}}\mathbf{V}$. Since $\overline{\mathbf{G}}'\overline{\mathbf{G}} = \mathbf{V}'\hat{\mathbf{G}}'\hat{\mathbf{G}}\mathbf{V} = I_k$, the maximization problem can be written as

$$\max_{\overline{\mathbf{G}}} \text{tr}(\overline{\mathbf{G}}'\mathbf{US}) \quad \text{subject to} \quad \overline{\mathbf{G}}'\overline{\mathbf{G}} = I_k. \tag{A5}$$

Assumptions i–iii of the proposition imply that $\mathbf{C}_y'\mathbf{WC}_x$ has full column rank so that $\mathbf{S}$ is a diagonal matrix with strictly positive diagonal elements. Thus since $\mathbf{U}'\mathbf{U} = I_k$, the maximization is achieved by $\overline{\mathbf{G}} = \mathbf{U}$. Working backward, we see that $\mathbf{G} = \mathbf{C}_y\mathbf{UV}'$, so that $\mathbf{\Sigma}_{xy} = \mathbf{C}_x\mathbf{G}' = \mathbf{C}_x\mathbf{VU}'\mathbf{C}_y'$.

Uniqueness follows since this choice of $\mathbf{\Sigma}_{xy}$ does not depend on the (arbitrary) choice of the matrix square roots, $\mathbf{C}_x$ and $\mathbf{C}_y$. To see this, let $\hat{\mathbf{C}}_y$ and $\hat{\mathbf{C}}_x$ denote other matrix square roots of $\mathbf{\Sigma}_y$ and $\mathbf{\Sigma}_x$. Then $\hat{\mathbf{C}}_y = \mathbf{C}_y\mathbf{R}_y$ and $\hat{\mathbf{C}}_x = \mathbf{C}_x\mathbf{R}_x$, where $\mathbf{R}_y$ and $\mathbf{R}_x$ are orthonormal matrices. From the analysis above, this yields $\hat{\mathbf{\Sigma}}_{xy} = \hat{\mathbf{C}}_x\hat{\mathbf{V}}\hat{\mathbf{U}}'\hat{\mathbf{C}}_y'$, where $\hat{\mathbf{U}}\hat{\mathbf{S}}\hat{\mathbf{V}}'$ is the singular value decomposition of $\hat{\mathbf{C}}_y'\mathbf{WC}_x$. By inspection, $\hat{\mathbf{U}} = \mathbf{R}_y'\mathbf{U}$, $\hat{\mathbf{S}} = \mathbf{S}$, and $\hat{\mathbf{V}} = \mathbf{R}_x'\mathbf{V}$, so that $\hat{\mathbf{\Sigma}}_{xy} = \mathbf{\Sigma}_{xy}$.

References

Akaike, H. "Information Theory and an Extension of the Maximum Likelihood Principle." In *Proceedings of the Second International Symposium on Information Theory,* edited by B. N. Petrov and F. Csaki. Budapest: Akademiai Kaido, 1973.

Altug, Sumru. "Time-to-Build and Aggregate Fluctuations: Some New Evidence." *Internat. Econ. Rev.* 30 (November 1989): 889–920.

Brillinger, David R. *Time Series: Data Analysis and Theory.* San Francisco: Holden-Day, 1981.

Campbell, John Y., and Shiller, Robert J. "The Dividend-Price Ratio and Expectations of Future Dividends and Discount Factors." *Rev. Financial Studies* 1, no. 3 (1988): 195–228.

Christiano, Lawrence J. "Why Does Inventory Investment Fluctuate So Much?" *J. Monetary Econ.* 21 (March/May 1988): 247–80.

Christiano, Lawrence J., and Eichenbaum, Martin. "Unit Roots in Real GNP: Do We Know and Do We Care?" *Carnegie-Rochester Conf. Ser. Public Policy* 32 (Spring 1990): 7–61.

———. "Current Real-Business-Cycle Theories and Aggregate Labor-Market Fluctuations." *A.E.R.* 82 (June 1992): 430–50.

Cochrane, John H. "Explaining the Variance of Price-Dividend Ratios." *Rev. Financial Studies* 5, no. 2 (1992): 243–80.

Durlauf, Steven N., and Hall, Robert E. "Measuring Noise in Stock Prices." Manuscript. Stanford, Calif.: Stanford Univ., 1989.

Geweke, John. "The Dynamic Factor Analysis of Economic Time-Series Models." In *Latent Variables in Socio-economic Models,* edited by Dennis J. Aigner and Arthur S. Goldberger. Amsterdam: North-Holland, 1977.

1040   JOURNAL OF POLITICAL ECONOMY

Haavelmo, Trygve. "The Probability Approach in Econometrics." *Econometrica* 12 (suppl.; July 1944): 1–115.
Hansen, Gary D. "Indivisible Labor and the Business Cycle." *J. Monetary Econ.* 16 (November 1985): 309–27.
Hansen, Gary D., and Sargent, Thomas J. "Straight Time and Overtime in Equilibrium." *J. Monetary Econ.* 21 (March/May 1988): 281–308.
Hansen, Lars Peter, and Jagannathan, Ravi. "Implications of Security Market Data for Models of Dynamic Economies." *J.P.E.* 99 (April 1991): 255–62.
Hansen, Lars Peter, and Sargent, Thomas J. "Formulating and Estimating Dynamic Linear Rational Expectations Models." *J. Econ. Dynamics and Control* 2 (February 1980): 7–46.
Hansen, Lars Peter, and Singleton, Kenneth J. "Generalized Instrumental Variables Estimation of Nonlinear Rational Expectations Models." *Econometrica* 50 (September 1982): 1269–86.
Hodrick, Robert J., and Prescott, Edward C. "Post-War U.S. Business Cycles: An Empirical Investigation." Manuscript. Pittsburgh: Carnegie Mellon Univ., 1980.
Howrey, E. Philip. "Stochastic Properties of the Klein-Goldberger Model." *Econometrica* 39 (January 1971): 73–87.
———. "Dynamic Properties of a Condensed Version of the Wharton Model." In *Econometric Models of Cyclical Behavior,* vol. 2, edited by Bert G. Hickman. New York: Columbia Univ. Press (for NBER), 1972.
King, Robert G.; Plosser, Charles I.; and Rebelo, Sergio T. "Production, Growth, and Business Cycles: Technical Appendix." Manuscript. Rochester, N.Y.: Univ. Rochester, 1987.
———. "Production, Growth and Business Cycles: I. The Basic Neoclassical Model." *J. Monetary Econ.* 21 (March/May 1988): 195–232. (*a*)
———. "Production, Growth and Business Cycles: II. New Directions." *J. Monetary Econ.* 21 (March/May 1988): 309–41. (*b*)
King, Robert G.; Plosser, Charles I.; Stock, James H.; and Watson, Mark W. "Stochastic Trends and Economic Fluctuations." *A.E.R.* 81 (September 1991): 819–40.
King, Robert G., and Rebelo, Sergio T. "Low Frequency Filtering and Real Business Cycle Models." *J. Econ. Dynamics and Control* (1993), in press.
Kydland, Finn E., and Prescott, Edward C. "Time to Build and Aggregate Fluctuations." *Econometrica* 50 (November 1982): 1345–70.
McCallum, Bennett T. "Real Business Cycle Models." In *Modern Business Cycle Theory,* edited by Robert J. Barro. Cambridge, Mass.: Harvard Univ. Press, 1989.
McFadden, Daniel. "Econometric Models of Probabilistic Choice." In *Structural Analysis of Discrete Data with Econometric Applications,* edited by Charles Manski and Daniel McFadden. Cambridge, Mass.: MIT Press, 1981.
Mankiw, N. Gregory. "Real Business Cycles: A New Keynesian Perspective." *J. Econ. Perspectives* 3 (Summer 1989): 79–90.
Mankiw, N. Gregory; Runkle, David E.; and Shapiro, Matthew D. "Are Preliminary Announcements of the Money Stock Rational Forecasts?" *J. Monetary Econ.* 14 (July 1984): 15–27.
Mankiw, N. Gregory, and Shapiro, Matthew D. "News or Noise: An Analysis of GNP Revisions." *Survey Current Bus.* 66 (May 1986): 20–25.
Manski, Charles F. *Analog Estimation Methods in Econometrics.* New York: Chapman and Hall, 1988.

Plosser, Charles I. "Understanding Real Business Cycle Models." *J. Econ. Perspectives* 3 (Summer 1989): 51–77.

Prescott, Edward C. "Theory Ahead of Business-Cycle Measurement." *Carnegie-Rochester Conf. Ser. Public Policy* 25 (Autumn 1986): 11–44.

Rotemberg, Julio J., and Woodford, Michael. "Oligopolistic Pricing and the Effects of Aggregate Demand on Economic Activity." *J.P.E.* 100 (December 1992): 1153–1207.

Sargent, Thomas J. "Two Models of Measurements and the Investment Accelerator." *J.P.E.* 97 (April 1989): 251–87.

Sargent, Thomas J., and Sims, Christopher A. "Business Cycle Modeling without Pretending to Have Too Much *a Priori* Economic Theory." In *New Methods in Business Cycle Research,* by Christopher A. Sims et al. Minneapolis: Fed. Reserve Bank, 1977.

Singleton, Kenneth J. "Econometric Issues in the Analysis of Equilibrium Business Cycle Models." *J. Monetary Econ.* 21 (March/May 1988): 361–86.

Soderlind, Paul. "Cyclical Properties of a Real Business Cycle Model." Manuscript. Princeton, N.J.: Princeton Univ., Dept. Econ., 1993.

Summers, Lawrence H. "Some Skeptical Observations on Real Business Cycle Theory." *Fed. Reserve Bank Minneapolis Q. Rev.* 10 (Fall 1986): 23–27.

Taylor, John B., and Uhlig, H. "Solving Nonlinear Stochastic Growth Models: A Comparison of Alternative Solution Methods." *J. Bus. and Econ. Statis.* 8 (January 1990): 1–17.

White, Halbert. "Maximum Likelihood Estimation of Misspecified Models." *Econometrica* 50 (January 1982): 1–25.

Woodford, Michael. "Stationary Sunspot Equilibria: The Case of Small Fluctuations around a Deterministic Steady State." Manuscript. Chicago: Univ. Chicago, 1986.

JOURNAL OF APPLIED ECONOMETRICS, VOL. 9, S123–S144 (1994)

STATISTICAL INFERENCE IN CALIBRATED MODELS

FABIO CANOVA

*Department of Economics, Universitat Pompeu Fabra, Balmes 132, 08008 Barcelona, Spain
and Department of Economics, Università di Catania, 95100 Catania, Italy, and CEPR*

SUMMARY

This paper describes a Monte Carlo procedure to assess the performance of calibrated dynamic general equilibrium models. The procedure formalizes the choice of parameters and the evaluation of the model and provides an efficient way to conduct a sensitivity analysis for perturbations of the parameters within a reasonable range. As an illustration the methodology is applied to two problems: the equity premium puzzle and how much of the variance of actual US output is explained by a real business cycle model.

1. INTRODUCTION

The current macroeconometrics literature has proposed two ways to confront general equilibrium rational expectations models with data. The first, an estimation approach, is the direct descendant of the econometric methodology proposed 50 years ago by Haavelmo (1944). The second, a calibration approach, finds its justification in the work of Frisch (1933) and is closely linked to the computable general equilibrium literature surveyed e.g. in Shoven and Whalley (1984).

The two methodologies share the same strategy in terms of model specification and solution. Both approaches start from formulating a fully specified general equilibrium dynamic model and in selecting convenient functional forms for preferences, technology, and exogenous driving forces. They then proceed to find a decision rule for the endogenous variables in terms of the exogenous and predetermined variables (the states) and the parameters. When the model is nonlinear, closed-form expressions for the decision rules may not exist and both approaches rely on recent advantages in numerical methods to find an approximate solution which is valid either locally or globally (see e.g. the January 1990 issue of the *Journal of Business and Economic Statistics* for a survey of the methods and Christiano, 1990, and Dotsey and Mao, 1991, for a comparison of the accuracy of the approximations).

It is when it comes to choosing the parameters to be used in the simulations and in evaluating the performance of the model that several differences emerge. The first procedure attempts to find the parameters of the decision rule that best fit the data either by maximum likelihood (ML) (see e.g. Hansen and Sargent, 1979, or Altug, 1989) or generalized method of moments (GMM) (see e.g. Hansen and Singleton, 1983, or Burnside *et al.*, 1993). The validity of the specification is examined by testing restrictions, by general goodness of fit tests or by comparing the fit of two nested models. The second approach 'calibrates' parameters using a set of alternative rules which includes matching long-run averages, using previous microevidence or *a priori* selection, and assesses the fit of the model with an informal distance criterion.

These differences are tightly linked to the questions the two approaches ask. Roughly speaking, the estimation approach asks the question 'Given that the model is true, how false is

CCC 0883–7252/94/0S0S123–22
© 1994 by John Wiley & Sons, Ltd.

Received July 1992
Revised August 1994

it?' while the calibration approach asks 'Given that the model is false, how true is it?' Implicit in the process of estimation is in fact the belief that the probability structure of a model is sufficiently well specified to provide an accurate description of the data. Because economic models are built with an emphasis on tractability, they are often probabilistically underspecified so that measurement errors or unobservable shocks are added at the estimation stage to complete their probability structure (see e.g. Hansen and Sargent, 1980, or Altug, 1989). By testing the model, a researcher takes the model seriously as a data-generating process (DGP) and examines what features of the specification are at variance with the data. A calibrationist takes the opposite view: the model, as a DGP for the data, is false. That is, as the sample size grows, it is known that the data are generated by the model will be at increasingly greater variance with the observed time series. An economic model is seen, at best, as an approximation to the true DGP which need not be either accurate or realistic and, as such, should not be regarded as a null hypothesis to be statistically tested (see Prescott, 1991, p. 5). In confronting the model with the data, a calibrationist wants to indicate the dimensions where the approximation is poor and suggest modifications to the theoretical model in order to obtain a better approximation.

Both methodologies have weak points. Model estimation involves a degree of arbitrariness in specifying which variables are unobservable or measured with error. In the limit, since all variables are indeed measured with error, no estimation seems possible and fruitful. In addition, tests of the model's restrictions may fail to indicate how to alter the specification to obtain a better fit. The limitations of the calibration approach are also well known. First, the selection criterion for parameters which do not measure long-run averages is informally specified and may lead to contradictory choices. Information used in different studies may in fact be inconsistent (e.g. a parameter chosen to match labour payments from firms in national account data may not equal the value chosen to match the labour income received by households) and the range of estimates for certain parameters (e.g. risk aversion parameter) is so large that selection biases may be important. Second, the outcomes of the simulations typically depend on the choice of unmeasured parameters. However, although some authors (see e.g. Prescott, 1991, p. 7, or Kydland, 1992, p. 478) regard a calibration exercise as incomplete unless the sensitivity of the results to reasonable perturbations of the parameters selected *a priori* or not well tied to the data is reported, such an analysis is not often performed. Third, because the degree of confidence in the results depends on both the degree of confidence in the theory *and* in the underlying measurement of the parameters and because either parameter uncertainty is disregarded or, when a search is undertaken, the number of replications typically performed is small, we must resort to informal techniques to judge the relevance of the theory.

This paper attempts to eliminate some of the weaknesses of calibration procedures while maintaining the general analytical strategy employed in calibration exercises. The focus is on trying to formalize the selection of the parameters and the evaluation process and in designing procedures for meaningful robustness analysis on the outcomes of the simulations. The technique we propose shares features with those recently described by Gregory and Smith (1991) and Kwan (1990), has similarities with stochastic simulation techniques employed in dynamic nonlinear large scale macro models (see e.g. Fair, 1991), and generalizes techniques on randomized design for strata existing in the static computable general equilibrium literature (see e.g. Harrison and Vinod, 1989).

The idea of the technique is simple. We would like to reproduce features of actual data, which is taken to be the realization of an unknown vector stochastic process, with an 'artificial economy' which is almost surely the incorrect generating mechanism for the actual data. The features we may be interested in include conditional and unconditional moments (or densities), the autocovariance function of the data, functions of these quantities (e.g. measures of relative volatility), or specific events (e.g. a recession). A model is simulated repeatedly using a Monte

Carlo procedure which randomizes over *both* the exogenous stochastic processes *and* the parameters. Parameters are drawn from a data-based density which is consistent with the information available to a simulator (which may include both time-series and cross-sectional aspects). We judge the validity of a model on its ability to reproduce a number of 'stylized facts' of the actual economy (see Friedman, 1959). The metric used to evaluate the discrepancy of the model from the data is probabilistic. We construct the simulated distribution of the statistics of interest and, taking the actual realization of the statistic as a critical value, examine (1) in what percentile of the simulated distribution the actual value lies and (2) how much of the simulated distribution is within a $k\%$ region centred around the critical value. Extreme values for the percentile (say, below $\alpha\%$ or above $(1 - \alpha)\%$) or a value smaller than k for the second probability indicates a poor fit in the dimensions examined.

The approach has several appealing features. First, it accounts for the uncertainty faced by a simulator in choosing the parameters of the model in a realistic way. Second, it has a built-in feature for global sensitivity analysis on the support of the parameter space and allows for other forms of conditional or local sensitivity analysis. Third, it provides general evaluation criteria and a simple and convenient framework to judge the relevance of the theory.

The paper is divided into six sections. The next section introduces the technique, provides a justification for the approach and describes the details involved in the implementation of the procedure. Section 3 deals with robustness analysis. Section 4 spells out the relationship with existing techniques. Two examples describing the potential of the technique for problems of practical interest appear in Section 5. Section 6 presents conclusions.

2. THE TECHNIQUE

A General Framework of Analysis

We assume that a researcher is faced with an $m \times 1$ vector of time series $\tilde{x}_t$, which are the realizations of a vector stochastic process $\bar{X}_t$ and that she is interested in reproducing features of $\bar{X}_t$ using a dynamic general equilibrium model. $\bar{X}_t$ is assumed to have a continuous but unknown distribution and moments up to the nth. For the sake of presentation we assume that the unconditional distribution of $\bar{X}_t$ is independent of t but shifts in the unconditional distribution of $\bar{X}_t$ at known points can easily be handled. $\bar{X}_t$ may include macro variables like GNP, consumption, interest rates, etc. We also assume that dynamic economic theory gives us a model expressing the endogenous variables X_t as a function of exogenous and predetermined variables Z_t (the states of the problem) and of the parameters β. Z_t may include objects like the existing capital stock, exogenous fiscal, and monetary variables or shocks to technologies and preferences. We express the model's functional relation as $X_t = f(Z_t, \beta)$. Under specific assumptions about the structure of the economy (e.g. log or quadratic preferences, Cobb–Douglas production function, full depreciation of the capital stock in the one-sector growth model), f can be computed analytically either by value function iteration or by solving the Euler equations of the model subject to the transversality condition (see e.g. Hansen and Sargent, 1979). In general, however, f cannot be derived analytically from the primitives of the problem. A large body of current literature has concentrated on the problem of finding approximations which are either locally or globally close to f for a given metric.[1]

---

[1]These include linear or log-linear expansions of f around the steady state (Kydland and Prescott, 1982; and King *et al.*, 1988), backward-solving methods (Sims, 1984; Novales, 1990), global functional expansions in polynomials (Marcet, 1992; Judd, 1992), piecewise linear interpolation methods (Coleman, 1989; Baxter, 1991) and quadrature techniques (Tauchen and Hussey, 1991).

Here we assume that either f is available analytically or that one of the existing numerical procedures has been employed to obtain a functional $\mathcal{F}$ which approximates f in some sense, i.e. $\| \mathcal{F}(Z_t, \gamma) - f(Z_t, \beta) \| < \varepsilon$, where $\gamma = \iota(\beta)$ and $\| . \|$ is a given norm. Given the model f, an approximation procedure $\mathcal{F}$, a set of parameters β, and a probability distribution for Z_t (denoted by $\kappa(Z_t)$), we can infer the model-based probability distribution for X_t.

Let $\mathcal{G}(X_t \mid \beta, f)$ be the density of the X_t vector, conditional on the parameters β and the model f, let $\pi(\beta \mid \mathcal{I}, f)$ be the density of the parameters, conditional on the information set $\mathcal{I}$ available to the simulator and the model f, and let $\mathcal{H}(X_t, \beta \mid f, \mathcal{I})$ be the joint density of simulated data and of parameters. $\mathcal{G}(X_t \mid \beta, f)$ represents the probability that a particular path for the endogenous variables will be drawn given a parametric structure for the artificial economy and a set of parameters, while $\pi(\beta \mid \mathcal{I}, f)$ summarizes the information on the parameters available to a researcher. Note that $\mathcal{G}$ is assumed to be independent of $\mathcal{I}$ and π may depend on f, i.e. if we are using a GE model we may want to use only estimates obtained with similar GE models. For a given β, X_t is random because Z_t is random, i.e. $\mathcal{G}(X_t \mid \beta, f)$ is a deterministic transformation of $\kappa(Z_t)$.

Throughout this paper we are interested in studying the behaviour of functions of simulated data (denoted by $\mu(X_t)$) under the predictive density $p(X_t \mid \mathcal{I}, f) = \int \mathcal{H}(X_t, \beta \mid f, \mathcal{I}) \, d\beta$, i.e. evaluating objects of the form:

$$E(\mu(X_t) \mid f, \mathcal{I}, \mathcal{A}, \mathcal{C}) = \int_{\mathcal{C}} \mu(X_t) p(X_t, \mathcal{I}, f) \, dX_t$$

$$= \int_{\mathcal{A}} \int_{\mathcal{C}} \mu(X_t) \mathcal{H}(X_t, \beta \mid \mathcal{I}, f) \, d\beta \, dX_t \tag{1}$$

where $\mathcal{A} \subset \mathcal{B}$ and $\mathcal{B}$ is the parameter space and $\mathcal{C}$ is the support of the exogenous variables. Let $h(\bar{x}_t)$ be the corresponding vector of functions of the actual data.

The problem of measuring the fit of the model can be summarized as follows. How likely is the model to generate $h(\bar{x}_t)$? To answer note that from equation (1) we can compute probabilities of the form $P(\nu(X_t) \in D)$, where D is a bounded set and $\nu(X_t)$ includes moments and other statistics of the simulated data. To do this let $\mu(X_t) = \chi(X_t, [X_t : \nu(X_t) \in D])$ where $\chi(X_t, S)$ is the indicator function, i.e. $\chi(X_t, S) = 1$ if $\nu(X_t) \in S$ and zero otherwise. Similarly, we can construct quantiles $q(X_t)$ by appropriately choosing D (see e.g. Geweke, 1989). Finally, we can also find a $\bar{h}$ satisfying $P[\nu(X_t) \leqslant \bar{h}] = \nu$ for any given vector ν, by appropriately selecting the indicator function.

Model evaluation then consists of several types of statements which are interchangeable and differ only in the criteria used to measure distance. First, we can compute $P[\nu(X_t) \leqslant h(\bar{x}_t)]$. In other words, we can examine the likelihood of an event (the observed realization of the summary statistics in the actual data) from the point of view of the model. Extreme values for this probability indicate a poor 'fit' in the dimensions examined. Alternatively, if we can measure the sampling variability of $h(\bar{x}_t)$, we can then choose the set D to include the actual realization of $h(\bar{x}_t)$ plus one or two standard deviations and either check whether $\bar{h}$ is in D or calculate $P[\nu(X_t) \in D]$.

Implementation

There are four technical implementation issues which deserve some discussion. The first concerns the computation of integrals like those in equation (1). When the (β, Z_t) vector is of high-dimension simple discrete grid approximations, spherical or quadrature rules quickly become infeasible since the number of function evaluations increases exponentially with the dimension of β and Z_t. In addition, unless the contours of $\mathcal{H}(X_t, \beta \mid \mathcal{I}, f)$ (and of $p(X_t \mid \mathcal{I}, f)$) are of ellipsoidal forms, grid evaluations may explore this density inefficiently. There are several feasible alternatives: one is the Monte Carlo procedure described in Geweke (1989), another is the data-augmentation procedure of Tanner and Wong (1987), a third is the 'Gibbs sampler' discussed in Gelfand and Smith (1990). Finally, we could use one of the quasi-random procedures proposed by Niederreiter (1988).

In this paper we adopt a Monte Carlo approach. After drawing with replacement i.i.d. β vectors and Z_t paths, we substitute sums over realizations for the integrals appearing in equation (1) and appeal to the strong law of large numbers for functions of i.i.d. random variables to obtain

$$\frac{1}{N} \sum_{i=1}^{N} \mu_i(X_t) \xrightarrow{\text{a.s.}} E(\mu(X_t)) \tag{2}$$

where N is the number of replications. Note that, although $\mathcal{H}$ (and p) are, in general, unknown, sampling from them can be conveniently accomplished by simulating the model repeatedly for random (Z_t, β), i.e. randomly drawing exogenous forces and selecting a parameter vector and using the decision rule to compute time paths for X_t.

Second, since in most cases the function f is unknown, $\mathcal{G}$ itself becomes unknown and the direct computation of equation (1) is infeasible. If the approximation $\mathcal{F}$ to f is accurate, we could simply neglect the error and proceed using $\mathcal{J}(X_t, \beta \mid \mathcal{I}, \mathcal{F})$ in place of $\mathcal{H}(X_t, \beta \mid \mathcal{I}, f)$ where $\mathcal{J}$ is the joint density of simulated data and parameters using the information set $\mathcal{I}$ and the approximation rule $\mathcal{F}$. However, since only little is known about the properties of approximation procedures and some have only local validity (see e.g. Christiano, 1990; Dotsey and Mao, 1991), we may want to explicitly account for the existence of an approximation error in conducting inference. In this case, following Geweke (1989), we would replace equation (1) with:

$$E(\mu(X_t) \mid f, \mathcal{I}, \mathcal{A}, \mathcal{C}) = \int_{\mathcal{A}} \int_{\mathcal{C}} \mu(X_t) \mathcal{J}(X_t, \beta \mid \mathcal{I}, \mathcal{F}) \mathcal{L}(\beta, f, \mathcal{F}) \, d\beta \, dX_t \tag{3}$$

where $\mathcal{L}(\beta, f, \mathcal{F})$ are weights which depend on the 'true' density $\mathcal{H}(X_t, \beta \mid \mathcal{I}, f)$ and on the approximation density $\mathcal{J}(X_t, \beta \mid \mathcal{I}, \mathcal{F})$. For example, if a quadratic approximation around the steady state is used, the density $\mathcal{L}$ can be chosen so that draws of Z_t inducing paths of X_t which are in the tails of $\mathcal{J}$ (i.e. paths which are very far away from steady states) receive a very small weight in the calculation of the statistics of interest.

Third, we must specify a density for the parameters of the model. We could select it on the basis of one specific data set and specify $\pi(\beta \mid \mathcal{I}, f)$ to be the asymptotic distribution of a GMM estimator (as in Burnside et al., 1993), of a simulated method of moments (SMM) estimator (as in Canova and Marrinan, 1993), or of a ML estimator of β (as in Phillips, 1991). The disadvantage of these approaches is that the resulting density measures the uncertainty surrounding β present in a particular data set and does not necessarily reflect the uncertainty faced by a researcher in choosing the parameters of the model. As Larry Christiano has pointed out to the author, once a researcher chooses the moments to match, the uncertainty surrounding estimates of β is small. The true uncertainty lies in the choice of moments to be matched and in the sources of data to be used to compute estimates.

A better approach would be to select $\pi(\beta \mid \mathcal{I}, f)$ so as to summarize efficiently all existing information, which may include point estimates of β obtained from different estimation techniques, data sets, or model specifications. El-Gamal (1993a,b) has formally solved the problem of finding such a $\pi(\beta \mid \mathcal{I}, f)$ using Bayesian methods. The resulting $\pi(\beta \mid \mathcal{I}, f)$ is the least informative pseudo-posterior density on the parameter space which is consistent with a set of constraints describing the information contained in various estimation experiments. El-Gamal suggests a Gibbs sampler algorithm to compute this density but, in practice, there are simpler ways to construct empirical approximations to this type of density. One would be to count estimates of β previously obtained in the literature and construct $\pi(\beta \mid \mathcal{I}, f)$ by smoothing the resulting histogram. For example, if one of the elements of the β vector is the risk aversion parameter, counting estimates obtained over the last 15 years from fully specified general equilibrium models and smoothing the resulting histogram, we would obtain a truncated (below-zero) bell-shaped density, centred around two and very small mass above four. Alternatively, we could take what the profession regards as a reasonable range for β and assume more or less informative densities on the support depending on available estimates. If theoretical arguments suggest that the maximum range for e.g. the risk aversion parameter is $[0, 20]$, we can put higher weights on the interval $[1, 3]$ where most of the estimates lie. If for some parameters previous econometric evidence is scant, measurement is difficult, or there are no reasons to expect that one value is more likely than others, we could assume uniform densities on the chosen support.

Available estimates of β are not necessarily independent (the same data set is used in many cases) and some are less reliable than others. Non-independent estimates are legitimate candidates to enter the information set as long as they reflect sampling variability or different estimation techniques. The influence of less reliable estimates or of estimates obtained with different model specifications can be discounted by giving them a smaller weight in constructing histograms (see also El-Gamal, 1993a,b).

Finally, in many applications the joint density of the parameter vector can be factored into the product of lower-dimensional densities. If no relationship across estimates of the various parameters exists, $\pi(\beta \mid \mathcal{I})$ is the product of univariate densities. If estimates of certain parameters are related (e.g. in the case of the discount factor and the risk aversion parameter in asset pricing models), we can choose multivariate densities for these dimensions and maintain univariate specifications for the densities of the other parameters.

To summarize, to implement the procedure we need to do the following:

- Select a reasonable (data-based) density $\pi(\beta \mid \mathcal{I}, f)$, where $\mathcal{I}$ represents the information set available to a researcher, and a density $\kappa(Z_t)$ for the exogenous processes.
- Draw vectors β from $\pi(\beta \mid \mathcal{I}, f)$ and z_t from $\kappa(Z_t)$.
- For each draw of β and z_t, generate $\{x_t\}_{t=1}^{T}$ and compute $\mu(x_t)$ using the model $x_t = f(z_t, \beta)$ or the approximation $x_t = \mathcal{F}(z_t, \gamma)$.
- Repeat the two previous steps N times.
- Construct the frequency distribution of $\mu(x_t)$, compute probabilities, quantiles and other measures of interest.

An Interpretation

The proposed framework of analysis lends itself to a simple Bayesian interpretation. In this case we treat $\pi(\beta \mid \mathcal{I}, f)$ as the prior on the parameters. The function $\mathcal{G}$ is entirely analogous to a classical likelihood function for X_t in a standard regression model. The difference is that $\mathcal{G}$ need not be the correct likelihood for $\bar{X}_t$ and need not have a closed form. Then equation (1) is the conditional expectation of $\mu(X_t)$ under the predictive density of the model and probability statements based on equation (1) can be justified using the arguments contained in Box (1980).

There is also a less orthodox interpretation of the approach which exchanges the role of $\pi(\beta \mid \mathcal{I}, f)$ and $\mathcal{G}(X_t \mid \beta, f)$ and is nevertheless reasonable. In this case $\mathcal{G}(X_t \mid \beta, f)$ is the prior and represents the *a priori* degree of confidence posed by the researcher on the time path generated by the model given the parameters while $\pi(\beta \mid \mathcal{I}, f)$ summarizes the information contained in the data. Then equation (1) is a 'pseudo-posterior' statement about the model's validity once the empirical evidence on the parameters is taken into account.

It is useful to note that, if we follow the first approach, we can relate the proposed construction of $\pi(\beta \mid \mathcal{I}, f)$ to the data-based priors employed in Meta-Analysis (see Wolf, 1986) and in the 'consensus literature' (see e.g. Genest and Zideck, 1986). El-Gamal (1993a) spells out in detail the connection with these two strands of literature.

3. ROBUSTNESS ANALYSIS

If we adopt a Monte Carlo approach to compute simulated densities for the statistics of interest, an automatic and efficient global sensitivity analysis is performed on the support of the parameter space as a by-product of the simulations. Sensitivity analysis, however, can take other more specific forms. For example, we may be interested in examining how likely $\mu(X_t)$ is to be close to $h(\bar{x}_t)$ when β is fixed at some prespecified value $\hat{\beta}$. This would be the case, for example, if β includes parameters which can be controlled by the government and $h(\bar{x}_t)$ is e.g. the current account balance of that country. In this case we could choose a path for Z_t and analyse the conditional distribution of $\mu(X_t)$ for the selected value(s) of β. Alternatively, we might wish to assess the maximal variation in $\mu(X_t)$ consistent, say, with β being within two standard deviations of a particular value. Here we choose a path for Z_t and construct paths for $\mu(X_t)$ for draws of β in the range. Finally, we may be interested in knowing which dimensions of β are responsible for particular features of the distribution of $\mu(X_t)$. For example, if the simulated distribution of $\mu(X_t)$ has a large spread or fat tails, a researcher may be interested in knowing whether technology or preference parameters are responsible for this feature. In this case we would partition β into $[\beta_1, \beta_2]$ and compute the simulated distribution of $\mu(X_t)$ conditional on $\beta_2 = \hat{\beta}_2$, where $\hat{\beta}_2$ is a prespecified value (or set of values).

So far, we have examined the robustness of the results to variations of the parameters within their support. In some cases it is necessary to study the sensitivity of the results to local perturbations of the parameters. For example, we may be interested in determining how robust the simulation results are to changes of the parameters in a small neighbourhood of a particular vector of calibrated parameters. To undertake this type of analysis we can take a numerical version of the average derivative of $\mu(X_t)$ in the neighbourhood of a calibrated vector (see Pagan and Ullah, 1991). Because global and local analyses aim at examining the sensitivity of the outcomes to perturbations in the parameters of different size they provide complementary information and should both be used as specification diagnostics for models whose parameters are calibrated.

4. A COMPARISON WITH EXISTING METHODOLOGIES

The framework of analysis in Section 2 is general enough to include simulation undertaken after the parameters are both calibrated and estimated via method of moments as special cases. To show this it is convenient to recall that $\mathcal{H}(X_t, \beta \mid \mathcal{I}, f)$ is a deterministic transformation of $Q(Z_t, \beta \mid \mathcal{I}, f) = \pi(\beta \mid \mathcal{I}, f) \kappa(Z_t)$. The two procedures can then be recovered by imposing restrictions on the shape and the location of $\pi(\beta \mid \mathcal{I}, f)$ and, in some cases, also on the shape and the location of $\kappa(Z_t)$.

S130   F. CANOVA

Calibration exercises impose a point mass for $\pi(\beta \mid \mathcal{I}, f)$ on a particular value of β (say, $\hat{\beta}$). One interpretation of this density selection is that a simulator is perfectly confident in the vector β used and does not worry about the cross-study or time-series uncertainty surrounding estimates of β. In certain situations a path for the vector of exogenous variables is also selected in advance either by drawing only one realization from their distribution or by choosing a z_t on the basis of extraneous information, e.g. inputting Solow's residuals in the model, so that $\kappa(Z_t)$ is also a singleton. In this instance, the density of $\mu(X_t)$ has a point mass and because the likelihood of the model to produce any event is either 0 or 1, we must resort to informal techniques to assess the discrepancy of simulated and actual data. In some studies the randomness in Z_t is explicitly considered, repeated draws for the exogenous variables are made for a fixed $\hat{\beta}$, and moments of the statistics of interest are computed by averaging the results over a number of simulations (see e.g. Backus *et al.*, 1989).

Simulation exercises undertaken with estimation of the parameters are also special cases of the above framework. Here $\pi(\beta \mid \mathcal{I})$ has a point mass at β^*, where β^* is either the GMM estimator, the SMM estimator (see Lee and Ingram, 1991), or the simulated quasi-maximum likelihood (SQML) estimator of β (see Smith, 1993). Simulations are typically performed by drawing one realization from $\mathcal{G}(X_t \mid \beta^*, f, \mathcal{I})$ and standard errors for $\mu(X_t)$ are computed using the asymptotic standard errors of β^* and the functional form for μ. In some cases, $\pi(\beta \mid \mathcal{I})$ is taken to be the asymptotic distribution of one of the above estimators (e.g. Canova and Marrinan, 1993). In this case, simulations are performed by drawing from $\mathcal{G}(X_t \mid \beta^*, f, \mathcal{I})\pi(\beta^* \mid \mathcal{I})$ and the distance of simulated and actual data is computed using measures of discrepancy like the ones proposed here.

In assessing the model's performance this last set of procedures has two advantages over calibration. First, they allow formal statements on the likelihood of selected parameter values to reproduce the features of interest. For example, if a four standard deviations range around the point estimate of the AR(1) parameter for the productivity disturbance is $[0\cdot84, 0\cdot92]$, then it is highly unlikely (with a probability higher than 99%) that a unit root productivity disturbance is needed to match the data. Second, they provide a set-up where sensitivity analysis can easily be undertaken (although not often performed).

These procedures, however, have also two major shortcomings. First, they impose a strong form of ignorance which does not reflect available *a priori* information. The vector β may include meaningful economic parameters which can be bounded on the basis of theoretical arguments but the range of possible β with GMM, SMM, or SQML procedures is $[-\infty, \infty]$. By appropriately selecting a hypercube for their densities a researcher can make 'unreasonable' parameter values unlikely and avoid *a posteriori* adjustments. Second, simulations conducted after parameters are estimated may not constitute an independent way to validate the model because the parameter estimates are obtained from the same data set which is used later to compare results.

Simulation procedures where parameters are selected using a mixture of calibration and estimation strategies have recently been employed by e.g. Heaton (1993) and Burnside *et al.* (1993). Here some parameters are fixed using extraneous information while others are formally estimated using moment (or simulated moment) conditions. Although these strategies allow a more formal evaluation of the properties of the model than pure calibration procedures, they face two problems. First, as in the case when the parameters are all selected using GMM, SMM, and SQML procedures, the evaluation of the model is problematic because measures of dispersion for the statistics of interest are based on one data set and do not reflect the uncertainty faced by a simulator in choosing the unknown features of the model. Second, as Gregory and Smith (1989) have pointed out, the small-sample properties of estimators obtained from these strategies may be far from reasonable unless calibrated parameters consistently estimate the true parameters. When this condition is not satisfied, estimates of the remaining parameters are sensitive to errors in pre-setting and results are misleading.

The Monte Carlo methodology we employ to evaluate the properties of the model is related to those of Kwan (1990) and Gregory and Smith (1991) but several differences need to be emphasized. First, Gregory and Smith take the model as a testable null hypothesis while this is not the case here. Second, they do not account for parameter uncertainty in evaluating the outcomes of the model. Third, because they take a calibrated version of the model as the 'truth', they conduct sensitivity analysis inefficiently, by replicating experiments for different calibrated values of the parameters. Kwan (1990) allows for parameter uncertainty in his simulation scheme, but, following an orthodox Bayesian approach, he chooses a subjective prior density for the parameters. In addition, he evaluates the outcomes of the model in relative terms by comparing two alternative specifications using a posterior-odds ratio: a model is preferred to another if it maximizes the probability that the simulated statistics are in a prespecified set.

The procedure for sensitivity analysis we proposed extends the approach that Harrison and Vinod (1989) used in deterministic computable general equilibrium models. The major difference is that in a stochastic framework parameter uncertainty is only a part of the randomness entering the model and the uncertainty characterizing the exogenous processes is important in determining the randomness of the outcomes.

To conclude, we should mention that, parallel to the literature employing Monte Carlo methods to evaluate calibrated models, there is also a branch of the literature which uses alternative tools to examine the fit of calibrated models. This is the case e.g. of Smith (1993), Watson (1993), and Canova et al. (1993) which assess the relevance of theoretical models with regression R^2's, tests based on restricted and unrestricted VARs, and encompassing procedures.

5. TWO EXAMPLES

The Equity Premium Puzzle

Mehra and Prescott (1985) suggest that an asset-pricing model featuring complete markets and pure exchange cannot simultaneously account for the average risk-free rate and the average equity premium experienced by the US economy over the sample 1889–1978 with reasonable values of the risk aversion parameter and of the discount factor.

The model they consider is a frictionless Arrow–Debreu economy with a single representative agent, one perishable consumption good produced by a single productive unit or a 'tree', and two assets, an equity share and a risk-free asset. The tree yields a random dividend each period and the equity share entitles its owner to that dividend in perpetuity. The risk-free asset entitles its owner to one unit of the consumption good in the next period only. The agent maximizes:

$$E_0 \sum_{t=0}^{\infty} \theta^t \left[\frac{c_t^{1-\omega} - 1}{1 - \omega} \right] \tag{4}$$

subject to:

$$c_t = y_t e_{t-1} + p_t^e(e_{t-1} - e_t) + f_{t-1} - p_t^f f_t \tag{5}$$

where E_0 is the mathematical expectation operator conditional on information at time zero, θ is the subjective discount factor, ω is the risk aversion parameter, c_t is consumption, y_t is the tree's dividend, p_t^e and p_t^f are the prices of the equity and the risk-free asset, and e_t and f_t are the agent's equity and risk-free asset holding at time t, Production evolves according to $y_{t+1} = x_{t+1} y_t$ where x_t, the gross growth rate, follows a two-state ergodic Markov chain with probability $P(x_{t+1} = x_j \mid x_t = x_i) = \phi_{ij}$. Defining the states of the problem as (c, i) where $y_t = c$ and $x_t = \lambda_i$, the period t equilibrium asset prices are

$$p^e(c, i) = \theta \sum_{j=1}^{2} \phi_{i,j} (\lambda_j c)^{-\omega} [p^e(\lambda_j c, j) + \lambda_j c] c^{\omega} \qquad (6)$$

$$p^f(c, i) = \theta \sum_{j=1}^{2} \phi_{i,j} \lambda_j^{-\omega} \qquad (7)$$

When the current state is (c, i), the expected equity return and the risk-free rate are:

$$R_i^e = \sum_{j=1}^{2} \phi_{i,j} \left(\frac{p^e(\lambda_j c, j) + \lambda_j c}{p^e(c, i)} - 1 \right) \qquad (8)$$

$$R_i^f = \frac{1}{p^f(c, i)} - 1 \qquad (9)$$

The unconditional (average) expected returns on the two assets are $R^e = \Sigma_{j=1}^{2} \pi_i R_i^e$, $R^f = \Sigma_{j=1}^{2} \pi_i R_i^f$, and the average equity premium is $EP = R^e - R^f$, where π_i are the Markov chain stationary probabilities, satisfying $\pi = \phi^T \pi$ and $\Sigma_i \pi_i = 1$, where $\phi^T = \phi_{j,i}$.

Mehra and Prescott specified the two states for consumption (output) to be $\lambda_1 = 1 + \mu + \nu$; $\lambda_2 = 1 + \mu - \nu$ and restricted $\phi_{1,1} = \phi_{2,2} = \phi$ and $\phi_{1,2} = \phi_{2,1} = 1 - \phi$. They calibrated the three technology parameters so that the mean, the standard deviation, and the AR(1) coefficient of the model's consumption match those of the growth rate of annual US consumption over the period 1889–1978 and searched for combinations of the preference parameters (θ, ω) in a prespecified interval to obtain values for the risk-free rate and the equity premium. Given that the average, the standard deviations, and the AR(1) coefficient of annual growth rate of US consumption are 1·018, 0·036, and −0·14, the implied values of μ, ν, and ϕ are 0·018, 0·036, and 0·43, respectively. The range for ω was selected to be [0, 10] and this choice was justified citing a number of empirical estimates of this parameter (see Mehra and Prescott, 1985, p. 154). The range for θ was chosen to be [0, 1], but simulations which produced a risk-free rate in excess of 4% were eliminated on the grounds that 4% constitutes an upper bound consistent with historical experience. The puzzle is that the *largest* equity premium generated by the model is 0·35%, which occurred in conjunction with a real risk-free rate of about 4%, while the US economy for the period 1889–1978 experienced an annual average equity premium of 6·18% and an average real risk-free rate of 0·80%.

Two hidden assumptions underlie Mehra and Prescott's procedure. First, they believe that technology parameters can be tightly estimated while the uncertainty surrounding the choice of preference parameters is substantial. Consequently, while the sensitivity of the results is explored to variations in θ and ω within the range, no robustness check is made for perturbations of the technology parameters. Second, by providing only the largest value generated, they believe that it is a sufficient statistic to characterize the puzzle.

Here we repeat their exercise with three tasks in mind: first, to study whether the uncertainty present in the selection of the technology parameters is important in determining the magnitude of the puzzle; second, to formally measure the discrepancy of the model from the data using a

STATISTICAL INFERENCE IN CALIBRATED MODELS S133

variety of statistics based on the probability distribution of outcomes of the model; third, to evaluate the contribution of two alleged solutions to the equity premium puzzle proposed in the literature.

This first example is particularly simple since we have an exact solution for the endogenous variables of the model. In addition, because the model produces values for the mean of R^f and EP, variations in X_t are entirely determined by variations in β, so that $\mathcal{H}(X_t, \beta \mid \mathcal{I}, f)$ is proportional to $\pi(\beta \mid \mathcal{I}, f)$. Therefore, once we have selected $\pi(\beta \mid \mathcal{I}, f)$, we can immediately determine the distribution of simulated means of the R^f–EP pair.

To select the density for the five parameters of the model we proceed in two steps. First, we choose a maximum range for the support of β on the basis of theoretical considerations.

Table I. Equity premium puzzle

(A) Parameter values

Basic case

θ Truncated normal, range [0·9523, 1·000], mode at 0·9708
ω $\chi^2(2)$ range [0, 10]

$$
\begin{array}{l}
\mu \\
\nu \quad \text{Uniform} \\
\phi
\end{array}
\begin{bmatrix}
-0{\cdot}0025 & 0{\cdot}0044 & 0{\cdot}0148 & 0{\cdot}0183 & 0{\cdot}0219 & 0{\cdot}0230 & 0{\cdot}0237 & 0{\cdot}0241 & 0{\cdot}0255 & 0{\cdot}0300 \\
0{\cdot}0528 & 0{\cdot}0307 & 0{\cdot}0100 & 0{\cdot}0357 & 0{\cdot}0252 & 0{\cdot}0490 & 0{\cdot}0100 & 0{\cdot}0140 & 0{\cdot}0531 & 0{\cdot}0397 \\
-0{\cdot}0700 & -0{\cdot}0500 & -0{\cdot}0100 & 0{\cdot}1100 & -0{\cdot}1800 & 0{\cdot}0600 & -0{\cdot}0400 & 0{\cdot}0400 & 0{\cdot}0700 & 0{\cdot}1100
\end{bmatrix}
$$

Experiment 1
β Truncated normal, range [0·9523, 1·040], mode at 0·9708

Experiment 2
ζ Exponential, range [0·0001, 0·2]

ξ $1 - \dfrac{\nu}{1+\mu}$ with prob ϕ; $\dfrac{1-\mu-\nu}{1+\mu}$ with prob $1 - \phi - \zeta$; $1 - \dfrac{\mu}{1+\mu}$ with prob ζ

(B) Statistics of the simulated distribution

	M-P case EP	R	Basic case EP	R	Alternative EP	R	Experiment 1 EP	R	Experiment 2 EP	R
Mean	0·0094	0·0913	0·0035	0·0702	0·0015	0·0670	0·032	−0·061	0·1087	−0·1519
S.D.	0·0067	0·0379	0·0073	0·0470	0·0032	0·0433	0·0066	0·0419	0·1808	0·3327
Skewness	0·35	−0·15	2·66	1·15	3·32	1·18	2·68	1·14	1·58	−1·57
Kurtosis	−1·08	−0·86	6·67	0·42	12·95	0·42	6·83	0·39	1·03	0·86
Maximum	0·022	0·167	0·034	0·215	0·022	0·203	0·031	0·061	0·747	0·224
5%	0·0005	0·028	0·00001	0·023	0·00001	0·023	0·00001	−0·107	0·00002	−0·938
Median	0·0084	0·094	0·0002	0·051	0·0001	0·0499	0·0001	−0·008	0·0098	0·022
95%	0·021	0·150	0·022	0·170	0·0079	0·159	0·019	0·020	0·511	0·068
Mode	0·0094	0·110	0·0008	0·052	0·0001	0·0478	0·0001	−0·074	0·007	−0·018
Pr 1	0·736		0·817		0·803		0·855		0·727	
Pr 2	0·99		0·99		0·99		0·95		0·62	
Pr 3 Q1	0·994		0·994		1·000		0·927		0·577	
Pr 3 Q2	0·000		0·000		0·000		0·000		0·295	
Pr 3 Q3	0·006		0·006		0·000		0·073		0·126	
Pr 3 Q4	0·000		0·000		0·000		0·000		0·002	

Note:
Pr 1 refers to the frequency of simulations for which the pair (R^f, EP) is in a classical 95% region around the actual values. Pr 2 reports the percentile of the simulated distribution where the actual (R^f, EP) pair lies. Pr 3 reports the probability that the model generates values in each of the four quadrants delimited by the actual pair of (R^f, EP). Q1 is the region where $R^{fs} > R^f$ and $EP^s < EP$, Q2 is the region where $R^{fs} > R^f$ and $EP^s \geqslant EP$, Q3 is the region where $R^{fs} \leqslant R^f$ and $EP^s < EP$ and Q4 is the region where $R^{fs} \leqslant R^f$ and $EP^s \geqslant EP$.

Second, we specify the joint density to be the product of five univariate densities and select each univariate density to be a smoothed version of the frequency distribution of estimates existing in the literature. The densities and their support are in panel A of Table I. The range for ω is the same as that of Mehra and Prescott and the chosen χ^2 density has a mode at 2, where most of the estimates of this parameter lie, and a low mass (smaller than 5%) for values exceeding 6. The range for θ reflects the results of several estimation studies which obtained values for the steady-state real interest rate in the range $[-0.005, 0.04]$ (see e.g. Altug, 1989; Dunn and Singleton, 1986; or Hansen and Singleton, 1983) and of simulation exercises which have a steady-state real interest rate in the range $[0, 0.05]$ (see e.g. Kandel and Stambaugh, 1990; or Mehra and Prescott, 1985). The density for θ is skewed to express the idea that a steady-state real interest rate of 2–3% or lower is more likely than a steady-state interest rate in excess of 4%. Note that although we assume that the densities of θ and ω are independent, many estimates of these two parameters are not. However, the rank correlation coefficient for the pairs of estimates is small and none of the results we present depends on this simplifying assumption.

To provide a density for μ, ν and ϕ we experimented with two procedures. The first, which is used in the basic experiment, involves taking the 10 sub-sample estimates of the mean, of the standard deviation, and of the AR(1) coefficient of the growth rate of consumption over 10-year samples contained in Mehra and Prescott (1985, p. 147) as characterizing reasonable consumption processes and then constructing a uniform discrete density over these triplets. The second involves dividing the growth rates of consumption over the 89 years of the sample into two states (above and below the mean), estimating a measure of dispersion for the first two moments and for the AR(1) coefficient of the growth rate of consumption in each state and directly inputting these estimates into the model. In this case simulations are performed by assuming a joint normal density for the mean, the standard deviation, and AR(1) coefficient in each state centred around the point estimate of the parameters and maximum support within two standard deviations of the estimate.

Figures 1–4 present scatterplots of the simulated pairs (R^f, EP) when 10,000 simulations are performed. We summarize the features of the joint distribution in panel B of Table I using a

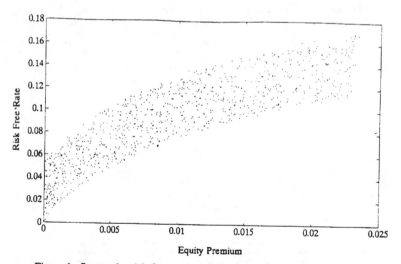

Figure 1. Scatterplot risk-free rate-equity premium: Mehra–Prescott case

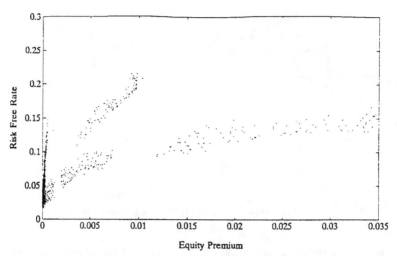

Figure 2. Scatterplot risk-free rate-equity premium: basic case

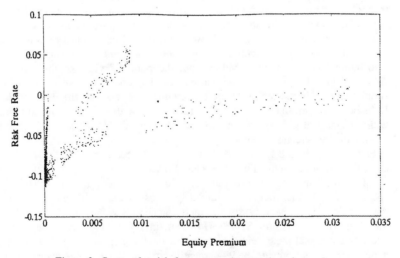

Figure 3. Scatterplot risk-free rate-equity premium: beta > 1 case

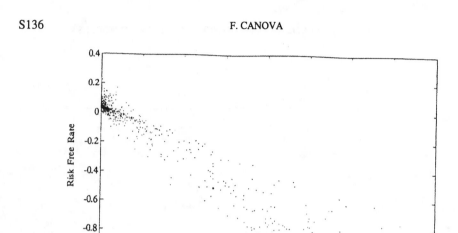

Figure 4. Scatterplot risk-free rate-equity premium: Reitz case

number of statistics. To evaluate the discrepancy of the model from the data we report (1) the probability that the model generates values for (R^f, EP) which fall within a two standard deviation band of the actual mean, (2) the percentile contour of the simulated distribution where the actual means of (R^f, EP) lies, and (3) the probability that the simulated pair is in each of the four quadrants of the space delimited by the actual means of (R^f, EP).

Figure 1 reports the scatterplot obtained with the Mehra and Prescott specification (i.e. when technology parameters are fixed and we draw replications from the densities of θ and ω only). It is necessary to check that the maximum value of the equity premium consistent with a risk free-rate not exceeding 4% is only 0·0030, confirming Mehra and Prescott's conclusion. Also for this specification,the distribution of the model's outcomes is uniform and the mode of the joint distribution (the most likely value from the point of view of the model) is at $R^f = 0·110$, $\text{EP} = 0·0094$. The probabilistic measures of discrepancy suggest that a large portion of the simulations are in the region where the simulated R^f exceeds the mean of R^f and the simulated EP is below the mean of EP we find in the data, that about 73% of the simulations produce pairs within a classical 95% ball around the actual means of (R^f, EP), and that the actual mean pair is outside the 99 percentile contour.

Figure 2 reports the scatterplot obtained with the basic specification of the model. Also in this case, the puzzle, as defined by Mehra and Prescott, is evident: if we set a 4% upper bound to the risk-free rate, the maximum equity premium generated is only 0·0038. However, with this specification, the distribution is bimodal and most of the simulated pairs lie on a ridge parallel to the R^f axis. The probability that the model generates values in a ball centred around the actual means of (R^f, EP) is now 81·4%. However, in 100% of the cases the simulated risk-free rate exceeds the actual mean and the simulated equity premium is below the actual mean and the actual pair still lies outside the 99 percentile contour of simulated distribution.

To examine whether the selection of the density for the technology parameters has effects on the results, we also conducted simulations using the alternative distribution for these parameters. No substantial changes emerge. For example, the probability that the model generates pairs in a ball centred around the actual means of (R^f, EP) is $80 \cdot 3\%$ and the maximum value for EP compatible with a R^f not exceeding 4% is $0 \cdot 0025$.

Several conclusions can be drawn from this first set of exercises. First, even after taking into account the uncertainty surrounding estimates of the technology parameters, the puzzle remains regardless of the way it is defined (maximum values, modes, or contour probabilities): the model cannot generate (R^f, EP) pairs which match what we see in the data. Second, once the uncertainty surrounding estimates of the technology parameters is taken into account, the simulated distributions are bimodal, highly left skewed, and have a fat left tail, indicating that lower than average values are more probable and that very small values have nonnegligible probability. Third, the simulated risk-free rate is always in excess of the actual one, a result that Weil (1990) has termed the risk-free rate puzzle. Fourth, while the model fails to generate values for (R^f, EP) which replicate the historical experience, in more than 80% of the simulations it produces pairs which are within two standard deviations of the actual means.

Next, we conduct two exercises designed to examine the contribution of the modifications suggested by Kocherlakota (1990), Benninga and Protopapadakis (1990), and Rietz (1988) to the solution of the puzzle. The first experiment allows the discount factor θ to take on values greater than 1. The justification is that, in a growing economy, reasonable values for the steady-state real interest rate can be obtained even with θ greater than 1. In this experiment we still maintain the truncated normal density for θ used in the baseline case but increase the upper value for its range to $1 \cdot 04$ and allow about 10% of the density in the region above 1.0.

The second experiment assumes the presence of a third unlikely crash state where consumption falls substantially.[2] The justification for including a third state is that in the Great Depression consumption fell substantially and excluding such a state may have important implications on the results (a conclusion denied by Mehra and Prescott, 1988). With this specification there are two new parameters which cannot be measured from available data: ζ, the probability of a crash state and ξ, the percentage fall in consumption in the crash state. Rietz (1988) searched over the *a priori* ranges of $[0 \cdot 0001, 0 \cdot 2]$ and $[\mu/(1+\mu), 1 - \nu/(1+\mu)]$ and examined the magnitude of the maximum simulated equity premium that the model consistent with a simulated risk-free rate below 4%. We maintain these ranges in our experiment and assume on these supports an exponential density for ζ and a three-point discrete density for ξ summarizing the three cases examined by Rietz.

Allowing the discount factor to take on values greater than 1 goes a long way towards reducing the discrepancy of the model from the data (see Figure 3) since it shifts the univariate distribution of R^f towards negative values (the minimum and maximum values of R^f are now $(-0 \cdot 084, 0 \cdot 0.092)$. For example, the probability that the model generates pairs in a ball centred around the actual means of (R^f, EP) is now $85 \cdot 7\%$ and in only $7 \cdot 4\%$ of the cases is the simulated risk-free rate in excess of the actual means. Because of this shift in the univariate distribution of R^f, the maximum value of EP consistent with a risk-free rate below 4% is now $0 \cdot 031$. Despite these differences, the location and the shape of the univariate distribution of EP are unaffected. Hence, although the equity premium puzzle is 'solved' when defined in terms of the maximum simulated EP consistent with a simulated R^f below 4%, it is still very evident when we look at the distributional properties of the simulated EP.

---

[2]The three consumption states are $\lambda_1 = 1 + \mu + \nu$, $\lambda_2 = 1 + \mu - \nu$, $\lambda_3 = \xi * (1 + \mu)$ and the transition matrix has elements: $\phi_{1,1} = \phi_{2,2} = \phi$; $\phi_{1,2} = \phi_{2,1} = 1 - \phi - \zeta$, $\phi_{1,3} = \phi_{2,3} = \zeta$, $\phi_{3,1} = \phi_{3,2} = 0.5$, $\phi_{3,3} = 0.0$. Note that the experiment is conceptually different from the previous ones since there are two extra degrees of freedom (the new parameters ξ and ζ) and no extra moments to be matched.

The second modification is much less successful (see Figure 4). It does shift the univariate distribution of EP to the right (the mode of 0·035) and increases the dispersion of simulated EPs but it achieves this at the cost of shifting the distribution of R^f towards unrealistic negative value (the mean is −0·15 and the 90% range is [−0·940, 0·068]) and of scattering the simulated (R^f, EP) pairs all over the place. For example, the probability that the simulated pair is in a ball centred around the actual means of (R^f, EP) decreases to 72·7% and the probabilities that the model generates values in each of the four quadrants delimited by the actual means of (R^f, EP) are almost identical. Finally, the maximum EP consistent with a R^f below 4% is 0·747. Therefore, adding a crash state shifts the mode and stretches and tilts the shape of the joint simulated distribution. Roughly speaking, too many (R^f, EP) configurations now have equal probability, and this weakens the ability of the theory to provide a coherent answer to the question posed.

Technology Shocks and Cyclical Fluctuations in GNP

Kydland and Prescott (1982) showed that a one-sector growth model driven by technology shocks calibrated to reproduce the statistical properties of Solow residuals explains about 70% of the variance of per capita US output. This result has spurred much of the subsequent literature which tries to account for business cycle regularities in models where monetary impulses play no role (the so-called real business cycle literature). Kydland and Prescott's initial estimate has been refined by adding and subtracting features to the basic model (see Hansen, 1985) but the message of their experiment remains: a model where technology shocks are the only source of disturbance explains a large portion of the variability of per capita US output.

Recently, Eichenbaum (1991) has questioned this assertion because 'decisions based solely on the point estimate of λ_y are whimsical (where $\lambda_y = \text{var}(y_t^s)/\text{var}(y_t)$ and $\text{var}(y_t^s)$ and $\text{var}(y_t)$ are the variance of the cyclical component of simulated and actual output) and suggests that 'the model and the data, taken together, are almost completely uninformative about the role of technology shocks in generating fluctuations in US output' (pp. 614–615). Using an exactly identified GMM procedure to estimate the free parameters, he finds that the model explains anywhere between 5% and 200% of the variance of per capita US output.

In this section we repeated Eichenbaum's exercise with three goals in mind. First, we are interested in knowing that is the most likely value of λ_y from the point of view of the model (i.e. in locating the mode of the simulated distribution). Second, we want to provide confidence bands for λ_y which reflect the uncertainty faced by a researcher in choosing the parameters of the model (not the uncertainty present in the data, as in Eichenbaum). Third, we wish to verify whether normal confidence bands appropriately describes the uncertainty surrounding point estimates of λ_y, and examine which feature of the model make deviations from normality more evident.

The model is the same as Eichenbaum's and is a simple variation of Hansen's (1985) model which allows for deterministic growth via labour-augmenting technological progress. The social planner of this economy maximizes

$$E_0 \sum_{t=0}^{\infty} \theta^t [\log(c_t) + \psi(T - h_t)] \qquad (10)$$

subject to:

$$c_t + k_{t+1} - (1 - \delta)k_t \leqslant A_t k_t^{1-\alpha} (\gamma^t h_t)^\alpha \qquad (11)$$

where c_t is per capital consumption, $T - h_t$ is leisure, and k_t the capital stock. When δ is different from 1, a closed-form stationary solution to the problem does not exist. Here we compute an approximate decision rule for the endogenous variables using a loglinear expansion around the steady state after variables have been linearly detrended as in King *et al.* (1988), but we neglect the approximation error in constructing probability statements on the outcomes of the model (i.e. we use $\mathcal{J}(X_t, \beta \mid \mathcal{I}, \mathcal{F})$ and no weighting).

There are seven parameters in the model, five deep (δ, the depreciation rate of capital; β, the subjective discount rate; ψ, leisure's weight in the utility function; α, labour's share in output; γ, the constant unconditional growth rate of technology) and two which appear only because of the auxiliary assumptions we made on the stochastic process for technology shocks (ρ, the AR parameter and σ the standard deviation of the shock). Hansen (1985) calibrated these seven parameters (the values are in the first column of panel A of Table II) and found that $\lambda_y \approx 1$. Eichenbaum (1991) estimated all parameters except β (which is calibrated) using a method of moments estimator (estimates and standard deviations are in the second column of panel A of Table II) and found (1) a point estimate of λ_y of 0·80, (2) a large standard deviation about the point estimate of λ_y due primarily to the uncertainty surrounding estimates of ρ and σ, and (3) a strong sensitivity of the point estimate of λ_y to small perturbations in the parameter vector used.

Table II. Technology shocks and cyclical fluctuations in GNP

(A) Parameter values

Hansen (1985)		Eichenbaum (1991)	Canova (1994)
θ	0·99	0·9926	Truncated normal, range [0·9855; 1·002], mode 0·9926
ϕ	2·60	3·6779 (0·0003)	Endogenous
α	0·64	0·6553 (0·0570)	Uniform [0·50; 0·75]
γ	1·00	1·0041 (0·0003)	Normal (1·0002, 0·001)
δ	0·25	0·0209 (0·0003)	Uniform [0·02; 0·03]
ρ	0·95	0·9772 (0·0289)	Normal (0·95, 0·01)
σ	0·00712	0·0072 (0·0012)	Truncated χ^2, range [0; 0·0091], mean 0·0073

(B) Statistics of the simulated distribution

Mean	0·8775
S.D.	0·7635
Skewness	1·9802
Kurtosis	4·4083
Minimum	0·1566
Maximum	7·2355
5%	0·2261
Median	0·5949
95%	2·6018
Mode	0·9046
Pr 1	0·427
Pr 2	0·673

Note:
Estimated standard errors are in parentheses. Pr 1 refers to the frequency of simulations for which the variance of simulated output is in a classical 95% region around the actual value of the variance of detrended output. Pr 2 reports the percentile of the simulated distribution where the point estimate of the actual variance of output lies.

S140   F. CANOVA

In the exercise we conduct, we assume that $\pi(\beta \mid \vartheta, f)$ is the product of seven univariate densities. Their specification appear in the third column of panel A of Table II. The range for the quarterly discount factor corresponds to the one implied by the annual range used in the previous example and the density is the same. δ is chosen so that the annual depreciation rate of the capital stock is uniformly distributed between 8% and 12% per year. The range is selected because in simulation studies δ is commonly set to 0·025, which corresponds to a 10% annual depreciation rate, while estimates of this parameter lie around this value (e.g. McGratten *et al.*, 1991, have a quarterly value of 0·0310 and a standard deviation of 0·0046, while Burnside *et al.*, 1993, have a quarterly value of 0·0209 and a standard deviation of 0·0003). The range for α reflects calculations appearing in Christiano (1988) where, depending on how proprietors' income is treated, the share of total output paid to capital varies between 0·25 and 0·43, and the estimate obtained, among others, in McGratten *et al.* (1991). We chose the densities for ρ and σ as in Eichenbaum because the econometric evidence on these two parameters is scant andthe values used in most simulation studies fall within a one standard deviation band around the mean of the assumed density (see e.g. Kydland and Prescott, 1982; Hansen, 1985). Finally, T is fixed at 1369 hours per quarter, the density for γ matches the quarterly distribution of unconditional quarterly growth rates of US output for the period 1950–1990, and ψ is endogenously chosen so that the representative household spends between one sixth and one third of its time working in the steady state.

We performed 1000 simulations with time series of length $T = 124$ and filtered both simulated and actual GNP data with the Hodrick and Prescott filter.[3] The results appear in panel B of Table II and in Figure 5, where we present a smoothed version of the simulated distribution of λ_y. The distribution is scaled so that with the point estimates of the parameters used by Eichenbaum $\lambda_y = 0·80$. The implied value of λ_y using Hansen's parameters is 0·84.

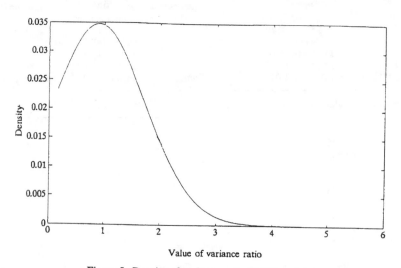

Figure 5. Density of variance ratio: HP filtered data

---

[3]We use the Hodrick and Prescott filter to maintain comparability with previous work. The results obtained when the data are linearly detrended or first-order differenced are not substantially different.

STATISTICAL INFERENCE IN CALIBRATED MODELS   S141

The mode of the distribution of λ_y is at 0.9046, the mean at 0.8775, and the median at 0.5949. The dispersion around these measures of location is very large. For example, the standard deviation is 0.7635 and the 90% range of the distribution is $[0.2261, 2.6018]$. The simulated distribution is far from normal and its right tail tends to be very long. Hence the range of reasonable values of λ_y is very large, and, as in Eichenbaum, small perturbations in the parameter vector induce large variations in the variance ratio. In addition, normal confidence bands do not appropriately characterize the uncertainty surrounding the outcomes of the model.

Several other features of the simulated distribution are worth mentioning. First, in 67·3% of the cases the variance of simulated output is smaller than the variance of actual output. Second, in 42·7% of the simulations the variance of simulated output is within a 95% confidence interval centred around the estimate of the variance of actual output. Third, if we select $v = 0.5$ and look for the $\hat{\lambda}$ satisfying $\Pr(\lambda_{y_i} \leqslant \hat{\lambda}) = 0.5$, i.e. $\hat{\lambda}$ is the median of the simulated distribution, we find that the median value of the variance of simulated GNP is outside the 95% normal confidence interval for the variance of actual GNP.

When we ask which parameter is responsible for the wide dispersion in the estimates of λ_y, we find that it is the location and width of the support of ρ which induce this feature in the distribution of λ_y. For example, assuming that the density of ρ has a point mass at 0.94 and maintaining the same densities for the other parameters, we find that location measures of the simulated distribution of λ_y decrease (the mode is now at 0.792) and the standard deviation drops to 0.529. Similar conclusions are obtained by shifting the range of ρ towards 0.90 or by cutting the range of possible ρ in half without changing the mean value. Hence, as in Eichenbaum, we find that it is the uncertainty present in the choice of the parameters of the exogenous processes rather than the uncertainty present in the selection of the deep parameters of the model that is responsible for the large spread in the distribution of λ_y.

6. CONCLUSIONS

This paper describes a Monte Carlo procedure to evaluate the properties of calibrated general equilibrium models. The procedure formalizes the choice of the parameters and the evaluation of the properties of the model while maintaining the basic approach used in calibration exercises. It also realistically accounts for the uncertainty faced by a simulator in choosing the parameters of the model. The methodology allows for global sensitivity analysis for parameters chosen within the range of existing estimates and evaluates the discrepancy of the model from the data by attaching probabilities to events a simulator is interested in characterizing. The approach is easy to implement and includes calibration and simulation exercises conducted after the parameters are estimated by simulation and GMM techniques as special cases. We illustrate the usefulness of the approach as a tool to evaluate the performance of theoretical models with two examples which have received much attention in the recent macroeconomic literature: the equity premium puzzle and the ability of a real business cycle model to reproduce the variance of actual US output. Finally, it is worth noting that for problems of moderate size, the computational complexity of the procedure is limited. For both examples presented the entire Monte Carlo routine required about a minute on a 486-33 MHz machine using RATS386 programs.

ACKNOWLEDGEMENTS

Part of this research was undertaken while the author was also associated with the European University Institute, Florence. The author has benefited from the comments and the suggestions

S142   F. CANOVA

of a large number of colleagues, including two anonymous referees, David Backus, Larry Christiano, Frank Diebold, Javier Diaz, Mahmoud El-Gamal, John Geweke, Eric Ghysels, Bruce E. Hansen, Gary Hansen, Jane Marrinan, Yaw Nyarko, Adrian Pagan, Franco Peracchi, Victor Rios, Gregor Smith, Herman Van Dijk, and Randall Wright. He would also like to thank the participants of seminars at Brown, European University Institute, NYU, Montreal, Rochester, Penn, University of Rome, Carlos III Madrid, Free University Bruxelles, CERGE, University of Minnesota, University of Maryland, Summer Meetings of the North American Econometric Society and the Conference on 'Econometric Inference Using Simulation Techniques' held in Rotterdam on 5–6 June 1992 for useful discussions.

REFERENCES

Altug, S. (1989), 'Time to build and aggregate fluctuations: some new evidence', *International Economic Review*, **30**, 889–920.

Backus, D., A. Gregory and A. Zin (1989), 'Risk premiums in the terms structure: evidence from artificial economies', *Journal of Monetary Economics*, **24**, 371–399.

Baxter, M. (1991), 'Approximating suboptimal dynamic equilibria: an Euler equation approach', *Journal of Monetary Economics*, **27**, 173–200.

Benninga, S. and A. Protopapadakis (1990), 'Leverage, time preference, and the equity premium puzzle', *Journal of Monetary Economics*, **25**, 49–58.

Box, G. (1980), 'Sampling and Bayes inference in scientific modelling and robustness', *Journal of the Royal Statistical Society*, Ser. A, **143**, 383–430.

Burnside, C., M. Eichenbaum and S. Rebelo (1993), 'Labor hoarding and the business cycle', *Journal of Political Economy*, **101**, 245–273.

Canova, F. and J. Marrinan (1993), 'Profits, risk and uncertainty in foreign exchange markets', *Journal of Monetary Economics*, **32**, 259–286.

Canova, F., M. Finn and A. Pagan (1993), 'Evaluating a real business cycle model', forthcoming, in C. Hargreaves (ed.), *Nonstationary Time Series Analyses and Cointegration*, Oxford: Oxford University Press.

Christiano, L. (1988), 'Why does inventory investment fluctuate so much?' *Journal of Monetary Economics*, **21**, 247–280.

Christiano, L. (1990), 'Solving the stochastic growth model by linear quadratic approximation and by value function iteration', *Journal of Business and Economic Statistics*, **8**, 23–26.

Coleman, W. (1989), 'An algorithm to solve dynamic models', Board of Governors of the Federal Reserve System, International Finance Division, Discussion Paper No. 351.

Dotsey, M. and C.S. Mao (1991), 'How well do linear approximation methods work? Results for suboptimal dynamic equilibria', *Journal of Monetary Economics*, **29**, 25–58.

Dunn, D. and K. Singleton (1986), 'Modelling the term structure of interest rates under non-separable utility and durability of goods', *Journal of Financial Economics*, **17**, 27–55.

Eichenbaum, M. (1991), 'Real business cycle theory: wisdom or whimsy?' *Journal of Economic Dynamic and Control*, **15**, 607–621.

El-Gamal, M. (1993a), 'The extraction of information from multiple point estimates', forthcoming in *Journal of Nonparametric Statistics*.

El-Gamal, M. (1993b), 'A Bayesian interpretation of extremum estimators', manuscript, California Institute of Technology.

Fair, R. (1991), 'Estimating event probabilities from macroeconomic models using stochastic simulations', Yale University, manuscript.

Friedman, M. (1959), *Essays in Positive Economics*, New York: Aldine Press.

Frisch, R. (1933), 'Propagation problems and impulse problems in dynamics economies', in *Economic Essays in Honor of Gustav Cassel*, London.

Geweke, J. (1989), 'Bayesian inference in econometric models using Monte Carlo integration', *Econometrica*, **57**, 1317–1339.

Gelfand, A. and A. Smith (1990), 'Sampling based approaches to calculating marginal densities', *Journal of the American Statistical Association*, **85**, 398–409.

Genest, C. and M. Zidak (1986), 'Combining probability distributions: a critique and an annotated bibliography', *Statistical Science*, **1**, 114–148.

Gregory, A. and G. Smith (1989), 'Calibration as estimation', *Econometric Reviews*, **9**(1), 57–89.

Gregory, A. and G. Smith (1991), 'Calibration as testing: inference in simulated macro models', *Journal of Business and Economic Statistics*, **9**(3), 293–303.

Haavelmo, G. (1944), 'The probability approach in econometrics', *Econometrica*, **12**, Supplement.

Hansen, G. (1985), 'Indivisible labor and the business cycle', *Journal of Monetary Economics*, **16**, 309–328.

Hansen, L. and T. Sargent (1979), 'Formulating and estimating dynamic linear rational expectations models', *Journal of Economic Dynamic and Control*, **2**, 7–46.

Hansen, L. and K. Singleton (1983), 'Stochastic consumption, risk aversion and temporal behavior of asset returns', *Journal of Political Economy*, **91**, 249–265.

Harrison, G. and H. D. Vinod (1989), 'Sensitivity analysis of applied general equilibrium models: completely randomized factorial sampling designs', University of New Mexico, manuscript.

Heaton, J. (1993), 'The interaction between time nonseparable preferences and time aggregation', *Econometrica*, **61**, 353–381.

Journal of Business and Economic Statistics, January 1990.

Judd, K. (1992), 'Projection methods for solving aggregate growth models', *Journal of Economic Theory*, **58**, 410–452.

Kandel, S. and R. Stambaugh (1990), 'Expectations and volatility of consumption and asset returns', *Review of Financial Studies*, **3**, 207–232.

King, R., C. Plosser and S. Rebelo (1988), 'Production, growth and business cycles: I and II', *Journal of Monetary Economics*, **21**, 195–232 and 309–342.

Kocherlakota, N. (1990), 'On the discount factor in growth economies', *Journal of Monetary Economics*, **25**, 45–48.

Kydland, F. (1992), 'On the econometrics of world business cycles', *European Economic Review*, **36**, 476–482.

Kydland, F. and E. Prescott (1982), 'Time to build and aggregate fluctuations', *Econometrica*, **50**, 1345–1370.

Kydland, F. and E. Prescott (1991), 'The econometrics of the general equilibrium approach to business cycles', *The Scandinavian Journal of Economics*, **93**(2), 161–178.

Kwan, Y. K. (1990), 'Bayesian calibration with an application to a non-linear rational expectation two country model', mimeo, University of Chicago Business School.

Lee, B.S. and B. Ingram (1991), 'Simulation estimators of time series models', *Journal of Econometrics*, **47**(2/3), 197–206.

Marcet, A. (1992), 'Solving nonlinear stochastic models by parametrizing expectations: an application to asset pricing with production', Universitat Pompeu Fabra, Working Paper 5.

Mehra, R. and E. Prescott (1985), 'The equity premium: a puzzle', *Journal of Monetary Economics*, **15**, 145–162.

Mehra, R. and E. Prescott (1988), 'The equity risk premium: a solution?' *Journal of Monetary Economics*, **22**, 133–136.

McGratten, E., R. Rogerson and R. Wright (1991), 'Estimating the stochastic growth model with household production', Federal Reserve Bank of Minneapolis, manuscript.

Niederreiter, H. (1988), 'Quasi Monte Carlo methods for multidimensional numerical integration', *International Series of Numerical Mathematics*, **85**, 157–171.

Novales, A. (1990), 'Solving nonlinear rational expectations models: a stochastic equilibrium model of interest rates', *Econometrica*, **58**, 93–111.

Pagan, A. and A. Ullah (1991), 'Nonparametric estimation', University of Rochester, manuscript.

Phillips, P.C.B. (1991), 'To criticize the critics: an objective Bayesian analysis of stochastic trends', *Journal of Applied Econometrics*, **6**(4), 333–354.

Prescott, E. (1991), 'Real business cycle theories: what have we learned?' Federal Research of Minneapolis, Working Paper 486.

Reitz, T. (1988), 'The equity risk premium: a solution', *Journal of Monetary Economics*, **22**, 117–132.

Shoven, J. and J. Whalley (1984), 'Applied general equilibrium models of taxation and international trade: an introduction and survey', *Journal of Economic Literature*, **22**, 1007–1051.

Sims, C. (1984), 'Solving nonlinear stochastic equilibrium models backward', University of Minnesota, manuscript.

Smith, T. (1993), 'Estimating nonlinear time series models using simulated VAR', *Journal of Applied Econometrics*, **8**, s63–s84.

Tanner, M. and W. Wong (1987), 'The calculation of posterior distributions by data augmentation', *Journal of the American Statistical Association*, **87**, 528–550.

Tauchen, G. and R. Hussey (1991), 'Quadrature based methods for obtaining approximate solutions to integral equations of nonlinear asset pricing models', *Econometrica*, 59, 371–397.

Watson, M. (1993), 'Measures of fit for calibrated models', *Journal of Political Economy*, **101**, 1011–1041.

Weil, P. (1990), 'The equity premium puzzle and the risk free puzzle', *Journal of Monetary Economics*, **24**, 401–421.

Wolf, F. (1986), *Meta-Analysis: Quantitative Methods for Research Synthesis*, Beverly Hills, CA: Sage.

INTERNATIONAL ECONOMIC REVIEW
Vol. 36, No. 2, May 1995

SENSITIVITY ANALYSIS AND MODEL EVALUATION IN SIMULATED DYNAMIC GENERAL EQUILIBRIUM ECONOMIES*

By Fabio Canova[1]

This paper describes a Monte Carlo procedure to evaluate dynamic nonlinear general equilibrium macro models. The procedure makes the choice of parameters and the evaluation of the model less subjective than standard calibration techniques, it provides more general restrictions than estimation by simulation approaches and provides a way to conduct global sensitivity analysis for reasonable perturbations of the parameters. As an illustration the technique is applied to three examples involving different models and statistics.

1. INTRODUCTION

A growing body of research in the applied macroeconomic literature uses simulation techniques to derive the time series properties of nonlinear stochastic general equilibrium models, to compare them to real world data and to evaluate policy options (see e.g. King, Plosser, and Rebelo 1988, or Cooley and Hansen 1990). In implementing numerical analyses of general equilibrium models, one has to overcome four hurdles. First, an economy must be specified and functional forms for its primitives selected. Second, a decision rule for the endogenous variables in terms of the exogenous (and predetermined) variables and of the parameters must be computed. Third, given the probability structure of the economy, values for the parameters must be chosen. Fourth, the closeness of functions of simulated and the actual data must be assessed in a metric which is relevant to the problem and policy conclusions, if any, should be drawn.

While models are often specified with an eye to analytical tractability and there has been progress in developing techniques to numerically approximate unknown decision rules for the endogenous variables (see e.g. Sims 1984, Coleman 1989, Novales 1990, Baxter 1991, Tauchen and Hussey 1991, Judd 1992, Marcet 1992 and the January 1990 issue of the *Journal of Business and Economic Statistics*), surprisingly little attention has been paid to the problems connected with the other two steps of the simulations. In particular, the selection of the parameters and the evaluation of the simulation results have been undertaken using procedures which

* Manuscript received October 1991; revised November 1994.

[1] I would like to thank David Backus, Javier Diaz, Frank Diebold, John Geweke, Eric Ghysels, Gary Hansen, Bruce E. Hansen, Jane Marrinan, Yaw Nyarko, Adrian Pagan, Franco Peracchi, Victor Rios-Rull, Gregor Smith, Herman van Dijk, Randall Wright, two anonymous referees, and the participants of seminars at Brown University, European University Institute, New York University, University of Montreal, University of Rochester, University of Pennsylvania, University of Rome and Carlos III Madrid for comments and suggestions.

lack statistical foundations (exceptions include Smith 1993, Burnside, Eichenbaum, and Rebelo 1993).

Starting with Kydland and Prescott (1982) it has been common to use a "calibration" methodology which typically consists of three steps: (i) select the parameters of the model using an array of criteria which range from matching long run averages, consistency with estimates obtained in the micro literature and a priori settings, (ii) represent the properties of actual data with simple statistics (the so-called "stylized facts") which are relatively insensitive to approximation and measurement errors, (iii) evaluate the quantitative properties of the model informally using a metric which is specific to the researcher and the question being asked (see Gregory and Smith 1993 and Kim and Pagan 1993 for detailed surveys of the methodology). Calibration procedures have been justified in different ways. Shoven and Whalley (1984) argue that calibration is a tractable procedure to convert general equilibrium structures from abstract representations into realistic models of actual economies. Jorgenson (1984) indicates that it is the only feasible alternative when it is impossible to simultaneously estimate the parameters without requiring an unrealistically large number of observations or overly severe identifying restrictions. Kydland and Prescott (1982) suggest that it is a reasonable way to assess the quality of a model when measurement errors are present and when its abstract nature is likely to result in a sure rejection when formally tested. Finally, Kydland and Prescott (1991) suggest that calibration is the natural heir of the original quantitative approach advocated by Frisch (1933).

Although popular among theorists, calibration procedures have always made econometricians uneasy. With the advent of modern computer technology, tractability and size limitations are no longer a stumbling block to the use of estimation methods. But apart from the issue of estimation (thoroughly discussed in Gregory and Smith 1989), there are other compelling reasons for considering the conclusions obtained with calibration procedures debatable.

The parameters used in simulations are typically chosen either to reproduce the long run properties of a particular data set or from existing econometric evidence. The former procedure is problematic since information used in different studies may be inconsistent (e.g. a parameter chosen to match average labor payments from firms in national account data may not equal the value chosen to match the average labor income received by households). The latter is dubious because existing evidence is contradictory and because the range of estimates for certain parameters (e.g. risk aversion) is so large that selection biases may be important. In addition, the micro studies that are cited to support particular parameter choices, may have obtained estimates using model specifications which are inconsistent with those imposed in the model under consideration (such as completeness versus incompleteness of markets or general versus partial equilibrium).

Because no uncertainty is typically allowed in the selection of the parameters and the number of replications typically performed is small, the results of the simulations can not be corroborated with formal statements on the range of possible outcomes of the model. Therefore, one must resort to informal techniques to judge the closeness of simulated and actual data and to evaluate policy alternatives. Moreover, although certain parameters are crucial in determining the conclusions of the study, results are often reported without any sensitivity analysis on how summary statistics change with reasonable perturbations of the parameters of interest. While these problems are well known in the static computable general equilibrium (CGE) literature (see e.g. Pagan and Shannon 1985) and partially recognized by Kydland and Prescott (1982), they were neglected by most of the subsequent literature.

The purpose of this paper is methodological. I propose a simulation methodology which formalizes the evaluation of properties of the model and allows for meaningful sensitivity analysis on the outcomes of the simulations. The methodology shares features with those recently proposed by Gregory and Smith (1991) and Kwan (1991b), can be justified using simple Bayesian tools (see Box 1980 and El-Gamal 1993) and has similarities with stochastic simulation techniques employed in dynamic nonlinear large scale macro models (see e.g. Fair 1991). Sims (1989), Smith (1992), Watson (1993) and Canova, Finn, and Pagan (1993) have suggested alternative procedures to formally measure the fit of calibrated models.

The idea of the procedure is simple. The model is recognized to be a *false* data generating process for the observed time series and the task is to know in which dimensions it is most at odds with actual data. The metric I use to evaluate the fit is probabilistic. I simulate the model repeatedly using a Monte Carlo procedure which randomizes over *both* the exogenous stochastic processes *and* the parameters. Parameters are drawn from a density consistent with the frequency distribution of estimates existing in the literature. I then construct the frequency distribution for the realizations of the statistics of interest and examine either in what percentile of the distribution of the simulated statistics the actual value lies or the percentage of simulated values which lie in a ball around the actual realization or both. Extreme values for the first percentile (say, below α percent or above $(1 - \alpha)$ percent) or a low value for the second percentile indicates that the model is particularly poor in the dimensions examined.

The approach I propose has several appealing features. First, it accounts for the uncertainty faced by a simulator in choosing the parameters of the model with a "realistic" Bayesian prior. This prior can be formally obtained using information theoretical measures and the outcomes of point estimation experiments (see El-Gamal 1993). Second, it has a built-in feature which allows for global sensitivity analysis on the support of the parameter space and generalizes techniques on randomized design for strata existing in the static CGE literature (see e.g. Harrison and Vinod 1989). Third, it provides a general evaluation criteria which attaches probabilities to events we are interested in characterizing (as in Box 1980). Finally, it provides a simple and convenient metric to judge the closeness of the simulated and the actual data.

The paper is divided in 6 sections. The next section reviews model building procedures and the criteria employed to examine the empirical relevance of dynamic economic models. Section 3 introduces the technique and describes the details involved in the implementation of the procedure. Section 4 spells out the relationship between the approach and existing techniques. Section 5 presents some examples. Section 6 concludes.

2. ON EVALUATING THE EMPIRICAL RELEVANCE OF ECONOMIC MODELS

The formulation, estimation and evaluation of dynamic general equilibrium macro models is a relatively recent undertaking. Hansen and Sargent (1979) pose the foundations for a maximum likelihood estimation of the "deep" (preference, technological) parameters of these models and for testing their validity. Hansen and Sargent face two basic problems. First, since closed form solutions for the endogenous variables in terms of exogenous variables and parameters do not always exist, they concentrate on parametric structures which deliver closed form solutions (linear-quadratic specifications for the primitives of the model and linear processes for the exogenous variables). Second, since many economic models do not provide a "realistic" statistical specification for the endogenous variables and will be discarded as empirically irrelevant in formal testing, Hansen and Sargent augment their models with additional random components (measurement errors, error in variables or unobserved components). Once a closed (final) form solution is obtained and there are enough sources of randomness in the economy to make the model "complete" in a probabilistic sense (see Haavelmo 1944), one proceeds to identify and estimate the parameters. The empirical relevance of the model is then judged by performing statistical goodness of fit tests or likelihood ratio tests for hypotheses concerning the parameters of interest.

Given the intrinsic limitations existing in the choice of linear quadratic specifications, Hansen (1982) proposed to estimate and test hypotheses concerning "deep" parameters directly from the Euler equations using simple moment conditions. Hansen's GMM-IV approach does not require a closed (or a final) form solution for the endogenous variables, is robust to any failure of the econometrician to have the same information set as agents (see Pagan and Ullah 1988) but still requires a fully specified probability structure for the model. The validity of the model is examined using standard goodness of fit tests (the J-tests).

Contemporaneously with the work of Hansen, Kydland, and Prescott (1982) suggested an alternative procedure to tackle the problem of the probabilistic underspecification of the model. Rather than augmenting an artificial economy with extraneous random components to obtain a richer statistical structure, they start from the observation that the model, as a data generating mechanism (DGP), is false. That is, it is known that, as the sample size grows, the data generated by the model will be at greater and greater variance with the observed time series. For Kydland and Prescott an economic model is neither an accurate nor a realistic description of the actual data but only an approximation to the stochastic process generating it. The task of an applied researcher is to indicate in what dimensions the approximation is poor and suggest ways to modify the artificial economy to obtain a better fit.

There are several logical consequences of this point of view. First, because the model is a false DGP for the actual data, classical estimation of the parameters is meaningless. In addition, classical hypothesis testing is inappropriate because a false model can not be regarded as a null hypothesis to be statistically examined (it can be rejected even before the test is undertaken). Similarly, standard Bayesian analysis is inapplicable because the (simulated) likelihood need not be the correct one, so that posterior statements for the parameters are worthless. In response to these deficiencies, researchers working in this area have adopted a two step approach which chooses the parameters so that the model replicates the data in some basic dimension of interest and evaluates the model on its ability to reproduce "stylized facts." For example, in an aggregate model of the business cycle, parameters are chosen so that the behavior of the endogenous variables in the steady state coincides with the long run behavior of the corresponding variables in the actual economy, and the model is evaluated on its ability to replicate variances and covariances of the cyclical component of macro variables. This first step of the approach is typically justified as a way to unify observations from different fields of economics but it should be noted that it is entirely analogous to the procedure employed in experimental sciences where the physical instrument used to measure some phenomenon is "calibrated" so as to reproduce some known result. For example, to measure the temperature of water a thermometer is calibrated so that in freezing water it gives a value of 32F and in boiling water it gives a value of 212F.

However, because the economy is not fully specified in a probabilistic sense and no measure of dispersion is attached to "calibrated" parameters, the metric employed to determine the quality of the approximation is left unspecified, inferential procedures are subjective to the researcher and, in general, lack statistical foundations. Continuing with the analogy with experimental sciences, if a measurement of 65F is reported it is hard to say if it is different from any value observed in real life or in any other experimental situation.

To overcome these problems Watson (1993) develops a classical procedure which makes evaluation less subjective in situations where the model is known to be a "false" description of the actual economy and the parameters are calibrated. The metric Watson uses is the relative contribution of the second order properties of the model to the second order properties of the actual data. A model fits the data well if the correlation between summary statistics of simulated and actual data in a particular range of frequencies is large (in a R^2 sense).

Sims (1989) and Smith (1992) have suggested a VAR metric to judge the fit of the model. Their approach applies to both situations where the parameters are calibrated or estimated. A VAR is a window which may only partially capture aspects of the data. A model is regarded as appropriate if the "distance" between the unrestricted VAR representations of simulated and actual data is small either in absolute terms or relative to the distance of other models to the actual data.

Finally, Canova, Finn, and Pagan (1993) use the restrictions implied by a calibrated model on the long and short run dynamics of the actual data to provide several general goodness of fit tests and an encompassing procedure to discriminate among models which pass the first round of goodness of fit tests. The procedure has some analogy to the one of Hansen and Sargent (1979) since it employs the restricted VAR representation implied by the model to examine exclusion restrictions for the actual data, and has the advantage of providing the information necessary to modify a model in response to its failure to pass the tests.

In developing an alternative framework of inference I follow Kydland and Prescott's philosophy very closely. I take the actual data to be the realization of an unknown underlying vector stochastic process. The task here is to reproduce features of the data with an "artificial economy," which is known to be almost surely a false generating mechanism for the actual data. The features of the actual data we may be interested in include conditional and unconditional moments (or the entire densities), the autocovariance function of the data and various functions of these quantities (e.g. measures of persistence or of relative volatility) and specific events (e.g. a recession or an average upward sloping term structure of interest rates). I recognize that "calibrating" the model to the actual data involves sampling error and, more importantly, that some judgmental decisions need to be made which lead to a whole range of calibrated values indexed by data sets, measurement techniques, model specifications and evaluation procedures. The presence of this cross sectional variability is the crucial ingredient to construct numerical measures of discrepancy between simulated and actual data. The inferential procedure adopted here follows Friedman (1959) and judges the validity of a model on its ability to reproduce, in a probabilistic sense, a selected number of facts of the actual economy. If the model is regarded to be a good approximation to the actual data generating process, it can be fruitfully used to evaluate policy options.

3. MODEL EVALUATION AND SENSITIVITY ANALYSIS

I assume that a simulator is faced with an $m \times 1$ vector of time series $\bar{x}_t$, which are the realizations of a vector stochastic process $\bar{X}_t$ and that she is interested in reproducing features of $\bar{x}_t$ using a dynamic general equilibrium model. The analysis of policy options will be discussed later on in this section. $\bar{X}_t$ is assumed to be a Markov process with absolutely continuous but unknown distribution and moments up to the nth. For the sake of presentation, I assume that the unconditional distribution of $\bar{X}_t$ is independent of t but there is nothing in the framework that prevents shifts in the unconditional distribution of $\bar{X}_t$ at known points. $\bar{X}_t$ may include variables like GNP, consumption, interest rates, exchange rates, etc. I also assume that dynamic economic theory gives us a model expressing the endogenous variables X_t as a function of exogenous and predetermined variables Z_t (the states of the problem) and of the parameters β. Z_t may include objects like the existing capital stock, exogenous fiscal and monetary variables or shocks to technology and preferences. I express the model's functional relation as $X_t = f(Z_t, \beta)$ where f is, in general, an unknown function. Under specific assumptions about the structure of the economy (e.g. log or quadratic preferences, Cobb-Douglas production function, full depreciation of the capital stock), f can be computed analytically either by value function iteration (see e.g. Bertsekas 1976) or by solving the Euler equations of the model subject to the transversality condition (see e.g. Hansen and Sargent 1979). Under general specifications, however, f can not be derived analytically from the primitives of the problem. A large body of current literature has concentrated on the problem of finding approximations which are either locally or globally close to f in a given metric.[2]

---

[2] Kydland and Prescott (1982), King, Plosser, and Rebelo (1988) for example, locally approximate the function f by linear or log-linear expansions of f around the steady state of the model. Sims (1984) and Novales (1990) employ a backward solution to recover the function f. Their idea is that although f is

SENSITIVITY ANALYSIS AND MODEL EVALUATION   483

Here I assume that either f is available analytically or that one of the existing numerical procedures has been employed so that a simulator has a functional $\mathscr{F}$ which approximates f in some sense, i.e. $\|\mathscr{F}(Z_t, \gamma) - f(Z_t, \beta)\| < \varepsilon$, where γ are functions of the parameters β and $\|\cdot\|$ is a given norm. Given the model f, an approximation procedure $\mathscr{F}$, a set of parameters β and a probability distribution for Z_t, one can infer the probability distribution of X_t from the model.

Let $\mathscr{G}(X_t|\beta, f)$ be the density of the X_t vector, conditional on the parameters β and the model f. $\mathscr{G}(X_t|\beta, f)$ represents the probability that a particular path for the endogenous variables will be drawn given a parametric model structure for the artificial economy and a set of parameters and is a deterministic (nonlinear) transformation of $\kappa(Z_t)$, the probability density of the exogenous variables. In other words, X_t is random because Z_t is random. The vector β is, in general, unknown. Let $\pi(\beta|\mathscr{I})$ be the density of the parameters of the model, conditional on the information set $\mathscr{I}$. $\pi(\beta|\mathscr{I})$ represents the information available to a simulator on the parameters of the model. Let $\mathscr{H}(X_t, \beta|f, \mathscr{I})$ be the joint density of simulated data and of parameters and let $p(X_t|f, \mathscr{I}, \mathscr{A}) = \int_{\mathscr{A}} \mathscr{H}(X_t, \beta|f, \mathscr{I}) \, d\beta$ be the simulated predictive density of X_t where $\mathscr{A} \subset \mathscr{B}$ is the parameter space.

A generic formulation for the problem we are interested in is to compute functions of simulated data under $p(X_t|f, \mathscr{I}, \mathscr{A})$, i.e. evaluating objects of the form:

(1)
$$E(\mu(X_t)|f, \mathscr{I}, \mathscr{A}, \mathscr{C}) = \int_{\mathscr{C}} \mu(X_t) p(X_t|f, \mathscr{I}, \mathscr{A}) \, dX_t$$

$$= \int_{\mathscr{A}} \int_{\mathscr{C}} \mu(X_t) \mathscr{H}(X_t, \beta|f, \mathscr{I}) \, d\beta \, dX_t$$

where $\mu(X_t)$ is the vector of functions of simulated data and $\mathscr{C}$ is the support of the exogenous variables. Let $h(\bar{x}_t)$ be the corresponding vector of functions of the actual data.

The problem of examining the fit of the model can be summarized with the following question: how likely is the model to generate $h(\bar{x}_t)$? To answer note that (1) allows us to compute probabilities of the form $P(\mu(X_t) \in D)$, where D is a bounded set. To do this choose, for example, the mth component of μ to be $\mu_m(X_t) = \chi(X_t : \mu(X_t) \in D)$ where χ is the indicator function, i.e. $\chi(\mu(X_t); D) = 1$ if $\mu(X_t) \in D$ and zero otherwise. From (1) one can also compute a value $\bar{h}$ satisfying $P[\mu(X_t) \leq \bar{h}] = \alpha$ for any given α, by appropriately selecting the indicator function.

---

impossible to compute, f^{-1} may be easier to find. In their approach, a process for the endogenous variables is selected and one seeks processes for the exogenous variables which may have generated them under f. Marcet's (1992) method of parametrizing expectations and Judd's (1992) minimum weighted method can be seen as choosing a set of known functions which globally approximate f in a given norm. Baxter's (1991) and Coleman's (1989) methods are grid procedures which obtain the function f by piecewise linear interpolation. Finally, Tauchen and Hussey's (1991) quadrature method is a grid approximation procedure which is appropriate for integral equations which are of Fredholm's second type.

Model evaluation then consists of several types of statements which are complementary and differ only in the criteria used to measure distance. For example, one can compute the probability that the model can generate a $\mu_m(X_t)$ less than or equal to $h_m(\bar{x}_t)$. In other words, we can examine the likelihood of an event (the observed realization of the summary statistics in the actual data) from the point of view of the model. Extreme values for this probability would indicate a poor "fit" in the dimensions examined. Alternatively, if one can measure the sampling variability of $h_m(\bar{x}_t)$, one can chose an α and compute the implied $\bar{h}$. Then, by choosing the set D to include the actual realization of $h_m(\bar{x}_t)$ plus one or two standard deviations around the point estimate, one can either see if $\bar{h}$ lies inside D or calculate the probability that the model generates functions $\mu_m(X_t)$ in the chosen set. If evaluation needs to be done in several dimensions of the $\mu(X_t)$ vector simultaneously, one can partition the simulated distribution of $\mu(X_t)$ into hyper-cubes and check the likelihood of the event $h(\bar{x}_t)$ from the point of view of the model. For example, if the task is to study the equity premium-risk free rate (EP-R) puzzle (see Merha and Prescott 1985), one could partition the space of simulated EP-R pairs into 4 quadrants with the origin on the actual mean values of the EP-R pair and check the proportion of simulated pairs which falls in each quadrant.

3.1. *Implementation.*   There are four technical issues regarding the implementation of the procedure that deserve some discussion. The first concerns the computation of integrals like those appearing in (1). If the (β, Z_t) vector is of high dimension simple discrete grid approximations, spherical or quadrature rules quickly become unfeasible since the number of function evaluations increases exponentially with the dimension of β and Z_t. In addition, unless the contours of $\mathcal{H}(X_t, \beta | \mathcal{I}, f)$ are of ellipsoidal forms, grid evaluations may miss most of the action of this density. There are several feasible alternatives available: one is the Monte Carlo procedure described in, e.g., Geweke (1989), another is the data augmentation procedure of Tanner and Wong (1987) or the "Gibbs sampler" discussed, e.g., in Gelfand and Smith (1990). Finally, one could use one of the quasi-random procedures presented in Niederreiter (1988).

In the examples of Section 5, I adopt a Monte Carlo approach. After drawing with replacement iid β vectors from $\pi(\beta | \mathcal{I})$ and Z_t paths from $\kappa(Z_t)$, I substitute sums over realizations for the integrals in (1) and appeal to the law of large numbers for functions of iid variables to show that

$$(2) \qquad \frac{1}{N} \sum_{i=1}^{N} \mu_i(X_t) \xrightarrow{\text{a.s.}} E(\mu(X_t))$$

where N is the number of replications. Note that, although $\mathcal{H}$ is unknown, sampling from $\mathcal{H}$ (or p) can be conveniently accomplished by simulating the model repeatedly for random (β, Z_t).

Second, since in most cases the function f is unknown, $\mathcal{G}$ itself becomes unknown and the direct computation of integrals like (1) is not feasible. If the approximation $\mathcal{F}$ to f is accurate, one could simply neglect the approximation error and proceed using $\mathcal{J}(X_t | \beta, \mathcal{F})$ in place of $\mathcal{G}(X_t | \beta, f)$. However, since only very little is known

SENSITIVITY ANALYSIS AND MODEL EVALUATION   485

about the properties of any of the approximation procedures and some have only local validity (see e.g. Christiano 1990 and Dotsey and Mao 1991), one may want to condition explicitly on the existence of an approximation error in conducting inference (as e.g. in Geweke 1989). In this case one would replace (1) with

$$(3) \quad E(\mu(X_t)|f, \mathcal{I}, \mathcal{A}, \mathcal{C}) = \int_{\mathcal{A}} \int_{\mathcal{C}} \mu(X_t) \mathcal{J}(X_t, \beta|\mathcal{I}, \mathcal{F}) \omega(\beta, f, \mathcal{F}) \, d\beta \, dX_t$$

where ω are weights which depend on the "true" density $\mathcal{G}(X_t, \beta|\mathcal{I}, f)$ and on the approximation density $\mathcal{J}(X_t, \beta|\mathcal{I}, \mathcal{F})$. Thus, the approximation problem can be posed in terms of choosing a procedure which makes the weights in (3) as close as possible to 1. In the example of Section 5 where the function f is unknown I simply neglect the approximation error.

Third, one must specify a density $\pi(\beta|I)$ for the parameters. One could choose this density to reflect the asymptotic distribution of a GMM estimator of β (as in Burnside, Eichenbaum, and Rebelo 1993), of a simulated method of moments (SMM) estimator of β (as in Canova and Marrinan 1993), or of a maximum likelihood (ML) estimator of β (as in Phillips 1991). Two disadvantages of this approach need to be noted: first, because the density of β is selected on the basis of one data set, it does not reflect all the information available to a simulator which includes estimates of β indexed by data sets, estimation procedures or model specifications. Second, and as a consequence of the above, the dispersion associated with the density may have little relationship with the true uncertainty faced by a simulator in choosing the parameters of a model.

The idea of the paper is to choose $\pi(\beta|\mathcal{I})$ so as to reflect all available cross-sectional information. El Gamal (1993) has shown how to do this formally, using information theoretical measures. The resulting $\pi(\beta|\mathcal{I})$ is the least informative (Bayesian) density consistent with available cross sectional information. Roughly speaking, the procedure amounts to counting estimates of β previously obtained in the literature and constructing $\pi(\beta|\mathcal{I})$ by smoothing the resulting histogram. For example, if one of the elements of the β vector is the risk aversion parameter, and one counts estimates over the last 15 years obtained from fully specified GE models and smooths the resulting histogram, one would obtain a truncated (below zero) bell-shaped density, centered around two with a small mass above four. If for some parameters previous econometric evidence is scant or there is no theoretical reason to expect that one value is more likely to occur than others, one could assume uniform densities on the chosen support.

Estimates of β available in the literature are not necessarily independent (the same data set is used in some cases), some are less reliable than others and many may be noncompatible as different definition of variables and model specification are used. Nonindependent estimates are legitimate candidates to enter into the information set as long as they reflect sampling variability or different estimation techniques. The influence of less reliable estimates or of estimates obtained with models which very are different from the theoretical framework used can be discounted by giving them a smaller weight in constructing histograms. In the examples of Section 5 I will choose a reasonable range for β based on theoretical considerations and current simulation practices and impose informative densities only in those dimensions where econometric evidence is rich.

Finally, in many applications the joint density of the parameter vector can be factored into the product of lower dimensional densities. If no relationship across estimates of the parameters exists, $\pi(\beta|\mathscr{I})$ is simply the product of univariate densities. If estimates of certain parameters are related (e.g. in the case of parameters describing the share of various intermediate goods in a production function), one can choose bivariate or trivariate densities for these dimensions and maintain univariate specifications for the densities of the other parameters.

3.2. *Sensitivity Analysis.* If one adopts a Monte Carlo approach to compute (1), an automatic global and efficient sensitivity analysis is performed on the entire support of the parameter space as a by-product of the simulations. Sensitivity analysis, however, can take other more specific forms. For example, one may be interested in examining how likely $\mu(X_t)$ is to be close to $h(\bar{x}_t)$ when $\beta = \hat{\beta}$ is a "cocktail party" estimate of β. In this case one could choose a path for Z_t and analyze the conditional distribution of X_t for the selected value(s) of β. Alternatively, one might wish to assess what is the maximal variation in $\mu(X_t)$ which is consistent, say, with β being in a two standard error band of a particular value. To answer this question one chooses a path for Z_t and constructs paths for x_t for draws of β in a particular range.

3.3. *Analysis of Policy Options.* Once a model has been validated, one can proceed to analyze policy options. The issue of policy analyses is subtle to deal with for two reasons. First, one has to decide how to model an intervention. Second, since many approximations to the decision rule are appropriate only locally, policy changes must be designed so that they belong to the region where approximations are valid.

The easiest case to analyze is when the component of Z_t we are interested in changing is deterministic (e.g. tax or tariff rates). In that case $\mathscr{H}(X_t, \beta|f, \mathscr{I}) \propto \pi(\beta|\mathscr{I})$ and only the randomness in the parameters affects the outcome of the experiment.

If the component of Z_t we are interested in is stochastic, but policy options do not involve changes in the distribution of the Z's, one can undertake an analysis of different policy options by simply comparing a band for $\mu(X_t)$ obtained by randomizing the β vector under the two policies. Finally, if a policy experiment involves changes in the entire distribution for Z_t one may want to compare $\mathscr{H}(X_t, \beta|f_1, \mathscr{I})$ with $\mathscr{H}(X_t, \beta|f_2, \mathscr{I})$ where f_1 and f_2 now represent two different specifications for Z_t. Differences in the outcomes can be examined using nonparametric methods as discussed in Pagan and Ullah (1991). In the example of Section 5 dealing with the evaluation of policy options, I will only consider deterministic policy changes.

4.   A COMPARISON WITH EXISTING PROCEDURES

The approach we have described in the previous section lends itself to a simple Bayesian interpretation and shares features with several existing Bayesian techniques.

SENSITIVITY ANALYSIS AND MODEL EVALUATION 487

We have already mentioned that our "prior" on the parameters can be justified formally as the least informative density which is consistent with the information contained in a variety of estimation experiments. The procedure we employ to construct this density is also tightly linked to the selection procedure used in the so-called "consensus literature" (see Genest and Zidek 1986), where the problem is to combine different subjective Bayesian priors into an overall (more objective) one, and to the one employed in "meta-analysis" (see Wolf 1986), where the outcomes of a number of hypothesis testing experiments are combined to reach a decision (accept or reject) based on the collection of experimental p-values.

Because $G(x_t|\beta, f)$ is not necessarily the correct "likelihood" of the data, our procedure shares features also with the limited information approach of Kwan (1991a), where an unknown density $\bar{G}$ is approximated with G on the basis of one or more statistics. As Kwan shows, the approximation is appropriate if and only if the statistic on which the approximated likelihood function is built is consistent and uniformly asymptotically normal. He uses these properties to construct a diagnostic check for the quality of the approximation. Because in our setup the statistic $\mu(X_t)$ need not be consistent, Kwan's diagnostic check is inapplicable.

Our inferential approach has direct connections with the one pioneered by Box (1980). Box used predictive densities and functions of the data to provide a diagnostic check for model adequacy, which may be used to either discredit or support posterior statements about the parameters. There are two major difference between that approach and ours: first, the predictive density need not be the correct predictive density for the actual data and second, it need not have a closed form expression. The lack of closed form expression for the predictive density prevents us from computing the probability of paths analytically, like Box does.

Our model evaluation procedure is also related to the ones proposed by Gregory and Smith (1991) and Kwan (1991b). However, a few differences need to be emphasized. Gregory and Smith take the model as a testable null hypothesis and compute the probability of type I error by simulation. Although the Monte Carlo methodology underlying their procedure is identical to ours, the interpretation of the results is different for three reasons. First, Gregory and Smith assume that the mod is the true DGP for the actual data while this is not the case here. Second, they do not account for parameter uncertainty in evaluating the outcomes of the model. Finally, because they take a calibrated version of the model as the "truth," they conduct sensitivity analysis inefficiently, by replicating the experiments for different calibrated values. Kwan, on the other hand, allows for parameter uncertainty in his simulation scheme. However, he chooses a subjective "prior" density for the parameters. In addition, he evaluates the outcomes in relative terms, by comparing two alternative model specifications using a posterior-odds ratio. A model is preferred to another if it maximizes the probability that the simulated statistics are in a given set (typically chosen to be of two standard deviations width around the point estimate of the actual statistics).

Finally, the procedure for sensitivity analysis proposed here extends the approach that Harrison and Vinod (1989) used in deterministic CGE models and is complementary to the local analysis of Canova, Finn, and Pagan (1993). To determine how robust simulation results are to "small" perturbations of the parameters around the calibrated values, they examine the magnitude of the local derivative of the statistic in the direction of interest. Because the two procedures measure the sensitivity of the results to perturbations in the parameters of different size and because they take a different point of view regarding the reliability of calibrated parameters, they provide complementary information and should both be used as specification diagnostics for simulated models.

It is simple to show that both "calibration" and "estimation by simulation" exercises appear as special cases of our simulation procedure. Calibration exercises can be seen as imposing a point mass for $\pi(\beta|\mathcal{I})$ on a particular value of β and, in certain cases, also selecting a particular path for the exogenous processes. One interpretation of this choice is that a simulator is perfectly confident that the vector β used is correct and does not worry about the cross-study or time series uncertainty surrounding estimates of β. Note that when the density of β is a singleton the marginal and the conditional density of X_t are identical. In addition, when a path for the vector of exogenous variables is selected in advance, either by drawing only one realization from their distribution or by choosing a z_t on the basis of extraneous information (for example, inputting Solow residuals in the model), the marginal for X_t has a point mass. In this last instance the likelihood of the model to produce any particular event is either 0 or 1 and one must resort to informal techniques to compare the closeness of functions of simulated and actual data. In some studies the randomness in Z_t is explicitly taken into account and repeated draws for the exogenous variables are made for a fixed value of β. In this case one computes moments of the statistics of interest by averaging the results over a small number of simulations (see, e.g., Backus, Gregory, and Zin 1989).

Simulation exercises conducted after parameters have been selected using a SMM or a GMM technique are also special cases of the proposed framework of analysis. Here $\pi(\beta|\mathcal{I})$ has a point mass at β^*, where β^* is either the SMM estimator of β (see Lee and Ingram 1990) or the SQML estimator of β (see Smith 1992) or the GMM estimator of β. In some cases, $\pi(\beta|\mathcal{I})$ is taken to be the asymptotic distribution of one of these estimators (see Canova and Marrinan 1993). Simulations are performed by drawing one or more realizations from $\mathcal{G}(X_t|\beta^*, f, \mathcal{I})$ (or from $\mathcal{H}(X_t, \beta|f, \mathcal{I})$, if the asymptotic distribution of β^* is used) and standard errors of $\mu(X_t)$ are computed using the asymptotic standard error of β^* and a linear approximation to μ.

In evaluating the model's performance these last procedures have two advantages over calibration. First, they allow formal statements on the likelihood of certain parameter values to reproduce the features of interest. For example, if the four standard error range around the point estimate of the AR(1) parameter for the productivity disturbance is [.84, .92], then it is highly unlikely (with probability higher than 99 percent) that persistent (in the sense of unit root) productivity disturbances are needed to match the data. Second, they provide a setup where sensitivity analysis to a reasonable perturbation of the parameters can easily be undertaken (although not often done).

Estimation procedures however, have two major shortcomings. First, they impose a strong form of ignorance on the simulator which does not reflect the available a priori information. The vector β may include meaningful economic parameters which can be bounded on the basis of theoretical arguments. For example, a priori it is known that a risk aversion parameter which is negative or in excess of, say 30, is very unlikely. With SMM, GMM or SQML procedures the range of possible β is $[-\infty, \infty]$. By appropriately selecting a hypercube for their densities a researcher can make "unreasonable" parameter values unlikely and avoid a posteriori adjustments. Second, simulations may not constitute an independent way to cross validate the model because the parameters used are obtained from the same data set which later will be used to compare results.

Procedures mixing calibration and GMM estimation and calibration and estimation by simulation recently employed by, e.g., Burnside, Eichenbaum, and Rebelo (1993), are also special cases of our approach. In this approach some parameters are fixed using extraneous information, while others are formally estimated using moment conditions. Although these strategies allow a more formal evaluation of the properties of the model than pure calibration procedures, they face several problems. First, parameters may be estimated regardless of their identifiability. Second, as for generic estimation procedures, the evaluation of the model is problematic because standard errors for the statistic of interest do not reflect the uncertainty faced by a simulator in choosing parameter values. Finally, as Gregory and Smith (1989) have pointed out, the small sample properties of estimators obtained from these procedures may be far from reasonable unless the parameters which are fixed in advance are consistent estimators of the true parameters. When this condition is not met, estimates of the remaining parameters may be sensitive to errors in pre-setting and close matching of simulated and actual moments may yield misleading inference.

5. SOME EXAMPLES

5.1. *A One Sector Growth Model.* The first example I consider is the Brock-Mirman one sector growth model. Here a social planner maximizes the discounted sum of utilities of the representative consumer subject to an economy wide resource constraint. The problem is of the form

$$(4) \qquad \max_{c_t} E_0 \sum_{t=0}^{\infty} \theta^t U(c_t)$$

subject to

$$(5) \qquad c_t + K_t - (1 - \delta)K_{t-1} \leq f(K_{t-1}, \varepsilon_t)$$

where $I_t = K_t - (1 - \delta)K_{t-1}$ is investment at t, K_t is the capital stock at t, δ is the depreciation rate, ε_t is a productivity shock and E_0 is the expectation operator. For computational convenience, I assume that the production function has the form $Y_t = f(K_{t-1}, \varepsilon_t) = K_{t-1}^{\xi}\varepsilon_t$ and that the instantaneous utility function has the form $U(c_t) = \ln(c_t)$.

For $\delta = 1$ a solution for consumption and investment in terms of the states of the problem (K_{t-1}, ε_t) exists and it is given by (see Sargent 1987)

$$(6) \qquad c_t = (1 - \xi\theta)K_{t-1}^{\xi}\varepsilon_t$$

$$I_t = \xi\theta K_{t-1}^{\xi}\varepsilon_t.$$

When $\delta \neq 1$ a closed form solution for c_t and I_t does not exist and numerical techniques must be used to compute an approximation to it. To avoid the issue of numerical approximations in this first example I will set $\delta = 1$. Therefore, there are two parameters in the model $\beta = (\theta, \xi)$ and one driving process $Z_t = \varepsilon_t$. Since there need not be any relationship between the range of possible θ and ξ, I assume that the density of β is the product of the densities of the two parameters.

Several studies have estimated the discount factor θ to be, for monthly data, in the neighborhood of 0.996 (see e.g. Hansen and Singleton 1983). Estimates of this parameter range across studies from 0.990 to 1.0022. Theoretically, it is known that in the steady state, the discount factor determines the real interest rate and that a reasonable range for the annualized real interest rate is $[-0.005, 0.05]$. In simulation studies various authors have used values of θ in the range [0.9951, 0.9992] (see e.g., Cooley and Hansen 1990 or Backus, Gregory, and Zin 1989). I capture these observations by choosing the density for θ to be truncated normal (with truncation on both sides) centered around 0.997 and with range [0.990, 1.0022]. Note that this distribution is skewed to express the idea that a real interest rate of 2 to 3 percent or lower is more likely than an interest rate in excess of 5 percent. I assume that ξ has a uniform distribution in the range [0, 1]. This range is consistent with either decreasing or constant returns to scale. Finally, to make simulations operative I draw ε_t as iid from a $\mathcal{N}(0, 1)$. Although the iid assumption is clearly unrealistic, it avoids the introduction of a nuisance (AR) parameter in the problem.

Since the model generates stationary paths for the endogenous variables, I take stationary inducing transformations of the real data. Suppose we are interested in the relative volatility of consumption to output as in, e.g. Deaton (1987). Using U.S. monthly data on the growth rate of personal consumption expenditure and income (as proxied by an index of industrial production) for the sample 1955–1985, I obtain a value of 0.56 for this ratio with a standard deviation of 0.21. Using (6) and the production function, I generate time series for c_t and Y_t using the level of the capital stock in the U.S. in 1954, 12 for k_0.

Figure 1 presents the estimated density of the statistic when 10000 random replications for the β, $\{\varepsilon_t\}_{t=1}^{T}$ pair are drawn. Estimates of the density are obtained nonparametrically using a kernel estimator with variable width as in Pagan and Ullah (1991).[3] A value of 0.56 lies in the 98th percentile of the density of the simulated statistics and only 25 percent of the simulated density mass lies within one standard deviation band around 0.56. Moreover, the mean value for the simulated density is 0.26, the median is 0.24, the mode is 0.02, the standard deviation is 0.12, the 90 percent range is [0.7, 0.49] and the minimum and maximum are 0.001 and 0.71. Therefore, it is unlikely that this parameterization of the one

---

[3] The use of the nonparametric density estimate in place of the empirical frequency density is of no consequence for the results obtained here and in the next two examples (see also Gregory and Smith 1991).

SENSITIVITY ANALYSIS AND MODEL EVALUATION   491

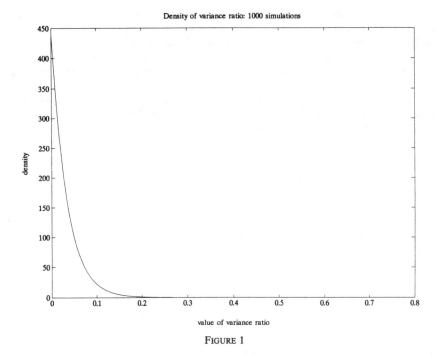

FIGURE 1

sector growth model is able to generate the relative variability of consumption to income we see in the U.S. data.

5.2. Profits from Uncovered Speculative Strategies.

The second example draws from Canova and Marrinan (1991) and (1993) who attempt to reproduce features of profits from uncovered speculative strategies in several foreign exchange markets and of holding premiums in the term structure of U.S. interest rates.

The economy they consider is characterized by two countries. Every period, each country i is endowed with Y_{it}, $i = 1, 2$ units of a nonstorable consumption good. There are two governments which consume G_{it} units of their own country's good. To finance these consumption requirements each government issues a country specific money, M_{it}, collects real lump sum taxes, T_{it}, levied equally on agents from both countries, and issues debt to finance any purchases in excess of money creation and tax collections. This debt is in the form of state contingent nominal bills of maturity k, $k = 1, 2, \ldots, K$, denominated in their own country's currency. Endowments, government consumption requirements and money supplies are exogenous and follow independent first order Markov processes with a stationary and ergodic transition function.

Countries are each populated by a representative household maximizing a time separable utility function defined over the two goods. Households are subject to both a wealth constraint and a liquidity constraint which compels them to purchase goods with cash. The timing of the model is such that asset markets open first and goods markets follow. At the beginning of each period the consumer enters the asset market and decides how to allocate her wealth among the productive assets of the 2 countries, currencies, and the state contingent nominal bonds issued by the 2 governments. After the asset market closes, the consumer enters the goods market and makes her consumption purchases with previously accumulated currency.

In equilibrium the expected nominal profits from holding a bond to maturity k for h periods relative to holding an h-period bond to maturity, defined as $HP^{k,h}_{i,t} = (k/h)r_{it,k} - ((k-h)/h)r_{it+h,k-h} - r_{it,h}$, are

$$(7) \quad HP^{k,h}_{i,t} = h^{-1} \left(\ln \left[\frac{E_t \theta^{k-h} Y_{it+k} (M_{it+k})^{-1} U_{it+k}}{Y_{it+h} (M_{it+h})^{-1} U_{it+h}} \right] - \ln \left[\frac{E_t \theta^k Y_{it+k} (M_{it+k})^{-1} U_{it+k}}{Y_{it} (M_{it})^{-1} U_{it}} \right] \right.$$

$$\left. + \ln \left[\frac{E_t \theta^h Y_{it+h} (M_{it+h})^{-1} U_{it+h}}{Y_{it} (M_{it})^{-1} U_{it}} \right] \right).$$

The approximate annualized percentage expected nominal profits from speculating in foreign exchange markets defined as $EP_{t,h} = (\log E_t\{S_{t+h}\} - \log\{F_{t,h}\})$, where $F_{t,k} = S_{t,k} e^{r_{1t,k} - r_{2t,k}}$ are

$$(8) \qquad EP_{t,h} = h^{-1} * \left(\log E_t \left\{ \left[\frac{Y_{2t+h} (M_{2t+h})^{-1} U_{2t+h}}{Y_{1t+h} (M_{1t+h})^{-1} U_{1t+h}} \right] \right\} \right.$$

$$\left. - \log \left\{ \frac{E_t [Y_{2t+h} (M_{2t+h})^{-1} U_{2t+h}]}{E_t [Y_{1t+h} (M_{1t+h})^{-1} U_{1t+h}]} \right\} \right).$$

Canova and Marrinan examine a wide array of functions of (7) and (8) for different h. Here I confine attention to the variability and first order autocorrelation of three month holding premium and three months profits from forward speculation. The reason is that the second order properties induced by similar general equilibrium models are, in general, so different from those of actual data that some authors (e.g. Campbell and Shiller 1987, Frankel and Froot 1987) have concluded that the simple version of the rational expectations-efficient market hypothesis is severely flawed. By describing the distribution of the outcomes of these second moments from the point of view of the model we can shed light on this issue. The standard deviation and the AR(1) coefficient for profits from holding 3 months a 6 month T-bill as compared to holding a 3 month T-bill to maturity for the period 1960–1988 are .221 and .792 respectively. The standard deviation and the AR(1) coefficient for profits from 3 month forward speculation on the dollar in the dollar/mark market for the period 1979–1987 are .042 and .785 respectively.

To obtain closed form solutions for (7) and (8), I take a second order Taylor expansion around $\eta_t = (\Delta \ln (Y_{1t}), \Delta \ln (Y_{2t}), \Delta \ln (M_{1t}), \Delta \ln (M_{2t}), \ln (1 - \psi_{1t}), \ln (1 - \psi_{2t})$ where $\psi_{it} = G_{it}/Y_{it}$. I assume that the conditional mean and conditional variance of η_t evolve according to

$$(9) \qquad\qquad E_t(\eta_{jt}) = A_{0j} + A_{1j}\eta_{jt-1} \quad j = 1, \dots, 6$$

$$(10) \quad E_t(\eta_{jt} - E_t(\eta_{jt}))^2 \equiv \sigma^2_{jt} = a_{0j} + a_{1j}\sigma^2_{jt-1} + a_{2j}\varepsilon^2_{jt-1}, j = 1, \dots, 6$$

where $\varepsilon_{jt} = \eta_{jt} - E(\eta_{jt}) \sim iid(0, \sigma_{jt}^2)$. Finally, I assume a utility function of the form $U(c_{1t}, c_{2t}) = (c_{1t}^\pi c_{2t}^{1-\pi})^{1-\gamma}/(1 - \gamma)$ where π is share of domestic goods in total consumption and γ is risk aversion parameter.

The problem under consideration is much more complex that the previous one since there are 6 exogenous sources of shocks (Y_{it}, G_{it}, M_{it}, $i = 1, 2$), 27 parameters to select and an approximation error to consider. Note that there are two types of parameters: preference parameters (π, γ) and "auxiliary" parameters, which enter expressions (7) and (8) only because of the particular time series model selected for the exogenous variables. For preferences parameters existing evidence is sufficiently rich to construct informative densities, while for the others the evidence is very slim and this forces us to choose uninformative densities for these parameters.

The density for $\beta = (\pi, \gamma)$ is assumed to be the product of univariate densities and it is selected as follows.[4] Since little is known about the mean value of π (the share of domestic good in total consumption) and different studies have used different values, I assume a uniform density over the range [0.5, 1.0]. I take the density for the risk aversion parameter to be truncated $\chi^2(4)$ and range [0, 20]. The rationale for this wide range is the large differences across studies for estimates of γ, which have obtained values between 0.5 and 3.0 (see e.g. Hansen and Singleton 1983 and Canova and Marrinan 1991) and recent simulation studies analyzing properties of financial data, which experimented with values ranging from 0.5 to 55 (see e.g. Merha and Prescott 1985, Backus, Gregory, and Zin 1989 and Kandel and Stambaugh 1990). Despite this diversity, there is enough consensus in the profession that $\gamma = 2$ is the most likely value. I capture this belief by selecting the mode of the density to take on this value. Finally, since the 95 percent range for a $\chi^2(4)$ is approximately [0.7, 10], no more than 1.5 percent of the mass of the distribution is in the region where $\gamma > 15$.

The remaining 25 parameters describe the conditional mean and variances of the exogenous processes. Based on the estimates of Stock and Watson (1989) and my own calculations I chose the ranges for A_{11}, A_{12} and A_{13} to be $[-.10, .00]$, $[-.06, .00]$, $[.45, 60]$ respectively. On the ranges for A_{11} and A_{12} I assume that 50 percent of the density mass is uniformly distributed below 0 and 50 percent is lumped at 0 (see Sims 1988 for a rationale for this choice) while on the range for A_{13} I assume a uniform density. Based on arguments provided in Canova and Marrinan (1993) and estimates of Hodrick (1989) I assume a uniform density for all GARCH parameters. a_{11}, a_{12}, a_{13} have support on $[-0.37, 0.13]$, $[-0.41, 0.19]$ and $[-0.14, -0.04]$, respectively while a_{21} and a_{22} both have support on $[0.00, 0.50]$ and a_{23} has support on $[0.17, 0.27]$.[5] The ranges for A_{01}, A_{02}, A_{03} and a_{01}, a_{02}, a_{03} are chosen endogenously so that the unconditional mean and the variance of the processes match the unconditional mean and variance of the growth rates of U.S. and OECD industrial production and of the monetary base in the U.S. For the remaining 10 parameters characterizing the behavior of government expenditure no

---

[4] Canova and Marrinan (1991) consider the case where the information about some of the parameters of the model is correlated. I will not examine this case here.

[5] The ranges for all the parameters are constructed from the point estimate for the period 64–88 plus or minus one standard error.

evidence exists because data on government expenditure shares in total output is not available at monthly frequency. Based on the quarterly estimates of Canova and Marrinan (1993) I assume that (A_{05}, A_{06}) have uniform densities in $[0.05, 0.30]$, the densities of (a_{05}, a_{06}) are uniform in $[0.05, 0.15]$. Finally, the densities of $(A_{15}, A_{16}, a_{15}, a_{16}, a_{25}, a_{26})$ are chosen to be uniform $[0, 1.0]$ but I eliminate all the paths for ψ_{it} which are too volatile or have a mean that lies outside of the cross sectional range of estimates of OECD countries.

For this problem I drew 5000 iid $(\beta, \{\eta_t\}_{t=1}^{T})$ vectors and neglect the approximation error due to the Taylor expansion by drawing η_t from a lognormal distribution. Estimates of the densities for the simulated variance and the simulated first autocovariance of the two series appear in Figure 2. For the holding profits series, the actual value of the standard deviation lies in the 28th percentile of the estimated density, while the actual value of the AR(1) coefficient is in 53th percentile. The means (modes) of the univariate distributions are 0.60, and 0.73 (0.18 and 0.35), the standard deviations are 0.53 and 0.22, 90 percent ranges are $[0.18, 1.74]$ for the standard deviation and $[0.35, 0.90]$ for the first order serial correlation. In 28 percent of the simulated values both the standard deviation and the AR(1) coefficient are below actual values, in 25 percent of the cases the variance is below the actual value but the AR(1) is greater than the actual value and in 47 percent of the cases both are greater than the actual values. For the risk profits series, the actual value of the standard error lies below all the simulated values, while the actual value of the AR(1) coefficient is in the 87th percentile. The means (modes) of the univariate distributions are 2.29 and 0.28 (1.14 and 0.57), the standard deviations are 1.36 and 0.32 and the 90 percent ranges are $[1.37, 5.37]$ for the standard deviation and $[0.07, 0.86]$ for the first order serial correlation. Finally, in 90 percent of the cases the standard deviation is above the actual value but the AR(1) is below than the actual value and in 10 percent of the cases they are both greater than the actual values.

In conclusion, the current model specification can generate on average more variability than what is found in the data but there are many reasonable parameter configurations for which the first order serial correlation coefficient is lower than what we see in the actual data.

5.3. *Optimal Taxation.* The final example considers the model employed by Cooley and Hansen (1990) and is chosen to illustrate how the procedure for sensitivity analysis outlined in the paper can be used to examine the consequences of policy options. The problem they examine is whether there is a combination of three different taxes which is less distorting than the actual U.S. taxation system.

The framework of analysis they employ is a closed economy model with production and two goods (cash and credit). To simplify the analysis, and because none of the conclusions depend on this, I assume that all goods are cash goods. The representative consumer maximizes lifetime utility given by

$$(11) \qquad E_0 \sum_{t=0}^{\infty} \theta^t [\log (c_t) + B*(1 - h_t)].$$

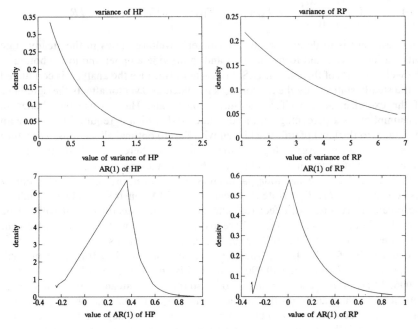

FIGURE 2

The cash-in-advance constraint and the wealth constraint are

$$(12) \qquad p_t c_t \leq m_{t-1} + (\xi_t - 1)m_{t-1}$$

$$(13) \quad T_{ct}c_t + I_t + \frac{m_t}{p_t} \leq (1 - T_{ht})w_t h_t + (1 - T_{kt})r_t K_t + T_{kt}\delta K_t + \frac{m_{t-1}}{p_t} + TR_t$$

where $\xi_t > \theta$ is the gross growth rate of the money supply, I_t is investment, h_t is hours, $w_t h_t$ is labor income, $r_t K_t$ is capital income, T_{ct}, T_{ht}, T_{kt} and TR_t are the consumption tax, labor income tax, capital income tax and net transfers at t, respectively. Capital is accumulated according to

$$(14) \qquad K_t = (1 - \delta)K_{t-1} + I_t.$$

There is a representative firm in the economy, owned by the consumer, maximizing profits

$$(15) \qquad PR_t = K_t^\alpha h_t^{1-\alpha} - w_t h_t - r_t K_t.$$

Finally, there is a government which taxes agents using four distortionary taxes (inflation, consumption, labor income and capital tax) and transfers the total back to agents in a lump sum fashion. The government budget constraint is

$$(16) \qquad (\xi_t - 1)\frac{M_{t-1}}{p_t} + T_{ht}w_t h_t + T_{kt}(r_t - \delta)K_t + T_c c_t = TR_t.$$

The task here is to determine how consumer's welfare varies in the steady state with various levels and forms of taxes and to provide a upper and lower bound to the welfare costs of the current U.S. tax system. Because the analysis is conducted in the steady states, only the randomness in selecting β vector affects the outcomes of the exercise. As a welfare measure, Cooley and Hansen use the change in consumption as a percentage of steady state GNP which is required to restore an individual to the level of utility achieved with Pareto optimal allocations. Therefore Δc solves: $\log(\hat{c} + \Delta c) - \log \bar{c} - B(\hat{h} - \bar{h}) = 0$ where $\bar{c}$ and $\bar{h}$ are the steady states values of consumption and hours when all taxes are zero.

In this model there are four parameters $\beta = (\theta, B, \alpha, \delta)$ and three policy instruments (T_c, T_k, T_h). Note that because the CIA constraint is always binding, the inflation tax does not affect real allocations in the steady state it will not be considered here. I compute the welfare losses associated with each tax instrument separately using a 10 point grid on $(0, 1)$ with 0.1 increments.

The density for the four parameters are as follows: θ is truncated normal, centered at 0.997 with range [0.990, 1.0022], α is uniform [0.25, 0.50], δ is uniform [0.006, 0.01] and B is endogenously chosen so that in the steady state agents spend between one-third and one-sixth of their time working. Choices for the range of θ has already been described. δ chosen so that the annual depreciation rate of the capital stock is between 8 and 12 percent per year. In simulation studies δ is commonly set to 0.025 which corresponds to a 10 percent annual depreciation rate. Cooley and Hansen chose a slightly lower value to match the value of the postwar investment-output ratio. In calculations I performed when quantities are not measured in per capita terms, I came up with a quarterly value for δ of 0.03. Finally, McGratten (1990) estimates δ to be 0.0226 with a standard error of 0.001. The range for α reflects calculations appearing in Christiano (1988) where, depending on how proprietors income is treated, the share of total output that is payment to capital varies between 0.25 and 0.43 and estimates obtained by, e.g., McGratten (1990).

Figure 3 plots the 90 percent bands for the welfare costs associated with each tax instrument when 10000 β vectors are drawn together with the median value of the distribution. The bands are, in general, large and nonmonotone, for a substantial portion of the grid the welfare costs of capital taxation include negative and zero values and the costs of consumption and income taxation are high for moderate tax rates. Note also that, in relative terms, the costs of capital taxation are smaller than with the other two taxes. The nonmonotonicity of the bands is due to the strong nonlinearities of Δc in the various tax rates. The fact that a low level of capital taxation yields negative welfare losses and that the costs of capital taxation appear to be smaller than with the other two taxes is related to the disincentive to work that capital taxation induces on agents. Therefore, the lower disutility of working is compensated by a lower level of consumption which needed to restore the agents to the nondistorted steady state level of utility.

To examine how far the U.S. economy is from an optimum, I compute the welfare losses using the values of the average tax rates on labor and capital obtained

SENSITIVITY ANALYSIS AND MODEL EVALUATION   497

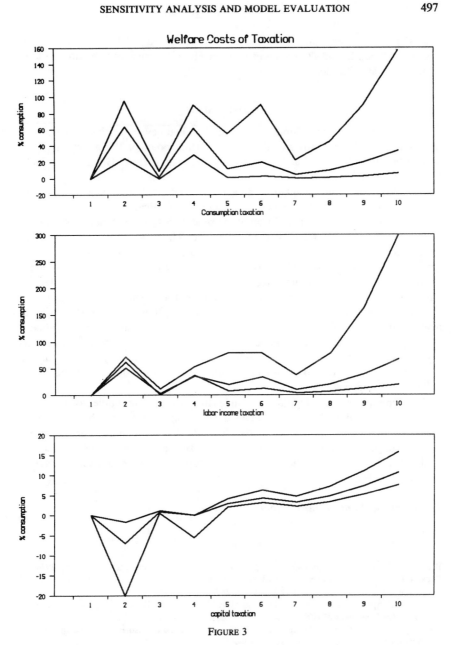

FIGURE 3

from Joines (1981) (0.23 and 0.50) and a consumption tax rate of zero. The 90 percent band for welfare losses corresponding to this tax vector is [0.12, 0.71], the median value of 0.25 and a mode of 0.52 (compared with a value of 0.31 obtained by Cooley and Hansen). Hence, if one takes the model seriously and believes

498   FABIO CANOVA

Joines' estimates, one can bound the distortions caused by the current U.S. tax system between 12 and 71 percent of U.S. steady state consumption with the most likely value at 52 percent.[6]

6. CONCLUSIONS

This paper describes a Monte Carlo approach to evaluate the properties of dynamic general equilibrium models. The starting point of the approach is the assumption that the model as DGP for the actual data is false. Given this point of view, standard classical inferential procedures are inappropriate and a new methodology for model evaluation is called for. The technique suggested in this paper can cope with the deficiencies of standard statistical analysis and provides formal foundations for the evaluation of the model via "stylized facts," which has been typical in the real business cycle literature. The procedure accounts for the uncertainty faced by a simulator in choosing the parameters of the model in a realistic way. The presence of this uncertainty becomes the key to provide a measure of dispersion for simulated statistics, a probabilistic metric to judge the closeness of the simulated and the actual data and an evaluation criteria for the model. The approach has a built-in feature which allows for global sensitivity analysis and several forms of conditional or local sensitivity analysis and evaluates the range of possibilities of the model by attaching probability statements to events a simulator may be interested in characterizing. Finally, the approach is easy to implement and includes existing calibration, estimation by simulation and GMM techniques as special cases.

The technique is applied to three examples involving different objectives, level of knowledge about the "deep" parameters and complexity and shows how to provide realistic conclusions to policy questions. Note also that computation considerations are not a major issue for problems of moderate size. For all the examples presented in this paper densities for the objects of interest were computed in a matter of minutes.

Universitat Pompeu Fabra, Spain

REFERENCES

BERTSEKAS, D., *Dynamic Programming and Stochastic Control* (New York: Academic Press, 1976).
BACKUS, D., A. GREGORY, AND S. ZIN, "Risk Premiums in the Terms Structure: Evidence from Artificial Economies," *Journal of Monetary Economics* 24 (1989), 371–399.
BAXTER, M., "Approximating Suboptimal Dynamic Equilibria: An Euler Equation Approach," *Journal of Monetary Economics* 27 (1991), 173–200.
BOX, G., "Sampling and Bayes Inference in Scientific Modelling and Robustness," *Journal of the Royal Statistical Society* Series A, 143 (1980), 383–430.
BURNSIDE, C., M. EICHENBAUM, AND S. REBELO, "Labor Hoarding and the Business Cycle," *Journal of Political Economy* 101 (1993), 245–273.

[6] McGratten (1990) shows that there are large differences in the time series properties for tax rates in the existing literature. Therefore both the magnitude of the band and its most likely value should be viewed with caution.

CANOVA, F., M. FINN, AND A. PAGAN, "Evaluating a Real Business Cycle Model," in C. Hargreaves, ed., *Nonstationary Time Series Analyses and Co-integration* (Oxford: Oxford University Press, 1993).

—— AND J. MARRINAN, "Reconciling the Term Structure of Interest Rates with the Consumption Based ICAP Model," *Journal of Economic Dynamic and Control* (forthcoming).

—— AND ——, "Profits, Risk and Uncertainty in Foreign Exchange Markets," *Journal of Monetary Economics* 32 (1993), 259–286.

CAMPBELL, J. AND R. SHILLER, "A Simple Account of the Behavior of Long Term Interest Rates," *American Economic Review, Papers and Proceedings* 74 (1987), 44–48.

CHRISTIANO, L., "Why Does Inventory Fluctuate so Much?" *Journal of Monetary Economics* 21 (1988), 247–280.

——, "Solving the Stochastic Growth Model by Linear Quadratic Approximation and by Value Function Iteration," *Journal of Business and Economic Statistics* 8 (1990), 23–26.

COLEMAN, W., "An Algorithm to Solve Dynamic Models," Discussion Paper No. 351, Board of Governors of the Federal Reserve System, International Finance Division, 1989.

COOLEY, T. AND G. HANSEN, "Tax Distortions in a Neoclassical Monetary Economy," Discussion Paper No. 38, Institute for Empirical Macroeconomics, Federal Reserve Bank of Minneapolis, 1990.

DEATON, A., "Life Cycle Models of Consumption: Is the Evidence Consistent with Theory?" in T. Bewley, ed., *Advance in Econometrics: Fifth World Congress*, Vol. 2 (New York: Cambridge University Press, 1987).

DOTSEY, M. AND C. S. MÁO, "How Well Do Linear Approximation Methods Work? Results for Suboptimal Dynamic Equilibria," *Journal of Monetary Economics* 29 (1991), 25–58.

EL-GAMAL, M., "The Extraction of Information from Multiple Point Estimates," *Nonparametric Statistics* (forthcoming 1993).

FAIR, R., "Estimating Event Probabilities from Macroeconomic Models Using Stochastic Simulations," manuscript, Yale University, 1991.

FRANKEL, J. AND K. FROOT, "Using Survey Data to Tests Standard Propositions Regarding Exchange Rate Expectations," *American Economic Review* 77 (1987), 133–159.

FRIEDMAN, M., *Essays in Positive Economics* (New York: Aldine Press, 1959).

FRISCH, R., "Propagation Problems and Impulse Problems in Dynamics Economics," in *Economic Essays in Honor of Gustav Cassel* (London: 1933).

GELFAND, A. AND A. SMITH, "Sampling Based Approaches to Calculating Marginal Densities," *Journal of the American Statistical Association* 85 (1990), 398–409.

GENEST, G. AND J. ZIDEK, "Combining Probability Distributions: A Critique and an Annotated Bibliography," *Statistical Science* 1 (1986), 114–148.

GEWEKE, J., "Bayesian Inference in Econometric Models Using Monte Carlo Integration," *Econometrica* 57 (1989), 1317–1339.

GREGORY, A. AND G. SMITH, "Calibration as Estimation," *Econometric Reviews* 9 (1989), 57–89.

—— AND ——, "Calibration as Testing: Inference in Simulated Macro Models," *Journal of Business and Economic Statistics* 9 (1991), 297–303.

—— AND ——, "Calibration in Macroeconomics," in G. S. Maddala, ed., *Handbook of Statistics*, Vol. 10 (Amsterdam: North Holland, 1993).

HAAVELMO, A., "The Probability Approach in Econometrics," *Econometrica* 12 (1944), Supplement.

HANSEN, L., "Large Sample Properties of Generalized Method of Moment Estimators," *Econometrica* 50 (1982), 1029–1054.

—— AND T. SARGENT, "Formulating and Estimating Dynamic Linear Rational Expectations Models," *Journal of Economic Dynamic and Control* 2 (1979), 7–46.

—— AND K. SINGLETON, "Stochastic Consumption, Risk Aversion and Temporal Behavior of Asset Returns," *Journal of Political Economy* 91 (1983), 249–265.

HARRISON, G. AND H. D. VINOD, "Sensitivity Analysis of Applied General Equilibrium Models: Completely Randomized Factorial Sampling Designs," manuscript, University of New Mexico, 1989.

HODRICK, R., "Risk, Uncertainty and Foreign Exchange Markets," *Journal of Monetary Economics* 23 (1989), 433–459.

JOINES, D., "Estimates of Effective Marginal Tax Rates on Factor Incomes," *Journal of Business* 54 (1981), 191–226.

500   FABIO CANOVA

JORGENSON, D., "Econometric Methods for Applied General Equilibrium Analysis," in H. Scarf and J. Whalley, eds., *Applied General Equilibrium Analysis* (New York: Cambridge University Press, 1984).

JOURNAL OF BUSINESS AND ECONOMIC STATISTICS (January 1990).

JUDD, K., "Projection Methods for Solving Aggregate Growth Models," *Journal of Economic Theory* 58 (1992), 410–452.

KANDEL, S. AND R. STAMBAUGH, "Expectations and Volatility of Consumption and Asset Returns," *Review of Financial Studies* 3 (1990), 207–232.

KIM, K. AND A. PAGAN, "The Econometric Analysis of Calibrated Macroeconomic Models," in H. Pesaran and M. Wickens, eds., *Handbook of Applied Econometrics*, Vol. 1 (London: Blackwell Press, 1993).

KING, R., C. PLOSSER, AND S. REBELO, "Production, Growth and Business Cycles: I," *Journal of Monetary Economics* 21 (1988), 195–232.

KWAN, Y. K., "Bayesian Analysis with an Unknown Likelihood Function: A Limited Information Approach," manuscript, University of Chicago Business School, 1991a.

———, "Bayesian Calibration with an Application to a Non-linear Rational Expectation Two Country Model," manuscript, University of Chicago Business School, 1991b.

KYDLAND, F. AND E. PRESCOTT, "Time to Build and Aggregate Fluctuations," *Econometrica* 50 (1982), 1345–1370.

——— AND ———, "The Econometrics of the General Equilibrium Approach to Business Cycles," *Scandinavian Journal of Economics* 93 (1991), 161–178.

LEE, B. S. AND B. INGRAM, "Simulation Estimators of Time Series Models," *Journal of Econometrics* 47 (1991), 197–206.

MARCET, A., "Solving Nonlinear Rational Expectations Models by Parametrizing Expectations," Working Paper No. 5, Universitat Pompeu Fabra, 1992.

MCGRATTEN, E., "The Macroeconomic Effects of Distortionary Taxation," Discussion Paper No. 37, Institute for Empirical Macroeconomics, Federal Reserve Bank of Minneapolis, 1990.

MERHA, R. AND E. PRESCOTT, "The Equity Premium: A Puzzle," *Journal of Monetary Economics* 15 (1985), 145–162.

NIEDERREITER, H., "Quasi Monte Carlo Methods for Multidimensional Numerical Integration," *International Series of Numerical Mathematics* 85 (1988), 157–171.

NOVALES, A., "Solving Nonlinear Rational Expectations Models: A Stochastic Equilibrium Model of Interest Rates," *Econometrica* 58 (1990), 93–111.

PAGAN, A. AND SHANNON, "Sensitivity Analysis for Linearized Computable General Equilibrium Models," in J. Piggott and J. Whalley, eds., *New Developments in Applied General Equilibrium Analysis* (Cambridge: Cambridge University Press, 1985).

——— AND A. ULLAH, "The Econometric Analysis of Models with Risk Terms," *Journal of Applied Econometrics* 3 (1988), 87–105.

——— AND ———, "Non-Parametric Estimation," manuscript, University of Rochester, 1991.

PHILLIPS, P.C.B., "To Criticize the Critics: An Objective Bayesian Analysis of Stochastic Trends," *Journal of Applied Econometrics* 6 (1991), 333–354.

SARGENT, T., *Dynamic Macroeconomic Theory* (Cambridge: Harvard Press, 1987).

SHOVEN, J. AND J. WHALLEY, "Applied General Equilibrium Models of Taxation and International Trade: An Introduction and Survey," *Journal of Economic Literature* 22 (1984), 1007–1051.

SIMS, C., "Solving Nonlinear Stochastic Equilibrium Models Backward," manuscript, University of Minnesota, 1984.

———, "Bayesian Skepticism on Unit Root Econometrics," *Journal of Economic Dynamic and Control* 12 (1988), 463–474.

———, "Models and Their Users," *American Journal of Agricultural Economics* 71 (1989), 489–494.

SMITH, T., "Estimating Non-Linear Time Series Models Using Simulated VAR: Two Approaches," *Journal of Applied Econometrics* 8 (1993), S63–S84.

STOCK, J. AND M. WATSON, "Interpreting the Evidence of Money-Income Causality," *Journal of Econometrics* 40 (1989), 161–182.

TANNER, M. AND W. WONG, "The Calculation of Posterior Distributions by Data Augmentation," *Journal of the American Statistical Association* 87 (1987), 528–550.

TAUCHEN, G. AND R. HUSSEY, "Quadrature Based Methods for Obtaining Approximate Solutions to Integral Equations of Nonlinear Asset Pricing Models," *Econometrica* 59 (1991), 371–397.

WATSON, M., "Measures of Fit for Calibrated Models," *Journal of Political Economy* 101 (1993), 1011–1041.

WOLF, F., *Meta-Analysis: Quantitative Methods for Research Synthesis* (Beverly Hills: Sage, 1986).

Part VI

Testing the real business cycle model

Federal Reserve Bank of Minneapolis
Quarterly Review   Spring 1990

Business Cycles: Real Facts and a Monetary Myth[*]

Finn E. Kydland
Professor of Economics
Graduate School of Industrial Administration
Carnegie–Mellon University

Edward C. Prescott
Adviser
Research Department
Federal Reserve Bank of Minneapolis
and Professor of Economics
University of Minnesota

Ever since Koopmans (1947) criticized Burns and Mitchell's (1946) book on *Measuring Business Cycles* as being "measurement without theory," the reporting of business cycle facts has been taboo in economics. In his essay, Koopmans presents two basic criticisms of Burns and Mitchell's study. The first is that it provides no systematic discussion of the theoretical reasons for including particular variables over others in their empirical investigation. Before variables can be selected, Koopmans argues, some notion is needed of the theory that generates the economic fluctuations. With this first criticism we completely agree: Theory is crucial in selecting which facts to report.

Koopmans' second criticism is that Burns and Mitchell's study lacks explicit assumptions about the probability distribution of the variables. That is, their study lacks "assumptions expressing and specifying how random disturbances operate on the economy through the economic relationships between the variables" (Koopmans 1947, p. 172). What Koopmans has in mind as such relationships is clear when he concludes an overview of Burns and Mitchell's so-called measures with this sentence: "Not a single demand or supply schedule or other equation expressing the behavior of men [i.e., people] or the technical laws of production is employed explicitly in the book, and the cases of implicit use are few and far between" (p. 163). Koopmans repeatedly stresses this need for using a structural system of equations as an organizing principle (pp. 169–70). Economists, he argues, should first hypothe-size that the aggregate time series under consideration are generated by some probability model, which the economists must then estimate and test. Koopmans convinced the economics profession that to do otherwise is unscientific. On this point we strongly disagree with Koopmans: We think he did economics a grave disservice, because the reporting of facts—without assuming the data are generated by some probability model—is an important scientific activity. We see no reason for economics to be an exception.

As a spectacular example of facts influencing the development of economic theory, we refer to the growth facts that came out of the empirical work of Kuznets and others. According to Solow (1970, p. 2), these facts were instrumental in the development of his own neoclassical growth model, which has since become the most important organizing structure in macroeconomics, whether the issue is one of growth or fluctuations or public finance. Loosely paraphrased, the key growth facts that Solow lists (on pp. 2–3) are

- Real output per worker (or per worker-hour) grows at a roughly constant rate over extended time periods.
- The stock of real capital, crudely measured, grows at a roughly constant rate which exceeds the growth rate of labor input.

---

[*]The authors thank the National Science Foundation for financial support.

- The growth rates of real output and the stock of capital goods tend to be similar, so the capital-to-output ratio shows no systematic trend.
- The rate of profit on capital has a horizontal trend.

These facts are neither estimates nor measures of anything; they are obtained without first hypothesizing that the time series are generated by a probability model belonging to some class. From this example, no one can deny that the reporting of growth facts has scientific value: Why else would Kuznets have received a Nobel Prize for this work? Or Solow, as well, for developing a parsimonious theory that rationalizes these facts—namely, his neoclassical growth model?

The growth facts are not the only interesting features of these aggregate time series. Also of interest are the more volatile changes that occur in these and other aggregates—that is, the cyclical behavior of the time series. These observations are interesting because they apparently conflict with basic competitive theory, in which outcomes reflect people's ability and willingness to substitute between consumption and leisure at a given point in time and between consumption at different points in time.

The purpose of this article is to present the business cycle facts in light of established neoclassical growth theory, which we use as the organizing framework for our presentation of business cycle facts. We emphasize that the statistics reported here are not measures of anything; rather, they are statistics that display interesting patterns, given the established neoclassical growth theory. In discussions of business cycle models, a natural question is, Do the corresponding statistics for the model economy display these patterns? We find these features interesting because the patterns they seem to display are inconsistent with the theory.

The study of business cycles flourished from the 1920s through the 1940s. But in the 1950s and 1960s, with the development of the structural system-of-equations approach that Koopmans advocated, business cycles ceased to be an active area of economic research. Now, once again, the study of business cycles, in the form of recurrent fluctuations, is alive. At the leading research centers, economists are again concerned with the question of why, in market economies, aggregate output and employment undergo repeated fluctuations about trend.[1]

Instrumental in bringing business cycles back into the mainstream of economic research is the important paper by Lucas (1977), "Understanding Business Cycles." We follow Lucas in defining *business cycles* as the deviations of aggregate real output from trend. We complete his definition by providing an explicit procedure for calculating a time series trend that successfully mimics the smooth curves most business cycle researchers would draw through plots of the data. We also follow Lucas in viewing the business cycle facts as the statistical properties of the comovements of deviations from trend of various economic aggregates with those of real output.

Lucas' definition differs importantly from that of Mitchell (1913, 1927), whose definition had guided students of business cycles up until World War II. Mitchell represents business cycles as sequences of expansions and contractions, particularly emphasizing turning points and phases of the cycle. We think the developments in economic theory that followed Mitchell's work dictate Lucas' representation of cycles.

Equipped with our operational definition of cyclical deviations, we present what we see as the key business cycle facts for the United States economy in the post–Korean War period (1954–1989). Some of these facts are fairly well known; others, however, are likely to come as a surprise because they are counter to beliefs often stated in the literature.

An important example of one of these commonly held beliefs is that the price level always has been procyclical and that, in this regard, the postwar period is no exception. Even Lucas (1977, p. 9) lists procyclical price levels among business cycle regularities. This perceived fact strongly influenced business cycle research in the 1970s. A more recent example of this misbelief is when Bernanke (1986, p. 76) discusses a study by King and Plosser (1984): "Although some points of their analysis could be criticized (for example, there is no tight explanation of the relation between transaction services and the level of demand deposits, and the model does not yield a strong prediction of price procyclicality), the overall framework is not implausible." Even more recently, Mankiw (1989, p. 88), in discussing the same paper, points out that "while the story of King and Plosser can explain the procyclical behavior of money, it cannot explain the procyclical behavior of prices." We shall see that, in fact, these criticisms are based on what is a myth. We show that during the 35 years since the Korean War, the price level has displayed a clear *countercyclical* pattern.

Other misperceptions we expose are the beliefs that

---

[1] The view of Hayek (1933, p. 33) in the 1930s and Lucas (1977, p. 7) in the 1970s is that answering this question is one of the outstanding challenges to economic research.

Finn E. Kydland, Edward C. Prescott
Business Cycles

the real wage is either countercyclical or essentially uncorrelated with the cycle and that the money stock, whether measured by the monetary base or by M1, leads the cycle.

The real facts documented in this paper are that major output components tend to move together over the cycle, with investment in consumer and producer durables having several times larger percentage deviations than does spending on nondurable consumption.

Alternative Views of Business Cycles

To many, when we talk about cycles, the picture that comes to mind is a sine wave with its regular and recurrent pattern. In economics and other sciences, however, the term *cycle* refers to a more general concept. One of the best-known examples of cycles is the sunspot cycle, which varies in length from under 10 years to nearly 20 years. The significant fact about cycles is the recurrent nature of the events.

In 1922, at a Conference on Cycles, representatives from several sciences discussed the cyclical phenomena in their fields. The participants agreed on the following definition (quoted in Mitchell 1927, p. 377) as being reasonable for all the sciences: "In general scientific use . . . the word (cycle) denotes a recurrence of different phases of plus and minus departures, which are often susceptible of exact measurement." Our definition of business cycles is consistent with this general definition, but we refer to departures as *deviations*.

Mitchell's Four Phases

In 1913, Wesley C. Mitchell published a major work on business cycles, in it reviewing the research that had preceded his own. The book presents his largely descriptive approach, which consists of decomposing a large number of time series into sequences of cycles and then dividing each cycle into four distinct phases. This work was continued by Mitchell (1927) and by Burns and Mitchell (1946), who defined business cycles as

> . . . a type of fluctuation found in the aggregate economic activity of nations that organize their work mainly in business enterprises: a cycle consists of expansions occurring at about the same time in many economic activities, followed by similarly general recessions, contractions, and revivals which merge into the expansion phase of the next cycle; this sequence of changes is recurrent but not periodic; in duration business cycles vary from more than one year to ten or twelve years; they are not divisible into shorter cycles of similar character with amplitudes approximating their own (p. 3).

From the discussion in their books, it is clear the authors view business cycles as consisting of four phases that inevitably evolve from one into another: prosperity, crisis, depression, and revival. This view is expressed perhaps most clearly by Mitchell ([1923] 1951, p. 46), who writes: "Then in order will come a discussion of how prosperity produces conditions which lead to crises, how crises run into depressions, and finally how depressions after a time produce conditions which lead to new revivals." Mitchell clearly had in mind a theoretical framework consistent with that view. In defending the use of the framework of four distinct cyclical phases, Mitchell later wrote that "most current theories explain crises by what happens in prosperity and revivals by what happens in depression" (Mitchell 1927, p. 472). (For an extensive overview of these theories and their relationship to Mitchell's descriptive work, see Haberler 1937.)

We now know how to construct model economies whose equilibria display business cycles like those envisioned by Mitchell. For example, a line of research that gained attention in the 1980s demonstrates that cyclical patterns of this form result as equilibrium behavior for economic environments with appropriate preferences and technologies. (See, for example, Benhabib and Nishimura 1985 and Boldrin 1989.) Burns and Mitchell would have been much more influential if business cycle theory had evolved in this way. Koopmans (1957, pp. 215–16) makes this point in his largely unnoticed "second thought" on Burns and Mitchell's work on business cycles.

In retrospect, it is now clear that the field of business cycles has moved in a completely different direction from the one Mitchell envisioned. Theories with deterministic cyclical laws of motion may a priori have had considerable potential for accounting for business cycles; but in fact, they have failed to do so. They have failed because cyclical laws of motion do not arise as equilibrium behavior for economies with empirically reasonable preferences and technologies—that is, for economies with reasonable statements of people's ability and willingness to substitute.

Frisch's Pendulum

As early as the 1930s, some economists were developing business cycle models that gave rise to difference equations with random shocks. An important example appears in a paper by Ragnar Frisch ([1933] 1965). Frisch was careful to distinguish between impulses in the form of random shocks, on the one hand, and their propagation over time, on the other. In contrast with proponents of modern business cycle theory, he emphasized damped oscillatory behavior. The concept of

5

equilibrium was interpreted as a system at rest (as it is, for instance, in the science of mechanics).

The analogy of a pendulum is sometimes used to describe this view of cycles. Shocks are needed to provide "energy in maintaining oscillations" in damped cyclical systems. Frisch reports that he was influenced by Knut Wicksell, to whom he attributes the following: "If you hit a wooden rocking horse with a club, the movement of the horse will be very different to that of the club" (quoted in Frisch [1933] 1965, p. 178). The use of the rocking horse and pendulum analogies underscores their emphasis on cycles in the form of damped oscillations.

The research of Frisch and Wicksell received considerable attention in the 1930s, but no one built on their work. Construction stopped primarily because the neoclassical growth model and the necessary conceptual tools (particularly the Arrow–Debreu general equilibrium theory) had not yet been developed. Since the tools to do quantitative dynamic general equilibrium analysis weren't available, whereas statistical time series techniques were advancing rapidly, it's not surprising that quantitative system-of-equation models—especially the Keynesian income-expenditure models—received virtually all the attention.

Slutzky's Random Shocks

An entirely different way of generating cycles is suggested by the statistical work of Eugen Slutzky (1937). Slutzky shows that cycles resembling business fluctuations can be generated as the sum of random causes—that is, by a stable, low-order, stochastic difference equation with large positive real roots.

The following exercise illustrates how Slutzky's method can generate cycles. Let the random variable e_t take the value 0.5 if a coin flip shows heads and -0.5 if tails. Assume that

$$(1) \quad y_{t+1} = 0.95y_t + e_{t+1}.$$

By repeated substitution, y_t is related to current and past shocks in the following way:

$$(2) \quad y_t = e_t + 0.95e_{t-1} + 0.95^2 e_{t-2} + \cdots$$
$$+ 0.95^{t-1}e_1 + 0.95^t y_0.$$

The y_t are geometrically declining sums of past shocks. Given an initial value y_0 and a fair coin, this stochastic difference equation can be used to generate a random path for the variable y.

Chart 1

Cycles Generated by Slutzky's Mechanism

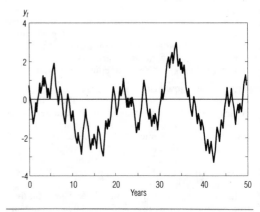

Chart 1 plots a time series generated in this way. The time series displays patterns that Burns and Mitchell (1946) would characterize as business cycles.[2] The amplitudes and duration of cycles are variable, with the duration varying from 1 to 12 years and averaging about 3½ years. The time series seems to display cycles in Mitchell's sense of expansions containing the seed for recessions and vice versa. But, by construction, recessions do not contain the seed of subsequent expansions. At each point in time, the expected future path is monotonic and converges to the zero mean, with 5 percent of the distance being closed in each quarterly time period.

Another demonstration of the role that random shocks can play appears in a paper by Adelman and Adelman (1959). Using the Klein–Goldberger model, they show that by adding random shocks to the model, it produces aggregate time series that look remarkably like those of the post–World War II economy of the United States. The deterministic version of this model converges almost monotonically to a point. This exercise forcefully demonstrates that a stochastic process can generate recurrent cycles while its deterministic version can converge monotonically.

Advancing to Lucas' Deviations

In the 1940s and the 1950s, while macroeconometric

---

[2]King and Plosser (1989) describe a well-defined, judgment-free scheme that successfully mimics the Burns and Mitchell procedure. The description of the cycles in the time series plotted in Chart 1 is based on this procedure.

Finn E. Kydland, Edward C. Prescott
Business Cycles

system-of-equations models were being developed, important theoretical advances were being made along entirely different fronts. By the early 1960s, economists' understanding of the way economic environments work in general equilibrium had advanced by leaps and bounds. The application of general equilibrium theory in dynamic environments led to theoretical insights on the growth of economies; it also led to important measurements of the parameters of the aggregate production function that formed the foundation for neoclassical growth theory. Thus, by the late 1960s, there were two established theories competing for dominance in aggregate economics. One was the behavioral-empirical approach reflected in the Keynesian system-of-equations models. The other was the neoclassical approach, which modeled environments with rational, maximizing individuals and firms. The neoclassical approach dominated public finance, growth theory, and international trade. As neoclassical theory progressed, an unresolvable conflict developed between the two approaches. The impasse developed because dynamic maximizing behavior is inconsistent with the assumption of invariant behavioral equations, an assumption that underlies the system-of-equations approach.

Not until the 1970s did business cycles again receive attention, spurred on by Lucas' (1977) article, "Understanding Business Cycles." There, Lucas viewed business cycle regularities as "comovements of the deviations from trend in different aggregative time series." He defined the business cycle itself as the "movements about trend in gross national product." Two types of considerations led Lucas to this definition: the previously discussed findings of Slutzky and the Adelmans, and the important advances in economic theory, especially neoclassical growth theory. We interpret Lucas as viewing business cycle fluctuations as being of interest because they are at variance with established neoclassical growth theory.

Another important theoretical advance of the 1960s and 1970s was the development of recursive competitive equilibrium theory. This theory made it possible to study abstractions of the aggregate economy in which optimizing economic behavior produces behavioral relations in the form of low-order stochastic difference equations. The role these advances played for Lucas' thinking is clear, as evident from one of his later articles discussing methods and problems in business cycle theory (see Lucas 1980).

In contrast with Mitchell's view of business cycles, Lucas does not think in terms of sequences of cycles as inevitable waves in economic activity, nor does he see a

need to distinguish among different phases of the cycle. To Lucas, the comovements over time of the cyclical components of economic aggregates are of primary interest, and he gives several examples of what he views as the business cycle regularities. We make explicit and operational what we mean by these terms and present a systematic account of the regularities. When that step is implemented quantitatively, some regularities emerge that, in the 1970s, would have come as a surprise—even to Lucas.

Modern Business Cycle Theory

In the 1980s and now in the early 1990s, business cycles (in the sense of recurrent fluctuations) increasingly have become a focus of study in aggregate economics. Such studies are generally guided by perceived business cycle regularities. But if these perceptions are not in fact the regularities, then certain lines of research are misguided.

For example, the myth that the price level is procyclical largely accounts for the prevalence in the 1970s of studies that use equilibrium models with monetary policy or price surprises as the main source of fluctuations. At the time, monetary disturbances appeared to be the only plausible source of fluctuations that could not be ruled out as being too small, so they were the leading candidate. The work of Friedman and Schwartz (1963) also contributed to the view that monetary disturbances are the main source of business cycle fluctuations. Their work marshaled extensive empirical evidence to support the position that monetary policy is an important factor in determining aggregate output, employment, and other key aggregates.

Since the early studies of Burns and Mitchell, the emphasis in business cycle theory has shifted from essentially pure theoretical work to quantitative theoretical analysis. This quantitative research has had difficulty finding an important role for monetary changes as a source of fluctuations in real aggregates. As a result, attention has shifted to the role of other factors—technological changes, tax changes, and terms-of-trade shocks. This research has been strongly guided by business cycle facts and regularities such as those to be presented here.

Along with the shift in focus to investigating the sources and nature of business cycles, aggregate analysis underwent a methodological revolution. Previously, empirical knowledge had been organized in the form of equations, as was also the case for the early rational expectations models. Muth (1960), in his pioneering work on rational expectations, did not break with this system-of-equations tradition. For that reason, his econometric program did not come to dominate. Instead, the program which has prevailed is the one that organizes empirical knowledge around preferences, technology, information structure, and policy rules or arrangements. Sargent (1981) has led the development of tools for inferring values of parameters characterizing these elements, given the behavior of the aggregate time series. As a result, aggregate economics is no longer a separate and entirely different field from the rest of economics; it now uses the same tools and empirical knowledge as other branches of economics, such as finance, growth theory, public finance, and international economics. With this development, measurements and quantitative findings in those other fields can be used to restrict models of business cycles and make our knowledge about the quantitative importance of cyclical disturbances more precise.

Business Cycle Deviations Redefined

Because economic activity in industrial market economies is characterized by sustained growth, Lucas defines business cycles as deviations of real gross national product (GNP) from trend rather than from some constant or average value. But Lucas does not define *trend*, so his definition of business cycle deviations is incomplete. What guides our, and we think his, concept of trend is steady state growth theory. With this theory there is exogenous labor-augmenting technological change that occurs at a constant rate; that is, the effectiveness of labor grows at some constant rate. Steady state growth is characterized by per capita output, consumption, investment, capital stock, and the real wage all growing at the same rate as does technology. The part of productive time allocated to market activity and the real return on capital remain constant.

If the rate of technological change were constant, then the trend of the logarithm of real GNP would be a linear function of time. But the rate of technological change varies both over time and across countries. (*Why* it varies is the central problem in economic development or maybe in all of economics.) The rate of change clearly is related to the arrangements and institutions that a society uses and, more important, to the arrangements and institutions that people expect will be used in the future. Even in a relatively stable society like the United States since the Second World War, there have been significant changes in institutions. And when a society's institutions change, there are changes in the productivity growth of that society's labor and capital. In the United States, the rate of

technological change in the 1950s and 1960s was significantly above the U.S. historical average rate over the past 100 years. In the 1970s, the rate was significantly below average. In the 1980s, the rate was near the historical average. Because the underlying rate of technological change has not been constant in the period we examine (1954–1989), detrending using a linear function of time is inappropriate. The scheme used must let the average rate of technological change vary over time, but not too rapidly.

Any definition of the trend and cycle components, and for that matter the seasonal component, is necessarily statistical. A *decomposition* is a representation of the data. A representation is useful if, in light of theory, it reveals some interesting patterns in the data. We think our representation is successful in this regard. Our selection of a trend definition was guided by the following criteria:

- The trend component for real GNP should be approximately the curve that students of business cycles and growth would draw through a time plot of this time series.

- The trend of a given time series should be a linear transformation of that time series, and this transformation should be the same for all series.[3]

- Lengthening the sample period should not significantly alter the value of the deviations at a given date, except possibly near the end of the original sample.

- The scheme should be well defined, judgment free, and cheaply reproducible.

These criteria led us to the following scheme. Let y_t, for $t = 1, 2, \ldots, T$, denote a time series. We deal with logarithms of a variable, unless the variable is a share, because the percentage deviations are what display the interesting patterns. Moreover, when an exponentially growing time series is so transformed, it becomes linear in time. Our trend component, denoted τ_t, for $t = 1, 2, \ldots, T$, is the one that minimizes

$$(3) \quad \sum_{t=1}^{T} (y_t - \tau_t)^2 + \lambda \sum_{t=2}^{T-1} [(\tau_{t+1} - \tau_t) - (\tau_t - \tau_{t-1})]^2$$

---

[3]The reason for linearity is that the first two moments of the transformed data are functions of the first two moments, and not the higher moments, of the original data. The principal rationale for the same transformation being applied to all time series is that it makes little sense to carry out the analogue of growth accounting with the inputs to the production function subject to one transformation and the outputs subject to another.

Finn E. Kydland, Edward C. Prescott
Business Cycles

for an appropriately chosen positive $\bar{\lambda}$. (The value of λ will be specified momentarily.) The first term is the sum of the squared deviations $d_t = y_t - \tau_t$. The second term is multiple λ of the sum of the squares of the trend component's second differences. This second term penalizes variations in the growth rate of the trend component, with the penalty being correspondingly larger if λ is larger.

The first-order conditions for this convex minimization problem are linear and can be solved for the τ_t.[4] We found that if the time series are quarterly, a value of $\lambda = 1600$ is reasonable. With this value, the implied trend path for the logarithm of real GNP is close to the one that students of business cycles and growth would draw through a time plot of this series, as shown in Chart 2. The remaining criteria guiding our selection of a detrending procedure are satisfied as well.

We have learned that this procedure for constructing a smooth curve through the data has a long history in both the actuarial and the natural sciences. Stigler (1978) reports that actuarial scientists used this method in the 1920s. He also notes that John von Neumann, who undoubtedly reinvented it, used it in the ballistics literature in the early 1940s. That others facing similar problems developed this simple scheme attests to its reasonableness. What is surprising is that economists took so long to exploit this scheme and that so many of them were so hostile to the idea when it was finally introduced into economics.[5]

Business Cycle Facts and Regularities

We emphasize that our selection of the facts to report is guided by neoclassical growth theory. This theory, currently the established one in aggregate economics, is being used not only to study growth and development but also to address public finance issues and, more recently, to study business cycles. The facts we present here are the values of well-defined statistics for the U.S. economy since the Korean War (1954–1989). We refer to consistent patterns in these numbers as business cycle *regularities*.

The statistics presented in Tables 1–4 provide information on three basic aspects of the cyclical behavior of aggregates:

- The amplitude of fluctuations
- The degree of comovement with real GNP (our measure of pro- or countercyclicality)
- The phase shift of a variable relative to the overall business cycle, as defined by the behavior of cyclical real GNP.

Chart 2

Actual and Trend of U.S. Real Gross National Product

Quarterly, 1954–1989

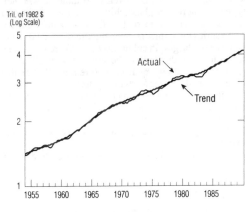

Source of basic data: Citicorp's Citibase data bank

We emphasize that, except for the share variables shown in Table 2, these statistics are percentage, not absolute, deviations. For instance, the percentage deviation of investment expenditures is more than three times that of total real GNP. Since this component averages less than one-fifth of real GNP, its absolute volatility is somewhat less than that of total output.

In the tables, the degree of contemporaneous comovement with real GNP is indicated in the $x(t)$ column. The statistics in that column are the correlation coefficients of the cyclical deviations of each series with the cyclical deviations of real GNP. A number close to one indicates that a series is highly *procyclical;* a number close to one but of the opposite sign indicates that a series is *countercyclical.* A number close to zero means that a series does not vary contemporaneously with the cycle in any systematic way, in which case we say the series is *uncorrelated* with the cycle.

The remaining columns of the tables also display

---

[4] A short FORTRAN subroutine that efficiently computes the trend and deviations components is available on request to the Research Department, Federal Reserve Bank of Minneapolis. The computation time required by this algorithm increases linearly with the length of the sample period, as do storage requirements.

[5] This approach was introduced in an unpublished paper by Hodrick and Prescott (1980).

correlation coefficients, except the series have been shifted forward or backward, relative to real GNP, by from one to five quarters. To some extent these numbers indicate the degree of comovement with GNP. Their main purpose, however, is to indicate whether, typically, there is a phase shift in the movement of a time series relative to real GNP. For example, if for some series the numbers in the middle of each table are positive but largest in column $x(t-i)$, where $i > 0$, then the numbers indicate that the series is procyclical but tends to peak about i quarters before real GNP. In this case we say the series *leads* the cycle. Correspondingly, a series that *lags* the cycle by $j > 0$ quarters would have the largest correlation coefficient in the column headed by $x(t+j)$. For example, productivity is a series that leads the cycle, whereas the stock of inventories is one that lags the cycle.

We let the neoclassical growth model dictate which facts to examine and how to organize them. The aggregate economy can be divided broadly into three sectors: businesses, households, and government. In the business sector, the model emphasizes production inputs as well as output components. Households allocate income earned in the business sector to consumption and saving. In the aggregate, there is an accounting relation between household saving and business investment. Households allocate a fraction of their discretionary time to income-earning activities in the business sector. The remaining fraction goes to nonmarket activities, usually referred to as leisure but sometimes (perhaps more appropriately) as input to household production. This time-allocation decision has received little attention in growth theory, but it is crucial to business cycle theory. The government sector, which is at the heart of public finance theory, also could play a significant role for business cycles.

Table 1

Cyclical Behavior of U.S. Production Inputs

Deviations From Trend of Input Variables
Quarterly, 1954–1989

Variable x	Volatility (% Std. Dev.)	Cross Correlation of Real GNP With										
		x(t−5)	x(t−4)	x(t−3)	x(t−2)	x(t−1)	x(t)	x(t+1)	x(t+2)	x(t+3)	x(t+4)	x(t+5)
Real Gross National Product	1.71	−0.03	0.15	0.38	0.63	0.85	1.00	0.85	0.63	0.38	0.15	−0.03
Labor Input												
Hours (Household Survey)	1.47	−0.10	0.05	0.23	0.44	0.69	0.86	0.86	0.75	0.59	0.38	0.18
Employment	1.06	−0.18	−0.04	0.14	0.36	0.61	0.82	0.89	0.82	0.67	0.47	0.25
Hours per Worker	0.54	0.08	0.21	0.35	0.49	0.66	0.71	0.59	0.43	0.29	0.11	−0.02
Hours (Establishment Survey)	1.65	−0.23	−0.07	0.14	0.39	0.66	0.88	0.92	0.81	0.64	0.42	0.21
GNP/Hours (Household Survey)	0.88	0.11	0.21	0.34	0.48	0.50	0.51	0.21	−0.02	−0.25	−0.34	−0.36
GNP/Hours (Establishment Survey)	0.83	0.40	0.46	0.49	0.53	0.43	0.31	−0.07	−0.31	−0.49	−0.52	−0.50
Average Hourly Real Compensation (Business Sector)	0.91	0.30	0.37	0.40	0.42	0.40	0.35	0.26	0.17	0.05	−0.08	−0.20
Capital Input												
Nonresidental Capital Stock*	0.62	−0.58	−0.61	−0.51	−0.48	−0.31	−0.08	0.16	0.39	0.56	0.66	0.70
Structures	0.37	−0.45	−0.51	−0.55	−0.53	−0.44	−0.29	−0.10	0.09	0.25	0.38	0.45
Producers' Durable Equipment	0.99	−0.57	−0.58	−0.53	−0.41	−0.22	0.02	0.26	0.47	0.62	0.70	0.71
Inventory Stock (Nonfarm)	1.65	−0.37	−0.33	−0.23	−0.05	0.19	0.50	0.72	0.83	0.81	0.71	0.53

*Based on quarterly data, 1954:1–1984:2.
Source of basic data: Citicorp's Citibase data bank

10

Finn E. Kydland, Edward C. Prescott
Business Cycles

The standard version of the neoclassical growth model abstracts from money and therefore provides little guidance about which of the nominal variables to examine. Given the prominence that monetary shocks have held for many years as the main candidate for the impulse to business cycles, it seems appropriate that we also examine the cyclical behavior of monetary aggre-gates and nominal prices.

Real Facts

□ Production Inputs

We first examine real (nonmonetary) series related to the inputs in aggregate production. The cyclical facts

Table 2

Cyclical Behavior of U.S. Output and Income Components

Deviations From Trend of Product and Income Variables
Quarterly, 1954–1989

Variable x	Volatility (% Std. Dev.)	Cross Correlation of Real GNP With										
		$x(t-5)$	$x(t-4)$	$x(t-3)$	$x(t-2)$	$x(t-1)$	$x(t)$	$x(t+1)$	$x(t+2)$	$x(t+3)$	$x(t+4)$	$x(t+5)$
Real Gross National Product	1.71	−0.03	0.15	0.38	0.63	0.85	1.00	0.85	0.63	0.38	0.15	−0.03
Consumption Expenditures	1.25	0.25	0.41	0.56	0.71	0.81	0.82	0.66	0.45	0.21	−0.02	−0.21
Nondurables & Services	0.84	0.20	0.38	0.53	0.67	0.77	0.76	0.63	0.46	0.27	0.06	−0.12
Nondurables	1.23	0.29	0.42	0.52	0.62	0.69	0.69	0.57	0.38	0.16	−0.05	−0.22
Services	0.63	0.03	0.25	0.46	0.63	0.73	0.71	0.60	0.49	0.39	0.23	0.07
Durables	4.99	0.25	0.38	0.50	0.64	0.74	0.77	0.60	0.37	0.10	−0.14	−0.32
Investment Expenditures	8.30	0.04	0.19	0.39	0.60	0.79	0.91	0.75	0.50	0.21	−0.05	−0.26
Fixed Investment	5.38	0.09	0.25	0.44	0.64	0.83	0.90	0.81	0.60	0.35	0.08	−0.14
Nonresidential	5.18	−0.26	−0.13	0.05	0.31	0.57	0.80	0.88	0.83	0.68	0.46	0.23
Structures	4.75	−0.40	−0.31	−0.17	0.03	0.29	0.52	0.65	0.69	0.63	0.50	0.34
Equipment	6.21	−0.18	−0.04	0.14	0.39	0.65	0.85	0.90	0.81	0.62	0.38	0.15
Residential	10.89	0.42	0.56	0.66	0.73	0.73	0.62	0.37	0.10	−0.15	−0.34	−0.45
Government Purchases	2.07	0.00	−0.03	−0.03	−0.01	−0.01	0.05	0.09	0.12	0.17	0.27	0.34
Federal	3.68	0.00	−0.05	−0.08	−0.09	−0.09	−0.02	0.03	0.06	0.10	0.19	0.24
State & Local	1.19	0.06	0.10	0.17	0.25	0.26	0.25	0.20	0.16	0.19	0.27	0.36
Exports	5.53	−0.50	−0.46	−0.34	−0.14	0.11	0.34	0.48	0.53	0.53	0.53	0.45
Imports	4.92	0.11	0.18	0.30	0.45	0.61	0.71	0.71	0.51	0.28	0.03	−0.19
Real Net National Income												
Labor Income*	1.58	−0.18	−0.02	0.18	0.42	0.68	0.88	0.90	0.80	0.62	0.40	0.19
Capital Income**	2.93	0.10	0.24	0.44	0.63	0.79	0.84	0.60	0.30	0.02	−0.19	−0.29
Proprietors' Income & Misc.†	2.70	0.11	0.24	0.38	0.55	0.62	0.68	0.46	0.29	0.11	0.02	−0.10

*Employee compensation is deflated by the implicit GNP price deflator.

**This variable includes corporate profits with inventory valuation and capital consumption adjustments, plus rental income of persons with capital consumption adjustment, plus net interest, plus capital consumption allowances with capital consumption adjustment, all deflated by the implicit GNP price deflator.

†Proprietors' income with inventory valuation and capital consumption adjustments, plus indirect business tax and nontax liability, plus business transfer payments, plus current surplus of government enterprises, less subsidies, plus statistical discrepancy.

Source of basic data: Citicorp's Citibase data bank

11

are summarized in Table 1. Since it is not unreasonable to think of the inventory stock as providing productive services, we include this series with the labor and capital inputs.

The two most common measures of the labor input are aggregate hours-worked according to the household survey and, alternatively, the payroll or establishment survey. We see in Table 1 that total hours with either measure is strongly procyclical and has cyclical variation which, in percentage terms, is almost as large as that of real GNP. (For a visual representation of this behavior, see Chart 3.) The capital stock, in contrast, varies smoothly over the cycle and is essentially uncorrelated with contemporaneous real GNP. The correlation is large, however, if the capital stock is shifted back by about a year. In other words, business capital lags the cycle by at least a year. The inventory stock also lags the cycle, but only by about half a year. In percentage terms, the inventory stock is nearly as volatile as quarterly real GNP.

The hours-worked series from the household survey can be decomposed into employment fluctuations on the one hand and variations in hours per worker on the other. Employment lags the cycle, while hours per worker is nearly contemporaneous with it, with only a slight lead. Much more of the volatility in total hours worked is caused by employment volatility than by changes in hours per worker. If these two subseries were perfectly correlated, their standard deviations would add up to the standard deviation of total hours. Although not perfectly correlated, their correlation is quite high, at 0.86. Therefore, employment accounts for roughly two-thirds of the standard deviation in total hours while hours per worker accounts for about one-third.

As a measure of the aggregate labor input, aggregate hours has a problem: it does not account for differences across workers in their relative contributions to aggregate output. That is, the hours of a brain surgeon are given the same weight as those of an orderly. This

Table 3

Cyclical Behavior of U.S. Output and Income Component Shares

Deviations From Trend of Product and Income Variables
Quarterly, 1954–1989

Variable x	Mean % of GNP	Volatility (% Std. Dev.)	Cross Correlation of Real GNP With										
			$x(t-5)$	$x(t-4)$	$x(t-3)$	$x(t-2)$	$x(t-1)$	$x(t)$	$x(t+1)$	$x(t+2)$	$x(t+3)$	$x(t+4)$	$x(t+5)$
Gross National Product													
Consumption Expenditures	63.55	0.58	0.29	0.15	−0.06	−0.32	−0.56	−0.78	−0.68	−0.52	−0.33	−0.17	−0.03
Nondurables & Services	54.79	0.70	0.06	−0.08	−0.27	−0.51	−0.72	−0.89	−0.73	−0.50	−0.23	0.01	0.18
Durables	8.76	0.33	0.36	0.43	0.48	0.54	0.56	0.53	0.36	0.15	−0.10	−0.31	−0.44
Investment Expenditures	15.85	1.07	0.03	0.18	0.36	0.56	0.75	0.87	0.71	0.47	0.18	−0.09	−0.30
Fixed Investment	15.16	0.56	0.11	0.25	0.40	0.57	0.74	0.81	0.77	0.61	0.40	0.14	−0.08
Change in Business Inventories	0.69	0.69	0.04	0.07	0.24	0.40	0.56	0.69	0.48	0.22	−0.05	−0.25	−0.40
Government Purchases	20.13	0.57	0.04	−0.09	−0.25	−0.40	−0.55	−0.61	−0.52	−0.36	−0.15	0.09	0.28
Net Exports	0.47	0.45	−0.51	−0.51	−0.48	−0.43	−0.37	−0.28	−0.17	0.00	0.17	0.30	0.38
Net National Income*													
Labor Income	58.57	0.47	−0.29	−0.36	−0.45	−0.52	−0.47	−0.39	−0.03	0.23	0.42	0.48	0.46
Capital Income	24.38	0.42	0.19	0.25	0.36	0.43	0.48	0.43	0.17	−0.13	−0.35	−0.48	−0.46
Proprietors' Income & Misc.	17.04	0.34	0.18	0.19	0.17	0.17	0.06	0.00	−0.16	−0.19	−0.20	−0.11	−0.11

*For explanations of the national income components, see notes to Table 2.
Source of basic data: Citicorp's Citibase data bank

12

Finn E. Kydland, Edward C. Prescott
Business Cycles

Chart 3

Deviations From Trend of U.S. Real Gross National Product
and Hours Worked*

Quarterly, 1954–1989

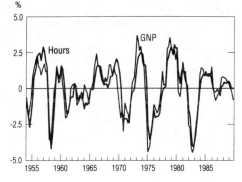

*The estimate of hours worked uses the establishment survey.
Source of basic data: Citicorp's Citibase data bank

disparity would not be problematic if the cyclical volatility of highly skilled workers resembled that of the workers who are less skilled. But it doesn't. The hours of the less-skilled group are much more variable, as established in one of our recent studies (Kydland and Prescott 1989). Using data for nearly 5,000 people from all major demographic groups over the period 1969–82, we found that, cyclically, aggregate hours is a poor measure of the labor input. When people were weighted by their relative human capital, the labor input for this sample and period varied only about two-thirds as much as did aggregate hours. We therefore recommend that the cyclical behavior of labor productivity (as reported by GNP/hours in Table 1) be interpreted with caution.

Since the human-capital-weighted cyclical measure of labor input fluctuates less than does aggregate hours, the implicit real wage (the ratio of total real labor compensation to labor input) is even more procyclical than average hourly real compensation. (For the latter series, see Table 1.) This finding that the real wage behaves in a reasonably strong procyclical manner is

Table 4

Cyclical Behavior of U.S. Monetary Aggregates and the Price Level

Deviations From Trend of Money Stock, Velocity, and Price Level
Quarterly, 1954–1989

Variable x	Volatility (% Std. Dev.)	Cross Correlation of Real GNP With										
		x(t−5)	x(t−4)	x(t−3)	x(t−2)	x(t−1)	x(t)	x(t+1)	x(t+2)	x(t+3)	x(t+4)	x(t+5)
Nominal Money Stock*												
Monetary Base	0.88	−0.12	0.02	0.14	0.25	0.36	0.41	0.40	0.37	0.32	0.28	0.26
M1	1.68	0.01	0.12	0.23	0.33	0.35	0.31	0.22	0.15	0.09	0.07	0.07
M2	1.51	0.48	0.60	0.67	0.68	0.61	0.46	0.26	0.05	−0.15	−0.33	−0.46
M2 − M1	1.91	0.53	0.63	0.67	0.65	0.56	0.40	0.20	−0.01	−0.21	−0.39	−0.53
Velocity*												
Monetary Base	1.33	−0.26	−0.15	0.00	0.22	0.40	0.59	0.50	0.37	0.22	0.08	−0.08
M1	2.02	−0.24	−0.19	−0.12	−0.01	0.14	0.31	0.32	0.27	0.20	0.10	0.00
M2	1.84	−0.63	−0.59	−0.48	−0.29	−0.05	0.24	0.34	0.40	0.43	0.44	0.43
Price Level												
Implicit GNP Deflator	0.89	−0.50	−0.61	−0.68	−0.69	−0.64	−0.55	−0.43	−0.31	−0.17	−0.04	0.09
Consumer Price Index	1.41	−0.52	−0.63	−0.70	−0.72	−0.68	−0.57	−0.41	−0.24	−0.05	0.14	0.30

*Based on quarterly data, 1959:1–1989:4.
Source of basic data: Citicorp's Citibase data bank

counter to a widely held belief in the literature. [For a fairly recent expression of this belief, see the article by Lawrence Summers (1986, p. 25), which states that there is "no apparent procyclicality of real wages."]

□ *Output Components*

Real GNP is displayed in Chart 4, along with its three major components: consumption, investment, and government purchases. These three components do not quite add up to real GNP, the difference being accounted for by net exports and change in business inventories. Because household investment in consumer durables behaves similarly to fixed investment in the business sector, we have added those two series. By far the largest component (nearly two-thirds) of total output is consumption of nondurable goods and services. This component, moreover, has relatively little volatility. The chart shows that the bulk of the volatility in aggregate output is due to investment expenditures.

The cyclical components (relative to cyclical real GNP) of consumer nondurables and services, consumer durable investment, fixed investment, and government purchases are reported in Table 2 and plotted in Charts 5–8. From the table and charts, we can see that all but government purchases are highly procyclical. Household and business investment in durables have similar

amplitudes of percentage fluctuations. Expenditures for consumer durables leads slightly while nonresidential fixed investment lags the cycle, especially investment in structures. Consumer nondurables and services is a relatively smooth series.

Some of the interesting features of the other components are that government purchases has no consistent pro- or countercyclical pattern, that imports is procyclical with no phase shift, and that exports is procyclical but lags the cycle by from six months to a year.

The cyclical behavior of the major output components, measured as shares of real GNP, is reported in Table 3. Using fractions rather than the logarithms of the series permits us to include some series that could not be used in Table 2 because they are negative during some quarters. We see that the change in business inventories is procyclical. Net exports is a countercyclical variable, with the association being strongest for exports shifted back by about a year.

□ *Factor Incomes*

Tables 2 and 3 also provide information about factor incomes, which are the components of national income. The cyclical behavior of factor incomes is described in terms of their levels (Table 2) and their shares of GNP (Table 3). Since proprietors' income includes labor and capital income, we treat this component (plus some small miscellaneous components) separately. We find that proprietors' income, as a share of national income, is uncorrelated with the cycle.

Table 2 shows that both labor income and capital income are strongly procyclical and that capital income is highly volatile. Table 3 shows that, measured as shares of total income, labor income is countercyclical while capital income is procyclical.

Nominal Facts

The statistical properties of the cyclical components of various nominal aggregates are summarized in Table 4, and four of these series along with cyclical real GNP are plotted on Charts 9–12.

□ *Monetary Aggregates*

There is no evidence that either the monetary base or M1 leads the cycle, although some economists still believe this monetary myth. Both the monetary base and M1 series are generally procyclical and, if anything, the monetary base lags the cycle slightly.

An exception to this rule occurred during the expansion of the 1980s. This expansion, so long and steady, has even led some economists and journalists to

Chart 4

U.S. Real Gross National Product and Its Components*

Quarterly, 1954–1989

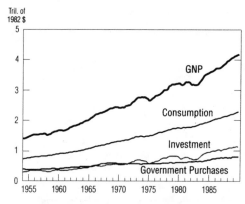

*Consumption includes nondurable goods and services. Investment is the sum of consumer durable investment and business fixed investment. Components do not add to total because net exports and the change in business inventories are excluded.

Source of basic data: Citicorp's Citibase data bank

14

Finn E. Kydland, Edward C. Prescott
Business Cycles

Charts 5–8

**Deviations From Trend of U.S. Real Gross National Product
and Its Components**

Quarterly, 1954–1989

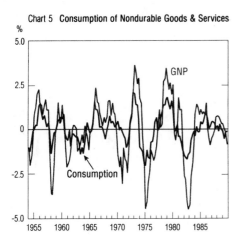

Chart 5   Consumption of Nondurable Goods & Services

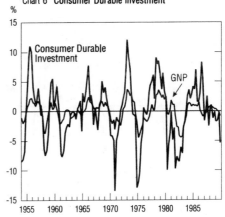

Chart 6   Consumer Durable Investment

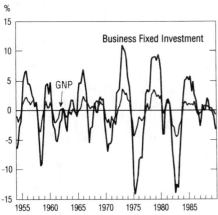

Chart 7   Business Fixed Investment

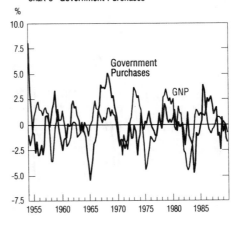

Chart 8   Government Purchases

Source of basic data: Citicorp's Citibase data bank

15

Charts 9–12

Deviations From Trend of U.S. Real Gross National Product
and Selected Nominal Aggregates

Quarterly, 1959–1989*

Chart 9   **Monetary Base**

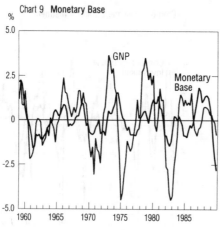

Chart 10   **M1**

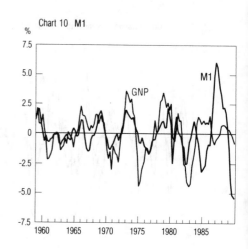

Chart 11   **M2**

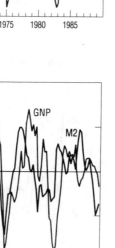

Chart 12   **Price Level (Consumer Price Index)**

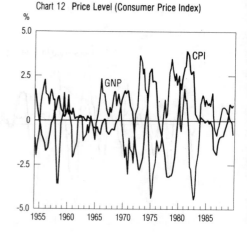

*For the price level, 1954–1989.
Source of basic data: Citicorp's Citibase data bank

16

Finn E. Kydland, Edward C. Prescott
Business Cycles

speculate that the business cycle is dead (Zarnowitz 1989 and *The Economist* 1989). During the expansion, M1 was uncommonly volatile, and M2, the more comprehensive measure of the money stock, showed some evidence that it leads the cycle by a couple quarters.

The difference in the behavior of M1 and M2 suggests that the difference of these aggregates (M2 minus M1) should be considered. This component mainly consists of interest-bearing time deposits, including certificates of deposit under $100,000. It is approximately one-half of annual GNP, whereas M1 is about one-sixth. The difference of M2 − M1 leads the cycle by even more than M2, with the lead being about three quarters.

From Table 4 it is also apparent that money velocities are procyclical and quite volatile.

☐ *Price Level*

Earlier in this paper, we documented the view that the price level is always procyclical. This myth originated from the fact that, during the period between the world wars, the price level *was* procyclical. But because of the Koopmans taboo against reporting business cycle facts, no one bothered to ascertain the cyclical behavior of the price level since World War II. Instead, economists just carried on, trying to develop business cycle theories in which the price level plays a central role and behaves procyclically. The fact is, however, that whether measured by the implicit GNP deflator or by the consumer price index, the U.S. price level clearly has been countercyclical in the post−Korean War period.

Concluding Remarks

Let us reemphasize that, unlike Burns and Mitchell, we are not claiming to measure business cycles. We also think it inadvisable to start our economics from some statistical definition of trend and deviation from trend, with growth theory being concerned with trend and business cycle theory with deviations. Growth theory deals with both trend and deviations.

The statistics we report are of interest, given neoclassical growth theory, because they are—or maybe were—in apparent conflict with that theory. Documenting real or apparent systematic deviations from theory is a legitimate activity in the natural sciences and should be so in economics as well.

We hope that the facts reported here will help guide the selection of model economies to study. We caution that any theory in which procyclical prices figure crucially in accounting for postwar business cycle fluctuations is doomed to failure. The facts we report indicate that the price level since the Korean War

moves countercyclically.

The fact that the transaction component of real cash balances (M1) moves contemporaneously with the cycle while the much larger nontransaction component (M2) leads the cycle suggests that credit arrangements could play a significant role in future business cycle theory. Introducing money and credit into growth theory in a way that accounts for the cyclical behavior of monetary as well as real aggregates is an important open problem in economics.[6]

---

[6]Two interesting attempts to introduce money into growth theory are the work of Cooley and Hansen (1989) and Hodrick, Kocherlakota, and D. Lucas (1988). Their approach focuses on the transaction role of money.

References

Adelman, Irma, and Adelman, Frank L. 1959. The dynamic properties of the Klein–Goldberger model. *Econometrica* 27 (October): 596–625.

Benhabib, Jess, and Nishimura, Kazuo. 1985. Competitive equilibrium cycles. *Journal of Economic Theory* 35: 284–306.

Bernanke, Ben S. 1986. Alternative explanations of the money-income correlation. In *Real business cycles, real exchange rates and actual policies*, ed. Karl Brunner and Allan H. Meltzer. Carnegie-Rochester Conference Series on Public Policy 25 (Autumn): 49–100. Amsterdam: North-Holland.

Boldrin, Michele. 1989. Paths of optimal accumulation in two-sector models. In *Economic complexity: Chaos, sunspots, bubbles, and nonlinearity*, ed. William A. Barnett, John Geweke, and Karl Shell, pp. 231–52. New York: Cambridge University Press.

Burns, Arthur F., and Mitchell, Wesley C. 1946. *Measuring business cycles.* New York: National Bureau of Economic Research.

Cooley, Thomas F., and Hansen, Gary D. 1989. The inflation tax in a real business cycle model. *American Economic Review* 79 (September): 733–48.

The Economist. 1989. The business cycle gets a puncture. August 5, p. 57.

Friedman, Milton, and Schwartz, Anna J. 1963. *A monetary history of the United States, 1867–1960.* Princeton: Princeton University Press (for NBER).

Frisch, Ragnar. [1933] 1965. Propagation problems and impulse problems in dynamic economics. In *Economic essays in honor of Gustav Cassel.* London: Allen and Unwin. Reprinted in *Readings in business cycles*, pp. 155–85. Homewood, Ill.: Richard D. Irwin.

Haberler, Gottfried. 1937. *Prosperity and depression: A theoretical analysis of cyclical movements.* Geneva: League of Nations.

Hayek, Friedrich August von. 1933. *Monetary theory and the trade cycle.* London: Jonathan Cape.

Hodrick, Robert J., and Prescott, Edward C. 1980. Postwar U.S. business cycles: An empirical investigation. Discussion Paper 451. Carnegie–Mellon University.

Hodrick, Robert J.; Kocherlakota, Narayana; and Lucas, Deborah. 1988. The variability of velocity in cash-in-advance models. Working Paper 2891. National Bureau of Economic Research.

King, Robert G., and Plosser, Charles I. 1984. Money, credit, and prices in a real business cycle. *American Economic Review* 74 (June): 363–80.

—————. 1989. Real business cycles and the test of the Adelmans. Unpublished manuscript, University of Rochester.

Koopmans, Tjalling C. 1947. Measurement without theory. *Review of Economic Statistics* 29 (August): 161–72.

—————. 1957. The interaction of tools and problems in economics. Chapter 3 of *Three essays on the state of economic science.* New York: McGraw-Hill.

Kydland, Finn E., and Prescott, Edward C. 1989. Cyclical movements of the labor input and its real wage. Research Department Working Paper 413. Federal Reserve Bank of Minneapolis.

Lucas, Robert E., Jr. 1977. Understanding business cycles. In *Stabilization of the domestic and international economy*, ed. Karl Brunner and Allan H. Meltzer, Carnegie-Rochester Conference Series on Public Policy 5: 7–29. Amsterdam: North-Holland.

—————. 1980. Methods and problems in business cycle theory. *Journal of Money, Credit and Banking* 12: 696–715. Reprinted in *Studies in business-cycle theory*, pp. 271–96. Cambridge, Mass.: MIT Press, 1981.

Mankiw, N. Gregory. 1989. Real business cycles: A new Keynesian perspective. *Journal of Economic Perspectives* 3 (Summer): 79–90.

Mitchell, Wesley C. 1913. *Business cycles.* Berkeley: University of California Press.

—————. [1923] 1951. Business cycles. In *Business cycles and unemployment.* New York: National Bureau of Economic Research. Reprinted in *Readings in business cycle theory*, pp. 43–60. Philadelphia: Blakiston.

—————. 1927. *Business cycles: The problem and its setting.* New York: National Bureau of Economic Research.

Muth, John F. 1960. Optimal properties of exponentially weighted forecasts. *Journal of American Statistical Association* 55 (June): 299–306.

Sargent, Thomas J. 1981. Interpreting economic time series. *Journal of Political Economy* 89 (April): 213–48.

Slutzky, Eugen. 1937. The summation of random causes as the source of cyclic processes. *Econometrica* 5 (April): 105–46.

Solow, Robert M. 1970. *Growth theory.* New York: Oxford University Press.

Stigler, S. M. 1978. Mathematical statistics in the early states. *Annals of Statistics* 6: 239–65.

Summers, Lawrence H. 1986. Some skeptical observations on real business cycle theory. *Federal Reserve Bank of Minneapolis Quarterly Review* 10 (Fall): 23–27.

Zarnowitz, Victor. 1989. Facts and factors in the recent evolution of business cycles in the United States. National Bureau of Economic Research Working Paper 2865.

18

INTERNATIONAL ECONOMIC REVIEW
Vol. 30, No. 4, November 1989

TIME-TO-BUILD AND AGGREGATE FLUCTUATIONS: SOME NEW EVIDENCE*

BY SUMRU ALTUĞ[1]

This paper presents maximum likelihood estimates and tests of a model similar to one Kydland and Prescott (1982) suggested. For this purpose, it derives equilibrium laws of motion for a set of aggregate variables as functions of the model's parameters and the innovation to the technology shock. The paper shows that a single unobservable index can explain the variability in the observed series, but identifying the single index with the innovation to the technology shock implies that per capita hours is not well explained. It also shows that time-separable preferences with respect to leisure are consistent with the data.

1. INTRODUCTION

In a paper that has received much recent attention, Kydland and Prescott (1982) presented a competitive equilibrium model of cyclical fluctuations. Using the one-sector optimal growth model to construct a prototype competitive economy, they argued that postwar U.S. business cycles could be explained in terms of the dynamic response of the aggregate economy to persistent technology shocks. To provide a more complicated propagation mechanism for such shocks, they modified the optimal growth model by introducing a time-to-build feature in investment and by allowing leisure to be a durable good.

This paper presents maximum likelihood estimates and tests of a model that is similar to Kydland and Prescott's, using postwar U.S. data for per capita hours and the growth rates of per capita output, per capita expenditures for the acquisitions of durable consumption goods and for the stocks of aggregate structures and equipment, respectively. It derives testable restrictions from the assumption that such time series are generated from the competitive equilibrium of an economy with the postulated preferences, technology, and stochastic environment. For this purpose, laws of motion describing the evolution of equilibrium quantities are calculated as functions of the underlying parameters of the model and the innovation to the technology shock.

* Manuscript received September 1986; revised October 1988.

[1] I received helpful comments and suggestions from Lars Peter Hansen, Robert Litterman, Kenneth Singleton, and an anonymous referee. In addition, I thank Thomas J. Sargent for his encouragement at various times. An earlier version of this paper entitled "Gestation Lags and the Business Cycle: An Empirical Analysis," 1983 was presented at seminars at Carnegie-Mellon University; Massachusetts Institute of Technology; Northwestern University; and the Universities of California (Los Angeles), Chicago, Minnesota, Rochester, and Southern California; as well as at the 1984 National Bureau of Economic Research Conference on Business Fluctuations and the 1984 North American Summer Meetings of the Econometric Society. A major part of the calculations for the current draft were done on the Cray 2 computer, on a grant from the Minnesota Supercomputer Institute.

Besides Kydland and Prescott, there have been other recent attempts to explain cyclical fluctuations of the postwar period in terms of the equilibrium behavior of simple dynamic economies. (See, for example, Long and Plosser 1983.) The analysis in these papers differs from mine by focusing on a small set of moments—typically, variances and low orders of serial and cross correlations—for matching the behavior implied by their model with actual data. There also exists the literature which uses Euler equations from the optimization problem of some representative consumer (or firm) to test restrictions for the covariation of aggregate quantities and prices. (For example, Eichenbaum, Hansen and Singleton 1988, and Mankiw, Rotemberg and Summers 1985, use representative consumer models to study the relationship between aggregate consumption, aggregate hours worked, aggregate compensation, and interest rates.) Although this paper does not use information on the behavior of equilibrium prices, it uses (approximate) equilibrium laws of motion for a subset of the quantity variables to derive as an econometric specification, a restricted index model in which the innovation to the random technology process appears as a common unobservable factor while serially uncorrelated measurement errors constitute specific disturbances. Hence, the estimation methodology in this paper utilizes restrictions implied by preferences and the production technology for equilibrium quantities. The empirical analysis also exploits restrictions originating from the nature of the uncertainty in the model. First, a test of the hypothesis that a single unobservable index can account for the covariation among a set of observable series is undertaken, incidentally providing a link to the purely statistical analyses of cyclical phenomena conducted earlier. (See, for example, Sargent and Sims 1973.) Second, endogenous stochastic trends for a subset of the quantity variables are derived from the assumption that the technology shock possesses a stochastic trend.

The economic model that forms the basis for the empirical analysis is described in Section 2. This model differs from Kydland and Prescott's specification in terms of disaggregating the physical capital stock as structures and equipment, where investment in the former is subject to time lags, and by assuming that there exists a dynamic technology for producing consumption services from current and past acquisitions of durable consumption goods. It also differs by assuming that the technology shock evolves with a stochastic trend. Because of the trend, the original nonstationary model must be replaced by its stationary counterpart to ensure the existence of a competitive equilibrium. The stationary model is obtained by removing a stochastic trend from a subset of the original variables and redefining preferences in terms of stochastically detrended consumption and the levels of leisure. Section 2 derives the stationary model and describes the methods used to calculate the (approximate) equilibrium laws of motion. Using these results, Section 3 formulates the econometric model and shows how maximum likelihood estimates of the parameters characterizing preferences and technology can be obtained from a frequency domain approximation to the exact likelihood function for the vector of observable series. Section 4 describes the data.

The empirical findings of this paper are in Section 5. First, frequency domain estimates of an unrestricted unobservable index model show that a single index is quite successful in explaining the variation in the observable series. Second, the empirical findings indicate that estimates of preference parameters, which are obtained by identifying the single index as the innovation to the technology shock and by imposing equilibrium restrictions for per capita quantities, are comparable to others obtained, for example, from Euler equation estimation. However, one notable difference is that while this paper does not find evidence against the intertemporal substitution of leisure hypothesis in terms of findings about the negative effect of past leisure time on current utility, it also cannot reject a time-separable form of preferences with respect to leisure. Results pertaining to the aggregate production technology and the nature of the time lags in the investment process are also presented. In relation to the former, it is indicated that the estimates are consistent with the assumptions of the underlying economic model. But when the estimated time series representation from this model is used to calculate the coherences of each element of the observable series with the innovation to the technology shock, it is shown that per capita hours is not well explained by the model. Section 6 concludes the paper by comparing the methods and results of Kydland and Prescott with those in this paper and by suggesting some possible directions for future research.

2. THE MODEL

2.1. *Specification.* The economy is populated by many identical consumers or, alternatively, by a single representative consumer who derives utility from alternative sequences of services from nondurable consumption goods and services, durable consumption goods and leisure, denoted $\{c_{1t}^*\}_{t=0}^{\infty}$, $\{c_{2t}^*\}_{t=0}^{\infty}$ and $\{l_t^*\}_{t=0}^{\infty}$, respectively, according to the utility functional described by equation (2.1):

$$(2.1) \qquad E_o \sum_{t=0}^{\infty} \beta^t \left[\frac{1}{\gamma} (c_{1t}^{*a} c_{2t}^{*b} l_t^{*c})^\gamma - \frac{1}{\gamma} \right].$$

Here $0 < \beta < 1$, $0 < a < 1$, $0 < b < 1$, $c = 1 - a - b$, $\gamma \leq 1$ and $\gamma \neq 0$. In this equation, β is the subjective discount factor and $E_o(\cdot)$ denotes expectation conditional on information at time zero. In terms of the composite service flow $c_{1t}^{*a} c_{2t}^{*b} l_t^{*c}$, utility is both separable and of the constant relative risk aversion type, with coefficient of relative risk aversion $(1 - \gamma)$. If $\gamma \neq 0$, utility is non-separable across c_{1t}^*, c_{2t}^* and l_t^*, while preferences are of the logarithmic variety—which is separable across the choice variables c_{1t}^*, c_{2t}^* and l_t^*—when $\gamma = 0$. Tastes are assumed to be constant and uninfluenced by exogenous random shocks.

Output of the single consumption model is produced according to the constant elasticity of substitution production function defined by equation (2.2):

$$(2.2) \qquad \lambda_t^\theta n_t^\theta [(1 - \sigma)k_{1t}^{-\nu} + \sigma k_{2t}^{-\nu}]^{-(1-\theta)/\nu}$$

with $0 < \theta < 1$, $0 < \sigma < 1$ and $-1 < \nu < \infty$. Here λ_t, n_t, k_{1t} and k_{2t} denote the shock to technology, total labor hours, and the services from two types of capital, respectively. The parameter ν determines the elasticity of substitution between the two types of capital. Since $\nu < \infty$, this elasticity is constrained to be less than the unit value of the Cobb-Douglas production function. θ measures the share of labor in aggregate output and σ the share of the second type of capital in the composite capital good $[(1 - \sigma)k_{1t}^{-\nu} + \sigma k_{2t}^{-\nu}]^{-\nu}$. The substitution elasticity between labor hours and the composite capital good, unlike the one for the two types of capital, is always unity.

Exogenous technological change, the driving force in this economy, is modelled in terms of a multiplicative shock λ_t to the production function. The technology shock is Hicks neutral and displays persistence, its logarithm evolving as a random walk with positive drift $\bar{\lambda}$. Equation (2.3) describes this process.

$$(2.3) \qquad\qquad \lambda_t = \lambda_{t-1} \exp(\bar{\lambda} + \varepsilon_t)$$

where $\{\varepsilon_t\}_{t=0}^{\infty}$ is a sequence of independently (and normally) distributed random variables with $E(\varepsilon_t) = 0$ and $\mathrm{Var}(\varepsilon_t) = \sigma^2$. Analyzing the residual from Solow's (1957) aggregate production function, Nelson and Plosser (1982) found that it could be well described as a random walk for the period of observation 1909–1949. While such a finding may provide some empirical support for (2.3), this support is somewhat tenuous because, as will become clear shortly, the technology shock in this paper is unobservable by an econometrician, so it cannot be measured directly as the residual from an estimated production function.

In the absence of additional assumptions restricting the investment process for the two capital goods or the service flow technology for consumption and leisure services, equations (2.1), (2.2), and (2.3) may be augmented with an aggregate market-clearing condition and laws of motion for the two capital stocks to form a slightly more complicated version of the one-sector optimal growth model described, for example, by Brock and Mirman (1972) or Mirman and Zilcha (1975). As in Kydland and Prescott, however, the model of this paper has features that induce richer forms of serial and cross-correlation for variables such as output, consumption, leisure hours, and investment expenditures than are possible within the standard framework.

One of these features is the "durability" of leisure. More precisely, it is assumed that current leisure services depend linearly on current and past values of leisure time, i.e.,

$$(2.4) \qquad l_t^* = l_t + \frac{\delta}{1 - (1 - \eta)L} l_{t-1}, \qquad 0 < \eta \le 1 \text{ and } \delta \text{ unrestricted.}$$

According to this specification, one unit of leisure time at date t contributes $\delta(1 - \eta)^{\tau-1}$ units of leisure services at date $t + \tau$. When δ is positive (as in Kydland and Prescott), leisure time today adds to leisure services in future periods, but the effect of current leisure time on future leisure services decays at the geometric rate η. For the special case of $\eta = 1$ but $\delta > 0$, (2.4) implies that current leisure time yields leisure services today and one period into the future. Now (2.4) can be expressed in an alternative way by defining the stock variable $a_t = \sum_{i=1}^{\infty} (1 - \eta)^{i-1} l_{t-i}$, i.e.,

$$(2.5a) \qquad\qquad l_t^* = l_t + \delta a_t$$

(2.5b) $$a_{t+1} = (1 - \eta)a_t + l_t.$$

While past leisure time may be expected to have positive (or negative) effects on current utility through the persisting effects of past leisure activities (consider, for example, the effects of a vacation at the beach or a night in the city), a more important source of durability is the durability of consumption goods. The specification that is adopted assumes that services from durable consumption goods is proportional to the purchases of durable consumption goods at date $t(c_{2t})$ plus the stock of durable goods held at that date (d_t). If Ψ denotes this factor of proportionality then c_{2t}^* can be expressed as

(2.6) $$c_{2t}^* = \Psi(c_{2t} + d_t) \qquad 0 < \mu < 1, \qquad 0 < \Psi < 1.$$

The law of motion for the stock of durable consumption goods is then derived by noting that the stock at the beginning of period t is equal to $c_{2t} + d_t$, less the amount consumed in period t to produce consumption services less the (physically) depreciated portion of the stock:

(2.7) $$d_{t+1} = (1 - \mu - \Psi)d_t + (1 - \Psi)c_2.$$

According to (2.7), μ denotes the physical rate of depreciation for the stock of durable consumption goods while $\mu + \Psi$ is the actual depreciation rate of the stock in each period.

While items that are classified as a nondurable or even a service—for example, a winter coat or a trip to the dentist—may produce services for several periods following the period when they were acquired, this paper assumes that service flows derived from nondurable consumption goods and services are identical to the acquisitions of nondurable consumption goods and services, i.e., $c_{1t}^* = c_{1t}$ where c_{1t} is the purchases of nondurables and services in period t. This is unlike some recent papers modeling the durability of consumption goods (see, for example, Eichenbaum and Hansen 1987, and Dunn and Singleton 1986), and was followed for computational reasons, which have to do with increasing the dimension of the system that must be solved and estimated.

The investment technology provides another departure from the standard formulation of the optimal growth model. Using a model of investment which dates back to the work of Frisch (1933) and Kalecki (1935), Kydland and Prescott assumed that production of one of the capital goods in their model requires multiple time periods. (See also Taylor 1982; and Park 1984.) In addition to labor and this capital good, they also assumed that (business) inventories entered as an input in the aggregate production function. By contrast, this paper disaggregates the physical capital stock as stocks of structures and equipment. (See Bernanke 1983 for a similar practice in the context of an adjustment cost model of investment). It assumes that investment in the second type of capital proceeds under standard neoclassical assumptions, with a constant depreciation rate $0 < \delta_2 < 1$ and an implied law of motion

(2.8) $$k_{2t+1} = (1 - \delta_2)k_{2t} + i_{2t}.$$

On the other hand, the construction of the first capital good requires several periods, a period being identified with a quarter in the subsequent empirical analysis. At a given point in time, there exist J types of the first capital good by stage of fabrication: $s_{jt}, j = 1, \ldots, J-1$, the number of investment projects which are j periods from completion; s_{Jt}, the new projects initiated in period t and the stock of capital k_{1t}. Abstracting from depreciation in the stocks of incomplete capital goods and assuming, as before, a constant depreciation rate $0 < \delta_1 < 1$ for the existing stock, the appropriate laws of motion are given by

$$(2.9) \qquad s_{j,t+1} = s_{j+1,t} \qquad j = 1, \ldots, J-1$$

$$(2.10) \qquad k_{1t+1} = (1 - \delta_1)k_{1t} + s_{1t}.$$

According to this model of investment, total investment expenditures at a given date t depend on the resources expended for the different incomplete projects. If the fraction of resources expended on a project j periods from completion is assumed constant and equal to ϕ_j, then total investment outlays for structures are given by

$$(2.11) \qquad i_{1t} = \sum_{j=1}^{J} \phi_j s_{jt}.$$

Even before solving for the optimal level of k_{1t+J}, it is possible to show the effect of the time-to-build assumption for generating interesting dynamics. For this purpose, define $g_0 = \phi_J, g_1 = \phi_{J-1} - (1 - \delta_1)\phi_J \ldots$ and $g_J = -(1 - \delta_1)\phi_1$, and use (2.9), (2.10), and (2.11) to obtain an accelerator-like equation for i_{1t} in terms of k_{1t+J}:

$$(2.12) \qquad i_{1t} = g_0 k_{1t+J} + g_1 k_{1t+j-1} + \cdots + g_J k_{1t}.$$

With nonzero values for ϕ_j, investment expenditures in structures form a distributed lag with the "desired capital stock" k_{1t+J} and covary with the stocks of structures chosen between t and $t - J$, i.e., with k_{1t+J} to k_{1t}.

2.2. *The Stationary Model.* In order to exploit the model's restrictions during estimation and testing, the equilibrium laws of motion describing the evolution of the model's variables must be computed. For the model of Section 2, this task is complicated by several factors. The first is the nonstationarity in the behavior of the technology shock: there may not exist a competitive equilibrium for this economy in which consumers solve well-defined individual optimization problems because the stochastic trend in the technology process will lead to unbounded growth in output and consumption. However, it is possible to show the existence of a competitive equilibrium for a stationary version of the model of Section 2. To do this, define the variables $\bar{q}_t = q_t/\lambda_t$, $\bar{c}_{1t} = c_{1t}/\lambda_t$, $\bar{c}_{2t}^* = \bar{c}_{2t}^*/\lambda_t$, $\bar{d}_t = d_t/\lambda_{t-1}$, $\bar{i}_{1t} = i_{1t}/\lambda_t$, $\bar{i}_{2t} = i_{2t}/\lambda_t$, $\bar{s}_{Jt} = s_{Jt}/\lambda_t$, $\bar{k}_{1t} = k_{1t}/\lambda_{t-J}$, $\bar{k}_{2t} = k_{2t}/\lambda_{t-1}$, $\bar{s}_{jt} = s_{jt}/\lambda_{t-J+j}$, $j = 1, \ldots, J-1, l_t^*$ and n_t. (Notice these variables are well-defined because the stochastic process for λ_t guarantees it is always positive). Using these definitions and the stochastic law of motion for λ_t given in (2.3), the production function may be rewritten as

$$(2.13) \qquad \bar{q}_t = n_t^\theta \left[(1 - \sigma) \left(\bar{k}_{1t} \exp \left(-\sum_{i=0}^{J-1} (\varepsilon_{t-i} + \bar{\lambda}) \right) \right)^{-v} \right.$$

$$\left. + \sigma (\bar{k}_{2t} \exp (-\bar{\lambda} - \varepsilon_t))^{-v} \right]^{[-(1-\theta)]/v}$$

Similarly, the constraints described by equations (2.6) and (2.7) are modified as

$$(2.14a) \qquad \bar{c}_{2t}^* = c_{2t}^*/\lambda_t = \Psi(c_{2t}/\lambda_t + d_t/\lambda_t)$$

$$= \Psi(\bar{c}_{2t} + \exp (-\varepsilon_t - \bar{\lambda}) \bar{d}_t)$$

and

$$(2.14b) \qquad \bar{d}_{t+1} = d_{t+1}/\lambda_t = (1 - \mu - \Psi)d_t/\lambda_t + (1 - \Psi)c_{2t}/\lambda_t$$

$$= (1 - \mu - \Psi) \exp (-\varepsilon_t - \bar{\lambda}) \bar{d}_t + (1 - \Psi)\bar{c}_{2t}.$$

The laws of motion for $(l_t^*$ and a_t are unchanged because leisure hours are independent of the stochastic trend in the technology process. To derive the laws of motion corresponding to (2.9) through (2.11), first use (2.9) and (2.3) for $j = 1, \ldots, J - 1$:

$$(2.15) \qquad s_{j,t+1}/\lambda_{t+1-J+j} = s_{j+1,t}/\lambda_{t-J+j+1}$$

or

$$\bar{s}_{j,t+1} = \bar{s}_{j+1,t}.$$

Then,

$$(2.16) \qquad \bar{k}_{1t+1} = k_{1t+1}/\lambda_{t-J+1} = (1 - \delta_1)k_{1t}/\lambda_{t-J+1} + s_{1t}/\lambda_{t-J+1}$$

$$= (1 - \delta_1) \exp (-\bar{\lambda} - \varepsilon_{t-J+1})\bar{k}_{1t} + \bar{s}_{1t}$$

and

$$(2.17) \qquad \bar{i}_{1t} = i_{1t}/\lambda_t = \sum_{j=1}^{J} \phi_j s_{jt}/\lambda_t$$

$$= \sum_{j=1}^{J-1} \phi_j \exp \left(-\sum_{i=j}^{J-1} (\varepsilon_{t-J+i+1} + \bar{\lambda}) \right) \bar{s}_{jt} + \phi_J \bar{s}_{Jt}.$$

Finally, divide through (2.8) by λ_t and use (2.3) to obtain

$$(2.18) \qquad \bar{k}_{2t+1} = (1 - \delta_2) \exp (-\bar{\lambda} - \varepsilon_t)\bar{k}_{2t} + \bar{i}_{2t}.$$

896   SUMRU ALTUĞ

Using the above results, consider the problem of maximizing the expected discounted utility of the representative consumer subject to the constraints imposed by the technology and stochastic environment for the stationary model. This is described by (2.19).

$$(2.19) \qquad \underset{\{z_t\}_{t=0}^{\infty}}{\text{maximize}} \ E_0 \left[\sum_{t=0}^{\infty} \left(\bar{\beta}^t \frac{1}{\gamma} (\bar{c}_{1t}^a \bar{c}_{2t}^{*b} l_t^{*c})^\gamma - \beta^t \frac{1}{\gamma} \right) \right]$$

subject to

$$\bar{c}_{1t} + \bar{c}_{2t} + \tilde{i}_{1t} + \tilde{i}_{2t} \leq \bar{q}_t$$

$$\bar{q}_t \leq n_t^\theta \left((1 - \sigma) \left[\bar{k}_{1t} \exp \left[- \sum_{i=0}^{J-1} (\varepsilon_{t-i} + \bar{\lambda}) \right] \right]^{-\nu} \right. $$
$$\left. + \sigma(\bar{k}_{2t} \exp(-\varepsilon_t - \bar{\lambda}))^{-\nu} \right)^{[-(1-\theta)]/\nu}$$

$$\bar{c}_{2t}^* = \Psi(\bar{c}_{2t} + \exp(-\varepsilon_t - \bar{\lambda})\bar{d}_t)$$

$$\bar{d}_{t+1} = (1 - \mu - \Psi) \exp(-\varepsilon_t - \bar{\lambda})\bar{d}_t + (1 - \Psi)\bar{c}_{2t}$$

$$l_t^* = l_t + \delta a_t$$

$$a_{t+1} = (1 - \eta)a_t + l_t$$

$$\bar{s}_{j,t+1} = \bar{s}_{j+1,t} \qquad j = 1, \ldots, J - 1$$

$$\bar{k}_{1t+1} = (1 - \delta_1) \exp(-\varepsilon_{t-J+1} - \bar{\lambda})\bar{k}_{1t} + \bar{s}_{1t}$$

$$\tilde{i}_{1t} = \sum_{j=1}^{J-1} \phi_j \exp\left(- \sum_{i=j}^{J-1} (\varepsilon_{t-J+i+1} + \bar{\lambda}) \right)\bar{s}_{jt} + \phi_J \bar{s}_{Jt}$$

$$\bar{k}_{2t+1} = (1 - \delta_2) \exp(-\varepsilon_t - \bar{\lambda})\bar{k}_{2t} + \tilde{i}_{2t}$$

$$\bar{c}_{1t} \geq 0, \quad \bar{c}_{2t}^* \geq 0, \quad l_t^* \geq 0, \quad \bar{s}_{Jt} \geq 0, \quad \tilde{i}_{2t} \geq 0, \quad n_t \geq 0, \quad \bar{k}_{1t} \geq 0, \quad \bar{k}_{2t} \geq 0,$$

given the initial conditions $\bar{d}_0$; a_0; $\bar{s}_{j0}, j = 1, \ldots, J - 1$; $\bar{k}_{10}$; $\bar{k}_{20}$; $\varepsilon_0, \varepsilon_{-1}, \ldots,$ ε_{-J+1} and the stochastic process for $\{\varepsilon_t\}_{t=0}^{\infty}$). Here, $\bar{z}_t = (\bar{c}_{1t}, \bar{c}_{2t}^*, l_t^*, \bar{s}_{Jt}, \tilde{i}_{2t}, n_t, \bar{k}_{1t}, \bar{k}_{2t})$ is the vector of decision variables chosen to depend only on information available at time t, i.e., on realizations of $\varepsilon_0, \varepsilon_1, \ldots, \varepsilon_t$.

Now (2.19) is the social planner's problem for the stationary economy. Notice that the discount rate for the transformed economy is no longer constant and equal to β. Instead, using the law of motion for λ_t, the discount rate at time t is defined by the random variable $\bar{\beta}_t$ where

TIME-TO-BUILD   897

$$\bar{\beta}_t \equiv \beta^t \lambda_0^{(a+b)\gamma} \exp\left(\sum_{i=0}^{t}(\varepsilon_{t-i}+\bar{\lambda})\right).$$

Notice also that the production function, the laws of motion for the capital stocks, and the technology for producing consumption services depend explicitly on the random variables $\tilde{\lambda}_t$ and $\tilde{\lambda}_t^{J-j}$, where

$$\tilde{\lambda}_t \equiv \exp(\varepsilon_t + \bar{\lambda})$$

and

$$\tilde{\lambda}_t^{J-j} \equiv \exp\left[\sum_{i=j}^{J-1}(\varepsilon_{t-i}+\bar{\lambda})\right], \qquad j = 0, \ldots, J-1.$$

Hence, extensions of standard results must be used to show that (2.19) has a (stationary) solution and a stationary stochastic steady state. (One approach is to use the results of Marimon 1984 for this purpose.) Once the existence of a solution to (2.19) is established, however, the arguments in Debreu (1954) may be used to show that this solution can be supported as a competitive equilibrium for the stationary economy. But there still remains the difficulty that due to the nonlinearity in the objective function and the constraint set, (2.19) does not admit a closed-form solution for the variables of interest. To deal with this additional problem, the social planner's problem for the stationary economy is approximated following a procedure similar to Kydland and Prescott's.

2.3. *The Approximate Equilibrium.* The approximation procedure replaces the objective function in (2.19) by a quadratic and linearizes its constraints in the neighborhood of the (stationary) model's steady state. The Appendix calculates this steady state as a function of the average growth rate of the technology process $\bar{\lambda}$ and the preference and technology parameters. It also formulates the approximate social planner's problem as a linear-quadratic dynamic optimization problem under uncertainty and solves it using methods described, for example, by Bertsekas (1976) and Hansen and Sargent (1981). This solution takes the form of a time-series representation showing the evolution of $\bar{y}_{1t} = (\bar{k}_{1t+J}, a_{t+1}, k_{2t+1}, \bar{d}_{t+1})'$ in equilibrium. The equilibrium representation for $\bar{y}_{2t} = (\bar{i}_{1t}, n_t, \bar{i}_{2t}, \bar{c}_{2t}, \bar{q}_t)'$ is obtained by using the law of motion for $\bar{y}_{1t}$ together with the linearized version of the CES production function and the (linear) laws of motion for $\bar{i}_{1t}, n_t, \bar{i}_{2t}, \bar{c}_{2t}$ derived in the Appendix. But representations for $\bar{y}_{1t}$ and $\bar{y}_{2t}$ are not useful for restricting actual data because the elements of $\bar{y}_{1t}$ and $\bar{y}_{2t}$ depend on values of the unobserved technology shock λ_t. The appendix shows that these representations may, nevertheless, be used to obtain (stationary) representations that do not depend on observations of λ_t. These are displayed by equations (2.20) and (2.21) below:

(2.20) $y_{1t} - T_1 y_{1t-1} = C(L)^{-1}B(L)\varepsilon_t + x^m \equiv K(L)\varepsilon_t + y_1^m$

(2.21) $y_{2t} = T_2 y_{2t-1} = [E(L)C(L)^{-1}B(L) + G(L)]\varepsilon_t + y_2^m \equiv H(L)\varepsilon_t + y_2^m.$

In these equations, $y_{1t} = (\log k_{1t+J}, \log a_{t+1}, \log k_{2t+1}, \log d_{t+1})'$ and $y_{2t} = (\log i_{1t}, \log n_t, \log i_{2t}, \log c_{2t}, \log q_t)'$, T_1 and T_2 are matrices of dimension 4×4 and 5×5, respectively, while $C(L)$ is a Jth-order matrix polynomial in nonnegative powers of L, such that the roots of det $C(z) = 0$ are greater than $\beta^{1/2}$ in modulus. The elements of $C(L)$, denoted $C_j, j = 0, \ldots, J$, are matrices of dimension 4×4. $B(L)$ and $E(L)$ are matrix polynomials of order $J + 1$ and J, respectively, in nonnegative powers of L and have elements of dimension 4×1 and 5×4, while the dimension of the Jth order matrix polynomial $G(L)$ is 5×1. $K(L)$ and $H(L)$ are infinite-order matrix polynomials with elements of dimension 4×1 and 5×1 respectively, defined from the right-hand side of (2.20) and (2.21). Finally, y_1^m and y_2^m are vectors of length 4×1 and 5×1.

The representations described by equations (2.20) and (2.21) embody restrictions implied by preferences and technology for the behavior of equilibrium quantities. For example, the time-to-build feature in investment and the durability of consumption goods and leisure time restricts the lag polynomials $E(L)$ and $C(L)$. Using the identity $C(L)^{-1} \equiv$ adj $C(L)/\det C(L)$, it is easy to see that the roots of det $C(L) = 0$ determine the (autoregressive) roots of these representations. It can be shown that the number of nonzero roots of det $C(L) = 0$ depends on the number of time periods required to build productive capital as well as on the fact that past leisure time and past acquisitions of durable consumption goods produce current utility. This yields a total of $J + 2$ autoregressive roots for the elements of y_{2t} (and y_{1t}). On the other hand, $B(L)$ reflects consumers' forecasts of future productivity, conditional on current and past realizations of $\bar{\lambda}_t$ and $\bar{\lambda}_t^J$. Since $B(L)$ is a matrix polynomial of order $J + 1$, both (2.20) and (2.21) display moving average components. These transitory components appear in the endogenous series because there are $J + 1$ shocks in the stationary version of the nonlinear economy, i.e., $\bar{\lambda}_t$ and $\bar{\lambda}_t^{J-j} = \Pi_{i=j}^{J-1}\bar{\lambda}_{t-i}, j = 0, \ldots, J - 1$. For the vector of stock variables, equation (2.20) shows that the moving average components in the endogenous series are at most of order $J + 1$. The order of the moving average polynomial for the elements of $y_{2t} - T_2 y_{2t-1}$ is greater due to the dependence of (2.21) on the Jth order matrix polynomial $E(L)$. For example, the coefficients of the accelerator-like representation for $\tilde{i}_{1t}$, i.e. $g_0, \ldots, g_J$, help to determine the moving average parts for investment in the first capital good. Likewise, the rates of decay of the remaining types of capital, namely, $\bar{k}_{2t+1}$, a_{t+1} and $\bar{d}_{t+1}$, determine the transitory effects of an innovation to the technology shock on the behavior or $\tilde{i}_{2t}$, n_t and $\bar{c}_{2t}$.

Another feature of (2.20) and (2.21) is that the stochastic trend in the technology shock also translates into a stochastic trend for a subset of the endogenous variables; for the elements of y_{1t} and y_{2t} that do evolve with a stochastic trend, the corresponding elements of y_1^m and y_2^m denote the average growth rates of these series. On the other hand, given the upper bound on total hours, per capita labor hours is independent of stochastic growth in technology; according to (2.21), it fluctuates randomly around a constant unconditional mean. Finally, notice that both $\{y_{1t}\}_{t=0}^\infty$ and $\{y_{2t}\}_{t=0}^\infty$ are stochastic processes with perfectly correlated elements, (or, equivalently, their variance-covariance matrix is singular). Since the singularity of these processes is sure to be rejected by actual data, the next section describes a way of giving empirical content to these representations.

3.   THE ECONOMETRIC MODEL

3.1. *Specification.* Consider equation (2.21), and let $\xi_t = (\xi_{1t}, \ldots, \xi_{5t})'$ denote the vector of measured series. One way of giving empirical content to (2.20) or (2.21) is to assume that the elements of ξ_t are noisy measures of the true series; that is,

$$(3.1) \qquad \xi_t = y_{2t} - T_2 y_{2t-1} + \nu_t = H(L)\varepsilon_t + y_2^m + \nu_t$$

where $\nu_t = (\nu_{1t}, \ldots, \nu_{5t})'$ are a vector of measurement errors and ν_{it} for $i = 1, \ldots, 5$ are defined to have mean zero, variance σ_i^2 and to be serially uncorrelated. Also, $E(\varepsilon_t, \nu_{it}) = 0$ and $E(\nu_{it}, \nu_{jt}) = 0$ for $i \neq j$ and $j = 1, \ldots, 5$. Under the latter assumption, (3.1) provides a restricted single-index representation for the observable series. Here any correlation between the elements of ξ_t arises from their mutual dependence on the unobservable innovation to productivity while the measurement errors constitute specific disturbances. While (3.1) was obtained under the assumption of a single aggregate technology, a similar representation may be derived under the assumption that there are a large number of firms differentiated only by the specific shocks to their otherwise identical technologies. Suppose, for example, that the random shock to the production function of an individual firm takes the form $\lambda_{it} = \lambda_{it-1} \exp(\varepsilon_t + \bar{\lambda} + \rho_{it})$ where $\{\rho_{it}\}_{t=0}^{\infty}$ are independent over time and over firms. Also, following the arguments of Eichenbaum, Hansen and Richard (1984), (3.1) may be modified to accommodate shocks to individual preferences and allow a simple form of heterogeneity among consumers who are differentiated by their initial endowments of physical capital stocks and by taste shocks. In this case, the nondiversifiable component of such preference shocks will appear as a second factor in the representation for ξ_t.

The single index representation for the observable series is subsequently tested in Section 5, without imposing any overidentifying restrictions on the lag polynomial linking the common shock to the observable series, using the so-called "exploratory" dynamic factor model. Equation (3.2) gives its formal statement.

$$(3.2) \qquad \xi_t = \bar{H}(L)\bar{\varepsilon}_t + \bar{y}^m + \bar{\nu}_t.$$

As before, $E(\bar{\nu}_{it}) = 0$, $\mathrm{Var}(\bar{\nu}_{it}) = \bar{\sigma}_i^2$, $E(\bar{\nu}_{it}, \bar{\nu}_{jt}) = 0$ and $E(\bar{\varepsilon}_t \bar{\nu}_{it}) = 0$ for $i \neq j$, $i = 1, \ldots, 5$ and $\bar{\varepsilon}_t$ is a scalar random variable with zero mean variance normalized as unity. In this representation, there are no restrictions on $\bar{H}(L)$ other than the requirement that it has an explicit expansion $\sum_{i=-\infty}^{\infty} \bar{H}_i z^i$ for any complex variable z. Nor are there any restrictions on the serial correlation properties of the specific disturbances.

A more important distinction between (3.1), on the one hand, and (3.2), on the other, involves the identification of the common unobservable factor as the innovation to the technology shock in the former representation. The restrictions that serve to identify ε_t in this way stem from the restrictions placed by the underlying economic model on the quadratic coefficients Q_{12} in the approximate utility function and on the coefficients of $\bar{\lambda}_t$ and $\bar{\lambda}_t^J$ in the linearized CES production function. Q_{12} is obtained from the off-diagonal of the matrix of quadratic coefficients Q calculated in the Appendix and by definition corresponds to the matrix of cross-partial derivatives of the nonlinear function in (B.1), showing how changes in $\bar{\lambda}_t$ and $\bar{\lambda}_t^J$ from their unconditional means affect changes in single-period utility due to deviations in $\bar{k}_{1t}$, a_t, $\bar{i}_{1t} + \bar{i}_{2t}$, $\bar{k}_{2t}$, n_t, $\bar{c}_{2t}$ and $\bar{d}_t$ from their steady-state values. Following the steps described in part C of the Appendix, it is easy to see that the elements of Q_{12} enter the formulas that define the moving-average polynomial $B(L)$ in equation (2.20). Hence, the restrictions placed by the underlying economic model on the elements of Q_{12} serve to identify the common shock in equation (3.1) as the innovation to the random technology process. By contrast, there are no restrictions in model (3.2) that yield an economic interpretation of the unobserved common factor.

3.2. *Estimation Strategy.* A frequency domain approximation to the exact likelihood function for a sample of observations on the $\{\xi_t\}_{t=0}^{\infty}$ process is used to estimate the unknown parameters in (3.1). Define the vector of parameters in (3.1) by $\underline{\theta}$, which includes the structural parameters (β, γ, b, η, δ, μ, Ψ, θ, ν, σ, ϕ_1, . . . , ϕ_J, δ_1, δ_2, $\bar{\lambda}$)' and the variances of the common shock and of the measurement error shocks (σ_ε^2, σ_1^2, . . . , σ_4^2, σ_5^2)'.

To derive the approximate likelihood function, let $\underline{\xi} = (\xi_1, . . . , \xi_T)'$ denote a $5T$ vector containing a sample of observations on the stationary stochastic process $\{\xi_t\}_{t=0}^{\infty}$ for $t = 1, . . . , T$ and define $\Gamma(\underline{\theta}) = E(\underline{\xi}\underline{\xi}')$ to be the variance-covariance matrix of $\underline{\xi}$ as a function of some parameter vector θ. Then the log-likelihood function for $\underline{\xi}$ can be expressed as

$$(3.3) \qquad L_T(\underline{\theta}) = -\frac{1}{2}(T + 5T) \log 2\pi - \frac{1}{2} \log [\det \Gamma(\theta)] - \frac{1}{2}\underline{\xi}'\Gamma(\theta)\underline{\xi}.$$

From the results derived by Hannan (1970), p. 378 and recently suggested by Hansen and Sargent (1980), the frequency domain approximation to $L_T(\theta)$, denoted $L_T^*(\theta)$, is given by

$$(3.4) \qquad L_T^*(\underline{\theta}) = -\frac{1}{2}(T + 5T) \log 2\pi - \frac{1}{2}\sum_{j=0}^{T-1} \log [\det S_\xi(\omega_j; \underline{\theta})]$$

$$-\frac{1}{2}\sum_{j=0}^{T-1} \text{trace } [S_\xi(\omega_j; \underline{\theta})^{-1}I(\omega_j)].$$

Here $\omega_j = 2\pi j/T$ for $j = 0, . . . , T - 1$ are the harmonic frequencies, $I(\omega_j)$ for $j = 0, . . . , T - 1$ is the periodogram for the sample of observations $\{\xi_t\}_{t=1}^{T}$, and $S_\xi(\omega_j; \underline{\theta})$ is the spectral density matrix of the $\{\xi_t\}_{t=0}^{\infty}$ process at frequency ω_j obtained by evaluating the covariance generating function of $\{\xi_t\}_{t=0}^{\infty}$ at $z = e^{i\omega_j}$. The periodogram

ogram summarizes the covariance properties of the sample of observations in the approximate likelihood function. Its ordinate at frequency ω_j is defined by

$$(3.5) \qquad I(\omega_j) = \frac{1}{2\pi T} \left[\sum_{j=1}^{T} \xi_t^{it\omega_j} \right] \left[\sum_{j=1}^{T} \xi_t'^{-it\omega_j} \right].$$

The spectral density matrix represents the restrictions of the underlying economic model for the covariances of the $\{\xi_t\}_{t=0}^{\infty}$ process at each frequency. If ξ_t evolves according to (3.1), the spectral density matrix $S_\xi(\omega_j; \theta)$ at frequency ω_j is defined by

$$(3.6) \qquad S_\xi(\omega_j; \underline{\theta}) = \frac{1}{2\pi} \left[\sigma_\varepsilon^2 H(\omega_j) H(\omega_j)^* + V \right]$$

$$= \frac{1}{2\pi} \{ \sigma_\varepsilon^2 [E(\omega_j) C(\omega_j)^{-1} B(\omega_j) + G(\omega_j)]$$

$$\times [E(\omega_j) C(\omega_j)^{-1} B(\omega_j) + G(\omega_j)]^* + V \}.$$

In equation (3.6), an asterisk (*) denotes both conjugation and transposition and $V = E(\nu_t \nu_t')$. Also, $H(\omega_j)$, $E(\omega_j)$, $C(\omega_j)$, $B(\omega_j)$, $F(\omega_j)$, and $\bar{H}(\omega_j)$ are the Fourier transforms of $H(L)$, $E(L)$, $C(L)$, $B(L)$, $F(L)$, and $\bar{H}(L)$, respectively. Subject to some regularity conditions, the results in Hannan (1970) can be used to show that the estimates obtained by maximizing (3.4) with respect to the vector of parameters θ are strongly consistent, asymptotically normal, and efficient and that the Wald and likelihood ratio test statistics have the usual distributions. Furthermore, these results hold even if the underlying distribution generating the observations is not normal.

The subsequent empirical analysis does not make use of the model's restrictions for the average growth rate (or means) of the actual series. This implies that the zero frequency is omitted when evaluating (3.4). To find the value of the approximate likelihood function for a given vector of parameters $\underline{\theta}$, $I(\omega_j)$ and $S_\xi(\omega_j; \underline{\theta})$ must be computed at the remaining frequencies. Since the periodogram does not depend on $\underline{\theta}$, it is computed only once and that value is used at every subsequent evaluation of the likelihood function. Determining the value of $S_\xi(\omega_j; \theta)$ requires more work. This is because the mapping from the vector of parameters $\underline{\theta}$ to $H(L)$ is not explicit. The expressions in part A of the Appendix for the deterministic steady states and equation (B.1) for the (indirect) single-period utility function are used to obtain the linear and quadratic coefficients W and Q of the approximate social planner's problem in terms of the given set of parameter values $\underline{\theta}$. The constraints in (2.19) are likewise linearized around the steady states of the relevant variables for each $\underline{\theta}$. The feedback polynomial $C(L)$ and the moving average polynomial $F(L)$ are obtained by iterating on the matrix Riccati difference equations defined in part C of the Appendix. Once $C(L)$ and $F(L)$ are determined, however, explicit formulas for $E(L)$ and $G(L)$ yield the value of $H(L)$ at $\underline{\theta}$.

4. DATA

So far, we have described a framework that restricts the joint time series behavior of a set of important aggregate variables, namely, expenditures for durable consumption goods, and for nondurables and services, total hours worked, investment expenditures for two types of capital, and total output. In order to interpret actual data within this framework, we need to make some further assumptions. First, we take the sample period to be 1948–1985 (I–IV). Second, in the absence of any theoretical restrictions, the length of a period in the model is equated to a quarter, and all series are seasonally adjusted and measured at annual rates. Third, according to the representative agent framework, the theoretical series correspond to per capita values of the measured series. Hence, all series are divided by the Bureau of Labor Statistics (BLS) measure of the civilian noninstitutional population, aged 16 and over, to obtain per capita values. Fourth, in terms of matching the theoretical variables with observed series, we identify investment in the two types of capital with investment in structures and equipment. Investment in structures is measured as the sum of investment expenditures for residential and nonresidential structures, including farm and nonfarm structures. Equipment investment is similarly defined as the sum of investment expenditures for residential and nonresidential producers' durable equipment. These data are obtained from the corresponding National Income and Product Accounts (NIPA) measures (see Survey of Current Business, Table 1.2). Likewise, the variable denoting expenditures for the purchases of consumer durables is measured by the corresponding NIPA series.

Next, output in the model is measured as GNP minus net exports of goods and services minus investment expenditures for business inventories minus total government expenditures. This definition is used because the model has no special features to account for the behavior of inventories or the foreign sector. Because the model does not distinguish between the behavior of government versus the behavior of private agents, one alternative to treating government expenditures as exogenous is to define the variables c_{1t}, c_{2t}, i_{1t} and i_{2t} as the sum of government expenditures for nondurables and services, for durables, etc. and private expenditures for these goods. But this practice introduces a further complication in that data on government capital (or investment) are typically available on an annual basis (see, for example, U.S. Department of Commerce Bureau of Economic Analysis publication, *Fixed Reproducible Tangible Wealth in the United States, 1925–1979*) and hence, must be interpolated to a quarterly basis in order to be used with the remaining data. Another possibility is to assume government expenditures are part of consumption. But this is also unsatisfactory because a large component of government purchases are for capital goods. Finally a measure of hours worked is obtained from 3-month averages of the monthly series "Total Employee Hours Worked in Nonagricultural Establishments," collected through the BLS Establishment Survey (see *Employment and Earnings* Table B.4). In the data, an important source of variation in total hours is due to variation in the number of persons working as well as the hours worked by those already employed (see, for example, Coleman 1984). With identical consumers, the former type of variation is absent from the theoretical series. While inconsistent with the model's assumptions, this measure of total hours is used because it represents more accurately the fluctuation in aggregate hours worked. (It also corresponds to the measure used by Kydland and Prescott 1982, and Eichenbaum, Hansen, and Singleton 1988). Another potential difficulty with the use of this hours data is that it creates a discrepancy between the measures of output and capital, on the one hand, and hours, on the other. While there exist separate series for hours worked in private versus government nonagricultural establishments collected through the BLS Establishment Survey, there are no comparable series for agricultural establishments. Similarly, data may be obtained for the total number of civilian employees and their average weekly hours from the BLS Household Survey, but no direct measure of hours worked in the private sector (including agriculture) is available. A final difficulty with this hours series is that incremental labor effort for inventory investment or export goods is assumed to have zero productivity. Since there is no tractable way of dealing with these difficulties given the framework in the paper, the empirical results that follow must be interpreted conditional on the choice of these data and any extensions left to future research.

Once the measures for the levels of the different variables have been constructed, the final step before the empirical implementation of the model is to stochastically detrend these variables using the stationarity-inducing transformation implied by the model. Recall that this involves differencing the logarithms of every variable except per capita hours. Hence, the series used in estimation refer to the logarithm of per capita hours and the logarithmic differences of the remaining series, namely, per capita expenditures for consumer durables, per capita investment expenditures for structures and for equipment, and per capita output.

5. EMPIRICAL RESULTS

5.1 *Estimates and Tests of Model (3.2)*. The single index representation implied by (3.1) is an important restriction for the behavior of the observable series. Before (3.1) is taken to data, this section tries to determine whether a single unobservable index can account for the covariation among the elements of ξ_t. Model (3.2) is used to derive the appropriate estimates and tests. It can be shown that the restrictions of this model for the $\{\xi_t\}_{t=0}^{\infty}$ process can be equivalently represented in terms of the covariation of the elements of ξ_t at each frequency ω, i.e.,

$$(5.1) \qquad S_\xi(\omega) = \bar{H}(\omega)\bar{H}(\omega)^* + \bar{V}(\omega).$$

In (5.1), the variance of ξ_t at frequency ω is decomposed according to the variance attributed to a low-dimensional vector of common latent factors and to the variance in a vector of specific disturbances, denoted by $\bar{H}(\omega)\bar{H}(\omega)^*$ and $\bar{V}(\omega)$, respectively.

Table 1 reports the χ^2 statistics for the hypothesis that, at the indicated frequencies, $S_\xi(\omega)$ decomposes according to a one-noise model versus the alter-

TABLE 1
TESTS OF MODEL (3.2) (ONE-NOISE TESTS): COHERENCES†

Frequency	Period (Quarters)	Ordinates	χ^2-Statistic*	Marginal Significance Level**	Output	Hours	Structures	Equipment	Consumer Durables
.0820π	28.8	7-16	22.4	0.021	0.995	0.539	0.883	0.890	0.834
.2578π	8.5	30-38	14.3	0.215	0.965	0.736	0.905	0.687	0.774
.4219π	4.9	51-59	9.6	0.561	1.000	0.194	0.672	0.471	0.525
.5859π	3.5	72-80	7.8	0.729	0.687	0.211	0.160	0.770	0.811
.7500π	2.7	93-101	17.1	0.104	1.000	0.041	0.328	0.088	0.575
.9141π	2.2	114-122	10.1	0.494	0.920	0.291	0.456	0.376	1.000
Overall	—	—	71.7		0.931	0.536	0.590	0.610	0.758

*For frequencies, $\chi^2(11)$; overall, $\chi^2(66)$.

**Defined as $\Pr[\chi^2(df) > c]$, where c is the value of the test statistic and df the number of degrees of freedom.

†Each row shows the coherence of the four series with the unobservable factor at the frequency listed in the first column. The overall coherence indicates the total proportion of the variance explained over all six bands.

native that $S_\xi(\omega)$ is merely positive definite.[2] In these tests, the degrees of freedom are $(n - k)^2 - n$ where n is the number of series. Since n is 5, k cannot exceed 2, otherwise (3.2) does not restrict the data. Because the estimators of $S_\xi(\omega)$ are asymptotically independent, an overall test of (3.2) can be constructed by summing the χ^2 statistics at the individual frequencies if $\bar{H}(\omega)$ and $\tilde{V}(\omega)$ are estimated from nonoverlapping bands of ordinates. Table 1 shows that the null hypothesis that a single factor accounts for the covariation among the elements of the measured series ξ_t cannot be rejected at conventional significance levels. This holds when the restrictions of (5.1) are considered overall as well as at the individual frequencies. Table 1 also presents the coherences of the elements of ξ_t with the common unobservable factor at the six listed frequencies. From (5.1), the coherence for the ith element of ξ_t at frequency ω is defined as

(5.2)
$$\text{coh}_i(\omega) = \frac{\bar{H}_i(\omega)\,\bar{H}_i(\omega)^*}{[S_\xi(\omega)]_{ii}}$$

where $\bar{H}_i(\omega)$ and $[S_\xi(\omega)]_{ii}$ denote the corresponding i^{th} elements of the 5×1 and 5×5 matrices $\bar{H}(\omega)$ and $S_\xi(\omega)$.

The single factor explains a large fraction of the variability of the growth rate of consumer durables and the growth rates of investment expenditures in structures and equipment. The overall proportion of variance explained for the respective series is 0.758, 0.590, and 0.610. For per capita hours, the common factor has the most explanatory power at the low frequencies, corresponding to cyclical components in this series with 8 quarters of more. The results for the output series deserve special mention: here the common factor accounts for 93 percent of the overall variance in the growth rate of output. Moreover, at some frequencies, namely frequencies associated with periods of 4.9 and 2.2 quarters, the proportion of variance explained is 100 percent. Another way of describing the same phenomenon is to note that the variance of the specific disturbances for the growth rate of output at those frequencies is zero. (A similar finding occurs for the consumer durables series at the sixth frequency band.) The occurrence of this event, referred to as the Heywood solution in the literature on maximum likelihood estimation of

---

[2] Geweke (1977) provides a comprehensive discussion of identification, estimation, and tests of models similar to (3.2). Briefly, to implement the test described in Section 5.1, calculate the finite Fourier transform of the sample of observations $\{\xi_t\}_{t=1}^T$ at the harmonic frequencies $\omega_j = 2\pi j/T$ for $j = 0, \ldots,$ $T - 1$. Denote this Fourier transform $w(j, T)$. Let ω_q be the frequency at which equation (3.2) is estimated and $(lq$ any positive integer. Also define the set of $(lq$ vectors $w(j_T + 1, T), \ldots, w(j_T + (lq, T)$, where j_T is chosen to minimize $\sum_{i=1}^{(lq} |2\pi(j_T + i) - \omega_q T|$. Then it can be shown that the joint distribution of the $(lq$ vectors converges to that of $(lq$ independent vectors, each possessing a complex normal distribution with mean zero and covariance matrix $S_\xi(\omega_q)$. If $\omega_q = 0$ or $\omega_q = \pi$, then this distribution is ordinary-normal. The complex likelihood function for $w(j_T + i, T)$ for $i = 1, \ldots, q$ is defined, for example, by Geweke (1977). Here, $q = 1, \ldots, Q$ defines the frequency band consisting of $(lq$ ordinates across which this complex likelihood function is evaluated. (3.2) is estimated at six frequencies: 0.820π, 0.2578π, 0.4219π, 0.5859π, 0.7500π, 0.9141π. The finite Fourier transform of the sample $\{\xi_t\}_{t=1}^T$ is calculated at a total of 128 harmonic frequencies between 0 and π. Out of this total of 128 ordinates, estimates of $\bar{H}(\omega)$ and $\tilde{V}(\omega)$ are obtained from disjoint bands of 9 periodogram ordinates each. In practice, all estimates and tests of the unrestricted frequency domain factor model are obtained using Robert Litterman's INDEX program.

906   SUMRU ALTUĞ

TABLE 2A
ESTIMATES OF $\bar{H}_i(\omega)\,\bar{H}_i(\omega)^*$ FOR $i = 1, \ldots, 5$

Frequency	Series				
	Output	Hours	Structures	Equipment	Consumer Durables
0.0820π	0.3571E-03	0.3149E-02	0.2944E-02	0.3148E-02	0.1968E-02
0.2578π	0.1927E-03	0.3029E-02	0.2201E-02	0.1986E-02	0.8382E-02
0.4219π	0.5148E-04	0.1146E-04	0.6923E-03	0.4805E-03	0.9619E-02
0.5859π	0.3877E-04	0.4693E-05	0.7408E-04	0.1245E-02	0.8594E-02
0.7500π	0.4494E-04	0.2962E-05	0.2836E-03	0.5547E-04	0.9253E-02
0.9141π	0.1124E-03	0.2664E-04	0.1943E-03	0.3097E-03	0.3927E-02

factor models (Joreskog 1967, 1969) and reported in earlier papers employing frequency domain factor analysis (Sargent and Sims 1977; Singleton 1980) implies that the tests of the one-noise model must be interpreted with some caution at the relevant frequencies because, in this case, the asymptotic distribution of minus twice the logarithm of the likelihood ratio statistic is unknown. However, Geweke and Singleton (1979) provide some Monte Carlo evidence showing that the effect of zero estimates for the variances of the specific disturbances at a given frequency is to shift the distribution of the corresponding χ^2 statistic rightward but, for sample sizes as large as the one in this paper, this problem is of little practical significance.

Table 2 presents estimates of $\bar{H}_i(\omega)\bar{H}_i(\omega)^*$ and $\bar{V}_i(\omega)$ which show the variance in each series attributed to its own specific disturbance at frequency ω. Notice that the values of $\bar{V}_i(\omega)$ for $i = 3, 4, 5$ (corresponding to the specific disturbance for the growth rates of structures, equipment, and consumer durables) are roughly of the same order of magnitude. Similarly, the variation in the values of $\bar{V}_2(\omega)$ (corresponding to the specific disturbance for hours) across the fourth to sixth frequency bands is within 40 percent of the largest value across those frequencies. However, there is a sharp decrease in the variance of ν_{2t} at the first frequency band relative to the others, suggesting that the specific disturbances for the hours series may follow a low-order autoregressive process.

The above results suggest that, aside from the behavior of the hours series, it is difficult to identify the variation in $\bar{V}_i(\omega)$ for the remaining series as being generated by simple autoregressive or moving average processes. Consequently, in what follows, the serial independence of the measurement errors together with the single

TABLE 2B
ESTIMATES OF $\bar{V}_i(\omega)$ FOR $i = 1, \ldots, 5$

Frequency	Series				
	Output	Hours	Structures	Equipment	Consumer Durables
0.0820π	0.1684E-05	0.2689E-02	0.3864E-03	0.3877E-03	0.3912E-03
0.2578π	0.6897E-05	0.1083E-03	0.2293E-03	0.9043E-03	0.2445E-03
0.4219π	0.0000	0.4735E-04	0.3375E-03	0.5397E-03	0.8685E-03
0.5859π	0.1764E-04	0.3389E-04	0.3873E-03	0.3701E-03	0.1993E-03
0.7500π	0.0000	0.6814E-04	0.5798E-03	0.5762E-03	0.6816E-03
0.9171π	0.9720E-05	0.6462E-05	0.2311E-03	0.5121E-03	0.0000

factor structure is imposed in (3.1) to determine whether the remaining restrictions of the economic model are supported by the data.

5.2 *Estimates and Tests of Model (3.1).* To derive the estimates of model (3.1), J, the number of periods required to build productive capital, was set equal to 4. Some justification for doing so exists in a survey by Mayer (1960), who found that the average time required for the completion of projects involving plants and structures was three to four quarters. This duration would seem a reasonable assumption for the completion of residential structures as well. For computational purposes, the subjective discount factor β and the depreciation rates δ_1 and δ_2 were also not estimated. The first was set at the value of 0.9909. The depreciation rate for structures was set at $\delta_1 = 0.02$. The rate for the depreciation of equipment was set as 0.03. These values are close to some estimates in the literature, although they are obtained from different models. For example, Hall and Jorgenson (1967) reported annual depreciation rates of 0.1471 and 0.1923 for equipment in manufacturing and nonfarm nonmanufacturing industries. The analogous rates reported for structures were 0.0625 and 0.0694.

The results of estimating (3.1) are reported in Table 3. These estimates are obtained by maximizing the likelihood function defined by equation (3.4) with respect to the remaining unknown parameters in $\underline{\theta}$.[3]

First, the estimates of γ, a, b, (and c) imply that the representative consumer's preferences are concave in $\bar{c}_{1t}$, $\bar{c}_{2t}^*$, and l_t^*. The point estimate for γ implies a moderate degree of risk aversion for the representative consumer, with a value of 1.5063 for the coefficient of relative risk aversion, defined by the expression $1 - \gamma$. However, the standard error of 0.7964 attached to this coefficient implies that the data cannot reject a logarithmic form for preferences, which occurs when $\gamma = 0$.

These results can be compared with the findings of Dunn and Singleton (1986) and Eichenbaum and Hansen (forthcoming 1990), who study relationships among real returns, durable good prices, expenditures for nondurable consumption goods and services, and expenditures for durable goods. The first paper reports point estimates of the concavity parameter γ that are all less than zero (but insignificantly different from the value of zero implied by logarithmic utility). The second paper finds that when single-period utility is constrained to be Cobb-Douglas in terms of services from nondurables and durables and the underlying growth process is

---

[3] This maximization problem involves maximizing a nonlinear objective function subject to inequality constraints because the model of Section 2 restricts the values of the preference and technology parameters. There are also restrictions of the form $\beta \exp(\bar{\lambda}(a + b)\gamma) < 1$ or, equivalently, $\gamma < \log(1/\beta)\bar{\lambda}(a + b)$. These ensure the existence of a positive real interest rate for the deterministic version of the stationary economy and, hence, that the deterministic steady-state equilibrium exists and the quadratic approximation procedure is well-defined. Finally, there are inequality constraints arising from the positivity of the variances for the innovation to the technology shock ε_t and the specific disturbances ν_{it}, $i = 1, \ldots, 5$. Instead of imposing these constraints directly, the estimates in Table 3 were obtained by searching over an unrestricted parameter space defined by H, F, M, A, B, T, S, P_1, P_2, P_3, SE, S_1, S_2, S_3, S_4, S_6, L, γ, ν, and δ and by defining the original parameters in the following way: $\Psi = [1 + \exp(F)]^{-1}$; $a = [1 + \exp(A)]$; $b = [1 + \exp(B)]^{-1}$; $\theta = [1 + \exp(T)]^{-1}$; $\sigma = [1 + \exp(S)]^{-1}$; $\phi_i = \exp(P_i)/D$ for $i = 1, \ldots, 3$; $\phi_4 = 1/D$; $\sigma_\varepsilon = (SE^2)^{1/2}$; $\lambda = \exp(L)$; $\sigma_i = [(S_i)^2]^{1/2}$ for $i = 1, \ldots, 5$; and $D = 1 + \exp(P_1) + \exp(P_2) + \exp(P_3)$.

TABLE 3
ESTIMATES OF MODEL (3.1)

Parameter	Estimate*
Preferences	
γ	−0.5063 (0.7964)
a	0.0767 (0.0704)
b	0.4538 (0.1173)
δ	0.2775 (0.4753)
η	0.9742**
Ψ	0.2269 (0.1721)
μ	0.0334**
Technology	
ν	1.5775 (1.000)
θ	0.7017 (0.2379)
σ	0.1915 (0.1541)
ϕ_1	0.1859 (0.0921)
ϕ_2	0.0851 (0.0551)
ϕ_3	0.3410 (0.0304)
ϕ_4	0.3878 (0.1115)
Technology Process	
$\bar{\lambda}$	0.2231**
σ_ε^2	4.8734 (0.5490)
Likelihood function $L_\tau^*(\underline{\theta})$	−724.8815
$\sum\limits_{j=1}^{T} \log\,[\det S_\xi(\omega_j;\theta)]$	−37.8600
$\sum\limits_{j=1}^{T} \text{trace}\,[S_\xi(\omega_j;\underline{\theta})^{-1}I(\omega_j)]$	−7.0007

*The numbers in parentheses are standard errors.
**Fixed during estimation.

modeled as one for which the stationarity-inducing transformation is logarithmic differencing (as it is in this paper), logarithmic separability of preferences cannot be rejected. Likewise, assuming a specification of preferences in which service flows from current and past values of leisure time and acquisitions of nondurable goods and services, Eichenbaum, Hansen and Singleton (1988) found little evidence against logarithmic separability when the service flow technology describing l_t^* was parameterized as $l_t^* = l_t + B_1 l_{t-1}$ with $B_1 > -1$.

The estimates of a and b imply that the share of total consumption services in current utility is about .53, which is greater than the value of 1/3 assumed by Kydland and Prescott (1982). On the other hand, the share of consumption from nondurable goods and services in current utility is estimated to be small relative to the share of consumption services from acquisitions of durable goods ($a = 0.0767$), but when its standard error is taken into account, it is consistent with the true value of this parameter being equal 0.1471. (This is approximately equal to the value Eichenbaum, Hansen and Singleton (1988) reported for the share of services from leisure time in their model.) The estimate of Ψ implies that 22 percent of the current purchases and stock of durable consumption goods are consumed per quarter but proportions between .05 and .40 are within one standard error of this value. For comparison purposes, it can be noted that Dunn and Singleton (1986) reported estimates for a similar parameter that range from 0.0025 to 0.0092 per month, with corresponding standard errors of 0.0094 and 0.0116. But they assumed that the physical depreciation rate for the stock of consumer durables was zero. In my case, the depreciation rate μ for the stock of consumer durables d_t turned out to be difficult to estimate; it was fixed during estimation at the value of 0.0334.

Of the remaining preference parameters, there is little evidence for the effect of past leisure choices on current utility. First, the estimate of 0.9742 for the parameter η, which is like a subjective depreciation rate for the stock of "accumulated leisure" a_t, implies that, in terms of its utility value, the stock of leisure time is almost depleted within a quarter. (This estimate does not possess a standard error because, like μ, it was fixed during estimation.) Second, although the estimate of δ (given by the value of 0.2775) is positive (implying that past leisure time contributes leisure services in the present), it is small and insignificantly different from zero when its standard error of 0.4753 is taken into account.

By contrast, Eichenbaum, Hansen and Singleton (1988) obtained negative and significant values for the parameter (analogous to δ in (2.4)) which governs the effect of past leisure choices on current utility. When they estimated their model using only the representative consumer's intertemporal Euler equation (which links marginal utilities of consumption across consecutive periods) as opposed to using the intratemporal Euler equation (which relates the marginal utility of consumption, the marginal utility of leisure, and the real wage), they found an estimate of 0.7062 (with a standard error of 0.6234) for a similarly defined parameter. Moreover, the results of specification tests seemed to indicate that failure of the overidentifying restrictions implied by their model could be attributed primarily to failure of the orthogonality conditions associated with the intratemporal Euler equation to hold in their sample. These authors suggested that their findings against the intertemporal substitution of leisure hypothesis (in terms of the finding that past leisure time contributes to leisure disservices in the present) could be due to the fact that the measures of compensation they used were error-ridden.

The above discussion suggests that aside from results relating to the time-separability of preferences with respect to leisure time (which may be due to the fact that this paper does not rely on aggregate wage or compensation data), the findings in this paper are qualitatively similar to those reported in studies employing the Euler equation methodology.

Turning to the results pertaining to the production technology, it is worthwhile to note that the statistical framework provided by (3.1) yields estimates of the technology parameters that are not subject to some of the biases encountered in static production function estimation. For example, it has been argued that if the capital utilization rate and man-hours are positively correlated, then failure to account for the former variable will lead to an upward bias for the estimate of the labor coefficient. Although this paper does not explicitly account for variations in the capital utilization rate, it controls for the correlation of the inputs in the aggregate production with the unobserved technology shock by making explicit the dependence of all endogenous variables on the innovation to this shock. In addition, because this paper does not use data on capital stocks directly to estimate the production function parameters but instead relies on information about (the growth rates of) investment in the relevant capital inputs, it indirectly allows for variations in capital utilization that are not captured by available measures of capital stocks. It also controls for the growth in the endogenous variables by linking the existence of a stochastic trend in a subset of these variables to the existence of a stochastic trend in the unobservable technology process. This is important as Nelson and Plosser (1982) show, neither the practice of representing technological change in terms of a time trend nor the practice of controlling for nonstationarity by means of population growth is sufficient to account for the growth in real GNP.

Taking into account these considerations, the parameter that determines the share of labor in the aggregate production, namely θ, is estimated to be 0.7017, but given the reported standard error, the true value of the parameter is consistent with values between 0.4638 and 0.9396. This point estimate of θ is somewhat larger than other reported labor share values. (The usual labor share value estimated from national income data is 0.64, which is also the value assumed by Kydland and Prescott 1982 for the labor share parameter in their model, while Hulten and Schwab 1984 report labor share values between 0.57 and 0.79 for manufacturing for several U.S. regions between 1951 and 1978.) On the other hand, it is consistent with diminishing returns with respect to labor hours and a positive marginal product for the composite capital good.[4] The estimate of σ implies that structures receive a larger share in the composite capital good relative to equipment: when the standard error of its estimate is taken into account, the value of this share parameter ranges between 0.617 and 0.9626. The estimate of ν (equal to 1.5775) implies that the quantity $1/(1 + \nu)$, which measures the elasticity of substitution between the two types of capital defined by the expression $1/(1 + \nu)$, is equal to 0.3879: this finding suggests that a Cobb-Douglas production function in hours, structures and equipment, with its unitary substitution elasticities, may not be a good approximation for describing the joint behavior of the relevant series.

The estimates of ϕ_j for $j = 1, \ldots, 4$ provide evidence about the importance of time lags in the investment for the stock of structures. According to the results of Table 3, these estimates increase with j, implying that a declining proportion of resources are allocated to investment projects closer to completion. These estimates also imply that over 70 percent of the resources needed to complete a given project are expended in the first two quarters. The standard errors of these coefficients indicate that the behavior of the structures series is not consistent with equal weights being assigned to the incomplete projects, i.e., with $\phi_j = 0.25$ for $j = 1, \ldots, 4$, which is the assumption made by Kydland and Prescott (1982). In particular, $\phi_2 = \phi_3 = 0.25$ can be rejected by the data. These results are similar to

---

[4] By contrast, many estimates from static production function estimation yield labor share values that imply (short-run) increasing returns to labor. (See Lucas 1970 for a summary of some of the earlier evidence.) More recently, Tatom (1980) reports a labor share value of 1.181 (with a capital coefficient of -0.048) for a Cobb-Douglas function with labor and nonresidential capital inputs, based on annual observations for the period 1948–73 for the private business sector. Usually, smaller labor elasticities of output are obtained only after correcting the capital input with some measure of capacity utilization. For example, using the Federal Reserve Board capacity utilization rate in manufacturing (as a proxy for the capital utilization rate) and imposing constant returns to scale, Tatom obtains a labor coefficient of 0.676.

the findings in Park (1984) and Taylor (1982). Using a flexible plan gestation lag model of investment in which the number of incomplete projects can be altered subject to some adjustment costs, Park (1984) finds that, with flexible plans and a maximum of three quarters allowed for the completion of new projects, 80 percent of all investment is completed in the first period. Taylor (1982) considers three types of projects, namely, nonresidential buildings in manufacturing industries which require up to three periods to complete. Using a survey of nonresidential construction conducted by the U.S. Census, he reports that a major fraction of the total value put in place occurs in the initial periods, i.e. for two period projects, 81 percent of the resources are expended in the first year while 85 percent of the resources are expended in the first two years for three year projects.

Since the technology shock is unobserved, it is somewhat difficult to evaluate the estimate of $\bar{\lambda}$ by comparing it with the mean of Solow's (1957) empirical stock of technology, for example. Nevertheless, the estimate of $\bar{\lambda}$ has some interest because $\exp(-\bar{\lambda})$ acts as a discount factor in the (linearized) laws of motion for the stationary economy. For example, the implied estimates for the undepreciated parts of the (stationary) stocks of structures and equipment, respectively defined as $(1 - \delta_1)\exp(-\bar{\lambda})$ and $(1 - \delta_2)\exp(-\bar{\lambda})$, are equal to 0.784 and 0.776. Likewise, the values of Ψ, μ and $\bar{\lambda}$ imply that the fraction of the (stationary) stock of consumer durables that remains undepreciated, i.e. $(1 - \Psi - \mu)\exp(-\bar{\lambda})$, is .60. Finally, the implied discount factor for the approximate social planner's problem is given by $\beta \exp(\bar{\lambda}(a + b)\gamma) = 0.9332$.

The estimate of the variance σ_ε^2 for the technology shock is also difficult to interpret because the approximation procedure implies that the estimated variance will not be invariant to normalizations involving the total leisure hours per quarter possessed by the representative consumer and the initial value of the technology shock λ_0.[5] Hence, in what follows, I focus on the proportion of variance explained by the innovation to the technology shock as a measure of the importance of such shocks in explaining the covariation of the observed series. For this purpose, I calculate the coherence of each element of ξ_t with ε_t across frequencies comparable to those in Table 1. These coherences are reported in Table 4. Likewise, instead of reporting the estimated variances for the measurement error shocks, Table 4 shows the overall proportion of variance in each series that can be attributed to variation in the innovation to the technology shock (this is a measure that is similar to a population R^2).

Table 4 indicates that among the different series, the variance of the measurement error shock for per capita hours is largest, relative to the total explained variance of these series. On the other hand, the coherences in Table 4 imply that the innovation to the technology shock can best account for the variability in the growth rate of output: aside from the very low frequencies, it can explain close to 90 percent of the total variance. It can also account for close to 50 percent of the explained variation in the growth rate for investment in structures and equipment. It is less successful in explaining the variation in the growth rate of expenditures for

---

[5] This point can be seen from the definition of the discount rate $\bar{\beta}_t$ for the stationary model and the indirect utility function (B.1) for the social planner's problem in (2.19).

TABLE 4

PROPORTION OF VARIANCE EXPLAINED BY ONE COMMON FACTOR:
COHERENCES FOR ξ_t FROM MODEL (3.1)

Frequency	Period (Quarters)	Output	Hours	Structures	Equipment	Consumer Durables
0.0405π	49.33	0.41598	0.11042	0.46423	0.46692	0.28057
0.0811π	24.66	0.70034	0.11567	0.49817	0.56789	0.28629
0.1216π	16.44	0.83380	0.11469	0.53087	0.56847	0.29550
0.1622π	12.13	0.88353	0.10551	0.54849	0.56876	0.30772
0.2027π	9.86	0.89928	0.09060	0.54434	0.56855	0.32235
0.2973π	6.72	0.91574	0.05820	0.46585	0.54830	0.36168
0.4054π	4.93	0.96856	0.06157	0.64640	0.34957	0.40664
0.5135π	3.89	0.85412	0.02444	0.77382	0.46911	0.44503
0.6216π	3.21	0.97545	0.00769	0.61911	0.67153	0.47175
0.7297π	2.74	0.98589	0.01627	0.48497	0.57440	0.49957
0.9459π	2.11	0.98453	0.10028	0.72847	0.80088	0.54038
π	2.00	0.9890	0.1318	0.7656	0.8303	0.5406
Overall	—	0.9654	0.0568	0.5631	0.6080	0.3652

consumer durables, especially at the lower frequencies where the coherences fall to 30–35 percent. It is least successful in accounting for the explained variation in per capita hours: here the largest coherences, which occur at the high frequencies, are less than 15 percent. These results show an overall similarity with those for the unrestricted frequency domain index model, reported in Table 1. There, as in Table 4, the largest coherences occur for the growth rate of output while per capita hours is the least well explained.

6. CONCLUSION

Taken together, the estimates of equations (3.1) and (3.2) imply that an aggregative model in which persistent technology shocks are the only driving force cannot rationalize the *joint* behavior of per capita hours with the remaining series. As one final question, it is worthwhile to ask how this finding compares with Kydland and Prescott's conclusions about the performance of their model. These authors concluded that "the fit of the model is very good, particularly in light of the model's simplicity" (p. 1363). Among other results, they reported that "the model is consistent with the large (percentage) variability in investment and low variability in consumption and their high correlation with output" (p. 1364). With respect to specific features of the model, they argued that "the dependence of current utility on past leisure choices . . . is crucial in making [the model] consistent with the observation that cyclical employment fluctuates substantially more than productivity does" (p. 1364). Although Kydland and Prescott's analysis could not be used to determine whether "technology shocks are adequate to generate output, employment, etc. fluctuations of the magnitude actually observed" (McCallum 1986) because they chose the variance of the innovation of the technology shock to make the variability of the output series generated by their model consistent with observed GNP variability, their comments nevertheless suggest the inability of their model to rationalize the relative variability of aggregate hours and productivity. Likewise, if we recall that one of the findings of the papers using the Euler equation estimation methodology was the failure of the intratemporal Euler equation between the marginal utility of leisure and the marginal utility of consumption to hold in the sample, then it appears that the findings in this paper are similar to the findings in related papers in so far as they point to the difficulties encountered in rationalizing the behavior of per capita hours (considered jointly with other quantity variables or with real wages or productivity).

There are several ways in which the current paper could be extended. One possibility is to allow for variability in the average work week of labor and to explicitly account for the behavior of individuals who do not participate each period. Another possibility is to separately model such components of GNP that we took as exogenous, namely, net exports, inventory investment, and government expenditures. These extensions would probably allow for a better test of the underlying hypothesis that an aggregative model driven by persistent technology shocks can explain the cyclical movement of a set of key series around some (stochastically) evolving trend. But these extensions would also take us far from the framework Kydland and Prescott originally presented and are hence the topic for future research.

University of Minnesota, U.S.A.

APPENDIX

This Appendix derives approximate equilibrium laws of motion describing the evolution of quantities for the economy of Section 2. This is accomplished in several steps. First, the steady states for the deterministic version of the stationary model are derived. Then the CES production function and the nonlinear social planner's problem in (2.19) are approximated around this steady state. Finally, the equilibrium laws of motion are obtained as the solution to a linear-quadratic dynamic optimization problem under uncertainty.

A. *The Deterministic Steady States.* To calculate the steady states for the deterministic economy, let $\bar{\lambda}_t = \exp(\bar{\lambda})$ and $\bar{\lambda}_t^{J-j} = \exp((J-j)\bar{\lambda})$ for $j = 0, \ldots,$ $J - 1$ for all t. Notice that this yields a deterministic version of the social planner's problem described by (2.19), such that all variables evolve as deterministic functions of the initial conditions. The first-order conditions for the deterministic version of (2.19) with respect to $\bar{c}_{1t}$, $\bar{c}_{2t}$, l_t, $\bar{k}_{1t+J}$, $\bar{k}_{2t+1}$ and n_t yield the relevant steady states. First, it can be shown that the steady-state interest rate and the shadow price for the first type of capital are given by

(A.1) $$r = \frac{1}{\beta \exp(\bar{\lambda}(a+b)\gamma)} - 1 \quad \text{and} \quad q = \sum_{j=1}^{J} (1+r)^{j-1} \phi_j \exp(-(J-j)\bar{\lambda}).$$

Given (A.1), the marginal cost for the two types of capital are defined as

(A.2) $q(1 + r - (1 - \delta_1) \exp(-\bar{\lambda}))$ and $1 + r - (1 - \delta_2) \exp(-\bar{\lambda})$, respectively. Equating the marginal product of each type of capital to its cost then yields the steady-state values for $\bar{k}_{1t+J}$ and $\bar{k}_{2t+1}$ as

(A.3) $\quad \bar{k}_2 = \left[\dfrac{q(1 + r - (1 - \delta_1)\exp(-\bar{\lambda}))}{1 + r - (1 - \delta_2)\exp(-\bar{\lambda})} \dfrac{\sigma \exp(\bar{\lambda}\nu)}{(1 - \sigma)\exp(J\bar{\lambda}\nu)}\right]^{1/(1+\nu)} \bar{k}_1 \equiv b_1 \bar{k}_1$

(A.4)

$$\bar{k}_1 = \left[\dfrac{(1-\sigma)(\exp(\bar{\lambda}J\nu)(1-\theta)((1-\sigma)\exp(J\bar{\lambda}\nu) + \sigma b_1^{-\nu}\exp(\bar{\lambda}\nu))^{-(1-\theta+\nu)/\nu}}{q(1 + r - (1 - \delta_1)\exp(-\bar{\lambda}))}\right]^{1/\theta} n$$

$$\equiv b_2 n.$$

In the deterministic steady state, both types of investment are a constant fraction of the relevant capital stocks, while the production function provides the steady-state value for output $\bar{q}$:

(A.5) $\quad \bar{i}_1 = (1 - (1 - \delta_1)\exp(-\bar{\lambda}))\left[\displaystyle\sum_{j=1}^{J} \phi_j \exp(-(J-j)\bar{\lambda})\right]\bar{k}_1 \equiv b_3 n$

(A.6) $\quad \bar{i}_2 = (1 - (1 - \delta_2)\exp(-\bar{\lambda}))\bar{k}_2 \equiv b_4 n$

(A.7) $\quad \bar{q} = [(1-\sigma)\exp(J\bar{\lambda}\nu) + \sigma b_1^{-\nu}\exp(\bar{\lambda}\nu)]^{-(1-\theta)/\nu} b_2^{1-\theta} n \equiv b_5 n.$

The steady-state value for hours n_t and for consumption from durable consumption goods $\bar{c}_{2t}$ is obtained by using the marginal rates of substitution of the two types of consumption for each other and for leisure and by assuming that the real wage equals the marginal product of labor. This yields

(A.8) $\quad \bar{c}_2 = \dfrac{b(1 + \mu\beta\exp(-\bar{\lambda}))(1 - (1 - \mu - \Psi)\exp(-\bar{\lambda}))}{a(1 - \beta(1 - \mu - \Psi)\exp(-\bar{\lambda}))(1 + \exp(-\bar{\lambda})\mu)} \quad \bar{c}_1 \equiv b_7 n$

(A.9) $\quad \bar{c}_2^* = \dfrac{(1 + \exp(-\bar{\lambda})\mu)\Psi\bar{c}_2}{1 - \exp(-\bar{\lambda})(1 - \mu - \Psi)} \qquad \bar{d} = \dfrac{(1 - \Psi)\bar{c}_2}{1 - \exp(-\bar{\lambda})(1 - \mu - \Psi)}$

and

(A.10) $\quad l^* = \dfrac{(\eta + \delta)l}{\eta} \qquad a = \dfrac{l}{\eta}$

(A.11) $\quad n = \left[1 + \dfrac{c(1 + \delta\beta - \beta(1 - \eta))\eta b_6}{a(1 - (1 - \eta)\beta)(\eta + \delta)\theta b_5}\right]^{-1}.$

The steady state value for consumption from nondurable goods and services $\bar{c}_{1t}$ is obtained using the aggregate market-clearing condition together with equation (A.8):

(A.12) $\quad \bar{c}_1 = (a(1 - \beta(1 - \Psi - \mu)\exp(-\bar{\lambda})(1 + \exp(-\bar{\lambda})\mu)[\bar{q} - \bar{i}_1 - \bar{i}_2])/$

$$(a(1-\beta(1-\Psi-\mu)\exp(-\bar{\lambda}))(1+\exp(-\bar{\lambda})\mu)$$

$$+b(1+\mu\beta\exp(-\bar{\lambda}))(1-(1-\mu-\Psi)\exp(-\bar{\lambda}))) \equiv b_6 n.$$

B. *The Approximate Social Planner's Problem.* To derive the approximate social planner's problem, use the constraints in (2.19) to substitute out for $\bar{c}^*_{1t}$, $\bar{c}^*_{2t}$ and l^*_t in the nonlinear objective function. Notice also that the nonsatiation of preferences with respect to consumption and leisure implies that the first three constraints in (2.19) will hold with equality. Using this fact, define the function

(B.1)
$$U(\bar{X}_t) \equiv \frac{1}{\gamma} \{[n_t^\theta[(1-\sigma)(\bar{k}_{1t}/\tilde{\lambda}_t^J)^{-\nu}$$

$$+ \sigma(\bar{k}_{2t}/\tilde{\lambda}_t)^{-\nu}]^{[-(1-\theta)]/\nu} - \tilde{i}_{1t} - \tilde{i}_{2t} - \bar{c}_{2t}]^a$$

$$\times [\Psi(\bar{c}_{2t} + \bar{d}_t/\tilde{\lambda}_t)]^b[1 + n_t + \delta a_t]^c\}^\gamma$$

where $\bar{X}_t = (\bar{k}_{1t}, a_1, \tilde{i}_{1t} + \tilde{i}_{2t}, \bar{k}_{2t}, \bar{n}_t, \bar{c}_{2t}, \bar{d}_t, \tilde{\lambda}_t, \tilde{\lambda}_t^J)'$ and λ_0 has been normalized as unity. Now approximate (B.1) around the vector of steady states $S = (\bar{k}_1, a, \tilde{i}_1 + \tilde{i}_2, \bar{k}_2, n, \bar{c}_2, \bar{d}, \exp(\bar{\lambda}), \exp(J\bar{\lambda}))'$, using the formulas provided by Kydland and Prescott (1982), pp. 1356–57. Similarly, linearize the laws of motion for $\bar{d}_{t+1}$, $\bar{k}_{1t+1}$, $\bar{k}_{2t+1}$, $\tilde{i}_{1t}$ and $\tilde{\lambda}_t^J$. This procedure yields an approximation to (2.19) which is exact at the deterministic steady states calculated in the previous section, i.e.,

(B.2)
$$\text{maximize } E_0 \left[\sum_{t=0}^{\infty} \beta^t \exp(t(\bar{\lambda})(a+b)\gamma)[(\bar{X}_t - S)'Q(\bar{X}_t - S) \right.$$
$$\left. \{z_t\}_{t=0}^{\infty} \right.$$

$$\left. + W'(\bar{X}_t - S) + U(S) \right]$$

subject to

$$\bar{d}_{t+1} = (1-\mu-\Psi)\exp(-\bar{\lambda})(\bar{d}_t - \exp(\bar{\lambda})\bar{d}) + (1-\Psi)(\bar{c}_{2t} - \bar{c}_2)$$

$$+ c_1(\tilde{\lambda}_t - \exp(\bar{\lambda})) + \bar{d}$$

$$a_{t+1} = (1-\eta)a_t + 1 - n_t$$

$$\bar{k}_{1t+1} = (1-\delta_1)\exp(-\bar{\lambda})(\bar{k}_{1t} - \exp(J\bar{\lambda})\bar{k}_1) + (\bar{s}_{1t} - \bar{s}_1)$$

$$+ c_2(\tilde{\lambda}_{t-J+1} - \exp(\bar{\lambda})) + \bar{k}_1 \exp((J-1)\bar{\lambda})$$

$$\bar{k}_{2t+1} = (1-\delta_2)\exp(-\bar{\lambda})(\bar{k}_{2t} - \exp(\bar{\lambda})\bar{k}_2) + (\tilde{i}_{2t} - \tilde{i}_2) + c_3(\tilde{\lambda}_t - \exp(\bar{\lambda})) + \bar{k}_2$$

$$\tilde{i}_{1t} = \sum_{j=0}^{J} d_j\left(\bar{k}_{1t+j} - \exp\left((J-j)\bar{\lambda}\right)\bar{k}_1\right) + \sum_{j=0}^{J-1} e_j(\tilde{\lambda}_{t-j} - \exp(\bar{\lambda})) + \tilde{i}_1$$

$$\bar{\lambda}_t^J = \sum_{j=0}^{J-1} f_j(\bar{\lambda}_{t+j} - \exp(\bar{\lambda})) + \exp(J\bar{\lambda})$$

given $\bar{d}_0; a_0; s_{j0}, j = 1, \ldots, J-1; \bar{k}_{10}; \bar{k}_{20}; \bar{\lambda}_j, j = 1, \ldots, J-1$ and the stochastic process for $\{\bar{\lambda}_t\}_{t=0}^{\infty}$. Likewise, linearize the CES production function as

(B.3)
$$\bar{q} = q_t/\lambda_t$$

$$= a_1(n_t - n) + a_2(\bar{k}_{1t} - \bar{k}_1) + a_3(\bar{k}_{2t} - \bar{k}_2)$$

$$+ a_4(\bar{\lambda}_t - \exp(\bar{\lambda})) + a_5(\bar{\lambda}_t^J - \exp(J\bar{\lambda})) + \bar{q}.$$

C. *Solution to the Approximate Social Planner's Problem.* The problem described by equation (B.2) is a linear-quadratic dynamic optimization problem under uncertainty. To obtain its solution, define $\bar{x}_t$ and $\bar{w}_t$ to be vectors of state and control variables such that

$$\bar{x}_t = (\bar{k}_{1t+J-1}, a_t, \bar{k}_{2t}, \bar{k}_{1t+J-2}, \ldots, \bar{k}_{1t}, \bar{d}_t, \bar{\lambda}_t, \ldots, \bar{\lambda}_{t-J+1}, 1)',$$

$$\bar{w}_t = \begin{bmatrix} \bar{k}_{1t+J} - (1 - \delta_1)\exp(-\bar{\lambda})k_{1t+J-1} \\ a_{t+1} - (1 - \eta)a_t \\ \bar{k}_{2t+1} - (1 - \delta_2)\exp(-\bar{\lambda})\bar{k}_{2t} \\ \bar{d}_{t+1} - (1 - \Psi - \mu)\exp(-\bar{\lambda})d_t \end{bmatrix}.$$

Using the constraints in (B.1) and omitting terms that do not involve $\bar{X}_t$, (B.1) can be equivalently expressed as

(C.1)
$$\underset{\{\bar{w}_t\}_{t=0}^{\infty}}{\text{maximize }} E_0 \sum_{t=0}^{\infty} \beta^t \exp(t\bar{\lambda}(a+b)\gamma)$$

$$\times [(\bar{x}_t'R\bar{x}_t + \bar{x}_t'S\bar{w}_t + \bar{w}_t'T\bar{w}_t + U_1'\bar{x}_t + U_2'\bar{w}_t])$$

subject to

$$\bar{x}_{t+1} = A\bar{x}_t + B\bar{w}_t,$$

given $\bar{x}_0$. Here, R, S, T, U_1 and U_2 are obtained from the appropriate elements of Q and W. Following Bertsekas (1976), the solution to this problem is obtained as

(C.2)
$$\bar{w}_t = -F\bar{x}_t, \quad t = 0, 1, 2 \ldots.$$

Using (C.2), the law of motion for $\bar{x}_{t+1}$ can be expressed as

(C.3)
$$\bar{x}_{t+1} = (A - BF)\bar{x}_t$$

where $A - BF$ has eigenvalues less than $\beta^{-1/2}$ in modulus. (See Hansen and Sargent 1981.) Now (C.3) can be used to obtain a convenient representation for the vector of stock variables $\bar{y}_{1t} \equiv (\bar{k}_{1t+J}, a_{t+1}, \bar{k}_{2t+1}, \bar{d}_{t+1})'$ as a function of current and past values of $\bar{\lambda}_t$, i.e.

(C.4) $$\bar{y}_{1t} = \bar{C}(L)^{-1}\bar{F}(L)\bar{\lambda}_t + \bar{m}_1$$

where $\bar{m}_1$ is a vector of constants and $\bar{C}(L)$ and $\bar{F}(L)$ are matrix polynomials in the lag operator L, with dimensions conformable with $\bar{y}_{1t}$ and $\bar{\lambda}_t$, such that

$$\bar{C}(L) \equiv I + \bar{C}_1 L + \cdots + \bar{C}_J L^J$$

and

$$\bar{F}(L) \equiv \bar{F}_0 + \bar{F}_1 L + \cdots + \bar{F}_{j-1} L^{J-1}.$$

To derive a representation for the flow variables $\bar{y}_{2t} = (\bar{i}_{1t}, n_t, \bar{i}_{2t}, \bar{q}_t)'$, use the linearized version of the CES production function (described by (B.3)) and the laws of motion for $\bar{k}_{1t+J}$, a_{t+1}, $\bar{k}_{2t+1}$, and $\bar{d}_{t+1}$ together with the representation for $\bar{y}_{1t}$, i.e.,

(C.5) $$\bar{y}_{2t} = \bar{E}(L)\bar{y}_{1t} + \bar{D}(L)\bar{\lambda}_t + \bar{m}_2$$

$$= [\bar{E}(L)\bar{C}(L)^{-1}\bar{F}(L) + \bar{D}(L)]\bar{\lambda}_t + \bar{m}_2$$

where

$\bar{E}(L) \equiv$

$$
\begin{bmatrix}
\bar{g}(L) & 0 & 0 & 0 \\
0 & 1 - (1-\eta)L & 0 & 0 \\
0 & 0 & 1 - (1-\delta_2)\exp(-\bar{\lambda})L & 0 \\
0 & 0 & 0 & \dfrac{1 - (1-\Psi-\mu)\exp(-\bar{\lambda})L}{(1-\Psi)} \\
a_1 \exp(J\bar{\lambda})L^J & a_2(1-(1-\eta)L) & a_3 \exp(\bar{\lambda})L & 0
\end{bmatrix}
$$

and

$$
\bar{D}(L) \equiv
\begin{bmatrix}
e_0 + e_1 L + \cdots + e_{t-1}L^{J-1} \\
0 \\
-c_3 \\
-c_1 \\
(a_4 + a_5 e_0) + a_5 e_1 L + \cdots + a_5 e_{J-1} L^{J-1}
\end{bmatrix}
$$

Now (C.4) and (C.5) provide representations for the variables of the stationary model, or equivalently, for the stochastically-detrended values of a subset of the variables from the original model. To eliminate the dependence of (C.4) and (C.5) on values of the unobserved technology shock λ_t, it is necessary to derive a logarithm approximation to (C.4) and (C.5). For this purpose, define

$$y_{1t} = (\log(k_{1t+J}), \log a_{t+1}, \log(k_{2t+1}), \log(d_{t+1}))',$$

$$y_{2t} = (\log(i_{1t}), \log n_t, \log(i_{2t}), \log(q_t))'$$

and let T_1 be a 4×4 diagonal matrix with $[T_1]_{11} = 1$ if $i \neq 2$ and $[T_1]_{22} = 0$ and $t_1 = (1\ 0\ 1\ 1)'$. Using these definitions and the fact that $\log(\tilde{\lambda}_t) = \varepsilon_t + \bar{\lambda}$, rewrite (C.4) as

$$(\text{C.6}) \qquad y_{1t} - t_1 \log \lambda_t = C_1 y_{1t-1} - C_1 t_1 \log \lambda_t + \cdots + C_J y_{1t-J}$$

$$- C_J t_1 \log \lambda_{t-J} + F_0(\varepsilon_t + \bar{\lambda}) + \cdots + F_{j-1}(\varepsilon_{t-J} + \bar{\lambda}) + m_1$$

where C_j, F_j and m_1 are the derivatives of $\log(\bar{y}_{1t} + \bar{C}_1 \bar{y}_{1t-1} + \cdots + \bar{C}_J \bar{y}_{1t-J})$ and $\log(\bar{F}_0 \tilde{\lambda}_{t-1} + \cdots + \bar{F}_{J-1} \tilde{\lambda}_{t-J-1} + \bar{m}_1)$ with respect to $\log \bar{y}_{1t-j}$, $\log \tilde{\lambda}_{t-j}$, and $\log \bar{m}_1$, respectively, evaluated at the steady-state values for the stationary economy. Subtracting $T_1 y_{1t-1}$ from both sides of this representation to eliminate its dependence on the nonstationary technology shock and rearranging terms implies

$$(\text{C.7}) \qquad y_{1t} - T_1 y_{1t-1} = t_1 \log \lambda_t - T_1 t_1 \log \lambda_{t-1} + C(L)^{-1}F(L)(\varepsilon_t + \bar{\lambda})$$

$$- T_1 C(L)^{-1}F(L)(\varepsilon_{t-1} + \bar{\lambda}) + m_1 - T_1 m_1$$

$$= (C(L)^{-1}F(L) + t_1)(\varepsilon_t + \bar{\lambda}) - T_1 C(L)^{-1}F(L)(\varepsilon_{t-1} + \bar{\lambda})$$

$$\equiv C(L)^{-1}B(L)\varepsilon_t + y_1^m.$$

Similarly, define the 5×5 matrix diagonal matrix T_2 with $[T_2]_{ii} = 1$ if $i \neq 2$ and $[T_2]_{22} = 0$, the vector $t_2 = (1\ 0\ 1\ 1\ 1)'$ and rewrite (C.7) as

$$(\text{C.8}) \qquad y_{2t} - t_2 \log \lambda_t = E(L)(y_{1t} - t_1 \log \lambda_t) + D(L) \log \lambda_t + m_2 - T_2 m_2$$

where E_j, D_j and m_2 are the derivatives of $\log(\bar{E}_0 \bar{y}_{1t} + \bar{E}_1 \bar{y}_{1t-1} + \cdots + \bar{E}_J \bar{y}_{1t-J} + \bar{D}_0 \tilde{\lambda}_t + \bar{D}_1 \tilde{\lambda}_{t-1} + \cdots + \bar{D}_{J-1} \tilde{\lambda}_{t-J-1} + \bar{m}_2)$ with respect to $\log \bar{y}_{1t-j}$, $\log \tilde{\lambda}_{t-j}$ and $\log \bar{m}_2$, respectively, evaluated at the appropriate steady states. Subtracting $T_2 y_{2t-1}$ from both sides implies

$$(\text{C.9}) \qquad y_{2t} - T_2 y_{2t-1} = E(L)y_{1t} - T_2 E(L)y_{1t-1} - E(L)t_1 \log \lambda_t$$

$$+ T_2 E(L)t_1 \log \lambda_{t-1} + D(L)(\varepsilon_t + \bar{\lambda})$$

$$- T_2 D(L)(\varepsilon_{t-1} + \bar{\lambda}) + t_2(\varepsilon_t + \bar{\lambda}) + m_2 - T_2 m_2.$$

Noting that $T_2 E(L) = E(L)t_1$ and $T_2 E(L)t_1 = E(L)t_1$, (C.11) can be rewritten as

$$(\text{C.10}) \qquad y_{2t} - T_2 y_{2t-1} = E(L)(y_{1t} - T_1 y_{1t-1}) + (D_0 - E_0 t_1 + t_2(\varepsilon_t + \bar{\lambda})$$

$$+ (D_1 - E_1 t_1 - T_2 D_0)(\varepsilon_{t-1} + \bar{\lambda}) + \cdots$$

$$+ (D_{J-1} - E_{J-1} t_1 - T_2 D_{J-2})(\varepsilon_{t-J+1} + \bar{\lambda})$$

$$- (E_J t_1 + T_2 D_{J-1})(\varepsilon_{t-J} + \bar{\lambda}) + m_2 - T_2 m_2.$$

Substituting for $y_{1t} - T_1 y_{1t-1} = C(L)^{-1}B(L)\varepsilon_t + y_1^m$ from (C.7) into the above expression and regrouping terms involving current and lagged values of ε_t into the polynomial $G(L)\varepsilon_t$ implies that

(C.11) $\quad\quad y_{2t} - T_2 y_{2t-1} = (E(L)C(L)^{-1}B(L) + G(L))\varepsilon_t + y_2^m.$

To simplify computations during the estimation, we identified C_j with $\bar{C}_j$, etc., when computing the lag polynomials in (C.13).

REFERENCES

BERNANKE, BEN S., "The Determinants of Investment: Another Look," *American Economic Review* 73 (1983), 71–75.

BERTSEKAS, DIMITRIS P., *Dynamic Programming and Stochastic Control* (New York: Academic Press, 1976).

BROCK, WILLIAM A. AND LEONARD MIRMAN, "Optimal Economic Growth and Uncertainty: The Discounted Case," *Journal of Economic Theory* 4 (1972), 479–513.

COLEMAN, T., "Essays on Aggregate Labor Market Business Cycle Fluctuations," Ph.D. Thesis, University of Chicago, 1984.

DEBREU, GERARD, "Valuation Equilibrium and Pareto Optimum," *Proceedings of the National Academy of Sciences* 40 (1954), 588–592.

DUNN, KENNETH B. AND KENNETH J. SINGLETON, "Modeling the Term Structure of Interest Rates Under Non-Separable Utility and Durability of Goods," *Journal of Financial Economics* 17 (1986), 27–56.

EICHENBAUM, MARTIN S. AND LARS PETER HANSEN, "Estimating Consumption Models with Intertemporal Substitution Using Aggregate Time Series Data," *Journal of Economic and Business Statistics* (forthcoming 1990).

——, —— AND SCOTT F. RICHARD, "The Dynamic Equilibrium Pricing of Durable Consumption Goods," Working Paper No. 2181, NBER, 1984.

——, ——, AND KENNETH J. SINGLETON, "A Time Series Analysis of Representative Agent Models of Consumption and Leisure Choice Under Uncertainty," *Quarterly Journal of Economics* 103 (1988), 51–78.

FRISCH, RAGNAR, "Propagation Problems and Impulse Problems in Dynamic Economics," in *Essays in Honor of Gustav Cassel* (London: Allen & Unwin, 1933).

GEWEKE, JOHN F., "The Dynamic Factor Analysis of Economic Time Series," in Dennis J. Aigner and Arthur S. Goldberger, eds., *Latent Variables in Socio-Economic Models* (Amsterdam: North-Holland, 1977).

—— AND KENNETH J. SINGLETON, "Interpreting the Likelihood Ratio Statistic in Factor Models When Sample Size is Small," *Journal of the American Statistical Association* 75 (1980), 133–137.

—— AND ——, "Maximum Likelihood 'Confirmatory' Factor Analysis of Economic Time Series," *International Economic Review* 22 (February 1981), 37–54.

HALL, ROBERT E. AND DALE W. JORGENSON, "Tax Policy and Investment Behavior," *American Economic Review* 57 (June 1967), 391–414.

HANNAN, E. J., Multiple Time Series (New York: Wiley, 1970).

HANSEN, LARS PETER AND THOMAS J. SARGENT, "Formulating and Estimating Dynamic Linear Rational Expectations Models," *Journal of Economic Dynamics and Control* 2 (1980), 7–46.

—— AND ——, "Linear Rational Expectations Models for Dynamically Interrelated Variables," in Robert E. Lucas, Jr. and Thomas J. Sargent, eds., *Rational Expectations and Econometric Practice*, Vol. 1 (Minneapolis: University of Minnesota Press, 1981), 127–158.

HULTEN, CHARLES R. AND ROBERT M. SCHWAB, "Regional Productivity Growth in U.S. Manufacturing: 1951–78," *American Economic Review* 74 (1984), 152–162.

JORESKOG, K. G., "Some Contributions to Maximum Likelihood Factor Analysis," *Psychometrika* 32 (1967), 443–482.

——, "Efficient Estimation in Image Factor Analysis," *Psychometrika* 34 (1969), 51–75.

KALECKI, M., "A Macrodynamic Theory of Business Cycles," *Econometrica* 3 (1935), 327–344.

KYDLAND, FINN E. AND EDWARD C. PRESCOTT, "Time to Build and Aggregate Fluctuations," *Econometrica* 50 (November 1982) 1345–1370.

LONG, JOHN B. AND CHARLES PLOSSER, "Real Business Cycles," *Journal of Political Economy* 91 (1983), 39–69.

LUCAS, ROBERT E., JR., "Capacity, Overtime, and Empirical Production Functions," *American Economic Review* 60 (May 1970), 23–27.

MANKIW, N. G., J. ROTEMBERG AND L. H. SUMMERS, "Intertemporal Substitution in Macroeconomics," *Quarterly Journal of Economics*, Vol. C, February (1985), 225–252.

MARIMON, RAMON, "General Equilibrium in Growth Under Uncertainty," Discussion Paper No. 624, Center for Mathematical Studies in Economics and Management Science, 1984.

MAYER, THOMAS, "Plant and Equipment Lead Times," *Journal of Business* 33 (April 1960), 127–132.

MCCALLUM, BENNET T., "On 'Real' and 'Sticky-Price' Theories of the Business Cycle," *Journal of Money, Credit and Banking* 18 (1986), 397–414.

MIRMAN, LEONARD J. AND ITZAK ZILCHA, "On Optimal Growth Under Uncertainty," *Journal of Economic Theory* 11 (1975), 329–339.

NELSON, CHARLES R. AND CHARLES I. PLOSSER, "Trends and Random Walks in Macroeconomic Time Series: Some Evidence and Implications," *Journal of Monetary Economics* 10 (September 1982) 139–162.

NERLOVE, MARC, DAVID M. GRETHER AND J. L. CARVALHO, *Analysis of Economic Time Series: A Synthesis* (New York: Academic Press, 1979).

PARK, JONG, "Gestation Lags With Variable Plans: An Empirical Study of Aggregate Investment," Ph.D. Thesis, Carnegie-Mellon University, 1984.

SARGENT, THOMAS J. AND CHRISTOPHER A. SIMS, "Business Cycle Modeling Without Pretending to Have Too Much A Priori Economic Theory," in *New Methods in Business Cycle Research: Proceedings from a Conference* (Minneapolis: Federal Reserve Bank of Minneapolis, 1977), 45–109.

SINGLETON, KENNETH J., "A Latent Time Series Model of the Cyclical Behavior of Interest Rates," *International Economic Review* 21 (1980), 559–575.

SOLOW, ROBERT M., "Technical Change and the Aggregate Production Function," *Review of Economics and Statistics* 39 (August 1957), 312–320.

U.S. DEPARTMENT OF COMMERCE, BUREAU OF ECONOMIC ANALYSIS, *Survey of Current Business*, various issues.

U.S. DEPARTMENT OF LABOR, BUREAU OF LABOR STATISTICS, Employment and Earnings, various issues.

TATOM, JOHN A., "The 'Problem' of Procyclical Real Wages and Productivity," *Journal of Political Economy* 88 (April 1980), 385–394.

TAYLOR, JOHN, "The Swedish Investment Funds System as a Stabilization Policy Rule," *Brookings Papers on Economic Activity* (1982), 57–99.

8

Evaluating a real business cycle model

Fabio Canova, Mary Finn and Adrian R. Pagan[*]

Most real business cycle models have been assessed by studying the correspondence of their predictions to a set of stylised facts. This paper argues that such tests are not extensive enough and proposes to evaluate the models using standard econometric procedures. Specifically it is argued that these models should be studied by eliciting the restricted VAR representation underlying them and comparing it with the VAR estimated in an unrestricted way from the underlying data. Allowance is made for cases where the driving forces are integrated and when they are stationary. When forces such as technology shocks are integrated these models produce a specific set of predictions about the cointegrating vectors as well as a set of restrictions upon the dynamics. The approach is illustrated using a real business cycle model estimated by Burnside, Eichenbaum and Rebelo. This model has been subjected to some formal testing based upon stylised facts, and it therefore seems an appropriate one upon which to utilize the formal econometric procedures.

1. INTRODUCTION

In the last decade, real business cycles (RBC) models have gone from the preliminary explorations of Long and Plosser (1983) and Kydland and Prescott (1982) to well developed and tested models such as Burnside, Eichenbaum and Rebelo (1993) and McGrattan (1991). Early models could be regarded as 'idealised', in the sense adopted in the philosophical literature summarised in

[*] Financial support from the U.K. Economic and Social Research Council under grant R000233447 is gratefully acknowledged by both authors. We are indebted to Neil Ericsson for helpful comments.

Hoover (1991*a*), in that they were 'simplifications that were designed to isolate an *essential* core' — in this instance, attempts to capture the characteristics of fluctuations within industrial economies. Given such an objective it was appropriate that the method employed to determine whether the 'essence' of an economy had been captured or not was the method of 'stylised facts'. In this procedure a certain number of key 'facts' are identified and subsequently used to gauge the performance of the model. Thus Long and Plosser concentrated upon the idea that business cycles generated co-movements between de-trended variables, and they asked whether it was possible to obtain such a feature with the very simple RBC model that they had constructed. Others have been somewhat more precise, asking if the variances and covariances between variables such as output, consumption and real wages observed in the US economy agreed with the predictions of their model. In extensions of this early work, e.g. King Plosser and Rebelo (1988), a similar strategy was adopted to that of Prescott and Kydland, but with a more extensive range of stylised facts to be explained.

Stylised facts are obviously a good way of evaluating idealised models. By their very nature the latter models are not meant to provide a complete description of any time series such as consumption or output, but rather attempt to emulate a few of the major characteristics of those variables. Nevertheless, even with such a limited objective, there still remains an important practical problem of determining just how well the models are emulating reality, and this necessitates the development of some 'metric' for that task. Because RBC models are explicitly stochastic a number of measures have been proposed that involve computing standard errors for the model predictions, either by analytic means or by computer based simulation, e.g. Gregory and Smith (1993), Canova (1990).

Early comparisons of model projections with stylised facts revealed that the models did not adequately account for the latter. Perhaps the most striking failures were the correlation of productivity with hours worked and of government consumption with the Solow residual. Stimulated by this fact, researchers in the area began to develop the models in a number of different directions, with the aim of getting a better match with the stylised facts. As discussed by Hoover (1991*a*) this development can be thought of as 'concretising ' the idealised models so as to make for a better correspondence with the 'real world'. 'Concretisation' has now been performed in many different directions and there has been substantial success in clearing up some of the striking failures of the early models.

The developments described above are reminiscent of early work with macroeconometric models. Initially, the desire was to explain some very broad characteristics of the data. As ambitions rose and simple models were replaced by large scale ones in an attempt to capture real world complexities, it was necessary to devise tests of the latter that were much more demanding, so as to try to isolate where the deficiencies of the models lay. It seems appropriate therefore that the attempts at evaluation via stylised facts, which have characterized most RBC studies to date, should also be replaced by more demanding and comprehensive tests, particularly since these models are progressively 'concretised' in order to account for specific 'stylised facts'. What makes this task different to the older econometric literature is that RBC models are models with a great deal of internal coherence, and it is very hard to evaluate the components separately; one is inevitably faced with the need to work with the whole model. Consequently, many of the 'single equation' tests that have been used so effectively when evaluating large scale macroeconometric models are difficult to apply, since one could not make a modification to a 'part' of the RBC model without affecting it somewhere else. Complete model evaluation methods are the logical way to proceed.

This paper is an attempt to do the requisite analysis along these lines. It is well known that RBC models involve a VAR in the variables — see Long and Plosser (1983) for example. Furthermore, as we observe in Section 2, it is a highly restricted VAR. Thus, just as for the rational expectations models considered by Sargent (1978), it seems as if a sensible way to evaluate the models is to test the restrictions on the implied VAR. Although the idea is straightforward, one has to be somewhat more cautious. Frequently, the driving forces in these models are integrated, and the VAR is actually a vector ECM, due to there being a smaller number of driving forces than variables being explained. If the driving forces are integrated, analysis suggests that there are two types of restrictions that might be tested. First, there are the cointegrating restrictions stemming from the fact that there are generally more variables to be modelled than there are independent integrated forcing processes. Second, there are restrictions upon the dynamics which apply to the system written after factoring out the cointegrating relations. Section 2 develops these ideas.

Section 3 of the paper takes a particular RBC model, that due to Burnside *et al.* and applies the ideas developed earlier to it. This model was chosen because there have been a number of concretising steps taken to make it emulate the real world, although there remains some doubt over whether it actually agrees with a comprehensive range of stylised facts. Our claim is that consideration of the two types of restrictions described above, and a determination of whether they are acceptable, can be a very useful input into a modelling exercise. In particular, such information can highlight deficiencies in the models and may suggest suitable re-specifications. In our example, we find that the BER model is strongly rejected by the data and we enquire into what changes might be made to the model to produce a VAR that more closely approximates what is seen in the data.

In Section 4, we ask the question of how well the RBC model functions relative to a simple model such as a multiplier-accelerator mechanism and discuss whether the latter is any more successful in reproducing the VAR than the RBC model is. The viewpoint of this section is that, ultimately, the relevant question pertains to the relative rather than absolute quality of a model. Such comparisons are also likely to yield better information about potential respecifications. Finally, Section 5 concludes with some suggestions about how the RBC model might be modified to produce a better fit to the data.

2. TESTING THE RESTRICTIONS OF AN RBC MODEL

Define y_t as the $(q \times 1)$ vector of variables of interest, z_t as the $(n \times 1)$ vector of controlled and uncontrolled state variables, and x_t as the $(p \times 1)$ vector of exogenous or forcing variables (the uncontrolled states). Most RBC models can be regarded as conforming to a linear structure of the form

$$y_t = Az_t \tag{1}$$

$$\dot{z}_t = Fz_{t-1} + Ge_t, \tag{2}$$

where e_t are the innovations into the forcing variables and G is a matrix showing. how these innovations impinge upon the state variables. Generally G is a matrix that only has rank p, i.e. there are more state variables than there are stochastic elements in (2). The linearity of the system stems from the fact that these systems are frequently solved by either linearising the Euler equations around the steady state, as in King, Plosser, and Rebelo (1988), or solving the Riccati equation associated with the linear/quadratic control problem, a method employed by McGrattan (1991). It is possible to argue that (1) and (2) are more general than they might appear to be in that some types of non-linearities might be accommodated, e.g. z_t might be functions of state variables. Some of the solution methods, such as Marcet (1989) or Chow (1992a), can allow this interpretation. Higher order dynamics can also be incorporated, but, since the application given later has first order dynamics, the discussion will focus upon the special case.

An especially important characteristic of many RBC models is that F and A are functions of a smaller number of parameters such as utility and production function parameters, and the latter are typically selected by some 'calibration' strategy. It is hard to be precise about exactly what the latter is as it ranges from selecting parameter values gleaned from micro or macro studies — estimated either by sample averages or by methods such as GMM and FIML — to 'guesstimates'. We will simply assume that A and F have precise numercial values assigned to them, so that an RBC model is both a set of relationships as in (1) and (2) and a specific set of values for the parameters A and F. Of course, this is true of any macroeconomic model. Nevertheless, one might argue over whether the parameter values should be taken as capturing the 'essence' of an economy or are simply concretising assumptions, i.e. perhaps what should be tested is the general format in (1) and (2) rather than the particular structure coming from specific values of A and F. As an example of the difference, suppose y_t was consumption and z_t was output. Then (1) can be interpreted as either saying that the average propensity to consume is *exactly* A or that the average propensity to consume is simply some unknown *constant* A. Although there are some testable implications of the latter viewpoint, they are obviously very weak, and it is likely that many models would yield such a prediction, e.g. there were many early consumption relations that were not intertemporal but which would imply constancy of the consumption ratio. Hence, as a way of distinguishing between different theories, it seems necessary to maintain that the numbers assigned to A and F are parts of the model. One could plausibly argue against this strategy if A and F were estimated directly from data, but since they are functions of a much smaller number of 'deep parameters', the power of the RBC model presumably derives from just this fact. Indeed that seems to have been an essential ingredient in the original arguments put forth for such models in Long and Plosser (1983) and by Prescott (1991) who imposes parameter values as a consequence of steady state relations.

It is necesssary to distinguish between two scenarios for (1) and (2) depending upon the nature of the forcing variables, x_t. In many applications of RBC models x_t are made I(1) processes, generally independent of each other, i.e.

$$x_t = x_{t-1} + e_t. \tag{3}$$

Under this specification, the structure of F is $F = \begin{bmatrix} \gamma & \delta \\ 0 & I_p \end{bmatrix}$ so that p of the eigen-values of F are unity while the remaining $(n - p)$ are the eigenvalues of γ. In RBC models the latter are less than unity, implying that there must be $(n - p)$ cointegrating vectors among the z_t. Defining the elements of z_t which exclude x_t as z_{1t}, if the z_{1t} are I(1) then it follows immediately that the cointegrating vectors are $[(I - \gamma) \quad -\delta]$; alternatively, if any of the z_{1t} is I(0), the corresponding row, $(\gamma_1 \quad \delta_1)$, must be a cointegrating vector. Identifying z_t with some observed data this would be a *first prediction* of the RBC model. It is also apparent that there are some Granger Causality predictions which stem from (2.3).

Equation (1) predicts that an exact relation should hold between y_t and z_t. Such an exact relation is unlikely to be observed with any set of data and it is important to weaken (1) so as to allow it to be non-exact. The most appropriate extension would seem to be to assume that $y_t - Az_t$ is an I(0) process. There are two arguments one might make in favour of this stance. The first is that the RBC model aims at capturing the essential mechanisms at work in the economy, and, *prima facie*, this suggests that what is left out should be distinguishable as something of less importance than what is retained. When z_t is integrated it is natural therefore to think that what has been ignored should be non-integrated. Second, if one thought of observed data as being different from the model constructs due to measurement error, it is natural to make the measurement error an I(0) process when the variable being incorrectly measured is I(1). Therefore, in terms of either argument, $(I_q - A)$ should be a set of cointegrating vectors, and this is a *second testable implication* of an RBC model. Note that what we have is not only the requirement that y_t and z_t be cointegrated but that they be cointegrated with the numerical values assigned to A.

A second set of restrictions implied by RBC models involves the dynamic structure, or what will be termed the 'non-cointegrating restrictions'. To derive these write (1) and (2) as

$$\Delta y_t = A\Delta z_t, \tag{4}$$

where

$$\Delta z_t = (F - I)z_{t-1} + Ge_t \tag{5}$$

$$= \Pi z_{t-1} + Ge_t \tag{6}$$

$$= \alpha\beta' z_{t-1} + Ge_t \tag{7}$$

and β are the cointegrating vectors existing among the z_t. Substituting (6) into (5) yields

$$\Delta y_t = A\alpha\beta' z_{t-1} + AGe_t \tag{8}$$

and, forming the cointegrating error $v_t = \beta' z_{t-1}$, we have

$$\Delta y_t = A\alpha v_{t-1} + AGe_t \tag{9}$$

which is a relation solely between I(0) variables. Defining $w_t' = (\Delta y_t' \; v_t')$ the VAR in w_t implied by an RBC model therefore has two characteristics. First, unless y_t is a state variable, Δy_{t-1} is excluded from it. Second, the coefficients of v_{t-1} are given by $A\alpha$. These are the *third set of testable predictions*, and they concern the non-cointegrating restrictions. Notice that the restrictions stem from the dynamic nature of the model, provided we have previously accepted that the cointegrating restrictions are valid ones.

When the forcing variables are not I(1) the distinction between the two types of restrictions ceases to be valid. In these cases, although (1) would still be a restriction, it would be very hard to test it, as any variables left out are of the same order of integration, zero, and one would be faced with the prospect of doing a regression in the presence of specification error. Hence, in these cases, it is logical to combine the two directly, substituting (1) into (2) to get

$$y_t = \mathrm{AF}z_{t-1} + \mathrm{AG}e_t. \tag{10}$$

Viewed as a VAR, now in the I(0) variables $\overline{w}_t' = (y_t'\, z_t')$, one finds a similar set of restrictions to the non-cointegrating set found above. Specifically, y_{t-1} does not appear in the VAR and the coefficients of z_{t-1} should be AF.

Basically, the argument for testing the restrictions upon the VAR advanced above is that it may be possible to identify suitable re-specifications of the RBC model in the event that rejections of the restrictions are encountered. For example, if the prediction that Δy_{t-1} is excluded from the VAR is false, attention is immediately directed to how the RBC model might be modified so as to induce such a variable into the implied VAR. The VAR is therefore being used as a 'reduced form' and, indeed, the evaluation strategy being followed here is the modern equivalent of the classical precepts laid down by the Cowles Commission researchers when testing the structural equation restrictions upon the reduced form — see Byron (1974). All that has changed is the substitution of the reduced form by its time series construct, the VAR. This idea has been mentioned or exploited by a number of authors, e.g. Spanos (1986), Monfort and Rabemananjara (1990) and Hendry and Mizon (1993), the latter being the most complete treatment in that it allows for variables to be either I(1) or I(0).

Although the systems approach to testing set out above is an attractive one, there may be advantages to focusing upon more restricted implications of the RBC model. One of these is the nature of the final equations for y_t, i.e. if y_t is a scalar, finding the ARMA process

$$C(L)y_t = D(L)\varepsilon_t \tag{11}$$

implied by (1) and (2). Comparing this derived equation to the ARMA models estimated from the data may be used to indicate how good a representation the RBC model is. Tinbergen (1939) was an early user of the final equations for summarising the properties of a system, and the idea was subsequently formalised and utilised in Zellner and Palm (1974), Wallis (1977) and Evans (1989). Cogley and Nason (1992) apply the idea to a variety of RBC models, showing that, with the exception of the Burnside *et al.* model, such models do not reproduce the higher order autocorrelation features of GDP data for the US. Obviously, such a comparison may be extremely valuable in revealing how well the system mimics the data on selected variables. Its principal disadvantage is that the information gleaned from such a comparison may be extremely difficult to use in re-specifying any RBC model, simply because $C(L)$ and $D(L)$ will inevitably be complex functions of all parts of the original model.

A related procedure, after making y_t a vector, is to determine the VAR in y_t alone, i.e. to reduce the VAR in y_t, z_t to one in terms of y_t alone. Such a construct may be of interest because of our familiarity with many bivariate and trivariate relations. For example, if y_t is composed of net investment and output, the accelerator mechanism is a well known bivariate relation linking those two variables, and it might therefore be profitable to enquire into whether there is an accelerator mechanism at work within RBC models. To perform this task requires a number of steps. First, after computing the autocovariances of y_t from (1) and (2), an approximating VAR can be fitted by solving the multivariate version of the Yule-Walker equations. This would lead to

$$C(L)y_t = \varepsilon_t. \tag{12}$$

Second, suppose that y_t was bivariate with elements y_{1t} and y_{2t}. To investigate relations like the accelerator necessitates relating y_{1t} to y_{2t} as well as their past histories. The error term in ε_t has to be decomposed to isolate the contemporaneous effect. To this end let the VAR in (12) be re-expressed as

$$y_{1t} = C_1(L)y_{t-1} + \varepsilon_{1t}$$
$$y_{2t} = C_2(L)y_{t-1} + \varepsilon_{2t}. \tag{13}$$

Owing to the linear structure ε_{1t} can be written as $\varepsilon_{1t} = \rho\varepsilon_{2t} + \eta_{1t}$, where $\rho = \sigma_{22}^{-1}\sigma_{12}$, $\sigma_{ij} = E(\varepsilon_{it}\varepsilon_{jt})$, and η_{1t} is an innovation with respect to $\{y_{t-j}, y_{2t}\}_{j=1}^{\infty}$. Consequently,

$$y_{1t} = [C_1(L) - \rho C_2(L)]y_{t-1} + \rho y_{2t} + \eta_{1t} \tag{14}$$

gives the desired relationship. In (13) the polynomials $C_j(L)$ and the correlation coefficient ρ are by-products from fitting the VAR (12) to the autocovariances of y_t coming from (1) and (2). Operationally, one simply has to decide upon the order of the approximating VAR. Of course, the relation under study might also be a trivariate one, e.g. if y_t contains real money, interest rates and output, a 'money demand function' could be elicited. Perhaps the main use of this device is when comparisons are made between RBC and alternative business cycle models such as multiplier-accelerator, as conversion of the RBC model to resemble the alternative model allows an easier assessment of the relative performance of the two contenders. Another use is if one wants to compute quantities such as the Kullback-Liebler Information Criterion (KLIC) in order to compare models. Because there are fewer shocks than variables in most RBC models, the density for z_t would be singular, and hence the KLIC is not defined. However, by restricting attention to a VAR system whose order equals the number of shocks one can define the KLIC for such a system.

Although what should be tested when evaluating RBC models seems to be fairly clear, exactly how it is to be done is much more controversial. The source of the controversy resides in the fact that the variables y_t and z_t in the model may not be accurately measured by data, i.e. there are errors in variables. When testing the cointegrating restrictions such a difficulty can be ignored, provided that the errors are I(0), but the same cannot be said for tests of the non-cointegrating restrictions. Here what is being tested is whether the coefficients of $v_{t-1} = \beta' z_{t-1}$ in (9) have the values predicted by the RBC model. But if the errors in z_t and y_t are linearly related to z_{t-1}, the observed value could validly deviate from that predicted by the RBC model. Without some statement about the mapping of the errors into z_{t-1}, it would therefore be impossible to follow the testing strategy outlined above. Within the literature on calibrated models, this point appears to be regarded as the critical one that prohibits formal econometric testing — Kydland and Prescott (1991) and Watson (1993). There is little that can be said about this objection. It could be applied to any model and, taken to its extreme, would result in nothing being testable. If it is adopted the only consistent attitude would seem to be one in which all quantitative modelling was eschewed. However, such consistency is a rare phenomenon; it is not uncommon to find proponents of RBC models rejecting competitive scenarios as incompatible with the data but failing to apply the same test to their preferred approach on the grounds that the models are too idealised. For example, Kydland and Prescott (1991) regurgitate the Lucas-Sargent criticism that large scale Keynesian models of the 1970's were inadequate due to a failure to correctly predict the observed unemployment-inflation correlations of that decade, but immediately exempt RBC models from a similar test by stating that 'the issue of how confident we are in the econometric answer is a subtle one which cannot be resolved by computing some measure of how well the model economy mimics historical data. The degree of confidence in the answer depends on the confidence that is placed in the economic theory being used'. (1991, p.171).

The only way out of this morass is to place some constraint upon the relationship of any errors in variables to z_{t-1}. Traditionally, this has been to insist upon the errors being white noise. Such errors in y_t would result in a white noise disturbance for (9), whereas a similar assumption for errors in z_t would create an MA(1) disturbance. In the first instance, estimation and testing would proceed in the normal way; in the second, some form of instrumental variables estimation would need to be performed to allow for the correlation between z_{t-1} and the MA(1) disturbance. Of course, the disturbance in (9) could be uncorrelated with z_{t-1} under weaker conditions than white noise in the errors in variables. The situation is reminiscent of rational expectations modelling where forward looking behaviour creates disturbance terms that are MA's but which are still orthogonal to any regressors that appear in agents' information sets. If this extension is envisaged allowance needs to be made for the effects of such serial correlation upon inferences by adopting robust measures of the variances of estimators.

If the errors in variables are to be allowed to be functions of z_{t-1}, it may still be possible to find some measures of fit of the model to data, even though inference is highly unlikely. This is Watson's (1993) approach. He takes the deviation between model output and data to be an 'error', u_t, and then finds an expression for it when the objective is to reproduce the autocovariance function (a.c.f.) of the data. Thus, distinguishing data by means of an asterisk, $y_t^* = y_t + u_t$ $= AFz_{t-1} + AGe_t + u_t$, and the task is to determine u_t. For convenience in exposition it will be assumed that z_t is perfectly measured and that y_t is a scalar. Approximating the observed a.c.f. of y_t^* with a VAR in y_t^* and z_t gives $y_t^* = C_1(L)y_{t-1}^* + C_2(L)z_{t-1} + \varepsilon_t$. By equating the two expressions for y_t^*, u_t is found to be $u_t = C_1(L)y_{t-1}^* + (C_2(L) - AF)z_{t-1} - AGe_t + \varepsilon_t$, and this choice of u_t means that the augmented model output reproduces the a.c.f. of the data (at least up to the chosen order of VAR). Watson's proposal is then to compute an $R^{2\prime}$, equal to $1 - (\text{var}(u_t) / \text{var}(y_t^*))$, as a measure of fit of the model. As it stands this latter measure is indeterminate as the var(u_t) depends upon an unknown, the covariance of ε_t with u_{t-j}. Because this is a free parameter, Watson proposes to choose it such that var(u_t) is minimised. To see how this is done take $C_1(L) = c_1 > 0$. Then the smallest value of σ_u^2 occurs when cov($\varepsilon_t u_{t-1}$) attains its largest negative value $-\sigma_\varepsilon \sigma_u$ (this corresponding to a correlation between the two variables y_t^* and y_t of -1). A low '$R^{2\prime}$' would presumably be taken as indicating that there is much left unexplained by the RBC model. In practice there are significant complications coming from the fact that y_t will generally be a vector, as the variance of u_t will become a matrix and there is no longer a unique measure of fit.

Watson's idea is certainly ingenious and, given the concern expressed about the idealised nature of these models, has to be useful information for anyone wishing to assess them. However, one cannot escape the feeling that the criterion has to be augmented with supplementary information. One problem that arises is the decision to take the minimum value of σ_u^2 as the basis of the 'R^2'. This is arbitrary, as many values of $\text{cov}(\varepsilon_t u_{t-1})$ would reproduce the a.c.f. of y_t^*, and it is unclear why the one minimising σ_u^2 is to be preferred. Obviously a model with a low R^2 would not be satisfactory, but it is conceivable that a high R^2 could be produced solely due to the particular selection made for $\text{cov}(\varepsilon_t u_{t-1})$, while other choices of this parameter may produce low R^2. Since the parameter, $\text{cov}(\varepsilon_t u_{t-1})$, has nothing to do with the model, and is essentially 'unidentified', it would seem misleading to conclude from the evidence of a high R^2 that the RBC model was satisfactory. At the very least it would seem important that the R^2 be provided for the values of $\text{cov}(\varepsilon_t u_{t-1})$ that both maximise and minimise R^2. If this range is narrow, and the minimum R^2 is a high one, it might be appropriate to conclude that, *prima facie*, the RBC model provides a satisfactory description of the data.

A second problem with the measure is that it does not provide information that may be useful in re-specifying the model. The variance of u_t may be large for a variety of reasons; a high σ_ε^2, a large gap between $C_2(L)$ and A, a large value for $C_1(L)$ etc., but this information is lost in the aggregative measure. However, our attitude towards the model is likely to be significantly affected by which one of these is the principal contributor. If it was due to a high value of $C_1(L)$, we would be led to enquire into whether the RBC model might be re-specified so as to induce the variable y_{t-1} into the VAR. In contrast, if it was a consequence of a large value for σ_ε^2, we are less likely to feel that there is something inadequate in the idealised model, as this parameter represents the extent to which variables exogenous to the model are unpredictable, and all models would have a similar deficiency e.g. a Keynesian model also has to make some assumption about how government expenditure is to evolve over time.

3. EVALUATING AN RBC MODEL

The model chosen for the evaluation exercise is due to Burnside, Eichenbaum and Rebelo (1990) (BER). It represents a modification of that described in Christiano and Eichenbaum (1992). Appendix 1 presents the principal equations underlying it. The controlled state variables are the capital stock and employment and the uncontrolled states are the technology and government expenditure shocks. When measured as deviations from a steady state growth path these variables are designated as k_t, n_t, a_t and g_t respectively. Other variables explained by the model, also as deviations from steady state, are output (y_t), private consumption (c_t), and investment (i_t). An assumption of the model is that the forcing factors are AR(1) processes. Parameter values for the model were estimated by BER from data over 1955(3) to 1984(1) using various moment conditions.

To evaluate the model BER compared the numerical values of selected variable correlations predicted by the model with the estimated values from the data. The vector of discrepancies can be formally compared with zero using the J-test of over-identifying restrictions. The principal comparison BER made involved the cross correlation of productivity and hours worked at L leads and lags. When all the sample was used there was strong rejection if $L = 2$ (the p value of the test being 0.001). This outcome encouraged them to split the sample at 1969(1) and to perform validation of the model on two different samples. They then concluded that the model seemed satisfactory for the first period (p-value = 0.278) but not for the second period (p-value = 0.001). Because of this diversity of outcomes the discussion below concentrates upon the two sub-samples separately. We also avoid the emphasis upon the relation between productivity and hours that characterizes BER's evaluation work, as an important ingredient of the way in which their model manages to emulate the data is by making the assumption that the employment data is subject to errors of measurement. That modification seems to be very important to their success along the productivity hours correlation dimension, even though it is hard to think of it as part of a 'model'.

3.1. Sample period 1955(3) to 1969(4)

As reviewed in the preceding section any RBC model makes a number of predictions, either about the cointegrating vectors expected to hold between variables or the dynamic behaviour of the variables. Our strategy will be to determine if the predictions made by the RBC model are consistent with the data.

A first item to check is whether the assumption made pertaining to the evolution of the uncontrolled states is valid. BER's point estimates for the AR(1) coefficients of a_t and g_t are 0.87 and 0.94 respectively. Although these are different from unity the ADF tests recorded in Table 1 point to the fact that the hypothesis of the series being integrated is accepted fairly easily. Furthermore, the correlation between the residuals from the AR(1)'s fitted to g_t and a_t is only 0.12, which suggests the processes are uncorrelated, as specified in BER's model. Based on this outcome, and the evidence of integration for k_t and n_t in Table 1, it is anticipated that the state vector comprising k_t, n_t, g_t and a_t should have two cointegrating vectors, as there are two common trends driving the RBC model (see

Table 1. Tests for Integration in Data using ADF(4)

Variable	Without trend	With trend
k_t	−1.43	−1.80
n_t	−1.25	−2.97
a_t	−2.44	−2.42
g_t	−2.13	−2.12
c_t	−2.19	−2.18
y_t	−2.21	−2.31
i_t	−2.37	−2.88
crit. val.	−2.92	−3.50

the brief description of the main features of the model in the Appendix).

Using the parameter values provided by BER it is possible to compute $F = \begin{bmatrix} \gamma & \delta \\ 0 & I_p \end{bmatrix}$ in (2) and hence to derive the predicted cointegrating vectors among vectors among the four states viz. $[(I - \gamma) \ -\delta]$. Logically, there are two distinct questions here. One is whether there are two cointegrating vectors or not. Using a VAR(4), Johansen's likelihood ratio test (LR) for the hypothesis of r cointegrating vectors easily indicates that there are two (the test of $r = 1$ versus $r = 2$ gives LR = 25.2 while $r = 2$ versus $r = 3$ has LR = 7.75, where the critical values corresponding to the 5% significance levels are 21.0 and 14.0 respectively). Exactly the same conclusion is reached with Johansen's trace test. Thus the number of cointegrating vectors agrees with the model prediction. A more demanding test is to assess whether the predicted numeric values (0.0435 −0.0295 −0.1434 0.0062) and (0.5627 1.0174 −1.5008 −0.1974) are compatible with the data. For this query, a likelihood ratio test of the restrictions gives a value of 45.53 which, when referred to a $\chi^2(4)$, soundly rejects the constraint. Consequently, a basic property of the model is rejected. Figure 1 plots $0.5627k_t + 1.0174n_t - 1.5008a_t - 0.1974g_t$, the projected second cointegrating error, and the lack of cointegration shows quite clearly (actually ADF tests applied to each cointegrating error separately shows that neither series is I(0)).

In addition to the state variables being I(1), Table 1 shows that three 'output' variables — consumption, output and investment — also possess this property. Therefore, RBC models conjecture that there are further cointegrating restrictions, now between the 'outputs' and the states — see (1). King *et al.* (1991) and Neusser

238   *Fabio Canova, Mary Finn and Adrian R. Pagan*

Figure 1. Plot of Projected Second Cointegrating Vector among States

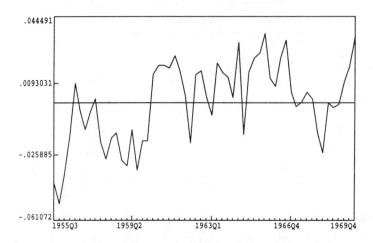

(1991) considered the long-run implications of neoclassical growth models for relations *between* the three 'output' variables above . In particular they argued that consumption and income and investment and income should be cointegrating pairs with cointegrating vectors $(1 -1)$. In this model it is consumption, income and government expenditure which should be cointegrated, as well as investment and output. Johansen's tests indicate that the first of these relations is satisfied, but the likelihood and trace tests are in conflict over whether investment and output are cointegrated.[1] Moreover, for two reasons, tests of an RBC model performed in this way are rather weak. First, information is being discarded. The RBC model makes a direct prediction about the cointegrating relations between states and 'outputs' but only an indirect one about the connection between 'outputs'. Thus we might have $c_t - z_t'\alpha_1$ and $y_t - z_t'\alpha_1$ both being I(0), so that $c_t - y_t$ is I(0), but the α_1 may not coincide with that indicated by the RBC model. Second, many models have the property that $c_t - y_t$ and $i_t - y_t$ are cointegrated, e.g. the multiplier accelerator model can be designed to produce this effect by an appropriate choice of ECM format, and therefore cointegration between 'output' variables cannot be taken as validating the RBC viewpoint. In summary, what should be tested are the *direct* implications of the RBC model and not the *indirect* ones.

---

[1] Robert King has suggested that this failure may well be a consequence of the way in which data is constructed by BER.

Evaluating a Real Business Cycle Model   239

Choosing BER's parameter values, the specific cointegrating relations from equation (1) are

$$c_t = 0.55k_t + 0.017n_t + 0.348a_t - 0.07g_t + \eta_{ct} \qquad (15a)$$

$$i_t = -0.65k_t + 1.12n_t + 5.45a_t - 0.24g_t + \eta_{it} \qquad (15b)$$

$$y_t = 0.13k_t + 0.31n_t + 1.64a_t + 0.07g_t + \eta_{yt}, \qquad (15c)$$

and our objective is to test if the η_t are I(1). This could be done in one of two ways.[2] A first possibility is to apply an ADF test to the errors from (15a–c); since no parameters are being estimated, many of the problems of using this test for cointegration are absent. An alternative is to use the fact that cointegration between variables means the existence of an ECM relationship — Engle and Granger (1985). Therefore, assuming (say) c_t and z_t are I(1) and cointegrated with vector $(1 \ -\alpha)$, an ECM of the form

$$\Delta c_t = a\Delta z_t' \alpha_1 + b(c_{t-1} - z_{t-1}' \alpha_1) \qquad (16)$$

would connect c_t and z_t. If c_t and z_t are not cointegrated, $b = 0$ making the t-ratio for $H_0 : b = 0$ a suitable test of no cointegration. This test is proposed in Banerjee *et al.* (1986) and has been dubbed the 'ECM test' by Kremers *et al.* (1992). The latter have argued that it has much better power than the ADF test whenever the latter imposes an invalid common factor restriction. Unfortunately, the distribution of the ECM test varies between the Dickey-Fuller density and the standard normal as $\text{var}[(a-1)\Delta z_t]/\text{var}(\Delta z_t)$ tends from zero to infinity. Because Δz_t in our situation is a vector it is difficult to determine exactly what the critical values are. One plan of action would be to be conservative and to adopt the DF critical values. Note that there are no tests of (15c). The reason is that the unobserved variable a_t is effectively computed from data on y_t, k_t etc. by inverting (15c), and therefore η_{yt} is identically zero. Unless a separate estimate of a_t can be made it is therefore impossible to test this cointegrating restriction in an RBC model.[3]

The evidence from Table 2 is that the cointegrating restrictions are most likely invalid. The problematic outcome is for consumption. Referred to an N(0,1) random variable one would opt for cointegration, but this would not be true if the comparison was made with a 5% critical value from the DF density (−2.91).

---

[2] A third method would be to employ Johansen's test, but the fact that the states do not have the co-integrating relations implied by the RBC model makes it more convenient to perform 'single equation' tests.

[3] Provided a unit root is specified for the a_t process it would be possible to generate data on a_t using a random number generator and thereupon one could test (15c). Smith (1990) advocates this approach when there is a latent variable.

Fabio Canova, Mary Finn and Adrian R. Pagan

Table 2. Tests of Cointegrating Relations in (15a) and (15b)

Variable	ADF(4) with trend	ECM Test
c_t	−3.12	−2.69
i_t	−2.66	−2.26
crit. val.	−3.50	

Nevertheless, Table 2 does hint at specification difficulties with the BER model. To see why the restrictions are being rejected it is useful to fit relations such as (15a–c) using the data to give

$$c_t = 0.89k_t + 0.12n_t + 0.56a_t - 0.03g_t \tag{17a}$$

$$i_t = -0.18k_t + 0.69n_t + 3.61a_t - 0.31g_t. \tag{17b}$$

Comparing (15a) and (15b) with (17a) and (17b), it seems as if the weight given to k_t in the model is too low for both variables, whereas the influence of a_t is too low for consumption but far too high for investment. As the R^2 from the regressions in (17a) and (17b) are 0.94 and 0.93 respectively, provided the series are I(1) there is likely to be only small bias in the estimated cointegrating vectors.[4]

Although it seems unlikely, let us suppose that the cointegrating restrictions are satisfied. Then the third set of restrictions imposed by an RBC model are those relating to dynamics — equation (8). These involve testing if the coefficients of the cointegrating errors v_{t-1} are $A\alpha$ in the regression of Δy_t on v_{t-1}. A simple way to compute the statistic for such a test is to regress Δy_t on z_{t-1} and test if the coefficients are equal to Π (equation (6)). One has to be careful to refer the resulting test statistic to a $\chi^2(2)$ since the distribution of $\hat{\Pi}$ is singular owing to the cointegration, i.e. as v_{t-1} is a 2×1 vector, only two coefficients are really being tested. With Δy_t set to Δc_t and Δi_t the test statistics are 3.5 and 98.3 respectively, showing that, although the dynamics of consumption seem to be accounted for, the investment dynamics are missed badly (there is some serial correlation in the regression for Δi_t but there is only a minor change in the value of the test statistic when computed robustly). Unlike the situation for cointegration tests, it is also possible to check the output dynamics, and the test statistic there is 28.58, again showing some problems with the model. Equations (18a–c) list the

---

[4] A more serious problem is that the parameters being estimated may not be identified. If there are only two stochastic trends then it is impossible to estimate the four parameters here as the number of identified parameters can be no larger than the number of trends.

predicted dynamic relations along with the estimated relations (in brackets) for each of the series

$$\Delta c_t = \underset{(-0.100)}{-0.033}\, k_{t-1} \underset{(-0.038)}{-0.001}\, n_{t-1} \underset{(0.086)}{+0.059}\, a_{t-1} \underset{(-0.017)}{+0.005}\, g_{t-1} \qquad (18a)$$

$$\Delta i_t = \underset{(-0.597)}{-0.603}\, k_{t-1} \underset{(-0.24)}{-1.16}\, n_{t-1} \underset{(-0.120)}{+0.877}\, a_{t-1} \underset{(+0.03)}{+0.24}\, g_{t-1} \qquad (18b)$$

$$\Delta y_t = \underset{(-0.19)}{-0.18}\, k_{t-1} \underset{(-0.086)}{-0.309}\, n_{t-1} \underset{(-0.075)}{-0.266}\, a_{t-1} \underset{(-0.016)}{+0.055}\, g_{t-1}, \qquad (18c)$$

As revealed by $(18a-c)$, the major problem with the RBC model in its forecasts of dynamics is that it ascribes far too much weight to the productivity shock and lagged employment.

It is now appropriate to consider some objections that might be made to the above analysis. One of these is that the restrictions being tested are found by using the parameter values in BER and these are $\rho_a = 0.8691$ and $\rho_g = 0.938$ rather than the values of unity needed if we are to argue that the series are I(1). For this reason it is logically more correct to re-compute what the implied restrictions would be if unit roots are imposed upon the two forcing processes and to then test if the resulting restrictions are compatible with the data. This means that $(15a-c)$ become

$$c_t = 0.55k_t + 0.017n_t + 0.888a_t - 0.14g_t + \eta_{ct} \qquad (19a)$$

$$i_t = -0.65k_t + 1.12\,n_t + 2.31\,a_t + 0.13g_t + \eta_{it} \qquad (19b)$$

$$y_t = 0.13k_t + 0.31n_t + 1.11\,a_t + 0.13g_t + \eta_{yt}. \qquad (19c)$$

Doing so does not change any of the conclusions reached previously however. For example, the ADF tests for cointegration among the states now become -2.89 and -3.32 (with a $\chi^2(4) = 44.79$ when testing using Johansen's estimator), while ADF test values of -1.19 (c_t) and -2.64 (i_t) are found when directly testing the restrictions in (19a) and (19b). Tests of the dynamic restrictions yield $\chi^2(2)$ test statistics of 3.0 (c_t), 118.4 (i_t) and 35.2 (y_t)

Another objection to the analysis could be that the series are not integrated and that the power of the ADF test is low. There is some merit to this argument. If $\rho_a = 0.8691$, simulation of the ADF(4) test (with trend) for 58 observations shows that 55% of the time one gets an ADF test larger than -2.44 (the value of the ADF tests using the data on a_t). Hence one would falsely conclude that the series is I(1) 55% of the time. In the same vein, with $\rho_g = 0.93$, one would invalidly conclude there was a unit root 45% of the time (using the ADF value of -2.13 found from

242   *Fabio Canova, Mary Finn and Adrian R. Pagan*

the data). Hence it may be more reasonable to conduct tests that assume the processes are I(0) rather than I(1). In this case we will test the restrictions from (9), i.e. that the coefficients of z_{t-1} are AF. Equations (20a–c) set out the theoretical coefficients for the 'reduced' VAR.

$$c_t = \quad 0.518k_{t-1} + 0.016n_{t-1} + 0.407a_{t-1} - 0.069g_{t-1} \qquad (20a)$$
$$i_t = -1.255k_{t-1} - 0.039n_{t-1} + 6.322a_{t-1} + 0.003g_{t-1} \qquad (20b)$$
$$y_t = -0.045k_{t-1} - 0.001n_{t-1} + 1.907a_{t-1} + 0.128g_{t-1}. \qquad (20c)$$

Corresponding empirical estimates (where we have added in missing terms from the VAR in (20a–c) if the t ratio was greater than 2) are

$$c_t = \quad \underset{(2.500)}{0.403} \ k_{t-1} + \underset{(0.570)}{0.026} \ n_{t-1} + \underset{(3.490)}{0.411} \ a_{t-1} \ \underset{(-1.800)}{-0.033} \ g_{t-1} + \underset{(2.6)}{0.433} c_{t-1} \quad (21a)$$

$$i_t = \quad \underset{(-2.870)}{-0.673} \ k_{t-1} + \underset{(0.260)}{0.047} \ n_{t-1} + \underset{(2.200)}{1.401} \ a_{t-1} \ \underset{(-1.320)}{-0.106} \ g_{t-1} + \underset{(3.57)}{0.579} i_{t-1} \quad (21b)$$

$$y_t = \quad \underset{(-0.430)}{-0.057} \ k_{t-1} + \underset{(2.670)}{0.222} \ n_{t-1} + \underset{(11.11)}{1.566} \ a_{t-1} + \underset{(1.570)}{0.056} \ g_{t-1} \qquad\qquad (21c)$$

The results in (21a–c) constitute a strong rejection of the restrictions implied by the RBC model. Testing that the parameters in (21a–c) equal those in (20a–c) gives χ^2 statistics of $\chi^2(5) = 104.1(c_t)$, $\chi^2(5) = 625.0(i_t)$, and $\chi^2(4) = 28.59(y_t)$. A comparison of the two sets of equations shows there are some variables missing from the former, c_{t-1} in the c_t equation, and i_{t-1} in the i_t — and that the model accords productivity too great an influence in determining investment and output. Others have remarked upon such a 'missing variable' feature, specifically for consumption (Chow, 1992b), but a casual comparison of the equations emphasises that there are many factors responsible for the failure of the model to explain output and investment variations.

The outcomes observed above bring to the fore a question raised in the introduction; is the rejection being caused by the model or by the parameter values being supplied to it? That is, does there exist an RBC model of this form that would be compatible with the data but which had a different set of parameter values? It might be argued that the essence of the model is the type of functional forms fed in and not the values of the parameters chosen to calibrate it. Earlier we remarked why we feel that this view should be rejected, but it is worth exploring what would happen if we adopted it. One can say immediately that the non-zero coefficients seen for c_{t-1} and i_{t-1} in (21a) and (21b) cannot be matched by calibration changes, as the model design automatically assigns a zero coefficient to these variables. Only re-specification of the RBC model would change this fact. Some of the other parameters in (21a–c) can be modified by changing the calibration settings. By studying the sensitivity of (21a–c) to variations in the parameters of BER's model, it was found that we could improve the approximation by increasing ρ_a and reducing α. However, it was necessary to make ρ_a almost unity if the weight on the productivity variable was to be reduced to the required magnitude. This would mean that we are dealing with processes that are very close to being integrated and so it would be appropriate to test the cointegrating restrictions. As mentioned earlier however, these are rejected when we impose I(1) behaviour upon the forcing variables. Hence, it does not seem as if the essentials of the economy are captured by the BER formulation. It is worth emphasising here that the rejections of the RBC model using the techniques above are far stronger than those encountered by BER, where what evidence there was against their model in this period was very mild. This fact emphasises that different types of information are being gathered by the different methods of evaluation.

3.2 Sample period 1970(1) to 1984(1)

In the second period there is evidence that the evolutionary pattern for the variables identified in the first period has changed. Looking first at the forcing processes, there is some doubt that they are now I(1). The ADF tests (with trend) are –3.40 and –2.85 for g_t and a_t respectively, while the ADF (without trend) for a_t of –2.86 is very close to the 5% critical value of –2.92. Examination of the estimates of the autoregressive parameters upon which the ADF test is based reveal them to be 0.47 (g_t) and 0.76 (a_t), below the values of 0.87 and 0.81 found in the first period. It seems very likely therefore that the processes are I(0); certainly one would only be comfortable with a single common trend, due to a_t, as the autoregressive parameter for g_t is far too low. Turning to the other series, here the evidence of I(1) behaviour is stronger, but even then the autoregressive parameter is (at best) just above 0.8.

What is to be done about these features? One possibility is to proceed with the tests outlined in the previous sub-section, maintaining that there is a single common trend. When this is done one encounters rejections of all the cointegrating restrictions. In the interests of economising on space, and recognizing the doubt raised over the integration properties of the data, our preference has been to only report results derived under the assumption that the series are all I(0). This means that we perform and report the tests of the dynamic restrictions appearing in (9).

Equations (22a–c) provide the estimated equations, along with the predicted values of the coefficients in brackets (variables not entering the model VAR have

244   *Fabio Canova, Mary Finn and Adrian R. Pagan*

been deleted if their t ratio is less than 2, while estimated intercept terms have also been suppressed).

$$c_t = \begin{array}{c} -0.112 \ k_{t-1} \\ (-0.535) \end{array} \begin{array}{c} -0.071 \ n_{t-1} \\ (0.014) \end{array} \begin{array}{c} -0.109 \ a_{t-1} \\ (0.396) \end{array} \begin{array}{c} -0.001 \ g_{t-1} \\ (-0.021) \end{array} \begin{array}{c} +1.153 c_{t-1} \\ (0) \end{array} \qquad (22a)$$

$$i_t = \begin{array}{c} -1.371 \ k_{t-1} \\ (-1.246) \end{array} \begin{array}{c} -0.537 \ n_{t-1} \\ (-0.034) \end{array} \begin{array}{c} -1.340 \ a_{t-1} \\ (6.363) \end{array} \begin{array}{c} -0.342 \ g_{t-1} \\ (-0.294) \end{array} \begin{array}{c} +1.970 c_{t-1} \\ (0) \end{array} \begin{array}{c} +1.033 i_{t-1} \\ (0) \end{array} \ (22b)$$

$$y_t = \begin{array}{c} -0.685 \ k_{t-1} \\ (-0.034) \end{array} \begin{array}{c} -0.153 \ n_{t-1} \\ (-0.001) \end{array} \begin{array}{c} -0.113 a_{t-1} \\ (1.913) \end{array} \begin{array}{c} -0.151 g_{t-1} \\ (0.027) \end{array} \begin{array}{c} +1.053 c_{t-1} \\ (0) \end{array} \begin{array}{c} +0.297 i_{t-1} \\ (0) \end{array} \ (22c)$$

The task is to determine whether the predicted and estimated parameters are significantly different from each other, and the resulting test statistics are $\chi^2(5) = 225.2$, $\chi^2(6) = 638.6$ and $\chi^2(6) = 91.7$ for c_t, i_t and y_t, respectively. If only the coefficients of k_{t-1}, n_{t-1}, a_{t-1} and g_{t-1} are tested for having their predicted values, the corresponding $\chi^2(4)$ statistics would be 110.3, 151.1 and 37.18. As before, this constitutes a very strong rejection of the model, although an important difference from the previous period is that the prediction of zero coefficients for c_{t-1} and i_{t-1} in the equations is now wildly at variance with the data, indicating that the dynamic structure of the model seems to have undergone some major shifts in the period. Looking at the estimates in (22a–c), the most striking feature is the fact that the technology shock a_t is estimated to have a *negative* impact on all variables in this period, which is in sharp contrast to the positive effect predicted by the model.

4. COMPARING MODELS

As mentioned in the introduction it is perhaps more reasonable to evaluate a model by its performance relative to others than to impose an absolute standard. For this reason it was decided to effect a comparison of the RBC model with a stylized version of the type of macro model that was popular in the 1960s. This generally featured a consumption relation dynamically connecting consumption and output, as well as an accelerator mechanism for investment. Although money featured in such models as well, here it is excluded in the interest of retaining comparability with the RBC model; the idea being to work with the same variables as BER did, but to provide a 'demand' rather than 'supply' side account of developments in the US economy.

Most of the models of the 1960s worked with levels of the variables and we therefore chose to do the same thing here. To make comparisons with the RBC model, the predictions of the latter had to be converted from deviations around steady state values back to levels. Levels of variables are distinguished by capital

Table 3. Estimates for Multiplier-Accelerator Model

Parameter	First Period	Second Period
α_1	0.695	0.848
β_1	0.135	0.128
β_2	−0.040	−0.106
c_1	352.3	362.7
ϕ_1	2.32	1.279
α_2	0.873	0.942
γ_1	0.267	0.430
γ_2	0.180	0.065
c_2	18.65	25.86
ϕ_2	0.523	−0.214
δ	0.020	0.022
ρ_g	0.934	0.560
c_3	62.32	583.1
ϕ_3	0.613	−0.469

letters. The multiplier-accelerator model (MPA) that was fitted is given in the equations below. No experimentation with lag lengths etc. was undertaken; the idea was just to take a simple model and to see how well it performs on the same data set. Some of the regressors in the equations were insignificant but were nevertheless retained.

$$C_t = \alpha_1 C_{t-1} + \beta_1 Y_t + \beta_2 Y_{t-1} + c_1 + \phi_1 t \tag{23a}$$

$$NI_t = \alpha_2 NI_{t-1} + \gamma_1 \Delta Y_t + \gamma_2 \Delta Y_{t-1} + c_2 + \phi_2 t \tag{23b}$$

$$NI_t = I_t - \delta K_{t-1} \tag{23c}$$

$$K_t = (1 - \delta)K_{t-1} + I_t \tag{23d}$$

$$G_t = \rho_g G_{t-1} + c_3 + \phi_3 t \tag{23e}$$

$$Y_t = C_t + I_t + G_t + D_t \tag{23f}$$

The variable D_t is needed to make the series on output satisfy the national income identity. It is always a small fraction of output Y_t and rarely reaches 1% of that variable, so that its introduction would not seem to produce any distorting factors. Table 3 gives the parameter estimates of the unknown parameters of the multiplier-accelerator model for each of the two periods. Estimation was done by OLS, as that was also the most common way of doing 'calibration' at that time.

It is interesting to first ask whether the MPA model makes correct predictions of the VAR coefficients. As can be seen, the MPA model implies that the data should be a VAR(2), and the coefficients of each lag can be worked out by solving (23a–f). The $\chi^2(10)$ statistics testing the adequacy of the model during the first period were 21.4, 23.4 and 42.3, for C_t, I_t and Y_t respectively. The corresponding test statistics in the second period were 73.0, 112.0 and 162.7. Although the fact that we are working with levels, and hence potentially integrated data, makes the actual distribution of these 'χ^2' statistics unlikely to be exactly that, their magnitude has to make one seriously question the MPA model as a good representation of the data. This conclusion is especially true of the second period, a feature that is consistent with the notion that 'Keynesian' models broke down in the 1970s. If one takes the size of the χ^2 statistics as an index of how good the model is, then both the RBC and MPA models have noticeably worse performance in the second period.

Figures 2(a–c) and 3(a–c) provide plots of the one step predictions of C_t, I_t and Y_t, from both models for each of the time periods. The overall impression is that the MPA model is more successful than the RBC model in tracking all series. Because the models are non-nested, imposing different restrictions upon the same VAR, one way to check the above impression is to enquire into whether the explanation of variables of interest given by the MPA model can be improved upon by using information from the RBC model. To this end we regress data on the variable being studied against the predictions of it made by both the MPA and RBC models; if the RBC model is correct then the coefficient on the predictions from the MPA model should be zero, and conversely. This test is in the spirit of Davidson and MacKinnon's (1981) J-test for non-nested models. Selecting C_t, I_t and Y_t as the variables of interest, the results are given below in (24a–c) for the first period and in (25a–c) for the second period, with t ratios in brackets.

First Period

$$C_t = \underset{(2.15)}{0.21}\ \hat{C}_{RBC,t} + \underset{(8.08)}{0.79}\ \hat{C}_{MPA,t} \tag{24a}$$

$$I_t = \underset{(1.74)}{0.09}\ \hat{I}_{RBC,t} + \underset{(15.94)}{0.90}\ \hat{I}_{MPA,t} \tag{24b}$$

$$Y_t = \underset{(2.41)}{0.18}\ \hat{Y}_{RBC,t} + \underset{(11.94)}{0.83}\ \hat{Y}_{MPA,t} \tag{24c}$$

Second Period

$$C_t = 0.14 \; \hat{C}_{RBC,t} + 0.88 \; \hat{C}_{MPA,t} \quad (25a)$$
$$ (1.63) \phantom{\; \hat{C}_{RBC,t} + \;} (11.57)$$

$$I_t = 0.15 \; \hat{I}_{RBC,t} + 0.82 \; \hat{I}_{MPA,t} \quad (25b)$$
$$ (3.45) \phantom{\; \hat{I}_{RBC,t} + \;} (14.47)$$

$$Y_t = 0.59 \; \hat{Y}_{RBC,t} + 0.52 \; \hat{Y}_{MPA,t} \quad (25c)$$
$$ (7.57) \phantom{\; \hat{Y}_{RBC,t} + \;} (8.34)$$

The evidence in the above equations is that the RBC model rarely adds a great deal to the explanatory power of the MPA model. Perhaps the most striking exception to this statement is in (25c); it would seem that output in the second period cannot be satisfactorily explained by a pure demand side model like MPA. Given the oil-price shocks of the 1970s, part of which would be reflected in the *ex-post* measurements of productivity, such a conclusion may not be too surprising.

One way to understand the difference in the two models is to ask what the RBC model would look like if turned into an MPA type model. To do this we use the ideas in Section 2 for reducing the VAR implied by the RBC model into bivariate VAR's between the pairs (consumption, output) and (investment, output). Equations (26a–b) and (27a–b) give the implied bivariate VARs for the two periods, with the estimated parameters in brackets.

First Period

$$c_t = 1.08 \; c_{t-1} - 0.09 \; c_{t-2} + 0.18 \; y_t - 0.19 \; y_{t-1} + 0.07 \; y_{t-2} \quad (26a)$$
$$ (0.79) \phantom{\; c_{t-1} -} (0.13) \phantom{\; c_{t-2} +} (0.24) (-0.12) \phantom{\; y_{t-1} +} (-0.08)$$

$$i_t = 0.87 \; i_{t-1} + 0.04 \; i_{t-2} + 3.17 \; y_t - 2.73 \; y_{t-1} - 0.317 \; y_{t-2} \quad (26b)$$
$$ (0.94) \phantom{\; i_{t-1} +} (-0.10) \phantom{\; i_{t-2} +} (0.98) (-0.20) \phantom{\; y_{t-1} -} (-0.63)$$

Second Period

$$c_t = 0.99 \; c_{t-1} - 0.05 \; c_{t-2} + 0.21 \; y_t - 0.21 \; y_{t-1} + 0.07 \; y_{t-2} \quad (27a)$$
$$ (1.12) \phantom{\; c_{t-1} -} (-0.16) \phantom{\; c_{t-2} +} (0.20) (-0.25) \phantom{\; y_{t-1} +} (0.05)$$

$$i_t = 0.73 \; i_{t-1} + 0.03 \; i_{t-2} + 3.31 \; y_t - 2.39 \; y_{t-1} - 0.24 \; y_{t-2} \quad (27b)$$
$$ (0.41) \phantom{\; i_{t-1} +} (0.12) \phantom{\; i_{t-2} +} (1.81) (-0.55) \phantom{\; y_{t-1} -} (-0.23)$$

These equations encapsulate most of the information in Figures 2 and 3 regarding the behaviour of consumption and investment. A succinct summary of the latter is that investment is much too volatile whilst consumption is too smooth. In terms of (26a–b) and (27a–b) the impact of output upon investment is seen to be too large, while the lag distribution of consumption response to income changes is longer for the RBC model. Another interesting feature of (26a–b) and (27a–b) is that the accelerator mechanism is very clear in the data of the first period but is not in evidence in the second (in the sense that the coefficients of y_t, y_{t-1} and y_{t-2} do not sum to zero). This provides one explanation for the MPA model's deterioration in performance during the second period.

5. CONCLUSION

This paper has set out a strategy for evaluating small linear models via the restrictions they impose upon the VAR in the variables they are meant to explain. Three types of restrictions were elicited. First, there are cointegrating restrictions implied among the state variables. Second, there are the cointegrating constraints existing between the state and 'output' variables. Finally, there are restrictions upon the dynamics of the model when all variables are transformed to be I(0). It was recommended that evaluation should proceed by examining the constraints sequentially. The technology was then applied to an RBC model that had performed reasonably well when assessed relative to a set of 'stylised facts'; failure on all three counts was evident, pointing to the need for some re-specification of the model.

A failure of the cointegrating restrictions is generally the hardest feature to rectify as some variables need to be added to the system. Candidates could be the effects of taxation upon capital accumulation, the impact of the external sector via terms of trade movements, or monetary factors. Although a complete study of this phenomenon is beyond the paper, understanding the source of the cointegration failures seems critical to determining what course of action should be followed. However, even if the cointegrating restrictions were made acceptable there also appears to be some difficulties with the 'short run' responses within the model. Results presented in Sections 3 and 4 make a strong case for introducing adjustment costs into investment in order to reduce the magnitude of its short run reponse to fluctuations in output. The opposite is true of consumption, where the impact of current income needs to be strengthened.

Evaluating a Real Business Cycle Model   249

Figure 2. First Period Values (—) and Predictions of them from the
            MPA (- - -) and RBC (·····) Models

(a) Consumption (C)

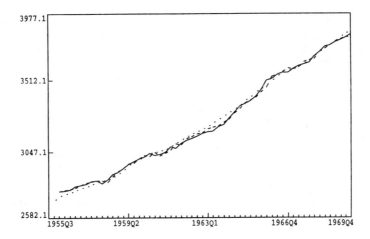

(b) Investment (I)

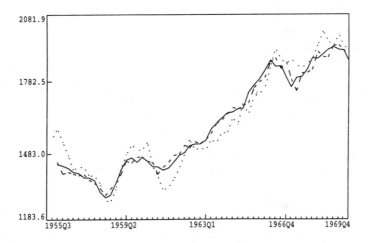

250   *Fabio Canova, Mary Finn and Adrian R. Pagan*

Figure 2. (continued)

(c) Income (Y)

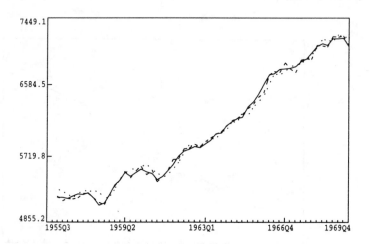

Figure 3. Second Period Values (—) and Predictions of them from the
MPA (- - -) and RBC (·····) Models

(a) Consumption (C)

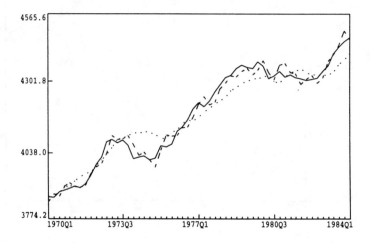

Evaluating a Real Business Cycle Model   251

Figure 3. (continued)

(b) Investment (I)

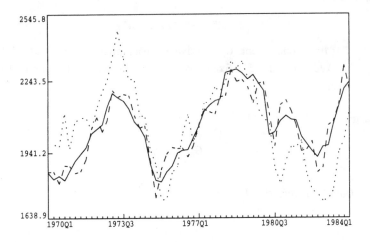

(c) Income (Y)

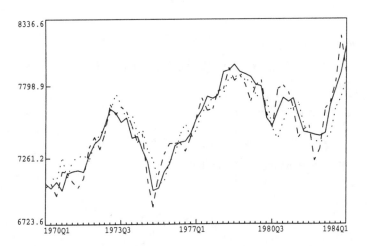

252   *Fabio Canova, Mary Finn and Adrian R. Pagan*

APPENDIX

The Burnside/Eichenbaum/Rebelo Model

Worker Utility

$$\ln(C_t^p) + \theta \ln(T - \xi - W_t f)$$

T = time endowment, C_t^p = private consumption, W_t = effort, f = hours worked per shift, ξ = fixed cost of work (in terms of hours of foregone leisure).

Non-Worker Utility

$$\ln(C_t^p) + \theta \ln(T)$$

Cobb-Douglas Production Function

$$Y_t = Z_t K_t^{1-\alpha} (N_t W_t f)^\alpha$$

Z_t = Technology, N_t = fraction of agents who are workers (the number of agents is normalized to unity), K_t = beginning of period capital stock.

Technology Change

$$Z_t = \gamma^{\alpha t} A_t$$

Productivity Shock

$$\ln(A_t) = (1 - \rho_a) \ln(A) + \rho_a \ln(A_{t-1}) + \varepsilon_t$$

Aggregate Resource Constraint

$$C_t^p + K_{t+1} - (1 - \delta) K_t + X_t \le Y_t$$

X_t = government consumption

Fiscal Rule

$$X_t = \gamma_g^t G_t$$

$$\ln(G_t) = (1 - \rho_g) \ln(G) + \rho_g \ln(G_{t-1}) + \mu_t$$

Table A. Parameter Values for the BER Model

Parameter	Period 1	Period 2
δ	0.0196	0.0221
θ	0.6593	0.6504
ρ_a	0.8691	0.8815
σ_ε	0.0042	0.0067
$\ln(A)$	8.4914	8.8733
$\ln(\gamma_y)$	0.0069	0.0015
$\ln(G)$	6.8090	7.1618
$\ln(\gamma_g)$	0.0073	−0.0013
ρ_g	0.938	0.6618
σ_μ	0.0143	0.0115

It is assumed that a social planner maximises

$$E_0 \sum_{t=0}^{\infty} \beta^t \left\{ \ln\left(C_t^p\right) + \theta N_t \ln\left(T - \xi - W_t f\right) + \theta(1 - N_t)\ln(T) \right\}$$

subject to the constraints above and K_0 by choice of contingency plans for $\{C_t^p, K_{t+1}, N_t, W_t : t \geq 0\}$. E_0 is the time 0 conditional expectations operator, β is the subjective discount rate, $0 < \beta < 1$.

Certain transformations are made to the problem before it is solved. These are to express the variables as deviations from deterministic steady state growth paths. Thus $\overline{C}_t^p = C_t^p / \gamma^t$, $\overline{Y}_t = Y_t / \gamma^t$, $\overline{K}_t = K_t / \gamma^t$, $\overline{X}_t = X_t / \gamma^t$ which means that the constraints on the optimisation can be reduced to

$$\gamma \overline{K}_{t+1} = A\overline{K}_t^{1-\alpha}(N_t W_t f)^\alpha - \overline{C}_t^p + (1 - \delta)\overline{K}_t - \overline{X}_t$$

while the optimand becomes

$$\sum_{t=0}^{\infty} \beta^t \log(\gamma^t) + E_0 \sum_{t=0}^{\infty} \beta^t \left\{ \ln(\overline{C}_t^p) + N_t \theta \ln(T - \xi - W_t f) + \theta(1 - N_t)\ln(T) \right\}$$

Finally small letters indicate deviations of variables from steady states. Thus $a_t = \log(A_t / A)$.

The solutions to this problem after linearization of the Euler equations are laws of motion for the state variables k_t, n_t, a_t and g_t as well as linear relations connecting other variables such as y_t, c_t^p to these states. With the parameter values in Table A it is possible to compute numerical values for these relations and they are presented in the text. The parameter σ_ν in the table arises from the assumption that there are measurement errors in hours worked.

REFERENCES

BANERJEE, A., J. J. DOLADO, D. F. HENDRY and G. W. SMITH (1986), 'Exploring Equilibrium Relationships Through Static Models: Some Monte Carlo Evidence', *Oxford Bulletin of Economics and Statistics*, 48, 3, pp. 253–77.

BURNSIDE, C., M. EICHENBAUM and S. REBELO (1993), 'Labor Hoarding and the Business Cycle', *Journal of Political Economy*, 101, pp. 245–73.

BYRON, R. P. (1974), 'Testing Structural Specification Using the Unrestricted Reduced Form', *Econometrica*, 42, pp. 869–83.

CANOVA, F. (1990), 'Simulating General Equilibrium Dynamic Models Using Bayesian Techniques', Mimeo, University of Rochester.

CHOW, G. C. (1992a), 'Dynamic Optimization without Dynamic Programming', *Economic Modelling*, 9, pp. 3–9.

—— (1992b), 'Statistical Estimation and Testing of a Real Business Cycle Model', Econometric Research Program Research Memorandum No. 365, Princeton University.

CHRISTIANO, L. J. and M. EICHENBAUM (1992), 'Current Real-Business-Cycle Theories and Aggregate Labor Market Fluctuations', *American Economic Review*, 82, pp. 430–50.

COGLEY, T. and J. M. NASON (1992), 'Do Real Business Cycle Models Pass the Nelson-Plosser Test?', Mimeo, University of British Columbia.

DAVIDSON, R. and J. G. MACKINNON (1981), 'Several Tests for Model Specification in the Presence of Alternative Hypotheses', *Econometrica*, 49, pp. 781–93.

EVANS, G. W. (1989), 'Output and Unemployment Dynamics in the United States: 1950–1985', *Journal of Applied Econometrics*, 4, pp. 213–37.

GREGORY, A. W. and G. W. SMITH (1993), 'Statistical Aspects of Calibration in Macroeconomics', in G. S. Maddala, C. R. Rao and H. D. Vinod (eds.), *Handbook of Statistics*, 11, pp. 703–19.

HENDRY, D. F. and G. M. MIZON (1993), 'Evaluating Dynamic Models by Encompassing the VAR', in P. C. B. Phillips (ed.), *Models, Methods and Applications of Econometrics*, Oxford: Basil Blackwell, pp. 272–300.

HOOVER, K. D. (1991a), 'Six Queries About Idealization in an Empirical Context', *Ponzan Studies in the Philosophy of Science and the Humanities* (forthcoming).

—— (1991b), 'Calibration and the Econometrics of the Macroeconomy', Mimeo, University of California at Davis.

KING, R. G., C. PLOSSER and S. REBELO (1988), 'Production, Growth and Business Cycles I: The Basic Neoclassical Model', *Journal of Monetary Economics*, 21, pp. 195–232.

KING, R. G., C. PLOSSER, J. STOCK and M. WATSON (1991), 'Stochastic Trends and Economic Fluctuations', *American Economic Review*, 81, pp. 819–46.

KREMERS, J. J. M., N. R. ERICSSON and J. J. DOLADO (1992), 'The Power of Cointegration Tests', International Finance Discussion Paper No. 431, Board of Governors of the Federal Reserve System.

KYDLAND, F. E. and E. C. PRESCOTT (1982), 'Time to Build and Aggregate Fluctuations', *Econometrica*, 50, pp. 1345–70.

—— (1991), 'The Econometrics of the General Equilibrium Approach to Business Cycles', *Scandinavian Journal of Economics*, 93, pp. 161–78.

LAIDLER, D. and B. BENTLEY (1983), 'A Small Macro-model of the Post-War United States', *Manchester School*, 51, pp. 317–40.

LONG, J. B. and C. I. PLOSSER (1983), 'Real Business Cycles', *Journal of Political Economy*, 91, pp. 39–69.

MARCET, A. (1989), 'Solving Non-linear Stochastic Models by Parameterizing Expectations', Mimeo, Carnegie-Mellon University.

MCGRATTAN, E. B. (1991), 'The Macroeconomic Effects of Distortionary Taxation', Discussion Paper No. 37, Institute for Empirical Macroeconomics.

MONFORT, A. and R. RABEMANANJARA (1990), 'From a VAR to a Structural Model, with an Application to the Wage Price Spiral', *Journal of Applied Econometrics*, 5, pp. 203–27.

NEUSSER, K. (1991), 'Testing the Long-Run Implications of the Neo-classical Growth Model', *Journal of Monetary Economics*, 27, pp. 3–37.

PRESCOTT, E. C. (1991), 'Real Business Cycle Theory: What Have We Learned?', Unpublished lecture, Latin American Meeting of the Econometric Society, Punta del Este, Uruguay.

SARGENT, T. J. (1978), 'Estimation of Dynamic Labour Demand Schedules Under Rational Expectations', *Journal of Applied Econometrics*, 4, pp. 213–37.

SPANOS, A. (1986), *Statistical Foundations of Econometric Modelling*, Cambridge University Press, Cambridge.

TINBERGEN, J. (1939), *Statistical Testing of Business Cycle Theories, Vol I: A Method and Its Application to Investment Activity*, League of Nations, Geneva.

WALLIS, K. F. (1977), 'Multiple Time Series Analysis and the Final Form of Econometric Models', *Econometrica*, 45, pp. 1481–97.

WATSON, M. W. (1993), 'Measures of Fit for Calibrated Models', *Journal of Political Economy*, 101, pp. 1011–41.

ZELLNER, A. and F. PALM (1974), 'Time Series Analysis and Simultaneous Equation Econometric Models', *Journal of Econometrics*, 2, pp. 17–54.

Journal of Monetary Economics 33 (1994) 405–438. North-Holland

Real business cycles and the test of the Adelmans*

Robert G. King
University of Virginia, Charlottesville, VA 22903, USA

Charles I. Plosser
University of Rochester, Rochester, NY 14627, USA

Received August 1992, final version received January 1994

This paper conducts a modern variant of the test proposed and carried out by Adelman and Adelman (1959). Using the methods developed by Burns and Mitchell (1946), we see if we can distinguish between the economic series generated by an actual economy and those analogous artificial series generated by a stochastically perturbed economic model. In the case of the Adelmans, the model corresponded to the Klein–Goldberger equations. In our case, the model corresponds to a simple real business cycle model. The results indicate a fairly high degree of coincidence in key economic aggregates between the business cycle characteristics identified in actual data and those found in our simulated economy.

Key words: Business fluctuations; Business cycles; Forecasting & simulation

JEL classification: E12; E32; E37

1. Introduction

The most prominent and detailed description of business cycle regularities is due to a generation of researchers assembled by Wesley Clair Mitchell at the

Correspondence to: Charles I. Plosser, William E. Simon Graduate School of Business Administration, University of Rochester, Rochester, NY 14627, USA.

*The authors thank Marianne Baxter, Mario Crucini, and Sergio Rebelo for discussion on substantive issues involved in this research project. We thank Anna J. Schwartz and Victor Zarnowitz for aiding us in understanding the opportunities provided by the work of Gerhard Bry and Charlotte Boschan (1971). None of the preceding individuals is, however, responsible for the contents of this paper. Plosser's support for this research is provided by the Olin Institute and The Bradley Policy Research Center at the W.E. Simon Graduate School of Business Administration. This paper is part of NBER's research program in Financial Markets and Monetary Economics. Any opinions expressed are those of the authors and not those of the National Bureau of Economic Research.

National Bureau of Economic Research (NBER) in New York in the 1940s and 1950s. These researchers pursued and expanded the research program initiated by Mitchell (1927) and Burns and Mitchell (1946). They analyzed hundreds of economic time series producing a wealth of information about the pace and pattern of economic activity in a variety of industrialized countries. This massive body of empirical work now provides the dominant background to most academic and policy discussion of macroeconomic developments.

It would be difficult to overstate the cumulative impact of this body of research. When we talk about business cycles, most of us have in mind one variant or another of the visual summary statistics produced by Burns, Mitchell, and their co-workers. To take one common example, when we think about the evolution of an industry's production over time, we frequently think about a plot of the time series with recession components highlighted by shaded areas. For another, our sense of how long expansion and recession episodes last is based on measurements that continue to be made by the NBER to this day, following the path of Burns and Mitchell. To cite yet a third example, our view of the extent to which particular economic variables move with the cycle in aggregate economic activity – for example, investment tightly related and real wages not so tightly linked – is heavily influenced by business cycle plots and conformity statistics of the type developed by Burns and Mitchell. In fact, these results are so much a part of our thinking that it is relatively common to evaluate models in terms of whether they *replicate* the stylized facts of business cycles as isolated by Burns and Mitchell.

Yet, from a modern perspective, the Burns and Mitchell procedures produced summary statistics with unknown distributional properties. This vacuum was primarily due to the complexity of the computations and macroeconomists' lack of detailed knowledge about the dynamic economic model generating the time series [Koopmans (1947)]. This paper is the first product of a research project that is designed to shed light on the character of the Burns and Mitchell procedures. In the current context, we are mainly interested in following the path of Adelman and Adelman (1959), using the Burns and Mitchell procedures to *evaluate* a specific economic model. Our intention, however, is to build on skills gained in execution of this project to ultimately provide a broader based evaluation of the procedures developed by Burns and Mitchell so that we may better understand the facts and figures that underlie our description of business cycles.

Although the NBER business cycle research was not designed to evaluate specific economic theories, it has of course been used – beginning with Mitchell (1927) – to guide the development of economic models because it represented a group of 'stylized facts' about economic fluctuations to which theories could be compared. This approach to model evaluation was made explicit by Adelman and Adelman (1959), who developed summary statistics based on the Burns and Mitchell methodology for the time series generated by a stochastically perturbed variant of the Klein–Goldberger (1959) model. Then, the Adelmans compared these statistics to those for the U.S. economy as reported in Mitchell (1951). As stated by Lucas (1980):

> 'the Adelmans posed, in a precise way, the question of whether an observer armed with the methods of Burns and Mitchell (1946) could distinguish between a collection of economic series generated artifically by a computer programmed to follow the Klein–Goldberger equations and the analogous series generated by an actual economy. The answer, to the evident surprise of the Adelmans (and, one suspects, of Klein and Goldberger, who had in no way directed their efforts to meeting this criterion) was *no*. This achievement signaled a new standard for what it means to understand business cycles. One exhibits understanding of business cycles by constructing a *model* in the most literal sense: a fully articulated economy which behaves through time so as to imitate closely the time series behavior of actual economies.'

More specifically, the Adelmans showed that only *one* of three types of displacements was capable of generating business cycle movements that resembled those isolated by the NBER researchers. Neither transitional responses from initial conditions nor sample variation in exogenous variables was capable of reproducing the stylized facts isolated by the NBER researchers. Rather, it was necessary to add random shocks to the structural equations of the Klein–Goldberger model. Then, the model's internal dynamic structure led to time series that resembled those of the U.S. economy from the perspective of an NBER researcher.

The objective of this paper is to conduct a modern variant of the Adelman's project, taking advantage of the development in economic theory, econometric method, and computing power that have occurred since the 1950s. First, we use a representative 'real business cycle model' that is driven by a stochastic process for total factor productivity as a basic example of a fully articulated model economy. Second, since the reduced form of this model is a system of log-linear difference equations, its time and frequency domain implications can be determined with precision. Third, drawing on work by Bry and Boschan (1971), we use computer algorithms for business cycle analysis that avoid some of the difficulties of replication that are evident in Burns and Mitchell's early work. Finally, given developments in computing power since 1959, it is possible for us to be more explicit about the *distribution* of the Burns and Mitchell measures than it was for the Adelmans. We generate time series from our real business cycle model and compute various summary measures, with an eye toward appraising the capacity of this artificial economy to mimic the time series of the U.S. economy.

In addition, a virtue of our approach is that it enables us to shed light on the mapping between the stochastic properties of an underlying economic model and the summary statistics of the Burns and Mitchell procedures. Articulation of this mapping is important because the Burns and Mitchell methods of business cycle analysis have not been previously subjected to this type of scrutiny. However, we defer until later a detailed and more complete evaluation of these business cycle methods.

Our discussion is organized as follows. In section 2, we provide a brief overview of business cycle research as described in Burns and Mitchell (1946) and codified by Bry and Boschan (1971). We discuss our variant of this approach – which can be mechanically applied to time series generated by an artificial economy.[1] Then, we present results of applying this method to the post World War II behavior of some major macroeconomic time series including the five series (measures of consumption, investment, output, labor input, and the real wage) we studied in a pair of recent papers on real business cycles [King, Plosser, and Rebelo (1988a,b)]. In section 3, we provide an overview of the basic real business cycle model that we employ in our analysis and summarize the model's stochastic properties. In section 4, we discuss the results of simulating this model and compare the business cycle characteristics of U.S. and model generated time series using the methods developed by Burns and Mitchell. In section 5, we make a crude comparison between the summary measure proposed by Burns and Mitchell and the more common statistical measures of standard deviation and correlation. The final section contains a summary and discussion of research plans.

2. Implementation of the Burns and Mitchell methodology

Burns and Mitchell's 1946 treatise, *Measuring Business Cycles*, provides the most complete description of their approach to processing information and summarizing the central characteristics of business cycles. In this section we briefly describe key aspects of the Burns and Mitchell method and our implementation of their procedures.

---

[1] The interested reader may also wish to refer to Hickman (1972). The studies reported in that volume were, in part, intended to evaluate a variety of then popular econometric models using the methods employed by the NBER which are closely related to the methods of Burns and Mitchell. After completion of this research, we became aware of two related unpublished studies. First, the thesis work of Scott Simkins (1988), who studies the business cycle implications of the Kydland–Prescott (1982) model. That research – as summarized in Simkins (1994) – differs from ours in a number of respects, notably the implementation of the NBER method and selection of Monte Carlo evidence discussed. Second, the manuscript of Litterman, Quah, and Sargent (1984) that studies business cycle implications of a particular index model. That research again differs in the implementation of the NBER method (both from our study and that of Simkins) and presentation of Monte Carlo evidence.

2.1. Reference cycle determination

In order to investigate and measure the characteristics of different series over the business cycle, it is necessary to define the business cycle and to determine when it occurs. Burns and Mitchell adopted the working definition proposed earlier by Mitchell:

> Business cycles are a type of fluctuations found in the aggregate economic activity of nations that organize their work mainly in business enterprises: a cycle consists of expansions occurring at about the same time in many economic activities, followed by similarly general recessions, contractions, and revivals which merge into the expansion phase of the next cycle; this sequence of changes is recurrent but not periodic; in duration business cycles vary from more than one year to ten or twelve years; they are not divisible into shorter cycles of similar character with amplitudes approximating their own.   [Mitchell (1927, p. 468)]

While vague, the definition does place restrictions on both duration and amplitudes that must be satisfied to qualify an episode as a business cycle. The first step, therefore, is to determine the periods of expansion and contraction in 'aggregate economic activity' or, in the terminology of Burns and Mitchell, to determine the dates or turning points for the reference cycle. Burns and Mitchell, however, were not satisfied with any of the measures of aggregate economic activity available to them so they did not wish to determine the reference cycle dates using only aggregate measures. Instead they relied primarily on two sorts of information: (i) descriptive evidence from business publications and general business conditions indexes and (ii) the 'specific cycles' found in many individual series and the tendency for the turning points from expansion to contraction (and vice versa) to sometimes cluster at certain dates. Based on this information a set of reference cycle dates were selected that specified the turning points (peaks and troughs) in 'aggregate economic activity'. This process was time-consuming and involved considerable researcher-specific judgement.

Our implementation of the Burns and Mitchell procedures, to the data of the post-war U.S. economy and to our simulated artificial real business cycle economy, differs only in the manner in which the reference cycle dates are selected. We depart from Burns and Mitchell in two ways. First, we determine the turning points in the reference cycle using a measure of aggregate economy activity such as real per capita GNP. Second, the actual turning points are selected using an algorithm developed by Bry and Boschan (1971). The advantage of the Bry and Boschan method is that it is quickly and easily implemented and can be readily replicated. The disadvantage, of course, is that it removes from the process the detailed knowledge and judgement of an experienced observer of business cycles.

Table 1

Procedure for programmed determination of turning points.[a]

I.   Determination of extremes and substitution of values

II.   Determination of cycles in 12-month moving average (extremes replaced)

    A.   Identification of points higher (or lower) than 5 months on either side
    B.   Enforcement of alternation of turns by selecting highest of multiple peaks (or lowest of multiple troughs)

III. Determination of corresponding turns in Spencer curve (extremes replaced)

    A.   Identification of highest (or lowest) value within $\pm$ 5 months of selected turn in 12-month moving average
    B.   Enforcement of minimum cycle duration of 15 months by eliminating lower peaks and higher troughs of shorter cycles

IV.   Determination of corresponding turns in short-term moving average of 3 to 6 months, depending on MCD (months of cyclical dominance)

    A.   Identification of highest (or lowest) values within $\pm$ 5 months of selected turn in Spencer curve

V.   Determination of turning points in unsmoothed series

    A.   Identification of highest (or lowest) value within $\pm$ 4 months, or MCD term, whichever is larger, of selected turn in short-term moving average
    B.   Elimination of turns within 6 months of beginning and end of series
    C.   Elimination of peaks (or troughs) at both ends of series which are lower (or higher) than values closer to end
    D.   Elimination of cycles whose duration is less than 15 months
    E.   Elimination of phases whose duration is less than 5 months

VI.   Statement of final turning points.

[a]This table is taken from Bry and Boschan (1971, p. 21).

The Bry and Boschan procedure for selecting turning points in any series is summarized in table 1. The general procedure, followed also by Burns and Mitchell, is to look for turning points in some smoothed version of a seasonally adjusted series so as not to be mislead by 'erratic' movements. Bry and Boschan implement this by beginning with a highly smoothed series (a 12-month moving average) to find initial estimates of the turning points. Using these initial estimates, a somewhat less smooth curve is investigated (a Spencer curve)[2] to refine the dates of the turning points. This process is repeated using a short-term (3-month) moving average. The final turning points are determined using the unsmoothed series and verifying that the turns satisfy a set of restrictions given

[2]The Spencer curve is a 15-month centered moving average with the terms near the center receiving the largest weight and the extreme terms receiving a negative weight. The actual weights on terms $t-7$ to $t+7$ are $[-0.0094, -0.0188, -0.0156, 0.0094, 0.0656, 0.1438, 0.2094, 0.2313, 0.2094, 0.1438, 0.0656, 0.0094, -0.0156, -0.0188, -0.0094]$.

in part V of table 1. Of particular interest is that business cycles must be no less than 15 months long and all phases (expansions and contractions) must be at least 5 months in duration.

Bry and Boschan present two types of evidence that are useful in evaluating their procedures. First, they study a series that was extensively studied by Burns and Mitchell; monthly bituminous coal production from 1914 to 1935. The 13 turning points selected by Burns and Mitchell correspond exactly to the ones selected by the program in all cases but one and this was a dating difference of 3 months. The only other discrepancy was that the programmed procedures isolated a minor cycle that was ignored by Burns and Mitchell. The second type of evaluation conducted by Bry and Boschan was to compare the turning points selected by their program in over 50 series covering the period 1947–1966 to the turning points selected by the National Bureau staff. Of the turns identified by the staff (435 in total) almost 95% of them were identified by the program and 90% had identical dates. The only systematic discrepancy arose because the program procedures tended to find about 15% more turns than the staff.

To illustrate these procedures we have computed the turning points for real GNP and per capita real GNP. One issue raised by these series is that they are quarterly rather than monthly series. Bry and Boschan handle quarterly data by simply setting each month of the quarter equal to the quarterly value and proceeding to treat the series as monthly. This interpolation procedure is similar, but not identical, to that employed by Burns and Mitchell. For subsequent analysis the turning point is arbitrarily assigned to the middle month of the quarter. The turning points are presented in figs. 1a and 1b. For comparison purposes we have labeled the turning points determined by the NBER business cycle dating committee. The NBER dates are not simply based on the behavior of GNP but on many series and thus there is no *a priori* reason the procedures should yield the same results.

There are two important observations to be made about fig. 1a. First, working solely from real GNP, the program procedures do not recognize the NBER recession that began in April 1960 and ended in February 1961. The smoothing process explicit in the programmed procedures effectively eliminates any evidence of a recession during this period. Second, the program procedure does not recognize the NBER recession that began in January 1980 and ended in July 1980. The reason arises from the phase duration restriction. The program recognized a peak in March 1980 and a trough in June 1980, but since it lasted less than 5 months it was rejected as a business cycle.[3]

Fig. 1b presents the turning points in real per capita GNP. While Burns and Mitchell did not consider per capita measures in their analysis, we do for the

---

[3]Consistent with the July 1980 selection, the NBER dates the trough as 1980.III even though real GNP was actually lower in 1980.II than in 1980.III.

412   *R.G. King and C.I. Plosser, Variant of the Adelmans' test*

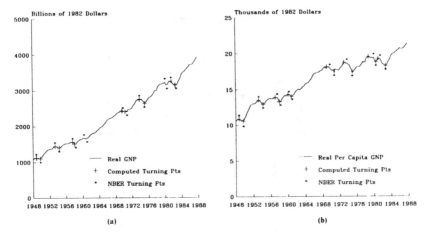

Fig. 1. Turning points in real GNP (a) and real per capita GNP (b).

simple reason that the sorts of representative agent models we are working with in section 3 are more naturally interpreted as describing per capita quantities. It is apparent, however, that real per capita GNP displays somewhat different cyclical patterns than real GNP. The reasons are easy to understand. By deflating by population, the peaks will tend to occur earlier than the peaks in total GNP. This holds true for 6 of the 8 peaks occurring in the post-war period. Working with the per capita measure also results in the return of the 1960 recession because the decline is more pronounced and the 1980 recession because the peak is identified so much earlier. Trough dates tend to correspond more closely because the typical rate of decline preceding a trough and the rate of increase following a trough are larger than the rate of increase preceding a peak. Thus deflating by population has little impact on the location of the trough.

Table 2 summarizes the turning points selected by the algorithm of Bry and Boschan and the business cycle peaks and troughs selected by the NBER. As can be seen from the table, the dates of the troughs coincide almost exactly, but the peaks in per capita GNP frequently lead the NBER selected peaks. The table also summarized the duration (in months) of the business cycles identified from real per capita GNP.

The average expansion lasted almost 40 months, the average contraction lasted just over 17 months, and the cycle averaged almost 57 months. As expected from the timing differences, these averages differ slightly from the NBER dates, where the average expansion is 45 months, average contraction is just over 11 months, and the cycle averaged 56 months.

Table 2

Comparison of turning points in the post-war period (1948–1987).

Turning points based on real per capita GNP		Reference cycle dates selected by the NBER		Timing differences (in quarters)		Duration (months)		
Trough	Peak	Trough	Peak	Trough	Peak	Expansion	Contraction	Cycle[a]
—	1948.IV	—	1948.IV	—	0	—	12	—
1949.IV	1953.II	1949.IV	1953.II	0	0	42	12	54
1954.II	1957.I	1954.II	1957.III	0	2	35	12	47
1958.I	1960.I	1958.II	1960.II	1	1	24	9	33
1960.IV	1969.I	1961.I	1969.IV	1	3	99	21	120
1970.IV	1973.I	1970.IV	1973.IV	0	3	27	24	51
1975.I	1978.IV	1975.I	1980.I	0	5	45	21	66
1980.III	1981.I	1980.III	1981.III	0	2	6	21	27
1982.IV	—	1982.IV	—	0	—	—	—	—
					Avg.	39.5	17.1[b]	56.6

[a]Cycle durations are computed on a trough-peak-trough (T-P-T) basis beginning with the trough in 1949.IV.

[b]The average contraction length is computed by ignoring the initial contraction from 1948.IV to 1949.IV to be comparable with the full cycle calculation. The average contraction length including the initial contraction is 15.9.

2.2. Summary measures of cyclical behavior

With the reference cycle defined by the turning points determined above, the basic measures of cyclical behavior, as developed by Burns and Mitchell, are easily computed. In this development we follow Burns and Mitchell as closely as possible. Our task has been simplified by Bry and Boschan, who programmed the summary statistics described below.

Reference cycle patterns and cycle relatives. Each reference cycle is divided into 9 stages. The initial stage (I) includes the 3 months centered on the initial trough, stage V is the 3 months centered on the reference cycle peak, and stage IX is the 3 months centered on the terminal trough. The expansion phase (stages I to V) is divided into 3 substages (II, III, and IV) of equal length (excluding those months included in stages I and V). The contraction phase is similarly divided to obtain stages VI, VII, and VIII. Since expansion and contraction are generally not of equal length, the number of months in the expansion stages (II, III, and IV) will not be the same as in the contraction stages (VI, VII, and VIII). Moreover, since reference cycle expansions (contractions) will be of differing lengths, stages II, III, and IV (VI, VII, and VIII) will not contain the same number of months across reference cycles. Breaking cycles into stages results in each reference cycle having associated with it 2 units of measurement; one is measured in calendar time and the other is measured in business cycle time.

In order to compare the behavior of different series over the cycle and across cycles, the series are typically converted to *cycle relatives.* This conversion is accomplished by computing the average value of the series over a particular reference cycle (the cycle base) and expressing each observation as a percentage of this average. Thus a cycle relative value of 100 is equivalent to the average value of the series over the cycle. The conversion to cycle relatives makes it possible to compare cycles at different points in time.[4] To do so, the Burns and Mitchell procedure eliminates an intercycle trend. But, the potential for an intracycle trend remains. Thus, if a series exhibits substantial growth over a cycle, the cycle relatives will have an upward drift.

A controversial step in the Burns and Mitchell procedures involves averaging cycle relatives at each stage across reference cycles. This results in an average cycle relative at each stage of the business cycle. Plots of these average reference cycle patterns are intended to show how different series behave, on average, over the business cycle. These *business cycle plots* provide an important graphical summary of the information contained in the Burns and Mitchell approach.

Amplitudes. One important summary measure that is easily discernible from the business cycle plots is the amplitude of a specific series over the reference cycle. Amplitudes are measured for both expansions and contractions as well as

---

[4]Cycle relatives are generally not appropriate for series that contain significant numbers of negative values. In such instances the analysis is usually carried out in the original units. This is the case, for example, for the yield spread and the inflation rate discussed in section 2.3 below.

the full cycle. The amplitude during expansion is simply the cycle relative at the peak (stage V) minus the cycle relative at the initial trough (stage I). For contractions, the amplitude is the cycle relative at the terminal trough (stage IX) minus the cycle relative at the preceding peak (stage V). Note that for a series that typically rises during expansions and falls during contractions the amplitude will be positive for expansions and negative for contractions. The full cycle amplitude is simply the expansion amplitude minus the contraction amplitude.

Conformity.   While the business cycle plots provide a useful visual impression of the degree to which a series moves with the business cycle, Burns and Mitchell developed a quantitative device for assessing this trait. This summary measure is called conformity and can be associated with expansions, contractions, and the full cycle. To compute the conformity of a series during reference cycle expansions, a value of 1 is assigned to each expansion for which the average per month change in the cycle relative from stage I to stage V (trough to peak) is positive. For those expansions where the average per month change is negative (that is the series falls during an expansion), a value of -1 is assigned. The average of this series of ones and minus ones (multiplied by 100) is the index of conformity. A conformity of $+100$ corresponds to a series that on average rises during each reference cycle expansion and a conformity of -100 corresponds to a series that on average falls during each reference cycle expansion. Conformity during contractions is measured in analogous fashion except that a value of $+1$ is assigned if the average per month change in the cycle relative from stage V to stage IX is negative. Conformity of $+100$ during contractions is associated with a series that on average declines during every reference cycle contraction.

Conformity for the full cycle is determined not by the average conformity during expansions and contractions, but by the relative behavior of the series during the two phases. A value of 1 is assigned to each cycle that the average per month change during the expansion phase exceeds the average per month change during the contraction phase. Thus a series might rise during every expansion and contraction so that confirmity is $+100$ during expansions and -100 during contractions, but if the rate of monthly increase in expansions exceeds that in contractions, the full cycle conformity would be $+100$.

2.3. Summary measures for the United States, 1948–1987

In this section we employ the methods of the Burns and Mitchell outlined above to characterize the business cycle in the post-war U.S. economy. Our primary focus is on 5 commonly discussed macroeconomic aggregates: per capita values of GNP, consumption of nondurables and services, gross fixed investment, average weekly hours, and a measure of the real wage.[5] These series

---

[5]See the appendix for a complete description of the data series.

also most closely correspond to the conceptual series generated by the real business cycle model discussed in section 3. Following Burns and Mitchell, no prior filtering or detrending of the data has been undertaken except for the implicit filtering implied by the use of seasonally adjusted data and per capita quantities.

Reference cycle dates are computed based on the methods of Bry and Boschan summarized in table 1 using aggregate real per capita GNP. In figs. 2a–2e, we plot the quarterly time series for our 5 macroeconomic quantities and indicate the reference cycle peaks and troughs based on real per capita GNP and those selected by the NBER business cycle dating committee. These pictures highlight the major features of the data familiar to macroeconomists: expansion phases are longer than contraction phases; contractions are accompanied by sharp changes in labor input and investment; and consumption responds far less than output to recession. In fig. 2f we have plotted the GNP deflator over the post-war period. It displays no special cyclical tendencies, instead rising during both expansions and contractions.

Next, we present a compendium of business cycle plots of the form employed extensively by Burns and Mitchell. These plots, presented in figs. 3a–3f, display the average behavior, in cycle relatives, over the 9 stages of the business cycle for each of the 6 macroeconomic time series. Each of these plots is constructed in the same manner and drawn to the same scale. They plot the average cycle relative for each stage where the average is taken over the 7 complete trough-peak-trough (T-P-T) cycles beginning with the trough in 1949.IV and ending with the trough in 1982.IV. The horizontal axis (T to T) measures the average duration of the business cycle in months (~ 57 months). The horizontal distance from T to P is the average length of expansion phases (~ 40 months) and from P to T it is the average length of contraction phases (~ 17 months). The vertical tick marks indicate the midpoints for each of the nine stages. Stage I coincides with the initial trough, stage V with the peak, and stage IX corresponds to the terminal trough. The average cycle relatives for each stage are plotted at these midpoints. The height of these tick marks is a measure of dispersion across cycles. More precisely they represent the mean absolute deviation across the 7 cycles at each stage and their magnitudes are read off the right-hand-side vertical axis. Note that both the right and left vertical axis in each figure have the same units and scale.

The business cycle behavior of per capita real GNP, of course, coincides with the reference cycle. At its peak, it is 5% higher than its reference cycle average, while the initial trough is about 7.5% below the reference cycle average. Per capita real consumption displays little responsiveness to contraction phases although there is evidence of slowing of its average monthly growth rate which is reflected in fig. 3b by the reduced slope during recessions. The cyclical behavior in investment is presented in fig. 3c. Investment tends to rise more sharply

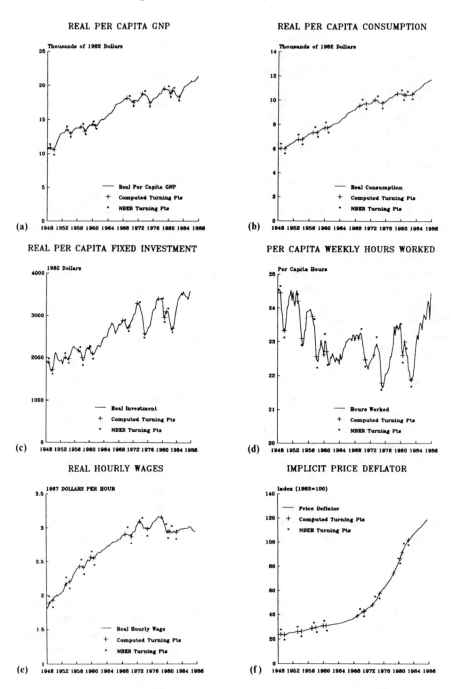

Fig. 2. Plots of quarterly time series for 5 macroeconomic quantities, (a)–(e), and of the GNP deflator over the post-war period, (f).

418   *R.G. King and C.I. Plosser, Variant of the Adelmans' test*

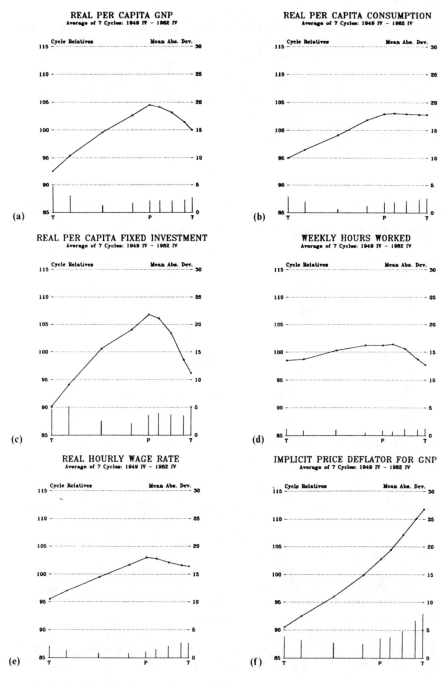

Fig. 3. Average behavior over 9 business cycle stages for 6 macroeconomic time series.

Table 3a

Burns and Mitchell cyclical measures for key quarterly aggregates, based on 7 cycles (1948–1987).

Series	Index of conformity[a]			Reference cycle amplitudes[b]		
	Expan-sions	Contrac-tions	Cycle	Expan-sions	Contrac-tions	Cycle
Quarterly series						
Real per capita GNP	+ 100	+ 100	+ 100	11.9/0.32 (6.9)	− 4.5/ − 0.27 (1.1)	16.4/0.30 (6.7)
Real per capita consumption of non-durables and services	+ 71	0	+ 85	7.9/0.17 (4.6)	− 0.1/ − 0.00 (1.0)	8.0/0.13 (0.41)
Real per capita fixed investment	+ 100	+ 100	+ 100	16.6/0.50 (7.6)	− 10.5/ − 0.59 (5.8)	27.1/0.52 (11.2)
Average weekly hours per capita	+ 100	+ 100	+ 100	2.7/0.10 (1.6)	− 3.6/ − 0.22 (1.2)	6.3/0.13 (2.5)
Real hourly wage	+ 71	+ 57	+ 85	7.6/0.19 (3.1)	− 1.6/ − 0.07 (2.1)	9.2/0.16 (3.3)
Implicit price deflator for GNP	+ 100	− 85	+ 35	12.3/0.39 (6.3)	9.0/0.44 (6.5)	3.3/0.03 (6.1)
Inflation rate[c]	+ 57	0	+ 28	1.4/0.06 (1.4)	− 0.9/ − 0.10 (2.7)	2.3/0.07 (3.9)

[a] The method for calculating the conformity index is detailed in the text. In general a conformity index of + 100 says that a series rises (falls) during each expansion (contraction) and rises at a faster rate during expansions than during contractions. An index of −100 indicates the opposite (e.g., a series that falls during every expansion would have a conformity of −100 for the expansion phase).

[b] The first amplitude measure indicates the total change in cycle relatives during each phase of the cycle. The number to the right converts that total change to a per month change. The number in parentheses below is the mean absolute deviation across seven cycles of the total change in cycle relatives for each phase.

[c] See footnote c to table 3b.

during expansion phases and decline more sharply during contraction phases than does either output or consumption. Labor input, as measured by weekly hours, is much smoother, but also moves with the cycle. Notably the real wage, fig. 3e, displays clear pro-cyclical tendencies, while the price level, fig. 3f, rises in during both expansion and contractions.

Table 3a presents the important summary measures of the business cycle characteristics of these 6 key macroeconomic series. The first group of statistics measures the conformity of each series to the reference cycle in GNP. Investment and hours display conformity of +100. The real wage is also pro-cyclical as seen from its business cycle plot, but does not conform perfectly. As seen in the plots, consumption conforms well during expansion phases, but displays neither positive nor negative conformity during contractions. The price level

Table 3b

Burns and Mitchell cyclical measures for some additional series of interest, based on 7 cycles (1948–1987).

Series	Index of conformity[a]			Reference cycle amplitudes[b]		
	Expansions	Contractions	Cycle	Expansions	Contractions	Cycle
Quarterly series						
Real per capita consumption of durables	+ 100	+ 85	+ 85	19.5/5.8 (12.0)	− 9.0/ − 4.8 (6.8)	28.5/0.48 (18.3)
Real per capita government expenditures	− 14	+ 14	+ 14	9.6/0.17 (16.7)	− 2.8/ − 0.17 (4.5)	11.3/0.17 (21.1)
Real per capita exports	+ 100	− 42	+ 14	16.1/0.48 (6.2)	2.0/0.06 (11.9)	14.1/0.34 (11.5)
Real per capita imports	+ 100	+ 42	+ 85	23.5/0.69 (10.9)	− 3.8/ − 0.24 (8.0)	27.3/0.53 (10.6)
Change in real per capita inventories[c]	+ 100	+ 100	+ 100	292.0/14.6 (70.5)	− 315.0/ − 19.7 (112.0)	608.0/13.8 (183.0)
Monthly series						
Yields on 3-month treasury bills	+ 100	+ 71	+ 100	63.8/2.6 (27.7)	− 41.2/ − 3.3 (31.2)	105.0/2.4 (49.2)
Yields on AAA corporate bonds	+ 71	+ 14	+ 28	17.5/0.64 (13.2)	5.3/0.09 (16.4)	12.2/0.33 (22.2)
Yield spread[c]	− 100	− 85	− 85	− 1.8/ − 0.13 (0.9)	2.1/0.12 (0.9)	− 3.9/ − 0.09 (1.7)
Ex post real rate on treasury bills[c]	− 42	− 42	− 14	0.2/0.17 (3.1)	1.2/0.06 (0.9)	− 0.9/0.01 (3.3)
Consumer price index	+ 100	− 85	− 14	10.3/0.33 (6.4)	10.5/0.52 (7.5)	− 0.3/ − 0.03 (5.8)
S&P 500 stock price index	+ 100	+ 14	+ 57	29.4/0.83 (12.1)	− 1.1/0.03 (16.5)	30.5/0.53 (26.0)
Unemployment rate[c]	− 100	− 100	− 100	− 1.9/ − 0.05 (0.87)	2.6/0.16 (0.62)	− 4.5/ − 0.09 (0.99)
Employment rate[c]	+ 100	+ 100	+ 100	1.5/0.05 (0.85)	− 1.3/ − 0.10 (0.51)	2.8/0.11 (1.06)
Real balances	+ 69	+ 23	+ 38	7.7/0.11 (7.7)	− 3.2/ − 0.13 (5.0)	10.9/0.14 (12.7)

[a]See footnote a to table 3a.

[b]See footnote b to table 3a.

[c]These amplitude measures are stated in original units rather than cycle relatives. For example, the yield spread, ex post real rates, and inflation rates are all stated in percent per annum. The unemployment rate and employment rate are stated in percentage points and the inventories measure is expressed in real per capita dollars.

actually conforms negatively during contractions, and thus displays little overall cyclical conformity.

Also summarized in table 3a are measures of each series' amplitude over the business cycle. As indicated previously, the phase amplitudes are measured (with exceptions discussed below) in the differences between cycle relatives at peaks and troughs and averaged across cycles. Thus real per capita GNP on average rises 11.9% of the cycle base during expansions and falls 4.5% of the cycle base during contractions. The full cycle amplitude is thus 16.4. The average absolute deviation across the 7 cycles is given in parentheses. Because these measures are in business cycle time, expansions that are very long and very short in calendar time are weighted equally. Thus the 11.9% is an average across expansions that range from 6 to 99 months. The number to the right of the / expresses the average amplitude in cycle relatives per month. Thus the GNP measure rises on average 0.32% of the cycle base per month during expansions. Looking at the full cycle amplitudes of our key series further highlights the relative volatilities of different series. The amplitude of consumption is approximately one-half that of output and investment's amplitude is about one and three-quarters that of output. Both hours and the real wage display less volatility than output. The inflation rate, which is very volatile in percentage terms, shows substantial variation across cycle as indicated by the large average absolute deviations.

In order to provide a somewhat broader perspective on post-war U.S. business cycles, we have constructed business cycle plots for several additional series focusing particularly several financial variables. These plots are presented in figs. 4a–4f and summary statistics for these variables are included in table 3b along with several additional series. All of the plotted series are monthly using the same scale (except figs. 4e and 4d), albeit a slightly different scale from the quarterly series in fig. 2.

The business cycle features of the yield on 3-month treasury bills are displayed in fig. 4a. It is a very pro-cyclical series displaying very large percentage changes (movements in cycle relatives). Note also the large average absolute deviations indicate variations in cyclical behavior. The peak in this short-term interest appears to occur after the peak in the reference cycle. Long-term rates as measured by the yield on AAA corporate bonds display much less conformity with the business as well as much less amplitude.

We have also constructed a measure of the ex post real rate of interest on the 3-month treasury bill and its business cycle characteristics are displayed in fig. 4c. Note that the scale is no longer plotted in cycle relatives, but in units of the series itself. The reason for this is that this series exhibits numerous negative and zero values that make it unsuitable for converting to cycle relatives. As can be seen in the plot and in the table, ex post real rates display little reliable conformity with the cycle. The conformity measures suggest that it is more frequently counter-cyclical than not, but the wide variety of cyclical behavior indicated by the large average absolute deviations makes such a conclusion very

422   *R.G. King and C.I. Plosser, Variant of the Adelmans' test*

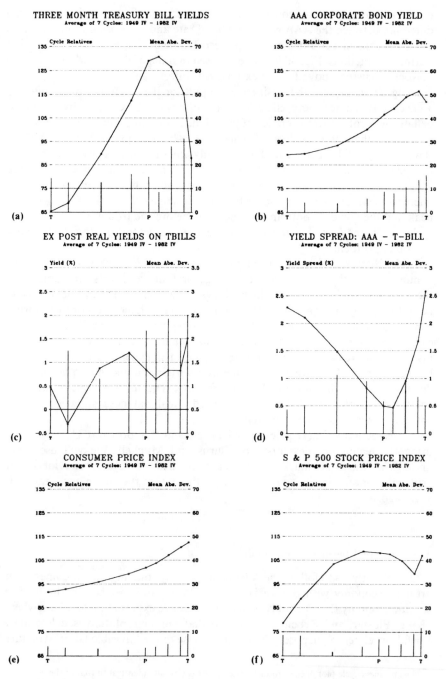

Fig. 4. Business cycle plots for additional serious focusing several financial variables.

dubious. We have also constructed a measure of the yield spread as the difference between the AAA corporate bond rate and the treasury bill rate. This series has a distinct counter-cyclical pattern, falling during expansions and rising during contractions. Fig. 4d is also expressed in units of the spread for the same reasons discussed above for the ex post real rate.

In fig. 4e we present the business cycle plot for the consumer price index as a check on whether the cyclical behavior of prices as exhibited by the GNP deflator was robust to the choice of price index. As is apparent from the plot, it is. In fact, there is even less evidence of pro-cyclical prices here than there is with the GNP deflator.[6] Fig. 4f graphically presents the business cycle characteristic of the stock prices. Two things are worth noting. First, stock prices are roughly pro-cyclical. Second, their timing, however, differs somewhat from the reference cycle. Stock prices appear to peak one stage prior to the reference cycle peak and they tend to bottom out one stage before the trough in the reference cycle. Thus they exhibit the sorts of leading indicator qualities frequently attributed to them.

Table 3b summarizes the behavior of the series in figs. 4a–4f along with a number of other series that are of general interest. First in table 3a is the quarterly inflation rate which shows little conformity in the post-war period – rising in as many contractions as it falls, hence conformity during contractions is zero. Other quarterly series reported in table 3b include per capita consumption of durables which has phase amplitudes that resemble investment more than consumption and government expenditures which exhibit little conformity. Inventories are expressed in original units and, to no surprise, display large amplitudes and high conformity. The unemployment rate and employment rate also behave as expected. Real balances show only mild conformity with the reference cycle.

In this section we have investigated 19 series for the post-war U.S. economy using the techniques developed by Burns and Mitchell. We will use these findings as the benchmarks to compare the business cycle behavior of an artificial economy in the spirit of the investigation of the Adelmans' nearly 30 years ago.

3. A basic real business cycle model

Our objective is to follow the Adelmans' path by studying the outcomes of an artificial economy with our variant of the Burns and Mitchell methods. The specific economy that we study is one that we have explored in detail elsewhere [King, Plosser, and Rebelo (1988a)], so that our presentation is deliberately brief. For reference purposes, the model is close to the 'divisible labor' structure

---

[6]The business cycle plot of the producer price index is virtually identical to that of the consumer price index.

of Hansen (1985) or that exposited by Prescott (1986) or Plosser (1989), differing only slightly in the selection of parameter values. In contrast to these other investigations, however, the specification studied here includes trend growth.

3.1. The basic neoclassical model

The preference, technology, and resource constraints – the deep structure of the model economy – are specified as follows:

Preferences: The representative agent values sequences of consumption (C_t) and leisure (L_t) according to

$$\sum_{t=0}^{\infty} \beta^t u(C_t, L_t),$$

where for simplicity we work with the momentary utility function $u(C_t, L_t) = \log(C_t) + \theta \log(L_t)$.

Technology: The production and accumulation technologies are

$$Y_t = A_t F(K_t, N_t X_t) \quad \text{and} \quad K_{t+1} = (1 - \delta)K_t + I_t,$$

where Y_t is output, N_t is labor output, K_t is capital, and I_t is investment. The function F is a constant returns-to-scale production function, chosen to be Cobb–Douglas, $F(K_t, N_t X_t) = [K_t^{1-\alpha}(N_t X_t)^{\alpha}]$, with $0 < \alpha < 1$. A trend in the series is induced by X_t, which is a labor-augmenting technological shift that satisfies $X_{t+1}/X_t = \gamma_x$. Fluctuations are induced by A_t, which is a stationary total factor productivity shift that satisfies $\log(A_t/\underline{A}) = \rho\log(A_t/\underline{A}) + \varepsilon_{At}$ with $\underline{A} > 0$, $\rho > 0$, $E(\varepsilon_{At}) = 0$, and $E(\varepsilon_{At})^2 = \sigma_\varepsilon^2$.

Resource constraints: The resource constraints for goods and leisure are

$$C_t + I_t = Y_t \quad \text{and} \quad N_t + L_t = 1.$$

Values for technology and preference parameters are given in table 4.

3.2. Approximate dynamics

The equilibrium quantities for consumption, investment, output, and capital along with real wages will fluctuate stochastically around a common deterministic trend induced by X_t. On the other hand, hours are stationary random

Table 4

Economic parameter values.

Depreciation rate	$\delta = 0.025$
Labor's share	$\alpha = 0.58$
Growth rate	$\gamma_x = 1.004$
Discount factor	$\beta = 1/(1 + 0.016) = 0.988$
Steady state fraction of time spent working	$N = 0.20$
Standard deviation of technological shifts	$\sigma_\varepsilon = 0.0075$
Persistence parameter	$\rho = 0.95$

variables in this stochastic steady state. Approximating this system,[7] we can develop a state space system for the logarithms of variables so that each variable can be written in the form $\log(Y_t) = \log(Y) + \log(X_t) + \hat{y}_t$, where $\hat{y}_t$ is interpretable as the deviation from trend. The state space system which then describes the vector $z_t = [\hat{y}_t \, \hat{c}_t \, \hat{N}_t \, \hat{i}_t \, \hat{w}_t]'$ is

$$z_t = \Pi s_t$$

with state evolution

$$s_{t+1} = M s_t + \varepsilon_{t+1}, \qquad M = \begin{bmatrix} \mu_1 & \pi_{kA} \\ 0 & \rho \end{bmatrix},$$

where $\hat{w}_t$ is deviations from trend of the log of the real wage rate, $s_t = [\hat{k}_t \, \hat{A}_t]'$ and $\varepsilon_{t+1} = [0 \, \varepsilon_{A,t+1}]$. Coefficients in the matrices Π and M – implied by the parameters in table 4 – are given in table 5. Stability of transitional dynamics ($\mu_1 < 1$) is assured by diminishing returns to capital (holding fixed labor input). Thus, s_t is stationary so long as A_t is stationary ($\rho < 1$).

It is relatively easy to compute the population moments of the economic variables, z_t and s_t, by the 2-step procedure common in state space systems. First, one computes the moments of the states and then one exploits the simple relations that are readily shown to exist for moments of the z variables. For example, if $V = E(s_t s_t')$ is the variance–covariance matrix of the states, then

---

[7]Our approximation method involves log-linear approximation in a way made precise in the technical appendix to King, Plosser, and Rebelo (1988a,b). The method is closely related to that of Christiano (1988), but there are slight differences in the strategies used to solve the log-linear system, which should be of minor importance in the current context (since no distortions are present). Either approach is capable of exactly replicating the closed form solution of Long and Plosser (1983).

Table 5

Parameters of the log-linear system.

	State variable	
	Capital	Technology shock
Consumption	$\pi_{ck} = 0.617$	$\pi_{cA} = 0.298$
Labor input	$\pi_{Nk} = -0.294$	$\pi_{NA} = 1.048$
Investment	$\pi_{ik} = -0.629$	$\pi_{iA} = 4.733$
Output	$\pi_{yk} = 0.249$	$\pi_{yA} = 1.608$
Real wage	$\pi_{wk} = 0.544$	$\pi_{wA} = 0.560$
Capital stock (next period)	$\mu_1 = 0.953$	$\pi_{kA} = 0.137$

$E(z_t z_t') = \Pi V \Pi'$ is the covariance matrix of the z variables. Results reported in table 6 involve application of these ideas in a straightforward manner. Constructed in the manner detailed in King, Plosser, and Rebelo (1988a), this table provides population moments for the baseline neo-classical model when a common deterministic trend is extracted from its trending series. Key pieces of information from this table are as follows: investment is almost twice as volatile as output, consumption and the real wage are about three fourths as volatile, and labor input is about one third as volatile. Generally, all series have high contemporaneous correlations with output, with consumption (0.91) and labor input (0.70) less strongly correlated than investment (0.92) and the real wage (0.95).

3.3. Simulating the system

To simulate the system, we assume that the innovations to technology are drawn from a normal distribution with zero mean and standard deviation $\sigma_\varepsilon = 0.0075$, which is taken from Prescott (1986). The autoregressive parameter governing technology is $\rho = 0.95$. As discussed above, this implies a variance–covariance matrix of the stationary distribution for the state vector. We assume that s_0 – the initial value of the state vector – is a random draw from its stationary distribution. Then, we draw a sequence of normal random variables for 160 quarters – the length of the post-war time period investigated in the preceding section – as innovations to the state vector. The results of one such simulation are given in figs. 5a–5e, which are comparable to the first set of plots explored in the prior section. We have indicated on these plots periods of recession which are determined by the turning point selected process of Bry and Boschan summarized in table 1 applied to the output measure of the simulated

Table 6

Population moments: Baseline model.

$\rho = 0.95$, $\sigma(\hat{A}) = 2.40$

Variable	Std. dev.	Std. dev. relative to $\hat{y}$	Autocorrelations			Cross-correlations with $\hat{y}_{t-j}$										
			1	2	3	12	8	4	2	1	0	-1	-2	-4	-8	-12
$\hat{y}$	4.45	1.0	0.97	0.93	0.87	0.66	0.76	0.87	0.93	0.97	1.0	0.97	0.93	0.87	0.76	0.66
$\hat{c}$	3.38	0.76	0.99	0.98	0.98	0.87	0.91	0.92	0.92	0.91	0.91	0.87	0.84	0.79	0.68	0.58
$\hat{\imath}$	8.49	1.91	0.93	0.86	0.80	0.34	0.48	0.67	0.78	0.84	0.92	0.89	0.86	0.80	0.70	0.61
$\hat{N}$	1.60	0.36	0.90	0.82	0.74	-0.01	0.15	0.38	0.52	0.61	0.70	0.67	0.65	0.61	0.54	0.46
$\hat{w}$	3.53	0.79	0.99	0.98	0.97	0.83	0.89	0.93	0.94	0.94	0.95	0.91	0.88	0.82	0.71	0.61

428   *R.G. King and C.I. Plosser, Variant of the Adelmans' test*

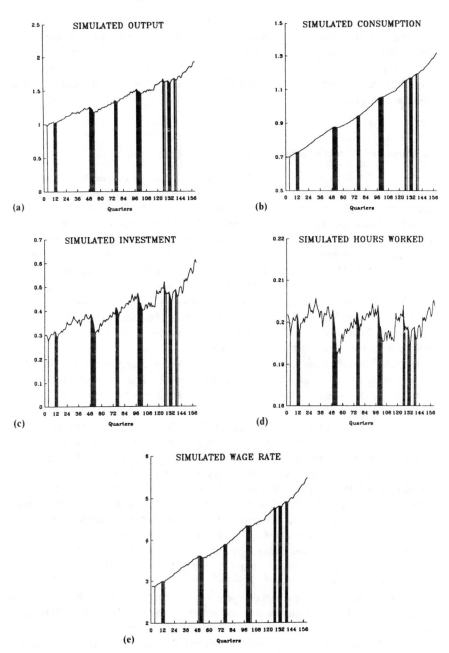

Fig. 5. Simulated economy for 160 quarters.

economy. The notable characteristics of this simulation include many that we saw for the post-war United States: (i) the tendency for business cycle expansions to be longer and visually more gradual than business cycle contractions, (ii) the sharp movements in investment during contraction episodes, (iv) the tendency for consumption to flatten out rather than to decline during contractions, etc.

4. Burns and Mitchell measures for simulated economies

Figs. 5a–5e show one realization of a 40-year history of quarterly data from a simple real business cycle model. The simulated series correspond to per capita measures of output, consumption, and investment along with a measure of hours worked and the real wage rate. While interesting, it does not convey detailed information about the nature of business cycle behavior that is capable of being generated by the model. To study the business cycle characteristics of the model more thoroughly we randomly generate 100 of these 40-year histories and investigate the distribution of the key business cycle measures of Burns and Mitchell. This exercise makes it possible for us to ask in a more precise way what would Burns and Mitchell likely have found using their methods if the economic data arose from a simple real business cycle model. This is, in fact, the same question that was posed by the Adelmans.

Prior to 1990 there have been 7 complete business cycles in the U.S. independent of whether one begins with the peak in 1948.IV and ends with the peak in 1981.III (peak-to-peak cycles) or begins with the trough in 1949.IV and ends with the trough in 1982.IV (trough-to-trough cycles). As a matter of convention, we will arbitrarily focus on the cycles defined from trough to trough (T-P-T cycles). These seven T-P-T cycles averaged just over 56 months. The first question we ask of our model is how many business cycles would a researcher find in a 40-year period of our simulated economy if he was armed with the techniques of Burns and Mitchell, as adapted by Bry and Boschan. Fig. 6 presents the frequency distribution of the number of complete T-P-T cycles found in our 100 simulated histories. The mean number of cycles found is 7.49 with a standard deviation of 1.63; the modal number of occurrences is 8. Of the simulations 45% exhibited either 7 or 8 cycles and 64% experience between 6, 7, and 8 cycles. The maximum number of cycles identified in any 40-year history is 12 and the minimum is 4.

The distribution of the average cycle duration for the 100 histories is presented in fig. 7. The mean average cycle length in the simulations in 56 months, almost identical to the U.S. post-war experience. The standard deviation is 12.78 months. As expected this distribution is skewed somewhat to the right because of the restrictions on duration imposed by Burns and Mitchell. The minimum average duration is 36 months and the maximum is 116 months.

T–P–T CYCLES IN 40 YEAR SAMPLE
Mean=7.49 Standard Deviation=1.63

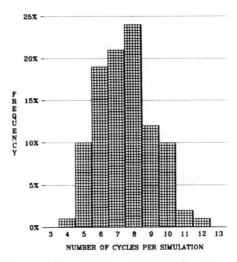

Fig. 6. Frequency distribution of the number of complete T-P-T cycles.

DURATION OF CYCLES (T–P–T)
Mean=56.08 Standard Deviation=12.78

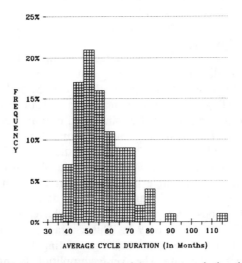

Fig. 7. Frequency distribution of the average cycle duration.

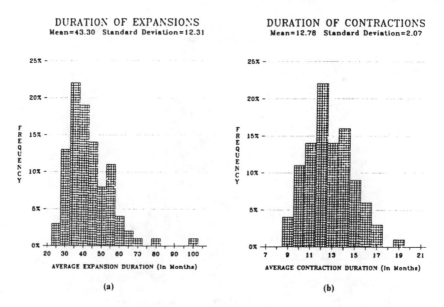

Fig. 8. Frequency distribution of expansion and contraction durations.

Figs. 8a and 8b break down the business cycle duration into the duration of the expansion and contraction phases. The duration of the average cycle expansion is 43.3 months with a standard deviation of 12.3 months. This corresponds to a value of 40 months for the post-war U.S. economy. The duration of the average cycle contraction is 12.78 months with a standard deviation of 2.07 months. This mean is close to the average post-war contraction of 11.4 months.

We have also computed the measures of amplitude for the different simulated series. Fig. 9a displays the frequency distribution of average output amplitudes for the 100 histories. The mean amplitude is 13.51 and the standard deviation is 2.44. This finding compares to a mean amplitude of 16.4 for per capita real GNP over the post-war period. Thus simulated output is slightly less variable than actual output. The mean consumption amplitude is 5.82 (fig. 9b) and the mean investment amplitude is 31.72 (fig. 9c). In the U.S. data these numbers compare to 8.0 and 27.1, respectively. This model yields slightly less variable consumption and slightly more variable investment, but the relative variability for these aggregates is identical to that found in the data.

In the U.S. post-war period real wages have larger amplitude than hours worked (6.3 compared to 9.2). This characteristic also carries over to the simulated data, but with the model generating a little less variability in hours than appears in the data. The average amplitude for hours is 6.09 compared to

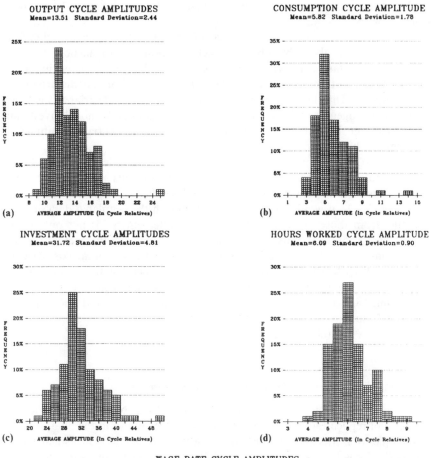

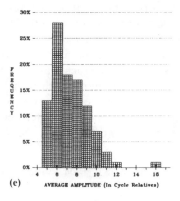

Fig. 9. Frequency distribution of cycle amplitudes.

6.3 for the U.S. data, and the average amplitude for real wages is 7.4 compared to 9.2 for the U.S. data.

It is interesting to recall that the Adelmans were able to generate significant differences in variability by subjecting each equation to a stochastic disturbance. However, the standard deviation of the stochastic disturbance shocking investment was about three times the standard deviation of the disturbance to consumption. Thus in the Adelmans' experiment differential variability is largely generated exogenously. By contrast, the real business cycle model investigated here is driven by only one disturbance. Thus all differential amplitudes are determined by the model.

A visual impression of the business cycle characteristics generated by our simple real business cycle model is provided in figs. 10a–10e. These business cycle plots have the same scale as those for the data. Comparing the pictures with figs. 3a–3e, it would be difficult to distinguish the simulated data's characteristics from those of the actual data. This statement holds not only for the general shape of these plots, but also for the magnitudes of the average absolute deviations as indicated by the height of the bars on the horizontal axis. We could show the distribution of conformity measures produced by the simulated economy, but it would simply show that all of these aggregates exhibit + 100 conformity in virtually all histories. Only consumption and the real wage deviate from this characterization and their average full cycle conformity is + 99 across the 100 histories.

5. Comparing alternative business cycle measurements

The previous section illustrates that a simple real business cycle model is capable of replicating major business cycle features found in the data using the techniques of Burns and Mitchell. In this section we begin an investigation that shifts the focus from evaluating a model as in the Adelmans' study to a more systematic investigation of the Burns and Mitchell procedures themselves and how they relate to more formal statistical procedures.

Table 7 presents a crude comparison between the Burns and Mitchell characterizations as summarized by their measures of amplitude and conformity and common statistical measures such as standard deviation and correlation. The Burns and Mitchell measures are constructed as we have described in previous sections. One feature of their procedures is that they are computed without regard to whether the moments of the series exist or not.[8] This raises some important questions regarding how one might interpret the statistical properties of these measures. Nevertheless, we can compare these measures with statistical

---

[8]Burns and Mitchell consciously made this trade-off because they did not wish to be constrained or mislead about business cycles based on purely statistic issues.

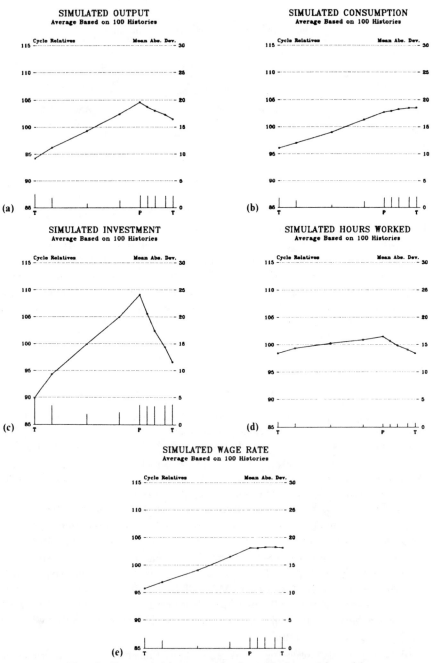

Fig. 10. Characteristics generated by the real business cycle model.

Table 7

Comparison of business cycle summary measures.

	United States	Simulated	United States	Simulated
	\multicolumn{4}{}{(A) *Cyclical variability*}			
Series	Std. deviations[a]		Amplitude[b]	
Output	5.62	4.45	16.4	13.5
Consumption	3.86	3.38	8.0	5.8
Investment	7.61	8.49	27.1	31.7
Hours worked	2.97	1.60	6.3	6.1
Real wage	6.49	3.53	9.2	7.4
	\multicolumn{4}{}{(B) *Cyclical conformity*}			
Series	Correlations with output[a]		Conformity[b]	
Output	1.00	1.00	+ 100	+ 100
Consumption	0.85	0.82	+ 71	+ 99
Investment	0.60	0.92	+ 100	+ 100
Hours worked	0.07	0.79	+ 100	+ 100
Real wage	0.76	0.90	+ 71	+ 99

[a] The sample and population measures of standard deviation and correlation with output are computed based on the percent deviations from trend rather than levels. The sample period is 1948 to 1987.

[b] The amplitude and conformity measures are computed using the Burns and Mitchell procedures outlined in section 2.

summary statistics that modern time series techniques might suggest. Measures such as standard deviation and correlation are useful but require some underlying assumptions if they are to be interpretable. For the simulated model, this is a straightforward exercise. The model generates series whose logged values are stationary fluctuations about a linear trend except for hours worked which is stationary. Thus standard deviations and correlations are computed based on these deviations from trend. Using the state space formulation presented in section 3 the population moments can be computed directly. The sample moments for the post-war U.S. data are computed as deviations from a common linear trend (in logs).

In part A of table 7 we report the standard deviations of both the simulated series and the data along with the corresponding amplitude measure constructed using the methods of Burns and Mitchell. One easy way of comparing these measures is to look at how the two procedures rank the variability of the series. As is easily verified, the ranking of the key series is identical whether one uses standard deviation or amplitude.

In part B of this table we make a crude comparison between Burns and Mitchell's measure of conformity and the simple correlation coefficient of each series with output. Here it is apparent that the conformity measure is a cruder metric, which does not necessarily imply a poorer measure. Remember, conformity over the entire cycle may be + 100 even though a series may rise during a contraction (thus negatively correlated with output during that period) as long as the per month rise during the expansion exceeds the per month rise during the contraction. Thus, while correlation and conformity clearly differ with respect to what they measure, it is unclear which method dominates the other. The answer clearly depends on the question at hand.

The correlation of hours worked with output in the post-war period (0.07) differs from what most macroeconomists take to be the 'fact' (see the conformity measure) that hours is a strongly procyclical series. This observation is discussed in King, Plosser, and Rebelo (1988a) and appears to be associated with the phenomenon that there are slow-moving components to either output or hours that interact in ways to alter the correlation. For example, while the overall correlation is 0.07, dividing the sample in 5-year subperiods produces correlation between 0.3 and 0.9 and averages almost 0.8. By looking at subperiods we effectively permit the means of the two series to vary from one period to the next. This sensitivity of the correlation raises some important questions involving appropriate methods of detrending and/or inducing stationarity in order to compute meaningful sample moments.[9]

6. Summary and future plans

In this paper we have attempted to follow the path laid out by the Adelmans. Using the methods laid out by Burns and Mitchell, we see if we can distinguish between the economic series generated by an actual economy and those analogous artificial series generated by a stochastically perturbed economic model. In the case of the Adelmans, the model corresponded to the Klein–Goldberger equations. In our case, the model corresponds to a simple real business cycle model. The results indicate a fairly high degree of coincidence in key economic aggregates between the business cycles characteristics identified in actual data and those found in our simulated economy.

This, it seems to us, is a necessary hurdle that any business cycle model must clear. It is a particularly important hurdle given the importance of the Burns and Mitchell stylized facts and their influence on macroeconomists' thinking about business cycles. Nevertheless, our findings leave us uncomfortable. While no one has claimed that the Adelmans' test or the one we have conducted here represent particularly powerful tests of a model, it is somewhat troubling to us that two models as different as the Klein–Goldberger model and a neoclassical real business cycle model are both able to pass this 'test'.

[9]For example, see Nelson and Plosser (1982) and King and Rebelo (1993).

There would appear to be two approaches to resolving this tension. First, it might well be the case that the findings of Burns and Mitchell are important stylized facts and that the implementation of the comparisons using their method have simply not been complete or thorough enough to help us distinguish among competing hypotheses. The second possibility is that the methods of Burns and Mitchell leads us to finding certain types of phenomenon regardless of the underlying model generating the data. If this latter possibility is the case, then macroeconomists must face the possibility that tests of the sort we conduct here are not only not powerful, but much of what we think we know about economic fluctuations as organized by Burns and Mitchell may be an artifact of their procedures. It would therefore seem critical to obtain a better understanding of the link between their methods and their stylized facts.

References

Adelman, Irma and Frank Adelman, 1959, The dynamic properties of the Klein–Goldberger model, Econometrica 4, 596–625.

Bry, Gerhard and Charlotte Boschan, 1971, Cyclical analysis of time series: Selected procedures and computer programs (NBER, New York, NY).

Burns, Arthur and Wesley C. Mitchell, 1946, Measuring business cycles (NBER, New York, NY).

Christiano, Lawrence J., 1988, Why does inventory investment fluctuate so much?, Journal of Monetary Economics 21, 247–280.

Hansen, Gary, 1985, Indivisible labor and the business cycle, Journal of Monetary Economics 16, 309–327.

Hickman, Bert, 1972, Econometric models of cyclical behavior (NBER, New York, NY).

King, Robert, Charles Plosser, and Sergio Rebelo, 1988a, Production, growth, and business cycles: I. The basic neoclassical model, Journal of Monetary Economics 21, 195–232.

King, Robert, Charles Plosser, and Sergio Rebelo, 1988b, Production, growth, and business cycles: II. New directions, Journal of Monetary Economics 21, 309–342.

King, Robert, Charles Plosser, James Stock, and Mark Watson, 1991, Stochastic trends and economic fluctuations, American Economic Review 81, 819–840.

King, Robert and Sergio Rebelo, 1993, Low frequency filtering and real business cycles, Journal of Economic Dynamics and Control 17, 207–231.

Klein, Lawrence and Arthur Goldberger, 1959, An econometric model of the United States, 1929–1952 (North-Holland, Amsterdam).

Koopmans, Tjalling, 1947, Measurement without theory, Review of Economics and Statistics 29, 161–172.

Kydland, Finn and Edward Prescott, 1982, Time to build and aggregate fluctuations, Econometrica 50, 1345–1370.

Litterman, Robert, Danny Quah, and Thomas Sargent, 1984, Business cycle analysis with unobservable index models and the methods of the NBER, Unpublished working paper.

Long, John and Charles Plosser, 1983, Real business cycles, Journal of Political Economy 91, 1345–1370.

Lucas, Robert E., Jr., 1977, Understanding business cycles, in: Karl Brunner and Allan H. Meltzer, eds., Stabilization of the domestic and international economy, Vol. 5 of the Carnegie–Rochester conference series on public policy (North-Holland, Amsterdam) 7–29.

Mitchell, Wesley C., 1927, Business cycles: The problem and its setting (NBER, New York, NY).

Mitchell, Wesley, C., 1951, What happens during business cycles? (NBER, New York, NY).

Nelson, Charles and Charles Plosser, 1982, Trends and random walks in macroeconomic time series, Journal of Monetary Economics 10, 139–167.

Plosser, Charles, 1989, Understanding real business cycles, Journal of Economic Perspectives 3:3, 51–77.

Prescott, Edward, 1986, Theory ahead of business cycle measurement, Carnegie–Rochester Conference Series on Public Policy 25, 11–66.

Simkins, Scott, 1988, Interpreting economic time series using the methods of Burns and Mitchell, Ph.D. thesis (University of Iowa, Iowa City, IA).

Simkins, Scott, 1994, Do real business cycles really exhibit business cycle behavior?, Journal of Monetary Economics, this issue.

JAMES HARTLEY

Mount Holyoke College
South Hadley, Massachusetts

KEVIN SALYER
STEVEN SHEFFRIN

University of California, Davis
Davis, California

Calibration and Real Business Cycle Models: An Unorthodox Experiment*

This paper examines the calibration methodology used in real business cycle (RBC) theory. We confront the calibrator with data from artificial economies (various Keynesian macroeconomic models) and examine whether a prototypical real business cycle model, when calibrated to these data sets using standard methods, can match a selected set of sample moments. We find that the calibration methodology does constitute a discriminating test in that the calibrated real business cycle models cannot match the moments from *all* the artificial economies we study. In particular, we find the RBC model can only match the moments of economies whose moments are close to actual U.S. data.

1. Introduction

Nearly a decade ago, Kydland and Prescott (1982) demonstrated that a simple optimal growth model subject to persistent technological shocks would exhibit characteristics that were similar in important respects to actual macroeconomic data. It is hard to exaggerate the practical importance of their finding. Not only did it begin an influential literature on business cycles (i.e., real business cycles) but it transformed the practice of other economists, both theoretical and applied, as well. It has become quite common now for many macroeconomists to begin with the real business cycle model as a basic framework and then use embellishments to highlight additional features of the data.

Critics of real business cycle models, however, have been uneasy about the empirical methodology used in support of the model. Specifically, these

*We are indebted to Ray Fair, Kevin Hoover, Stephen LeRoy, James Nason, Linda Tesar and Randy Wright for insightful comments and suggestions.

Journal of Macroeconomics, Winter 1997, Vol. 19, No. 1, pp. 1–17

1

James Hartley, Kevin Salyer and Steven Sheffrin

criticisms have focused on the calibration methods used in RBC analysis. The defining characteristics of the calibration approach are: (i) the parameters of a model are not estimated but instead determined by long-run (i.e., steady-state) behavior of the economy and (ii) given these parameters, the characteristics of the model's unconditional equilibrium distribution for the endogenous variables are compared to that of the data. This comparison typically involves a limited set of second moments. Recently, due to this criticism, several alternative real business cycles have been estimated rather than calibrated.[1] Kydland and Prescott (1991), in response to this criticism, strongly defend calibration as a scientific method. In addition, Hoover (1995) also finds some virtues in this approach on philosophical and methodological grounds.

Proponents of estimation point to the possibility of testing overidentifying restrictions as a virtue of this method. But Kydland and Prescott have emphasized the importance of accounting for pervasive measurement error in economic data. Once one allows for measurement errors, testable overidentifying restrictions can easily disappear. Moreover, a decade of experience of estimating macro models with complex, cross-equation restrictions has not been comforting. Models often fail these restrictions. When they do not fail these restrictions, it is often because the fit of the model was so poor to begin with that the restrictions do not matter.

Watson (1993) and Canova, Finn, and Pagan (1994) have advocated alternative strategies for evaluating real business cycle models. Watson estimates the variance of measurement errors (at different frequencies) which are necessary to reconcile the models with the data. Canova, Finn, and Pagan examine whether the time series properties of the data (for example, the number of co-integrating vectors) match those implied by the model. Both approaches provide useful diagnostics and are important contributions to evaluating specific calibrated models.

However, we are still left with a basic question. Is it just an accident that calibrated real business cycle models seem to resemble actual economies in important respects or is there something truly fundamental underlying this correspondence? This paper tries to address this question with an unorthodox experiment using economic models.

We begin by demonstrating that a typical Keynesian model, for which we chose the Fairmodel (developed by Ray Fair), will generate sample moments similar to both U.S. data and a real business cycle model calibrated to U.S. data. Furthermore, if real business cycle practitioners were confronted with artificial data generated from the Fairmodel, they would choose parameters similar to those that are chosen to match U.S. data.

---

[1] See Altug (1989) and Christiano and Eichenbaum (1992) as examples.

We then use a version of the Fairmodel modified to generate different aggregate time series. From these time series, we calibrate real business cycle models using such data as factor shares and the calculated Solow residuals. We then ask if the calibrated real business cycle moments match the moments of the modified Keynesian model. This experiment addresses the question of whether real business cycle models can be successfully calibrated to mimic any model.

Our basic finding is that the RBC model and the calibration methodology does indeed limit the range of data characteristics which can be generated within the model. Specifically, the intertemporal optimization framework inherent in all RBC models sharply constrains the relative volatilities and correlations among investment, consumption, and output. Moreover, this behavior, as noted by RBC practitioners, is similar to that observed in U.S. data. This result, while comforting to those studying U.S. macroeconomic conditions, may prove problematic if RBC models are confronted with data from other countries. To elaborate on this point, recent research by Backus and Kehoe (1992) has highlighted the variety of correlation properties exhibited in aggregate time-series across countries as well as sample periods. Our results suggest that conventional RBC models cannot easily match the broad range of data characteristics reported in their study.

The next section describes our simulations with the Fairmodel and reports the estimated sample moments for selected variables. The following section uses the simulated data from two versions of the artificial economy to calibrate real business cycle models and determine if they can match the moments of artificial economies. Throughout our discussion we highlight the critical nature that commonly employed assumptions have in determining the goodness of fit of these models.

2. Moments of a Keynesian Macro Model

In this section, we first demonstrate that a typical Keynesian macro model will generate sample moments similar to those observed in U.S. data. In the following section, we use simulations from this Keynesian model to generate artificial time series to be used in calibration exercises.

We chose the Fairmodel for our simulations.[2] The Fairmodel consists of 128 equations of which 98 are identities. There are 128 endogenous and over 100 exogenous variables. The 30 behavioral equations were individually estimated by two-stage least squares, with the data series starting in the first quarter of 1954. The model is explicitly Keynesian in design; for example, disequilibrium possibilities are built into the model via a labor constraint

---

[2]For a detailed description, see Fair (1990) and Fair (1994).

James Hartley, Kevin Salyer and Steven Sheffrin

TABLE 1.   *Autocorrelation of Output: Actual and Artificial Economies*

	Leads and Lags			
	±1	±2	±3	±4
U.S.[1]	0.84	0.57	0.27	−0.01
FM (reaction function)	0.89	0.65	0.39	0.15
FM (M1 exog.)	0.92	0.75	0.54	0.34
King Plosser, Rebelo[2]	0.93	0.86	0.80	0.74

NOTES: [1]From Kydland and Prescott (1982), Table II, p. 1364.
[2]From King, Plosser, and Rebelo (1988), Table 5, p. 224.

variable. In short, the Fairmodel bears little resemblance to a typical real business cycle model.

To generate artificial data, the Fairmodel was used to produce forecasts over the period 1968:*i* to 1977:*iv* under two assumptions regarding monetary policy. One set of data was produced under the assumption that the monetary aggregate, M1, is exogenous and equal to the historical data. Another was constructed using the Fairmodel's interest rate reaction function. Given these exogenous time series, the Fairmodel generated time series for the remaining endogenous variables through dynamic simulation. Of the 128 endogenous variables in the model, we restrict our attention to the critical set of output, consumption, investment, and labor input. Specifically, the logarithms of per capita GNP (y), consumption (c), investment (i), and hours worked (n) generated by the model were regressed on a constant and a time trend.[3] The residuals from these regressions, which can be interpreted as the percentage deviations from trend, are the series we examine.

We first determine whether the model generates the correct autocorrelations in output. Table 1 contains these values. While the fit appears to be quite close, as noted earlier, there is no standard metric to gauge the degree of fit. Hence, for comparison, the output from a real business cycle model studied by King, Plosser, and Rebelo (1988) is also reported. Under both assumptions about monetary policy, the Fairmodel output is less autocorrelated than the data from the real business cycle model and matches quite well the pattern observed in the actual data.

Table 2 compares the cyclical volatility of the Fairmodel series to the

[3]If the growth model with constant, exogenous technological growth is taken seriously, then output, consumption, and investment should be detrended using a common trend. However, since we are examining only ten years of data, this restriction is too severe. Also, even though per-capita labor in the growth model does not have a trend in steady state, we nonetheless linearly detrended this series as well.

Calibration and Real Business Cycle Models

TABLE 2.   *Descriptive Statistics for U.S. Economy and Artificial Economies*

	σ_y	σ_c/σ_y	σ_i/σ_y	σ_h/σ_y	$Corr(y, c)$	$Corr(y, i)$	$Corr(y, h)$
U.S. Data[1]	0.017	0.49	3.02	0.96	0.76	0.80	0.88
Fairmodel (reaction function)	0.012	0.40	2.16	0.70	0.35	0.89	0.80
Fairmodel (M1 exogenous)	0.020	0.65	3.60	0.80	0.79	0.93	0.96
Hansen[2]	0.018	0.29	3.24	0.77	0.87	0.99	0.98
Kydland & Prescott[3]	0.018	0.35	3.58	0.58	0.94	0.80	0.93
King, Plosser, Rebelo Model[4]	0.043	0.64	2.31	0.48	0.76	0.85	0.73

NOTES: [1]From Kydland and Prescott (1990), Tables I and II, p. 10–11.
[2]Hansen (1985) indivisible labor model, see Table 1, p. 321.
[3]Kydland and Prescott (1982) time-to build model, Table III, p. 1364.
[4]Taken from King, Plosser, Rebelo (1988), Table 5, p. 224. Both Hansen and Kydland and Prescott pass model data through the Hodrick-Prescott filter.

data; in addition the contemporaneous correlations of all variables with output are reported for the U.S. and model output. For comparison, the sample moments from three real business cycle models are also given for comparison.[4] None of the models matches perfectly the entire set of sample moments, but the Fairmodel seems to do qualitatively as well as the other models.[5] In particular, output from the model replicates the observed volatilities of consumption, investment, and labor relative to that of output reasonably well.

These results demonstrate that the Fairmodel is able to match a limited set of sample moments at least as well as typical real business cycle models. There may be some question, however, as to whether this is particularly surprising. Since the Fairmodel was estimated using data from the actual economy, the parameter values may incorporate these sample moments into the model's structure.

[4]Because the cited papers used different detrending procedures on the model data, quantitative comparison of the reported sample moments is problematic.

[5]Because the Fairmodel was used to generate data over a relatively small sample period (9 years), the moments reported in Table 2 are somewhat sensitive to the choice of forecast period. For instance, the correlations of consumption, investment and hours with output produced by the reaction function model over the period 60:*i*–69:*iv* are 0.83, 0.90, and 0.90, respectively. Over this period, the same moments under the assumption of exogenous M1 are 0.66, 0.83, and 0.73. However, the relative volatilities, which are the primary focus of the next section, are not as sensitive to the particular forecasting period.

James Hartley, Kevin Salyer and Steven Sheffrin

To be more precise, in some cases, standard econometric methods can be viewed as "matching moments." As Bollen (1989) discusses in detail, latent variable models and models with errors of measurement can most easily be estimated by matching theoretical and sample covariances. For simultaneous equation models, full information maximum likelihood estimation is equivalent to minimizing a function of the sample and theoretical covariances. Methods-of-moments estimators, of course, also are based on "matching" moments.

Fair, however, estimated his model using single-equation methods, typically, 2SLS with corrections for serially correlated errors. This method of estimation does not necessarily lead to close fits between actual and sample moments. Moreover, the moments that the real business cycle literature examines (and we employ in this paper) are based on detrended data. Thus, there is even less reason to expect a close correspondence between actual and simulated sample moments.

The demonstration that the Fairmodel roughly matches U.S. sample moments is useful for our purposes. It means that in our base case both the Fairmodel and a real business cycle model calibrated to U.S. data produce joint distributions for the endogenous variables that have similar second moment characteristics. In the next section, we use the Fairmodel to generate artificial data and then examine the properties of a RBC model calibrated to this data.

3. Calibrating a RBC Model to the Fairmodel Data

The claim that RBC models should be taken seriously as a useful description of the U.S. economy is often supported by the model's ability to duplicate two basic characteristics of U.S. time series: investment is two to three times as volatile as GNP, while consumption exhibits half the volatility of output. The following quote from a recent article by Hansen and Wright (1992) is typical:

> The model predicts that consumption will be less than half as volatile as output, that investment will be about three times as volatile as output, and that consumption, investment, and employment will be strongly positively correlated with output, just as in the postwar U.S. time series. In this sense, the real business cycle approach can be thought of as providing a benchmark for the study of aggregate fluctuations (p. 2).

The conviction that these particular features of RBC models constitute telling evidence of their relevance is reflected in the response of RBC practitioners to the original model's noted failure in describing labor market activity. Specifically, its counterfactual predictions about the correlations between labor supply, productivity, and GNP resulted in modifications to the basic model (e.g., Hansen's 1985 introduction of indivisible labor, the modeling of government-produced output by Christiano and Eichenbaum 1992 and the introduction of a home production sector by Benhabib, Rogerson, and Wright 1991) rather than a refutation of the underlying paradigm.

But how compelling is this evidence? That is, might it be possible that the growth model and calibration methodology are sufficiently malleable to permit duplication of these variance-covariance relations from a broad range of model economies; in particular, economies whose underlying structure is vastly different from that of the growth model? To put the question more bluntly, Are real business cycles the truth or just truly good chameleons? To answer that question, the Fairmodel described in the previous section was used to generate aggregate time series. We conduct the experiment of whether a growth model calibrated to this data can successfully duplicate the volatilities of consumption, investment and output.

Once again, the Fairmodel was used to generate data over the period 68:*i*–77:*iv*. For this exercise it was assumed the money stock, M1, was exogenous and determined by the historical record. This produces the same set of sample moments reported in Table 2; for convenience, these statistics are repeated in Table 3.

With these characteristics noted, a real business cycle model (identical to Hansen's 1985 divisible labor model) was calibrated to the Fairmodel output. Specifically, it was assumed that the time path of the economy was characterized as the solution to the following social planner problem:

$$\max \quad E_0 \left\{ \sum_{t=0}^{\infty} \beta^t [\ln c_t + A \ln (1 - h_t)] \right\} \tag{P}$$

subject to

$$c_t + k_{t+1} \le \lambda_t k_t^\theta h_t^{1-\theta} + k_t(1 - \delta) ; \tag{1}$$

$$\ln \lambda_{t+1} = \gamma \ln \lambda_t + \varepsilon_{t+1} ; \tag{2}$$

where k_t denotes beginning-of-period capital, β is agents' discount factor, θ is capital's share, δ the depreciation rate of capital, and $A > 0$ represents the importance of leisure in utility. The variable $\lambda_t > 0$ denotes the technology shock; its motion is described by the AR(1) process in Equation (2). It is assumed that ε_τ is independently and identically distributed with a standard deviation of σ_ε and a mean such that $E(\lambda_t) = 1$.

7

James Hartley, Kevin Salyer and Steven Sheffrin

As is well known, if depreciation is less than 100% then no analytic solution to problem (P) exists, thus necessitating the use of numerical approximation methods. We employed the approach described in King, Plosser, and Rebelo (1988) which involves taking a first-order Taylor series expansion of the necessary equilibrium conditions around the steady state (i.e., non-stochastic) equilibrium values. The resulting linear expectational difference equations will have a unique solution because of the saddle path properties implied by the typical growth model with constant returns to scale. The solution is represented by a set of functions that express the choice variables at time t (consumption, labor, and investment) in terms of the current state variables (capital and the technology shock). Moreover, the linear structure in the approximated economy implies that the solutions will also be linear. The equilibrium characteristics of the model can then be studied through simulation methods.

In order to solve for the steady state, the parameter values describing tastes (β, A) and technology (θ, δ, λ, γ, σ_s) must be stipulated. In accordance with RBC methodology, these were chosen (i.e., calibrated) so that the implied steady-state behavior of the artificial economy was similar to the long-run characteristics of the Fairmodel data. Specifically, labor's share of GNP averaged 63% in the Fairmodel output implying a value for θ of 0.37. In addition, agents spent roughly 22% of their time in work activity; this implies a value for A of 3. The autocorrelation of $\ln \lambda_t$ and the standard deviation of the residual, σ_s, were determined by studying the time-series properties of the Solow production residual defined as

$$\ln Z_t = \ln y_t - 0.37 \ln k_t - 0.63 \ln h_t .\tag{3}$$

The series $\ln Z_t$ was linearly detrended and $\ln \lambda_t$ was defined as the deviations from trend. Assuming the AR(1) process in Equation (2) for this constructed series produced estimates for γ of 0.91 and σ_s of 0.005. As in virtually all RBC models, the remaining two parameters, β and δ, were assumed to be 0.99 and 0.025, respectively.[6]

With these parameter values, the RBC model was used to generate artificial time series. The sample length was assumed to be 2000 observations in order to minimize spurious behavior of the random technology shock. Since the model implies all series are stationary (and without trend), the artificial data was not detrended. The sample variances and covariances from the artificial economy are reported in Table 3.

---

[6]Together with θ, the parameters β and δ determine the steady-state capital output ratio. The implied ratio is roughly 12 (with GNP measured as a quarterly flow) which is consistent with U.S. data.

8

Calibration and Real Business Cycle Models

TABLE 3.   *Sample Moments from Fairmodel and Calibrated RBC Model*

Variable	Fairmodel			RBC model		
	σ_x	σ_x/σ_y	$\sigma(x, y)$	σ_x	σ_x/σ_y	$\sigma(x, y)$
y	0.020	1.00	1.00	0.022	1.00	1.00
c	0.013	0.65	0.79	0.013	0.59	0.80
i	0.072	3.60	0.93	0.060	2.73	0.93
n	0.016	0.80	0.96	0.011	0.50	0.84

It is clear from Table 3 that the calibrated RBC model duplicates quite closely the behavior of the Fairmodel as reflected in the reported sample moments. In addition to the cross-correlations and volatilities relative to GNP, the RBC model also matches the absolute variances of output and consumption. Based on the success of the calibration exercise it is likely that a RBC theorist, if presented with data from the Fairmodel, would incorrectly conclude that a stochastic growth model accurately describes the structure of the economy. This potential error, however, is not necessarily a criticism of RBC models and the calibration methodology but, instead, should be interpreted as a demonstration of observational equivalence. That is, the previous section showed that the Fairmodel can duplicate the variances and correlations of U.S. aggregate time series; and it is well known that RBC models exhibit this property as well. Hence, this calibration exercise illustrates the *consistency* of these two models. Given this illustration, we are now ready to engage in the primary test of this paper.

4. The Range of the Real Business Cycle Model

The Fairmodel is now modified in order to generate time series with different characteristics (as reflected in the moments reported in Table 3) than that of U.S. data. The calibration methodology is then used to examine whether a standard real business cycle model, calibrated to this new data, can produce similar second moments. While this exercise directly tests the range of second moments that a calibrated RBC model can produce, the test is clearly limited in scope: the RBC model we employ is relatively simple and only one set of parameter changes in the Fairmodel is studied. From this perspective, our analysis is best viewed as is an illustrative inquiry into the calibration approach rather than a thorough test; indeed, the altered parameters were chosen specifically for this purpose.[7] That is, we sought

[7]We examined several different modifications (e.g., changing the parameter which governs

James Hartley, Kevin Salyer and Steven Sheffrin

modifications to the Fairmodel that not only produced the desired variations in model output but also represented a thought experiment familiar to macroeconomists; at the same time, we wished to highlight the discriminating aspects of the calibration methodology.

To generate the new artificial economy, we changed the value of two important coefficients in the Fairmodel. These parameters were chosen in order to exploit the Keynesian monetary transmission mechanism within the economy. This aspect of the model is similar to a textbook IS-LM framework in which the real consequences from a change in the money supply depends critically on the interest rate response induced by the money shock (i.e., the slope of the LM curve) and the corresponding reaction of investment demand (the slope of the IS curve). In light of this structure, we dramatically increased the interest rate elasticity of households' money demand (Equation [9] in the Fairmodel). Specifically, the interest rate coefficient was changed from -0.0033 to -0.09, a roughly 30-fold increase.[8] As a consequence of this change, interest rate fluctuations due to variations in the money supply are greatly reduced. In order to produce fluctuations in investment demand even though interest rates exhibit low volatility, we increased the coefficient on interest rates that enters into the demand for consumer durables (Equation [3]). (The sum of consumer durables, firm investment, and residential housing is defined as investment). Specifically, this coefficient was changed from -0.0037 to -0.1.[9] Within an IS-LM framework, these changes imply a flattening of both the LM and IS curves.

In order to illustrate the impact that these modifications have on equilibrium behavior, some impulse response functions are presented in Figure 1. These are constructed in the following manner: the money stock initially is assumed to follow its historical path over the sample period (68:*iv*–77:*iv*). Under this restriction, the original (denoted FM1) and modified (denoted FM2) Fairmodels are used to generate a forecast for the endogenous vari-

---

the responsiveness of the price level to output changes) but none produced much variation in the moments reported in Table 3. This clearly does not imply that the Fairmodel is insensitive to parameter variation but reflects the limited data characteristics we studied. Our focus on the relative volatilities and contemporaneous correlations of model output is fairly standard in RBC analysis.

[8]A change in the interest rate coefficient requires a corresponding change in the equation's intercept term so that the forecast errors remain centered on zero. If this is not done, the constructed forecast confounds cyclical behavior with a transition path. The intercept term in Equation (9) was changed, therefore, from 0.0767 to 0.48. We thank Ray Fair for bringing this issue to our attention; our ignoring it in an earlier draft resulted in our misinterpreting equilibrium dynamics.

[9]As noted in the previous footnote, the constant term must also be changed so that the forecast errors from the model are centered around zero. The constant in Equation (3) was changed from -0.000315 to 0.61.

Calibration and Real Business Cycle Models

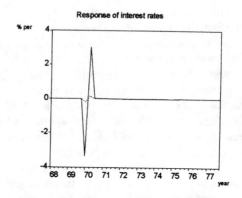

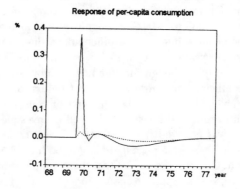

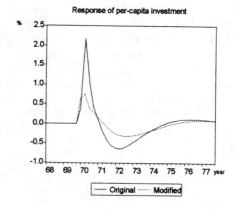

Figure 1.
Impulse Response Functions: Original and High Interest Rate Elasticity Models
(1% Change in M1 in 1970:*i*)

11

James Hartley, Kevin Salyer and Steven Sheffrin

TABLE 4.   *Sample Moments from Modified (High Interest Rate Elasticity) Fairmodel and Calibrated RBC Model*

Variable	Fairmodel			RBC model		
	σ_x	σ_x/σ_y	$\sigma(x, y)$	σ_x	σ_x/σ_y	$\sigma(x, y)$
y	0.019	1.00	1.00	0.022	1.00	1.00
c	0.002	0.11	0.51	0.013	0.59	0.80
i	0.061	3.21	0.87	0.060	2.73	0.93
n	0.018	0.95	0.87	0.011	0.50	0.84

ables. The model is then solved under the assumption that M1 follows the same path except for an increase of 1% in the first quarter of 1970. Taking the difference between the forecasts produces the desired impulse response functions. The three graphs in Figure 1 present these impulse response functions from the two economies for a key interest rate (top panel), consumption (middle panel), and investment (lower panel). The effects of the increased interest rate elasticities are fairly dramatic—in the original economy the money shock results in a significant fall in interest rates while interest rates are almost constant in the modified economy. This difference is reflected in the behavior of consumption (which is affected by interest rate changes through implied capital gains) and investment. The greater interest rate elasticity of investment in the modified economy is illustrated in the third panel. This is reflected in the fact that the investment response due to a money shock is much greater than the interest rate effect. The left-hand columns of Table 4 present the now familiar set of sample moments that are generated from solving the modified Fairmodel. And it is clear from the numbers that consumption in the new economy is extremely stable; this is reflected in the fact that the standard deviation of consumption is only 11% as large as GNP volatility.

In order for the output from a calibrated RBC model to produce relative volatilities like that observed in the modified Fairmodel, the calibration exercise must generate different parameter values for the RBC model. However, while the greater interest rate elasticities in the modified economy result in different equilibrium dynamics, they do not affect the type of equilibrium behavior measured by the RBC parameters. In particular, labor's share in the modified economy is still roughly 63% (implying a constant value for θ of 0.37) and the fraction of time spent in work activity is still about 21% so that the parameter A is unchanged. By assumption (β, δ) are constant so the only parameters remaining are those describing the stochastic process for the shock. But again, constructing the Solow residual and analyzing the

TABLE 5.   *Postwar Volatilities of Consumption and Investment and Correlations with Output*

Country	(σ_c/σ_y)	(σ_i/σ_y)	$\sigma(c, y)$	$\sigma(i, y)$
Japan	1.25	2.01	0.65	0.61
Norway	2.90	5.50	0.76	0.42
Sweden	1.17	2.10	0.52	0.55
U.S.	0.65	2.60	0.82	0.88

serial correlation properties of the detrended series shows that the autocorrelation parameter is virtually unchanged ($\gamma = 0.92$ in the modified economy rather than the original value of 0.91). As a consequence, the relative volatilities from a RBC model calibrated to the high interest rate elastic Fair-model output would not mimic that economy but instead generate sample moments virtually identical to the original calibrated model. For this reason, the moments reported in Table 4 for the RBC model are the same as those in Table 3.[10]

This exercise demonstrates that the calibration methodology places important restrictions on the parameter choices for an RBC model; moreover these restrictions imply a limited set of equilibrium characteristics which can be duplicated by the calibrated model. A substantial body of research has established consistency between the time series characteristics of the U.S. economy and the RBC approach. It remains to be seen, however, whether the broad range of volatilities and correlations seen in international data can be produced within this framework. This diversity was reported by Backus and Kehoe (1992); some of their statistics are reproduced below in Table 5 (taken from their Table 3, p. 875).

The low volatility of consumption and highly procyclical nature of consumption and investment in the U.S. are clearly not seen in the other countries. Since, as noted above, these features are precisely those which are generated within the RBC framework, its ability to match international data is suspect. That is, the properties of the model are determined entirely by

---

[10]It is important to note that the method of choosing the parameter values (the calibration of the model) that we employ is standard; most real business cycle theorists presented with our data would choose roughly the same values. This consistency is ensured by the requirement that the computed steady state of the model replicates the sample averages of key economic variables; i.e., the steady state of the model mimics the long-run features of the data. For the model studied here, the sample averages of labor's share of output, the return on capital, the fraction of time spent working, and the capital-output ratio uniquely determine the preference parameters (β, A) and the technology parameters (δ, θ).

James Hartley, Kevin Salyer and Steven Sheffrin

the values of the parameters describing tastes (β, A) and technology (θ, δ, γ, σ_ε). Internationally, the time spent working (which determines A) and capital's share (θ), while different, do not vary dramatically. It is also difficult to justify wide ranges in the rate of depreciation of capital (δ). Hence, the values for the remaining parameters, i.e., those which describe the autocorrelation (γ) and volatility (σ_ε) of the technology shock are critical in differentiating the equilibrium characteristics across nations. With respect to the relative volatilities of consumption, investment, and output, the most crucial parameter is the autocorrelation of the technology shock. In order to generate greater volatility in consumption (relative to income) than observed in U.S. data, the shock must be significantly less autocorrelated than what is observed in the U.S. due to the implied income and substitution effects. Recently, Backus, Kehoe, and Kydland (1992) measured this autocorrelation parameter (for a constructed aggregate of European output) to be 0.90 (recall that the value used for our analysis was 0.91). Hence, while more empirical research in this area is necessary, we conclude tentatively that the international relevance of the standard RBC approach is questionable.

5. Conclusion

The purpose of this research was to assess the quality of the evidence offered in support of real business cycle analysis. This evidence takes the form of a comparison between the second moments implied by an artificial economy and those observed in the data; consequently, our assessment was from two different perspectives. We first asked whether a Keynesian artificial economy can duplicate the variances and covariances observed in the U.S. economy. Not surprisingly, using the Fairmodel as the artificial economy, we demonstrated that it did. We then calibrated a RBC model to the output from two versions of the Fair model and checked for consistency in terms of the absolute and relative volatilities of GNP and its components. The first version used to generate data was the unmodified (i.e., estimated) Fairmodel; upon calibrating a growth model to this data set we concluded that the RBC model could indeed replicate the volatilities of consumption and investment relative to output produced within the Fairmodel. We then modified the Fairmodel so that the resulting output did not have the same characteristics as observed in actual data. Calibrating the RBC model to this data set led to significant inconsistencies.

We are left with the question we started with: Do these results enhance or diminish one's confidence in RBC models? While it is premature to answer this question definitively, it appears that the permanent income framework and implicit intertemporal prices that constitute the core structure of standard RBC models do impose fairly stringent restrictions on the prop-

14

Calibration and Real Business Cycle Models

erties of equilibrium. This feature has positive as well as negative aspects. On the one hand, it insures that real business cycle models are not pure chameleons—that is, they cannot mimic any model. On the other hand, it means that it may be difficult to match the full range of moments and correlations from industrialized economies as presented by Backus and Kehoe (1992).

Received: November 1994
Final version: February 1996

References

Altug, Sumru. "Time-to-Build and Aggregate Fluctuations: Some New Evidence." *International Economic Review* 30 (November 1989): 889–920.

Backus, David K., and Patrick J. Kehoe. "International Evidence on the Historical Properties of Business Cycles." *The American Economic Review* 82 (1992): 864–88.

Backus, David K., Patrick J. Kehoe, and Finn Kydland. "International Real Business Cycles." *Journal of Political Economy* 100 (August 1992): 745–75.

Benhabib, Jess, Richard Rogerson, and Randall Wright. "Homework in Macroeconomics: Household Production and Aggregate Fluctuations." *Journal of Political Economy* 99 (December 1991): 1166–87.

Bollen, Kenneth A. *Structural Equations with Latent Variables.* New York: John Wiley & Sons, 1989.

Canova, Fabio, Mary Finn, and Adrian Pagan. "Evaluating a Real Business Cycle Model" In *Nonstationary Time Series Analysis and Cointegration,* edited by C. Hargreaves. Oxford: Oxford University Press, 1992.

Christiano, Lawrence J., and Martin Eichenbaum. "Current Real-Business Cycle Theories and Aggregate Labor-Market Fluctuations." *American Economic Review* 82 (June 1992): 430–50.

Fair, Ray C. *Fairmodel User's Guide and Intermediate Workbook.* Southborough, Massachusetts: Macro Incorporated, 1990.

Testing Macroeconomic Models. Cambridge, MA: Harvard University Press, 1994.

Hansen, Gary D. "Indivisible Labor and the Business Cycle." *Journal of Monetary Economics* 16 (November 1985): 309–28.

Hansen, Gary D., and Randall Wright. "The Labor Market in Real Business Cycle Theory." Federal Reserve Bank of Minneapolis *Quarterly Review* (Spring 1992): 2–12.

Hoover, Kevin D. "Fact and Artifacts: Calibration and the Empirical As-

James Hartley, Kevin Salyer and Steven Sheffrin

sessment of Real-Business Cycle Models." *Oxford Economic Papers* 47 (1995): 24–44.

King, Robert G., Charles Plosser, and Sergio Rebelo. "Production Growth and Business Cycles I: The Basic Neoclassical Model." *Journal of Monetary Economics* 21 (March/May 1988): 195–232.

Kydland, Finn, and Edward C. Prescott. "Business Cycles: Real Facts and a Monetary Myth." Federal Reserve Bank of Minneapolis *Quarterly Review* 14 (1990): 3–18.

———. "Time to Build and Aggregate Fluctuations." *Econometrica* 50 (1982): 1345–70.

———. "The Econometrics of the General Equilibrium Approach to Business Cycles." *Scandinavian Journal of Economics* 93 (1991): 161–78.

Watson, Mark W. "Measures of Fit for Calibrated Models." *Journal of Political Economy* 101 (1993): 1011–41.

Data Appendix

All of the data used in this paper was that provided with the Fairmodel. For further information, consult the *FAIRMODEL User's Guide*.

The following variables from the Fairmodel were used in our simulations:

> CN = Real consumer expenditures for nondurable goods.
> CD = Real consumer expenditures for durable goods.
> COG = Federal government purchases of goods (Fiscal policy variable).
> CS = Real consumer expenditures for services.
> GNPD = GNP deflator.
> GNP = Nominal gross national product.
> GNPR = Real gross national product.
> HF = Nonresidential fixed investment by firms.
> IHH = Residential investment by households.
> IKF = Nonresidential fixed investment by firms.
> JF = Number of jobs in the business sector.
> M1 = Money supply, end of quarter (Monetary policy variable).
> POP = Noninstitutional population over 16 years old.
> PROD = Output per paid for worker hour.
> WF = Average hourly earnings excluding overtime of workers in business sector.

The above variables were used to generate the following:

16

Calibration and Real Business Cycle Models

Consumption (C) = ln((CN + CS)/POP)
Hours (N) = ln((JF*HF)/POP)
Investment (I) = ln((IKF + IHH + CD)/POP)
Real Output (Y) = ln(GNPR/POP)

Journal of Economic Dynamics and Control 15 (1991) 607–626. North-Holland

Real business-cycle theory*

Wisdom or whimsy?

Martin Eichenbaum

Northwestern University,
NBER and The Federal Reserve Bank of Chicago

Received January 1990

This paper assesses the empirical plausibility of the view that aggregate productivity shocks account for most of the variability in post-World War II US output. We argue that the type of evidence forwarded by proponents of this proposition is too fragile to be believable. The answer could be 70% as Kydland and Prescott (1989) claim, but the data contain almost no evidence against either the view that the answer is really 5% or that the answer is really 200%. Moreover point estimates of the importance of technology shocks are extremely sensitive to small perturbations in the theory. Depending on the sample period investigated, allowing for labor-hoarding behavior in an otherwise standard RBC model reduces the ability of technology shocks to account for aggregate fluctuations by between 30% to 60%.

This paper discusses two questions which are of fundamental importance to macroeconomists. First – how important have aggregate technology shocks been as sources of fluctuations to post-war US aggregate output? Second, how reliable are existing answers to the first question?

The answers to these questions obviously matter from the perspective of optimal public policy. But just as important, the *perceived* answers also matter because they influence the research agenda of macroeconomists. Around 1977 it seemed just as obvious to the representative graduate student as it was to Milton Friedman or Robert Lucas that monetary instability is a

*This paper is based on an invited talk, presented at the Society of Economic Dynamics and Control Meeting in Minneapolis, Minnesota, on June 29th, 1990. The author is very grateful to Craig Burnside, Lawrence Christiano, and Sergio Rebelo for their advice and help in preparing this paper. Thomas Sargent and Mark Watson provided numerous useful comments.

critical determinant of aggregate output fluctuations. Granted there was substantial disagreement about the nature of the relationship between monetary and real phenomena. But the critical point is that those years were marked by enormous amounts of research aimed at understanding the propagation mechanisms by which monetary policy affects aggregate economic activity. That this was a critical item for business-cycle research was, by and large, simply taken for granted.

The situation has clearly changed. Since Kydland and Prescott's (1982) apparent demonstration that productivity shocks can account for *all* output variability in the post-war US, the need for an adequate theory of monetary and fiscal sources of instability has come to seem much less pressing. Not surprisingly, the amount of research devoted to these topics has declined precipitously.

Does the evidence *in fact* provide such overwhelming support in favor of the basic claim of existing Real Business Cycle (RBC) theories so as to rationalize this fundamental shift in our view of the business cycle? In my view it does not. This is because the evidence in favor of the proposition that productivity shocks can account for most of the variability in post-World War II US output is simply too fragile to be believable:

(1) Small perturbations to the theory alter the conclusion in a basic way.

(2) Small changes in the statistical methods used alter the conclusion in a basic way.

(3) Changes in the sample period alter the conclusion in a basic way.

(4) And most importantly, our confidence in the conclusion is fundamentally affected once we abandon the convenient fiction that we actually *know* the true values of the structural parameters of standard RBC models.

Indeed, once we quantify the uncertainty in model predictions arising from uncertainty about model parameter values, calibrated or otherwise, our view of what the data is telling us is affected in a first-order way. Even if we do not perturb the standard theory and even if we implement existing formulations of that theory on the standard postwar sample period and even if we use the stationary inducing transformation of the data that has become standard in RBC studies – even then the strong conclusions which mark this literature are unwarranted. What the data are actually telling us is that, while technology shocks almost certainly play some role in generating the business cycle, there is simply an enormous amount of uncertainty about just what percent of aggregate fluctuations they actually do account for. The answer could be 70% as Kydland and Prescott (1989) claim, but the data contain almost no evidence against either the view that the answer is really 5% or that the answer is really 200%.

Under these circumstances, the decision to drastically de-emphasize the importance of traditional impulses like monetary and fiscal shocks in business-cycle research ought to be viewed as whimsical, in the sense that Leamer (1983) uses that term. An inference is just not believable if it is fragile. And a decision based on a fragile inference is whimsical.

In this paper I discuss the first and fourth of the aforementioned contentions. In addition I briefly touch upon the third contention.[1] Most of the quantitative results used to support my arguments are taken from Burnside, Eichenbaum, and Rebelo (1990).[2] In order to be concrete it is useful to consider the quantitative implications of one widely used RBC theory – the indivisible-labor model associated with Hansen (1985) and Rogerson (1988). According to this model, the time series on the beginning of period t capital stock, k_t, time t consumption, c_t, and time t hours worked, n_t, correspond to the solution of a social planning problem which can be decentralized as a Pareto optimal competitive equilibrium. The planner ranks streams of consumption services and leisure, $T - n_t$, according to the criterion function:

$$E_0 \sum_{t=0}^{\infty} \beta^t \{\ln(c_t) + \theta(T - n_t)\}. \tag{1}$$

Here T denotes the representative agent's time endowment, E_0 is the time 0 conditional expectations operator, θ is a positive scalar, and β is the subjective discount rate, $0 < \beta < 1$.

There are at least two interpretations of the term involving leisure in (1). First, it may just reflect the assumption that individual utility functions are linear in leisure. The second interpretation builds on the assumption that there are indivisibilities in labor supply, so that individuals can either work some fixed positive number of hours or not at all. Assuming that agent's utility functions are separable across consumption and leisure, Rogerson (1988) shows that a market structure in which individuals choose the probability of being employed rather than actual hours worked will support the Pareto optimal allocation. Under these circumstances, criterion function (1) represents a reduced-form preference ordering which can be used to derive the Pareto optimal allocation using a fictitious social-planning problem. The parameter θ places no restriction on the elasticity of labor supply at the micro level of the individual agent.

Output, y_t, is produced via the Cobb–Douglas production function

$$y_t = A_t k_t^{1-\alpha} (\gamma^t h_t)^\alpha, \tag{2}$$

---

[1] For a discussion of contention 2, see Christiano and Eichenbaum (1990a).

[2] The reader is referred to that paper for a more careful discussion of the methodology used to generate the results as well as additional findings which pertain to points 1, 3, and 4.

where $0 < \alpha < 1$, γ^t is the constant unconditional growth rate of technology, and A_t is an aggregate shock to technology which has the time-series representation

$$A_t = A_{t-1}^{\rho_a} \exp(\varepsilon_t). \tag{3}$$

Here ε_t is a serially uncorrelated i.i.d. process with mean ε and standard error σ_ε, and ρ_a is a scalar satisfying $|\rho_a| < 1$.

The aggregate resource constraint is given by

$$c_t + k_{t+1} - (1 - \delta)k_t \le y_t. \tag{4}$$

The parameter δ, which governs the depreciation rate on capital, is a positive scalar satisfying $0 < \delta < 1$.

To discuss the quantitative implications of the theory, it is convenient to denote the model's structural parameters by the vector Ψ. Given a value for Ψ, it is straightforward to deduce the model's implications for a wide variety of moments which might be of interest. For example, the analyst might be interested in understanding the model's quantitative implications for an object like the variance of aggregate output. Existing RBC studies do this by conditioning on a particular value for Ψ, say $\hat{\Psi}$, and then compare the model's prediction for the variance of output with an estimate of the corresponding data moment. When RBC analysts say that the model accounts for $\lambda\%$ of the variance of output, what they mean is that their model yields a value of λ given by

$$\lambda = \sigma_{ym}^2(\hat{\Psi}) / \hat{\sigma}_{yd}^2. \tag{5}$$

Here the numerator denotes the variance of model output, calculated under the assumption that Ψ is equal to $\hat{\Psi}$, and the denominator denotes an estimate of the variance of actual US output. The claim that technology shocks account for most of the fluctuations in postwar US output corresponds to the claim that λ is a large number, with the current estimate being between 0.75 and 1.0, depending on exactly which RBC model is used [see for example Hansen (1988)].

To evaluate this claim, we abstract, for the moment, from issues like sensitivity to small perturbations in the theory. As decision makers, some obvious things we might want to know are:

How much information is there in the data about λ?
Is our calculation of λ sensitive to small perturbations in $\hat{\Psi}$?
And just what is a small perturbation in $\hat{\Psi}$?

Unfortunately, the existing RBC literature does not offer much help in answering these questions. Basically this is because that literature makes little use of formal econometric methods, either at the stage when model parameters values are selected, or at the stage when the fully parameterized model is compared to the data. Instead a variety of informal techniques, often referred to as 'calibration' are used. Irrespective of what other virtues or defects calibration techniques may possess – one limitation is clear. Objects like λ are random variables. By ignoring the sampling uncertainty which is inherent in such objects, calibration exercises do not provide any information about how loudly the data speak on any given question.

That there is sampling uncertainty in variables like λ follows from the simple fact that they are statistics in the sense defined by Prescott (1986), i.e., they are real-valued functions of the time series. In the case of λ, the precise form of that dependency is defined jointly by the functions defining $\hat{\sigma}_{yd}^2$ and $\hat{\Psi}$, and the model which maps any given value of Ψ into a value for σ_{ym}^2. Sampling uncertainty in either $\hat{\Psi}$ or $\hat{\sigma}_{yd}$ implies the existence of sampling uncertainty in λ. In fact both $\hat{\Psi}$ and $\hat{\sigma}_{yd}^2$ are subject to sampling uncertainty. We do not *know* the actual variance of US output. This is a population moment which must be estimated using the data. But the same observation holds for $\sigma_{ym}^2(\hat{\Psi})$ – it too is a statistic in Prescott's sense, if only because $\hat{\Psi}$ itself is a statistic. To be concrete consider an element of Ψ like α. Calibrators typically pick a value for α which implies that the model is consistent with the 'observed' share of labor in national income. But we do not observe the population value of labor share's in national income. That object must be estimated as some well defined function of the data. Since the estimator defined by that function is subject to sampling uncertainty so is $\hat{\Psi}$. Consequently $\sigma_{yd}^2(\hat{\Psi})$ ought to be viewed as a random variable. By ignoring the sampling uncertainty inherent in $\hat{\Psi}$, calibration exercises do not lead, in any natural way, to a definition of what a small perturbation in $\hat{\Psi}$ is. And this precludes the possibility of quantifying the sampling uncertainty inherent in model predictions or diagnostic statistics like λ.

In recent work Lawrence Christiano and I discuss one way to circumvent these problems, in a way that is similar in spirit to existing analyses of RBC models, but which uses formal econometric tools [see Christiano and Eichenbaum (1990a)]. The basic idea is to use a version of Hansen's (1982) Generalized Method of Moments procedure in which the estimation criterion is set up so that, in effect, the estimated parameter values succeed in equating model and sample first moments of the data. As it turns out these values are very similar to the values employed in existing RBC studies. For example, most RBC studies [see for example Prescott (1986)] assume that the quarterly depreciation rate, δ, and the share of capital in the aggregate production function, $(1 - \alpha)$, equal 0.025 and 0.36, respectively. Our procedure yields point estimates of 0.021 and 0.35, respectively.

The key difference between the procedures does not lie so much in the point estimates of Ψ. Rather the difference is that, by using formal econometrics, our procedure allows us to translate sampling uncertainty about the functions of the data which define our estimator of Ψ into sampling uncertainty regarding $\hat{\Psi}$ itself. This information leads to a natural definition of what a small perturbation in $\hat{\Psi}$ is. In turn this makes it possible to quantify uncertainty about the model's second-moment implications. The net result is that it is possible to convey how much confidence we have in statements like:

The model accounts for $\lambda\%$ of the variability of output.

Before reporting the results of implementing this procedure for the model discussed above I must digress for one moment and discuss the way in which growth is handled. In practice empirical measures of objects like y_t display marked trends, so that *some* stationary inducing transformation of the data must be adopted. A variety of alternatives are available to the analyst. For example, according to the balanced-growth model described above, the data ought to be trend-stationary, with the ln of real variables, excluding per capita hours worked, growing as a linear function of time. So one possibility would be to detrend the time series emerging from the model as well as the actual data assuming a linear time trend and calculate the moments of the linearly detrended series.

A different procedure involves detrending model time series and the data using the filter discussed in Hodrick and Prescott (1980). Although our point estimates of the vector Ψ were *not* obtained using transformed data, diagnostic second-moment results were generated using this transformation of model time series and US data.

I do this for three reasons. First, many authors in the RBC literature report results based on the Hodrick–Prescott (HP) filter [see, for example, Kydland and Prescott (1982), Hansen (1985), Prescott (1986), Kydland and Prescott (1988), and Backus, Kehoe, and Kydland (1989)]. In order to evaluate their claims, it seems desirable to minimize the differences between our procedures. Second, the HP filter is in fact a stationary inducing transformation for trend-stationary processes [see King and Rebelo (1988)]. So there is nothing logically wrong with using HP transformed data. Using it just amounts to the assertion that you find a particular set of second moments interesting as diagnostic devices. And third, all of the calculations reported in this paper were also done with linearly detrended data as well as growth rates. The qualitative results are very similar, while the quantitative results provide even stronger evidence in favor of the points I wish to make. So presenting results based on the HP filter seems like an appropriate conservative reporting strategy.

Table 1

Standard indivisible-labor model – summary statistics.

	σ_ε	ρ_a	σ_{ym}	λ
Standard model (constant government)	0.0089 (0.0013)	0.986 (0.026)	0.017 (0.007)	0.78 (0.64)
Standard model (variable government)	0.0089 (0.0013)	0.986 (0.026)	0.017 (0.007)	0.82 (0.64)

The first row of table 1 reports results for the baseline indivisible-labor model in which the only shocks to agents' environments are stochastic shifts in the aggregate production technology. Here, σ_ε denotes the standard error of the innovation to the ln of A_t, the linearly detrended Solow residual, ρ_a denotes the autoregressive coefficient of the ln of A_t, and σ_{ym} denotes the standard error of the ln of output. The statistic λ denotes the ratio of the variance of the ln of per capita output implied by the model to the ratio of the variance of the ln of HP filtered per capita postwar real output.[3] Numbers in parentheses denote the standard errors of the corresponding statistics. All uncertainty in model statistics reflects only uncertainty regarding the values of the structural parameters.[4]

Three key features of these results deserve comment. First, the standard error associated with our point estimate of ρ_a is quite large. This is important because the implications of RBC models are known to be sensitive to changes in this parameter, especially in a neighborhood of ρ_a equal to one [see Hansen (1988) and Christiano and Eichenbaum (1990b)]. Second, the standard error on our estimate of σ_ε is quite large. Taken together, these results indicate substantial uncertainty regarding the population values of the parameters governing the evolution of technology shocks. This is the case despite the fact that the standard error of our point estimate of the coefficient on capital in the production function is very small (see footnote 4). Third, our point estimate of λ equals 82%. This is consistent with claims that technology shocks explain a large percentage of the variability in postwar US output. But notice that the standard error of λ is very large. There is simply an *enormous* amount of uncertainty regarding what percent of the variability of output the model accounts for. As it turns out, this uncertainty almost

[3] Our point estimate of σ_{yd}^2 is 0.019 with standard error of 0.002.

[4] The data and econometric methodology underlying these estimates are discussed in Burnside, Eichenbaum, and Rebelo (1990). Our point estimates of α, θ, δ, ρ_a, and σ_ε equal 0.655 (0.006), 3.70 (0.040), 0.021 (0.0003), 0.986 (0.0026), and 0.0089 (0.0013). Numbers in parentheses denote standard errors.

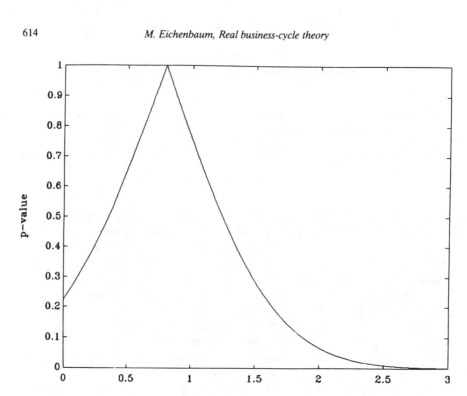

Variance of Y (Model) / Variance of Y (Data)

Fig. 1. Standard model (constant government).

completely reflects uncertainty regarding ρ_a and σ_ε, and hardly at all uncertainty regarding the values of the other parameters of the model.[5]

A different way to summarize this uncertainty is to consider the graph of the confidence interval of λ, depicted in fig. 1. Each point on the graph is generated by fixing λ at a specific value, λ^*, and then testing the hypothesis that $\sigma_{ym}^2 = \lambda^* \sigma_{yd}^2$. The vertical axis reports the probability value of our test statistic for the corresponding value of λ. To see just how little information this model and the data contain regarding λ, consider the question: What values of λ could we reject at the 5% significance level? The answer is: Not many. Even granting that our algorithm breaks down when calculating probability values for negative values of λ, we ought to be very comfortable believing that the model explains *anywhere* between 5% and 200% of the variance in per capita US output. Evidently, the model and the data, taken

[5]See Burnside, Eichenbaum, and Rebelo (1990).

together, are almost completely uninformative about the role of technology shocks in generating fluctuations in US output.[6] Decisions based solely on the point estimate of λ are whimsical in the extreme. If you thought that monetary policy was the key impulse in the business cycle – there is virtually no evidence here to change your mind.

What about the point estimate itself of λ? Just how sensitive is it to small perturbations in the theory?

One interesting perturbation is to consider the effects of labor hoarding on the analysis. Existing RBC studies interpret all movements in measured total factor productivity as being the result of technology shocks or, to a much smaller extent, as reflecting classical measurement error in hours worked. Various authors, ranging from Summers (1986) to Lucas (1989) have conjectured that many of the movements in the Solow residual which are labelled as productivity shocks are actually an artifact of labor-hoarding-type phenomena.[7] To the extent that this is true, empirical work which identifies technology shocks with the Solow residual will systematically overstate their importance to the business cycle.

In fact, there is a substantial amount of evidence that the time-series properties of Solow residuals are inconsistent with the notion that they represent exogenous technology shocks. For example Hall (1988) has argued that if Solow residuals represent exogenous technology shocks, then under perfect competition, they ought to be uncorrelated with different measures of fiscal and monetary policy. As it turns out this implication is counterfactual. Evans (1990) has pointed out that the Solow residual is actually highly correlated with different measures of the money supply. Hall (1988) himself presents evidence they are also correlated with the growth rate of military expenditures. In interpreting his results as evidence of imperfect competition, Hall argues that labor hoarding alone will not produce significant procyclical behavior in the Solow residual, given perfect competition and flexible prices.

In ongoing research, Craig Burnside, Sergio Rebelo, and I have tried to assess the sensitivity of inference based on Solow residual accounting to the Lucas/Summers critique. The model that we use incorporates a particular type of labor hoarding into a perfect-competition, complete-markets RBC model. Its purpose is to demonstrate, in a quantitative way, the fragility of

---

[6]Our method for estimating the model's structural parameters amounts to using an exactly identified version of Hansen's (1982) Generalized Method of Moments procedure. Presumably the confidence interval could be narrowed by imposing more of the model's restrictions, say via a maximum-likelihood estimation procedure or an overidentified Generalized Method of Moments procedure. Using such procedures could result in substantially different estimates of Ψ, making comparisons with the existing RBC literature very difficult. See Christiano and Eichenbaum (1990a) for a discussion of this point.

[7]For a more general critique of RBC models, see McCallum (1989).

existing claims about the cyclical role of technology shocks. Our basic findings can be summarized as follows:

(I) RBC models can, in fact, be quite sensitive to the possibility of labor hoarding. Allowing for such behavior reduces our estimate of the variance of technology shocks by roughly 60%. Depending on the sample period investigated, this reduces the ability of technology shocks to account for aggregate output fluctuations by 30% to 60%.

(II) We find that Hall's (1988) conjecture notwithstanding, labor hoarding with perfect competition and complete markets, is fully capable of accounting for the observed correlation between government consumption and the Solow residual.

Our model setup can be described as follows. Suppose, as in the standard indivisible-labor model, that if an individual goes to work there is a fixed cost, ξ, denominated in terms of hours of foregone leisure. If a person does go to work, he stays there for a fixed number of hours, h. The time t criterion of this person is given by

$$\ln(c_t^p) + \theta \ln(T - \xi - e_t h). \tag{6}$$

Here c_t^p denotes time t privately purchased consumption and e_t denotes the level of time t effort. The time t criterion function of a person who does not go to work is simply given by

$$\ln(c_t^p) + \theta \ln(T). \tag{7}$$

The aggregate production technology is given by

$$y_t = A_t k_t^{1-\alpha} (\gamma^t N_t e_t h)^\alpha. \tag{8}$$

Here N_t denotes the total number of persons going to work at time t.

Proceeding as in Rogerson (1988) it is easy to show that, since agents' criterion functions are separable across consumption and leisure, the social planner will equate the consumption of employed and unemployed individuals. The Pareto optimal competitive equilibrium corresponds to the solution of the social-planning problem

$$\max \mathrm{E}_0 \sum_{t=0}^\infty \beta^t \{\ln(c_t^p) + \theta N_t \ln(T - \xi - e_t h) + \theta(1 - N_t)\ln(T)\}, \tag{9}$$

subject to the aggregate resource constraint

$$A_t k_t^{1-\alpha} \left(\gamma^t N_t e_t h \right)^\alpha = c_t^p + g_t + k_{t+1} - (1-\delta) k_t. \tag{10}$$

Here g_t represents time t government consumption, which evolves according to

$$g_t = \left(\gamma^{\alpha t} \right) g_{t-1}^{\rho_g} \exp(\mu_t), \tag{11}$$

where μ_t is a serially uncorrelated i.i.d. process with mean μ and standard error σ_μ, while ρ_g is a scalar satisfying $|\rho_g| < 1$.[8]

If we assume that the social planner sees the time t realization of the technology shock and government consumption *before* he chooses N_t and e_t, then this model is observationally equivalent to the standard indivisible-labor model, modified to incorporate government consumption into the aggregate resource constraint. The second row of table 1 reports the results of incorporating g_t alone into the analysis.[9] While the effect of this perturbation is very important for statistics like the correlation between hours worked and real wages [see Christiano and Eichenbaum (1990a)], its effect on statistics like σ_{ym} or λ is minimal.

How can we perturb the model so as to capture labor-hoarding-type behavior? One particularly simple way to do this, which does not change the nonstochastic steady state of the model, is to just change the information structure facing agents when they make their work decisions. In particular, suppose that N_t must be chosen *before*, rather than *after*, time t government consumption and the level of technology is known. To provide a bound for the effects of labor hoarding in this setup, we maintain the assumption that the shift length, h, is constant.

The basic idea underlying this perturbation is that it is costly for firms to vary the size of their work force. In the limit it is simply not feasible to change employment in response to *every* bit of new information regarding the state of demand and technology. One way to capture this is to consider environments where firms must make their employment decisions conditional on their views about the future state of demand and technology, and then adjust, within a period of fixed time, to shocks along other dimensions. In our model this adjustment occurs by varying labor effort and is costly because

---

[8]See Aiyagari, Christiano, and Eichenbaum (1989) for a discussion of the effects of government purchases in the stochastic one-sector growth model.

[9]Our point estimates of α, θ, δ, ρ_a, σ_ε, ρ_g, and σ_g equal 0.655 (0.0057), 3.70 (0.040), 0.021 (0.0003), 0.986 (0.029), 0.0089 (0.0013), 0.979 (0.021), and 0.0145 (0.0011). See Burnside, Eichenbaum, and Rebelo (1990) for details.

workers care about *effective* hours of work.[10] More generally, incorporating unobserved time-varying effort into the model can be thought of as capturing, in a rough manner, the type of measurement error induced by the fact that in many industries reported hours worked do not vary in a one-to-one way with actual hours worked. This explanation of procyclical productivity has been emphasized by various authors like Fair (1969).

Burnside, Eichenbaum, and Rebelo (1990) show that, in this model, the ln of the Solow residual S_t^*, the ln of the true technology shock, A_t^*, and the ln of effort, e_t, are, in equilibrium, tied together via the relationship

$$S_t^* = A_t^* + \alpha e_t^*. \tag{12}$$

Here the superscript asterisk denotes the deviation of the ln of a variable from its steady-state value. The equilibrium law of motion for e_t^* is of the form

$$e_t = \pi_1 k_t^* + \pi_2 N_t^* + \pi_3 A_t^* + \pi_4 g_t^*, \tag{13}$$

where the π's are nonlinear functions of the structural parameters of the model.

Given our estimates of the structural parameters, obtained using data spanning the period 1955:3–1984:4, both π_3 and π_4 are positive.[11] This implies that, other things equal, it is optimal to work harder when faced with a positive innovation in government purchases or technology, i.e., *effort will be procyclical*. Consequently naive Solow residual accounting systematically overestimates the level of technology in booms, systematically underestimates the level of technology in recessions, and systematically overestimates the variance of the true technology shock.

Granted that this result is based on a model which does not allow for variations in the degree to which capital is utilized. However, allowing for such effects would only strengthen our conclusions. While poorly measured, capital-utilization rates are clearly procyclical. Consequently, the measurement error involved in using the stock of capital for the purpose of calculating Solow residuals would also be procyclical. The same sorts of impulses which cause labor effort to increase presumably also induce increases in capital-utilization rates. To the extent that this is true, the setup considered here understates the sensitivity of RBC models to more general types of 'hoarding' behavior.

---

[10] It follows that labor must be compensated for working harder. We need not be precise about the exact compensation scheme because the optimal decentralized allocation can be found by solving the appropriate social-planning problem for our model economy.

[11] For this model our point estimates of α, θ, δ, ρ_a, σ_ε, ρ_g and σ_g equal 0.655 (0.0057), 3.68 (0.033), 0.021 (0.0003), 0.977 (0.029), 0.0072 (0.0012), 0.979 (0.021), and 0.0145 (0.0011). See Burnside, Eichenbaum, and Rebelo (1990) for details.

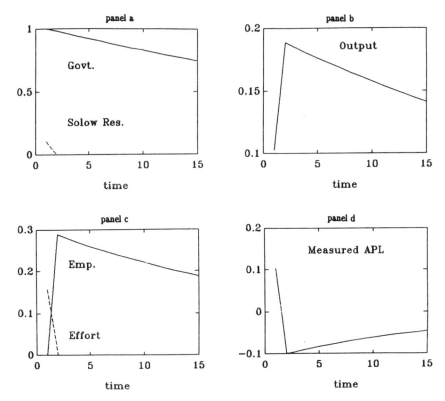

Fig. 2. Shock to government.

To understand the dynamic properties of the model, it is useful to consider the impulse-response functions of the system, evaluated at our estimates of the model's structural parameters. Excluding the parameters which govern the law of motion of the *true* technology shock, these estimates are almost identical to those of the standard indivisible-labor model (see footnotes 9 and 11). Fig. 2 presents the response of the system to a 1% innovation in government consumption. By assumption employment cannot immediately respond to this shock. However, effort rises by over 15% in the first period and then reverts to its steady-state level. Panel a shows the implied movement in the Solow residual. Since effort has gone up in the first period but total hours of work hasn't changed, the Solow residual increases by about 0.25%. This is true *even though there has been no technology shock whatsoever*. Naive Solow residual accounting falsely interprets the increase in average productivity to a shift in technology rather than an exogenous increase in government consumption. As panel d shows, productivity rises in the first period by 0.1% in response to the 1% innovation in government

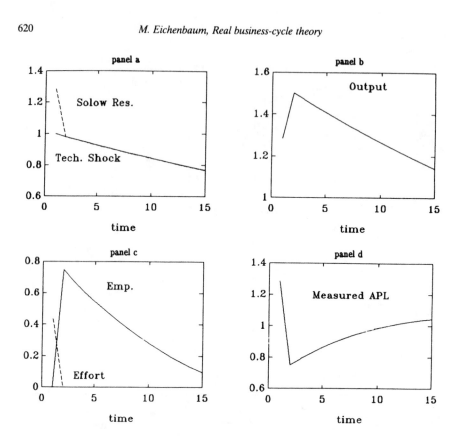

Fig. 3. Shock to technology.

consumption. Like the mechanisms embedded in Lucas (1970) or Hansen and Sargent (1988), this simple perturbation of the model provides, at least in principle, an alternative to technology shocks as the sole explanation for the procyclical behavior of average productivity.

Fig. 3 shows how the system responds to a 1% innovation in technology. Given agents' willingness to intertemporally substitute effective leisure over time, they respond to the shock in the first period by increasing effort by about 0.4 of a percent. As a result the Solow residual rises by 1.3% in response to the 1% technology shock. Again naive Solow residual accounting exaggerates the true magnitude of the technology shock.

How do these considerations translate into inferences regarding λ? As it turns out, the answer to this question, depends to some extent on the sample period investigated. Given our assumptions, the variables in the model are trend-stationary stochastic processes. Conditional on that view, there is substantial reason to believe that there is a break in the data. Numerous researchers have documented the fact that the growth rate of average

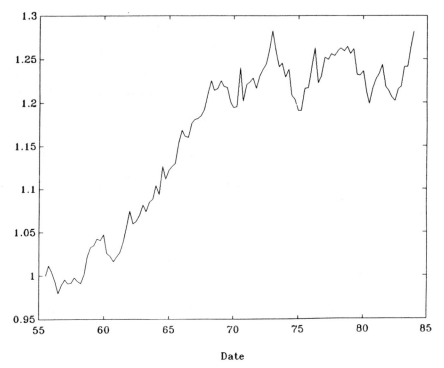

Fig. 4. Solow residuals.

productivity slowed down substantially in the late 1960's. This can be seen from fig. 4 where we graph the log of the Solow residual.[12] To document the likelihood of a 'break' in the process, Burnside, Eichenbaum, and Rebelo (1990) perform a series of iterative Chow tests. Using these tests, they find that the null hypothesis of no break is rejected at very high significance levels at all dates during the interval 1966:1–1974:2. The actual break point which they choose corresponds to 1969:4. Fortunately, their results are not sensitive to the precise breakpoint used.

Burnside, Eichenbaum, and Rebelo (1990) discuss at some length the impact of allowing for a break in the sample on their estimates of the structural parameters. Table 2 displays a subset of their results obtained using both the whole sample period and the two subsample periods. Basically there are four important important differences in the parameter values across

[12] The Solow residual was calculated using the formula $\ln(S_t) = \ln(Y_t) - (1 - \alpha)\ln(K_t) - \alpha \ln(h_t)$ and the point estimate of α equal to 0.655 obtained by Burnside, Eichenbaum, and Rebelo (1990). The variable h_t denotes time t aggregate hours worked.

the different sample periods. First, the estimated values of the unconditional growth rate of the Solow residual in the first and second sample periods, 0.0069 and 0.0015, respectively, are quite different. Second, the estimated value of ρ_a is quite sensitive to the sample period. For example, using the standard indivisible-labor model, the estimated value of ρ_a over the whole period is 0.986, whereas it equals 0.86 and 0.88 in the first and second sample periods, respectively. The fact that the point estimate of ρ_a is substantially larger when the whole sample period is used is exactly what we would expect if there were indeed a break in the Solow residual process [see Perron (1988)]. Third, the estimated value of σ_ε equals 0.0060, 0.0101, and 0.0089, in the first, second, and whole sample periods, respectively. Evidently, estimates of the standard error of the innovation to technology are also quite sensitive to the choice of sample period. Fourth, the estimates of γ_g (the growth rate in government consumption), ρ_g, and σ_μ are affected in the same qualitative ways as the analog parameters governing the evolution of the Solow residual. However, the quantitative differences are even larger.

Burnside, Eichenbaum, and Rebelo (1990) investigate the implications of this parameter sensitivity on the models' implications for standard diagnostics moments like volatility of consumption and investment relative to output. Their results indicate that the standard model and the labor-hoarding model do quite well in reproducing estimates of the analog data moments when the whole sample is used. However, they also find that the models' performance deteriorates quite dramatically once we allow for a break in the sample. Evidently claims regarding the ability of RBC models to reproduce the relative volatility of key aggregate variables are quite fragile in the sense that they depend sensitively on the choice of sample period.

Given this fragility, we report the impact of labor hoarding on λ, allowing for a break in the sample period. From table 2 we see that over the whole sample period, introducing time-varying effort causes λ to decline by 28% from 0.81 to 0.58. The sensitivity of λ is even more dramatic once we allow for a break in the sample. Labor hoarding reduces λ by 58% in the first sample period and by 63% in the second period. As it turns out the sensitivity of λ to labor hoarding is primarily due to the impact of time-varying effort on our estimates of σ_ε. While allowing for time-varying effort reduces our estimate of ρ_a, the main effect is a large reduction in σ_ε. Based on the whole sample period the variance of the innovation to technology shocks drops by roughly 25%. In the first- and second-period samples, this variance drops by 48% and 56%, respectively. A different way to assess this sensitivity is to consider the unconditional variance of the stationary component of the technology shocks, σ_a^2.[13] Allowing for time-varying effort reduces the volatility

---

[13]This variance was calculated using the formula $\sigma_a^2 = \sigma_\varepsilon^2/(1 - \rho_a^2)$.

M. Eichenbaum, Real business-cycle theory   623

Table 2

	$\ln(\gamma)$	σ_ε	ρ_a	$\ln(\gamma_g)$	ρ_g	σ_μ	σ_y	λ
				Labor-hoarding model[a]				
Whole sample	0.0041 (0.0003)	0.0072 (0.0012)	0.977 (0.029)	0.0021 (0.0004)	0.979 (0.021)	0.014 (0.001)	0.015 (0.001)	0.58 (0.14)
Sample period 1	0.0069 (0.0004)	0.0042 (0.0006)	0.869 (0.043)	0.0073 (0.007)	0.938 (0.047)	0.014 (0.001)	0.011 (0.001)	0.71 (0.20)
Sample period 2	0.0015 (0.0003)	0.0067 (0.0006)	0.882 (0.061)	−0.0013 (0.0003)	0.662 (0.077)	0.012 (0.001)	0.017 (0.001)	0.52 (0.12)
				Standard model (variable government)				
Whole sample	0.0041 (0.0001)	0.0089 (0.0013)	0.986 (0.026)	0.0021 (0.0004)	0.979 (0.021)	0.014 (0.001)	0.017 (0.006)	0.81 (0.56)
Sample period 1	0.0069 (0.0004)	0.0060 (0.0022)	0.862 (0.071)	0.0073 (0.0007)	0.938 (0.047)	0.014 (0.001)	0.017 (0.007)	1.69 (1.51)
Sample period 2	0.0015 (0.0003)	0.0101 (0.0015)	0.884 (0.065)	−0.0013 (0.0003)	0.662 (0.077)	0.012 (0.001)	0.028 (0.005)	1.42 (0.65)

[a]Whole sample corresponds to data over the period 1955:3–1984:4. Sample period 1 corresponds to data over the period 1955:3–1969:4. Sample period 2 corresponds to data over the period 1969:5–1984:4.

of technology shocks by 58% in the whole sample, 49% in the first sample period, and 57% over the second sample period.

Before leaving my discussion of the labor-hoarding model – let me point to one more bit of subsidiary evidence in favor of that model relative to existing RBC models. Hall (1988, 1989) has emphasized the fact that the Solow residual appears to be correlated with a variety of objects like government consumption as measured by military expenditures.[14] Suppose that we regress the growth rate of the Solow residual on the growth rate of government consumption. According to existing RBC models, this regression coefficient ought to equal zero. In fact it equals 0.184 with a standard error of 0.076. Interestingly, our labor-hoarding model implies that this regression coefficient ought to equal 0.104 with a standard error of 0.026.[15] Taking sampling uncertainty into account one cannot reject, at conventional significance levels, the view that, over whole sample period, the model fully succeeds in

[14]Hall (1989) argues that time-varying effort is not a plausible explanation for explaining this correlation. To argue this, he first calculates the growth rate of effective labor input required to explain all of the observed movements in total factor productivity. From this measure he subtracts the growth rate of actual hours work to generate a time series on the growth rate in work effort. He argues that the implied movements in work effort are implausibly large. This calculation does not apply to our analysis because it presumes that there are *no* shocks to productivity, an assumption which is clearly at variance with our model.

[15]This standard error reflects sampling uncertainty on our estimates of the model's structural parameters.

accounting for the observed correlation between the Solow residual and government consumption.[16] Standard RBC models obviously cannot.[17]

After all is said and done, what is my answer to the question advertised in the title of this paper: 'Real Business-Cycle Analysis: Wisdom or Whimsy?'. My answer is – both. On the whimsy side, I have tried to convince you that the substantive claims in this literature regarding the cyclical role of technology shocks are exceedingly fragile. Decisions based on those claims ought to be viewed as whimsical.

On the wisdom side we *have* learned that dynamic stochastic general equilibrium models can be used to successfully organize our thoughts about the business cycle in a quantitative way. We *have* learned that technology shocks play *some* role in the business cycle. But we have not learned just how large that role is. Finally, to its great credit, work on quantitative Real Business Cycle models has reminded us that empirical work whose *sole* purpose is to answer the question 'Is the model true?' is not likely to be very useful. Of course the model is not true. That much should have been obvious before we started. And it has been obvious to theorists all along. To take an obvious example – nobody objects to Lucas' (1972) model of the Phillips curve because old people aren't randomly whisked away in the middle of the night via unobservable helicopters. A formal statistical test which rejected the model because of that fact wouldn't be very useful or change anybody's mind about anything.

Convincing structural empirical work ought to address the question: 'Does the model succeed *quantitatively* in accounting for those features of the data it was designed to shed light on?' But good empirical work also ought to tell us just how loudly the data speak in favor of a given hypothesis. And just as importantly, it also ought to help us understand – at what cost did we succeed? What *didn't* we explain? What steps appear to be the most promising in the inevitable and ongoing interaction between data and theory?

I conclude by trying to draw one final lesson from the way in which theorists proceed. Theorists are often told to be leery of econometricians bearing free parameters. They already know that they ought to be leery of qualitative conclusions which emerge *only* under highly specialized assumptions. Their response to this problem is to engage in *theoretical* fragility

---

[16] The labor-hoarding model's performance is more mixed when we allow for a break in the sample. Burnside, Eichenbaum, and Rebelo (1990) find virtually no evidence against the model along this dimension in the first subsample. However, there is considerable evidence against this aspect of the model in the second sample period.

[17] Burnside, Rebelo, and I are currently pursuing our labor-hoarding model to see whether it is quantitatively consistent with (a) the fact that average productivity leads the cycle, i.e., average productivity is positively correlated with future output and hours worked, and (b) the fact that average productivity tends to fall at the end of expansions [see Gordon (1979)]. McCallum (1989) points out that existing RBC models fail to account for the dynamic correlations between average productivity and output.

analyses. Indeed, Lucas' (1989) paper on 'The Effects of Monetary Shocks when Prices Are Set in Advance' provides an excellent example of this type of analysis. In motivating his paper Lucas writes:

> Models of monetary economies necessarily depend on the assumed conventions about the way in which business is conducted in the absence of complete markets, about who does what, when, and what information he has when he does it. Such conventions are necessarily highly specific, relative to the enormous variety of trading practices we observe. Do the various rigid price models have enough in common to have useful empirical or policy implications, or does everything hinge on the accuracy of assumptions in constructing each specific example?

Lucas concludes that the substantive implications which emerge from this class of models are, in fact, quite robust. Whether one agrees or not is not germane here. What is germane is the effort to address the question.

Unfortunately, despite some important exceptions, notably Cooley and LeRoy's (1981) research on money demand, Leamer's (1984) work on international trade, and recent work by Hansen, Sargent, and Roberds (1990) on the time-series implications of martingale models of consumption and taxes, it's hard to think of many analog examples in the empirical literature. The time has come for more empiricists to follow suite. Absent a greater willingness to engage in empirical fragility analysis, structural empirical work will simply cease to be relevant. We may continue to publish, but our influence will surely perish.

References

Backus, David K., Patrick J. Kehoe, and Finn E. Kydland, 1989, International trade and business cycles, Working paper 425 (Federal Reserve Bank of Minneapolis, MN).

Blanchard, Oliver J., 1989, A traditional interpretation of macroeconomic fluctuations, American Economic Review 79, 1146–1164.

Burnside, Craig, Sergio T. Rebelo, and M. Eichenbaum, 1990, Labor hoarding and the business cycle, Manuscript (Northwestern University, Evanston, IL).

Christiano, Lawrence J. and Martin Eichenbaum, 1990a, Current real business cycle theories and aggregate labor market fluctuations, Manuscript (Northwestern University, Evanston, IL).

Christiano, Lawrence J. and Martin Eichenbaum, 1990b, Unit roots in real GNP – Do we know and do we care?, Carnegie–Rochester Conference Series on Public Policy 32, 7–62.

Cooley, Thomas F. and Stephen F. LeRoy, 1981, Identification and estimation of money demand, American Economic Review 71, 825–844.

Evans, Charles L., 1990, Productivity shocks and real business cycles, Manuscript (University of South Carolina, Columbia, SC).

Fair, Ray, 1969, The short run demand for workers and hours (North-Holland, Amsterdam).

Gordon, Robert J., 1979, The end-of-expansion phenomenon in short-run productivity behavior, Brookings Papers on Economic Activity 2, 447–461.

Hall, Robert E., 1988, The relation between price and marginal cost in U.S. industry, Journal of Political Economy 96, 921–947.

Hall, Robert E., 1989, Invariance properties of the Solow residual, NBER working paper 3034.

Hansen, Gary D., 1985, Indivisible labor and the business cycle, Journal of Monetary Economics 16, 309–328.

Hansen, Gary D., 1988, Technical progress and aggregate fluctuations, Manuscript (University of California, Los Angeles, CA).

Hansen, Gary D. and Thomas J. Sargent, 1988, Straight time and over-time in equilibrium, Journal of Monetary Economics 21, 281–308.

Hansen, Lars P., Thomas J. Sargent, and William Roberds, 1990, Implications of expected present value budget balance: Application to postwar data, Manuscript (University of Chicago, Chicago, IL).

Hansen, Lars P., 1982, Large sample properties of generalized method of moments estimators, Econometrica 50, 1029–1054.

Hodrick, Robert J. and Edward C. Prescott, 1980, Post-war U.S. business cycles: An empirical investigation, Manuscript (Carnegie-Mellon University, Pittsburgh, PA).

King, Robert G. and Sergio T. Rebelo, 1988, Low frequency filtering and real business cycles, Manuscript (University of Rochester, Rochester, NY).

Kydland, Finn E. and Edward C. Prescott, 1982, Time to build and aggregate fluctuations, Econometrica 50, 1345–70.

Kydland, Finn E. and Edward C. Prescott, 1988, The work week of capital and its cyclical implications, Journal of Monetary Economics 21, 343–360.

Kydland, Finn E. and Edward C. Prescott, 1989, Hours and employment variation in business cycle theory, Discussion paper 17 (Institute for Empirical Economics, Federal Reserve Bank of Minneapolis, MN).

Leamer, E.E. 1983, Let's take the con out of econometrics, American Economic Review 73, 31–43.

Leamer, E.E., 1984, Sources of international comparative advantage: Theory and evidence (MIT Press, Cambridge, MA).

Lucas, Robert E. Jr., 1970, Capacity, overtime, and empirical production functions, American Economic Review, Papers and Proceedings 6, 1345–1371.

Lucas, Robert E. Jr., 1972, Expectations and the neutrality of money, Journal of Economic Theory 4, 103–124.

Lucas, Robert E. Jr., 1988, The effects of monetary shocks when prices are set in advance, Manuscript (University of Chicago, Chicago, IL).

McCallum, Bennett T., 1989, Real business cycle models, in: Robert J. Barro, ed., Modern business cycle theory (Harvard University Press, Cambridge, MA) 16–50.

Perron, P., 1988, The Great Crash, the oil price shock and the unit root hypothesis, Econometrica 55, 277–302.

Prescott, Edward, C., 1986, Theory ahead of business cycle measurement, Federal Reserve Bank of Minneapolis Quarterly Review 10, 9–22.

Rogerson, R., 1988, Indivisible labor, lotteries, and equilibrium, Journal of Monetary Economics 21, 3–17.

Summers, Lawrence J., 1986, Some skeptical observations on real business cycle theory, Federal Reserve Bank of Minneapolis Quarterly Review 10, 23–27.

Did Technology Shocks Cause the 1990–1991 Recession?

By GARY D. HANSEN AND EDWARD C. PRESCOTT*

Real-business-cycle theory has been used to determine the statistical properties of aggregate fluctuations induced by technology shocks. The finding is that technology shocks have been an important contributor to fluctuations in the U.S. economy. For example, Finn E. Kydland and Prescott (1991) estimate that if the only impulses were technology shocks, the U.S. economy would have been 70 percent as volatile as it has been over the postwar period. In this paper we employ the theory to answer the question "Did technology shocks cause the 1990–1991 recession?"

Answering this question requires the determination of the effects of technology shocks on the *path* of the economy. The procedure that we use to make this determination is as follows. First, we construct a model economy and calibrate it so that its steady-state matches actual 1987 values. Data for other years are used to determine the realizations of the shocks and the nature of the stochastic processes generating these shocks. Given these stochastic processes, the equilibrium decision rules for our calibrated economy are computed. We then construct the path for the economy implied by the model for the period 1984:1–1992:3. We set 1984:1 model values of the state variables equal to actual 1984:1 values and use the decision rules and the *realized* shocks to construct this path. Fi-

nally, we examine whether the model economy experiences a recession in 1991 as did the U.S. economy.

Business cycles are variations in output per adult that are in large part accounted for by variation in the per-adult time allocated to market production. Figure 1 plots the time path of the per-adult labor input. During the 1983:1–1989:1 period there was a remarkable 12-percent increase in the labor input per adult. Beginning in 1990:2 there has been a decline of nearly 6 percent in this per-adult labor input. An unusual feature of the recovery subsequent to the 1990–1991 recession is that this labor-input variable has continued to decline well into the recovery. This unusual behavior leads to a related question, "Did technology shocks cause the slow recovery?"

We found it necessary to modify the standard real-business-cycle model in four ways in order to answer the posed question. First, given the enormous changes in the relative prices of durables as depicted in Figure 2, we could not treat technology change as being neutral with respect to different types of final goods. Following John B. Long and Charles Plosser (1983) and Jeremy Greenwood et al. (1992) we consider multiple production sectors with technology change differing across sectors. Second, we assume that there is a technology employed within the household sector that produces a consumption flow from the stock of consumer durables. Third, we consider land to be a factor of production in addition to labor and capital. Our fourth modification is to introduce population growth.

I. What Are These Technology Shocks?

By definition, technology shocks are changes in the production functions or, more generally, the production possibility sets of the profit centers. In a growing economy we observe positive technology change over

*Hansen: University of California-Los Angeles and Department of Economics, University of Pennsylvania, Philadelphia, PA 19104-6297; Prescott: Research Department, Federal Reserve Bank of Minneapolis, Minneapolis, MN 55401, and University of Minnesota. We thank Fernando Alvarez and Terry Fitzgerald for their more than able assistance and the NSF for financial support. The views expressed herein are those of the authors and not necessarily those of the Federal Reserve Bank of Minneapolis or the Federal Reserve System.

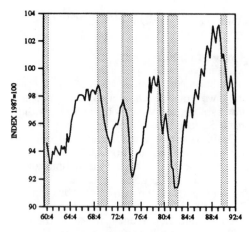

FIGURE 1. HOURS WORKED PER ADULT

Notes: The variable plotted is the Citibase measure of the seasonally adjusted total hours at work in all industries (LHOURS) divided by the civilian noninstitutional population aged 20 and older. The jaggedness beginning in 1984 indicates a problem with the seasonal adjustment procedure used by Citibase.

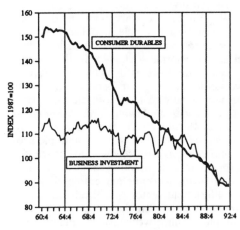

FIGURE 2. PRICES OF INVESTMENT GOODS
RELATIVE TO CONSUMPTION

time with these production possibilities sets shifting out as production processes are improved or new ones invented. One factor leading to this change is growth of public scientific and technical knowledge. This knowledge can, in principle, be accessed and used by firms in any country to develop a new technology and to improve upon an existing one. Thus, this factor does not account for the differences in the relative per capita wealth of nations at a point in time. The reason why India has a per capita income only one-twentieth the U.S. value cannot be because India is in some other world with a much smaller stock of technical knowledge.

Similarly, changes in this stock of knowledge cannot account for the business cycles observed within a country over time. Although the rate at which inventions and discoveries are made may vary over time, the stock of knowledge should not decrease. Thus, these variations are not likely to account for the negative growth rates sometimes observed. If technology shocks are shown to cause the 1991 recession, and if changes in knowledge are not responsible, what is?

Every nation has a set of rules and regulations that govern the conduct of business. These have consequences for the incentives to adopt more advanced technologies and for the resources required to operate an existing one. Bureaucracies that assist in the adoption of new technologies, say, by making available technical information to businesses, foster technological growth. Systems that divert entrepreneurial talent from improving technologies to rent-seeking activities have an adverse effect on growth. The reason for the huge difference between the United States and India must be that India has been less successful than the United States in setting up economic institutions conducive to development. It would not be surprising then, that changes in the legal and regulatory system within a country often induce negative as well as positive changes in technology.

A related source of technology shocks originates from the fact that we can only measure outputs and inputs that are actually traded in markets and have associated prices. In part, the set of traded factors of production and commodities is also dependent upon the economic institutions in place. For example, if the legal system is such that there is a market for pollution rights, then these rights become a measured factor of production. There is a rental price of these rights like there is a rental price of land. If the government purchases some of these rights in order to reduce the amount of pollution produced, there is no technology change but simply a reduction in the endowment of a particular factor of production. If, on the other hand, pollution rights are not traded and the government imposes constraints on firms with regard to the amount of pollution per unit of output, this represents a technology shock, since the amount of output that can be produced from given quantities of market inputs changes.

An important consequence of our interpretation of these technology shocks is that, although they are exogenous to the profit centers, they are not exogenous to the society as a whole. If technology shocks are an important contributor to business cycles, then changes in the political system and the institutions created by it are also important.

II. The Model Economy

The model economy employed is a three-sector stochastic growth model consisting of a consumption-good sector producing consumer services, nondurables, and government consumption; a consumer-durables sector; and a producer-durables sector. The technologies associated with each sector are as follows:

$$(1) \qquad C_t \le Z_t K_{1t}^{\theta_1} h_{1t}^{\theta_2} L_{1t}^{1-\theta_1-\theta_2}$$

$$X_{dt} \le Z_{dt} Z_t K_{2t}^{\theta_1} h_{2t}^{\theta_2} L_{2t}^{1-\theta_1-\theta_2}$$

$$X_{kt} \le Z_{kt} Z_t K_{3t}^{\theta_1} h_{3t}^{\theta_2} L_{3t}^{1-\theta_1-\theta_2}$$

where all variables are per capita values. K_{it}, h_{it}, and L_{it} are the stock of capital, hours worked, and land employed in sector i in period t and C_t, X_{dt}, and X_{kt} are consumption, investment in consumer durables, and investment in productive capital, respectively. The variable Z_t is the consumption sector technology shock while Z_{dt} and Z_{kt} are the investment-goods-sector technology shocks relative to the consump-

tion-good-sector shock. The inverses of Z_d and Z_k are the equilibrium relative prices of consumer durables and capital in terms of consumption.

Define K_t to be $\Sigma_i K_{it}$ and h_t to be $\Sigma_i h_{it}$. In addition, the per capita stock of land is fixed and set equal to 1, so $\Sigma_i L_{it} = 1$. The stocks of durables evolve according to the following laws of motion:

$$(2) \quad N_{t+1} D_{t+1} = N_t[(1-\delta_d) D_t + X_{dt}]$$

$$N_{t+1} K_{t+1} = N_t[(1-\delta_k) K_t + X_{kt}]$$

where N_t is the population size at time t.

The technology shocks Z, Z_d, and Z_k are modeled as follows:

$$(3) \quad Z_t = \lambda^t z_t \qquad Z_{dt} = \lambda_d^t z_{dt} \qquad Z_{kt} = \lambda_k^t z_{kt}$$

where

$$\log z_{t+1} = (1-\rho)\log \bar{z} + \rho \log z_t + \varepsilon_{t+1}$$

$$\log z_{d,t+1} = \rho_d \log z_{dt} + \varepsilon_{d,t+1}$$

$$\log z_{k,t+1} = \rho_k \log z_{kt} + \varepsilon_{k,t+1}.$$

Here ρ, ρ_d, and ρ_k are each greater than 0 but less than or equal to 1; ε, ε_d, and ε_k are independently and identically distributed random variables with 0 mean; and λ, λ_d, and λ_k are each greater than or equal to 1.

Optimality implies that the value marginal product of each input will be equalized across sectors. Given that identical Cobb-Douglas production functions are assumed, this implies that there exist fractions, ϕ_{1t}, ϕ_{2t}, and ϕ_{3t}, where $\Sigma_i \phi_{it} = 1$, such that $K_{it} = \phi_{it} K_t$, $h_{it} = \phi_{it} h_t$, and $L_{it} = \phi_{it}$ for each i. Using this result, it is possible to aggregate over sectors to obtain the resource constraint

$$(4) \qquad C_t + \frac{X_{dt}}{Z_{dt}} + \frac{X_{kt}}{Z_{kt}} \le Z_t K_t^{\theta_1} h_t^{\theta_2}.$$

The population consists of a continuum of identical households of measure N_t that grows at the rate $\eta - 1$. The utility of a household in period t is given by

$$(5) \quad u(C_t, D_t, h_t)$$

$$= \sigma \log C_t + (1 - \sigma) \log D_t - \alpha h_t$$

where the second term reflects the utility from the service flow provided by the stock of durables. The fact that utility is linear in hours worked results from assuming that labor is indivisible (households can work some $\hat{h}$ hours or not at all) and that labor is allocated through a market for employment lotteries as in Richard Rogerson (1988) and Hansen (1985).

Since there are no distortions in this economy, an equilibrium can be computed by solving a social-planning problem in which the objective function of the social planner is $E\{\Sigma_t \beta^t N_t u(C_t, D_t, h_t)\}$. The numerical methods we use to solve this problem, which are described in detail in Hansen and Prescott (1993), require that there be no secular trends in the variables. Therefore, we transform the model as follows. Let

$$c_t = C_t/\gamma^t \quad x_{dt} = X_{dt}/(\gamma\lambda_d)^t \quad x_{kt} = X_{kt}/(\gamma\lambda_k)^t$$

$$d_t = D_t/(\gamma\lambda_d)^t \quad k_t = K_t/(\gamma\lambda_k)^t$$

where $\gamma = [\lambda\lambda_k^{\theta_1}]^{1/(1-\theta_1)}$. After this transformation, the social planning problem can be represented by the following stationary dynamic program:

$$(6) \quad v(z, z_d, z_k d, k)$$

$$= \max\{\sigma \log c + (1 - \sigma)\log d - \alpha h$$

$$+ E[\beta\eta v(z', z'_d, z'_k, d', k')]\}$$

subject to

$$c + \frac{x_d}{z_d} + \frac{x_k}{z_k} = zk^{\theta_1}h^{\theta_2}$$

$$\eta\gamma\lambda_d d' = (1 - \delta_d)d + x_d$$

$$\eta\gamma\lambda_k k' = (1 - \delta_k)k + x_k$$

and equations (3).

III. Model Calibration

The parameters of the model that need to be assigned values include parameters describing the exogenous shock processes ($\bar{z}$, ρ, ρ_d, ρ_k, λ, λ_d, and λ_k), factor income shares (θ_1 and θ_2), rates of depreciation for durables (δ_d and δ_k), and parameters describing preferences (β, σ, and α). The quarterly growth rate of the population, η, is taken to be 1.0032. For the most part, parameters are assigned so that the steady state of the model corresponds to actual data for the first quarter of 1987 (1987:1).

The parameters of the shock processes are obtained by examining the empirical counterparts to Z, Z_d, and Z_k. The variables Z_d and Z_k are equal to the inverses of the relative prices of consumer durables and capital investment shown in Figure 2. Estimates of the linear trends in the logs of these variables from 1975:1 to 1992:3 provided values for λ_d and λ_k equal to 1.0051 and 1.0026, respectively. In addition, examination of these series led us to choose values for ρ_d and ρ_k equal to 1.

Equation (4) is used to obtain an empirical counterpart to the realized technology shocks, Z_t. To compute Z, however, empirical counterparts to C, X_d, X_k, h, and K are needed as well as values for the parameters θ_1 and θ_2. The first three variables are taken from the national income and product accounts. The variable C is consumption of nondurables and services plus government consumption, X_d is expenditures on consumer durables, and X_k is the difference between GNP and the first two components. Each of these components is measured in 1987 dollars and is divided by N_t, which is taken to be the population aged 20 and older. The labor input is weekly hours at work per adult, scaled so that h_t is equal to its steady-state value in the first quarter of 1987.[1] The steady-state value used is 0.305,

---

[1] The hours series used is a smoothed version of the series plotted in Figure 1. The smoothing was done to better seasonal adjustment and to reduce sampling error problems.

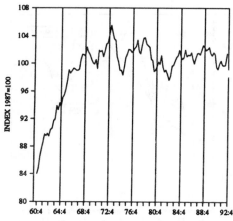

FIGURE 3. CONSUMPTION-SECTOR TECHNOLOGY
PARAMETERS (Z)

model:[3]

$$[(1+r)/\gamma - 1]L + [(1+r)\lambda_k - 1 + \delta_k]K$$
$$= (1 - \theta_2)\text{GNP}.$$

Given this value for r, we set $\theta_1 = [(1+r)\lambda_k - 1 + \delta_k]K/\text{GNP} = 0.26$.

Using these values, we are able to construct a time series for Z_t. Figure 3 plots the realized consumption-sector technology-shocks path. Examining this series led us to set $\lambda = 1$ and $\rho = 0.95$. The parameter $\bar{z}$ was chosen so that the realized value of z_t is equal to its value in 1987:1. Finally, the parameters of preferences, α, β, and σ, were chosen in a manner similar to θ_2: the parameters were calibrated so that steady-state conditions are satisfied using 1987:1 observations as steady-state values.[4]

IV. Findings

Figure 4 contains a plot of quarterly GNP in 1987 prices for the model economy given the realizations of the shocks for the U.S. economy from 1984:4 to 1992:3 and the expected value of the shocks from 1992:4 to 1993:4. Also plotted is the actual path of U.S. GNP through 1992:3. The key finding is that the model economy had a recession in the 1990–1991 period. Not only does the timing of the recessions match, but the amplitude and duration of the downturns match as well. The second finding is that technology shocks did not cause the slow recovery.

There are some differences between the behavior of the model economy and the behavior of the U.S. economy during this period. One difference is that the model economy reacts more strongly to productivity shocks with adjustments being more rapid. As a result, the path of GNP for the model is more jagged and fluctuates about

implying that just over 30 percent of a household's substitutable time is spent engaged in market activities. The capital series is constructed by setting $N_t K_t$ ($t = 1959:1$) equal to the stock of fixed private capital taken from John Musgrave (1992) for the end of 1958 and iterating forward using equation (2) and the empirical series X_k. The depreciation rate δ_k was chosen so that the capital stock for $t = 1987:1$ matches the number for 1986 as reported by Musgrave (1992). A similar procedure was used to calibrate δ_d.

The parameter θ_2, which is labor's share of income, was set equal to 0.69 using national income data for 1987:1, which we take to be the steady state.[2] Given the stock of land, stock of fixed private capital, and GNP for 1987:1 and assuming that land does not depreciate, we can obtain a value for the real interest rate (for the consumption good) from the following equation which holds in the steady state for our

---

[2] We assign all compensation of employees, fraction θ_2 of proprietors' income, fraction θ_2 of the statistical discrepancy, and one-half of indirect business taxes to labor income.

[3] The price of land relative to the consumption good grows in the steady state at rate $\gamma - 1$, which is the rate at which per-adult consumption grows.

[4] The calibrated parameter values are $\lambda = 1.000$, $\lambda_d = 1.005$, $\lambda_k = 1.003$, $\rho = 0.95$, $\rho_d = 1.00$, $\rho_k = 1.00$, $\bar{z} = 0.0331$, $\delta_d = 0.051$, $\delta_k = 0.014$, $\theta_1 = 0.26$, $\theta_2 = 0.69$, $\beta = 0.98$, $\sigma = 0.88$, $\alpha = 2.625$, and $\eta = 1.0032$. Rates are quarterly.

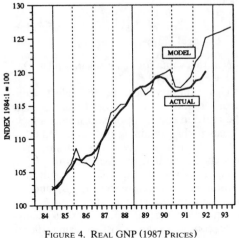

FIGURE 4. REAL GNP (1987 PRICES)

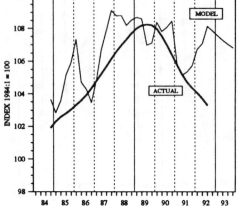

FIGURE 6. LABOR INPUT PER ADULT

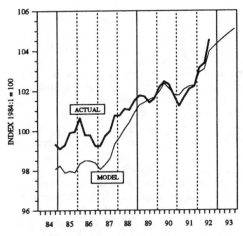

FIGURE 5. LABOR PRODUCTIVITY

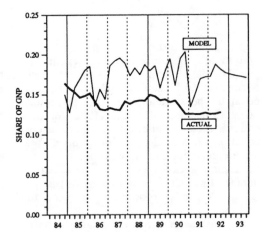

FIGURE 7. BUSINESS INVESTMENT SHARE

the path for the U.S. economy. This was expected given the nature of the abstraction that we employed. Model economies with some cost of people moving between sectors, time-to-build, and time-to-train and with more curvature on the utility function would have resulted in slower responses (see Kydland and Prescott, 1991).

The paths of labor productivity are similar for the two economies, as shown in Figure 5. Actual labor productivity was higher than that of the model in the early part of the period and grew more rapidly in 1991

and 1992. The reason for this can be seen in Figure 6, which plots the paths of the labor input per adult for the two economies. In the early period the labor input increased more rapidly in the actual economy than it did in the model. In the model, hours worked per adult increase in the 1991:2–1992:3 period, while in the actual economy they continued to decline. Another difference in the behavior of the model and the actual economy is the behavior of business investment share. As can be seen in Figure 7, business investment as a share of GNP is higher in the model economy except in the early part of the sample.

V. Discussion

The recovery from the recession in the U.S. economy has not been as fast as in the model economy. As we have pointed out, the model economy tends to adjust more quickly than the actual economy to technology shocks. In addition, there are factors other than technology shocks that have real consequences and may have inhibited the recovery. Perhaps changing demographics and life-cycle factors leading to lower savings rates are partly responsible for the slow recovery. Perhaps public-finance shocks are responsible. For example, people may be expecting the effective marginal tax on capital income to be higher in the future. Alternatively, people may be anticipating the institution of investment tax credits that will lower the effective price of new capital, and as a result, businesses are deferring investments.

Insofar as there are no significant public-finance shocks, this quantitative theoretical exercise leads us to forecast reasonably rapid growth for a few quarters as real GNP converges to the path predicted by the model. In addition, if future technology shocks are of average values, the longer-run prognosis is not so optimistic. This can be seen in the predicted path of GNP for the model economy beyond 1992:3, as shown in Figure 4. Of course, if technology shocks continue to be above average, the United States will experience a boom; if the shocks in the coming year are below average, we can expect a recession. The final outcome depends on the nature of the economic institutions —the legal, regulatory, and political environment—currently in place and on changes that occur over the next year or so.

REFERENCES

Greenwood, Jeremy, Hercowitz, Zvi and Krusell, Per, "Macroeconomic Implications of Investment-Specific Technological Change," Institute for Empirical Macroeconomics Discussion Paper No. 76, Federal Reserve Bank of Minneapolis, 1992.

Hansen, Gary D., "Indivisible Labor and the Business Cycle," *Journal of Monetary Economics*, November 1985, *16*, 309–27.

_____ **and Prescott, Edward C.,** "Recursive Methods for Computing Equilibria of Business Cycle Models," Institute for Empirical Macroeconomics Discussion Paper No. 36, Federal Reserve Bank of Minneapolis, 1993.

Kydland, Finn E. and Prescott, Edward C., "Hours and Employment Variation in Business Cycle Theory," *Economic Theory*, 1991, *1* (1), 63–81.

Long, John B. and Plosser, Charles, "Real Business Cycles," *Journal of Political Economy*, February 1983, *91*, 39–69.

Musgrave, John, "Fixed Reproducible Tangible Wealth in the United States," *Survey of Current Business*, January 1992, *72*, 106–37.

Rogerson, Richard, "Indivisible Labor, Lotteries, and Equilibrium," *Journal of Monetary Economics*, January 1988, *21*, 3–16.

Part VII

The Solow residual

TECHNICAL CHANGE AND THE AGGREGATE PRODUCTION FUNCTION*

Robert M. Solow

IN this day of rationally designed econometric studies and super-input-output tables, it takes something more than the usual "willing suspension of disbelief" to talk seriously of the aggregate production function. But the aggregate production function is only a little less legitimate a concept than, say, the aggregate consumption function, and for some kinds of long-run macro-models it is almost as indispensable as the latter is for the short-run. As long as we insist on practicing macro-economics we shall need aggregate relationships.

Even so, there would hardly be any justification for returning to this old-fashioned topic if I had no novelty to suggest. The new wrinkle I want to describe is an elementary way of segregating variations in output per head due to technical change from those due to changes in the availability of capital per head. Naturally, every additional bit of information has its price. In this case the price consists of one new required time series, the share of labor or property in total income, and one new assumption, that factors are paid their marginal products. Since the former is probably more respectable than the other data I shall use, and since the latter is an assumption often made, the price may not be unreasonably high.

Before going on, let me be explicit that I would not try to justify what follows by calling on fancy theorems on aggregation and index numbers.[1] Either this kind of aggregate economics appeals or it doesn't. Personally I belong to both schools. If it does, I think one can

draw some crude but useful conclusions from the results.

Theoretical Basis

I will first explain what I have in mind mathematically and then give a diagrammatic exposition. In this case the mathematics seems simpler. If Q represents output and K and L represent capital and labor inputs in "physical" units, then the aggregate production function can be written as:

$$Q = F(K,L;t). \tag{1}$$

The variable t for time appears in F to allow for technical change. It will be seen that I am using the phrase "technical change" as a shorthand expression for *any kind of shift* in the production function. Thus slowdowns, speedups, improvements in the education of the labor force, and all sorts of things will appear as "technical change."

It is convenient to begin with the special case of *neutral* technical change. Shifts in the production function are defined as neutral if they leave marginal rates of substitution untouched but simply increase or decrease the output attainable from given inputs. In that case the production function takes the special form

$$Q = A(t)f(K,L) \tag{1a}$$

and the multiplicative factor $A(t)$ measures the cumulated effect of shifts over time. Differentiate (1a) totally with respect to time and divide by Q and one obtains

$$\frac{\dot{Q}}{Q} = \frac{\dot{A}}{A} + A\frac{\partial f}{\partial K}\frac{\dot{K}}{Q} + A\frac{\partial f}{\partial L}\frac{\dot{L}}{Q}$$

where dots indicate time derivatives. Now define $w_k = \dfrac{\partial Q}{\partial K}\dfrac{K}{Q}$ and $w_L = \dfrac{\partial Q}{\partial L}\dfrac{L}{Q}$ the relative shares of capital and labor, and substitute in the above equation (note that $\partial Q/\partial K = A\,\partial f/\partial K$, etc.) and there results:

$$\frac{\dot{Q}}{Q} = \frac{\dot{A}}{A} + w_K\frac{\dot{K}}{K} + w_L\frac{\dot{L}}{L}. \tag{2}$$

---

* I owe a debt of gratitude to Dr. Louis Lefeber for statistical and other assistance, and to Professors Fellner, Leontief, and Schultz for stimulating suggestions.

[1] Mrs. Robinson in particular has explored many of the profound difficulties that stand in the way of giving any precise meaning to the quantity of capital ("The Production Function and the Theory of Capital," *Review of Economic Studies*, Vol. 21, No. 2), and I have thrown up still further obstacles (ibid., Vol. 23, No. 2). Were the data available, it would be better to apply the analysis to some precisely defined production function with many precisely defined inputs. One can at least hope that the aggregate analysis gives some notion of the way a detailed analysis would lead.

From time series of $\dot{Q}/Q$, w_k, $\dot{K}/K$, w_L and $\dot{L}/L$ or their discrete year-to-year analogues, we could estimate $\dot{A}/A$ and thence $A(t)$ itself. Actually an amusing thing happens here. Nothing has been said so far about returns to scale. But if all factor inputs are classified either as K or L, then the available figures always show w_K and w_L adding up to one. Since we have assumed that factors are paid their marginal products, this amounts to assuming the hypotheses of Euler's theorem. The calculus being what it is, we might just as well assume the conclusion, namely that F is homogeneous of degree one. This has the advantage of making everything come out neatly in terms of intensive magnitudes. Let $Q/L = q$, $K/L = k$, $w_L = 1 - w_K$; note that $\dot{q}/q = \dot{Q}/Q - \dot{L}/L$ etc., and (2) becomes

$$\frac{\dot{q}}{q} = \frac{\dot{A}}{A} + w_K \frac{\dot{k}}{k}. \qquad (2a)$$

Now all we need to disentangle the technical change index $A(t)$ are series for output per man hour, capital per man hour, and the share of capital.

So far I have been assuming that technical change is neutral. But if we go back to (1) and carry out the same reasoning we arrive at something very like (2a), namely

$$\frac{\dot{q}}{q} = \frac{1}{F}\frac{\partial F}{\partial t} + w_k \frac{\dot{k}}{k} \qquad (2b)$$

It can be shown, by integrating a partial differential equation, that if $\dot{F}/F$ is independent of K and L (actually under constant returns to scale only K/L matters) then (1) has the special form (1a) and shifts in the production function are neutral. If in addition $\dot{F}/F$ is constant in time, say equal to a, then $A(t) = e^{at}$ or in discrete approximation $A(t) = (1 + a)^t$.

The case of neutral shifts and constant returns to scale is now easily handled graphically. The production function is completely represented by a graph of q against k (analogously to the fact that if we know the unit-output isoquant, we know the whole map). The trouble is that this function is shifting in time,

so that if we observe points in the (q,k) plane, their movements are compounded out of movements along the curve and shifts of the curve. In Chart 1, for instance, every ordinate on the curve for $t = 1$ has been multiplied by the same factor to give a neutral upward shift of the production function for period 2. The problem is to estimate this shift from knowledge of points P_1 and P_2. Obviously it would be quite misleading to fit a curve through raw observed points like P_1, P_2 and others. But if the shift factor for each point of time can be estimated, the observed points can be corrected for technical change, and a production function can then be found.[2]

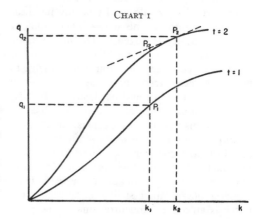

CHART I

The natural thing to do, for small changes, is to approximate the period 2 curve by its tangent at P_2 (or the period 1 curve by its tangent at P_1). This yields an approximately corrected point P_{12}, and an estimate for $\triangle A/A$, namely $\overline{P_{12}P_1}/q_1$. But $k_1P_{12} = q_2 - \partial q/\partial k \triangle k$ and hence $\overline{P_{12}P_1} = q_2 - q_1 - \partial q/\partial k \triangle k = \triangle q - \partial q/\partial k \triangle k$ and $\triangle A/A = \overline{P_{12}P_1}/q_1 = \triangle q/q - \partial q/\partial k \ (k/q) \triangle k/k = \triangle q/q - w_k \triangle k/k$ which is exactly the content of (2a). The not-necessarily-neutral case is a bit more complicated, but basically similar.

[2] Professors Wassily Leontief and William Fellner independently pointed out to me that this "first-order" approximation could in principle be improved. After estimating a production function corrected for technical change (see below), one could go back and use it to provide a second approximation to the shift series, and on into further iterations.

An Application to the U.S.: 1909–1949

In order to isolate shifts of the aggregate production function from movements along it, by use of (2a) or (2b), three time series are needed: output per unit of labor, capital per unit of labor, and the share of capital. Some rough and ready figures, together with the obvious computations, are given in Table 1.

The conceptually cleanest measure of aggregate output would be real net national product. But long NNP series are hard to come by, so I have used GNP instead. The only difference this makes is that the share of capital has to include depreciation. It proved possible to restrict the experiment to private non-farm economic activity. This is an advantage (a) because it skirts the problem of measuring government output and (b) because eliminating agriculture is at least a step in the direction of homogeneity. Thus my q is a time series of real private non-farm GNP per man hour, Kendrick's valuable work.

The capital time series is the one that will really drive a purist mad. For present purposes, "capital" includes land, mineral deposits, etc. Naturally I have used Goldsmith's estimates (with government, agricultural, and consumer durables eliminated). Ideally what one would like to measure is the annual flow of capital services. Instead one must be content with a less utopian estimate of the stock of capital goods in existence. All sorts of conceptual problems arise on this account. As a single example, if the capital stock consisted of a million identical machines and if each one as it wore out was replaced by a more durable machine of the same annual capacity, the stock of capital as measured would surely increase. But the maximal flow of capital services would be constant. There is nothing to be done about this, but something must be done about the fact of idle capacity. What belongs in a production function is capital in use, not capital in place. Lacking any reliable year-by-year measure of the utilization of capital I have simply reduced the Goldsmith figures by the fraction of the labor force unemployed in each year, thus assuming that labor and capital always suffer unemployment to the same percentage. This is undoubtedly wrong, but probably gets

closer to the truth than making no correction at all.[3]

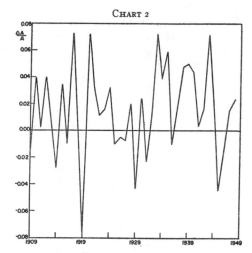

CHART 2

The share-of-capital series is another hodgepodge, pieced together from various sources and ad hoc assumptions (such as Gale Johnson's guess that about 35 per cent of non-farm entrepreneurial income is a return to property). Only after these computations were complete did I learn that Edward Budd of Yale Univer-

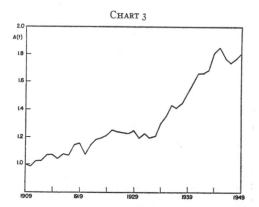

CHART 3

sity has completed a careful long-term study of factor shares which will soon be published. It seems unlikely that minor changes in this ingredient would grossly alter the final results,

[3] Another factor for which I have not corrected is the changing length of the work-week. As the work-week shortens, the intensity of use of existing capital decreases, and the stock figures overestimate the input of capital services.

TECHNICAL CHANGE AND PRODUCTION FUNCTION   315

but I have no doubt that refinement of this and the capital time-series would produce neater results.

In any case, in (2a) or (2b) one can replace the time-derivatives by year-to-year changes and calculate $\triangle q/q - w_k \triangle k/k$. The result is an estimate of $\triangle F/F$ or $\triangle A/A$, depending on whether these relative shifts appear to be neutral or not. Such a calculation is made in Table 1 and shown in Chart 2. Thence, by arbitrarily setting $A(1909) = 1$ and using the fact that $A(t+1) = A(t) (1 + \triangle A(t)/A(t))$ one can successively reconstruct the $A(t)$ time series, which is shown in Chart 3.

TABLE 1. — DATA FOR CALCULATION OF $A(t)$

Year	% labor force employed (1)	Capital stock ($ mill.) (2)	Col. 1 x Col. 2 (3)	Share of property in income (4)	Priv. nonfarm GNP per manhour (5)	Employed capital per manhour (6)	$\triangle A/A$ (7)	$A(t)$ (8)
1909	91.1	146,142	133,135	.335	$.623	$2.06	−.017	1.000
1910	92.8	150,038	139,235	.330	.616	2.10	.039	.983
1911	90.6	156,335	141,640	.335	.647	2.17	.002	1.021
1912	93.0	159,971	148,773	.330	.652	2.21	.040	1.023
1913	91.8	164,504	151,015	.334	.680	2.23	.007	1.064
1914	83.6	171,513	143,385	.325	.682	2.20	−.028	1.071
1915	84.5	175,371	148,188	.344	.669	2.26	.034	1.041
1916	93.7	178,351	167,115	.358	.700	2.34	−.010	1.076
1917	94.0	182,263	171,327	.370	.679	2.21	.072	1.065
1918	94.5	186,679	176,412	.342	.729	2.22	.013	1.142
1919	93.1	189,977	176,869	.354	.767	2.47	−.076	1.157
1920	92.8	194,802	180,776	.319	.721	2.58	.072	1.069
1921	76.9	201,491	154,947	.369	.770	2.55	.032	1.146
1922	81.7	204,324	166,933	.339	.788	2.49	.011	1.183
1923	92.1	209,964	193,377	.337	.809	2.61	.016	1.196
1924	88.0	222,113	195,460	.330	.836	2.74	.032	1.215
1925	91.1	231,772	211,198	.336	.872	2.81	−.010	1.254
1926	92.5	244,611	226,266	.327	.869	2.87	−.005	1.241
1927	90.0	259,142	233,228	.323	.871	2.93	−.007	1.235
1928	90.0	271,089	243,980	.338	.874	3.02	.020	1.226
1929	92.5	279,691	258,714	.332	.895	3.06	−.043	1.251
1930	88.1	289,291	254,865	.347	.880	3.30	.024	1.197
1931	78.2	289,056	226,042	.325	.904	3.33	.023	1.226
1932	67.9	282,731	191,974	.397	.879	3.28	.011	1.198
1933	66.5	270,676	180,000	.362	.869	3.10	.072	1.211
1934	70.9	262,370	186,020	.355	.921	3.00	.039	1.298
1935	73.0	257,810	188,201	.351	.943	2.87	.059	1.349
1936	77.3	254,875	197,018	.357	.982	2.72	−.010	1.429
1937	81.0	257,076	208,232	.340	.971	2.71	.021	1.415
1938	74.7	259,789	194,062	.331	1.000	2.78	.048	1.445
1939	77.2	257,314	198,646	.347	1.034	2.66	.050	1.514
1940	80.6	258,048	207,987	.357	1.082	2.63	.044	1.590
1941	86.8	262,940	228,232	.377	1.122	2.58	.003	1.660
1942	93.6	270,063	252,779	.356	1.136	2.64	.016	1.665
1943	97.4	269,761	262,747	.342	1.180	2.62	.071	1.692
1944	98.4	265,483	261,235	.332	1.265	2.63	.021	1.812
1945	96.5	261,472	252,320	.314	1.296	2.66	−.044	1.850
1946	94.8	258,051	244,632	.312	1.215	2.50	−.017	1.769
1947	95.4	268,845	256,478	.327	1.194	2.50	.016	1.739
1948	95.7	276,476	264,588	.332	1.221	2.55	.024	1.767
1949	93.0	289,360	269,105	.326	1.275	2.70	. . .	1.809

NOTES AND SOURCES:

Column (1): Percentage of labor force employed. 1909–26, from Douglas, *Real Wages in the United States* (Boston and New York, 1930), 460. 1929–49, calculated from *The Economic Almanac*, 1953–54 (New York, 1953), 426–28.

Column (2): Capital Stock. From Goldsmith, *A Study of Saving in the United States*, Vol. 3 (Princeton, 1956), 20–21, sum of columns 5, 6, 7, 9, 12, 17, 22, 23, 24.

Column (3): (1) x (2).

Column (4): Share of property in income. Compiled from *The Economic Almanac*, 504–505; and Jesse Burkhead, "Changes in the Functional Distribution of Income," *Journal of the American Satistical Association*, Vol. 48 (June 1953), 192–219. Depreciation estimates from Goldsmith, 427.

Column (5): Private nonfarm GNP per man hour, 1939 dollars. Kendrick's data, reproduced in *The Economic Almanac*, 490.

Column (6): Employed capital per man hour. Column (3) divided by Kendrick's man hour series, *ibid*.

Column (7): $\triangle A/A = \triangle (5)/(5) - (4) \times \triangle (6)/(6)$.

Column (8): From (7).

I was tempted to end this section with the remark that the $A(t)$ series, which is meant to be a rough profile of technical change, at least looks reasonable. But on second thought I decided that I had very little prior notion of what would be "reasonable" in this context. One notes with satisfaction that the trend is strongly upward; had it turned out otherwise I would not now be writing this paper. There are sharp dips after each of the World Wars; these, like the sharp rises that preceded them, can easily be rationalized. It is more suggestive that the curve shows a distinct levelling-off in the last half of the 1920's. A sustained rise begins again in 1930. There is an unpleasant sawtooth character to the first few years of the $\triangle A/A$ curve, which I imagine to be a statistical artifact.

The Outlines of Technical Change

The reader will note that I have already drifted into the habit of calling the curve of Chart 2 $\triangle A/A$ instead of the more general $\triangle F/F$. In fact, a scatter of $\triangle F/F$ against K/L (not shown) indicates no trace of a relationship. So I may state it as a formal conclusion that over the period 1909–49, shifts in the aggregate production function netted out to be approximately neutral. Perhaps I should recall that I have defined neutrality to mean that the shifts were pure scale changes, leaving marginal rates of substitution unchanged at given capital/labor ratios.

Not only is $\triangle A/A$ uncorrelated with K/L, but one might almost conclude from the graph that $\triangle A/A$ is essentially constant in time, exhibiting more or less random fluctuations about a fixed mean. Almost, but not quite, for there does seem to be a break at about 1930. There is some evidence that the average rate of progress in the years 1909–29 was smaller than that from 1930–49. The first 21 relative shifts average about 9/10 of one per cent per year, while the last 19 average 2¼ per cent per year. Even if the year 1929, which showed a strong downward shift, is moved from the first group to the second, there is still a contrast between an average rate of 1.2 per cent in the first half and .9 per cent in the second. Such *post hoc* splitting-up of a period is always dangerous. Perhaps I should leave it that there is some

evidence that technical change (broadly interpreted) may have accelerated after 1929.

The over-all result for the whole 40 years is an average upward shift of about 1.5 per cent per year. This may be compared with a figure of about .75 per cent per year obtained by Stefan Valavanis-Vail by a different and rather less general method, for the period 1869–1948.[4] Another possible comparison is with the output-per-unit-of-input computations of Jacob Schmookler,[5] which show an increase of some 36 per cent in output per unit of input between the decades 1904–13 and 1929–38. Our $A(t)$ rises 36.5 per cent between 1909 and 1934. But these are not really comparable estimates, since Schmookler's figures include agriculture.

As a last general conclusion, after which I will leave the interested reader to his own impressions, over the 40 year period output per man hour approximately doubled. At the same time, according to Chart 2, the cumulative upward shift in the production function was about 80 per cent. It is possible to argue that about one-eighth of the total increase is traceable to increased capital per man hour, and the remaining seven-eighths to technical change. The reasoning is this: real GNP per man hour increased from \$.623 to \$1.275. Divide the latter figure by 1.809, which is the 1949 value for $A(t)$, and therefore the full shift factor for the 40 years. The result is a "corrected" GNP per man hour, net of technical change, of \$.705. Thus about 8 cents of the 65 cent increase can be imputed to increased capital intensity, and the remainder to increased productivity.[6]

Of course this is not meant to suggest that the observed rate of technical progress would have persisted even if the rate of investment had been much smaller or had fallen to zero. Obviously much, perhaps nearly all, innovation must be embodied in new plant and equipment to be realized at all. One could imagine this process taking place without net capital for-

[4] S. Valavanis-Vail, "An Econometric Model of Growth, U.S.A. 1869–1953," *American Economic Review, Papers and Proceedings*, XLV (May 1955), 217.

[5] J. Schmookler, "The Changing Efficiency of the American Economy, 1869–1938," this REVIEW (August 1952), 226.

[6] For the first half of the period, 1909–29, a similar computation attributes about one-third of the observed increase in GNP per man-hour to increased capital intensity.

TECHNICAL CHANGE AND PRODUCTION FUNCTION   317

mation as old-fashioned capital goods are replaced by the latest models, so that the capital-labor ratio need not change systematically. But this raises problems of definition and measurement even more formidable than the ones already blithely ignored. This whole area of interest has been stressed by Fellner.

For comparison, Solomon Fabricant [7] has estimated that over the period 1871–1951 about 90 per cent of the increase in output per capita is attributable to technical progress. Presumably this figure is based on the standard sort of output-per-unit-of-input calculation.

It might seem at first glance that calculations of output per unit of resource input provide a relatively assumption-free way of measuring productivity changes. Actually I think the implicit load of assumptions is quite heavy, and if anything the method proposed above is considerably more general.

Not only does the usual choice of weights for computing an aggregate resource-input involve something analogous to my assumption of competitive factor markets, but in addition the criterion output ÷ a weighted sum of inputs would seem tacitly to *assume* (a) that technical change is neutral and (b) that the aggregate production function is *strictly* linear. This explains why numerical results are so closely parallel for the two methods. We have already verified the neutrality, and as will be seen subsequently, a strictly linear production function gives an excellent fit, though clearly inferior to some alternatives.[8]

[7] S. Fabricant, "Economic Progress and Economic Change," *34th Annual Report of the National Bureau of Economic Research* (New York, 1954).

[8] For an excellent discussion of some of the problems, see M. Abramovitz "Resources and Output Trends in the U.S. since 1870," *American Economic Review, Papers and Proceedings*, XLVI (May 1956), 5–23. Some of the questions there raised could in principle be answered by the method used here. For example, the contribution of improved quality of the labor force could be handled by introducing various levels of skilled labor as separate inputs. I owe to Prof. T. W. Schultz a heightened awareness that a lot of what appears as shifts in the production function must represent improvement in the quality of the labor input, and therefore a result of real capital formation of an important kind. Nor ought it be forgotten that even straight technical progress has a cost side.

The Aggregate Production Function

Returning now to the aggregate production function, we have earned the right to write it in the form (1a). By use of the (practically unavoidable) assumption of constant returns to scale, this can be further simplified to the form

$$q = A(t)f(k,1), \qquad (3)$$

which formed the basis of Chart 1. It was there noted that a simple plot of q against k would give a distorted picture because of the shift factor $A(t)$. Each point would lie on a different member of the family of production curves. But we have now provided ourselves with an estimate of the successive values of the shift factor. (Note that this estimate is quite *independent* of any hypothesis about the exact shape of the production function.) It follows from (3) that by plotting $q(t)/A(t)$ against $k(t)$ we reduce all the observed points to a *single* member of the family of curves in Chart 1, and we can then proceed to discuss the shape of $f(k,1)$ and reconstruct the aggregate production function. A scatter of q/A against k is shown in Chart 4.

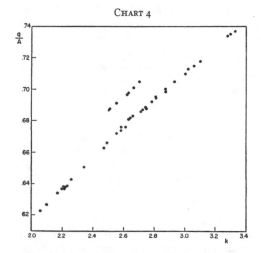

CHART 4

Considering the amount of *a priori* doctoring which the raw figures have undergone, the fit is remarkably tight. Except, that is, for the layer of points which are obviously too high. These maverick observations relate to the seven last years of the period, 1943–49. From the way they lie almost exactly parallel to the main scatter, one is tempted to conclude that in 1943 the aggregate production function simply shifted. But the whole earlier procedure was designed to purify those points from shifts in the function, so that way out would seem to be closed. I suspect the explanation may lie in some systematic incomparability of the capital-in-use series. In particular during the war there was almost certainly a more intensive use of capital services through two- and three-shift operation than the stock figures would show, even with the crude correction that has been applied. It is easily seen that such an underestimate of capital inputs leads to an overestimate of productivity increase. Thus in effect each of the affected points should really lie higher and toward the right. But further analysis shows that, for the orders of magnitude involved, the net result would be to pull the observations closer to the rest of the scatter.

At best this might account for 1943–1945. There remains the postwar period. Although it is possible that multi-shift operation remained fairly widespread even after the war, it is unlikely that this could be nearly enough to explain the whole discrepancy.[9] One might guess that accelerated amortization could have resulted in an underestimate of the capital stock after 1945. Certainly other research workers, notably Kuznets and Terborgh, have produced capital stock estimates which rather exceed Goldsmith's at the end of the period. But for the present, I leave this a mystery.

In a first version of this paper, I resolutely let the recalcitrant observations stand as they were in a regression analysis of Chart 4, mainly because such casual amputation is a practice I deplore in others. But after some experimentation it seemed that to leave them in only led to noticeable distortion of the results. So, with some misgivings, in the regressions that follow I have omitted the observations for 1943–1949. It would be better if they could be otherwise explained away.

Chart 4 gives an inescapable impression of curvature, of persistent but not violent dimin-

ishing returns. As for the possibility of approaching capital-saturation, there is no trace on this gross product level, but even setting aside all other difficulties, such a scatter confers no particular license to guess about what happens at higher K/L ratios than those observed.

As for fitting a curve to the scatter, a Cobb-Douglas function comes immediately to mind, but then so do several other parametric forms, with little to choose among them.[10] I can't help feeling that little or nothing hangs on the choice of functional form, but I have experimented with several. In general I limited myself to two-parameter families of curves, linear in the parameters (for computational convenience), and at least capable of exhibiting diminishing returns (except for the straight line, which on this account proved inferior to all others).

The particular possibilities tried were the following:

$$q = a + \beta k \tag{4a}$$
$$q = a + \beta \log k \tag{4b}$$
$$q = a - \beta/k \tag{4c}$$
$$\log q = a + \beta \log k \tag{4d}$$
$$\log q = a - \beta/k. \tag{4e}$$

Of these, (4d) is the Cobb-Douglas case; (4c and e) have upper asymptotes; the semilogarithmic (4b) and the hyperbolic (4c) must cross the horizontal axis at a positive value of k and continue ever more steeply but irrelevantly downward (which means only that some positive k must be achieved before any output is forthcoming, but this is far outside the range of observation); (4e) begins at the origin with a phase of increasing returns and ends with a phase of diminishing returns — the point of inflection occurs at $k = \beta/2$ and needless to say all our observed points come well to the right of this.

The results of fitting these five curves to the scatter of Chart 4 are shown in Table 2.

The correlation coefficients are uniformly so high that one hesitates to say any more than

---

[9] It is cheering to note that Professor Fellner's new book voices a suspicion that the postwar has seen a substantial increase over prewar in the prevalence of multi-shift operation. See *Trends and Cycles in Economic Activity* (New York, 1956), 92.

[10] A discussion of the same problem in a different context is to be found in Prais and Houthakker, *The Analysis of Family Budgets* (Cambridge, England, 1955), 82–88. See also S. J. Prais, "Non-Linear Estimates of the Engel Curves," *Review of Economic Studies*, No. 52 (1952–53), 87–104.

TECHNICAL CHANGE AND PRODUCTION FUNCTION   319

TABLE 2

Curve	α	β	r
4a	.438	.091	.9982
b	.448	.239	.9996
c	.917	.618	.9964
d	−.729	.353	.9996
e	−.038	.913	.9980

that all five functions, even the linear one, are about equally good at representing the general shape of the observed points. From the correlations alone, for what they are worth, it appears that the Cobb-Douglas function (4d) and the semilogarithmic (4b) are a bit better than the others.[11]

Since all of the fitted curves are of the form $g(y) = a + \beta\, h(x)$, one can view them all as linear regressions and an interesting test of goodness of fit proposed by Prais and Houthakker (ibid., page 51) is available. If the residuals from each regression are arranged in order of increasing values of the independent variable, then one would like this sequence to be disposed "randomly" about the regression line. A strong "serial" correlation in the residuals, or a few long runs of positive residuals alternating with long runs of negative residuals, would be evidence of just that kind of smooth departure from linearity that one would like to catch. A test can be constructed using published tables of critical values for runs of two kinds of elements.

[11] It would be foolhardy for an outsider (or maybe even an insider) to hazard a guess about the statistical properties of the basic time series. A few general statements can be made, however. (a) The natural way to introduce an error term into the aggregate production function is multiplicatively: $Q = (1 + u)F(K,L;t)$. In the neutral case it is apparent that the error factor will be absorbed into the estimated $A(t)$. Then approximately the error in $\Delta A/A$ will be $\Delta u/1 + u$. If u has zero mean, the variance of the estimated $\Delta A/A$ will be approximately $2(1 − \rho)$ var u, where ρ is the first autocorrelation of the u series. (b) Suppose that marginal productivity distribution doesn't hold exactly, so that $K/Q\partial Q/\partial K = w_k + v$, where now v is a random deviation and w_k is the share of property income. Then the error in the estimated $\Delta A/A$ will be $v\, \Delta k/k$, with variance $(\Delta k/k)^2$ var v. Since K/L changes slowly, the multiplying factor will be very small. The effect is to bias the estimate of $\Delta A/A$ in such a way as to lead to an overestimate when property receives less than its marginal product (and k is increasing). (c) Errors in estimating $A(t)$ enter in a relatively harmless way so far as the regression analysis is concerned. Errors of observation in k will be more serious and are likely to be large. The effect will of course be to bias the estimates of β downward.

This has been done for the linear, semilogarithmic, and Cobb-Douglas functions. The results strongly confirm the visual impression of diminishing returns in Chart 4, by showing the linear function to be a systematically poor fit. As between (4b) and (4d) there is little to choose.[12]

A Note on Saturation

It has already been mentioned that the aggregate production function shows no signs of levelling off into a stage of capital-saturation. The two curves in Table 2 which have upper asymptotes (c and e) happen to locate that asymptote at about the same place. The limiting values of q are, respectively, .92 and .97. Of course these are both true asymptotes, approached but not reached for any finite value of k. It could not be otherwise: no analytic function can suddenly level off and become constant unless it has always been constant. But on the other hand, there is no reason to expect nature to be infinitely differentiable. Thus any conclusions extending beyond the range actually observed in Chart 4 are necessarily treacherous. But, tongue in cheek, if we take .95 as a guess at the saturation level of q, and use the linear function (4a) (which will get there first) as a lower-limit guess at the saturation level for k, it turns out to be about 5.7, more than twice its present value.

But all this is in terms of gross output, whereas for analytic purposes we are interested in the net productivity of capital. The difference between the two is depreciation, a subject about which I do not feel able to make guesses. If there were more certainty about the meaning of existing estimates of depreciation, especially over long periods of time, it would have been better to conduct the whole analysis in terms of net product.

However, one can say this. Zero net marginal productivity of capital sets in when gross marginal product falls to the "marginal rate of depreciation," i.e. when adding some capital adds only enough product to make good the depreciation on the increment of capital itself. Now in recent years NNP has run a bit over

[12] The test statistic is R, the total number of runs, with small values significant. For (4a), $R = 4$; for (4b), $R = 13$. The 1% critical value in both cases is about 9.

320   THE REVIEW OF ECONOMICS AND STATISTICS

90 per cent of GNP, so capital consumption is a bit under 10 per cent of gross output. From Table 1 it can be read that capital per unit of output is, say, between 2 and 3. Thus annual depreciation is between 3 and 5 per cent of the capital stock. Capital-saturation would occur whenever the gross marginal product of capital falls to .03–.05. Using (4b), this would happen at K/L ratios of around 5 or higher, still well above anything ever observed.[13]

Summary

This paper has suggested a simple way of segregating shifts of the aggregate production function from movements along it. The method rests on the assumption that factors are paid their marginal products, but it could easily be extended to monopolistic factor markets. Among the conclusions which emerge from a crude application to American data, 1909–49, are the following:

1. Technical change during that period was neutral on average.

2. The upward shift in the production function was, apart from fluctuations, at a rate of about one per cent per year for the first half of the period and 2 per cent per year for the last half.

3. Gross output per man hour doubled over the interval, with $87\frac{1}{2}$ per cent of the increase attributable to technical change and the remaining $12\frac{1}{2}$ per cent to increased use of capital.

4. The aggregate production function, corrected for technical change, gives a distinct impression of diminishing returns, but the curvature is not violent.

---

[13] And this is under relatively pessimistic assumptions as to how technical change itself affects the rate of capital consumption. A warning is in order here: I have left Kendrick's GNP data in 1939 prices and Goldsmith's capital stock figures in 1929 prices. Before anyone uses the β's of Table 2 to reckon a yield on capital or any similar number, it is necessary to convert Q and K to a comparable price basis, by an easy calculation.

Journal of Economic Perspectives— Volume 3, Number 3—Summer 1989—Pages 79–90

Real Business Cycles:
A New Keynesian Perspective

N. Gregory Mankiw

The debate over the source and propagation of economic fluctuations rages as fiercely today as it did 50 years ago in the aftermath of Keynes's *The General Theory* and in the midst of the Great Depression. Today, as then, there are two schools of thought. The classical school emphasizes the optimization of private economic actors, the adjustment of relative prices to equate supply and demand, and the efficiency of unfettered markets. The Keynesian school believes that understanding economic fluctuations requires not just studying the intricacies of general equilibrium, but also appreciating the possibility of market failure on a grand scale.

Real business cycle theory is the latest incarnation of the classical view of economic fluctuations. It assumes that there are large random fluctuations in the rate of technological change. In response to these fluctuations, individuals rationally alter their levels of labor supply and consumption. The business cycle is, according to this theory, the natural and efficient response of the economy to changes in the available production technology.

My goal in this essay is to appraise this newly revived approach to the business cycle. I should admit in advance that I am not an advocate. In my view, real business cycle theory does not provide an empirically plausible explanation of economic fluctuations. Both its reliance on large technological disturbances as the primary source of economic fluctuations and its reliance on the intertemporal substitution of leisure to explain changes in employment are fundamental weaknesses. Moreover, to the extent that it trivializes the social cost of observed fluctuations, real business cycle theory is potentially dangerous. The danger is that those who advise policy-makers might attempt to use it to evaluate the effects of alternative macroeconomic policies or to conclude that macroeconomic policies are unnecessary.

■ *N. Gregory Mankiw is Professor of Economics, Harvard University, and Research Associate, National Bureau of Economic Research, both in Cambridge, Massachusetts.*

Walrasian Equilibrium and The Classical Dichotomy

The typical undergraduate course in microeconomics begins with partial equilibrium analysis of individual markets. A market for a good is characterized by a downward sloping demand curve and an upward sloping supply curve. The price of the good is assumed to adjust until the quantity supplied equals the quantity demanded.

The course then builds up to Walrasian general equilibrium. In this Walrasian equilibrium, prices adjust to equate supply and demand in every market simultaneously. The general equilibrium system determines the quantities of all goods and services sold and their relative prices. The most important theoretical result, after the existence of such a Walrasian equilibrium, is the "invisible hand" theorem: the equilibrium is Pareto efficient.

Courses in microeconomics thus show how employment, production, and relative prices are determined without any mention of the existence of money, the medium of exchange. The simplest way to append money to the model is to specify a money demand function and an exogenous money supply. Money demand depends on the level of output and the price level. The level of output is already determined in the Walrasian system. The price level, however, can adjust to equate supply and demand in the money market.

Introducing money in this way leads to the classical dichotomy (Patinkin, 1956). Real variables, such as employment, output, and relative prices, including the real interest rate, are determined by the Walrasian system. Nominal variables, such as the price level, the nominal wage, and the nominal interest rate, are then determined by the equilibrium in the money market. Of course, since nominal variables do not affect real variables, the money market is not very important. This classical view of the economy suggests that, for most policy discussions, the money market can be ignored.

The professor of macroeconomics must in some way deal with the classical dichotomy. Given the assumptions of Walrasian equilibrium, money is largely irrelevant. The macroeconomist must either destroy this classical dichotomy or learn to live with it.

Keynesian macroeconomics destroys the classical dichotomy by abandoning the assumption that wages and prices adjust instantly to clear markets. This approach is motivated by the observation that many nominal wages are fixed by long-term labor contracts and many product prices remain unchanged for long periods of time. Once the inflexibility of wages and prices is admitted into a macroeconomic model, the classical dichotomy and the irrelevance of money quickly disappear.

Much of the early work in the new classical revolution of the 1970s attempted to destroy the classical dichotomy without abandoning the fundamental axiom of continuous market clearing (Lucas, 1972; 1973). These models were based on the assumption that individuals have imperfect information regarding prices. These individuals therefore confuse movements in the overall price level (which under the classical dichotomy should not matter) with movements in relative prices (which should matter). An unanticipated decrease in the money supply leads individuals to infer that the relative prices of the goods they produce are temporarily low, which induces them to reduce the quantity supplied. While the fascination with this sort of story was substantial in the 1970s, it has attracted relatively few adherents in the 1980s. It is hard to believe that confusion about the price level is sufficiently great to generate the large changes in quantities observed over the business cycle.

In contrast to both the Keynesian and the early new classical approaches to the business cycle, real business cycle theory embraces the classical dichotomy. It accepts the complete irrelevance of monetary policy, thereby denying a tenet accepted by almost all macroeconomists a decade ago. Nominal variables, such as the money supply and the price level, are assumed to have no role in explaining fluctuations in real variables, such as output and employment.

Real business cycle theory thus pushes the Walrasian model farther than it has been pushed before. In evaluating whether it provides a successful explanation of recessions and booms, two questions naturally arise. First, why are there such large fluctuations in output and employment? And second, why do movements in nominal variables, such as the money supply, appear related to movements in real variables, such as output?

Classical and Keynesian Views of Economic Fluctuations

The only forces that can cause economic fluctuations, according to real business cycle theory, are those forces that change the Walrasian equilibrium. The Walrasian equilibrium is simply the set of quantities and relative prices that simultaneously equate supply and demand in all markets in the economy. To understand how real business cycle theory explains the business cycle, it is necessary to look into the fundamental forces that change the supplies and demands for various goods and services.

Many sorts of macroeconomic disturbances can in principle generate fluctuations in real business cycle models. For example, changes in the level of government purchases or in the investment tax credit alter the demand for goods and therefore affect the Walrasian equilibrium. Changes in the relative price of oil alter the equilibrium allocation of labor among alternative uses. Many of the macroeconomic disturbances that receive much attention among Keynesian macroeconomists will also have important effects in real business cycle models. There is, however, substantial disagreement between the two schools regarding the mechanisms through which these disturbances work.

Consider the case of a temporary increase in government purchases. Almost all macroeconomists agree that such a change causes an increase in output and employment, and the evidence, mainly from wartime experience, supports this prediction. Yet the explanations of this effect of government purchases differ greatly.

Real business cycle theory emphasizes the intertemporal substitution of goods and leisure (Barro, 1987). It begins by pointing out that an increase in government purchases increases the demand for goods. To achieve equilibrium in the goods market, the real interest rate must rise, which reduces consumption and investment. The increase in the real interest rate also causes individuals to reallocate leisure across time. In particular, at a higher real interest rate, working today becomes relatively more attractive than working in the future; today's labor supply therefore increases. This increase in labor supply causes equilibrium employment and output to rise.

While Keynesian theory also predicts an increase in the real interest rate in response to a temporary increase in government purchases, the effect of the real interest rate on labor supply does not play a crucial role. Instead, the increase in employment and output is due to a reduction in the amount of labor unemployed or underutilized. In most Keynesian theory, the labor market is characterized as often in a state of excess supply. In contrast, the Walrasian approach of real business cycle theory does not allow for the possibility of involuntary unemployment.

Both real business cycle theory and Keynesian theory thus conclude that increases in government purchases increase output and employment. This example shows that some of the prominent implications of Keynesian models also come out of intertemporal Walrasian models. Macroeconomists face a problem of approximate observational equivalence: many observed phenomena are consistent with both the classical and Keynesian paradigms.

The Central Role of Technological Disturbances

While many sorts of macroeconomic disturbances can in principle cause economic fluctuations in real business cycle models, most attention has focused on technological disturbances. The reason is that other sorts of disturbances are unlikely to generate fluctuations in real business cycle models that resemble actual economic fluctuations.

An obvious but important fact is that over the typical business cycle, consumption and leisure move in opposite directions. When the economy goes into a recession, consumption falls and leisure rises. When the economy goes into a boom, consumption rises and leisure falls. Explaining this phenomenon is potentially problematic for real business cycle theory: consumption and leisure would often be expected to move together, since both are normal goods. In the example of a temporary increase in government purchases, both consumption and leisure should fall. Many other changes in the demand for goods, such as a change due to a temporary investment tax credit, also should cause consumption and leisure to move together.

Real business cycle theory must explain why individuals in a recession find it rational to increase the quantity of leisure they demand at the same time they decrease the quantity of goods they demand. The answer must be that the price of leisure relative to goods, the real wage, falls in a recession. Hence, a crucial implication of real business cycle theory is that the real wage is procyclical.[1]

---

[1]Alternatively, one could explain the observed pattern without a procyclical real wage by positing that tastes for consumption relative to leisure vary over time. Recessions are then periods of "chronic laziness." As far as I know, no one has seriously proposed this explanation of the business cycle.

If the production function were unchanging and demand shocks were the source of fluctuations, real business cycle theory would have trouble generating a procyclical real wage. Since labor input is low in a recession, one would expect that the marginal product of labor and thus the real wage should be high. With an unchanging production function, diminishing marginal returns to labor would produce a counter-cyclical real wage, not the procyclical real wage necessary to explain the fluctuations in consumption and leisure.

Real business cycle theorists therefore assume that there are substantial fluctuations in the rate of technological change. In a recession, the available production technology is relatively unfavorable. The marginal product of labor and thus the real wage are low. In response to the low return to working, individuals reduce consumption and increase leisure.

Since real business cycle theory describes economic fluctuations as a changing Walrasian equilibrium, it implies that these fluctuations are efficient. Given the tastes of individuals and the technological possibilities facing society, the levels of employment, output, and consumption cannot be improved. Attempts by the government to alter the allocations of the private market, such as policies to stabilize employment, at best are ineffective and at worst can do harm by impeding the "invisible hand."

Of all the implications of real business cycle theory, the optimality of economic fluctuations is perhaps the most shocking. It seems undeniable that the level of welfare is lower in a recession than in the boom that preceded it. Keynesian theory explains the reduction in welfare by a failure in economic coordination: because wages and prices do not adjust instantaneously to equate supply and demand in all markets, some gains from trade go unrealized in a recession. In contrast, real business cycle theory allows no unrealized gains from trade. The reason welfare is lower in a recession is, according to these theories, that the technological capabilities of society have declined.

The Evidence on Technological Disturbances

Advocates of real business cycle theories have trouble convincing skeptics that the economy is subject to such large and sudden changes in technology. It is a more standard presumption that the accumulation of knowledge and the concurrent increase in the economy's technological opportunities take place gradually over time. Yet to mimic observed fluctuations, real business cycle theorists must maintain that there are substantial short-run fluctuations in the production function.

Edward Prescott (1986) has offered some direct evidence on the importance of technological disturbances. He examines changes in total factor productivity for the United States economy—the percent change in output less the percent change in inputs, where the different inputs are weighted by their factor shares. This "Solow residual" should measure the rate of technological progress. Prescott points out that there are substantial fluctuations in the Solow residual, a finding which suggests a potentially important role for technological disturbances as a source of business cycle fluctuations.

Figure 1
Solow Residuals and Output Growth

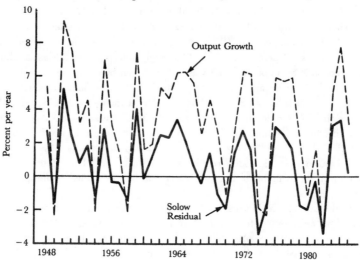

Figure 1 presents my calculation of the Solow residual and the percent change in output yearly since 1948. (Both variables are for the private economy less agriculture and housing services.) Like Prescott, I find substantial fluctuations in measured total factor productivity. For example, in 1982 total factor productivity fell by 3.5 percent, while in 1984 it rose by 3.4 percent. One might interpret these numbers as showing that the economy's ability to convert inputs into outputs—the aggregate production function—varies substantially from year to year.

Figure 1 also shows that measured productivity is highly cyclical. In every year in which output fell, total factor productivity also fell. If the Solow residual is a valid measure of the change in the available production technology, then recessions are periods of technological regress.

The Solow residual need not be interpreted as evidence regarding exogenous technological disturbances, however. The standard explanation of cyclical productivity is that it reflects labor hoarding and other "off the production function" behavior. Productivity appears to fall in a recession because firms keep unnecessary and underutilized labor. In a boom the hoarded laborers begin to put out greater effort; output increases without a large increase in measured labor input.[2]

---

[2]A related explanation of the procyclical behavior of the Solow residual has recently been proposed by Hall (1987). Hall points out that if price exceeds marginal cost because of imperfect competition, then the measured Solow residual will appear procyclical even if the true production technology is unchanging. Alternatively, the Solow residual could reflect endogenous changes in technology due to demand shocks: such endogeneity might arise if, for example, learning-by-doing is important.

An examination of the data from the early 1940s appears to support this standard explanation of the cyclical behavior of productivity. The increase in output associated with the World War II build-up is most plausibly a demand-driven phenomenon. Yet from 1939 to 1944 measured total factor productivity grew an average of 7.6 percent per year. (By contrast, the most productivity has grown in any year since then is 5.2 percent in 1950.) One might interpret this finding as showing that the economic boom of the 1940s was in fact driven by supply shocks rather than demand shocks. A more appealing interpretation is that the Solow residual is not a good measure over short horizons of changes in the economy's technological abilities.

Once the Solow residual is rejected as a measure of year-to-year changes in the available production technology, there is no longer any direct evidence for substantial technological disturbances. Yet to generate fluctuations that mimic observed fluctuations, real business cycle models require such disturbances. The existence of large fluctuations in the available technology is a crucial but unjustified assumption of real business cycle theory.

An advocate of real business cycle theory might respond that economic models often rely on assumptions for which there is no formal evidence. Yet more casual evidence also does not give plausibility to the assumption of substantial technological disturbances. Recessions are important events; they receive widespread attention from policy-makers and the media. There is, however, no discussion of declines in the available technology. If society suffered some important adverse technological shock, we would be aware of it. My own reading of the newspaper, however, does not lead me to associate most recessions with some exogenous deterioration in the economy's productive capabilities.

The OPEC energy price changes of the 1970s illustrate that when the economy experiences large real shocks, these shocks are easily identifiable and much discussed. Figure 1 indeed shows that the economy experienced large negative Solow residuals in 1974 and 1979, as one might have expected.[3] Yet the five other recessions in the postwar period also exhibit large negative Solow residuals. To explain these Solow residuals as adverse changes in the aggregate production function, one would need to find events with the economic significance of the OPEC price increases. The apparent absence of such events is evidence that these recessions cannot be easily attributed to exogenous real shocks.[4]

Labor Supply and Intertemporal Substitution

Real business cycle theorists assume that fluctuations in employment are fully voluntary. In other words, they assume the economy always finds itself on the labor

[3] Whether changes in energy prices affect the Solow residual computed from GNP depends on a variety of issues involving the construction of index numbers like GNP. See Bruno and Sachs (1985, p. 43) for a discussion.
[4] Hamilton (1983) finds oil price changes are also associated with the pre-OPEC recessions. Yet these price changes are much too small to explain plausibly such large declines in productivity.

supply curve. Yet over the typical business cycle, employment varies substantially while the determinants of labor supply—the real wage and the real interest rate—vary only slightly. To mimic this observed pattern, real business cycle models require that individuals be very willing to reallocate leisure over time. Individuals must significantly reduce the quantity of labor they supply in response to small temporary reductions in the real wage or in response to small decreases in the real interest rate.

It is unlikely, however, that individuals are so responsive to intertemporal relative prices. Econometric evidence on labor supply typically finds that the willingness of individuals to substitute leisure over time is slight. If leisure were highly intertemporally substitutable, as real business cycle theorists assume, then individuals facing expected increases in their real wage should work little today and much in the future. Individuals facing expected decreases in their real wage should work hard today and enjoy leisure in the future. Yet studies of individual labor supply over time find that expected changes in the real wage lead to only small changes in hours worked (Altonji, 1986; Ball, 1985). Individuals do not respond to expected real wage changes by substantially reallocating leisure over time.

Personal experience and introspection provide another way to judge the behavioral responses on which real business cycle models rely. One key behavioral response is that quantity of labor supplied reacts substantially to the real interest rate. Without such intertemporal substitution, real business cycle models are unable to explain how a temporary increase in government purchases increases output and employment. Yet such a behavioral response does not seem plausible. The real interest rate is simply not a significant consideration when individuals decide to leave their jobs or to accept new employment. While economists can easily convince laymen and students that the quantity of apples demanded depends on the price of apples, it is much harder to convince them that labor supply depends on the real interest rate. The implication I draw from this observation is that the intertemporal substitutability of leisure is very likely far too weak to get real business cycle models to work.

Real Business Cycle Theories with Multiple Sectors

The real business cycle theories I have been discussing so far treat production as if it takes place in a single industry. This abstraction, however, is not characteristic of all real business cycle theories.

Some real business cycle theories emphasize changes in the technologies of different sectors, rather than economy-wide changes in technology (Long and Plosser, 1983). These models highlight the interactions among the sectors. Even if the shocks to the different sectors are independent, the outputs of the different sectors move together. For example, an adverse shock to one sector reduces the wealth of the individuals in the economy; these individuals respond by reducing their demand for all goods. An observer would see an aggregate business cycle, even without a single aggregate shock.

To get these real business cycle models to work, however, the number of independent sectoral shocks cannot be too great. If there were many independent sectoral shocks and labor were mobile between sectors, then the law of large numbers would guarantee that these shocks and their effect on the aggregate economy would average out to zero. To get an aggregate business cycle, these models therefore require that there be only a few sectors and that these sectors be subject to large technological disturbances. These models are therefore similar to the single-sector theories and suffer from the same weaknesses: the absence of any direct evidence for such large technological disturbances and the implausibility of strong intertemporal substitutability of leisure.

A second type of sectoral shock theory emphasizes the costly adjustment of labor among sectors (Lilien, 1982). These models, which depart more from the Walrasian paradigm, assume that when a worker moves from one sector to another, a period of unemployment is required, perhaps for job search. In this case, independent shocks across many sectors do not offset each other. Recessions are, according to these theories, periods of more sectoral shocks and thus greater intersectoral adjustment.

This type of real business cycle theory may appear more plausible than those relying on substantial aggregate productivity shocks and intertemporal substitution. It is perhaps easier to imagine that recessions are characterized by an unusually great need for intersectoral reallocation than by some sort of major technological regress that makes leisure unusually attractive. Yet the available evidence appears not to support this intersectoral story. If workers were unemployed voluntarily in recessions because they were moving to new jobs in other sectors, we would expect to find high unemployment coinciding with high job vacancy. Yet observed fluctuations have just the opposite pattern: high unemployment rates coincide with low levels of help wanted advertising (Abraham and Katz, 1986). Moreover, in contrast to the prediction of this theory, the measured mobility of workers between sectors is strongly procyclical (Murphy and Topel, 1987). This real business cycle theory is also unable to be plausibly reconciled with observed economic fluctuations.

Money and Prices over the Business Cycle

Before real business cycle theory entered the macroeconomic debate in the early 1980s, almost all macroeconomists seemed to agree on one conclusion: money matters. Both historical discussions of business cycles (Friedman and Schwartz, 1963) and more formal econometric work (Barro, 1977) pointed to the Federal Reserve as an important source of macroeconomic disturbances. While there was controversy as to whether systematic monetary policy could stabilize the economy, it was universally accepted that bad monetary policy could be destabilizing.

It is ironic that real business cycle theory arose in the wake of Paul Volcker's disinflation. Many economists view this recent experience as clear confirmation of the potency of monetary policy. Volcker announced he was going to slow the rate of money growth to achieve a lower rate of inflation; the rate of money growth in fact slowed down; and one of the deepest postwar recessions followed, as did an eventual reduction in the rate of inflation. This set of events is easy to explain within the context of Keynesian theory with its emphasis on the gradual adjustment of wages and prices. It is less easy to explain within the context of real business cycle theory.[5]

Robert King and Charles Plosser (1984) explain the historical association between money and output by arguing that the money supply endogenously responds to fluctuations in output. Standard measures of the money supply such as M1 are mostly inside money, that is, money created by the banking system. King and Plosser suggest that the transactions services of inside money should be viewed as simply the "output" of one sector of the economy, the banking sector. Just as one should expect the outputs of different sectors to move together within a multi–sector real business cycle model, one should expect the output of the banking sector to move with the outputs of other sectors. An increase in productivity in any sector will tend to increase the demand for transactions services; the banking system responds by creating more inside money. Hence, the procyclical behavior of standard monetary aggregates cannot necessarily be interpreted as evidence that changes in outside money caused by the monetary authority have real effects.

While the story of King and Plosser can explain the procyclical behavior of money, it cannot explain the procyclical behavior of prices. It is a well-documented fact that, in the absence of identifiable real shocks such as the OPEC oil price changes, inflation tends to rise in booms and fall in recessions. This famous Phillips curve correlation played a central role in the macroeconomic debate of the 1960s, and it was the primary empirical motivation for the early new classical theories in the 1970s (Friedman, 1968; Lucas, 1972). Yet since the model of King and Plosser generates procyclical money through the demand for transactions services, these fluctuations in money will be associated with fluctuations in real balances not with fluctuations in prices. The short-run Phillips curve has thus been left without an explanation by real business cycle theorists.[6]

The Tradeoff Between Internal and External Consistency

A good theory has two characteristics: internal consistency and external consistency. An internally consistent theory is one that is parsimonious; it invokes no *ad hoc* or peculiar axioms. An externally consistent theory is one that fits the facts; it makes empirically refutable predictions that are not refuted. All scientists, including economists, strive for theories that are both internally and externally consistent. Yet

---

[5]The recent disinflation is not unusual. Romer and Romer (1989) show that output typically falls after the Fed makes an explicit decision to reduce inflation, which they interpret as evidence against real business cycle theory.

[6]Indeed, as King and Plosser point out, their model makes the counterfactual prediction that the price level should be countercyclical: since the demand for real outside money probably rises in a boom, and it is the outside money stock that pins down the price level, equilibrium in the market for outside money requires that the price level fall in a boom.

like all optimizing agents, scientists face tradeoffs. One theory may be more "beautiful," while another may be easier to reconcile with observation.

The choice between alternative theories of the business cycle—in particular, between real business cycle theory and new Keynesian theory—is partly a choice between internal and external consistency. Real business cycle theory extends the Walrasian paradigm, the most widely understood and taught model in economics, and provides a unified explanation for economic growth and economic fluctuations. New Keynesian theory, in its attempt to mimic the world more accurately, relies on nominal rigidities that are observed but only little understood. Indeed, new Keynesians sometimes suggest that to understand the business cycle, it may be necessary to reject the axiom of rational, optimizing individuals, an act that for economists would be the ultimate abandonment of internal consistency.

The tension between these two goals of science will undoubtedly continue. Each school of macroeconomic thought will highlight its strengths while trying to improve on its weaknesses. My own forecast is that real business cycle advocates will not manage to produce convincing evidence that there are substantial shocks to technology and that leisure is highly substitutable over time. Without such evidence, their theories will be judged as not persuasive. New Keynesians, however, have made substantial progress in recent years toward providing rigorous microeconomic foundations, the absence of which was the fatal flaw of the Keynesian consensus of the 1960s. While real business cycle theory has served the important function of stimulating and provoking the scientific debate, it will, I predict, ultimately be discarded as an explanation of observed fluctuations.

■ *I am grateful to Lawrence Ball, Susanto Basu, Marianne Baxter, Mark Bils, Lawrence Katz, Deborah Mankiw, David Romer, Joseph Stiglitz, Lawrence Summers, Timothy Taylor, David Weil, and Michael Woodford for helpful discussions and comments, and to the National Science Foundation for financial support.*

References

Abraham, Katharine G., and Lawrence F. Katz, "Cyclical Unemployment: Sectoral Shifts or Aggregate Disturbances?" *Journal of Political Economy*, June 1986, *94*, 507–522.

Altonji, Joseph G., "Intertemporal Substitution in Labor Supply: Evidence from Micro Data," *Journal of Political Economy*, June 1986, Part 2, *94*, S176–S215.

Ball, Laurence, "Intertemporal Substitution and Constraints on Labor Supply: Evidence from Panel Data," manuscript, M.I.T., 1985.

Barro, Robert J., "Unanticipated Money Growth and Unemployment in the United States," *American Economic Review*, 1977, *67*, 101–115.

Barro, Robert J., *Macroeconomics.* New York: Wiley, 1987.

Bruno, Michael, and Jeffrey Sachs, *Economics of Worldwide Stagflation.* Cambridge, MA: Harvard University Press, 1985.

Friedman, Milton, "The Role of Monetary Policy," *American Economic Review*, 1968, *58*, 1–17.

Friedman, Milton, and Anna Schwartz, *A Monetary History of the United States.* Princeton, NJ: Princeton University Press, 1963.

Hall, Robert E., "Market Structure and Macroeconomic Fluctuations," *Brookings Papers on Economic Activity*, 1987:1, 285–322.

Hamilton, James D., "Oil and the Macroeconomy since World War II," *Journal of Political Economy*, April 1983, *91*, 228–248.

King, Robert G., and Charles I. Plosser, "Money, Credit, and Prices in a Real Business Cycle," *American Economic Review*, June 1984, *74*, 363–380.

Lilien, David M., "Sectoral Shifts and Cyclical Unemployment," *Journal of Political Economy*, August 1982, *90*, 777–793.

Long, John B. Jr., and Charles I. Plosser, "Real Business Cycles," *Journal of Political Economy*, February 1983, *91*, 39–69.

Lucas, Robert E. Jr., "Expectations and the Neutrality of Money," *Journal of Economic Theory*, 1972, *4*, 103–124.

Lucas, Robert E. Jr., "International Evidence on Output-Inflation Tradeoffs," *American Economic Review*, 1973, *63*, 326–334.

Murphy, Kevin M., and Robert H. Topel, "The Evolution of Unemployment in the United States: 1968–1985," *NBER Macroeconomics Annual*, 1987.

Patinkin, Don, *Money, Interest, and Prices: An Integration of Monetary and Value Theory*, Evanston, Ill.: Row, Peterson, 1956.

Prescott, Edward, "Theory Ahead of Business Cycle Measurement," *Carnegie-Rochester Conference on Public Policy*, Autumn 1986, *25*, 11–44.

Romer, Christina, and David Romer, "Does Monetary Policy Matter: A New Test in the Spirit of Friedman and Schwartz," *NBER Macroeconomics Annual*, 1989, forthcoming.

Journal of Economic Literature
Vol. XXXIV (September 1996), pp. 1324–1330

The Discovery of the Residual:
A Historical Note

ZVI GRILICHES

National Bureau of Economic Research
and *Harvard University*

THE CONCEPT OF total productivity and the notion that labor is not the only factor of production, that other factors such as capital and land should also be taken into account in a wealth of the nation calculation or a measure of its productivity, were discussed repeatedly in the literature of the 1930s. Two major strands of research came together, ultimately, in what was to become total factor productivity measurement and growth "accounting": The first developed out of the national income measurement tradition, based largely on the work of NBER and what was later to become the BEA.[1] The second was influenced by Paul Douglas's work on production functions. His work had been largely cross-sectional, but as time series data became available it was an obvious generalization to add trend-like terms to the function and allow it to shift over time.[2] This re-search tradition had a more econometric background and did not accept, necessarily, the various compromises and assumptions embedded in the national income accounts. It found a fertile soil in agricultural economics, spurred by the presence and teaching of Tintner at Iowa State University (Tintner 1944) and the later work of Earl Heady (see Heady and John Dillon 1961, ch. 1, for an early review of this literature). The two traditions came together in the work of Solow (1957), in some of my own early papers (Griliches 1960 and 1963), and especially in Dale Jorgenson and Griliches (1967). But they have also kept drifting apart.

The first mention of what might be called an output-over-input index that I can find appears in Morris Copeland (1937).[3] Once one started thinking about "real" national income and worrying how to deflate it, it was a relatively short step to the idea that the two different sides of these accounts (product receipts and fac-

---

[1] This tradition and the data bases it developed, together with the development of Keynsian economics, also contributed to the rise of growth theory in the works of Roy Harrod, Evsey Domar, and Robert Solow. But that is a different story.

[2] Douglas had been criticized earlier for not allowing for some kind of trend factor in his estimation equation, especially by Horst Mendershausen (1938), a criticism that Jan Tinbergen endorsed in his *Econometrie* textbook, published in Dutch in 1941. Given the increasing availability of time series data and the general advice of that time to use "de-trended" data, it was not long before trend

variables began to appear in production function estimation. The first one to do so, as far as I can tell, was Victor Smith in 1940, in his Northwestern Ph.D. dissertation on the productivity of the steel industry, followed by Gerhard Tintner in a number of papers based on data for U.S. agriculture (Tintner 1944 and 1946).

[3] More thorough research may unearth even earlier references.

tor payments) could be deflated separately, with their own specific deflators, yielding measures of real product and real input, and an associated measure of economic efficiency.[4] A year later the idea was much more fleshed out in Copeland and E. M. Martin (1938) who said:

> construct an index of the physical volume of wealth used in production each year and weight it by the total property income in the period selected for the determination of weights. This weighted plant-hour series might then be added to a correspondingly weighted man-hour series to measure physical input for the economic system. (p. 104)

> . . . divergence is likely to appear between the movements of a series representing the physical volume of input [and output] and . . . this divergence is a rough measure of changes in the efficiency of our economic system. (p. 132)

In commenting on this paper, Milton Friedman, in one of his earliest appearances on the scene, interprets the authors as saying "that a comparison of the two types of indices [output and input] provides a basis for estimating the degree of technical change" (p. 126).[5]

[4] "Income derived from an area may be deflated to show changes in the physical volume of services of labor and wealth employed by the economic system. . . . the deflated distributive shares may be compared with the deflated consumed and saved income to show changes in the efficiency of operation of the economic system" (Copeland 1937, p. 31).

[5] Friedman also raised a series of doubts about the empirical feasibility of this approach. After discussing the substitution bias that is implicit in any fixed weight index construction, he goes on to say: "Add to this [the substitution bias] the necessity of assuming 'constant tastes,' if the comparison is to be meaningful, and the difficulty of obtaining an adequate measure of the quantity of capital, . . . as well as the lesser difficulties with the other factors of production, and the possibility of actually employing the procedure suggested by . . . Copeland and Martin seems exceedingly small. The derivation of a measure of 'real input' that would provide an adequate basis for measuring changes in economic efficiency is even more complicated and difficult than the measurement of 'real output'; for the former involves the latter and

John Hicks, while considering a similar approach to "efficiency" measurement in 1940, added an explicit discussion of index number biases, noting that the problem "is much worse when we allow for increasing returns and imperfect competition" (p. 121). He also asked whether taxes should be included in the weights (yes for output indexes, no for input).

Actual measurement was initiated by several people, working independently but subject to the same intellectual milieu. Whether they measured it as a shifter of the production function (Tinbergen 1942; Tintner 1944; D. Gale Johnson 1950; Solow 1957) or as an output-over-total-input index (George Stigler 1947; Glen Barton and Martin Cooper 1948; Jacob Schmookler 1952;

other difficulties as well. . . . We can . . . ask the question—to what extent is the change in output over some specified period a result of a change in the quantity of available resources, . . . [or] the way these resources are employed. [This separation is to a considerable extent artificial: technological change affects not only the way in which resources are employed but also the quantity and the character of the resources themselves.] In order to answer this question it would be necessary to determine the volume of 'real output' that *would* have been produced had techniques remained unchanged. A comparison of this series with the actual 'real output' then provides a measure of the change in efficiency" (pp. 126–27).

Copeland and Martin responded: "The measurement difficulties about which Mr. Friedman is concerned do not seem to have deterred others to the same extent. Dr. Kuznets has already provided measures of deflated national income in an output sense. Dr. Kuznets' measures of capital formation necessarily involve measurements of the quantities of all kinds of capital . . . Moreover, . . . estimates of total man-years of employment have been developed. Thus . . . the two main elements for measurements of changes in social input (except . . . for non-reproducible wealth . . .) are admittedly at hand. . . .

It must . . . be conceded that [such] measurements . . . are certain to be rough under present conditions. However, those who insist on a high degree of precision had best choose some field of activity other than estimating national wealth and income" (p. 134).

Remember, this discussion is taking place in 1937!

Solomon Fabricant 1954; Vernon Ruttan 1954 and 1956; John Kendrick 1955 and 1956; Moses Abramovitz 1956), they did not claim any particular originality for it. They were making illuminating calculations for a concept that was obviously already there. Credit for the earliest explicit calculation clearly belongs to Tinbergen, who in a 1942 paper, published in German, generalizes the Cobb-Douglas production function by adding an exponential trend to it, intended to represent various "technical developments."[6] He computed the average value of this trend component, calling it a measure of "efficiency," for four countries: Germany, Great Britain, France, and the U.S., using the formula $t = y - 2/3n - 1/3k$, where y, n, and k are the average growth rates of output, labor, and capital respectively and the weights are taken explicitly from Douglas. Note how close this is to Solow who will let these weights change, shifting the index number formula from a fixed-weight geometric to an approximate Divisia form. Nobody seems to have been aware of Tinbergen's paper in the U.S. until much later.[7]

The developments in the U.S. originated primarily at the NBER where a program of constructing national income

and "real" output series under the leadership of Simon Kuznets was expanded also to include capital series for major sectors of the economy, with contributions by Daniel Creamer, Fabricant, Raymond Goldsmith, Alvin Tostlebe, and others. It seemed reasonably obvious to try and use such capital numbers in a more general productivity calculation.[8] The first such published calculation appears in 1947 in Stigler's book on *Trends in Output and Employment* where, after working pretty hard on the output and employment data, he presents (on p. 49), off-handedly, what looks like a "back of the envelope" calculation of efficiency, which he says "is usually defined as Output/(Input of Labor + Input of Other Resources)," for 12 manufacturing industries. In 1952, Schmookler, who had been Kuznets' student at the University of Pennsylvania, published a detailed article on the "Changing Efficiency of the American Economy" in which he constructs an output over total input index with the intent "to describe the pattern and magnitude of technical change."[9]

The "raw-materials" assembled by the NBER were used repeatedly in sub-

---

[6] The fact that an occupied Dutchman was publishing in Germany in 1942 caused some comment after the war. This was an example of trying to keep "science" going despite the circumstances. A position that was tenable in 1942 when much of what was happening was not yet widely known.

[7] Stefan Valavanis-Vail (1955) mentions Tinbergen but, it is obvious from the context, not this paper. Following a suggestion attributed to Arnold Harberger, he uses average factor shares to compute a Cobb-Douglas type total input index and a residual which he then uses to estimate the trend coefficient for an aggregate production function, yielding an estimate of 0.75 percent per year for the 1869–1953 period. This is essentially equivalent to what Tinbergen did, but with weights based on income shares rather than estimated production function coefficients. Solow does reference Valavanis-Vail, but obviously neither of them is aware of Tinbergen (1942) at that point.

[8] This was clearly foreshadowed in the earlier exchange between Copeland and Friedman quoted above.

[9] There are two major components in Schmookler's dissertation on which this article was based. The primary task of the thesis was the assembly and examination of a consistent series on patenting in the U.S., interpreting it as a measure of inventive activity. This part was published as Schmookler (1954). It is clear that the intent was to bring these two parts together, with the patent series "explaining" the growth in input-over-output series. In a third, unpublished, chapter Schmookler tries to do just that and gets nothing. It is interesting to note that as the result of this outcome he left the productivity measurement field and concentrated on the analysis of patent data, perhaps feeling that they are closer to and a more tangible reflection of the actual processes of invention and innovation that he wanted to study. A generation later I will pursue the same mirage (Griliches 1990).

TABLE 1
EARLY ESTIMATES OF THE "RESIDUAL" IN U.S. GROWTH.
(Percentage of Growth not Accounted for by Conventional Inputs)

	Total Economy				Agriculture	
Source	Period	In output	In output per man or manhour	Source	Period	In output
Tinbergen (1942)	1870–1914	27	100			
Stigler (1947), Selected manuf. ind's	1904–1937	n.a.	median 89	Barton and Cooper (1948)	1910–45	57
Schmookler (1952) manuf.	1869–1938	37	n.a.	Johnson (1950)	1900–20	24
	1869–1928	31	88		1923–29	50
					1940–48	50
Fabricant (1954)	1870–1950	n.a.	92	Ruttan (1956)	1910–50	
					beg. wts.	88
					end wts.	71
Kendrick (1955) manuf.	1899–1948		87			
Abramovitz (1956)	1869–1878 to 1944–53	48	86			
Solow (1957)	1909–1949	52	88			

n.a. — not available
beg. wts. — beginning period weights
end wts. — end of period weights

sequent studies, and in 1953 Kendrick was asked to systematize and develop this line of measurement more explicitly. Calculations based on his preliminary work were made by Fabricant in 1954, who may have been the first to emphasize loudly that most of the growth in output per unit of input has not been explained and hence, "it follows that the major source of our economic advance has been a vastly improved efficiency" (p. 8). In 1956, a more detailed analysis of basically the same data was published by Abramovitz, who identified productivity with his computed index of "output per unit of utilized resources" and observed that "the lopsided importance which it appears to give to productivity increase" (in accounting for the growth

in output per manhour) "should be . . . sobering, if not discouraging, to students of economic growth" and labeled the resulting index "a measure of our ignorance." Kendrick's own similar results were already reported in the 1955 NBER Annual Report (Kendrick 1955, pp. 44–47), but his magnum opus did not come out until 1961 (Kendrick 1961) and in the end he was overshadowed and did not get enough credit, in my opinion, either for providing the data to his "interpreters" or for the detailed data construction effort behind it. Some of these computations, and the parallel ones made for agriculture, are summarized in Table 1.

At the same time that the NBER was assembling data for the U.S. economy as a whole and for several of its major sectors, a parallel measurement effort was proceeding at the Bureau of Agricultural Economics of the USDA directed at the measurement of farm output and efficiency. In 1948, Barton and Cooper published a fully articulated and detailed output per unit of input index for the U.S. agriculture. Without computing such an index explicitly, Johnson (1950) used their data to estimate the magnitude of the shifts in the aggregate agricultural production function in different periods, based on weights from estimated production functions, both linear and linear in the logarithms of the variables.[10] Theodore Schultz (1953) used the Barton and Cooper index to compute the return to public investments in agricultural research. Ruttan (1954), as part of his dissertation at the University of Chicago, constructed linear and geometric output over input indexes for meat packing plants, interpreting these indexes as approximations to shifts in the underlying production function. He used base and end period weights to bound them, and included a reasonably complete discussion of the potential biases in such a construction. An extension of this work to the measurement of "The Contribution of Technological Progress to Farm Output" was published in Ruttan (1956).

Against this historical background the 1957 paper by Solow may appear to be less original than it really was. Not the question, nor the data, nor the conclusion was new. Nor did using a geometric input index with shifting weights affect the results all that much. What was new and opportune in it, the "new wrinkle" (p. 312), was the explicit integration of economic theory into such a calculation and the use of calculus, which by then

was being taught to most graduate students. It showed that one need not assume stable production function coefficients to make such calculations and provided an approximation formula for any constant returns production function and, by implication, also an interpretation of the earlier work that did not use this formula. This clarified the meaning of what were heretofore relatively arcane index number calculations and brought the subject from the periphery of the field to the center. It also connected it, indirectly, to Solow (1956) and growth theory and macroeconomics as it was to develop, and had an immense influence on subsequent work in both macro and micro economics.

All of the pioneers of this subject were quite clear about the tenuousness of such calculations and that it may be misleading to identify the results as "pure" measures of technical progress. Abramovitz worried about possible measurement errors in his labor and capital series, especially the omission of intangible capital accumulation through education, nutrition, and R&D, and also about not allowing for increasing returns to scale. Kendrick (1956) noted the omission of intangible capital, such as R&D, from his total input construction. Solow emphasized that he used "the phrase 'technical change' for *any kind of shift* in the production function" (emphasis in the original). He commented on the absence of good measures of capital utilization and he credited Schultz for "a heightened awareness that a lot of what appears as shifts in the production function must represent improvement in the quality of labor input, and therefore a result of real capital formation of an important kind" (fn. 6). Schultz, as mentioned earlier, actually attributed such numbers to public R&D and used them to compute a rate of return to them, influencing my subsequent work on returns to hybrid corn

[10] Johnson credits Tintner with stimulating his interest in this approach (personal communication).

research (Griliches 1958). Most writers echoed Abramovitz's conclusion that such calculations should be interpreted, primarily, as providing an "indication of where we need to concentrate our attention."

At this point the gauntlet had been thrown: even though it had been named "efficiency," "technical change," or most accurately a "measure of our ignorance," much of observed economic growth remained unexplained. It was now the turn

[11] The search for "explanations" of such residual measures of productivity growth (technical change) will be the topic of the sequel to this note.

of the explainers.[11]

REFERENCES

ABRAMOVITZ, MOSES. "Resource and Output Trends in the United States since 1870," *Amer. Econ. Rev.*, May 1956, 46(2), pp. 5–23.
BARTON, GLEN THOMAS AND COOPER, MARTIN R. "Relation of Agricultural Production to Inputs," *Rev. Econ. Statist.*, 1948, 30(2), pp. 117–26.
COPELAND, MORRIS A. "Concepts of National Income," in *Studies in income and wealth*. Vol. 1, New York: National Bureau of Economic Research, 1937, pp. 3–63.
COPELAND, MORRIS A. AND MARTIN, E. M. "The Correction of Wealth and Income Estimates for Price Changes," in *Studies in income and wealth*. Vol. 2. New York: National Bureau of Economic Research, 1938, pp. 85–135; including discussion with MILTON FRIEDMAN.
FABRICANT, SOLOMON. *Economic progress and economic change*. 34th Annual Report. New York: NBER, 1954.
GRILICHES, ZVI. "Research Cost and Social Returns: Hybrid Corn and Related Innovations," *J. Polit. Econ.*, Oct. 1958, 66(5), pp. 419–31.
———."Measuring Inputs in Agriculture: A Critical Survey," *J. Farm Economics*, Dec. 1960, 42(5), pp. 1411–27.
———. "The Sources of Measured Productivity Growth: United States Agriculture, 1940–1960," *J. Polit. Econ.*, Aug. 1963, 71(4), pp. 331–46.
———. "Patent Statistics as Economic Indicators: A Survey," *J. Econ. Lit.*, Dec. 1990, 28(4), pp. 1661–1707.
HEADY, EARL O. AND DILLON, JOHN L. *Agricultural production functions*. Ames, Iowa: Iowa State U. Press, 1961.
HICKS, JOHN R. "The Valuation of the Social Income," *Economica*, N. S., May 1940, 7, pp. 105–24.

JOHNSON, D. GALE. "The Nature of the Supply Function for Agricultural Products," *Amer. Econ. Rev.*, 1950, 40(4), pp. 539–64.
JORGENSON, DALE W. AND GRILICHES, ZVI. "The Explanation of Productivity Change," *Rev. Econ. Stud.*, June 1967, 34(3), pp. 249–83.
KENDRICK, JOHN W. "Productivity," in *Government in economic life*. Ed.: SOLOMON FABRICANT. 35th Annual Report, New York: NBER, 1955, pp. 44–47.
———. *Productivity trends: Capital and labor*. New York: NBER, 1956.
———. *Productivity trends in the United States*. Princeton, NJ: Princeton U. Press, 1961.
MENDERSHAUSEN, HORST. "On the Significance of Professor Douglas' Production Function," *Econometrica*, Apr. 1938, 6(2), pp. 143–53.
RUTTAN, VERNON W. *Technological progress in the meatpacking industry, 1919–47*. Washington, DC: USDA, 1954.
———. "The Contribution of Technological Progress to Farm Output: 1950–75," *Rev. Econ. Statist.*, 1956, 38(1), pp. 61–69.
SCHMOOKLER, JACOB. "Invention and Economic Development." Unpub. Ph.D. dissertation, U. of Pennsylvania, Philadelphia, 1951.
———."The Changing Efficiency of the American Economy: 1869–1938," *Rev. Econ. Statist.*, 1952, 34(3), pp. 214–321.
———. "The Level of Inventive Activity," *Rev. Econ. Statist.*, May 1954, 36, pp. 183–90.
SCHULTZ, THEODORE W. *The economic organization of agriculture*. New York: McGraw-Hill, 1953.
SMITH, VICTOR E. "An Application and Critique of Certain Methods for the Determination of a Statistical Production Function for the Canadian Automobile Industry, 1917–1930." Unpublished Ph.D. dissertation, Department of Economics, Northwestern U., Evanston, IL, 1940.
SOLOW, ROBERT M. "A Contribution to the Theory of Economic Growth," *Quart. J. Econ.*, Feb. 1956, 70, pp. 65–94.
———."Technical Change and the Aggregate Production Function," *Rev. Econ. Statist.*, 1957, 39(3), pp. 312–20.
STIGLER, GEORGE J. *Trends in output and employment*. New York: NBER, 1947.
TINBERGEN, JAN. *Econometrie*. Gorinchem: J. Noorduijn en zoon n. v., 1941.
———. "Zur Theorie der Langfristigen Wirtschaftsentwicklung," *Weltwirts. Archiv*. 1, Amsterdam: North-Holland Pub. Co., 1942, pp. 511–49; reprinted in English translation in JAN TINBERGEN. *Selected papers*. North-Holland, 1959.
TINTNER, GERHARD. "A Note on the Derivation of Production Functions from Farm Records," *Econometrica*, Jan. 1944, 12(1), pp. 26–34.
———."Some Applications of Multivariate Analysis to Economic Data," *J. Amer. Statist. Assoc.*, Dec. 1946, 41, pp. 472–500.
U.S. DEPARTMENT OF LABOR. BUREAU OF LA-

BOR STATISTICS. *Trends in multifactor productivity, 1948–81.* Bulletin No. 2178. Washington, DC: U.S. Department of Labor, 1983.

VALAVANIS-VAIL, STEFAN. "An Econometric Model of Growth: U.S.A. 1869–1953," *Amer. Econ. Rev.*, 1955, *45*(Sup), pp. 208–21

Output Dynamics in Real-Business-Cycle Models

By Timothy Cogley and James M. Nason *

The time-series literature reports two stylized facts about output dynamics in the United States: GNP growth is positively autocorrelated, and GNP appears to have an important trend-reverting component. This paper investigates whether current real-business-cycle (RBC) models are consistent with these stylized facts. Many RBC models have weak internal propagation mechanisms and must rely on external sources of dynamics to replicate both facts. Models that incorporate labor adjustment costs are partially successful. They endogenously generate positive autocorrelation in output growth, but they need implausibly large transitory shocks to match the trend-reverting component in output. (JEL E32, C52)

There is an extensive empirical literature on the time-series properties of aggregate output. For example, prominent univariate studies include papers by Charles R. Nelson and Charles I. Plosser (1982), Mark W. Watson (1986), John Y. Campbell and N. Gregory Mankiw (1987), John H. Cochrane (1988), and James D. Hamilton (1989). Multivariate analyses include papers by Olivier Jean Blanchard and Danny Quah (1989), Robert G. King et al. (1991), and Cochrane (1994). This literature documents two stylized facts about output dynamics in the United States. First, GNP growth is positively autocorrelated over short horizons and has weak and possibly insignificant negative autocorrelation over longer horizons (e.g.,

Nelson and Plosser, 1982; Cochrane, 1988). Second, GNP appears to have an important trend-reverting component that has a hump-shaped impulse-response function (e.g., Blanchard and Quah, 1989; Cochrane, 1994).

This paper links the empirical literature on output dynamics with the theoretical literature on real-business-cycle (RBC) models. In particular, it considers whether various RBC models are consistent with these stylized facts. Our approach is similar in spirit to the "test of the Adelmans" (e.g., Irma Adelman and Frank L. Adelman, 1959; King and Plosser, 1994; Scott P. Simkins, 1994), except that we concentrate on a different set of stylized facts.[1,2] We ask how often an econometrician armed with the techniques used in the time-series literature would observe the same kind of stylized facts in data generated by RBC models. To

* Economic Research Department, Federal Reserve Bank of San Francisco, 101 Market St., San Francisco, CA 94105, and Department of Economics, University of British Columbia, 1873 East Mall, Vancouver, BC V6T 1Z1, respectively. We are grateful to two referees for their comments; we have also benefited from discussion and correspondence with Jack Beebe, John Cochrane, Roger Craine, Allan Gregory, Thomas Sargent, Anthony Smith, Gregor Smith, Richard Startz, and George Tauchen. Desiree Schaan provided exceptional research assistance. Much of this work was done while the authors were visiting the Haas School of Business at UC-Berkeley, whose hospitality is gratefully acknowledged. Opinions expressed in this paper do not necessarily represent the views of the Federal Reserve Bank of San Francisco or the Federal Reserve System.

[1] These authors consider whether various models can replicate Burns-Mitchell stylized facts.

[2] There is also an extensive literature on testing for unit roots. All the models that we study replicate the univariate persistence found in U.S. GNP. This follows directly from the specification of technology shocks. In models where technology shocks are difference-stationary, output has a unit root. In models where technology shocks are trend-stationary, output has a near unit root that conventional tests cannot distinguish from unity.

be specific, we generate artificial data by simulating a variety of RBC models, we compute autocorrelation and impulse-response functions for each artificial sample, and then we count the fraction of artificial samples that yield results like those found in U.S. data. Formally, our procedure can be regarded as a specification test of a particular RBC model. Alternatively, one can regard this as an informal guide to model reformulation.[3]

We find that standard RBC models must rely heavily on exogenous sources of dynamics in order to replicate both stylized facts. Many RBC models have weak endogenous propagation mechanisms and do not generate interesting output dynamics via their internal structure.[4] For example, in models that rely on capital accumulation and intertemporal substitution to spread shocks over time, output dynamics are essentially the same as impulse dynamics. Hence, these models must rely on impulse dynamics to replicate observed autocorrelation and impulse-response functions.

Other RBC models incorporate gestation lags or costs of adjusting the capital stock. For example, time-to-build models assume that it takes several quarters to install new capital (e.g., Finn E. Kydland and Edward C. Prescott, 1982), while q-theoretic models assume that the marginal cost of installing new capital is an increasing function of the rate of investment (e.g., Marianne Baxter and Mario J. Crucini, 1993). Gestation lags and quadratic adjustment costs have little effect on output dynamics. Although these factors alter the flow of investment, the change in the flow is very small relative to the stock of capital. Hence gestation lags and capital adjustment costs have little effect on the trajectory of the capital stock. Since the capital stock is what matters for

production, these factors do not generate business-cycle dynamics in output. Therefore, time-to-build and simple q-theoretic models must also rely on impulse dynamics to replicate observed output dynamics.

Finally, we examine RBC models that incorporate lags or costs of adjusting labor input. For example, Craig Burnside et al. (1993) assume that firms are subject to a one-quarter lag in adjusting employment. We also consider dynamic labor-demand models in which the marginal cost of adjusting employment is an increasing function of the rate of change in employment. These models are partially successful. They endogenously generate positive autocorrelation in output growth and a small hump in the transitory impulse-response function. However, they must rely on implausibly large transitory shocks in order to match the large hump found in the transitory component of GNP.

Our discussion is organized as follows. Section I replicates the time-series evidence and motivates our interest in it. Section II discusses models that abstract from gestation lags, employment lags, and costs of adjustment. Section III examines the effects of incorporating gestation lags and capital adjustment costs, and Section IV investigates employment lags and labor adjustment costs. The final section summarizes our results.

I. Stylized Facts about Output Dynamics

According to Prescott (1986), the "business-cycle phenomenon" has three dimensions: the periodicity of output, comovements of other variables with output, and the relative volatilities of various series. This paper provides information on the first dimension by comparing output dynamics in RBC models with stylized facts reported in the time-series literature.

Before proceeding to this comparison, we undertake two preliminary tasks. First, since the data used in the empirical literature differ in a number of ways from the customary treatment in RBC models, we replicate the time-series evidence so that it is conformable with the RBC literature. Second,

---

[3]Allan W. Gregory and Gregor W. Smith (1991) discuss various aspects of this approach to analyzing macroeconomic models.

[4]For example, see Lawrence J. Christiano (1988) or King et al. (1988a,b).

494   THE AMERICAN ECONOMIC REVIEW   JUNE 1995

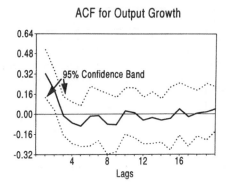

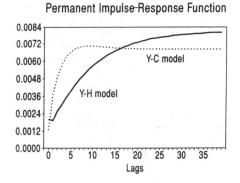

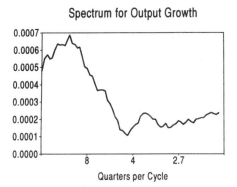

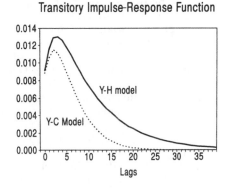

FIGURE 1. STYLIZED FACTS ABOUT GNP DYNAMICS

we explain why students of the business cycle might care about these stylized facts.

A. *The Autocorrelation Function for Output Growth*

Nelson and Plosser (1982) and Cochrane (1988) report that output growth is positively and significantly autocorrelated over short horizons and negatively but insignificantly autocorrelated over longer horizons. While their results are based on annual data, RBC models are typically calibrated to generate quarterly data. There are two ways to reconcile the difference in sampling frequency. One is to time-aggregate data generated by RBC models, and the other is to replicate the time-series evidence using quarterly data. Since temporal aggregation

involves a loss of information, we prefer to do the latter.

The upper left panel of Figure 1 reports the autocorrelation function (ACF) for real per capita GNP growth, 1954:1–1988:4, along with bands that mark plus and minus two standard errors.[5] At lags of 1 and 2 quarters, the sample autocorrelations are positive and statistically significant. At higher lags, the autocorrelations are mostly negative and statistically insignificant. This is basically the same pattern as found in annual data.

---

[5]The starting date was chosen to match other RBC simulations (e.g., Prescott, 1986). The standard errors are robust to serial correlation and heteroscedasticity in output growth.

The economic significance of the autocorrelation function becomes apparent when it is transformed into frequency domain. The lower left panel of Figure 1 shows the spectrum for output growth, which was estimated by smoothing the periodogram using a Bartlett window. The spectrum decomposes the variance of output growth by frequency. A peak in the spectrum indicates that the corresponding periodic components have greater amplitude than other components and therefore contribute a greater portion of the variance. The spectrum for output growth has a broad peak that ranges from approximately 2.33 to 7 years per cycle, with maximum power at roughly 3.2 years per cycle. Thus a relatively large proportion of the variance of output growth occurs at business-cycle frequencies.

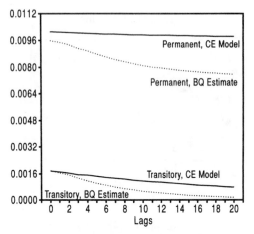

FIGURE 2. ESTIMATED AND POPULATION IMPULSE-RESPONSE FUNCTIONS FROM THE BLANCHARD-QUAH (BQ) TECHNIQUE AND THE CHRISTIANO-EICHENBAUM (CE) MODEL

B. Impulse-Response Functions for Output

While the autocorrelation function provides some information about business-cycle periodicity, it also masks differences in the dynamic response of output to various kinds of shocks. This problem does not arise in one-shock RBC models. However, in multi-shock RBC models, the autocorrelation function is a complicated function of the various impulse-response functions. Since these models imply that output responds differently to different kinds of shocks, the impulse-response functions contain additional useful information about output dynamics.

To estimate impulse-response functions, we use the structural VAR technique developed by Blanchard and Quah (1989). They use information on output growth and the unemployment rate to decompose GNP into permanent and transitory components. In particular, they assume that there are two kinds of orthogonal shocks, one that has a permanent effect on output and another that has only a transitory effect, and these assumptions are sufficient to identify the two components.

RBC models do not generate data on the unemployment rate. To make the Blanchard-Quah model conformable with RBC models, we substitute per capita

hours worked for the unemployment rate. Balanced-growth RBC models imply that per capita hours are stationary, so the modified VAR satisfies the Blanchard-Quah assumptions. A second-order VAR was estimated for per capita output growth and hours over the period 1954:1–1988:4, and impulse-response functions were estimated using the Blanchard-Quah technique. The solid lines in the right-hand panels of Figure 1 illustrate the results. In response to a permanent shock, output rises gradually and reaches a plateau after about six years. In response to a transitory shock, output rises for a few quarters and then returns to its stochastic trend. A substantial portion of the variation in output growth is due to transitory fluctuations. Thus, output appears to have an important trend-reverting component.

As a robustness check, we also estimated impulse-response functions by applying the Blanchard-Quah technique to a vector error-correction model for output and consumption. The results are shown as dotted lines in the right-hand side of Figure 1, and they are quite similar to those obtained from the output–hours model. For example, the contemporaneous correlation between the permanent innovations in the two models is 0.89. Output rises more quickly in response to a permanent shock, and the transitory impulse-response function is a bit smaller in magnitude, but these differences do not affect any of the results reported below. To save space, we focus on results derived from the output–hours model.

Finally, when applied to data generated by two-shock difference-stationary RBC models, the Blanchard-Quah decomposition extracts reasonable estimates of the population impulse-response functions. For example, Figure 2 compares the population impulse-response functions from the model of Christiano and Martin Eichenbaum (1992) with the mean estimate from 1,000 Monte Carlo replications. The estimated impulse-response functions exhibit the right qualitative pattern, but they are biased downward due to the usual small-sample bias in time series.[6] Nonetheless, for the multishock models that we consider, the Blanchard-Quah method allows us to estimate reasonable sample analogues to the population impulse-response functions.

II. Baseline Real-Business-Cycle Models

Broadly speaking, RBC models rely on three kinds of propagation mechanisms: capital accumulation, intertemporal substitution, and various kinds of adjustment lags or costs. This section studies a number of models that abstract from adjustment lags or costs and that rely entirely on capital accumulation and intertemporal substitution to spread shocks over time. Our list includes the models of King et al. (1988b), Jeremy Greenwood et al. (1988), Gary D. Hansen (1989), Jess Benhabib et al. (1991), Christiano and Eichenbaum (1992), and R. Anton Braun (1994).

These models have similar structures and parameter values, and they generate similar output dynamics. For expositional purposes, it will be convenient to discuss our results in terms of a single model and then to indicate how the results for other models differ. We begin by outlining the Christiano-Eichenbaum model. In this model, there is a representative agent whose preferences are given by

$$(1) \qquad E_t \left\{ \sum_{j=0}^{\infty} \beta^j \left[\ln(c_{t+j}) + \gamma(N - n_{t+j}) \right] \right\}$$

where c_t is consumption, N is the total endowment of time, n_t is labor hours, and β is the subjective discount factor. Following Christiano and Eichenbaum, we assume that $\beta = 1.03^{-0.25}$ and $\gamma = 0.0037$.

There is also a representative firm that produces output by means of a Cobb-Douglas production function:

$$(2) \qquad y_t = k_t^\theta (a_t n_t)^{1-\theta}$$

where y_t is output, k_t is the capital stock, and a_t is a technology shock. The capital stock obeys the usual law of motion:

$$(3) \qquad k_{t+1} = (1-\delta)k_t + i_t$$

where δ is the depreciation rate and i_t is gross investment. Christiano and Eichenbaum (1992) estimate that $\theta = 0.344$ and $\delta = 0.021$.

The model is driven by technology and government spending shocks. Technology shocks are assumed to be difference-stationary, but none of our results depends on this assumption.[7] We initially assume that technology shocks follow a random walk with drift and that government spending shocks evolve as a persistent AR(1) process

---

[6] The reduced-form VAR has a near unit root, and the estimated root is biased downward in finite samples. This causes the estimated impulse-response functions to decay faster than the population impulse-response functions. We obtain similar results for the other two-shock models studied in this paper.

[7] We have also studied trend-stationary representations for each of the models discussed in the paper, and the results are essentially the same.

around the stochastic technology trend:

$$(4) \qquad (1 - L)\ln(a_t) = \mu + \varepsilon_{at}$$

$$(5) \qquad \ln(g_t) - \ln(a_t) = \bar{g} + \varepsilon_{gt}/(1 - \rho L)$$

where g_t denotes government spending and ε_{at} and ε_{gt} are the technology and government spending innovations, respectively. Later we consider models with more complicated impulse dynamics. Christiano and Eichenbaum (1992) estimate $\mu = 0.004$, $\bar{g} = 0.177$, and $\rho = 0.96$. We assume that the relative volatility of the two shocks is the same as in Christiano and Eichenbaum (1992), but we rescale the innovation variances so that the model matches the sample variance of per capita GNP growth. This yields $\sigma_a = 0.0097$ and $\sigma_g = 0.0113$.

The model has a balanced-growth equilibrium. The natural logarithm of per capita output inherits the trend properties of total factor productivity and is therefore difference-stationary. Preferences are restricted so that technical progress has no long-run effect on labor supply. Hence per capita hours follow a stationary process.

The other models in the group differ in various ways. The King et al. (1988b), Hansen (1989), and Greenwood et al. (1988) models assume that technology shocks are the only source of fluctuations. Greenwood et al. also assume that technology shocks affect new capital goods but not existing capital and that firms vary capacity utilization in response to variation in the user cost of capital. Braun (1994) extends the Christiano-Eichenbaum model by including distortionary taxes on labor and capital. Finally, Benhabib et al. (1991) study a two-sector model in which goods are produced at home as well as in the market. These variations have important effects on co-movements and relative volatilities, but in most cases they have little influence on output dynamics.[8]

The remainder of this section considers whether these models are consistent with the stylized facts discussed in the previous section. Our statistical approach is based on Monte Carlo simulation. The models were used to generate artificial data over a time horizon of 140 quarters, which matches the length of the sample period, 1954:1–1988:4. Each model was simulated 1,000 times. Autocorrelation and impulse-response functions were estimated for each artificial sample, and the results were collected into empirical probability distributions. The empirical distributions were then used to calculate the probability of observing the statistics estimated from U.S. data under the hypothesis that the data were generated by a particular RBC model.

A. *Autocorrelation Functions*

Our first question is whether the models replicate the autocorrelation function for output growth. To test the match between sample and theoretical autocorrelation functions, we compute generalized Q statistics, which are defined as follows:

$$(6) \qquad Q_{\text{acf}} = (\hat{c} - c)' \hat{V}_c^{-1} (\hat{c} - c).$$

The vector $\hat{c}$ is the sample autocorrelation function, and c is the model-generated autocorrelation function. The latter was estimated by averaging autocorrelations across

---

[8]In replicating these models, we follow the original construction as closely as possible. For example, we use the same preference and technology parameter values as in the original. However, in the Greenwood et al.

(1988) model, the original specification generates time series that are stationary around a steady-state equilibrium. We transform this to a sustained-growth economy by adding nonstationary technical progress. Similarly, in the Benhabib et al. (1991) model, the original specification generates series that are stationary around a deterministic trend. We transform this to a difference-stationary model by assuming that market technology shocks follow a random walk with drift. Finally, we rescale the shocks in all the models so that they match the sample variance of output growth. A technical appendix, which is available from the authors upon request, provides details about the model specifications and parameter values, and it discusses the numerical techniques used to solve the models.

the ensemble of artificial samples:

$$c = (1/N) \sum_{i=1}^{N} c_i \tag{7}$$

where c_i is the autocorrelation function on replication i, and $N = 1,000$ is the number of replications. The covariance matrix, $\hat{V}_c$, is estimated by taking the ensemble average of the outer product of the autocorrelation function for simulated data:

$$\hat{V}_c = N^{-1} \sum_{i=1}^{N} [c_i - c][c_i - c]'. \tag{8}$$

Generalized Q statistics are approximately chi-square with degrees of freedom equal to the number of elements in c. As with an ordinary Q statistic, some judgment is required in choosing the number of lags. Since the autocorrelations die out at high-order lags, too high a choice will diminish the power of the test. We report results for a lag order equal to 8, but the results are not sensitive to this choice.

The first column of Table 1 reports Q_{acf} statistics for each model, with chi-square probability values shown in parentheses. A large value of Q_{acf} indicates that the theoretical autocorrelation function is a poor match for the sample autocorrelation function. The models are all rejected at roughly the 1-percent level or better.

The upper left panel of Figure 3 illustrates the results for the model of Christiano and Eichenbaum (1992). The solid line shows the sample autocorrelation function, and the dotted line shows the model-generated autocorrelation function. The dotted line is hard to see because it lies on top of the horizontal axis. Since the model-generated autocorrelations are all close to zero, output growth is close to being white noise. The main discrepancy between the sample and theoretical autocorrelations is the absence of positive dependence at lags 1 and 2.

Further insight can be obtained by looking at the problem in frequency domain. The lower left panel of Figure 3 compares the sample power spectrum, which is shown

TABLE 1—BASELINE REAL-BUSINESS-CYCLE MODELS

Model	Q_{acf}	Q_{irf}	
		y_P	y_T
King et al. (1988b)	23.0 (0.003)	—	—
Hansen (1989)	20.5 (0.008)	—	—
Greenwood et al. (1988)	25.7 (0.001)	—	—
Christiano and Eichenbaum (1992)	22.1 (0.005)	50.1 (0.018)	449.3 (0.000)
Benhabib et al. (1991)	31.2 (0.0001)	23.0 (0.064)	163.9 (0.001)
Braun (1994)	19.9 (0.011)	25.2 (0.054)	194.3 (0.001)

Notes: This table reports test statistics for the autocorrelation and impulse-response functions. The statistics Q_{acf} and Q_{irf} are defined by equations (6)–(8) and (9)–(11), respectively. The variable y_P refers to the permanent component of output, and y_T refers to the transitory component. The autocorrelation and impulse-response functions are truncated at lag 8, and probability values are in parentheses.

by the solid line, with the model-generated spectrum, which is shown by the dotted line. The dashed lines show upper and lower 2.5-percent probability bounds implied by the model.[9] The Christiano-Eichenbaum model does not generate business-cycle periodicity in output growth. Instead, its spectrum is quite flat, which indicates that business-cycle components are no more important than other periodic components. Further, the disparity between sample and theoretical spectra cannot be dismissed as sampling error, since the business-cycle peak in the sample spectrum lies well above the 2.5-percent upper probability bound implied by the model. Data generated by this model rarely exhibit business-cycle peaks of this magnitude.

These results also apply to four of the other five models in this group. The Benhabib et al. (1991) model is the only one

---

[9] The theoretical spectrum was estimated by smoothing the ensemble averaged periodogram with a Bartlett window. Upper and lower probability bounds were computed using the approximation given by theorem 5.5.3 in David R. Brillinger (1981).

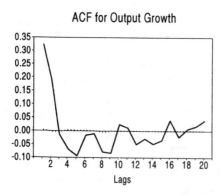

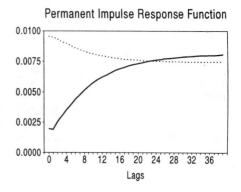

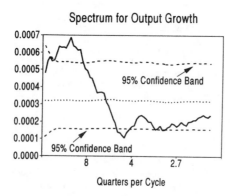

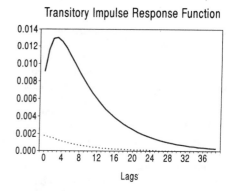

FIGURE 3. THE CHRISTIANO-EICHENBAUM MODEL

Note: Solid lines show sample moments, and dotted lines show moments that are generated by the Christiano-Eichenbaum model.

that endogenously generates serial correlation in output growth, but it generates *negative* autocorrelation and is rejected even more strongly than the others (see the fifth row of Table 1).

B. *Impulse-Response Functions*

Our second question is whether the baseline models replicate observed impulse-response functions. To test the match between sample and model-generated impulse-response functions, we compute the following statistic:

$$(9) \qquad Q_{\text{irf}} = (\hat{\mathbf{r}} - \mathbf{r})' \hat{\mathbf{V}}_{\mathbf{r}}^{-1} (\hat{\mathbf{r}} - \mathbf{r}).$$

The vectors $\hat{\mathbf{r}}$ and $\mathbf{r}$ are the sample and model-generated impulse-response functions, respectively. Theoretical impulse-response functions are estimated by averaging across the ensemble of artificial samples,

$$(10) \qquad \mathbf{r} = (1/N) \sum_{i=1}^{N} \mathbf{r}_i$$

where $\mathbf{r}_i$ is the impulse-response function on iteration i. The covariance matrix, $\hat{\mathbf{V}}_{\mathbf{r}}$, is estimated by taking the ensemble average of the outer product of the simulated impulse response functions:

$$(11) \qquad \hat{\mathbf{V}}_{\mathbf{r}} = N^{-1} \sum_{i=1}^{N} [\mathbf{r}_i - \mathbf{r}][\mathbf{r}_i - \mathbf{r}]'.$$

Again, since we are interested in short-run dynamics, we truncate at lag 8.[10]

The second and third columns of Table 1 report impulse-response statistics for the Christiano-Eichenbaum, Benhabib et al., and Braun models, with Monte Carlo probability values shown in parentheses. (The other models in this group are driven by a single shock, so their bivariate VAR's have stochastic singularities.) These models have some success matching the permanent impulse-response function but do not match the transitory impulse-response function. On this dimension, the models are rejected at better than the 1-percent level.

The right-hand panels of Figure 3 illustrate the results for the model of Christiano and Eichenbaum. The solid lines show the sample impulse-response functions, and dotted lines show model-generated impulse-response functions. The model strongly damps transitory shocks, so most of the variation in output growth is due to permanent movements. Furthermore, while GNP first rises and then falls in response to a transitory shock, the model generates monotonic decay. Thus the model does not generate an important trend-reverting component in output. Similar results apply to the Braun (1994) and Benhabib et al. (1991) models.

C. Impulse and Propagation

These results can be interpreted in terms of the model's impulse dynamics and propagation mechanisms. First consider the information in the autocorrelation function. In the Christiano-Eichenbaum model, technology shocks account for most of the variation in output growth. So far, we have assumed that technology shocks follow a random walk, which implies that the autocorrelations for growth in total factor productivity

are zero. Figure 3 shows that the autocorrelations for output growth are also close to zero. Thus the dynamics of output growth are essentially the same as the dynamics of total factor productivity growth. This suggests that the model has weak propagation mechanisms.

The impulse-response functions provide additional information. In the Christiano-Eichenbaum model, the permanent component of output can be written as:

$$(12) \quad y_P(t) = \left[\frac{\varepsilon_a(t)}{1-L} \right] \left[(1.04) \left(\frac{1-0.87L}{1-0.94L} \right) \right]$$

(see Cogley and Nason, 1993). The right-hand side is partitioned so that the first term shows shock dynamics and the second term shows propagation effects. The permanent component inherits a random-walk term from the technology shock and an ARMA(1, 1) term from the propagation mechanisms. However, the ARMA(1, 1) term contains near common factors. Since these roughly cancel, the propagation effects nearly vanish. Hence the model weakly propagates technology shocks.

The transitory component of output can be written as

$$(13) \quad y_T(t) = \left[\frac{\varepsilon_g(t)}{1-0.96L} \right] (0.16).$$

This is also partitioned so that the first term shows shock dynamics and the second term shows propagation effects. The transitory impulse-response function inherits the AR(1) dynamics of the government spending shock. Propagation mechanisms damp government spending shocks but do not alter their dynamics. Hence there are no dynamic propagation effects on government spending shocks.

In the Christiano-Eichenbaum model, output dynamics are determined primarily by impulse dynamics, with little contribution from propagation mechanisms. Since propagation mechanisms are weak, the model does

---

[10] If the chosen lag order is too low, we lose information about the shape of the transitory impulse-response function. Choosing too high a lag order reduces the power of the test because the transitory impulse-response function dies out and the standard errors for the permanent impulse response grow large.

not endogenously generate business-cycle dynamics in output. Similar results apply to four of the other five models in this group.

The Benhabib et al. (1991) model is the only one in this group that has a strong propagation mechanism, but it generates *negative* autocorrelation in output growth. This arises from intersectoral labor flows, which enhance intertemporal substitution into and out of market employment. To understand how this works, it is useful to think about the response of market output to Cholesky innovations.[11] A transitory shock is defined as a one-unit increase in home productivity, while a permanent shock consists of a one-unit increase in market productivity plus a fractional increase in home productivity.

In response to a temporary increase in home productivity, labor flows out of the market and into the home sector, causing market output to fall at impact. Home productivity shocks follow an AR(1) process, so home productivity peaks at impact and then begins to decline. As it falls, labor gradually returns to the market, and measured output rises back toward its stochastic trend. Thus, in response to a transitory shock, measured output falls at impact and then rises back toward trend, generating negative autocorrelation in the transitory component of output growth.

The response to a permanent shock is a combination of the responses to home and market innovations. Output rises in response to a positive innovation in market productivity, but the impact effect is partially damped by a positive innovation in home productivity, which draws some labor out of the market sector. Subsequently, as home productivity declines, labor gradually returns to the market, generating further small increases in output. The positive impact effect on market output is followed by a sequence of further small increases, and this generates modest positive autocorrela-

tion in the permanent component of output growth.

The autocorrelation function for output growth depends on both effects. But since the permanent-growth component involves partially offsetting effects, the negative autocorrelation in the transitory-growth component dominates. Therefore the home-production model generates negative autocorrelation in output growth.

D. External Sources of Dynamics

Models that have weak propagation mechanisms must rely on external sources of dynamics to replicate observed output dynamics. This section briefly considers three possible candidates: temporal aggregation, serially correlated increments to total factor productivity, and higher-order autoregressive representations for transitory shocks. While all three are sufficient to generate positive serial correlation in output growth, the first two do not generate a hump-shaped transitory impulse-response function. Furthermore, all three require shock dynamics that are counterfactual in some dimension.

We investigate these issues in the context of the Christiano-Eichenbaum model. We first consider whether temporal aggregation might account for observed output dynamics. Suppose, for example, that households and firms make decisions on a weekly basis. To convert from a quarterly to a weekly model, we followed the procedure of Christiano (1989). The parameters with time dimensions, such as the discount rate, 1 minus the depreciation rate, and the autoregressive coefficients, were adjusted by raising them to the 1/13 power. The time endowment and means of the disturbances were divided by 13, and the innovation variances were rescaled so that the time-aggregated data match the sample variance of output growth. The modified model was used to generate weekly data, the weekly data were flow-averaged to generate quarterly series, and autocorrelation and impulse-response functions were estimated from the temporally aggregated quarterly data. The first row of Table 2 reports test

---

[11] Home and market technology shocks are positively correlated, and this thought experiment implicitly accounts for the covariance term.

TABLE 2—EXTERNAL SOURCES OF DYNAMICS

Source	Q_{acf}	Q_{irf}	
		y_P	y_T
Temporal aggregation	7.7	11.6	803.7
	(0.467)	(0.182)	(0.000)
ARIMA(1,1,0)	8.6	117.7	152.1
technology shocks	(0.376)	(0.003)	(0.003)
AR(2) government	5.5	23.2	14.4
spending shocks	(0.705)	(0.070)	(0.126)

Notes: This table reports test statistics for the autocorrelation and impulse-response functions. The statistics Q_{acf} and Q_{irf} are defined by equations (6)–(8) and (9)–(11), respectively. The variable y_P refers to the permanent component of output, and y_T refers to the transitory component. The autocorrelation and impulse-response functions are truncated at lag 8, and probability values are in parentheses.

statistics, and the top panels of Figure 4 show the impulse-response functions.

On a weekly basis, output is well approximated by a random walk, which implies that quarterly output is well approximated by an ARIMA(0, 1, 1) process with first-order autocorrelation equal to 0.25. Thus the temporally aggregated model easily passes the autocorrelation test (see the first row of Table 2, column 1). However, while the model generates roughly the right degree of autocorrelation in output growth, it generates too much autocorrelation in total factor productivity growth. In U.S. data, the first-order autocorrelation for growth in total factor productivity is −0.015, whereas the mean autocorrelation in the time-aggregation model is 0.234. The difference is significant at the 0.2-percent level.

Furthermore, the impulse-response functions show that temporal aggregation operates primarily on the permanent component and has little effect on the transitory component. Time aggregation improves the model's ability to replicate the permanent impulse-response function but does not generate a hump-shaped transitory impulse-response function. On the latter dimension, the model is still rejected at better than the 1-percent level. Thus, temporal aggregation does not account for the trend-reverting component found in U.S. data.

Next we consider whether serial correlation in total factor productivity growth might account for observed output dynamics. We return to the quarterly model but now assume that technology shocks follow an ARIMA(1, 1, 0) process with autoregressive coefficient equal to 0.2. Output growth inherits the AR(1) structure of total factor productivity growth, so this model also passes the autocorrelation test (see the second row of Table 2). But this specification also generates too much autocorrelation in total factor productivity growth. Furthermore, since technology shocks drive the permanent component of output, this modification does not generate a hump-shaped transitory impulse response (see the second row of Fig. 4). The model is still rejected on these dimensions.

To replicate both stylized facts, the model needs a high-variance transitory shock that has a hump-shaped moving-average representation. Hump-shaped shock dynamics are needed to match the shape of the sample impulse-response function, and a high variance is needed to match its magnitude. For example, suppose that government spending shocks follow an AR(2) process with roots equal to 0.9 and 0.45.[12] Also suppose that the standard error of the innovation to government spending is 3.5 times larger than in the baseline model. (To match the sample variance of output growth, the standard error of technology shocks must then be reduced by roughly 30 percent.) In this case, the transitory component of output inherits a large hump-shaped impulse-response function from the transitory shock (see the bottom panels of Fig. 4). This generates positive low-order autocorrelation in output growth, so the model also passes the autocorrelation test (see the third row of Table 2).

While this specification can replicate both stylized facts, it must rely on partially counterfactual shock dynamics to do so. The

---

[12] These are roughly the same as the AR roots for the transitory component of GNP.

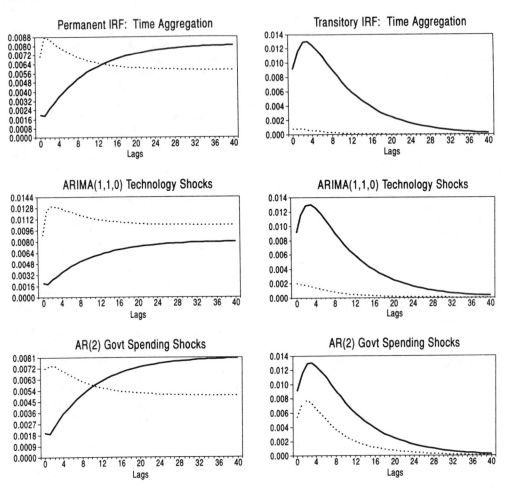

FIGURE 4. EXTERNAL SOURCES OF DYNAMICS

Note: Solid lines show sample impulse-response functions, and dotted lines show model-generated impulse-response functions.

specification for Solow residuals is plausible, but the representation for government spending is problematic. In U.S. data, government spending is better approximated by an AR(1) process around the productivity trend. If one fits an AR(2) model to these data, the second root is equal to 0.07 with a standard error of 0.05. Furthermore, the assumed innovation variance for government spending is much larger than in the data, so the government-spending shocks are implausibly large.

III. Gestation Lags and Capital Adjustment Costs

In the baseline models, there are no costs or time lags associated with adjusting the capital stock. This section studies two models that incorporate these features. The first is a time-to-build model, which assumes that firms face multiperiod gestation lags when installing new capital and that there are no markets for capital goods in process. The second is a *q*-theoretic model, which

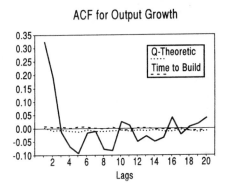

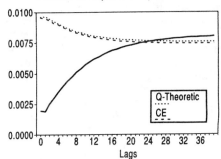

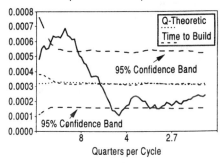

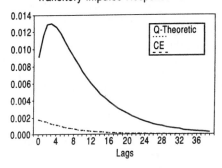

FIGURE 5. GESTATION LAGS AND CAPITAL ADJUSTMENT COSTS

Note: Solid lines show sample moments, and dashed and dotted lines show model-generated moments.

assumes that the marginal cost of installing new capital is an increasing function of the rate of investment.

The time-to-build model closely resembles the one studied by K. Geert Rouwenhorst (1991). In this model, technology shocks are the only source of fluctuations. Preferences and technology are restricted so that there is a balanced-growth equilibrium, and firms face a 3-quarter gestation lag when installing new capital. We follow Rouwenhorst's specification because it isolates the role of the time-to-build technology and because it has a balanced-growth equilibrium when driven by labor-augmenting technical progress.

The q-theoretic model is a variant of the Christiano-Eichenbaum model in which the production function is modified so that there are quadratic costs of adjusting the capital stock. In particular, the production function becomes

$$(14)\quad \ln(y_t) = \ln[f(k_t, a_t n_t)] $$
$$ - (\alpha_k/2)[\Delta k_t/k_{t-1}]^2 $$

while all the other aspects of the model remain the same. This specification implies that the marginal cost of adjusting the capital stock is a linear function of the rate of net investment, and it is similar to the specifications used by Matthew D. Shapiro (1986) and Baxter and Crucini (1993).[13]

The parameter α_k is calibrated from estimates in Shapiro (1986). Using his parameter estimates, the marginal cost of a 1-percent increase in the capital stock amounts to roughly 2.2 percent of a quarter's output. Hence the baseline value for α_k is 2.2. To check whether the results are sensitive to the choice of α_k, we also simulated the model for α_k equal to 2.2/4, 2.2/2, 2×2.2, and 4×2.2, and we found that the results were not sensitive to the size of the adjustment-cost parameter.

Figure 5 summarizes output dynamics in the time-to-build and baseline q-theoretic models, and Table 3 reports test statistics. The left-hand panels of Figure 5 report autocorrelation functions and power spectra for output growth, with solid lines showing sample moments and dashed and dotted lines showing model-generated moments. Gestation lags and capital adjustment costs do not generate serial correlation or business-cycle periodicity in output growth. As in the baseline RBC models, time-to-build and q-theoretic models imply that output growth is approximately white noise, and this implication is rejected at better than the 1-percent level (see the first column of Table 3).[14]

---

[13]There are two superficial differences between our specification and that of Baxter and Crucini. First, Baxter and Crucini subtract the adjustment cost from the flow of investment rather than the flow of output. Second, they start with a general functional form for adjustment costs and then linearize the marginal adjustment-cost function when approximating the model's first-order conditions. The two formulations yield similar output dynamics.

[14]The main difference between our specification and that of Rouwenhorst is that he assumes that technology shocks are trend-stationary. This has a minor effect on the results. In the trend-stationary specification, the autocorrelation function for output growth exhibits slowly decaying, low-amplitude, period-3 oscillations (the spectrum has a small peak at 3 quarters per cycle). This arises directly from the gestation lag. A positive technology shock generates an increase in output. The increase is temporary, so the representative consumer saves much of it, thus generating a relatively large increase in new project starts. Three periods hence, the new projects come on line as productive

TABLE 3—GESTATION LAGS AND CAPITAL ADJUSTMENT COSTS

Model	Q_{acf}	Q_{irf} y_P	y_T
Time-to-build	20.6 (0.008)	—	—
Q-theory, $\alpha_k = 2.2$	20.1 (0.008)	57.4 (0.015)	419.3 (0.000)
Sensitivity analysis:			
$\alpha_k = 2.2/4$	21.8 (0.005)	40.1 (0.028)	410.8 (0.000)
$\alpha_k = 2.2/2$	21.4 (0.006)	40.0 (0.028)	406.5 (0.000)
$\alpha_k = 2(2.2)$	19.0 (0.015)	71.1 (0.008)	385.9 (0.000)
$\alpha_k = 4(2.2)$	16.4 (0.036)	95.9 (0.005)	387.1 (0.000)

Notes: This table reports test statistics for the autocorrelation and impulse-response functions. The statistics Q_{acf} and Q_{irf} are defined by equations (6)–(8) and (9)–(11), respectively. The variable y_P refers to the permanent component of output, and y_T refers to the transitory component. The autocorrelation and impulse-response functions are truncated at lag 8, and probability values are in parentheses. The parameter α_k governs the marginal cost of a 1-percent change in the capital stock [see equation (14) and the discussion in Section III].

The q-theoretic model is driven by technology and government spending shocks, and the two impulse-response functions are shown in the right-hand panels of Figure 5. For the sake of comparison, the impulse-response functions for the original model of Christiano and Eichenbaum (1992) are also shown. The addition of capital adjustment costs has almost no effect on the model's impulse-response functions. As in the original Christiano-Eichenbaum model, output dynamics are determined primarily by impulse dynamics. Since capital adjustment costs do not help to propagate shocks over time, the q-theoretic model does not endogenously generate business-cycle dynamics in output. Thus, the q-theoretic model must also rely on external dynamics to match the sample impulse-response functions.

---

capital, generating a secondary increase in output, and so on. Since gestation lags are typically assumed to be three or four quarters, time-to-build cycles do not account for U.S. business cycles.

This result may seem counterintuitive. Initially, our intuition was that gestation lags and capital adjustment costs would help to propagate shocks by spreading the response of investment over time and that this might generate interesting output dynamics. This intuition is half right. Gestation lags and capital adjustment costs do alter the flow of investment relative to the baseline model, but the change in the flow is small relative to the stock of capital. Quarterly net investment is only 0.4 percent of the capital stock, on average, so gestation lags and capital adjustment costs would have to have huge effects on investment in order to have significant effects on the short-term dynamics of capital. Since these factors have only modest effects on investment, they have very little effect on the path of the capital stock. The capital stock is what matters for production, so gestation lags and capital adjustment costs have little effect on the short-term dynamics of output.

IV. Employment Lags and Labor Adjustment Costs

Baseline RBC models also abstract from employment lags and labor adjustment costs, and this section examines two models that incorporate these features. The first is a difference-stationary version of the labor-hoarding model of Burnside et al. (1993). They assume that firms must choose the size of the labor force before observing the current state of the economy but can vary the intensity of work effort after observing the current state. Although employment adjustment costs are not explicitly modeled, one can interpret this as the reduced form of a model in which it is infinitely costly to make current-quarter adjustments on the extensive margin (e.g., by hiring, layoffs, or overtime). Thus firms choose to make all their current-quarter adjustments on the intensive margin (i.e., by varying effort). Since the ability to vary work effort only partially compensates for the inability to make current-quarter employment adjustments, these assumptions introduce a one-period lag in adjusting labor input, and this helps to propagate shocks over time.

We also consider a dynamic labor-demand model which assumes that the marginal cost of adjusting employment is a linear function of its rate of change. This model extends the previous section's q-theoretic model to include quadratic costs of adjusting labor input. In particular, the production function now becomes

$$(15) \quad \ln(y_t) = \ln[f(k_t, a_t n_t)]$$
$$- (\alpha_k/2)[\Delta k_t/k_{t-1}]^2$$
$$- (\alpha_n/2)[\Delta n_t/n_{t-1}]^2$$

while the other elements of the model remain the same. For α_k, we use the previous section's benchmark value of 2.2, but the results do not depend on the value of this parameter.

The labor-adjustment parameter, α_n, is calibrated using Shapiro's estimates. He distinguishes between adjustment costs for production and nonproduction workers and finds that the latter are substantial but that the former are negligible. In particular, the marginal cost of a 1-percent change in the number of nonproduction workers is roughly 0.36 percent of a quarter's output, while the marginal cost of a 1-percent change in the number of production workers cannot be distinguished from zero.

Since our model has only one kind of worker, it is a bit difficult to translate Shapiro's (1986) estimates directly into a value of α_n. If employment of production and nonproduction workers varied in the same proportion, one could simply set α_n equal to 0.36. However, employment of production workers appears to be more cyclically sensitive than employment of nonproduction workers. If employment adjustments occur primarily on the production-worker margin, α_n should be less than 0.36. We take $\alpha_n = 0.36$ as our benchmark case, but we recognize that this probably overstates the size of aggregate labor adjustment costs. We do sensitivity analysis to deal with the resulting ambiguity. Fortunately, the results are robust to the choice of α_n.

must be joined with large transitory shocks in order to generate an important trend-reverting component in output.

V. Conclusion

The time-series literature on aggregate output dynamics documents two stylized facts about U.S. GNP. The first is that GNP growth is positively autocorrelated in the short run and weakly negatively autocorrelated over longer horizons. The second is that GNP appears to have an important trend-reverting component that has a hump-shaped moving-average representation. This paper considers whether various RBC models can replicate these stylized facts.

We find that existing RBC models must rely heavily on exogenous factors to replicate both stylized facts. Many RBC models have weak internal propagation mechanisms and do not generate interesting dynamics via their internal structure. In particular, in models that rely on intertemporal substitution, capital accumulation, and costs of adjusting the capital stock, output dynamics are nearly the same as impulse dynamics. Hence, these models must rely on impulse dynamics to replicate the dynamics found in U.S. data. Models that rely on lags or costs of adjusting labor input are partially successful. Although they endogenously generate the right pattern of autocorrelation in output growth and a small hump in the transitory impulse-response function, they must rely on implausibly large transitory shocks to match the large transitory impulse response found in the data.

From the perspective of the literature of the 1970's and early 1980's, it is perhaps surprising that RBC propagation mechanisms do not generate business-cycle dynamics in output. For example, in response to James Tobin's (1977) criticism that equilibrium monetary business-cycle models fail to deliver serially correlated movements in output, Robert E. Lucas and Thomas J. Sargent (1981) noted that capital accumulation and costs of adjustment could turn serially uncorrelated shocks into serially correlated movements in output. Although RBC theorists have explored this idea in great detail, the propagation mechanisms embodied in current models do not generate the right kind of output dynamics. Our results suggest that RBC theorists ought to devote further attention to modeling internal sources of propagation.

DATA APPENDIX

Output is defined as real gross national product, and population is measured by the civilian noninstitutional population aged 16 or older. Labor input is measured by hours worked by all workers in all industries, and consumption is defined as real personal consumption expenditures. Government spending is measured by real purchases of goods and services by federal, state, and local governments. The capital stock measure that was used to compute Solow residuals was constructed by summing net private investment in equipment and structures, which was measured by subtracting the capital consumption allowance and the change in business inventories from gross private domestic investment. The initial value for the quarterly capital stock series was taken from the annual series on the stock of private residential and nonresidential capital. The data are available on the Federal Reserve System's FAME Economic Database and on CITIBASE.

REFERENCES

Adelman, Irma and Adelman, Frank L. "The Dynamic Properties of the Klein-Goldberger Model." *Econometrica*, October 1959, *27*(4), pp. 596–625.

Baxter, Marianne and Crucini, Mario J. "Explaining Saving–Investment Correlations." *American Economic Review*, June 1993, *83*(3), pp. 416–36.

Benhabib, Jess; Rogerson, Richard and Wright, Randall. "Homework in Macroeconomics: Household Production and Aggregate Fluctuations." *Journal of Political Economy*, December 1991, *99*(6), pp. 1166–87.

Blanchard, Olivier Jean and Quah, Danny. "The Dynamic Effects of Aggregate Demand and Supply Shocks." *American Economic Review*, September 1989, *79*(4), pp. 655–73.

Braun, R. Anton. "Tax Disturbances and Real Economic Activity in the Postwar United States." *Journal of Monetary Economics*, June 1994, *33*(3), pp. 441–62.

TABLE 4—EMPLOYMENT LAGS AND LABOR
ADJUSTMENT COSTS

Model	Q_{acf}	Q_{irf}	
		y_P	y_T
Burnside et al. (1993)	6.7	31.5	72.7
	(0.469)	(0.035)	(0.014)
Adjustment costs in labor and capital:			
$\alpha_n = 0.36$, $\alpha_k = 2.2$	9.2	34.6	76.0
	(0.326)	(0.031)	(0.012)
Sensitivity analysis:			
$\alpha_n = 0.36/4$, $\alpha_k = 2.2$	12.9	37.0	193.7
	(0.116)	(0.031)	(0.005)
$\alpha_n = 0.36/2$, $\alpha_k = 2.2$	9.8	39.2	123.1
	(0.224)	(0.024)	(0.008)
$\alpha_n = (0.36)2$, $\alpha_k = 2.2$	9.0	37.1	52.4
	(0.339)	(0.024)	(0.021)
$\alpha_n = (0.36)4$, $\alpha_k = 2.2$	10.1	48.7	54.8
	(0.257)	(0.016)	(0.018)

Notes: This table reports test statistics for the autocorrelation and impulse-response functions. The statistics Q_{acf} and Q_{irf} are defined by equations (6)–(8) and (9)–(11), respectively. The variable y_P refers to the permanent component of output, and y_T refers to the transitory component. The autocorrelation and impulse-response functions are truncated at lag 8, and probability values are in parentheses. The parameters α_n and α_k govern the marginal cost of a 1-percent change in labor and capital, respectively [see equation (15) and the discussion in Section IV].

fort). Since effort adjustments are more costly than employment adjustments, the marginal cost of a contemporaneous change in labor input is greater than the marginal cost of a deferred change.

Thus, when firms experience a positive technology shock, the optimal response is to spread labor adjustments over time. Firms complete part of their adjustment in the current quarter, by increasing work effort, and defer the rest to the subsequent quarter when it becomes feasible to adjust employment and thus less expensive to increase labor input. Output rises at impact, both because of the direct effect of the technology shock and because of the increase in work effort, and it rises again in the subsequent quarter because of the delayed increase in employment. Eventually, the income effect of a technology shock begins to offset the substitution effect, causing per capita hours to revert to the mean and

output to decline from its peak. This generates a hump-shaped response of output to technology shocks (see the upper right panel of Fig. 6). If we take first differences, we find that output growth has positive low-order autocorrelation and weak negative high-order autocorrelation.[15]

The propagation mechanism in the cost-of-adjustment model operates in a similar fashion, except that the cost of a contemporaneous change in employment is finite and the cost of a future change is positive. Thus, the impact effect of a technology shock is somewhat larger than in the Burnside et al. model, and the lagged effects are somewhat smaller. This generates weaker serial correlation in output growth.

Although the labor-hoarding and cost-of-adjustment models account for serial correlation in output growth, they are less successful at replicating the impulse-response functions (see the right-hand panels of Fig. 6 and the second and third columns of Table 4). Both models overstate the short-term response of output to technology shocks and understate its response to transitory shocks. In particular, conditional on the baseline parameterization of the transitory shock, neither model generates an important trend-reverting component in output. On this dimension, the models are rejected at the 1–3-percent level. Although the models generate the right qualitative response to transitory shocks, it is strongly damped and much too small in magnitude. In order to match the magnitude of the transitory impulse response, the innovation variance of government-spending shocks would have to be considerably larger than the value found in the data. Thus, the labor-hoarding and adjustment-cost models

---

[15] If the constraint on current-quarter employment adjustments were relaxed, firms would immediately raise employment and would not increase work effort. In this case, the Burnside et al. model would become observationally equivalent to the Christiano-Eichenbaum model and thus would not generate serial correlation in output growth. Therefore, the constraint on contemporaneous employment adjustments is critical for generating serial correlation in this model.

ACF for Output Growth

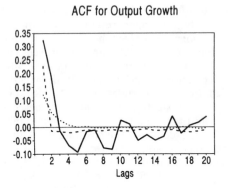

Permanent Impulse Response Function

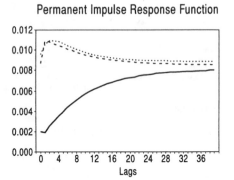

Spectrum for Output Growth

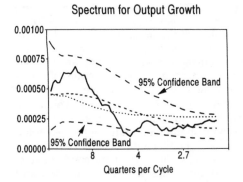

Transitory Impulse Response Function

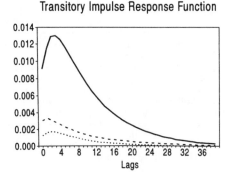

FIGURE 6. EMPLOYMENT LAGS AND LABOR ADJUSTMENT COSTS

Note: Solid lines show sample moments, dotted lines show moments generated by the cost-of-adjustment model, and dashed lines show moments generated by the Burnside et al. (1993) model.

Figure 6 summarizes the output dynamics in the labor-hoarding and adjustment-cost models, and Table 4 reports test statistics. The upper left panel of Figure 6 shows the sample- and model-generated autocorrelation functions. In contrast to the other models studied in this paper, the labor-hoarding and adjustment-cost models endogenously generate positive autocorrelation in output growth. In the Burnside et al. (1993) model, output growth is positively autocorrelated at lag 1 and has modest negative autocorrelation at higher-order lags, and the model easily passes the autocorrelation test (see the first row of Table 4, column 1). In the adjustment-cost model, output growth is well approximated by an AR(1) representation, with positive autocorrelation at lag 1 and

monotonic decay at higher-order lags. Although the adjustment-cost model generates rather modest serial correlation, it still passes the autocorrelation test (see the second row of Table 4). This result is robust to changes in the value of α_n; for example, the model passes even when $\alpha_n = 0.09$ (see the third row of Table 4).

The propagation mechanism in the Burnside et al. (1993) model derives from the assumption that employment is predetermined. Although firms can vary work effort, this is relatively costly, both because wages are higher (firms have to pay a premium in order to compensate workers for supplying greater effort) and because the marginal product is lower (there are sharply diminishing marginal returns to greater ef-

Brillinger, David R. *Time series: Data analysis and theory*. San Francisco, CA: Holden-Day, 1981.

Burnside, Craig; Eichenbaum, Martin and Rebelo, Sergio T. "Labor Hoarding and the Business Cycle." *Journal of Political Economy*, April 1993, *101*(2), pp. 245–73.

Campbell, John Y. and Mankiw, N. Gregory. "Are Output Fluctuations Transitory?" *Quarterly Journal of Economics*, November 1987, *102*(4), pp. 857–80.

Christiano, Lawrence J. "Why Does Inventory Investment Fluctuate So Much?" *Journal of Monetary Economics*, March/May 1988, *21*(2/3), pp. 247–80.

_____. "Consumption, Income, and Interest Rates: Reinterpreting the Time Series Evidence: Comment," in Olivier Jean Blanchard and Stanley Fischer, eds., *NBER macroeconomics annual: 1989*. Cambridge, MA: MIT Press, 1989, pp. 216–33.

Christiano, Lawrence J. and Eichenbaum, Martin. "Current Real-Business-Cycle Theories and Aggregate Labor-Market Fluctuations." *American Economic Review*, June 1992, *82*(3), pp. 430–50.

Cochrane, John H. "How Big Is the Random Walk in GNP?" *Journal of Political Economy*, October 1988, *96*(5), pp. 893–920.

_____. "Permanent and Transitory Components of GNP and Stock Prices." *Quarterly Journal of Economics*, February 1994, *109*(1), pp. 241–65.

Cogley, Timothy and Nason, James M. "Impulse Dynamics and Propagation Mechanisms in a Real Business Cycle Model." *Economics Letters*, December 1993, *43*(4), pp. 77–81.

Greenwood, Jeremy; Hercowitz, Zvi and Huffman, Gregory W. "Investment, Capacity Utilization, and the Real Business Cycle." *American Economic Review*, June 1988, *78*(3), pp. 402–17.

Gregory, Allan W. and Smith, Gregor W. "Calibration as Testing: Inference in Simulated Macroeconomic Models." *Journal of Business and Economic Statistics*, July 1991, *9*(3), pp. 297–303.

Hamilton, James D. "A New Approach to the Economic Analysis of Non-Stationary Time Series and the Business Cycle." *Econometrica*, March 1989, *57*(2), pp. 357–84.

Hansen, Gary D. "Technical Progress and Aggregate Fluctuations." Department of Economics Working Paper No. 546, University of California, Los Angeles, 1989.

King, Robert G. and Plosser, Charles I. "Real Business Cycles and the Test of the Adelmans." *Journal of Monetary Economics*, April 1994, *33*(2), pp. 405–38.

King, Robert G.; Plosser, Charles I. and Rebelo, Sergio T. "Production, Growth, and Business Cycles: I. The Basic Neoclassical Model." *Journal of Monetary Economics*, March/May 1988a, *21*(2/3), pp. 195–232.

_____. "Production, Growth, and Business Cycles: II. New Directions." *Journal of Monetary Economics*, March/May 1988b, *21*(2/3), pp. 309–42.

King, Robert G.; Plosser, Charles I.; Stock, James H. and Watson, Mark W. "Stochastic Trends and Economic Fluctuations." *American Economic Review*, September 1991, *81*(4), pp. 819–40.

Kydland, Finn E. and Prescott, Edward C. "Time to Build and Aggregate Fluctuations." *Econometrica*, November 1982, *50*(6), pp. 1345–70.

Lucas, Robert E. and Sargent, Thomas J. "After Keynesian Macroeconomics," in Robert E. Lucas and Thomas J. Sargent, eds., *Rational expectations and econometric practice*. Minneapolis, MN: University of Minnesota Press, 1981, pp. 295–319.

Nelson, Charles R. and Plosser, Charles I. "Trends and Random Walks in Macroeconomic Time Series." *Journal of Monetary Economics*, September 1982, *10*(2), pp. 139–62.

Prescott, Edward C. "Theory Ahead of Business-Cycle Measurement." *Carnegie-Rochester Conference Series on Public Policy*, Autumn 1986, *25*, pp. 11–44.

Rouwenhorst, K. Geert. "Time to Build and Aggregate Fluctuations: A Reconsideration." *Journal of Monetary Economics*, April 1991, *27*(2), pp. 241–54.

Shapiro, Matthew D. "The Dynamic Demand for Capital and Labor." *Quarterly Journal of Economics*, August 1986, *101*(3), pp. 513–42.

Simkins, Scott P. "Do Real Business Cycle

Models Really Exhibit Business Cycle Behavior?" *Journal of Monetary Economics*, April 1994, *33*(2), pp. 381–404.

Tobin, James. "How Dead Is Keynes?" *Economic Inquiry*, October 1977, *15*(4), pp. 459–68.

Watson, Mark W. "Univariate Detrending Methods with Stochastic Trends." *Journal of Monetary Economics*, July 1986, *18*(1), pp. 49–76.

Part VIII

Filtering and detrending

ROBERT J. HODRICK
EDWARD C. PRESCOTT

Postwar U.S. Business Cycles:
An Empirical Investigation

We propose a procedure for representing a time series as the sum of a smoothly vary-ing trend component and a cyclical component. We document the nature of the com-ovements of the cyclical components of a variety of macroeconomic time series. We find that these comovements are very different than the corresponding comovements of the slowly varying trend components.

THE PURPOSE OF THIS ARTICLE is to document some features of aggregate economic fluctuations sometimes referred to as business cycles. The investigation uses quarterly data from the postwar U.S. economy. The fluctuations studied are those that are too rapid to be accounted for by slowly changing demo-graphic and technological factors and changes in the stocks of capital that produce secular growth in output per capita.

As Lucas (1981) has emphasized, aggregate economic variables in capitalist econ-omies experience repeated fluctuations about their long-term growth paths. Prior to Keynes' *General Theory*, the study of these rapid fluctuations, combined with the attempt to reconcile the observations with an equilibrium theory, was regarded as the main outstanding challenge of economic research. Although the Keynesian Rev-

Support of the National Science Foundation is acknowledged. We also acknowledge helpful com-ments by the participants at the 1979 Summer Warwick Workshop on Expectation and the money work-shops at the Universities of Chicago and Virginia and at Carnegie-Mellon University. In particular, we thank Robert Avery, V.V. Chari, Lars Peter Hansen, Charles R. Nelson, Thomas J. Sargent, Kenneth J. Singleton, and John H. Wood for comments. We also thank the Wharton Economic Forecasting Associ-ates for providing the data.

This paper is substantially the same as our 1981 working paper. The only major change to the paper is the addition of an Appendix of Tables that mirror our originals and contain data ending in 1993. Since we did not update the citations, we apologize to the many authors who have used the Hodrick-Prescott filter and studied its properties in the intervening eighteen years since its original development.

ROBERT J. HODRICK *is Nomura Professor of International Finance at the Graduate School of Business, Columbia University.* EDWARD C. PRESCOTT *is Regents' Professor at the Univer-sity of Minnesota and Advisor to the Federal Reserve Bank of Minneapolis. Both are research associates of the National Bureau of Economic Research.*

Journal of Money, Credit, and Banking, Vol. 29, No. 1 (February 1997)
Copyright 1997 by The Ohio State University Press

olution redirected effort away from this question to the one of determining the level of output at a point in time in disequilibrium, the failure of the Keynesian Theory in the 1970s has caused many economists to want to return to the study of business cycles as equilibrium phenomena. In their search for an equilibrium model of the business cycle, modern economists have been guided by the insights of Mitchell (1913) and others who have used techniques of analysis that were developed prior to the development of modern computers. The thesis of this paper is that the search for an equilibrium model of the business cycle is only beginning and that studying the comovements of aggregate economic variables using an efficient, easily replicable technique that incorporates our prior knowledge about the economy will provide insights into the features of the economy that an equilibrium theory should incorporate.

This study should be viewed as documenting some systematic deviations from the restrictions upon observations implied by neoclassical growth theory.[1] Our statistical approach does not utilize standard time series analysis. Our prior knowledge concerning the processes generating the data is not of the variety that permits us to specify a probability model as required for application of that analysis. We proceed in a more cautious manner that requires only prior knowledge that can be supported by economic theory. The maintained hypothesis, based upon growth theory considerations, is that the growth component of aggregate economic time series varies smoothly over time. The sense in which it varies smoothly is made explicit in section 1.

We find that the nature of the comovements of the cyclical components of macroeconomic time series are very different from the comovements of the slowly varying components of the corresponding variables. Growth is characterized by roughly proportional growth in (per capita) output, investment, consumption, capital stock and productivity (output per hour), and little change in the hours of employment per capita or household. In contrast, the cyclical variations in output arise principally as the result of changes in cyclical hours of employment and not as the result of changes in cyclical productivity or capital stocks. In the case of the cyclical capital stocks in both durable and nondurable manufacturing industries, the correlation with cyclical output is even negative. Another difference is in the variability of components of aggregate demand. Cyclical consumption varies only one-half and investment three times as much as does cyclical output.

Section 2 presents our findings regarding the comovements of these series with the cyclical component of real GNP, as well as an examination of the cyclical components of prices, interest rates, and nominal and real money balances. Section 3 examines the serial correlation properties of a number of the series.

Several researchers, using alternative methods, have added and are adding to our knowledge of aggregate economic fluctuations.[2] Our view is that no one approach dominates all the others and that it is best to examine the data from a number of different perspectives. We do think our approach documents some interesting regularities.

---

1. Lucas (1980) interprets the work of Mitchell (1913) in a similar light.

2. Examples include Litterman and Sargent (1979), Nelson and Plosser (1980), Neftci (1978), Sargent and Sims (1977), Sims (1980, a, b), and Singleton (1980).

1. DECOMPOSITION PROCEDURE

The observed time series are viewed as the sum of cyclical and growth components. Actually, there is also a seasonal component, but as the data are seasonally adjusted, this component has already been removed by those preparing the data series. If growth accounting provided estimates of the growth component with errors that were small relative to the cyclical component, computing the cyclical component would be just a matter of calculating the difference between the observed value and the growth component. Growth theory accounting (cf. Denison 1974), in spite of its considerable success, is far from adequate for providing such numbers. If our prior knowledge were sufficiently strong so that we could model the growth component as a deterministic component, possibly conditional on exogenous data, plus a stochastic process and the cyclical component as some other stochastic process, estimating the cyclical component would be an exercise in modern time series analysis. Our prior knowledge is not of this variety, so these powerful methods are not applicable. Our prior knowledge is that the growth component varies "smoothly" over time.

Our conceptual framework is that a given time series y_t is the sum of a growth component g_t and a cyclical component c_t:

$$y_t = g_t + c_t \qquad \text{for } t = 1, \ldots, T. \tag{1}$$

Our measure of the smoothness of the $\{g_t\}$ path is the sum of the squares of its second difference. The c_t are deviations from g_t and our conceptual framework is that over long time periods, their average is near zero. These considerations lead to the following programming problem for determining the growth components:

$$\min_{\{g_t\}_{t=-1}^{T}} \left\{ \sum_{t=1}^{T} c_t^2 + \lambda \sum_{t=1}^{T} [(g_t - g_{t-1}) - (g_{t-1} - g_{t-2})]^2 \right\} \tag{2}$$

where $c_t = y_t - g_t$. The parameter λ is a positive number which penalizes variability in the growth component series. The larger the value of λ, the smoother is the solution series. For a sufficiently large λ, at the optimum all the $g_{t+1} - g_t$ must be arbitrarily near some constant β and therefore the g_t arbitrarily near $g_0 + \beta t$. This implies that the limit of solutions to program (2) as λ approaches infinity is the least squares fit of a linear time trend model.

Our method has a long history of use, particularly in the actuarial sciences. There it is called the Whittaker-Henderson Type A method (Whittaker 1923) of graduating or smoothing mortality experiences in constructing mortality tables. The method is still in use.[3] As pointed out in Stigler's (1978) historical review paper, closely related methods were developed by the Italian astronomer Schiaparelli in 1867 and in the ballistic literature in the early forties by, among others, von Neuman.

---

3. We thank Paul Milgrom for bringing to our attention that the procedure we employed has been long used in actuarial science.

Value of the Smoothness Parameter

The data analyzed, with the exception of the interest rates, are in natural logarithms so the change in the growth component, $g_t - g_{t-1}$, corresponds to a growth rate.

The growth rate of labor's productivity has varied considerably over this period (see McCarthy 1978). In the 1947–53 period, the annual growth rate was 4.20 percent, in the 1953–68 period, 2.61 percent, in the 1968–73 period, only 1.41 percent, and in the subsequent period it was even smaller. Part of these changes can be accounted for by a changing capital-labor ratio and changing composition of the labor force. But, as shown by McCarthy, a sizable and variable unexplained component remains, even after correcting for cyclical factors. The assumptions that the growth rate has been constant over our thirty-year sample period, 1950–79, is not tenable. To proceed as if it were would result in errors in modeling the growth component and these errors are likely to be nontrivial relative to the cyclical component. For this reason, an infinite value for the smoothness parameter was not selected.

The following probability model is useful for bringing to bear prior knowledge in the selection of the smoothing parameter λ. If the cyclical components and the second differences of the growth components were identically and independently distributed, normal variables with means zero and variances σ_1^2 and σ_2^2 (which they are not), the conditional expectation of the g_t, given the observations, would be the solution to program (2) when $\sqrt{\lambda} = \sigma_1/\sigma_2$.

As this probability model has a state space representation, efficient Kalman filtering techniques can be used to compute these g_t.[4] By exploiting the recursive structure, one need not invert a $(T + 2)$ by $(T + 2)$ matrix (T is the number of observations in the sample) as would be necessary if one solved the linear first-order conditions of program (2) to determine the g_t. The largest matrix that is inverted using the Kalman filtering computational approach is 2 by 2. If T is large, this is important because inverting large matrices is costly and there can be numerical rounding problems when implemented on computers. Kalman filtering can be performed with computer packages that are widely available.

Our prior view is that a 5 percent cyclical component is moderately large, as is a one-eighth of 1 percent change in the growth rate in a quarter. This led us to select $\sqrt{\lambda} = 5/(1/8) = 40$ or $\lambda = 1,600$ as a value for the smoothing parameter. One issue is, how sensitive are the results to the value of λ that is selected? To explore this issue, various other values of λ were tried. Table 1 contains the (sample) standard deviations and autocorrelations of cyclical real GNP for the selected values of the smoothing parameter as well as statistics to test for the presence of a unit root in the cyclical components.[5] These numbers change little if λ is reduced by a factor of four

---

4. This minimization has two elements, g_0 and $g_0 - g_{-1}$, which are treated as unknown parameters with diffuse priors. The Kalman smoothing technique (see Pagan 1980) was used to compute efficiently the conditional expectations of the g_t, given the observed y_t. The posterior means of g_0 and $g_0 - g_{-1}$ are the generalized least squares estimates. The conditional expectation of the g_t for $t \geq 1$ are linear functions of these parameters and the observations.

5. The tests for the presence of a unit root are augmented Dickey-Fuller tests in which the change in the cyclical component is regressed on a constant, the level of the cyclical component, and six lags of the

TABLE 1

STANDARD DEVIATION AND SERIAL CORRELATIONS OF CYCLICAL GNP FOR DIFFERENT VALUES OF THE SMOOTHING PARAMETER; SAMPLE PERIOD: 1950.1–1979.2

	$\lambda = 400$	$\lambda = 1600$	$\lambda = 6400$	$\lambda =$ infinity
Standard Deviations	1.56%	1.80%	2.03%	3.12%
Autocorrelations				
Order 1	.80	.84	.87	.94
Order 2	.48	.57	.65	.84
Order 3	.15	.27	.41	.73
Order 4	−.14	−.01	.17	.61
Order 5	−.32	−.20	.00	.52
Order 6	−.39	−.30	−.11	.44
Order 7	−.42	−.38	−.20	.38
Order 8	−.44	−.44	−.27	.31
Order 9	−.41	−.44	−.31	.25
Order 10	−.36	−.41	−.32	.20
Unit-Root Test	−5.02	−4.47	−3.57	−1.15

to 400 or increased by a factor of four to 6,400. As λ increases, the standard deviation increases and there is greater persistence, with the results being very different for $\lambda = \infty$. It is noteworthy that only the results for the linear detrending violate the assumption that no unit root is giving rise to nonstationarity in the cyclical component.

With our procedure for identifying the growth component ($\lambda = 1,600$), the annual rate of change of the growth component varied between 2.3 and 4.9 percent over the sample period, with the minima occurring in 1957 and in 1974. The maximum growth rate occurred in 1964, with another peak of 4.4 percent in 1950. The average growth rate over the period was 3.4 percent. The differences between our cyclical components and those obtained with perfect smoothing ($\lambda = \infty$) are depicted in Figure 1, along with the cyclical component. The smoothness of the variation in this difference, relative to the variation in the cyclical component, indicates that the smoothing parameter chosen is reasonable. We caution against interpreting the cyclical characteristic of the difference as a cycle of long duration. Such patterns can appear as artifacts of the data analysis procedure.

The same transformation was used for all series: that is, for each series j

$$g_{jt} = \sum_{i=1}^{T} w_{it}^{T} y_{ji},$$ (3)

where T is the length of the sample period. If the sample size were infinite, it would not be necessary to index these coefficients by t and

$$g_{jt} = \sum_{i=-\infty}^{\infty} w_{i}^{\infty} y_{j,t+i}$$ (4)

change in the cyclical component. One rejects the presence of a unit root in the cyclical component if the t-statistic for the coefficient on the level of the cyclical component is more negative than the critical value of -2.89 (5 percent) or -3.50 (1 percent).

6 : MONEY, CREDIT, AND BANKING

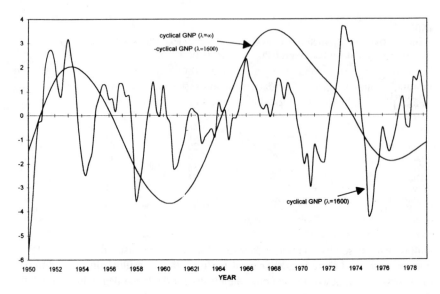

FIG. 1.

where

$$w_i^\infty = 0.8941^i \, [0.056168 \cos(0.11168 \, i) + 0.055833 \sin(0.11168 \, i)] \qquad (5)$$

for $i \geq 0$ and $w_i = w_{-i}$ for $I < 0$.[6] For t, far from either the end or the beginning of the sample, the w_{it}^T are near w_{t-i}^∞, so our method is approximately a two-way moving average with weights subject to a damped harmonic. The advantage of using the exact solution is that observations near the beginning and the end of the sample period are not lost.

The above makes it clear that the data are being filtered. As any filter alters the serial correlation properties of the data, the reported serial correlations should be interpreted with caution. The results do indicate that there is considerable persistence in the rapidly varying component of output. When using the statistics reported here to examine the validity of a model of the cyclical fluctuations of an artificial economy, the serial correlation of the rapidly varying component of the model's aggregate output series should be compared to these numbers. That is, the model's output series should be decomposed precisely as was the data for the U.S.

---

6. See Miller (1946) for a derivation. There are certain implicit restrictions on the y_t sequence when the sample is infinite. Otherwise, the g_{jt} may not exist. We require that the $\{y_t\}$ sequence belongs to the space for which

$$\sum_{t=-\infty}^{\infty} .8941^{|t|} |y_{jt}| < \infty .$$

economy. Only then, would the model's statistics and those reported here be comparable.

As the comovement results were not particularly sensitive to the value of the smoothing parameter λ selected, in the subsequent analysis only the statistics for λ = 1,600 are reported. With a larger λ, the amplitudes of fluctuations are larger, but the relative magnitudes of fluctuations of the series change little. We do think it is important that all series be filtered using the same parameter λ.

2. VARIABILITY AND COVARIABILITY OF THE SERIES

The components being studied are the cyclical components and subsequently all references to a series relate to its cyclical component. The sample standard deviations of a series is our measure of a series's variability, and the correlation of a series with real GNP is our measure of a series's covariability. These measures are computed for the first half and the second half of the sample, as well as for the entire sample. This is a check for the stability of the measures over time.

A variable might be strongly associated with real output, but lead or lag real output. Therefore, as a second measure of the strength of association with real output, the R-squared for the regression

$$c_{jt} = \alpha_j + \sum_{i=-2}^{2} \beta_{ji} GNP_{t-i} \tag{6}$$

for each series j was computed.

The ratio of the explained sum of the squares for this regression to the explained sum of squares for the regression when the coefficients are not constrained to be equal in the first and the second halves of the sample is our measure of stability. It is a number between zero and one, with one indicating that the best-fit equation is precisely the same in the first and second halves of the sample.

We chose this measure rather than applying some F-test for two reasons. First, we do not think the assumption of uncorrelated residuals is maintainable. Second, even if it were, it is very difficult to deduce the magnitude of the instability from the reported test statistic.

Aggregate Demand Components

The first set of variables studied are the real aggregate demand components. The results are summarized in Tables 2 and 3. The series that vary the least are consumption of services, consumption of nondurables and state and local government purchases of goods and services. Each of these has standard deviation less than the 1.8 percent value for real output. The investment components, including consumer durable expenditures, are about three times as variable as output. Covariabilities of consumption and investment with output are much stronger than the covariability of government expenditures with output.

TABLE 2

AGGREGATE DEMAND COMPONENTS: STANDARD DEVIATIONS AND CORRELATIONS WITH GNP
SAMPLE PERIOD: 1950.1-1979.2

	Standard Deviations in Percents			Correlations with Real Output			Average Percent of Real GNP
	Whole	First Half	Second Half	Whole	First Half	Second Half	
Real GNP	1.8	1.7	1.9	—	—	—	—
Total Consumption	1.3	1.2	1.4	.739	.503	.917	61.7
Services	.7	.7	.6	.615	.441	.781	26.8
Nondurables	1.2	1.0	1.3	.714	.575	.808	26.5
Durables	5.6	6.1	5.0	.574	.298	.884	8.4
Total Invest. Fixed	5.1	4.2	5.9	.714	.454	.884	14.2
Residential	10.7	8.5	12.4	.436	.123	.637	4.4
Nonresidential	4.9	4.4	5.3	.684	.554	.777	9.7
Equipment	5.8	5.6	5.9	.707	.642	.760	6.0
Structures	4.5	3.8	5.1	.512	.225	.698	3.7
Total Government	4.8	6.5	2.2	.258	.353	.152	22.6
Federal	8.7	11.6	4.2	.266	.377	.125	10.8
State and Local	1.3	1.6	1.0	−.170	−.408	.131	11.8

Factors of Production

The second set of variables considered are the factors of production and productivity which is output per hour. These results are summarized in Tables 4 and 5. There is a strong and stable positive relationship between hours and output. In addition, the variability in hours is comparable to the variability in output. The contemporaneous association between productivity and output is weak and unstable with the standard deviation of productivity being much smaller than the standard deviation of output. It is interesting to note that when lead and lag GNPs are included, the

TABLE 3

AGGREGATE DEMAND COMPONENTS: STRENGTH OF ASSOCIATION WITH GNP AND MEASURE
OF STABILITY
SAMPLE PERIOD: 1950.1-1979.2

	Correlation with Real Output Squared	R^2 for Regression $c_{jt} = \alpha_j + \sum_{i=-2}^{2} \beta_{ji} GNP_{t+1}$	Stability Measure
Total Consumption	.546	.620	.922
Services	.378	.424	.877
Nondurables	.510	.589	.968
Durables	.329	.415	.829
Total Invest. Fixed	.509	.552	.785
Residential	.190	.441	.809
Nonresidential	.468	.602	.831
Equipment	.500	.631	.908
Structures	.262	.367	.834
Total Government	.067	.119	.509
Federal	.071	.129	.482
State and Local	.029	.095	.298

ROBERT J. HODRICK AND EDWARD C. PRESCOTT : 9

TABLE 4

FACTORS OF PRODUCTION: STANDARD DEVIATIONS AND CORRELATIONS WITH GNP
SAMPLE PERIOD: 1950.1-1979.2

	Standard Deviations in Percents			Correlations with Real Output		
	Whole	First Half	Second Half	Whole	First Half	Second Half
Real GNP	1.8	1.7	1.9	—	—	—
Capital Stocks						
Inventory	1.7	2.0	1.4	.507	.686	.309
Capital Stock Durables	1.2	1.4	1.0	−.210	−.178	−.274
Capital Stock Nondurables	.7	.7	.7	−.236	−.185	−.297
Hours	2.0	2.1	1.8	.853	.896	.824
Work Week	.5	.6	.5	.820	.854	.800
Employees	1.4	1.6	1.2	.773	.831	.732
Productivity	1.0	1.0	1.1	.100	−.231	.361

association between GNP and productivity increases dramatically with the R-squared increasing from .010 to .453.

Capital stocks, both in durable goods and nondurable goods industries, are less variable than real output and negatively associated with output. Inventory stocks, on the other hand, have a variability comparable to output, and their correlations with output are positive. Further, the strength of association of inventories with GNP increases when lag and lead GNPs are included in the regression. This is indicated by the increase in the R-squared from .257 to .622.

Monetary Variables

Results for the final set of variables are presented in Tables 6 and 7. Correlations between nominal money, velocity, and real money with GNP are all positive. The differences in the correlations in the first and second halves of the sample, with the exception of nominal M1, suggest considerable instability over time in these relationships. A similar conclusion holds for the short-term interest rate. The correlations of GNP with the price variables are positive in the first half of the sample and

TABLE 5

FACTORS OF PRODUCTION: STRENGTH OF ASSOCIATION WITH GNP AND MEASURE OF STABILITY
SAMPLE PERIOD: 1950.1-1979.2

		R^2 for Regression	
	Correlation with Real Output Squared	$c_{jt} = \alpha_j + \sum_{i=-2}^{2} \beta_{ji} GNP_{t+1}$	Stability Measure
Capital Stocks			
Inventory	.257	.622	.828
Capital Stock Durables	.044	.235	.782
Capital Stock Nondurables	.056	.129	.740
Hours	.728	.838	.954
Work Week	.672	.700	.513
Employees	.600	.801	.935
Average Product of Labor	.010	.453	.773

10 : MONEY, CREDIT, AND BANKING

TABLE 6

MONETARY AND PRICE VARIABLES: STANDARD DEVIATIONS AND CORRELATIONS WITH GNP
SAMPLE PERIOD: 1950.1-1979.2

	Standard Deviations in Percents			Correlations with Real Output		
	Whole	First Half	Second Half	Whole	First Half	Second Half
Real GNP	1.8	1.7	1.9	—	—	—
M1						
Nominal Value	.9	.8	1.0	.661	.675	.649
Velocity	1.6	2.0	1.0	.614	.801	.415
Real Value	1.5	1.2	1.7	.565	.079	.865
M2						
Nominal	1.1	.9	1.3	.480	.175	.665
Velocity	1.9	2.4	1.2	.529	.818	.131
Real Value	1.8	1.4	2.1	.432	−.221	.828
Interest Rates						
Short	.24	.27	.19	.510	.738	.255
Long	.06	.06	.06	.193	.640	−.175
Price Indexes						
GNP Deflator	1.0	1.0	1.1	−.239	.490	−.814
CPI	1.3	1.3	1.3	−.316	.223	−.799

negative in the second half with the correlation for the entire period being small and negative.

3. SERIAL CORRELATION PROPERTIES OF DATA SERIES

A sixth-order autoregressive process was fit to a number of the series which displayed reasonable stable comovements with real output. Figure 2 presents plots of the unit impulse response functions for GNP and nine other series for the estimated

TABLE 7

MONEY AND PRICE VARIABLES: STRENGTH OF ASSOCIATION WITH GNP AND MEASURE
OF STABILITY
SAMPLE PERIOD: 1950.1-1979.2

	Correlation with Real Output Squared	R^2 for Regression $c_{jt} = \alpha_j + \sum_{i=-2}^{2} \beta_{ji} GNP_{t+1}$	Stability Measure
M1			
Nominal Value	.437	.445	.378
Velocity	.378	.408	.281
Real Value	.319	.495	.678
M2			
Nominal Value	.230	.371	.749
Velocity	.280	.376	.650
Real Value	.187	.428	.684
Interest Rates			
Short	.260	.506	.748
Long	.037	.381	.724
Price Index			
GNP Deflator	.057	.261	.567
CPI	.010	.330	.481

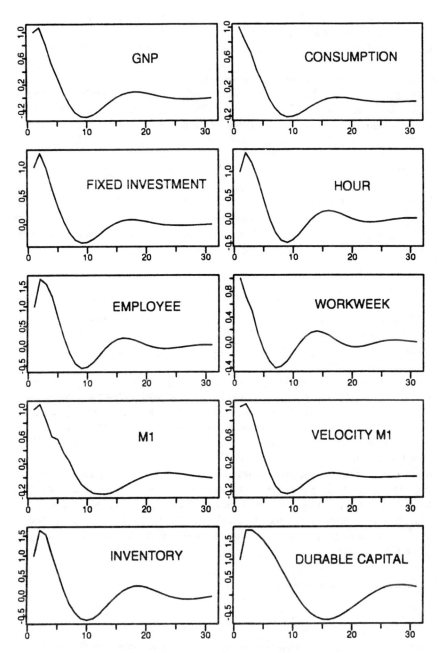

FIG. 2. Unit Impulse Response Function

autoregressive function.[7] The function for GNP increases initially to a peak of 1.15 in period one and has a minimum of $-.39$ in period eight. The patterns for consumption and investment are similar except that the peak for consumption is in the initial period. The function for consumption and each of its three components (not pictured) are similar to the one for the aggregate.

The pattern for total hours and the number of employees, except for the greater amplitude, is very similar to the pattern for GNP. The average work-week pattern, however, begins to decline immediately and the period of damped oscillation is shorter. The monetary variables have very different response patterns, indicating serial correlation properties very different than those of real output.

There is a dramatic difference in the response pattern for the capital stock in durable goods industries. The maximum amplitude of the response is much greater, being about 3.6, and occurs slightly over a year subsequent to the unit impulse. The pattern for the capital stock in the nondurable goods industries (not pictured) is similar though the maximum amplitude is smaller, being 2.8. For both capital stocks the peaks in the unit response function are in period five.

APPENDIX

All the data from the original paper were obtained from the Wharton Economic Forecasting Association Quarterly Data Bank. The short-term interest rate was the taxable three-month U.S. Treasury bill rate, and the long-term interest rate, the yield on U.S. Government long-term bonds.

Tables A.1–A.7 contain data from 1947.1 to 1993.4. All data for Tables A.1–A.3 come from the National Income and Product Accounts: Historical NIPA Quarterly Data, Survey of Current Business, U.S. Department of Commerce. The capital stock data in Tables A.5 and A.6 come from the Survey of Current Business as annual series. We used quarterly investment series from the NIPA with the annual capital stocks to construct quarterly series. All labor data in Tables A.5 and A.6 come from Citibase. Data for the price series in Tables A.6 and A.7 also come from Citibase. The interest rate series are from the Federal Reserve Bulletin and are constructed from the monthly series in Tables 1.33 and 1.35. Real M1 and Real M2 were obtained from the Business Cycle Indicators Historical Diskette, published by the U.S. Department of Commerce. Nominal series were calculated by multiplying by the GNP deflator.

7. Letting a_t be the innovations and

$$c_t = \sum_{i=0}^{\infty} \theta_i a_{t-i}$$

be the invertible moving average representation, parameter θ_i equals the value of the unit response function in period i. One must take care in interpreting the response pattern. Two moving average processes can be observationally equivalent (same autocovariances function) yet have very different response patterns. We chose the invertible representation because it is unique. It is just one way to represent the serial correlation properties of a covariance stationary stochastic process. Others are the spectrum, the autoregressive representation, and the autocovariance function.

TABLE A1

STANDARD DEVIATION AND SERIAL CORRELATIONS OF CYCLICAL GNP FOR DIFFERENT VALUES
OF THE SMOOTHING PARAMETER. SAMPLE PERIOD: 1947.1-1993.4

	$\lambda = 400$	$\lambda = 1600$	$\lambda = 6400$	$\lambda =$ infinity
Standard Deviations	1.47%	1.80%	2.14%	4.94%
Autocorrelations				
Order 1	.81	.86	.90	.96
Order 2	.53	.64	.73	.91
Order 3	.22	.39	.53	.86
Order 4	−.03	.16	.34	.80
Order 5	−.21	−.05	.18	.74
Order 6	−.32	−.27	.02	.69
Order 7	−.39	−.30	−.09	.63
Order 8	−.43	−.37	−.19	.58
Order 9	−.40	−.40	−.26	.52
Order 10	−.35	−.40	−.28	.47
Unit-Root Test	−6.52	−5.91	−4.98	−2.34

TABLE A2

AGGREGATE DEMAND COMPONENTS: STANDARD DEVIATIONS AND CORRELATIONS WITH GNP
SAMPLE PERIOD: 1947.1-1993.4

	Standard Deviations in Percents			Correlations with Real Output			Average Percent of Real GNP
	Whole	First Half	Second Half	Whole	First Half	Second Half	
Real GNP	1.8	1.8	1.8	—	—	—	—
Total Consumption	1.2	0.9	1.4	.719	.511	.875	61.7
Services	0.7	0.7	0.8	.685	.544	.810	31.2
Nondurable	1.2	1.0	1.3	.707	.558	.827	24.5
Durables	5.5	5.4	5.6	.457	.112	.787	6.9
Total Invest. Fixed	5.5	4.5	6.4	.732	.470	.927	15.2
Residential	10.9	9.1	12.6	.462	.755	.745	5.1
Nonresidential	5.1	4.6	5.6	.746	.659	.820	10.1
Equipment	6.1	5.8	6.4	.798	.715	.871	6.1
Structures	4.8	3.8	5.6	.469	.397	.528	4.0
Total Government	3.9	5.4	1.2	.350	.515	−.012	21.6
Federal	6.9	9.5	1.9	.348	.540	−.164	10.7
State and Local	1.5	1.9	1.1	−.216	−.453	.015	10.8

TABLE A3

AGGREGATE DEMAND COMPONENTS: STRENGTH OF ASSOCIATION WITH GNP AND MEASURE
OF STABILITY
SAMPLE PERIOD: 1947.1-1993.4

		R^2 for Regression	
	Correlation with Real Output Squared	$c_{jt} = \alpha_j + \sum_{i=-2}^{2} \beta_{ji} GNP_{t+1}$	Stability Measure
Total Consumption	.517	.571	.808
Services	.469	.512	.873
Nondurables	.500	.520	.872
Durables	.209	.324	.669
Total Invest. Fixed	.536	.580	.796
Residential	.213	.482	.731
Nonresidential	.557	.662	.929
Equipment	.637	.702	.955
Structures	.220	.396	.792
Total Government	.123	.229	.500
Federal	.121	.224	.436
State and Local	.047	.080	.200

TABLE A4

FACTORS OF PRODUCTION: STANDARD DEVIATIONS AND CORRELATIONS WITH GNP
SAMPLE PERIOD: 1947.1-1993.4

	Standard Deviations in Percents			Correlations with Real Output		
	Whole	First Half	Second Half	Whole	First Half	Second Half
Real GNP	1.8	1.8	1.8	—	—	—
Capital Stocks						
Inventory	2.1	2.4	1.8	.510	.547	.475
Capital Stock Durables	1.2	1.1	1.2	.510	.387	.619
Capital Stock Nondurables	1.0	1.0	0.9	−.055	−.125	.021
Hours	1.8	1.9	1.7	.883	.860	.911
Work Week	1.1	1.1	1.0	.778	.778	.783
Employees	1.5	1.6	1.5	.828	.808	.850
Productivity	0.9	1.0	0.8	.239	.151	.360

TABLE A5

FACTORS OF PRODUCTION: STRENGTH OF ASSOCIATION WITH GNP AND MEASURE OF STABILITY
SAMPLE PERIOD: 1947.1-1993.4

	Correlation with Real Output Squared	R^2 for Regression $c_{jt} = \alpha_j + \sum_{i=-2}^{2} \beta_{ji} GNP_{t+1}$	Stability Measure
Capital Stocks			
Inventory	.260	.373	.801
Capital Stock Durables	.260	.728	.967
Capital Stock Nondurables	.003	.356	.874
Hours	.779	.869	.992
Work Week	.605	.764	.994
Employees	.685	.858	.989
Average Product of Labor	.057	.465	.933

TABLE A6

MONETARY AND PRICE VARIABLES: STANDARD DEVIATIONS AND CORRELATIONS WITH GNP
SAMPLE PERIOD: 1947.1-1993.4

	Standard Deviations in Percents			Correlations with Real Output		
	Whole	First Half	Second Half	Whole	First Half	Second Half
Real GNP	1.8	1.8	1.8	—	—	—
M1						
Nominal Value	2.1	1.3	2.7	.368	.542	.318
Velocity	2.7	2.1	3.1	.328	.680	.104
Real Value	2.7	1.6	3.4	.347	.219	.436
M2						
Nominal	1.8	1.4	2.2	.337	.324	.357
Velocity	2.5	2.5	2.6	.404	.672	.151
Real Value	2.4	1.8	2.9	.319	.058	.491
Interest Rates						
Short	1.1	0.6	1.5	.324	.335	.358
Long	0.6	0.2	0.8	.032	.228	−.020
Price Indexes						
GNP Deflator	1.0	1.0	1.0	−.156	.327	−.635
CPI	1.6	1.4	1.7	−.222	.247	−.585

TABLE A7

MONEY AND PRICE VARIABLES: STRENGTH OF ASSOCIATION WITH GNP AND MEASURE
OF STABILITY
SAMPLE PERIOD: 1947.1-1993.4

		R^2 for Regression	
	Correlation with Real Output Squared	$c_{jt} = \alpha_j + \sum_{i=-2}^{2} \beta_{ji} GNP_{t+1}$	Stability Measure
M1			
Nominal Value	.135	.229	.783
Velocity	.108	.280	.747
Real Value	.120	.270	.738
M2			
Nominal Value	.114	.291	.782
Velocity	.163	.377	.755
Real Value	.102	.321	.707
Interest Rates			
Short	.105	.336	.701
Long	.001	.191	.701
Price Index			
GNP Deflator	.024	.199	.430
CPI	.049	.248	.485

LITERATURE CITED

Denison, Edward F. *Accounting for United States Growth, 1929–1969*. Washington, D.C.: The Brookings Institute, 1974.

Keynes, John Maynard. *The General Theory of Employment, Interest, and Money*. London: Macmillan, 1936.

Litterman, Robert, and Thomas J. Sargent. "Detecting Neutral Price Level Changes and the Effects of Aggregate Demand with Index Models." University of Minnesota Working Paper, 1979.

Lucas, Robert E., Jr. "Methods and Problems in Business Cycle Theory." *Journal of Money, Credit, and Banking* 12 (1980), 696–715.

———. *Studies in Business Cycle Theory*. Cambridge, Mass.: The MIT Press, 1981.

McCarthy, Michael D. "The U.S. Productivity Growth Recession: History and Prospects for the Future." *The Journal of Finance* 33 (1978), 977–89.

Miller, M. D. *Elements of Graduation*. New York: Actuarial Society of America and American Institute of Actuaries, 1946.

Mitchell, Wesley C. *Business Cycles*. Berkeley, Calif.: University of California Press, 1913.

Neftci, Salih N. "A Time-Series Analysis of the Real Wage-Employment Relationship." *Journal of Political Economy* 86 (1978), 281–91.

Nelson, Charles L., and Charles I. Plosser. "Trends and Random Walks in Macroeconomic Time Series." University of Washington Discussion Paper, 1980.

Pagan, Adrian. "Some Identification and Estimation Results for Regression Models with Stochastically Varying Coefficients." *Journal of Econometrics* 13 (1980), 341–64.

Sargent, Thomas J., and Christopher A. Sims. "Business Cycle Modeling without Pretending to Have Too Much a Priori Economic Theory." In *New Methods in Business Cycle Research: Proceedings from A Conference*. Minneapolis: Federal Reserve Bank of Minneapolis, 1977.

Sims, Christopher A. "Macroeconomics and Reality." *Econometrica* 48 (1980a), 1–48.

————. "Comparison of Interwar and Postwar Business Cycles: Monetarism Reconsidered." *American Economic Review* 70 (1980b), 250–57.

Singleton, Kenneth J. "Real and Nominal Factors in the Cyclical Behavior of Interest Rates, Output, and Money." Carnegie-Mellon University Working Paper, 1980.

Stigler, Stephen M. "Mathematical Statistics in the Early States." *Annals of Statistics* 6 (1978), 239–65.

Whittaker, Edmund T. "On a New Method of Graduations." *Proceedings of the Edinburgh Mathematical Society* 41 (1923), 63–75.

JOURNAL OF APPLIED ECONOMETRICS, VOL. 8, 231–247 (1993)

DETRENDING, STYLIZED FACTS AND THE BUSINESS CYCLE

A. C. HARVEY

Department of Statistics, London School of Economics, Houghton Street, London WC2A 2AE, UK

AND

A. JAEGER

Austrian Institute of Economic Research, A-1103 Vienna, PO Box 91, Austria

SUMMARY

The stylized facts of macroeconomic time series can be presented by fitting structural time series models. Within this framework, we analyse the consequences of the widely used detrending technique popularised by Hodrick and Prescott (1980). It is shown that mechanical detrending based on the Hodrick–Prescott filter can lead investigators to report spurious cyclical behaviour, and this point is illustrated with empirical examples. Structural time-series models also allow investigators to deal explicitly with seasonal and irregular movements that may distort estimated cyclical components. Finally, the structural framework provides a basis for exposing the limitations of ARIMA methodology and models based on a deterministic trend with a single break.

1. INTRODUCTION

Establishing the 'stylized facts' associated with a set of time series is widely considered a crucial step in macroeconomic research (see e.g. Blanchard and Fischer, 1989 chapter 1). For such facts to be useful they should (1) be consistent with the stochastic properties of the data and (2) present meaningful information. Nevertheless, many stylized facts reported in the literature do not fulfil these criteria. In particular, information based on mechanically detrended series can easily give a spurious impression of cyclical behaviour. Analysis based on autoregressive-integrated-moving average (ARIMA) models can also be misleading if such models are chosen primarily on grounds of parsimony.

We argue here that structural time-series models provide the most useful framework within which to present stylized facts on time series. These models are explicitly based on the stochastic properties of the data. We illustrate how, when these models are fitted to various macroeconomic time series, they provide meaningful information and serve as a basis for exposing the limitations of other techniques. These arguments have, to some extent, been made before (Harvey, 1985, 1989; Clark, 1987). They are further elaborated here. In addition, we examine the consequences of the mechanical detrending method suggested by Hodrick and Prescott (1980), which has recently started to become popular in macroeconomics (see e.g. Danthine and Girardin, 1989; Backus and Kehoe, 1989; Kydland and Prescott, 1990; Brandner and Neusser, 1992). We show that the uncritical use of mechanical detrending can lead investigators to report spurious cyclical behaviour. This point has also been made by Cogley

0883–7252/93/030231–17$13.50
© 1993 by John Wiley & Sons, Ltd.

Received September 1991
Revised June 1992

(1990). We argue that the structural framework provides further insights and that trends and cycles should be fitted simultaneously to avoid such pitfalls.

The plan of the paper is as follows. In Section 2 we lay out the basic framework of structural time-series modelling in this context. Section 3 provides an analysis of the consequences of detrending using the Hodrick–Prescott filter approach. Section 4 considers modelling and detrending of several macroeconomic time series. Section 5 discusses several issues including seasonal adjustment, trends with deterministic break points, and spurious cross-correlations between inappropriately detrended series. Section 6 draws together the main conclusions.

2. THE TREND PLUS CYCLE MODEL

Structural time-series models are set up explicitly in terms of components that have a direct interpretation (see Harvey, 1989). In the present context we postulate the appropriate model to be

$$y_t = \mu_t + \psi_t + \varepsilon_t, \qquad t = 1, \dots, T \tag{1}$$

where y_t is the observed series, μ_t is the trend, ψ_t is the cycle, and ε_t is the irregular component. The trend is a local linear trend defined as

$$\mu_t = \mu_{t-1} + \beta_{t-1} + \eta_t \qquad \eta_t \sim \text{NID}(0, \sigma_\eta^2) \tag{2}$$

$$\beta_t = \beta_{t-1} + \zeta_t \qquad \zeta_t \sim \text{NID}(0, \sigma_\zeta^2) \tag{3}$$

where β_t is the slope and the normal white-noise disturbances, η_t and ζ_t, are independent of each other. The stochastic cycle is generated as

$$\psi_t = \rho \cos \lambda_c \psi_{t-1} + \rho \sin \lambda_c \psi_{t-1}^* + \chi_t \tag{4}$$

$$\psi_t^* = -\rho \sin \lambda_c \psi_{t-1} + \rho \cos \lambda_c \psi_{t-1}^* + \chi_t^* \tag{5}$$

where ρ is a damping factor such that $0 \leqslant \rho \leqslant 1$, λ_c is the frequency of the cycle in radians, and χ_t and χ_t^* are both $\text{NID}(0, \sigma_\chi^2)$. The irregular component is $\text{NID}(0, \sigma_\varepsilon^2)$ and the disturbances in all three components are taken to be independent of each other.

The trend is equivalent to an ARIMA(0,2,1) process. However, if $\sigma_\zeta^2 = 0$, it reduces to a random walk with drift. If, furthermore, $\sigma_\eta^2 = 0$ it becomes deterministic, that is, $\mu_t = \mu_0 + \beta t$. When $\sigma_\eta^2 = 0$, but $\sigma_\zeta^2 > 0$, the trend is still a process integrated of order two, abbreviated $I(2)$, that is, stationary in second differences. A trend component with this feature tends to be relatively smooth. An important issue is therefore whether or not the constraint $\sigma_\eta^2 = 0$ should be imposed at the outset. We argue that there are series where it is unreasonable to assume a smooth trend *a priori* and therefore the question whether or not σ_η^2 is set to zero is an empirical one. The examples in Section 4 illustrate this point.

The cyclical component, ψ_t, is stationary if ρ is strictly less than one. It is equivalent to an ARMA(2,1) process in which both the MA and the AR parts are subject to restrictions (see Harvey, 1985, p. 219). The most important of these is that the AR parameters are constrained to lie within the region corresponding to complex roots. Since the purpose is to model the possible occurrence of stochastic cycles, imposing this constraint *a priori* is desirable.

Estimation of the hyperparameters, $(\sigma_\eta^2, \sigma_\zeta^2, \sigma_\chi^2, \rho, \lambda_c, \sigma_\varepsilon^2)$, can be carried out by maximum likelihood either in the time domain or the frequency domain. Once this has been done, estimates of the trend, cyclical, and irregular components are obtained from a smoothing algorithm. These calculations may be carried out very rapidly on a PC using the STAMP package.

DETRENDING AND BUSINESS CYCLE FACTS   233

The model in equation (1) can be extended to deal with seasonal data. Thus there is no need to use data that may have been distorted by a seasonal adjustment procedure. Furthermore, if we are interested in stylized facts relating to seasonal components, structural time-series models provide a ready tool to determine these components without imposing a deterministic structure on the seasonal pattern (see e.g. Barsky and Miron, 1989).

3. THE HODRICK–PRESCOTT FILTER

Nelson and Kang (1981) have drawn attention to the distortions that can arise from fitting deterministic trends to series actually driven by stochastic trends. Similarly, it has long been known that the mechanical use of moving average filters can create a wide range of undesirable effects in the data (see Fishman, 1969). The filter adopted by Hodrick and Prescott (1980), hereafter denoted HP filter, has a long tradition as a method of fitting a smooth curve through a set of points. It may be rationalized as the optimal estimator of the trend component in a structural time-series model

$$y_t = \mu_t + \varepsilon_t \qquad t = 1, \ldots, T \tag{6}$$

where μ_t is defined by equation (2) and (3) but with σ_η^2 set equal to zero. [1]

Of course, the reason for estimating the trend in the present context is to detrend the data. The optimal filter which gives the detrended observations, y_t^d, is, for large samples and t not near the beginning or end of the series

$$y_t^d = \left[\frac{(1 - L)^2 (1 - L^{-1})^2}{q_\zeta + (1 - L)^2 (1 - L^{-1})^2} \right] y_t \qquad q_\zeta > 0 \tag{7}$$

where $q_\zeta = \sigma_\zeta^2 / \sigma_\varepsilon^2$ and L is the lag operator. This expression can be obtained as the optimal estimator of ε_t in equation (6) by means of the standard signal extraction formulae which, as shown by Bell (1984), apply to non-stationary, as well as stationary, time series. [2]

If equation (6) was believed to be the true model, q_ζ could be estimated by maximum likelihood as outlined in the previous section. However, the whole reason for applying the HP filter is the belief that detrended data consist of something more than white noise. Thus, a value of q_ζ is imposed, rather than estimated. We will denote this value of q_ζ by $\bar{q}_\zeta$. From the point of view of structural time-series modelling, HP filtering is therefore equivalent to postulating model (1) and imposing the restrictions $\sigma_\zeta^2 / \sigma_\varepsilon^2 = \bar{q}_\zeta$, $\sigma_\eta^2 = 0$, and $\psi_t = 0$. The HP estimate of the cyclical component is then simply given by the smoothed irregular component.

Given a particular model for y_t, the process followed by the HP detrended series, y_t^{HP}, and hence its dynamic properties, may be determined by substituting for y_t in equation (7). Suppose that we specify y_t as an ARIMA(p,d,q) process, possibly representing the reduced form of a structural time-series model such as equation (1). That is,

$$(1 - L)^d y_t = \varphi^{-1}(L) \theta(L) \xi_t, \qquad \xi_t \sim \text{NID}(0, \sigma^2) \tag{8}$$

where $\varphi(L)$ and $\theta(L)$ denote the AR and MA polynomials in the lag operator. Then

$$y_t^{HP} = \left[\frac{(1 - L)^{2-d} (1 - L^{-1})^2}{\bar{q}_\zeta + (1 - L)^2 (1 - L^{-1})^2} \right] \frac{\theta(L)}{\varphi(L)} \xi_t \tag{9}$$

---

[1] The continuous time version of this model can be used to rationalize a cubic spline fitted to data which may not be regularly spaced. See Wecker and Ansley (1983).

[2] The exact solution is given by the smoother obtained from the state space model. A fast algorithm is given in Koopman (1991). Such a smoother is valid even if the trend is deterministic, that is, $q_\zeta = 0$.

As noted by King and Rebelo (1989), y_t^{HP} is a stationary process for $d \leqslant 4$.

The autocovariance generating function (a.c.g.f.) of y_t^{HP} is given by

$$g_{HP}(L) = \left[\frac{(1-L)^{4-d}(1-L^{-1})^{4-d}}{[\bar{q}_\zeta + (1-L)^2(1-L^{-1})^2]^2} \right] g_y(L) \qquad (10)$$

where $g_y(L)$ is the a.c.g.f. of $\Delta^d y_t$ and $\Delta = 1 - L$.

Note that if y_t is specified in terms of unobserved components, $g_y(L)$ may be obtained directly without solving for the ARIMA reduced form. Setting $L = \exp(i\lambda)$ gives the spectrum of y_t^{HP}, $f_{HP}(\lambda)$.[3] The spectrum may be calculated straightforwardly and it provides particularly useful information if we wish to study the possible creation of spurious cycles.

Specifying y_t to be a structural time-series model of the form (1) gives insight into the effects of detrending, since the contribution of each of the unobserved components to the overall spectrum, $f_{HP}(\lambda)$, can be assessed. To this end, rewrite model (1) in the single-equation form

$$y_t = \frac{\zeta_{t-1}}{\Delta^2} + \frac{\eta_t}{\Delta} + \psi_t + \varepsilon_t \qquad (11)$$

The first term is integrated of order two, abbreviated as $I(2)$, the second term is $I(1)$, and the last two terms are stationary or $I(0)$. From model (10) we have

$$f_{HP}(\lambda) = \tau(\lambda)\{\sigma_\zeta^2 + 2(1 - \cos \lambda)\sigma_\eta^2 + 4(1 - \cos \lambda)^2 [g_\psi(\lambda) + \sigma_\varepsilon^2]\} \qquad (12)$$

where

$$\tau(\lambda) = \frac{1}{2\pi} \frac{4(1 - \cos \lambda)^2}{[\bar{q}_\zeta + 4(1 - \cos \lambda)^2]^2}$$

and $g_\psi(\lambda)$ is the spectral generating function of ψ_t.

More generally, suppose we have any unobserved components model with $I(2)$, $I(1)$, and $I(0)$ components. Then the transfer function for an $I(d)$ component is

$$\tau_d(\lambda) = 2^{(2-d)}(1 - \cos \lambda)^{2-d}\tau(\lambda) \qquad d = 0, 1, 2 \qquad (13)$$

The transfer function tells us the effect of the filter on the spectrum of the dth difference of an $I(d)$ component. Note that $\tau_2(\lambda) = \tau(\lambda)$.

For the macroeconomic series they study, Kydland and Prescott (1990) set $\bar{q}_\zeta = 0 \cdot 000625$. Figures 1(a) to 1(c) show the transfer functions for $I(0)$, $I(1)$, and $I(2)$ components assuming this value for $\bar{q}_\zeta$ plotted against a period over the range $0 \leqslant 2\pi/\lambda \leqslant 4$. The filter for $I(0)$ components removes the very low frequency components, but frequencies corresponding to periods of less than 20 are virtually unaffected. Multiplying $\tau(\lambda)$ by $2(1 - \cos(\lambda))$, on the other hand, produces a transfer function $\tau_1(\lambda)$, with a peak at

$$\lambda_{max} = \arccos[1 - \sqrt{0 \cdot 75 \bar{q}_\zeta}] \qquad (14)$$

which for $\bar{q}_\zeta = 0 \cdot 000625$ corresponds to a period of about 30. Thus applying the standard HP filter to a random walk produces detrended observations which have the characteristics of a business cycle for quarterly observations. Such cyclical behaviour is spurious and is a classic example of the Yule–Slutzky effect.

Spurious cycles can also emanate from the $I(2)$ component. The transfer function in Figure 1(c) has a peak at a frequency corresponding to a period of about 40. The nature of any spurious cyclical behaviour in the detrended observations depends on the relative importance

---

[3] Neglecting factors of proportionality.

DETRENDING AND BUSINESS CYCLE FACTS   235

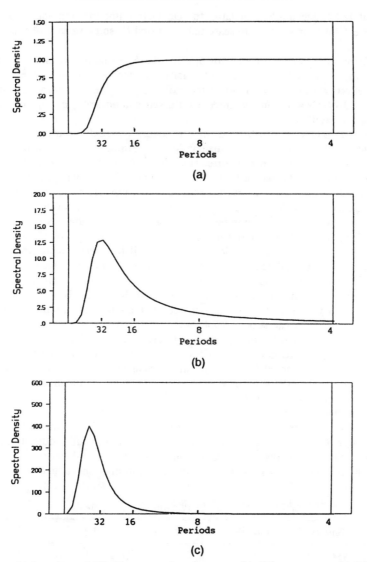

Figure 1. Transfer functions of HP filter. (a) $I(0)$ component; (b) $I(1)$ component; (c) $I(2)$ component

of $I(1)$ and $I(2)$ components. For data generated by (1) the peaks created in the spectrum are of similar height if $\sigma_\zeta^2/\sigma_\eta^2 \approx 25$. In this case they tend to merge together, and the overall effect is of a transfer function with a single peak corresponding to a period between 30 and 40.

4. MACROECONOMIC TIME SERIES

We now examine the stylized facts that can be produced by different techniques when applied to quarterly macroeconomic time series (all in logarithms). The series are US, real GNP,

Austrian real GDP, the implicit deflator for US GNP, and the nominal value of the US monetary base.[4] All four series were seasonally adjusted by some variant of the Census X-11 program.

The HP filter was always applied with $\bar{q}_\zeta = 0 \cdot 000625$. Attempts to estimate this ratio by applying maximum likelihood to model (6) usually produced a very high value of q_ζ, leading to the trend effectively picking up most of the movements in the stationary part of the series. Thus unless model (1) is a reasonable model for the series in question, q_ζ must be fixed in order to obtain sensible results.

Details of the results of fitting structural time-series model (1) are shown in Table I. Estimation was carried out in the frequency domain. Estimation in the time domain gave similar results and so these are not reported. Goodness of fit can be assessed by means of the estimated prediction error variance (σ^2), or, equivalently, by R_D^2 which is the coefficient of determination with respect to first differences. The Box–Ljung statistic, $Q(P)$, is based on the first P residual autocorrelations. The degrees of freedom for the resulting χ^2 statistic should be taken to be $P + 1$ minus the number of estimated hyperparameters (see Harvey, 1989, chapter 5). Tests for normality and heteroscedasticity were also carried out. They are not reported in Table I and are only mentioned in the text if they were significant.

Estimating model (1) for real US GNP gives $\tilde{\sigma}_\eta^2 = 0$. Thus the result of unrestricted estimation is a relatively smooth trend. Furthermore, since $\tilde{\sigma}_\epsilon^2 = 0$, the series effectively decomposes into a smooth trend plus a cycle (see Figure 2(a)). This is not surprising since $\tilde{\sigma}_\zeta^2$ is small and, coupled with the zero for $\tilde{\sigma}_\eta^2$, this means there is little contamination from non-stationary components in the series. Application of the HP filter yields a detrended series which is difficult to distinguish from the cycle extracted from the structural model (see Figure 2(b)). Thus applying the HP filter to real US GNP data is practically equivalent to estimating the structural time-series model (1). The striking coincidence between the estimated business cycle component and the HP cycle suggests that the HP filter is tailor-made for extracting the business cycle component from US GNP.

The close similarity between estimated and HP cycle reported for US GNP may not necessarily obtain for output series from other countries. To illustrate this point, we estimated model (1) using real Austrian GDP. Attempting to estimate the full model, (1), leads to the cyclical component virtually disappearing and we are led to a local linear trend model. On the other hand, if we impose $\sigma_\eta^2 = 0$ on (1) we obtain a smooth trend and a cycle. A graph of

Table I. Estimates of structural time-series models

Series	Time range	Restrictions	σ_ζ^2	σ_η^2	$\sigma_\varkappa^2$	ρ	$2\pi/\lambda_c$	σ_ϵ^2	σ^2	R_D^2	$Q(P)$
US GNP	1954 : 1–89 : 4	None	8	0	625	0·92	22·2	0	937	0·05	8·01
Austrian GDP	1964 : 1–88 : 4	None	9	578	0	—	—	244	1126	0·05	13·63
		$\sigma_\eta^2 = 0$	21	—	36	0·97	13·0	438	1071	0·09	7·46
US Prices	1954 : 1–89 : 4	None	28	94	0	—	—	0	161	0·64	5·78
		$\sigma_\eta^2 = 0$	19	—	79	0·94	27·5	3	160	0·65	4·27
US monetary base	1959 : 1–89 : 4	None	40	63	3	0·98	5·6	0	151	0·64	7·89
		$\sigma_\eta^2 = 0$	47	—	25	0·73	6·0	0	153	0·64	10·68

Notes: All variance estimates have been multiplied by 10^7. $2\pi/\lambda_c$ is period (in quarters). $Q(P)$ is Box–Ljung statistic based on first P residual autocorrelations. $P = 12$ for US Series and $P = 10$ for Austrian GDP.

---

[4] The US series are taken from Citibase data bank. Austrian GDP data are taken from the data bank of the Austrian Institute of Economic Research.

the cycle shows it to be relatively small (see Figure 3(a)); it rarely deviates from the trend by more that 2 per cent. However, the cycles do coincide with the Austrian experience of somewhat muted booms and recessions. The cyclical component obtained from HP filtering, shown in Figure 3(b), is more volatile and quite erratic because it includes the irregular movements in the series which appear to be substantial.

The cyclical model obtained by imposing a smooth trend by setting $\sigma_\eta^2 = 0$ has a slightly better fit than the local linear trend model. The explanation lies in the fact that the local linear trend model emerges as a limiting case of the smooth trend and cycle model as $\rho \to 0$ and $\lambda_c \to 0$. Thus, when σ_x^2 is quite small, as it is here, it is difficult to pick out the cycle in an

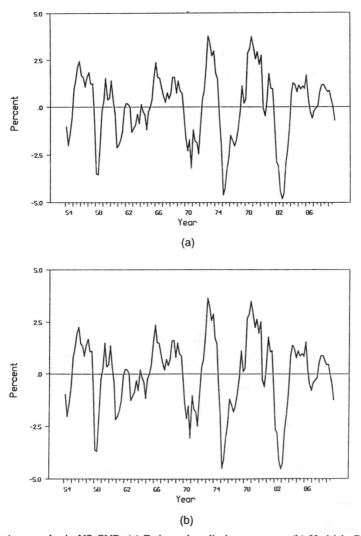

(a)

(b)

Figure 2. Business cycles in US GNP. (a) Estimated cyclical component; (b) Hodrick–Prescott cycle

unrestricted model since the likelihood function is very flat. The fact that the cycle model would be rejected on grounds of parsimony does not mean that it does not provide a valid description of the data. Furthermore, if we feel *a priori* that the underlying trend should be smooth then the cycle model is to be preferred over the more parsimonious local linear trend.

The two examples considered so far are based on real output series. Next we look at a price series and a nominal money stock series. Unrestricted estimation of model (1) for the implicit US GNP deflator leads quite clearly to a random walk plus noise model in first differences. This very simple model is also consistent with the correlogram of the second differences which is -0.47 at lag 1 and -0.07, 0.04, 0.05, -0.01 for lags 2 to 5. Thus Box–Jenkins

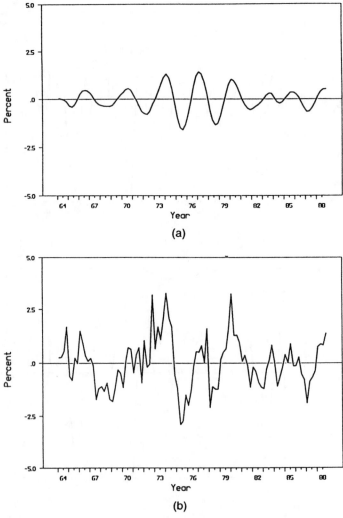

Figure 3. Business cycles in Austrian GDP. (a) Estimated cyclical component; (b) Hodrick–Prescott cycle

methodology would almost certainly select an equivalent model, namely ARIMA(0,2,1). Nevertheless, setting $\sigma_\eta^2 = 0$ does give a cycle and the model has essentially the same fit. It would clearly be rejected on grounds of parsimony, but it is consistent with the data and so cannot be dismissed, just as we could not dismiss the smooth trend/cycle model for Austrian GDP. However, while it may be reasonable to argue that a real series, such as GDP, contains a smooth trend, such an argument is less convincing for prices. Abrupt upwards or downwards movements in the price level can easily arise from indirect tax changes or oil price shocks, suggesting that the underlying trend is not smooth and contains an $I(1)$ component.

Applying the HP filter to the US price series yields what Kydland and Prescott (1990)

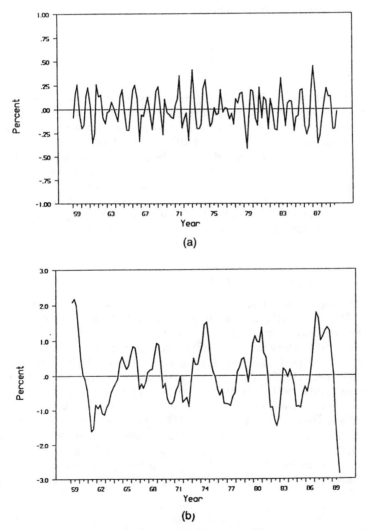

(a)

(b)

Figure 4. Business cycles in US monetary base. (a) Estimated cyclical component; (b) Hodrick–Prescott cycle

identify as cyclical movements. While we cannot rule out the possibility that the price level contains cycles, we note that the transfer function for our preferred model, the random walk plus noise in first differences, has a peak since it is a combination of the $\tau_2(\lambda)$ and $\tau_1(\lambda)$ filters shown in Figures 1(b) and 1(c). It is therefore possible that the price cycle identified by Kydland and Prescott (1990) is spurious.

For the US monetary base series, the unrestricted structural model is a local linear trend with a very small cycle. Setting $\sigma_\eta^2 = 0$ gives a model with basically the same fit and a cycle with a somewhat larger amplitude (see Figure 4(a)). The HP filter procedure imposes a smaller variance on the trend component and gives rise to a large cycle (see Figure 4(b)). This provides an illustration of how HP filtering may change substantially the volatility and periodicity properties of an estimated cyclical component.

5. FURTHER ISSUES

5.1. Seasonality

In common with most studies, the results reported above used seasonally adjusted data. Such data may not always have desirable properties, particularly if the seasonality pattern changes in some way, and is not of a kind that a standard adjustment method, such as the Bureau of the Census X-11, handles well. Data on real GDP for the United Kingdom provide a good example.[5] With the seasonally adjusted data and the restriction $\sigma_\eta^2 = 0$ imposed we estimated the cyclical component given in Figure 5(b). This cycle is not well defined and does not coincide particularly well with the known booms and recessions in the UK. On the other hand, seasonally unadjusted data produce much better results when a seasonal component[6] is added to model (1) (compare Figure 5(a) with 5(b)). The estimated seasonality pattern given in Figure 5(c) changes quite noticeably and the adjustment procedure presumably creates distortions in the series in attempting to cope with it.

5.2. ARIMA Methodology and Smooth Trends

ARIMA methodology usually results in the stylized fact that real output series are $I(1)$. Informal Box–Jenkins identification as well as formal root tests support this notion. For example, the first five autocorrelations of the first differences of real US GNP are $0 \cdot 29$, $0 \cdot 19$, $-0 \cdot 02$, $-0 \cdot 10$, $-0 \cdot 01$. These autocorrelations show no need for second differencing of the data. A standard augmented Dickey–Fuller test rejects the null hypothesis of a second unit root in US GNP quite clearly. The relevant t-statistic is around $-6 \cdot 0$, the precise value depending on the number of lags included. Thus, an ARIMA model of order $(0,1,2)$ with a constant might be a reasonable selection. If we restrict attention to pure autoregressions and test down from a high number of lags an ARIMA(1,1,0) model with constant is obtained.

Neither of the above models is consistent with the structural time-series model (1) which has an ARIMA(2,2,4) reduced form. However, since σ_ζ^2 is relatively small, the $I(2)$ component may be difficult to detect by ARIMA methodology given typical sample sizes. To verify this conjecture we conducted two small Monte Carlo experiments. The data-generating process for

---

[5] The series run from 1960:1 1987:4. The seasonally adjusted series is taken from the OECD Main Economic Indicator data bank whereas the seasonally unadjusted series from the OECD Quarterly National data bank.
[6] The estimated seasonal component is modelled using the trigonometric formulation described in Harvey (1989, pp. 42–3).

DETRENDING AND BUSINESS CYCLE FACTS   241

both experiments is the estimated structural time series model for real US GNP reported in Table I. Table II reports the sample autocorrelations up to lag eight for the first differences of the generated series using sample sizes 100 and 500, respectively. Table III reports the empirical size of augmented Dickey–Fuller tests at the 5 per cent level for the null hypothesis that the first difference of the generated data has a unit root. The numbers of lags included in the Dickey–Fuller regression is fixed at 4, 8, and 16. The experiments are based on 500 replications. The results for $T = 100$ in Table II, confirm that much longer time series would be needed than commonly available to detect small but persistent changes in growth rates using ARIMA methodology. As regards the results for unit root tests reported in Table III, the findings of Schwert (1989) and Pantula (1991) are clearly applicable. They demonstrate that

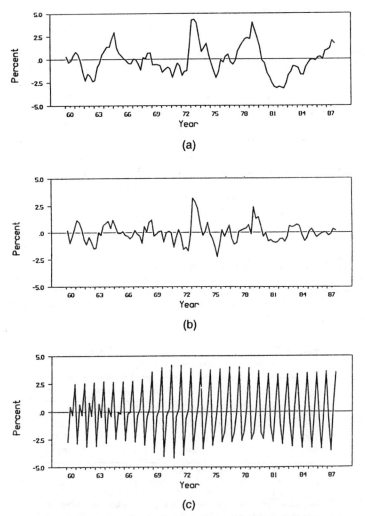

Figure 5. Business cycles in UK GDP. (a) Estimated cycle in seasonally unadjusted data; (b) estimated cycle in seasonally adjusted data (c) estimated seasonal component

242   A. C. HARVEY AND A. JAEGER

if, after first differencing, we have an MA process which is close to being non-invertible, standard unit root tests will tend to reject the null hypothesis that a unit root is present with much higher frequency than the nominal test size. This tendency appears to be even more pronounced in a situation where a smooth local linear trend model (6) is appropriate since the reduced-form ARIMA (0,2,2) model will then have two roots close to the unit circle. For example, the results in Table III show that with a sample size of 100 and the number of lags in the Dickey–Fuller regression fixed at 8, the empirical size of the test is $0 \cdot 74$, exceeding the nominal 5 per cent size of the test substantially.

For purposes of short-term forecasting a parsimonious ARIMA model, such as ARIMA (1,1,0), may well be perfectly adequate compared with a trend plus cycle model. But as a descriptive device it may have little meaning and may even be misleading. For example, it may lead to a rejection of cyclical behaviour when such behaviour is, in fact, quite consistent with the data (see Harvey, 1985). Perhaps more important is the concept of 'persistence' associated with the identification of $I(1)$ models. A trend plus cycle model of the form (1) with $\sigma_\eta^2 = 0$ has stationary components with no persistence and a smooth $I(2)$ trend with infinite persistence. But since the trend is reflecting slow long-term changes in growth rates, perhaps

Table II. Autocorrelations of first differences of $I(2)$ process

Sample	Autocorrelation at lag							
	1	2	3	4	5	6	7	8
100	$0 \cdot 41$	$0 \cdot 30$	$0 \cdot 19$	$0 \cdot 09$	$0 \cdot 01$	$-0 \cdot 05$	$-0 \cdot 09$	$-0 \cdot 11$
	$(0 \cdot 12)$	$(0 \cdot 12)$	$(0 \cdot 11)$	$(0 \cdot 12)$	$(0 \cdot 13)$	$(0 \cdot 13)$	$(0 \cdot 14)$	$(0 \cdot 14)$
500	$0 \cdot 58$	$0 \cdot 50$	$0 \cdot 42$	$0 \cdot 34$	$0 \cdot 28$	$0 \cdot 23$	$0 \cdot 18$	$0 \cdot 18$
	$(0 \cdot 11)$	$(0 \cdot 13)$	$(0 \cdot 15)$	$(0 \cdot 17)$	$(0 \cdot 18)$	$(0 \cdot 20)$	$(0 \cdot 20)$	$(0 \cdot 20)$

Notes: This table presents the results of a Monte Carlo experiment. The data generating process is given by the estimated structural time-series model for US GNP. The table reports the mean of the autocorrelations of the first differences, and, in parentheses, standard deviations of the estimates. The results are based on 500 replications.

Table III. Empirical size of 5 per cent ADF-test for unit root in first differences of $I(2)$ process

Sample size	Empirical size		
	$k = 4$	$k = 8$	$k = 16$
100	0.90	0.74	0.25
500	0.99	0.94	0.38

Notes: This table presents the results of a Monte Carlo experiment. The data generating process is given by the estimated structural time-series model for US GNP. The table reports the empirical size of the 5 per cent level augmented Dickey–Fuller test of the null hypothesis of a unit root in the first differences. k denotes the numbers of lags included in the Dickey–Fuller regressions. The results are based on 500 replications.

arising from demographic changes, innovations in technology, changes in savings behaviour, or increasing integration of capital and goods markets, the shocks which drive the smooth trend may have no connection with short-term economic policy. Following the extensive literature on the productivity slowdown phenomenon, we may well argue that understanding the reasons for persistent changes in growth rates is one of the key problems in macroeconomics.

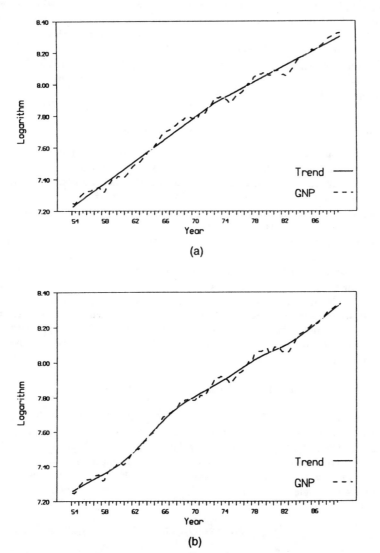

Figure 6. Segmented trends in US GNP. (a) Deterministic trend with break in 1973 : 1; (b) estimated trend component

5.3. Segmented Trends

It is sometimes argued that the trend component in economic time series is deterministic, but with a break at one or more points. We do not find the argument for such a trend particularly persuasive but if the data were really generated in this way, it is worth noting that a smooth trend within a structural time-series model would adapt to it. Thus the structural time series model would still give a good indication of the appropriate stylized facts. Indeed it is interesting to note that the trend component we estimated for US GNP shows a slowdown in the underlying growth rate in the late 1960s (see Figure 6(b)) and not in the first quarter of 1973 as maintained by Perron (1989) (see Figure 6(a)).[7] The imposition of exogenously determined breakpoints could therefore be potentially misleading and subject to many of the pitfalls associated with fitting deterministic trends to the series as a whole.

Making segmented trends more flexible by allowing several endogenously determined breaks also has a limited appeal. Such an approach is unnecessarily complicated and the conclusions could be very sensitive to the method used to choose the breaks. Structural models are not only likely to be more robust, but are also easier to fit.

5.4. Spurious Cross-correlations Between Detrended Series

The illustrative examples in Section 4 cast serious doubt on the validity of the cycles in the detrended price and monetary base series obtained using the HP filter. For US data, Kydland and Prescott (1990) draw wide-ranging conclusions about macroeconomic behaviour based on such data by examining sample cross-correlations. In particular, they argue that mainstream macroeconomic theory is inconsistent with a negative contemporaneous correlation of about -0.50 for US data between HP detrended prices and real GNP.

In this section we use some of the results developed in Section 3 to study the possibility of spurious sample cross-correlations between spurious cycles. From the point of view of the structural time-series model (1), arbitrary cross-correlations can arise if one or both of the cyclical components is absent and the shocks of the trend components are correlated across series. In the following, we focus our attention on the analytically tractable case where spurious HP cycles are imposed on two series and the two series are independent by construction. First, note that the asymptotic distribution of the sample cross-correlations between two independent stationary series is asymptotically normal (AN) and given by (see e.g. Brockwell and Davis, 1987, p. 400)

$$\hat{r}_{12}(h) \sim \text{AN}\left(0, T^{-1}\left(1 + 2 \sum_{j=1}^{\infty} r_1(j)r_2(j)\right)\right) \tag{15}$$

where $\hat{r}_{12}(h)$ is the sample cross-correlation at lag h between two series with sample size T and $r_1(j)$ and $r_2(j)$ are the autocorrelations of the two sta tionary processes at lag j, respectively. The standard deviation of $\hat{r}_{12}(h)$ can be used to evaluate the probability of finding large spurious sample cross correlations between spurious cycles imposed on independent series. To evaluate the standard deviation of the sample cross-correlations we need the autocorrelations of the spurious HP cycles. As a benchmark case, assume we have two independent random walk processes

$$(1 - L)y_{i,t} = \xi_{i,t}, \qquad \xi_{i,t} \sim \text{NID}(0, \sigma_i^2) \tag{16}$$

---

[7] In fact, Nordhaus (1972) published a paper entitled 'The recent productivity slowdown' before the assumed breakpoint.

where $i = 1, 2$ and the $\xi_{i,t}$ are uncorrelated with each other. From equation (12), the spectra of the two HP filtered random walk processes are

$$f_{c,i}(\lambda) = \frac{8(1 - \cos \lambda)^3}{[\bar{q}_\varsigma + 4(1 - \cos \lambda)^2]^2} \frac{\sigma_i^2}{2\pi} \tag{17}$$

The autocovariances of the HP-filtered processes may be calculated by taking the inverse Fourier transform of equation (17)

$$c(j) = \frac{\sigma_i^2}{2\pi} \int_{-\pi}^{\pi} \frac{\cos(\lambda j) 8(1 - \cos \lambda)^3}{[\bar{q}_\varsigma + 4(1 - \cos \lambda)^2]^2} \, d\lambda \qquad j = 0, 1,\dots \tag{18}$$

and the autocorrelations are therefore given as $r(j) = c(j)/c(0)$ for $j = 1, \dots.$ Setting $\sigma_i^2 = 1 \cdot 0$, the autocorrelations can be calculated by numerical integration up to some maximum lag j_{max}.

Line 1 in Table IV reports the asymptotic standard deviations for the chosen benchmark case. Sample sizes T are 25, 100, and 500; $\bar{q}_\varsigma$ is fixed at $0 \cdot 000625$; and the first 100 autocorrelations are used to approximate the infinite sum for the asymptotic variance defined in equation (15). If the sample size T is 100, the standard deviation for the sample cross-correlations $\hat{r}_{12}(h)$ is $0 \cdot 20$. Thus, given a normal distribution there is about a 30 per cent chance of finding spurious cross-correlations exceeding $0 \cdot 20$ in absolute value. To reduce the chance of finding spurious cross-correlations to about 5 per cent, cross-correlations have to exceed $0 \cdot 40$ in absolute value. If the sample size is as low as $T = 25$, the standard deviation increases to $0 \cdot 41.$[8] Even if the sample size is as large as 500, there is still a chance of about 5 per cent that the sample cross-correlations will exceed 0.18 in absolute value. If the two independent processes are specified as doubly integrated random walks, $(1 - L)^2 y_{i,t} = \xi_{i,t}$, appropriately modified versions of equations (17) and (18) give the standard deviations reported in line 2 of Table IV. For $T = 100$, the standard deviation is $0 \cdot 34$ and so values of sample cross-correlations which are quite high in absolute value may easily arise under this specification for the two independent processes. These examples illustrate that the danger of finding large sample cross-correlations between independent but spurious HP cycles is not negligible. Furthermore, they strongly indicate that research on stylized business cycle facts should report standard errors in addition to point estimates of cross-correlations.[9]

Table IV. Asymptotic standard deviation of sample cross-correlations

	Standard deviation		
Process	$T = 25$	$T = 100$	$T = 500$
$(1 - L)y_{i,t} = \xi_{i,t}$	$0 \cdot 41$	$0 \cdot 20$	$0 \cdot 09$
$(1 - L)^2 y_{i,t} = \xi_{i,t}$	$0 \cdot 67$	$0 \cdot 34$	$0 \cdot 15$

Notes: This table reports the asymptotic standard deviations for the sample cross-correlations between two independent spurious HP cycles. $\bar{q}_\varsigma$ is fixed at $0 \cdot 000625$.

---

[8] Monte Carlo experiments indicate that the asymptotic distribution in equation (15) approximates the actual small sample distribution well for sample sizes as low as $T = 25$.

[9] As an exception, Brandner and Neusser (1992) suggest the rule of thumb that cross-correlations between detrended series exceeding $2/\sqrt{T}$ in absolute value are significant at the 5 per cent level. From equation (15), however, this rule of thumb is misleading because it implicitly assumes that at least one of the detrended series is white noise.

A. C. HARVEY AND A. JAEGER

6. CONCLUSIONS

Given the nature of macroeconomic time series, it is almost impossible to unambiguously obtain stylized facts from a single series. Instead we must be content with the less ambitious objective of extracting sets of stylized facts that are consistent with the data. It will often be possible to obtain several sets of stylized facts for a series and these may have very different implications. In such cases it is necessary to look for corroborating evidence from other sources.

We have argued in this article that because structural time-series models are formulated in terms of components that have a direct interpretation, they are a particularly useful way of presenting stylized facts. Furthermore, they provide a framework for assessing the limitations of stylized facts obtained by other methods. Our principal conclusions are as follows:

(1) ARIMA models fitted on the basis of parsimony may be uninformative and are sometimes misleading. A process integrated of order 2, or $I(2)$, is unlikely to be chosen in small samples using correlogram and standard unit root tests. The net result are simple $I(1)$ representations which are not consistent with a smooth trend plus cycle representation. If the latter representation is believed to be appropriate, measures of persistence associated with $I(1)$ models have little meaning.

(2) Pure autoregressive models are even more unlikely than ARIMA models to be consistent with trend plus cycle models. Furthermore, they have virtually no hope of adequately modelling the kind of changing seasonality that is to be found in the UK GDP series. These points need to be borne in mind when making inferences from vector autoregressions.

(3) The Hodrick–Prescott filter may create spurious cycles and/or distort unrestricted estimates of the cyclical component. This property of the Hodrick–Prescott filter may lead to misleading conclusions being drawn on the relationship between short-term movements in macroeconomic time series. A proper presentation of the stylized facts associated with a trend plus cycle view needs to be done within the framework of a model that fits both components at the same time.

ACKNOWLEDGEMENTS

We would like to thank Robert Kunst, Klaus Neusser, George Tiao, and Mark Watson for helpful comments on the original draft of this paper.

REFERENCES

Backus, D. K., and P. J. Kehoe (1989), 'International evidence on the historical properties of business cycles', Working Paper 402R, Federal Reserve Bank of Minneapolis.

Barsky, R. B., and J. A. Miron (1989), 'The seasonal cycle and the business cycle', *Journal of Political Economy*, **97**, 503–35.

Blanchard, O. J., and S. Fischer (1989), *Lectures in Macroeconomics*, MIT Press, Cambridge.

Bell, W. (1984), 'Signal extraction for nonstationary time series', *The Annals of Statistics*, **12**, 646–664.

Brandner, P., and K. Neusser (1992), 'Business cycles in open economies: Stylized facts for Austria and Germany', *Weltwirtschaftliches Archiv*, **128**, 67–87.

Brockwell, P. J., and R. A. Davis (1987), *Time Series: Theory and Methods*, Springer, New York.

Clark, P. (1987), 'The cyclical component of U.S. economic activity', *Quarterly Journal of Economics*, **102**, 797–814.

Cogley, T. (1990), 'Spurious business cycle phenomena in HP filtered time series', Mimeo, University of Washington.

Danthine, J. P., and M. Girardin (1989), 'Business cycles in Switzerland. A comparative study', *European Economic Review*, **33**, 31–50.

Fishman, G. S. (1969), *Spectral Methods in Econometrics*, Harvard University Press, Cambridge.

Harvey, A. C. (1985), 'Trends and cycles in macroeconomic time series', *Journal of Business and Economic Statistics*, **3**, 216–27.

Harvey, A. C. (1989), *Forecasting, Structural Time Series Models and the Kalman Filter*, Cambridge University Press, Cambridge.

Hodrick, R. J., and E. C. Prescott (1980), 'Postwar U.S. business cycles: An empirical investigation', Discussion Paper No. 451, Carnegie-Mellon University.

King, R. G., and S. T. Rebelo (1989), 'Low frequency filtering and real business cycles', Working Paper No. 205, University of Rochester.

Koopman, S. (1991), 'Efficient smoothing algorithms for time series models', Mimeo, London School of Economics.

Kydland, F. E., and E. C. Prescott (1990), 'Business cycles: Real facts and a monetary myth', *Federal Reserve Bank of Minneapolis Quarterly Review*, **14**, 3–18.

Nelson C. R., and H. Kang (1981), 'Spurious periodicity in inappropriately detrended time series', *Econometrica*, **49**, 741–51.

Nordhaus, W. D. (1972), 'The recent productivity slowdown', *Brookings Papers on Economic Activity*, **3**, 493–546.

Pantula, S. G. (1991), 'Asymptotic distributions of unit-root tests when the process is nearly stationary', *Journal of Business and Economic Statistics*, **9**, 63–71.

Perron, P. (1989), 'The great crash, the oil shock, and the unit root hypothesis', *Econometrica*, **57**, 1361–1401.

Schwert, G. W. (1989), 'Tests for unit roots: A Monte Carlo investigation', *Journal of Business and Economic Statistics*, **7**, 147–160.

Wecker, W. E., and C. F. Ansley (1983), 'The signal extraction approach to nonlinear regression and splint smoothing', *Journal of the American Statistical Association*, **78**, 81–9.

ELSEVIER

Journal of Economic Dynamics and Control
19 (1995) 253–278

JOURNAL OF
Economic
Dynamics
& Control

Effects of the Hodrick–Prescott filter on trend and difference stationary time series Implications for business cycle research

Timothy Cogley*,[a], James M. Nason[b]

[a] *Research Department, Federal Reserve Bank of San Francisco, San Francisco, CA 94120, USA*
[b] *Department of Economics, University of British Columbia, Vancouver, B.C., V6T 1Z1, Canada*

(Received April 1993; final version received September 1993)

Abstract

When applied to persistent time series, the Hodrick–Prescott filter can generate business cycle dynamics even if none are present in the original data. Hence the presence of business cycles in HP filtered data does not imply that there are business cycles in the original data. For example, we show that standard real business cycle models do not generate business cycle dynamics in pre-filtered data and that the business cycles observed in HP filtered data are due to the filter. As another example, we show that under plausible assumptions HP stylized facts are determined primarily by the filter and reveal little about the dynamics of the underlying data.

Key words: Business fluctuations; Time series models; Model evaluation and testing
JEL classification: E32; C22; C52

1. Introduction

Macroeconomic time series often have an upward drift or trend which makes them nonstationary. Since many statistical procedures assume stationarity, it is

---

*Corresponding author.

We thank Roger Craine, Jon Faust, Andrew Harvey, Stephen LeRoy, Charles Nelson, Adrian Pagan, Kenneth West, and a referee for helpful comments. Much of this research was done while Cogley was visiting the Haas School of Business at U.C. Berkeley, and their hospitality is gratefully acknowledged. Opinions expressed in this paper do not necessarily represent the views of the Federal Reserve Bank of San Francisco or the Federal Reserve System.

often necessary to transform data before beginning analysis. There are a number of familiar transformations, including deterministic detrending, stochastic detrending, and differencing. In recent years, methods for stochastic detrending have received much attention (e.g., Hodrick and Prescott, 1980; Beveridge and Nelson, 1981; Watson, 1986). This paper studies the Hodrick–Prescott (HP) filter, which has become influential in the real business cycle literature. Kydland and Prescott (1982) used this technique in their seminal 'Time to Build' paper, and it has been widely adopted by subsequent authors.

The HP filter is a two-sided symmetric moving average filter, and a number of authors have studied its basic properties. Singleton (1988) shows that it operates like a high pass filter when applied to stationary time series.[1] King and Rebelo (1993) show that it can transform series which are integrated of order 4 or less into stationary series. They also characterize a class of unobserved components models for which the HP filter is the optimal Wiener filter, but they suggest that it is an uninteresting class. These authors also give a number of examples which demonstrate that the dynamics of HP filtered data can differ dramatically from the dynamics of detrended or differenced data.

This paper builds on earlier work by distinguishing the HP filter's effects on trend- and difference-stationary time series (TS and DS, respectively). Many previous results on the HP filter rely on theorems which assume that the original data are stationary. This assumption is problematic, since the filter is typically applied to nonstationary data. We show that Singleton's result extends in a straightforward manner when the data are TS. In this case, HP filtering is conceptually equivalent to a two-step operation: linearly detrend the data and then apply the HP filter to deviations from trend. Thus the HP filter operates like a high pass filter on deviations from trend.

When the data are DS, the filter does not operate like a high pass filter. In this case, the HP filter is equivalent to a two-step linear filter: difference the data to make them stationary and then smooth the differenced data with an asymmetric moving average filter. The smoothing operation amplifies growth cycles at business cycle frequencies and damps long- and short-run fluctuations. As a consequence, the filter can generate business cycle periodicity and comovement even if none are present in the original data. In this respect, applying the HP filter to an integrated process is similar to detrending a random walk (Nelson and Kang, 1981).[2] This has an important practical

---

[1] A stationary time series can be decomposed into orthogonal periodic components. A high pass filter removes the low frequency or long cycle components and allows the high frequency or short cycle components to pass through.

[2] Nelson and Kang show that a detrended random walk exhibits spurious cycles whose *average* length is roughly two-thirds the length of the sample. Thus there are important transitory fluctuations in the detrended series even though there are none in the original data.

T. Cogley, J.M. Nason / Journal of Economic Dynamics and Control 19 (1995) 253–278   255

implication: if an applied researcher is reluctant to detrend a series on account of the Nelson–Kang result, she should also be reluctant to apply the HP filter.

We use these results to study two applications of the HP filter. One is in studies which describe stylized facts about business cycles (e.g., Kydland and Prescott, 1990). The problem with using the HP filter for this purpose is that it is subject to the Nelson–Kang critique. Since the HP filter can generate spurious cycles when applied to integrated processes, it is not clear whether the results should be interpreted as facts or artifacts. We show that if U.S. data are modeled as DS, stylized facts about periodicity and comovement primarily reflect the properties of the implicit smoothing filter and tell us very little about the dynamics of the underlying data.

A second application is in real business cycle (RBC) simulations. Many authors use the HP filter to transform data generated by RBC models. When passed through the HP filter, artificial data display business cycle periodicity and comovement. These fluctuations depend on three factors: impulse dynamics, propagation mechanisms, and the HP filter. We investigate the role the filter plays in generating these dynamics. Using a conventional RBC model, we show that the combination of persistent technology shocks and the HP filter is sufficient to generate business cycles in artificial data. Propagation mechanisms are unnecessary, and in many models they do not play an important role.[3]

Finally, we consider how HP filtering affects judgments about goodness of fit. The great majority of papers in the RBC literature rely on informal, subjective comparisons of population and sample moments. Such informal judgments are not robust to alternative data transformations. In particular, post-HP filter dynamics often seem to match well even when pre-filter dynamics do not. Thus, on the 'eyeball metric', the HP filter can mask important differences between sample and theoretical dynamics. Since results based on informal comparisons are sensitive to HP filtering, it is important to develop methods which are robust. We show how to construct goodness of fit statistics which are invariant to HP filtering, and we apply them to a standard model.

Our discussion is organized as follows. Section 2 describes the HP filter and analyzes its effects on TS and DS processes. Section 3 considers the problem of interpreting stylized facts, and Section 4 examines the filter's role in generating periodicity and comovement in RBC models. Section 5 discusses the problem of evaluating goodness of fit in filtered data. Section 6 concludes.

---

[3] Cogley and Nason (1992) provide an extensive analysis of the role of propagation mechanisms in RBC models.

2. Effects on trend- and difference-stationary time series

The HP filter decomposes a time series into cyclical and growth components: $y(t) \equiv g(t) + c(t)$, where $y(t)$ is the natural logarithm of the observed series, $g(t)$ is the growth component, and $c(t)$ is the cyclical component. To identify the two components, Hodrick and Prescott minimize the variance of $c(t)$ subject to a penalty for variation in the second difference of the $g(t)$,[4]

$$\min_{g(t)} \left\{ \sum_{t=-\infty}^{\infty} [y(t) - g(t)]^2 + \mu \sum_{t=-\infty}^{\infty} [g(t+1) - 2g(t) + g(t-1)]^2 \right\},$$

where μ controls the smoothness of the growth component.[5] The solution to this problem is a linear time-invariant filter which maps $y(t)$ into $c(t)$. The HP cyclical component can be written as $c(t) = H(L)(1-L)^4 y(t)$, where $H(L)$ equals

$$(|\rho|^2/L^2)[1 - 2\text{Re}(\rho)L + |\rho|^2 L^2]^{-1}[1 - 2\text{Re}(\rho)L^{-1} + |\rho|^2 L^{-2}]^{-1}.$$

The parameter $1/\rho$ is a stable root of the lag polynomial $[\mu^{-1}L^2 + (1-L)^4] = 0$, $\text{Re}(\rho)$ denotes the real part ρ, and $|\rho|^2$ is its mod-square.[6] The proper interpretation of the filter's effects depends on the nature of original data. Suppose that $y(t)$ is stationary and mixing.[7] In this case, $y(t)$ has a Cramer representation, which means that it can be decomposed into orthogonal periodic components. When the HP filter operates on a stationary series, the spectra for the input and output series satisfy $f_{cc}(\omega) = |HP(\omega)|^2 f_{YY}(\omega)$, where $f_{cc}(\omega)$ is the spectrum for $c(t)$, $f_{YY}(\omega)$ is the spectrum for $y(t)$, and $|HP(\omega)|^2$ is the squared gain of the filter $(1-L)^4 H(L)$. The gain indicates how the filter affects the amplitude of the periodic component of $y(t)$ at frequency ω. If $|HP(\omega)| > 1$, then the filter increases the amplitude of the frequency ω component of $y(t)$. Similarly, if $|HP(\omega)| < 1$, the filter decreases the amplitude of the frequency ω component. The function $|HP(\omega)|^2$ is shown in the top panel of Fig. 1 (taken from Singleton, 1988). When applied to stationary series, the HP

---

[4] They actually formulate a related finite horizon problem, the solution to which is a time-varying filter. In the finite horizon case, the moments of $\Delta g(t)$ and $c(t)$ depend on time and hence are nonstationary. The solution to the infinite horizon problem is a time-invariant filter which generates covariance stationary processes for $\Delta g(t)$ and $c(t)$ for the input processes studied in this paper. Since the filters are otherwise quite similar, we prefer to analyze the version which generates stationary output processes.

[5] As μ increases, $g(t)$ becomes smoother. In the limit, $g(t)$ becomes a linear deterministic trend. When applied to quarterly data, μ is almost always set equal to 1600.

[6] That is, $|\rho|^2 = \rho\bar{\rho}$, where $\bar{\rho}$ is the complex conjugate of ρ.

[7] The latter condition ensures that the data have a short span of dependence.

T. Cogley, J.M. Nason / Journal of Economic Dynamics and Control 19 (1995) 253–278   257

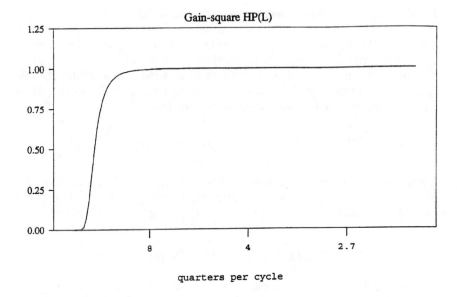

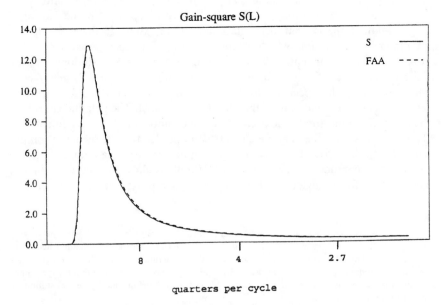

Fig. 1. Transfer functions.

filter operates like a high pass filter, damping fluctuations which last longer than eight years per cycle (in quarterly data) and passing shorter cycles without change.

This result relies fundamentally on the Cramer representation of a stationary time series. Since a stationary series can be decomposed into orthogonal periodic components, it is meaningful to analyze how the filter operates on its periodic components. This result has limited practical value, however, because the HP filter is typically applied to nonstationary time series, which do not have Cramer representations (Priestley, 1988). It is not meaningful to analyze the periodic components of $y(t)$ when $y(t)$ does not have a periodic decomposition!

An alternative approach is useful when the data are nonstationary. Decompose the filter into two operations, one which renders $y(t)$ stationary by an appropriate transformation and another which operates on the resulting stationary series. Then it is possible to determine the filter's effect on the stationary component of $y(t)$ by analyzing the properties of the second operation. We use this approach to analyze the HP filter's effect on TS and DS processes. We also consider the special case of a near unit root, TS process.[8]

2.1. Trend-stationary processes

Suppose that $y(t)$ is TS: $y(t) = \alpha + \beta t + z(t)$, where $z(t)$ is stationary and mixing. Applying the HP filter term by term yields

$$c(t) = H(L)(1 - L)^4 z(t).$$

Applying the HP filter to a TS process is conceptually equivalent to a two-step operation: linearly detrend $y(t)$ to make it stationary and then apply the HP filter to the deviations from trend, $z(t)$. Since $z(t)$ is stationary and mixing, Singleton's characterization extends in a straightforward manner. The HP filter works like a high pass filter on deviations from trend.

2.2. Difference-stationary processes

Now suppose that $y(t)$ is DS: $\Delta y(t) = \alpha + v(t)$, where $v(t)$ is stationary and mixing. In this case, the HP filter operates like a two-step linear filter. Difference $y(t)$ to make it stationary, and then smooth $\Delta y(t)$ with an asymmetric moving average filter:

$$c(t) = S(L)\Delta y(t),$$

---

[8] Harvey and Jaeger (1993) use this approach to compare the HP filter with the optimal Wiener filter for an unobserved components model of trend and cycle.

T. Cogley, J.M. Nason / Journal of Economic Dynamics and Control 19 (1995) 253–278   259

where

$$S(L) = H(L)(1 - L)^3.$$

Since $\Delta y(t)$ is stationary and mixing, we can apply the usual theorems on linear filters to analyze the properties of $S(L)$. The solid line in the bottom panel of Fig. 1 shows its squared gain.[9]

$S(L)$ is not a high pass filter. When applied to quarterly data, it amplifies growth cycles at business cycle frequencies and damps long- and short-run components. Its gain has a maximum at 7.6 years per cycle and increases the variance of this frequency component by a factor of 13. $S(L)$ also amplifies neighboring frequencies. For example, it increases the variance of growth cycles lasting between 3.2 and 13 years by more than a factor of 4.

To illustrate the filter's effect on DS processes, we conduct a variant of the Nelson–Kang (1981) experiment. Consider the effect of applying the HP filter to a pair of random walks. Specifically, assume that $\Delta y_1(t)$ and $\Delta y_2(t)$ are white noise variates which are correlated at lag zero but uncorrelated at all other leads and lags. The spectral density matrix for the vector $c(t)$ is $f_{cc}(\omega) = |S(\omega)|^2 f_{\Delta\Delta}(\omega)$, where $f_{\Delta\Delta}(\omega)$ is the spectral density matrix for the vector $\Delta y(t)$.[10] The elements of $f_{\Delta\Delta}(\omega)$ are constants, so $f_{cc}(\omega)$ inherits the spectral shape of $S(L)$.

Since the power spectrum for an HP filtered random walk is proportional to $|S(\omega)|^2$, it has a peak at 7.6 years per cycle. Hence there is business cycle periodicity in the elements of $c(t)$ even though the elements of $y(t)$ are random walks. The cross-spectrum is also proportional to $|S(\omega)|^2$, so the elements of $c(t)$ also display comovements over business cycle horizons.[11]

Fig. 2 translates this information into time domain. The top panel shows the autocorrelation function for an HP filtered random walk. It has strong positive autocorrelation at short horizons and negative autocorrelation at long horizons. This pattern is similar to the autocorrelation function for a detrended random walk. The bottom panel shows cross-correlation functions for HP filtered random walks. The contemporaneous correlations between the pre-filtered series are set equal to $\frac{3}{4}, \frac{1}{2}$, and $\frac{1}{4}$, respectively. The cross-correlation function has

---

[9] This is drawn for $\mu = 1600$. As μ increases, the peak becomes larger, narrower, and moves to lower frequencies. The dotted line in Fig. 1 will be discussed below.

[10] Let $d_y(\omega)$ denote the frequency ω component of the vector time series $y(t)$. The spectral density matrix is proportional to the covariance matrix for the complex random vector $d_y(\omega)$.

[11] We do not claim that $S(L)$ *always* generates business cycle comovement in DS processes. For example, if $\Delta y_1(t)$ and $\Delta y_2(t)$ are uncorrelated at all leads and lags, $c_1(t)$ and $c_2(t)$ are also uncorrelated at all leads and lags. But this exception is irrelevant to macroeconomists, since dynamic economic models rarely generate series which are uncorrelated at all leads and lags. Our example is relevant, since the assumed cross-correlations are similar to comovements which arise in many RBC models.

260   *T. Cogley, J.M. Nason / Journal of Economic Dynamics and Control 19 (1995) 253–278*

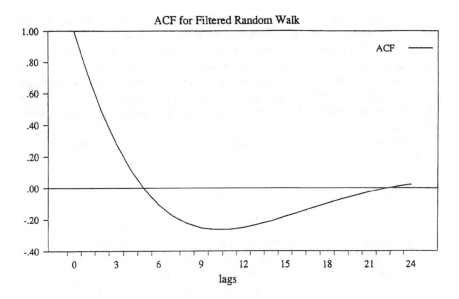

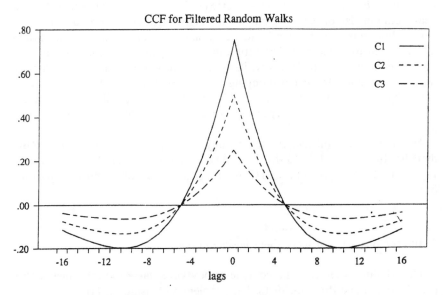

Fig. 2. Auto- and cross-correlation functions for HP filtered random walks.

T. Cogley, J.M. Nason / Journal of Economic Dynamics and Control 19 (1995) 253–278 261

the same shape as the autocorrelation function, with the scale depending on the size of the contemporaneous correlation between $\Delta y_1(t)$ and $\Delta y_2(t)$.

One might think that HP filtered dynamics reflect business cycle periodicity and comovement. In the short run, there is positive dependence over time and across series, and there is trend reversion and error correction in the long run. However, in this example, the business cycle dynamics of $c(t)$ are artifacts of the filter. This shows that HP filtered data can exhibit periodicity and comovement over business cycle horizons even if none are present in the input series. Hence the presence of business cycle dynamics in $c(t)$ does not imply business cycle dynamics in $y(t)$.

2.3. A special case: Near unit root TS processes

If macroeconomic time series are modeled as TS processes, deviations from trend have large autoregressive roots. As one might expect, the effect of the HP filter on near unit root processes is much like its effect on unit root processes. To see why, let $\tilde{z}(t) = (1 - \phi L)z(t)$, where ϕ is the largest autoregressive root of $z(t)$; ϕ is close to but less than one. The HP cyclical component is $c(t) = \{(1 - L)/(1 - \phi L)\}S(L)\tilde{z}(t)$. The term in brackets is a near common factor whose gain has a narrow trough near frequency zero and is close to one at all other frequencies. Since its gain is close to one at high and medium frequencies, it has little influence on the high and medium frequency dynamics of $c(t)$. Further, its influence near frequency zero is largely negated by the low frequency damping effect of $S(L)$. Thus $c(t)$ is well approximated by $S(L)\tilde{z}(t)$. Since $\tilde{z}(t)$ is quasi-differenced $z(t)$, it typically has a relatively flat spectrum. Therefore the spectrum for $c(t)$ has roughly the same shape as $|S(\omega)|^2$.

As an example, consider the technology shock process used in many RBC models: $A(t) = \gamma t + (1 - 0.95L)^{-1}\varepsilon(t)$. The dotted line in the bottom panel of Fig. 1 graphs the spectrum for HP filtered $A(t)$. It is nearly indistinguishable from $|S(\omega)|^2$.

3. Interpreting stylized facts about business cycles

The HP filter is sometimes used to describe stylized facts about business cycles (e.g., Kydland and Prescott, 1990). The problem with using the HP filter for this purpose is that it is subject to the Nelson–Kang critique. Since the HP filter can generate spurious cycles in DS processes, it is not clear whether the results should be regarded as facts or artifacts. Hence the interpretation of stylized facts depends on assumptions about the nature of the input series. King and Rebelo (1993) consider how to interpret HP stylized facts when the data are assumed to

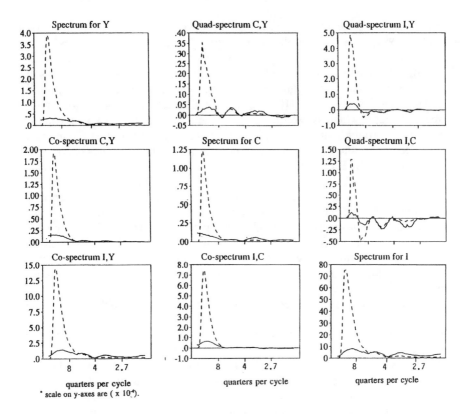

Fig. 3. Spectral density matrices, before and after filtering.

be TS.[12] This section complements their work by considering the interpretation of stylized facts when the data are modeled as DS.

Although it is customary to summarize periodicity and comovement by reporting auto- and cross-correlations, it is more convenient for our purpose to examine spectral density matrices. The spectral density matrix contains the same information as auto- and cross-correlations and makes it easier to interpret the effects of filtering.

Fig. 3 shows estimated spectral density matrices for quarterly U.S. real GNP, real personal consumption expenditures, and real gross private domestic fixed

[12] Briefly, since TS representations of macroeconomic time series have near unit roots, most of the variation is due to low frequency components. Since the HP filter damps low frequency fluctuations in detrended data, it reduces the amplitude and average length of cycles.

investment. All three series are measured in per capita units, and the sample period is 1954–1991. The graphs on the diagonal are power spectra, the graphs below the diagonal are co-spectra (the real part of cross-spectra), and the graphs above the diagonal are quadrature spectra (the imaginary part of cross-spectra). The solid lines are the elements of $f_{\Delta\Delta}(\omega)$, and the dotted lines are the elements of $f_{cc}(\omega)$.[13]

This figure shows that HP cyclical components have their own 'typical spectral shape' which is essentially the same as the $|S(\omega)|^2$. Experimentation with other variables and sample periods verifies that this is robust. To interpret this, decompose the dynamics of $c(t)$ into two parts: the dynamics of $\Delta y(t)$ and the effects of $S(L)$. Pre- and post-smoothing spectral density matrices are related by the equation $f_{cc}(\omega) = |S(\omega)|^2 f_{\Delta\Delta}(\omega)$. Since the elements of $f_{\Delta\Delta}(\omega)$ are flat relative to $|S(\omega)|^2$, the elements of $f_{cc}(w)$ inherit the shape of $|S(\omega)|^2$. Hence the smoothing filter is the primary determinant of the dynamics of $c(t)$. Growth dynamics have only a secondary influence. Since the spectra for HP filtered data mainly reflect the shape of $|S(\omega)|^2$, auto- and cross-correlations of HP filtered data reveal more about the properties of the smoothing operation than about the properties of $\Delta y(t)$. In the DS case, HP stylized facts are determined primarily by the filter.

The literature on HP stylized facts suffers from the same problem as Kuznets' (1961) work on long swings in growth. In looking for evidence of long swings, Kuznets employed a filter which was designed to remove business cycles from the data, and he found evidence of 20-year cycles in the filtered data. Adelman (1965) and Howrey (1968) later analyzed the properties of the Kuznets filter and found that it would generate 20-year cycles even if the original data were white noise or white noise around a deterministic trend. Thus the presence of 20-year cycles in Kuznets filtered data does not imply that there are 20-year cycles in the original data. Long swings might simply be an artifact of filtering. Similarly, since the HP filter can generate spurious business cycles, the presence of business cycles in HP filtered data does not imply that there are important transitory fluctuations in the original data.

4. Sources of periodicity and comovement in RBC models

Business cycle theorists are interested in periodicity, comovement, and relative volatility (e.g., Lucas, 1987; Prescott, 1986). In this section, we focus on periodicity and comovement.[14] In the RBC literature, periodicity is usually

---

[13] The spectral density matrix for $\Delta y(t)$ was estimated by smoothing the matrix periodogram using a Bartlett window. This was multiplied by $|S(\omega)|^2$ to obtain the spectral density matrix for $c(t)$.

[14] King and Rebelo (1993) show that the HP filter alters relative volatilities, increasing the relative volatility of investment and hours and decreasing that of consumption and real wages.

264   *T. Cogley, J.M. Nason / Journal of Economic Dynamics and Control 19 (1995) 253–278*

measured by the autocorrelation function of output, and comovements are summarized by cross-correlations between output and variables such as consumption, investment, and hours. Since most macroeconomic data are nonstationary, some transformation is needed in order to make second moments finite. Following Kydland and Prescott (1982), many authors use the HP filter to induce stationarity.

When artificial data are passed through the HP filter, they display periodicity and comovement over business cycle horizons. These fluctuations depend on three factors: the exogenous impulse dynamics which drive the model, the endogenous propagation mechanisms which spread shocks over time, and the HP filter. This section investigates the role the HP filter plays in generating periodicity and comovement. Using a conventional RBC model, we show that the combination of persistent technology shocks plus the HP filter is sufficient to generate business cycle periodicity and comovement. Propagation mechanisms are unnecessary, and, in many cases, do not play an important role.

We study TS and DS representations of the Christiano–Eichenbaum (CE) (1992) model. Its dynamics are essentially the same as those of many other RBC models, so the results reported below apply to many other models.[15]

4.1. The difference-stationary model

The CE model is driven by technology and government spending shocks. In the DS version, the natural logarithm of technology follows a random walk with drift, and the natural logarithm of government spending evolves as a stationary process around the technology shock. The natural logarithms of output, consumption, and investment inherit the unit root in the technology shock, while the natural logarithm of hours worked follows a stationary process. Since output, consumption, and investment are DS, we compare HP filtering with first differencing. Hours are stationary, so no preliminary transformation is needed.

4.1.1. Periodicity
The top row of Fig. 4 reports autocorrelation functions and power spectra for output growth. The solid lines show results for data generated by the CE model, and the dotted lines show results for U.S. data (1954–1991).[16] There are two

---

[15] Previous drafts of this paper showed that these results also hold for the models of King, Plosser, and Rebelo (1988a,b), Hansen (1989), and Kydland and Prescott (1988). The results in Cogley and Nason (1992) imply that the results on periodicity hold for several other prominent RBC models as well.

[16] Theoretical autocorrelations are calculated by simulating the model 1000 times and averaging autocorrelations across replications. Theoretical spectra are estimated by simulating the models 1000 times, averaging periodograms across replications, and then smoothing the ensemble averaged periodogram using a Bartlett window. The artificial data are scaled so that output growth has the same variance as in U.S. data.

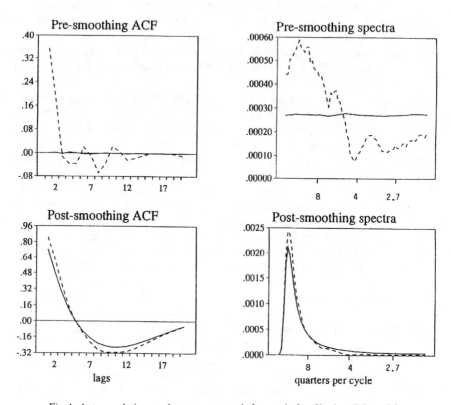

Fig. 4. Autocorrelations and power spectra, before and after filtering (DS model).

interesting facts about artificial output dynamics. The first is that the model does not generate business cycle periodicity. Output growth is very weakly autocorrelated at all lags, and its spectrum is quite flat. Fluctuations at business cycle frequencies are no more important than fluctuations at any other frequency.

Second, the periodicity of output growth is determined primarily by shock dynamics, with little contribution from the model's endogenous propagation mechanisms. Output growth is well approximated by a white noise variate, and total factor productivity growth is also white noise. Since output dynamics are essentially the same as impulse dynamics, it follows that the model's internal propagation mechanisms are weak.

The bottom row of Fig. 4 shows the effects of HP filtering on autocorrelations and power spectra. Since output growth is nearly white noise in the CE model, the spectrum for HP filtered output inherits the shape of $|S(\omega)|^2$. Transforming $|S(\omega)|^2$ into time domain produces positive autocorrelation for four quarters, followed by negative dependence for several years. In this model, the source of business cycle periodicity in HP filtered data is the HP filter! An RBC model can exhibit business cycle periodicity in HP filtered data even if it does not generate business cycle periodicity in output growth.

4.1.2. Comovement

Figs. 5a and 5b report cross-correlation functions and cross-spectra, before and after filtering. The solid lines show results for artificial data, and the dotted lines are for U.S. data. The first two rows of Fig. 5a report comovements of consumption and investment growth with output growth. In the CE model, consumption and investment growth are very highly correlated with output growth at lag zero (0.91 for consumption and 0.99 for investment) and nearly uncorrelated at nonzero leads and lags. In frequency domain, the theoretical cross-spectra are flat everywhere except near frequency zero.

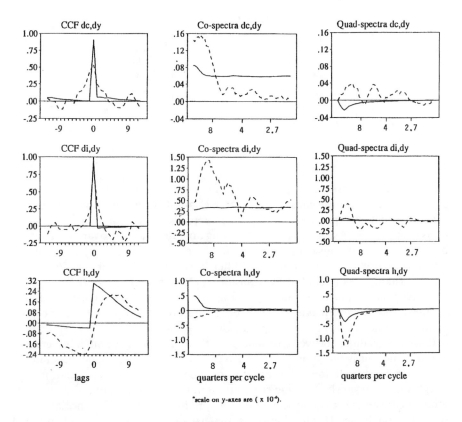

*scale on y-axes are (x 10⁴).

Fig. 5a. Pre-filter comovements (DS model).

T. Cogley, J.M. Nason / Journal of Economic Dynamics and Control 19 (1995) 253–278 267

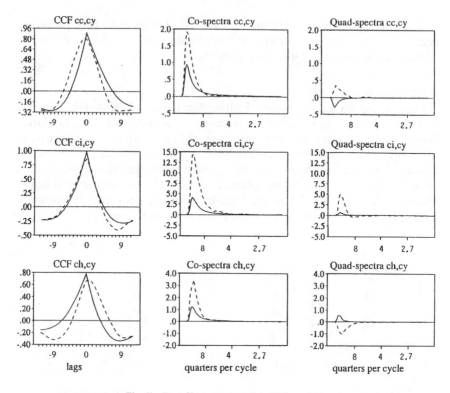

Fig. 5b. Post-filter comovements (DS model).

The CE cross-correlation functions for consumption and investment growth conform closely to those considered in the Nelson–Kang experiment in Section 2.2. From that example, we know that $S(L)$ spreads contemporaneous correlations over periods of several years, thus giving an impression of covariation over business cycle horizons. Since the pre-filter cross-spectra are relatively flat (except near frequency zero), the post-filter cross-spectra inherit the shape of $|S(\omega)|^2$. Taking the inverse Fourier transform of $|S\omega)|^2$ produces the bell-shaped cross-correlation functions shown in Fig. 5b. An RBC model can exhibit business cycle comovements in HP filtered data even when pre-filter comovements are almost entirely contemporaneous.

Cross-correlations between output growth and hours exhibit a different pattern, and this is shown in the third row of Fig. 5a. The CE model generates weak negative correlation at low order leads, a contemporaneous correlation of roughly 0.3, and slowly decaying correlations at low order lags. In this case, the model does generate dynamic covariation in pre-filtered data. After the data are passed through the HP filter, however, the cross-correlation function exhibits

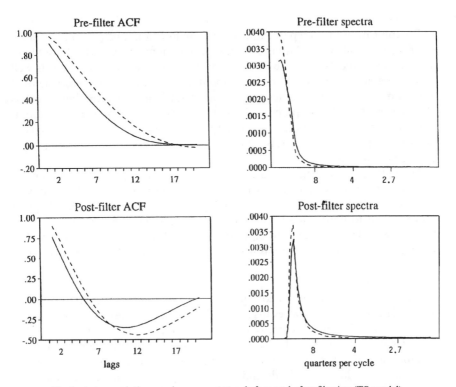

Fig. 6. Autocorrelations and power spectra, before and after filtering (TS model).

the characteristic bell shape (see the third row of Fig. 5b). The cross-spectra show that post-filter dynamics are determined primarily by $S(L)$. Since the smoothing operation dominates the dynamics of HP filtered data, the filter can also obscure interesting comovements in the original data.

4.2. The trend-stationary model

In the TS version of the CE model, the natural logarithm of technology follows a persistent AR(1) process about a linear deterministic trend, and the natural logarithm of government spending evolves as a stationary process around the technology trend. The natural logarithms of output, consumption, and investment inherit a deterministic trend from the technology shock, so we compare HP filtering with linear detrending. As before, hours follow a stationary process, so no preliminary transformation is needed.

T. Cogley, J.M. Nason / Journal of Economic Dynamics and Control 19 (1995) 253–278   269

4.2.1. Periodicity

The top row of Fig. 6 reports autocorrelation functions and power spectra for detrended output. The solid lines are theoretical moments, and the dotted lines are sample moments.[17] In the TS CE model, one can show that output is well approximated by an AR(1) process about trend with an AR coefficient of approximately 0.95 (e.g., Cogley and Nason, 1993). Since the technology shock is also a persistent AR(1) process about trend, we again observe that output dynamics are essentially the same as impulse dynamics. Output periodicity is determined primarily by impulse dynamics with little contribution from propagation mechanisms.

The bottom row of Fig. 6 reports autocorrelations and power spectra for HP filtered data. Since output has a near unit root in this model, the results of Section 2.3 apply. The spectrum for HP filtered output inherits the shape of $|S(\omega)|^2$. Transforming $|S(\omega)|^2$ into time domain produces the usual autocorrelation pattern. The combination of a near unit root in technology and the HP filter is sufficient to generate business cycle periodicity in HP filtered output.

4.2.2. Comovement

Figs. 7a and 7b report cross-correlation functions and cross-spectra for the TS model. The solid lines show results for artificial data, and the dotted lines are for U.S. data. Fig. 7a reports comovements of detrended consumption, detrended investment, and hours with detrended output. In the CE model, all three variables are highly correlated with output at lag zero, and cross-correlations decay slowly at low-order leads and lags. In frequency domain, the co-spectra have peaks near zero, and the quad-spectra indicate that there are fairly substantial phase shifts in consumption and hours and a minor phase shift in investment.

Fig. 7b reports comovements for HP filtered data. After filtering, the cross-spectra inherit the shape of $|S(\omega)|^2$. Transforming into time domain generates the characteristic bell-shaped cross-correlation function. HP filtered data have their own typical spectral shape, and this pattern comes from the filter $S(L)$.

5. Evaluating goodness of fit

This section considers the problem of evaluating goodness of fit in HP filtered data. In the RBC literature, most authors do not report formal test statistics. Instead, it is common to rely on informal, subjective comparisons of population

---

[17] Theoretical moments are calculated by simulating the model 1000 times and averaging across replications. The artificial data are scaled so that detrended output has the same variance as in sample.

270   T. Cogley, J.M. Nason / Journal of Economic Dynamics and Control 19 (1995) 253–278

and sample moments. Since this practice is pervasive, our first task is to consider whether such informal judgments are sensitive to the choice of data transformation. We show that informal judgments are not robust. Researchers who employ different data transformations would often reach different conclusions. In particular, HP filter dynamics often seem to match well even when pre-filter dynamics do not.

Since this is rather unsatisfactory, our second task is to develop methods which are robust. We show how to construct goodness of fit statistics which are invariant to HP filtering, and we apply them to the CE model.

5.1. The 'eyeball metric'

Suppose that two researchers were interested in determining whether an RBC model could replicate patterns of periodicity and comovement found in U.S.

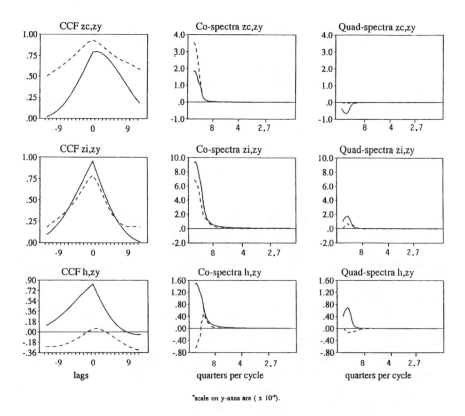

*scale on y-axes are (x 10⁻⁴).

Fig. 7a. Pre-filter comovements (TS model).

T. Cogley, J.M. Nason / Journal of Economic Dynamics and Control 19 (1995) 253–278   271

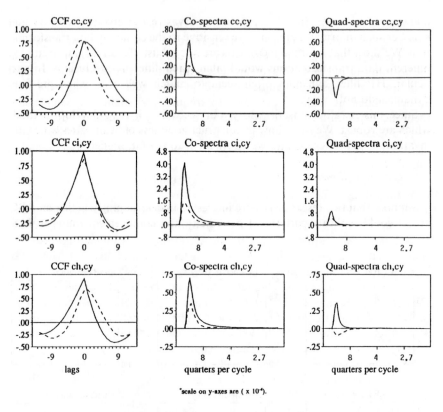

Fig. 7b. Post-filter comovements (TS model).

data. One transformed the actual and artificial data by applying the HP filter, and the other transformed the data in accordance with the model's trend specification (i.e., detrending the data when studying the TS model and differencing when studying the DS model). Would they reach the same conclusion?

5.1.1. Periodicity

Fig. 4 reports results relevant to the DS model. A researcher analyzing differenced data would produce the graphs shown in the top row. The sample autocorrelation function for output growth is positive at lags 1 and 2 and weakly negative at higher-order lags. The sample spectrum has a broad peak ranging from roughly 3 to 12 years per cycle, with maximum power at 5.5 years per cycle. This indicates that there is business cycle periodicity in U.S. output growth. In contrast, the theoretical autocorrelations are close to zero at all lags, and the theoretical spectrum is flat. Since the DS model does not generate

272   *T. Cogley, J.M. Nason / Journal of Economic Dynamics and Control 19 (1995) 253–278*

business cycle periodicity, a researcher analyzing these results would probably conclude that the model fails to replicate the dynamics of U.S. output growth.

A researcher analyzing HP filtered data would produce the graphs shown in the bottom row of Fig. 4. This researcher would observe that actual and artificial data are both positively autocorrelated at low-order lags and negatively autocorrelated at higher-order lags. In frequency domain, the sample and theoretical spectra both have large peaks at roughly 7.5 years per cycle. Since there appears to be an excellent match between sample and theoretical moments, this researcher would be likely to conclude that the model matches sample output dynamics quite well.

Fig. 6 reports results relevant to the TS model. A researcher analyzing detrended data would produce the graphs shown in the top row. Both actual and artificial data are well approximated by persistent autoregressive processes. However, while the artificial data are well approximated by an AR(1) process, U.S. data are well approximated by an AR(2) process with two positive real roots.[18] Thus the model generates less persistence than observed in sample. In other words, the model generates too little low frequency power.

A researcher studying HP filtered data would produce the graphs shown in the bottom row. Since the HP filter eliminates low frequency information in TS processes, the low frequency discrepancy observed in detrended data vanishes. A researcher analyzing HP filtered data would probably conclude that the model matches sample output dynamics quite well.

Researchers who employ different data transformations are likely to reach different conclusions about periodicity. Researchers who analyze HP filtered data would be likely to draw favorable conclusions, while those who analyze differenced or detrended data would not. The reason why actual and artificial HP filtered data appear to have common dynamic properties is that they inherit common dynamic factors from the filter. After filtering, actual and artificial spectra look alike because they both display the spectral shape of $|S(\omega)|^2$. Autocorrelation functions for HP filtered data look alike because they display the characteristic HP pattern, which is the inverse Fourier transform of $|S(\omega)|^2$. Thus, on the 'eyeball metric', the periodicity of HP filtered output appears to match well even though pre-filter measures of periodicity do not.

5.1.2. Comovement

Figs. 5a and 5b report results for the DS model. A researcher analyzing differenced data would study the graphs shown in Fig. 5a. The first two rows summarize results for consumption and investment. The DS model predicts that consumption and investment growth are very highly correlated with output ·

---

[18] E.g., see Cogley and Nason (1993). This difference is easier to see when looking at partial autocorrelations.

growth at lag zero and are very weakly correlated at other leads and lags. In contrast, observed comovements are spread out over several quarters. Sample cross-correlations are lower than predicted at lag zero (0.54 for consumption and 0.8 for investment) and larger than predicted at low-order leads and lags (roughly 0.25 to 0.35). A researcher analyzing differenced data might have doubts about the nearly perfect contemporaneous relation between these variables.

A researcher analyzing HP filtered data would study the graphs shown in the first two rows of Fig. 5b. In this case, the cross-correlations for consumption and investment appear to match quite well. In particular, they have the same bell shape. Thus a researcher analyzing HP filtered data would be more likely to come to a favorable conclusion about the model's ability to replicate the sample comovements of consumption and investment with output.

The frequency domain graphs show that the bell shape pattern comes from $S(L)$. Before filtering, the cross-spectra are flat relative to $S(L)$. Therefore, when actual and artificial data are passed through $S(L)$, they inherit its spectral shape (Fig. 5b). Transforming $|S(\omega)|^2$ into time domain produces bell-shaped cross-correlation functions.

Comovements between output and hours are summarized in the third row of Figs. 5a and 5b. Before filtering, the theoretical cross-correlation function has modest negative correlation at low-order leads, a peak of roughly 0.3 at lag 0, and slowly decaying correlations at low-order lags. The sample cross-correlation function has a similar shape, but the contemporaneous correlation is close to zero, and the peak occurs at lags 5 through 7. A researcher analyzing differenced data would note a significant discrepancy between sample and theoretical lead/lag relations. In U.S. data, an increase in output growth is associated with an increase in hours, but this occurs with a lag of 5 to 7 quarters. In the CE model, hours respond contemporaneously.

After filtering, the sample and theoretical cross correlation functions have the characteristic bell shape, with peaks at lags 1 and 0, respectively. A researcher analyzing HP filtered data would be likely to conclude that the model generates the right qualitative comovements but has a relatively minor discrepancy in lead/lag relations.

Figs. 7a and 7b report results for the TS model. The first two rows summarize comovements of consumption and investment with output. Investment/output comovements match well both before and after filtering. Consumption/output comovements seem to match fairly well in a qualitative sense, but there appears to be rather large quantitative discrepancies. In this case, researchers analyzing detrended and HP filtered data would be likely to reach the same conclusions.

The third row reports results for output and hours. Before filtering, the match between sample and theoretical cross-correlations is quite poor. In particular, the predicted correlations between hours and detrended output are much too high. On the other hand, after filtering, the match is much improved. A researcher analyzing unfiltered data would be likely to conclude that the model's implications for hours/output comovements are grossly inconsistent with the data, while a researcher analyzing HP filtered data would be likely to conclude that the model produces a reasonable qualitative match.

5.2. Filter-invariant goodness of fit statistics

The results of the previous section highlight the desirability of developing goodness of fit measures which are invariant to HP filtering. This section constructs invariant spectral goodness of fit statistics. The basic idea is to work with ratios of sample and theoretical spectra. The HP filter multiplies numerator and denominator by the same number, so these ratios are invariant to HP filtering.[19] We investigate the model's implications for periodicity by computing statistics based on power spectra. We investigate comovement implications by computing statistics based on coherence.[20]

5.2.1 Periodicity

Let $R_T(\omega) = I_T(\omega)/f(\omega)$, where $I_T(\omega)$ denotes the sample periodogram and $f(\omega)$ denotes the population, model generated spectrum for pre-filtered data. 'Pre-filtered' refers to detrended data when studying TS models, and it refers to differenced data when studying DS models. Let $U_T(\omega)$ be proportional to the partial sums of $R_T(\omega)$: $U_T(2\pi j/T) = (2\pi/T)\sum_{i=1}^{j} R_T(2\pi i/T)$. The variable $U_T(\omega)$ is invariant to HP filtering, since the numerator and denominator of all the elements in the sum are both multiplied by the squared gain of the filter:

$$U_T^{HP}(2\pi j/T) = (2\pi/T) \sum_{i=1}^{j} \frac{G(2\pi i/T)I_T(2\pi i/T)}{G(2\pi i/T)f(2\pi i/T)}$$

$$= (2\pi/T) \sum_{i=1}^{j} \frac{I_T(2\pi i/T)}{f(2\pi i/T)}$$

$$= U_T(2\pi j/T),$$

where $G(\omega) = |HP(\omega)|^2$ in the TS case and $G(\omega) = |S(\omega)|^2$ in the DS case. Since $U_T(\omega)$ is invariant to HP filtering, any statistic based on $U_T(\omega)$ is also invariant.

Under the hypothesis that the data are drawn from a population governed by $f(\omega)$, $U_T(\omega)$ converges to a uniform distribution function. Thus goodness of fit

---

[19] Watson's (1993) approach is similar, but his overall goodness of fit statistic is not invariant to linear filtering, and its statistical properties are unknown.

[20] Coherence is the frequency domain analog to correlation, and it is defined as $|f_{12}(\omega)|^2/f_{11}(\omega)f_{22}(\omega)$, where $f_{11}(\omega)$ and $f_{22}(\omega)$ are the power spectra for series 1 and 2 and $f_{12}(\omega)$ is the cross-spectrum.

Table 1
HP filter-invariant goodness of fit tests

	TS model		DS model	
	KS	CVM	KS	CVM
(1) *Periodicity of output*				
	1.03	0.52	2.44	2.45
	(0.239)	(0.036)	(1.3E-05)	(0.000)
(2) *Coherence with output*				
(c, y)	1.29	0.81	1.12	0.64
	(0.000)	(0.000)	(0.000)	(0.000)
(i, y)	0.53	0.14	0.50	0.13
	(0.000)	(0.000)	(0.000)	(0.000)
(h, y)	0.89	0.29	1.16	0.51
	(0.000)	(0.000)	(0.000)	(0.000)

This table reports Kolmogorov–Smirnov and Cramer–von Mises statistics for TS and DS versions of the Christiano–Eichenbaum (1992) model. Asymptotic probability values are shown in parentheses.

statistics for uniform distributions can be applied to $U_T(\omega)$. For example, these include the Kolmogorov–Smirnov and Cramer–von Mises statistics:

$$KS = \max |B_T(\tau)|,$$

$$CVM = \int_0^1 B_T^2(\tau)\, d\tau,$$

where

$$B_T(\tau) = (\sqrt{2T}/2\pi)[U_T(\pi\tau) - \tau U_T(\pi)] \quad \text{and} \quad 0 \le \tau \le 1.$$

Dzhaparidze (1986) shows that these statistics converge to functionals of a Brownian bridge, and their limiting distributions are tabulated in Shorack and Wellner (1987).

The top panel of Table 1 reports Kolmogorov–Smirnov and Cramer–von Mises statistics for the TS and DS CE models, with asymptotic probability values in parentheses. The hypothesis being tested is that the sample spectrum matches the theoretical spectrum. The TS version of the model fares better than the DS version. In the TS case, the Kolmogorov–Smirnov statistic fails to reject the CE model, while the Cramer–von Mises test rejects at the 3.6 percent level. In the DS case, both tests reject at very high significance levels. It is interesting to note that these results appear to be consistent with informal comparisons based on inspection of detrended and differenced data, but contradict informal judgments based on inspection of HP filtered data.

5.2.2. Comovement

Coherence goodness of fit statistics can be constructed in an analogous fashion. Let $R_T(\omega) = c_T(\omega)/c(\omega)$, where $c_T(\omega)$ denotes the sample coherence and $c(\omega)$ denotes the theoretical coherence, and let $U_T(\omega)$ be proportional to the partial sums of $R_T(\omega)$: $U_T(2\pi j/T) = (2\pi/T)\sum_{i=1}^{j} R_T(2\pi i/T)$. Since coherence is invariant to nonzero linear filtering, the HP filter has no effect on $U_T(\omega)$. Thus any statistic based on $U_T(\omega)$ is invariant to HP filtering.

The bottom panel of Table 1 reports Kolmogorov–Smirnov and Cramer–von Mises statistics based on coherence functions. The null hypothesis is that the sample coherence matches the theoretical coherence. In this case, the limiting distributions are unknown, so we compute them numerically.[21] Coherence goodness of fit tests strongly reject the comovement implications of both versions of the model. Both versions imply very high coherence at all frequencies. Observed coherences are not nearly as tight, especially at high frequencies.

6. Conclusion

This paper extends earlier work on the HP filter by analyzing its effects on trend- and difference-stationary time series. The paper's main result is that the HP filter is subject to the Nelson–Kang critique. When applied to integrated processes, the HP filter can generate business cycle periodicity and comovement even if none are present in the original data. Thus, if a researcher is reluctant to detrend a data series on account of the Nelson–Kang result, she should also be reluctant to apply the HP filter.

We consider the implications of this result for two applications. The first is in studies which describe stylized facts about the business cycle. Since the HP filter can generate spurious cycles in some cases, the interpretation of HP stylized facts depends on assumptions about the nature of the input series. If the data are assumed to be DS, stylized facts about periodicity and comovement primarily reflect the properties of the filter and tell us very little about the dynamic properties of the underlying data.

---

[21] We draw 1000 random realizations of $c_T(\omega)$ from its asymptotic distribution, compute KS and CVM statistics for each draw, and then compile the results into an asymptotic distribution. Since the asymptotic distribution for $c_T(\omega)$ depends on nuisance parameters, the distributions for KS and CVM statistics have to be re-calculated for each coherence function. This is an efficient algorithm for computing these distributions.

T. Cogley, J.M. Nason / Journal of Economic Dynamics and Control 19 (1995) 253–278   277

A second application is in RBC simulations. When artificial data are passed through the HP filter, they exhibit business cycle periodicity and comovement. We inquire into the source of these fluctuations. We show that RBC models can exhibit business cycle dynamics in HP filtered data even if they do not generate business cycle dynamics in pre-filtered data. The combination of a unit root or near unit root in technology and the HP filter is sufficient to generate business cycle dynamics. Propagation mechanisms are unnecessary, and in many RBC models they do not play an important role.

Finally, we consider the problem of evaluating a model's goodness of fit. In the RBC literature, it is common to rely on informal judgments based on inspection of sample and theoretical moments. Conclusions based on informal comparisons are sensitive to the choice of data transformation. Researchers who analyse HP filtered are often likely to reach different conclusions from researchers who analyze differenced or detrended data. Since actual and artificial data inherit common dynamic factors when they are passed through the filter, HP filtered dynamics can appear to match well even if pre-filter dynamics do not. We show how to circumvent this problem by computing filter-invariant goodness of fit statistics.

References

Adelman, I., 1965, Long cycles: Fact or artifact?, American Economic Review 55, 444–463.

Beveridge, S. and C.R. Nelson, 1981, A new approach to decomposition of economic time series into permanent and transitory components with particular attention to measurement of the business cycle, Journal of Monetary Economics 7, 151–174.

Christiano, L.J. and M. Eichenbaum, 1992, Current real business cycle theories and aggregate labor market fluctuations, American Economic Review 82, 430–450.

Cogley, T. and J.M. Nason, 1992, Do real business cycle models pass the Nelson–Plosser test?, Mimeo. (Federal Reserve Bank of San Francisco, CA).

Cogley, T. and J.M. Nason, 1993, Impulse dynamics and propagation mechanisms in a real business cycle model, Economics Letters 43, 77–81.

Dzhaparidze, K., 1986, Parameter estimation and hypothesis testing in the spectral analysis of stationary time series (Springer-Verlag, New York, NY).

Hansen, G.D., 1989, Technical progress and aggregate fluctuations, Department of Economics working paper no. 546 (University of California, Los Angeles, CA).

Harvey, A.C. and A. Jaeger, 1993, Detrending, stylized facts, and the business cycle, Journal of Applied Econometrics 8, 231–247.

Hodrick, R. and E.C. Prescott, 1980, Post-war U.S. business cycles: An empirical investigation, Mimeo. (Carnegie-Mellon University, Pittsburgh, PA).

Howrey, E.P., 1968, A spectrum analysis of the long–swing hypothesis, International Economic Review 9, 228–260.

King, R.G. and S.T. Rebelo, 1993, Low frequency filtering and real business cycles, Journal of Economics Dynamics and Control 17, 207–232.

King, R.G., C.I. Plosser, and S.T. Rebelo, 1988a, Production, growth, and business cycles I: The basic neoclassical model, Journal of Monetary Economics 21, 195–232.

King, R.G., C.I. Plosser, and S.T. Rebelo, 1988b, Production, growth, and business cycles II: New directions, Journal of Monetary Economics 21, 309–342.

Kuznets, S.S., 1961, Capital in the American economy: Its formation and financing (National Bureau of Economic Research, New York, NY).

Kydland, F.E. and E.C. Prescott, 1982, Time to build and aggregate fluctuations, Econometrica 50, 1345–1370.

Kydland, F.E. and E.C. Prescott, 1988, The workweek of capital and its cyclical implications, Journal of Monetary Economics 21, 343–360.

Kydland, F.E. and E.C. Prescott, 1990, Business cycles: Real facts and a monetary myth, Federal Reserve Bank of Minneapolis Quarterly Review 14, 3–18.

Lucas, R.E., 1987, Models of business cycles (Basil Blackwell, Oxford).

Nelson, C.R. and H. Kang, 1981, Spurious periodicity in inappropriately detrended time series, Econometrica 49, 741–751.

Priestley, M.B., 1988, Non-linear and non-stationary time series analysis (Academic Press, New York, NY).

Prescott, E.C., 1986, Theory ahead of business cycle measurement, Carnegie–Rochester Conference Series on Public Policy, 11–66.

Shorack, G.R. and J.A. Wellner, 1987, Empirical processes with applications to statistics (Wiley, New York, NY).

Singleton, K.J., 1988, Econometric issues in the analysis of equilibrium business cycle models, Journal of Monetary Economics 21, 361–368.

Watson, M.W., 1986, Univariate detrending methods with stochastic trends, Journal of Monetary Economics 18, 49–76.

Watson, M.W., 1993, Measures of fit for calibrated models, Journal of Political Economy 101, 1011–1041.

Index